Nineteenth-Century Literature Criticism

Topics Volume

Guide to Gale Literary Criticism Series

For criticism on	Consult these Gale series
Authors now living or who died after December 31, 1999	*CONTEMPORARY LITERARY CRITICISM (CLC)*
Authors who died between 1900 and 1999	*TWENTIETH-CENTURY LITERARY CRITICISM (TCLC)*
Authors who died between 1800 and 1899	*NINETEENTH-CENTURY LITERATURE CRITICISM (NCLC)*
Authors who died between 1400 and 1799	*LITERATURE CRITICISM FROM 1400 TO 1800 (LC)* *SHAKESPEAREAN CRITICISM (SC)*
Authors who died before 1400	*CLASSICAL AND MEDIEVAL LITERATURE CRITICISM (CMLC)*
Authors of books for children and young adults	*CHILDREN'S LITERATURE REVIEW (CLR)*
Dramatists	*DRAMA CRITICISM (DC)*
Poets	*POETRY CRITICISM (PC)*
Short story writers	*SHORT STORY CRITICISM (SSC)*
Literary topics and movements	*HARLEM RENAISSANCE: A GALE CRITICAL COMPANION (HR)* *THE BEAT GENERATION: A GALE CRITICAL COMPANION (BG)* *FEMINISM IN LITERATURE: A GALE CRITICAL COMPANION (FL)* *GOTHIC LITERATURE: A GALE CRITICAL COMPANION (GL)*
Asian American writers of the last two hundred years	*ASIAN AMERICAN LITERATURE (AAL)*
Black writers of the past two hundred years	*BLACK LITERATURE CRITICISM (BLC)* *BLACK LITERATURE CRITICISM SUPPLEMENT (BLCS)* *BLACK LITERATURE CRITICISM: CLASSIC AND EMERGING AUTHORS SINCE 1950 (BLC-2)*
Hispanic writers of the late nineteenth and twentieth centuries	*HISPANIC LITERATURE CRITICISM (HLC)* *HISPANIC LITERATURE CRITICISM SUPPLEMENT (HLCS)*
Native North American writers and orators of the eighteenth, nineteenth, and twentieth centuries	*NATIVE NORTH AMERICAN LITERATURE (NNAL)*
Major authors from the Renaissance to the present	*WORLD LITERATURE CRITICISM, 1500 TO THE PRESENT (WLC)* *WORLD LITERATURE CRITICISM SUPPLEMENT (WLCS)*

ISSN 0732-1864

Volume 212

Nineteenth-Century Literature Criticism

Topics Volume

Criticism of Various
Topics in Nineteenth-Century Literature,
including Literary and Critical Movements,
Prominent Themes and Genres, Anniversary
Celebrations, and Surveys of National Literatures

Kathy D. Darrow
Project Editor

GALE
CENGAGE Learning

Detroit • New York • San Francisco • New Haven, Conn • Waterville, Maine • London

Nineteenth-Century Literature Criticism, Vol. 212

Project Editor: Kathy Darrow

Editorial: Dana Barnes, Elizabeth Cranston, Kristen Dorsch, Jeffrey W. Hunter, Jelena O. Krstović, Michelle Lee, Thomas J. Schoenberg, Lawrence J. Trudeau

Content Conversion: Katrina D. Coach, Gwen Tucker

Rights and Acquisitions: Barb McNeil, Timothy Sisler, Sara Teller

Composition and Electronic Capture: Gary Oudersluys

Manufacturing: Cynde Bishop

Associate Product Manager: Marc Cormier

For product information and technology assistance, contact us at **Gale Customer Support, 1-800-877-4253.**
For permission to use material from this text or product, submit all requests online at **www.cengage.com/permissions.**
Further permissions questions can be emailed to **permissionrequest@cengage.com**

Gale
27500 Drake Rd.
Farmington Hills, MI, 48331-3535

LIBRARY OF CONGRESS CATALOG CARD NUMBER 84-643008

ISBN-13: 978-1-4144-3410-0
ISBN-10: 1-4144-3410-3

ISSN 0732-1864

Printed in the United States of America
1 2 3 4 5 6 7 13 12 11 10 09

Contents

Preface vii

Acknowledgments xi

Literary Criticism Series Advisory Board xiii

Preface

Since its inception in 1981, *Nineteenth-Century Literature Criticism* (*NCLC*) has been a valuable resource for students and librarians seeking critical commentary on writers of this transitional period in world history. Designated an "Outstanding Reference Source" by the American Library Association with the publication of is first volume, *NCLC* has since been purchased by over 6,000 school, public, and university libraries. The series has covered more than 500 authors representing 38 nationalities and over 28,000 titles. No other reference source has surveyed the critical reaction to nineteenth-century authors and literature as thoroughly as *NCLC*.

Scope of the Series

NCLC is designed to introduce students and advanced readers to the authors of the nineteenth century and to the most significant interpretations of these authors' works. The great poets, novelists, short story writers, playwrights, and philosophers of this period are frequently studied in high school and college literature courses. By organizing and reprinting commentary written on these authors, *NCLC* helps students develop valuable insight into literary history, promotes a better understanding of the texts, and sparks ideas for papers and assignments. Each entry in *NCLC* presents a comprehensive survey of an author's career or an individual work of literature and provides the user with a multiplicity of interpretations and assessments. Such variety allows students to pursue their own interests; furthermore, it fosters an awareness that literature is dynamic and responsive to many different opinions.

Every fourth volume of *NCLC* is devoted to literary topics that cannot be covered under the author approach used in the rest of the series. Such topics include literary movements, prominent themes in nineteenth-century literature, literary reaction to political and historical events, significant eras in literary history, prominent literary anniversaries, and the literatures of cultures that are often overlooked by English-speaking readers.

NCLC continues the survey of criticism of world literature begun by Gale's *Contemporary Literary Criticism* (*CLC*) and *Twentieth-Century Literary Criticism* (*TCLC*).

Organization of the Book

An *NCLC* entry consists of the following elements:

- The **Author Heading** cites the name under which the author most commonly wrote, followed by birth and death dates. Also located here are any name variations under which an author wrote, including transliterated forms for authors whose native languages use nonroman alphabets. If the author wrote consistently under a pseudonym, the pseudonym will be listed in the author heading and the author's actual name given in parenthesis on the first line of the biographical and critical information. Uncertain birth or death dates are indicated by question marks. Single-work entries are preceded by a heading that consists of the most common form of the title in English translation (if applicable) and the original date of composition.

- The **Introduction** contains background information that introduces the reader to the author, work, or topic that is the subject of the entry.

- The list of **Principal Works** is ordered chronologically by date of first publication and lists the most important works by the author. The genre and publication date of each work is given. In the case of foreign authors whose works have been translated into English, the list will focus primarily on twentieth-century translations, selecting those works most commonly considered the best by critics. Unless otherwise indicated, dramas are dated by first performance, not first publication. Lists of **Representative Works** by different authors appear with topic entries.

- Reprinted **Criticism** is arranged chronologically in each entry to provide a useful perspective on changes in critical evaluation over time. The critic's name and the date of composition or publication of the critical work are given at the beginning of each piece of criticism. Unsigned criticism is preceded by the title of the source in which it appeared. All titles by the author featured in the text are printed in boldface type. Footnotes are reprinted at the end of each essay or excerpt. In the case of excerpted criticism, only those footnotes that pertain to the excerpted texts are included. Criticism in topic entries is arranged chronologically under a variety of subheadings to facilitate the study of different aspects of the topic.

- A complete **Bibliographical Citation** of the original essay or book precedes each piece of criticism.

- Critical essays are prefaced by brief **Annotations** explicating each piece.

- An annotated bibliography of **Further Reading** appears at the end of each entry and suggests resources for additional study. In some cases, significant essays for which the editors could not obtain reprint rights are included here. Boxed material following the further reading list provides references to other biographical and critical sources on the author in series published by Gale.

Indexes

Each volume of *NCLC* contains a **Cumulative Author Index** listing all authors who have appeared in a wide variety of reference sources published by Gale, including *NCLC*. A complete list of these sources is found facing the first page of the Author Index. The index also includes birth and death dates and cross references between pseudonyms and actual names.

A **Cumulative Nationality Index** lists all authors featured in *NCLC* by nationality, followed by the number of the *NCLC* volume in which their entry appears.

A **Cumulative Topic Index** lists the literary themes and topics treated in the series as well as in *Classical and Medieval Literature Criticism, Literature Criticism from 1400 to 1800, Twentieth-Century Literary Criticism,* and the *Contemporary Literary Criticism* Yearbook, which was discontinued in 1998.

An alphabetical **Title Index** accompanies each volume of *NCLC*, with the exception of the Topics volumes. Listings of titles by authors covered in the given volume are followed by the author's name and the corresponding page numbers where the titles are discussed. English translations of foreign titles and variations of titles are cross-referenced to the title under which a work was originally published. Titles of novels, dramas, nonfiction books, and poetry, short story, or essay collections are printed in italics, while individual poems, short stories, and essays are printed in roman type within quotation marks.

In response to numerous suggestions from librarians, Gale also produces an annual paperbound edition of the *NCLC* cumulative title index. This annual cumulation, which alphabetically lists all titles reviewed in the series, is available to all customers. Additional copies of this index are available upon request. Librarians and patrons will welcome this separate index; it saves shelf space, is easy to use, and is recyclable upon receipt of the next edition.

Citing *Nineteenth-Century Literature Criticism*

When citing criticism reprinted in the Literary Criticism Series, students should provide complete bibliographic information so that the cited essay can be located in the original print or electronic source. Students who quote directly from reprinted criticism may use any accepted bibliographic format, such as University of Chicago Press style or Modern Language Association style.

The examples below follow recommendations for preparing a bibliography set forth in *The Chicago Manual of Style,* 14th ed. (Chicago: The University of Chicago Press, 1993); the first example pertains to material drawn from periodicals, the second to material reprinted from books:

Franklin, J. Jeffrey. "The Victorian Discourse of Gambling: Speculations on *Middlemarch* and *The Duke's Children*." *ELH* 61, no. 4 (winter 1994): 899-921. Reprinted in *Nineteenth-Century Literature Criticism*. Vol. 168, edited by Jessica Bomarito and Russel Whitaker, 39-51. Detroit: Thomson Gale, 2006.

Frank, Joseph. "*The Gambler*: A Study in Ethnopsychology." In *Freedom and Responsibility in Russian Literature: Essays in Honor of Robert Louis Jackson,* edited by Elizabeth Cheresh Allen and Gary Saul Morson, 69-85. Evanston, Ill.: Northwestern University Press, 1995. Reprinted in *Nineteenth-Century Literature Criticism*. Vol. 168, edited by Jessica Bomarito and Russel Whitaker, 75-84. Detroit: Thomson Gale, 2006.

The examples below follow recommendations for preparing a works cited list set forth in the *MLA Handbook for Writers of Research Papers,* 6th ed. (New York: The Modern Language Association of America, 2003); the first example pertains to material drawn from periodicals, the second to material reprinted from books:

Franklin, J. Jeffrey. "The Victorian Discourse of Gambling: Speculations on *Middlemarch* and *The Duke's Children*." *ELH* 61.4 (Winter 1994): 899-921. Reprinted in *Nineteenth-Century Literature Criticism*. Eds. Jessica Bomarito and Russel Whitaker. Vol. 168. Detroit: Thomson Gale, 2006. 39-51.

Frank, Joseph. "*The Gambler*: A Study in Ethnopsychology." *Freedom and Responsibility in Russian Literature: Essays in Honor of Robert Louis Jackson*. Eds. Elizabeth Cheresh Allen and Gary Saul Morson. Evanston, Ill.: Northwestern University Press, 1995. 69-85. Reprinted in *Nineteenth-Century Literature Criticism*. Eds. Jessica Bomarito and Russel Whitaker. Vol. 168. Detroit: Thomson Gale, 2006. 75-84.

Suggestions are Welcome

Readers who wish to suggest new features, topics, or authors to appear in future volumes, or who have other suggestions or comments are cordially invited to call, write, or fax the Associate Product Manager:

Associate Product Manager, Literary Criticism Series
Gale
27500 Drake Road
Farmington Hills, MI 48331-3535
1-800-347-4253 (GALE)
Fax: 248-699-8054

Acknowledgments

The editors wish to thank the copyright holders of the criticism included in this volume and the permissions managers of many book and magazine publishing companies for assisting us in securing reproduction rights. Following is a list of the copyright holders who have granted us permission to reproduce material in this volume of *NCLC*. Every effort has been made to trace copyright, but if omissions have been made, please let us know.

COPYRIGHTED MATERIAL IN *NCLC*, VOLUME 212, WAS REPRODUCED FROM THE FOLLOWING PERIODICALS:

African American Review, v. 39, spring/summer, 2005 for "'Civil' War Wounds: William Wells Brown, Violence, and the Domestic Narrative" by Jennifer James/v. 41, summer, 2007 for "'When Dey 'Listed Colored Soldiers': Paul Lawrence Dunbar's Poetic Engagement with the Civil War, Masculinity, and Violence" by Jennifer Terry. Copyright © 2005 Jennifer James, 2007 Jennifer Terry. Both reproduced by permission of the author.—*American Periodicals*, v. 11, 2001. Copyright © 2001 by University of North Texas Press. Reproduced by permission.—*Anales Galdosianos*, v. XXXVII, 2002. Reproduced by permission.—*Brontë Society Transactions*, v. 21, 1994. Copyright © 1994 The Incorporated Brontë Society. Reproduced by permission.—*Bulletin of the John Rylands Library*, v. 71, autumn 1989. Copyright © 1989 The John Rylands University Library of Manchester. Reproduced by courtesy of the Director and University Librarian, the John Rylands University Library of Manchester.—*Criticism*, v. XVI, summer, 1974. Copyright © 1974 Wayne State University Press. Reproduced with permission of the Wayne State University Press.—*Dickens Quarterly*, v. VIII, June, 1991. Copyright © 1991 by the Dickens Society. Reproduced by permission.—*English Studies*, v. XLVII, 1966 for "The Novel as Fairy Tale: Dickens' *Dombey and Son*" by Harry Stone. Reproduced by permission of Taylor & Francis, Ltd., http//:www.tandf.co.uk/journals, and the author.—*Lion and the Unicorn*, v. 23, September, 1999. Copyright © 1999 by The Johns Hopkins University Press. Reproduced by permission.—*Nineteenth Century Theatre*, v. 21, summer, 1993 for "The Construction of Racial Type: Caricature, Ethnography, and Jewish Physiognomy in Fin-de-Siècle Melodrama" by Shearer West. Copyright © 1993 *Nineteenth Century Theatre*. Reproduced by permission of the publisher and author.—*Prose Studies*, v. 27, April-August, 2005 for "Cripple, Soldier, Crippled Soldier: Alfred Bellard's Civil War Memoir" by William Etter. Copyright © 2005 Taylor & Francis Group Ltd. Reproduced by permission of Taylor & Francis, Ltd., http//:www.tandf.co.uk/journals, and the author.—*Southern Quarterly*, v. XXXVII, winter, 1999. Copyright © 1999 by the University of Southern Mississippi. Reproduced by permission.—*Southern Studies*, v. II, summer, 1991. Copyrighted © 1991 by Southern Studies Institute. Reproduced by permission.—*Studies in Short Fiction*, v. 16, fall, 1979. Copyright © 1979 by *Studies in Short Fiction*. Reproduced by permission.—*Studies in the Literary Imagination*, v. XII, fall, 1979. Copyright © 1979 Department of English, Georgia State University. Reproduced by permission.—*Texas Studies in Literature and Language*, v. V, winter, 1964 for "Dickens and Some Motifs of the Fairy Tale" by Shirley Grob. Copyright © 1964 by the University of Texas Press. All rights reserved. Reproduced by permission of the publisher and the author.—*Theatre Notebook*, v. L, 1996. Reproduced by permission.—*Victorian Studies*, v. 24, spring, 1981. Copyright © 1981 Indiana University Press. Reproduced by permission.—*Walt Whitman Quarterly Review*, v. 20, winter/spring, 2003; v. 23, summer/fall, 2005. Copyright © 2003, 2005 by the University of Iowa. Both reproduced by permission.—*War, Literature, & the Arts*, v. 14, 2002 for "Obscured Hurts: The Civil War Writing of Henry James and Ambrose Bierce" by Adrian Hunter. Reproduced by permission of the author.—*Women and Language*, v. 28, spring, 2005. Reproduced by permission of the publisher.

COPYRIGHTED MATERIAL IN *NCLC*, VOLUME 212, WAS REPRODUCED FROM THE FOLLOWING BOOKS:

Anderson, Victoria. From "Investigating the Third Story: 'Bluebeard' and 'Cinderella' in *Jane Eyre*," in *Horrifying Sex: Essays on Sexual Difference in Gothic Literature*. Edited by Ruth Bienstock Anolik. McFarland, 2007. Copyright © 2007 Ruth Bienstock Anolik. All rights reserved. Reproduced by permission of McFarland & Company, Inc., Box 611, Jefferson NC 28640, www.mcfarlandpub.com.—Berland, Kevin. From "Inborn Character and Free Will in the History of Physiognomy," in *Physiognomy in Profile: Lavater's Impact on European Culture*. Edited by Melissa Percival and Graeme Tytler. University of Delaware Press, 2005. Copyright © 2005 by Rosemont Publishing & Printing Corp. All rights reserved. Reproduced by permission.—Blamires, David. From "A Workshop of Editorial Practice: The Grimms' *Kinder- und Hausmärchen*," in *A Companion to the Fairy Tale*. Edited by Hilda Ellis Davidson and Anna Chaudhri. D. S. Brewer,

Gale Literature Product Advisory Board

The members of the Gale Literature Product Advisory Board—reference librarians from public and academic library systems—represent a cross-section of our customer base and offer a variety of informed perspectives on both the presentation and content of our literature products. Advisory board members assess and define such quality issues as the relevance, currency, and usefulness of the author coverage, critical content, and literary topics included in our series; evaluate the layout, presentation, and general quality of our printed volumes; provide feedback on the criteria used for selecting authors and topics covered in our series; provide suggestions for potential enhancements to our series; identify any gaps in our coverage of authors or literary topics, recommending authors or topics for inclusion; analyze the appropriateness of our content and presentation for various user audiences, such as high school students, undergraduates, graduate students, librarians, and educators; and offer feedback on any proposed changes/enhancements to our series. We wish to thank the following advisors for their advice throughout the year.

The American Civil War in Nineteenth-Century Literature

The following entry presents critical discussion of the American Civil War in nineteenth-century literature. For further information on the American Civil War, see *NCLC*, Volume 32.

INTRODUCTION

Fought for four years over several issues, most notably the preservation of the union of states and the practice of slavery, the American Civil War is considered by many historians to be the first modern strategic war and the most costly conflict in American history in terms of human lives and natural resources. Although generally regarded as a dominant period in American letters, the Civil War years also prompted numerous personal narratives whose historical and literary significance are recognized today.

The production and consumption of Civil War literature between the 1860s and the early 1900s took place in a kind of literary ecosystem involving writers, critics, and readers. Periodicals regularly published fiction, poetry, commentary, and serialized novels dealing with the war and its legacies, and included Civil War commentary written by such prominent authors as Mark Twain and Henry James. With most of the American reading public focusing on news reports of the war's progress, the market for fiction and poetry declined from 1861 to 1865, and little of the literature published in the United States during that time receives notice today. Many Southern literary magazines were forced to cease publication for financial reasons, but magazines such as *Harper's New Monthly* and *Godey's Lady's Book* offered sentimental poetry and short stories that centered on the reunions of soldiers with their wives and loved ones. Some periodicals featured stories that treated, often metaphorically, the civilian lives of soldiers who sustained crippling and disfiguring physical injuries in battle, as well as those who suffered emotional and psychological trauma. Northern newspapers and magazines had the resources to send artists to the field and a wide-reaching readership, thus becoming the mainstays upon which anxious Americans came to rely for information about the war; scholarly and personal reflections were contributed as well. Coverage of the American Civil War in the French press was heavily steeped in stereotypical images of Americans, which were used to bolster or undermine various French political aims. The war further evoked a broad spectrum of narrative responses in the decades that followed it. Some authors retreated into fantasies of a Southern golden age, while others imagined the reunion of North and South as a romance culminating in marriage. Many chose to focus upon particular aspects of the war, rather than trying to capture it holistically; others opted to employ a gothic approach to the subject matter, or offered straightforward and realistic accounts of battles and other events.

While many authors confronted and depicted the horrors of slavery or gave voice to their own views on the issue, the direct treatment of the topic of slavery was avoided in a good portion of literature written during the Civil War, despite the institution's role as one of the war's main causes. Many periodical editors and individual authors focused instead upon the idea of reconciling the North and the South, and their avoidance of the issue of race is read by critic Janet Gabler-Hover as an indication of pervasive racism and resistance to racial equality in American society. African-American novelist William Wells Brown's *Clotel; or, The President's Daughter: A Narrative of Slave Life in the United States* (1853) was a popular success upon its publication and the original version, published in England, created something of a scandal. Drawing on the legend that Thomas Jefferson had fathered many children with enslaved African-American women, Brown cast his heroine, Clotel, as Jefferson's daughter. Critics have maintained that Brown illustrates, simply and effectively, both the horror and the irony of the institution of slavery in a system that would allow the daughter of a president to be sold into bondage. For the American editions of *Clotel,* which were published several years after the original, Brown chose not to suggest presidential parentage for his heroine and instead concentrated on the heroism of the African-Americans during the American Civil War as they fought for their freedom. Brown's history, *The Black Man; His Antecedents, His Genius, and His Achievements* (1863), is composed of two major sections. Part one, "Antecedents," is prefaced by a comparison between Anglo-Saxon and African civilizations and outlines the reasons for and benefits of the abolition of slavery in America. Part two, which forms the bulk of *The Black Man,* is composed of fifty-three biographical sketches, mostly of noteworthy African Americans. Commentators have stressed the importance of *The Black Man* in terms of its advocacy of African Americans and its capacity to delineate the important role that African Americans played in American culture in the years following the Civil War. Brown's history, *The Negro in the American Rebellion:*

His Heroism and His Fidelity (1867), offered what critics have called a realistic portrayal of Civil-War-era military life that exposes the psychological and physical assaults that African-American soldiers endured at the hands of both Union and Confederacy, and highlights the dignity and bravery of these soldiers. African-American poet Paul Laurence Dunbar has also been noted by critics as capturing the extraordinary challenges facing African-American men during the Civil War by using the form of dialect poetry. Dunbar, according to critics, reveals the dignity, power, and resolve of black soldiers, illustrates their achievements, and highlights the sacrifices they made in pursuit of justice and equality.

Although commonly and critically regarded as one of America's premier poets, Walt Whitman remains in some ways a controversial figure. *Leaves of Grass,* a collection of poetry written between 1855 and 1892—and almost universally considered Whitman's masterpiece—was revolutionary both in its style and content, praising the divinity of the self, of the common individual. First published in 1855, the text was expanded, revised, and reissued in subsequent editions, the last in 1892. Because Whitman's poetry was so innovative and included realistic imagery and candid discussions of sexuality, it was dismissed as vulgar and indecent by Whitman's contemporaries, with the exception of Ralph Waldo Emerson and Henry David Thoreau. Whitman wrote entirely in free verse, and combined the traditional historical subject matter of epic poetry with the personal, subjective focus of lyric poetry. His themes were especially notable: Whitman celebrated the creation and restless spirit of America, particularly its westward expansion, and embraced the different experiences of the country's diverse population, including slaves and recent immigrants, in his vision. Over time Whitman attracted a growing number of readers who appreciated both his artistic achievement and his depiction of a multicultural and democratic America. In the essays and journal entries that comprise his *Specimen Days & Collect* (1882-83), Whitman constitutes what might be considered a poet's workshop of images and memories of his activities in Washington, D.C., from 1862 to 1865, when he worked as a government clerk and volunteer hospital aide. Although *Specimen Days* is autobiographical, it is highly experimental in form. The sketches describe the aftermath of battles, hospital scenes, camp life, conversations with soldiers, and glimpses of President Abraham Lincoln. Critics have observed that in these works Whitman serves as a mediating consciousness and sometimes as a participant in the events he describes. In this sense, *Specimen Days* anticipates the mythic vision of Whitman portrayed in his collection of Civil War poems *Drum-Taps* (1865), which was incorporated into a later edition of *Leaves of Grass,* and upon which Whitman worked throughout the last quarter-century of his life. Scholars have maintained that the Civil War greatly changed the nature and content of Whitman's poetry, and that in expanding and reorganizing the poems in *Drum-Taps,* as well as in his other works treating the Civil War, Whitman displays a gradually evolving but notably different, less idealized, vision of America and democracy at the end of his life.

The American Civil War required American women, both intentionally and unintentionally, to defy nineteenth-century cultural and social norms. Whether women became the victims of war-time occupation, resettlement, or violence, the conflict imposed a new set of tensions on them. Often the feminine reaction was to examine roles that would allow them to assist their fathers, husbands, and brothers in a supportive capacity both behind and on the front lines. Women wrote volumes about the effects of the conflict on their particular geographic areas of the country. Most of these writings appeared in the form of diaries that now serve as valuable historical documents to use in analyzing the events of the period. In 1861, Mary Chesnut began a diary that recorded the explosive happenings around her during the years of the Civil War. Following her husband on his duties in the South, she provided a firsthand view of the political world of the Confederacy. As the battles were waged, Chesnut soon began to write of the horrors she and her contemporaries witnessed, including tending sick and wounded soldiers and mourning the losses of family members, friends, and acquaintances. Chesnut strongly criticized the decisions of Southern leaders, and she complained about her lack of power as a woman in the South. It wasn't until 1905 that the first edition of her work appeared under the title *A Diary from Dixie,* and early editors of Chesnut's diary took great liberties in removing material they thought inappropriate or unnecessary. But even its incomplete form, the diary became extremely popular for the unique insight that it offers into the difficulties of Southern life during the Civil War, and reveals strong support of women's rights, as Chesnut suggested that Southern women were disenfranchised by the traditional Southern patriarchy. A complete edition of Chesnut's diary was published in 1981 as *Mary Chesnut's Civil War.* Sarah Emma Edmonds impersonated a male soldier and fought during the American Civil War; her novel, *Nurse and Spy in the Union Army* (1865), created a scandal when it was published. A popular fictionalized account of Edmonds's experiences in the Union Army, *Nurse and Spy* was the first of several narratives to chronicle the exploits of women masquerading as men and serving in the military during the American Civil War. While the text is based on historically documented evidence of Edmonds's soldiering, critics have maintained that its embellishments consign it to a more speculative mode. Considered by scholars as a skillfully written propaganda novel, Augusta Jane Evans's *Macaria; or, Altars of Sacrifice* (1863) depicts two Southern women's journey toward self-realization through their service to the

Confederacy. The novel promotes Southerners' desire to preserve their culture, which included slavery as an integral part of plantation life, and reflects Southern values as they were at that time. *Macaria*, which was originally printed on wrapping paper and bound with wallpaper, was smuggled into the North to try to undermine public support for the war among Northerners. It was also circulated among Northern troops to incite animosity and was so successful in this regard that some Union officials thought it should be banned.

The American Civil war as a literary topic continued to garner widespread popular interest throughout the twentieth century, and present-day artistic fascination with this war continues. Hundreds of works of fiction, films, and songs have treated the American Civil War, many of them highly melodramatic and romanticized. The 1990 Public Broadcasting System (PBS) documentary *The Civil War*, created and directed by Ken Burns, gained tremendous popularity and prompted the reissuing of memoirs by Generals Ulysses S. Grant and William Tecumseh Sherman. The highly-acclaimed film *Glory* (1989), directed by Ed Zwick, was based on the actual experiences of Union Army Colonel Robert Gould Shaw, who led America's first all-black volunteer company. This film, along with Burns's documentary, fueled popular and academic interest in the significant contributions of African Americans and women to the war effort.

REPRESENTATIVE WORKS

Louisa May Alcott
Hospital Sketches (letters and sketches) 1863

Ambrose Bierce
Tales of Soldiers and Civilians (short stories) 1891; also published as *In the Midst of Life*, 1892
The Collected Works of Ambrose Bierce. 12 vols. (short stories, sketches, poetry, essays, and satire) 1909-12
The Collected Writings of Ambrose Bierce [edited by Clifton Fadiman] (short stories, sketches, poetry, essays, and satire) 1996

William Wells Brown
Clotel; or, The President's Daughter: A Narrative of Slave Life in the United States (novel) 1853; revised as *Miralda; or, The Beautiful Quadroon: A Romance of American Slavery, Founded on Fact*, 1861-62; also revised as *Clotelle: A Tale of the Southern States*, 1864; also revised as *Clotelle; or, The Colored Heroine*, 1867
The Black Man; His Antecedents, His Genius, and His Achievements (history) 1863

The Negro in the American Rebellion: His Heroism and His Fidelity (history) 1867

George Washington Cable
The Grandissimes: A Story of Creole Life (novel) 1880

Mary Chestnut
A Diary from Dixie [abridged edition] (diary) 1905; unabridged edition published as *Mary Chestnut's Civil War*, 1981

Stephen Crane
The Red Badge of Courage (novel) 1896

John W. De Forest
Miss Ravenel's Conversion from Secession to Loyalty (novel) 1867

Paul Laurence Dunbar
The Complete Poems of Paul Laurence Dunbar (poetry) 1913
The Collected Poetry of Paul Laurence Dunbar [edited by Joanne M. Braxton] (poetry) 1993

Sarah Emma Edmonds
Nurse and Spy in the Union Army (novel) 1865

Augusta Jane Evans
Macaria; or, Altars of Sacrifice (novel) 1863

William Dean Howells
The Rise of Silas Lapham (novel) 1885

Henry James
†*The Bostonians: A Novel*. 3 vols. (novel) 1886
Notes of a Son and Brother (autobiography) 1914

Herman Melville
Battle-Pieces and Aspects of the War (poetry) 1866

Emma Dorothy Eliza Nevitte Southworth
‡*Fair Play; or, The Test of the Lone Isle* (novel) 1868
‡*How He Won Her: A Sequel to Fair Play* (novel) 1869

Mark Twain
The Adventures of Huckleberry Finn (novel) 1884

Walt Whitman
Leaves of Grass (prose and poetry) 1855, 1856, 1860-61, 1867, 1871, 1876, 1881-82, 1888, 1891, 1892
§*Drum-Taps* (poetry) 1865
§*Sequel to Drum-Taps* (poetry) 1865-66
Memoranda during the War (journal, poetry, and essays) 1875-76
Specimen Days & Collect (journalism, essays, and criticism) 1882-83; revised as *Specimen Days in America*, 1888

The Wound Dresser: A Series of Letters Written from the Hospitals in Washington during the War of the Rebellion (letters) 1898

*This work was originally published serially in *Century Magazine* in 1884.

†This work was originally published in *Century Magazine,* 1885-86.

‡These works were serialized as *Britomarte, the Man-Hater,* 1865-66.

§These works were incorporated in later editions of *Leaves of Grass.*

OVERVIEWS

Dominique A. Laurent (essay date 2001)

SOURCE: Laurent, Dominique A. "The American Civil War in the French Press." In *National Stereotypes in Perspective: Americans in France, Frenchmen in America,* edited by William L. Chew, III, pp. 187-208. Amsterdam, Netherlands: Rodopi, 2001.

[*In the following essay, Laurent surveys the various depictions of the American Civil War in nineteenth-century French periodicals, and highlights the reliance upon and purpose of stereotypes in these narratives.*]

'War for liberty', 'Southern barbarity,' these were some of the terms used by the U.S. correspondent of the republican newspaper *Le Temps* to comment on the outbreak of the American Civil War. Support for the Union's fight against slavery, however, was not universal in the French press under Napoleon III. Conservative newspapers presented a radically different image of the war. *Le Consitutionnel,* for instance, portrayed the Confederacy in the most flattering terms, praising the gallantry of the Southern gentry in their fight against the 'tyranny' of the Federal government. The official newspaper of Napoleon III's regime, *Le Moniteur universel,* while critical of Lincoln and the Union, adopted a more moderate position reflecting the French government's declaration of neutrality in the conflict. Each newspaper thus interpreted the American Civil War in a different way. This research examines how these diverse interpretations—and by extension America's portrayal in the French press—were determined by domestic political considerations.

The three newspapers mentioned above were chosen because they represent the major political tendencies in France at the time. In order to compare their coverage of the Civil War, three significant events have been selected: the outbreak of the war after the bombardment of Fort Sumter on April 12, 1861; the battle of Gettysburg on July 1-3, 1863; and Lincoln's assassination on

April 14, 1865, a few days after General Lee's surrender at Appomattox Court House. This article first examines the state of the French press during the Second Empire. Articles from each newspaper are then analyzed, beginning with the outbreak of the war and proceeding chronologically. Special attention is given to the political and diplomatic context and its influence upon the positions of the newspapers. The content analysis concentrates on the images and stereotypes used to represent both camps to French readers. Finally, conclusions are drawn on the image of America in the French press and on the permanence of stereotypes in inter-national representations.

THE FRENCH PRESS IN THE EARLY 1860's

Among the despotic regimes of nineteenth-century France the Second Empire is perhaps the one which paid the closest attention to the press. On the very night of the December 2, 1851 coup, Louis-Napoleon Bonaparte ordered the police and the military to occupy the offices of the major Parisian newspapers.[1] A censorship bureau was quickly set up and the authorized press was placed under the close scrutiny of the Interior Ministry. In 1852 the regime passed a decree that established the new statute of the press. Among other strict regulations, newspapers had to pay a very high *droit de caution* (security deposit) as well as a tax of 6 centimes for each issue published.[2] A system of *avertissements* (warnings) was also established to keep journalists and editors in check.[3] If an article displeased the authorities, the newspaper was given a warning. After two warnings the newspaper was suspended for two months—a penalty that often proved financially fatal to the newspapers. A third warning brought about the closure of the newspaper. In addition to these repressive measures, the regime applied financial pressure by rewarding docile newspapers with subsidies, government subscriptions, or the authorization to publish administrative announcements.[4] The government also controlled the distribution of the news through the Havas press agency which served 307 newspapers in France with the telegraph. By means of heavy subsidies, the authorities encouraged Havas to publish the regime's propaganda, to transform or even to suppress news that was unfavorable to the Emperor or his government.[5] The regime's close scrutiny of the press was also exercised in France's regions where the *préfets* (government-appointed chief administrators) were ordered to send periodical reports on the press in their cities to the Paris Press Bureau.

After the December 2 Coup, Louis-Napoleon had inherited *Le Moniteur universel* as the official government newspaper. The authorities soon set about to reorganize it and turn it into an instrument of official propaganda. The price of each issue was lowered by two-thirds and some prominent writers were lured into writing articles for *Le Moniteur* in exchange for high honors or remunerations. Théophile Gautier, Auguste Sainte-Beuve, and Champfleury, to name a few, thus began to contribute regular articles to the newspaper.[6] Another source of prestige for *Le Moniteur* was the fact that as the official newspaper it had the exclusive right to publish government news and dispatches.

Le Moniteur's official statute, however, limited its efficiency as an instrument of propaganda. The authorities therefore decided to encourage the development of a non-official press, so long as it only published articles that were not critical of the regime. Of the various daily newspapers selected for that task, the most prominent was perhaps *Le Consitutionnel*. Directed by Doctor Véron and financed by Adolphe Thiers, *Le Consitutionnel* had been an Orleanist (moderate conservative) newspaper during the Second Republic (1848-1852). Thinking that it could easily be turned into a pro-government newspaper, Louis-Napoleon forced Véron to hire one of his ardent supporters, the journalist Granier de Cassagnac. Cassagnac had served as a *député* (representative) from the Antilles during the reign of Louis-Philippe (1830-1848) thanks to the support of the slave-owning French planters of the Antilles in whose defense he had written an essay called *De l'affranchissement des esclaves*. The 1848 Revolution and the Second Republic having frustrated his political ambitions, Cassagnac had become violently anti-republican. Once in power, Louis-Napoleon rewarded Cassagnac's support by finding him a job at *Le Consitutionnel*. Opposed to the strident tone of Cassagnac's articles, Véron sold the newspaper to a pro-Bonaparte businessman by the name of Mirès in 1852. By 1857, *Le Consitutionnel* was France's third largest newspaper with a distribution of 24,000 behind *La Presse* and *Le Siècle*.[7] *La Presse* and *Le Siècle* were opposition newspapers. That opposition, however, was only superficial since Napoleon could exert financial pressure on both newspapers through his cousin, Prince Napoleon, and his half-brother, the Duc de Morny, who owned large portions of their stocks. In addition Morny, who was Napoleon's *Ministre de l'Intérieur* (security minister), had many friends among the newspapers' other shareholders. It was Morny himself who had suggested to Napoleon to allow these newspapers to continue publication so long as their criticism remained moderate.[8] The year 1857 marked a turnaround for *La Presse* under the leadership of Auguste Nefftzer, a liberal journalist from the Alsace region. *La Presse* decided to express its opposition more openly by supporting republican candidates in the legislative elections. *Le Siècle* did likewise and both newspapers promptly received an avertissement from the authorities. Nefftzer was fired from *La Presse* and the paper also received a two-month suspension from which it never quite recovered. *Le Siècle* remained the only major opposition newspaper, but after that episode it became very cau-

tious in its opposition. In fact, Natalie Isser claims that the 'government came to regard *Le Siècle* as its own republican voice'.[9]

In 1859, Napoleon decided to loosen his control over the press. Many political prisoners were liberated, among them journalists who quickly became active again. Several opposition newspapers were created, others reappeared. Ever the champion of liberalism, Auguste Nefftzer seized the opportunity to create *Le Temps,* a newspaper that was soon to become the herald of the republican opposition.

In spite of the slight liberalization of Napoleon's regime in 1859, freedom of the press was still limited and opposition newspapers were forced to express their criticism of the regime in an indirect manner. As Case and Spencer explain, the press could—and often did—offer praise for the democratic regime in the United States.[10] A far away and little known country to most French people, the young American Republic constituted a 'safe' topic for the liberal press. Journalists could extol the values of democracy in America without having to fear reprisals from the imperial authorities. *Le Temps*'s praise and support for the United States government was to become even more vibrant as the very existence of the Republic was endangered by civil war and its capital threatened by General Lee. *Le Temps* would especially insist on the fact that the Confederates defended slavery and that such a cause was morally indefensible.

Unlike *Le Temps* and other opposition newspapers, the anti-republican press, Bonapartist and royalist, regarded the United States as the embodiment of a political regime they despised. When the American Republic was destabilized by the Confederate rebellion, the anti-republican press chose to support the Rebels who were trying to destroy—or at the very least weaken—the democratic regime in America. *Le Consitutionnel,* the leading anti-republican newspaper, completely ignored the question of slavery and placed the responsibility for the war on the Federal government which had, it argued, violated the Declaration of Independence by refusing to allow the Southern states to secede.[11] *Le Consitutionnel* would henceforth endeavor to prove that in spite of its claims the United States government was in fact undemocratic and that it was suppressing freedom.[12] By the same token the Confederates were to be portrayed as gallant heroes fighting to defend their country's freedom against Northern aggression.

The American Civil War thus became the focal point of a French political fight. As is often the case in similar situations, the view of America was to be considerably affected by the newspapers' political biases. Events and people would therefore be distorted so as to serve the needs of various political discourses.

THE OUTBREAK OF THE WAR

Three days after the bombardment of Fort Sumter by General Beauregard's Confederate troops on April 12, 1861, President Lincoln signed a decree for the drafting of 75,000 Union soldiers from the various state militias. The goal of this mobilization was to help the Federal army put down the rebellion and enforce the law in the Southern states. Jefferson Davis, President of the Confederacy, replied by hiring privateers to attack Union ships. On April 19 President Lincoln declared a blockade of Confederate harbors in retaliation.

News of the outbreak of hostilities reached France only on April 27. *Le Moniteur universel* was the first to announce the beginning of the war to its readers. On April 29, the newspaper published a commentary from its London correspondent which stressed the fact that the British deeply regretted the outbreak of the war. According to that correspondent, Britain's regret was augmented by Lincoln's alleged declaration to the effect that he was now free to reconquer Virginia. This observation evoked the image of a conquering and warlike Abraham Lincoln, which was to be used again and again in the anti-republican press. Another critical image of the United States government can be found in a *Moniteur* article on April 30. The newspaper commented on Jefferson Davis's use of privateers by stressing the irony of the fact that the United States government would be the first victim of that 'barbaric usage', which it was vainly asked to reject by the signatories of the Treaty of Paris. Further on the article derided the Monroe Doctrine as an 'alleged rule that the U.S. is the only country to observe'.[13] Both passages thus suggested the idea that the United States government did not play by the rules by which other civilized nations abided. In fact the word 'barbaric' was even used, evoking the stereotype of a semi-civilized country quite ready to use warfare methods from another age.

The criticism of the United States government was even more direct in *Le Constitutionnel*. In an article published on April 29th, the newspaper clearly accused Abraham Lincoln of being responsible for the war, of having prepared for it for a long time and having placed his partisans in all the key positions in the administration. The South had simply responded to Lincoln's hostility with resolve. The theme of Lincoln's aggressiveness was repeated in an April 30 article of *Le Constitutionnel,* which stressed the president's bellicose attitude, but omitted to explain that the first shots had in fact been fired by the Rebels. On May 7, a *Constitutionnel* columnist, Edouard Gaulhiac, published a long defense of the Confederacy on the front page of the newspaper. The article presented some of the major stereotypes that would be used by the newspaper throughout the war. Gaulhiac stressed the 'chivalrous conduct' of the Confederate troops during the attack on Fort Sumter. That conduct was contrasted with the bellicose tone of the New York press. Gaulhiac went even further by accusing Lincoln of having refused to let the U.S. Navy rescue Fort Sumter so as to make the war inevitable, thereby placing all the blame on the Rebels. Furthermore, Lincoln's decision to treat all privateers hired by the Confederacy as pirates was not only illegal, according to Gaulhiac, it was a repudiation of the Union's diplomatic tradition. Even King George III had not acted that way towards American patriots during the Revolution, he concluded. This argument once more depicted the U.S. government as a completely undemocratic one, acting in an uncivilized way. On the other hand, the columnist defended the South's use of privateers as an act of self-defense after the U.S. Navy had established a blockade of its ports. This argument was in fact erroneous, since the blockade was ordered by Lincoln in response to the use of privateers by Jefferson Davis, not the other way around. This may have been a simple mistake on Gaulhiac's part, but it is nevertheless reflective of the newspaper's attitude towards Lincoln. Gaulhiac also dismissed the slavery argument. The Federal government, he wrote, cared little about slaves who had very few friends in Washington. Stressing again the illegality of the Federal government's action, an article in the May 9 edition of *Le Constitutionnel* announced that Governor Ellis of North Carolina had refused to lend troops to the Union army because, according to him, the drafting of Federal troops to subjugate the Southern States, was 'a violation of the Constitution and an usurpation of power'. The article described several incidents reflecting the hostility of the population of various border states to the Union army.

These articles suggest that *Le Constitutionnel* was describing the Civil War as a conflict between Southern noblemen—by soul if not by birth—courageously defending their freedom and their country against the brutal aggression of a lawless and completely discredited Federal government.

As can be expected, *Le Temps* gave a very different interpretation of the situation. The outcome of the war would determine the credibility of the democratic regime which all French republicans hoped to see in France. Support for Lincoln was therefore essential. On May 1 *Le Temps* responded to the accusations made against Lincoln by the anti-democratic press in France. For the liberal newspaper the drafting of Federal troops was a legitimate action. *Le Temps* placed the entire responsibility for the War on South Carolina. In opposition to *Le Constitutionnel,* which stressed the lack of support for the Federal government in border states, *Le Temps* described the unanimity with which the Northern states supported Lincoln. As proof, *Le Temps* announced that the head of the Democratic opposition in Congress, Judge Stephen Douglas, had declared his unconditional support for the President. *Le Temps* also responded to the claim made by *Le Constitutionnel* that the situation of the Federal government was precarious since it was surrounded by unsupportive states. Citing Governor Curtin of Pennsylvania, *Le Temps* maintained that 100,000 Pennsylvania soldiers could be sent to defend Washington within 48 hours, should this become necessary.

The most dramatic article of the period was published on the front page of *Le Temps* on May 4. It was a letter that the newspaper's special correspondent in the U.S. had written on April 13, immediately after the bombardment of Fort Sumter. In a very emotional tone the journalist described the hope felt by all abolitionists now that the might of the Federal government was finally on their side. The abolitionist movement had not chosen violence, he wrote, violence had been forced upon them. Placing the responsibility for the war squarely on the Southern rebels, the author took up the challenge and declared that the partisans of liberty were ready to make any sacrifice for this most righteous of causes. A war for freedom, he continued, was better than participation in the horrors of slavery. Democracy would not be 'engulfed by Southern barbarity'. Finally, vowing to persevere in the fight for freedom, the correspondent declared: 'We shall not let any traitor, in the North or in the South, forget what the price of this struggle is, nor what the blood which is going to be shed is destined to redeem'.

The tone of this article was quite eloquent and very reminiscent of that of a preacher. Indeed the conflict was presented in religious terms: it was seen as a crusade against evil; blood would redeem the Union from its original sin.

THE BATTLE OF GETTYSBURG

Two years later the war had not turned to the Union's advantage. In late spring of 1863, after several victories, General Lee was preparing for the invasion of Pennsylvania with the Army of Northern Virginia, some 70,000 strong. Lee had several goals. First he wanted to relieve Virginia, hitherto the theater of many battles, by carrying the war to enemy territory. Such a move would have the additional advantage of boosting Southern morale. Lee also coveted the vast agricultural resources of Pennsylvania which his army so badly needed. Furthermore, the Confederate general hoped that once Pennsylvania had been conquered, he could push his troops through Maryland and cut off Washington from the North. Finally the Confederates hoped that a resounding victory over the Union would give them international recognition and might convince some European powers to abandon their neutrality. The stakes were high and their importance had not escaped Union strategists. Washington therefore sent the Army of the Potomac—93,000 strong—under the command of General Joseph

Hooker, to stop Lee.[14] The clash of the two armies occurred on July 1-3, 1863, a few miles south of the little town of Gettysburg.

In another part of the North American continent the year before, Napoleon III had sent French troops to occupy the port city of Vera Cruz in order to force the Mexican government to repay its debts. Britain and Spain initially took part in the invasion, but withdrew after a few months. Probably influenced by his most conservative and religious advisers, including Empress Eugenie herself, Napoleon III decided to take advantage of the temporary weakness of the United States to invade Mexico and set up a pro-French Roman Catholic regime that would balance the growing power of the U.S.[15] In June 1863 the French expeditionary forces entered Mexico City, but the Mexicans, under the leadership of President Benito Juarez, continued the fight against the French invaders. Eager to get French diplomatic and military support, the Confederate government hinted that it might ignore this violation of the Monroe Doctrine and accept the French presence in Mexico in exchange for French official recognition of the Confederate regime as a legal government. By July 1863 Napoleon III was beginning to show signs that he might be tempted by such a quid pro quo and abandon the neutral position that France had adopted until now, along with Britain. The tone of the Bonapartist newspapers in France became noticeably more favorable to the Confederates, reflecting the French diplomatic shift.

On July 2, as the battle was raging, *Le Moniteur* informed its readers of the imminence of the battle. On three columns published on the front page, the newspaper gave a detailed analysis of the tactics of both armies. The imperial newspaper refrained from taking sides overtly, but clearly indicated that it was Lee who had the initiative and that Federal troops were on the defensive. On July 14, *Le Moniteur* devoted another four columns of its front page to the situation in America. That article was more favorable to Lee and hailed his 'extreme audacity'. On the other hand, General Hooker's decision to withdraw the Army of the Potomac from its position in the Shenandoah Valley to defend Washington was deemed a 'grave mistake'.[16] *Le Moniteur* noted the 'apathy and lassitude' displayed by the population of the many cities conquered by the Confederates in Pennsylvania and Maryland. The article praised the impeccable conduct of Lee's troops and contrasted it with the brutal attitude of Northern troops, even on their own soil. For *Le Moniteur* the lack of hostility—and at times even the friendliness—displayed by the population of Pennsylvania and Maryland towards the Confederates was a bad omen for Washington. If Philadelphia was occupied, the population might side with the Rebels and make it impossible for Washington to pursue the war. Even in New York, the article concluded, the population appeared indifferent to the latest events.

On July 19, *Le Moniteur* published an article describing the situation in Baltimore, where a Confederate attack was expected. The article indicated that the Federal military authorities had declared martial law; it also described the resulting difficulties endured by the civilian populations. *Le Moniteur* suggested that in reality martial law had been declared to intimidate the population—which according to the newspaper was predominantly favorable to the South—rather than to face a real danger. Once more the imperial newspaper raised the image of a government rejected by the people and forced to resort to despotic measures to maintain its control. News of the battle was published on July 22. *Le Moniteur* gave a detailed account of the various phases of the battle and announced that Union forces, under the command of General George Meade had won. The article immediately mitigated that declaration by explaining that it was not so much a defeat for Lee as a 'failed attack', since the Southern general had always had the initiative and that his withdrawing army had not been pursued. In fact, the article explained, the Northern army had suffered as much as Lee's and was 'far less prepared for pursuit than the Rebels were for withdrawal'. In conclusion *Le Moniteur* announced that the Gettysburg victory had been received with complete indifference in New York. The newspaper again conjured up the image of a Federal government disavowed by its own citizens, emphasizing that despite the victory resistance to conscription continued and Washington was forced to raise the enrollment bonus in order to attract more volunteers.

On July 3, 1863, *Le Consitutionnel* announced Lee's invasion of Pennsylvania to its readers in a sarcastic tone. The conservative newspaper ridiculed the panic created in Philadelphia by what it described as a mere incursion by a small column of supply troops to gather fodder. Like *Le Moniteur*, *Le Consitutionnel* insisted on the Southern troops' 'scrupulous respect for the private property' of individual citizens and the complete apathy of the population of Pennsylvania towards the war. That theme was repeated in a July 8 article explaining that Federal troops were not greeted with enthusiasm anywhere. Similarly, *Le Consitutionnel* stressed the difficulty the Federal government had in recruiting soldiers. On July 9, it was even announced that two entire regiments from New Jersey had simply returned home because of the way they were treated by the population of Pennsylvania. The same article again contrasted the Southern soldiers' good conduct with the 'arson, plunder, and devastation' by which Northern soldiers usually distinguished themselves.

On July 10, *Le Consitutionnel* published an interesting article quoting Richmond newspapers. According to that article, these newspapers had declared that if it was in the 'interest' of the North to favor the Mexicans in their fight against Napoleon III, it was the 'solemn duty'

of the South to support the French. The choice of words in this article is interesting: the North, it said, was motivated by 'interest', whereas the South was bound by its 'solemn duty'. These words again evoked the stereotypes of the 'noble' Southerners and the 'interest-driven/ plutocratic' Northerners. *Le Constitutionnel* went even further in that article by suggesting that the North's support for Mexican president Benito Juarez made the Federal government the de facto enemy of France and, conversely, the Confederates her allies.

On July 13, the newspaper announced the replacement of General Hooker by General Meade and commented that such a major change in Northern ranks showed the complete confusion in the Union Army. A brief article on July 17 described the beginning of the battle and the movement of troops. On July 19 news of the Union victory finally reached *Le Constitutionnel*. The conservative newspaper refused to believe in Lee's defeat and conjured up another stereotype to discredit Washington's claims of victory. In order to properly assess the veracity of those claims, the article explained, one had to keep in mind that the Union's victory was announced on July 4. That date was the celebration of patriotism in the United States. On July 4 religious and political orators gave 'long-winded harangues' to 'overexcited masses'. In the most outrageous language they prophesied that the United States eagle would gain 'domination of the universe'. Thus the news from Washington had no credibility. As further proof, *Le Constitutionnel* explained, the previous year on that date, the fall of Richmond was announced in the North just as McClellan's army was being disastrously defeated on the banks of the James River (in the Seven Days' Battles around Richmond). This article raised the image of an arrogant and aggressive nationalistic America with imperialistic designs for world domination.

Finally on July 22, the outcome of the battle was quite clear and *Le Constitutionnel* curtly announced that since it was currently impossible to verify the Federal version of the battle, it would only publish Meade's report to Lincoln. No more mention of the battle of Gettysburg would be published by the newspaper.

The beginning of Lee's Pennsylvania campaign was announced by *Le Temps* on July 1. The article examined the movements of both armies and tried to determine their current positions. Contradicting *Le Moniteur* and *Le Temps* explained that Washington and Baltimore were in no danger and that the population of Pennsylvania would 'vigorously defend' the Susquehanna river and prevent Lee's troops from crossing it in order to attack Philadelphia. The article thus contradicted the anti-republican newspapers' portrayal of the population of Pennsylvania as apathetic or even hostile to the Union. *Le Temps* also gave a radically different image of Lee's soldiers. Whereas *Le Consitution-*

nel and *Le Moniteur* praised the Rebels' noble conduct, *Le Temps* insisted upon the devastation wreaked upon Pennsylvania by the invaders. With a lyrical tone the article bemoaned the 'generous blood' shed to vanquish the 'savage might' of slavery and prevent it from 'bringing anarchy upon a continent made for peace, prosperity and the greater development of human brotherhood'. *Le Temps* here contrasted two stereotypes: the savagery of Southern slavery and the peace and brotherhood of the Union. Contrary to the image given by the conservative newspapers, *Le Temps* insisted upon the profound division in the South where many Unionists wanted to take up arms against the Rebel government. With the help of 'thousands of deserters' these Unionists were in the process of forming armies. In a July 10 article entitled 'The Situation in the United States' André Cochut described the terrible economic conditions in the South and concluded that Lee's invasion of Pennsylvania was an attempt to remedy the various shortages in the Confederacy. The second half of that article appeared in the July 14 edition of *Le Temps*. It analyzed the various components of society in the South. A small but all-powerful oligarchy of slave-owners at the top controlled every aspect of life in the South. At the bottom was the slave population and in between, the largest section, the 'small whites', too poor to own slaves. To depict these poor whites Cochut conjured up a stereotype of 'half-savages' too proud to work, living in the countryside and surviving through 'hunting, fishing, and larceny'. Such a population, the journalist concluded, could never form a nation. Nor could the 'monstrous novelty' of a slave-empire become a reality, even if European powers tried to encourage it. The image of Southern atrocities was again used in a July 15 article. *Le Temps* announced to its readers that Lee's incursion was in fact a full-fledged invasion of Pennsylvania. The liberal newspapers explained that everywhere they went, Lee's soldiers kidnapped all colored freemen. Long columns of black women and children were thus driven back to the South along with all the goods looted in Pennsylvania. While those crimes were being committed, explained *Le Temps,* the Union army had not been inactive and General Meade's first measures had forced the Rebel army 'to leave the plains of Maryland and regroup in the mountains'. The Susquehanna valley was no longer threatened by the Confederate army which was 'withdrawing south, towards Carlisle'. A major clash was imminent in the area of Hannover and Gettysburg. *Le Temps* praised the valor of black regiments and contrasted the black soldiers' noble conduct to that of the Confederates', who 'have turned into children- and women-kidnappers'. Repeating the theme of Southern cruelty, *Le Temps* compared (General Lee to 'an ancient tyrant' since his victories always meant the enslavement of the people he defeated. On July 17 the republican newspaper announced to its readers that the Union had prevailed. The news was all the more credible, the article explained, since it was announced by the conservative newspapers themselves. On July 21, the Federal victory was certain, the Republic was safe. *Le Temps* stressed that it had been the first French newspaper to announce the Federal victory at Gettysburg. The good news from America boosted the morale of all French republicans who had been discouraged by so many Northern defeats. *Le Temps* castigated the 'prophets of doom' who had predicted the end of the United States and it declared its certainty about the final victory of democracy. The Federal government, it added, would forever have the 'imperishable glory of having freed a race, sustained a terrible war, defeated the evil designs of Europe, without ever, not even for one hour, stifling freedom under dictatorship'. The end of this article was in direct response to the anti-republican press's frequent argument that the American democracy could not face the crisis without turning into a dictatorship. Gettysburg had just proven that democracy was indeed strong enough to prosecute a war successfully without abandoning its fundamental respect for freedom and human rights. The cause of democracy all over the world, and in particular in France, was reinforced by the recent ordeal.

ABRAHAM LINCOLN'S ASSASSINATION

Although defeated at Gettysburg, Lee was still capable of defending the Confederacy. The war dragged on for another two years. At last, its economy in ruins, its troops decimated, and an ever increasing portion of its territory in Federal hands, the Confederacy was forced to capitulate after Lee's surrender at Appomattox Court House, on April 9, 1865. Five days later, on the evening of April 14, President Lincoln was assassinated by John Wilkes Booth. Secretary of State William Henry Seward was also targeted by one of Booth's co-conspirators, but miraculously survived. The news of the President's death reverberated throughout the nation and the rest of the world, causing dismay and sadness everywhere.

In 1865 Napoleon III and his ministers had given up any hope of victory for the Confederacy. Everyone knew that the Union would prevail and the French government was eager to get back into Washington's good graces. Paris feared that once the war was over, the U.S. government would be free to turn its attention to international affairs and especially to the French occupation of Mexico. In 1864 already many people had demonstrated in the North to protest against the French violation of the Monroe Doctrine.[17] Napoleon III was therefore trying to adopt a conciliatory attitude towards Washington.

This diplomatic shift was reflected in the imperial press. *Le Moniteur universel,* for instance, was now lauding the merits of Federal troops whose conduct in the South 'was worthy of the greatest praises'. This view was in sharp contrast with what the same newspaper had written about Union troops two years before.

The news of Lincoln's assassination was announced in *Le Moniteur* on April 28. The newspaper also reported, albeit erroneously, that Secretary of State Seward had been murdered by the conspirators. This was disastrous news for Napoleon, for Seward had adopted a moderate position about France's occupation of Mexico. David P. Crooke notes that Seward had assured France of U.S. neutrality on the Mexican question even after the end of the Civil War.[18] In spite of their hostility to the French invasion of Mexico and many official declarations to that effect, Lincoln and Seward had decided to maintain a neutral position in the conflict so long as the French themselves remained neutral in the American Civil War. Even in 1865, as the Union's victory appeared certain, Lincoln and Seward had no desire to launch into another war and preferred instead to settle the controversy through diplomatic means.[19] The announcement of Lincoln's and Seward's death meant the demise of the moderate faction in Washington and possibly the arrival of a new administration far less favorably inclined towards Paris. *Le Moniteur* called Lincoln's death an 'odious event' the gravity of which eclipsed all the good news that was coming from every front. On May 2 the Bonapartist newspaper described the mourning of the whole nation and expressed its faith in America's future. The American people, the article explained, had a deep faith in their institutions, and the death of any single man—admirable though he may have been—was only relatively important. Lincoln's greatest merit was 'the faithfulness with which he fulfilled the mandate given to him by his fellow citizens'. Such an expression of faith in the strength of the democratic system was surprising in the columns of Napoleon III's official newspaper. It can only be understood in the diplomatic context of the moment.

A similar attitude and tone can be observed in *Le Consitutionnel*. On April 27, the newspaper announced that the President had been assassinated by a 'demented secessionist' and that Vice-President Andrew Johnson had been sworn into office. The following day, the conservative newspaper published a more detailed account of the 'abominable actions'. *Le Consitutionnel* commented that Lincoln's last speech on April 11 was 'full of wise and conciliatory views towards the South'. Another article from the London correspondent of the Havas news agency described Booth as 'a talented actor' but 'a most dishonorable man devoid of any morality'. On April 29 Paulin Limayrac, the editor of the newspaper, wrote a front page tribute to the slain president. Limayrac expressed the pain and indignation caused by the 'horrible assassinations' among honest people throughout France and Europe regardless of their political opinions. Lincoln's death was a loss for the entire civilized world. Limayrac then listed the many qualities that everyone recognized in Lincoln: uprightness, honesty, and practical wisdom, but even more so, the president's greatest honor was in the moderation, benevolent

disposition, and conciliatory views he displayed at the very moment of victory.

As can be expected, Lee's surrender was treated with a lot of enthusiasm by *Le Temps*. Surrender was portrayed as the ultimate victory of the abolitionist cause and of the republican regime, which *Le Temps* had never ceased to champion even in the darkest hours of the war. The liberal newspaper therefore celebrated the victory of its cause with jubilation. On April 21, the New York correspondent of the newspaper, A. Le François, thanked his readers for their faithful and unremitting support even during the 'dark hours when the cause of the North seemed doomed'. Le François then paid a tribute to the American people who had never questioned the righteousness of their cause. The example of a 'great people saved by its faith in itself' must not, he continued, be lost on the French. 'When justice is on your side, when you feel you are going in the way of progress and civilization, the day must come when fate is defeated and when might is forced to serve right'. This message of hope to French republicans once more evoked the stereotype of America as the country of Liberty leading the rest of mankind towards progress and civilization. That important article covered three columns on the front page of the newspaper. In the following days, *Le Temps* published more details on the fall of Richmond and announced that shortly before the arrival of Federal troops, the city had been sacked by its own defenders, which reinforced the newspaper's repeated portrayal of Southern troops as a 'half-savage' rabble. On April 23, *Le Temps* joyfully announced that the first Federal troops to enter Richmond were black soldiers. The theme of Washington's magnanimity was again echoed on April 24. *Le Temps* indicated that Lee's soldiers had been allowed to return home with their hand weapons. The next day the republican newspaper dispelled the idea that a Southern guerrilla might continue fighting; the mass of the population, it explained, had been dragged into the war by a small group of rich slave-owners; no one would fight for them anymore. On April 26 *Le Temps* published a warning to all Southerners 'on this side of the ocean' and especially in England. Despite reassuring declarations from Lincoln and Seward, those 'who know their own wrongdoings' must be afraid. A socialist stereotype was used to describe the enemies of the Republic: 'Aristocratic England, the England of the governing classes is preoccupied'. Clearly this warning was directed at Napoleon III and his regime who, like England, had long favored the South. Analyzing reactions in England in another article, Le François observed that the working class masses had always supported the North.[20]

The news of Lincoln's death was announced by *Le Temps* on April 27. The commentary stressed the horror of that crime but also its uselessness since 'the United States' providential mission does not depend upon any single man and the freedom which created M. Lincoln and which he served, will find worthy successors'. The reference to the 'providential mission' was consistent with the religious tone the newspaper had been using to comment on the war since 1861, but it is also interesting because it showed that *Le Temps* was using the American 'auto-stereotype' of manifest destiny. The next day nearly the whole front page of *Le Temps* was devoted to Lincoln's death. On page 2 the newspaper described the president's humble origin. A child of the people, he had raised himself through 'intelligence, hard work, and probity'. This passage evoked another American 'auto-stereotype': the land of opportunity where a child from the most humble household can rise to the highest position.

Another theme treated in *Le Temps* in the context of Lincoln's death was that of the stability of the democratic regime. The president's assassination had not affected the democratic institutions of the country. America, the liberal newspaper explained on April 30, was the only country in the world where no single person could control the destiny of an entire nation. It was the country where instead of shouting 'the king is dead, long live the king!', people could shout 'a man is dead, long live the people!'.

Le Temps devoted four columns on its front page to the United States on May 2. Again the newspaper stressed the fact that the constitutional process had functioned normally despite the gravity of the situation. The tribute to Abraham Lincoln continued with veiled attacks against the French emperor as was often the case in *Le Temps*: the greatest tribute to Lincoln was the fact that, even though he came to power in a tormented time, he did nothing to make himself indispensable and that his death in no way threatened 'the [political] stability which is too often attached to the life of a single man'. *Le Temps* published a letter adressed to the President of the United States and signed by the publishers, editors, and journalists of *Le Temps, Le Siècle, L'Opinion nationale,* and *L'Avenir national.* The letter repeated now familiars themes as it praised the American Constitution for protecting democracy and establishing the reign of Liberty and the rule of law. The authors of the letter expressed their admiration for Abraham Lincoln, the 'great man of the people', who through hard work had 'reached his country's highest office and had remained a faithful servant of the law'. This last phrase was of course another attack against Napoleon III who, like Lincoln, had been a democratically elected president, but who had betrayed his mission in the 1851 coup. The letter concluded with a cry of victory: 'Slavery is dead, freedom shall never perish, the triumph of this great republic is assured!'. This was another instance of the liberal newspaper using American patriotic stereotypes.

The stereotypical images of the Confederacy and of Southerners are of lesser importance since any reference to that regime disappeared from the news after the Union victory. More interesting are the stereotypes used to describe the Federal government and the majority of the American population. Those stereotypes are either unfavorable or favorable. Among the unfavorable stereotypes the most common image that appeared in the press was that of a warlike and brutal government refusing to abide by the rules observed by the rest of the civilized world and behaving as a semi-barbaric power. Another frequent negative stereotype stressed the fact that the Federal government, despite its claims to the contrary, violated its own constitution and was in fact undemocratic, even illegal. Also criticized was the U.S. government's arrogance and imperialism, as revealed by its desire to spread its domination in the world. The American population was portrayed as a vastly apathetic mass, which could sometimes be aroused into chauvinistic frenzy by religious or political orators. Union soldiers were sometimes ridiculed as uniformed buffoons, but more often depicted as brutish rabble. Less frequently one also finds the stereotypes of an interest-driven government and of a racist population.

On the positive side, the most frequent stereotype was that of the champion of liberty and democracy. The cause of freedom for which the United States government was fighting was portrayed in religious terms as a crusade against evil. America was the City on a Hill, the support and the inspiration for democrats the world over. Linked with these images was the image of the stability and strength of the American constitution, which occurred frequently especially after Lincoln's assassination and the smooth transition to Andrew Johnson's presidency. Abraham Lincoln himself was the embodiment of another stereotype: that of the land of opportunity. The press stressed the slain president's humble origins as proof that in the U.S., through hard work and honesty even a working-class child could reach the highest office. Lincoln's determination and his military response to the Rebellion evoked the image of a firm and courageous leader. Finally the stereotype of the Great Democracy was brandished by the liberal newspaper as a threat to the ruling classes of the Old World.

The first observation one can make from this study is about the versatility of stereotypes which can often be used in a negative or a positive way depending upon the political tendency of the newspaper or the diplomatic context of the time. America's quasi-religious faith in its mission of liberation could also be interpreted as self-righteousness and zealotry by its enemies. Likewise the American people's desire to champion democracy throughout the world was—and continues to be—viewed as arrogance and imperialism by its detractors. Finally, what was belligerence and war-mongering for some was firmness and determination for others. The second observation is the permanence of the stereotypes. French newspapers in the past two or three years, whether they deal with the United States' policy on Iraq or Kosovo to name only two, have employed much of the same stereotypes as their predecessors over a century ago. Stereotypes are indeed useful tools for newspapers; they never become obsolete and they can very often be used to fit the newspapers' particular needs at any given moment. These observations tend to confirm the idea that politics plays a major role in the way the French perceive the United States. To the French the United States is a gigantic Rorschach test; its coverage in the press reveals at least as much about the French themselves as it does about Americans.

Notes

1. René Mazedier, *Histoire de la presse parisienne* (Paris, 1945), 117.

2. Ibid., 118.

3. Clyde Thogmartin, *The National Daily Press of France* (Birmingham, 1998), 60.

4. Natalie Isser, *The Second Empire and the Press* (The Hague, 1974), 14-15.

5. Ibid., 14.

6. Ibid., 19.

7. Ibid., 25.

8. Ibid., 26.

9. Ibid., 27.

10. Lynn M. Case & Warren M. Spencer, *The United States and France: Civil War Diplomacy* (U of Pennsylvania P, 1970), 40.

11. Ibid., 41-42.

12. Philippe Roger, *Rêves et cauchemars américains. Les Etats-Unis au miroir de l'opinion publique française (1945-1954)* (Presses universitaires du Septentrion, 1996), 30.

13. All translations are mine.

14. On June 28, 1863, three days before the battle of Gettysburg, President Lincoln named General George Meade as commander of the Army of the Potomac in replacement of Joseph Hooker.

15. Jean-Baptiste Duroselle, *La France et les Etats-Unis des origines à nos jours,* (Paris, 1976), 61-62. See also: Henry Blumenthal, *France and the United States. Their Diplomatic Relations 1789-1914* (New York, 1972), 107.

16. This piece of information was inaccurate, since Hooker's army was not in the Shenandoah Valley

in the first place; it had in fact remained east of the Blue Ridge Mountains, along the Rappahannock River, after it had been defeated by Lee at the battle of Chancellorsville earlier in May. Hooker had little choice but to move north and follow Lee's movement in order to protect Washington. As in the May 7, 1861, article in *Le Constitutionnel* about the Union naval blockade of Southern ports, it seems that in their zeal to criticize the North the conservative newspapers failed to verify the accuracy of their information or worse, were willing to distort the facts.

17. David P. Crooke, *The North, the South, and the Powers 1861-1865* (New York, 1974), 354.

18. Ibid., 358.

19. Blumenthal, op. cit. 111.

20. Even though the shortage of cotton brought about by the war had caused the closure of many textile factories and the laying-off of thousands of workers in Britain and in France.

Kathleen Diffley (essay date 2002)

SOURCE: Diffley, Kathleen. "Daily Emergency: Civil War Stories of the War Generation." In *To Live and Die: Collected Stories of the Civil War, 1861-1876,* edited by Kathleen Diffley, pp. 1-24. Durham, N.C.: Duke University Press, 2002.

[*In the following essay, an introduction to* To Live and Die, *an anthology of Civil War stories, Diffley provides an overview of Civil War stories published in American periodicals during the nineteenth century.*]

Dawn comes slowly to Charleston in April. When a storm threatens, as it did on the morning of April 12, 1861, freighted clouds make the darkness linger, though on that morning few people kept to their beds. At 3:20 A.M., Major John Anderson had received an official warning that Fort Sumter would be fired on within the hour. It was thus no surprise when a 10-inch shell flashed red against the night sky and cannon across the fortressed harbor began to boom. As dawn spread, the sky began filling with smoke, and from the shore it grew difficult to see how the fight was progressing. But on roofs and church steeples, in city streets and along the Battery, people crowded to watch the exploding shells, the embattled harbor, and the sudden spectacle of war. As "The House-Tops in Charleston during the Bombardment of Sumter" (frontispiece) reveals, they were themselves becoming part of a riveting scene, part of a national drama that was already underway.

For the next four years, it was a drama that newborn magazines were poised to share. With the resources to send artists to the field and the readership to ensure that many would see the smoke of battle secondhand, illustrated journals like *Harper's Weekly* quickly became mainstays on which anxious Americans came to rely. Before, during, and after the war's tumultuous events, magazines of various sorts continued to crop up and to find as willing an audience as Charleston's bombarded fort. When the special artists who later sketched battlefields and camp scenes, glory and longing, finally came home in 1865, *Harper's Weekly* would declare: "All over the country thousands and thousands of the faces and events which the war has made illustrious are tacked and pinned and posted upon the humblest walls."[1] So fetching was magazine artistry, in fact, that the dismay of Charleston's spectators is still palpable, even though the engraving testifies more to art department imagination than to the documented euphoria of the city's crowds. What magazines made sense of was the anxiety of their readers, who were often far from reported events. More than newspaper bulletins and broadside appeals, new weeklies and monthlies offered ways of seeing the war, in pictures and in prose, for growing numbers of subscribers who passed their pages along.

So when Daniel Aaron complained years ago that the Civil War was "unwritten," he was only partly right. True, there were plenty of personal accounts and memoirs, even a fair enough range of poetry, commentary, and latter-day fiction from William Faulkner and the Southern Agrarians to give Aaron's *The Unwritten War: American Writers and the Civil War* (1973) both reasonable heft and remarkable shelf life. What he lamented, however, was the absence of a transcendent American masterpiece, an epic with sufficient distance on Appomattox to enable scope, with sufficient ambition to ferret out the causes of the war, and with sufficient honesty to tackle race. The problem, countered Leslie Fiedler, was that Aaron was looking for the real war in all the wrong places and, arguably, all the wrong genres.

In his turn, Fiedler proposed an "inadvertent epic" running from Harriet Beecher Stowe through Thomas Dixon and D. W. Griffith and Margaret Mitchell to Alex Haley. His effort to recognize history's rumble in the groundswell of popular texts missed wartime responses, to be sure, but the resulting genre was boldly domestic, polyvocal, and engaged in tackling race head-on.[2] Fiedler's *The Inadvertent Epic: From "Uncle Tom's Cabin" to "Roots"* (1979) was intent on achieving scope across haunted time and "many hands," one sure way of tracking the Civil War's racial legacy beyond the constitutional abolition of slavery in 1865. And yet even his synthetic approach neglected the one right place for discovering what many Americans imagined while cannon were still hot and losses were piling up, the one right place for unearthing the alarms, misgivings, and settling purposes of wartime life, the one right

place that Stowe herself sought once *Uncle Tom's Cabin* was underway: namely, midcentury magazines.

Delving into these at last, *To Live and Die* retrieves thirty-one stories of secession and its aftermath, stories culled from the hundreds that circulated in popular magazines between the fall of Fort Sumter in 1861 and the celebration of the American Centennial in 1876. These were among the earliest efforts to make creative sense of domestic crisis, when first the war and then Reconstruction were still in progress. Assembled here, out of their original welter, they constitute what might be called an "inadvertent novel" of the times, a collective narrative that provides a first seismic reading of the war's upheaval. When stories published even after the war are arranged to plot the country's unfolding drama, as they are in the pages to come, the war they register is still close, still one of sudden confrontations, backwater misfortunes, and the peculiarities of ordinary dislocation that could be shared for the first time in print. As imaginative ventures, these stories favor exactly those "pedestrian details" that Aaron saw choking epic sublimity, but that readers may once again find catching them up in the wartime clash first seen from the housetops of Charleston.

In 1861, those housetops were alive with memories of the country's first war. Even New York's *Harper's Weekly* acknowledged the near revolutionary grounds on which Southern states would fight. "They are thoroughly persuaded that they are right, and that their cause is the cause of God and independence," the magazine editorialized just one page after Charleston's harbor view.[3] Across the years of war and rebuilding, the revolution's legacy remained a public preoccupation, so much so that Thomas Nast's double-page illustration for "The Nation's Birthday" in 1876 pictured Columbia as the "Teacher of Liberty" coupling the Declaration of Independence with the Emancipation Proclamation to spread the country's example throughout the world. Between the fall of Fort Sumter and the Centennial celebrations, between the Charleston housetops in 1861 and the country's lesson some fifteen years later, the revolution's legacy was strikingly reconceived in ways that the stories of *To Live and Die* illuminate.

At Gettysburg especially, both the lessons of war and the readiness to inscribe them were insistent. Not only were more magazine stories written about the three-day battle than any other, but the urge to commemorate the Confederacy's sharpest inroad and the Union's bravest rebuff led to a sculptural commission that helps to define a period of transformation. On July 1, 1869, exactly six years after the battle began, the Gettysburg Monument to the Union soldiers who fell was dedicated on the spot where Abraham Lincoln delivered his eloquent address. As *Harper's Weekly* noted when engraving a photograph of the occasion, the massive tribute to the "unknown dead" was large enough to include several allegorical figures.[4] At the monument's base were four statues representing War, History, Peace, and Plenty, as well as their gendered relations: the soldier appeared to tell the story of war to the muse of history, listening with "stylus" in hand, while the mechanic of peace seemed to join the goddess of plenty carrying the "fruits of the earth" (458). Above them rose a fifth statue representing the "Genius of Liberty," which was most immediately defined by the laurels of victory held in one hand and the sheathed sword of power held in the other, and yet that "colossal" figure significantly rested on its allegorical base. The commemorative message in 1869 was that liberty had been won through the force of arms but would be grounded on the force of words amid the peace and plenty that the occasion's spectators already enjoyed, a message that Lincoln's moving sense of "unfinished work" anticipated and this collection amplifies.

In *Harper's Weekly,* the dedicated monument retained some of its scaffolding, a useful reminder that the meaning of "liberty" was still under construction between 1861 and 1876, when stories of the war were first told. The figure of War also predominated in the magazine's engraving, where History was caught in shadow to the side and Peace with its Plenty was effectively hidden. That, too, can be significant for any effort to recollect how the war was initially seen, since its events were as insistent as the monument's soldier. For that reason, chronology and thus narrative setting in this collection are uppermost, rather than the dates of story publication and the peacetime negotiations that always seem out of sight just around the corner. Still, Pennsylvania's parochialism in recognizing only the Union dead has been set aside in these pages for a wider acknowledgment of the war's expense and its manifold opportunities. Because the stories in this volume come from literary magazines across the South and West as well as the culturally dominant Northeast, they trace a "real" war that ultimately joins Northern and Southern allegiances with a Western slant, that integrates battlefield and home front, that reckons fitfully but insistently with race, that points to the ascendancy of paramount national citizenship, and that marks a new colloquial vitality in prose. At Gettysburg, a muse with a stylus shadowed a soldier with a rifle to guarantee the foundations of American liberty, a vision that Daniel Aaron missed and that this inadvertent novel restores. Yet it is wise to remember that the story of an abolitionist parson in prewar Kansas that opens this volume was published in 1874, within weeks of the "true story" that closes the collection in the remembered words of an outspoken black cook. If the war's events are justifiably insistent, the social "progress" they suggested in the stories writers told was at best uncertain and tantalizing.

For many, the details of these recovered stories may be most striking in their idiosyncrasy, like the magazines from which the stories have come. The voices of the Civil War were diverse and clamorous, it turns out, especially when more regional publications came to jostle the general interest monthlies that were established just before the war began. Some of the periodicals that were filling with war stories are as familiar today as the *Atlantic Monthly* in Boston and *Harper's New Monthly Magazine* in New York, both founded during the 1850s. Others emerged in just such publishing centers but earned more fleeting reputations, like Boston's *Continental Monthly* (1862-1864), New York's *Galaxy* (1866-1878) and the revitalized *Putnam's* (1868-1870), and Philadelphia's *Lippincott's* (1868-1916). Still others spread across the country to challenge the commemorative sway of the Northeast: periodicals like the *New Eclectic* (1866-1868) in Richmond and then the *Southern Magazine* (1868-1875) in Baltimore, the *Southern Monthly* (1861-1862) in Memphis, the *Land We Love* (1866-1869) in Charlotte, the *Overland Monthly* (1868-1875) in San Francisco, the *Lakeside Monthly* (1869-1874) in Chicago, and Frederick Douglass's *New National Era* (1870-1874) in Washington, D.C. Less cosmopolitan writers in their pages noticed stranger people in messier places at odder moments: a pawnshop owner whose bombazine morning gown and grizzly beard in Chauncey Hickox's "Job and the Bug" only partly disguise his secret agenda, a Southern scout who hides with his buckhorn knife among the bullfrogs off an island in the Potomac in William H. Kemper's "The Sergeant's Little Story," a frontier regiment along the Gulf coast in Richard M. Sheppard's "Sentenced and Shot" that inches toward mutiny during the war's final months. Away from the time-honored battlefields of Virginia and the sheltered cottages of Massachusetts, theirs is a surreptitious war that the urban *Harper's Weekly* (1857-1916) just began to suggest, despite circulating far more stories to far more readers than any other magazine could claim.

It is fair to say that other collections might have been assembled to illustrate how the war generation responded to widespread disruption. If coverage and circulation ought to count for more than regional disparity in the statistical scale for example, then the sheer number of contributions to *Harper's Weekly* might have weighed more heavily when choices were made. In addition to on-the-scene reports, the magazine published more than a hundred Civil War stories, largely unsigned, before turning its attention and huge readership to other events after 1866. Many of these narratives concern matters that claim only a small part of *To Live and Die,* where guerrilla demands, mistaken casualty reports, family sacrifice, and substitute soldiers appear less often. Because *Harper's Weekly* on the eve of civil war had a subscriber list of well over one hundred thousand, and an audience of several times that number once issues read aloud were passed around, it is worth noting these recurring emphases. They reveal whose war more Americans were first invited to see. There is also the matter of brevity; in the shorter narratives that *Harper's Weekly* preferred, there was more outspoken opinion from a disproportionate number of Southern Unionists, lady teachers, soldier letters, and newspaper reports, which may simply underline the ready politics and brisk composition of a weekly news-magazine. By contrast, literary monthlies were distinctly less partisan, and they published better-crafted fiction whose greater length suggested a more complicated war and a better-heeled if less numerous reading public.

A different collection might also have arisen from the cultural life that was evidently shared across the Mason-Dixon line. No matter where magazines were published, there were plenty of unusual references that went unexplained in one story or another to suggest a ready knowledge that has since melted away, references to such things as Bob Ridleys, Shaker bonnets, Julien soup, the rebel cheat counties of West Virginia, jade-hoppers, and "sure enough" coffee. During a time when the Union and the Confederacy faced off at gunpoint, when the peace made at Appomattox was subsequently enforced through military districting and the reoccupation of the South, so common a culture raises intriguing questions. Who once sang "Ever of Thee" or "Her Bright Smile" or "Safe in the Kingdom" so regularly that a hymn title or a snatch of lyrics could jog the memories of readers without fuss? What cultural trafficking made Belshazzer, Mrs. Jarley's wax-work show, Alonzo and Imogen, Chang the giant, Bill Sling, Japan lilies, corn-dodgers, the waters of Marah, and the Ellsler twirl (for instance) a relatively simple and undeciphered stock-in-trade for mid-century writers on their way to national memory of the war? Another collection might be made from such things held in common, from secret society pins and shared watering holes, and from the cultural custodians whose bricks and straw came so readily and now so mysteriously to hand.

But the story of civil war as daily emergency and liberty's crucible showed up in literary magazines consistently, more than enough to upset easy distinctions between North and South, male and female, free and enslaved, even Standard English and unlettered dialect. When neglected regional journals are examined beside familiar sources, recollections of the war take on an intensity that prompts more significant questions. Until recently, for example, the distance between battlefields and cottages has tended to grow when historians have looked back to the Civil War. At the time, however, violence and sanctuary seemed much more entangled. In magazine stories, bushwhackers carry the war to the most out-of-the-way homesteads, spies work households from the inside, journeying paymasters rely on the kindness of border women, and soldiers turn out to

be girls. Ellen D. Larned's "Three Days of Terror" brings the New York draft riots and class-bound threat to the doors of Twenty-Second Street; Rebecca Harding Davis's "Ellen" shows what the open road of war-time removals means to an abandoned girl in search of her enlisted brother. The widespread dismay these stories reveal makes it harder to isolate the home front from blundering disaster and harder to detach captains, lieutenants, and civil servants from the amenities of home.

Further complicating the routine separation of gendered spheres is the narrative fate of slaves and their sporadic but undeniable claim on magazine readers after 1861, especially as the cries for liberty and justice gathered strength. *To Live and Die* opens with a prewar vigilante attack on the underground railroad and a Kansas parson in Henry King's "The Cabin at Pharaoh's Ford"; the collection ends with a black cook's loss of her remaining son in Mark Twain's "A True Story," a narrative sustained by dialect as a freedwoman speaks out where King's fugitives mutely slip away. Between silent exodus and personal joy in this patchwork novel, a poor white woman defends emancipation in "A Letter from the Country," a slave family abandons a Virginia plantation to follow the Union army in M. Shele De Vere's "The Freedman's Story," and a black private in "Buried Alive" climbs out of Fort Pillow's massacre of colored artillery troops and a living grave. That desperate soldier struggling to free himself anticipates Twain's resilient cook serving Union officers in a confiscated plantation kitchen, an image of Southern sanctuary blasted on behalf of newly paramount national liberties and the fresh promise of rights unhampered by race.

Ultimately, since most of these narratives are taken from literary magazines, they are about the evocative power of language as well as the particular ways in which the nineteenth century's colloquial verve took hold, even in the dialogue given once silent slaves. Some stories are comparatively bleak: in Ross Guffin's description of the Western war on smugglers in "A Night on the Mississippi," the escalating danger of a Union detail's trip to a snowbound island derives from a closely watched material world, where wisps of breath freeze instantly. Other stories turn suddenly comic: in Confederate Gray's "T. J.'s Cavalry Charge," a horse rolls over and a disheveled volunteer complains, "There now, won't Betsy give me particular fits!" Still others seem to run on sheer talk, like that of Twain's Aunt Rachel declaring, "Den I was just a-*bilin'*! Mad? I was jist a-*boomin'*!" As early as the 1860s, narratives like these chronicled a war whose hard surfaces and verbal rhythms would prevail in American fiction for years to come.

This is the world the storytellers made, and theirs was a mediated war that helped patch together a nation reconceived in liberty. It was a nation that readers could literally envision. At a time when special artists traveled with the armies and photographic operatives hauled costly equipment to nearby battlefields, representative patches were often pictures, at least on other magazine pages. Although short American fiction was not generally illustrated mid-century, a collective narrative like this one that recalls how the war was first seen deserves to be read as *Harper's Weekly* once was, for the pictures as well as the prose. Not surprisingly, those period pieces varied. Most were drawn for magazine publication by artists like Alfred Waud, Winslow Homer, Thomas Nast, and Frank Vizetelly, whose work reappears on the following pages. Some were alternately redrawn for the wood block from photographs, like "The Harvest of Death—Gettysburg" that here accompanies General John D. Imboden's account of the defeated Lee. But the wood engraving of the photograph's littered field misses the shock of Gettysburg's rotting corpses, because the art department combined three separate photographs, whose empty skies, lonely corpses, and abandoned detritus were not nearly as stark when recomposed as a single engraved view. Such mistranslation recurred when photographic landscapes, rather than simpler portraits, were engraved, and for that reason new wet collodion images competed at a disadvantage in wartime magazines. Because *To Live and Die* is attentive to magazine culture rather than to the new visual technologies that had not yet overturned art department habits, the war's startling photographs make as fitful an appearance in the following pages as they once did in the newsmagazines that favored cheap reproduction over silvered detail.

The more telling contrast in these selected illustrations should lie between the wartime images of *Harper's Weekly* and those of the *Illustrated London News,* which began its transatlantic coverage in the North. When artist-correspondent Frank Vizetelly sketched the Union rout at Bull Run in disturbing detail, however, he lost permission to travel with the Army of the Potomac; after waiting fruitlessly for a reprieve, he joined Confederate forces and covered the war for British readers from a Southern perspective. The engravings made from his sporadic drawings accompany some of the stories appearing here from Southern magazines or those set along the Potomac, generally stories first published without the pictures that most magazines could ill afford. More than once, as it happens, Vizetelly's view of the Confederacy actually graced the pages of *Harper's Weekly,* which printed his intercepted drawings while adding substitute prose. His eyewitness work for "Bursting of a Shell in the Streets of Charleston, South Carolina" appeared intact during January 1864, for example, but the Harpers merely credited "an English artist" after passing the drawing along to London, and they trimmed his inconvenient caption: "The Federals Shelling the City of Charleston—Shell Bursting in the Streets."[5] For Vizetelly, it was the independence of the Confederacy

and the liberty of Southerners that were under attack, as his later account of the siege for the *Cornhill Magazine* demonstrated. Neither of those concerns was glossed by the pirating *Harper's Weekly* when the "same" illustration appeared, a sign of how much prose can count in the war readers think they see.

How widely conflicting messages were once disseminated thus depends on the particular journals in which contributions were published and the particular agendas of journal editors, which had long intersected with public debates and market concerns in strikingly different ways. As far back as 1835, when President Jackson asked Congress to forbid the postal circulation of volatile abolitionist papers, William Lloyd Garrison had been outraged and Louis A. Godey must have shrugged. As editor of the weekly *Liberator* (1831-1865), Garrison had declared that he would be "as harsh as truth, and as uncompromising as justice" on the subject of slavery. He wanted his voice to be heard beyond the narrow streets of Boston, and he welcomed the slave insurrections and mob violence that white Southerners increasingly feared. Godey, by contrast, wanted the widest possible circulation for his *Lady's Book* (1830-1898), which was launched in Philadelphia and already on its way to reaching the 150,000 readers in the North, South, and West who would subscribe by the eve of the Civil War. For the "fair Ladies" to whom he appealed, Godey designed "a magazine of elegant literature," steadfastly sidestepping the kind of censorship that Garrison protested and that even Andrew Jackson could not finally turn into law.[6] As more literary journals began to appear around the country by midcentury, they ranged self-consciously along a political spectrum from zeal to serenity that Garrison and Godey had long since laid out.

Closest to Garrisonian agitation were the *Atlantic Monthly* and the *Continental Monthly,* both Boston journals that were founded on antislavery principles, though they were as different in literary circles as giant and dwarf. More agile and less stern were several magazines in New York: *Harper's Monthly* favored literary neutrality over the *Weekly*'s outspoken opinion, but both magazines were temperate "family" forums by Boston standards. *Putnam's* was more thoroughly committed to encouraging original literature and Republican policy in its postwar years, while the *Galaxy* sought greater vitality if less rectitude in promoting writers from across the emerging nation. Still, reconstructing Southerners found their warmest Northern reception in *Lippincott's,* a Philadelphia journal that willingly stepped in for the reticent *Godey's* to welcome ex-Confederates hoping to be paid for their work.[7]

That was scarcely an option in the South, during or after the war's devastation. The *Southern Monthly* flared early and boisterously in Memphis before disappearing when Union gunboats arrived, a fate that the *New Eclectic* avoided by assembling its often pirated pages in postwar Richmond and then moving to Baltimore. Greater originality, absorbing Charlotte's the *Land We Love,* and an upcoming affiliation with the new Southern Historical Society prompted a change of name to the *Southern Magazine,* but the journal's coffers were still not robust enough in the 1870s to compete with Northern pay. The lure of greater compensation in Boston also enticed editor Bret Harte away from San Francisco and the *Overland Monthly,* but he left behind a brash Western magazine that remained as alert to the peculiar echoes of upheaval as Chicago's *Lakeside Monthly* was to the war's odd ambivalences. By comparison, as the following pages reveal, the *New National Era* in the nation's capital was more attuned to shorter, anecdotal fare that gained dimension when published in Frederick Douglass's postwar journal for mainly freeborn blacks. Although the magazine's literary material was often copied from larger journals with greater resources and presumably white contributors, the snatches of narrative on Douglass's pages then appeared cheek by jowl with sharp political essays by black commentators whose editorial aims could also transform the way stories were read.[8] In the literary marketplace of the 1860s and 1870s, the lesson of Vizetelly's intercepted drawings is worth remembering since no reprinted and thus migrating story was ever quite the same.

Of course, stories migrated from magazine to magazine less often when established authors were paid for their contributions and competing editors respected such arrangements. Yet, between the attack on Fort Sumter and the end of Reconstruction, few better-paid American authors wrote Civil War stories. At $200 and more per contribution, Harriet Beecher Stowe was earning premium rates for submissions to the *Atlantic Monthly,* considerably more than the $300 she had received for serializing *Uncle Tom's Cabin* in the *National Era* (1851-1852). During the 1860s, however, Stowe was more drawn to spiritual grace and serialized *Agnes of Sorrento* in the *Atlantic* (1861-1862); thereafter, she wrote about ministers and oldtown folks, chimney corners and home papers, Sojourner Truth and Lady Byron, but infrequently about the war. Similarly, *Putnam's* paid Herman Melville the magazine's highest rate in the 1850s, $5 per printed page for stories like "Benito Cereno," up from the $3 that other writers received. But in the 1860s, Melville turned from fiction to the poetry that appeared occasionally in *Harper's Monthly* before being published as *Battle-Pieces and Aspects of the War* in 1866.

At about that time, the *Galaxy* commissioned Walt Whitman's "Carol of Harvest for 1867," a poem about the war's passing blue-clad armies that the magazine paid $60 to publish in September of that year; with similar largesse, the *Galaxy* also brought out Whitman's essays "Democracy" (December 1867) and "Personalism" (May 1868), which would become the better part of *Democratic Vistas* by 1871. In these several genres and throughout the postwar years, Whitman called upon his experiences as a wartime nurse, but he had left short fiction behind with the temperance tales of "Walter Whitman" in the 1840s. Nathaniel Hawthorne, who died in 1864, contributed an essay entitled "Chiefly about War Matters" (July 1862), for which the *Atlantic Monthly* was pleased to pay top dollar and then double that figure for the essays on contemporary English life that Hawthorne submitted after wartime inflation pushed rates up in 1863.[9] Hawthorne, Whitman, Melville, and Stowe had all written earlier stories as the antebellum genre evolved, but none of them contributed Civil War stories to the magazines of the 1860s and 1870s. By then, reputations were more often in the making as short war fiction first began to appear, and lower "tyro" rates for newcomers plus the pressure of hasty promises and subsequent book publication meant that Civil War stories could still be read more than once and in substantially different contexts.

A handful of authors on the cusp of national reputation may reveal how protean midcentury tyros could be, how elusive name recognition was for many, and how much more context could count when their stories were read. Rebecca Harding Davis, for example, had only begun her magazine career when "Ellen" (*Atlantic Monthly,* July 1865) was published, after the lively success of her now classic "Life in the Iron Mills" revealed Wheeling's factory conditions to the *Atlantic*'s readers in 1861. During the magazine's war years, Davis contributed several remarkable home front stories while also writing headlong and near anonymously for *Peterson's,* a Philadelphia women's magazine that had topped the circulation of rival *Godey's* by the time war was declared. In July 1863, an earlier version of "Ellen" appeared in *Peterson's* as part of an issue that opened with plenty of engravings (of a lace cape, a "senorita dress," hair styles, and children's fashions), as well as sheet music for Alice Hawthorne's "Yes, I Would the War Were Over" and patterns for a handkerchief border. Davis would later insist that this first submission was a fictionalized version of the incidents she then retooled for Boston publication, but the story of a trusting sister who seeks an Ohio regiment in the fractious border country south of Wheeling was close enough to look like plagiarism to the editors of the *Atlantic Monthly* before matters were resolved. When the revised "Ellen" was linked in their prestigious pages to "the author of 'Life in the Iron-Mills'" and surrounded in 1865 by contributions written with greater care, such as John G. Whittier's poem "The Changeling" and Bayard Taylor's "Winter Life in St. Petersburg," the refashioned narrative seemed purposely fragmentary, its addled heroine disturbing, and Davis's story of the war's first months entirely different in its import.[10] Like wandering women on subsequent magazine roads, this later Ellen is led into a world of bewildering uncertainty and a twice-told story of unraveling narrative guarantees far from the *Peterson's* reassurance of ready-made patterns.

By comparison, Louisa May Alcott's hospital ward in "The Brothers" (*Atlantic Monthly,* November 1863) is orderly, feminized, and recuperative, though her wartime scene offers less of the familial reassurances to come in *Little Women* (1868-1869) and more of the unsettling logic that Alcott gave her early, pseudonymous stories for less distinguished magazines. The reason became clearer after the author's postwar rise to fame, when "The Brothers" was reprinted with her *Hospital Sketches* in 1869 and retitled "My Contraband." In both versions of the story, Alcott pits Northern principle against Southern transgression by pitting a slave soldier against his master and half-brother. But where her earlier title emphasizes familial and then sectional clash, which is narratively resolved when the colored 54th Massachusetts assaults Fort Wagner, "My Contraband" as a title foregrounds the story's unexpected triptych, the "mistress" inserted between the two brothers, and therefore what Elizabeth Young terms a shift "from male injury to female healing."[11] Where Davis points to the shared blood that holds families together in precarious times, Alcott takes the violated safety of slave cabins as fundamental, with almost as much national consequence in the *Atlantic Monthly* as a white nurse's gentle hand. The bad blood of reckless plantations suited the abolitionist cause that put a liberty cap on the magazine's rippling banner in 1865, but the migrating story's later title and the postwar volume's recurring hospital nurses indicate who was gently angling to assume the Southern master's authority.

Outside the *Atlantic Monthly,* it was certainly possible to achieve professional success without the hurried writing for which both Davis and Alcott got paid, but it was that much harder to make a living and particularly so for Southerners, no matter how often their work appeared in print. Richard Malcolm Johnston published his first tale of rural Georgia life in a New York sporting journal called *Porter's Spirit of the Times* (December 1857). He then collected the tale with three more for Augusta publication as *Georgia Sketches* (1864), reworked these and wrote others for Baltimore's *New Eclectic* (1869-1870) and the *Southern Magazine* (1871-1872), and collected these again in several arrangements as the *Dukesborough Tales* (1871, 1874), published likewise in Baltimore. But only after New York's *Scribner's Monthly* began accepting his stories in 1879 did he sign his own name and receive any recompense, and only after sixteen migrating stories were collected yet again by Harper Brothers in 1883 did he become a national sensation. In this wayward saga, "Mr. Williamson Slippey and His Salt" (*New Eclectic,* October 1870)

was sometimes quietly ignored; it was the only story set as late as the Civil War and as far from central Georgia eccentricity as commercial Atlanta, peculiarities skewing the otherwise affable sketches that were picked up in the North more readily.[12]

Not that earlier fame would necessarily have helped. While Johnston was scraping together a living, Mark Twain was already much better known. At $20 per printed page, he was also much better rewarded when "A True Story" first appeared in the *Atlantic Monthly* (November 1874). That was actually the problem. Twain's reputation for humor so influenced reviews of his subsequent *Sketches, New and Old* (1875) that *Atlantic* editor and reviewer William Dean Howells felt he had to rescue the story of Aunt Rachel from misreading. Well before *Huckleberry Finn* was excerpted in the *Century* (1884-1885) and *Pudd'nhead Wilson* was serialized in the same magazine (1893-1894), Twain signaled his unanticipated moral reckoning by republishing "A True Story" with "Facts Concerning the Recent Carnival of Crime in Connecticut" (1877), a more serious companion in a volume advertising the stately Little Classics series and the smaller Vest-Pocket Series that circulated such writers as Emerson, Whittier, and Hawthorne.[13] As both Johnston and Twain discovered, the impact of any migrating story had a great deal to do with the company it kept, the same lesson that Davis and Alcott had learned by heart.

These four tyros were not the only members of a new literary generation to write about wartime crisis, and even their later celebrity is not reason enough by itself to include their stories in a volume of the war's first literary traces. After all, Henry James published several Civil War stories in the *Atlantic Monthly,* as did John W. De Forest and Rose Terry. But James's interest in detailed psychological study makes his war narratives as inert as his war heroes and as coolly removed from events. Instead, it was magazine unknowns such as William H. Kemper and Richmond Wolcott who acknowledged the desperate times that more willing volunteers could not escape. De Forest's short fiction, which also appeared in *Harper's Monthly* and the *Galaxy,* has the snap of Fred B. Perkins's story about Wall Street speculators or the otherworldly appeal of the *New National Era*'s "Believe in Ghosts!" But his attention often focuses on Reconstruction's complexities rather than the war's intrusions. Rose Terry reveals how distant the war could seem when its events figure so peripherally in the domestic life of her New England characters, a useful reminder but one that does not touch the challenge Daniel Aaron raised or mitigate the tumbling immediacy of war in narratives from less touted authors or in less predictable magazines. Although some of the war's first stories migrate once again anonymously in the following pages, where forgotten writers like Chauncey Hickox and Ellen D. Larned are about as opaque as "Izilda" and "Confederate Gray," it is worth remembering that Twain himself was so unfamiliar to the Eastern audiences devouring magazines in the 1860s that *Harper's Monthly* attributed his first published submission to "Mark Swain."

For magazine subscribers, Civil War stories were usually less about their authors than about their settings, especially when editorial policy could make periodical fare less attributable to individuals than to magazines. *Harper's Weekly,* the *New National Era,* and many of the Southern journals specifically resisted crediting authors; even magazines that did help build reputations would not often describe the little-known American contributors of short fiction and would sometimes delay revealing their names until issues were bound with a table of contents. Consequently, regimental veterans who had never written much magazine fiction could revise firsthand accounts with some marketplace success, but they could not always be distinguished from the publishing authors who relied on news bulletins or the occasional contributors who remain unfamiliar to this day. In magazine prose shaped by both inherited conventions and unanticipated events, by readerly expectations and wartime loss, it was less particular tellers than particular tales that helped make the war make sense. Above all, it was the narrative practice of entangling invention and evidence that counted when events were raw and that counts again as *To Live and Die* recalls the war's rough chronology.

Traditionally, because most readers and editors lived in the East, the war's story begins with the election of Abraham Lincoln, the secession of Southern states, and the firing on Fort Sumter, when the war's big guns first rolled into play. The clash of arms in the battles that followed is for many synonymous with the Civil War, and the distant smoke of military engagement is still as riveting as it once was for the citizens of Charleston on their housetops. As Gary Gallagher has observed, battlefield news was eagerly consumed throughout the war, a good reason now to privilege what Gallagher sees as "the vital ways in which military events influenced the homefront."[14] So the trajectory of the war in *To Live and Die* is also defined by its unfolding battles: the sudden rout at Bull Run in 1861, the unexpected expense of Antietam in 1862, Pickett's frontal assault at Gettysburg in 1863, and Spotsylvania's nighttime offensive in 1864.

But where war correspondents hammered out newspaper copy with summary leads and thus breaking information, contemporary magazines told battle stories with a more protracted difference: Chauncey Hickox's "Job and the Bug" arrives at the road to Bull Run through the Washington miasma of doubtful allegiances and the pawnshop suspicions of a ragtag boatman's son; "On the Antietam" follows part of a Union regiment to a ne-

glected corner of the Maryland field. Stories with a further difference arise from the Southern perspective on such engagements, the martial euphoria that sends Confederate regiments to Virginia in Izilda's "A True and Simple Tale of '61" and the hasty ride that sends a rebel courier out of Maryland in Kemper's "The Sergeant's Little Story." The later Confederate drive into Pennsylvania can also be recalled contrapuntally: the panoply of Pickett's charge when seen by Union soldiers along Cemetery Ridge in "The Fourteenth at Gettysburg" gives way to the logistical nightmare of spiriting Lee's army trains south in General Imboden's "Lee at Gettysburg." If Davis's "Ellen" is twice-told in mid-century literary magazines, the war's military trajectory is double-voiced there and in the pages to come.

Such a pairing of stories is most revealing when the damaged, rain-swept Spotsylvania of "A Night in the Wilderness" is read against the light-hearted Western skirmishing of Richmond Wolcott's Shiloh in "Hopeful Tackett—His Mark," both exceptions that prove a curious narrative rule. No matter what slaughter took place on Eastern battlefields, the stories told about them tend to follow heroic soldiers; no matter how essential the war in the West was to eventual Union victory, its stories tend to be ruthless, lowdown, and closer to damaged homes, even in this collection. And yet, exactly the opposite happens in these paired stories. What makes "A Night in the Wilderness" unforgettable are the "bodies chopped and hacked by balls" that litter the grim Virginia woods, as they did the Gettysburg plain in photographer Timothy O'Sullivan's "Harvest of Death" and the Antietam cornfields that witnessed the single bloodiest day in American military history. Yet magazine stories about Gettysburg and Antietam regularly substituted tidier landscapes and just as regularly transferred the war's unnerving brutality to Kansas cabins, Missouri bushwhackers, Mississippi smuggling, Tennessee massacre, or Louisiana mutiny. The practice persisted even when magazines in Chicago and San Francisco began publishing war stories after Confederate forces admitted defeat. Although all of these portraits of a Western war are authentic, it is also true that the Tennessee battle at Shiloh church ended the war's first year with staggering casualties, and yet Hopeful Tackett volunteers to fight for the star-spangled "banger" like many other Northerners without shoulder straps. One explanation may be that Wolcott's story appeared in Boston's *Continental Monthly* just a few months after the battle while the war was still in progress; it is also worth noting that Massachusetts regiments and the magazine's abolitionist readers paid far less of the cost for Western victory than Wolcott's own 10th Illinois. By contrast, "A Night in the Wilderness" was published after the war in the less ideological *Galaxy,* where Spotsylvania's grueling attack could become part of Grant's Western "butchery" as he approached Richmond.

At the very least, magazine storytelling consistently suggests that it matters who was telling which story when and to whom, matters enough in this collection to augment the paired stories of battlefield clash with the troubling stories of home gone wrong that befuddle traditional tallies of victory and defeat. Shifting perspective makes the fall of New Orleans in April 1862 both the whopping opportunity of New York merchants in Perkins's "Thomas Elliott's Speculations" (*Harper's Monthly*, February 1863) and the disquieting hint in Nora Perry's "Mrs. F.'s Waiting Maid" (*Harper's Monthly*, June 1867) of an occupied people's resistance well into Reconstruction. Female soldiers, prison despair, draft riots, and slave family migrations all once prompted stories that further defamiliarize a conventional military narrative by insisting on the war's relentless intrusions. Instead of Lincoln's house divided, what emerged in the ongoing magazine war was a house invaded, sometimes comically. In Richmond, a confidential secretary in Edward Everett Hale's "The Skeleton in the Closet" learns that the discarded hoopskirts of his womenfolk have tripped couriers, clogged gunboats, and worse, much worse. More often, however, such stories suggest the war's permanent wounds, like the amputations in Silas Weir Mitchell's "The Case of George Dedlow" or the lingering malice of the Old Dominion in "Believe in Ghosts!" Gathering urgency in postwar magazines, the figure of the house invaded reveals both an abiding Victorian conservatism and a sharp Reconstructive break with the founding premises of the country's Constitution.

The fundamental and yet half-hidden significance of race in the magazine world of *To Live and Die* is finally worth confirming and is actually part of the book's title, which inaugurates this collection's inadvertent plot in much the same way that Lincoln's inauguration in 1861 hurried the events of the war. The line comes from the minstrel song "Dixie," which was written in the antebellum North and appropriated by the wartime South after its popularity spread across the country. "Dixie" was so widely sung, in fact, that Lincoln requested the band to play it when he heard that Lee had surrendered at Appomattox. More recently, thanks to the research of Howard L. Sacks and Judith Rose Sacks for *Way Up North in Dixie*, it has become clearer that the song emerged in rural Ohio, where the black Snowden family made music and where minstrel Dan Emmett first heard the jingle of notes and colloquial longing that would forever be part of his legend.[15]

All three claims to "Dixie," from the minstrel North and the wartime South as well as a black oral tradition long ignored, suggest the braiding preoccupations of this volume, whose stories stretch from abolition to assassination, from Boston to San Francisco, from wedding parties to mangled corpses, and from state glory to national citizenship. Their unfolding plot rightly ends after the armies disbanded and rightly begins during the 1850s in the Western territories, as the *Overland Monthly* once persuasively demonstrated. Taking its cue from regional challenge, then, this patchwork novel opens in Kansas, where relocating Northerners, Southerners, and slaves first stake their claims on national destiny and first discover at Parson Brewster's "ark" who would live and who would die.

Notes

1. *Harper's Weekly* (3 June 1865): 339.

2. Fiedler began *The Inadvertent Epic: From "Uncle Tom's Cabin" to "Roots"* (New York: Simon and Schuster, 1979) with a determination to rescue Stowe's best-selling novel from the literary critics and aesthetic judgments that Aaron valued, particularly when measuring "artistic creativeness" in *The Unwritten War: American Writers and the Civil War* (1973; rpt. Madison: University of Wisconsin Press, 1987). Edmund Wilson ranged more widely in *Patriotic Gore: Studies in the Literature of the American Civil War* (1962; rpt. New York: Norton, 1994), a substantial volume that considers diaries and journals as well as more public texts; but Wilson's attention to prose style and literary endeavor tends to favor a thoughtful few, much like George M. Fredrickson's *The Inner Civil War: Northern Intellectuals and the Crisis of the Union* (1965; rpt. Urbana: University of Illinois Press, 1993). More recently, Fiedler's challenge to reconsider popular reading habits has been taken up in my own *Where My Heart Is Turning Ever: Civil War Stories and Constitutional Reform, 1861-1876* (Athens: University of Georgia Press, 1992), as well as by scholars like Jim Cullen in *The Civil War in Popular Culture: A Reusable Past* (Washington, DC: Smithsonian Institution Press, 1995), Elizabeth Young in *Disarming the Nation: Women's Writing and the American Civil War* (Chicago: University of Chicago Press, 1999), and Alice Fahs in "The Feminized Civil War: Gender, Northern Popular Literature, and the Memory of the War, 1861-1900," *Journal of American History* 85 (March 1999): 1461-94, and *The Imagined Civil War: Popular Literature of the North and South, 1861-1865* (Chapel Hill: University of North Carolina Press, 2001). All of these studies are more cordial to what Robert A. Lively once called "the mass product" in *Fiction Fights the Civil War: An Unfinished Chapter in the Literary History of the American People* (Chapel Hill: University of North Carolina Press, 1957), his survey of 512 Civil War novels.

3. "The War," *Harper's Weekly* (4 May 1861): 274. The vista from "The House-Tops in Charleston during the Bombardment of Sumter" appeared on

the issue's cover and was the magazine's first view of the outbreak of hostilities.

4. "The Gettysburg Monument," *Harper's Weekly* (17 July 1869): 458. The several pages devoted to the festivities that Theodore R. Davis sketched for the magazine include engravings of "relic-seekers" and the "Gettysburg Spring Hotel" that suggest how quickly the battlefield became a Civil War mecca.

5. See *Harper's Weekly* (9 January 1864): 15, as well as the *Illustrated London News* (5 December 1863): 561, and Vizetelly's later account of the Union siege in "Charleston under Fire," *Cornhill Magazine* 10 (July 1864): 99-110. The best discussion of Vizetelly's venture into the Confederacy remains W. Stanley Hoole, *Vizetelly Covers the Confederacy* (Tuscaloosa, AL: Confederate Publishing, 1957), 19-48. See, too, William P. Campbell, *The Civil War: A Centennial Exhibition of Eyewitness Drawings* (Washington, DC: National Gallery of Art, 1961), especially 11-13, 29, 36-39, 43, 51, 53, 61, 80, 107, 134-38; and my "'Musquitos,' Rattlesnakes, and Perspiration: The Civil War's Special Artist for the *Illustrated London News*," *Books at Iowa* 63 (November 1995): 3-13.

6. The contested use of the mails during 1835 is thoughtfully considered in Richard R. John, *Spreading the News: The American Postal System from Franklin to Morse* (Cambridge, MA: Harvard University Press, 1995), 257-83; Donna Lee Dickerson, *The Course of Tolerance: Freedom of the Press in Nineteenth-Century America* (New York: Greenwood, 1990), 81-113; and W. Sherman Savage, *The Controversy over the Distribution of Abolition Literature, 1830-1860* (Washington, DC: Association for the Study of Negro Life and History, 1938), 9-81. For Garrison's editorial policies and the *Liberator*'s strategic function in the fight against slavery, see Robert A. Fanuzzi, "'The Organ of an Individual': William Lloyd Garrison and the *Liberator*," *Prospects* 23 (1998): 107-27; David Paul Nord, "Tocqueville, Garrison, and the Perfection of Journalism," *Journalism History* 13 (summer 1986): 56-63, and his sketch in the *Dictionary of Literary Biography* 43 (1985): 232-47; Donald M. Jacobs, "William Lloyd Garrison's *Liberator* and Boston's Blacks, 1830-1865," *New England Quarterly* 44 (1971): 259-77; and Frank Luther Mott, *A History of American Magazines* (Cambridge, MA: Harvard University Press, 1938-1968), 2: 275-96. Garrison's own declaration appears in "To the Public," *Liberator* (1 January 1831): 1, and the remarks on Godey's *Lady's Book* were made by Sarah Josepha Hale in "Louis A. Godey," *Godey's*

(February 1850): 87. For an overview of that magazine during its early years, see Isabelle Lehuu, "Sentimental Figures: Reading *Godey's Lady's Book* in Antebellum America," in Shirley Samuels, ed., *The Culture of Sentiment: Race, Gender, and Sentimentality in Nineteenth-Century America* (New York: Oxford University Press, 1992), 73-91, as well as her *Carnival on the Page: Popular Print Media in Antebellum America* (Chapel Hill: University of North Carolina Press, 2000), 102-25; Edward H. Sewell Jr., "Louis A. Godey," *DLB* 73 (1988): 139-45; Allison Bulsterbaum's sketch in Edward E. Chielens, ed., *American Literary Magazines: The Eighteenth and Nineteenth Centuries* (Westport, CT: Greenwood, 1986), 144-50; Mott, *A History of American Magazines,* 1: 580-94; and Lawrence Martin, "The Genesis of *Godey's Lady's Book*," *New England Quarterly* 1 (1928): 41-70. For persuasive arguments that "a magazine of elegant literature" was nonetheless politically charged, see Amy Kaplan, "Manifest Domesticity," *American Literature* 70 (1998): 581-606; and Patricia Okker, *Our Sister Editors: Sarah J. Hale and the Tradition of Nineteenth-Century American Women Editors* (Athens: University of Georgia Press, 1995), 38-58.

7. For detailed coverage of all these magazines, see Diffley, *Where My Heart Is Turning Ever,* xxi-xlii. More specifically, for discussions of Boston's *Atlantic Monthly,* whose circulation high in 1866 surpassed fifty thousand, see Ellery Sedgwick, *The Atlantic Monthly: Yankee Humanism at High Tide and Ebb* (Amherst: University of Massachusetts Press, 1994), especially 68-159, and "The Atlantic Monthly," in Chielens, *American Literary Magazines,* 50-57; Louis J. Budd, "Howells, the *Atlantic Monthly,* and Republicanism," *American Literature* 24 (1952): 139-56; and Mott, *A History of American Magazines,* 2: 493-515. For the *Continental Monthly,* whose unspecified circulation was comparatively small, see Mott, *A History of American Magazines,* 2: 540-43.

Useful treatments of New York's *Harper's Monthly* appear in Sheila Post-Lauria, "Magazine Practices and Melville's *Israel Potter*," in Kenneth M. Price and Susan Belasco Smith, eds., *Periodical Literature in Nineteenth-Century America* (Charlottesville: University Press of Virginia, 1995), 115-32; my "Home on the Range: Turner, Slavery, and the Landscape Illustrations in *Harper's New Monthly Magazine,* 1861-1876," *Prospects* 14 (1989): 175-202; Barbara M. Perkins's sketch in Chielens, *American Literary Magazines,* 166-71; Eugene Exman, *The House of Harper: One Hundred and Fifty Years of Publishing* (New York: Harper and Row, 1967), 69-79; and Mott, *A*

History of American Magazines, 2:383-405, which notes that by 1864 the magazine's circulation had returned to its prewar high of about two hundred thousand. For *Harper's Weekly,* see Andrea G. Pearson, "*Frank Leslie's Illustrated Newspaper* and *Harper's Weekly*: Innovation and Imitation in Nineteenth-Century American Periodical Reporting," *Journal of Popular Culture* 23 (1990): 81-111; Exman, *The House of Harper,* 80-93; and Mott, *A History of American Magazines,* 2: 469-87, where the magazine's circulation is said to have reached 160,000 by 1872. Useful information about *Putnam's* may be found in Ezra Greenspan, *George Palmer Putnam: Representative American Publisher* (University Park: Pennsylvania State University Press, 2000), especially ch. 12, "G. P. Putnam and Sons (and Daughters), 1867-72," where Greenspan corrects Mott's error to set average circulation at twelve thousand to fifteen thousand; also see Post-Lauria, "Magazine Practices"; Kent Ljungquist, "*Putnam's Monthly Magazine,*" in Chielens, *American Literary Magazines,* 328-33; and Mott, *A History of American Magazines,* 2:428-30. The *Galaxy* achieved a circulation high of over twenty-three thousand in 1871, according to Chielens's sketch in *American Literary Magazines,* 139-44; for additional coverage, see Robert J. Skolnick, "The *Galaxy* and American Democratic Culture, 1866-1878," *Journal of American Studies* 16 (1982): 69-80; Justus R. Pearson, "Story of a Magazine: New York's *Galaxy* 1866-1878," *Bulletin of the New York Public Library* 61 (1957): 217-37, 281-302; and Mott, *A History of American Magazines,* 3:361-81.

Philadelphia's *Lippincott's,* which refused to cite circulation figures during its early and unprofitable years, is discussed in Rayburn S. Moore, "Paul Hamilton Hayne and Northern Magazines, 1866-1886," in James Woodress, ed., *Essays Mostly on Periodical Publishing in America: A Collection in Honor of Clarence Gohdes* (Durham, NC: Duke University Press, 1993), 134-47; and Mott, *A History of American Magazines,* 3: 396-401.

8. Useful remarks about the *New National Era* appear in Roland E. Wolseley, *The Black Press, U.S.A.* (Ames: Iowa State University Press, 1990), 35; Martin E. Dann, ed., *The Black Press, 1827-1890: The Quest for National Identity* (New York: Putnam's, 1971), 91-99; Constance McLaughlin Green, *The Secret City: A History of Race Relations in the Nation's Capital* (Princeton, NJ: Princeton University Press, 1967), 94-113; and Mott, *A History of American Magazines,* 3: 283-84. Although Douglass eventually lost as much as $10,000 on the magazine, perhaps one reason why circulation reports remain unavailable, the weekly

was recognized by Washington's *Daily Republican* as "a brave and forcible champion of the race for which it speaks." See "What the Press Say of the New Era," *New National Era* (3 February 1870): 2.

Further south, magazine circulations were likewise rarely discussed as magazines rarely succeeded for long and subscribers were often in arrears. The *Southern Monthly,* whose subscription agents were at least active throughout the South, is considered more fully in Sam G. Riley, *Magazines of the American South* (Westport, CT: Greenwood, 1986), 247-49; and Mott, *A History of American Magazines,* 2: 111. For the *New Eclectic,* which went on to absorb the *Land We Love* and become the *Southern Magazine,* see my "Home from the Theatre of War: The *Southern Magazine* and Recollections of the Civil War," in Price and Smith, *Periodical Literature in Nineteenth-Century America,* 183-201; Ray M. Atchinson's sketch in Chielens, *American Literary Magazines,* 395-99; and Mott, *A History of American Magazines,* 3: 46. For the *Southern Magazine* in the wider field of Southern periodicals, see Jay B. Hubbell, *The South in American Literature, 1607-1900* (Durham, NC: Duke University Press, 1954), 716-26; and Elisabeth Muhlenfeld, "The Civil War and Authorship," in Louis D. Rubin Jr., ed., *The History of Southern Literature* (Baton Rouge: Lousiana State University Press, 1985), 178-87.

To the west, the *Overland Monthly* in its postwar years is discussed in George Rathmell, "The *Overland Monthly*: California's Literary Treasure," *Californians* 8, no. 6 (1991): 12-21; Hank Nuwer's sketch in Sam G. Riley and Gary W. Selnow, eds., *Regional Interest Magazines of the United States* (Westport, CT: Greenwood, 1991), 241-46; William M. Clements's sketch in Chielens, *American Literary Magazines,* 308-13; Franklin Walker, *San Francisco's Literary Frontier* (New York: Knopf, 1939), 256-83; and Mott, *A History of American Magazines,* 3: 402-9, where the magazine's early peak circulation of ten thousand is noted. For the *Lakeside Monthly,* which reached a circulation of fourteen thousand in 1873 before that year's economic panic, see Michael Hackenberg's sketch in Chielens, *American Literary Magazines,* 199-203; Mott, *A History of American Magazines,* 3: 413-16; "The Life-Story of a Magazine," *Dial* 54 (16 June 1913): 489-92; and Herbert E. Fleming, "The Literary Interests of Chicago," *American Journal of Sociology* 11 (1906): 377-408.

9. The rates paid to Stowe and Hawthorne are discussed in Sedgwick, *Atlantic Monthly,* 74-76; par-

ticular attention to Stowe's market value may be found in Susan Coultrap-McQuin, *Doing Literary Business: American Women Writers in the Nineteenth Century* (Chapel Hill: University of North Carolina Press, 1990), 96-99. For Melville's success with short fiction in *Putnam's,* see Greenspan, *George Palmer Putnam,* ch. 9, "*Putnam's Magazine* and 'the Putnam Public'"; and Lea Bertani Vozar Newman, *A Reader's Guide to the Short Stories of Herman Melville* (Boston: G. K. Hall, 1986). The *Galaxy*'s continuing interest in Whitman is documented in Jerome Loving, *Walt Whitman: The Song of Himself* (Berkeley: University of California Press, 1999), 317-19. For general rates of payment to midcentury contributors, see Mott, *A History of American Magazines,* 2: 19-25, and 3: 12-17.

10. The reincarnation of "Ellen" and Davis's double life in *Peterson's* and the *Atlantic Monthly,* soon to be complicated by the *Galaxy* and *Lippincott's,* are discussed in Jane Atteridge Rose, *Rebecca Harding Davis* (New York: Twayne, 1993), 37-51; and Sharon M. Harris, *Rebecca Harding Davis and American Realism* (Philadelphia: University of Pennsylvania Press, 1991), 103-51. For fuller commentary on Davis's wartime writing for literary magazines, see Jean Pfaelzer, *Parlor Radical: Rebecca Harding Davis and the Origins of American Social Realism* (Pittsburgh: University of Pittsburgh Press, 1996), 76-106.

11. Young, *Disarming the Nation,* 94. As Young makes clear (329 n. 64), Alcott herself preferred "My Contraband" and reclaimed that title when her story was reprinted in *Hospital Sketches and Camp and Fireside Stories* (1869); see 69-108 for her incisive discussion of Alcott's story in the context that later re-publication invited. The initial title change seems to have been the suggestion of *Atlantic* assistant Howard Ticknor, who wanted to avoid confusion with a story by Mary E. Dodge called "Our Contraband" that *Harper's Monthly* had published in August 1863; see Joel Myerson, Daniel Shealy, and Madeleine B. Stern, eds., *The Journals of Louisa May Alcott* (Boston: Little, Brown, 1989), 124 n. 31. Further discussion may be found in Sarah Elbert, introduction, to *Louisa May Alcott on Race, Sex, and Slavery* (Boston: Northeastern University Press, 1997), xl-xliv; Betsy Klimasmith, "Slave, Master, Mistress, Slave: Genre and Interracial Desire in Louisa May Alcott's Fiction," *ATQ* 11 (1997): 115-35; and Diffley, *Where My Heart Is Turning Ever,* 34-39. For the pervasive shiver of desire in such narratives, what Karen Sanchez-Eppler calls "anti-slavery fiction's fascination with miscegenation," see her *Touching Liberty: Abolition, Feminism, and the Politics of the Body* (Berkeley: University of Cali-

fornia Press, 1993), 14-49. For Alcott's "The Brothers" as a step in her early magazine career, see Madeleine B. Stern, *Louisa May Alcott: From Blood & Thunder to Hearth and Home* (Boston: Northeastern University Press, 1998), 114-26; and Richard Brodhead, "Starting Out in the 1860s: Alcott, Authorship, and the Postbellum Literary Field," in *Cultures of Letters: Scenes of Reading and Writing in Nineteenth-Century America* (Chicago: University of Chicago Press, 1993), 69-106.

12. The publication history of Johnston's single story of the war is actually more complicated: before "Philemon Perch" published a revised version in the *New Eclectic,* the tale had appeared as "The Last Day of Mr. Williamson Slippey, Salt Merchant" in Augusta's *Southern Field and Fireside* (28 March 1863) but was not included the next year in *Georgia Sketches,* which thus remained insouciantly antebellum. For the particulars of Johnston's kaleidoscopic career with the *Dukesborough Tales,* see Bert Hitchcock, *Richard Malcolm Johnston* (Boston: Twayne, 1978), 44-67, as well as his sketch in *DLB* 74 (1988): 232-37; Jimmy Ponder Voyles, "Richard Malcolm Johnston's Literary Career: An Estimate," *Markham Review* 4 (February 1974): 29-34; Hubbell, *The South in American Literature,* 777-82; and three related essays by Francis Taylor Long on "The Life of Richard Malcolm Johnston in Maryland, 1867-1898": "Pt. 1 Country Gentleman, Teacher, and Writer, 1867-1881," *Maryland Historical Magazine* 34 (December 1939): 305-24; "Pt. 2 Some Literary Friendships—The Lecture Platform, 1882-1889," *Maryland Historical Magazine* 35 (September 1940): 270-86; and "Pt. 3 The Closing Years, 1889-1898," *Maryland Historical Magazine* 36 (March 1941): 54-69.

13. Unlike Davis and Alcott, and certainly unlike Johnston, Twain was offered twice the normal rate for "A True Story" and more than the *Atlantic Monthly* paid anyone else, one measure of reputation's sure if bedeviling power. For discussion of a story that Tom Quirk calls "a vernacular tour de force," see his *Mark Twain: A Study of the Short Fiction* (New York: Twayne, 1997), 57-62; Diffley, *Where My Heart Is Turning Ever,* 44-53; and James D. Wilson, *A Reader's Guide to the Short Stories of Mark Twain* (Boston: G. K. Hall, 1987), 267-73. To discover how much of Twain's story is "repeated word for word," see Herbert A. Wisbey Jr., "The True Story of Auntie Cord," *Mark Twain Society Bulletin* 4 (June 1981): 1, 3-5. For Twain's "Forty-Three Days in an Open Boat" (*Harper's Monthly,* December 1866) and his initial fumble with Eastern audiences, before *Innocents Abroad* (1869) and a scintillating humor department for

the *Galaxy* (1870-1871), see Twain's own recollection in "My Debut as a Literary Person," *Century* 59 (November 1899): 76-88.

14. Gary W. Gallagher, *The Confederate War* (Cambridge, MA: Harvard University Press, 1997), 8.

15. Howard L. Sacks and Judith Rose Sacks, *Way Up North in Dixie: A Black Family's Claim to the Confederate Anthem* (Washington, DC: Smithsonian Institution Press, 1993).

Ian Frederick Finseth (essay date 2006)

SOURCE: Finseth, Ian Frederick. "Introduction: The Written War." In *The American Civil War: An Anthology of Essential Writings,* edited by Ian Frederick Finseth, pp. 1-15. New York: Routledge, 2006.

[*In the following essay, an introduction to* The American Civil War, *an anthology of primary documents related to the Civil War, Finseth surveys the impact of the American Civil War on the literature produced during that era.*]

THE RATIONALE AND DESIGN OF THIS BOOK

The purpose of this anthology is to encourage attention to the most significant or compelling writings produced both during the Civil War and in the decades after. By gathering together a generous variety of these works, I have tried to provide readers with an original and dynamic arrangement of writings illustrating the war's influence on the literary imagination and cultural politics of nineteenth-century America.

Surprising though it may be—given the rate at which university and trade presses continue to publish historical and critical studies on the Civil War—there has not yet appeared a single volume devoted to the wide range of primary materials dealing with the war. Single-genre and single-author collections exist, along with scholarly editions of correspondence, memoirs, and documentary material, but thus far one could search in vain for an anthology presenting, in one place, Lincoln's Gettysburg Address and Ambrose Bierce's fiction, Herman Melville's war poetry and Mary Chesnut's diary entries, Louisa May Alcott's short stories and Ulysses S. Grant's memoirs, Frederick Douglass's speeches and Julia Ward Howe's song lyrics.

Taken singly, these writings do not always, or even frequently, convey the full measure of the Civil War's psychic and social impact. Taken together, however, they attain something of the effect of a symphony, in which all the instruments contribute to the musical experience.

It is a central argument of this book that Civil War writings, including those of canonical authors such as Walt Whitman or Stephen Crane, are best understood in relation to one another, and in the context of the full range of literary expression that the war stimulated. The piccolo or the tuba when unaccompanied is a lonely voice; in concert with other instruments, they are indispensable.

Deciding what to include, however, and what to leave out, proved a remarkably difficult undertaking. Some choices were obvious, such as Lincoln's second inaugural address or Whitman's "The Real War Will Never Get in the Books." But many more decisions could have gone either way, and for each text that made the cut, several others could not. The sheer volume of available material meant that many early selections had to be borne from the field, casualties of the editorial process, and the ones left standing are the survivors of that process. In the end, this anthology represents just one possible configuration of Civil War writings; ten other editors would have produced ten different collections.

The result is far from random, however. A number of active principles guided the selection of texts. First, priority has been given to literature in which the meanings of the war are not simplified, but explored in their fuller psychological and cultural complexity. Daniel Aaron may be correct in arguing that the Civil War produced no undisputed masterpiece of fiction, and that American writers had trouble assimilating it, but his conclusion that the war was "not so much unfelt as unfaced" does an injustice to the literary record.[1] Certainly the war prompted a good deal of essentially propagandistic writing, along with a slew of indigestible novels and a scattering of literary scraps and shards. Yet it also called forth an impressive number of free-spirited works that took seriously the job of exploring different aspects of the war and its aftermath: the experience of combat, the complexities of race, the implications of violence, and peace, for relationships and families. Epic they are not. But, each in its own way, these more focused writings are passionate, conflicted, amazed, humorous, brooding, and tragic.

Chronologically, the texts range from 1859 (Daniel Emmett's "Dixie") to 1903 (W. E. B. Du Bois's *The Souls of Black Folk*). They include some material only tangentially related to the war itself, but directly related to the war's aftermath and the difficulties of national reconciliation. Throughout the late nineteenth century and into the twentieth, the Civil War made itself felt, both directly and indirectly, not only in the country's literature but in a variety of professional disciplines: philosophy, medical science, psychology, journalism. Here, I have emphasized short stories, poetry, essays, and oratory which reflect a committed imaginative engagement with the Civil War, and which illustrate how the conflict could be soberly interpreted, and creatively reinterpreted, for a variety of audiences. These works represent a range of social perspectives: Southern and Northern, African American and European American, male and female, patrician and plebeian.

In the spirit of inclusiveness and the interest of breadth, this collection includes both canonical works and many less familiar writings by authors whose renown grows dim. There is a double benefit to this approach. The more famous pieces, such as Walt Whitman's "When Lilacs Last in the Dooryard Bloom'd," are brought into sharper relief when restored to the full context of Civil War literary interpretation and remembrance. At the same time, the great variety of noncanonical works help to provide a rich sense of the war's impact on American culture, and a fresh perspective on the development of American literature during the crucial decades before World War I.

To the degree possible, the selection process has been ideologically neutral, valuing literary quality more than literary correctness, but I am also aware that any anthology represents an implicit thesis about its subject matter—in this case, an implicit narrative of American history. To lay the cards on the table, then, it is worth observing up front that this book gives weighty emphasis to the conflicts of race and slavery that lay at the heart of the Civil War and that hardly abated in its echoing aftermath. That is actually not a very eccentric or controversial statement, but it might shed light on certain editorial decisions—on why, for instance, "African American Experience" forms the collection's largest section. More importantly, however, I have tried to design the architecture of this anthology such that there are both resonances among the texts and a built-in tension among different viewpoints. The goal has been a dynamic balance of harmony and discord. The anthology will have succeeded, in part, if rather than simply reproducing the familiar polemics, it conveys a sense of the various meanings the Civil War quickly acquired, and of how thoughtful observers both shaped and navigated those meanings.

As for the many necessary exclusions, several considerations prevailed. With a few exceptions of notable merit or cultural importance, such as Ulysses S. Grant and Mary Chesnut, I have avoided memoirs, autobiographies, and diaries, preferring to include works in their entirety whenever possible. Novels, for the same reason, do not appear here, although a number of interesting ones did emerge from the Civil War—notably Rebecca Harding Davis's *Waiting for the Verdict* (1867), John W. De Forest's *Miss Ravenel's Conversion from Secession to Loyalty* (1867), Elizabeth Phelps's *The Gates Ajar* (1868), S. Weir Mitchell's *In War Time* (1885), Paul Laurence Dunbar's *The Fanatics* (1901), and, of course, Stephen Crane's *The Red Badge of Courage* (1896). Other kinds of writing, finally, have been excluded for reasons of space and originality: soldiers' correspondence; antebellum antislavery or proslavery literature; documentary narratives, such as *Battles and Leaders of the Civil War*; and works that are commonly anthologized elsewhere, such as Ambrose Bierce's "Chickamauga."

Organizationally, the anthology is divided into six broad categories meant to give clear definition to a large body of literature by highlighting certain natural connections among the writings. Within each section—"Origins," "Battlefields," "African American Experience," "The Civil War in Song" "The Home Front," and "Remembrance and Forgetting." The texts appear for the most part chronologically, although some writings belonged next to one another regardless of their date of publication. Despite its advantages, the drawbacks of a thematic approach are worth acknowledging. Primarily, it entails a certain pigeon-holing of works and authors. Many works could plausibly fit into more than one category, and some are simply hard to categorize, such as John Wilkes Booth's correspondence or Harriet Beecher Stowe's "The Chimney-Corner." Complex works operate on multiple levels, and the particular organizational decisions here by no means foreclose on alternative ways of conceptualizing the material. In that spirit, the anthology does not segregate African American writers into their own category, even as it is important to highlight African American participation in and perceptions of the war and reconstruction. Accordingly, the section "African American Experience" includes some works by white writers, such as Louisa May Alcott and Thomas Wentworth Higginson, while some works by black writers are included in other groupings, such as George Moses Horton's war poems (in "Battlefields") or Frederick Douglass's "Address on the Unknown Dead" (in "Remembrance and Forgetting").

What this anthology offers, then, is a portrait of war in its broad dimensions. It represents just a fraction of the totality of Civil War literature, but in their psychological, ideological, and stylistic diversity, the writings here should convey something of the scope of the war's influence on American literature and culture.

WAR AND LANGUAGE

Writing about war—about the organized killing of people, the complex forces that go into that killing, and the profound consequences that flow from it—is almost as old as war itself. War fascinates, appalls, and defies those who would put words to it. It stretches the language we have, and demands that we come up with new language to describe the ever-startling face it shows us.

The essential material of writing is language, and the essential material of war is violence, or what Whitman called "the red business," and these materials, language and violence, intertwine in complex ways. On the one hand, writing seems the apex of civilization, the triumph of culture over nature, while war seems to confirm the survival of a primal, even animalistic, savagery. Social theorists and philosophers of violence have taught us that physical violence, in its overwhelming literalness, can warp and constrain language, which depends on abstraction and metaphor. The suffering of extreme violence so radically departs from ordinary individual experience that it thwarts the human impulse to give voice to that suffering, whether as participant or observer. And violence thrives on the breakdown of language, erupting at the moment when dialogue, negotiation, and self-expression stumble and fail. As long as people are talking, to put it simply, they are not fighting. At the same time, words and war have a long and intimate history, and that history has much to do with how language is used in the furtherance of violence. Elementally, the destructive power of language—in war or in daily life—involves the use of dehumanizing epithets that remove a person from the circle of human empathy, and makes them, so to speak, fair game. In a more general sense, language establishes the full conceptual framework within which a conflict proceeds. It sets the terms by which people understand the violence (including, frequently, the contractual terms governing the conduct of participants); it promotes ideological coherence amidst the chaos of violence; and, in a very practical sense, it enables the planning and coordination necessary for organized violence.[2]

For all that, however, the violence of war is one of the most powerful of stimuli to the creative imagination. Even as violence stymies language, it requires that we use language to represent it—and thus is born the literature of war.

Generalizations about war literature are perilous, but we might hazard a few. To write about war is to write about a human experience that is horrific and yet all too routine. It is to try to communicate something of the moral ambiguity of deliberate killing; of the feelings of soldiers and civilians; of the unexpected artistry of war. Writing about war is to heroize a nation or an ethnic group; to absolve oneself of cowardice or incompetence; or to anatomize a socio-historical moment. It means evaluating the social relations between the men (and women) who fight, their changed relations to those left at home, and the transformation of personality that can take place in combat. It means weighing the pain and the horror against the visceral thrill and sense of glory that war can invoke, and making room for the random absurdities that cling to all wars. And above all, to write about war is to offer some interpretation, implicit or explicit, of what the conflict means for the present.

We can approach these issues as they apply to the Civil War by considering two other defining wars in American history. In her study of King Philip's War, a brutal conflict involving English colonists and Algonquian tribes in 1675-1676, Jill Lepore has explained the impulse to build language out of the destruction of war:

> At first, the pain and violence of war are so extraordinary that language fails us: we cannot name our suffering and, without words to describe it, reality itself becomes confused, even unreal. But we do not remain at a loss for words for long. Out of the chaos we soon make new meanings of our world, finding words to make reality real again. . . . War twice cultivates language: it requires justification, it demands description.[3]

This "cultivation" of language often leads in the direction of propaganda, toward a restricted and manipulative interpretation of what the war entailed. For the Puritans, in this case, writing about King Philip's War became a means of securing their own English identity over and against both the Native Americans and other European societies. Yet the literary response to war can also lead in more creative, open-ended directions—if a writer chooses to explore the deeper, uncertain meanings of the conflict.

Some three centuries after King Philip's War, Tim O'Brien looked back on his experience in Vietnam and described both the need to articulate that experience and the difficulty in doing so:

> Partly catharsis, partly communication, [telling stories] was a way of grabbing people by the shirt and explaining exactly what had happened to me, how I'd allowed myself to get dragged into a wrong war, all the mistakes I'd made, all the terrible things I had seen and done. . . . By telling stories, you objectify your own experience. You separate it from yourself. You pin down certain truths. You make up others. You start sometimes with an incident that truly happened . . . and you carry it forward by inventing incidents that did not in fact occur but that nonetheless help to clarify and explain.[4]

This blending of imagination and reportage—even when the goal is "objectivity"—has been a universal feature of the literature of war. From the *Iliad* to *Catch-22* to *Safe Area Gorazde,* communicating the truths of war has required more than the objective transcription of events and details, if such a thing were even possible. It has required many different voices, and a willingness to bend language and to enlist the imagination in order to get at the deeper nerve centers of human experience.

And yet, it is precisely this imaginative dimension of war literature that raises difficult moral questions. Can we rely on the imagination to find the "real story" behind the cold hard facts of war? What do we make of a subjective response to war masquerading as general human truth? Do the aesthetic qualities of literature help to bring home the horrors of war, or make them more remote? Is figurative language a path to understanding or a glorified form of escapism?

LITERATURE OF THE CIVIL WAR

In his second inaugural address, given about a month before the peace settlement at Appomattox, Lincoln observed that neither North nor South had expected the Civil War to become the kind of conflict it grew into: "Each looked for an easier triumph, and a result less fundamental and astounding." The war had stunned and transformed the nation, with a force that the imagination found hard to reckon, and at a cost difficult to fathom. In the literature of the Civil War—even the literature produced during the war itself—one can sense the feeling of staggered awe with which American authors contemplated the wreckage of the conflict. Yet one can also hear other notes: humor, outrage, perplexity, denial, forgiveness, guilt, revenge.

The war evoked a spectrum of writerly responses in the decades that followed. Some authors retreated into fantasies of a Southern golden age; others imagined the reunion of North and South as a romance culminating in marriage. A few writers handled it analytically, even sociologically; many more treated it obliquely, folding it into works whose principal focus lay elsewhere. A number of authors approached the war in its fragments rather than its totality. Some concentrated on its gothic qualities, while others thought its truths were best reported straight, in realistic accounts of battles and episodes. What late nineteenth-century writers found hard to do was to avoid the war altogether.

Literature was a mode of both psychological and social reconstruction. As James Dawes has suggested, the Civil War fundamentally "challenged the communicative and deliberative procedures of the republic," so writing about the war represented a means of repairing and reinforcing those traditions. "The struggle to talk during and after violence," Dawes writes, "is language's struggle to regain mastery over violence, whether manifest in the individual's attempt to speak her trauma or a culture's attempt to produce a literary record."[5] For authors whom the war had affected most directly, such as Ambrose Bierce or Oliver Wendell Holmes, Jr., putting language to their experiences could serve as a probing or a closing of personal wounds. For authors too young to fight in or remember the war, as were many of those represented here, turning to the war enabled them to write about the society the war had created: increasingly consolidated, more economically and politically powerful than ever before, yet still riven by the faultlines of social class and race. The challenge was to discern in the Civil War a source of meaning for the postbellum period, a pattern of cause and effect, right and wrong, that would serve as philosophical and emotional ballast for Americans who lived in its turbulent wake.

This does not mean that writing about the Civil War or its aftermath was simply an exercise in social healing or a good-faith effort to reinvigorate the traditions of American public discourse. In some cases, war literature became a second front on which the festering conflicts could be fought anew, or on which old scores could be settled. The military phase of the conflict had concluded, but the struggle to define American culture had by no means waned—even when it appeared to be submerged under an outpouring of nostalgia and reconciliationist sentiment. The old adage that history is written by the victors was not entirely borne out by the late nineteenth-century American literary scene. Magazines, novels, newspapers, public speeches, autobiographies—all formed an interpretive arena in which the meanings of the war, and of the racial, political, and economic conflicts that gave rise to the war, were up for grabs. The stakes were high, for what kind of country the United States would become depended in large measure on what kind of war Americans imagined they had fought.

In wars fought between different nations or cultures, with different languages and histories, the process of post-war interpretation does not have the same closed, impacted quality as it does after a civil war. In this case, the veterans, partisans, and commentators inhabit the same political territory, speak the same language, share the same cultural reference points, and look back to the same past, all of which are nonetheless fought over. After King Philip's War, the English colonists did not have to compete with or accommodate Native American interpretations of the conflict; they had only to work out amongst themselves how the war would be remembered. After the Civil War, by contrast, writers from a more or less reintegrated North and South drew from the same bag of cultural tropes and icons and narratives (the martyrdom of Lincoln, the beckoning frontier, the plantation fallen into disrepair), even if they had very different purposes in doing so—and they had to negotiate the expectations of the same publishing industry and of overlapping, increasingly self-aware reading publics.

The production and consumption of Civil War literature between the 1860s and the early 1900s did not take place in a vacuum, but rather in a kind of literary ecosystem involving writers, editors, publishers, distribution syndicates, critics, and readers. It thrived, indeed, in a burgeoning periodical culture in which the number of American newspapers rose from about 4,000 in 1860 to almost 19,000 in 1899, while the number of other periodicals rose from about 700 in 1865 to more than 3,000 in 1885.[6] Newspapers, illustrated weeklies, and monthly magazines regularly published fiction, poetry, commentary, and, in serial form, novels dealing with the war and its legacies—including the work of such major authors as Mark Twain, Kate Chopin, Henry James, and many others. Significantly, not only the newspapers but the big literary magazines represented a far-reaching geographic diversity: the *Atlantic Monthly*

(Boston), *Putnam's Monthly Magazine, Harper's Monthly,* the *Century,* and the *Galaxy* (all New York); the *Southern Magazine* (Baltimore), the *Overland Monthly* (San Francisco), and the *Lakeside Monthly* (Chicago), to name just a few of the most prominent. Kathleen Diffley has estimated that between 1861 and 1876, some sixteen literary magazines, representing the Northeast, the South, and the West, printed more than 300 pieces of short fiction about the Civil War.[7] Given the large circulations of many of these periodicals, and given the relatively high rate of American literacy in the late nineteenth century, writings about the Civil War worked down into the capillary level of American culture, reaching millions of readers, in scores of towns and cities, representing a wide range of social backgrounds.

By the same token, Civil War writings had to be responsive to the pressures of the literary marketplace. Social values and expectations became business considerations, and business considerations in turn weighed on editorial and authorial decisions. For this reason, the ideological diversity of Civil War literature was to a certain degree constrained by a subtle yet pervasive cultural desire to avoid the most difficult subjects, such as race, or war guilt. All writings on the war communicated, perforce, a particular vision of the nation's past and future, whether implicitly or explicitly. They engaged in a titanic, slow-motion struggle with each other to determine how the nation would understand regionalism, civil rights, economic growth, and moral responsibility for the war and its aftermath. Yet even when it broke into acrimony, this struggle went forward on the basis of a shared national identity, against the backdrop of a reconciliationist national mood, and within the same national system of commerce.[8]

At one end of this relatively narrow spectrum, some Civil War writings were openly reconciliationist. The best example of this may be *Battles and Leaders of the Civil War,* a compendium of generals' and veterans' accounts, representing both Northern and Southern perspectives, published serially in the *Century* magazine between 1884 and 1887, and issued in book form in 1887-1888. At the other end of the spectrum, some literature was aggressively vindicationist, such as the publications of the Southern Historical Society, the brainchild of Gen. Jubal Early dedicated to keeping the Confederate point of view alive and in the public consciousness.

In the midst of the histories and the memoirs, other American authors turned to a variety of literary modes or genres in an effort to get at the lingering mysteries of the conflict. Frequently they had to navigate the crosscurrents of the literary marketplace in order to find a publisher, let alone a receptive audience, and Civil War literature often reveals how a writer could work both

within and against the conventions of any particular form or tradition. Hence we see Charles Chesnutt, for instance, in response to the popular plantation and dialect fiction of Thomas Nelson Page and Joel Chandler Harris, submitting to magazines short stories that invoke the antebellum plantation not romantically, but for the purpose of representing slavery's unique fusion of economics and cruelty. In like fashion, Sarah Morgan Bryan Piatt turned to the well-worn conventions of sentimental poetry not as a retreat from emotional candor but in order to reimagine the feelings of women whose experiences and loyalties resisted easy classification. In short, much Civil War literature can be read against the grain of dominant literary tastes and cultural values. We should read it with an eye toward the recurrent fissures and omissions in its treatment of national identity, toward the unacknowledged or imperfectly suppressed African American presence in its picture of American life, toward the psychological tics and conflicts that belie the notion of a hale postwar culture. Much American literature reduced the war to its simplicities—and, it might be noted, some of this literature did so in a perversely illuminating way—but many other writings struggled against themselves, and against the cultural tide, in order to come to terms with some piece of the war or with its aftermath. The Civil War became many civil wars when refracted through the prism of literary style. The war can look very different depending on whether we approach it through William T. Sherman's factualism, Oliver Wendell Holmes's heroic romanticism, Lucy Larcom's ironic sentimentalism, or Hamlin Garland's regionalism. Each of these styles brings to the fore different meanings and perspectives; each renders just an aspect of the war, however sweeping a writer's ambition may be; and our impression of the war will vary from one to the next. Local color, humor, naturalism: all will imply certain attitudes toward or perceptions of the war's impact on people. At issue is not only subject matter (military tactics vs. domestic tribulation) but the worldview, the moral sense, and the epistemology embodied in different ways of using the language. What distinguishes a tabulation of regimental losses, for instance, from an elegiac poem goes beyond genre to embrace a fundamentally different view of human mortality.

The ascendancy of "realism" in late nineteenth-century American culture is of particular significance for the development of Civil War literature. While there were (and are) competing theories of realism, and as many practitioners as there were ideas of what constituted "reality" in the first place, signal patterns emerge across the era's fiction, non-fiction, and visual art. Realism of the nineteenth-century variety is generally oriented less toward the heroic individual than toward the representative type. It concerns itself with the details and material conditions of everyday life—with how people look, sound, interact, entertain themselves, earn a living, face the day—in a carefully wrought social context. The realist novel, painting, or photograph often has political overtones, reflecting a progressive concern with the plight of the "common man." Particularly in its early years, realism retained a belief in a universal moral order that transcended and compensated for the brutalities of the economic and social order. In its local color or regionalist varieties, realism focused on the lives of unusual people in the less familiar areas of the country—coastal Maine, New Orleans, rural Wisconsin—and on the cultural adhesives that held together a geographically diverse nation. In the strain of realism that evolved into naturalism, we find a concern with the forces working in an individual life, from within and without, as biology or culture. Realism, broadly conceived, was an effort to apprehend the textures and operating principles of a world whose startling complexity both the social scientists and the natural scientists made more evident every day.[9]

Realism in the arts and literature was nurtured by a heightened demand for and an increased supply of information, and the Civil War contributed to both. In 1860, the United States was well on its way to becoming an information culture, and the war accelerated that process by stimulating the public's appetite for reliable knowledge about military and political matters, and by encouraging the improvement of communication networks. It quickly became the most visible, accessible war in American history, with photographers and print journalists recording almost every imaginable fact and facet of the conflict, and distributing their findings to a knowledge-hungry public.

The rise of reproducible images and syndicated news reports as dominant modes of public knowledge had profound implications for how nineteenth-century Americans understood the world. Along with the proliferation of news outlets and the increasing professionalization of journalism, improvements in photographic and lithographic technology made the representation of "reality" a matter of course. The photograph, seemingly, could not lie, and it set a standard for reliability that the canons of professional journalism echoed by emphasizing "objectivity" as a core principle of the reporter's craft. More than ever before, information became a commodity, and quick, seemingly accurate knowledge of the world could be had for a penny. Yet both the photograph and the news story have the strange effect of making the world at once more available and more remote. Photographs, in John Berger's words, "offer appearances—with all the credibility and gravity we normally lend to appearances—prised away from their meaning." The photographic image "offers information, but information severed from all lived experience."[10] In strikingly similar terms, Alan Trachtenberg has made the same point about newspapers in the Gilded Age: "the dailies dramatized a paradox of metropolitan life

itself: the more knowable the world came to seem as information, the more remote and opaque it came to seem as experience."[11]

Writings about the Civil War, "literary" or otherwise, can be read partly for how they respond to these problems of realism and the culture of information. On the one hand, both fiction and nonfiction bear the imprint of the era's photographic and journalistic norms in their concern with detail, panorama, visual impact, and the detached point of view. It is not coincidental that many of the major authors of the late nineteenth century—Crane, Bierce, Frank Norris, Mark Twain, and Harold Frederic, among others—were also professional journalists. This was an age, by and large, when the brooding romances of Hawthorne, the elaborate idealism of Emerson, and the stylistic excesses of Melville seemed less in keeping with the hard-nosed, no-nonsense culture the United States imagined itself becoming. Imaginative symbolism, flights of fancy, and other forms of authorial self-indulgence did not always seem well-suited to communicating the difficult truths and social nuances of an increasingly complex culture.

On the other hand, postbellum American literature—both fiction and nonfiction—often reveals an uncertainty about the adequacy of realism, about the capacity of writing to get at the deeper truths of the war, or of society more broadly. The conventions of linear narrative, expository description, character development, conflict resolution, and so forth, gave literary texts their form and coherence, but at what cost? The sober factuality of military memoirs, orthodox histories, and occasional speeches was indispensable to capturing the war's meaning, but was it sufficient? These questions hung in the air, and they help to explain why much of the salient literature of the period—from S. Weir Mitchell's medical fiction to Bierce's gothic gems—extravagantly violates the norms of "realistic" representation, even as it borrows freely from the realist palette. If imagination had to supplement or trump reportorial objectivity, so be it.

For realism's confounding challenge was violent death. The central reality of the Civil War that Americans had to assimilate was the unprecedented level of trauma and bereavement: more than 620,000 dead and more than one million wounded. The numbers have become somewhat numbing in their familiarity, but we need to remember that civil war brought death on a scale, and with a ferocity, wholly new to Americans. It is true, as Lewis Saum writes, that in the antebellum era "death was an ever present fact of life," and that Americans had "an immediate, not a derivative or vicarious, awareness" of it.[12] But the Civil War marked a quantum shift, not only in the numbers of dead (about 2 percent of the population, or the equivalent of about six million Americans today), but in its spectacular disbursement of agony and disfigurement. How does one put words to such suffering without either trivializing, heroizing, or otherwise falsifying the experience? Memorial Day tributes to the fallen? Elegiac verse? Earnest personal testimony? Stories of battles, triumphs, hospitals, widows, and reunions? Where the carnage lies raw, unburied and unforgotten, the most effective realism may be one that embodies the failure of words, a realism akin to what Mitchell Breitwieser has discerned in Mary Rowlandson's narrative, which "is a realistic work, not because it faithfully reports real events, but because it is an account of experience that breaks through or outdistances her own and her culture's dominant means of representation, and because it is itself a continuation of that breakthrough rather than a fully composed and tranquilized recollection."[13]

Americans are good at burial; thus Saum sees in nineteenth-century American thought "a seeming insouciance, a capacity to register without questioning."[14] This ability to hold death at a remove would have helped both soldiers and civilians get through the scenes they encountered, and the war had the paradoxical effect of rendering death both shockingly present and increasingly impersonal, through the statistical banality of the body count and through the accumulation of the "unknown dead." From this perspective, the power and the obligation of realism might be to startle its audience out of that unquestioning insouciance. "Realism," Philip Fisher writes in connection to Baudelaire, "surprises us into unwanted moments or necessary moments of confronted sight. We face [the] carrion, and by means of the object, face what lies behind it, decay and death, the fate of the body in its relation to beauty."[15] It takes a rare art to accomplish that, however. How far does graphic description—"The greater part of the forehead was torn away, and from the jagged hole the brain protruded"—take us? Do the symmetries of verse—"Two white roses upon his cheeks, / And one, just over his heart, blood red!"—take us any further? Perhaps the desperation of the living is the most vivid mark of the fearsomeness of mortality: "A hundred ghastly fears and fancies strutted a moment, pecking at the young girl's naked heart, like sandpipers on the weltering beach."[16] The dilemma can be sensed even in these brief passages, and it was essentially this: Even for writers who wanted to confront mortality honestly, writing about death is like chasing one's own shadow, the experience itself always flitting away before the net of words.

Those who wrote about the Civil War wrote about a social earthquake whose aftershocks reverberated through American culture, politics, psychology, and literature. In its technical innovations and its violent reorganization of American society, the war marked the advent of a new age and audaciously challenged Americans' sensibilities and moral certainties. The nation's economic and political life was forever altered, and emancipation hardly solved the grinding conflicts of race in the United States. It is not surprising, perhaps, that many Americans and many writers lapsed into platitudes or silence. Yet others made the effort to rise to the occasion—made the effort, that is, to overcome the shock in order to reach and represent the deeper experiences of war, to find the soft tissue and the hard feelings beneath the banalities of press reportage and gauzy reminiscence. They did so even as American society had much to occupy itself with between the 1860s and the 1910s: class antagonism and labor strikes; the final push against the Native Americans in the West; a steady influx of European immigrants; the radical expansion of American geopolitical power during the Spanish-American War; an ongoing effort to reconcile religious orthodoxy with new forms of science.

In the midst of such upheaval, Americans did what came naturally: they embraced both tradition and the modern world. Michael D. Clark has written that tradition, especially for the elite, "could be a psychological anodyne offering a sense of stability in the midst of unsettling change and the feeling of time-hallowed certainty in the face of religious or metaphysical doubt." At the same time, "[s]ome Americans came to view tradition as extending rather than merely limiting the possibilities of individual and collective life," and it was therefore "the problem of tradition to find the middle ground, or the linkages, which would plausibly bind immediate to transcendent, past to present, local to imperial."[17] Anne C. Rose, stressing the importance of religious change, has also found in Victorian American culture a capacity for preserving or updating the old ways and the old beliefs in the face of widespread social transformation:

> The Victorians were not unaware of the trials and horrors of war. They felt keen disappointment at the failure of the founder's republicanism and saw clearly the suffering of soldiers and civilians alike. But the war's prospects of personal glory and shared idealism contested their soberer judgment, drew them powerfully toward the conflict, and came to dominate their recollections of war. To the extent that the Victorians' relentless search for meaning in secular activities finally achieved resolution, it was the Civil War, conceived as a struggle over profound issues, that convinced them that human effort even without clear supernatural references still had value.[18]

The literature of the American Civil War did not always reach that same conclusion. But as much as anything else, these writings represented part of the wider cultural effort to come to terms with the changes the United States underwent during the late nineteenth century. That was actually inevitable, for these changes depended, to no small degree, on the conduct and the outcome of the war.

If language and literature are forms of social and personal reconstruction, what they were able to accomplish in the fifty years after the Civil War was precarious, imperfect, and incomplete. Indeed, it is a sign of that precariousness that Americans are still coming to terms with the Civil War. The war settled the defining constitutional crisis of the country's history, and yet in other respects it seems to have resolved so little. The political tensions involving race and region, federal power and states' rights, modernity and tradition, continue to make themselves felt across the cultural landscape, from presidential campaigns to landscape conservation to civil rights. In its continuing hold on the national psyche, the Civil War has become a touchstone for understanding modern American culture, but it means very different things to different people. An essential part of coming to terms with its unresolved status in the American imagination is to explore how earlier generations came to terms with it—and that is best done through an exploration of the writings they left us.

Notes

1. Daniel Aaron, *The Unwritten War,* p. 328.

2. These issues are treated at much greater length in a number of classic works, including: Elaine Scarry, *The Body in Pain: The Making and Unmaking of the World* (New York: Oxford University Press, 1985); Hannah Arendt, *On Violence* (New York: Harvest, 1970); and Jürgen Habermas, *Moral Consciousness and Communicative Action* (Cambridge: MIT Press, 1990). More recently, see James Dawes, *The Language of War: Literature and Culture in the U.S. from the Civil War through World War II* (Cambridge: Harvard University Press, 2002); and Judith Butler, *Excitable Speech: A Politics of the Performative* (New York: Routledge, 1997).

3. Jill Lepore, *The Name of War: King Philip's War and the Origins of American Identity* (Vintage, 1999), p. x.

4. Tim O'Brien, *The Things They Carried* (Broadway Books, 1998), pp. 157-58.

5. Dawes, *The Language of War,* p. 4, p. 11.

6. Charles Johanningsmeier, *Fiction and the American Literary Marketplace: The Role of Newspaper Syndicates,* 1860-1900 (Cambridge: Cambridge University Press, 1997), pp. 2-3; Patricia Okker, *Social Stories: The Magazine Novel in Nineteenth-Century America* (Charlottesville: University of Virginia Press, 2003), ch. 1, ch. 5.

7. Kathleen Diffley, "Home from the Theatre of War: The *Southern Magazine* and Recollections of the Civil War," in Kenneth M. Price and Susan Belasco Smith, eds., *Periodical Literature in Nineteenth-Century America* (University of Virginia Press, 1995), pp. 183-201, p. 184.

8. See Lawrence Buell, "American Civil War Poetry and the Meaning of Literary Commodification: Whitman, Melville, and Others" in Steven Fink and Susan S. Williams, eds., *Reciprocal Influences: Literary Production, Distribution, and Consumption in America* (Columbus: Ohio State University Press, 1999).

9. Recent relevant studies of realism include Phillip Barrish, *American Literary Realism, Critical Theory, and Intellectual Prestige, 1880-1995* (Cambridge: Cambridge University Press, 2001); Augusta Rohrbach, *Truth Stranger than Fiction: Race, Realism, and the U.S. Literary Marketplace* (New York: Palgrave, 2002); Philip Fisher, *Still the New World: American Literature in a Culture of Creative Destruction* (Cambridge: Harvard University Press, 1999), esp. Part IV.

10. John Berger, "Uses of Photography," in *About Looking* (New York: Pantheon, 1980; New York: Vintage, 1991), pp. 55-56.

11. Alan Trachtenberg, *The Incorporation of America: Culture and Society in the Gilded Age* (New York: Hill and Wang, 1982), p. 125.

12. Lewis O. Saum, "Death in the Popular Mind of Pre-Civil War America," in David E. Stannard, ed., *Death in America* (Philadelphia: University of Pennsylvania Press, 1975), p. 32.

13. Mitchell Breitwieser, *American Puritanism and the Defense of Mourning: Religion, Grief, and Ethnology in Mary White Rowlandson's Captivity Narrative* (Madison: University of Wisconsin Press, 1990), p. 10.

14. Saum, p. 35.

15. Fisher, *Still the New World,* p. 199.

16. Ambrose Bierce, "Chickamauga"; Henry Wadsworth Longfellow, "Killed at the Ford"; Henry James, "The Story of a Year."

17. Michael D. Clark, *The American Discovery of Tradition, 1865-1942* (Baton Rouge: Louisiana State University Press, 2005), p. 16, p. 17, p. 20.

18. Anne C. Rose, *Victorian America and the Civil War* (New York: Cambridge University Press, 1992), p. 5.

Suggested Reading

Aaron, Daniel. *The Unwritten War: American Writers and the Civil War.* New York: Alfred A. Knopf, 1973.

Blanton, De Anne and Lauren M. Cook. *They Fought Like Demons: Women Soldiers in the Civil War.* New York: Vintage, 2003.

Cullen, Jim. *The Civil War in Popular Culture: A Reusable Past.* Washington, DC: Smithsonian Institution Press, 1995.

Dawes, James. *The Language of War: Literature and Culture in the U.S. from the Civil War through World War II.* Cambridge: Harvard University Press, 2002.

Diffley, Kathleen. *Where My Heart Is Turning Ever: Civil War Stories and Constitutional Reform.* Athens: University of Georgia Press, 1992.

Eiselein, Gregory. *Literature and Humanitarian Reform in the Civil War Era.* Bloomington: Indiana University Press, 1996.

Fahs, Alice. *The Imagined Civil War: Popular Literature of the North and South, 1861-1865.* Chapel Hill: University of North Carolina Press, 2001.

Fahs, Alice and Joan Waugh, eds. *The Memory of The Civil War in American Culture.* Chapel Hill: University of North Carolina Press, 2004.

Frederickson, George. *The Inner Civil War: Northern Intellectuals and the Crisis of the Union.* New York: Harper and Row, 1965.

Gardner, Sarah E. *Blood and Irony: Southern White Women's Narratives of the Civil War, 1861-1937.* Chapel Hill: University of North Carolina Press, 2004.

Jimerson, Randall C. *The Private Civil War: Popular Thought during the Sectional Conflict.* Baton Rouge: Louisiana State University Press, 1988.

Madden, David. *Beyond the Battlefield: The Ordinary Life and Extraordinary Times of the Civil War Soldier.* New York: Simon & Schuster, 2000.

Lively, Robert A. *Fiction Fights the Civil War.* Chapel Hill: University of North Carolina Press, 1957.

Long, Lisa A. *Rehabilitating Bodies: Health, History, and the American Civil War.* Philadelphia: University of Pennsylvania Press, 2004.

Rose, Anne C. *Victorian America and the Civil War.* New York: Cambridge University Press, 1992.

Samuels, Shirley. *Facing America: Iconography and the Civil War.* New York: Oxford University Press, 2003.

Sizer, Lyde Cullen. *The Political Work of Northern Women Writers and the Civil War, 1850-1872.* Chapel Hill: University of North Carolina Press, 2000.

Sweet, Timothy. *Traces of War: Poetry, Photography, and the Crisis of the Union.* Baltimore: Johns Hopkins University Press, 1990.

Wilson, Edmund. *Patriotic Gore: Studies in the Literature of the American Civil War.* New York: W. W. Norton, 1994; Farrar, Straus and Giroux, 1962.

Woodworth, Steven E. *While God Is Marching On: The Religious World of Civil War Soldiers.* Lawrence: University Press of Kansas, 2001.

GENDER ROLES

Suzy Clarkson Holstein (essay date summer 1991)

SOURCE: Holstein, Suzy Clarkson. "'Offering up Her Life': Confederate Women on the Altars of Sacrifice." *Southern Studies* 2, no. 2 (summer 1991): 113-30.

[*In the following essay, Holstein studies how the impact of the Civil War on women, especially the ideal "Southern belle," was depicted in works by Augusta Jane Evans and Mary Chesnut.*]

History is the winner's story; it has also been, until very recently, the male story. The voices of women committed to losing causes have been heard, if at all, as distortion or romance. But if we listen to those voices, we hear new notes that give greater fullness to the sounds of the past. At the same time, the defeated women's stories also call attention to the defeated woman herself, and we begin to understand the peculiarity of her position. When Johnny comes marching home as the vanquished, not the victor, how must the woman respond? Or, phrased another way, what does war—more specifically the loss of war—cost a woman? The Southern white woman faced this question during and after the Civil War, and she learned that she had lost more than just a military struggle. As she watched an old culture die, she began to learn the terrible price of the doomed cause—a price she would continue to pay for decades.

The South's perceived need for an inviolate identity, for unquestioning loyalty to the cause, exacted a heavy toll from women as well as men, and two works written by women during the war demonstrate this cost in different ways. For Augusta Jane Evans, author of the novel *Macaria,* the South's predicament meant a curtailing of ambiguity. The latter third of that novel, completed in 1863, takes place during the war, and the search for women's proper sphere which dominates the book becomes sharpened and redefined by the onset of hostilities. For Evans, to publish a work during the course of the war mandates cutting off loose ends of doubt in order to shore up morale and faith in the cause. *Macaria* is highly conscious propaganda and, thus, requires the elimination of ambivalent feelings and troubling complexity. Evans works to solidify a political position, one that was already in severe jeopardy as she wrote. Consequently, her finished novel presents a flattened portrait of the war-torn South that allows her female characters even less freedom and complexity than Evans herself enjoyed. *Macaria,* then, assists in crystallizing the myth of Southern womanhood.

For Mary Chesnut, the childless wife of a high-ranking official from South Carolina, the individual cost was different. During James Chesnut's distinguished career as U. S. Senator, aide to Jefferson Davis, and Confederate General, his wife freely expressed herself in private journals. Mrs. Chesnut gives vent to all the ambiguities she feels concerning the underlying causes of the war, the conduct of the battles, women's roles, and the social structure. Yet she was never able to revise her notes and present them in a final form that she felt justified publication.[1] Some of Chesnut's difficulties in finishing, of course, arose from the straitened economic conditions of her life, from her own idiosyncratic perception of what the finished product should look like, and from her relatively early death. In addition, Mary Chesnut must have had some doubts as to the audience for her work—doubts confirmed by R. M. T. Hunter, a man for whom she had utmost respect. He told her in 1876 that "if published just now by a So. Ca. lady, such a work might make the world a little too hot to hold her" (*Civil War,* xxi-xxii). Though Woodward, her most recent editor, treats as almost accidental the fact that the Chesnut diary was not published until twenty years after her death (and forty years after the war's end), certainly we must attribute at least part of Chesnut's difficulty to the fact that her work could not conform to the shape of the Southern myth. As Woodward notes, "Miss Martin [one of the original editors] was intensely concerned that Chesnut passages out of line with the current Southern version of Confederate legend be deleted" (*Civil War,* xxviii). Undoubtedly, part of the problem was located in the genre itself, one which transforms private reflection into public document. But Chesnut's observations had an especially difficult time becoming a public work because they entertained extensive questioning of the antebellum Southern myth. Only the passage of nearly one hundred years could pave the way for Chesnut's ambivalent tone to find an audience. By that time, the patterns laid down by the myth of the "Lost Cause" were well-woven into the fabric of post-bellum Southern life. As we shall see, Evans's sacrifice of complexity and Chesnut's unwillingness or inability to complete the public version of her experience provide a gloss for the role adopted by Southern womanhood during the Civil War, and predict the future of the post-bellum Southern woman. Both writers' decisions reflect the pattern of the female Southerner—namely, relinquishing any actions or sentiments that did not fit the ideal form of Southern womanhood. The myth of the unquestioning, fragile lady, the Southern belle whom Southern soldiers were fighting to protect, was too important to be undermined by publicly presenting an opposing model.

Macaria and *Mary Chesnut's Civil War* share a special perspective, for not only are they written by Southern women about Southern women, but both works are written in the context of a fervent yearning for a Southern victory, without knowledge of the war's outcome.[2] Even so, while both books repeatedly hope for the best (Evans dedicates *Macaria* to the Army of the Confederacy and writes expressly to bolster morale), there is an elegiac, doomed quality tinging the works. Indeed, both contain explicit references to Cassandra. Chesnut, in particular, recognizes the coming defeat as early as April, 1862 (*Civil War,* 330), and Evans's projections of a bright future in *Macaria* are noticeably feeble. Death and destruction loom large throughout the novel's last one hundred pages.[3] As a result, the authors are caught in a contradictory position, one of many tensions we will see in the roles of real and fictional women. Both writers long for a victorious South and believe fervently in their cause. Yet neither writer can escape the foreboding sense of doom, so that their works reveal a curious split vision: hopefulness that realizes hope is futile. Like their contemporaries, they are women caught between powerful myth and unavoidable reality. Further, because defeat and the loss of a way of life haunt these works, we may also trace the embryonic mythological identification of women within the framework of the "Lost Cause." That is, the defeated South that each author unwillingly reveals through her work relies heavily for sustenance on the inner strength and outward docility of the mythical Southern lady. As the myth of the Lost Cause crystallizes, so too does the idealized identity of Southern womanhood that supports the myth.

The image of the Southern belle, the mythic figure that endures into the present, may seem at first glance a flat stereotype. But beneath the exterior, the image usually reveals itself to be oxymoronic: the Southern lady's velvet glove covers a fist of steel. Chesnut tells a story which perfectly exemplifies this paradoxical ideal:

> Mrs. Preston was resplendent in diamonds, point lace, velvet train, & c. There is a gentle dignity about Mrs. Preston which is very attractive, and her voice is low and sweet. And her will is iron. (I have grown devotedly attached to her.) She is an exceedingly well-informed person, but exceedingly quiet, retiring, and reserved. Indeed, her apparent gentleness almost amounts to timidity. [At a ball,] Governor Manning said to me: "Look at sister Caroline! Does she look as if she had the pluck of a heroine?" "How?" A little while ago, William came to tell her that John Walker was drunk in the cellar—mad with drink—and that he had a carving knife which he was brandishing in his drunken fury and keeping everybody from their business, because he threatened to kill anyone who dared go in the basement. They were like a flock of frightened sheep down there. She did not speak to one of us but followed William down to the basement, holding up her skirts. She found the servants scurrying everywhere, screaming and shouting that John was crazy and going to kill them. John was bellowing like a bull of

Bashan, knife in hand, chasing them at his pleasure. Mrs. Preston walked up to him.

"Give me that knife." He handed it to her. She laid it on the table.

"And now come with me," she said, putting her hand on his collar. She led him away to the empty smoke-house. And then she locked him in and put the key in her pocket. And she returned, without a ripple on her placid face to show what she had done. She told me of it, smiling and serene, as you see her now.

(*Civil War,* 348-49)

This passage suggests at least two troubling questions: why did women's life in the Civil War South give rise to such contradictions? Further, why and how did the Southern woman allow these contradictions to be simplified and reduced into a caricature that belied the difficulty of integrating disparate parts of a self and even denied certain elements of women's personalities? Examining *Mary Chesnut's Civil War* and *Macaria* will help us begin to answer these questions.

A Southern lady in 1860 and the years following could not avoid the contradictions and tensions of her role. Slavery, often seen as the central issue of the war, represented both Southern identity and an onerous burden to the women of the South. Chesnut reports of writing a letter to her husband as early as 1842 denouncing slavery (*Civil War,* 246) and she claims that most of the women she knows share her opinion. An overseer tells her, "In all my life I have only met one or two women-folk who were not abolitionists in their hearts—and hot ones too." A Northern sympathizer is described as an abolitionist, and another woman replies that she "never saw a true woman who was not" (*Civil War,* 255, 718). When the war ends and Mrs. Chesnut considers her bleak prospects—"poverty—no future, no hope," a friend adds, "but no slaves—thank God!" (*Civil War,* 796).[4]

Despite these strong feelings, Chesnut and her sisters feel themselves powerless to speak out or to avert the coming disaster. "Our votes are not counted—women, alas!" She also responds to Mrs. Johnston, a friend who tells her that she (Mrs. Johnston) would never own slaves: "I might say the same thing. *I* never would. *Mr.* Chesnut does" (*Civil War,* 256, 729, emphasis mine). She makes several explicit connections between being a slave and being a woman: "All married women, all children, and girls who live on in their fathers houses are slaves!" (*Civil War,* 729). Yet in spite of her recognition of her own "slavery" and her abhorrence of the day-to-day reality of the institution, her loyalty to the Southern war effort never flags. She lives her life in the contradictory and difficult position of despising the foundation of the social system she vigorously upholds.[5]

If we turn to the novelist's presentation of Southern womanhood to help us understand this tension, we will be immediately disappointed. Evans writes of slaves (called, as in *Civil War,* "servants"), but we see no acknowledgment of the inherent contradictions that surround Mrs. Chesnut and her friends. Irene Huntington, the heiress in *Macaria,* owns slaves and treats them well. The novel rarely mentions the servants, and when they do appear, they are all-wise and devoted. One even dies on the field of battle, serving his master. But Evans presents us with neither an apology for slavery nor a clear ideological stand opposing slavery while upholding states' rights; the peculiar institution seems almost completely ignored. This omission would be remarkable enough in a Southern book which is written and takes place during the Civil War, but it is especially noteworthy in a novel that frequently occupies itself with long philosophical and theoretical discussions about many other issues. Clearly, Evans avoids the subject intentionally and for rather obvious reasons. Propaganda mandates certainty and an unambiguous presentation.[6] Evans's fiction removes the tension we find in Chesnut's diary and replaces it with only one mention of the institution of slavery. Irene, discussing the future of the post-war Confederacy, recognizes that slavery is only viable in an agrarian economy. She asserts, therefore, "*If* our existence as a republic depends upon the perpetuity of the institution of slavery, then, it seems to me, that the aim of our legislators should be to render us *par excellence* an agricultural people.'"[7] Evans deals with contradictions by ignoring them. As we shall see later, this tactic predicts her handling of contradictions within her characters' lives. Fiction allows her to align all the images in the same direction rather than acknowledging the multiple messages evident in Chesnut's account.[8]

The two writers do, however, share certain perceptions about the war and its roots. Both reject the primacy of slavery as the cause of the war: Chesnut argues explicitly against those who assert that the "war is an attempt to extend the area of slavery" (*Civil War,* 153), while Evans makes the argument implicit as she speaks of the war as a struggle for freedom. Both women also perceive Lincoln as the personification of evil: Chesnut attacks his awkwardness and ignorance, and Evans labels him a tyrant and criticizes his wartime measures, including the repeal of *habeas corpus.* But their attitudes toward Lincoln also reveal a glimpse at a contrast similar to the one reflected in their depictions of slavery. Evans's stance remains relentlessly one-sided, while Chesnut's allows tolerance and complexity. Chesnut cannot avoid some grudging admiration for Lincoln and occasionally quotes him approvingly. In addition, she sees parallels in attacks on Jefferson Davis and attacks on Lincoln: "In our democratic republic, if one rises to be its head, whoever he displeases takes a Turkish revenge—defiles the tombs of his father and mother. His father a horse thief and his mother no better than she should be . . . It is all hurled at Lincoln or Jeff Davis indiscriminately" (*Civil War,* 627).

When we examine each work's portrayal of the war effort and of Northerners, the difference between the perceptions intensifies. The narrator of *Macaria* implies that New Englanders would shoot at women, and she repeatedly labels Yankees as murderers (*Macaria*, 407, 436). She also challenges the bravery of Yankee generals and offers no indication that Northerners display virtue or are made to suffer by the war (*Macaria*, 452). The Northern family that Irene loves become Southern sympathizers, and their devout son becomes a chaplain in a Texas regiment because he cannot support the North's attempts at coercion nor its abridgement of rights (*Macaria*, 438). (This unflinching one-sidedness represents the other half of the view in Louisa May Alcott's *Work*, for in that novel everything Northern is glorious and everything Southern is infamous.) Chesnut also avows a deep hatred of Yankees and of the North; she proclaims North and South divorced and asserts "we hated each other so" (*Civil War*, 25). Frequently, she insists that the South wishes to be rid of Yankees at any price, and part of her anger stems from her belief that the North makes all the money from slavery (with the tariff) while the South gets "all the opprobrium" (*Civil War*, 80). "I would gladly go to Liberia—worse, to Sahara—than to live in a country surrendered to Yankees!" she vows in 1862 (*Civil War*, 325). But Chesnut's diary also reveals frequent recognition that Northern and Southern individuals endure parallel plights, and certain of her actions and observations indicate that she feels emotions other than simple, unyielding hatred. She admits that it must be difficult to live in the enemy camp, and recognizes that if she were in the North, she would be a "heavy handful." As a result, she "makes allowances" for Northern wives living in the South (*Civil War*, 351). Indeed, several of her acquaintances have Northern sympathies, and she does not refrain from socializing with them. Throughout the diary, there are scattered instances of the Chesnuts' considerate treatment of individual Northerners (e.g., *Civil War*, 115, 351), and when the war ends, Mary Chesnut also reports several examples of Yankee kindness (e.g., *Civil War*, 783). On a larger scale, she recognizes that prisoners of war on both sides of the Mason-Dixon line are subject to similar horrors (*Civil War*, 150, 606). Unlike Christie Devon in Alcott's *Work*, Mary Chesnut recognizes that "women—wives and mothers—are the same everywhere." When Northern papers print lies about the South, she responds, "It ought to teach us not to credit what our papers say of them" (*Civil War*, 108, 121).

Yet for all her understanding of the war's complexities, Chesnut's public rhetoric remains as strictly anti-north as that of the characters in *Macaria*. An awareness of this discrepancy between thought and action might not surprise Mary Chesnut herself. She admits the necessity during such a critical period for public language that may not mirror individual, private belief. When someone asserts that Fort Sumter was left undefended to tempt the South into attacking it, Chesnut remarks, "We think it sheer stupidity to make this public statement, and that it is in all probability perfectly true" (*Civil War*, 218). This observation provides further insight into the nature of the differences we perceive in Evans's novel and Chesnut's diary. One is written as a public statement on the nobility of the Confederacy; the other is a more private document of one woman's experience. Consequently, *Macaria* must eliminate uncertainty and second-guessing about the enemy and the war, while *Civil War* allows the writer the freedom to explore the inconsistencies and flaws in the public posture. But just as Chesnut saw it as "sheer stupidity" openly to refute Southern mythology, she recognizes that her observations had to remain private, that her thoughts and doubts could not be published at the time. Indeed, as I have suggested, her inability to present the diary publicly during her lifetime indicates the pervasive power of the myth and the enduring tension of the Southern woman's position.

Within the confines of her chosen genre, the personal journal, Chesnut is able to express inconsistencies even within her inconsistencies. Fiercely loyal to Jefferson Davis, she repeatedly castigates those who attack him. She recognizes factionalism as a serious internal threat to the Confederacy, even before the war begins: "We are abusing one another as fiercely as ever we abused Yankees. It is disheartening" (*Civil War*, 20). Later, she predicts "'factions among themselves'—the rock on which we split" (*Civil War*, 314). But despite this insistence on unity and loyalty, she frequently questions military decisions. In 1864 she cries, "surely there is horrid neglect or mismanagement somewhere!" and maintains that "we have shown the weakness and imbecility of our arrangement" (*Civil War*, 578, 579). She criticizes the army for retreating (e.g., *Civil War*, 555) and repeatedly laments the top-heaviness of the Confederate Army: after the surrender, a nephew refers to her as "you who moaned that generals were so cheap and privates so dear!" and she replies, "Yes, I have been for four years snowed up with generals" (*Civil War*, 820). Further, she clearly feels the tension between believing in a cause fervently and doubting whether it is acceptable to sacrifice the lifeblood of a country for that cause. "Is anything worth it? This fearful sacrifice—this awful penalty we pay for war?" (*Civil War*, 625). "I do not believe a genuine follower of Christ can be a soldier. It is a trade which calls for all that he forbids. There!" (*Civil War*, 261). Chesnut's final exclamatory word reveals her understanding that her feeling is subversive, something that should be hidden but that she can hide no longer. It is as if her words have broken free and relieved her of a burden. Here, as elsewhere, Chesnut recognizes sharply the disjunction between her private feelings and her role as a Confederate General's wife.

Macaria displays no equivalent counting of the cost or questioning. For its narrator, the war simply enobles its Southern participants: "Mothers closed their lips firmly to repress a wail of sorrow as they buckled on the swords of their first-born," and one character forgets his lifelong hatred and jealousy of another as "patriotism throttled all the past in her grasp." (*Macaria*, 348, 378). Both Evans's and Chesnut's works are filled with reports of death, but *Macaria*'s highly idealized battlefield death scenes uniformly reveal men glad to die for their country (*Macaria*, 385). Further, all the battles Evans describes are victories, all the generals brave and good. She responds to the horrible cost of the war by asserting that casualties prove the necessity of the separation, not its folly: "national, like individual life, (sic) which is not noble, is not worth the living" (*Macaria*, 412). Again, the fictional portrait arranges all its figures into a consistent, uniform image. Doubt and disturbing complexity must be banished.

The uncritical acceptance of all Confederate policies and values demonstrated in *Macaria* also differs strikingly from Augusta Evans's own freely expressed views. She wrote frequently to General Beauregard and to an Alabama Congressman, discussing military and political matters. She criticized specific battle strategies of Jefferson Davis, she deplored making slave ownership a criterion for exemption from military service, and she argued that the talents of women were being overlooked as a source of assistance in the Confederate struggle.[9] Clearly, then, her fiction was not intended to represent the diversity of Southern existence during the war nor simply to reflect her own positions on the conflict. Instead, *Macaria* presents a carefully manipulated, idealized image in order to undergird support for the Southern cause. As a Southern woman writing during the war, she chose to present fictional models that denied women the complexity she herself displayed. For the perceived good of the South, Augusta Evans's fiction argued for the absolute submergence of women's private endeavors under her public docility and role as symbol.

The contradictions between the public image and the private concerns that I have traced enable us to understand more thoroughly the striking oxymoron which typified descriptions of Southern women. Enmeshed in a troubling social system, caught up in a desperate and devastating war, women knew that public dissent endangered the strength of the cause. As a result they expressed their dissatisfaction only in private. But the discrepancy between external appearance and internal perception becomes even more glaring in the image of the Southern lady. Perhaps suppressing her discontent about other matters taught her to suppress her ambivalence about the role: in any case, the Southern woman chose not to rebel openly against the image. Just as she learned to ignore troubling aspects of the war, so the

Southern woman represented by Evans and Chesnut learned to embrace the mythical identity she was given. All her reservations about her role, like her other reservations about the war effort, had to be submerged and only admitted to privately, if at all. Her inner strength had to be covered by outward fragility, both to inspire the Southern man and to obviate any potential threat to his tenuous power. Thus, Chesnut's descriptions of her own and her friends' feminine roles reveal surfaces which often comply with the romantic, chivalric codes the South needed for its identity while undercurrents of discontent rumble fiercely below the shining exterior of the descriptions. Evans does not ignore these undercurrents, but how she chooses to deal with them is rather remarkable, and her treatment exposes much about the persistence of certain aspects of the Southern woman's image.

Observations about the frustration and powerlessness of being a wife abound in *Mary Chesnut's Civil War*. Chesnut chafes at her dependence upon her husband for even small sums of money. She remarks, after a conversation among her friends, "What a blessed humbug domestic felicity is—eh? At every word, the infatuated fool of a woman recoils as if she had received a slap in the face. And for dear life, she begins to excuse herself for what is no fault of hers. And explains the causes of failure, which he knows beforehand as well as she does. She seems to be expected to put right every wrong in the world" (*Civil War*, 407-08). Frequently, Mrs. Chesnut disagrees with her husband, yet she always submits to his will and guards against any overt rebellion. When he forbids her to throw any more parties, she gives in, styling herself "the obedient wife": "he is the master of the house—to hear is to obey" (*Civil War*, 499, 503). The irony that a modern reader hears in Chesnut's tone is real, but so is the absolute submission. Chesnut emphatically recognizes the tension: "It was very nice of J. C. to take no notice, for my conduct at dinner had been open to criticism. And all the comfort of my life depends on his being in a good humor." Her comparisons of marriage to slavery, already mentioned, are also compelling: "There is no slave, after all, like a wife" (*Civil War*, 514, 59). Yet by all accounts (including her own), Mary Chesnut's marriage was a good one. Ben Williams, who edited the 1949 edition of the diary, says it contains "the lively and heart-warming story of the deep, fine love between Mrs. Chesnut and her husband."[10] While Williams surely ignores much of the material at his disposal, still his remark provides evidence of how carefully Mary Chesnut manages the surface of her life. For a reader not sensitive to feminist concerns or discrepancies in tone, it may be possible to see only the exterior that Chesnut's social circle saw: the charming, witty wife of a gallant, quiet, intelligent soldier. But *Civil War* surely displays also the cost of maintaining that exterior.

Chesnut's critique goes beyond simple complaints about her own marriage, as she displays how the war has widened the gap between men and women and maneuvered women into the position of domestic symbol. Throughout the diary, she comments on the inequity of male and female positions. Discussing the search and seizure of women spies, she says "to men, [war brings] glory, honor, praise, and power—if they are patriots. To women—daughters of Eve—punishment comes in some shape, do what they will" (*Civil War,* 172). She complains bitterly of the sexual double standard and of the plantation owners' frequent and uncondemned fathering of illegitimate black children among the slaves. In a powerful indictment of her home state, she asserts that "South Carolina as a rule does not think it necessary for women to have any existence out of their pantries or nurseries. If they have none, let them nurse the bare walls. But for men! The pleasures of all the world are reserved!" (*Civil War,* 569).

Similarly, the female characters in Augusta Evans's fiction are not brainless beauties who never aspire to anything beyond a husband: Evans's central characters, at some point, display strength and present decided opinions. Like Mary Chesnut and some of her friends, the women of Evans's novels reveal intelligence and ambition. In *Macaria,* the two most important women both pronounce themselves as independent: Irene states (more than once) "I belong to God and myself," and Electra Grey, the poor, aspiring artist says, "I must depend upon myself" (*Macaria,* 25, 78). Both women give themselves over to the pursuit of excellence in fields outside the domestic sphere: Irene avidly studies astronomy in her observatory and Electra goes to New York and Italy to pursue an artistic career. Halfway through the novel, Irene explains her passion for science in graphic and physical terms: "I take my heart, my intellect, and my life, and offer all upon the altar of [astronomy's] penetralia." Electra, facing a life apart from the man she loves unrequitedly, is asked by another suitor if she can be happy with her artistic renown. She replies, "I will grapple fame to my empty heart, as women do other idols" (*Macaria,* 194, 163). Further, when Evans discusses astronomy and painting, she does so eagerly and with genuine understanding and appreciation. The novelist shows remarkable range and depth of knowledge in these subjects, as well as in several other areas outside the traditional sphere of the sentimental novel. She does not simply set up a weak straw man to be overcome easily by "true love" or a sudden recognition of woman's "proper role." Consciously or not, Evans allows her characters seriously to explore alternative possibilities for women. In addition, Electra and Irene are extremely active during the war, and some of their behavior differs sharply from the passive female stereotype. Irene oversees the plantation and makes changes in its management, while Electra smuggles documents from Europe in her paintings. Both

work as volunteer nurses in Richmond and plan to open a school of design after the war, in order to provide new careers for women left destitute by the conflict.

Yet despite the impressive independence and strength Evans depicts in these characters, the author demonstrates that Irene attains peace and a degree of happiness only by learning to accept a subservient role, and at the end of the novel Electra hopes to be able to follow her lead. Interestingly enough, neither woman marries (both love the same man, who is killed in the war), yet Evans still has them learn that woman can be happy only in her appointed domestic sphere. Irene comes to believe this doctrine shortly before the war, when she begins to take care of the poor on "Factory Row." She undertakes this work because her socially active life has left her feeling useless and empty. After she begins her charitable work for others, her pursuit of astronomy is barely mentioned. She does not forsake it, but clearly it no longer governs her life. In an earlier novel, *Beulah,* Evans creates a strong character, a woman writer, who argues throughout the book for the validity of her own career, then capitulates near the end of the novel to Dr. Guy Hartwell:

> He folded his arms about her, clasped her to his heart with a force that almost suffocated her, and bending his head, kissed her passionately. Suddenly his arms relaxed their clasp; holding her off, he looked at her keenly, and said: "Beulah Benton, do you belong to the tyrant Ambition, or do you belong to that tyrant, Guy Hartwell? Quick, child, decide."
>
> "I have decided," said she. Her cheeks burned; her lashes drooped.
>
> "Well?"
>
> "Well, if I am to have a tyrant, I believe I prefer belonging to you!"[11]

Similarly, Evans has the Civil War teach Irene the necessity of sublimating one's "selfish" interests for the good of society. Irene does not trade her pursuit of scientific knowledge for a husband, but she does yield herself up completely to the needs of others, consciously burying all traces of self-interest in her chosen domestic role. She acknowledges that at first glance this loss may seem large, but then she says, "When disposed to lament the limited sphere of woman's influence, I am reminded of Pascal's grand definition: 'A sphere of which the center is everywhere, the circumference nowhere;' and I feel encouraged to hope that, after all, woman's circle of action will prove as sublime and extended" (*Macaria,* 358). In Evans's framework, the course of the war leads Irene consciously to change or repress central aspects of her personality. She becomes submissive and concerned only for the welfare of others—especially others' spiritual welfare. By sacrificing her independence of thought, she becomes a holy exemplar. Like many of the women Mary Chesnut describes, this fictional character consciously accepts a subservient role as her contribution to the war effort. Chesnut refers to her own return to the plantation as "offering up my life on the altar of country" (*Civil War,* 5).

And an "offering up" is exactly how the women perceive most of their own "best" actions. The alternate title of *Macaria* is "Altars of Sacrifice," and the novel is replete with characters who give up something they cherish for the sake of a higher good. The climax of the work occurs when Irene confesses her long-hidden love to Russell as he marches off to war, and explains her devotion: "Of old, when Eurystheus threatened Athens, Macaria, in order to save the city and the land from invasion and subjugation, willingly devoted himself (sic) a sacrifice upon the altar of the gods. Ah, Russell! that were an easy task, in comparison with the offering I am called upon to make. I can not, like Macaria, by self-immolation, redeem my country; from that great privilege I am debarred; but I yield up more than she ever possessed. I give my all on earth—my father and yourself—to our beloved and suffering country. My God! accept the sacrifice, and crown the South a sovereign, independent nation!" (*Macaria,* 371-72) But this sacrifice—yielding up the loved one to the battle—signifies only the beginning for the Southern woman, and the immolation of the Greek woman Macaria that Irene describes serves as emblem for the post-war South. Instead of yielding up her physical life, however, the woman of the defeated South was called upon to sacrifice her independent intellectual and emotional life. That is, like the fictional models created by Evans, the women of the South yielded to the overpowering imagery of sacrifice and restricted themselves to the genteel domestic sphere. Just as Evans and Chesnut deliberately subordinated private ideas to public expression, so the Southern lady deliberately subordinated herself to the Southern man. By allowing herself to serve as an ideal symbol, the Southern woman believed herself to be fulfilling her duty to her country. She had to fit herself carefully and completely into the mold provided to produce the myth around which the South could rally.

This largely unconscious decision differed somewhat from similar "sacrifices" made by Southern women before the war. First, the Civil War forced women into more active roles than they had held previously, and the heavy casualties inflicted by the conflict seriously depleted the manpower of the South during Reconstruction. Therefore, Southern women stood in a position to attempt to establish a more equitable, less patriarchal system than the Old South had been. But the Southern men who did return were defeated, and their way of life had been destroyed. A power struggle would have emasculated them still further. Even more critically, the tradition of the Southern lady stood central to the South's definition of itself as a Cavalier society. As slavery and every other pillar to support the aristocratic myth

crumbled, the image of the ideal, dependent woman had to become unassailable. As a recent historian has argued, the defeated South spawned two myths simultaneously: the Lost Cause and the flawless "Southern woman."[12] That is, as the war was being lost, the mythology of magnolias, fair ladies, and gallant gentlemen had to be created, and the myth's relation to the actual conditions of the antebellum South remains problematic. Nevertheless, the Southern lady became the living embodiment of all that was precious about the Old South. The steel forged in her character by the war *had* to fit into the velvet glove—otherwise, it represented too great a threat to the fragile male ego and male social order. The lady had to allow her ambivalences and complexities to be simplified into a stereotype that presented a docile, gracious face. In an amazing tour-de-force, both the strength the women were forced to exercise because of the war and women's own strong inclinations to rebel at the assigned roles were harnessed and transformed into quiet power that worked only to undergird the social structure.

Augusta Evans's portrayal of Irene's struggle represents the chosen model for Southern womanhood. All the fierce independence and intellectual or artistic abilities a woman might cultivate add to her inner strength. But that strength must always remain under the surface, never threatening the rightful male dominance. Again and again, the narrator of *Macaria* asserts that each man and woman has his or her specific God-oriented task—and the gender distinctions within tasks are clearly marked. "Practically, women should have as little to do with politics as men with darning stockings or making puff-paste; but we should be unworthy of the high social *status* which your chivalry accords us were we indifferent to the conduct of public affairs." She continues:

> Man for the field, and woman for the hearth:
> Man for the sword, and for the needle she:
> Man with the head, and woman with the heart:
> Man to command, and woman to obey.
>
> (*Macaria,* 309)

Irene, the woman who offers this ideal division of labor, has ridden high-spirited horses, become an expert astronomer, successfully defied her father's choice of husband for her, and single-handedly cared for several factory poor. The message stands out sharply: no matter how bright and talented a woman may be, her place must be subservient to man. The Southern woman accepts this role partially because it preserves the social order and partially because the myth generates a cluster of compensations. *Macaria* contains many passages explaining the special privileges this role grants to women:

> It is not woman's place to obtrude herself in the pulpit,
> or harangue from the rostrum; such an abnormal course

levels the distinction which an all-wise God established between the sexes, but the aggregate of her usefulness is often greater than man's.

(122)

It is woman's province and prerogative to gather up the links of beauty, and bind them as a garland round her home.

(237)

Women have a knack of intertwining stems and grouping colors; our fingers were ordained for all such embroidery on the coarse grey serge of stern, practical every-day life.

(205)

Early in her journal, Mary Chesnut asks, "Why am I so frightfully ambitious? Now will I set out from henceforth to care only for my country's salvation." (*Civil War*, 151). Though Chesnut never fully succeeds in such self-abnegation, Augusta Evans's fictional heroines do learn to put their country's salvation before their own aspirations in precisely the way Chesnut describes here. Like Electra, Irene, and Beulah, the woman of the South learns to yield ambition and power, but she gains, according to Evans, the opportunity to beautify and enoble her environment. *Macaria* ends with a poem that represents the apotheosis of this compensatory vision, and of the yoking of velvet and steel:

> Rise, woman, rise!
> To the peculiar and best altitudes
> Of doing good and of enduring ill,
> Of comforting for ill, and teaching good,
> And reconciling all that ill and good
> Unto the patience of a constant hope.
>
> Henceforward, rise, aspire,
> To all the calms, and magnanimities,
> The lofty uses and the noble ends,
> The sanctified devotion and full work,
> To which thou are elect for evermore!

(*Macaria*, 469)

Unlike her Northern sisters, the Southern woman could not perceive man as "the other" because she identified with him in mutual grief over their loss and mutual fear of their future. Thus, the Yankee became her "other."[13] Perhaps more than any other single factor, this need to remain linked with the Southern man in a defeated land against all outside enemies sealed the fate of the Southern lady. Her services as a symbol were required to maintain a sagging cultural structure, and she acquiesced to her role.

Notes

1. The publishing history of Chesnut's diary is somewhat complicated. Mary Chesnut kept extensive and very private journals during the war and then attempted two revisions, once in 1875 and then

again in the 1880s. In the latter version, she expanded and transformed her material so that it was no longer, strictly speaking, a dairy. That is, she did not produce a literal record of her experiences day by day. Instead, as her most recent editor observes, "sometimes dates get shifted around, entries telescoped, speakers switched, and words and ideas originally attributed to the writer herself are put into the mouths of others." (Mary Boykin Chesnut, *Mary Chesnut's Civil War*, ed. C. Vann Woodward [New Haven and London: Yale Univ. Press, 1981], p. xxv). But her essential perceptions did not change—she did not add the dissatisfaction with slavery, the pessimism about the war, or the proto-feminist observations as hindsight. Those elements are found in the original journals. Therefore, for the purposes of this essay, I will employ *Mary Chesnut's Civil War* as an accurate record of her reflections during the war years.

Though Chesnut seemed genuinely interested in publishing her book, she wrote to a friend in 1883 that the diary was not yet ready to be printed and that she wanted to "overhaul it again—and again" (*Civil War*, xxiv). Subsequent events including Chesnut's unexpected death three years later prevented such revision, and the work lay unpublished in any form until 1905, when Isabella Martin and Myrta Lockett Avary used the 1880's manuscript to produce a drastically abridged work entitled *A Diary from Dixie*. Ben Ames Williams, editor of the 1949 edition, used the same title. He added much controversial material that the first editors had omitted, but the work was still a shortened and changed version of Chesnut's manuscript.

C. Vann Woodward has produced the most recent and most extensive edition. He states his general purpose as follows: "to publish *what* the author wrote and *how* she wrote it" (*Civil War*, emphasis in original). Woodward argues convincingly that the title *A Diary from Dixie* is inappropriate, and thus calls the book *Mary Chesnut's Civil War*. This work will be the one cited in this essay, and subsequent references to it will appear in the text as *Civil War*.

2. This is true of Chesnut's journals, the raw material for the work under discussion.

3. The book itself could only be published on brown wrapping paper in Richmond because Confederate supplies were extremely low. (Anne Goodwyn Jones, *Tomorrow Is Another Day* [Baton Rouge and London: Louisiana State Univ. Press, 1981], p. 59).

4. The journals and diaries of Southern women provide abundant examples of this same sentiment.

See, for example, Anne Firor Scott's *The Southern Lady: From Pedestal To Politics 1830-1930* (Chicago and London: Univ. of Chicago Press, 1970), pp. 45-53 and Jones, *Tomorrow*, pp. 29-30.

5. Chesnut's response to slavery is further complicated by her attitude toward blacks, for whom she simultaneously manifests affection, empathy, fear, and hatred. After the murder of Betsy Witherspoon by her own slaves, Chesnut ponders: "Hitherto I had never thought of being afraid of negroes. I had never injured any of them. Why should they want to hurt me? Two thirds of my religion consists in trying to be good to negroes because they are so in my power, and it would be so easy to be the other thing. Somehow today I feel that the ground is cut away from under my feet. Why should they treat me any better that they have done Cousin Betsy Witherspoon?" (*Civil War*, 199). She maintains a steadfastly dual vision about blacks, deeming them "placid, docile, kind, and obedient. Also as lazy and dirty as ever" (*Civil War*, 233).

6. That Evans does not present a fully developed pro-slavery argument may possibly be seen as an unwillingness on her part to articulate a belief she finds repugnant or politically unpopular.

7. Augusta J. Evans (Wilson), *Macaria* (New York: John Bradburn, 1864), p. 414, first emphasis mine. Subsequent references to this edition will appear in the text.

8. Evans, of course, is not the only novelist who simplifies in order to make a political point. Mary Chesnut frequently complains that Harriet Beecher Stowe's presentation of the South ignores the complexity of plantation lives and especially the trials of white women. Chesnut also accuses Northern abolitionists of using anti-slavery to advance their own careers (*Civil War*, 245). Upon overhearing a story of an eccentric mistress, Chesnut and a friend wonder what Mrs. Stowe would make of it. The diarist decides "Mrs. Stowe would feel exactly as we do, but she would take an extraordinary freak of nature as a specimen of class—a common type" (*Civil War*, 311).

9. Bell Irvin Wiley, *Confederate Women* (Westport, Connecticut: Greenwood Press, 1975), p. 173. Mary Chesnut also deplored the failure to capitalize on the victory at First Manassas, but she did not blame Jeff Davis (*Civil War*, 124-25).

10. Ben Ames Williams, ed., *A Diary from Dixie* (Boston: Houghton Mifflin Co., 1949), p. viii.

11. Augusta J. Evans, *Beulah* (1859; rpt. New York: New York Book Company, 1909), p. 174.

12. John Carl Ruoff, "Frivolity to Consumption: or Southern Womanhood in Antebellum Literature," *Civil War History*, XVLI (1972), 229.

13. Jones, *Tomorrow*, p. 25.

Karen Tracey (essay date winter 1999)

SOURCE: Tracey, Karen. "Recasting Women's Roles: Southworth's *Britomarte, the Man-Hater* as Civil War Fiction." *Southern Quarterly* 37, no. 2 (winter 1999): 5-15.

[*In the following essay, Tracey explores Emma Dorothy Eliza Nevitte (E.D.E.N.) Southworth's treatment of the Civil War's effect on gender roles and women's identity in her novel,* Britomarte, the Man-Hater.]

E.D.E.N. Southworth's post-Civil War serial *Britomarte, the Man-Hater*, published in two volumes as *Fair Play; or, The Test of the Lone Isle* (1868) and *How He Won Her* (1869), includes the typical features of Southworth's bestselling novels: action-adventure plots that alternate and intersect with sentimental domestic plots, courageous and unconventional heroines that contrast with traditional true women, and realistic descriptions and events that are interwoven with highly improbable sensational episodes. The fact that much of the second volume of the narrative is set during the Civil War might appear to be merely incidental to Southworth's story; she suggests as much herself: "I shall not burden this light and simple story with the politics of civil war. I shall only allude to it where it immediately concerns the people of whom I am writing" (*Fair Play* 354). But where the war "immediately concerns the people" of whom Southworth writes, it also immediately concerns the people *for* whom she writes. In addition to promoting her own pro-Union politics, the Britomarte serial investigates how the Civil War acted upon those aspects of American life that had interested Southworth in her antebellum novels: the lack of security for women within the home, the restrictive nature of gender roles, and the consequent and profound importance of marrying wisely.

Southworth's Civil War novel, though presented as merely another entertaining narrative, participated in the crucial cultural work undertaken by Americans as they attempted to understand, explain, define, and control the momentous impact of the war. The war created havoc or at least disruption in almost every area of life, and conventional nineteenth-century distinctions between the genders were no exception. The notion of "separate spheres" and generalizations about the distinct attributes of woman (ruled by the heart) and of man (ruled by the head) never did reflect reality even for the privileged white classes. But as the Civil War disrupted homes and forced women to take on new roles, it became difficult to protect even the linguistic fiction that men and women inhabited different spheres or that they could be defined by different characteristics. Southworth's narrative explores the effect on four heroines when civil war shatters the fragile, and artificial, barriers that had been rhetorically constructed between public and private worlds, political and domestic spheres. No one could pretend any longer that the domestic space could be protected from the rough male world. Categories treated as naturally separate in antebellum language collapsed under the pressures of war. Love and courtship could not be kept distinct from political loyalties. In fact, women themselves were no longer always distinguishable from men. The task of Southworth's pair of novels was, in part, to use multiple courtship plots to examine the disruptions war forced onto the characters' lives, to chart new paths for women in the territory opened by the destruction of old barriers, and to negotiate marriages that would heal personal and national wounds, helping to reconstruct a domestic and public order in which women could retain some of the responsibilities and privileges that they had proven they deserved during the war.

Southworth's post-war serial capitalizes upon war-born changes in women's lives to demonstrate that women are stronger and more complex than conventional ideology allowed. She set her story largely in Washington which, as a border city and the seat of federal government, was a strategic location for a story about how the Civil War disrupted domestic life in both northern and southern families. Four heroines—Alberta Goldsmith, Erminie Rosenthal, Elfie Fielding, and Britomarte Conyers—open the narrative dressed alike in white graduation gowns, planning futures that are subsequently disrupted by the war in a variety of ways, demonstrating how thoroughly the Civil War may have redirected and redefined women's roles, and women's understanding of those roles. Each of Southworth's heroines is given a dramatic courtship plot, and conventional gender ideology would have suggested that since women are ruled by the heart, their political commitments would be subject to their emotional ones. Not so for these heroines. Southworth suggests that while women do indeed love passionately, they are at least as passionate about their political convictions.

To make this point without violating the conventions of popular women's fiction, Southworth historicized her adventure tale while disavowing interest in writing about the war: "It would be presumptuous in a mere story-writer to dwell upon these magnificent themes, so much beyond her power of treatment. This story does not pretend to be a history of the campaign or of any portion of it; it is only a simple narrative" (*How He Won Her* 468). Despite such disclaimers, Southworth interlaces her "simple narrative" with references to par-

ticular battles, significant dates, and historical figures, invoking enough conventional history to remind a reader that the story is set in quite real, and quite recent, times. She alludes gingerly, for example, to the assassination of Lincoln, enhancing her novel with the "seriousness" of history even as she excuses herself for mentioning it: "Let us reverently pass over that awful calamity of April the fourteenth, which followed so swiftly upon the winged feet of Victory, quenching all her lights of joy and of triumph in darkness and in blood. The Nation's holy sorrow is too sacred a subject to be treated here" (*How He Won Her* 480). And when Southworth describes a Confederate prison "as I saw it in May, 1865," she vouches for her own historical veracity. She even invites her readers to call upon their own memories: "Everyone knows how hopefully the campaign of the Spring of 1864 opened. In almost every engagement the Union arms triumphed" (366).

But Southworth is selective in invoking history and does not encourage her readers to think about the pressing problem of race. In the wake of emancipation, she fails to imagine a role for freedmen, even though in one of her antebellum novels, *Mark Sutherland* (1853), serialized as *India; or the Pearl of Pearl River,* she had celebrated a character who chose to sacrifice his wealth and free his slaves. Southworth joins many of her contemporaries in imagining the Civil War to be about the dis-union and re-union of a white America. Nina Silber finds that white northerners, sympathizing with the defeated planter class, "eventually cast southern blacks outside their reunion framework altogether" (6), while Kathleen Diffley has observed that black characters in Civil War stories usually die on the battlefield protecting whites or continue as servants in white households (53). Diffley's second category describes the one black character who appears regularly in *Britomarte.* Southworth devotes just one-half of one page to acknowledging emancipation and the black contribution to the Union war effort: Britomarte is freed from a Richmond prison by black Union soldiers who are being joyously welcomed "by the colored population on the sidewalk" (*How He Won Her* 476). Southworth is more than ready to gloss over issues of race in order to promote the particular interests of white women and, more generally, the progress of white reconciliation.

Thus Southworth's central subject is the impact of the Civil War on gender roles as the genteel white classes had conventionally defined them. She presents the war as an arena in which women could take, in fact had no choice but to take, aggressive roles. Her novels reveal the same patterns of expanded opportunity for women during the war and varying degrees of retrenchment after the war that have been discovered and examined in recent years by social historians. A woman's war job was to "keep the home fires burning," but in the absence of men, she also had to supply the fuel. In the border states and in the South, she moreover often found herself watching the home itself burn down unless she could defend it. Planter class women frequently took control of plantations, managing overseers and slaves, and directing agricultural and financial operations. Occupations were opened to women in the North and South as men were absorbed by the armies, and labor was needed to supply soldiers with the necessities of war and civilians with the necessities of life. Many women who did not work for wages extended traditional domestic skills into the public realm. Many of them organized large volunteer groups, thus demonstrating impressive managing skills. Others broke a strong taboo by nursing wounded soldiers in public hospitals. By choice or by necessity, thousands of women breached convention to serve their men, their country, or their own desire for expanded liberty. Whether individuals embraced gender transformation or had it thrust upon them, the war forced reconsideration of conventional gender roles in both the North and South.[1] Southworth's *Man-Hater* narrative provides us with one contemporary exploration of the very trends that have only recently been researched by historians.

For one of her four heroines the break with convention results in tragedy. Alberta Goldsmith, the heiress of a wealthy planter, rejects her family to marry the itinerant Italian Corsoni. She does not, however, reject her southern upbringing. On the contrary, she inspires her husband to fight for the Rebel cause, and both are killed by one bullet when a Union force attacks their guerilla band. Southworth's depiction of Alberta Goldsmith's fate is a cautionary fable about the tragic end of the "model young lady of her set" (*Fair Play* 31), a southern belle who is raised only to ornament family circles, and therefore does not internalize the moral standards that motivate the other three heroines. As the narrator puts it, "So far from having any affinity or mission on this earth, she had scarcely a sentiment or an opinion of her own" (31). A woman who is such a blank slate is vulnerable, at the mercy of her passions, and unable to reason on serious moral or political issues. But with the outbreak of the war, Alberta commits herself to both her husband and her Confederacy. Southworth's "model" southern belle comes to a tragic end, but not because she abandoned traditional feminine passivity. Rather, she dies because she acted for a mistaken cause.

Consider the contrast of Erminie's story, which uses the circumstances of war to argue that the ideal "true woman" of the North may have strength untested by her usual domestic employments, and to suggest that the country would benefit from a revised understanding of true womanhood. Erminie has a contented home life. Although her mother is dead, her father is a benevolent patriarch and her brother a loving protector. When she leaves school, she falls in love with Colonel Eastworth, a "distinguished son of South Carolina" (57) whose good looks, heroic military background, and "superiority in age" attract her because "reverence was so large an element" in her love (72). They are quickly betrothed, but her father asks them to wait two years because Erminie is too young to marry. Had the Civil War not intervened, she would have been peacefully transferred from loving patriarchal father to loving patriarchal husband. But instead, Southworth gives Erminie a courtship and marriage that is emblematic of the division and reunion between North and South.

The war disrupts the courtship and challenges Erminie to prove she is more than a simple domestic creature. Eastworth is blinded by ambition and by secessionist propaganda, becoming embroiled in a (failed) plot to prevent Lincoln from taking office. When discovered, he escapes South to serve as a general in the Confederate army. He takes advantage of his residence in the Rosenthal's home to carry on clandestine activities. Neither Erminie nor her father, both committed Unionists who assume Eastworth is on their side, notice anything amiss; Erminie does not even catch on when Eastworth becomes upset over her rendition of "The Star Spangled Banner" (371-73). The Rosenthal household, like much of the North perhaps, failed to take secessionist talk seriously, and Erminie, "who was no more of a politician than her father, and had no more misgivings about the safety of the national union than she had about the certainty of her own union with the husband of her choice, went gaily about her household business" (369). Erminie is still bound by her domestic space, but the narrator foreshadows the conflict that will disrupt both national and private unions.

Domestic ideal though she is, Erminie is no more fully defined by her conventional gender role than was Alberta, the model (and misguided) southern belle. In Erminie, Southworth offers an embodiment of the traditional "true woman," yet the heroine has strengths and convictions not accounted for by typical true woman ideology. When she discovers that Eastworth is a Rebel, she refuses to elope with him to the South as he expects her to do. Eastworth assumes that Erminie can easily transfer her allegiances, personal and political, from father to husband because she is a domestic creature. He tells her that "daughter-like, you take your opinions from your father, and, parrot-like, repeat the words he uses, without attaching much meaning to them" (450). He is wrong. He attempts to "plead the cause of Secession with all the arguments by which astute leaders influence the opinions of people. . . . But they made no impression on the mind of Erminie Rosenthal" (452-53). The simplicity of her faith, rather than making her pliable, makes her strong: "I see this all too clearly to deceive myself. I have loved this Union so much! . . . And would you aim a death-blow at her? . . . I would give my life—almost my soul—to save you from this vortex!" (452). Eastworth departs for the South while

Erminie remains in Washington to volunteer as a nurse. Like many historical women, Erminie extends her role as nurturer beyond the bounds of the home, testing and extending her own endurance. Erminie refers to the hospital as "a great school for the spirit" (*How He Won Her* 41-42). When Eastworth returns at the end of the war, defeated, humbled, and mutilated, Erminie has grown from a naive girl into a strong woman, and she plans to continue her active role to help heal her country.

The parallel between Erminie's "union" and the country's "Union" is sustained throughout her plot. Reconciliation is possible because General Eastworth recants his Confederate convictions. Erminie welcomes Eastworth back, to his amazement: "What a welcome, and how unworthy I am to receive it! Do angels always welcome returning sinners so, Erminie?" (495). He protests that he is "old and gray and broken and mutilated," having lost his right arm "in a bad cause"; furthermore, he is "poor and penniless. . . . My once spotless name is stained with reproach" (496). All this makes no difference to Erminie, and "these two were reconciled, and this was but the forerunner of a deeper and broader reconciliation yet to come" (496). Southworth obviously hopes that the North, like Erminie, will welcome the South back into the Union without rancor. Once married, Eastworth and Erminie go to Virginia, planning to work to "restore order and industry in their own section of country, and to promote peace and goodwill between the North and the South" (511). This fictional representative of a cultural icon has been strengthened by asserting herself as a political as well as a domestic creature. In narrating the story of Erminie's war experiences, Southworth redefines the concept of "true woman," suggesting that the many domestic women who proved themselves during the war should be understood as having a substantial post-war role to play in healing both their own families and their country. Southworth appears to have understood a phenomenon explained by Whites, who writes that women's war work "served to reveal the way in which their own domestic labors literally created, or at least underpinned, the public position of their men" (136-37). Erminie's story suggests that the country will benefit by allowing women to continue to extend their domestic labors beyond the home.

This argument itself is not new. Southworth is writing in the tradition of domestic writers who envisioned the home as a positive and active influence on the public realm. Harriet Beecher Stowe's *Uncle Tom's Cabin* is perhaps the most famous example of a novel in which domestic influence is exerted for political ends. The writers in the woman's fiction tradition identified by Nina Baym were, along similar lines, "thinking about a social reorganization wherein their special concept of home was projected out into the world" (48). Baym

adds that the "decade of the 1850s was the high point of their fiction because the motives of self-development and social reform could run together so smoothly" (49). The Civil War provided Southworth the opportunity for women to prove that domesticity had the strength antebellum novelists had claimed for it. When Eastworth first proposes to Erminie, he arrogantly assumes that she is exclusively a domestic creature, and although appreciative of how adept she is at arranging rooms and planning meals, he fails to recognize the depth and strength of her convictions and the clarity of her sense of political as well as domestic duty. He understood the domestic role to be entirely subordinate to the political interests of the head of household, whereas Erminie had a more inclusive vision. When she welcomes him back, with her love unchanged in spite of his humiliation, he recognizes her moral superiority and sees the strength and clear-mindedness that goes with it. Through the extended courtship, Southworth negotiates a marriage that will strengthen the woman's role and humble the man so that he recognizes and must rely on that strength.

The progressive impetus of Southworth's courtship plot becomes clearer when her story is contrasted with other post-Civil War writing that imagined national reunion through private unions. Diffley's study found that approximately one-fourth of romance stories of the period "aligned courtship rituals with sectional politics," but that such tales usually featured a northern suitor and a southern heroine, thus implying that the conquered South must submit to the government of the North (62-63). Silber finds the gendered reunion metaphor to be pervasive in both fiction and nonfiction. She argues that the "image of marriage between northern men and southern women stood at the foundation of the late nineteenth-century culture of conciliation and became a symbol which defined and justified the northern view of the power relations in the reunified nation" (6-7). For Southworth's contemporaries, then, reunion stories typically presented the South as conquered and submissive, and therefore feminine, and the North as triumphant and dominant, and therefore masculine. Southworth's Erminie and Eastworth union inverts this power relationship, as the male represents the defeated South who must be forgiven, while the female stands for the strong and true North, waiting patiently for her wayward partner to repent and acknowledge her moral superiority.

Thus while Southworth's narrative implies on one level that men will benefit from women's extended role, she also reveals her awareness that increased power for women involves decreased power for men. In the defeated South, surviving men were often physically mutilated as well as economically and ideologically stripped. Eastworth, with arm amputated and secessionist politics recanted, suggests the fate of planter class men, who were forced to dismantle the slave system upon which they had founded their claims of racial and gender superiority. According to historian George Rable, when southern men failed to successfully defend themselves and their homes, they were perceived as "no longer men," while at the same time, women gained strength because, through their contributions to the war, they "no longer saw themselves as passive victims" (137). Apparently, Southworth comprehended how the war had opened possibilities for extended women's roles and more egalitarian marriages, and, under the protection of a conventional courtship closure, she inverts the typical reunion courtship and marries the chastened Eastworth to the strengthened Erminie. Southworth thus manipulates literary conventions and Reconstruction politics to recast gender roles.

Elfie Fielding's courtship plot examines the relationship of a second politically divided couple who never reconcile their political commitments, although they are briefly reconciled in marriage. Both Elfie and her suitor, Albert Goldsmith, are southerners, but Elfie remains loyal to the Union while Albert conspires with Eastworth before joining the band of Confederate guerrillas led by Alberta Goldsmith's husband Corsoni. Elfie is forced to flee to Washington as a refugee because she displays the Union flag and shoots a man who tries to take it down; she reports that the "first public act of my life resulted in getting our house burned over our heads!" (404). Her public acts continue. She discovers the Rebel plot brewing in the Rosenthal house when Albert, assuming that she is on the Confederate side, unwittingly discusses it with her. Elfie breaks her engagement, denouncing secession in terms that articulate her understanding of a continuity between political and domestic relations:

> If a state has the right to secede from the Union, a county has the same right to secede from a state; and a township to secede from a county; and a farm from a township; and the barn from the farm; and the husband from the wife, and the child from the father!—and there you have disintegration and anarchy!
>
> (*Fair Play* 429)

Albert wants to marry Elfie immediately and take her South, but she refuses: "She loved him and hated him at the same moment; her heart was breaking, and she wished for death. But she never dreamed of flinching from her duty!" (428). Elfie links her private decision to terminate her courtship with political rhetoric: "If I were fool enough to marry you this week, why, next week, or next month you might secede from *me*!" (431). She reports Eastworth's plot to the government, although in so doing she endangers the man she loves. She then attempts to get herself drafted by the Union using her androgynous middle name "Sydney"; her father refuses to let her go to war, but he does buy a substitute for her.

Albert, like Eastworth, refuses to believe that a woman's political loyalties could be stronger than her private affections. He kidnaps Elfie and, in spite of her violent opposition (she nearly tears his ears off with her bare hands) forces her through a marriage ceremony while promising not to consummate that marriage without her consent: "You shall be as sacred to me as my sister" until "you will forgive me and love me" (*How He Won Her* 272). Elfie is rescued by Union forces and returns to Washington, where she helps Erminie in the hospitals. Albert, like Eastworth, is badly wounded and loses a limb (in his case a leg). Elfie, overcome by grief and love, dons her hated wedding ring and acknowledges her marriage so that she may nurse him. Each recognizes the other's right to a different opinion; Albert tells Elfie that "diametrically opposed as we are, we are each of us true to our firmest convictions of duty. . . . And so far each of us is right" (348). But because Albert dies, he and Elfie are never faced with the problem of reconciling their marriage with their irreconcilable political divisions.

No doubt the North, like Elfie, finds the fallen and disarmed (or dis-legged) Rebel easier to love than a Rebel in arms:

> When I saw *him* at the head of his band; strong, rampant, insolent; in arms against the government; doing his arrogant will with everybody, and with myself among the rest, I *hated* him. . . . And now, when I see him stretched, broken, helpless, and writhing in agony in that bed, as if it was a rack, I feel as if my cruel prayers had been granted, and I had brought him to it!
>
> (*How He Won Her* 332-33)

But only converted Rebels and those true to the Union are left to promote reconciliation; Southworth cannot envision a union between characters whose public commitments are not compatible. Elfie can only express her love for Albert when he admits her right to hold to her own convictions, and when he can no longer exert "his arrogant will" over her. In this courtship, again featuring a couple whose sectional allegiances invert the more common motif, the North (coded female) survives while the unrepentant South (coded male) dies. In addition to pointing out that Confederate ideology is doomed, Southworth conflates history and narrative to suggest that, given the death of so many men, the reunified nation must rely on its strengthened women for survival.

While Alberta, Erminie, and Elfie all illustrate ways in which women could be politicized and energized by the war, the fourth heroine, the "Man-hater" Britomarte Conyers, is the most aggressively political and action-oriented of them all. Her prolonged courtship with Justin Rosenthal (Erminie's brother) is resolved only after the Civil War has offered the heroine the opportunity to display the courage and bravery of which she is capable. Britomarte has "rebelled against the fate that made her woman and the law that limited her liberty to woman's sphere" (*Fair Play* 29), and vows never to marry and therefore to subject herself to laws and customs that circumscribe her freedom. She draws unabashedly feminist conclusions about "not only the rights of married women to the control of their own property and custody of their own children, but the rights of all women to a competition with men in all the paths of industry and a share with them in all the chances of success" (53). Justin finds in her words "much of right, strongly asserted" ("strong" probably carrying the pejorative connotation associated with "strong-minded women") and quickly falls in love with her. Britomarte, to her dismay, returns his passion, but "she combatted that love with all the strength of her strong will" (111). Britomarte and Justin survive a shipwreck, build a home on a deserted island ("chaperoned" by the Irish servant Judith), fight against a pirate ship, and then return home to act in the theater of the Civil War.

Fair Play contains well-argued and passionate articulations of women's wrongs and their need for political protection. Britomarte lectures Justin and Erminie's father, the gentle but firm patriarch Dr. Rosenthal, when he claims to have had "no hand in making these laws or encouraging these customs"; the heroine points out, "You live under these laws without raising pen or voice to modify them. You profit by these customs without ever remembering that you do so" (125). Her concerns for women go beyond her class, and at least tentatively beyond her race, and she draws on personal observation and statistics to prove her case. She deplores the unequal working conditions and pay for working-class women that exist because "your diabolical laws and customs have not only barred against woman in almost every field of labor, but have reduced her to the lowest pittance of wages in those few fields in which you permit her to work" (122); she asks that her listener "take into consideration the humanity of freeing the poor white slave women of the cities" in addition to "the slaves of the plantations" (124). She further notes that among the "semi-professional classes. . . . the male teacher gets from ten to twelve hundred dollars a year, the female, for teaching the same branches and doing the same amount of work, gets but two hundred and fifty or three hundred" (122-23). Britomarte vows to live a life of protest rather than to submit to the unfair play of laws and customs:

> In the first place, so long as the barbarous law in changing a woman to a wife makes her a nonentity, I will not marry. . . . In the second place, so long as your barbarous customs close half of woman's legitimate field of labor, and open the other half only to admit her to work at degrading rates of wages, I will not work for any wages whatever. . . . In the third place so long as man continues to wrong woman, I will never accept assistance from any man whomsoever.
>
> (125)

Britomarte moderates her hatred of men gradually, talking less of women's rights as circumstances give her more opportunities to act.

The transition between the two volumes of the serial, as the action moves from fantasy island to historicized war, suggests what Southworth, as a writer interested in women's lives, found so valuable in the changes brought about by the Civil War. In order to put antebellum heroines in positions where they could display their strengths, she created fantastic situations. Her best-known heroine, Capitola Black of *The Hidden Hand,* dressed as a boy to survive the streets of New York, fought a duel in defense of her own honor, rescued a maiden from a forced marriage, and captured a dreaded outlaw. And while Capitola's transgressive adventures clearly comment upon contemporary gender roles and restrictions, they of necessity carry an air of the fabulous which is underscored by the wild, even gothic, settings in which they take place and by the quest romance language Southworth uses to describe them. When the men in that novel go to fight in the Mexican War, the narrator reluctantly leaves Cap at home, commenting that "our little domestic heroine, our brave little Cap . . . when women have their rights, shall be a lieutenant-colonel herself. Shall she not, gentlemen?" (348). The Civil War offered Southworth the opportunity denied in the earlier conflict. Using the cross-dressing and role-playing strategies that made Capitola successful, and working herself for a time when "women have their rights," Britomarte does indeed fight in battles and rise in rank (to Captain) in a man's army. The fantastic adventures of Southworth's earlier fiction continue, but are now historically situated.

Britomarte says that the war allowed men to prove their heroism and therefore earn her regard, but it also offered opportunities for women. While many women remained in their home communities to tend the house and participate in local volunteer efforts, others, both northern and southern, went to war even if the war was not coming to them. Most often, they worked as nurses or other support personnel for soldiers, but also, more frequently than has been suspected, they became soldiers themselves. Historians have documented that many women served dressed as men in Union and Confederate armies (both as enlisted soldiers and as officers), and that many women who served as nurses, daughters of the regiment, or vivandieres came under fire. Catherine Clinton notes that "over four hundred women were discovered posing as soldiers" (85), and Richard Hall suggests that women perhaps made a much greater contribution than that, because (like Southworth's Britomarte) they kept their secret during and after the war whenever possible; one Civil War veteran was discovered to be female in 1911 (20-26).[2] As Elfie announces: "Nothing but our crinoline, if that is to stand for our sex, keeps thousands of us out of the army!"

(*How He Won Her* 338). Hundreds did breach convention, abandon their crinoline, and enter the army, as Elfie attempts to do, and as Britomarte succeeds in doing, demonstrating "patriotism, courage, fortitude, and self-devotion" (*How He Won Her* 509) as valiantly as any male soldier.

Whereas Erminie's work in the hospitals and Elfie's heroic defense of her own home, effort to be drafted, and willingness to betray her lover to the federal authorities attest to women's heroism and patriotism, Britomarte's actions outdo them both. While her adventures are more harrowing and dramatic than were Capitola's, many parts of Britomarte's story might have been drawn from historical accounts. Confederate soldier Amy Clarke joined the army with her husband and suffered two wounds before being taken prisoner, re-dressed in women's clothes, and returned to her home (Faust 203). And Emma Edmonds entered the Union army as a man, later assuming various disguises to penetrate Confederate lines on spying missions (Sizer 117). Britomarte's adventures recall the experiences of both these women. Dressed as a man, she enlists in Justin's regiment and becomes his aide; she later dons other disguises as an undercover agent for the Union. She participates heroically in armed conflict, at times leading charges into the teeth of enemy fire, and she spies for information that leads to the capture of the Rebel guerilla band. The heroine is finally caught and imprisoned; she was "more than a suspected spy in the hands of the enemy, and as such, she was only saved from the usual fate of a spy by that consideration for her sex which restrained her captors from putting a woman to death for anything less than a capital crime proved upon her . . . by direct testimony" (469-70).

Southworth justifies Britomarte's "unwomanly" behavior in the war by tying it to her great love for Justin, deflecting criticism that might be directed at how Britomarte cross-dresses, lives with men in army camps, fights in battles, and spies on enemies: "Justin, my beloved, I abjured my womanhood, disguised myself and followed you to battle; I have been by your side on twenty well fought fields; I have dared what woman never dared before, that I might be ever with you!" (440); in other words, Britomarte is more, not less womanly, for having "transformed and disfigured" herself (441). Southworth's rhetoric has shifted; whereas she once called her readers to admire the "brilliant Amazon" because of her strength and talents, she now adds to that heroine's character the trait of supreme selfless love. The "manly" strengths Britomarte demonstrates throughout the novels are derived from, rather than existing in spite of, her "womanly" traits. The story of Britomarte and Justin best represents the possibilities for expanded roles for women, and for progressive marriage within this new order, even an order in which unjust marriage laws are still in effect.

Yet Southworth is not excessively optimistic about the increased power women might be able to take in marriage, or about the increased respect they might be able to command as a result of their heroic activities during the war. She must have been aware of the desperate efforts at retrenchment undertaken by men who returned from war longing to reassert their dominance over the domestic sphere. The reassertion was particularly crucial in the South, as Whites explains: "Confederate men looked to the domestic arena as their one remaining location of legitimate domination just as the same war that had defeated them on all other terrains had increased, however painfully, the autonomy of their women" (136). And Leonard finds that in the North, women had to struggle to maintain the advances they made during the war, for early post-war historians were creating "a carefully constructed postwar image of Yankee womanhood designed to circumscribe the social and political consequences of wartime stresses on the gender system" (182). To a degree, the conclusion of Southworth's novel seems to follow the same design, to participate in the common historical pattern wherein, following the disruption to domestic life caused by war, women and men return with relief to household relations reflecting conservative pre-war ideologies of gender.[3] Following their wedding, Justin asks Britomarte, "How about Woman's Rights now, sweet wife?" to which she responds with a protest that sounds like a younger Britomarte, but with a disclaimer: "While I live . . . I will advocate the rights of woman—*in general*. But for my individual self, the only right I plead for is woman's dearest right—to be loved to my heart's content all the days of my life!" (512). Britomarte compromises her political convictions by accepting happiness for herself in marriage to her beloved fellow-soldier. Elfie does not recant her unionist convictions, but she does accept her Rebel suitor as a husband so that she can fulfill her wifely role as nurse and death-bed attendant. And Erminie envisions her future domestic role as promoting the healing of national wounds, but does, after all, marry her reformed Confederate soldier. The *Man-Hater* narratives may work in part to restrain post-war anxiety about women's increasing power by intimating that women had always been political as well as domestic creatures, and that despite this truth, women were ready to fulfill their old duties as well as to claim some new ones. Perhaps the title change between serial publication and two-volume novel signifies most strongly the conservative shift. The serial title, *Britomarte, the Man-Hater,* focuses on the single heroine as women's rights activist, while the novel titles, *Fair Play* and *How He Won Her,* stress the courtship and foreshadow the marriage ending.

But for two thick volumes Southworth celebrates Britomarte's strength and independence, and the images of Britomarte the Man-hater, the soldier, and the spy far outweigh the brief final pages during which, in the afterglow of wartime glory, she accepts marriage. And in history as in these novels, returning to pre-war conditions or ideas is not so easy. Many women appreciated the increased liberty and strength they gained during the war, and were reluctant to return to a sphere as circumscribed as it had been before the war. Others, deprived of male support, were forced to fend for themselves and their children whether they wanted it that way or not. Still others, particularly in the South, having discovered they could not rely on men to defend and support them, retained a degree of independence in self-defense. And many of the men left by the war were weakened, physically and/or economically, and therefore forced to rely on the work of their women. Thus the widened horizons of possibilities for women combined with the demands of rebuilding the Union could not be controlled by revisionary post-war rhetoric; popular works such as Southworth's would make sure that reactionary post-war voices did not go unchallenged. A "simple story" like Southworth's had all the potential influence wielded by popular literature cast in historical context:

> This is the power of popular culture: to offer large numbers of people explanations of why things are the way things are—and what, if anything, can be done about it. Infuse this power with history—explanations of how things came to be the way they are—and you have a potent agent for influencing the thinking, and thus the actions, of millions of people.
>
> (Cullen 13)

Despite her protestations to the contrary, Southworth's voice spoke through her narrative to a popular audience about the meaning of the war. Out of the confusion the Civil War infused into conventional concepts of gender roles, Southworth's novels redefine traditional feminine virtues by recasting woman's sphere as both political and domestic, and by advocating marriages that are built on this broadened definition of woman's role. As Britomarte's final words remind the reader, women "in general" need and have earned increased political and legal rights. Their heroic behavior during the Civil War should help to convince doubters that women are fit to participate in public spheres of action, and that, in fact, the survival and healing of the nation depends on the growing strength of its women.

Notes

1. Nina Silber concludes that "the Civil War had wreaked havoc on the stability and rigidity of the Victorian code of gender. . . . women everywhere had assumed new responsibilities and new roles which ran counter to accepted notions of the feminine sphere" (28). Elizabeth Leonard's *Yankee Women: Gender Battles in the Civil War* reveals in detail how three northern women capitalized on the needs and opportunities brought to women by the war, while LeeAnn Whites's *The Civil War As A Crisis in Gender* explores how the privileged white community of Augusta, Georgia, confronted threats to gender roles and redefined them to protect as best they could the southern notions of gender roles and white identity that were thrown into disarray by the Civil War. Leonard writes that the Civil War "rapidly made untenable the strict adherence of northern, middle-class Americans, at least, to this very particular, and in many minds apparently fixed and perfectly harmonious web of ideals about the social roles and relative power of men and women and about their proper interaction" (xxii). Whites finds that "gender roles as well as gender relations played a critical role in the initial outbreak of the war, as well as in its course, its conduct, and its eventual outcome in the 'reconstruction' of the South. For individual men and women, this moment of gender transformation in the social order at large created a crisis in the very way that they perceived their appropriate gender roles" (3). Drew Gilpin Faust argues that while southern women did develop new identities because of their accomplishments during the war, their experiences should not be construed as positive: "This new sense of self was based not in the experience of success but in desperation, in the fundamental need simply to survive" (243).

2. Hall surveys women's roles as vivandieres, daughters of the regiment, and nurses; Lyde Cullen Sizer and Hall discuss the role of women spies in the Civil War. Marilyn Mayer Culpepper collects and analyzes extensive primary materials that reveal how women acted in and were acted upon by the Civil War.

3. Karen Lystra's study of nineteenth-century courtship letters suggests that private correspondence registered the same kinds of war-related disruption in gender relations that historians have documented and that Southworth's novels explored:

> Although men's and women's outward role behavior may not have changed greatly, evidence indicates there was more tension over sex roles from the Civil War to the end of the century than in the antebellum period. Certainly the Civil War itself may be a factor in what appears to be a new level of sex-role insecurity in postbellum male-female relationships.
>
> (147)

Works Cited

Baym, Nina. *Woman's Fiction: A Guide to Novels By and About Women in America, 1820-1870*. Ithaca: Cornell UP, 1978.

Clinton, Catherine. *The Other Civil War: American Women in the Nineteenth Century*. New York: Hill and Wang, 1984.

Cullen, Jim. *The Civil War in Popular Culture: A Reusable Past.* Washington: Smithsonian Institution P, 1995.

Culpepper, Marilyn Mayer. *Trials and Triumphs: Women of the American Civil War.* East Lansing: Michigan State UP, 1991.

Diffley, Kathleen. *Where My Heart is Turning Ever: Civil War Stories and Constitutional Reform, 1861-1876.* Athens: U of Georgia P, 1992.

Faust, Drew Gilpin. *Mothers of Invention: Women of the Slaveholding South in the American Civil War.* Chapel Hill: U of North Carolina P, 1996.

Hall, Richard. *Patriots in Disguise: Women Warriors of the Civil War.* New York: Paragon, 1993.

Leonard, Elizabeth D. *Yankee Women: Gender Battles in the Civil War.* New York: Norton, 1994.

Lystra, Karen. *Searching the Heart: Women, Men, and Romantic Love in Nineteenth-Century America.* New York: Oxford UP, 1989.

Rable, George. "'Missing in Action': Women of the Confederacy." *Divided Houses: Gender and the Civil War.* Ed. Catherine Clinton and Nina Silber. New York: Oxford UP, 1992. 134-46.

Silber, Nina. *The Romance of Reunion; Northerners and the South, 1865-1900.* Chapel Hill: U of North Carolina P, 1993.

Sizer, Lyde Cullen. "Acting Her Part: Narratives of Union Women Spies." *Divided Houses: Gender and the Civil War.* Ed. Catherine Clinton and Nina Silber. New York: Oxford UP, 1992. 114-33.

Southworth, Emma D. E. N. *Fair Play; or, The Test of the Lone Isle.* Philadelphia: T. B. Peterson, 1868.

————. *The Hidden Hand; or, Capitola the Madcap.* 1859. Ed. Joanne Dobson. New Brunswick: Rutgers UP, 1988.

————. *How He Won Her. A Sequel to "Fair Play."* Philadelphia: T. B. Peterson, 1869.

Whites, LeeAnn. *The Civil War as a Crisis in Gender: Augusta, Georgia, 1860-1890.* Athens: U of Georgia P, 1995.

Jane E. Schultz (essay date 2001)

SOURCE: Schultz, Jane E. "Performing Genres: Sarah Edmonds' *Nurse and Spy* and the Case of the Cross-Dressed Text." In *Dressing Up for War: Transformations of Gender and Genre in the Discourse and Literature of War,* edited by Aránzazu Usandizaga and Andrew Monnickendam, pp. 73-91. Amsterdam, Netherlands: Rodopi, 2001.

[In the following essay, Schultz analyzes the cultural ideals of gender identity and gender roles that informed Sarah Edmonds' cross-dressing Civil War narrative, Nurse and Spy.]

Sarah Edmonds' *Nurse and Spy in the Union Army* was the first of several narratives to chronicle the exploits of female military cross-dressers active during the American Civil War.[1] Published in 1864 in the midst of the war, Edmonds and her three publishers hoped to capitalize on the public hunger for war stories then sweeping the nation. Louisa May Alcott had tested the waters a few months earlier with *Hospital Sketches*—her account of six weeks in a Washington military hospital—and despite modest sales, launched a writing career by imagining herself "the son of the house" going off to war.[2] Edmonds alludes to *Hospital Sketches* in her own narrative (75, 237)[3] intimating her familiarity with it. Instead of adopting military language as Nurse Periwinkle does, however, Edmonds does one better by literally becoming a Union soldier.

Postwar testimony from members of a Union regiment and service records at the U. S. National Archives confirm that a soldier named Franklin Thompson joined the Second Michigan Infantry in the spring of 1861, as the war was getting underway and thousands of soldiers were enlisting.[4] Twenty years after the war, Edmonds revealed that she had been that soldier. The cursory medical exams administered to Union recruits made it relatively easy for women to slip into the ranks; soldiers were not always required to disrobe, and Edmonds, who had cross-dressed as a bookseller before the war, had already cultivated masculine mannerisms.[5] Private Thompson's performance, though unusual, was not unique: wartime observers maintained that several hundred women passed as men in the ranks.[6] Even Edmonds' tentmate, R. H. Halsted, claimed not to have known that Thompson was a woman until her revelation. However, the regiment's assistant surgeon, Jerome Robbins, knew the secret and kept it. Having sustained a serious leg injury and fearing discovery, Edmonds deserted after the battle of Fredericksburg late in 1862, her disguise intact.[7] In *Nurse and Spy,* Edmonds neither divulges her assumed name nor the unit with which she enlisted, presumably to dodge the controversy that would have ensued had these facts been known before the end of the war.

I am grateful to Claire Tylee of Brunel University (United Kingdom) and Elizabeth Leonard of Colby College (United States) for their helpful comments on an earlier draft of this essay. I also extend thanks to Elizabeth Young of Mount Holyoke College (United States), whose ideas have been very influential in shaping my own.

Although it resembles a wartime nursing narrative—Edmonds dedicated her work to "the sick and wounded soldiers of the Army of the Potomac" and assumed a rhetorical piety befitting the evangelical mission of many other volunteer relief workers[8]—*Nurse and Spy*'s authenticity as historical narrative is dubious at best. In the course of the narrative, Edmonds' performances become increasingly outlandish, inviting readers to suspend their disbelief and interpret *Nurse and Spy* as a fiction. While the text is based on historically documented evidence of Edmonds' soldiering, its embellishments consign it to a more speculative mode. Of course, men and women have cross-dressed throughout human history, but in *Nurse and Spy* it is a question of how *textual* role play translates into cultural meaning.[9] When we shift the point of inquiry from historical authenticity to literary invention, we are free to examine the cultural work of cross-dressing.[10] We can ask, for example what myths Edmonds' series of masks drew upon. Or whether the gendering of Edmonds' disguises suggested a wider cultural dissatisfaction with feminine prescriptions. Or if Edmonds' performances of masculinity and racial and ethnic others betokened a solidarity born of marginalization or were in themselves opportunistic and exploitative? Finally, we can reflect on the rigidity or fluidity of a gender system that prompted such flights of fancy.

Nurse and Spy had fictional antecedents in the early nineteenth century. *The Female Marine* (1815-18) was a tremendously popular narrative of cross-dressing in which a young woman rises above seduction and prostitution by masking herself as a sailor; she is ultimately rewarded with wealth and marriage.[11] Popular domestic novelist E. D. E. N. Southworth created Capitola Black who supported herself by dressing as a boy in *The Hidden Hand* (1859)—a story widely known on the eve of the Civil War. Edmonds later told readers that her imagination had been fired in adolescence by reading *Fanny Campbell, the Female Pirate Captain* (1844), the tale of a young woman who cross-dresses to save an imprisoned lover during the American Revolution.[12] The picaresque plots of these fictions were parallel: a young woman of low status falls into a precarious situation from which she is able to extricate herself only by assuming the identity of a man. She discovers that the disguise gives her an unanticipated freedom of movement that builds self-esteem and provides an antidote to the socially perceived vulnerability of women. The heroine not only becomes accustomed to masculine performance, she is thrilled by it, acting the parts of ladies' man, confidence man, and even swashbuckler. Her masquerade ultimately yields the monetary rewards that allow her to reassume her feminine identity, understood in the context of nineteenth-century fictions of cross-dressing as the appropriate subject position for a woman.[13]

This formula fiction was popular well into the 1870s in the United States. Cuban-born Loreta Janeta Velazquez published a narrative with resonances similar to Edmonds' in 1876: *The Woman in Battle* is Velazquez's pseudo-autobiographical account of a young woman who follows her husband to war with the Confederate

States and subsequently passes as an officer and a spy to advance the southern cause. Like Edmonds, Velazquez moves almost imperceptibly between disguises, equally at home in the skin of men and women, southerners and northerners, and elites and servants. More self-conscious about her performances than Edmonds, Velazquez burlesques her role as male suitor. S/he makes love indiscriminately to aggressively romantic belles without concealing her homophilic admiration, and by the end of the story has wed four times, as man and woman, and borne four children. Elizabeth Young has shown in a marvelous analysis of *The Woman in Battle* the "cultural destabilization" that cross-dressing represented in Civil War America. Young notes that "military masquerade in this text functions as a metaphorical point of exchange for intersections between individual bodies and the body politic," suggesting that the body's physical or sartorial presentation becomes a symbolic repository of national identity fraught with discursive conflict.[14] An intimate relation between the crossed-dressed body and the wartime body politic also exists in *Nurse and Spy,* as Edmonds plays roles on both sides of the line that gender, race, region, class, and ethnicity demarcate. But instead of emphasizing how the nineteenth-century female body absorbed the turbulence of contemporary political discourse, I want to examine how the genre of such narratives reflects the physical dynamics of disguise attempted by the narrator.[15] By looking into how the narrator of *Nurse and Spy* construes genre and textuality, we gain additional insight into the arbitrariness of gender constructions and the creative use of sexual alternatives on the part of those who felt constrained by the rigidity of their social roles.

If one is tempted to think of *Nurse and Spy in the Union Army* as a conventional wartime nursing narrative, one need look no further than the titles by which the work was known. The yoking of "spy" with "nurse" in the Hartford edition of 1864 lured those interested in the "thrilling adventures" genre, as did the title given it by a Boston publisher in the same year—*The Female Spy of the Union Army.* A third edition, published in Philadelphia as *Unsexed; or, the Female Soldier: The Thrilling Adventures, Experiences and Escapes of a Woman, as Nurse, Spy and Scout, in Hospitals, Camp and Battlefields,* titillated readers with the illicit nature of feminine soldiering.[16] Titles marketed to achieve a sensation bespoke *Nurse and Spy*'s generic difference from the likes of Alcott's *Hospital Sketches,* Jane Hoge's *The Boys in Blue* (1867), Sophronia Bucklin's *In Hospital and Camp* (1869), and scores of other accounts written by northern nurses.[17] So did the sales figures: *Nurse and Spy* and its alternately titled editions sold over 175,000 copies—a figure three times greater than any nursing narrative.[18]

Despite Edmonds' leanings toward picaresque fiction, she saw rhetorical advantages in adopting the literary conventions of the nursing narrative. Allegiance with Alcott and the emerging war genre would bring a measure of respectability to an otherwise lurid tale. Nursing narratives featured paeans to patriotism, often in the form of dedications such as Edmonds'. Her Hartford publisher, W. S. Williams, linked Edmonds' patriotism with the purity of her motives in his introduction: "Should any of her readers object to some of her disguises," he intoned, "it may be sufficient to remind them it was from the purest motives and most praiseworthy patriotism, that she laid aside, for a time, her own costume, and assumed that of the opposite sex, and hazard[ed] her life for her adopted country, in its trying hour of need" (6). Williams diverts the question of purity from a description of Edmonds to the book itself two paragraphs later, constructing a connection between the human text and the literary one: "The moral character of the work—being true to virtue, patriotism, and philanthropy . . . will, we trust, render it an interesting and welcome visitor at every fireside" (6). The personification of the book as a "welcome visitor" "true to virtue" blurs the gendered and generic texts.

The celebration of male courage and the concomitant minimizing of the authorial subject in narratives such as Edmonds' helped authenticate the ideals of self-sacrifice and humility to which middle-class women in the United States aspired during this period. With its references to cross-dressing and the pleasure derived from successful performance, *Nurse and Spy* aggrandized its authorial subject even as it apologized for transgressing feminine decorum—a contradiction that fed its generic hybridity. Deathbed conversion scenes, another convention of most nursing narratives, illustrated the female caregiver's moral influence over truant soldiers.[19] This staging of Edmonds' piety comes early in the narrative, as if to build readers' confidence in the storyteller before their credulity is put to the test. Like other nineteenth-century deathbed watchers for whom death was spiritually liberating, Edmonds is transported in her narration.[20] When a soldier dying of typhoid is asked, "What is the foundation of your hope of Heaven?" Edmonds writes, "His face was calm and beautiful in its expression, and his splendid dark eyes lit up with holy confidence and trust, as he replied, 'Christ—Christ!' These were his last words. Glorious words for a dying soldier" (27). For all of Edmonds' religious rapture, however, readers could not fail to notice that the "nurse" played her most rewarding role in military intelligence, disguising herself eleven times in the course of the tale.

Judith Butler's theory of the performativity of gender provides a useful framework for interpreting the cultural meaning of Edmonds' disguises and through which we can examine the extent to which wartime social identity was a fluid commodity based on performance.

Butler holds that gender identities are inherently unstable and that individuals learn gender by observing the performances of others.[21] Edmonds' multiple performances as white male nurse, Union soldier, courier, civilian, and intelligence agent; black male laborer, Irish female domestic, and black female cook render not only gender unstable but a host of other social categories. Such instability sets the audience free to explore alternative identities within the safe bounds of fiction, where readers have the opportunity to try on "foreign" selves without penalty. As one observer has suggested about Civil War and Reconstruction-era readers, if fictions of cross-dressing did not represent real power gains for women, then they at least created "the *fantasy* of such power."[22] In this sense, Edmonds' costume changes serve metaphorically the performance of the text while the text frees readers for imaginative performance.

The text, I will argue, is itself cross-dressed because it inhabits the third space—the place, as Marjorie Garber has proposed, that disrupts the binarity of categorization.[23] Not wholly a nursing narrative or an adventure story, *Nurse and Spy* inscribes generic dissonance on the text of war. Its "category crisis" (Garber's words) parallels the narrator's own indeterminate identity. Both Edmonds' performance and the performance of the text are epistemologically related: war provides the opportunity to suspend, to experiment with, to re-form social order. A social order in transition—in this case brought about by war—is one in which both new sexual and textual paradigms may emerge. As the author discovers the power of performing new or unconventional sexualities, her representation of these diverse roles will necessarily transgress generic boundaries. Insofar as *Nurse and Spy* exploits elements of adventure fiction *and* historical narrative, it may be considered a generic hybrid in which the "unsexed" soldier-agent and the obedient transgendered nurse coexist in dynamic tension. If nineteenth-century women cross-dressed to achieve greater freedom of movement, as historians have noted, then war certainly accelerated this calculus for Edmonds.[24] The easing of social restriction during the war was appealing to women of all classes. Many welcomed household autonomy and the opportunity to assume men's work roles.[25] Edmonds found satisfaction in military cross-dress where she could access more powerful male roles and in the same stroke elude the prescriptions of feminine vulnerability.[26] Civil war promoted an even greater degree of movement when we consider that civilians' sectional proclivities were not easily discernible. Edmonds could pass as northerner or southerner without exciting more than the usual suspicion accorded to strangers. Her Canadian citizenship added a further layer of complexity to this profile. A native of New Brunswick, the teenage Edmonds had emigrated to the US around 1859, presumably to escape an arranged marriage.[27] So in addition to performing maleness, she performed nationality—a disguise perhaps made easier by her assumed gender in light of the US call to arms in 1861.

Edmonds carries her masculine performance into the narration of *Nurse and Spy.* Instead of retaining a woman's perspective on the military world through which she moves, Edmonds sees as a man. Male subjectivity is everywhere present: she displays uncommon knowledge of horsemanship and ballistics, reproduces the language of official dispatches, and even goes fishing to provide for a sick patient. She tells us that she answered the President's call for 75,000 *men* and that she was "furnished with all the necessary equipments" (19), despite her assignment as a nurse. Her confession that she is teary-eyed at the prospect of war does little to alter the image of martial competency that emerges (18). When applying to the secret service for a position in intelligence, Edmonds must attest to her marksmanship before a board of generals: "In that department," she proclaims confidently, "I sustained my character in a manner worthy of a veteran" (106). The editorial lip service devoted to Edmonds' feminine credentials is not enough to counteract her having "penetrated the enemy's lines . . . always with complete success and without detection" (5)—language that similarly represents masculine assertion.

Even before Edmonds goes under cover, she assumes a masculine role in a depredation against a Confederate home. As a Union nurse foraging for food, Edmonds encounters a suspicious-looking woman who fires a pistol at her as she departs. In the engraving of this incident, Edmonds' gender identity is ambiguous: she may indeed be a man and there is no pictorial suggestion that two women are fighting.[28] By leaving open this space for interpretation, Edmonds can urge readers to see her as male. Enraged that she has been fired on, she draws her own pistol and wounds the woman in the hand. The fact that she is successful in wounding her foe and that the rebel is not contrasts masculine know-how with feminine incompetence. This testosterone moment continues as Edmonds restrains the struggling woman and drags her behind her horse. Her description of these events smacks of masculine solicitude: "I bound up her hand with my handkerchief, gave her my scarf to throw over her head, and assisted her to the saddle. I marched along beside her, holding tight to the bridle rein all the while" (95). Not only strong verbs but literal strength is apparent when Edmonds catches her prisoner in a fall from her horse. Conciliatory as only a gentleman can be (especially one who has just shot a woman), Edmonds fetches water in her hat. Having subdued her opponent, Edmonds now converts her to Unionism and renames her—two other powers that men-at-war may claim. Impressed with "Nellie's" fidelity as a nurse, Edmonds writes that "she was the only real lady in personal appearance, education, and refinement,

that I ever met among the females of the peninsula" (97). Making the distinction between "females" and "ladies" is clearly a masculine prerogative: the power of naming extends to seizing bodies for the state.

As engaging as Edmonds' male performance might be, however, she does not attempt to conceal qualities that her contemporary readers would have gendered female. Laura Laffrado has observed that Edmonds "consistently reinforces cultural constructions . . . that guard her self-definition as a heterosexual woman."[29] In doing her duty, proclaiming the purity of her motives, and wondering at her luck in having eluded the costume police, Edmonds is attempting to appease precisely those who would have equated her masculine disguise with the mortification of her femininity and also might have questioned her sexual motives. Thus the narrator's ambiguous sexing helps offset the charge that her male disguises "unsex" her, assures readers of her heteronormativity, and perhaps most importantly allows her the liminal and liberating identity of a sexual go-between—one who defies both gender and sexual categorization.

The ease of Edmonds' performance of masculinity is comparable to civilian men's performance of martial roles. It is no more a challenge for her to play a man than it is for men to march off to war and transform themselves from peace-abiding citizens to killers. Throughout *Nurse and Spy,* Edmonds is hyper-aware of the performance of disguise and uses dramatic tropes to reveal her awareness. "What part am *I* to play in this great drama?" she asks at the outset (18); her various intelligence assignments become "debuts" (106, 148); and she worries about not being "able to successfully act [the] part" of an Irish peddler when the perils of exposure compromise her "Hibernian" accent (156).

The success of disguise rests as well on convincing props, and these Edmonds "procures" in abundance. She never travels without a pocket mirror, carries chalk to alter her skin color—from white to black and from black to white again, and stops at nothing to garb herself authentically. She "captures" the uniform of a rebel prisoner after a skirmish so that she can complete an intelligence mission behind enemy lines (312), and gets a Union postmaster, who believes her to be a contraband laborer, to purchase a Negro wig for her in Washington when she is unable to find one at Fortress Monroe (107). The layers of artifice are striking here, especially the exigency that she be racially disguised in order to perfect her costume. The white woman with masculine sensibilities, under cover among peers who must not suspect her, poses as a black man to enlist the aid of a white man, who might not be so cooperative were Edmonds a white woman or white man.[30] Edmonds' triple crossing of gender, race, and class boundaries, typical of her dramatic range, suggests that at its very core gender, not to mention other social categories, are about performance and not biological essence.

Dialect becomes for Edmonds a crucial part of the cosmetics of disguise. She refers in the same breath to "procuring" the brogue of an Irish peddler and a new suit of clothes, and packs up "a set of Irish phrases" in the same hamper where she stores cakes and pies (147-48). With stock phrases at the ready, speech becomes a material part of disguise—adopted as quickly as the "little time [it took] to don my new disguise, and feel at home in the clothes" (148). However, when Edmonds becomes ill, she thinks of those "fine phrases" differently; as having "taken so much pains to learn" (150). When performance is threatened—as it is here and later while she nurses a dying rebel soldier—its linguistic catalyst is not as efficacious.

Edmonds' performance of contraband dialect is apparently so convincing that friends and associates (like the postmaster) do not detect her whiteness. Even Edmonds' nursing companion, Mrs. B., does not recognize her when she comes to the hospital as "Ned," the cook. When Edmonds' pigment begins to bleed, no white person is the wiser—a sign more of the invisibility of blackness among white spectators in nineteenth-century America than of Edmonds' dramatic expertise.[31] The African-American contraband laborers are, of course, not fooled: they see through her performance of race, if not of gender. In spite of this, they admire the grit of her performance and express their solidarity by easing her burden of manual labor and showing "brotherly kindness" as the sable tint fades (114-16). Edmonds can return the favor later in the narrative, both as a white orderly assisting hospitalized blacks and as a female contraband behind Confederate lines. Symbolically, Edmonds' liminal position puts her in league with other outsiders. White dismissal of the racially marginal contrasts with the warm reception Edmonds gets from those who honor even the appearance of blackness.

This reverse "passing," which sensitizes Edmonds to the social costs of racial difference, may also be understood as an act of exploitation.[32] She passes as black to avoid detection, confident that black subjectivity is invisible to most whites. But she never considers how black "originals" may perceive her disguise, or that their keen vision may blow her cover. From this perspective, Edmonds has vastly underestimated her black "peers," having no conception of her luck in incurring their amusement instead of their wrath, and thereby revealing her whiteness. The laborers' benevolence results significantly from Edmonds' successful obfuscation: even though her racial masquerade is transparent, her gender remains veiled. What she liberally understands as social parity or brotherhood might have an uglier face were the full extent of the masquerade known. Thus, appearing to the laborers as "one of them" merely conceals another layer of pretense.

The measure of Edmonds' heightened consciousness may be seen at Antietam, where she herself becomes the benevolent unmasker. During the battle, while she is acting as aide-de-camp for a Union general, Edmonds meets a fallen comrade-incognito. Here only gender is disguised instead of race and gender, which may account for the moment of transcendence that unmasker and unmasked share. All it takes is one "earnest gaze" from the sweet-faced youth for Edmonds to suspect a kindred spirit and "look more closely":

> The little trembling hand beckoned me closer, and I knelt down beside him and bent my head until it touched the golden locks on the pale brow before me; I listened with breathless attention to catch every sound which fell from those dying lips, the substance of which was as follows:
>
> "I can trust you, and will tell you a secret. I am not what I seem, but am a female. I enlisted from the purest motives, and have remained undiscovered and unsuspected. . . . I have performed the duties of a soldier faithfully, and am willing to die for the cause of truth and freedom. My trust is in God, and I die in peace. I wish you to bury me with your own hands, that none may know after my death that I am other than my appearance indicates." Then looking at me again in that earnest, scrutinizing manner, she said: "I know I can trust you."

(271-72)

The soldier's twice repeated words of trust communicate the cross-dresser's code to Edmonds, who knows, before the wounded soldier tells her, that he is a woman. Likewise, the code obviates the need for Edmonds herself to be revealed. The resonating experience of the cross-dressers brings them into rare alignment: their spiritual affinity silently promises confidentiality and affirms labor in the third space, the invisible space between, where conventional gender identity does not figure.

Moments of trans-gendered and trans-racial contact are, by their very nature, transitory because transgressive power must not be paraded before the powerful. Like other marginal social actors for whom performance may be liberating, the cross-dresser, be she transvestite or trickster, risks the wrath of majority observers if she is detected.[33] Even during wartime when a more carnivalized atmosphere eases social restriction, vigilanteism and guerrilla tactics increase the danger of discovery for the cross-dresser.[34] But there are also instances in the American Civil War of men dressing as women to provide other men dance partners during parties—a gender reversal that manifests the more benevolent forms of carnivalization. Although American war historians have argued that the purpose of such transvestism was not burlesque but evidence of men's reverence for absent women, I would argue that social burlesques did not compromise manhood and that there was a freer range of sexual expression available to men before homosexuality was labeled a perversion and aberration later in the nineteenth century.[35] Neither can we discount the likelihood of pleasure to all parties in these staged events. Just as importantly, in a climate where men could dress as women with impunity, women's own transgressions of gender borders were not always scorned by men—particularly those in the rank and file who respected a woman with grit.[36]

Still, the question of loyalty during a civil war raises the stakes of "outing" whether one is male or female. Although Edmonds does finally "come out" to Mrs. B.—here a sign of female solidarity—she maintains her male disguise before her military colleagues lest she jeopardize her sexually inviolable status. The danger she averts is erotically charged in a way that resembles male soldiers' performance as women: though the danger men experience masked as women is manufactured through dramatic discourse without the real possibility of dismissal that the female cross-dresser faces, danger and eroticism are linked whether or not trans-gendered play has serious consequences. The prophylaxis of performance in Edmonds' case heightens pleasure because her disguise puts her at an advantage over those who do not suspect it.[37]

We see these dynamics in her reunion with Lt. V., a Canadian compatriot whom Edmonds meets by chance during the war. Lt. V. does not recognize her after a five-year hiatus because Edmonds has changed her name and is dressed as a Union soldier. "I was glad that he did not know me," she writes, and I "took peculiar pleasure in remaining unrecognized" (99). A rehearsal of her own former history undergirds the new friendship and creates sexual tension, "for I was obliged," she confides, "to listen to a recapitulation of my own former conversations and correspondence with him, which made me feel very much like an eavesdropper" (99). Here the pleasure is voyeuristic because the cross-dresser meets an earlier version of herself at the same moment that she exerts a powerful hold on Lt. V. precisely because of her strangeness. It is her experience of herself as unfamiliar through the eyes of Lt. V. that feeds Edmonds' pleasure.

The double and sometimes triple layers of disguise in Edmonds' repertoire allow us to consider how categories of difference may give rise to unexpected social realities—especially during wars, when social identity is more fluid. How, for example, do Edmonds' ethnic and class marginality enable or disable performance? How does the performance of masculinity aid or harm the performance of blackness? And what impact do the performances of gender and race—individually or together—have on class crossings? Edmonds' brush with death when she is dressed as a white male orderly in the Army of the Potomac illustrates how these catego-

ries collide and sometimes provide cross-fertilization. On assignment to deliver a message to General McClellan's headquarters in the rear, Edmonds establishes masculine authority with an inexperienced picket by chastising him for divulging the countersign. Her lecture, which instructs him in the proper way to hold his gun (a not-so-subtle demonstration of phallic authority), and her knowledge of enemy positions up the line excites the interest of the assembled troops, who concede to Edmonds an even broader share of authority (292-93). But these advantages are undermined as soon as Edmonds resumes the trip to the front, her gender authority canceled as it were by her elite military responsibilities. That is, when she is expected to perform in a privileged capacity, her duty to class supersedes her solidarity with the rank and file, and she loses the chance to make even more of her manhood.

A day later, her gender and class positions align serendipitously when a group of Union cavalrymen shelter her from hunger and fatigue. But despite their kindness to the bedraggled courier, the unit is ambushed by rebel guerrillas. Here it would appear that regional aggression dwarfs the combined affect of gender and class disguise inasmuch as the Union soldiers' genteel manhood is not enough to purchase their immunity. During the skirmish, Edmonds' horse goes down with her under it, and although drenched with the horse's blood, she has not sustained a bullet wound herself. Now she performs by "playing possum" (295), for the guerrillas return to the site to loot the bodies. When one plunges his saber into one of Edmonds' dead comrades, she fears that her turn will come next. By chance the guerrillas ride away, impressed by the bloody and lifeless appearance of Edmonds' body. But before she can extricate herself, another raider appears, takes hold of her feet, and empties the contents of her pockets without ever realizing that she is (a) not a man and (b) not dead. Edmonds' performance of death ironically saves her life: her performed maleness and martial valor contribute nothing to her deliverance.

The action of *Nurse and Spy* is driven by military performance, but the efficacy of performance diminishes with the aggregate of disguises; that is, as the Confederates become aware of Edmonds' con game. Her departure from the potent Army of the Potomac and her reassignment to plainclothes detective work in the western theater literally and symbolically undress her. And if clothes make the man—a phrase that Edmonds has invoked earlier in the narrative—then to undress the man makes him a woman. After her last performance as a young man seeking training in the Confederate intelligence network, Edmonds is unmanned by the unexpected explosion of a shell outside her tent. The sudden ferocity of what appears to be a benign shell reprises the immediate danger that she herself has always been in through potential detection. "All my soldierly qualities seemed to have fled," she confesses, "and I was again a poor cowardly, nervous, whining woman; . . . I could do nothing but weep hour after hour" (359). Here detonation and detection are linked: something finally explodes inside of Edmonds (her successful performance of masculinity perhaps) and she is returned to a feminine reality consonant with loss.

Reverence for male-identified valor and heroism during the American Civil War encouraged cross-dressers like Edmonds to celebrate masculinity through military channels. The celebration of manhood both eased the reception of Edmonds' performances of white and black masculinity and discouraged public vigilance of her two feminine disguises, which in turn made them more effective. For the same reasons, Edmonds' racial performances gave her added mobility, her blackness (like her womanhood, comparatively speaking) marking her as insignificant and ineffectual. At the same time, the wish to cross-dress as a man is closely related to the wish to escape womanhood, at least for a time. Even if Edmonds had no intention of denying her femininity in masculine cross-dress, the fact that she assumed a male identity must be seen in larger cultural terms as a critique of the restrictions upon mid-century womanhood.[38] It is not therefore surprising that Edmonds' suspension of her cross-dressing, the loss of her war of identity, is represented through feminization. Even though the war made possible advances in female independence and autonomy, postwar attempts to restore manhood to its former glory surely compromised any feminist agenda.[39]

Whether Edmonds wore patriotism like a mask of opportunity is difficult to say. "Fond of adventure" though she was, Edmonds claims that "*patriotism* [not adventure] was the grand secret of my success" (121). Whether she would have become a cross-dresser without a war as backdrop is even more uncertain. That she did not cross-dress after the war seems to suggest that war was a powerful inducement to try on social identities without fear of reprisal. Indeed, as Elizabeth Young has concluded, "gender masquerade" distills the social dislocations of war, and "is both its own form of revolt and a protean metaphor for myriad forms of misrule."[40] The protean identity of the military cross-dresser required a woman with an unencumbered status who was willing to stand against convention to risk the pleasure of invention. Taking care of herself and standing alone were the cross-dresser's "inevitables"—a profile in concert with a world at war from which men might not return.

Ultimately *Nurse and Spy* poses as a piece of nationalism—something that many texts of the war and postwar period of reunion exploited. In this context, individuals—especially those on the social margins—may use the state for their own ends. But the question of what those ends are is a troubling one if social experimenta-

tion and evolution do not survive the war. Perhaps the representation of such performances is inherently valuable, even when the work of social change cannot be sustained, because it allows spectators to cross-dress themselves, if only in the imagination. The real challenge for those who value the personal agency made possible by wars—and which Sarah Edmonds herself discovered through the text—is to develop a structure in which multiple forms of social identity may thrive even after the guns are silent.

Notes

1. The other autobiographical accounts were Belle Boyd's *Belle Boyd in Camp and Prison* (London and New York, 1865) and Loreta Janeta Velazquez's *The Woman in Battle: A Narrative of the Exploits, Adventures, and Travels of Madame Loreta Janeta Velazquez,* ed. C. J. Worthington (Richmond, 1876). Among contemporary fictional accounts were Madeline Moore's *The Lady Lieutenant* (Philadelphia, 1862); and Rachel Longstreet's *Remy St. Remy; or, the Boy in Blue* (New York, 1866).

2. See Alcott, *Hospital Sketches* (New York: Garland, 1984) 11. For information on the publication of *Hospital Sketches* (Boston: Redpath, 1863) see Ednah D. Cheney, *Louisa May Alcott: Her Life, Letters, and Journals* (Boston: Little, Brown, 1928) 125-26.

3. *Nurse and Spy in the Union Army* was published in 1864 by W. S. Williams in Hartford. The same text was brought out under different titles by publishers in Philadelphia and Boston in 1864. In addition to the 1864 imprint, Williams put out editions in 1865 and 1867. By 1900, three more editions had been published, including one in German. I am using the Williams edition of 1865. All references to this edition of the novel will be given parenthetically after quotations in the text.

4. See pension file of Sarah Edmonds Seelye (#526889), Record Group 15, Veterans Administration, U. S. National Archives, Washington, D. C. See also J. R. Miller to Frank Moore, February 1866, Frank Moore Papers, Duke University, Durham, North Carolina. For secondary sources on Edmonds' soldierhood, see Elizabeth Leonard, *All the Daring of the Soldier* (New York: Norton, 1999) 170-81; Edmonds, *Nurse and Spy in the Union Army,* ed. Elizabeth Leonard (DeKalb, Ill.: Northern Illinois U P, 1999) introduction; and Richard Hall, *Patriots in Disguise: Women Warriors of the Civil War* (New York: Paragon, 1993) 85-97.

5. Laura Laffrado has argued that Edmonds' childhood transgressions of gender scripts prepared her

to assume her adult passing as a man. See Laffrado, "'I Am Other than My Appearance Indicates': Sex-Gender Representation in Women's Nineteenth-Century Civil War Reminiscences," *Over Here* 17. 2 (Winter 1997): 167. See also George Worthington Adams, *Doctors in Blue: The Medical History of the Union Army in the Civil War* (Dayton: Morningside Press, 1985) 12-13; and frontispiece of the Williams 1865 edition of *Nurse and Spy,* which features an engraving of Edmonds in a dress.

6. See Mary Livermore, *My Story of the War* (Hartford, Conn.: A. D. Worthington, 1889), 116-20; my own dissertation, "Women at the Front: Gender and Genre in Literature of the American Civil War," (University of Michigan, 1988); Lauren Cook Burgess, ed., *An Uncommon Soldier: The Civil War Letters of Sarah Rosetta Wakeman* (Pasadena, Md.: Minerva Center, 1994); Elizabeth D. Leonard, *All the Daring of the Soldier* (New York: Norton, 1999); and DeAnne Blanton, "Women Soldiers of the Civil War," *Prologue* 25 (Spring 1993): 27.

7. See correspondence of R. H. Halsted and Sarah Edmonds Seelye, Clarke Historical Library, Central Michigan University, Mount Pleasant, Michigan; and Jerome Robbins Diary, November 11, 1861, Michigan Historical Collections, Bentley Historical Library, University of Michigan, Ann Arbor, Michigan. See also Betty Fladeland, "Alias Franklin Thompson," *Michigan History* 42. 4 (December 1958): 435-62; and "New Light on Sarah Emma Edmonds, Alias Franklin Thompson," *Michigan History* 47. 4 (December 1963): 357-62.

8. For information on the evangelical motives of northern relief workers, see, for example, Charles Stillé, *History of the United States Sanitary Commission* (Philadelphia: Lippincott, 1866); Frank Moore, *Women of the War; Their Heroism and Self-Sacrifice* (Hartford, Conn.: Scranton, 1866); Phillip Shaw Paludan, *A People's Contest: The Union and Civil War* (New York: Harper's, 1988); and Ralph Gordon, "Nashville and the U. S. Christian Commission in the Civil War," *Tennessee Historical Quarterly* 55. 2 (Summer 1996): 98-111.

9. See Vern and Bonnie Bullough, *Cross-Dressing, Sex, and Gender* (Philadelphia: U of Pennsylvania P, 1993) especially the introduction and chapter 1.

10. Elizabeth Young uses a similar logic in her analysis of Velazquez' 1876 narrative of cross-dressing in the Civil War, *The Woman in Battle*: "When we treat this work as a picaresque nineteenth-century novel rather than as an evidentiary account of the Civil War, . . . [it] becomes a productive site for an extended inquiry into the meanings of cross-dressing, as constructed by the intersecting axes of gender, sexuality, race, region, and nation." See Young, "Confederate Counterfeit: The Case of the Cross-Dressed Civil War Soldier" in *Passing and the Fictions of Identity,* Elaine Ginsberg, ed. (Durham and London: Duke U P, 1996) 185.

11. Daniel A. Cohen notes that nineteen editions of *The Female Marine* were published in Boston between 1815 and 1818 and that over 300 related pamphlets were ultimately published. See Daniel A. Cohen ed., *The Female Marine and Related Works: Narratives of Cross-Dressing and Urban Vice in America's Early Republic* (Amherst: U of Massachusetts P, 1997) 3, 25.

12. See Hall 75-76; and Maturin Murray Ballou, *Fanny Campbell, the Female Pirate Captain, a Tale of the Revolution* (Boston: F. Gleason, 1845).

13. See Karen Halttunen's discussion of what the "painted woman" gains from her masquerade in *Confidence Men and Painted Women: A Study of Middle-Class Culture in America, 1830-1870* (New Haven: Yale U P, 1982). In a more recent study of the female trickster, Lori Landay has argued that "in their pursuit of autonomy and active participation in the world around them, [popular heroines] deploy trickster tactics such as deception, disguise, duplicity, subversion, feigned submission, parody, and impersonation." Edmonds uses all of these tactics in *Nurse and Spy*. See Lori Landay, *Madcaps, Screwballs, and Con Women: The Female Trickster in American Culture* (Philadelphia: U of Pennsylvania P, 1998) 30.

14. Young 183, 185.

15. In a related project, Margaret Higgonet has characterized the political conflicts of civil war as a template for social and particularly gender conflict, which ultimately results in redirection and redefinition. See Higgonet, "Civil Wars and Sexual Territories," in *Arms and the Woman: War, Gender, and Literary Representation,* ed. Helen Cooper, Adrienne Munich, and Susan Squier (Chapel Hill: U of North Carolina P, 1989) 80-96.

16. The Boston publisher was De Wolfe, Fiske; and the Philadelphia Publishing Company was the third publisher to come out with Edmonds' memoir in 1864.

17. I have estimated in *Women at the Front: Female Hospital Workers in the American Civil War* (Chapel Hill: University of North Carolina, 2001) that 66 women wrote monographs about military relief work and that 42 of them sought publication. Of the 42, 11 were former Confederate, 31 former Union citizens.

18. For publication information on *Nurse and Spy,* see Earl W. Fornell, "A Woman in the Union Army,"

American-German Review 26-27 (February-March 1961): 13-15. Publication figures also quoted in Lide Cullen Sizer, "Acting Her Part: Narratives of Union Women Spies" in *Divided Houses: Gender and the Civil War,* ed. Catherine Clinton and Nina Silber (New York: Oxford, 1993) 126. The next most commercially successful account, Mary Livermore's *My Story of the War* (1887), sold 60,000 copies. See Mary Livermore, *My Story of the War,* ed. Nina Baym (New York: Da Capo, 1995) xii. Edmonds also claimed to have donated the proceeds from the work to the U. S. Sanitary Commission and the Christian Commission (military relief agencies), wishing to head off charges that her only motive in producing the book had been profit. See Edmonds pension file.

19. See, for example, Harriet Eaton Diary, October 18, 1862, Southern Historical Collection, University of North Carolina, Chapel Hill; Amy Morris Bradley Diary and Letterbook, August 17, 1862, Duke University, Durham, North Carolina; and Esther Hill Hawks, *A Woman Doctor's Civil War,* ed. Gerald Schwartz (Columbia: U of South Carolina P, 1984) 51-52.

20. I am thinking here of Ann Douglas' observations about the death of Little Eva in Stowe's *Uncle Tom's Cabin* (1852) and her chapter on "The Domestication of Death" in *The Feminization of American Culture* (New York: Knopf, 1977) 3-13, 200-226.

21. Judith Butler, *Gender Trouble: Feminism and the Subversion of Identity* (New York: Routledge, 1990).

22. See Young 189.

23. Marjorie Garber, *Vested Interests: Cross-Dressing and Cultural Anxiety* (New York: Routledge, 1992) 13.

24. See, for example, Lillian Faderman, *Surpassing the Love of Men* (New York: Morrow, 1981), 17, chapter 4; and Kathleen De Grave, *Swindler, Spy, Rebel: The Confidence Woman in Nineteenth-Century America* (Columbia: U of Missouri P, 1995) 14.

25. For discussions of women's altered work roles during the American Civil War, see, for example, Mary Elizabeth Massey, *Bonnet Brigades* (New York: Knopf, 1966); and Drew Gilpin Faust, *Mothers of Invention: Women of the Slaveholding South in the American Civil War* (Chapel Hill: U of North Carolina P, 1996).

26. Edmonds' publisher even suggested that "it makes but little difference what costume she assumes while in the discharge of her duties.—Perhaps she should have the privilege of choosing for herself whatever may be the surest protection from insult and inconvenience in her blessed, self-sacrificing work" (6). Such a view excused cross-dressers from seeking personal safety through gender disguise. For more on the subject of women's motives for cross-dressing during the Civil War and war more generally, see Julie Wheelwright, *Amazons and Military Maids: Women Who Dressed as Men in the Pursuit of Life, Liberty, and Happiness* (London: Pandora, 1989); and my dissertation, "Women at the Front: Gender and Genre in Literature of the American Civil War" (University of Michigan, 1988) chapter 5.

27. Leonard cites an interview with Edmonds in the Fort Scott, Kansas *Weekly Monitor,* January 17, 1884, in which she reveals these motives. See Leonard's introduction to *Nurse and Spy.*

28. The illustrations, or "embellishments" as they are called in the text, were a series of wood engravings done by R. O'Brien. The single exception is the portrait of Edmonds with which the narrative begins—a steel engraving done by George E. Perine.

29. Laffrado 168-69.

30. Marjorie Garber has argued that "transvestism can be a trickster strategy for outsmarting white oppression." Although Garber makes the statement in the context of blacks passing as whites, Edmonds applies another layer as a white posing as a black manipulating the cooperation of a white. Thus, instead of a black passing as a white, she plays the reverse role in hope of gaining the same object. See Garber 303.

31. Kathleen De Grave also notes that Edmonds makes herself invisible through marginalizing her identity, but how this is possible when Edmonds "'eliminat[ed] the feminine' rather than heightening it" is not clear. See De Grave 137-38.

32. Laffrado has read the episode of Edmonds' cross-dressing as an African-American laborer in similar terms. She writes, "Edmonds's impersonations invert conventions of nineteenth-century passing narratives which characteristically use disguise to pass higher (as opposed to Edmonds's lower) in the class hierarchy and which typically portray passing in front of a less observant upper-class to be easier than deceiving a watchful underclass." See Laffrado 166.

33. There was harsh criticism of cross-dressers in Edmonds' day. See, for example, the New York *Herald,* November 5, 1861, and September 23, 1863; and *Frank Leslie's Illustrated Magazine,* November 5, 1864. De Grave notes that "the final, if un-

conscious aim of the con woman is to step outside her restrictive role as commodity and achieve a personal sense of selfhood, no matter how socially unacceptable that self might be." See De Grave 14; and Landay 11.

34. Michael Fellman discusses the lack of predictable gender relations in the context of guerrilla war. See Fellman, *Inside War: The Guerrilla Conflict in Missouri During the American Civil War* (New York: Oxford, 1989); and "Women and Guerrilla Warfare," in *Divided Houses: Gender and the Civil War*, ed. Catherine Clinton and Nina Silber (New York: Oxford, 1993) 147-165.

35. For instances of male transvestism during the American Civil War, see Reid Mitchell, *The Vacant Chair: The Northern Soldier Leaves Home* (New York: Oxford, 1993), 71. For theories on the construction of homosexuality as deviant, see the work of David Halperin; Eve K. Sedgwick, *Epistemology of the Closet* (Berkeley: California, 1990); and Eve K. Sedgwick and Andrew Parker, eds., *Performativity and Performance* (London: Routledge, 1995).

36. See, for example, Charles Woodruff to D. O. Woodruff, May 1, 1863, D. O. Woodruff Papers, Michigan Historical Collections, Bentley Historical Library, University of Michigan, Ann Arbor, Michigan. In this letter, the young Woodruff tells his father of an incident in which a known crossdresser is hired by his commanding officer because of her impressive manners and bearing.

37. Elizabeth Young explores the homoerotic implications of a female cross-dresser's appeal to southern women in "Confederate Counterfeit," 185, 193-97. In citing early twentieth-century work on transvestism, Marjorie Garber observes that an unusually large number of people in the military have cross-dressed compared to people in the general population, the frequency of which suggests the unacknowledged popularity of male bonding, homosexual desire, and "the erotics of same-sex communities." See Garber 55-56.

38. Laffrado comes to a related conclusion: "The mixed cultural responses that allowed representations of women's wartime cross-gender impersonation to appear without full censure highlight for that culture and our own a false rigidity of conventional sex-gender scripts for women and men." See Laffrado 180.

39. Many scholars have recognized the gendering of political discourse and particularly the presence of masculine metaphors in the postwar era. See, for example, Nina Silber, "Intemperate Men, Spiteful Women, and Jefferson Davis," in *Divided Houses:*

Gender and the Civil War, eds. Catherine Clinton and Nina Silber (New York: Oxford 1993) 283-305; and Lee Ann Whites, *The Civil War as a Crisis in Gender: Augusta, Georgia, 1860-1890* (Athens: U of Georgia P, 1995).

40. Young 209.

Adrian Hunter (essay date 2002)

SOURCE: Hunter, Adrian. "Obscured Hurts: The Civil War Writing of Henry James and Ambrose Bierce." *War, Literature, and the Arts* 14, nos. 1-2 (2002): 280-92.

[*In the following essay, Hunter maintains that both the fiction of Henry James and Ambrose Bierce reveal the presence of post-traumatic stress disorder among Civil War soldiers, and how the psychological—rather than the physical—wounding conflicts with nineteenth-century masculine gender ideals.*]

In his renowned study of Civil War literature, Daniel Aaron classes Henry James, along with Henry Adams, William Dean Howells and Mark Twain, among the "malingerers."[1] In so doing, Aaron favors the psychological interpretation of the notorious "obscure hurt" that James said prevented him from serving. According to this line of thought, James had in fact neither "castrated himself nor developed a hernia, but . . . had suffered a psychic wound."[2] In contrast to the "malingerers," Aaron gives us the "combatants," among them Ambrose Bierce, whose writing on the War is a model of clarity, "uncanny visual sense," and relish for "the details of the soldier's "trade"."[3] For Aaron, Bierce's fiction contains the kind of "solidity of specification" James claimed to admire yet failed to deliver. But are James and Bierce so very different in their treatment of the War as Aaron says? Distinguishing between them on the basis of their divergent experiences of the conflict obscures important similarities in their writing, while marking a factitious border between the "fighter" and the "stay-at-home," the man of action and the man of thought. In their depictions of the Civil War, at home and at the front, James and Bierce have much in common. In particular, they are both concerned with the spectacle of the war-traumatized male, and they both struggle to deal with this figure in terms of their culture's definition of masculinity. The strategies they devise in their writing in order to disguise the presence of the hysterical man reveal the impact the War had on late-19th-century versions of American manhood.

The bulk of James' Civil War writing is found in his late retrospective memoir, *Notes of a Son and Brother.*[4] There he reflects on what it was like to be a stay-at-home during the War, mysteriously enfeebled, hindered from violence, cut off from the age. It was, he writes, a matter of "living inwardly, compared, that is, to the immense and prolonged outwardness, outwardness naturally at the very highest pitch, that was the general sign of the [Civil War] situation" (227). In his few War stories, James returns to the idea of a population of "inwards" left behind during this defining episode in American history. Largely, of course, the "inwards" are women. Gertrude Whittaker, in the story "Poor Richard," defines the role of such women in relation to the War: they register its momentum, account for it in the heart; in short, they *think* about it:

> War is an infamy, Major, though it *is* your trade. It's very well for you, who look at it professionally, and for those who go and fight; but it's a miserable business for those who stay at home, and do the thinking and the sentimentalizing. It's a miserable business for women; it makes us more spiteful than ever.[5]

By contrast, the world of the male combatant is deliberately thought*less,* destitute of depth or sentiment. For the soldiers in James' stories, emotion amounts to a self-inflicted wound in the combat zone. As young officer Jack Ford, in "The Story of a Year," tells his fiancée, Lizzie Crowe, "if I find your memory makes a milksop of me, I shall thrust you out of the way without ceremony" (23). What really goes on at the front line, between men, is beyond James' reckoning, and he doesn't propose to imagine it. In this respect, Lizzie is not the only absentee from the world of exclusively male contest: the narrator, too, misses out: "I have no intention of following Lieutenant Ford to the seat of war," he tells us: "My own taste has always been for unwritten history, and my present business is with the reverse of the picture" (30).[6]

It was with the "reverse of the picture," the "unwritten history" of the stay-at-home, that James was concerned in his *Notes of a Son and Brother.* There the one left behind was a man, James himself, the cause of his confinement the infamous "wound." Precisely what the "wound" consisted in, by what mechanism it occurred, and in what ways it disabled the author are not made clear. Instead, James stirs up confusion at the scene by conflating his personal hurt and the nation's embattlement:

> Beyond all present notation the interlaced, undivided way in which what had happened to me, by a turn of fortune's hand, in twenty odious minutes, kept company of the most unnatural—I can call it nothing less—with my view of what was happening, with the question of what might still happen, to everyone about me, to the country at large: it so made of these marked disparities a single vast visitation. One had the sense, I mean, of a huge comprehensive ache, and there were hours at which one could scarce have told whether it came most from one's own poor organism, still so young and so meant for better things, but which had

suffered particular wrong, or from the enclosing social body, a body rent with a thousand wounds and that thus treated one to the honor of a sort of tragic fellowship.

(277)

James' device is to collapse his own minor hurt into the national plight, proposing that he is unable to distinguish one from the other. The ache is "comprehensive" in the sense that it contains all points of origin, personal and political; it is not, however, "comprehensive" as that word relates to "understanding," for the hurt is to remain, as he has already told us, "obscure." The blur James creates in this passage is to allow for the improbable conclusion he wishes to draw, namely that he was in a "sort of tragic fellowship" with those who fought. He avoids specifying the nature of his injury in this passage by enacting a ratio upon it, placing the event itself and his response to it at the time within a larger narrative about the national significance of the War.

The explanation Leon Edel gives for James' mysterious malady is that he was suffering from an attack of neurotic anxiety such as his father had suffered when Henry was a boy. According to Edel, the physical injury sustained at Newport amounted to little more than a strained back; indeed, Henry Sr.'s Boston physician is said to have found nothing at all the matter with the young man. Edel goes on to describe James as one "[t]emperamentally unsuited for soldiering, unable to endure violence," having long since "substituted acute and close observation of life for active participation in it.'"[7] The implication is that the physical injury was conjured up in order to mask the reality of a psychological indisposition. Now, the obvious reason for James' conversion of his anxiety into a bodily lameness is that it offered to preserve his honor as well as his life; as Kelly Cannon puts it, the injury allowed James to meet "the social expectations of manhood."[8] But a more precise motivation is evident in the *Notes,* and that is his desire to maintain "a sort of tragic fellowship" with those actually fighting the war. Throughout the memoir, James recounts his determined efforts to establish adequate homosocial relations with fighting men. Recalling a visit paid to a regiment of Union soldiers at Portsmouth Grove, he reflects that the "great point" of his meeting with the troops was not just that he achieved intimacy with them, but that he did so by observing their own strict codes of personal engagement, their "pathetically 'knowing' devices" (292). He recognizes the importance of reticence among men, firm boundaries in speech, a limited expressiveness conducted indirectly through "rueful humor," "stoic reserve," an "esoteric vernacular" (292-3). James is watchful of his own natural loquacity because he understands how delicate the contract is that exists between these men, how much it depends on keeping the self in check. Thinking back on the perplexing account of the "wound," it can be argued that in order to preserve this "fellowship" with other men, and to maintain his likeness to them *as men*, James casts his disabling anxiety, his fear, as something else: in Freudian terms, he converts it into a physical symptom—the "wound." For the Freudian, the extent of James' awareness of the process of conversion is not important; rather, the crucial thing is to appreciate, as Elaine Showalter describes, that neurosis is a compromise established by the psyche between the instinct towards self-preservation (i.e. the desire not to go to war) and the "prohibitions against deception or flight" imposed by society and its ideals of "duty, patriotism, and honor."[9] In other words, James produces an "acceptable" physical condition, rather than the culturally *unacceptable* affliction of anxiety, in order to free himself from this predicament. He converts his internal condition into an external one, the better to manage it.

In the *Notes* and in the stories, the stay-at-home male struggles to live up to the version of masculine conduct that fighting men promote. The only way he can do this is to establish the identity of his condition with theirs, carrying a bodily wound as they do, curbing his hysterical, effeminate talkativeness in favor of their manly taciturnity. James depicts himself as an intensely committed participant in the national calamity, a sharer in the contagious tension of the time, engaged from his supine position in what he calls "a negative of combat . . . firmly parallel to action in the tented field" (281). He invokes the idea of the stay-at-home's experience as the flip-side of combat, the "reverse of the picture." He too is a veteran; his state of "inwardness" is not different from the "outwardness" to which his soldier-friends are compelled, but coterminous with it. Similarly, in the stories "Poor Richard" and "The Story of A Year," both the principal male characters express their wish to belong to the "tragic fellowship" of War veterans. At one point, Richard, in his tale, finds himself in competition for Gertrude's hand with two officers of the Union Army. He senses his inadequacy in comparison with these men and so enlists in order to correct the deficit. For Richard, adopting the discipline of war is a way of curbing the disfiguring emotionalism he suffers from. By inclination a stay-at-home, he is naturally confessional, sentimental, talkative, repeatedly declaring his love for Gertrude. After the war, he is far more restrained (repressed, one might say), calling on Gertrude "dutifully and respectfully" (178), content in the knowledge that no woman would ever again be able to afflict him as she once had. In "The Story of a Year," as we have seen, Jack finds it a necessary condition of his soldiering to banish all thoughts of Lizzie and what her love might mean to him, for fear that it will make him susceptible of injury by other men.

I dwell on James because his complex evasiveness over the matter of his anxiety, his strategic conversion of the psychological into the physical, is a feature too of Am-

brose Bierce's Civil War writing. Bierce, of course, had a very different experience of the War from James. He saw action, volunteering for the Union Army in 1861 and mustering out a lieutenant. Nevertheless, he shares with James a deep interest in the dynamics of male relationships, and particularly in how forms of male anxiety undermine or threaten the normal codes of masculine socialization. Despite the ubiquity of the hysterical or battle-traumatized male in his fiction, Bierce, like James, consistently disavows what Peter Middleton terms the "inward gaze."[10] In his writing, the successful soldier is only reckoned with in terms of his outward conduct: indeed, his very identity as a combatant depends on not investigating his mind. Conversely, the soldier who fails to perform adequately in battle has his failure explained in terms of his excessive "inwardness." In both cases, competent masculinity is presented as a triumph of deed over thought. The stories I will look at below all demonstrate how Bierce diverts attention from the psychological content of his soldiers' behavior.

"Killed at Resaca" is the story of Lieutenant Herman Brayle, the best man in an Ohio regiment, narrated by one of his comrades. Brayle is a kind of national ideal for the narrator, "more than six feet . . . with light hair and gray-blue eyes . . . a gentleman's manners, a scholar's head, and a lion's heart."[11] What is more, he has risen discreetly in the ranks during a time of shrill "loquacity" (40). Brayle is noted in particular for his spectacular acts of heroism on the battlefield, deeds that increasingly border on the downright foolhardy and senseless, to the point that he endangers the security of the regiment. Despite this, he is admired by his comrades for the manner of his courage:

> Let me do justice to a brave man's memory; in all these needless exposures of life there was no visible bravado nor subsequent narration. In the few instances when some of us had ventured to remonstrate, Brayle had smiled pleasantly and made some light reply, which, however, had not encouraged a further pursuit of the subject. Once he said:
>
> "Captain, if ever I come to grief by forgetting your advice, I hope my last moments will be cheered by the sound of your beloved voice breathing into my ear the blessed words, 'I told you so'."
>
> (42)

Brayle's quality is his lack of "narration," his taciturnity: he is a doer, not a talker. Elsewhere he is praised for lacking "affectation" and for being "intensely dramatic, but in no degree theatrical" (43). It is not simply that he is brave, but that his courage comes unblemished by expressiveness, by any effeminate loquacity. The soldier is noted for his bluff masculinist humor, the same quality James took pleasure in among the troops at Portsmouth Grove. (In Stephen Crane's *The Red*

Badge of Courage, young Henry Fleming—another Civil War combatant whose anxiety imperils his manly identity—has his inadequacy defined in terms of his exclusion from the bleak humor of his comrades: he cannot understand how they "move with glee, almost with song"[12] in the face of such horror.) The function of self-effacing humor among these fighting men is to encode fear, to firm up the boundaries of their masculinity by not giving way to a potentially damaging "excess" of feeling. The man who says too much, the leaky vessel, is viewed with suspicion in this environment. As Ben Knights observes, masculinity is defined in such narratives "by a high degree of management over the calls the world makes upon a man's identity and inner resources."[13] In Bierce's stories in particular, introspection is displaced by humor or, more commonly, by action; male character is defined and endorsed in terms of its "outwardness." The narrator's analysis of Brayle's madcap conduct in "Killed at Resaca" is tellingly limited in this way:

> It is easy to condemn this kind of thing [Brayle's reckless conduct], and not very difficult to refrain from imitation, but it is impossible not to respect, and Brayle was liked none the less for the weakness which had so heroic an expression. We wished he were not a fool, but he went on that way to the end, sometimes hard hit, but always returning to duty about as good as new.
>
> (43)

The "respect" for Brayle's conduct marks a refusal to deal with him psychologically. His behavior is reckless, suicidal, dissociative, yet "foolishness" is as far as the narrator is prepared to probe into Brayle's motivations. It is as though to admit the psychological would be to threaten the terms of his identity as a soldier. The ending to the story is explicable in the same terms. There the narrator visits Marian Mendenhall, Brayle's former lover. We discover that Brayle's madcap courage was the product of his once being convicted of cowardice by her. She wrote to him then:

> "Mr Winters, whom I shall always hate for it, has been telling that at some battle in Virginia, where he got his hurt, you were seen crouching behind a tree. I think he wants to injure you in my regard, which he knows the story would do if I believed it. I could bear to hear of my soldier lover's death, but not of his cowardice."
>
> These were the words which on that sunny afternoon, in a distant region, had slain a hundred men. Is woman weak?
>
> (45)

It is an interesting final question, displacing the enquiry from male to female weakness. The narrator is in no doubt that Brayle was the bravest man he ever saw; but was he not in fact the greatest hysteric he ever saw? Surely Brayle's actions were not a cancellation of his formerly fearful behavior, but a further manifestation of

it. Yet the significance of Brayle's behavior is missed by the narrator because of his absolute adherence to the codes of reticent, selfless masculinity. He considers Brayle "the truest and bravest heart that ever beat" (45), when in fact he was a man spurred to a frightful self-destructiveness because of the intolerable demands of the role he must act up to. The narrator refuses to tell Marian Mendenhall of the "heroic" nature of Brayle's death because he thinks she is not deserving of this knowledge. Those who really "knew" Brayle were his comrades and even the Confederate troops who "honored the fallen brave" (44) by a cessation of hostilities on the battlefield when he died. The irony Bierce seems to want us to grasp is that Brayle's heroism was triggered by the complacent thoughtlessness of a vacuous woman. But this irony evades the issue of Brayle's psychological state by placing responsibility for his actions in the hands of an external agent, Marian Mendenhall; to adopt the phrase I used in discussion of James, Bierce enacts a ratio upon male interiority by converting the story into a tale of betrayal by woman. The convenience of the betrayal explanation is that Brayle's masculinity emerges intact, if not revitalized, by his subsequent conduct on the battlefield, and the issue of his earlier cowardice is cancelled out.

Throughout his war stories, Bierce, like James, considers the admission of psychological weakness a threat to masculine character itself. In "Killed at Resaca" this means he must divert attention from the inward to the outward in order still to affirm Brayle. Yet eccentric, traumatized behavior by men in battle is a repeated concern of his writing, as stories such as "George Thurston," "A Horseman in the Sky," "One Officer, One Man," and "A Son of the Gods" make clear. In the last of these, a combatant narrator tells of a young officer who rides out on to the front line in full dress uniform, atop a white stallion, in order to draw the enemy's fire and so reveal their position to the Union infantry. He is shot to pieces, and to add insult the "vain devotion" (29) of this "gallant man—this military Christ" (27) brings about only the death and defeat of his comrades. This bitter concluding irony is a characteristic gesture of Bierce's War fiction, telling of the destitution of the old myths of heroism and presenting a fatalistic, defeatist vision of battle in which the noble and the simple-minded alike are consumed, or consume themselves. But in order for that irony to succeed, the young officer's actions need to be read as gallant: it is not the soldier but this complex modern war that has robbed the world of heroism. Yet for us to read the officer as heroic, as the narrator does, we need to need to close off the troubling aspects of his behavior that lurk in the text:

> Galloping rapidly along in the edge of the open ground comes a young officer on a snow-white horse. His saddle blanket is scarlet. What a fool! No one who has

ever been in action but remembers how naturally every rifle turns toward the man on a white horse; no one but has observed how a bit of red enraged the bull of battle. That such colors are fashionable in military life must be accepted as the most astonishing of all the phenomena of human vanity. They would seem to have been devised to increase the death-rate.

The young officer is in full uniform, as if on parade. He is all agleam with bullion—a blue-and-gold edition of the Poetry of War. A wave of derisive laughter runs abreast of him all along the line. But how handsome he is!—with what careless grace he sits his horse!

(25)

The derision soon gives way to pure admiration as the young officer presents himself to certain death. But what is he doing dressed in full ceremonial garb? Why this effete splash of color on the disconsolate battlefield? The young officer is suicidal; at best he is acting in a dissociative manner. John Talbott, in an article on combat trauma in the Civil War, has found evidence of this kind of behavior in several high-ranking officers in the Union army. As he describes, dissociation "is an adaptive strategy" which "allows a person under stress to continue functioning, although often in an autonomic and sometimes inappropriate way."[14] But in order for the ironic structure of Bierce's story to function, and for the young officer to be construed as heroic rather than damaged, the narration must draw a blank on the content of his mind. We are therefore left with this fleeting image of horrified madness while Bierce diverts to his wider story about the futility of warfare. Once again, interiority is refused, and a ratio enacted upon the issue of male psychological trauma.

The complexity of this relationship between masculinity and psychology in Bierce's writing is perhaps best displayed in "One Officer, One Man," a story that differs from "Killed at Resaca" and "A Son of the Gods" because it does not offer any endorsement of its central character. The story tells of a young Captain Graffenreid in his first encounter on the battlefield with an armed enemy. Early on we are told that Captain Graffenreid is suspected of inadequacy by his men because the privilege of a military education has kept him from the front line until now. Greffenreid is therefore keen to earn the "respect of his men and the companionship of his brother officers" (91). In the event, faced with the first bombardment from the enemy he experiences an attack of hysterical anxiety, exhibiting symptoms including mutism, temporary loss of consciousness and uncontrollable movements of the limb. Rooted to the spot with terror when a corpse falls at his feet, Greffenreid's one decisive act in the battle is his last: he kills himself by falling on his sword.

As in James' stories, and "Killed at Resaca," "One Officer, One Man" depicts the anxious or hysterical soldier as one who fails to act due to his excessive and disfiguring "inwardness." We are told that Graffenreid is disabled by too much thought: "From inaction had come introspection. He sought rather to analyze his feelings than distinguish himself by courage and devotion. The result was profoundly disappointing" (93). Again, it is the failure of the man to engage with the world, to develop a strategy of action for displacing his anxiety, that is seen as the cause of his inadequacy. In contrast to Graffenreid's messy, self-polluting intellectualism—his "fancy" (94)—is the narrator's severe ironic self-containment. For the narrator, the incapable soldier lacks definition in the world: he is permeable, disorderly, inward, unable to take control of his environment through decisive action. The effective man, on the other hand, is readily locatable, and appropriately speechless:

An army in line-of-battle awaiting attack, or prepared to deliver it, presents strange contrasts. At the front are precision, formality, fixity, and silence. Toward the rear these characteristics are less and less conspicuous, and finally, in point of space, are lost altogether in confusion, motion and noise. The homogeneous becomes heterogeneous. Definition is lacking; repose is replaced by an apparently purposeless activity; harmony vanishes in hubbub, form in disorder. Commotion everywhere and ceaseless unrest. The men who do not fight are never ready.

(90)

Graffenreid's weakness finds it correlative in the gossipy disarray of the rear ranks whose "apparently purposeless activity" presumably includes such episodes of introspection as the young officer is said to have indulged. An opposition is therefore established between Graffenreid and Bierce's narratorial voice. The latter's ironic detachment is meant to define by contrast Graffenreid's failing by showing us the mode of conduct that *can* survive the battleground; and that mode is purposely *un*reflective. The story observes the symptoms of the young officer's trauma—the "strain upon his nervous organism was insupportable. He grew hot and cold by turns. He panted like a dog, and then forgot to breathe . . ." (94)—but there is no consideration of these symptoms as produced by the intolerable demands of combat; rather, it is implied that Graffenreid's gathering hysteria is produced by his temperamental unsuitability to battle, by his failure to maintain a "manly" control over his emotions and behavior.

During the Civil War there was, as John Talbott explains, "no label like shell shock, battle fatigue or posttraumatic stress disorder to help explain and legitimize a mysterious condition, no category short of lunacy to account for peculiar behavior."[15] That failure to "legitimize" combat trauma was a failure to name it, to differentiate it from known categories such as lunacy, malingering, dereliction or cowardice. Bierce's stories reveal the same dependence on the conventional descriptors of male behavior in order to produce their ironic commentary on the futility of modern warfare. Despite the fascination evident throughout his work with the subject of anxiety and war neurosis, Bierce refuses to examine how it might be produced by the very intolerable ideals of male conduct that make the prosecution of war possible.

To return to Daniel Aaron, the Civil War was for him "unwritten" because of the reluctance of many American writers to deal with the fundamental issue of the conflict—race. But the War was "unwritten" in another sense too, as I have shown here, even by those who addressed it directly. Both James and Bierce are evasive about the way war inflicts psychological and emotional damage on men, whether active in service or not. Both writers find it necessary to convert internal conflict into stories of wounds and the making of men—coherent narratives of "outwardness." In this, they reflect their culture's struggle to square mental frailty with conventional definitions of manhood. The spectacle of the hysterical man threatened what Showalter calls the late Victorian "ideology of absolute and natural difference between women and men."[16] Hysteria was considered a "female malady," a product of the susceptible feminine constitution, hence the euphemisms such as "railway spine" devised in order to emphasize the distinctly physiological (as opposed to psychological) male condition. It is telling that Silas Weir Mitchell's infamous "rest cure" (initially developed, ironically enough, from his treatment of Civil War veterans) was applied to women rather than to men, the belief being that male maladies of the mind should be prescribed a dose of vigorous physical exercise. The 1890s doctrine of "strenuous life" advocated by Theodore Roosevelt among others represents a further subordination to the body of the male psyche. In fact, it is not until the First World War that physicians in Europe and America come to acknowledge that men involved in war may suffer injury that is not simply or wholly physical, and the diagnosis of "shell-shock" is finally made. Reading James and Bierce, we see how significant the will to make that diagnosis is, not only to the history of modern warfare, but to the story of masculinity itself.

Notes

1. Daniel Aaron, *The Unwritten War: American Writers and the Civil War* (New York: Knopf, 1973).

2. Aaron, 107. For Leon Edel's account of the wound, on which Aaron draws, see Leon Edel, *Henry James: The Untried Years 1843-1870* (London: Rupert Hart-Davis, 1953), 171-86.

3. Aaron, 183-4.

4. Henry James, *Notes of a Son and Brother* (London: Macmillan, 1914). Subsequent references to this text are parenthetical.

5. Henry James, *The Tales of Henry James Volume 1,* Maqbool Aziz, ed. (Oxford: Clarendon Press, 1973), 166. Subsequent references to this volume are parenthetical.

6. On James's interest in characters and narrators who are absented, excused, or excluded from conventional arenas of masculinity, see, for example, Eve Kosofsky Sedgwick's *Epistemology of the Closet* (Berkeley, CA: University of California Press, 1990), and Kelly Cannon's *Henry James and Masculinity: The Man at the Margins* (Basingstoke and London: Macmillan, 1994).

7. Edel, 174.

8. Cannon, 37.

9. Elaine Showalter, *The Female Malady: Women, Madness, and English Culture, 1830-1980* (London: Virago, 1987), 170.

10. Peter Middleton, *The Inward Gaze: Masculinity and Subjectivity in Modern Culture* (London and New York: Routledge, 1992).

11. Ambrose Bierce, *The Collected Writings of Ambrose Bierce,* Clifton Fadiman, ed. (New York: Citadel Press, 1996), 41. Subsequent references to this volume are parenthetical.

12. Stephen Crane, *The Red Badge of Courage: An Episode of the American Civil War,* Henry Binder, ed. (New York: W. W. Norton, 1979), 12.

13. Ben Knights, *Writing Masculinities: Male Narratives in Twentieth-Century Fiction* (London and Basingstoke: Macmillan, 1999), 126.

14. John Talbott, "Combat Trauma in the American Civil War," *History Today 46* (March 1996): 42. Elaine Showalter, in a chapter on shell-shock in World War I, points out that officers, such as Siegfried Sassoon, whose "psychological stability was shaky," often dealt with their fear "by reckless acts of combat" (Showalter, 179).

15. Talbott, 41.

16. Showalter, 167-8.

Works Cited

Aaron, Daniel, *The Unwritten War: American Writers and the Civil War* (New York: Knopf, 1973).

Bierce, Ambrose, *The Collected Writings of Ambrose Bierce,* Clifton Fadiman, ed. (New York: Citadel Press, 1996),

Cannon, Kelly, *Henry James and Masculinity: The Man at the Margins* (Basingstoke and London: Macmillan, 1994).

Crane, Stephen, *The Red Badge of Courage: An Episode of the American Civil War,* Henry Binder, ed. (New York: W. W. Norton, 1979).

Edel, Leon, *Henry James: The Untried Years 1843-1870* (London: Rupert Hart-Davis, 1953).

James, Henry, *Notes of a Son and Brother* (London: Macmillan, 1914).

———. *The Tales of Henry James Volume 1,* Maqbool Aziz, ed. (Oxford: Clarendon Press, 1973).

Knights, Ben, *Writing Masculinities: Male Narratives in Twentieth-Century Fiction* (London and Basingstoke: Macmillan, 1999).

Middleton, Peter, *The Inward Gaze: Masculinity and Subjectivity in Modern Culture* (London and New York: Routledge, 1992).

Sedgwick, Eve Kosofsky, *Epistemology of the Closet* (Berkeley, CA: University of California Press, 1990).

Showalter, Elaine, *The Female Malady: Women, Madness, and English Culture, 1830-1980* (London: Virago, 1987).

Talbott, John, "Combat Trauma in the American Civil War," *History Today* 46 (March 1996): 41-7.

Linda Czuba Brigance (essay date spring 2005)

SOURCE: Brigance, Linda Czuba. "Ballots and Bullets: Adapting Women's Rights Arguments to the Conditions of War." *Women and Language* 28, no. 1 (spring 2005): 1-7.

[*In the following essay, Brigance illustrates how two leading figures in the women's suffrage movement, Elizabeth Cady Stanton and Susan B. Anthony, utilized rhetorical opportunities afforded by the Civil War to advance their cause.*]

Introduction

Slaves, immigrants, those without property, people of color, and adherents to certain religious beliefs have been excluded from the rights and responsibilities of full citizenship at various times in American history. As Anna Yeatman (1993) explains it, "the dominant discourses of modern citizenship are predicated on systemic exclusions of those who are othered by these discourses" (quoted in Kingfisher, 1998, p. 128). When "woman" is added to the previously mentioned descriptors, another layer of exclusion is added. For example, the Fifteenth Amendment to the U.S. Constitution, enacted after the Civil War, granted suffrage rights to black men, but excluded women of all races.

The citizenship of those whose civic status is already ambiguous becomes even more troublesome in times of war. This is because war challenges not only the material and human resources of a nation, but also its collective identity. Contemporary consequences of ambiguous citizenship status include the internment of American citizens of Japanese ancestry during World War II and the post 9-11 treatment of citizens of Middle Eastern heritage. Because the rights and responsibilities of citizenship that are emphasized in war (such as public policy making and military service) are activities from which women traditionally have been excluded, the idea of woman-as-citizen is even more problematic during times of war than it is during times of peace. For women who engage in challenges against the status quo, wartime presents particular difficulties, because dissent against the government is often characterized as unpatriotic. Thus, throughout U.S. history, wartime has presented extraordinary challenges for women's rights advocates.

This paper examines the discourse of women's rights activists during and after the Civil War in order to better understand how the rhetoric of social reform can take advantage of the circumstances of war to advance activists' causes. This analysis focuses on the Civil War because it was the first war that women's rights activists faced after the 1848 Seneca Falls women's rights convention. Therefore, it provides the first example of the rhetorical strategies used in wartime by an organized women's movement in the United States. I argue that some women's rights advocates in the Civil War era, specifically movement leaders Susan B. Anthony and Elizabeth Cady Stanton, did not abandon their gender equality agenda to the war effort; rather, they adapted to the rhetorical situation presented to them by the war.

Women's Rights War Rhetoric

It is impossible to separate the beginning of the women's rights movement in the United States from many of the issues that led to Civil War, because the leaders acquired their social reform consciousness and strategies through their involvement in the abolition movement. Indeed, it was their exclusion from the World Anti-Slavery conference in England in June, 1840, that motivated Elizabeth Cady Stanton and Lucretia Mott to call the first women's rights conference in Seneca Falls, New York, in 1848 (Stanton, 1898/1971, p. 82).

During the years leading up to the Civil War, the campaign for women's rights was small compared to the abolition and temperance crusades. The movement could be characterized as being situated at the margins of a reform agenda that was itself at the political margins. Nevertheless, these years were profitable ones for the budding movement. The primary tool for raising the level of social consciousness about women's legal inequality and for recruiting activists to the cause was a series of conventions held throughout the Northeast. These conventions served as "public forums for the testing and formulation of an ideology" (Campbell, 1989, p. 50) and focused on "violation of natural rights; disabilities of married women; religious discrimination; and denials of opportunity for individual development" (Campbell, 1989, p. 53).

Although the movement was limited in nature, there were significant gains. For example, one of the most consequential victories came in March, 1860, when the New York legislature passed a Married Women's Property Rights Law, granting married women the right to own property, keep earned wages and petition for custody of their children in the case of divorce.[1] However, despite such legislative efforts and growing attendance at the conventions, women's rights was not a national issue before the Civil War, and the majority of American women and men showed little interest in the cause (Buhle, 1979, p. 13).

When the war started in 1861, the most visible women's rights activity, the conventions, were discontinued. Many accounts of the movement during this time suggest that the goals of the movement were abandoned temporarily. Gurko (1974) represents this perspective when she decisively declares, "with the coming of the Civil War, all woman's rights activities stopped" (p. 208). Other scholars have contributed to this view by explicitly dividing the activities of this First Wave of American feminism into "before" and "after" the Civil War, skipping over the war years or focusing solely on women's auxiliary war activities. For example, neither Karlyn Kohrs Campbell (1989) in her volume of "key texts of the early feminists" nor Ellen Carol DuBois (1981) in her edited volume of speeches and letters of Elizabeth Cady Stanton and Susan B. Anthony include any texts from the years 1862 through 1866. This pattern of overlooking women's political rhetoric during the Civil War years is further illustrated in Miriam Schnier's (1972) collection of "essential historical [feminist] writings" which jumps from a 1860 convention speech by Ernestine Rose (p. 125) to a statement by Sojourner Truth in 1867 (p. 128).

While many activists did redirect their efforts toward the war, Elizabeth Cady Stanton and Susan B. Anthony did not. They resisted this course of action and urged the active continuation of demands for women's rights, because they feared that women's concerns would be completely lost in the climate of war (Stanton, 1898/1971, p. 254; Gurko, 1974, p. 208.) An examination of the discourse of Anthony and Stanton during this period indicates that they kept the movement alive by rhetorically adapting to the wartime situation by linking the war, the anti-slavery movement and their own movement in ways that served their calls for women's equality. Their rhetorical strategies included (1) binding women's rights to negro[2] rights; (2) positioning women as vital to victory; and (3) constructing women as independent political actors. The use of these strategies contributed to the evolution of the women's rights movement from a position at the fringes of the abolitionist movement before the war to a full-fledged, independent social reform movement after the war.

BINDING WOMEN'S RIGHTS TO NEGRO RIGHTS

In 1860, as the possibility of civil war escalated, Stanton was invited as "the foremost representative of American feminism" (DuBois, 1981, p. 22) to speak to the annual meeting of the American Anti-Slavery Society. Her speech illustrates a primary rhetorical strategy of women's rights advocates during the war years—linking the plight of the American woman with the plight of American negroes. Stanton accomplished this through a series of rhetorical shifts that presented the syllogistic argument that to be anti-slavery was to be pro-women's rights. She began her argument by broadening the goal of the anti-slavery movement:

> This [organization] is generally known as the platform of one idea—that is negro slavery. In a certain sense this may be true but the most casual observation of this whole anti-slavery movement, of your lives, conventions, public speeches and journals, show this one idea to be a great humanitarian one.
>
> (Stanton, 1860, p. 79)

Here, Stanton offered delegates the premise that the nature of their cause encompassed more than a narrow focus on slavery. She explained that their commitment was to all of humanity, not just the slave.

Having established the true breadth of their social reform agenda, she then presented the premise that their commitment to humanity necessarily included a commitment to women:

> The motto of your leading organ, 'The world is my country and all mankind my countrymen,' proclaims the magnitude and universality of this one idea, which takes in the whole human family, irrespective of nation, color, caste or *sex* [emphasis added], with all their interests, temporal and spiritual.
>
> (Stanton, 1860, p. 79)

Having specified sex, along with race, as a category of inclusion of humanitarian concerns, Stanton then provided evidence for her claim that to support the negro's cause was to support the woman's cause. She did this by detailing the similarities between negroes as a class and women as a class:

> . . . [a woman is] more fully identified with the slave than [the white] man can possibly be, for she . . . learns the misfortune of being born an heir to the crown

of thorns, to martyrdom, to womanhood. For while the [white] man is born to do whatever he can, for the woman and the negro there is no such privilege. There is a Procrustean bedstead ever ready for them, body and soul, . . . the black man and the woman are born to shame. The badge of degradation is the skin of sex.

(Stanton, 1860, p. 83)

After linking the subject position of (white) women with that of negro men, Stanton drove home the point of women's special circumstance (and, therefore, special obligation of support by the reformers) by detailing the plight of those who suffered because of race *and* gender: the female slave. She said,

Are not nearly two million of native-born American women, at this very hour, doomed to the foulest slavery that angels ever wept to witness? Are they not doubly damned as immortal beasts of burden in the field, and sad mothers of a most accursed race? Are not they raised for the express purposes of lust? Are they not chained and driven in the slave-coffle at the crack of the whip of an unfeeling driver? Are they not trained up in ignorance of all laws, both human and divine, and denied the right to read the Bible?

(Stanton, 1860, p. 84)

Stanton knew that this series of rhetorical questions would be answered by abolitionists in only one way; by answering in the affirmative, social reformers were left with no logical means of withholding support for women's rights.

After identifying the broad social agenda of the anti-slavery movement and stipulating the concerns of both negroes and white women as an inherent element of that agenda, she then presented her inevitable conclusion:

No, the mission of the Radical Anti-Slavery Movement is not to the African slave alone, but to the slaves of custom, creed and sex, as well . . . If you would have us teach our sons a sacred reverence for law, so frame your constitutions and your codes that, in yielding obedience to their requirements, they are not false to the holy claims of humanity.

(Stanton, 1860, p. 81)

In this rousing conclusion to her argument, Stanton returned to her opening claim that the anti-slavery movement was in actuality a humanistic movement and, as such, must be as interested in women as it was in negro men.

Ultimately, this rhetorical strategy proved to be the most controversial, and its adoption by Anthony and Stanton foreshadowed the split in the women's movement in the period immediately after the war. At the heart of the breech between the New York contingent (led by Anthony and Stanton) and the Boston contingent (led by Lucy Stone) was controversy over support

for the Fifteenth Amendment which granted the right to vote regardless of "race, color, or previous condition of servitude," but left out the issue of gender.

During the war, Stone had supported the linkage of women's and negro rights. In 1863, for example, she declared,

while you [government leaders] are going through this valley of humiliation, do not forget you must be true alike to the women and the negroes. We can never be truly "loyal" if we leave them out.

(Anthony, Stanton and Gage, 1891, "The Woman's National . . ." p. 65)

However, after the war, she parted ways with Anthony and Stanton because she was not willing to sacrifice negro suffrage for woman suffrage by opposing the Fifteenth Amendment, stating that she was "thankful in my soul" for any expansion of voting rights (Gurko, 1974, p. 232).

Others, however, led by Elizabeth Cady Stanton, Susan B. Anthony and Lucretia Mott refused to support the separation of woman suffrage from negro suffrage after working so diligently to link them together. As Stanton wrote in *The Revolution* in 1868, "Now is the hour— not the negro's hour alone, but everybody's hour."

POSITIONING WOMEN AS VITAL TO VICTORY

A second rhetorical strategy used by women's rights activists to forward their political and social agenda was to prove that women were capable of contributing to the nation as fully as were men—even in a time of war. They did this by reminding the public of women's contributions to the war in terms of traditionally feminine activities as well as battlefield exploits. In addition, they identified examples of women who surpassed men's military achievements.

Ever since the Revolutionary War, American women have been expected to serve their country, but primarily from the domestic sphere. As Woloch (1984) explains, "the conflicts that began in the 1760s drew attention to women's household work and upgraded the value of their domestic contributions—as producers of homespun, boycotters of imports, and enthusiasts of the cause (p. 80). Women on both sides of the Civil War continued this tradition. As Anthony, Stanton, and Gage (1881) explained:

At this eventful hour the patriotism of woman shone forth as fervently and spontaneously as did that of man; and her self-sacrifice and devotion were displayed in as many varied fields of action . . . Think of the busy hands from the Atlantic to the Pacific, making garments, canning fruits and vegetables, packing boxes, preparing lint and bandages for soldiers at the front;

think of the mothers, wives and daughters on the far-off prairies, gathering in the harvests, that their fathers, husbands, brothers, and sons might fight the battles of freedom.

("Woman's Patriotism . . ." p. 1)

This litany of women's contributions served as a reminder that victory was as dependent on the work of women in the home as it was on the work of men in battle.

In addition to pointing out women's many domestic contributions to victory, the leaders of the women's rights movement also made the case that women could perform successfully on the battlefield along side of men. As one account described it:

Hundreds of women marched steadily up to the mouth of a hundred cannon pouring out fire and smoke, shot and shell, mowing down the advancing hosts like grass; men, horses, and colors going down in confusion, disappearing in clouds of smoke; the only sound, the screaming of shells, the crackling of musketry, the thunder or artillery, through all this women were sustained by the enthusiasm born of love of country and liberty.

(Anthony, Stanton and Gage, 1881, "Women as Soldiers" p. 21)

Details of the battlefield exploits of women such as Elizabeth Compton, Ellen Goodridge, Pauline Cushman, Frances Hook, and others were offered as evidence of women's successful performance of this most masculine obligation of citizenship. Based on these examples they argued, "in all the great battles of the past woman as warrior in disguise has verified her right to fight and die for her country by the side of man . . . she has shown equal skill and capacity with him" (Anthony, Stanton and Gage, 1881, "Woman Earned . . . ," p. 89). This argument concluded with the claim that women were vital participants in the public sphere, even during wartime, and, therefore, deserved the rights and obligations of citizenship granted to men. As they explained, "were proof of woman's love of freedom [or] of the right to freedom needed, the history of our civil war would alone be sufficient to prove that love, to establish that right" (Anthony, Stanton and Gage, 1881, "Women as Soldiers," p. 18).

While the previously mentioned examples were presented as proof that women could perform on an equal footing with men in a time of war, other arguments established that women could actually outperform men. One such example was Anna Ella Carroll. In 1861, Carroll criticized a planned military excursion down the Mississippi River and offered an alternative that was adopted and proved successful. Activists reported that an English expert on military history ranked the battle that ensued, based on Carroll's military strategy, as the sixteenth "most decisive battle in world history" (Anthony, Stanton and Gage, 1881, "Anna Ella Carroll," p. 9).

Like other patriotic feats by women in the Civil War, Carroll's story was directly linked to demands for full citizenship:

It has been well said: 'That assumption of man that as feud is the origin of all laws; that as woman does not fight she shall not vote, that her rights are to be forever held in abeyance to his wishes, was forever silenced by the military genius of Anna Ella Carroll in planning this brilliant campaign. Proving, too, that as right is of no sex, so genius is of no sex.'

(Anthony, Stanton and Gage, 1881, "Anna Ella Carroll," p. 9)

Through this rhetorical strategy, Anthony and Stanton attacked the powerful tradition of separate spheres and the premise that different types of civic performance justifies different classes of citizenship—concepts that grounded women's ambiguous citizenship status throughout the ages. This separate spheres/separate civic status argument dates back to Plato's *Republic* where he concluded that only women sufficiently freed from domestic duties were free to handle to obligations of leadership and rule equally with men (Okin, 1979, p. 38). Anthony and Stanton attacked this ideology by arguing that women's and men's wartime contributions were *not* of different spheres. They wanted all types of women's war work understood as legitimate military service. Once redefined in that manner, the only logical conclusion was that women's citizenship status should be no different than men's.

CONSTRUCTING WOMEN AS INDEPENDENT POLITICAL ACTORS

The third rhetorical strategy that Anthony and Stanton employed during the Civil War era focused on defining women as independent political actors. One of the most visible vehicles for this goal was the Woman's National Loyal League, founded by Stanton and Anthony in May, 1863. One might ask "to what cause were the women of the Loyal League being asked to pledge their loyalty?" In her autobiography, Stanton succinctly summed up the purpose of the Loyalty League; the purpose was not limited to winning the Civil War. As she explained, "this Woman's Loyal League voiced the solemn lessons of the War: Liberty to all: national protection for every citizen under our flag; universal suffrage, and universal amnesty" (Stanton, 1898/1971, p. 235). Nowhere was what Anthony and Stanton expected as the outcome of the war more clearly articulated than in a resolution proposed by Anthony and adopted by the Loyal League which read, "Resolved, There never can be a true peace in the Republic until the civil and political rights of all citizens of African descent and all women are practically established" (Stanton, 1898/1971, p. 238).

These passages made it clear that the founders of the Loyal League envisioned it as a vehicle for attaching their women's rights message to the national discourse about the war. The rhetorical strategy employed by Anthony and Stanton included explaining their definition of an independent political actor, arguing that women were capable of independent political thought, and instructing women on how to enact their independent political status.

In their "Call to the Woman's National Loyal League Meeting," Anthony and Stanton framed the purpose as a reassessment of women's civic role during war. As they explained,

> To man, by common consent, is assigned the forum, camp, and field. What is woman's legitimate work, and how she may best accomplish it, is worthy of our earnest counsel one with another.
>
> (Anthony, Stanton and Gage, 1881, "The Woman's National . . ." p. 53)

Inherent in declaring that there was a need to have a public discussion of the civic role of women was the following argument. First, the ability to make deliberate choices about civic matters is a hallmark of an independent political actor. Second, women are capable of making choices about civic matters; otherwise, there would be no need for the type of public discussion they advocated. These two premises led to their conclusion: women were capable of being independent political actors.

To reinforce this conclusion, Anthony and Stanton argued that women were as culpable as men for the circumstances that led to the Civil War. This was an important part of their argument. It would have been far easier to argue that women had little responsibility for the state of the nation because they were barred from holding elective office, could not vote, and were rarely consulted as experts in civic matters. However, to argue that women had choices would be an empty argument if they also argued that women had no responsibility for the consequences of those choices. In the call for the founding of the organization, they declared, "woman is equally interested and responsible with man in the final settlement of this problem of self-government; therefore let none stand a spectator now" (Anthony, Stanton and Gage, 1881, "The Woman's National . . ." p. 53). Later, in the opening session of the organization's first meeting, on May 14, 1863, Anthony asserted women's responsibility for the war:

> Had the women of the North studied to know and to teach their sons the law of justice to the black man, regardless of the frown or the smile of pro-slavery priest and politician, they would not now be called upon to offer the loved of their households to the Bloody Moloch of war.
>
> (Anthony, Stanton and Gage, 1881, "The Woman's National . . .," p. 58)

By arguing that women should not hide behind others, even authorities such as priests and politicians, Anthony was defining an independent political actor as someone who "assume[s] her God-given responsibilities . . . [and] no longer [is] the mere reflector, the echo of the worldly pride and ambition of men" (Anthony, Stanton and Gage, 1881, "The Woman's National . . ." p. 58).

After rhetorically framing women as: (1) having a choice in terms of their war service and, (2) bearing responsibility for the state of civic affairs, she explained how to best channel independent thinking:

> And now, women of the North, I ask you to rise up with earnest, honest purpose, and go forward in the way of right, fearless, as independent human beings, responsible to God alone for the discharge of every duty, for the faithful use of every gift the good Father has given you. Forget conventionalism, forget what the world will say, whether you are in your place or out of your place; think your best thoughts, speak your best words, do your best works, looking to your own conscience for approval.
>
> (Anthony, Stanton and Gage, 1881, "The Woman's National . . .," p. 58)

After reiterating that women were responsible to no one but themselves and God, Anthony urged them to enact their citizenship by challenging the status quo. She instructed them to move beyond the wartime roles that had been prescribed for them by others. After all, the reason for the formation of the Loyalty League was for women to "counsel one with another" about the issue of "what is woman's legitimate [war] work," not to seek the counsel of others (Anthony, Stanton and Gage, 1881, "The Woman's National . . ." p. 53). In a tone that is almost pleading, Anthony told women not only to think for themselves, but to speak up for their ideas and then turn those ideas into actions. The admonition to "speak your best words" is perhaps the most unconventional direction of all, as this was a period in which women's engagement in public address still evoked ridicule and scorn. Anthony and Stanton, by their own example as well as their words, communicated the importance of inserting the voice and concerns of women into the national discourse—the very discourse that defined them as "other" in order to exclude them from full citizenship.

Throughout the meetings of the Loyal League, Anthony and Stanton continued to offer instructions to women about how to enact their autonomy. For example, Anthony said,

> It is high time for the daughters of the revolution, in solemn council to unseal the last will and testament of the Fathers—lay hold of their birthright of freedom, and keep it a sacred trust for all coming generations.
>
> (Anthony, Stanton and Gage, 1881, "The Woman's National . . .," p. 53)

In this passage they made two clear points about the ways in which women should assert their political independence. First, women should not wait to be handed full citizenship; rather they should actively take it. The commands to "unseal" and "lay hold" are strong words that connote taking charge of the circumstances women find themselves in regarding their citizenship status. Second, Anthony and Stanton identified another means of enacting citizenship—securing benefits for future generations. Implicit in this type of action is that women have the capacity to make judgements about what is best for the collective and how to best bring it about.

CONCLUSION: JOINING THE NATIONAL DISCOURSE

When the Civil War ended on April 9, 1865, the immediate question facing the nation was "the political status of the negro" (Stanton, 1898/1971, p. 241). The issue was not a simple one nor was it limited to the circumstances of former slaves. As Stanton (1898/1971) explained, "to demand his [the negro man's] enfranchisement on the broad principle of natural rights was hedged about with difficulties, as the logical result of such action must be the enfranchisement of all ostracized classes" (p. 241), which included women. Women's rights activists were dismayed by the ratification of the Fourteenth Amendment in 1866, because it added, for the first time, the qualifier "male" to constitutionally guaranteed rights.[3] The subsequent passage and ratification of the Fifteenth Amendment in 1869 and 1870, that protected the rights of citizens against discrimination "on account of race, color, or previous condition of servitude" severed women's rights from negro rights. As previously discussed, irreconcilable differences over support for these amendments led to a splintering of the women's rights movement. The May, 1869, meeting of the Equal Rights Association (formed in 1866 to supports universal rights) "broke wide open on the [amendment] issue" (Flexner, 1974, p. 152). Stanton and Anthony, who opposed supporting any measure that excluded support for women rights, immediately formed the National Woman Suffrage Association, the first U.S. national women's rights organization. Later that year, Lucy Stone and others who supported the amendments formed the American Woman Suffrage Association.[4]

It was another fifty-one years before women were granted the right to vote by the Nineteenth Amendment. Neither Stanton nor Anthony lived to see their dream realized. While Stanton's and Anthony's rhetoric during the Civil War years did not result in the immediate enfranchisement of women, it did represent a crossroads in the women's rights movement. By recognizing that the circumstances of war offered a unique rhetorical moment in the nation's history and by creating strategies that took advantage of those circumstances, they guaranteed that women's voices became part of the national discourse in a way they were not prior to the war.

This analysis of the wartime rhetoric of women's rights activists began with two assumptions. The first claims that particular social groups are constructed as "other" by the national discourse about citizenship, and that women have traditionally been among those excluded groups. The second assumption states that times of war present particular rhetorical difficulties for those who voice complaints against the status quo. The latter assumption was recognized by many women's rights activists in the period of the American Civil War, motivating them to discontinue their social reform conventions and, instead, turn to efforts in support of the war. They did this because of the belief that the nation would express its gratitude for their loyalty by granting women the right to vote.

Anthony's and Stanton's rhetoric during this period suggests that while they recognized the second assumption, they were primarily motivated by the first. Instead of curtailing their women's rights rhetoric either out of a fear of being labeled unpatriotic or a belief that suffrage could be earned by good works alone, they recognized the opportunity the circumstances of war offered to social reformers. They took this opportunity to present arguments that challenged women's ambiguous citizenship status. All three of their rhetorical strategies focused on women's equality with men in terms of rights responsibilities and obligations of citizenship. By challenging the ideology of separate spheres/separate status, they attacked the rationality for denying women full citizenship status.

By binding women's rights to negro's rights, positioning women as vital to victory, and constructing women as independent political actors, Anthony and Stanton changed the national discourse about both women's rights and the war. They positioned victory against slavery as victory for women's rights; sacrifices for the war effort as sacrifices in the name of women's rights; and battles against the Confederacy, as battles against the inequalities black and white women faced in the North and the South. The result was that when the military hostilities of the Civil War formally concluded, the civil war over women's rights did not. It was fought with more vitality, solicited more heated public discussion, and ultimately met with more successes, than before the war.

In addition to keeping women' rights movement alive during the war and ensuring its growth after the war, the rhetorical strategies of Anthony and Stanton have served as a models for subsequent women rights activists. While opposition against the government in times of war still carries risks, women's rights reformers continue to take advantage of the unique rhetorical moments created by the circumstances of war. For example, in the final years of the suffrage movement, another generation of women's rights activists successfully adapted their arguments to wartime. In 1917, members of the National Woman's Party, under the leadership of Alice Paul became the first group to picket the

White House. They stood silently holding banners pointing out the "hypocrisy . . . [involved in] . . . fighting for democracy in Europe while denying American women the right to vote" (Ford, 1995, p. 290).

Even after suffrage was granted in 1920, women's rights activists continued to strategically use wartime to advance their concerns. During World War II, for example, labor activists feared women working in traditionally male positions would lose their jobs when the men returned from the battlefields. Echoes of Anthony and Stanton about the value of women's contributions can be heard in the words of Mary Anderson of the Women's Bureau, who argued that the nation's stated postwar goal of full employment had to benefit "not only men but women workers whose services and sacrifices are essential factors in winning the peace" (quoted in Daniel, 1983, p. 131). While an analysis of the many wars that have followed the Civil War is beyond the scope of this analysis, women's full equality continues to be a political issue and the rhetoric of women's rights, war, and citizenship during the Korean War, Vietnam, Gulf War, and wars in Afghanistan and Iraq provide rich examples of strategies of adaptation utilized by women's rights activists.

Language does more than represent our circumstances and concerns. Used strategically, it constructs our understanding of fundamental concepts like "citizenship." By insisting that the concerns of women be part of the civic discourse during and after the Civil War, Anthony and Stanton provided those who are systematically excluded from such discourse lessons about entering the discussion, changing the discussion, and, therefore, expanding national conceptualizations of who is a citizen.

Notes

1. This victory was short-lived. The New York state legislature rescinded the law only a few years later (Sherr, p. 47).

2. The term "negro" was used during this time period to denote people of African descent. For the sake of consistency, I use this term throughout the essay.

3. Section 2 of the Fourteenth Amendment reads ". . . when the right to vote at any election for the choice of electors for President and Vice President of the United States, Representatives in congress, the executive and Judicial officers of a State, or the members of the Legislature thereof, is denied to any of the male inhabitants of such State, being twenty-one years of age, and citizens of the United States, or in any way abridged, except for participation in rebellion, or other crime, the basis of representation therein shall be reduced in the proportion which the number of such male citizens shall bear to the whole number of male citizens twenty-one years of age in such State."

4. The two organizations adopted difference goals and strategies in their campaigns for women's rights. For example, the National Woman's Suffrage Association banned men from holding office and worked for a federal suffrage amendment, while the American Woman's Suffrage Association welcomed the participation of men, even electing Henry Blackwell as president, and focused on state and local suffrage rights. Due in large part to the efforts of Stone and Blackwell's daughter, Alice Stone Blackwell, the two organizations merged in 1890 to form the National American Woman Suffrage Association with Stanton as its first president.

References

Anthony, S., Cady Stanton, E., and M. J. Gage. (1881). Woman's patriotism in the war. *History of Woman Suffrage, Vol. II.* Rochester, NY, p. 1-3.

Anthony, S., Cady Stanton, E., and M. J. Gage. (1881). Anna Ella Carroll: The Tennessee Campaign. *History of Woman Suffrage, 1861-1876.* Rochester, NY, p. 3-11.

Anthony, S., Cady Stanton, E., and M. J. Gage. (1881). Women as soldiers. *History of Woman Suffrage, 1861-1876.* Rochester, NY, p. 18-22.

Anthony, S., Cady Stanton, E., and M. J. Gage. (1881). The Woman's National Loyal League. *History of Woman Suffrage, 1861-1876.* Rochester, NY, p. 50-78.

Anthony, S., Cady Stanton, E., and M. J. Gage. (1881). Woman earned her right to vote. *History of Woman Suffrage, 1861-1876.* Rochester, NY, p. 88-89.

Buhle, P. and Buhle, M. J. (1979). *The concise history of woman suffrage.* Urbana: University of Chicago Press.

Campbell, K. K. (1989). *Man cannot speak for her: Key texts of the early feminists.* New York: Praeger.

Daniel, R. L. (1987). *American women in the 20th century: The festival of life.* New York: Harcourt Brace Jovanovich.

DuBois, E. C. (Ed.) (1981). *Elizabeth Cady Stanton, Susan B. Anthony: Correspondence, writings, speeches.* New York: Schocken.

Flexner, E. (1974). *Century of struggle: The woman's rights movement in the United States.* New York: Atheneum.

Ford, L. G. (1995). Alice Paul and the triumph of militancy. In M. S. Wheeler (Ed.) *One woman, one vote: Rediscovering the woman suffrage movement.* Troutman, OR: New Sage, p. 277-294.

Gurko, M. (1974). *The Ladies of Seneca Falls: the birth of the woman's rights movement.* New York: Schocken.

Keyssar, A. (2000). *The right to vote: The contested history of democracy in the United States.* New York: Basic Books.

Kingfisher, C. P. (1998). Citizenship. In E. B. Amico (Ed.) *Reader's guide to women's studies.* Chicago: Fitzroy, p. 127-128.

Okin, S. M. (1979). *Women in western political thought.* Princeton: Princeton University Press.

Schnier, M. (Ed.) (1972). *Feminism: The essential historical writings.* New York: Random House.

Sherr, L. (1995). *Failure is impossible: Susan B. Anthony in her own words.* New York: Random House.

Stanton, E. C. (1860). Speech to the Anniversary of the American Anti-Slavery Society. In DuBois, E. C. (Ed.) (1981). *Elizabeth Cady Stanton, Susan B. Anthony: Correspondence, writings, speeches.* New York: Schocken, p. 79-85.

Stanton, E. C. (1898/1971). *Eighty Years and More: Reminiscences, 1815-1897.* New York: Schocken.

Woloch, N. (1984). *Women and the American experience.* New York: Alfred A. Knopf.

Yeatman, A. (1993). *Postmodern revisioning of the political.* New York: Routledge.

RACE AND SLAVERY

Janet Gabler-Hover (essay date 1995)

SOURCE: Gabler-Hover, Janet. "The North-South Reconciliation Theme and the 'Shadow of the Negro' in *Century Illustrated Magazine*." In *Periodical Literature in Nineteenth-Century America,* edited by Kenneth M. Price and Susan Belasco Smith, pp. 239-56. Charlottesville: University Press of Virginia, 1995.

[In the following essay, Gabler-Hover studies the extent to which the theme of reconciliation between the North and South affected the view of race in the Civil War fiction published in the nineteenth-century periodical, The Century.*]*

> "We all white folks al'ays set heap o' sto' by one nurr."
> —Thomas Nelson Page, "Meh Lady"

In 1885 *Century Illustrated Magazine* published installments or excerpts from three American masterworks: Henry James's *The Bostonians,* William Dean How-

ells's *The Rise of Silas Lapham,* and Mark Twain's *Adventures of Huckleberry Finn.* I have wondered persistently how readers of the time might come upon these serials. How might they have read these installments in the context of other essays and literature appearing in the *Century?* The question is irrelevant with *The Bostonians,* which remained unknown to the majority of *Century*'s audience. In a famous 1886 anecdote, senior editor L. Frank Tooker overheard an editor on the *Century* ask another if *The Bostonians* would finish serialization in February. "'Yes,' [he] replied, not looking up from his own work. 'James says it does, and so does Tooker, and they ought to know: they are the only ones who have ever read it.'"[1]

Strangely enough, the plot of the once unread *Bostonians* speaks eloquently today about the context of the *Century* in the 1880s. One reason James may have been disappointed that *The Bostonians* failed, for example, was that he had changed his New England-bound hero from a Westerner into a Mississippian specifically to accommodate and take advantage of an enfant terrible in the pages of the *Century*—the popular Civil War series running concurrently.[2] James's seemingly casual use of the Civil War series provides a key for readers today to the text and subtext of the *Century* magazine and its fiction in the 1880s. For one thing, James used the Civil War theme to try to make *The Bostonians* more popular, and profitability was an incentive to *Century* writers to use the series or its accompanying theme of North-South reconciliation.[3]

James's Civil War novel, insofar as it was one, also followed the other predictable pattern of the North-South reconciliation theme in the *Century*; oddly—or perhaps not so oddly—treatment of the war between the North and South was marked by no mention of the African-American presence for whom the war was at least in part ostensibly fought. From its inception, the Civil War series in the *Century* was conceived with the ethical motive of reconciling the white North and South; profitability was presented as a minor happy consequence. Unfortunately, the *Century* ethics of reconciliation was an exclusionary ethics. If the presence of African Americans was not so dominant in the 1880s *Century,*[4] then it might not be so apparent how much this presence was resisted by the Northern editors who continued to deny in *Century* editorials that racial injustice in the South was still a problem. Indeed, there are eloquent arguments made in prose and fiction during this time in the *Century* for the fair treatment of African Americans, but ironically, these arguments are usually made by Southern writers invited into the *Century* for their profitability and endorsed by the enthusiasm of antisectional fervor. Although there are a plurality of voices in the *Century* that would suggest an openness to engagement and controversy on the issue of Euro-American treatment of African Americans during the 1880s, the influential pervasiveness of the reconciliation theme indicates a strong psychological pull toward ethnic homogeneity and a resistance and denial of racial difference. Hence, a notable characteristic of the contextual ambience of the *Century* in the 1880s was a pathological attitude toward the African-American race and its place in America. This pathology extended to the pages of *Century*'s fiction, even to *The Bostonians, Silas,* and the selection of excerpts from *Huckleberry Finn.*

I

To understand the environment of the 1880s *Century,* one must first turn to the *Century*'s Civil War series. By the mid 1880s, the *Century* had become the forum for the first real North-South discussion of the Civil War. The Civil War series, which took up a good third of each monthly issue of approximately 160 pages, ran in the *Century* from November 1884 through November 1887.[5] As explained by associate editor Robert Underwood Johnson, it "included contributions from nearly all the surviving officers of high command on both sides of the struggle—Grant, Sherman, McClellan, Pope, Rosecrans, Franklin and many others on the Union side, with Beauregard, Joseph E. Johnston, Longstreet, Hill, Wheeler, Law, and other leaders of the Confederates" on the other.[6]

The Civil War series, launched as an experiment, was an astounding financial success. Tooker commented on the initial reserve of wily business manager Roswell Smith about the project: "Now, though Mr. Roswell Smith was a man of far-sighted mental vision and bold almost to the point of riskiness . . . he doubted that the proposed War Series would be of material advantage to the magazine, which he thought had attained its potential growth." Yet, remarkably, in the series's second year, *Century*'s circulation rose from 127,000 to 225,000. Tooker remembers that "there were times when the normally quiet editorial rooms were like the headquarters of an army on the eve of a great battle, with generals and privates, Confederates and Federals, coming and going."[7]

Proceeds from the series and subsequent published volumes ultimately earned more than $1 million for the *Century* company. But with the Civil War series the *Century* took on not only a financial boon but an accompanying sense of mission. The full consequence of the series for the *Century* can only be understood by remembering that culture in late-nineteenth-century America, especially lucrative culture, could not be justified by profit margins alone. *Century* editors (perhaps more than their audience) had to be convinced that moral purpose was the driving force behind their art. One scholar notes the paradoxical conflation between art, morality, and economics in late-nineteenth-century America. America saw "the emergence of a rhetoric that deployed the 'cultural' and the 'aesthetic' as advertising slogans, as part of a naive but nevertheless effective strategy for advertising commodities that would at once glorify and efface the act of consumption itself by grounding even the most mundane acquisitive choices in the nonmaterial realm of transcendent value designated by the aesthetic."[8] The idea of North-South reconciliation "saved" the Civil War series with its transcendent mission of reconciling the regions and hence creating a post-Civil War unity. Actually, reconciliation was so embedded in the series as its motivating force that it is not altogether clear that the moral urge did not precede profit motive as the series's inspiration.

The editors certainly realized early on that, with timely albeit perhaps unwitting brilliance, they had tapped into a great need in the still regionally divided country for a moral catharsis. Exposed was the still-raw wound of North-South division and perhaps the North's need to absolve itself of the responsibility of decimating the South. The series, confirms one editor, "did more to bring together North and South than anything that had happened since they were torn apart in 1861."[9] Editors later reminisced about the ethical goal of their Series, to "soften controversy"[10] between the North and the South. General editor Richard Watson Gilder used this ethical argument in his solicitation of contributors: "Please," he begged one officer, "don't say 'no' to our war series request! This is the time for the 'unveiling of all hearts.' If the North can see the heart of the South, and the South of the North's, they will love each other as never before! This is truth and no sentimentalism."[11]

But even with North-South reconciliation as the series's guiding force, it seems almost inevitable that, once a Pandora's box of profit motive was opened, the ethical reasons for urging North-South reconciliation were complicated considerably. A more sophisticated member of *Century*'s audience certainly might feel cynical about the basis for the series. One society friend of editor in chief Richard Watson Gilder—Mariana Griswold van Rensselaer, to be specific—commented slyly to her friend in personal correspondence about the gold mine that the series had provided: "What would you all have done if the contemporaries of the last war had used up all the material at the time instead of letting [it] lie in camphor for you?"[12]

As revealed above, ethical motives aside, the Civil War series and its implicit goal of reconciling North and South was of tremendous financial importance to the *Century*. Gilder explained in a letter in 1886 that "what makes a magazine 'go' in a business and moneyed point of view" is the combination of materials in its pages: "We put a poem or an artistic story in next to a war article and that number of the magazine has a huge circulation, but it is the war article that gives it the circulation and is the power to pay authors, rather than the individual story."[13] Gilder and the rest of the staff had come to depend on the series. It had gained the power of an addiction; withdrawn, Gilder may well have feared for the *Century*'s prosperity. Tooker commented ruefully on his own provisional stability after the end of the series: "To learn every detail of the routine work of the office appeared highly advisable, for the flood-tide of activity and prosperity that the War Series had caused was certain to be followed by the ebb, when poorly piloted craft might be stranded."[14]

The *Century*'s mixture of economic and moral reasons for the Civil War series can be seen in the editorial attitude about how to package it. The Civil War series was the invention and subsequent responsibility of associate editor Johnson. Johnson came on board after Gilder succeeded founding editor Josiah Gilbert Holland as the editor in 1881. Holland had been the morally conservative co-owner, with business manager Smith, of the original *Scribner's Monthly Magazine,* which changed its name to the *Century* after the periodical owners split with Scribner's so that they could have their own publishing company.[15] A Gilder biographer notes that although "Gilder had been a liberal influence on Holland [as his assistant editor], . . . Johnson was probably the most prudish editor on the staff of *The Century*."[16] And Johnson apparently orchestrated the reconciliatory tone of the series. Johnson wrote to Gilder during the series's halcyon days, "Dear RWG: We have come across a most excellent Ms. account of life with the Army of the [?] by the author of our Andersonville article—full of color and humor and with fine descriptions of the fighting at Fredericksburg, Antietam, Gettysburg and in the Peninsula. It is *exactly the sort of thing we want the generals to write*" (italics his).[17] It is disconcerting to find Johnson not only approving but mandating that battle accounts of Gettysburg and Antietam be filled with color and with humor. Undoubtedly Johnson is striving for a reconciliatory effect, however; it would be impolitic to linger too long on the negative. Given the moral agenda of reconciliation, Johnson's formula of mixing battle accounts with humor seems targeted toward transforming the potentially bitter memories of *Century*'s sectional audiences into nostalgic reminiscences.

The *Century* war series proofs on file at the New York Public Library are not complete; one cannot determine how much prepublication editing took place at the *Century*: the extant article editing, which seems to be in Gilder's handwriting, relates to wordiness and historical accuracy. Probably much of the encouragement for a reconciliatory tone in the articles happened verbally, in pre-writing correspondence or in the office of the *Century*. Johnson explained that many "acrimonious" controversies sprang up between generals and soldiers during the course of the series, "particularly on the

Confederate side." Yet because the controversies were apparently subdued by the *Century* staff, "the general reader never knew the violence of them." Johnson recalled the instance when Generals J. E. Johnston and P. G. T. Beauregard argued over the victory at Bull Run: "In the heat and flame of such discussions Buel [the assistant editor] and I would recall to each other, humorously, from the public announcement of the series, the statement that one of its aims would be to 'soften controversy.' As between the warring parties, this was true, since the contemplation of sacrifice, resourcefulness and bravery in foes (upon which we took every occasion to lay stress) became an element of intersectional reconciliation. This was promoted, if not insured by our rigid enforcement of our main principle, the exclusion of political questions."[18] This sort of reconciliatory rhetoric even appears in the *Century* article "The Battle of Shiloh" by Ulysses S. Grant. Although Grant cannot help himself from confrontationally calling the Union troops "National" and the Southern troops the "so-called Confederate," he later temporizes: "The troops on both sides were American, and united they need not fear any foe. It is possible that the Southern man started in with a little more dash than his Northern brother; but he was correspondingly less enduring" (Feb. 1885, 593, 609).

II

The *Century*'s open-door policy toward southerners in the Civil War series extended to southern fiction writers. Nowhere is the Gilded Age's fascination with America's diverse regions—which included the outermost regions of the far-flung world—more evident than in the *Century,* which navigated a fine line between being the arbiter of fine taste and expressing the currents of popular judgment. Of all these diverse places, the *Century* most aggressively pursued the South. About the time of the Civil War series, the *Century* welcomed impoverished southern writers into its pages, and for the new regional writers of the South, such as Joel Chandler Harris, George Washington Cable, and Thomas Nelson Page, the *Century*'s endorsement meant refuge in northern magazines from the dry southern markets.

The *Century*'s tradition of opening the door to and reconciling with the "Great South" actually began with a special series bearing that name by Edward King in the 1870s under the editorship of Holland. Robert Scholnick has noted that "the 'Great South' series was widely acknowledged to be a most successful publication, demystifying the region and establishing the grounds for the reconciliation of the former antagonists."[19] The phrase "Great South," amended by Sidney Lanier in *Scribner's* in 1880 as the "New South,"[20] implied among other things a South reformed in its attitude toward slavery. The "New South" would have to possess changed attitudes toward African Americans if the North were to open itself up to southern writers: the *Century* inherited the legacy of moral views of pre-Civil War abolitionist rural New England.[21]

The "New South" concept included a South reformed from racism. The *Century* extended this impression in the later 1880s. With Gilder and Johnson as editors, the *Century* became increasingly conscious of the profitability as well as ethical dimensions of imagining the New South as reformed. The editors tended to minimize, in editorials and in their consideration of the work of southern writers, sectional disagreement on racial questions. In June 1880, despite the optimism of the New South series, Holland wrote candidly about racial problems in the United States: "The shadow of the negro," Holland wrote in his editorial of the same title, "lies upon the North as upon the South. . . . It cannot be disputed that the great obstacle that stands to-day in the way of the negro is the white man, North and South" (*Scribner's,* June 1880, 304).[22] By January 1885, however, Gilder wrote much more temperately and consolingly about America's racial problems: "There are, indeed, many indications . . . that the old lines of color, and of geography also, are soon (though none too soon) to fade from sight in American politics" (*Century,* Jan. 1885, 462). This optimism obviously flew squarely in the face of the facts, even as they were being addressed by southern writers in the *Century.*

Century's optimism about the South and racism allowed northern readers to turn their gaze, without compunction, to a consideration of the South. There are a variety of possible reasons why northern readers wanted to do so. At a time when America was fascinated with its diverse regions, interest in the South is not surprising. Perhaps more fundamentally, however, the North felt a prurient and exculpatory fascination with the land that they had conquered and an unconscious guilt for privileging a "foreign" element—African Americans—over their own white brethren in the South. Perhaps on an even more sinister level of unconsciousness, northerners were themselves resisting the "shadow of the Negro."

Century's acceptance of the fiction of Thomas Nelson Page is one example of how it gave wide berth to its own stated commitment to anti-slavery sentiment. Although Page had published dialect poetry in *Scribner's* in 1877, his two most famous stories appeared in the *Century,* "Marse Chan" in April 1884 and "Meh Lady" in June 1886, both during the run of the Civil War series. Tooker disclosed in his memoirs that Johnson suggested to Page the North-South reconciliation theme of "Meh Lady"—"the happily ending love-story of a Virginian girl and a Northern soldier."[23] Meh Lady, her brother, Marse Phil, and the Mistis suffer the travails of a Southern plantation-owning family during the Civil

War. Phil is killed fighting bravely in battle, his sister and mother travel against odds to the battle site to give him final alms, and Meh Lady is finally reduced to teaching "niggers" in the nearby school and faces the anxiety of losing the plantation, while her declining mother languishes away in increasing dependency upon her daughter. Salvation comes from the Yankee Captain Wilton, who just happens to be half-Virginian, distantly related to Meh Lady's family, and in love with Meh Lady. Wilton had extended all the courtesies of the South during the war, protecting Meh Lady's plantation from Yankee marauders. Meh Lady, predictably, falls in love with him after she nurses him back from ailing health. However, only on Mistis's death bed does Mistis release Meh Lady to marry a Yankee. Wilton returns one final time to the plantation not to be rebuffed, and the day is saved.

Northern readers, of course, noticed that Page had made his hero not quite a Yankee, but "Northern readers, however, had shown no partizan feeling, and had accepted the compromise in their eagerness to believe that the breach between the two erstwhile hostile regions was closed."[24] And "Meh Lady" certainly obliged. The tone of appeasement in General Grant's lauding of the bravery of both sides in the Civil War is also present here: "Meh Lady she ax one de doctors ef many o' de cav'lry wuz into de fight, an' he say she'd think so ef she'd been dyah; dat de cav'lry had meck some splendid charges bofe sides."[25]

Present also but unacknowledged by delighted northern readers, was the profound irony that Page's telling the story of the fall of southern aristocracy through the voice of an ex-slave makes for a better story. Thanks to Shelley Fisher Fishkin's consciousness-raising about the presence of the African-American voice in *Huckleberry Finn,* we can see how much of the lyricism of the southern voice comes from its African-American influence, a point that nineteenth-century American authors such as Page, Harris, Cable, and Twain seemed to intuit. Although "Meh Lady" is framed in brief by a presumably white nonvernacular southern speaker sometime after the Civil War, the storyteller in this tale about fallen southern aristocracy is the ex-slave Uncle Billy, who in old age still identifies himself as one of the "boys—Meh Lady's" (78).

Billy exhibits traits of African-American dialect that Fishkin notes make African-American storytelling so interesting, including a proliferation of "slang and figurative expressions," for example, that make for a speaker's "lucidity and directness," and his lyricism, his "breath of life caught from his surroundings," as one linguist put it.[26] Here is one example of figurative language from the African-American persona in "Meh Lady": "'Well, suh, dat night de plantation wuz fyah 'live wid soldiers—our mens; dee wuz movin' all night long, *je' like ants,* an' all over todes de gre't road *de camp-fires* look *like stars*; an' nex' morning' dee wuz movin' 'fo' daylight, gwine 'long' down de road, an' 'bout dinner-time hit begin, an' from dat time tell in de night, right down yander way, *de whole uth wuz rockin'.* You'd a-thought *de wull wuz splittin open* an' sometimes ey you'd listen right good you could *heah 'em yellin', like folks in de harves'-fiel' holleri' after a ole hyah'"* (italics added) (96).

Page's narrators also mark tense nonredundantly, a trait of African-American dialect, according to Fishkin. Nonredundant narration applies tense shifts erratically as long as a stabilizing time cue denoting the real time is established.[27] African-American dialect also includes the use of serial verbs, or "the tendency to describe every detail of an action or event from start to finish with its own special verb, a trait that has been traced to a number of African languages."[28] The following example from "Meh Lady" illustrates both nonredundant and serial narration: "De Cap'n he *wuz* [past tense cue] in he room and he head me, and he *come* [shift to present tense, nonredundant] out wid he cap on, *bucklin'* on Marse Phil' s'o'de whar he done *teck* down off de wall, and he *order* me to come 'long, and *tell* Meh Lady not to come out; and down de steps he *stride* out and 'cross de yard out th'oo de gate in de road to whar de mens wuz wid meh horses at de fence. . . . Well, suh, de Cap'n' eye *flash*; he ain' *say* a wud; he jes *rip* out Marse Phil' s'o'de an' *clap* it up 'ginst dar man' side, and *cuss* him once" (serial and nonredundant verbs in italics) (104).

I do not intend here to authenticate Page's use of African-American dialect or to prove that the narrators in Page's "Marse Chan" and "Meh Lady" are African American. Obviously, unlike Huck, these narrators are established as such in Page's tales. Page's appropriation of the African-American voice to tell the Southern story is certainly offensive: not only does Billy in "Meh Lady" empty out his identity by empathizing with his enslavers—condemning the black slave Ananias as a "weevly black nigger" because he tells the Yankees where the plantation horses are and joins the Yankee forces (109), devoting his life to the romantic happiness of Meh Lady—but he also abandons himself by identifying himself as white ("like we all white folks" [133] and "We all white folks al'ays set heap o' sto' by one nurr" [105]).

Perhaps as egregious because more insidious is Page's relaying of his propaganda through the African-American voice—"the new and picturesque dialect."[29] Such use of dialect was invariably patronizing in an age that equated grammaticality with social and moral stature.[30] Yet, paradoxically, a great part of the charming simplicity that northerners enjoyed in "Meh Lady" and "Marse Chan" is created by the "indescribably sugges-

tive" ("Meh Lady," 7) lyrical point of view of the world as focalized through Billy in "Meh Lady" and Sam in "Marse Chan." It might seem paradoxical, then, to say that African-Americans are absent in these stories, but the African-American voice is more than absent. "Marse Chan" is a story told by former slave Sam about his young Master Channing, to whom Sam is still devoted. Although Sam is the focalizer of the story, the value-centered character in the story is the young white plantation master. Although in Sam's dialect, which is exploited for its storytelling properties, the tale is in effect read through to hear the story of Master Channing. In essence, African-Americans are absent in this fiction, which is relayed right through them as if they were invisible.

"Marse Chan" stereotypes the African-American slave as naive, simple, kind, and devoted to his master, with whom he is engaged in a benevolent patriarchal relationship. As such, the story represents the Old South rationale against which the North fought so vocally. "Meh Lady" and "Marse Chan" are unreconstructed southern stories that pretend that slaves are back in their place and that the Civil War has not even been fought: "Marse Chan's" outer frame narrator literally dreams himself back into the story of the Old South, where "time was of no consequence to them,"[31] and Billy in "Meh Lady" says his story "cyars me back sometimes, I mos' furgit de ain' nuver been no war nor nuttin'" (79). One would assume that post-Civil War northern readers would strongly resist such a message.

Yet famous post-Civil War readers loved the story. The abolitionist Henry Ward Beecher was moved to tears when "Marse Chan" was read to him. Thomas Wentworth Higginson also cried over the story, perhaps because "'Marse Chan' was a story of a vanished way of life so remote in time and space that [it] had a romantic charm. Or perhaps [this story] recalled to readers in huge Northern cities memories of a simpler life they had known or heard their parents or grandparents speak of."[32] How we shudder today to read the fond description by one "antislavery" *Century* editor of a story like "Marse Chan": such stories present "the hospitable, patriarchal life; the new and picturesque dialect; the half-humourous clashes between master and man; the heroic devotion shown to 'ol' Miss' and the children by faithful old servitors even at the moment of the dissolution of the bond that held them together—all these things the Northerner read with delight, and with a half-conscious softening of his former hostility. And the Southerner, awakened to hope, and thrilled by the successes of his latest conquest, felt a new glow of fraternity. Justification seemed no longer necessary."[33]

The northern reader's oversimplification of the racist nuances in "Marse Chan" can be juxtaposed with the way it was understood by some of Page's unreconstructed contemporary southern readers, who imputed to "Marse Chan" the value of a historical document that justified, as one southern woman put it, "the slave plantation and made the lost cause seem in many ways the right one."[34] That African Americans would have rejected the implications in this story about the benevolent Marse is suggested by the only known essay by an African-American that appeared in the 1880s *Century*: "My Master," says Frederick Douglass scornfully, in "My Escape from Slavery," with quotation marks around the word "master" (Nov. 1881, 128).

Both in yearning for an agrarian past that was simpler and in relegating southern patriarchal treatment of African Americans to "distance," northern readers and *Century* critics unconsciously expressed a desire to transcend the fragmented self. Beecher's reconciliatory yearning for the Old South days represents an Anglo-American myth of sameness and a desire for a simplifying plenitude that would deny that the nation was fractured by internal division. In the positing of unity, something is, of necessity, repressed. What was repressed in this "cathartic recapitulation of a plenitude of being?"[35] The shadow of the Negro.

Perhaps the phrase the "shadow of the Negro," used by Holland in his 1880 *Century* editorial, came originally from George Washington Cable's *The Grandissimes,* which was accepted by the *Century* in 1879 and was serialized beginning that November. Cable was discovered by King during his Great South series. Given the startlingly radical nature of the novel's pronouncements about racism, one wonders whether the novel would have been accepted for serialization during the run of the Civil War series. Lawrence Berkove notes that Cable exposed in *The Grandissimes* "the travesty of equality that blighted the lives" of free men of color, both before and after the Civil War. Cable's novel, Berkove suggests, influenced antiracist works serialized in the *Century* by Mark Twain and Joel Chandler Harris.[36]

The Grandissimes is a story about honor, love, and caste prejudice in old New Orleans to which I cannot do justice here. There are, indeed, the requisite white southern belles and southern heroes. But the novel also features Bras-Coupe, an African slave of royal lineage in love with the beautiful mulatto Palmyra, who is in turn in love with the white Honore Grandissime and who plots to use Bras-Coupe's love to incite insurrection. Through Bras-Coupe and his tragedy readers see "a type of all Slavery, turning into flesh and blood the truth that all Slavery is maiming."[37]

Yet it is the black Honore—half-brother to the white—who is referred to as the "shadow" in a lengthy and monumental passage between the white Honore and the apothecary-narrator Frowenfeld. It is a reference made so prominently in *The Grandissimes* that it would have

been difficult for Holland to miss it. The white Honore sees his half-brother and remarks to Frowenfeld that "civilization [is] sitting in a horrible darkness, my-de'seh!" Frowenfeld immediately responds, "The shadow of the Ethiopian," and the white Honore responds that he "had said the very word": "Ah! my-de'-seh, when I try sometimes to stand outside and look at it, I am *ama-aze* at the length, the blackness of that shadow! . . . It is the *Nemesis* w'ich, instead of coming afteh, glides along by the side of this morhal, political, commercial, social mistake! . . . It brheeds a thousan' cusses that nevva leave home but jus' flutter-h up an' rhoost, my-de'seh, on ow *heads*; an' we nevva know it!" (155-56). The phrase is subsequently internalized into the narrative frame to describe "the other Honore . . . like [the white Honore's] shadow" (185).

This connection between African Americans and the image of the shadow powerfully suggests the way in which blacks in Anglo-American culture and literature sometimes become not just the "type" of slavery but emblematic of Anglo-Americans' own archetypal guilt. One sees a kind of biblical sense of this, for example, in the writings of William Faulkner. In addition to Holland's and Cable's use of "shadow" during the nineteenth century, William Dean Howells also labeled slavery the "dark shadow of our shameful past" in an 1886 *Harper's Monthly.*[38] He reiterated the phrase possibly because of his intimate acquaintance with the *Century*'s use of it when Howells worked with the magazine in the early '80s. Perhaps nothing is intrinsically wrong with this archetype. Indeed, conceiving of African Americans as shadows constitutes an acknowledgment of historical guilt for the ill treatment of slaves. Nevertheless, this phrase and the thinking it implies suggests the objectification of black people as something less than complex human beings; as shadows, their quintessence is reduced to an allegorical function for someone else.

One possible repercussion of this way of thinking is that African Americans become enslaved to whites' impressions of themselves, in particular to the unpleasant, guilt-ridden parts that they might likely seek to repress. Cable's speaker fixates on the blackness of that shadow as if it were some sort of horror with a life external to that of the speaker. Hence, the evil within becomes expelled and becomes the shadow without. In an odd twist of fate, the shadow, African Americans, becomes responsible for the guilt, which is expunged by a fantasy of white homogeneity.

If such conceptualization of the shadow with its accompanying repression and denial brings to mind for the reader the psychoanalysis of Carl Jung, this is not surprising. Jung himself remarked in 1912, "I have frequently observed in the analysis of Americans that the inferior side of the personality, the 'shadow,' is represented by a Negro or an Indian, whereas in the dream of a European it would be represented by a somewhat shady individual of his own kind."[39] The African-American writer Frances Watkins Harper invoked this psychoanalytical iconography of shadow in *Iola Leroy or Shadows Uplifted* (1892). Harper uses "shadow" with overwhelming rapidity in the novel in a confusing—confuting—number of ways. Harper's ingenuity deserves an essay of its own. Suffice it to say here that Harper firmly reattaches shadow to the person who "owns" it, regardless of ethnicity, and that the shadow is something clearly outside African-American ethnicity in a historical, global sense.

III

Cable's *Grandissimes* aside, more often than not the *Century* editorial strategy during the run of the Civil War series was to relegate racial intolerance to the antebellum South and to deny that in the New South racial injustices still existed. At no time was this affirmation of a white homogenous way of thinking more fervent than in 1885, as is evident in a sudden surge of *Century* editorials and open letters about African Americans during this time. These essays, in line with the reconciliation theme, reiterated the mutual gallantry of the North and South in Civil War battle; they suggested that this recognition could now be made because there was a New South of racial tolerance.

The *Century* printed a letter from a "Southern Democrat" in January 1885 that even praised the South for its past of slavery: "There is not a thinking man at the North who will not admit that American slavery seems to have been a provision of Providence for the advancement of a large part of the negro race. This is a phase of the slavery question worthy the attention of reflecting minds. The negroes came to this country barbarians. They were savages; but they were not savages when freedom found them out" (471). Gilder in "Let Us Have Peace" wrote in the succeeding month that there was an "improved condition and spirit [in] the South, and [a] new era of common interests and mutual sympathy and respect" (Feb. 1885, 638). Later in the year Gilder again wrote appeasingly about the "need for patience and tolerance in judging the movements of Southern opinion upon this question [of racism]. It is clear that the cause of the negro may safely be left to such champions as those who have now risen up on Southern soil to defend his rights" (Oct. 1885, 967).

The 1885 date of these editorials was probably strategic. They mediated between Cable's agitationist writings, which Gilder perhaps printed in deference to his longtime contributor, and the vehement Southern response to Cable's work. The tinder for the political fire was the 1883 U.S. Supreme Court decision that rendered unconstitutional the Civil Rights Act of 1875,

which had given African-American citizens unconditional access to public accommodations. Suddenly, the North in its legal collusion seemed no more enlightened than the South. As W. E. B. Du Bois observed about the late 1880s, "The rich and dominating North . . . was not only weary of the race problem, but was investing largely in Southern enterprises, and welcomed any method of peaceful cooperation."[40]

It took a Southerner, Cable, in his two *Century* essays, "The Freedman's Case in Equity" (Apr. 1885, 409-18) and "The Silent South" (Aug. 1885, 674-91), to enjoin both North and South to take notice that the "separate but equal" policy imposed in the South was just a more subtle and insidious version of African-American enslavement based on the same southern belief that the black race was inherently inferior. Thinkers in the South were furious at Cable. As Jay Hubbell notes, "Even Southern liberals like Henry W. Grady found altogether unacceptable the views of the Negro question which Cable was freely expressing—[Southern] conservatives regarded him as a traitor to the South."[41] The *Century*, which invited *Atlanta Constitution* editor Grady to write a rebuttal on behalf of southern sentiment, continued nevertheless to support Cable. Yet the support ended after these three articles. Gilder rejected Cable's suggestion that Charles Chesnutt's voice be added to the discussion: "Mr. Chesnutt's paper—'The Negro's Answer to the Negro Question,' is a timely political paper. So timely and *so* political—in fact so partisan—that we cannot handle it. It should appear at once somewhere." Herbert Smith observes of this response, "Editors do not *enjoy* printing unprofitable and controversial articles in the pages of their magazines, and Gilder was no exception."[42]

The *Century* persisted with its claim that race prejudice was a bygone issue for both the North and the South. In its desire to deflect focus from divisive controversy, the *Century* consistently refused to acknowledge racism. And the northern readers, who Cable insisted shared in the more insidious racism of post-Reconstruction America, "even tinctured by that race feeling whose grosser excesses it would so gladly see suppressed" (*Century*, Jan. 1884, 409), turned away from the "shadow of the Negro" as much as their Southern counterparts. Ironically, it was two Southerners, Harris in his fictional "Free Joe and the Rest of the World" (*Century*, Nov. 1884, 117-23) and Cable in his essays, who exposed the old South slave-master ideology for the exploitative system that it was and who uncovered still lurking in the collective unconscious of the entire nation the implicit racist assumptions.

Nevertheless, even Cable and Harris were not immune from the effects of northern apologistic rhetoric. Regardless of how one presently judges the level of racism, intentional or otherwise, in Harris's "Uncle Remus" tales, a review in the *Century* understood the tales from a racist, apologistic perspective: the stories presented "a type familiar to us all—the old plantation negro. . . . The gentle old darky—shrewd, yet simple-minded, devoted to the people who once owned him as a slave. . . . Even the occasional mild little apologies for the patriarchal system which the author scatters through his work will offend no one. They lend it a pleasant old-time, 'befo'-the-wah' flavor; so to speak, they give the picture 'distance'" (Apr. 1881, 961).

It is also true that *The Grandissimes* was an early '80s serial and that Cable's *Dr. Sevier* finished serialization in the *Century* only one month before the beginning of the Civil War series. Is it coincidental that a central theme of *Dr. Sevier* is North-South reconciliation? In *Dr. Sevier,* southerner John Richling is disinherited before the war because of "simple sectional prejudice": he marries a northerner.[43] The last third of the novel takes up the reunion of John and his wife, Mary, behind enemy lines and concentrates also on the bravery of the Southern troops. The one nod to the Northern faction that its "cause [was] just" (377) provoked angry Southern response, which suggests how volatile sectional difference still was during this time of supposed appeasement.[44] Just as noteworthy is the fact that this novel by the creator of Bras-Coupe makes African Americans barely a minor footnote in this work, Cable's novel of the Civil War.

IV

The question of the absence of African Americans can be put, finally, to the great works by Twain, Howells, and James that can now be read within the context of the North-South reconciliation theme in the mid-1880s *Century*. Where did these works stand on the "shadow of the Negro?" The *Huckleberry Finn* excerpts chosen by Gilder[45] included the Sheperdson-Grangerford feud, the episodes with the duke and the king, and Huck and Jim's conversation about the wisdom of King Solomon. Although there is certainly an intertextual challenge in Twain's debunking chapter on the Grangerfords (1885) to Page's glorification of southern chivalry in his '84 "Marse Chan," Gilder's selection of this excerpt takes no chances with racial questions. When the slave Jim is involved in the excerpts that Gilder apparently selected, his presence serves as minstrel farce or plot enabler. And, significantly, the section in the duke-king episode that in Fishkin's reading "signifies" Jim's humanity beyond the minstrel tropes—Jim's discussion of his deaf daughter and his own human pain—is edited out for the *Century*.[46] Absent is the one clear instance in these scenes where Jim's humanity is shown and Huck forced to acknowledge it.

In Howell's *The Rise of Silas Lapham,* although one could argue that the presence of the Civil War theme in the novel is so minimal that such questions as have

been considered in this essay need not be addressed, one might recall that the subplot of the novel is fueled by the hero's debt to a Civil War soldier who sacrificed his own life for the hero. This kind of Civil War heroism and nobility was central to the ideology of the Civil War series, so it is a significant omission that there is no mention of the moral issue that compelled the Civil War.

Finally, in James's *The Bostonians,* southerner Basil Ransom speaks in tribute to the fallen Union heroes who are honored in Harvard's Memorial Hall. Though the North-South reconciliation theme is predictably problematized by James, and thus in one sense *The Bostonians* implicitly undermines the *Century* ideology, there remains a notable absence of African Americans in this novel and a predictable valorization, vis-à-vis the reconciliation theme, of the Anglo-Americans who fought on both sides of the Civil War. One could conclude that these works, as serialized in the *Century,* are as Anglocentric as were the northern readers fixated on Anglo-American presence and ignoring the "shadow of the Negro."

Nevertheless, as Toni Morrison has so eloquently informed us,[47] even through omission the African-American presence is manifested in American literature, as it was in the 1880s *Century*. When Henry James wrote of his white southern hero that "his discourse was pervaded by something sultry and vast, something almost African in its rich, basking tone, something that suggested the teeming expanse of the cotton field,"[48] James goes one step further than the southern writers of his time by actually appropriating African-American dialectical identity to enhance the character of his Anglo-American hero. No more strongly, one could argue, could the need of an Anglo-American writer for identity cancel out and simultaneously exploit the African-American presence.

Notes

1. L. Frank Tooker, *Joys and Tribulations of an Editor* (New York: Century, 1924), 227.

2. See Herbert F. Smith and Michael Peinovich, "*The Bostonians*: Creation and Revision," *Bulletin of the New York Public Library* 73 (1969): 300.

3. For a complete discussion of the popular subgenre of Civil War novels, see Robert A. Lively, *Fiction Fights the Civil War* (Chapel Hill: Univ. of North Carolina Press, 1957).

4. Articles on African-American ethnicity included Henry King, "A Year of the Exodus in Kansas," *Scribner's* 20 (1880): 211-18; "In the M. E. African," *Scribner's* 20 (1880): 423-29; Eugene V. Smalley, "In and Out of the New Orleans Exposition," *Century* 30 (1885): 185-99; George Wash-

ington Cable, "The Dance in Place Congo," *Century* 31 (1886): 517-53.

5. Tooker, *Joys and Tribulations,* 321.

6. Robert Underwood Johnson, *Remembered Yesterdays* (Boston: Little, Brown, 1923), 190.

7. Tooker, *Joys and Tribulations,* 190, 46.

8. Jonathan Freedman, *Professions of Taste: Henry James, British Aestheticism, and Commodity Culture* (Stanford, Calif.: Stanford Univ. Press, 1990), 108-9.

9. William Webster Ellsworth, *A Golden Age of Authors* (Boston: Houghton Mifflin, 1919), 233.

10. Johnson, *Remembered Yesterdays,* 194.

11. Rosamund Gilder, *Letters of Richard Watson Gilder* (Boston: Houghton Mifflin, 1916), 130-31.

12. Van Renssalaer to Gilder, 8 June 18??, Richard Watson Gilder Letter-Press Book 1 (16 Nov. 1880-13 Jan. 1886), Gilder Collection, New York Public Library.

13. Quoted in Carol Klimick Cyganowski, *Magazine Editors and Professional Authors in Nineteenth-Century America* (New York: Garland, 1988), 190.

14. Tooker, *Joys and Tribulations,* 112.

15. For an account of the origins of *Scribner's/Century,* see, for example, Cyganowski, *Magazine Editors,* 179-227; or "The Century Magazine 1870-1924," *Pan-American Magazine* 37 (1924): 341-45.

16. Herbert F. Smith, *Richard Watson Gilder* (New York: Twayne, 1970), 154.

17. Johnson to Gilder, 7 July 1884, Gilder Papers, New York Public Library.

18. Johnson, *Remembered Yesterdays,* p. 194.

19. Robert Scholnick, "*Scribner's Monthly* and the 'Pictorial Representation of Life and Truth' in Post-Civil War America," *American Periodicals* 1 (1991): 61.

20. "The New South," *Scribner's* 20 (1880): 840-51.

21. Scholnick, "*Scribner's Monthly,*" 50.

22. One should note, however, that although Holland could speak in such an enlightened manner about the condition of African Americans, *Scribner's* published more than a dozen poems in black dialect by Irwin Russell between 1875 and 1880 that "assumed an unbridgeable gulf between blacks and whites," as Elsa Nettels observes in "The Problem of Negro Dialect in Literature," in *Language, Race, and Social Class in Howells's America* (Lexington: Univ. Press of Kentucky, 1988), 73.

23. Tooker, *Joys and Tribulations,* 203.

24. Ibid.

25. Thomas Nelson Page, "Meh Lady," in *In Ole Virginia or Marse Chan and Other Stories* (New York: Scribner's, 1968), 98. Further references to this work are to this edition and will be cited in the text.

26. Shelley Fisher Fishkin, *Was Huck Black? Mark Twain and African-American Voices* (New York: Oxford Univ. Press, 1993), 43, 44.

27. Ibid., 44-45.

28. Ibid., 47.

29. Tooker, *Joys and Tribulations,* 42.

30. See Nettels, *Language, Race, and Social Class,* 7-40.

31. Thomas Nelson Page, "Marse Chan," in *In Ole Virginia or Marse Chan and Other Stories* (New York: Scribner's, 1968), 1.

32. Jay Hubbell, *The South in American Literature, 1607-1900* (Durham, N.C.: Duke Univ. Press, 1954), 801-2.

33. Tooker, *Joys and Tribulations,* 42.

34. Hubbell, *South in American Literature,* 802.

35. Psychoanalytic phrasing quoted from Donna Przybylowicz, *Desire and Repression: The Dialectic of Self and Other in the Late Works of Henry James* (University: Univ. of Alabama Press, 1986), 23.

36. Lawrence Berkove, "The Free Man of Color in *The Grandissimes* and Works by Harris and Mark Twain," *Southern Quarterly* 18: (1980): 60-61.

37. George Washington Cable, *The Grandissimes, A Story of Creole Life* (New York: Sagamore, 1957), 171. Further references to this work are to this edition and will be cited in the text.

38. "Dostoevski Discovered," in *W. D. Howells as Critic,* ed. Edwin R. Cady (Boston: Routledge and Kegan Paul, 1973), 95.

39. Carl Jung, "The Origin of the Hero," in *Symbols of Transformation,* trans. R. F. C. Hull (Princeton: Princeton Univ. Press, 1976), 183.

40. W. E. B. DuBois, "Of Mr. Booker T. Washington and Others," in *The Souls of Black Folk* (New York: Vintage, 1990), 42.

41. Hubbell, *South in American Literature,* 815.

42. Smith, *Richard Watson Gilder,* 71.

43. George Washington Cable, *Dr. Sevier* (New York: Garrett, 1970), 449. Further references to this work are to this edition and are cited in the text.

44. See, for example, "Old Questions and New," *Century* 29 (1885): 471-72.

45. See Cyganowski, *Magazine Editors,* which suggests that Gilder chose the selections.

46. See "Royalty on the Mississippi," *Century* (Feb. 1885): 544-67. The episode begins several pages into chapter 19 with the arrival of the duke and king. On p. 553, one notes that the entire end of chapter 23 is deleted. The *Century* text stops after what would be the second paragraph of p. 202 in the *Adventures of Huckleberry Finn,* ed. Walter Blair and Victor Fischer (Berkeley: Univ. of California Press, 1986), and picks up with chapter 24, p. 203.

47. Toni Morrison, *Playing in the Dark: Whiteness and the Literary Imagination* (Cambridge: Harvard Univ. Press, 1992).

48. Henry James, *The Bostonians* (New York: Random House, 1956), 5.

George Hutchinson (essay date winter-spring 2003)

SOURCE: Hutchinson, George. "Race and the Family Romance: Whitman's Civil War." *Walt Whitman Quarterly Review* 20, nos. 3-4 (winter-spring 2003): 134-50.

[*In the following essay, Hutchinson argues that Whitman's exclusion of African Americans from his Civil War discourse reveals a widespread desire on the part of white Americans to focus on issues such as states' rights and national unity, rather than on issues such as slavery and the rights of African Americans.*]

Whitman often spoke of the importance of the Civil War to *Leaves of Grass.* He told his disciple Horace Traubel in his later years that it was "the very centre, circumference, *umbillicus,* of [his] whole career."[1] In the poem "To Thee Old Cause," he wrote, "My book and the war are one"; and elsewhere he wrote that his poems turned on the war as a wheel on its axle.[2] What Whitman liked to call the "Four Years War" indeed represented for the poet a pivotal event in universal history, a sacred conflict between democracy and its internal as well as external antagonists. It proved his poetry's validity and anchored his personal history, with all its private anguish, to the public life of the nation.

I would like to examine the implications of Whitman's experience of the Civil War as a familial tragedy, remembering Whitman as a member of a white, New York working-class family that was experiencing continuous trauma throughout the war years, even as Whitman immersed himself in the trauma of the Union hospitals in Washington and developed surrogate family relationships there. Familial metaphors pervade his written responses to the War—indeed, some of his most moving (and neglected) writing of the period can be found in letters to his own family, or to the families of sick and dying soldiers. I will try to weave together Whitman's response to the Civil War as one of the "common people" directly affected by it, his wartime correspondence, and his striking transformation of the poetry of war into a poetry of primary relationships, attachment and loss. I will then suggest that one chief reason Whitman leaves the relation of African Americans to the Civil War almost entirely unspoken, unrepresentable, is that they do not belong to the national "family" Whitman imagined and addressed. Relegated to the periphery of Whitman's imagination, they become a repressed element, uncanny, a source of dread. A peculiar correspondence arises between his inability to question the "meaning" he ascribed to the Civil War as the birth of American democracy and his inability to face squarely the issue of African Americans' relationship to it, to his own identity. In his and the nation's process of recovery from the trauma of war, much was left unspoken, undiagnosed, and unhealed in the heart of the democratic experiment.

It is difficult to understand Whitman's response to the war without understanding both his despair for the country before hostilities broke out and the depth of his attachment to the idea of American nationhood. Whitman believed the causes of the war lay not in Southern secessionism alone but rather in lingering "feudal" elements and corruption that infected both the South and the North. Hence, like Lincoln, Whitman viewed it as a war within one identity. Moreover, this identity was, for Whitman, shaped to a great degree by a kind of national family romance, in relation to the Founding Fathers, that had extraordinary resonance in his poetic imagination.[3] Two of his brothers, after all, were named George Washington and Thomas Jefferson Whitman. As a youth Walt was always eager to hear about Revolutionary War days, and in his earliest journalism he participated in the intense idealization of figures like Washington and Jefferson, holding them up as paternal models to American youth.

An exaggerated sentimentality pervades Whitman's references to Washington, in which the general appears as a sensitive parent spreading his mantle of love over the American people and particularly the young "sons" given over by families to his care in the Revolutionary War. In "The Sleepers" of 1855, for example, Washington "cannot repress the weeping drops" at the sight of his soldiers dying in battle at Brooklyn (Whitman's home town): "He sees the slaughter of the southern braves confided to him by their parents."[4] The poet sets the scene from the nation's family history against a backdrop of his native landscape; drawing attention to the sacrifice of "southern braves," he implicitly strives to stave off the growing schism in the "American" family of his own day. He redirects the emotional current inherent in the suffering of sons toward affirmation of "family" bonds—a feature we will find central to his later writing on the Civil War. Whitman repeatedly portrays the Revolutionary hero as a father or elder companion—a role he would later carve out for himself in relation to the young soldiers of the Civil War. Just so, he came to see the Civil War as superseding the Revolution in the birth of the democratic nation.[5]

The greater the threat to the Union, the more Whitman regressively drew on materials from the nation's "family romance." In his visionary poems of the 1850s, the crisis of the Union continually drives the poetic persona to a despair filled with oedipal and familial resonances, a despair that gives way to ecstatic prophecy and imaginary resolutions to the threat of betrayal. The Civil War he always dreaded, a fact in history, opened up an abyss beneath Whitman's deepest faith; but the Union victory would seem to close that abyss once and for all, with the painful emergence of the integral identity of the nation. After "When Lilacs Last in the Dooryard Bloom'd," in which the "dark mother" enfolds Lincoln and all the dead of the Civil War in her arms, we find no more ecstatic descents to the underworld, no more crises of faith in Whitman's poetry. With the Inferno behind him, the poet retreats from further immersion in history's endless betrayals and denials.[6]

It is important to recognize, as Ed Folsom and Martin Klammer have, how closely identified the oppression (and defiance) of black slaves was to Whitman's fears about the "abyss" in the years before the war, when *Leaves of Grass* emerged.[7] In some of the earliest fragments known to have been written in Whitman's new free verse manner, the evocative figure of "Black Lucifer" takes shape—identified with a whale in the ocean whose "tap is death"—and seems to signify a fundamental challenge to American society. The passage, as it finally appears in 1855, provides a kind of premonition of the Civil War:[8]

> I have been wronged. . . . I am oppressed. . . . I
>   hate him that oppresses me,
> I will either destroy him, or he shall release me.
> Damn him! How he does defile me,
> How he informs against my brother and sister and
>   takes pay for their blood,
> How he laughs when I look down the bend after the
>   steamboat that carries away my
>   woman.
> Now the vast bulk that is the whale's bulk. . . . it
>   seems mine,
> Warily, sportsman! Though I lie so sleepy and slug-
>   gish, my tap is death.[9]

I agree with those who find in Whitman's early poems for *Leaves of Grass* not only intense anxiety about the future of democracy but, paralleling that, an unusual level of empathy for black slaves. Such passages help explain Whitman's appeal to later African American authors.[10] If anything, it is the very uniqueness of his use of African Americans in the pre-war poetry that makes one wonder what happened between that period and Reconstruction. "Did Whitman's Black Lucifer go on, after emancipation, to become a citizen, to vote?" Ed Folsom asks. "The question seems faintly ridiculous, because Lucifer fails to evolve in Whitman's work; the poet creates no black characters, not a hint of a representation that offers a place or role for the freed slaves in reconstructed America."[11] Whitman's need for reintegration following the war may have something to do with this. If dominant notes of his 1855 and 1856 editions are rebellion and fear for the nation's future, in the wake of the "war of attempted secession" he had his heart set on other things.[12]

To Whitman, the war not only preserved the Union; it proved as well that American democracy was breeding what he termed a "race" of heroes in the common people—a new type of human being. This proof Whitman found through personal experience in the hospitals, in the way the boys and men (in Whitman's view at least) faced suffering and death without complaint or fear, in the way they expressed selfless affection for each other and, indeed, for Walt Whitman—despite the incompetence, "feudalism," and cruelty of many commissioned officers and politicians, the state-designated officials whom Whitman mostly despised.

WHITMAN'S FAMILY AND THE WAR

Until the very end of 1862, Whitman had no direct experience of the war, for all his interest in it; and he never took up arms. (He was forty-two when it broke out.) Whitman remained in New York during the first year and more, occasionally visiting a hospital for the sick and wounded, and following the conflict in the newspapers. His brother George, on the other hand, enlisted early and would fight in many of the war's major battles yet emerge practically unscathed.

On December 16, 1862, the Whitmans learned that George had been wounded at Fredericksburg, Maryland, and Walt set off to find him. Thus it was a search for a family member that sent Whitman into the space of the hospitals that would be the center of his experience of the war—and in his mind the spiritual center of the nation itself, "America brought to hospital in her fair youth."[13] After canvassing the hospitals in Washington, Walt found George still with his company across the Rappahannock from Fredericksburg, his cheek pierced by shrapnel but on the mend. Walt stayed with his brother slightly over a week, witnessed the dead on the battlefield, visited the wounded in hospitals, and toured the camps. Throughout the war, Whitman's mother depended on Walt to keep up with the movements of George's regiment as it fought through many harrowing battles, keeping the family in a constant state of anxiety.

In fact, throughout the war Whitman's family was in continual crisis, and he had to take on some of the functions of both a father and an intermediary (Walter Whitman senior having died about the time the first edition of *Leaves of Grass* went to press in 1855). After a brief stint in the army, his brother Andrew died of a painful throat disease in late 1863, leaving a young son and a wife five months pregnant, who soon after giving birth became one of Brooklyn's many wartime prostitutes.[14] Another brother, Ed, was always unable to care for himself, apparently afflicted with Down's Syndrome. Walt's one older brother, Jesse, went mad from syphilis in the course of the war, to the point of physically assaulting family members, until Walt finally came to New York and committed him to an insane asylum in December 1864. By that date, the family knew brother George was missing in action—actually a prisoner of war, as they later found out, at which point Walt would begin pulling strings to secure his release through prisoner exchange. Meanwhile, his sister Hannah's health broke down to the point that for five months she could not stand up. The one dependable source of support other than Walt's aging mother and absent Walt himself was his brother Jeff, who was in danger of being drafted, an event that would spell, as Whitman wrote his mother, "the downfall almost of our entire family."[15] He began saving money to buy a substitute if necessary. This was a characteristic mediating role for Whitman, a role that took on larger significance in the context of his nursing and literary work. For the most part, Whitman observed the war and participated in it from the point-of-view of nurses behind the lines, between the battlefield and the homeplace. For Whitman would mediate between the battlefront and the civilian sphere, the living and the dead, the immediate bodily reality and its poetic inscription for all later generations. Such mediation took a variety of forms—physical and social activity, correspondence, journalism, and poetry.

WALT IN WASHINGTON

All the time that Whitman's own family was falling apart, with Walt constantly monitoring the situation through correspondence, he was in a sense creating surrogate relationships in Washington that helped sustain him. Here he settled into a rooming-house where an acquaintance, William Douglas O'Connor, was staying with his wife Nellie, and took meals with them. His relationships with these two became among the most important of his career as they formed the nucleus of his first circle of fervent supporters and, in the end, helped make him famous.

After finding a part-time job as a copyist in the army paymaster's office, Whitman was able to support himself and visit the soldiers in the hospitals. Soon he began to find his real calling in the war—providing aid, comfort, and encouragement to the sick, wounded, and dying. At the same time he wrote journalistic pieces for the New York papers describing the conditions of the hospitals and, more movingly, the emotional condition of the hospitalized. As M. Wynn Thomas has pointed out, from his first sight of the camp where he had found his brother George, Whitman "realized, with a shock that galvanized his whole being and irrevocably altered his imagination, that the soldiers and civilians lived worlds apart from each other, separated by a gulf of fearful unknowing."[16] Much of his work for the rest of the war was to connect these worlds.

Whitman's routine was to rest after his office-work, bathe, dress in fresh clothes, eat a good meal, and put in four to five hours touring the hospitals. He would often pack a knapsack with fruit, tobacco, paper, envelopes, and the like for individual distribution to the soldiers—materials chiefly paid for with money raised from relatives and friends. He entered the hospitals well-rested, sweet-scented, and cheerful in appearance. He was not so much a "wound-dresser," as his poem of that title suggests, as he was a healer of the spirit, an affectionate comrade or "uncle," whose curative abilities were nonetheless deeply respected at a time when doctors' interventions often did more harm than good. Whitman never read his poetry to the men—in fact, he apparently never told them he was a poet—but he would recite Shakespeare or passages from the Bible. He would also hold the men's hands, kiss them, write letters for them. As William Douglas O'Connor put it: "His theory is that these men, far from home, lonely, sick at heart, need more than any thing some practical token that they are not forsaken, that someone feels a fatherly or brotherly interest in them."[17] His notebooks listing soldiers' names and their condition frequently also list the names and addresses of relatives whom Whitman intended to write. He would feed some of the "boys" their dinners. They would put their hands on his knee as they rested for hours at a time; he would kiss them as they went to sleep, and hold their hands as they died. He would write his mother about particular soldiers he was nursing and keep her up-to-date on their condition from week to week; and he would talk of his mother to the men, who would ask him to send her their love.

Many of the men looked upon Whitman explicitly as a father or uncle. Thus Elijah Fox, whom Whitman addressed as "son" and "comrade" addressed Whitman "Dear Father," and wrote, "Walt, you will be a second Father to me won't you, for my love for you is hardly less than my love for my natural parent."[18] When Whitman fell ill in July of 1864, broken down from the strain of his hospital work, Fox wrote to say he wished he could come to nurse him, for "I am sure no Father could have cared for their own child, better than you did me."[19]

Some of Whitman's most admirable prose can be found in letters informing parents of the exact circumstances and manner of the death of a son. In one extraordinary letter to the mother and father of Erastus Haskell, Whitman recounts the young man's suffering, describing his manners and speech and gestures through the period of sickness and death. The letter then shifts from narrative to a direct address to the dead: "Poor dear son, though you were not my son, I felt to love you as a son, what short time I saw you sick & dying here—it is well as it is, perhaps better—for who knows whether he is not better off, that patient & sweet young soul, to go, than we are to stay? So farewell, dear boy—it was my opportunity to be with you in your last rapid days of death—no chance as I have said to do any thing particular, for nothing [could be done—only you did not lay] here & die among strangers without having one at hand who loved you dearly, & to whom you gave your dying kiss."[20] Here Whitman takes up a position between the living and the dead, in communion with both, between the strangers and the parents. Mr. Haskell's gratitude for this letter drove him to look up Whitman's family in Brooklyn and visit them. On more than this occasion Whitman undertook the role that Wynn Thomas has aptly called "surrogate mourner of the dead," holding a vigil over the lifeless body and keeping remembrance when family members could not.[21]

Such experiences, melded with stories he heard of actual events after battles, inform such poems as "Vigil Strange I Kept on the Field One Night":

> Vigil strange I kept on the field one night;
> When you my son and my comrade dropt at my side
>   that day,
> One look I but gave which your dear eyes return'd
>   with a look I shall never forget,
> One touch of your hand to mine O boy, reach'd up as
>   you lay on the ground,
> Then onward I sped in the battle, the even-contested
>   battle,
> Till late in the night reliev'd to the place at last again
>   I made my way,
> Found you in death so cold dear comrade, found your
>   body son of responding kisses,
>   (never again on earth responding,)
>   . . . . .
> Vigil of silence, love and death, vigil for you my son
>   and my soldier,
>   . . . . .
> Vigil final for you brave boy, (I could not save you,
>   swift was your death,
> I faithfully loved you and cared for you living, I think
>   we shall surely meet again,). . . .[22]

Whitman gave his greatest attention to the young men without family or companions near, the most forlorn,

and the emotional rewards for him were extraordinary. To William S. Davis he wrote, "I find often young men, some hardly more than children in age yet—so good, so sweet, so brave, so decorous, I could not feel them nearer to me if my own sons or young brothers—Some cases even I could not tell any one, how near to me, from their yearning ways & their sufferings—it is comfort & delight to me to minister to them, to sit by them—some so wind themselves around one's heart, & will be kissed at parting at night just like children—though veterans of two years of battles & camp life."[23] Whitman's family-like relationships with the soldiers created hopes in him for long-term bonds. Such relationships take familial intimacy beyond the traditional nuclear family to long-term relationships between men who live together bound by love. To Thomas Sawyer he wrote, "I don't know how you feel about it, but it is the wish of my heart to have your friendship, and also that if you should come safe out of this war, we should come together again in some place where we could make our living, and be true comrades and never be separated while life lasts."[24] And to Elijah Douglas Fox: "Dearest son, it would be more pleasure if we could be together just in quiet, in some plain way of living, with some good employment & reasonable income, where I could have you often with me, than all the dissipations & amusements of this great city—O I hope things may work so that we can yet have each other's society—for I cannot bear the thought of being separated from you."[25]

Mental and emotional collapses brought on by the hospital work forced Whitman on two occasions to go home to Brooklyn to recuperate. From there he sent stories of civilian and domestic life, stitching together the home and the hospitals, mediating between them—"My loving comrades, I am scribbling all this in my room in my mother's house."[26] He shared stories of the soldiers with his mother, and when at home would write to the soldiers in the hospitals tender letters sending his mother's love as well as his own. He promised in October 1863, "Mother, when I come home I will show you some of the letters I get from mothers, sisters, fathers & c., They will make you cry."[27] Most wrenching of all were the cases of soldiers dying entirely unknown, as in the case of a young man who died on a stretcher being taken to a hospital ward, with no identification and no one to identify him: "Mother, it is enough to rack one's heart, such things—very likely his folks will never know in the world what has become of him—poor poor child, for he appeared as though he could be but 18."[28] The death of an unknown soldier, without family or friends or anyone even able to establish his identity—an identity absolutely obliterated, without witness—throws the language of human meaning and connection into crisis.[29] Such painful reflections would lead Whitman to further ruminations threatening any redemptive notions concerning the war; the callous indifference to the sufferings of the common soldiers particularly saddened and infuriated Whitman: "even the dying soldier's money stolen from his body by some scoundrel attendant, or from sick ones, even from under his head, which is a common thing—& then the agony I see everyday, I get almost frightened at the world."[30] These are feelings, by the way, that Whitman did not record in his poetry.

POEMS AND EPISTLES

Although he left out of his published poems the most damnable abuses he witnessed, Whitman tried to imbue his poetry of the war with the emotional intimacy and immediacy that the trauma in the hospitals had demanded of him. *Drum-Taps* is saturated with the intimacy and actual rhythms and phrasing, as well as scenes and images, we find in Whitman's notes and correspondence of the time. In fact, as Jerome Loving has pointed out, "Some of the greatest poems of *Drum-Taps* were conceived near the very battlefield they effectively describe."[31] According to Loving, both "Vigil Strange I Kept on the Field One Night" and "A Sight in Camp in the Daybreak Gray and Dim" are based on a Christmas night Whitman spent at Fredericksburg, Virginia, when he was looking for his brother. Moreover, most of the *Drum-Taps* poems were never revised after their first publication (although their positions in *Leaves of Grass* did change over time)—which makes them very unusual in the Whitman canon. Whitman began drafting some of the poems in the same notebooks in which he took down the names of soldiers he met in the hospitals or recorded his activities of the day.

As he tried in his nursing and in his letter-writing to mediate between the soldiers' sphere and that of their (and his) families, so in his poetry he tried, paradoxically, to eliminate the conventional distance inherent in aesthetic mediation, to make the poems not substitute for reality but somehow keep the war's reality real for all time, to bridge the gap between that cluster of years and all later ones. In this attempt he knew he could not succeed. Yet in Whitman's war writing, taken altogether, one finds a peculiar series of linkages between the actual experience; the note taken at the hospital, blood-stained and tear-spotted; the letter written to a parent or spouse; and the poem, often itself a sort of epistle—to whom?

Civilians can never, Whitman asserts, know the actuality of the suffering bodies; even so, he tried to provoke understanding, at times with graphic descriptions, as in "The Wound-Dresser":

> From the stump of the arm, the amputated hand,
> I undo the clotted lint, remove the slough, wash off
>   the matter and blood,
> Back on his pillow the soldier bends with curv'd neck
>   and side-falling head,
> His eyes are closed, his face is pale, he dares not look
>   on the bloody stump,

> And has not yet look'd on it.[32]

But what finally cannot be represented, most importantly, for Whitman is a kind and depth of emotion that is both too traumatic to recapture and inestimably dear. It is the bond of one human being to another—mother, father, brother, son, loving comrade—revealing its primal value at the point when death intervenes, fused with a cause so sacred that the contradiction threatens to open up an ethical abyss. One ends up fighting for the very meaning of those primary bonds of attachment that the work of battle perpetually annihilates—unless this world connects with one beyond, unless identity and attachment survive.

Even when the emotion concatenates around a battle flag, what the flag represents is more than nationality or a political principle but simultaneously a bond of human attachment, of comrades to each other, often inflected with the feeling of a child for its mother, the flag a substitute for the mother (as a child's blanket is) and this feeling thoroughly (perhaps perversely, pathetically) absorbed into the sense of the cause. Whitman himself was given a little flag by one of the wounded who expected to die—the flag had been captured by the "Rebs" and then rescued in a little skirmish that "cost 3 men's lives," "all just for the name of getting their little banner back again—this man that got it was very badly wounded, & they let him keep it—I was with him a good deal, he wanted to give me something he said, he didn't expect to live, so he gave me the little banner as a keepsake."[33]

In "Song of the Banner at Daybreak," the poet imagines a banner, associated with the mother, speaking to a child and calling him to leave his home for war, over the father's objections:

> So loved—O you banner leading the day with stars
>   brought from the night!
> Valueless, object of eyes, over all and demanding all—
>   (absolute owner of all)—O
>   banner and pennant!
> I too leave the rest—great as it is, it is nothing—
>   houses, machines are nothing—I see
>   them not,
> I see but you, O warlike pennant! O banner so broad,
>   with stripes, I sing you only,
> Flapping there in the wind.[34]

The connection Whitman felt among the soldiers between primary bonds of attachment and the banner or cause may explain the strange fact that in the original *Drum-Taps,* just before "Vigil Strange," Whitman included a poem called "Mother and Babe," of only two lines: "I see the sleeping babe, nestling the breast of its mother; / The sleeping mother and babe—hush'd, I study them long and long."[35] Seemingly incongruous in a collection of war poems, it is the mother-child bond that in fact irradiates all of the *Drum-Taps* cluster with its unusual combination of tenderness and terror.

And paradox. For what bond challenges the authority of the nation or the cause over the body of the child more radically than that of the mother? So Whitman himself seems to acknowledge in the poem "Come Up from the Fields Father," in which he imagines a midwestern farm family receiving just the sort of letter Whitman himself often wrote about a sick or wounded boy/soldier:

> Open the envelope quickly,
> O this is not our son's writing, yet his name is sign'd,
> O a strange hand writes for our dear son, O stricken
>   mother's soul!
> All swims before her eyes, flashes with black, she
>   catches the main words only,
> Sentences broken, *gunshot wound in the breast, cav-
>   alry skirmish, taken to hospital,*
> *At present low, but will soon be better.*
>
> Ah now the single figure to me,
> Amid all teeming and wealthy Ohio with all its cities
>   and farms,
> Sickly white in the face and dull in the head, very
>   faint,
> By the jamb of a door leans.
>   . . . . .
>
> Alas poor boy, he will never be better, (nor may-be
>   needs to be better, that brave and
>   simple soul,)
> While they stand at home at the door he is dead al-
>   ready,
> The only son is dead.
>   . . . . .
>
> But the mother needs to be better,
> In the midnight waking, weeping, longing with one
>   deep longing,
> O that she might withdraw unnoticed, silent from life
>   escape and withdraw,
> To follow, to seek, to be with her dear dead son.[36]

The greatest heroism of the war, Whitman sometimes stated, was that of mothers such as his own, often not knowing for weeks or months on end the fate of their children whom they knew to have been engaged in harrowing battles.[37]

For all his faith in the cause, Whitman seeks, as John Carlos Rowe has written, "a more profound justification for the human damage he witnesses" than patriotism or transcendental idealism can provide.[38] He finds it in qualities of feeling. If the war appears as an infernal experience, it is also one that evokes depths of emotion and filial affections that no peacetime pleasures can match. For Whitman, it seems to confirm a profundity of human attachment undreamed of before the war, and, to his peculiar way of thinking, a proof of the theory of democracy.

ASSASSINATION AND SUTURE

The Saturday after Good Friday in 1865, Whitman and his family learned of Lincoln's assassination on one of the poet's visits home. They literally read the newspaper aloud to each other, passing it back and forth across his mother's kitchen table. Walt and his mother, Louisa, did not eat that day but sat silently as the sky darkened and the rain fell in dreary accompaniment to their sorrow. Whitman came quickly to believe that the assassination of the President encapsulated the entire meaning of the war and proved its sacred quality: "The whole involved, baffling, multiform whirl of the Secession period," he would write, came to a head in that single "fierce deed."[39] It proved the universal significance of the war; it was democracy's originary moment, its rite of crucifixion. Whitman ceased thinking of the nation as having been born during the Revolution; he began to see the Civil War and assassination as America's true "parturition and delivery"; the nation had been "born again, consistent with itself."[40] In all his post-war work, Democracy and America are figured as a Mother. Thus was the suffering redeemed.

But what if Whitman's reading of the War, and with it Lincoln's death, were wrong? If the poet had deceived himself and democracy had not been truly and permanently saved, then America, he believed, would be a spectacular failure and his life's work wasted—both nation and poet victims of "a destiny . . . equivalent in its real world to that of the fabled damned," as he wrote in *Democratic Vistas*.[41] Fear of such self-deceit is one of the keys to Whitman's later years. He avoided any radical questioning of the motion of history, which helps explain the dramatic shift in his poetry away from personal crisis and ecstasy to stoic detachment, reminiscence, and meditation.

In incorporating *Drum-Taps* into *Leaves of Grass* and, throughout the last quarter-century of his life, expanding as well as reorganizing that work into a cathedral-like form, Whitman gave the Civil War a central position.[42] He devoted the heart of his autobiography, *Specimen Days,* to his memoranda from the war period. Yet Whitman does not provide a comprehensive view of the war; most glaring is an almost total absence of reflection upon slavery and emancipation, except for the awkward "Ethiopia Saluting the Colors" (which, nonetheless, would be much admired by some black writers of later years).

This may be connected with his view of the war as a "family" drama; the ideology of "race" as "family" made it impossible for Whitman to conceive of the Civil War as centrally involving African Americans (although it must be said that he showed interest in the involvement of black troops, and registered the evidence of their competence and courage). To Whitman, African Americans were beside the point, for the point was a "family" crisis, and Whitman could not think of black people as part of his "family." As Ed Folsom has pointed out, in the text of a speech late in life that spoke in the warmest tones of national reconciliation,

Whitman wrote, "To night I would say one word for that South—the whites. I do not wish to say one word and will not say one word against the blacks—but the blacks can never be to me what the whites are. Below all political relations, even the deepest, are still deeper, personal, physiological and *emotional* ones, the whites are my brothers & I love them."[43] The presence of African Americans in the national household is not addressed but generally covered up in Whitman's rhetoric of national solidarity and healing. Just what African Americans had to do with the coming of the war (dreadfully hinted at in the "Black Lucifer" passage quoted earlier) is completely avoided by a narrative of fratricide in which the "brothers" are all white—as are the "fathers" over whose heroic legacy they quarrel, under the eyes of the surviving Mother, democracy. Certainly, Whitman believed slavery was evil, but it was only one of the great threats to democracy that the war, in Whitman's view, addressed. The reintegration of the national household takes place with blacks basically left out, or forming a mysterious puzzle. A hint of this problem occurs in Whitman's description of troops on review in 1864, passing under Lincoln's gaze: "The 9th Corps made a very fine show indeed—there were I should think five very full regiments of new black troops under Gen Ferrero, they looked & marched very well—It looked funny to see the President standing with his hat off to them just the same as the rest as they passed by."[44] In the spring of 1867, Whitman would write his mother, "Washington is filled with *darkies*. The men and women & wenches swarm in all directions—(I am not sure but the North is like the man that won the elephant in a raffle)."[45]

Only one poem in the original *Drum-Taps* cluster— "Pioneers! O Pioneers!," which looks to the settlement of the West as a way of transcending sectional animosity, turning battle-axes into woodsman's tools—included any reference to slavery (but not specifically to black people).[46] In 1867, Whitman wrote the poem "Ethiopia Saluting the Colors"; much later, in 1881, he added it to the *Drum-Taps* cluster. It is one of the most awkward poems he ever wrote, and completely alien to his poetic style. Some critics have assailed the poem for stereotypical description, but what is more striking to me is the dread implicit in the questions with which the poem closes, six years after the Civil War had actually ended. "What is it fateful woman, so blear, hardly human? / Why wag your head with turban bound, yellow, red and green? / Are the things so strange and marvelous you see or have seen?"[47] These words, it is true, are ostensibly spoken by a persona, a white soldier in Sherman's army; nonetheless, much is revealed in Whitman's awkwardness and irresolution here—an irresolution quite atypical of the postwar poet, who often expressed the belief that democracy in America had nothing more to fear, having, in his opinion, defeated its internal demons.[48] That the whole epic story of black Americans'

experience of the conflict lies outside Whitman's reach reveals much not only about himself but about the limits of the white poetic imagination as the nation emerged from its most traumatic experience, intent on healing, on sewing up its wounds.[49]

We see in Whitman's work in this respect, and in the nation, an example of the sort of "suturing" that has been described recently within film and narrative theory. Surgical suturing reconnects torn or cut flesh, after an operation or in the repair of a wound. But out of Lacanian psychoanalysis and related theories has developed the notion that, in the words of Robert Leigh Davis, "works of art expose and then cover over the inadequacies of their subject. They promote an awareness of wounding in order to relieve it, to suture it, in a way that stabilizes the viewer or reader within a pre-existing social order. The more intense the threat of negation and loss, the more intense the desire for closure."[50] The issue of African Americans' relation to the American household could not really be a part of the calculus for Whitman, for they belonged to another "family."[51] He rarely imagined them in relation to the family romance, and the reintegration of the country after the war meant for him chiefly the reintegration of Southern and Northern whites. Indeed, during the war itself, although Whitman was not unfriendly to black soldiers in the hospitals, he generally did not minister to them; and he avoided the "Contraband" hospitals: "There is a limit to one's sinews & endurance & sympathies, & c.," he wrote his mother.[52] While the war gradually revealed for some white people, like Lincoln, the profound significance of the existence of African Americans as slaves or ex-slaves within the nation, for others this was an issue best avoided. And so the healing of the wounds of the war came at the expense of probing further the nature of problems that, as Whitman's pre-war verse occasionally hinted, had made the war irrepressible.

Joel Williamson, among others, has pointed out that the Civil War resulted in a crucial drama in the development of American racial culture, for one of its results was to precipitate a formalization of racial difference on a bipolar model and on a national scale. Differences by state concerning racial identification disappeared, anti-miscegenation laws spread, and the "Race War" moved North in the early twentieth century, which in turn nourished a growing sense of black national identity as distinct from white American identity.[53] The correlation of "race" with "family"—or rather, the subordination of family to race, the utter suppression of potential "family" relations that crossed the color line—became increasingly adamant and nationalized, setting up the basic vectors of modern American racial formation. The question of whether the war was fought over equality and black emancipation or over states' rights versus national union was settled in favor of the latter. And we have lived with the consequences of that answer—a failure of imagination, of love and recognition—ever since.

Notes

1. Horace Traubel, *With Walt Whitman in Camden,* 9 vols. (various publishers, 1914-1996), 3:95.

2. Whitman, "To Thee Old Cause," in *Leaves of Grass* [Abbreviated *LG*], Comprehensive Reader's Edition, ed. Harold W. Blodgett and Sculley Bradley (New York: New York University Press, 1965), 5.

3. See George Hutchinson, *The Ecstatic Whitman: Literary Shamanism and the Crisis of the Union* (Columbus: Ohio State University Press, 1986), 1-16.

4. "The Sleepers," *LG,* 429.

5. For further discussion of the filiopiety in Whitman's imaginary relationship to the revolutionary generation, see Hutchinson, *Ecstatic Whitman,* 1-8. A work that sheds much light on the subject generally is George B. Forgie, *Patricide in the House Divided* (New York: Norton, 1979).

6. George Hutchinson, "Whitman's Confidence Game: The 'Good Gray Poet' and the Civil War," *South Central Review* 7 (1990), 20-35.

7. Martin Klammer, *Whitman, Slavery, and the Emergence of Leaves of Grass* (University Park: Pennsylvania State University Press, 1995); and Ed Folsom, "Lucifer and Ethiopia: Whitman, Race, and Poetics before the Civil War and After," in *A Historical Guide to Walt Whitman,* ed. David S. Reynolds (Oxford: Oxford University Press, 2000), 46-53. See also Folsom, "Walt Whitman's Working Notes for the First Edition of *Leaves of Grass,*" *Walt Whitman Quarterly Review* 16 (1998), 91.

8. Hutchinson, *Ecstatic Whitman,* 66.

9. Whitman, *Complete Poetry and Collected Prose,* ed. Justin Kaplan (New York: Library of America, 1982), 113.

10. In some poems such as "To You (Whoever You Are)" he uses the condition of the slave as representative of the condition of his audience. The "you" of his songs, if it is to apply to all readers, must apply to slaves, those most graphically denied the right to self-determination. Eschewing pity for admiration and love, the poet projects upon his reader a spiritual freedom that will ensure self-fulfillment: "The hopples fall from your ankles, you find an unfailing sufficiency, / Old or young, male or female, rude, low, rejected by the rest, whatever you are promulges itself" (*LG,* 235). I discuss passages like this and Whitman's appeal to black modernist poets in "Langston Hughes and the 'Other' Whitman," in *The Continuing Presence of Walt Whitman: The Life After the Life,* ed. Robert K. Martin (Iowa City: University of Iowa Press, 1992), 16-27.

11. Folsom, "Lucifer and Ethiopia," p. 52.

12. Christopher Beach comments that "symbolically, Whitman turns increasingly to a vision of 'reconciliation' that would unite the white 'brothers' of North and South while obliterating the black race entirely" (*The Politics of Distinction: Whitman and the Discourses of Nineteenth-Century America* [Athens: University of Georgia Press, 1996], 97).

13. Whitman to Ralph Waldo Emerson, January 17, 1863, in *The Correspondence* [Abbreviated *Corr.*], ed. Edwin Haviland Miller (New York: New York University Press, 1961), 1:69. A fine article on the importance of George Whitman to Walt's response to the war is M. Wynn Thomas, "Fratricide and Brotherly Love: Whitman and the Civil War," in Ezra Greenspan, ed., *The Cambridge Companion to Walt Whitman* (New York: Cambridge University Press, 1995), 27-44.

14. Jerome Loving, *Walt Whitman: The Song of Himself* (Berkeley: University of California Press, 1999), 11. Other excellent sources on Whitman's family in the Civil War include Gay Wilson Allen, *The Solitary Singer* (1955, rev. 1967; Chicago: University of Chicago Press, 1985); and David S. Reynolds, *Walt Whitman's America: A Cultural Biography* (New York: Knopf, 1995). For the most part, for biographical information I draw in this essay from Loving and from Whitman's correspondence of the period.

15. Whitman to Louisa Van Velsor Whitman, July 15, 1863, in *Corr.,* 1:117-118.

16. Thomas, 31.

17. Quoted in Loving, 265.

18. Quoted in Loving, 277.

19. Quoted in Loving, 188, note 72.

20. Whitman to Mr. And Mrs. S. B. Haskell, August 10, 1863, in *Corr.,* 1:129.

21. Thomas, 35.

22. *LG,* 303-304.

23. Whitman to William S. Davis, October 1, 1863, in *Corr.,* 1:152-153.

24. *Corr.,* 1:93.

25. Whitman to Elijah Douglass Fox, November 21, 1863, in *Corr.,* 1:187-188.

26. Whitman to Lewis K. Brown and others, November 9, 1863, in *Corr.,* 1:181.

27. Whitman to Louisa Van Velsor Whitman, October 27, 1863, in *Corr.,* 1:173.

28. Whitman to Louisa Van Velsor Whitman, March 29, 1864, in *Corr.,* 1:205.

29. Thomas, 35; and Keith V. Comer, *Strange Meetings: Walt Whitman, Wilfred Owen, and the Poetry of War* (Lund: Lund University Press, 1996), 23.

30. Whitman to Louisa Van Velsor Whitman, March 29, 1864, in *Corr.,* 1:205.

31. Loving, 19.

32. *LG,* 310.

33. *Corr.,* 1:210.

34. *LG,* 290-291.

35. Whitman, "Mother and Babe," in *Drum-Taps* (New York, 1865), 41.

36. *LG,* 303.

37. See, e.g., Whitman to Ellen O'Connor, November 15, 1863, in *Corr.,* 1:183.

38. Rowe, "Whitman's Body Poetic," in Kathryne V. Lindberg and Joseph G. Kronick, ed., *America's Modernisms: Revaluing the Canon* (Baton Rouge: Louisiana State University Press, 1996), 175.

39. Whitman, "Death of Abraham Lincoln," in Roy P. Basler, ed., *Walt Whitman's Memoranda During the War [&] Death of Abraham Lincoln* (Bloomington: Indiana University Press, 1962), 11.

40. "Death of Abraham Lincoln," 12.

41. *Democratic Vistas,* in Mark Van Doren, ed., *The Portable Walt Whitman* (New York: Viking, 1973), 380.

42. Hutchinson, "Whitman's Confidence Game," 31-32.

43. Quoted in Folsom, "Lucifer and Ethiopia," 82, from Edward F. Grier, ed., *Notebooks and Unpublished Prose Manuscripts* (New York: New York University Press, 1984), 6:2160.

44. Whitman to Louisa Van Velsor Whitman, April 26, 1864, in *Corr.,* 1:211-212.

45. *Corr.,* 1:323.

46. The reference to "all the masters with their slaves" (*LG,* 231) in "Pioneers" does not clearly include these persons among the pioneers themselves, but seems to refer to them as among the groups who are urging the pioneers—the "beloved race" of "resolute children"—onward.

47. *LG,* 318-319.

48. For an intensive investigation of the poem and its context, see Ed Folsom's discussion in "Lucifer and Ethiopia," 53-77. One thing Folsom's extensive analysis and historical reconstruction suggests to me is how thoroughly Whitman sublimated the African American experience and presence through the figure of this one aged woman. Folsom's careful research into the dramatic contemporary accounts about African Americans shadowing Sherman's march in South Carolina suggests that Whitman could not have been ignorant of the subject.

49. For an influential argument about the relationship of racism and racial ambivalence to the inability of American authors to adequately address the Civil War, see Daniel Aaron, *The Unwritten War: American Writers and the Civil War* (New York: Knopf, 1973).

50. Robert Leigh Davis, *Whitman and the Romance of Medicine* (Berkeley: University of California Press, 1997), 127. Davis ingeniously applies theories of suture to Whitman's work to demonstrate that while Whitman seeks to heal and stabilize identity, he "affirms the value of what cannot be fully treated, sutured, comprehended, or closed off." Unfortunately, it seems to me, when it came to nationality and race, Whitman fell short of such affirmation in the post-war period. Luke Mancuso, I should add, has argued otherwise in *The Strange Sad War Revolving: Walt Whitman, Reconstruction, and the Emergence of Black Citizenship, 1865-1876* (Columbia, SC: Camden House, 1997).

51. Ed Folsom (65-66) points out that Whitman wrote positively in 1862 of "Aunty Robinson, a colored nurse" in an article on the Broadway Hospital; the "Aunty" moniker in this case I take to be typical of a racially specific form of respectful usage at the time, applied chiefly to mature, respectable, and non-threatening blacks, who generally were not addressed as "Mr." and "Mrs." by whites.

52. Whitman to Louisa Van Velsor Whitman, July 7, 1863, in *Corr.,* 1:115.

53. Joel Williamson, *New People: Miscegenation and Mulattoes in the United States* (New York: The Free Press, 1980).

Jennifer James (essay date spring-summer 2005)

SOURCE: James, Jennifer. "'Civil' War Wounds: William Wells Brown, Violence, and the Domestic Narrative." *African American Review* 39, nos. 1-2 (spring-summer 2005): 39-54.

[*In the following essay, James delineates William Wells Brown's portrayal of the African American soldiers' experience during the Civil War and how the author promotes his anti-slavery stance in his works.*]

In 1867, William Wells Brown, the first published black American novelist, wrote a fictionalized account of the Civil War, becoming also, it appears, the first black American war novelist in the process. However, *Clotelle, The Colored Heroine, A Tale of the Southern States* was not a war novel in its origins. Brown, who manifested an unparalleled talent for repetition throughout his career, took one of his several revisions of the 1853 *Clotel, or The President's Daughter* and added four chapters dealing with the Civil War. Brown admits in his preface that all but these chapters were completed "before the breaking out of the recent rebellion" (4). Approximately six months before the publication of *Clotelle,* Brown had also become the first black American to publish a book-length historical account of the Civil War, *The Negro In the American Rebellion: His Heroism and His Fidelity* (1867).

The 1867 version of Brown's revisions of *Clotel* brings the fugitive slaves Clotelle (the re-named daughter of the Clotel of the first novel) and her black husband Jerome home from their refuge in France to participate in the Civil War. Joining the Louisiana "Native Guards," one of the first black regiments raised to fight in the war, Jerome is killed off four paragraphs into the Civil War section of the narrative when a white general asks that his black subordinates charge into an onslaught of bullets and shells to retrieve the body of another (presumably white) officer. Four by four, they are fed into the fire until, on the fourth try, the body has been rescued. Very nearly out of danger, Jerome is decapitated by a shell. What Brown labels "human sacrifice" (106), was, of course, "black sacrifice"; black men willingly—and here, forcibly—laying down their bodies at the altars of freedom and citizenship. Jerome does not die in sacrificial glory, as Frances Harper's slave-martyr Tom will in the Civil War novel *Iola Leroy* (1892), saving black and white men alike; Jerome's death is senseless and the scene absurd. Moreover, Jerome's commanding officer is not the concerned abolitionist/commander both Harper and memoirist Susie King Taylor will both put to use in their war texts, but "a sorry tribute to [white] humanity" (106).[1]

This episode is a fictionalized representation of an event in the war that apparently had made a deep impression on Brown. In *The Negro in the American Rebellion,* the writer allots the incident an entire chapter, rendering it in explicit, excruciating detail. In historical actuality, a non-commissioned black officer, Captain Andre Callioux, whom Brown describes in the most elevated terms of black masculinity—"the blackest man in the Crescent City. . . . Finely educated, polished in his manners . . . bold, athletic and daring"—was killed in a poorly planned attack on the rebel works at Port Hudson, Louisiana (169). Although it was evident that the works could not be taken without extraordinary loss of life, a General Dwight ordered that the mission continue. His subordinate, Colonel Nelson, made seven charges of the Confederate batteries, each unsuccessful, and each bringing more deaths and casualties. "Humanity," Brown writes, "will never forgive Gen. Dwight . . . for he certainly saw he was throwing away the lives of his men. But what were his men? 'Only Niggers'" (170). Brown's narrator asks the relevant question: "But had they accomplished anything more than the loss of many of their brave men?" Unwilling to let the query hang too long, he answers it quickly and affirmatively. "Yes: they had," the author writes, explaining that the bravery of the black troops "created a new chapter in American history for the colored man" (172). His assurance seems more than a little disingenuous. Brown indeed is trying to have it both ways: these black lives were both carelessly disposed of in battle *and* honorably preserved by historical record—not just his, but also that of the dominant culture, which, Brown writes, "paid . . . tribute" to these men (172). In his own preface to the *Negro in the American Rebellion,* Brown acknowledges "Feeling anxious to preserve for future reference an account of the part which the Negro took" in the Slaveholder's Rebellion. Thus, Brown's insistence that the blood of black lives lost, even those lost in this most obscene manner, had *already* written this "chapter in American history" appears more hopeful than truthful.

Brown's attempt to "have it both ways" underscores the difficulty he faced in creating a usable African American history of the Civil War: writing a realistic portrayal of black military life that exposes the psychological and physical assaults that blacks endured at the hands of both the Union and Confederacy (aspects that Harper will later forgo) while at the same time idealizing the dignity and bravery of the troops. The Civil War was nothing if not a conflict rife with conflicts: a war that was and was not about slavery, that freed some slaves but not others, in which blacks were used as both Union and Confederate soldiers, and in which those blacks who did don Union uniforms were paid no more than fugitive slave laborers. It was a war the end of which seemed to promise total liberation, but brought about a freedom so limited that many blacks were left to wonder whether emancipation had come at all. Looking at Brown as a Civil War writer, I am intrigued by his troubled endeavors to produce and manage a black body that can negotiate this contradictory historical terrain. As I will explain, Brown used his early texts to create male and female heroic bodies that could take their proper places within an evolutionary, linear narrative of black historical progress, a narrative designed to combat the devolutionary temporal narratives that would preclude blacks from inhabiting national space. In a work published during the Civil War, *The Black Man: His Antecedents, His Genius and His Achievements* (1863), Brown argues that blacks, who belong "to the great family of man," are not debilitated by a "natural inferiority" that would prevent them from achieving equality "on this continent with the white man" (31). The argument that belonging to the same evolutionary time should secure blacks the right to live with whites in the nation, rather than to be expatriated or expelled to a more "backward" elsewhere, is a variation of the claim he had used to demand the abolition of slavery. Throughout his lectures and speeches Brown maintains that blacks, if indeed degraded, were made that way from the intellectual and physical deprivations of bondage, and given time, they will (re)emerge as enlightened, capable beings.

For Brown, that linear narrative of black progress almost always crosses the threshold of the domestic, the allegorical space where he enacts his fantasies of national inclusion. The manner in which Brown constantly moves his hero and heroine across geography and circumstance—from the United States, to Europe, back to the United States; from slavery to freedom—demonstrates that Brown's particular notion of a politically useful domesticity relies less on the creation of a perfected material space than on an idealized heterosexual union whose hallmark is its very mobility: black men and women forming a political alliance that is impervious to time, space, and history. For African Americans, whose historical experience has been defined by geographical movement, displacement, and loss, the notion of a moveable "homespace" defends against the "lack" implied by an inability to construct a stable physical domesticity. This holds particularly true for Brown, who was a fugitive slave. His sketch of Madison Washington, the instigator of the revolt on the slave ship *Creole,* included in *The Black Man,* articulates Brown's notion of a black progress within the trope of a mobilized matrimony. While Frederick Douglass's fictionalized version, *The Heroic Slave,* has Washington's wife dying before the insurgency takes place, Brown places Washington's beautiful "mulatta" companion ("marbled" skin, "mild blue eyes," a "finely chiseled mouth") within the group of slaves freed by her husband (81). As Richard Yarborough observes, Brown's realization of liberation results in "a restoration of the integrity of the domestic circle," revising Douglass's idealization of a solitary male heroic figure (173). As I argue below,

Brown was intent on creating a decidedly black and a decidedly heroic male protagonist who could access public male power and perform domesticity at once.[2]

However, as the 1867 *Clotelle* demonstrates, a marked shift takes place in the narrative Brown produced after the war. In abandoning the heterosexual domestic imaginary, and with it, the powerful set of meanings it had accrued within his work, Brown questions whether the cultural vocabulary most dominant in 19th-century America can function within postbellum black protest fiction. He raises a similar question in abandoning the black corporeal fantasy embodied by the hero and heroine he sculpted so meticulously for the *Clotel* novels: Can highly stylized, aestheticized representations of blackness still perform the political work necessary for African Americans in post-Civil War United States? In *Clotelle* Jerome's magnificent body is very certainly "transformed," but the equally magnificent "mulatta" Clotelle is also altered, nullified, as it were, through Brown's linguistic neglect. In these chapters, he refuses to enshroud her in the idealizing terms standard for the literary figure whose very comeliness had come to represent the political and social promise of the black nation. Focusing on the alterations made to these bodies and the alterations to the *Clotel* narratives, I will argue that Brown's unwillingness to provide Jerome and Clotelle with either a protective domestic narrative or a protective corporeal language in the Civil War section of the 1867 revision reflects the writer's disillusionment in the years following the conflict, a disillusionment that led him to create a depiction of the "Rebellion" that rejects the laws that govern sentimentality for the laws that govern the frankly unsentimental project of war.

It almost seems unnecessary to explain the degree of optimism the war inspired in black Americans, and therefore, the corresponding degree of disappointment that African Americans experienced when their hopes for prosperous lives as freed people were dashed repeatedly. Long before the abolition of slavery was declared an official war aim, and well before the Emancipation Proclamation, most blacks understood that any war between the northern and southern states would turn on the issue of slavery. Brown, a tireless antislavery activist, had ample reason to believe that everything he had worked for throughout his entire adult life would come to fruition. At the end of 1865, the Congress both ratified the Thirteenth Amendment abolishing slavery and enacted legislation establishing the Freedman's Bureau. However, the opportunities the Bureau provided were all too often negated by the "Black Laws" that many states, north and south, had first rushed to enact in the wake of the Emancipation Proclamation, hoping to keep contra-band from securing employment. Most of these laws appeared after the war, when free(d) blacks were seen as even more of a threat to white labor. Called "Black Codes" in the South, they imposed restrictions in nearly all aspects of African American life, giving whites the opportunity to reign over blacks with impunity. Blacks in South Carolina, for instance, one of the states most devastated by the war, could not marry if "paupers"; orphaned black children were forced into indentured apprenticeships (Mullane 301, 302).

Brown transcribes some of these laws in his Civil War history, commenting acerbically on what he views as their absolute hypocrisy: "And yet Connecticut, with her proscription of the negro, and receiving their aid in fighting her battles, retains her negro 'black laws' upon her statutebook by a vote of more than six thousand" (Brown, *Negro* 143). The war within the war that Martin Delany, Frederick Douglass, and other black activists had waged to force the Union to accept black soldiers had already given blacks an inkling of the obstacles they would face as freedpeople. Indeed, Brown, who had been vocal in this movement, and who later recruited blacks to join Union forces after Lincoln agreed to raise African American troops in 1862, resigned his post in 1864 in anger at the Union's refusal to grant adequate wages to black soldiers.

I return, then, to the dilemma that *The Negro in the American Rebellion* presented to Brown in 1867 as he sought to write a "non-fiction" history that balanced the real and the ideal, and as he strove to present a black male body capable of transforming physical and psychic humiliation into a transcendent state of heroism. He tries to solve this problem by re-imagining the conflict as a race war taking place almost exclusively between black men and their oppressors, attempting to construct a black male body in which two modes of violence are reconciled: a body that is both injured and injuring.

Calling the war the "Slaveholders' Rebellion" in his introduction, Brown begins his chronology with Crispus Attucks, the fugitive slave who was the first to fall in the Boston Massacre. Writing of Attucks's escape from bondage in one sentence and the massacre at Boston in the next, Brown represents Attucks's slave-break and his involvement in the war in one fluid movement, from fugitive to revolutionary, collapsing the distinction between slave and patriot. He devotes the next three chapters to Nat Turner, Denmark Vesey, and Madison Washington, each of whom planned a slave revolt. He follows these installations with "The Growth of Slave Power," a chapter characterizing the expanding proportions of slavery as an overfed "monster" (40). The next chapter describes John Brown's raid on Harper's Ferry, emphasizing the roles played by John Copeland and Shields Green, the only two blacks captured alive. Quoting an article in the *Baltimore Sun* that marvels at Copeland's "unwavering fortitude" before his execution, Brown adds that Shields "behaved with equal heroism" (49).

He concludes: "Shields Green . . . died as he had lived, a brave man, and expressing to the last his eternal hatred to human bondage, prophesying that slavery would soon come to a bloody end" (49).

In Brown's book, the Civil War begins thereafter, with black men heeding (albeit unsuccessfully) Lincoln's call for 75,000 Union volunteers. By positioning black soldiers along a continuum of American slave revolutionaries, Brown transforms the Civil War into the greatest in a series of slave revolts, placing the black male in direct, armed confrontation with his master/monster: "an opportunity of settling with the 'ole boss' for a long score of cruelty" (157). Far from being something as removed from African American life as a conflict over "state's rights," the war instead becomes slavery's bloody finale, the inevitable conclusion to an inhumane institution prophesied decades before by a black man with his dying breath. Indeed, in his 1854 meditation on the slave revolution in Santo Domingo and its leader Toussaint L'Ouverture, Brown predicted that if slaves rose up, then "the God of Justice would be on their side" (qtd. in Levine 502). Thus, he defines revolt as a morally righteous materialization of R/republican ideology and divine retribution, and envisions such uprising as the completion of the "revolution that was commenced in 1776" (502). In the 1853 *Clotel*, Brown had already fused the philosophies of black slave "revolt" and white American "revolution." There, George Green, on trial for insurgency, provocatively asks, "Did not American revolutionists violate the laws when they struck for liberty? They were revolters, but their success made them patriots—we were revolters, and our failure makes us rebels" (226). Thus, while the history of slave revolts left many "failed" bodies—wounded, wrecked, and even obliterated by violence—it was nevertheless a heroic violence of slaves' own making, in which they forcefully asserted selves that centuries of enslavement had attempted to de-create. These bodies, then, represented willing and necessary forfeitures in the making of a manly race and, as Brown sees it, in the making of a black American.

But the powerful association Brown makes between the war and slave revolution obscures a simple fact: the Civil War was not a slave revolt, and at Port Hudson, these men did not volunteer for the charges—a crucial fact that Brown alters within his novel when he writes that the black soldiers were *asked,* not commanded, to put themselves in harm's way. The fictionalized account in *Clotelle* therefore becomes puzzling. Within the space of the imaginary, Brown could have chosen to portray many less bloody and less tragic events of the war. He could have chosen events that showed an emerging fraternity among white officers and their black subordinates. In other words, he could have used his "nonfiction" to construct an uncompromised heroic black manhood, the decision Douglass made in depicting in

The Heroic Slave a black man who wages a successful revolt, rather than a fictionalized version of, say, Nat Turner, whose body ended up dangling from a noose. Instead, Brown apparently felt so distressed by white wounding of black male subjectivity (on many terrains) that he himself re-violates the black male body: "His head entirely torn off by a shell," Jerome is simply and unceremoniously snuffed out (106). Images of slaying, Kenneth Burke observes in an analysis of Milton's heroes, are acts of transformation; "the killing of something is the changing of it" (179). Brown willfully presents a grotesque where once stood a "whole" black man.

Certainly, then, this seems an odd fate for a character the writer had carefully chiseled across the span of four versions of his novel. Indeed, Brown did not initially construct his hero as a man physically dark enough to be Andre Callioux's double. Named George in the first *Clotel,* he more phenotypically resembles the white aristocrats in the first text, Henry Morton and Antoine Devenant—who marry mixed race women—than he resembles most of the other prominent black males in the narrative. In part, George's phenotypic whiteness serves one of the same fundamental purposes as the mulatta's: it renders him a reasonable facsimile of the chivalric heroes of white sentimental literature generally, and within *Clotel* specifically, it allows him to supplant the white male figures who form ultimately unsuccessful relationships with Brown's mixed race heroines. Influenced perhaps by the appearance of what Delany called the "New negro" black male in his serialized novel *Blake, or the Huts of America* (1859-62)—a hero defined by the combination of his undeniably black skin, powerful intellect, great strength, and, most supremely, his commitment to instigating global black revolution—Brown apparently concluded that George was too white to signify black manhood, physically and ideologically. More than a bulked up, colorized version of George, Jerome consolidates the two distinct manifestations of black heroic masculinity in the novel: the ultra-light-skinned black romantic hero who marries the mulatta heroine and is allowed access to the domestic sentimentalized narrative, and the ultra-black slave-revolutionary, whose acts place him within a different narrative, one that distinctly disallows for domestic stability.

In fact, in *Clotel,* it appears that physical proximity to the darker-skinned African ancestors to a large measure determines revolutionary potential; thus, as a light-skinned rebellious hero, George is an odd man out, standing apart from the other black men in the texts who also engage in overt acts of resistance against the system of slavery, particularly the figures of Nat Turner and Picquilo (whose messianic blackness is coded in opposition to the minstrel blackness of the comic folk in Brown's work). Showing no hint of "African blood," George possesses hair "straight, soft, fine and light,"

but William, the slave who ushers Clotel to freedom and flees to Canada, is "tall, full bodied" (224, 171). George had a "prominent" nose and "thin" lips; Turner is "full-blooded" (224, 213). Brown reserves his most detailed description of a black man's body for the cat-like, stealthy Picquilo, "large, tall, full-blooded Negro with a stern and savage countenance . . . his step oblique, his look sanguinary" (213, 214). For Brown, the tribal marks on this African's skin were signs of inner power made visible, as if they were carved from the "bold spirit" of his interior (214).

It is no wonder, then, that after George takes part in a slave insurrection at the end of the original *Clotel,* he arrives in the next version physically inscribed by revolution: "This slave, whose name was Jerome, was of pure African origin, perfectly black" (Takaki 289). Brown enacts another change; the racialized defiance that lands George in jail is downgraded from insurgency to insolence—from participation in a slave revolt to a refusal to be whipped by his master.[3] While these modifications might seem minor when compared to his wholesale purging of the extratextual documents woven into the first narrative, they nonetheless represent a profound change in the way that Brown represents his primary figure of heroic black masculinity. An act of will replaces insurgency, but elicits the same consequences; revolution, Brown appears to say, can take place on a small scale.

The writer is nevertheless playing it safe. In replacing insurgency with insolence, Brown reconfigures Jerome as a character who does not commit a revolutionary act so implicitly violent that it would risk situating him permanently outside of civil law and evolutionary discourse, and therefore outside the permissible boundaries of domestic sentimentality. A fugitive slave who has run from his master's cruelty can be freely reintegrated into civil society; a fugitive slave who has murdered whites would remain a fugitive for life, even if no longer a slave. Moreover, while Brown and other abolitionists celebrated the San Domingo uprising, whites terrified by the prospect of rebellion in North America pointed to the bloodshed as a sign of black savagery. Ever cognizant of the ways the dominant culture perceived African Americans, Brown might have been reluctant to corroborate theories of the beast lurking within the black. These two significant alterations to the narrative, merging divergent manifestations of African masculinity—the sentimental hero and the black revolutionary—and reducing the gravity of Jerome's rebellion allow the black heroic figure to fulfill two narrative functions. Jerome can participate in the creation of the idealized social imaginary that republican domesticity signifies in the sentimental text and simultaneously represent a fierce blackness, with the implicit threat that messianic blackness carries.

The transformation of Jerome is just one of many changes the writer made in revising *Clotel*. Ironically, Brown, a man of so many "firsts," appeared to delight in seconds and thirds, repeating characters, plots, and passages verbatim from one text to another. And not only did the writer borrow from his own historical publications for the 1867 *Clotelle*; as a basis for a subplot for the 1853 version, he used a panel from the guide to the 1850 panorama he had staged while a fugitive in Britain, *A Description of William Wells Brown's Original Panoramic Views of the Scenes in the Life of An American Slave, From His Birth in Slavery to His Death or His Escape to His Home of Freedom on British Soil* (Levine 306).

That Brown mined his own historical material for his novels is interesting but not especially surprising: historical fiction is inherently a return to prior representation. More compelling is the nature of Brown's returns. We must ask what that echoing might signify within the body of the writer's work, a body filled with echoes. And although it remains true that Brown often repeats without revision, Brown's instances of repetition can be thought of as similar but never as the same. For example, in *Clotel,* Brown includes the part of Andrew Jackson's 1814 address that recommends commendations for blacks who participated in the War of 1812. He embeds the document within a discussion between Mrs. Carlton and her husband, who are debating plans to manumit their slaves. During this discussion, Mrs. Carlton remarks upon the ineffectiveness of Jackson's declaration: "And what did these noble men receive in return for their courage, their heroism? Chains and slavery" (164). Recontextualized and reprinted by Brown in 1867 as part of *The Negro in the American Rebellion,* Jackson's address becomes something else altogether: evidence that Brown offers to argue that white Americans have always understood and valued blacks' contributions to the US military.[4] What is revealed here is, of course, the inherently unstable condition of any text; replaced, the text itself accrues altered meanings. In light of the now familiar poststructuralist argument that "history" is only text, a discursive recreation of "the thing itself," Brown's act—taking a document produced from a historically messy moment and attempting to impose a tidy evolutionary reading on it, beating back previous interpretations with his newer one—shows us how Brown might have approached the writing of America's slave past, not only in *The Negro,* but in his imaginative works as well (especially since Brown insisted on blurring any distinctions between the two).

Brown recognized the instability of both text and interpretation: Jackson's letter, and thus the fruits of black military labor, could read/be read differently in 1853 than in 1867. It follows, then, that in the case of the *Clotel* novels, the writer's compulsion to repeat and re-vise is, in part, an attempt to retroactively ascribe meaning to previous incarnations of the work. Throughout the versions written before 1867, he faithfully adheres to the most significant aspects of the plot of the first *Clotel,* adding more elements, such as the reunion of Clotelle with her slaveholding father, that show Brown anticipating positive historical developments, and in my speculation, anticipating the possibility that he at last might be able to ground Jerome and Clotelle in a stable, integrated home on domestic soil. Each subsequent novel appears as an evolution made along a linear narrative of progress that was moving, if slowly, toward liberation. As an anti-slavery polemicist, Brown's mission had been indisputably clear: to use the medium of the novel as an abolitionist tool. In the tumultuous, contradictory state of the nation in the years immediately following the war, his mission became less certain, and his outlook grew increasingly bleak. The final *Clotelle* registers these psychological and ideological changes, and powerfully so: as the severing of Jerome's head from his torso suggests, the four chapters completing the 1867 publication represent a break from the other narratives that is so drastic that it can only be described as complete.

If the "killing" of Jerome is one marker of the writer's shifting perspective, so, then, are the alterations he makes to his heroine. After the hero's death, the black protagonist who remains in the narrative is the widowed Clotelle, dubbed "the Angel of Mercy" for her ministrations to the suffering. But Brown will not have her take center stage in the narrative. Grief-stricken, Clotelle "withdrew from the gaze of mankind" (106). More than a self-imposed act of mourning within the story, her withdrawal signals Brown's desire to cloak the mulatta body. He takes the "impassioned and voluptuous" form he had described in detail on the first page of the novel, the woman who stood upon an auction block with a crowd "gazing and feasting" upon her, the creature locked in a cell as onlookers "gazed at her" and hides this figure from the audience/spectator (5, 43, 74). Moreover, he has her "pass" for white, as a "rebel lady" in Georgia, then again in Alabama (107, 112). Clotelle hidden, the gaze is reversed as she becomes a spectator to the kind of "repulsive" scene the reader has witnessed in the episode of Jerome's decapitation. In the Georgia hospitals, she sees "emaciated Union prisoners, worn down to skin and bone with disease and starvation, with their sunken eyes and wild looks . . . hideous in the extreme" (107); in Alabama, she is taken in by a black woman whose husband lopped his hand off rather than serve in the Confederate Army. As is true of Brown's other disjointed, episodic, and strange incarnations of this narrative, it is difficult to determine just what Brown is up to. One possible interpretation is that placing the highly-charged (feminized) figure of the mixed race body out of the reader's view, a body already overly determined by the multiple sexual and racial ideologies ascribed to it, allows him to redirect that gaze to the spectacle of disfigured bodies (and nation) produced by war.

While that very well might stand as one interpretive possibility, Brown himself complicates it in *The Negro in the American Rebellion*. It would seem that his historical account of the Civil War—a patchwork of newspaper articles, first hand narratives, rumor, and information from other historians—would be no place to insert the tale of (yet another) beautiful "mulatta" who is part of (yet another) idealized "domestic" union. That, however, is exactly what "The Colored Historian" does. In Chapter 31, Brown addresses the massacre at Fort Pillow, which, because of its vast scope and calculated execution, came to symbolize Confederate atrocities in the war. On April 13, 1864, a group of soldiers led by Nathan Bedford Forrest (who would later found the Ku Klux Klan) entered the Tennessee fort with the intention of slaughter. Although it had been captured already, blacks did not have the option to surrender and were summarily shot; some were "burned alive" (Franklin 216). Although whites were also killed, at least 100 African Americans were murdered, some of whom were women and children. A black New Yorker wrote the Secretary of War, suggesting that black soldiers be allowed to kill an equal number of Confederate prisoners of war (Berlin 465-66). The Union government made the requisite noise about punishing the Confederates, but did nothing. Brown, after including the lengthy and detailed report of the Committee on the Conduct of War on the Fort Pillow Massacre, tags on the story that I abbreviate here:

> When the murderers returned, the day after the capture, to renew their fiendish work upon the wounded and dying, they found a young and beautiful mulatto woman searching among the dead for the body of her husband. She was the daughter of a wealthy and influential rebel residing at Columbus. With her husband, this woman was living near the fort when our forces occupied it, and joined the Union men to assist in holding the place. Going from body to body with all the earnestness with which love could inspire an affectionate heart, she at last found the object of her search. He was not dead; but both legs were broken. The wife had succeeded in getting him out from among the piles of dead, and was bathing his face. . . . At the moment she was seen by this murderous band; and the cry was at once raised, "Kill the wench[!]" The next moment the sharp crack of a musket was heard, and the angel of mercy fell a corpse on the body of her wounded husband, who was soon after knocked in the head by the butt-end of the same weapon.

> (247)

Whether or not this woman's story is true becomes secondary to a greater consideration: why the novelist would insert this overdetermined body into what many historians agree forms the most tragic single episode of the war, particularly since he announces in the preface that faced with abundant information about the Civil War, he "did not feel bound to introduce an account of every little skirmish in which colored men were engaged" (vi). The mulatta figure, however, survives Brown's rigorous selection process to finish off a factual chronicle of carnage. Brown's decision transforms a field of blood into a page straight from a sentimental novel: his own. Like the heroines in the *Clotel* novels, this young woman character is also the daughter of a "wealthy and influential" white father of high society (though not a President nor a senator). And as he does her counterparts, Brown also labels the unnamed heroine of his 1867 text "the angel of mercy." Given these similarities, it seems appropriate to read this war story in relationship to the *Clotel* narratives.

In the era when Brown was writing about the Civil War, the white female body of Columbia functioned as the corporeal symbol of the Republic.[5] Not so for Brown, who embodies the nation in the figure of the mulatta, "the representation of two races" standing for a republic ancestrally linking two racial identities—a symbolism that will become even more important as Harper makes use of this figure in *Iola Leroy* (Brown, *The Black Man* 81). The dual ancestry of the mulatta does not render her a unified ideal; as a figure both black and white in a country divided by race, the biracial female will not live an un-embattled condition until both of her racial identities can co-exist within the boundaries of her nation/body. Thus, despite the manner in which the endings of the novels taken together produce an evolutionary narrative—each revision another cautious step toward freedom—each of the *Clotel* novels also repeatedly defers closure, ending tentatively with the heroine's ultimate fate undetermined.

At the end of the first *Clotel*, written three years after the Fugitive Slave Law was passed, Mary is trapped in Europe with George, unable to come home lest she fall prey to slave catchers. By 1861, when a version of *Clotel* was serialized in *The Weekly Anglo African* under the name *Miralda; or the Beautiful Quadroon: A Romance of American Slavery, Founded on Fact*, the nation had divided over the issue of slavery. Brown closes his novel with a statement voicing his optimism that "in the world to come," equality would reign (Fabi 648). The nation was still warring when *Clotelle, A Tale of the Southern States* was published in 1864; consequently, Brown leaves his heroine safely in Europe, reconciled with her father, who is making plans to free his slaves and to "end his days in the society of his beloved daughter" (Takaki 340). Still recovering from the war in 1867, the "new" nation is under construction, and we find Clotelle correspondingly performing the work of Reconstruction as a schoolteacher in New Orleans.

As idyllic as this scenario might appear, the route that Clotelle has taken home belies any genuine sense of narrative stability or closure. After Clotelle is accused of helping a female Union sympathizer in Alabama, she defiantly announces her allegiance to the North. Clotelle learns from a slave woman that she will be jailed for her offense; the heroine, still passing as white, is whisked away in the dead of night by a black servant, and taken to the cabin home of Jim and Dinah, an embattled black couple with whom Clotelle hides for a week.[6] Brown draws a rather unflattering picture of the U/union that has replaced Clotelle and Jerome's in the narrative. Describing the hero and heroine's state of matrimonial bliss, he writes that "Few unions had been more productive of harmonious feelings" (106); however, this uneducated, unrefined couple bickers incessantly, their fights ending when Jim, who has purchased his wife, threatens to sell her back into enslavement. It is in this "place of concealment," a physically violent space where the folk are unmercifully taunted by slavery, that Clotel reemerges as black, not, as in the other narratives, on a boat sailing safely away from her former position as chattel (114). Reinhabiting her black subjectivity thusly, in the slave cabin, she later purchases the land where she herself once lived in bondage, "where at this writing—now June, 1867—resides the 'Angel of Mercy'" (114). Far from being the end of anything, or even the originary moment leading to a definitive conclusion, Clotelle is still suspended, still in present tense, and still on the geographic terrain of slavery.

The differences between the "close" of this final *Clotelle* and the closure of the story that Brown attaches to the Fort Pillow massacre report further reveal his struggle with interpreting the war in terms of its ability to secure a future for black Americans. In the Fort Pillow narrative, he turns his reader's attention to the mulatta figure's physicality by calling her expressly "a young beautiful mulatto," the very corporeality he subsequently attempts to conceal in the Civil War chapters of *Clotelle*. In addition, while Clotelle, the other "angel of mercy," who, in her capacity as nurse, is positioned as a *spectator* to the "hideous" bodies of Union men, the Fort Pillow "angel" plows through piles of mangled dead and dying bodies and dies herself intermingled with them. The very gruesomeness of the situation that this character (and Brown) encounters necessitates her specific embodiment as a "young beautiful mulatto," a corporeal code that signifies a spiritual and physical fecundity that stands in frank opposition to death.

Five years before *Clotelle, the Colored Heroine* and *The Negro in the American Rebellion* were published, Brown remained sanguine about changes that the Civil War might bring to African American civil life. In 1862, Brown assured members of the New York Branch of the Anti-Slavery Society that freedpeople would prosper—on their own—if permitted "the opportunity to exercise their own physical and mental abilities" (Aptheker

470). Using himself as an example, Brown boasted that he "did not ask society to take me up. . . . All I asked of the white people was, to get out of the way . . ." (470). As Ronald Takaki notes, on the first anniversary of the Emancipation Proclamation, a still forward-looking Brown characterized the war as an opportunity for racial union: "This rebellion will extinguish slavery in our land, and the Negro is henceforth and forever to be a part of the nation. His blood is to mingle with that of his former oppressor, and the two races blended into one will make a more peaceful, hardy race . . . than America has ever seen before" (227). Brown's psyche, shaped by his own mulatto body and its traumatic origins, insists upon a corporeal understanding of nation, so much so that even the unsettling image of black blood spilling into a common stream with his oppressors' proved comforting to the writer. The excess of the mulatta figure's "impassioned and voluptuous" form stands as a less painful version of this liberational paradigm. As a material manifestation of Brown's unwavering faith that "God hath made one blood of all nations for men to dwell on the face of the earth," the bountiful, ripe figure who in Brown's imagination has always been able to bring forth a "hardy" "blended" race without the violence of war symbolizes a nation ready to deliver peacefully the promise of both God and the Republic. Therefore, giving the "angel of mercy" the (re)productive corporeality he later disposes of in the 1867 *Clotelle* enables Brown to present that body as a reminder of that promise. Figuring the "mulatta" dead atop a heap of wounded, or destroyed, black masculinity enables Brown to depict the purposeful and violent slaughter of the promise her body represents. In the same way, a black wife dead atop her prostrate husband figures as Brown's matrimonial ideal.

Indeed, at the point that Brown returns to the mulatta body in *Clotelle,* the tears in his veil of optimism had become visible. It is not the body he had circulated within the first and second versions of *Clotel,* or even in the chapters leading up to the Civil War in the third. Throughout Brown's fiction, this figure's beauty is both asset and detriment; if it causes her to be objectified and coveted by white men, it also rescues her from the auction block and wins her the lifelong devotion of the narrative's black hero. Her beauty is also transcendent. Even when Mrs. Miller, her jealous mistress, chops off her hair to diminish her allure, she still radiates; disguised as a male to escape slavery, her fine "Spanish" looks attract a group of female admirers. Most certainly, her ability to mesmerize was Brown's manner of making her inferior to no white woman, but, as a representative of the miscegenated nation, her comely face parallels the promises of her corporeal excess.

However, in the 1867 *Clotelle,* her beauty is not merely hidden behind masquerades, but permanently extinguished. Brown, who hardly lets a passage about Clotelle pass without remarking on some aspect of her attractiveness, makes not a single mention of it in the Civil War section of the 1867 narrative. The only comment made about Clotelle's physical appearance is Dinah's remark as Clotelle emerges from a storm looking like a "drownd [sic] rat" (112). Brown does not expressly say that this old woman is the same grinning Dinah who conspires with Mrs. Miller in the violent haircutting scene—"'Gins look like a nigger, now'" (40)—but he underscores her name in the novel's concluding chapter: "Dinah," he writes, "for such was her name" (113). In forging this link, Brown highlights the difference in his heroine's "before" and "after" appearance: before and after the Civil War had altered Brown's authorial disposition. In the span of four short chapters, Jerome, the "very fine looking" defiant hero of the antebellum portion of the novel is transformed into a decapitated torso; Clotelle, the "'beautiful quadroon',," into a rodent.

In eradicating mentions of her beauty and cloaking her form, Brown dislocates the mulatta figure from her body; in killing Clotelle's second husband and leaving both her son and her long-lost father abandoned in Europe, he wipes out her family. The noncommittal yet definitely sentimentalized endings of the other *Clotel* works give way to an ending that undercuts domestic sentimentality by refusing the heroine the safety of heteronormative union and family. Attached to no man conjugally and bereft of (patrilineal) blood kin, her primary ties to the domestic narrative have been severed. Brown provides his heroine with an alternative to her previous life of domesticity: a life dedicated to work. The romanticized antidote Brown provides in the part of the novel written before the war stands in stark contrast to the more sober, practical remedy offered in the section written thereafter. This change is explained by the fact that Brown actually has written two very different novels posing as one. The first belongs to the school of sentimentalized abolitionism, invested with moral, social, and civil pedagogical instructives of domesticity; the second is a war narrative, questioning a pedagogy that posits overly simplified answers to problems that grew increasingly complex in postbellum America. Brown apparently realized that neither fictive depictions of black heroism on the battlefield nor idealized representations of black matrimony would effect black equality in real, rather than imagined, worlds.

Brown's four short chapters on the Civil War stand as an important contribution to African American war literature—and an aberration within that tradition—precisely because of what the writer has refused to do.[7] Within war writing in general, the wound serves an essential metaphor, linking physical trauma to the body to the psychological trauma suffered by all whom war has affected, directly and indirectly. The nature of the wound (its site, its severity, its effects on the body's many functions) can be interpreted as an index of the nature of psychic trauma inflicted to other bodies elsewhere, inside and outside of the text: those bodies represented by the particular fleshly incarnation that the writer chooses to depict as assaulted. In this understanding, Jerome's wound, and therefore, the wound to the black body politic, becomes even more severe, for the damage done to his body is not simply severe, but irreversible.

Moreover, before the destructive capabilities of the modern weapons used in the Civil War had made such an injury far too common, a head blown from a body was a relatively unfamiliar form of wounding. This unfamiliarity adds to its symbolic potency: Jerome's decapitation renders anti-black violence appropriately shocking and strange precisely because it is offered to the reader in less recognizable form than, say, the lynching of the unnamed black man that Brown details in the 1853 novel. Adding to the strangeness of the decapitation is its very legal appropriateness, which distinguishes it from the lynching: it is a "civil" war wound, inflicted within the bounds of "civil" law, sanctioned and authorized by a representative of the State. Though Brown sees the General's order as an undeniably deadly racist calculus in which 16 black bodies are "sacrificed" for a single dead white one—described by Brown as inhumane choice—the act hides within the bounds of civil law, becoming, in the rules of war, something other altogether.

Although Brown invests his characters with little interior motivation, we can assume that Jerome's decision to fight for the Union parallels the thousands of black men who did the same. Throughout the history of warfare on the American continent, before even the Revolutionary War "made" a nebulous geography into a nation, African Americans had offered their lives to be recognized as human beings, who in turn deserved to be recognized as citizens. This method of "recognition" is, of course, ironic: not simply because of its seeming futility, but because of what a body becomes in violent death—unrecognizable in relation to what it was before. Elaine Scarry argues that a civilization embeds itself in the body; a handshake, a gait, a wave are signs of that civilization carried within an individual human form. The inherent contradiction in the concept of "dying for one's country" lies within the radical deconstruction of the body slain on a battlefield. When "the chest is shattered," the nation is emptied from the body; "the civilization as it resides" in the body is unmade (122). Any notion of the Republic inside of Jerome's form exited through his headless neck.

Even if we reject Scarry's theory, the idea that postbellum African American war literature might repeat Brown's narrative—resulting in works full of black bodies "dying" for their country—is nevertheless disconcerting. The desire to be recognized as a citizen expresses one's desire to be considered a "speaking subject" rather than an object spoken "for." Drawing energy from Benedict Anderson's reading of the rise of French nationalism, Sharon Holland makes a simple but significant observation: "The ability of the emerging nation to speak hinges on its correct use of the 'dead' in the service of its creation" (28). A dead body very quickly surrenders its agency (hence, for example, the note attached to a suicidal body in an effort to ensure the "meaning" of its death). Anderson's analysis itself examines how one of the more influential French historians of the eighteenth century, Jules Michelet, reads the bodies of those who died in the violence of the French Revolution. Speaking *for* them, as Anderson notes, on their behalf, Michelet pronounces them sacrifices in making the French nation although "these sacrifices were not understood as such by the victim" (198). In a similar manner, Brown speaks for his construct (Jerome's dead form), but not as a mouthpiece for the State. When Brown labels Jerome both a "hero" and a "sacrifice" to the General's inhumanity, he disrupts the post-war official language that tended to speak of dead black Union bodies as uniformly "heroic" (in the same leveling way that nations honor *all* of their soldiers as "heroic"), a language that failed to acknowledge the specificity of what it meant for a black body to fight and die in the war: a language that did not, in effect, endeavor to ascertain what a black body might say from the grave.

While Brown's decision to represent Jerome as injured and killed raises many intriguing questions—possibly more interesting than if this character had lived—after Brown, graphic, specific depictions of the wounded black male body and representations of the grotesque will virtually disappear until the middle of the twentieth century.[8] Given the powerful link between corporeal and psychic wounding, the presentation of a physically damaged black male body, the body Brown willingly describes, poses a political and social risk to African American writers. Within the black masculinist war novel in particular, African American male writers accept the (live) body Brown derives from Douglass and Delany, to construct a brown-skinned, full-bodied, vigorous soldier-citizen—a "manly" black self—who refutes the dominant culture's feminized construction of the black male body as degraded, passive, and weak.[9] This newer model of black masculinity is fueled by the necessity of imagining a body poised to represent the black body politic, a masculine preserve, in its quest for citizenship rights.[10]

The reluctance to depict violence to the black male body in the black American war novel, a public text, responds in part to a historical legacy of routinized torture and mutilation of the black body. The black body

objectified and diminishing before their very eyes constituted a transformational power of violence that whites could witness. As many historians have documented, photographs of lynchings were routinely mailed and traded as postcards, and severed black body parts displayed as trophies. Earlier, anti-slavery activists had depended on displays and photographs of the scarred and deformed black body to provide material evidence of the barbarity of slavery; anti-slavery literature offered its literary equivalent. Even if the use of the wounded body in anti-slavery efforts asked on-lookers and readers to gaze not too long upon the body itself, but instead to turn that gaze upon the spectral image refracted by the body—in other words, the slaveholder—the wounded black form was intended to linger in audiences' minds, that ocular lingering necessary for arousing a desire for change. The risk of specularity is apparent: the body is at risk of being imagined in a permanent state of damage or injury. The absence of the wound in novels after Brown's can be read therefore as an attempt to shield the violated black male body from the gaze of the spectator-audience.

In comparing the issue of injury in African American war literature to anti-slavery literature (and also anti-lynching literature), the very source of the infliction further complicates the meaning of the wound for these writers, as Brown's work aptly demonstrates. If violence to the enslaved or lynched body can be read as "unjust" and "non-consensual," the injury stemming from battle resists similar cultural interpretation, particularly as many of the wounded men who *are* depicted in African American war literature volunteer to place themselves in a position where their bodies might be readily deformed or destroyed. The involuntary wound, in other words, was efficiently mobilized in a "useful" capacity. The symbolic potential of the voluntarily, "consensually" disfigured or disabled black body produced by war has less accusative power in a tradition of war literature that is very much accusatory, operating in the same vein as anti-slavery literature: as evidence of the dominant culture's unwillingness to extend to African Americans civil and human rights. Thus the brilliance of Brown's decapitation of Jerome—his "civil" war wound(ing)—lies in the writer's successful elision of the differences between non-consensual and consensual injury, between slavery and war, allowing the wound to exist somewhere between the voluntary sacrifice of battle and the involuntary injury inflicted by the oppressor.

Protective domesticity, the second element that Brown rejects in his war narrative, returns when Harper, who borrows as freely from Brown as he does from himself, reconstructs the ending of Brown's 1867 *Clotelle* in her 1892 novel *Iola Leroy*. While Harper's Iola, like Clotelle, chooses a public life of work, Harper will rebuild for her the domestic structure Brown has dismantled, constructing correct black marriages as political unions stronger than the reconstituted nation itself. The idea of black matrimony as the basis of civilization and a politically committed union as "the consummation" of the couple's "desire" to be racially rather than sexually engaged will dominate the African American literature of that period (Tate 125). Harper will follow those literary edicts, even as she strives to write about war.

Notes

1. In my larger project, I argue that the "concerned abolitionist/commander" is a characterization that allows Harper and Taylor to invest Union officers with anti-slavery sentiments when such sentiments were certainly not always the case historically. See Taylor.

2. I am indebted in this article to M. Guilia Fabi's work on the *Clotel* novels.

3. See Bentley.

4. Brown introduces this document just 10 pages into his work as part of a chapter on blacks who served in the Revolutionary War. He precedes it with Jackson's first 1814 letter imploring free blacks to participate in the 1812 conflict. "That colored men were equally serviceable in the last war with Great Britain is true," Brown writes, "as the following historical document will show" (9). The first letter, addressed to the "Free Coloured Inhabitants of Louisiana," promises black men who volunteer "the same in bounty, in money and lands, now received by the white soldiers of the United States . . ." and freedom from "unjust sarcasm" (9). The second address, given three months later, lauds their service: "The President of the United States shall be informed of your conduct on the present occasion; and the voice of the Representatives of the American nation shall applaud your valor . . ." (11). The exact wording of both speeches varies according to source; William Cooper Nell's citation in *Services of Colored Americans in the Wars of 1776 and 1812* (1851) differs from Brown's.

5. For one of many works that read this figure, see Warner.

6. Reid-Pharr offers a similar reading of Clotelle's racial reinterpellation and the significance of Jim and Dinah to the 1867 *Clotelle* in *Conjugal Union: The Body, the House and the Black American.*

7. To argue that there is a discernable "tradition" of black war writing, I trace many recurring elements found within African American war writing to William Nell's expansion of the aforementioned 1851

Services of Colored Americans, Colored Patriots of the American Revolution (1855), the first full length history of black participation in warfare. I demonstrate how the greater part of African American autobiography, fiction, and poetry written before the desegregation of the military in 1948 echoes Nell's concerns: establishing a corrective public military history inclusive of blacks; narrating acts of black patriotism and valor to show that blacks are fit for full and equal enfranchisement; and finally, using the nationalist discourses of liberation that accompany American warfare to argue for citizenship rights. Moreover, a shift occurs in black American literature written after the Vietnam War, as African Americans question the usefulness of warfare as a political tool and the military as a means of social advancement and civic inclusion. While American war literature has long been analyzed, even those wide-sweeping generic considerations of literature such as Wayne Charles Miller's *Armed in America: Its Face in Fiction,* John Limon's *Writing After War* (1994), and Helen Cooper, Adrienne Auslander Munich, and Susan Merill Squire's collection of essays, *Arms and the Woman* (1989) generally have ignored war writing by black Americans. Some critics have analyzed a few pre-Vietnam texts—Susan Schweick's and Ann Folwell Stanford's insightful analyses of Gwendolyn Brooks's war poetry (*A Gulf So Deeply Cut: American Women Poets and the Second World War,* 1991; "Dialectics of Desire: War and Resistive Voice in Gwendolyn Brooks's 'Negro Hero' and 'Gay Chaps at the Bar,'" 1992), J. L. Greene's brief analysis of African American WWI fiction in *Blacks in Eden: The African American Novel's First Century* (1996). There have been, of course, numerous analyses of Chester Himes's brilliant homefront novel *If He Hollers Let Him Go* (1945). However, black literary war content has been sidelined in favor of other critical perspectives. For instance, before Elizabeth Young's extensive treatment of *Iola Leroy* in her book on American women war writers, *Disarming America, Women's Writing and the American Civil War* (2000), Harper's work had been studied primarily as an early effort in the African American novel, usually within the framework of black women's sentimental fiction. In *The American Soldier in Fiction 1880-1963,* Peter Aichinger offers a useful definition of the war novel that extends the genre beyond depictions of the battlefield proper, arguing that the war novel is "any long work of fiction in which the lives and actions of the characters are principally affected by warfare or the military establishment" (6). By this definition, a work such as Harper's *Iola Le-*

roy, which features very few battle scenes, can be considered a work of war. For a recent analysis of the collection by Helen Cooper, et al., see Ernest.

8. For instance, in *Iola Leroy* Harper references two black male soldiers' respective wounds, and even calls one "severe," but she does not attempt to describe them. Each wound remains dislocated, unanchored, abstract, and therefore materially separate from the black body that it should "realistically" mark. Gwendolyn Brooks's sonnet sequence "Gay Chaps at the Bar" in *A Street in Bronzeville* (1945) marks a turning point in the black war tradition, purposefully, presenting psychologically and physically disabled bodies in a set of poems that arguably assert an anti-war ideology.

9. The black masculinist war novel's main concern is to present the black soldier-citizen as the epitome of manliness: honorable, ethical, powerful, and sexual. Although the first masculinist war novel I have been able to identify, F. Grant Gilmore's *The Problem: A Military Novel* (1915), wavers between conventions of sentimentalism and conventions of realism, the works in this tradition mark the African American war novel's break from sentimental discourse. Most of these novels include depictions of the "front." The front generally operates in two ways: first, it adds a dimension of realism; secondly, it serves as a backdrop against which the black soldier-citizen can demonstrate his patriotism, and more significantly, his manhood. The novels invariably include a white antagonist, generally a superior officer who, through intense racial provocation, tests the soldier's commitment to military principles, and by extension, his commitment to the nation that he has sworn to protect. The heterosexual love plot becomes less about imaginings domestic-sentimental notions of "civility" (as in the black sentimental war novel) than about reaffirming denied masculinities. The pre-Vietnam war versions of these novels include Gilmore's work on The Spanish-Cuban-American Wars and the Wars against the Philippines, Victor Daly's 1932 novel *Not Only War: A Story of Two Great Conflicts* (WWI), William Gardner Smith's 1948 book *Last of the Conquerors* (WWII), and John Oliver Killens's 1962 epic *And Then We Heard the Thunder* (WWII).

10. Thus Harper must "kill off" the slave-martyr Tom, who, while "Herculean" in his strength, cannot enlist as a soldier because of his unnamed "physical defects" (40). His defective body arguably unfits him to represent the evolved black masculinity that Harper fashions for a post-slavery political milieu. A physically "disabled" body is a politically "disabled" one as well.

Works Cited

Aichinger, Peter. *The American Soldier in Fiction 1880-1963.* Ames: Iowa State UP, 1975.

Anderson, Benedict. *Imagined Communities: Reflection on the Origins and Spread of Nationalism.* New York: Verso, 1991.

Aptheker, Herbert. *A Documentary History of the Negro People in the United States,* Vols. 1-5. New York: Carol P, 1990.

Bentley, Nancy. "White Slaves: The Mulatto Hero in Antebellum Fiction." *Subjects and Citizens: Nation, Race, and Gender from* Oroonko *to Anita Hill.* Eds. Michael Moon and Cathy Davidson. Durham: Duke UP, 1995. 195-218.

Berlin, Ira. *Free At Last: A Documentary History of Slavery, Freedom and the Civil War.* New York: New P, 1992.

Brown, William Wells. *The Black Man, His Antecedents, His Genius, His Achievements.* New York: Thomas Hamilton, 1863. 11 Sept. 2000 <http://metalab.unc.edu./docsouth/brown.html>.

———. *Clotel, or the President's Daughter: A Narrative Life in the United States.* New York: Carol, 1995.

———. *Clotelle; or The Colored Heroine. A Tale of the Southern States.* Miami: Mnemosyne P, 1969.

———. *The Negro in the American Rebellion: His Heroism and His Fidelity.* Miami: Mnemosyne P, 1969.

Burke, Kenneth. *On Symbols and Society.* Chicago: U of Chicago P, 1989.

Ernest, John. *Liberation Historiography: African American Writers and the Challenge of History, 1794-1861.* Chapel Hill: U of North Carolina P, 2004.

Fabi, M. Guilia. "The 'Unguarded Expressions of the Feelings of the Negros': Gender, Slave Resistance, and William Wells Revisions of *Clotel,*" *African American Review* 27 (1993): 639-54.

Franklin, John Hope, and Alfred A. Moss, Jr. *From Slavery to Freedom: A History of African Americans.* New York: McGraw Hill, 1994.

Harper, Frances E. W. *Iola Leroy, Or Shadows Uplifted.* New York: Oxford UP, 1990.

Holland, Sharon. *Raising the Dead: Readings of Death and (Black) Subjectivity.* Durham: Duke UP, 2000.

Levine, Robert, ed. *Clotel, or the President's Daughter.* New York: Bedford/St. Martin's, 2000.

Mullane, Deidre. *Crossing the Danger Water: Three Hundred Years of African-American Writing.* New York: Doubleday, 1993.

Reid-Pharr, Robert. *Conjugal Union: The Body, the House and The Black American.* New York: Oxford UP, 1999.

Scarry, Elaine. *The Body in Pain: The Making and Unmaking of the World.* New York: Oxford UP, 1985.

Takaki, Ronald. *Violence and the African American Literary Imagination.* New York: Oxford UP, 1992.

Tate, Claudia. *Domestic Allegories of Political Desire.* New York: Oxford UP, 1992.

Taylor, Susie King. *Reminiscences of My Life in Camp with the 33d United States Colored Troops Late 1ˢᵗ S. C. Volunteers.* 1902. *Collected Black Women's Narratives.* Ed Anthony Barthelmy. New York: Oxford UP, 1988.

Warner, Marina. *Monuments and Maidens: The Allegory of the Female Form.* Berkeley: U of California P, 1985.

Yarborough, Richard. "Race, Violence and Manhood: The Masculine Ideal in Frederick Douglass's 'The Heroic Slave.'" *Haunted Bodies: Gender and Southern Texts.* Eds. Anne Goodwyn Jones and Susan V. Donaldson. Charlottesville: UP of Virginia, 1997. 159-84.

Jennifer Terry (essay date summer 2007)

SOURCE: Terry, Jennifer. "'When Dey 'Listed Colored Soldiers': Paul Laurence Dunbar's Poetic Engagement with the Civil War, Masculinity, and Violence." *African American Review* 41, no. 2 (summer 2007): 269-75.

[*In the following essay, Terry demonstrates how in his poetry treating the Civil War, Paul Laurence Dunbar "gives extraordinary voice to African American experiences, positions, and protests."*]

Paul Laurence Dunbar's poetic treatment of the Civil War and its legacies explores heroism, patriotism, citizenship, death, mourning, and trauma. In reflecting on the war, considered a worthy and elevated national theme, the author found an acceptable yet powerful way to set black suffering alongside white, to testify to African American contributions and sacrifices, to figure a form of haunting bound up with the sin of racial slavery, and to pass comment on the disappointments and abuses of the post-Reconstruction era. Through readings of the poems, "When Dey 'Listed Colored Soldiers," "The Colored Soldiers," "The Unsung Heroes," "Robert Gould Shaw," and "The Haunted Oak," with particular attention to gender construction and imagery of vio-

lence, this analysis will demonstrate how Dunbar gives extraordinary voice to African American experiences, positions, and protests.[1]

The preoccupation of the Civil War may seem a strange one for an African American poet writing in the North in the 1890s and early 1900s. Yet, this topic enables Dunbar to enter into dialogue with prior literary representations and, with varying degrees of success, to form a critique of contemporary racial injustices. Composed against a backdrop of rising anti-black violence and the widespread collapse and reversal of political and legal gains made by African Americans during the post-war period, Dunbar's poetry might be considered alongside the turn of the century prose interventions of Frances E. W. Harper, Pauline Hopkins, and W. E. B. Du Bois.[2] In different ways, these works address questions of black identity, uplift, and self-determination in light of the legacies of slavery and the Civil War. Yet in his revisitation of the national conflict, Dunbar, too, looks to earlier European American poetic engagements with war to shape his own voicing.[3] Whether in dialect or standard English, the verse under consideration here works to reaffirm the Civil War as inextricably tied up with racial oppression, thus distancing itself from nostalgic reflections on the Lost Cause of the South, and to build a case for the equal claim of African Americans to belonging and liberty in the here and now.

The subjects of slavery and the Civil War are treated explicitly in the dialect poem "When Dey 'Listed Colored Soldiers" (Dunbar, *Collected* 182-84). Here Dunbar creates the powerful first-person voice of an enslaved black woman whose beloved, 'Lias, joins the Union army to fight for freedom. The poem parallels white and black experiences of war, in large part, through an exploration of racial identity and fitness to fulfil dominant gender roles. Indeed, in this instance, gendered behaviors and codes are key to the claim to African American citizenship and full personhood. While the form of "When Dey 'Listed Colored Soldiers" consists of regular long lines and rhyming couplets, it also relies on a familiar and black vernacular voicing that lends to the crafting of the warmth and humanity of the speaker.

The poem's narrative sequence takes us from 'Lias's enlistment and departure to battle, through the experiences of the women left behind—both black and white—and to their responses to loss and mourning. The repeated line "W'en dey 'listed colo'ed sojers" (ll. 16, 24, 40) centers our attention on the decision to let blacks join the Union ranks during the Civil War. Simultaneously, it makes us aware of their previous exclusion from the fighting forces, the white perception of their unreliability both with arms and in the face of danger, and also the non-admittance of African American men into a particular mode of masculinity. 'Lias's enlistment hence signals both a pressing desire to obtain liberty for his people and entry into a male military sphere bound up with ideals of honor, duty (it is the slave's "conscience" that calls him), strength, valor, and sacrifice for a noble cause. 'Lias wishes to fight "For de freedom dey had gin him an' de glory of de right" (l. 12), but his pride, and the speaker's, is tied up with his uniformed and parading appearance: "so strong an' mighty in his coat o' sojer blue" (l. 22). This pride is indicative of newly marshalled masculine attributes including bravery and physical power as well as efficient participation in a disciplined and regulatory order perceived as very different from that of slavery. The significance of this induction is reinforced by the speaking persona's emotional and bolstering cry of "Step up, manny." Her later drawing of an equivalence between the departure of her Confederate master and that of 'Lias dismantles the racial hierarchy of the time which, in conjunction with dominant gender constructions, opposed the emasculation and animalization of black men to a model of white male control, honor, and patriarchal potency. The fate of 'Lias, laid to rest in southern soil "wid de flag dat he had fit for shinin' daih acrost his breast" (l. 38), confirms his place as war hero, his alignment with a suitable form of US nationalism and, perhaps most importantly for Dunbar here, his rightful claim to full citizenship, if before doubted or unrecognized, now proven by his sacrifice.

Another key focus of the poem is the speaker's own position and identity as a black female, which is explored in relation to white womanhood as represented by the Mistress and her daughter. Dunbar juxtaposes their respective experiences of loss when male partners or relatives leave to fight in the war. In women of both races, we find a mixture of pride and grief at their men's enlistment and an emphasis on the capacity for true feeling. When the Master and his son first leave, despite her expression of sympathy, the slave woman is denied understanding of her white superiors' distress. She herself can only speculate on the women's emotions: "dey only *seemed* mo' proudah" (l. 28; emphasis mine) and she is informed that, as a slave, she cannot fully empathize: "I didn't know dey feelin's is de ve'y wo'ds dey say" (l. 26).[4] When 'Lias enters into a masculinized role as combatant and hero, however, the black woman, too, enacts conventionally gendered behaviors, promising to be true in a sentimental farewell, enduring his absence as a kind of martyrdom with a stricken heart and eventually weeping and mourning at the passing of her "loved un." Now the loss of the dead, whether Confederate or Union, is felt "thoo an' thoo" (l. 35).

If here we witness the speaker gaining access to a sphere of feminine empathy, right feeling, and suffering that contests the view of slaves as lacking human sensitivity or fully realized interpersonal bonds, Dunbar perhaps goes further, positioning her as possessing a more comprehensive and refined capacity for understanding than the featured representatives of white womanhood. Her simple and sincere voice contributes to the heartfelt nature of the poetic enunciation just as the persona's cry to her soldier is all the more choked and charged with emotion as it comes from a throat "so' an' raw" (l. 23).[5] The poem concludes with the black woman's compassion for her Mistress's loss, an apparently unreciprocated response, and this subversive ascendancy to a contemporary feminine ideal is furthered by a gracious grief that can accommodate, even take solace in, renunciation of a beloved in the service of a greater cause framed as both patriotic and religious: "whut Gawd had called him for" (l. 39). While the burial of 'Lias with the respect due a military hero stands in favorable contrast to the roadside abandonment of young Ned's body and the shameful return of the Master, "broke for life," the speaker's closing empathy and ennobled feeling elevates her above the limited sensitivity of the mourning white women.

We thus find the subject of the Civil War enabling Dunbar to validate and assert black American identity, albeit through rather narrowly defined gender codes. This recourse to the masculine and feminine qualities privileged within the patriarchy of the time can be seen as a powerful, if for today's readership compromised, strategy. Not only do such compositions as "When Dey 'Listed Colored Soldiers" prompt a re-evaluation of the writer's work in the light of western traditions of war poetry, but they also express a register of discontent at injustice, forming an important part of his wider, and increasingly recognised, legacy as a protest poet.

The preoccupation with the participation of ex-slaves in the Civil War and the concomitant celebration of black male bravery can be further witnessed in the two longer poems "The Colored Soldiers" and "The Unsung Heroes" (Dunbar, *Collected* 50-52, 196-98). In both, Dunbar rejects dialect for a more standard voicing on the need for song to commemorate hitherto unacknowledged heroic deeds and selfless sacrifice. The earlier poem, "The Colored Soldiers," employs a first person speaker suggestive of Dunbar himself. While this speaker is aligned with African American identity, his use of direct address throughout implies a white audience being held to account, for example, of black volunteers commenting, "In the early days *you* scorned them" (l. 9; emphasis mine). Recounting the initial dismissal of a black role in "the white man's [battles]," the subsequent "distress" of "the nation," the vigorous response of "the colored soldiers" to the eventual Union call and "the life blood of their thousands" spent to obtain freedom, the poem can be read as a straightforward paean of praise. Yet Dunbar incorporates in the tribute a forceful cry for contemporary recognition and equality as well as subtle constructions of color and masculinity.

"The Colored Soldiers" appears to establish a familiar symbolic opposition between darkness and light, that is between polluting dust, the "funeral pall" of war and "the depths of slavery's night," and the illumination of day and freedom: "Their muskets flashed the dawning, / And they fought their way to light" (ll. 55-56). Yet the poem's imagery proves more complex and invokes a second somewhat different opposition between color, here associated with African American identity, and whiteness. The actual word "white" is used only in the second stanza in the context of blindness to the potential of black troops. Color, in contrast, is implicitly present in the flags, banners, and standards under threat of being dulled by dust and defeat, in the skin of the African American forces themselves and in the fiery imagery of battle ("blazing breach," "hot wrought spirits," and so on). In addition, the use of "unblanched" in the fourth stanza to describe the black soldiers' bravery works powerfully in the poem, linking color with male valor and paleness, even white identity, with fading, fear and perhaps also a rather feminized form of weakness.[6] This association inverts, if only temporarily, dominant codifications of manhood and race and the final flushed color imagery of blood that has "cleansed completely / Every blot of Slavery's shame" (ll. 73-74) further disrupts expectations as bloodshed causes not a dark stain but rather washes away the mark of the oppressive white institution. Dunbar's call for racial equality gains force also from an unusual invocation of the "commingling" of blood, perhaps more commonly associated with the taint and threat of miscegenation, yet here forming a part of a patriotic vision of interracial brotherhood on the battlefield.[7] Indeed, the speaker argues that having shared ordeals and losses during the war, having once ranked as "citizens and soldiers," surely blacks have earned civil rights and recognition in the post-war period.[8] He pointedly asks, presumably of a white northern audience, "They were comrades then and brothers, / Are they more or less today?" (ll. 57-58) thus rendering this "song heroic" of unequivocal and provocative contemporary relevance.[9]

"The Unsung Heroes" from the outset poses itself as a revisionary voicing for the unacknowledged "who rose in the country's need" (l. 1). Like "The Colored Soldiers," this poem foregrounds black agency, courage, and blood sacrifice during the war, in particular focusing on the proof of previously doubted manhood. Indeed, observing combatants' actions and "might," God is said to have pronounced, "I have made them men." Racial pride is found in mention of the soldiers' "sinews brown" and in the rekindling of "the old free fires of their savage sires," an image that suggests the rediscovery of the spirit and bravery of their unenslaved African ancestors.[10] Such affirmation and the wishing of "hate of race . . . obsolete" keep injustices against black Americans to the front of this engagement with the Civil War. This poem, however, lacks the more radi-

cal gesture regarding contemporary inequality located in "The Colored Soldiers." Here the leap from the bygone conflict to Dunbar's own day is not as effectively achieved as the past tense predominates and it is left to the following war poem to contest, through bitter condemnation, continuing prejudice.

Dunbar's sonnet "Robert Gould Shaw" can be fruitfully read alongside a wider body of American poetry that pays tribute to the heroic dead of the Civil War and sometimes to Shaw himself (Dunbar, *Collected* 221).[11] For the purposes of this essay, however, I will focus on Dunbar's movement from the past conflict to contemporary disappointments. As already observed, with its direct address and shift from "then" to "today," "The Colored Soldiers" offers a more forceful critique than "The Unsung Heroes." "Robert Gould Shaw" initially presents a rather oblique approach, at length asking of Shaw himself why he left "the classic groves" of academia "To lead th' unlettered and despised droves / To manhood's home and thunder at the gate?" (ll. 7-8). Such formulations obviously return us to issues of degradation and of race and gender. In the second stanza, however, war is figured in a less allegorical and more violently disturbing manner as the "hot terror of a hopeless fight" (l. 11). The efforts and sacrifices of the Union soldiers "for right" were, "the Present teaches, but in vain!" (l. 14). The poem thus articulates a bitter sense of failure that undercuts previous evocations of glory. This bleak vision parallels that of the speaker of Melville's earlier "Lee in the Capitol," who considers a post-war "desolted land" and "harvest large of doubt and dread" (ll. 114, 119): "A voice comes out from these charnel-fields, / A plaintive yet unheeded one: / 'Died all in vain? both sides undone'" (ll. 133-35). However, while here the tragedy is ongoing division and "rancor" between North and South, in Dunbar's work the disappointment lies in continuing racial oppression, even after the devastating sacrifices of the conflict. In "Robert Gould Shaw" we also find an elliptical timeframe as the "hopeless fight" of the war is described as *this* hot terror," "*This* . . . endurance" (ll. 11, 12; emphasis mine), so eroding the distance between the struggles of the earlier national strife and those of the here and now. Such an effect is reinforced by the use of the formulation "Have died" rather than died; Shaw and his men, Dunbar suggests, have given their lives in an ongoing and seemingly futile war. This construction marks out somewhat different territory to previously discussed celebrations of black service, offering a bleaker portrait of waste and a lack of victorious resolution or social change.[12] The address to a deceased white soldier rather than contemporary communities is perhaps of significance in this, Dunbar feeling compelled neither to present a message of hope and pride nor to rebuff charges of African American inferiority. The expressed continuity between the antebellum and postbellum situations is picked up by my final poetic selection.

In "The Haunted Oak," Dunbar employs the ballad form to treat the theme of lynching (Dunbar, *Collected* 219-20). It is my contention that, through imagery of suffering and rift originating from the Civil War, the issue of anti-black violence, painfully significant to African Americans in the 1890s, is tied up with a shameful *national* heritage and responsibility. Here we find the racial tensions and abuses of the post-Reconstruction era explored through the powerful figure of a damaged roadside oak tree. The poem's construction involves a complex layering of voicings and addresses that renders a movement from the particular to a more widely shared form of trauma and haunting. In spite of not explicitly confronting civil conflict, "The Haunted Oak" hence does handle the legacies of slavery and of aggressive division within US society.

The central image of the poem is that of the withered bough from which an innocent man was strung up by vigilantes. Although the text employs few overt racial markers, we are told that the "guiltless victim" was "charged . . . with the old, old crime" (ll. 8, 13), a phrase which, within the loaded lexicon of race relations in America, implies his alleged rape, as a black man, of a white woman. The persecutory nature of the hanging is reinforced by the perpetrators' circumvention of the law and heartless laughter. Even more provocative perhaps on Dunbar's part is the exposure of the lynchers as figures of authority and responsibility within the white community, as "the judge," "the doctor," and "the minister" (who, in bringing along "his oldest son," completes the image of the masked riders as the four horsemen of the apocalypse).

The forceful effect of "The Haunted Oak" is achieved through several mechanisms, including recourse to notions of the uncanny and the evocation of physical sensation and bodily disruption. The oak is a gothic site bearing the ongoing "curse" of a past atrocity, a marker of violence and death still imbued with the power to trouble and disturb. Indeed, the tree itself is encoded with history as it bears witness to the final terror and pain experienced by the wronged man. This witness is wrought through a kind of substitution or equation of corporeal forms as the oak, and in particular the bough used in the hanging, not only "feel[s]" the abrasion of the rope against its "bark" as if against skin, but also shudders with the victim's "gurgling moan" and last "throe" as "The touch of [its] own last pain" (ll. 53, 14, 55, 56). With such sensitivity, the branch becomes "bare," "burned with dread . . . dried and dead" (ll. 1, 59). The figure of the tree thus does not merely stand as a haunted gallows site, but actually speaks to the physical sensation and damage suffered, so emblematizing a more broadly shared wound. Indeed, the withered bough offers an analogy for the cleft and injured post-Civil War nation, most famously envisioned in Lincoln's second inaugural address.[13] The death on the oak of an innocent black man loosely refigures the Crucifixion and perhaps also echoes Melville's suggestive poem about the execution of anti-slavery campaigner and insurrectionist John Brown, "The Portent": "Hanging from the beam, / . . . Gaunt the shadow on your green, / . . . The meteor of the war" (ll. 1, 3, 14). The central image of the tree itself feeling and remembering, too, echoes Melville's "Malvern Hill," in which the local elms recall the violence and losses of this Civil War engagement.[14]

Key to the movement from an individual tragedy to a shared curse or affliction in "The Haunted Oak" is the question of voice. For most of the poem, the oak tree itself speaks in the first person, relating the incident and consequences of the lynching. Within this voicing is the reported speech of the lynchers, who use "lying words" to poach the victim from jail. This example of deception through language throws into relief the oak tree's own unusual but presumably more reliable telling; its account, unlike those of the judge, doctor and minister, can be trusted and, through shared feeling, a process of substitution, can give voice to the experiences of the now silenced. The tree's enunciation, however, is first prompted by the enquiry of yet another speaker in the opening stanza. This persona is a passer-by who, having addressed the tree about its damaged bough, becomes the tree's addressee in the telling of the tale. In the final stanza, the poem returns to this speaker, who has himself been affected by the story of the blighted oak; this time, however, he addresses not the tree, but an implied wider audience that includes the reader. This voicing constitutes a rhetorical device that renders complicit and haunted an entire nation and is backed up by further bodily equation.

As established, the tree feels the suffering of the lynched man, but his "weight," surely representative of the burden of the crime, is also borne by the oak and, in addition, the perpetrators. In an image that calls up distinctly black diasporic belief systems such as voodoo or candomblé, we are told of the judge "ever another *rides* his soul / In the guise of a mortal fear" (ll. 55-56; emphasis mine). The judge is possessed, dragged down by the spirit of his victim, the verb "to ride" also referring back to the aforementioned vengeful four horsemen. The significance of this reference becomes yet clearer when the framing persona, he who has heard the tree's story, in conclusion says that "ever the man he rides *me* hard / . . . I *feel* his curse *as* a haunted bough, / On the trunk of a haunted tree" (ll. 57, 59-60; emphasis mine). Here the listener takes on the rider of the lyncher, the burden of the oak; he, too, shares in the "curse," becoming a substitute body in bearing such a load. The gesture is completed when readers realize that as fellow listeners to the poem, like the tree's addressee, they may have to assume the weight of past wrongs.[15] This device alone implies wider complicity, but the suggestion is reinforced by the extended metaphor of the damaged oak, presenting an image of the wounded nation riven by the blight of slavery and war and still feeling, still "burned" by the painful and haunting effects.[16]

The subject of the Civil War is a recurring one for Dunbar and one that opens up a significant space for black voicing and critique shaping. Some of the poems I have considered are based on the drawing out of parallels, whether that be how the bravery, sacrifice, and masculine aggression of black soldiers, although often unacknowledged, equalled that of whites or, in the case of "When Dey 'Listed Colored Soldiers," how keenly felt loss elevates the humble speaker to a dominant feminine ideal. Such sharing of experience, then, often provides a foundation for the call for contemporary equality, recognition, and citizenship. In the case of "The Colored Soldiers" and "Robert Gould Shaw," this call is reinforced by the clever use of address and shifts in tense. "The Haunted Oak," while exploring the theme of postbellum violence, involves the reader in past injustice, through corporeal substitution and layered articulations that recall national strife and imply a form of shared haunting and guilt. Dunbar's poetic engagements revisit earlier literary representations of the Civil War, pointedly keeping to the fore African American experience and enabling concomitant celebration, affirmation, mourning, and bitter recrimination. As Shelley Fisher Fishkin has observed, "Slavery was being erased from the story being told about why the Civil War was fought" and Dunbar's writing, and indeed this reading, works to counter such silences (284).

Notes

1. Further study might also encompass "Ode for Memorial Day," "Dirge for a Soldier," "Black Samson of Brandywine," "The Conquerors: The Black Troops in Cuba," and "Lincoln."

2. I am thinking of the politically aware romance novels *Iola Leroy* (1893) and *Contending Forces* (1900), by Harper and Hopkins, respectively, and Du Bois's provocative cultural and sociological study *The Souls of Black Folk* (1903).

3. The handling of division and loss in the poetry of Walt Whitman and Herman Melville provides an illuminating point of reference here.

4. This is reinforced by the lines, "But I t'ought dat I could sorrer for de losin' of 'em too, / But I couldn't, for I didn't know de ha'f o' whut I saw" (ll. 30-31).

5. The individualized depiction of black womanhood found here provides a counterpoint to that within,

for example, Whitman's "Ethiopia Saluting the Colors" from his 1865 volume of war poetry, *Drum-Taps* (Whitman 343).

6. The ferocity of the troops is also reinforced by a metaphor of, in this case apparently positively weighted, animality: "like hounds unleashed and eager." This Image recalls "the dogs of war" of Shakespeare's *Julius Caesar* (III.I).

7. The "life blood" of both blacks and whites has soaked into and enriched the soil of the South.

8. Dunbar here establishes a very different perspective from that found in Melville's *Battle Pieces* (1866). In "A Meditation," for example, in pleading for the reconciliation of white kinsmen from the North and South, Melville has them together ask: "Can Africa pay back this blood / Spilt on Potomac's shore?" (ll. 21-22).

9. For further readings of "The Colored Soldiers," see Braxton xix-xx and Leonard 71-75.

10. Such "sinews brown" might recall Whitman's lines from "Eighteen Sixty-One": "Saw I your gait and saw I your sinewy limbs clothed in blue, bearing / weapons, robust year" (ll. 19-20).

11. Most obviously, "Ode to the Union Dead," by James Russell Lowell (1865), "Ode to the Confederate Dead," by Allen Tate (1928), and, more recently, "For the Union Dead," by Robert Lowell (1960). It has been examined with other black authored poems dedicated to Shaw, the white commander of the first black regiment, the 54th Massachusetts, who died with his men in 1863 (see Flint).

12. A similar sentiment can be found in parts of "To the South On Its New Slavery": "What, was it all for naught, those awful years / That drenched a groaning land with blood and tears?" (ll. 61-62).

13. "Let us strive on to finish the work we are in, to bind up the nation's wounds, to care for him who shall have borne the battle" (Lincoln 1580).

14. For example, "Does the elm wood / Recall the haggard beards of blood?" (Melville ll. 19-20).

15. The tree's witness is here aligned with white identity in taking on the guilt of the lyncher. The device might be intended to implicate European American readers in a similar way while for African Americans the burden might rather be one of an inescapable history of trauma.

16. Parallel imagery is presented in "Lincoln": "Hurt was the nation with a mighty wound" (l. 1).

Works Cited

Braxton, Joanne M. Introduction. Dunbar, *Collected* ix-xxxvi.

Dunbar, Paul Laurence. *The Collected Poetry of Paul Laurence Dunbar.* Ed. Joanne M. Braxton. Charlottesville: U of Virginia P, 1993.

———. *The Life and Works of Paul Laurence Dunbar: Containing His Complete Poetical Works, His Best Short Stories, Numerous Anecdotes and A Complete Biography of the Famous Poet.* By Linda Keck Wiggins. Nashville: Winston-Derek, 1992.

———. *The Sport of the Gods and Other Essential Writings.* Eds. Shelley Fisher Fishkin and David Bradley. New York: Random House, 2005.

Fishkin, Shelley Fisher. "Race and the Politics of Memory: Mark Twain and Paul Laurence Dunbar." *Journal of American Studies* 40 (2006): 283-309.

Flint, Allen. "Black Response to Colonel Shaw." *Phylon* 45 (1984): 210-19.

Leonard, Keith D. *Fettered Genius: The African American Bardic Poet from Slavery to Civil Rights.* Charlottesville: U of Virginia P, 2006.

Lincoln, Abraham. "Second Inaugural Address, March 4 1865." *The Norton Anthology of American Literature.* Vol 1. Ed. Nina Baym, et al. New York: Norton, 1994. 1579-80.

Melville, Herman. *Battle-Pieces and Aspects of the War.* 1866. 18 Sept. 2006. <http://www.gutenberg.org/etext/12384>.

Whitman, Walt. *The Complete Poems.* Ed. Francis Murphy. London: Penguin, 1975.

PHYSICALITY AND MORTALITY

Valerie DeBrava (essay data 2001)

SOURCE: DeBrava, Valerie. "The Offending Hand of War in *Harper's Weekly.*" *American Periodicals* 11 (2001): 49-64.

[*In the following essay, DeBrava centers on Civil War stories published in the nineteenth-century periodical* Harper's *that reveal "a fascination with dismemberment that is played out in the romantic context of courtship."*]

Between 1861 and 1865, *Harper's Weekly* published dozens of short stories about Northern men who returned from the Civil War with missing limbs. Published anonymously—like so many of the literary pieces in mid-nineteenth-century American magazines—these stories can be read on an immediate level as a collective representation of one of the most outstandingly horrific aspects of the war. As many historians have observed, unsanitary conditions in Civil War hospitals and the consequent prevalence of infection led to an unprecedented number of amputations—more amputations than in any other war in American history. In the southern city of Richmond in 1862, surgeons performed 580 amputations during a two-month period (Wright 202). Read in the full complexity of their narrative preoccupation, however, the *Harper's* stories point to more than a simple concern with one of the war's most troubling realities. Without exception, these stories share a fascination with dismemberment that is played out in the romantic context of courtship. The loss of limb is embedded in the marital hopes and disappointments of the soldiers as they strive to win the affection of a particular woman.

Returning home from the front minus a leg or an arm, the always unmarried Union soldiers depicted in these tales leave behind the conflict of battle only to engage in a sexualized conflict that pits autonomous masculinity against heterosexual interdependence. Typically, the wounded soldier has a previous attachment to a woman from whom he was separated by the war. Upon his return to the home front, his injury sets the stage for an internal struggle with notions of male self-sufficiency, and with the idea of depending on a woman he once hoped to protect and govern. Rendered at least partially reliant on his beloved by his amputation, the Union soldier must come to terms with a compromised sense of his independence and an altered conception of female dependence. Likewise, the soldier's injury often sets the stage for another contest—that of the wooed woman who (for a variety of reasons) wrestles with misgiving, and who usually overcomes her doubts in a matrimonial acceptance of the wounded lover. For both the soldier and his beloved, the missing limb is a phantom displacement of conflict from the martial to the prospectively marital, and usually leads to a literal and figurative resolution in the offer and acceptance of the conjugal hand.

The stories in *Harper's Weekly* examined here present soldiers whose particular injury is the loss of a hand or an arm—soldiers distinguished by (to use a recurring, identifying phrase) an "empty sleeve."[1] While there are many tales depicting men who have lost a leg in the war, the stories presenting veterans with "empty sleeves" are more numerous and more striking in their articulation of gender issues than the works about legless men. The arm and hand, moreover, are symbolically more resonant in their disappearance than the leg, as diminished manual power apparently translates into diminished man power. The absence of the hand suggests a loss of dexterity, of control, of the authority conveyed in the iron fist. The loss of the hand is apparently a loss of the agency that makes a man the active, capable figure he typically cuts in Victorian ideology. At the same time, the loss of the hand threatens to signify the reduced capability of the soldier as spouse. The only hand the soldier has to offer in marriage is the phantom hand of the invalid, a mere vestige of the guiding, protective companionship expected in a husband. That which the wounded veterans in these stories offer to their loved ones is merely an "empty sleeve" to lean on.

Unable to guide a plow, drive a carriage, or pen a love letter, the injured soldiers in *Harper's Weekly* are most poignantly incapable—at least in their own minds—of serving as worthy mates. Amputation is experienced by these men as emasculation, both on the narrative level of presumed incompetence (whether as farmers, driving companions, letter writers, or physical protectors) and on the symbolic level of castration. The loss of the hand or arm is a distinct manifestation of male lack, so that the "empty sleeve" becomes the hollow sheath of an illusory manhood. Consequently, the veterans ask the women they love to become their wives with an agonized conviction of their own unworthiness as husbands. They make their marriage proposals with a guilty sense of uselessness and inadequacy.

In one story, "An Arm For a Heart," the wounded soldier refers to himself as "a miserable cripple" unworthy of love. Subsequently, when he is out site-seeing with his beloved, he laments "the loss of his arm because of the idle, aimless life to which it would compel him." With the loss of this soldier's arm goes the loss of "his power of usefulness," that component of his identity that has been gleaned from an ideal of vigorous, productive manhood. In a tale entitled "The Heart of Miriam Clyde," a soldier returns from the war looking like the living dead. He arrives unannounced, "his face pale as death, his figure attenuated, one sleeve empty at his side, and only the old smile curving his mustached lip to tell [his beloved] it was not his wraith." When the young man asks the girlfriend whether she will "take a husband with one arm," the girlfriend expresses her willingness with the half-joking response that he "will be easier to manage" than with two arms—a kidding assertion of the man's at least partial disempowerment. In "Leap-Year," another tale about a one-armed veteran, the soldier and would-be husband refers to himself repeatedly as "a common private with only one arm." Indeed, when he proposes marriage to his beloved, he asks softly and piteously, ". . . would you sacrifice your bright young life to a common private with only one arm?" The wounded soldier in "Devereux Dare, Private" proposes a second time to a woman who spurned him when he was uninjured. "I put on this ring before with my right hand," he says. "I had a strong arm then to shield and support you. Do you care to wear my token, when I have only my left hand to put it on with?" The answer, not surprisingly, is a resounding, tearful "yes."

Despite the self-doubting, self-deprecating language of these Union soldiers, their marriage proposals are almost always accepted. The soldier who laments the "idle, aimless life" to which his injury will compel him is met with the whispered confession of his future wife's affection, an affection she was not able to acknowledge before the young Captain Revere returned from battle "a miserable cripple." The young woman who responds to her maimed suitor's proposal with the jocular claim that he will be "easier to manage" than when he had two arms betrays beneath her frivolity a sincere attachment intensified by separation and the threat of death. "I learned how much I wanted you," she says, "by finding how much I missed you." To "the common private with only one arm" the much admired Harriet Deane responds with compassionate devotion quite unlike the arch reserve that characterized her earlier relationship with the man. "I would devote [my life] to the noblest hero who ever spilled his blood for his country!" she pronounces when asked if she would marry the wounded John Carlyle. The soughtafter Clara Gage, meanwhile, reacts to the offer of her one-armed soldier with the assertion that she would be his if he "think[s] [her] good enough to wear the honor of [his] name." Referring to his "empty sleeve," she says, "I shall only be prouder of my hero because he bears about with him a token of how dear he held his country and his manhood."

While the language of these marriage proposals suggests an acute sense of compromised masculinity, the rhetoric of the responses conveys an ideological reinstitution of manhood as patriotic lack, as absence that is a token of devotion and self-sacrifice. The function of these offers and their reception is on one level at least a propagandistic celebration of one of the war's grisly consequences, the ideological packaging of a horrible reality that will embolden men to fight in the war and encourage women to embrace these men on their return from the front. In this respect, these narratives catalyze the defining power of gender with the direct goal of perpetuating Union fervor. Real men are not afraid to bear the token of their devotion to their country, while real women are honored to be united with the battle-maimed.

As the terms "lack," "self-sacrifice," and "devotion" imply, however, the gender types that these narratives employ in their propagandistic capacity are not straightforward enhancements or re-articulations of masculinity and femininity. Joined with the symbolic resonance of amputation as emasculation, the idea of a sacrificing dedication to something other or larger than oneself evokes the Victorian prototype of womanhood. The soldier whose lack of an arm—which from a post-Freudian perspective connotes the chronic lack of female genitalia—identifies him as a self-sacrificing figure is, in a curious negotiation of stereotypes, a woman. Compelled to an idle life and more manageable than a veteran with two arms, the one-armed soldier is the ornamental wife who defers to the preferences and opinions of her husband. The beloved or the fiancée, on the other "hand," is the male figure whose affection is finally won by the docility and inclination of the soldier to be kept. From this perspective, the uselessness and malleability of the wounded male is as appealing to the girlfriend left at home as the gentle, self-effacing femininity of unmarried women is to the suitors in most popular narratives about courtship. The girlfriend on the home front is, indeed, empowered by the new dependent status of the lover, promoted to a position of managerial authority that, from the propagandistic standpoint, enlists the enthusiasm of women readers with a vision of sexual reversal and subversion.

Three stories in particular—"Aunt Debby's Brown Cottage," "Sally's Choice," and "The Empty Sleeve at Newport"—present the wounding of the soldier in a context of sexual fluidity and sentimentalized, feminized maleness. The first of these tales, "Aunt Debby's Brown Cottage," tells the story of Captain James Hunt, a Union soldier without any kin. Unlike the other soldiers, who receive mail from an extensive network of family members, Captain Hunt has but one correspondent, an elderly woman who had been a friend of his father's, and whom he affectionately calls "Aunt Debby." Aunt Debby is the actual aunt of a young woman named Lucy Larcom, whom the Captain has never met, but who sends her regards through Aunt Debby in a gesture of universal friendship with all Northern military men. Captain Hunt, in a thoughtful moment that presages a deep attachment, reflects on this Lucy Larcom who is widely considered to be one of the most brilliant, handsome, and cultivated young women in the North. As it happens, Lucy's brother, Ned, is also fighting in the war. In keeping with the many conveniences and coincidences of sentimental fiction, Ned is wounded on a battlefield where Captain Hunt is also fighting. The captain encounters the injured boy during a skirmish, and, struck by the prone figure of the youth, is inspired to carry the boy to safety despite the danger this poses to himself. The moment of this encounter is described thus: "There was something in the face of the wounded boy which instantly attracted Captain Hunt; and gathering him in his arms, with the aid of a soldier he carried him at once out of danger, when, leaving the boy in charge of the other, he hurried away for [the] regimental surgeon, whom finding, he dispatched at once to the relief of the stranger." Meant to foreshadow the attraction that the army officer will feel toward Lucy Larcom when he finally meets her, Captain Hunt's immediate attraction to Ned also serves

to destabilize gender roles, to question the understanding of masculinity in a narrative predicated on bourgeois heterosexuality. Captain Hunt gathers Ned in his arms in what inevitably registers as a moment of tenderness, thus summoning simultaneously the possibilities of homoeroticism and—within the parameters of heterosexuality—the feminization of one of the males. That it is the older man who, in effect, becomes a woman is indicated in a figurative causality by the fact that, moments after rescuing Ned, Captain Hunt sustains the injury that will lead to his symbolic lack. After leaving the youth in the care of the surgeon, the captain returns to the battlefield and is soon struck by "a brace of rebel bullets," a misfortune that transforms his phallic fervor into the passivity of a nagging absence. Captain Hunt's feminization is confirmed, moreover, by his reactions later in the story when he and Ned meet again in Aunt Debby's hometown. Listening to Ned recount to various townspeople how he rescued the youth at Gettysburg, Captain Hunt does what a Victorian woman would do—he blushes. "[H]ow brave Captain Hunt blushed like a girl at hearing his praises so warmly sounded," the narrator tells us, while again when the youth mentions his sister's name, "a quick flush [creeps] into the Captain's face." Like a bride whisked away to a prepared nest, the officer is then provided with a domestic sanctuary in Aunt Debby's cottage. "[H]ow Ned told [Captain Hunt] of Aunt Debby's alarm for his safety, and how he carried him away at last to the brown cottage, supporting him on his stronger arm as he went—all this is recorded in the history of that day in Riverton chronicles." How Captain Hunt became a woman so that—in essence—Lucy Larcom could become a man is chronicled, meanwhile, in the pride and joy she expresses when asked to marry this man who has "given one arm . . . to [his] country." The elation of acceptance suggests a subtle boost of testosterone as Lucy, like so many other heroines of the period, takes a manageable, dependent husband.

In "Sally's Choice," a young woman is pressured by her mother to marry Major Brewer, rather than the orderly with whom she is in love. Mrs. Snow and the Major conspire to convince Sally to forget her working-class beau, but neither parent nor suitor can wrest the affections of the young woman from John Cutter. When Sally boldly admits that she is longing for a man other than the Major, Mrs. Snow replies coolly—without ever mentioning John Cutter's name—, "It's no use. His thirteen dollars a month and his being taught that he is a machine, has demoralized him before this." The "this" referred to here is the courtship orchestrated by parent and officer, while the "being taught that he is a machine" is Mrs. Snow's estimation of the relatively lowly place that John Cutter occupies in the army. The position of orderly, combined with his meager income, have in effect already emasculated Sally's beau in the opinion of Mrs. Snow. The final demoralization of a competing, public courtship only serves to reinforce the already obvious unmanliness of John Cutter. Sally, however, is not persuaded by her mother's view that her favored lover is not a true man—the binary consequence of which is that her affection for Cutter persists while, according to the figurative logic that requires her to marry a feminized man and assume the empowered place of a masculinized woman, the option of marriage with Cutter is foreclosed. Sally, in other words, gives in to the pressure to marry Major Brewer even as her heart remains devoted to Cutter. In another example of fictional coincidence, the orderly encounters Major Brewer on the battlefield after the latter has been mortally wounded. Instead of spurning his rival, Cutter adopts a stance of feminine sentimentality and takes the dying officer's watch as a memento for Sally. Only after Major Brewer bestows a final kiss on the watch does the orderly pocket it. The watch is not enough to preserve the emotional momentousness of the occasion, however. After the Major breathes his last breath, Cutter decides to cut a lock of the dead officer's hair with his jackknife. As he is preparing to take the lock of hair in a paradigmatic gesture of emotion, "a ball [strikes] him on the elbow, [sending] the knife spinning and [shattering] his arm to pieces." As with the juncture of tenderness and injury in the case of Captain Hunt, the display of feminine sentimentality in the cutting of the dead man's lock of hair is made permanent in the symbolic transformation of the orderly into a woman through the misfortune of his injury. The knife—a phallic object—is sent spinning from John Cutter's grasp as the arm that had embodied manual and manly power is destroyed— all at the precise moment when sentiment is at its peak. This feminization of the orderly is, of course, permanent, and is signified not only in the amputation of Cutter's arm, but in his weeping at the sight of Sally when he returns home. The masculinization of Sally, meanwhile, is demonstrated in her unprecedented assertion of her own mind against her mother's wishes. Sally insists that she will now marry John Cutter, and that she will take a job, if necessary, to support herself and her spouse. Mr. and Mrs. Snow decide to let the newlyweds live with them on the farm where Cutter, spared a life of complete dependence, eventually learns to drive the oxen with his left hand.

"The Empty Sleeve at Newport; or, Why Edna Ackland Learned to Drive" is another tale that employs shifting gender roles in its depiction of a veteran with an amputated arm. Unlike "Aunt Debby's Brown Cottage" and "Sally's Choice," "The Empty Sleeve at Newport" does not represent the moment at which the soldier is injured. Instead, the narrative focuses on Captain Harry Ash's arrival in Newport after his right arm has been amputated, a circumstance that allows the anonymous author to explore the subjective struggle in a soldier's emasculation. And, indeed, the author wastes no time in presenting the Captain's hardship and healing as an epi-

sode in re-genderification. The first thing Harry Ash sees when he arrives in Newport for a period of convalescence, the narrator tells us, is the woman he had once admired and hoped to marry driving a carriage. Standing in the park with his "left sleeve pinned empty to his breast," Captain Ash watches Edna Ackland race past, handling a pair of ponies with evident skill and enjoyment. Too caught up in the emotional and physical rush of the ride to notice the wounded soldier, Edna becomes the dynamic prototype of an independent and active womanhood that threatens to disregard all the old attractions of manhood. She, with fifty or so other "girlish drivers," races through the park in a confident display of "the new feminine accomplishment." From the perspective of the ignored Captain, however, the accomplishment is not feminine at all. In fact, the "pretty picture" of Edna at the reins only demonstrates her unwomanliness. An indiscriminate spectacle for the crass admiration of fops and servants, Edna's flushed face and leaning figure are the image of female promiscuity—which amounts to the negation of true womanhood. Harry Ash had loved Edna Ackland "because she had seemed so womanly and gentle—a dainty thing to be watched over and guarded from harm." But now here she is, "driving with the daring eyes of fops and roués turned upon her, eager for their praise and admiration, forgetful of him and his opinion." Preferring "womanly women" who—as the irksome thought of Edna's obliviousness suggests—do not forget their beaux, Harry Ash instantly resolves to distance himself from Edna, who now falls into the category of "girls [who] . . . with their loud laughter and bold eyes, and ambition to be 'fast,' often shocked him." While Edna Ackland grows independent and bold, the Captain slips into a domestic dependence that is strikingly feminine. "What was he," the narrator asks, "[but] a helpless, one-armed fellow, shut off from the manly sports for life at twenty-six—an invalid to be nursed and tended, who needed so much and could give so little . . . ?"

Discouraged by the losses of his love and an active, manly existence, Captain Ash retires to a reclusive life of idleness. For weeks, neither the "occasional raid[s] of masculine friends" nor the prospect of encountering his former love are able to lure him from his seclusion. Finally, though, the Captain ventures out, unable to bear the oppressive confinement of his room any longer. Not surprisingly, Harry Ash soon finds himself in Edna's presence, having his first conversation with that "fast," "bold" woman since his return from the war. When Edna chides him for not calling or even sending a message, the Captain reminds her of his new (i.e., feminized) status as an invalid. Moments later, he chides her for her behavior—that is, for having learned to drive a carriage. "I grieve to see a woman unwomanly," he says by way of reprimand. To which the young woman responds by explaining that she learned to manage the ponies only so that she could drive her one-armed suitor through the park. "[O]ld Mark taught me to drive," she says, "and I learned, as I have learned many things, for love of you."

Conventionally enough, the couple reconciles when Edna presents her autonomy as a service to her lover. She is apparently redeemed from her "unwomanliness" with the confession that her independence is merely a twist to her role as helpmate. After Harry and Edna marry, the narrator tells us they are often seen riding together on "pleasant August afternoons." "Her hands guide the reins, and he sits with his empty sleeve beside her. Yet, for all that, his eye is on the road and his voice guides her; so that, in reality, she is only his left hand, and he, the husband, drives." "The Empty Sleeve at Newport" ends with a reversal of the reversal that made Edna Ackland independently mobile and Captain Harry Ash dependent and confined.

Or so the pat conclusion appended to this story—nearly as an afterthought—would have us believe. This static, almost trite resolution to Edna's "unwomanliness," however, stands in unconvincing contrast not only to the sustained and energetic problem of the text (how does an unmanly veteran come to terms with his unwomanly girlfriend?), but also to the remarkably dynamic and subversive illustration accompanying the story. Drawn by Winslow Homer, this illustration seriously questions whether Edna Ackland realizes that she is "only" her husband's "left hand." The staunch control she exerts, not merely over the horses but over the direction in which she and Harry are heading, combines with the almost huddled posture of her husband to suggest that Edna is the left hand and the phantom right hand both. The young wife stares resolutely ahead, while her husband's sidelong gaze suggests that he has yielded to her determination. The captain's head, in fact, is surrounded by Edna's billowing veil, a detail that subtly feminizes Harry Ash and confirms his attitude of submission. If we must take the narrative at its word in the representation of marital interdependence, therefore, we can at least assume that Edna is the dominant figure in the relationship. She is, at least, the right hand—an idea confirmed by her position at Harry's right in Homer's illustration.

This image of interdependence, so compelling in this story and in another tale, "Recaptured" (February 14, 1863), in which the soldier must rely on his beloved as his amanuensis, connotes a union of contrary forces that is a vision of Northern victory in the war. The success of the Union would be a yoking together of opposites—North and South—into an interdependent relationship as cooperative yet inegalitarian as the tie between male veteran and female helpmate. Accepting for a moment the literal subordination of Edna to her husband, the South becomes the weaker hand of the woman who has been restored to her proper "womanly"

place, while the North is the guiding male whose vision and voice (read here as a metaphor for superior technologies of communication) dictate where the carriage will go.

If the interdependence of man and woman conveys the promise of Union victory in these tales, the question naturally arises how the ongoing struggle of the war—the present conflict preceding future reconciliation—is depicted. What images and language in these narratives convey the frenzied destruction of the Civil War? The answer to this question shifts our attention back from the interdependent embrace of man and woman to the body of the male soldier itself. While reconciliation is envisioned in the heterosexual slippage between husband and wife, the strife itself is imaged in the discrete bodily existence of the soldier. The corporal fate of the veteran is, in essence, a metaphor for the political state that has gone awry. Keeping in mind David H. J. Morgan's observation that military training requires the shaping of "the individual body and the self that is identified with that body . . . into the collective body of men," the wounded soldier who comes back from the front becomes—militarily and in the sense of a body politic—the aggregate potency and disablement of a nation (167). The amputee becomes the embodiment of all American males at war. Of course, it must be conceded that the amputee in these stories is an embodiment of conflict Bowdlerized for the middle-class families reading *Harper's Weekly,* a bodily representation disemboweled of memory and disillusionment. The gruesomeness leading to amputation occurs beyond the narrative confines of these tales, just as the horror of battle itself occurred beyond the confines of the parlors in which *Harper's Weekly* was so often read. Nonetheless, the wraithlike veteran who is cut off from a lifetime of "manly sports" serves as a powerful picture of a national populace undermining its own vitality and camaraderie.

This brings us to the question of the civil nature of the strife depicted. We should remember that the conflict represented in the pages of *Harper's Weekly* is the threatened disintegration of a single nation, the attempted dissolution of the Union. Had *Harper's* been a Southern establishment, it would have presented the war as a struggle between two nations. The conflict would have been publicized as the monopolizing aggression of the Northern States, and the self-defense of a separate entity—the Confederate States. The editorial stance of *Harper's Weekly* denied the legitimacy of such separation from the outset of the war, however. Responding in 1861 to the declining subscriptions and the angry letters of its Southern audience, the editors at *Harper's* made a bold Unionist stand:

> As for *Harper's Weekly,* it will continue, as heretofore, to support the Government of the United States, the Stars and Stripes, and the indivisible union of thirty-

four States. We know no other course consistent with the duty of citizens, Christians, and honest men. If any subscriber to this journal expects us to give our aid or countenance to rebellion against the Government, he will be disappointed. . . . The proprietors of *Harper's Weekly* would rather stop this journal tomorrow than publish a line in it which would hereafter cause their children to blush for the patriotism or the manhood of their parents.

(25 May 1861: 322)

The result of this editorial position, filtered into the imaginative milieu of the periodical's fiction, is an understanding of the Civil War as a form of reflexive violence. Compelled to offer an image of the national body as one figure, bearing evidence of frenetic, reflexive engagement, *Harper's Weekly* presented again and again the image of the man with "the empty sleeve." The amputee, in other words, symbolizes not simply American males at war, but a conflict that is self-imposed. The amputee is, in an ultimate sense, violated by his own self.

The sexual dynamics underpinning the *Harper's* stories take a turn here. While the interaction between the amputees and the women they love points to an influential—if sometimes unstable—heterosexuality, the amputee himself points to a metaphorical subtext of autoeroticism. A particularly threatening form of reflexive activity in the minds of nineteenth-century Americans, the "solitary vice" of masturbation was epitomized by the "offending hand." The figure of the amputee, in fact, is an emblem of what Sylvester Graham calls "crippled nature," the sexual and ultimately social economy whose "renovating, vital" influences have been disrupted by self-absorption (*Lecture* 68). The man with "the empty sleeve" is best understood, therefore, within the context of the pervasive cautionary lore warning men (and the intended audience for most anti-masturbation treatises *was* men) about the effects of self-abuse and squandered semen. The body of prescriptive and restrictive material on masturbation, which includes works by Graham, John Todd, William Andrus Alcott, George Peck, and Timothy Shay Arthur, serves as a kind of didactic reservoir of images for these narratives about debilitating self-engagement and recuperation through hetero-eroticism.[2]

To the Victorians, masturbation was an acting upon and against oneself that undermined health and entailed a loss of self-control. As Michael Kimmel observes, middle-class Americans became obsessed with "gaining control over the body, often imagined in . . . advice books as a well of carnal desires and diffuse energy." The writers of advice manuals counseled their readers to control their desires and channel their physical appetites toward productive goals. In particular, Kimmel

continues, advice book writers were "frantically concerned about masturbation, which would sap men's vital energies and enervate them for the tasks ahead" (10).

The devastating potential of the "solitary vice" in fact called to the minds of the Victorians the annihilating effects of war. Graham considered male sexuality, particularly when turned in upon itself, as a major obstacle to public order. Writing of "self-pollution" in his *Lecture to Young Men,* Graham claims that because the "secret and solitary vice . . . requires the consent of no second person . . . the practice has little to prevent its frequency." Consequently,

> the practice almost inevitably becomes more and more frequent, . . . until it sometimes reaches the most ruinous excess, and acquires a power which irresistibly urges on the unhappy sufferer in the voluntary course of self-destruction.
>
> (44)

The "unhappy sufferer," so secretly bent on self-destruction, is plagued by a loss of "manly confidence" that hinders his ability to mingle with "virtuous females." His "practice" excludes him from the company of moral women who "stimulate young men to pursue the course of ennobling refinement, and mature them for the social relations and enjoyments of life" (46). How, Graham wonders, can society function if many of its male members are barred from the uplifting, socializing influence of women? Even former masturbators who have "become married men, and respectable members of society" carry the seeds of anarchy within them in their recurring "shamefacedness" (46).

William Andrus Alcott, in *The Young Man's Guide,* writes of marriage as a duty that the individual must perform in the interest of social order. A gauge of collective stability, the prevalence (or paucity) of marriages, Alcott writes, "points out the condition of society . . . as accurately as a thermometer shows the temperature of the surrounding atmosphere" (251). The implied opposite of marriage, which for Alcott is not celibacy but the "solitary vice," is an equally accurate gauge—of collective *in*stability and malaise. Alcott emphasizes for the reader who may succumb to the "solitary vice" that the damage resulting from masturbation is not confined to the practitioner alone. The physiological effects of the vice, which include a general weakening of the constitution, are transmitted to future generations as debility and disease. "Would it were true that they [masturbators] injured none but *themselves*! Would there were no generations yet unborn to suffer by inheriting feeble constitutions, or actual disease, from their progenitors!" (324). The truth for Alcott, however, is that the "solitary vice" affects many people, transforming populations in its physiological corruption.

One minister, revealing a connection in his own thinking between the "solitary vice" and the social vice of civil strife, even maintained that "masturbation had claimed more healthy lives than the [Civil] war" (Kimmel). To many, the link between the most private form of sexuality and the vast dissolution of public conflict found its paradigm in *Genesis,* where Onan's "spilling" of his "semen on the ground" and his subsequent slaying at the hands of the Lord evoke the combative syntax of spilled blood on the battleground and consequent death.

The association of autoeroticism with debility and disease generally was made almost universal during the antebellum period by an array of publications, two of which dated back to the eighteenth century. By 1750, 38,000 copies of the anonymous book, *Onania, or the Heinous Sin of Self-Pollution,* had been sold. Readers of *Onania* were taught that masturbation was not merely a moral problem, but a medical problem as well. An alleged cause of epilepsy, hysteria, and sterility, masturbation was for the first time presented as a health problem that could potentially undermine the vitality of an entire population. Samuel Tissot's 1758 work, *Onanism, or, A Treatise upon the Disorders Produced by Masturbation,* appeared in its American edition in 1832, and laid the foundations for a number of advice manuals identifying the threat to American manhood posed by the "solitary vice." Graham, in particular, offered a vivid, repulsive, and yet fascinating depiction of what would become of the sensualist who indulged in the "solitary vice." The masturbator in Graham's depiction becomes

> a confirmed and degraded idiot, whose deeply sunken and vacant, glossy eye, and livid shrivelled countenance, and ulcerous, toothless gums, and fetid breath, and feeble, broken voice, and emaciated and dwarfish and crooked body, and almost hairless head—covered perhaps with suppurating blisters and running sores—denote a premature old age! A blighted body—and a ruined soul.
>
> (*Lecture* 58)

Alcott describes one masturbator—a thirty-five-year-old Pennsylvania resident whose name we need not know—as a victim of "premature old age." The man's "bending and tottering form, wrinkled face, and hoary head might be traced to solitary and social licentiousness," Alcott maintains—as will be the emaciated and tottering frames of fledgling masturbators in the years to come (315-16). Given the popularity of these advice books, the man in *Harper's* who comes back from the war looking wraithlike and emasculated must have roused a particular alarm in readers schooled to detect the wasted youth as a practitioner of the "solitary vice." Readers of *Harper's Weekly* would have recognized this wasted figure from Alcott's *Physiology of Marriage* and its companion volume—advertised in the *Weekly* in

1857 and 1866—*The Moral Philosophy of Courtship and Marriage.*[3] At the same time, the wraithlike amputee must have reminded readers of the prospect of recovery and reform inherent in any prescriptive delineation of a vice. The absence of the "offending hand" in the *Harper's* stories suggests an attitude of penance and restraint that, with the inevitable turn to matrimony, betokens a permanent move away from destructive self-involvement. The lopping off of the offending member—Old Testament style—signals a resolution to quit the vice, to bring to an end the wasting effects of a reflexive passion.

If the vulnerabilities of the amputees in the *Harper's* stories differ from the tottering weaknesses of the prematurely aged masturbator, then, it is because the amputee is the sensualist on the road to recovery. Bearing in mind some of the measures proposed (not just by Graham) for the remedying of self-indulgence, amputation does not seem beyond the realm of prescriptive possibility! Some writers advised the use of straightjackets to prevent masturbation, while a more subtle solution might be the use of "cork cushions" to keep the thighs from rubbing against the genitals. A patent was even issued for a "genital cage" that sounded an alarm if its wearer experienced an erection (Kimmel 13)! The amputation of the hands was itself never proposed, but the bizarre, punitive dimensions of these remedies makes such a solution seem at least remotely possible.

From this point of view, the amputee who takes a wife is as much the Reconstructable South as he is the redeemable masturbator. The man with the missing hand is the collective possibility of penance and redemption, of the recovery of a nation racked by the frenetic loss of self-control. The hero in these stories represents a frenzy that occurs beyond the vision of the reader in the parlor—whether on a distant, southern battlefield, or behind the locked door of an upstairs bedroom. At the same time, though, the hero represents the reach of a vision anticipating a regimen of correction and the promise of healing. In this respect, the struggle of "the common private" to gain the esteem of his beloved—which is also the struggle of the common privates to fix their potency on the higher activities of marriage—is rewarded with a union (always in these stories a *re*union) built on the recognition of difference and complementarity. The heteroerotic amputee in *Harper's Weekly* embodies an unspeakable history of self-engagement, transformed into the healing prospect of an interactive sexuality. Peace, ultimately, is to be counted on as much as the reliable Victorian scenario of the "happily ever after."

Notes

1. I would like to thank Mary Leech, formerly of Harp Week, for calling to my attention the abun-

dance of tales in *Harper's Weekly* depicting amputee veterans. I would also like to acknowledge my own affiliation with Harp Week, an electeronic publishing company specializing in the digitization of *Harper's Weekly*.

2. Besides Graham's 1834 *A Lecture to Young Men,* the most popular advice books include his 1839 *Lectures on the Science of Human Life* and John Todd's *The Student's Manual,* published in 1835. William Andrus Alcott's *The Young Man's Guide,* George Peck's *The Formation of a Manly Character,* and Timothy Shay Arthur's *Advice to Young Men*—all dating from the 1850s—were enormously popular as well.

3. *The Moral Philosophy of Courtship and Marriage* was also reviewed in the pages of *Harper's Weekly* in 1857. *The Physiology of Marriage* was referred to in the text of *Harper's Weekly* twice in 1857.

Works Cited

Alcott, William Andrus. *The Young Man's Guide.* Boston: T. R. Marvin, 1851.

"An Arm for a Heart." *Harper's Weekly,* 22 Nov. 1862: 746.

Arthur, Timothy Shay. *Advice to Young Men on their Duties and Conduct in Life.* Boston: Phillips, Sampson, 1847.

"Aunt Debby's Brown Cottage." *Harper's Weekly,* 9 April 1864: 234-35.

"Devereux Dare, Private." *Harper's Weekly,* 13 Sept. 1862: 587.

Graham, Sylvester. *A Lecture to Young Men on Chastity.* Providence, RI: Weeden and Cory, 1834.

———. *Lectures on the Science of Human Life.* Boston: Marsh, Capen, Lyon and Webb, 1839.

"Leap-Year." *Harper's Weekly,* 23 April 1864: 266.

Morgan, David H. J. "Theater of War: Combat, the Military, and Masculinities." *Theorizing Masculinities.* Eds. Harry Brod and Michael Kaufman. Thousand Oaks, CA: Sage Publications, 1994.

Onania, or, The Heinous Sin of Self-Pollution. London, 1710.

Peck, George. *Formation of a Manly Character.* New York: Carlton and Porter, 1853.

"Sally's Choice." *Harper's Weekly,* 30 May 1863: 342.

"The Empty Sleeve at Newport: or, Why Edna Ackland Learned to Drive." *Harper's Weekly,* 26 August 1865: 534.

"The Heart of Miriam Clyde." *Harper's Weekly,* 27 Feb. 1864: 135.

Tissot, Samuel Auguste David. *Onanism, or, A Treatise Upon the Disorders Produced by Masturbation.* London, 1758.

Todd, John. *The Student's Manual: Designed, by Specific Directions, to Aid in Forming and Strengthening the Intellectual and Moral Character and Habits of the Student.* Northampton: J. H. Butler, 1835.

Wright, Mike. *What They Didn't Teach You About the Civil War.* Novato, CA: Presidio Press, 1996.

Franny Nudelman (essay date 2004)

SOURCE: Nudelman, Franny. "'This Compost': Death and Regeneration in Civil War Poetry." In *John Brown's Body: Slavery, Violence, and the Culture of War,* pp. 71-102. Chapel Hill: North Carolina University Press, 2004.

[*In the following essay, Nudelman emphasizes the belief that physical sacrifice would bring about rebirth and renewal that informs the treatment of death and disfigurement in the Civil War poetry of Walt Whitman and other American authors.*]

Whitman's 1856 "Poem of Wonder at the Resurrection of the Wheat" begins "Something startles me where I thought I was safest." Sickening at the sudden realization that the earth teems with rotting corpses, the poet withdraws from the natural world. Suspecting that he has been deceived by the earth's apparent bounty, he decides to turn up the soil and "expose some of the foul meat" lying underneath. He finds, however, that the "sour dead" are wonderfully transformed. Far from contaminating the soil, they are the source of new life: "What chemistry!" The poet celebrates the process of organic renewal that turns death into life with an exultant description of spring's arrival: new wheat rises, calves are born, birds resume their song, and the poet is free to return to the natural world to bathe, eat, and loaf. Yet in the wake of this happy resolution the poem takes another sudden turn. Reassured, the poet is also "terrified" by the earth, which "grows such sweet things out of such corruptions." In the final lines of the poem Whitman describes the earth as a machine that "turns harmless and stainless on its axis" as it produces "sumptuous crops" from "endless successions of diseas'd corpses." In the end, the poet succumbs to the power of a machine able to unite life and death, health and disease, ugliness and beauty in a process of consumption and reproduction that proceeds without end.[1]

"Poem of Wonder" appears to prophesy the spectacle of mass death that would, five years later, leave hundreds of thousands of corpses rotting beneath the earth's surface. During the Civil War, the disposal and commemoration of the dead became a national project. Describing new life as the result of death, organic metaphor affiliates two of the chief aims of wartime culture: mourning the dead and mobilizing the living. Uniting the ritual observance of loss—the burial of the dead—with nature's power to produce, representations of the dead body as a source of fertility consoled grieving individuals while helping to reconstitute the fragile bonds of national community. In order to continue to fight, die, and grieve, people needed to believe that something worthwhile, even beautiful, could grow from their suffering. The plant life that springs up from the graves of dead soldiers provides a ready image for the willingness of soldiers and civilians to continue to support the war effort in the face of massive losses. At the same time, by projecting expansion—in the form of growth—as the natural trajectory of political community, organic metaphors characterize violent death as the source of the nation's increasing strength.

After the war, Whitman renamed the poem "This Compost," thus emphasizing not only the corpse's materiality (as opposed to the miraculous appearance of new wheat) but also the process of decomposition through which death would renew the natural world. During the war, organic metaphors were used to construe violence as an instrument of natural progress and, on this basis, to lend mass death an aura of beauty and inevitability. Although it is tempting to imagine that Whitman's graphic and erotically charged portrayals of dead and wounded bodies resist institutional efforts to categorize, and rationalize, war-torn flesh, it seems to me that Whitman was determined to give death a transcendent purpose that is very much in keeping with the interests of the state.[2] The specificity of his descriptions of the wounded and dead, while they suggest the difficulty of finding redemptive meaning in the massive casualties of wartime, do not detract from this effort. Whitman's wartime poetry and prose at once renders wounded and dead bodies in detail and uses the figure of the anonymous or unknown soldier to abstract them. Representing the harm done to individual bodies, Whitman treats the wounded and dead with great tenderness while placing them in an overarching scheme that sentimentalizes the state as the apotheosis of wartime heroism.

If Whitman uses the metaphor of composting to describe the burial of the dead as a means to collective renewal, he prescribes silence as the appropriate attitude of the mourner in the face of these losses. Indeed, an organic model of national community often went hand in hand with a rhetoric of unrepresentability that interpreted silence as evidence of the gravity and grandeur of death in war. Declaring that the Civil War could not be described, writers and politicians implied that the public performance of silence was one way that citizens could participate in a regenerated national community.

Abraham Lincoln, who appeared at Gettysburg dressed in mourning for his own young son, told the assembled that words could not possibly compete with the deeds of dead soldiers. At his own funeral, large and silent crowds provided further evidence of the martyr's power to create political community. Canvassing the art of the Civil War, we find that representations of unanimity, so vital to the state's objectives, use silence to signify the devotion of citizens to the cause of war.

In this [essay], I will consider Whitman's contribution to a nationalist aesthetic of silence and abstraction, founded on the bodies of the wounded and the dead, as well as occasional poetry that resists abstraction by focusing on the material conditions of war and the mechanics of cultural production in constrained circumstances. While Whitman's war writing takes the disappearance of the dead into the earth as a central figure for the production of nationhood out of individual suffering, a vast body of poetry authored by anonymous, or virtually unknown, occasional poets attempts, more modestly, to document the circumstantial detail of war. Viewing the conflict through the lens of specific places and events, anthologies of occasional poetry, published in the years following the war, short-circuit the rhetoric of transformation that will make easy use of corpses. Though many individual poems celebrate the war effort, taken together these poems convey a fragmentary account of the conflict that cuts against the grain of nationalist representations of common purpose and institutional expansion. The mourner who pauses, humbled, at the soldier's grave, provides a model for the reader of Whitman's poetry, as well as for the student of Civil War history, awed by a spectacle she cannot fully comprehend. The imprisoned Southern colonel who scribbles a poem on the wall of his cell before committing suicide suggests a very different kind of poetic practice: executed in a state of emergency, occasional poetry uses simple and highly accessible conventions to describe the extraordinary circumstances of war. Documenting not only the conditions of war, but also the mechanics of transmitting them, these poems trade a rhetoric of commonality for a record of experiential diversity.

Recalling Henry James's comment that the war was an "immense and prolonged outwardness" that made it difficult to "live inwardly," Neil Schmitz observes that "the text the Civil War principally produced is a vast photography, an archive of views we are still assembling and sorting. What significant writing there is— several speeches, brief takes, small pieces, short poems—scans like photography, is other-directed, memorial, documentary."[3] Scholars have described the Civil War as a catalyst for the development of postwar realism. According to this view, the war produced seismic changes in technology and social organization that, in turn, demanded new modes of representation. Confronting Americans with bloodshed on an unprecedented scale, the conflict shook artists out of a transcendentalist reverie, in which they contemplated the affinity of self, nature, and God, and urged them to document a rapidly changing world.

If we pause to consider representations of the dead before and during the war, however, arguments concerning the advent of realism in the postbellum period appear partial. Antebellum Americans surrounded themselves with images of dead people that are so graphic that they often offend contemporary viewers. An antebellum "culture of death" beautified and objectified the dead body in the process of memorializing it. Grieving relatives displayed the dead body, carefully tended, before burial; they gathered keepsakes from the corpse, making jewelry, for example, out of the hair of the deceased; they took postmortem photographs that portrayed the dead—eyes open, sitting erect—as if they were still alive. Mourning portraits, sometimes drawn from daguerreotypes of the subject, were also characterized by a meticulous attention to physical detail: in some instances, the corpse was carefully measured so that the portrait would be life-size.[4]

Antebellum mourners employed a realist aesthetic to repress death's material effects. Lingering over the dead body, they cultivated its lifelike appearance, thus expressing their ongoing emotional attachment to the dead. The circumstances of death in war did not, however, conform to realist modes of representation. Once the war began, the military found it difficult to identify the bodies of dead soldiers, let alone transport them home for burial.[5] As a result, Northern civilians often mourned soldiers in the absence of their corpses. As I have argued, to be unclaimed in death was an anathema that differentiated disenfranchised people from those more secure in the comforts of middle-class domesticity. The uncertain fate of soldiers' corpses intensified the anguish of grieving families, and it may at times have raised uncomfortable questions about the status of soldiering itself.

At the same time that the war made it difficult for Northern civilians to individuate the dead, it challenged them to imagine mass death and to feel sorrow, if they could, for countless unidentified bodies. The unprecedented scale of war violence called for forms of representation that could help people grieve for a large, undifferentiated group. If antebellum death rituals helped mourners remember the dead in vivid detail, during the war descriptions of the dead tended toward a universalizing abstraction.[6] Organic images that described the regenerative effect of the decaying body located the significance of wartime death not in the body-as-object but in the gradual deterioration of body's form. In this way, they offered a commemorative figure that might encompass all the absent dead.

Addressing the impact of war on Whitman's career, Betsy Erkkila remarks that it "had the effect of jolting literary America out of romance and into realism," and transforming Whitman, the "poet-prophet," into a "poet-historian." In discussing Whitman's war poems, Erkkila, like Schmitz, emphasizes the ascendance of the image. She writes, "The immediacy and brutality of the war shocked Whitman into a new realism in which painting and the snapshot rather than oratory and opera became the primary artistic analogues of his poems."[7] Indeed, *Specimen Days,* which recounts Whitman's experience tending the sick, wounded, and dying in Washington's military hospitals, contains some of the most graphic representations of wounded and dead bodies to be found in the literature of the Civil War. Unlike mourning portraiture, however, which uses the dead body to produce an enduring image of a living person, Whitman's descriptions of the dead fuel a nationalist romance in which the remains of the body are absorbed by a greater whole. Although Whitman describes the scenes of war in great detail, an emphasis on the documentary aims of his wartime prose and poetry overlooks the ease with which he used a model of organic transformation to incorporate the seemingly intractable particulars of war into a narrative of national regeneration.

In "The Million Dead, Too, Summ'd Up," the penultimate entry in the war-related section of *Specimen Days,* Whitman surveys the "varieties of strayed dead" left behind by the war. The entry experiments with different ways of imagining what becomes of dead bodies. Whitman writes, "The dead in this war—there they lie, strewing the fields and woods and valleys and battlefields of the south—Virginia, the Penin sula—Malvern hill and Fair Oaks—the banks of the Chickahominy—the terraces of Fredericksburgh—Antietam bridge—the grisly ravines of Manassas—the bloody promenade of the Wilderness."[8] Whitman begins by emphasizing the massive extent of death, giving the impression that bodies fill the Southern landscape. Dashes pile locations, like bodies themselves, one on top of another, conveying a sense of disorder and neglect. Whitman interrupts this list with a parenthetical aside in which he rehearses the War Department's own count of the unburied, or inadequately buried, dead: "(the estimate of the War department is 25,000 national soldiers kill'd in battle and never buried at all, 5,000 drown'd—15,000 inhumed by strangers, or on the march in haste, in hitherto unfound localities—2,000 graves cover'd by sand and mud by Mississippi freshets, 3,000 carried away by caving-in of banks, & c.,)" (800). The horror entailed by the particulars of the body's disappearance is played off against the "& c.," which implies the callousness of institutional efforts to count the dead, as well as their futility: this list, it seems, could go on indefinitely. As well as signifying the government's inability to account for the dead, "& c." calls for a different kind of institutional approach to commemoration, one that acknowledges, even elevates, the impossibility of representing dead soldiers. Whitman concludes "The Million Dead, Too, Summ'd Up" by describing the "soldiers Cemeteries of the Nation" that pervade "all the peaceful quarters of the land" in the years following the conflict. In these cemeteries, "we see, and ages yet may see, on monuments and gravestones, singly or in masses, to thousands or tens of thousands, the significant word UNKNOWN" (801).

"Counting," James Dawes writes, "is the epistemology of war." While numbers contain an otherwise "borderless trauma," they also convey the massive extent of death in war.[9] Dawes praises Whitman for avoiding sentimental strategies that reinterpret mass violence by way of individual suffering. Instead, Whitman attempts "to create a new genre of war writing, a genre appropriate to the unprecedented multiplicative array of national action." He continues, "For Whitman, a national memory properly constituted must body forth from a skeletal structure built out of numbers rather than narration, out of counting rather than history" (54-55). Dawes offers "The Million Dead, Too, Summ'd Up" as an example of Whitman's effort to communicate the extent of war violence through enumeration rather than individuation. And yet the number Whitman arrives at—one million dead—is grossly exaggerated.[10] Numbers mount toward an apocalyptic figure that impresses by virtue of its inaccuracy. Throughout, Whitman conveys the breadth of death in war by converting its hard particulars—words or numbers—into capacious abstractions. In the end, "UNKNOWN" provides another way of "summing up" when numbers fail and intimates one powerful aim of Whitman's wartime writing: not to know the dead but to unknown them, to enumerate the particulars of dying and death in order to arrive at a sum that is truly greater than its parts—the awesome whole that in its entirety resists description.

Whitman's final war entry announces that "future years will never know the seething hell and the black infernal background of countless minor scenes and interiors." He continues, "*And it is best they should not*—the real war will never get into the books" (802, emphasis mine). *Specimen Days* begs the question: how to reconcile the assertion that the war should not be represented with the graphic nature of Whitman's descriptive prose? Shuttling, as so much of Whitman's writing does, between the particular and the abstract, "The Million Dead, Too, Summ'd Up" suggests an answer to this question. On the one hand, Whitman presents us with material remnants of the dead: one might yet discover the "bleach'd bones, tufts of hair, buttons, fragments of clothing" left behind in secluded spots where soldiers "crawl'd to die, alone" (801). On the other hand, he describes the complete disappearance of the dead into a landscape "saturated, perfumed, with their impalpable

ashes' exhalation in Nature's chemistry distill'd" (801). While commemorative objects embody the dead, organic metaphor allows Whitman to represent the influence of the dead—manifest "in every future grain of wheat and ear of corn, and every flower that grows, and every breath we draw"—as it grows and changes over time.

Whitman describes (at the very least) two different ways of conceptualizing the dead and our relation to them: we can hold tightly to the relic, the material trace (however inscrutable) of a particular life; or, we can take the absence of the corpse—most powerfully signified by the land's fertility and beauty—as an occasion to affirm the ongoing presence of the dead. Here and elsewhere Whitman uses the figure of decay to imagine these two modes of commemoration as part of a single process. While the body decomposes and disappears into the soil, fragments are left behind. These fragments, in turn, force us to recognize what cannot be fully known or remembered. The claim that the real war will never get into the books, generally taken to indicate the inadequacy of language, signals instead its power; the elaboration of detail produces an intense, nearly visceral experience of all that falls outside the realm of observation and memory. Whitman uses fragments of the dead body—amputated limbs or scraps of clothing—to indicate his own inability to represent the dead. In doing so, he demonstrates the power of documentary representation to produce a keen awareness of its own limits. In the end, "& c." intimates the particulars that have been lost to time and circumstance. When dignified with the "significant word UNKNOWN," this absence attaches the mourner more firmly to an idealized nation that translates the lives of individuals into a motivating aura—impossible to describe—of life without end.

Whitman's "The Million Dead, Too, Summ'd Up" could be describing the War Department's own efforts to figure out how to best commemorate the dead under new and trying conditions. During wartime, responsibility for tending and burying the dead fell to the state. The task of honoring hundreds of thousands of corpses was inextricably related to the state's ability to produce enthusiasm for the war effort: how to dispose of the dead in a way that would dignify the war itself, ensuring the continued contribution of soldiers and civilians? In 1863, the Gettysburg and Antietam battlefields became the first national cemeteries for the Union dead. They provide examples of state-sponsored culture struggling to invest dead bodies with common meaning. Whereas antebellum commemorative practices celebrated the particulars of character, identity, and appearance, the national cemetery at Gettysburg eschewed precise identification, honoring the individual soldier by assigning him a place in a well-ordered assembly. William Saunders, the architect appointed to design the cemetery, held that in order to "produce an expression of grandeur" it would be necessary to "avoid intricacy and great variety of parts."[11] Accordingly, the dead were buried in graves of uniform size that were grouped by state and marked by identical headstones that recorded name, company, and regiment. Saunders abandoned an aesthetic of specificity out of necessity—many of the dead could not be identified. Yet by representing the subordination of dead individuals to a greater cause these generic headstones served a political purpose.

While nineteenth-century headstones typically recorded a history of particulars—date of birth, relation to loved ones, a line from a favorite poem—the war dead ware commemorated en masse. During the Civil War, an emphasis on the corpse's particular features was supplanted by a tendency to view the dead as featureless, or unknown: the elaboration of anonymity as a function of national identity is perhaps the national cemetery's most important contribution to the art of war. A democratic gesture that refuses to reinstate military (and implicitly class) hierarchy, the anonymity of state burial also implies the leveling effect of death itself. It seems possible, however, that the generic cast of the cemetery at Gettysburg could be taken as a sign of indifference on the part of the state that failed to recognize dead individuals. Perhaps to avoid any appearance of callousness in the design, David Wills, Pennsylvania governor Andrew Curtin's representative in Gettysburg, asked Lincoln to attend the cemetery's commemoration in order to assure soldiers that they would be well treated in death. Lincoln's presence, he wrote, would "kindle anew in the breasts of the comrades of these brave dead, who are now in the tented field or nobly meeting the foe in the front, a confidence that they who sleep in death on the battle-field are not forgotten by those highest in authority; and they will feel that, should their fate be the same, their remains will not be uncared for."[12]

Forgoing any elaboration of the particulars of the battle, Lincoln's "Gettysburg Address" mirrored the design of the cemetery itself.[13] Lincoln attempted to justify this approach by explaining, "The world will little note, nor long remember what we say here, but it can never forget what they did here."[14] While the speech uses language to spectacular effect, it elevates the actions of the dead by denigrating the power of the living to "consecrate" the war in words. We might imagine that the much-noted brevity of Lincoln's speech was the closest he could come to calling for a moment of silence. Indeed, when the speech was over (almost as soon as it was begun) the audience was left dumbstruck. The scene at Gettysburg—simple headstones arranged in orderly ranks, the president paying homage to a generic heroism—suggests the contours of a nationalist aesthetic that favors abstraction over detail and vies with commemorative traditions that dwell on the material properties of the corpse.

The claim that the Civil War stimulated the development of postwar realism stands, somewhat uneasily, alongside the contention that it failed to produce "great" art. Even as they attempt to account for the interesting, if occasional, texts that the war left behind, literary critics note that many of the nineteenth century's most celebrated American writers remained silent on the subject of war. Most notably, Daniel Aaron's *The Unwritten War* offers an exhaustive survey of literary responses to the conflict while maintaining that writers failed to say anything "revealing" about the causes, or the meaning, of the Civil War.[15] In Aaron's view, the inability of writers to illuminate the war testifies to its monumental violence and the paralyzing impact this violence had on the imagination. He writes, "The thrill of fear after the first exultation and the abrupt change from haphazard engagements to massive and machine-made slaughter stunned the imagination. . . . It took time . . . to adjust to the enormous scale of the War and to tally its material and human cost" (336).

While Aaron does not dwell on the effect that technological change had on cultural production at any length, scholars who study the wars and genocides of the twentieth century have theorized this relationship more fully. Discussions of modern war describe the ways that the advent of new killing technologies, designed to destroy ever-larger groups of people more efficiently, alternately paralyzed the imagination and provoked it to invent new forms. Attempting to convey disorientation, disbelief, and mental and emotional paralysis, twentieth-century writers often rejected representational conventions designed to make the world appear ordered and coherent.[16] Indiscriminate and far-reaching destructiveness found formal expression as artists tried to communicate the power of war to cripple and destroy language. Represented silence offered one way to convey the failure of language in the face of pain and suffering.

Analyses of twentieth-century representations of war, which emphasize both the power of war to deconstruct language and artistic attempts to reconstruct it in new and politicized ways, are instructive in their failure to describe the literature of the Civil War. Indeed, what remains disquieting about the culture of this war is how rarely, and incompletely, it protests war violence. Civil War writing does not regard silence as evidence of the debilitating effect of violence on the individual's power of self-expression, but rather as testimony to the war's monumentality—its power not to shock and disturb but to awe and inspire. If twentieth-century authors often broke with literary conventions in an attempt to describe the impact of trauma on individual consciousness, Civil War writers used highly conventionalized declarations of the war's unrepresentability to express grief and pay homage to the war effort.

Forsaking the abundant detail of *Specimen Days,* Whitman's wartime poetry aestheticizes the carnage of war.

In *Drum-Taps,* Whitman uses the informal, often improvised burials that occurred on the battlefield and in the hospital to structure a narrative of triumphant nationalism. While the volume as a whole narrates the emergence of a robust, unified nation from the chaos of war, poems that describe the burial of the dead demonstrate the role of ritualized silence in establishing the citizen's attachment to the state. Unlike *Specimen Days,* which devotes a great deal of attention to the dying soldier, *Drum-Taps* focuses on the spectator who "beholds" the war and, particularly, the mourner who contemplates the bodies of the wounded and the dead. Poems of death and mourning offer up simple, unelaborated images of the dead. Formulating a poetic practice commensurate with the claim that the real war should not get into the books, these poems conjure brief moments of silence amid the cacophony of the conflict as a means of ordering war's diversity and directing its affective power.

As scholars have argued, *Drum-Taps* expresses Whitman's deep ambivalence about the Civil War.[17] Clearly, it was difficult for him to reconcile the grandeur of the war effort with the dead and wounded bodies it produced: while some poems celebrate the advent of war others recoil from its horrors. Over time, however, Whitman reworked the volume in significant ways, using poems of death and mourning to enlarge, rather than detract from, a sense of the war's overarching purpose. Ruminating on war in retrospect, the final edition of *Drum-Taps* uses the reverential encounter between mourner and corpse to structure and dignify a narrative of war as the mechanism of national progress.

Michael Moon takes the tension between "war-rhetoric" and "elegiac rhetoric," which characterizes the first edition of *Drum-Taps,* to indicate how Whitman's view of war changed when he began working in Washington military hospitals.[18] During the first two years of the war, Whitman anticipated a brief and successful conflict at a safe distance from the battlefield. During these years he produced his patriotic poems, which urge participation in the war effort. "First O Songs for a Prelude" (called "Drum-Taps" in the original edition), which opens both early and late versions of *Drum-Taps,* provides one example. This poem re-creates the cacophony of the early days of the conflict as whole cities shift their attention from the routines of daily life to the project of war. Against the backdrop of the Manhattan cityscape, people emerge from interior spaces—houses, workshops, stores, and churches—to congregate in the street. As the title implies, sound provides the main motif for the poem: this noisy scene reminds us of a chorus warming up, testing its lungs with the round, empty "O" of the poem's title. What we hear in the rumble of artillery, the cheers of the crowd, the drum struck lightly is not the orchestrated tune but the "mutter of preparation."[19]

After his arrival in Washington, where he spent three years nursing soldiers, Whitman's outlook changed: the poetry of these years focuses on the sick, wounded, and dead. If the recruitment poems take marching as their central image for the engagement of individuals in the war effort and the consequent progress of the nation as it moves forward in history, these later poems pause the action of war in order to describe the soldier-spectator who gazes on the dead. The earlier poems emphasize sound as they strive to re-create the invigorating accompaniment of martial tunes; the later poems emphasize visual detail as they portray the poet's silent encounter with damaged bodies.[20]

In its two earliest versions—published in a separate volume as *Drum-Taps and Sequel to Drum-Taps* in 1865 and annexed to *Leaves of Grass* in 1867—the collection is marked by an unsteadiness of tone and purpose. Poems that celebrate the war effort clash with somber meditations on dead bodies. These are awkwardly juxtaposed to very brief descriptive poems that seem to bear little or no relevance to the subject of war ("Mother and Babe," "A Farm Picture," "The Torch"). While the volume as a whole captures the sense of excitement and restless energy that, in Whitman's view, characterizes the early days of the war, it defies the order and steady rhythm of the military march—the volume's ostensible framing device. Indeed, because the poems seem to follow one another in nearly arbitrary ways the volume has a staccato quality—like tap-tapping on a drum—but these bursts of sound, and attendant pauses, never cohere in a fluid and sustainable rhythm.

By contrast, the final edition of *Drum-Taps* (1891-92) represents the mourner's encounter with the dead as a necessary, if painful, step in the development of national community.[21] This volume takes on a narrative shape that moves from the "militant exultation" of the recruitment poems, to the imagistic, highly controlled poems of death and mourning, to the final poems, which offer a "justification of the war as part of the 'throes of democracy' in its march toward the future."[22] Whitman helps to achieve this effect by bringing together—and placing them near the center of the volume—four poems that describe the poet-soldier's confrontation with the dead and wounded: "Vigil Strange I Kept on the Field One Night," "A Sight in Camp in the Daybreak Gray and Dim," "As Toilsome I Wander'd Virginia's Woods," and "A March in the Ranks Hard Prest." In each of these poems, the narrator is brought up short by an unexpected encounter with a dead body. He pauses to pay tribute and then continues on his way. In "Vigil Strange," for example, a soldier sees his comrade drop on the battlefield. He continues fighting and then, during the night, returns to find that his friend has died. He sits all night with the body and buries it at dawn. He does not cry or speak ("not even a long-drawn sigh") but gazes on the corpse in silence. The word "vigil," repeated throughout, suggests both devotional watching and wakefulness, implying that even in mourning the soldier remains alert to danger. At daybreak the soldier "rose from the chill ground," wrapped his friend in a blanket, "And buried him where he fell."[23]

In describing a mourner paying homage to a corpse before moving on, these poems enact a ritual devotion that bridges the need to honor the dead with the need to keep fighting. The structure of these poems—movement that pauses and then resumes—is mirrored by the structure of the whole: this cluster of poems works to slow the progress of the volume by building a devotional pause into the triumphant forward motion of the whole. They help Whitman to structure this narrative of war as a well-ordered procession that moves, in a simple, elegant rhythm, from past (innocence) to present (death) to future (unity). In the final version of *Drum-Taps,* the double meaning of the title is realized and put to use: the slow, sad cadence of the funeral march structures and dignifies the progress of war.[24]

As Whitman's wartime writing demonstrates, close scrutiny of the dead does not necessarily temper the project of nation building through war. In "Turn O Libertad," the penultimate poem in *Drum-Taps,* the nation emerges from war "expanding, doubting no more, resolute, sweeping the world."[25] In a wartime setting, mourning often involves a ritualized forgetting that paves the way for future conflict. As the poet-soldier who gazes on the body of his enemy in the poem "Reconciliation" remarks, "Beautiful that war and all its deeds of carnage must in time be utterly lost" (453). Once the dead are buried and forgotten, Whitman can turn to celebrating a robust nation poised for "wars to come" (457). The imperial imagination is the beneficiary of wartime commemoration: a country unified by abstract losses—the untold suffering of unknown soldiers—can more easily project itself into a limitless future.

After burying his friend, the narrator of "Vigil Strange" rises up to return to the work of war. As I have argued, organic metaphor provided a way to describe the living invigorated by wartime death: some went so far as to imagine that violence would produce new populations—masses of people as well as the common identity that united them. Written by James Sloan Gibbons in 1862, "We Are Coming, Father Abraham, Three Hundred Thousand More" describes recruits rising up, like new wheat, from the ground where the dead lie buried:

> We are coming, Father Abraham, three hundred thousand more,
> From Mississippi's winding stream and from New England's shore;
> We leave our plows and workshops, our wives and children dear,
> With hearts too full for utterance, with but a silent tear;

> We dare not look behind us, but steadfastly before,
> We are coming, Father Abraham, three hundred thousand more.
> Chorus:
>
> We are coming, coming our union to restore,
> We are coming, Father Abraham, with three hundred thousand more.
> If you look across the hilltops that meet the northern sky,
> Long moving lines of rising dust your vision may descry;
> And now the wind an instant, tears the cloudy veil aside,
> And floats aloft our spangled flag in glory and in pride;
> And bayonets in the sunlight gleam, and bands brave music pour,
> We are coming, Father Abraham, three hundred thousand more.
> If you look all up our valleys, where the growing harvests shine,
> You may see our sturdy farmer boys fast forming into line;
> And children from their mothers knees are pulling at the weeds,
> And learning how to reap and sow, against their country's needs;
> And a farewell group stands weeping at every cottage door,
> We are coming, Father Abraham, three hundred thousand more.
> You have called us and we're coming, by Richmond's bloody tide,
> To lay us down for Freedom's sake, our brother's bones beside;
> Or from foul treason's savage group to wrench the murd'rous blade,
> And in the face of foreign foes its fragments to parade;
> Six hundred thousand loyal men and true have gone before—
> We are coming, Father Abraham, three hundred thousand more![26]

Gibbons wrote this song in response to Lincoln's request for 300,000 new volunteers. He uses Lincoln's own viewpoint to portray recruitment as a breathtaking natural spectacle: the president, who scans the horizon in anticipation, is barely able to distinguish new recruits from the landscape that appears to produce them. The song also describes the soldier's sad departure from home. We catch a glimpse of the mother left behind teaching her children to pull up weeds, "learning how to reap and sow against their country's needs." Images of fertility link landscape, home, and army in a vision of natural abundance; Gibbons imagines the emergence of 300,000 volunteers as a function of a fertile and well-tended national landscape.

Although "We Are Coming" begins with 300,000 living men growing up from the earth, it ends with them laying themselves down "for freedom's sake, our brothers' bones beside." The "more" of the title acknowledges that these men follow others who have already died in the conflict; the final stanza names the "six hundred thousand loyal men" who have "gone before." As this song demonstrates, wartime culture not only compensates loss with images of prosperity, productivity, and well-being but also imagines death itself as the source of such bounty. Representations of the dead body, gradually decaying, as the source of national identity, find their complement in representations of the miraculous appearance of new populations that give nationhood its public expression.

Benedict Anderson observes that nationalism and religion both provide ways of imagining life without end.[27] While religion offers the promise of immortality to the individual soul, nationalism projects the ongoing life of an abstract "people" and the institutions that govern them. In Gibbons's song the nation's immortality is expressed by its ability to produce fighting men. Lincoln himself imagined that the country could produce an infinite supply of soldiers. In his Annual Messages to Congress, Lincoln celebrated national expansion—territorial, economic, and industrial. On December 6, 1864, he linked these forms of expansion to the growth of "the most important branch of national resources—that of living men." Presenting a detailed comparison between the election returns of 1860 and 1864, Lincoln asserts that despite the mounting death toll the country's population is on the rise: the "important fact remains demonstrated, that we have *more* men *now* than we had when the war *began*; that we are not exhausted, nor in process of exhaustion; that we are *gaining* strength, and may, if need be, maintain the contest indefinitely." Referring to both men and material, he concludes that "national resources, then, are unexhausted, and, as we believe, inexhaustible."[28] Lincoln imagines the war as a generative force that, like a powerful machine or like the earth itself, can produce fighting men "in endless succession."

Lincoln's Annual Message, which describes the production of bodies during wartime as evidence of national strength, implies his broader effort to rethink the nature of state authority. Rejecting British governance, founding authors asserted the primacy of contractual association; the Declaration of Independence insisted that the textual elaboration of collective grievances and common interests legitimated the new nation. In order to neutralize obvious analogies between colonists and secessionists, Unionists needed to demonstrate the failure of the founding texts—especially the Constitution—as a basis for political community and to offer an alternative. They often turned to an organicism that viewed bodies, like plants, as part of a regenerative cycle in order to imagine a nation that preceded, and would outlast, the consent of its citizens. Although Lincoln at times insisted that protecting the Constitution was his chief object, his First Inaugural Address describes the

Constitution as an outgrowth of the Union. He argues, in a maddeningly circular fashion, that it is "safe to assert that no government proper, ever had a provision in its organic law for its own termination" (217). Lincoln's "new" nationalism, born of necessity, trades an Enlightenment emphasis on rational consent for an ill-defined "organic law" that takes expansion, rather than stability, as the natural trajectory of political community.

During times of war, and especially civil war, a nation's legitimacy and its future are called into question. Insisting that the nation was producing men at an increased clip, Lincoln refused to acknowledge that, at points, the machine of state nearly ground to a halt. His Annual Message, like Gibbons's song, masks the crisis of authority faced by a government unable to count on the enthusiastic participation of its citizens. After all, Lincoln had to ask for volunteers because the example of many thousands dead was not inspiring enough: the enlargement of federal power during the war was occasioned by a shortage, rather than an abundance, of manpower.

The Civil War witnessed the marked and permanent expansion of federal authority. James McPherson describes this remarkable structural transformation: "The old federal republic in which the national government had rarely touched the average citizen except through the post-office gave way to a more centralized polity that taxed the people directly and created an internal revenue bureau to collect these taxes, drafted men into the army, expanded the jurisdiction of federal courts, created a national currency and a national banking system, and established the first national agency for social welfare—the Freedmen's Bureau."[29] Lincoln was the principal agent, as well as the chief theorist, of these changes. Three important instances of the controversial exercise of state power occurred during the second year of the war (1862-63): the first military draft in U.S. history, the nationwide suspension of the writ of habeas corpus, and the Emancipation Proclamation. At Gettysburg Lincoln asserted that the dead had the power to "dedicate" the living to the "unfinished work" of war.[30] In fact, quite the opposite was true. All three measures were, according to Lincoln, responses to a crisis in manpower. In 1862, the Union army was depleted, and potential recruits were far from eager to join up. Losses from combat, disease, and desertion were compounded by the expiration of enlistments. In response to this short-age of fighting men, Lincoln undertook the expansion of federal power that he regarded as necessary to obtain and retain new soldiers.

Lincoln's wartime writing is characterized by a certain contradiction: does the soldier's self-sacrifice renew and expand the influence of the state, as Lincoln suggests at Gettysburg, or does the state, which needs more fighting men, enlarge itself by finding ways to obtain them? In his Opinion on the Draft, written in September 1863, Lincoln justified the draft as a military necessity. He wrote, "We already have, and have had in the service, as appears, substantially all that can be obtained upon this voluntary weighing of motives. And yet we must somehow obtain more. . . . To meet this necessity the law of the draft has been enacted. You who do not wish to be soldiers, do not like this law."[31] Lincoln described emancipation as, like the draft, a response to a labor shortage. In numerous letters, he explains that he issued the Emancipation Proclamation in order to provide the army with a new source of recruits. On April 4, 1864, he writes that faced with the prospect of "surrendering the Union, and with it, the Constitution," he decided instead to place a "strong hand upon the colored element." Over a year later, the military "shows a gain of quite a hundred and thirty thousand soldiers, seamen, and laborers." He concludes, "We have the men; and we could not have had them without the measure" (586). In light of his remarks on conscription and emancipation, the production of fighting men appears not to be the expression of a prolific national landscape fertilized by dead soldiers, but rather the result of decisive and unorthodox assertions of state power.

The assassination of Abraham Lincoln, and the subsequent spectacle of national mourning, contributed enormously to the belief that death in war produced national unity. In "Death of Abraham Lincoln" (1887), a lecture that Whitman delivered annually on the anniversary of Lincoln's assassination, the poet claims that Lincoln's death gave birth to a "homogenous Union, compact, born again, consistent with itself."[32] Toward the end of the lecture he turns to Lincoln's "prairie-grave," where "Crumbled and wordless now lie his remains long buried," to describe the awesome influence of Lincoln's death. Whitman writes, "The final use of a heroic-eminent life—especially of a heroic-eminent death—is its indirect filtering into the nation. . . . Then there is a cement to the whole People, subtler, more underlying, than any thing in written Constitution, or courts or armies—namely, the cement of a first-class tragic incident thoroughly identified with that People, at its head, and for its sake. Strange, (is it not?) that battles, martyrs, blood, even assassination, should so condense— perhaps only really, lastingly condense—a Nationality" (12). Once again, the Constitution comes up short when compared to that "subtler, more underlying" form of social cohesion produced by blood sacrifice. The president's death stands in for the myriad individual losses of wartime, and his power to orchestrate war pales in comparison to his representative vulnerability.

Whitman, like Lincoln, imagined that violence would produce an infinite supply of living soldiers. Echoing Lincoln's claim that "national resources, then, are unexhausted, and, as we believe, inexhaustible," Whitman wrote, "I strengthen and comfort myself much with the certainty that the capacity for just such regiments, (hundreds, thousands of them) is inexhaustible in the United States, and that there isn't a county nor a township in the republic—nor a street in any city—but could turn out, and, on occasion, would turn out, lots of just such typical soldiers, whenever wanted."[33] Descriptions of the living who rise up in the wake of the dead metaphorize death as growth, inverting the material effects of war. During war, soldiers kill people. They rape women, demolish buildings, burn crops, and destroy culture. But while war obliterates bodies, objects, and memories, it also produces meaning—the sense of a worthy cause—that compensates for material losses. Whitman's claim that the "United States" can generate an infinite supply of "typical soldiers" not only represses war's destruction but also provides a powerful figure for the genesis of meaning; these masses embody the mobilizing influence of nationalist abstractions disseminated by wartime culture.

I would suggest that people were able to use the dead body as an occasion for collective rededication because they believed that dead people would be reborn, that the body retained some essential significance that was not extinguished in death but was freed to circulate. Lincoln's death provides a case in point. While James Gibbons describes "father Abraham" straining to see 300,000 soldiers mustering in the distance, at least that number went out of their way to catch a glimpse of the dead president as his body made its way across the countryside. Concluding a period of civil conflict, Lincoln's death occasioned an outpouring of nationalist feeling as enormous, peaceful crowds gathered in Northern cities to pay their respects. Over the course of two weeks, Lincoln's funeral procession, which began in Washington, D.C., stopped in Baltimore, Harrisburg, Philadelphia, New York, Albany, Buffalo, Cleveland, Columbus, Indianapolis, and Chicago, before arriving in Springfield. In each city, people turned out in unprecedented numbers for street processions and stood in line for many hours in order to have a chance to file past Lincoln's open casket.[34] All along the route, they gathered in groups, small and large, to sing and pray. These crowds provided evidence of Lincoln's authority, now disseminated through the body politic in the form of common feeling.[35]

Visual depictions of the event stress the impressive spectacle of these huge, peaceful crowds. While photographs show Lincoln's catafalque surrounded by an unwieldy mass of people, prints and wood engravings give form and structure to the crowds. Like visual representations, first-person accounts dwell on the size of the crowds that gathered to mourn the president. They emphasize the length of the lines, attempt to estimate the number of people in attendance, and often marvel at the silence that characterized these huge and potentially unruly groups. Describing Washington on the day of Lincoln's funeral, one spectator remarked that "the scene in the White House, the street, and the Capitol today, was the strongest evidence the war afforded of the stability of our institutions and the worthiness and magnanimous power of our people."[36] Representations of Lincoln's funeral procession, in which enormous and immobile crowds gather to pay their respects, exemplify, in microcosm, the power of the dead to produce civic unity out of civil war.

While representations of Lincoln's death affirmed a popular narrative of the regenerative effect of self-sacrifice, a great deal of wartime art did not readily contribute to this vision of a unified and inexhaustible public. In the years following the war, anthologists gathered a diverse body of poetry that cannot be read through the lens of homogenizing nationalist abstractions. Rather than describing a mass of people animated by a single will, these anthologies investigate a wide range of responses to the war. Sallie Brock prefaced her anthology of Southern wartime poetry, *The Southern Amaranth,* with the following remarks: "The design of this work was conceived in an individual desire to offer a testimonial of gratitude to the memories of the brave men who perished in the late ineffectual effort for SOUTHERN INDEPENDENCE; as well as in a wish to render to my Southern sisters some assistance in gathering up the remains of the CONFEDERATE DEAD, from the numberless battle-fields over which they were scattered, and placing them where the rude ploughshares may not upturn their bleaching bones, and where sorrowing friends may at least drop a tear and lay a flower upon the grass-covered hillocks that mark their resting places."[37] Analogizing these collected poems to bone fragments, Brock describes the process of recovering obscure, occasional poems, written in a time of crisis, as a form of mourning that was not possible during the war. Published in New York in 1869, *The Southern Amaranth* is one of many anthologies that appeared in the years following the Civil War. These collections use the occasional expressions of wartime culture in an effort to rebuild national community. Unlike Whitman, who assimilates the particulars of war into a narrative of triumphant national unity, these anthologies narrate the war through the accumulation and juxtaposition of discrete instances of poetic expression. Attempting to recover the homely particulars of wartime poetry, they reverse the process of abstraction vital to the development of Civil War nationalism.

Mary Louise Kete has examined the role that poetry played in shaping community during the nineteenth century. She describes the production and exchange of sentimental poetry as a form of mourning that helped middle-class Americans shore up their sense of self and community in the face of death and dislocation. Her analysis centers on "Harriet Gould's Book": originally

blank, Gould's book was filled with occasional verse, inscribed by family and friends, over the course of a lifetime. Containing poems to mark a variety of occasions, such books chronicled an individual's life through the words of her intimate circle. Some of the poems in Gould's book are original, some are copied from other sources, and some are lifted and rewritten without attribution. It seems that these poems were not valued for their originality, or viewed as the property of individual authors. Instead, they were gifts that strengthened communal bonds as they passed from hand to hand.[38] In important respects, anthologies of war poetry resemble the albums that Kete discusses. In order to include poems by famous authors and anonymous ones, devotional poems and irreverent satires, poems that applaud the war and those that call it into question, anthologists cast a wide net. They subordinate coherence to comprehensiveness and representative genius to idiosyncratic self-expression.

Introducing a retrospective account of the war that proceeds by way of accumulation rather than synthesis, these anthologies necessarily meditate on the relationship between war and art, implicitly asking what kind of poetry best represents, and most respectfully commemorates, the events of war. Instead of imagining a community constituted by representative acts of suffering, they stress the material nature of poetry itself, asserting, as "Harriet Gould's Book" does, that culture is produced by individuals, as well as groups, on particular occasions. Far from applauding art for transcending circumstance, they describe circumstance as the ground of culture. Indeed, anthologists defended wartime poetry against the attacks of critics, real or imagined, who valued formal refinement too dearly. While Daniel Aaron notes that "almost immediately after Appomattox Northern commentators began to complain about the failure of American writers to do justice to the recent strife," some complained about those who mounted such criticism.[39] Oliver Wendell Holmes, for example, began his lecture on the poetry of war, delivered on November 21, 1865, by addressing "those who would save me all trouble by the assertion that there has been no real poetry produced during the war."[40] Holmes does not leap to defend the literary merit of war poetry, or to call standards of judgment into question. Instead, he maintains that the unique circumstances of wartime, particularly advances in the technologies that produce and circulate print material, call for a certain kind of poetry. Unlike the days when "everything had to be written out by hand, and . . . parchment was very dear," now "printing is cheap; paper is cheap. The gods are dethroned, men are less exclusive, and the columns of the daily, weekly and monthly press require a standing army of moderately good poets" (3). Punning on "columns," Holmes links advances in the publishing industry to efforts to wage war on the cultural front, and argues that the poetry of a democratic war, implicitly a war waged against the "exclusive" institution of slavery, will be authored by amateur poets.

As Holmes suggests, the vast body of wartime poetry was published in daily newspapers and illustrated magazines. These poems were written with a sense of urgency—often in response to a particular battle or event—and rushed off for publication. Those who witnessed the war firsthand wanted to convey their experience to civilians, while civilians translated secondhand accounts of the war that they found in newspapers, magazines, and bulletins into poetry.[41] The hasty production and mass publication of a lot of poetry was part of a much larger effort to maintain communication between the battlefield and the home front—a process inevitably plagued by rumor and hypothesis. In keeping with these conditions, anthologists asserted that the value of occasional poetry lay not in its beauty, its complexity, or its ability to transmute the circumstances of war, but rather in the power of the poems, when collected, to reproduce war's cacophony.

Drawing attention to the unevenness and inconsistency of their volumes, anthologists suggested that in order to adequately convey the reality of war a collection of poems *must* be mediocre. Introducing a volume of his own poems that had already been published in newspapers, Henry Howard Brownell remarks that because his poems were "penned, for the most part, on occasion, from day to day," and often in the midst of crisis, his collection will be marred by "instances of diffuseness, contradiction, or repetition."[42] Introducing his 1866 anthology, Richard White acknowledges that in selecting a representative collection of Civil War verse "poetical merit has not been the only consideration." Indeed, "fastidiousness in these respects would be much out of place." Rather than choosing his poems on the basis of literary merit, he has "looked through the street ballads as well as the monthly magazines, and . . . taken as readily what was printed upon a broadside, or written for negro minstrels, as what came from Bryant, Longfellow, Lowell, or Boker."[43] Anthologists do not, however, forgo claims to representativeness. They insist that when gathered together these poems convey the will and the mood of the American people during wartime. Thus aesthetic mediocrity goes hand in hand with a volume's power to embody the evanescent spirit of a people at a particular moment in time. Brownell describes his verse as "spray . . . flung up by the strong Tide-Rip of Public Trouble" which will "present the Time more nearly, perhaps, than they do the writer" (iii). And White portrays his volume as a "poetical reflex of the mind of a whole people under the excitement of a war lasting four years."[44]

Anthologies do not embody a people at war by synthesizing, abstracting, or homogenizing the conflict's particulars but rather by collecting individual poems, each indebted to its own urgent occasion, and letting them stand side by side. In the aftermath of the Civil War, these anthologies suggest how difficult it was to arrive at a common understanding of the recent conflict. Their response to the nationalist imperative of shared remembrance is hesitant at best: proposing the accumulation of occasional verse, in all its diversity and artistic unevenness, as the best way to describe the war, these collections trade a vision of seamless union for an account of political community that remains divided by circumstance.

When reading through collections of Civil War poetry, however, I hardly feel that I am brought face to face with the conditions of war. Ideologically motivated and highly conventional, these poems often blend into one another. Those that stand out, able to convey a sense of immediacy over time, are distinguished not by content but by context. For example, "What tho' These Limbs," written by a Confederate prisoner of war, appeared in the anthology *War Lyrics and Songs of the South* (1866):

> What tho' these limbs be bound with iron cords,
> Still I am free!
> For liberty can dwell amidst the clank of chains,
> And in the gloom of dungeons,
> As well as 'neath the leafy arches
> Of the boundless forest.
> Who can fetter the undying spirit,
> Or circumscribe the limits of the mind?
> Far out beyond these prison walls
> I roam adown the vistas
> Of imagination—and still am free![45]

This poem pivots on the conventional trope of slavery and freedom often found in Confederate and Union poetry. What will catch a reader's attention, however, is the brief description that precedes the poem: "Written by Col. Ben Anderson of Louisville, Kentucky, on the prison wall in Cincinnati, shortly before committing suicide." The fact that this poem was written by a prisoner of war, or that it was intended as a suicide note, can only heighten its affective power. The emotional intensity produced by these particulars is inseparable from the poem's dramatic appearance on the wall of a prison cell. Similarly, an editorial note that introduces "Too Good to Be Lost"—a poem that meditates on the worthlessness of Confederate currency—explains that "the following lines were found written on the back of a five hundred dollar Confederate note."

These contextualizing remarks draw attention to the importance of spatial settings—actual and imagined—to the production and reproduction of war poetry. Whether or not Colonel Anderson actually wrote his verse on the wall of a prison cell, this text imagines that wartime poets write in desperate circumstances, making use of all available surfaces. Poetry is not an instrument of refined expression but a form that responds impulsively to an unprecedented crisis and proceeds by way of improvisation. The reality of war, in this context, does not attach to the graphic representation of bodily pain but to the production of poetry itself. In contrast to Whitman's efforts to convey the failure of representation, this poetry takes an optimistic view of the power of language to record the circumstances of war. While the dead body, subject to certain decay, is the appropriate object for an aesthetics of forgetfulness, the materiality of unlikely spaces of production furthers the anthologist's effort to secure the war in memory.

I would like to turn now to a particular compilation of occasional poetry that documents the war's symbolic conclusion—the assassination of Abraham Lincoln. In the days after Lincoln was killed, an observer walked, pen in hand, through the streets of Manhattan and recorded in a notebook all the occasional poetry and sketch art that appeared in the windows of storefronts, churches, schools, and homes.[46] Although this is a private document, most likely not intended for publication, it underscores the role that carefully recorded detail plays in helping to orient the observer in a world suddenly transformed by violence. Reading this notebook, one begins to imagine the streets of New York papered with expressions of sorrow, shock, and revenge.[47] Most frequently, the poems express sadness. In the window of Frederick's Gallery: "In sorrowing tears the nation's grief is spent / Mankind has lost a friend, and we a President." At 843 Broadway: "The tear that we shed, / Though in secret it rolls, / Shall long keep his memory / Green in our souls." Many verses are, like these, lilting and predictable in their rhymes; others, like this one, are more awkward: "A martyr to the cause of man / His blood is freedom's eucharist / And in the world's great hero list, / His name shall lead the van." Threats of revenge also appear with frequency, though not in poetic form. At 663 Broadway a sign reads: "Woe to the hand that shed this costly blood." More pointedly, 18 Bowery declares, "Death to Assassins." Throughout, poetry is accompanied by discursive prose that tends to be somewhat more idiosyncratic. At 544 Broadway: "There was in this man something that could create, subvert, or reform: an understanding, a spirit, and an eloquence, to summon mankind to society, or to break the bonds of slavery asunder, and to rule a wilderness of free minds with unbounded authority, something that could establish and overwhelm an empire, and strike a blow in the world that resound [*sic*] through the universe." In addition, we find drawings of weeping willows and tombstones, quotes from Shakespeare, and a passage from a speech by Andrew Johnson announcing that if he were president all traitors would be arrested and hanged.[48]

This anthologist also recorded the context in which these poems, drawings, and aphorisms appeared, not only noting the street address and often the type of es-

tablishment where they were posted, but also the relationship of a given text to its material context. One verse is followed by a note remarking that it appeared in "white letters on black ground"; a passage from Lincoln's Second Inaugural Address is surrounded by a sketch of a wreath and then, in handwriting, "green wreath"; a written description of an image accompanies a poem—"Goddess of Liberty holding the olive branch, the frame was draped with black crape and white rosettes with this inscription." The anthologist tries to reproduce as nearly as possible the public space of the city filled with the particulars of occasional art. The blurring of forms—poetry, prayer, drawing, aphorism—is accompanied by the blurring of the boundaries between the text and the physical context in which it appears.

In the wake of Lincoln's assassination, the streets and storefronts of New York resembled the pages of "Harriet Gould's Book," covered with an eclectic array of poetry and prose that favored quotation and juxtaposition over originality. In *City Reading,* Kevin Henkin describes the proliferation of ephemeral public texts in antebellum New York: "Disparate urban texts marked the streets as a site of public reading, a palimpsest of shared information upon which claims to personal authority blurred into one another and receded into a larger verbal collage."[49] According to Henkin, the expressions of grief and rage that filled New York after Lincoln's death were reproduced in the city's major newspapers. Like the private notebook I have described, the *New York Times* not only reprinted messages posted in windows and on storefronts but also tried to convey a sense of the varied settings in which these texts appeared: "From every window in every street . . . from the spires of our churches, from the domes of our halls, from every flag-staff, from every pane of glass, on the lappel [*sic*] of the millionaire, about the arm of the laborer . . . are the insignia of grief."[50]

As Henkin demonstrates, during the nineteenth century public culture was increasingly permeated by anonymous and ephemeral printed texts. Insisting that occasional poetry must exceed the bounds of great art if it were to capture the reality of war, anthologists also scrambled distinctions between high and low art, between poems by famous authors and those by anonymous authors, between poetry and song. In recording poems with an eye to context—where and how did these poems originally appear?—anthologists drew attention not only to the material properties of occasional poems but also to the difficulty of producing art during wartime. In the view of anthologists, the real war did not, as Whitman claimed, fail to get into the books. Instead, it was captured by poetry of a certain sort—poetry that responded to the exigencies of the moment by recording the events of war on the page, in the margins of the page, on the walls of prison cells, and on city streets.

Published in 1866, Herman Melville's *Battle-Pieces and Aspects of the War* is dedicated "To the Memory of the Three Hundred Thousand who in the War for the Maintenance of the Union Fell Devotedly under the Flag of Their Fathers."[51] This dedication might prepare us for a narrative of suffering and redemption, but while Melville does pay tribute to the heroism of soldiers and the grand purpose of the war in some poems, in others he laments war's pointlessness. Like the volumes of occasional poetry that I have discussed, and like the first edition of *Drum-Taps,* this book is willfully eclectic: drawing on various poetic styles and popular forms, Melville refuses to unify the scenes of war. In composing *Battle-Pieces,* Melville relied on *The Rebellion Record,* a thirteen-volume collection of newspaper articles, speeches, maps, and other sources.[52] His poems not only feature well-known battles, military leaders, and events, they also draw on the forms of communication—photographs, ballads, newspaper reports—that gave descriptions of the war their particular texture. The fragmented quality of the work—emphasized by the "pieces" and "aspects" of its title—is one effect of its documentary method.

Foregrounding his dependence on an array of external sources, Melville acknowledges the mediated and indeterminate nature of his relation to the Civil War. Throughout, he calls attention to the inconclusive particulars of war, repudiating an organicist vision of war as part of a natural cycle of death and regeneration.[53] Whitman's war writing is characterized by a momentum that breeds interconnection: soldiers march, the death toll mounts, memory recurs, as the war builds toward its inevitable conclusion. Combining an easy antiformalism with a romantic investment in the feeling subject, many of the poems in *Drum-Taps* produce a sense of linguistic and emotional abundance. The poems in *Battle-Pieces,* by contrast, are "grim, carefully crafted, aesthetic objects."[54] Despite Melville's claim that he simply drew on themes that "chanced to imprint themselves upon the mind," the volume's formal diversity, adherence to prescribed poetic form, and obvious debt to other sources communicate the effort that goes into writing these poems.[55]

If Melville's wartime poetry stands in stark contrast to Whitman's, it is formally, if not ideologically, affiliated with popular poetry of the period. The anthologies I have discussed are embedded in circumstances that cannot be reduced to, or redeemed by, political unities; *Battle-Pieces* intensifies the eclectic and improvisational nature of the genre. But unlike popular anthologies in which such diversity, taken to characterize the mood of the people, is an end in itself, *Battle-Pieces* uses formal multiplicity to reflect on redemptive narratives like Whitman's own.

If *Drum-Taps* takes the intimacy between the living and the dead as a source of political unity, *Battle-Pieces* takes the standoff between North and South to characterize relations of many sorts—between civilian and soldier, observer and object, reader and text, past and future—as conflicted and incomplete. The poem "Donelson," drawn from *The Rebellion Record* accounts of the battle at Fort Donelson, takes the difficulty of conveying information from the battlefield to the home front as its subject. Describing a group of people who gather around a bulletin board during a winter storm to find out what is happening in the battle over Fort Donelson, the poem dramatizes the imprecise nature of wartime communication.[56] It is divided between sections that describe civilians responding to a series of news bulletins and sections that comprise the reports, narrating the battle itself. Throughout, an attention to context runs counter to the representation of unanimity or coherence. We are reminded of the reporter who does his best to compile his dispatch "from varied sources" and of the vagaries of technology when transmission is disrupted by a storm in the west (41, 49). Melville emphasizes the unreliability of communication and, by extension, the unbridgeable distance between battle and home fronts.

The divide that separates soldiers and civilians also characterizes the relationship between the living and the dead. Far from sentimentalizing battlefield death as a source of civic commitment, Melville stresses the difference between the living and the dead by objectifying corpses and mocking the conventions meant to elevate them. Unlike the narrator of Whitman's "Reconciliation," who leans over to kiss the lips of his dead enemy, Melville's "Magnanimity Baffled" describes the Northern "victor" who reaches out to his Southern foe only to find himself grasping the hand of a corpse (156).

In much of the popular culture of war, the absence of the corpse, and of language commensurate to its demise, allows the mourner's feelings of affection and longing for the dead to be transferred to the state. This displacement of feeling obscures the workings of power as well as the historicity of the circumstances that produce suffering. But the reconstruction of historical context, which situates suffering in place and time, may fail to do justice to wartime experiences that do not conform to the observations of documentary description any more than they conform to nationalist narratives of heroism and transcendence. As Margot Norris has observed, survivors witness "the deconstruction not only of their material world but also of their conceptual universe." As a result, when one is documenting war, the "effects of irreality" may become tools of "historical explanation."[57]

At times, Melville uses images of the body's resistant materiality to produce this very effect. In "Donelson," a dozen wounded soldiers freeze to death on the battlefield. Melville describes their "ice-glazed corpses, each a stone" (43). This image of bodies frozen solid neatly links the two worlds of the poem: they remind the reader of the "shards" of freezing rain that pummel civilians gathered for news, as well as the fragments of information they receive. Melville's corpses fail to yield knowledge or consolation. At one point, Melville describes the civilian's emotional response to death in war as a brittle object not unlike the corpses of dead soldiers, or Melville's own poems. Having read the latest posting from the front, the reader looks "To find in himself some bitter thing, / Some hardness in his lot as harrowing / As Donelson" (46). Rather than using a rhetoric of transformation to harmonize the living and the dead, Melville uses the dead body's material and epistemological recalcitrance to describe the fragmenting effect of violence on the survivor's consciousness.

While collections of occasional poetry focus on detail in an attempt to reproduce context, they do not use these details to describe the war's impact on perception. Using brittle fragments—stone, shards, ice—to depict both external conditions and internal states, Melville contemplates the impact of physical violence on subjectivity, reminding us of modernist efforts to use the shards of language—curtailed and incomplete—to describe war's effect on the mind. In my view, the representations that most powerfully convey the damage done by the war are those that in their emphatic materiality resist narration or contextualization, thus communicating the alien and incomprehensible nature of wartime suffering. Defying assimilation of any kind, these texts imply that death is final and loss cannot be redeemed. I find one example in the collection of photographs taken by Reed Bontecue, Civil War physician and photographer, at Harewood Hospital in Washington. Portraying sick and wounded soldiers, who look at the camera or refuse to meet its stare, these portraits meditate on the power and limits of the diagnostic gaze; graphically portraying wounded body parts while also studying the powerfully expressive faces of these soldiers, they consider the impact of amputation and disfigurement on the psychologized subject.[58]

One unusual photograph, however, portrays the result of wounding in the absence of appropriate context: it presents a fragment of bone mounted on a small pedestal. If this image were not accompanied by a written description, and juxtaposed to photographs of amputees, John Miller's leg bone would appear a stray piece of stone, a geologist's find. We might wonder where it came from and why someone saw fit to photograph it. Then again, its interest might be self-evident: a brittle substance, riddled with pockmarks, with an oval hole in the middle, and tapered to a point. Reading the caption that originally accompanied the photograph, we learn that this is a bone fragment, six inches in length, "drawn from the end of the stump" of one John Miller, a private in the 118th Pennsylvania Volunteers who was shot in the knee in October 1864 somewhere near Petersburg, Virginia. These details do not qualify the impenetrable materiality of this photograph. If anything, they exaggerate it. Looking at this piece of bone one comes no closer to imagining what it was like to fight in Petersburg on an October day, or to be wounded there. In their resistant ahistoricity, such fragments reproduce a fundamental disorientation on the part of the viewer that, if it does not resemble the disorientation of wartime experience, certainly testifies to the impact of time on historical inquiry: this bone fragment reminds us that the thing that we are looking for—John Miller, his experience of war, the war itself—no longer exists. In this instance, the referential content of the wounded body floats free, suggesting that war is best expressed by pieces of the broken body that cannot be reassembled, let alone resurrected.[59]

While Whitman's "This Compost" points toward the war's stupendous death toll and rehearses the narrative of organic transformation that will help to rationalize it, the poem also suggests a certain tension in wartime culture. Time and again in poems and songs, essays and speeches, battlefield death is viewed as one stage in an inevitable, and virtually unaccountable, natural process. Yet in the midst of these affirmations we sometimes hear the hum of a sturdy machine—the machine of state—at work. When we do, it is difficult not to pause and observe that state-sanctioned death may not lead forward—to redemption, renewal, or even social progress—but may, to the contrary, be an end in itself. Melville concludes "Donelson" not by envisioning the body's fruitful decomposition but rather by evoking the decaying machinery of war:

> The battle flag-staff fall athwart
> The curs'd ravine, and wither; naught
>   Be left of trench or gun;
> The bastion, let it ebb away,
> Washed with the river bed; and Day
>   In vain seek Donelson.
>
> (52)

Melville imagines the power of nature turned against the instruments of war. Unlike Whitman, who uses organic imagery to ennoble state power, Melville is glad that the machines that produce wounded and dead bodies will, in time, erode and disappear. His poetry of brittle particulars reveals that there is no object, belief, or figure commensurate with the war; instead, such poetry intimates the debris war leaves behind, fragments that, at the very least, dissociate the act of interpretation from the affirmation of triumphant rebirth.

Notes

1. Walt Whitman, *Leaves of Grass* (Brooklyn, N.Y., 1856), 202-5.

2. See Katherine Kinney, "Making Capital: War, Labor, and Whitman in Washington, D.C.," in *Break-*

ing Bounds: Whitman and American Cultural Studies, ed. Betsy Erkkila and Jay Grossman (New York: Oxford University Press, 1996), 174-89.

3. Neil Schmitz, "Refiguring Lincoln: Speeches and Writings: 1832-1865," *American Literary History* 6 (Spring 1994): 104.

4. See Phoebe Lloyd, "Posthumous Mourning Portraiture," in *A Time to Mourn: Expressions of Grief in Nineteenth Century America,* ed. Martha V. Pike and Janice Gray Armstrong (Stony Brook, N.Y.: Museums at Stony Brook, 1980), 71-106; and Jay Ruby, *Secure the Shadow: Death and Photography in America* (Cambridge, Mass.: MIT Press, 1995).

5. As the war progressed, attempts to identify the dead and bury them in marked graves were increasingly successful. Many bodies, however, never received an adequate burial. In the aftermath of the conflict the War Department placed white wooden headboards on more than 300,000 graves, and these were replaced during the 1870s with more durable marble and granite markers. See David Sloane, *The Last Great Necessity: Cemeteries in American History* (Baltimore: Johns Hopkins University Press, 1991), 114.

6. On the discontinuity between antebellum death ritual and the "impersonal and disembodied national narrative" used to commemorate the dead during wartime, see Lisa Long, "'The Corporeity of Heaven': Rehabilitating the Civil War Body in *The Gates Ajar*," *American Literature* 69 (December 1997): 794.

7. Betsy Erkkila, *Whitman the Political Poet* (New York: Oxford University Press, 1989), 205, 214.

8. Walt Whitman, *Poetry and Prose,* ed. Justin Kaplan (New York: Library of America, 1996), 800.

9. James Dawes, *The Language of War: Literature and Culture in the U.S. from the Civil War through World War II* (Cambridge, Mass.: Harvard University Press, 2002), 29, 32.

10. My thanks to Stephen Cushman for this observation.

11. Qtd. in Sloane, *The Last Great Necessity,* 115.

12. Henry Sweetser Burrage, *Gettysburg and Lincoln: The Battle, the Cemetery, and the National Park* (New York: G. P. Putnam's Sons, 1906), 91.

13. In *Lincoln at Gettysburg: The Words That Remade America* (New York: Simon and Schuster, 1992), 19-40, Garry Wills describes the aftermath of the battle of Gettysburg, the design of the national cemetery, and the occasion of Lincoln's famous speech.

14. Abraham Lincoln, *Speeches and Writings, 1859-1865,* ed. Don Fehrenbacher (New York: Library of America, 1989), 536.

15. As Elizabeth Young has argued in response to Aaron and others, this represented absence is a critical fiction that exposes the process of canonization as it works to elevate certain texts and eliminate others. Young draws our attention to a longstanding critical preoccupation with the (failed) representational efforts of white male authors that has facilitated the glaring absence of women's war writing from this canon. Like wartime writers who claimed that the war could not be described, critics have taken the silence of certain authors as testimony to the war's immensity and significance while sidelining an enormous body of wartime writing. Like Young, Kathleen Diffley and Alice Fahs also take Aaron's "unwritten war" as the point of departure for their investigations of the vast and diverse popular culture of the Civil War. Daniel Aaron, *The Unwritten War: American Writers and the Civil War* (New York: Alfred A. Knopf, 1973), xix; Elizabeth Young, *Disarming the Nation: Women's Writing and the American Civil War* (Chicago: University of Chicago Press, 1999), 2-3; Kathleen Diffley, *Where My Heart Is Turning Ever: Civil War Stories and Constitutional Reform, 1861-1876* (Athens: University of Georgia Press, 1992); Alice Fahs, *The Imagined Civil War: Popular Literature of the North and South, 1861-1865* (Chapel Hill: University of North Carolina Press, 2001).

16. Jahan Ramazani discusses modern poets who reshape the elegy by working against the grain of its idealizing conventions. Taking the work of Geoffrey Hill as his example, Ramazani discusses Holocaust poems that "refuse the closure, rebirth, and substitution traditional in the elegiac genre, lest they seem to impose sense and purpose on mass murder." Jahan Ramazani, *Poetry of Mourning: The Modern Elegy from Hardy to Heaney* (Chicago: University of Chicago Press, 1994), 8. On twentieth-century war writing, see also Allyson Booth, *Postcards from the Trenches: Negotiating the Space between Modernism and the First World War* (Oxford: Oxford University Press, 1996); Dawes, *The Language of War*; Margot Norris, *Writing War in the Twentieth Century* (Charlottesville: University Press of Virginia, 2000).

17. Susan Sontag beautifully describes this ambivalence when she writes, "Though far from enthusiastic about this war, which he identified with fratricide, and for all his sorrow over the suffering on both sides, Whitman could not help but hear war's epic and heroic music. This ear kept him martial,

albeit in his own generous, complex, amatory way." Susan Sontag, *Regarding the Pain of Others* (New York: Farrar, Straus and Giroux, 2003), 52.

18. Michael Moon, *Disseminating Whitman: Revision and Corporeality in "Leaves of Grass"* (Cambridge, Mass.: Harvard University Press, 1991), 173.

19. Whitman, *Poetry and Prose,* 416.

20. Stephen Cushman describes the "discrepancy" between "loud belligerence" and "quieter watching" that characterizes *Drum-Taps.* Like Erkkila and Schmitz, Cushman is interested in the impact of photography on Whitman's wartime writing and believes that the best poems in *Drum-Taps* are distinguished by their visual emphasis. He cautions, however, against the view that the Civil War "engendered" either photographic or literary realism, suggesting that "it makes much more sense to say that some of the conditions that combined to produce war in North America during the nineteenth century also combined to produce realism there." Stephen Cushman, *Bloody Promenade: Reflections on a Civil War Battle* (Charlottesville: University Press of Virginia, 1999), 236, 240.

21. Whitman made his last revisions of *Drum-Taps* for the 1881 edition of *Leaves of Grass.*

22. Erkkila, *Whitman the Political Poet,* 212.

23. Whitman, *Poetry and Prose,* 438-39.

24. Erkkila, *Whitman the Political Poet,* 213.

25. Whitman, *Poetry and Prose,* 457.

26. C. A. Browne, *The Story of Our National Ballads* (New York: Thomas Y. Crowell, 1919), 216.

27. Benedict Anderson, *Imagined Communities: Reflections on the Origin and Spread of Nationalism,* rev. ed. (New York: Verso, 1991), 11.

28. Lincoln, *Speeches and Writings, 1859-1865,* 659-60.

29. James McPherson, *Battle Cry of Freedom: The Civil War Era* (1988; New York: Ballantine Books, 1989), 859.

30. Lincoln, *Speeches and Writings, 1859-1865,* 536.

31. Ibid., 505. Likewise, Lincoln argued that the suspension of the writ of habeas corpus was a military necessity aimed at detaining agitators intent on discouraging recruitment. See "To Erastus Corning and Others, June 12, 1863," 454-63.

32. Walt Whitman, *"Memoranda during the War"* [and] *"Death of Abraham Lincoln,"* ed. Roy P. Basler (Bloomington: Indiana University Press, 1962), 12.

33. Whitman, *Poetry and Prose,* 799.

34. Gary Laderman informs us that although Lincoln's body was embalmed it began to show signs of putrefaction while on display. The paradoxical relationship between decay and continuity was inscribed on the president's corpse through the partial failure, or incomplete success, of this new technology. Once again, the nationalist abstraction of undying continuity, meant to deny the material effects of violence, played out against the backdrop of the body's decomposition. Laderman, *Sacred Remains,* 160-63.

35. Edward Steers estimates that 7 million people—one in four Americans—turned out to pay their respects to the dead president. For descriptions of the funeral tour, see Ralph Borreson, *When Lincoln Died* (New York: Appleton-Century, 1965), 78, 103; Dorothy Meserve Kunhardt and Philip B. Kunhardt Jr., *Twenty Days: A Narrative in Text and Pictures of the Assassination of Abraham Lincoln and the Twenty Days and Nights That Followed* (New York: Harper and Row, 1965); Steers, *Blood on the Moon: The Assassination of Abraham Lincoln* (Lexington: University Press of Kentucky, 2001), 293.

36. Borreson, *When Lincoln Died,* 69.

37. Sallie Brock, *The Southern Amaranth* (New York: Wilcox and Rockwell, 1869).

38. Mary Louise Kete, *Sentimental Collaborations: Mourning and Middle-Class Identity in Nineteenth-Century America* (Durham, N.C.: Duke University Press, 2000). See also Mary Loeffelholz, "The Religion of Art in the City at War: Boston's Public Poetry and the Great Organ, 1863," *American Literary History* 13 (Summer 2001): 212-41.

39. Aaron, *The Unwritten War,* xv.

40. Oliver Wendell Holmes, "The Poetry of War," first delivered to the Dowse Institute, Cambridge, Mass., November 21, 1865, Special Collections Department, University of Virginia, Charlottesville, Va.

41. See Mark L. Walston, "Voices of the Holy War: Occasional Verse of the American Civil War," *Victorians Institute Journal* 15 (1987): 93-104.

42. Henry Howard Brownell, *Lyrics of a Day; or, Newspaper-Poetry* (New York: Carleton, 1864), iii.

43. Richard White, *Poetry Lyrical, Narrative, and Satirical, of the Civil War* (New York: American News Company, 1866), vi-vii.

44. Ibid., vii. Likewise, Walston argues that the mediocrity of Civil War poetry—characterized by "dif-

fuseness, contradiction, or repetition"—establishes it as a reflection of "the unrehearsed feelings of Americans in a period of great upheaval" and provides an unmediated expression of "the character of a people at war." Walston, "Voices of the Holy War," 103.

45. *War Lyrics and Songs of the South* (London: Spottiswoode, 1866).

46. I have not found any account of the notebook or its author. The notebook is held at Brown University's John Hay Library. As it is unpaginated, I will not refer to page numbers here.

47. After September 11, the streets of New York were again full of occasional poetry and art. Dan Barry, reporting for the *New York Times,* described messages written in the dust that covered the area near ground zero: "Perhaps a formal memorial will be built someday. For now there are the walls and windows of Lower Manhattan, where thousands of messages have been inscribed in the gray snow of destruction that fell two weeks ago today." Dan Barry, "Ephemeral Notes from a World Lost Bear Witness to the Unspeakable," *New York Times,* September 25, 2001.

48. An anthology of poetry written in response to Lincoln's death sounds similar themes and provides an interesting companion to this notebook. See *Poetical Tributes to the Memory of Abraham Lincoln* (Philadelphia: J. B. Lippincott, 1865).

49. Kevin Henkin, *City Reading: Written Words and Public Spaces in Antebellum New York* (New York: Columbia University Press, 1998), 3.

50. Qtd. in Henkin, *City Reading,* 98.

51. Herman Melville, *Battle-Pieces and Aspects of the War* (1866; New York: Da Capo, 1995).

52. Timothy Sweet, *Traces of War: Poetry, Photography, and the Crisis of the Union* (Baltimore: Johns Hopkins University Press, 1990), 167.

53. Sweet argues that Melville's war poems reflect critically on the tendency of other wartime artists, most especially Whitman, to "aestheticize the effects of violence and to evade questions about the historical contingency of politics." Melville, by contrast, rejects "conventional inscriptions that harmonize nature, the human body, and ideology." Sweet, *Traces of War,* 165.

54. Michael Rogin, *Subversive Genealogy: The Politics and Art of Herman Melville* (1979; Berkeley: University of California Press, 1985), 260.

55. Melville, preface to *Battle-Pieces,* v.

56. On the function of these bulletin boards in relation to the circulation of information during the Civil War, see Menahem Blondheim, *News over the Wires: The Telegraph and the Flow of Public Information in America, 1844-1897* (Cambridge, Mass.: Harvard University Press, 1994), 29; Fahs, *The Imagined War,* 19; Henkin, *City Reading,* 168-70.

57. Norris, *Writing War,* 24-25.

58. My account of these photographs, housed at Yale University's Medical Library, is indebted to Kathy Newman's essay "Wounds and Wounding in the American Civil War: A (Visual) History," *Yale Journal of Criticism* 6 (Fall 1993): 63-86.

59. Alan Trachtenberg also juxtaposes Melville's *Battle-Pieces* with medical photographs of wounded soldiers. He finds a determined objectivity, which aims to capture the part rather than the whole, in the episodic quality of Melville's volume and in the "sullen" gaze of soldiers who "watch themselves being watched." These provide examples of the fragmentation that characterizes representations of the Civil War. The unusual portrait of John Miller's leg bone allows me to argue that this kind of observation occasionally produced images of fragmentation so intense that they are able to convey the impossibility of trying to comprehend, let alone narrate, the war. Alan Trachtenberg, *Reading American Photographs: Images as History, Mathew Brady to Walker Evans* (Hill and Wang, 1989), 116.

William Etter (essay date April-August 2005)

SOURCE: Etter, William. "Cripple, Soldier, Crippled Soldier: Alfred Bellard's Civil War Memoir." *Prose Studies* 27, nos. 1-2 (April-August 2005): 80-92.

[*In the following essay, Etter uses Civil War veteran Alfred Bellard's memoir to offer a scholarly analysis of how the treatment of physical difference and disability inform disabled veterans' identity as well as national identity and ideology.*]

The disabled Civil War veteran was a freak of nationalism. A patriot who neither died in the service of reuniting his country nor continued fighting for it, a citizen who had actively shaped the postbellum nation yet now seemed the exemplar of passivity and dependence imagined as the very antithesis of the self-reliant "American," an individual who engaged in the most masculine of endeavors in battle yet who did not seem to be fully a "man," he was both a reservoir of nationalist capital and a perceived national liability. His maimed body inspired symbolic interpretations of the relationship between the body and the creation of the nation, and yet such symbolism threatened to undermine nationalistic fantasies about the beneficent relationship between the Union and its citizens. "Reconstitution" and "unity," and the more ambivalent "fragmentation," were all terms central to both the injured soldier's body and the Civil War-era United States. In four years the Civil War literally constructed between 300,000 and 350,000 permanently disabled individuals. Vexing questions regarding what really constituted an "American citizen" were, at least partially, negotiated in the cultural work performed by the figure of the disabled veteran in prose works of the period like Louisa May Alcott's quasi-autobiographical *Hospital Sketches* (1863), John W. De-Forest's novel *Miss Ravenel's Conversion* (1867), and Walt Whitman's memoir *Specimen Days* (1882). These texts conventionally strove to transcend the abnormal bodies of disabled veterans, render them irrelevant to the project of constituting national unity, or utilize them to reinforce the resilient "normal" bodies of the majority of American subjects in a time of national chaos. A little-known memoir by one disabled Union soldier, however, offers powerful alternative visions of a veteran's unique sense of self. Private Alfred Bellard's text charts his development of an identity that blends nationalistic ideology with disabled subjectivity and thereby offers us insights into the historical relationship between Americans with disabilities and their nation that can be productively applied to the United States of the present day.

Alfred Bellard was a forgotten but essential figure who participated in efforts to reimagine the identity of the disabled solder in the Civil War era. The son of British immigrants who relocated to New Jersey shortly after his birth, Bellard was an 18-year-old carpenter's apprentice when the war started. Though foreign born and fighting in a company in which two-thirds of the members were native Irish or German, Bellard watched the war end from the self-constructed perspective of a disabled, American veteran. While serving as a private first in the Union army and later in the Invalid Corps and Veterans Reserve Corps (units established by the United States government for injured soldiers), the young man regularly mailed letters and, what was more unusual, his own sketches home to his parents; at Bellard's request, his father collected all of this data in a notebook. When Bellard became old and infirm and moved into a Soldiers' Home to be cared for by the state, he composed his private memoirs (which he apparently never intended for publication) from the information contained in this notebook, the pocket diary he carried with him as a soldier, and letters written by his comrades. He completed the memoir before he died in 1891, absolutely and unjustly unknown as opposed to his contemporaries Herman Melville (who died the same year) and Walt Whitman (who died only a few months later). Extraordinary for its detailed portrait of the quotidian elements of life in the Army of the Potomac, Bel-

lard's autobiography is unique in also being one of the few lengthy Civil War memoirs by a common member of the Invalid Corps or Veterans Reserve Corps. Unlike the wartime works by Whitman, Alcott, or DeForest, Bellard's text offers invaluable insight into disabled and convalescent soldiers' own attempts to reconstitute an identity for themselves that derives its value from both the bodily abnormality produced by military service and the unity of nationalism.[1]

To the extent to which Bellard's memoirs can be said to have a plot independent of the chronology of the war, the narrative progresses from the chaos of physical dissolution in battle to the uncertainty of medical treatment to, finally, the restoration of order in the hearty acceptance of bodily abnormality within the institutional structures of the federal government. Approximately the first third of the text is strewn with wounded, maimed, and annihilated bodies. Most of the fighting in which Bellard participated took place in Virginia, and during the Richmond campaign he reports seeing an artilleryman with his leg blown off at the knee, and whole regiments "with their legs or arms shot off . . . with the top or side of the head cut off as with a knife."[2] Tumbling shells clipped off hands and feet. Even the attempt to offer such bodies the civilized, spiritual compensation of burial results in physical destruction during this campaign for exposure of corpses to the summer sun "turn[s] them as black as ink." Whenever the survivors try to bury such corrupted bodies, "the instand [sic] it went over the edge . . . in nearly all cases it burst" (85).[3] When casualties of war are not literally cut into pieces or dissolving before the narrator's eyes, Bellard's description of them often makes them appear as though they were. Because rain continually follows afternoons of heavy fighting and hasty burial in the Richmond campaign, "every morning a detail was sent out to cover up arms, legs and heads that had protruded from the ground during the night" (86). This image of a landscape of chaotic body pieces conveys in symbolic form the crucial initial, though formally unstated, assertion of Bellard's text: all those who fought in the Civil War experienced, whether directly or as witnesses, the destruction of any conventional understanding of physical normality.

Though Bellard's text appears to have been intended as a private and not a public endeavor, one can see its author deliberately striving to construct a polished text, to remain true to this assertion, and to maintain the logic of his narrative. One element of Bellard's book that makes it unique among Civil War memoirs is the number and quality of its pencil and colored ink freehand illustrations, all composed by the author himself. Quite often these illustrations foreground the physical abnormality produced by the war; for example, Bellard draws, in a sketch colored almost entirely in black and Union blue, a maimed artilleryman supported by two comrades, with no background scenery, yet the artist places the amputated limb, highlighted as a brilliant red spot, at the center of the image (68). While Bellard's prose at times reflects the distanced perception of a veteran re-writing his war experiences two decades after the fact, the illustrations that accompany the text testify to the immediate chaos of mangled flesh cast aside in the wake of battle. In an illustration representing the second day of fighting in the Richmond campaign Bellard portrays a mass of dead horses from Confederate cavalry, "a horrible sight," bloody with their legs broken and dis-jointed, framed by a handful of Confederate fatalities (84). Typically, Bellard is more attentive than other art-ists of the period—excluding photographers—to the devastating effects of the war on animals, but such at-tentiveness is most likely not the result of any special sensitivity to non-human life on his part. The written text supplementing Bellard's stunning depiction of an-nihilated horses coolly relates that when his regiment came across these creatures' bodies, the horses were simply "covered over with brush and fence rails and burnt . . . we cooked our coffee over their ribs" (85-6). Far more important to Bellard than the identities of in-dividuals wounded and killed in the war (very few of whom are named), or even their species is the fact of wartime bodily damage itself to which the surviving soldiers must emotionally and practically respond.

The memoir, in large part, concerns the act of seeing injury, disability, and destruction. In Bellard's narrative disability and death frequently appear as the spectacles they commonly were in Civil War-era photography. In-deed, in roughly the first half of the text Bellard's his-torically valuable descriptions of Civil War casualties are often presented as the observations of an inquisitive audience of soldiers centered, not surprisingly, around Bellard himself. At times, Bellard the narrator is the sole observational figure of damaged bodies. "Having a curiosity to see the wounded," our author relates, "I paid a visit to a church that was used for a hospital, and little way from our camp. The building was filled with wounded, and as I got there, our regimental surgeon was just finishing the amputation of a victim's arm, and was engaged in tying up the arteries and sewing the flaps of flesh together" (144-5). Bellard typically de-picts his observations of wartime disability as formed at the immediate moment in which the intersection of com-bat wounds and medical intervention occurs. Shortly af-ter this event, while wandering about their camp he and a few friends observe "some surgeons opperating . . . One of them had his leg cut off above the knee, and when we arrived the surgeon was tying up the arteries. The stump looked like a piece of raw beef. The other man had a part of his foot taken off. Neither of them seemed to be under the influence of cloreform, but were held down" (46). This narrative approach—which Bel-lard will amend once he himself is wounded in battle—fixes these disabilities in space (just as photographs of

the period do) so they manifest themselves to the reader as portraits. In doing so, he implies they have distinct points of historical and social origin, moments in which the wounded soldier is not constituted individually but emerges before the eyes of the battlefield surgeon who operates upon him as well as those of (non-wounded) spectators and, in a much broader sense, the national activity of waging war.

Bellard's descriptions of his first year in the army are striking in their capacity to render disability and death as a spectacle fixed in time. To achieve this effect Bel-lard often likes to depict bodies killed in quotidian pos-tures, such as his regiment's discovery of a rebel sitting "on a door step inclining forward as if he was asleep. One of our men thinking that he was so, called to him, but receiving no answer, he shook him by the shoulder, when the body fell over dead as a door nail" (86). As with a similar portrait of a rebel fatally shot when reach-ing into a cracker box—a shot that freezes his body into a paradox of deliberate action and the permanent inaction of death—the image of the sitting rebel is ac-companied by a color illustration. This approach to nar-rating the physical damage produced by the war is not an idiosyncratic element of Bellard's text alone but a convention of representations of war in this period that suggested combat disabilities and death were abnormal events that simply "happened" without anyone or any-thing culpable for them. Crucial to the rhetorical con-struction of the disabled veteran in American photogra-phy and literature was the portrait of the freakishly sudden injury, of disability abruptly fixed in time. This convention, particularly as deployed in the frozen me-dium of the photographic image, not only rendered the war's wounding an established fact of national history but also necessarily figured disability as permanent and irreversible.

In his novel *Miss Ravenel's Conversion,* John W. De-Forest depicts the bizarre death of a man accidentally hit by a ball while reading the newspaper; the leisurely reclining posture into which he is frozen by death causes his comrades for a long time to ignore him under the mistaken belief he is merely asleep. One also finds nu-merous photographs taken during the war depicting scenes equally graphic and startling: gunshot injuries to the lower face. The nature of these wounds meant they often healed into a position that seemed to freeze the moment of injury in time: the mouth permanently forced open in an expression of surprise or pain, the lines of the chin fixed into marks of implosion.[4] In its apparent irrationality and unpredictability, this mode of portray-ing the disabled body also helped reduce the responsi-bility of the two competing nations for individual de-struction. Disability was something that simply "happened"; it was an historically real event involving an historical personage but devoid of an historical agent.

The period in Bellard's life when he himself was wounded in the leg and removed from the front seems to have been the origin of his understanding that Civil War injury could exist as a spectacle that complicates the conventionally hierarchical relationship between the maimed soldier and the "normal" viewer of his body, necessitating the revision of personal identity. Not only was this incident undoubtedly significant in fact, Bellard—as elderly autobiographer—locates this event as a turning point in his text, a moment in which Alfred—the young private—undergoes a transition from common man to disabled veteran, all the while retaining his identity as a soldier. Bellard does relate that, while serving in the regular army during the early years of the war (before his battlefield injury), he was "occasionally troubled" by an unspecified childhood injury to his foot, an injury which isolates him (literally) from his comrades on at least two occasions when he must march more slowly than they due to "mud and the tight boots" (*Gone for a Soldier*, 70). Yet despite the fact Bellard refers to himself as "lame" on both occasions, he does not provide further details about his impairment or any long-term effects caused by it. In these early sections of the autobiography this injury is not employed for any significant narrative purpose or represented as characterizing Bellard as a subject. The author seems most interested in using his troublesome foot to lampoon the camp physician's mishandling of simple injuries with ineffective, confused prescriptions of pills and "liniment" for Bellard's foot, "at the same time reporting me fit for duty," though Bellard's commanding officers know full well he should be given light tasks around camp for the day. A serious wound to the knee from a musket ball at Chancellorsville, however, proves to be the single most significant personal event of the narrative as it drives Bellard to reimagine himself as a disabled soldier in his visual and written self-portraits.

Bellard's subjective position as both chronicler of the physical "abnormality" produced by the war and physically disabled individual gives him a unique perspective on the relationship between the bodies of Civil War soldiers and the institutional structures within which they were immediately placed once wounded: the surgeon, the hospital, the Invalid/Veteran's Reserve Corps, and civilian society. The professional competence of a central figure in the reinforcement of dominant ideologies of the body during the Civil War—the corps surgeon—is repeatedly derided in Bellard's text for egregious misdiagnoses and haphazard treatments. Given scornful nicknames by the men they serve—Bellard's regiment called their surgeon "Old Pill Garlic" due to his ignorance of the effects of the drugs he prescribed—military physicians were ridiculed for their ill-informed pessimism or feared for their willingness to put their patients through agonizing and, many soldiers believed, unnecessary and dangerous procedures. One soldier "badly wounded in the groin" was told by the examining physician "it was

no use doing anything for him," yet, Bellard reports as though it were a punchline, "About 3 weeks after the same man went home" in good health (82-3). Like his fellow recruits, Bellard came to understand that "These military hospitals were a fine field for young M.D.'s to practice in" after witnessing grueling treatments in which extensive "probing and cutting" for lodged balls "with no success" simply ended in the doctors "cut-[ting] off the leg, and w[inding] up the job" (227). This assessment was certainly shared by many Americans of the period. On 30 July 1862 the *New York Tribune* protested

> against the free use of the surgeon's knife and saw on the legs and arms of our wounded soldiers. That there is just cause for complaint we have the assurance of medical men . . . Young aspirants for distinction in the profession of surgery easily persuade themselves that the wounded or shattered limb of a soldier is a proper subject on which to practise the science of amputation.[5]

Louisa May Alcott stated in 1863 that hospital nurses were frequently shocked to observe experienced surgeons "whipping off legs like an animated guillotine."[6] When he himself is wounded at Chancellorsville Bellard thus avoids consulting the camp physicians who understandably cause him great anxiety and waits to care for himself despite the excessive discomfort and danger in letting his wound go untreated for too long: "The next morning I got some bandages from the hospital steward and dressed the wound myself, for I was afraid from the looks of the wound, which had turned black, that the doctors would want to experiment on it and perhaps cut it off altogether" (*Gone for a Soldier*, 218). Soldiers with physical impairments, Bellard suggests, knew more about their own bodies than the physicians who treated them, though the latter most often ignored their patients' opinions.

In addition to employing personal experience as an injured soldier as a means of questioning the capabilities of the military medical establishment to diagnose and treat him properly, Bellard uses his unique position as a disabled spectator of disabled bodies to establish his narrative authority. At the same time he complicates the specular dynamic of "normal" institutional viewer and "deviant" maimed soldier conventional to the army's medical approaches to disability. During the war, hospitals, particularly those in the nation's capital, were regularly open to members of the public who wished to tour them and see their inmates, a demand that only grew after the war ended. In the 1860s and 1870s, the Army Medical Museum began publishing advertisements depicting "Curiosities" in line drawings, such as "A Withered Arm" found sun-dried in a tree, to encourage attendance. In 1875 an estimated "twenty-five thousand people visited the Museum annually."[7] Bellard was one of these sorts of tourist. Once, while still only performing light duties around the army hospitals at which they were still patients, Bellard and his comrades gain passes to visit the "Citizens' Volunteer Hospital" in Philadelphia where they notice that "lots of people came there out of mere curiosity to see the place and the patients. A squad of men had been detailed for the purpose of escorting them round and showing them the different points of interest" (*Gone for a Soldier,* 231). In one sense the Hospital serves the same purpose for Bellard and his friends as it does for the tourists they encounter: it is one tourist stop among many in one of the largest cities in the nation.

Yet at the same time Bellard and his friends cannot be said to occupy the same perspective as these other touring citizens for they are these patients' peers. True, the men in Bellard's group have advanced to a different stage of treatment or recovery and are permitted to leave their hospital on occasion, but they are still classified "convalescents" and have not yet been discharged or placed in the Invalid Corps. Perhaps even more important than the author's highlighting of this reconfiguration of this specular dynamic by replacing the merely presumed "normal" spectator with a "maimed" one is his validation of the entire persona of the disabled soldier as a part of the Invalid Corps following such experiences.

With General Order 36 in 1862 and General Order 69 in 1863, the Union authorized the appointment of "wounded or feeble men" as cooks, clerks, nurses, and hospital attendants while they were still carried on regimental rolls (a policy novelists John W. DeForest and Louisa May Alcott harshly criticized). Later, when greater numbers of free blacks and "contrabands" were made available for these duties, the "Invalid Corps" (or "IC") was established. Composed of two battalions divided according to degree of impairment—the first authorized to carry weapons while the second served as nurses, cooks, and prison guards or were assigned the tasks of "keeping drunken and rowdy soldiers from misbehaving in theaters and on the streets" and brothels in Washington—the IC was officially established in April 1863 and by January 1864 boasted 491 officers and 17,764 men.[8] Notably, whereas states organized their own companies composed solely of citizens from the same region, the government attempted to make the IC "a truly Federal force" by distributing members from different states among its various divisions. Ironically, the soldiers who could no longer be members of the Union's regular armies thus came in a sense to represent a broader conception of the "United States" than those individuals directly fighting to preserve the nation.[9] Curiously, despite its contribution to the Union cause, the IC became the butt of a great deal of ridicule from both society at large and the military, indicating a notable disunity in the Union and demonstrating the degree to which various facets of the nation remained doubtful about the place of the disabled veteran in the body politic. Jokes traveled about the camps that the "IC" of "Invalid Corps" stood for "Inspected-Condemned," the same initials stamped on faulty government equipment. The jokes became so embarrassing that the government officially changed the name of the organization to the "Veterans Reserve Corps" (or "VRC"). Even within the administrative structure governing the activities of the IC/VRC confusions about how to define and organize individuals with varying degrees of disability resulted in a vague, almost comically inept, system of classifying "fit" and "unfit" soldiers.[10]

An anxious indeterminacy haunted the disabled soldier of the Civil War, even when he was absorbed into the army's ever-expanding bureaucracy. Bellard bemusedly reports that "Examinations were made every week by orders of the head surgeons for the purpose of clearing out the hospitals . . . The well men were sent to their regts., while all those who were fit to do duty round the hospitals, but not fit for a march, were transferred to the Invalid Corps," and then redistributed into first or second battalions (or discharged entirely). Nevertheless, physicians frequently quarreled over determinations of physical status. After being declared not "fit for active service," Bellard himself was then stuck in limbo by a second examination board which "had quite a discussion, w[h]ether to discharge me or not" and, after some dispute, "finally came to the conclusion to put me in the first battalion of invalids" (*Gone for a Soldier,* 231-2, 235). After an extensive period spent in limbo at hospitals and thus prevented from seeing any sort of combat, Bellard delightedly recalls the pride he felt in donning the blue and black uniform of the Invalid Corps and serving on guard duty: "I found myself detailed for the first time in five months" (Bellard later ended his military career as a member of the VRC) (238). The service of the disabled IC soldier, Bellard's comment suggests in its comparison of being "detailed" as part of a regular New Jersey regiment with being placed on duty in the IC, was equivalent to that of any Union soldier.

This perspective has merit, for members of the IC/VRC did see combat, and in his narrative Bellard repeatedly makes a point of stressing the labor demanded of members of the Invalid Corps. He tells us that even the Second Battalion (men deemed the most "unfit" of the IC), in which Bellard served for a short time, typically marched 16 miles a day, performed patrol duty in the nation's capital for six hours daily even during the 100-degree heat of the summer, and did so on at most only six hours' rest. Many of the divisions also regularly performed the ceremonial offices of the regular army to demonstrate the North's military might and unity; they marched through Washington, DC on review and three regiments of the Veterans' Reserve Corps, including Bellard's, even passed "through the White House grounds . . . [and] made a very creditable display, large numbers of citizens and soldiers looking on" (247).

One of these reviews is said to have garnered an estimated audience of two to three thousand people. Yet this equivalence between the regular army and the IC/VRC on the grounds that both are "soldiers" on active duty—in terms of both labor and national symbolism—so frequently stressed by Bellard in the later sections of his autobiography is an equivalence with a difference, for Bellard just as readily stresses the latter's distinct identity as *disabled* soldiers on active duty.

The disabled soldier could be imagined as marking the distinction between the actively "loyal," courageous, self-sacrificing American citizen and the individual who failed to participate in the construction and defense of the nation, thereby reinforcing the legitimacy of the national war machine. Bellard offers this sort of defense when he reports wounded and disabled soldiers' response to the news of the 1863 draft riots: "At the time the riots took place in New York, all the boys in the hospital who could walk, volunteered to form a company or regt. and proceed to New York, but were not allowed to do so by the doctors. The verdict of the soldiers were that whenever one of them was caught, to string him up at once" (232). In other regions, some wounded soldiers got their wish when General James Fry marshaled men from the First Battalion of the Invalid Corps to Vermont to arrest opponents of the draft; in the latter half of the war, the Corps saw similar action in Michigan and Pennsylvania.[11] During the war it became popular for both sides of the conflict to understand the figure of the selfless, injured soldier as saliently indicating the shamefully unpatriotic existence of the non-combatant or the individual who opposed the national engagement in war.[12]

Though Bellard's Civil War letters and journal were initially read only by friends and family, his memoir bespeaks a keen awareness of the social perceptions of disabled soldiers as well as the attempt to offer a counter-narrative of a distinct disabled identity which is nevertheless fully amenable and loyal to the Union war effort and its ideals. Reflections by non-disabled individuals on the potential "unfitness" of the Veterans Reserve Corps for military duty are immediately followed by descriptions of VRC members asserting control over military personnel. Washington, DC was "full of soldiers," Bellard relates, and "It seemed to be a good joke for them to call us condemned yanks, and jeer at us while marching across the street. Coming across some members of the 69th Pen. (an Irish Regt.) one day, they gave us a good deal of talk, and the Lieut. arrested one of them." When the individual in question pulls a revolver, Bellard angrily "grab[s] him by the neck and pin[s] him against the wall," keeping his bayonet on the prisoner on the long walk back to the regimental guard house (*Gone for a Soldier,* 255). At the end of that month the VRC, charged with keeping order at a ball, must forcibly intervene when one of its own is physi-

cally assaulted: "some citizen struck the Lieut. and as he only had one arm to defend himself with, he called for the guard to arrest them" (259). Even missing a limb the Lieutenant retains his power of command; an enraged Bellard pursues the offender, who is ultimately captured and imprisoned, in fulfillment of the commander's order. As described by Bellard this incident depicts a disabled individual who exercises power because, and not in spite, of his own physical impairment. As the Lieutenant could not sufficiently defend himself physically, he employs the institutional structure of the military chain of command to do so, using the vehicle placed at his disposal by his government: a cadre of disabled soldiers.

The recognition and acceptance of oneself as a disabled veteran offered a means by which one might participate in the construction of one's own independent and historically significant identity, complementing the practical power granted by participation in the military. The structure of Bellard's narrative suggests he himself arrived at this self-concept by evolving from identifying some affinities between himself and other disabled soldiers, to appreciating the extent to which disabled individuals participated in the war effort, to understanding himself as a soldier and a compatriot of soldiers who experienced permanent injury in battle; the latter vision of identity constituted a new social role. Traveling in a hospital wagon for treatment immediately following his wounding at Chancellorsville, Bellard's experience of his body prompts him to perceive commonality between he and "a badly wounded man" for "every jolt of the ambulance over the corduroy road would make him cry with pain" and "it was not very pleasant even for me" (222). Yet at this initial stage in Bellard's experience with his newly acquired disability the reader still notices the author's subtle differentiation between himself and the "wounded" in his application of degrees of injury and discomfort. Shortly after leaving the ambulance for treatment, Bellard proudly relates in a letter to his father he "said nothing" and "did not kick up a rumpus" when a hospital nurse poured liquor on his wound while the presumably weaker patient in the neighboring bunk "yelled as if he was getting killed when it was poured on him" (227). In Bellard's case the ability to endure pain, to battle his own body quietly and successfully, gives him a sense of self-worth while writing to family members whom he wishes to be proud of him. The soldier's impaired body is the enemy of himself as well as those attempting to mitigate his suffering and thus merely a reified pain.

After months of witnessing first-hand military and civilian hospitals and serving in the IC/VRC, however, Bellard comes to understand the extent and significance of the presence of "maimed men" in the war, a fact he registers in narrative by discussing the physically disabled authorities with whom he comes into close contact while he himself moves among the contexts into which wounded soldiers were placed. Michael Schaffel, who lost an arm at Fredericksburg and was placed in command of a division of the VRC, was also a one-eyed major. Colonel William Sewell, who commanded Bellard's New Jersey Company B in the regular army and was wounded at Chancellorsville along with Bellard, returned to action only to be wounded again at Gettysburg and eventually received a disability discharge in 1864. Perhaps the most famous disabled soldier Bellard claims to have encountered is Dan Sickles; though Bellard essentially only mentions Sickles in passing, the latter was notorious to nineteenth-century Americans as the mentally unbalanced one-legged general who had shot his wife's lover in Washington, DC in 1859 only to be acquitted of murder in what is believed to be "the first successful plea of temporary insanity in the history of American jurisprudence" and who managed to live long enough to witness the beginning of World War I.[13] While it is going too far to call Bellard's text a conscious effort at revisionary history (reinserting the disabled, famous and infamous alike, into the story of the United States), his approach certainly demonstrates a personal revision which presents the experience of the Civil War as an evolution into a conception of the disabled self for Private Bellard.

Indeed, Bellard repeatedly distinguishes the self-images of disabled soldiers from impressions of them held by soldiers in the regular armies, using the former's comfortable acceptance of these self-images as a point of distinction. On board a railcar transporting them to another encampment in Virginia, Bellard and his fellow hospital patients "passed the 7th N. Y. militia . . . Some of them wanted to know what brigade that was on the train. One of the cripples sung out 'The Cripple Brigade' but the 7th didn't seem to understand" (*Gone for a Soldier,* 229). Significantly, this event occurs before Bellard musters out in the Invalid Corps. Standard administrative procedure for Union armies during the war dictated that soldiers being treated for wounds or illness in the hospital remained on the rosters of their original regiments (organized by state and subdivided by regions within states) even if they spent months in the hospital, until they were discharged for disability, transferred to a different regiment, or transferred to the Invalid Corps/Veterans Reserve Corps. The call, "The Cripple Brigade," however, imaginatively places all the disabled soldiers aboard the car in a single unit despite the fact that many came from different regiments and thus reorganizes identification within the military along lines of physical difference more than state and national divisions. At the same time this call asserts a continued commitment of patriotic members of the "Brigade" to the Union's war effort. Moreover, the ridicule directed at the IC/VRC (recall the play on initials with "Inspected-Condemned") depicted so often by Civil War historians as lamentable intolerance on the part of

"normal" soldiers and callous members of the popular press was in fact casually appropriated by Bellard and his peers as appropriate means of description. With an unconcerned, factual, even non-judgmental air Bellard relates that "the boys [of the regular army] called us Condemned Yanks" when they encountered members of the IC/VRC on guard duty or serving as military police in the nation's capital (238). Bellard similarly unhesitatingly deploys seemingly derogatory terms as simple descriptors in his text; after a tedious day spent guarding military prisoners he relates that "the cripples [were] sent back to quarters, tumbling into our bunks about five o'clock a.m.," notably asserting his own identification with the label of disability and its human referents with the phrase "our bunks" which counters the potential distance between author and disabled subjects suggested in the adoption of the conventional appellation "the cripples" (243).

Because Bellard and his comrades' assertion of a shared sense of disability as an essential component of their identity is not designed to challenge dominant national ideologies, does not explicitly aim to redefine disability, and is not narratively extended by the author beyond the immediate circumstances of war, it would be inaccurate to see it as a fully politicized form of solidarity. Certainly the Veterans Reserve Corps and postwar veterans' organizations like the Grand Army of the Republic and federal and state "Soldiers' Homes" put individuals with a wide variety of disabilities within shared organizational contexts and thus could foster the recognition of rudimentary "cross-disability coalitions" that might later promote the establishment of a more definitive minority group consciousness, but it does not appear this often occurred. The communal mindset Bellard encounters and subsequently adopts and represents does, however, represent a rough mid-nineteenth century manifestation of a minority-group consciousness among people with disabilities, a consciousness that would much later emerge to offer truly powerful and thoroughly politicized dissent in late-twentieth and twenty-first century America.[14]

As his drawings of his own wartime injury indicate, Bellard eventually came to understand himself as essentially disabled as well as essentially the soldier he enthusiastically imagined himself to be when he first enlisted. While a drawing apparently made shortly after the battle in which he was wounded rather clinically depicts a depersonalized knee marked by two bloody holes, drawings made later in the war—after Bellard became part of the Invalid Corps—reveal an illustrator not only comfortable with his physical condition but even going so far as to assert it as a badge of distinction. A few months after receiving his injury, Bellard composes visceral illustrations of amputations performed at corps field hospitals, the most notable of which depicts a soldier with a wound precisely the same as Bellard's undergoing an amputation while lying on a table above an unconcealed pile of limbs (*Gone for a Soldier,* 221). Illustrating Bellard's implicit identification with other "maimed" soldiers this drawing demonstrates that, despite the recognition that his own injury could have been far worse (Bellard calls himself "a lucky dog," all things considered) he willingly makes abnormal bodies, including his own, focal points of his narrative in such a way as to make the story of the Civil War as much about its living casualties as about its unmaimed heroes and its dead sacrificial victims. In a striking revision of popular Civil War-era folk songs like "When Johnny Comes Marching Home" and, at the other extreme, magazine accounts of the families of fallen soldiers destined to never see their loved ones again like "The Children of the Battlefield," Bellard closes his memoirs with his return home to New Jersey. His self-portrait shows himself with unshaven face and untucked shirt—a wearied, common citizen-veteran—looking at his house from a distance. This representation, with its posture of leaning against a fence to support his injured leg and carrying a cane over his shoulder, asserts that the returning soldier is the disabled soldier (277).

Bellard's autobiographical narrative of the refashioning of his identity is not the standard story of the dehistoricized "self-made" man. Far more interesting than that, it is the tale of an individual who learns to understand himself in terms of his relationship to physical and social circumstances and national ideologies that quite often, and quite powerfully, influence him. Indeed, the self-concept he develops—which incorporates elements of the dominant culture through a military and nationalistic discourse along with elements of Bellard's experience as a member of a unique class of Americans through his discussion of his own disability—calls to mind the negotiations of multicultural and multinational subjectivities within the intersecting dynamics of public and private identities that form such an important component of the postmodern conception of "the American." Bellard's memoirs therefore provide modern scholars with a resource for studying not only Civil War America but also contemporary concerns: literary and visual registers of the multiplicity of human experience, diverse modes of perceiving American culture, and the relationship of human "difference" to democratic politics.

By the end of the war Bellard's composite identity was fully established. When in an idle moment he sketched out a personal battle-flag for himself at this time he listed on it all the conflicts in which he participated but placed Chancellorsville (the site of his wounding) at the center, vertically aligned with his name (x). Like his narrative, Bellard's flag represents the symbolic confluence of the wounded surviving veteran with the newly reunited nation, the figure of the disabled veteran inti-

mately tied to nationalistic ideologies. This figure tested understandings of citizenship, the relationship between "normal" and "abnormal" Americans amidst conditions of widespread violence, and the reconfigurations of the operations and responsibilities of the federal government.

Alfred Bellard's memoir offers us insights into the historical and sociopolitical relationship between Americans with disabilities and their nation, insights that can be applicable to the present-day United States. His engagement with the representation of disability as something that simply "happened," a historically real event without an agent, for instance, encourages us to consider the ways in which disability continues to be figured as irrational and unpredictable and how social or national responsibility for disability can be excused or simply elided as a result. As sociologist and disability rights advocate Michael Oliver has recently stressed, when one understands disability as "some terrible chance event which occurs at random to unfortunate individuals," one tends to ignore "society's failure to provide appropriate services and adequately ensure the needs of disabled people are fully taken into account in its social organization."[15] This vision of disability in turn impacts medical approaches to disability, programs of economic assistance for people with disabilities, and the concept of disability "rights." Reading Alfred Bellard's memoir today reminds us that developing a fuller understanding of the historical continuities of cultural visions of disability and disabled people's efforts to forge unique identities embedded within these historical trends remains one of our most compelling reasons for studying disability in narrative prose.

Notes

1. Historical information on Bellard in addition to that provided by the memoirs themselves has largely been compiled by David Herbert Donald, the first historian to authenticate Bellard's text through extensive research.

2. Alfred Bellard, *Gone for a Soldier,* ed. David Herbert Donald (Toronto: Little, Brown and Company, 1975), 68. Subsequent references to this text will be cited parenthetically.

3. Bellard makes very few attempts to make his spelling consistent in his memoirs except when relating proper names. As his references are nearly always clear without correction, I have chosen to quote his text as it stands in every instance.

4. See William Davis and William A. Frassanito, eds., *Touched by Fire: A Photographic Portrait of the Civil War,* 2 vols. (Boston, MA: Little, Brown, 1985), 2: 250; and *The Medical and Surgical History of the War of the Rebellion,* 3 vols., Surgeon General Joseph K. Barnes, Director (Washington, DC: Government Printing Office, 1870), 1: 371ff.

5. Quoted in Allan Nevins, *War Becomes Revolution: 1862-1863* (New York: Collier, 1960), 141-2.

6. Louisa May Alcott, *Hospital Sketches* in *Alternative Alcott,* ed. Elaine Showalter (New Brunswick, NJ: Rutgers University Press, 1988), 71. Alcott was not simply being sensational; reliable studies of Civil War medicine currently available conservatively place the number of amputations performed during the war at 30,000 (see Lisa A. Long, "'The Corporeity of Heaven': Rehabilitating the Civil War Body in *The Gates Ajar,"* *American Literature* 69/4 [Dec. 1997], 786). This figure is not surprising given that the Surgeon General's office determined "Shot wounds of the upper arm, forearm, and hand were, perhaps, the most common accidents of battle" (*Medical and Surgical History,* 2: 471).

7. Katherine Kinney, "Making Capital: War, Labor, and Whitman in Washington, D.C.," in: *Breaking Bounds: Whitman and American Cultural Studies,* ed. Betsy Erkkila and Jay Grossman (New York: Oxford University Press, 1996), 184-5.

8. Bellard, *Gone for a Soldier,* 248; Byron Stinson, "The Invalid Corps," *Civil War Times Illustrated* 10/2 (1971), 25.

9. Stinson, "The Invalid Corps," 23.

10. Members of the IC/VRC thoroughly manifested their martial contributions to the national cause. From their official records Byron Stinson estimates no less that 82% of VRC officers "had been literally shot to pieces" or were paralyzed in some fashion as a result of battle (see Stinson, "The Invalid Corps," 25). DeForest, who at one point was declared unfit for the regular army and began composing his novel *Miss Ravenel's Conversion* as a virtual invalid, later became the Corps' last commander. Furthermore, when they engaged in combat themselves members of the IC/VRC were known to have performed admirably. In 1863, for instance, an Ohio soldier (who was not a member of the Corps) wrote that he observed Morgan's Raiders "so roughly handled by a force of invalids . . . that they hastily withdrew" (quoted in Stinson, "The Invalid Corps," 25).

11. Stinson, "The Invalid Corps," 24.

12. A drawing published in *Harper's Weekly* just after the Civil War ended demonstrates the nation's insistent use of this figure to symbolize "national" principles, national sacrifice, and patriotism. Titled "And Not This Man?" and intended to advance the cause of black male suffrage the drawing depicts the interior of a marble temple draped with decorations reminiscent of the American flag, apparently meant to represent the US Capitol building. On the left an African-American uniformed soldier stands supported by crutches, his right leg missing at the knee, the aisle rug beneath him also adorned with stars. Gesturing imploringly towards this disabled veteran a classical robed maiden (symbolizing Liberty) looks towards an unseen group of viewers at the end of the aisle (theoretically the US Congress or, more generally, the American voters). In this image an individual type who is imagined as possessing a great deal of symbolic nationalistic capital is deployed in support of the argument that African-Americans are "men" useful to their country and thus should be considered "citizens."

13. James M. McPherson, *Battle Cry of Freedom* (New York: Ballantine, 1988), 641.

14. For an overview of minority-group consciousness in disability communities in recent times, see Paul K. Longmore, *Why I Burned My Book and Other Essays on Disability* (Philadelphia, PA: Temple University Press), 2003, especially Introduction and chapters 1 and 5; and Joseph P. Shapiro, *No Pity: People with Disabilities Forging a New Civil Rights Movement* (New York: Times Books), 1993.

15. Michael Oliver, *Understanding Disability: From Theory to Practice* (New York: St Martin's Press, 1996), 32.

Daneen Wardrop (essay date summer-fall 2005)

SOURCE: Wardrop, Daneen. "Civil War Nursing Narratives, Whitman's *Memoranda During the War,* and Eroticism." *Walt Whitman Quarterly Review* 23, nos. 1-2 (summer-fall 2005): 26-47.

[*In the following essay, Wardrop studies the eroticism in the relationship between nurse and patient in the context of Walt Whitman's* Memoranda During the War, *and compares this with other nursing narratives written by women authors.*]

"All flesh is grass."

—Peter I, 1:24.

Bodies of soldiers "had gone down as Grass falls below the scythe."

—Civil War veteran

"[At Gettysburg] every grass-blade seemed to have been stained with blood."

—Sophronia Bucklin[1]

Whitman's *Memoranda During the War* has recently begun to be considered within the historical framework of the many Civil War nursing narratives that proliferated during and after the war. While Whitman's *Memoranda* is not solely a nursing narrative—for it offers depictions of other aspects of the war—and while he served during the war as a nurse "in my own style"[2] as much as an official appointee of the Christian Commission, his memoir shares with the nursing narratives that preceded his work some important aspects of style and tone. A genre of prose that arose during and after the war, the nursing narrative was written most often by women who wished to offer the female version of service in the hospitals and on the field. Narratives written by Union nurses that appeared before Whitman's 1875-1876 *Memoranda During the War* include Louisa May Alcott's *Hospital Sketches,* Georgeanna Woolsey's *Three Weeks at Gettysburg,* the anonymous 1864 *Notes of Hospital Life,* Sarah Emma Edmond's *Nurse and Spy in the Union Army,* Elvira Powers' *Hospital Pencillings,* Anna Morris Holstein's *Three Years in Field Hospitals of the Army of the Potomac,* Sophronia Bucklin's *In Hospital and Camp,* and Jane Stuart Woolsey's *Hospital Days,* all published before or in 1870. A full cultural assessment of Whitman's *Memoranda* depends at least partially upon discerning the ways in which he constructed his memoir within the context of those previous memoirs, utilizing themes of democracy, the typical American, motherhood, and, in the primary focus of this essay, the eroticism that forms between nurse and patient.[3]

Nursing narratives were well received by the general public. Alcott's 1863 *Hospital Sketches,* for example, proved so popular that it inaugurated her literary career. Whitman's interest in Alcott's book, in fact, was responsible for his query to his friend and Alcott's publisher, James Redpath, whom he contacted concerning his own prospective narrative. Alcott's account of her Civil War nursing experiences first appeared serially in the Boston *Commonwealth* from May 22 through June 26, 1863, and then, later in 1863, in book form through the press of Redpath. Whitman wrote Redpath on October, 1863, about his narrative, as an idea "worthy the time,—something considerably beyond hospital sketches."[4] The phrase "hospital sketches" probably refers at least obliquely to Alcott's narrative and, even if generic, reflects Alcott's achievement in that within a few months her title had become absorbed and restated into casual parlance for Whitman.

Given its wide following among the general populace, Whitman would have been likely also to have at least perused Sarah Emma Edmonds' 1865 *Nurse and Spy in the Union Army. Nurse and Spy* was eagerly consumed for Edmonds' portrayals of herself as a nurse, if at times contested for her depictions of herself as a spy. Georgeanna Woolsey's 1863 *Three Weeks at Gettysburg,* written specifically "for the purpose of stimulating sewing circles to keep sending supplies,"[5] saw the distribution of ten thousand copies. It is hard to tell exactly which nursing narratives Whitman might have read (though it is unlikely he encountered Jane Stuart Woolsey's narrative, only 100 copies of which were printed [Austin, 118]). The fact is incontestable, nonetheless, that the genre had developed significantly and primarily through the auspices of female nurses by the time Whitman published his *Memoranda During the War* in 1875-1876.

Though the memoirs of female nurses were to continue to grow more popular in the later decades on the nineteenth century, they had already lodged themselves into the consciousness of the nation in the decade after the war. Frank Moore's *Women of the War; Their Heroism and Self-Sacrifice* appeared in 1867, and its nearly 600 pages described the contributions of some thirty-eight nurses and a handful of women soldiers during the war; a year later, L. P. Brockett and Mary Vaughan's similarly encyclopedic volume described the contributions of at least as many women nurses, with a chapter on the four Woolsey sisters that included nearly the full text of Georgeanna Woolsey's narrative.[6] In offerings like these, and especially in the proliferating narratives written by women themselves, Whitman had access to a plethora of material that might serve as a model for a nursing memoir with a general and large readership.

In *Memoranda,* Whitman extended the nursing narratives' style of nineteenth-century bricolage—that is, of notes composed on the spot and put together so as to retain the immediacy of the experience. Even a cursory glance at the narratives' titles indicates such immediacy: *Sketches, Three Weeks, In Hospital and Camp, Notes, Pencillings, Three Years, Hospital Days.* In one such instance of the technique of note-taking, the narrator of the anonymous 1864 *Notes of Hospital Life* states at the outset: "These notes were jotted down as the incidents occurred; they are a simple statement of facts simply stated."[7] The caveat—or boast—of on-the-pulse informality is one that Whitman, too, would claim ten years later. All the titles offer a necessary informality, giving notice that the author wrote in the rush of experience, offering a pastiche of observations running day-to-day or week-to-week. While Whitman was a self-trained journalist and had certainly honed the skills of *in medias res* reporting, still his *Memoranda*—composed from notes he wrote while at the site of the hospital or camp—were compiled, revised, and augmented in the years after the war, in the wake of the newly developing genre of nursing narratives.[8]

Whitman's newspaper reporting, however, in which he recounts some of his hospital experiences, precedes all the nursing narratives (except Alcott's serialized book). As early as August 16, 1863, Whitman published articles in various newspapers such as *The New York Times* that he later incorporated into *Memoranda.*[9] In the *New York Times,* for example, he noted a sleeping soldier so handsome that "one must needs go nearer him," and he also wrote of a dying soldier, "He behaved very manly and affectionate. The kiss I gave him as I was about leaving, he returned fourfold."[10] Whitman reported his involvement with his patients as early as 1864, but the scenes of erotic attraction in *Memoranda* appeared in a more detailed manner in 1875; that is to say, Whitman's project of eroticism was well-established, if not particularly well-read, by the time of the Civil War, but the scenes in *Memoranda* carry Whitman's distinctive voice while also locating themselves within the burgeoning sweep of the popular new genre of nursing narratives.

In addition, a prepossessing concern of the nursing narratives predating *Memoranda* was the need to show a kind of union of humanity that could transcend and outlast the division and cruelty of the war. Here, too, Whitman's writings of the 1850s and early 1860s including his war journalism—concerned as they are in a profound way with American unity—predate almost all of the early nursing narratives. The early nursing narratives, however, provide a means by which Whitman could subtly reframe his already prominent concerns. This he did by individualizing attraction to soldier patients, and by doing so in an accepted and popular way. The nursing narratives are characterized in part by a subterranean magnetism that acknowledges unity by revealing occasional scenes of eroticism, either explicit or coded. *Memoranda* shares in such a need to demonstrate union in this visceral and powerful way.

In his 1864 *New York Times* article, Whitman described the great importance of "personal love, caresses and the magnetic flood of sympathy and friendship" involved in nursing, and he also stated that the "American soldier is full of affection, and the yearning for affection."[11] What he achieves in *Memoranda,* then, is to personalize the portrayal of that affection. Hardly representing a sea change in attitude, *Memoranda* is rather a subtle extension and more intimate recounting of Whitman's already longstanding convictions. He could extend these convictions in part because of the successful examples of affection found in the nursing narratives of 1863-1870. The success and popular reception of those narratives afforded Whitman the confidence to cite in *Memoranda* the existence of particular men—men whose names and places in their communities and fighting units he for the first time recorded in full.[12] Whitman stated the unequivocal attraction he felt towards these individual men, directing his affection toward real and named human beings who were present and palpable to him.

My position here furthers Alice Fahs's argument that popular Civil War literature insisted on a sympathetic humanity that recognized individual suffering, defined as sentimental literature: "Both a popular mode of thought and language of expression in mid-nineteenth-century America, sentimentalism emphasized the central importance of emotion in the individual's life" (94). Fahs identifies this sentimentalism as that which allows "powerful feelings [to structure] individual identity," and that which "fused patriotism and Christianity" (94, 95). Gregory Eiselein, too, states the importance of compassion, seeing the efforts of Alcott and Whitman to develop a kind of humanitarian praxis as providing "a critical examination of the patient/agent relation [which] illuminated the overlooked issue of power in this dynamic, and suggested the need for an eccentric humanitarian practice" (79). I would emphasize yet another pattern delineating the interactions between nurses and patients. This interaction also falls into the realm of powerful feelings, but not specifically in the realm of patriotism and Christianity, and gathers as a more subliminal aspect of the nursing narratives preceding *Memoranda.* That is to say, an undeniable magnetism in some scenes of hospital life exists so as to privilege sensual connection and eschew division, and this magnetism exists outside of the available rhetorical structures of morality and thus subversively insists on its own validity.

When eroticism exists as an underlying force in significant moments of a memoir, it enables, whether by conscious design of the narrator or not, both the narrator's own prodigious individualism and an undeniable and overarching union of humanity. The outlook of soldiers and nurses, necessarily strained nearly beyond endurance in the daily tension between duty to country and horror at the atrocity of war, proved one of unutterable complexity. In some cases nurses needed to develop an emotive dynamic that would allow them to continue to function and exist as integrated selves. If compassion forms the sentimental Christian and patriotic side of nursing narratives, then passion forms an intensive erotic facet of some nurse-patient dynamics.

My focus in this essay is on the central scene of an erotic attraction to a patient. While women's early nursing narratives remain true to their titles, indicating sketchiness and flickers of scenes that comprise a compendium of scattershot stories and observations, the erotic scene often forms a relatively small proportion, but a significant weight, in each account. Sometimes it exercises more narrative integrity than other reportings in the memoirs; the scene lengthens as the narrator lingers on the import of physical attraction. To the extent that the narrating is conscious, the narrator may develop the scene of erotic attraction to underscore, as in the case of Alcott, a brace of humanity, and in other cases, to illustrate a devotion to the democratic principles of multiplicity and diversity in America.[13] To the extent that it is not altogether conscious, the erotic scene may show a highly individualized self distinguished by the inarguable sweep and force of desire.

The theme of unity—or, in more Whitmanian terms, merging—was hardly new to Whitman, but it was newly available as popular literature in these memoirs, and as such provided a form he could refashion for his own project. In 1875 Whitman presented the dynamic of erotic unity in his memoir, with the added confidence of having written within a newly acclaimed genre.

Two questions attend the inception of this inquiry: why would Whitman have chosen to enter such a primarily female vocation as nursing, and why would he choose to draw partially upon the genre of the nursing narrative? In regard to the first question—why he entered the primarily female vocation of nursing—the answer is, he didn't. Nursing as an occupation in prewar United States was primarily a male pursuit; trained nurses in prewar United States were a rarity, and most nurses were patients who had stayed on in the institution of the hospital because they could not afford to leave. Only in the home did nursing prove almost altogether female—where it wasn't seen as a vocation or even an avocation at all. Nursing or domestic care at home was provided almost exclusively by women, because a sick person "usually obtained nursing care from female relatives,"[14] and the majority of the population never left home to visit a hospital.

In wartime situations previous to the American Civil War, nurses were male and usually drawn from convalescing patients, but in the Civil War, organized nursing opportunities for women opened up, and nursing and the conception of the nurse changed drastically. After the high volume of casualties in the battle of First Bull Run, the shortage of nurses became acute and apparent, and "just about anybody who could apply a lint bandage" was allowed to tend to soldiers, including "undesirable soldiers, . . . convalescents, invalids, prisoners, those too young or old for military service, relatives, and recruited females."[15] To put the need for nurses dramatically, the situation following the outbreak of the war was as follows: "The Army Medical Department, which consisted of fewer than one-hundred doctors at the outbreak of the war, had no general hospitals; its largest facility was a post hospital in Leavenworth, Kansas, with only forty beds," and as a result the medical bureau converted hotels, colleges, and even a jail into makeshift medical facilities.[16] There were very few professionally trained nurses of either gender in relation to the prodigious number of wounded and sick.

While statistics concerning nurses have been historically elastic—for instance, a convalescent soldier might perform nursing duties for a week and then be sent back to the front; a mother might arrive to help her sick son, then stay on as a nurse for years; another nurse might come through the bureaucracy of the Sanitary Commission or Christian Commission and stay but a month or two—Jane Schultz's recent study sets the number of female nurses in service much higher than previously acknowledged. Whereas John Brumgardt stated that there were approximately 2,000 women nurses, North and South, in the Civil War, and Stewart Brooks stated that between 3,000 and 4,000 women served in Union hospitals alone, Schultz puts the figure at upwards of 20,000, and that is just for Northern nurses who were paid: "The Carded Service Records of Union hospital attendants, compiled in 1890 by the U.S. Record and Pension Division as Congress debated granting pensions to women, list the names of 21,208 women."[17] Of course this number does not include Southern nurses nor does it include nurses who donated their services.

As for the second question—why would Whitman align himself with a primarily female genre to write *Memoranda*?—the answer is that the alignment is not so surprising, given that Whitman had from the beginning of his writing career been intensely interested in and aligned with women as thinkers and writers. Roy P. Basler, in his introduction to *Memoranda,* notices Whitman's "sensitive, almost feminine spirit" (2), as have others. Sherry Ceniza, Vivian Pollak, and David Reynolds, among others, have shown the influences of women and the feminine upon Whitman's production.[18] Notably, Whitman used Fanny Fern's *Fern Leaves,* the title and cover of which influenced *Leaves of Grass.* Highly aware of genre and women's literature in the early decades of his career, Whitman in *Memoranda* also relies on women's literature.

Whitman, however, did differentiate between male and female nurses, as when he specifically mentions Mrs. G of Ward F as a "lady nurse," a designation that suggests the relative novelty of females in the hospitals. He also devotes a short section to the description of a "lady named Miss or Mrs. Billings, who has long been a practical friend of soldiers and nurse in the army" and who asked to be buried among the soldiers she served.[19] The request was granted, and Whitman, by dint of including the account—detailing her fine service as well as the salute fired over her grave—seemed to admire her. He usually finds the accounts of female nurses' duties moving, especially as those duties intersect with his ideas of unity, motherhood, and erotic magnetism as a healing force.

Such unity, maternalism, and magnetism converge in erotic moments in nursing narratives. A hospital forms the site wherein the primacy of the body remains indisputable, where certainly the worst is seen of the body but also the best, as when a patient almost miraculously recovers through the care of good nursing. Often, moments of sensual intensity form the center of early nursing narratives, a kind of indelible, inexplicable hub of desire from which the rest of the text radiates and borrows energy. The scene of erotic attraction in nursing narratives draws in part from the significance of democracy as it functioned with unstated immediacy in the lives of the hospital workers. A hospital scene of erotic attraction emphasizes the desire of human beings, the pull of individual magnetism, regardless of class or political alignment, and depends upon the uprooted and chaotic circumstances of wartime activities. It marks a state of affairs nearly impossible to apprehend or organize in other more routine ways. The presence of erotic attraction is one that may surprise and discomfit readers of nursing narratives, yet it seems to be nearly universal, sometimes pressing implicitly if unconsciously for tolerance or unity and always existing in raw power.

Consider, for example, a Whitman letter describing an intimate and romantic attraction, relating to friends the situation of a "poor boy" whose leg had been amputated: "our affection is quite an affair, quite romantic—sometimes when I lean over to say I am going, he puts his arm round my neck, draws my face down, & c."[20] Such sensual intensity almost equals the intensity of the ineluctably physical nature of war, as when Alcott's sympathy toward her charges extends to the sympathy she feels physically. She experiences pain not only as a meeting of minds but as a meeting of bodies, admitting, "I often longed to groan for them."[21] Whitman detailed his erotic attractions more directly and personally in *Memoranda* than he had before in his public writings. Hardly devoid of erotic scenes, Whitman's poems glory in lavish, passionate descriptions, such as those from the famous fifth section of *Song of Myself,* the "Calamus" poems, and to some extent the *Drum-Taps* poems. In *Memoranda,* however, Whitman develops even more personal scenes, naming specific individuals and sketching the particular beloved in a more personal manner than ever before. The men he is attracted to have names, regiments, companies, families, communities, and exist as nonhypothetical and highly individual human beings.

In one intimate, erotic encounter in *Memoranda,* Whitman attends to a badly hurt, beautiful soldier whose name is "Thomas Haley, Co. M, Fourth New York Cavalry—a regular Irish boy, a fine specimen of youthful physical manliness." Whitman then refers to Thomas as Tom, a patient whom Whitman thought could not survive twelve hours yet after three days "looks well enough in the face to a casual observer." The soldier Tom, Whitman reports, "lies there with his frame exposed above the waist, all naked, for coolness, a fine built man, the tan not yet bleach'd from his cheeks and neck." The soldier acknowledges for a moment the presence of Whitman, then falls asleep again, remaining unaware of Whitman's almost ghostly yet reassuring presence:

> Poor youth, so handsome, athletic, with profuse beautiful shining hair. One time as I sat looking at him while he lay asleep, he suddenly, without the least start, awaken'd, open'd his eyes, gave me a long, long steady look, turning his face very slightly to gaze easier—one long, clear silent look—a slight sigh—then turn'd back and went into his doze again. Little he knew, poor death-stricken boy, the heart of the stranger that hover'd near.[22]

The "long, long steady look" from an individual, Thomas Haley, registers as no look in Whitman's work has registered before. The Whitmanian perspective here occurs in an almost otherworldly way, the hovering "heart of the stranger" that emphasizes the romantic inevitability and attraction that overlaps with the horror attendant upon life in the hospitals. Such a scene contributes to the complex character of the erotic moment during war experience.

The *Ur*-story of erotic Civil War experience, however, undoubtedly belongs to Louisa May Alcott's *Hospital Sketches,* as she tells at length of the attachment she feels to the exemplary soldier, John. Alcott's John, a working class blacksmith whom she differentiates in terms of class by dint of his speech patterns and especially grammar, represents the very type of the American working man, possessing character, dignity, and serenity. Alcott describes him by using the following words: courageous, sober, self-denying, stately, uncomplaining, tranquil, earnest, faithful, true, excellent, natural, frank, brave, and upright. He is the perfectly attractive man, for a "most attractive face he had, framed in brown hair and beard, comely featured and full of vigor, as yet unsubdued by pain; thoughtful and beautifully mild. . . ." He is "a large, fair man, with a fine face, and the serenest eyes I ever met," has "'bonny brown hair'" and is unquestionably the "manliest man" among her patients. Not only admired by Nurse Periwinkle, John is nearly worshiped by virtually all of the men, and before he dies his comrade and he "kissed each other, tenderly as women" (Alcott, 38-44).

John represents the fine democratic American male in every way for just about everyone who sees him, combining as he does the types of a mythological Paul Bunyan, a tragic character from Shakespeare, and an American Jesus. He functions, too, as a kind of mate for Nurse Periwinkle who almost creates him by way of sympathetic forces; indeed, he is overdetermined as a character, being made to hold the efflux of sensory and sensual repression, the nonverbal locus for pain, the hope for an as yet idealized democratic nation, and the complex vortices of family relationships under the dire stresses put upon them by the conflagration of the war. Nurse Periwinkle understands many of these complications, admitting that she knew she "was the poor substitute for mother, wife, or sister" (41), a set of substitutions including what to a twenty-first-century audience might seem the uncomfortable polar opposites of mother and wife.[23]

Further, Nurse Periwinkle is perhaps at her most revealing when she admits, upon writing a letter for John, that she cannot subdue "an irrepressible glimmer of feminine curiosity" about whether the recipient of the letter is his mother or his wife. This reveals much about the nurse but also much about the patient, for John's home life back in Virginia incorporates these very polar opposites—mother and wife—in his relationship with his widowed mother. In his own words, he acts as "father to the children and husband to the dear old woman, if I can." John wears a ring he deems of great importance, one given him by his mother, as he says, "to keep me steady," a plain ring he touched "and often turned thoughtfully on his finger when he lay alone" (Alcott, 42).

It is important to emphasize that such complications in relationships were in part viewed differently in nineteenth-century American culture than in our time; Alcott's nurse sees John as admirable in acting as both son and husband to his mother. As John is husband to his mother and father to his siblings, Nurse Periwinkle is in turn mother, wife, and sister to him. This situation is far from unusual and in fact somewhat typical of nursing narratives, whereby the nurse sees herself in a complex of relationships to some patients, in both maternal and erotic connection with a wounded and dying soldier. Such an overloaded relationship does not admit of easy emotional filing, and because of this difficulty the connection resists categorization and remains a quintessential characteristic of nurses' memoirs. This relationship evokes compassion in a narrative otherwise characterized by sass and wit, and the story of John provides the most extended moment of tragedy in Alcott's *Hospital Sketches*.

It also provides ample passion, as Schultz observes: "Though few women openly admitted romantic attachments, a number obliquely acknowledged the sexual energy that infused their work. Louisa May Alcott's description of Virginia blacksmith John Suhre's death (her 'manliest' patient) invoked maternal imagery, but was full of grasping, clutching, and other sexual cues" (94-95). The intimacy established between John and Nurse Periwinkle continues until his death, when "to the end [he] held my hand close, so close that when he was asleep at last, I could not draw it away" (Alcott, 45). Death and life are conjoined in a handclasping from which she finds it difficult to extricate her fingers. "I could not but be glad," she says, "that through its touch, the presence of human sympathy, perhaps, had lightened that hard hour" (45). Alcott allows Nurse Periwinkle to overcome sorrow through sympathy and to feel the electrical wave of physical contact, both maternal and sensuous. Indeed, the maternal may function as a sometime cover-up for the sensual, as Schultz notes, in that nurses "could, in fact, admit the affection they felt for soldiers through the mask of the maternal without jeopardizing reputation" (95). At the end of the scene, Alcott makes herself "happy with the thought, that . . . he would not be without some token of love which makes life beautiful and outlives death" (33). The need to mention a token of love suggests a reason for the eroticization of a patient—the need to signify into memory the belief that touch and contact can reconcile loss.

Alcott wrote the most extended moment of erotic attraction and sympathy among the narratives preceding Whitman's *Memoranda,* but she is certainly not the only nurse to report such passion. Alcott's wanting to groan for her patients shows an extraordinary movement of compassion and a kind of physical countertransference as regards her attendance upon her patients. Sophronia Bucklin in her narrative, too, reports the groans of her men in a remarkable way, noting that the "groans of suffering men echoing on all sides, aroused me to the highest pitch of excitement" (48), an excitement, of course, of sympathy, yet also, as she says, of arousal. Such pairing of arousal and death—a conjoining that perhaps sits uncomfortably with the reader when a sensual connection is involved—nonetheless exists notably in such Civil War nursing accounts, showcasing unpretending erotic moments.

The parallels between Alcott's and Whitman's scenes are manifold: both see the soldier as physically beautiful; both see him as infantilized;[24] both note that the dying man looks well on the surface of things even though they know differently; both portray the wounded man as possessing a magnetism; and both seem to be the sole sympathizers provided for the soldier. While Alcott includes one extended scene, Whitman includes numerous brief instances of erotic attraction in *Memoranda*—numerous undoubtedly because they underscore the nature of a conflict that afflicts such multitudes. Like Alcott, he offers the detail of the patient's first name, but offers further detail in providing the last name as well. For instance, Whitman relates the last days of Corporal Frank Irwin, whose left knee was wounded and subsequently amputated. In *Memoranda* Whitman records a letter he wrote to Irwin's family about Frank, who was fond of Whitman and was "sweet and affectionate." Whitman elaborates that Frank was "good and well-behaved, and affectionate, I myself liked him very much. I was in the habit of coming in afternoons and sitting by him, and soothing him, and he liked to have me—liked to put his arm out and lay his hand on my knee—would keep it so a long while." Near the close of the letter Whitman states that "I loved the young man, though I but saw him immediately to lose him" (51).

Like Alcott and Bucklin, Whitman cues the exchange of sympathy through a kind of underlying passion, conflating the presence of the suffering body and the erotic body so as to show mortification and attraction in conjunction. It may have been the most profound challenge of his writing career. He marks physical anguish and beauty at the same time, for instance, in the person of Thomas Lindly, of the First Pennsylvania Cavalry who, suffering "horribly" and dosed with morphine, is given "a large handsome apple" by Whitman. Whitman shows, too, the conjoining of suffering and beauty in a description not technically from the hospital: he offers the "fine sight" of a passing cavalry force made up of "the gallant bearing, fine seat, and bright faced appearance of a thousand and more handsome young American men, [who] where so good to see—quite set me up for hours." But almost directly afterward—he briefly describes two more passing forces—Whitman notes the ambulances moving the other way "up Fourteenth street north, slowly wending along, bearing a large lot of wounded to the hospitals," so that each procession is in marked contrast to the other, moving in different directions, but occurring on the same street (*Memoranda,* 18-19).

About the long-suffering cases, Whitman remarked that they needed "special sympathetic nourishment. These I sit down and either talk to, or silently cheer them up. They always like it hugely, (and so do I). . . . Some of the poor young chaps, away from home for the first time in their lives, hunger and thirst for affection. This is sometimes the only thing that will reach their condition" (*Memoranda,* 30-31). It is important for Whitman to report that both sides enjoy the attention, which he perceives as mutual. The phrase, "hunger and thirst for affection," demarcates a need as strong as the need for nourishment. Affection and attraction provide staples of hospital life for Whitman, Alcott, Bucklin, Powers, and other nurse narrators. For these hospital workers, perhaps eroticization of the body in pain is one of the few things that a nurse can do in the face of death. The erotic may provide a means by which a patient or nurse can attempt to override pain, replacing one physical phenomenon, one bodily experience, with another.

The exacerbated condition of pain deserves scrutiny here. Pain, as investigated by Elaine Scarry in *The Body in Pain,* is immediate in nature and necessarily attended by inarticulation. By the time health and comfort return and pain might be articulated, the immediacy is of necessity gone and thereby inexpressible in a direct form. Scarry suggests that the difficult relationship of pain to language is part of the reason that pain-inducing experiences such as war and torture can be manipulated by power and governmental structures and thus be allowed to continue. She suggests, too, that the fact of pain is essentially isolating and invisible because of such a relationship: "Invisible in part because of its resistance to language, it [the fact of pain] is also invisible because its own powerfulness ensures its isolation, ensures that it will not be seen in the context of other events, that it

will fall back from its arrival in language and remain devastating."[25] Probably the isolation of the sufferer is a situation witnessed if not usually acknowledged by medical staff members, for if suffering on a day-to-day basis were felt on the pulse of the worker as acutely as upon the pulse of the patient, then no aid or relief would be possible, due to the crippling empathy experienced by the workers.

However, the pain experienced by patients is at least partially felt by the nurses, if momentarily or subconsciously.[26] Patients' suffering, absorbed by ministering nurses, may register as physical response—body to body—in a manner that allows pain almost to be translated, the isolation of the patient to be alleviated, and the nurse to enter into a sympathy that has extended its own logic. As such it assures the nurse of her vital existence within the entropy and enormity surrounding her. Erotic attraction provides a way for a narrator to spotlight, emotionally, an interaction of meaning in the middle of chaos, in the middle of violence that cannot be predicted or controlled. "When one hears about another person's physical pain," states Scarry, "the events happening within the interior of that person's body may seem to have the remote character of some deep subterranean fact, belonging to an invisible geography that, however portentous, has no reality because it has not yet manifested itself on the surface of the earth" (3). An erotic connection does not register that invisible geography fully but it does, in a seismic way, attend to it, body to body. Eroticization of a patient in pain may be one means by which to register exacerbated experience, given the circumstance that the body resists language. Through Scarry's recognition of such resistance the body is made visible, in an entelechy of human sympathy, or a kind of democratic *misericordia* felt in the body.

The unrepresentability of pain stands in necessary conjunction with an inimical political utilization of that condition whereby such political force may assert its own rhetoric. As Sweet interprets Scarry, "the displacement of the body by ideology is possible because wounds are referentially unstable and thus can be appropriated rhetorically as signs of the legitimacy of an ideological position." I agree that *Memoranda* attempts, as Sweet says, "to find aesthetic and ideological solutions" after posing the "representational problems" that war brings forth.[27] To the extent that repressive political organizations make use of and depend upon the unrepresentability of pain in order to polarize power, the nurse who in her or his narrative attempts to foreground the body may be engaging, almost certainly unconsciously, in an act of political resistance.

It is an aesthetic act, too. Time and again nurses speak lovingly of one or two or several particular soldiers, usually those men noble or handsome or in some way enhanced through a lover's eye. Beauty is often mentioned, and to the extent that beauty is usually equated with health it must have alleviated stress for hospital workers to feel attraction to patients. Bucklin, for example, emphasizes the beauty of some of the soldiers she attends, calling a soldier a "beautiful boy," and in another case confessing that she "could hardly turn my fascinated eyes from this feast of beauty" that was a wounded soldier. Another soldier calls Bucklin by a woman's name not her own and asks if she will stay through the night with him, possibly mistaking her for his wife (Bucklin, 106, 265, 203-204). The Quaker nurse Cornelia Hancock (who did not write a memoir but recorded incidents in her letters) somewhat disturbingly reports the fact that doctors she worked with would, after the deaths of certain handsome soldiers, embalm the soldiers' bodies, after which she and the doctors would periodically visit the mausoleum to admire their beauty.[28] Georgeanna Woolsey describes the death of an attractive man, a "fair-haired, blue-eyed young lieutenant, a face innocent enough for one of our own New England boys."[29] The lieutenant is actually a rebel soldier, a significant fact in the ability for a nurse to represent the eroticisation of pain in terms of restating the goals of reunion of the nation.

The goal of union of the nation is powerful if understated in the narratives written by women; the narrators tend rather toward demonstrating union than asserting it rhetorically. For example, many rings are given in the accounts of nurses. Jane Stuart Woolsey, for one, exclaims, "What hospital nurse has not a bone ring or trinket carved by her men in the wards or in prison?" and lists the many types of rings and the icons carved on them, including a wooden ring carved by a thankful rebel soldier. Woolsey tells the story of Hunter, not a rebel but "a loyal Tennessean" (135), who gave her a little ring. Though Hunter fights on the union side he hails from the south, and he recounts the conflict of joining the Union army while watching his southern home jeopardized by that same army, his capture and imprisonment, and his carving of the ring while in a Macon jail. The ring bears "'two clasped hands to mean *True till Death,* or something like that,'" he explains, as he asks her to take the ring. Woolsey says to her reader, "Let those who have one of these rings with two clasped hands to mean 'True till Death,' keep it as a sacred relic."[30] Woolsey uses the image of the ring, often a sign of erotic and romantic attraction, to show the strength of the Union cause, which includes Southerners, in a symbol that does double duty in representing union: the symbol of the ring itself of course shows union, and the clasped hands emphasize union, too. Bucklin describes bone rings and also a ring given to her that was made of a shell fuse found from the rebels' firing attack on her hospital (300). While these rings are

not always romantic, as can be seen by the fact that they are also sent to mothers and daughters,[31] they are at the very least intimate. Elvira Powers receives a ring from a man referred to as "Kentucky," with her name engraved on it, and it fits perfectly because he had contrived in advance, through painstaking and ingenious measures, to discover her ring size.[32] Charlotte McKay, whose 1876 narrative is contemporaneous with Whitman's, recounts a rebel giving her a ring carved of bone, "in token of his gratitude."[33]

A particularly powerful scene of ring-giving is offered in Sarah Emma Edmonds' *Nurse and Spy.* This scene rivals Alcott's portrayal of John and Nurse Periwinkle, because in both books the erotic scene unfolds in a more extended and heightened narrative space than the rest of the episodes. Edmonds finds herself receiving a ring from a wounded soldier to whom she is attracted; she presents this soldier as owning some of the same admirable qualities possessed by Alcott's John. An important distinction inheres, however: this soldier is a Confederate. Edmonds's attraction proves additionally titillating because the interaction occurs not in a supervised hospital but in the literal no-man's land of space between the North and South lines. In this uninhabited space Edmonds comes upon a deserted house where she wishes to regroup before her next surveillance mission, and discovers that the house is the shelter for a mortally wounded rebel soldier. She cooks food and feeds him before she tends to her own needs, describing the soldier as "a very pleasant and intelligent looking man" and noting that "it is strange how sickness and disease disarm our antipathy and remove our prejudices."[34]

Edmonds enjoys attending to him and easing his pain and more than once refers to his beauty with phrases such as, "those beautiful eyes," "those beautiful windows of the soul," and "lovely in death." His dying action is to give her a ring and ask her to keep it in memory: "taking a ring from his finger he tried to put it on mine, but his strength failed." The moment has hallmarks of the erotic but also of the maternal, with Edmunds perceiving the soldier "as a little child" folding his hands in prayer as "he would do at his mother's knee" (89-91). Edmunds's encounter with the rebel soldier proves charged, erotic, unchaperoned, between lines. The intimacy is intense and undeniable.

While Whitman experiences many intensified intimate encounters in his nursing narrative, probably the most healing of such encounters comes in the final pages of *Memoranda* where, like Sarah Emma Edmonds, he presents a rebel soldier he loves. Needless to say, Whitman's project of eroticized democracy is his own and had been at least since the 1855 *Leaves of Grass.* Whitman, always impassioned about human unity as commensurate with national unity, may nonetheless have discerned in the early nursing narratives a way to further his project. The nursing narratives' maternal and erotic structuring of desire bespoke unification and found legitimization for union. Whitman placed his longstanding project within this new context of a popularly received and admired genre that detailed intimate relationships with real human beings, at least in part as a way to make his primary project more accessible to a general readership.

For instance, he describes "a young Baltimorean, aged about 19 years, W. S. P., (2nd Md. Southern)," whose right leg had been amputated. The young man was dying, sleepless, and under the influence of morphine:

> Evidently very intelligent and well bred—very affectionate—held on to my hand, and put it by my face, not willing to let me leave. As I was lingering, soothing him in his pain, he says to me suddenly, "I hardly think you know who I am—I don't wish to impose upon you—I am a rebel soldier." I said I did not know that, but it made no difference. . . . I loved him much, always kiss'd him, and he did me.
>
> (53)

This depiction of devotion, handclasping, and kissing is marked by tenderness and affection. The account is set apart, as is that of Edmonds, by the fact that the man is a Secessionist. Furthermore, in the next ward Whitman found the man's brother, a Union soldier, hit in the same battle and also mortally wounded; this second soldier is identified as a brave Union soldier, "Col. Clifford K. Prentiss, Sixth Md. Infantry." The two brothers were "brought together" in their dying, and "each died for his cause" (*Memoranda*, 53). Here Whitman accentuates his espousal of a post-war democracy, attributing equal valor and dignity to each side in the war.

He admires Union and Secession soldier alike in a remarkable reverence that crescendos in the last sections of *Memoranda*. His respect for the soldiers of both sides proves notable in the reunion of the two brothers from the North and South, one of whom was the rebel Whitman kissed and loved. He states, after the anecdote about the Northern and Southern brothers, "I can say that in my ministerings I comprehended all, whoever came in my way, Northern or Southern, and slighted none" (56). Whitman uses the word "comprehended" to form the same movement characteristic of his earlier works: he not only understands the wounded in a deep and intimate way but he is part of them all, and assumes them all into himself comprehensively.[35] It is in response to the fractured condition of the country during and after the war that Whitman reintroduces in nar-

rative form his aesthetic of maternal, erotic, and homosexual merging. This aesthetic operates in response to the bifurcated sense of the American self, pulled between North and South, and allows Whitman to achieve a perspective that engenders tenderness.

For all the erotic traces underscoring unity in the accounts of Civil War nursing memoirs, however, the potential for female and male nurses to become romantic figures was hardly identical. Whereas the position of the female nurse in tending to male patients was controversial in the nineteenth century, and female nurses were sometimes seen as potential seekers of romance and marriage, the motivation of the male nurse would have been scrutinized far less rigorously.[36] Homosexuality in nineteenth-century United States was for the most part unnoticed or perceived ambiguously (British writers such as John Addington Symonds notwithstanding). The reception of Whitman's "Calamus" poems of mutual male attraction or adhesiveness was largely unruffled, for instance; such reception stands in marked contrast to the scandalized reaction to Whitman's poems of heterosexual attraction, "Children of Adam." Because of relatively vague conceptions of homosexuality in the mid-nineteenth century, Whitman's attractions to male patients might have intensified without the need to register any "staggered" reaction, as did Alcott's nurse upon first needing to bathe a naked male soldier.[37]

Thus Whitman could use the tenderness of the early nursing narratives and the maternal imperative that went unquestioned in the popular conception of the female nurse, and, further, he could skirt the perceived difficulties concerning heterosexual eroticism. "Whitman presents the in-betweenness of the homosexual healer as a therapeutic habit of mind, a habit of mind capable of sustaining the uncertainties of medicine, capable of 'being in uncertainties,' as Keats said of the poet," states Robert Leigh Davis, and Lawrence Buell, too, posits the existence during the Civil War of Whitman's "maternal/erotic tenderness for beautiful young men."[38] Subtly undercutting assumptions about preference in terms of passion, Whitman in his adhesive eroticism continues in this "therapeutic habit of mind" in order to be able to discover a way to heal the nation.

From the context of female nursing narratives of 1863-1870, Whitman displays the maternal strain evidenced almost universally therein, effecting an intimate relationship both "motherly" and romantic. Importantly, it is a relationship the nation was willing to accept and valorize. Nowhere is that tenderness more prominent than in his role as nurse in *Memoranda*. It may be that in portraying himself as both maternal and erotic he can find an ambient formula that approximates the expression of homosexuality in a culture that distrusts or resists or is blind to it. Whitman defines his aesthetic by positioning himself in his role as nurse and attending to attraction more directly and specifically than ever before in his career.

If my emphasis upon the erotic in this essay seems overloaded, consider the views of authorities at the time who registered fear of the attraction that might occur by admitting women to the occupation of nursing. There existed a general sexual anxiety about women's roles in tending to the body, including not only a fear that American women might faint if exposed to wounded men, but also "a usually unstated fear [that] involved exposure of young women to the naked male body" (Freemon, 52). In addition, fears about sexuality caused authorities to conceive of nursing as an occupation befitting older women, for "the exposure of an older motherly woman to naked bodies, especially those of men, was deemed neither shocking nor arousing."[39]

Superintendent of nurses, Dorothea Dix, famous for barring young and pretty women from duty as hospital nurses, turned away thousands of women because they were "too attractive." Female nurses were required to be over thirty years of age and to be unremarkable in appearance.[40] Dix announced that "no woman under thirty years need apply to serve in the government hospitals. All nurses are required to be very plain-looking women. Their dresses must be brown or black, with no bows, no curls, or jewelry, and no hoop-skirts" (Brown, 54, 303). Clearly, such governmental stipulations spoke to a fear of heterosexual attraction and eroticism. Florence Nightingale, too, in her work in the Crimean War, stressed that nurses' training "had to eliminate any hint of eroticism."[41]

For example, the anonymous narrator of the 1864 *Notes of Hospital Life* describes an erotic interchange with a patient who tells her that she can help him assuage his loneliness. He says to her, "Sure, and it's lonely I am, so very lonely; and it's some one to love that I'm wanting." He observes that the lady nurses are there exactly to supply such want, to which the narrator, somewhat amused, retorts, "I do not find wives among the list of luxuries on our diet-table" (25). In *Pencillings,* Powers too notes these preconceptions at the outset of her narrative and presents them in order to poke fun. When she and her two companions arrive at the wards to visit patients, they joke that they will "notice only the good looking ones" (2). Later, Powers reports that once she had "the audacity to pay special attention to a young corporal from Massachusetts, fifteen years her junior, by accompanying him to church one Sabbath evening, and came very near being discharged for the same" (157-158).

An awareness of the body—the body that is magnetic because it arouses maternal sympathy and because it arouses erotic urgings—is crucial to a full understanding of nursing. One of Whitman's aesthetic tasks in *Memoranda* was to embrace the body as fully and vigorously, yet even more specifically, than he had in "Song of Myself" and the 1860 "Calamus" poems. The body in *Memoranda* is the body of the male soldier, of course, which is now diseased, disfigured, amputated, putrefying, weakened, or dying. Never was Whitman's need to celebrate the body so dire as it was at this crux. By and large the strategy he used remained the same as the strategy he used at the outset of his career—the assertion of merging. In the 1875 *Memoranda During the War,* however, unlike in "Song of Myself" twenty years earlier, the test for merging was severe and the strain palpable. Timothy Sweet points out that "in Whitman's experience of army hospitals, the adhesive love that had made his poetic self 'completely satisfied' in the 'Calamus' poems had to find its object in the violated bodies of soldiers" (64). The erotic attraction was disjunctive, as was the experience of visiting tent to tent, as was the experience of the wounded, fragmented body. Whitman's project of adhesiveness and erotic merging had never been more thoroughly tested as in the hospital tents of the Civil War. The sense of purpose that the war afforded to Whitman caused him to reclaim the primacy of his commitment to the cause of union and democracy in America, and this redoubled commitment infused his prose writing. Indeed, important to all early nursing narratives is the concept that healing the soldiers might also "heal the country," as Dorothea Dix, Superintendent of nurses, believed (Brown, 274). Whitman attempted to heal the fragmentation of a national and political conflagration in his role as a lover of patients and as a writer of the nation's hospitals.

It is the achievement of *Memoranda During the War* that Whitman was able to put forward a kind of antiwar tract that included the atrocity of war at the same time that he offered a hopeful statement about the tenderness of humankind, and to affirm the United States as a nation, as well. Ed Folsom points out that Whitman's remarkable prose "could turn the war inside out, . . . bring America to the hospital that its war had created . . . [and] recenter the war on what had previously been its marginal and ignored aspects," such as infection, amputation, and other incidents deemed unmentionable before.[42] Whitman refused to flinch from the horror of war at the same time that he refused to exclude the presence of erotic attraction in the midst of such horror. In the final three words of the narrative, Whitman honors the memory of the dead, from both the North and the South, to whom he chooses to "dedicate my book" (*Memoranda,* 58).

He believes the kisses that he and the soldiers exchange—and the love these kisses represent—can bring reconciliation (and so it is fitting that in his poem "Reconciliation," he concludes by kissing his "enemy [who] is dead . . . the white face in the coffin").[43] Whitman sees, together, devastation and healing. He worked hard for his *Leaves of Grass* to signal, once again, democratic impulses so as to save a nation. Like Sophronia Bucklin, who said of the aftermath of Gettysburg, that "every grass-blade seemed to have been stained with blood" (189), Whitman did not turn away from the enormity of the Civil War. He realized in a visceral way in 1875 that each blade of grass had been blood-stained and labored under the onus of dedicating the leaves of grass (and his *Leaves of Grass*) to the fallen war dead. At the same time, however, he submitted once again that tenderness might heal the nation's division. Placing his memoir, in part, within the context of popular nursing narratives published in the decade before his, he attempted to validate his vision in the democratic mind. To further his own already well-established aesthetic of passion and commitment to unity, he rediscovered in his prose an erotic positioning as a means to heal a rift so wide an embrace could hurt.

Notes

1. The three epigraphs are from Peter I, 1:24; Hard Holzer and Mark E. Neely, Jr., *Mine Eyes Have Seen the Glory: The Civil War in Art* (New York: Orion Books, 1993), 197; and Sophronia E. Bucklin, *In Hospital and Camp: A Woman's Record of Thrilling Incidents among the Wounded in the Late War* (Philadelphia: John E. Potter and Company, 1869), 189. This essay is an expanded version of a paper delivered at a symposium, "The (R)Evolution of Walt Whitman," at Texas A & M University in April 2004. I wish to thank M. Jimmie Killingsworth especially for inviting me to write and deliver the paper.

2. *New York Times,* December 11, 1864. See Kenneth M. Price, "Whitman's Journalism," in Price, Martin G. Murray, and Robert K. Nelson, *Whitman's Memory* (http://www.iath.virginia.edu/fdw/volume2/price/memoranda/journalism/).

3. See, for works on Civil War nursing: Robert Leigh Davis, *Whitman and the Romance of Medicine* (Berkeley: University of California Press, 1997); Gregory Eiselein, *Literature and Humanitarian Reform in the Civil War Era* (Bloomington: Indiana University Press, 1996); Alice Fahs, *The Imagined Civil War: Popular Literature of the North & South, 1861-1865* (Chapel Hill: University of North Carolina Press, 2001); Elizabeth D. Leonard, *Yankee Women: Gender Battles in the Civil War* (New York: W. W. Norton, 1994); Lisa Long, *Rehabilitating Bodies: Health, History, and the American Civil War* (Philadelphia: University of Pennsylvania Press, 2004); Jane E. Schultz, *Women at the Front: Hospital Workers in Civil War America* (Chapel Hill: The University of North Carolina Press, 2004); Ann Douglas Wood, "The War within the War: Women Nurses in the Union Army," *Civil War History* 18 (1972), 197-212; and Elizabeth Young, *Disarming the Nation: Women's Writing and the American Civil War* (Chicago: University of Chicago Press, 1999). See also Libra Rose Hilde, "Worth a Dozen Men: Women, Nursing, and Medical Care During the American Civil War" (Ph.D. Dissertation, Harvard University, 2003). In general, most of these critics acknowledge Whitman's memoir in the light of Alcott and sometimes Edmonds, but less often or not at all with Jane Stuart Woolsey, Georgeanna Woolsey, Powers, Holstein, and Bucklin, and not as an exploration of how the nuances of narrative style are used and developed. My project distinguishes itself from the above works by concentrating intensively on the narratives preceding Whitman's, and investigating the tone and style of those early narratives through 1876.

4. Cited in Roy P. Basler, "Introduction," in *Walt Whitman's Memoranda During the War [&] Death of Abraham Lincoln* (Bloomington: Indiana University Press, 1962), 11.

5. Anne L. Austin, *The Woolsey Sisters of New York: A Family's Involvement in the Civil War and a New Profession (1860-1900)* (Philadelphia: American Philosophical Society, 1971), 94.

6. See L. P. Brockett and Mrs. Mary C. Vaughan, *Woman's Work in the Civil War: a Record of Heroism, Patriotism and Patience* (Philadelphia: Zeigler, McCurdy & Co., 1868); and Frank Moore, *Women of the War; Their Heroism and Self-Sacrifice* (Hartford, Connecticut: S. S. Scranton & Co., 1867).

7. Anonymous, *Notes of Hospital Life* (Philadelphia: Lippincott, 1864), xiii.

8. Such note-taking styles, however, are also anticipated, for example, in the works of Irving, Dickens, and Thackeray.

9. For Whitman's journalism preceding *Memoranda,* I've relied on Price, "Whitman's Journalism," *Whitman's Memory* website.

10. *New York Times,* December 11, 1864.

11. *New York Times,* December 11, 1864.

12. He names individuals in one article from December 11, 1864: D. F. Russell, Company E; Charles Miller, Company D; and Oscar F. Wilder, Company G, who returned Whitman's kiss fourfold, as mentioned earlier—also William Cohn, the handsome sleeping soldier also mentioned earlier, whose name Whitman makes a point to discern, along with a couple others. This one article (though another article on February 23, 1863, has initials of one soldier, JAH) is closest to what *Memoranda* will become, though still without the protraction of detail and depth of affection registered in 1875.

13. Alcott, however, is an exception to the theme of using hospital experience to unify democratically. She refused to restrain herself in the first version of her narrative from unleashing vitriol on the rebel soldier. On Alcott's subsequent revisions, see Young, 89-90.

14. Freemon, Frank R. *Gangrene and Glory: Medical Care during the American Civil War* (London: Associated University Presses, 1998), 51.

15. Stewart Brooks, *Civil War Medicine* (Springfield, IL: Charles C. Thomas, 1966), 51.

16. Thomas J. Brown, *Dorothea Dix: New England Reformer* (Cambridge: Harvard University Press, 1998), 287.

17. John R. Brumgardt, ed., *Civil War Nurse: The Diary and Letters of Hannah Ropes* (Knoxville: University of Tennessee Press, 1980), 3. Also Brooks, 54; and Schultz, 20.

18. See Sherry Ceniza, *Walt Whitman and Nineteenth-Century Women Reformers* (Tuscaloosa: University of Alabama Press, 1998); Vivian R. Pollak, *The Erotic Whitman* (Berkeley: University of California Press, 2000); David Reynolds, *Walt Whitman's America: A Cultural Biography* (New York: Knopf, 1995); and Daneen Wardrop, *Word, Birth, and Culture in the Poetry of Poe, Whitman, and Dickinson* (Westport, CT: Greenwood Press, 2002), for Whitman's alignments with women.

19. Whitman, *Memoranda During the War* (Camden, NJ: 1875-1876), 39.

20. Edwin Haviland Miller, ed., *The Correspondence* (New York: New York University Press, 1961), 1:81.

21. Louisa May Alcott, *Hospital Sketches,* in *Alternative Alcott,* ed. Elaine Showalter (New Brunswick: Rutgers University Press, 1988), 29. Concerning the physical, Alcott also notes her preoccupation with the activities of a seasoned doctor: "There was an uncanny sort of fascination in watching him, as he peered and probed into the mechanism of those wonderful bodies, whose mysteries he understood so well."

22. Walt Whitman, *Memoranda During the War* (Camden, NJ: 1875-1876), 16-17.

23. Alcott, though, often seems to familialize her characters' objects of desire.

24. Eiselein and other critics have noted Civil War nurses' tendency to infantilize patients.

25. Elaine Scarry, *The Body in Pain: The Making and Unmaking of the World* (New York: Oxford University Press, 1985), 61.

26. Nearly all of these Civil War nurses became seriously ill at some point in their service, often suddenly or, as in Whitman's case, experiencing life-threatening illnesses afterwards. These reactions must have been at least partly due to a reception of suffering on an unconscious level.

27. Timothy Sweet, *Traces of War: Poetry, Photography, and the Crisis of the Union* (Baltimore: Johns Hopkins University Press, 1990), 2, 46.

28. Cornelia Hancock, *South after Gettysburg: Letters of a Civil War Nurse,* ed. Henrietta Stratton Jaquette (Lincoln: University of Nebraska Press, 1998).

29. Georgeanna Woolsey, *Three Weeks at Gettysburg* (New York: Anson D. R. Randolph, 1863), 16.

30. Jane Stuart Woolsey, *Hospital Days* (New York: Van Nostrand, 1870), 135, 137.

31. Bucklin, 240; Anna Morris Holstein, *Three Years in Field Hospitals of the Army of the Potomac* (Philadelphia: Lippincott, 1867), 23.

32. Elvira J. Powers, *Hospital Pencillings; Being A Diary while in Jefferson General Hospital, Jeffersonville, Ind., and Others at Nashville, Thennessee, as Matron and Visitor* (Boston: Edward L. Mitchell, 1866), 201-202.

33. Charlotte E. McKay, *Stories of Hospital and Camp* (Philadelphia, 1876), 120.

34. Sarah Emma Edmonds, *Memoirs of a Soldier, Nurse and Spy: A Woman's Adventures in the Union Army,* ed. Elizabeth D. Leonard (DeKalb: Northern Illinois University Press, 1999), 87.

35. From the very beginning of *Memoranda*—indeed in the first paragraph—Whitman defines soldiers as "Not Northern soldiers only . . . [but] many a

Southern face and form, pale, emaciated, with that strange tie of confidence and love between us, welded by sickness, pain of wounds" (3). Early on, too, he proposes a kind of universal hero in a fallen "altogether unnamed" Southern boy (13). At the end of the narrative, this theme gains in force.

36. There were those, however, who disliked Whitman's treatment of patients, so that "the poet's attachment to soldiers raised concerns in some quarters. Two women nurses [Amanda Akin and Harriet Foote Hawley] reacted to Whitman in very negative ways, disliking his presence and disapproving of his charged relationships with men" (Price, Introduction, on *Whitman's Memory* website).

37. For her first task, Alcott's nurse is directed by Miss Blank to wash and scrub the bodies of the patients, and responds with shock: "If she had requested me to shave them all, or dance a hornpipe on the stove funnel, I should have been less staggered; but to scrub some dozen lords of creation at a moment's notice, was really—really—" (23).

38. Davis, 14. Lawrence Buell, "American Civil War Poetry and the Meaning of Literary Commodification: Whitman, Melville, and Others," in *Reciprocal Influences: Literary Production, Distribution, and Consumption in America,* ed. Steven Fink and Susan S. Williams (Columbus: Ohio State University Press, 1999), 132.

39. Susan M. Reverby, *Ordred to Care: The Dilemma of American Nursing, 1850-1945.* (Cambridge: Cambridge University Press, 1987), 20.

40. Bucklin flouted this stipulation, and found herself in the personal presence of Dix, who said she was "altogether too young for a nurse" (Brooks, 60), but Dix let her stay on anyway. Other nurses, too, delighted in trying to resist Dix's stipulations, and many did so successfully.

41. For Nightingale, however, the concern "was not the fixation of a sexually repressed Victorian, but rather an attempt to limit any male claim on a woman through the sexual exchange" (Reverby, 43). See also Florence Nightingale, *Notes on Nursing: What It Is, and What It Is Not,* ed. Virginia M. Dunbar (New York: Dover, 1969).

42. Ed Folsom, *Walt Whitman's Native Representations* (Cambridge: Cambridge University Press, 1994), 126.

43. Whitman, *Sequel to Drum-Taps* (Washington, DC: 1865-1866), 23.

FURTHER READING

Criticism

Hall, Julie E. "At the Crisis of Our Fate: Sophia Peabody Hawthorne's Civil War." In *Reinventing the Peabody Sisters,* edited by Monika M. Elbert, Julie E. Hall, and Katharine Rodier, pp. 61-76. Iowa City: University of Iowa Press, 2006.
> Illustrates how Sophia Peabody Hawthorne's letters to her husband, Nathaniel Hawthorne, and to her friend, Annie Adams Fields, during the Civil War provide insight into the experience of Northern women during the war.

Juncker, Clara. "Confederate Languagescapes: Kate Stone's *Brokenburn*." *Southern Quarterly* 34, no. 4 (summer 1996): 37-42.
> Examines the expression—by Kate Stone in her journal, *Brokenburn*—of feminist rhetoric and gender identity within the Confederate world.

Larson, Kelli A. "Bierce's 'Chickamauga': A Lesson in History." *Midwestern Miscellany* 27 (spring 1999): 9-22.
> Highlights Ambrose Bierce's various critiques of the grave errors made by leaders during the Battle of Chickamauga.

Mariani, Giorgio. "Ambrose Bierce's Civil War Stories and the Critique of the Martial Spirit." *Studies in American Fiction* 19, no. 2 (autumn 1991): 221-28.
> Discusses the curious dual nature of Ambrose Bierce's relationship to warfare, as the author was fiercely anti-war, and yet largely preoccupied with the impassioned depiction of combat in his works.

Mullins, Maire. "Stopping History in Walt Whitman's *Drum-Taps*." *Walt Whitman Quarterly Review* 17, nos. 1-2 (summer-fall 1999): 4-14.
> Concentrates on the concept of isolated, "frozen" periods of time as depicted in Walt Whitman's poetry in Drum-Taps.

Nabers, Deak. "Victory of Law: Melville and Reconstruction." In *Victory of Law: The Fourteenth Amendment, The Civil War, and American Literature, 1852-1867,* pp. 19-46. Baltimore, Md.: Johns Hopkins University Press, 2006.
> Studies Herman Melville's concern with the abolition of slavery and the fourteenth amendment to the U.S. Constitution as evidenced in *Battle-Pieces and Aspects of the War.*

Owens, David M. "Early War Stories: 1861, West Virginia." In *The Devil's Topographer: Ambrose Bierce and the American War Story,* pp. 21-37. Knoxville: University of Tennessee Press, 2006.

Full-length, chronological study of the historical context surrounding Ambrose Bierce's detailed fictional narratives of the Civil War.

Parker, Alice. "The Civil War Journal of Julia LeGrand Waitz (1861-1863)." *New Orleans Review* 15, no. 1 (spring 1988): 69-72.

    Discusses the treatment of gender, race, identity, and class in a 1911 edition of a journal kept by Julia LeGrand Waitz during the occupation of New Orleans by Federal troops during the Civil War.

Rowe, John Carlos. "Whitman's Body Poetic." In *America's Modernisms: Revaluing the Canon: Essays in Honor of Joseph N. Riddel,* edited by Kathryne V. Lindberg and Joseph G. Kronick, pp. 168-81. Baton Rouge: Louisiana State University Press, 1996.

    Analyzes how Walt Whitman's treatment of the damage inflicted upon human bodies during the Civil War changes from the original edition of *Drum Taps* and the *Sequel to Drum Taps.*

Schaefer, Michael W. "Ambrose Bierce on the Construction of Military History." *War, Literature, and the Arts* 7, no. 1 (spring-summer 1995): 1-13.

    Examines Ambrose Bierce's awareness and treatment of the manner in which government and military leadership's accounts of war always seem to overshadow those of individual soldiers' accounts in the eyes of the public.

Sullivan, Walter. "Civil War Diaries and Memoirs." In *The History of Southern Women's Literature,* edited by Carolyn Perry and Mary Louise Weaks, pp. 109-18. Baton Rouge: Louisiana State University Press, 2002.

    Surveys various journals written by Southern women during the Civil War period.

Szczesiul, Anthony. "The Maturing Vision of Walt Whitman's 1871 Version of *Drum-Taps.*" *Walt Whitman Quarterly Review* 10, no. 3 (winter 1993): 127-41.

    Illustrates Walt Whitman's changing views regarding the overall impact and importance of the Civil War on his own life and on the United States as a nation by studying various versions of Whitman's *Drum-Taps.*

Young, Elizabeth. "Confederate Counterfeit: The Case of the Cross-Dressed Civil War Soldier." In *Passing and the Fictions of Identity,* edited by Elaine K. Ginsberg, pp. 181-217. Durham, N.C.: Duke University Press, 1996.

    Focuses upon cross-dressing—by women pretending to be Civil War soldiers—in the context of gender identity during the nineteenth century.

Fairy Tales and Nineteenth-Century Literature

The following entry presents critical commentary on the treatment of fairy tales in nineteenth-century literature.

INTRODUCTION

Although some fairy tales have literary sources, most belong to an oral tradition, and all are recognized by their recurring subject matter and narrative patterns. Certain character types, such as innocent young people, various villains, and fairy godmothers or other supernatural powers, dominate the stories, with someone or something in the latter group intervening on behalf of the young people. The enchanted settings provide a backdrop for magic, animism, and some form of transformation of people or things. The typical narrative pattern presents an innocent young man or woman whose adversary is a villain. When intervention arrives on behalf of the innocent character, he or she achieves victory over the villain and the result is a happy ending. Fairy tales entertain and offer moral lessons, but their reception and interpretation has been at times controversial.

The eighteenth century saw the collection and translation of many fairy tales into English, but the prevailing rationalism and didacticism of the era prevented the tales from becoming approved literature for children. As a result, the tales in England began to disappear. By the time the German authors Jacob and Wilhelm Grimm began to collect fairy tales in the early nineteenth century, they found only a few extant tales in England. Scholars have advanced several theories to explain England's paucity of tales, such as the pushing out of native English tales by the French and German ones, Puritanism's objection to the tales' frivolity, the rationalists' objection to their falsity, and others' objection to their lack of sophistication. The fairy-tale genre nevertheless had its defenders, such as Samuel Taylor Coleridge, Charles Lamb, William Wordsworth, and John Ruskin, all of whom believed that fairy tales were good for children's imagination. Most critics credit the restoration of the fairy tale in England to the Grimm brothers and their *Kinder- und Hausmärchen* (1812-1815; *German Popular Stories* or *Grimm's Fairy Tales*). The scholarship that the Grimms employed in compiling their collection and its subsequent editions, as well as the printing of the tales, generated a newfound respect for the genre. Each edition of the Grimms's seven editions differs from others in the collection because of text that was added or deleted, stories that were altered as new versions came along, and stylistic changes that were made. The year 1823 marked the first English translation of the tales, and the various revisions and reprints of the old stories inspired British authors to write new ones. As fairy tales became more available, Victorians began to recognize and appreciate their psychological and entertainment value. The tales allowed a form of escape from real life, they helped relieve the anxieties of children and adults, and the combination of entertainment and moral lessons finally gained the tales' acceptance as children's literature. Even so, not all of the new tales written in the nineteenth century were received positively.

Oscar Wilde, contributing to this expanding genre, wrote fairy tales for his children and for the "child-like," but controversy marked their critical reception. The tales, so different from his other works, baffled the critics. Many did not perceive his stories as fairy tales and considered them more appropriate for adults than for children. They saw his tales as subversive, asserting that good children's literature should be conservative. Some categorized his stories as allegories of homosexual repression, while others dismissed them altogether. Recent critics have considered the tales from a more personal perspective, such as Wilde's exploration of his spirituality or his commentary on contemporary political and moral concerns. Despite their controversial reception, Wilde's stories have always been popular with adults and children, and most have been included in reprint editions and children's anthologies.

Although Hans Christian Andersen wrote in many genres, he is remembered primarily as one of the most distinguished writers of fairy tales (see Further Reading). Many of these tales, such as "Den grimme Ælling" (1843; "The Ugly Duckling"), "Keiserens nye Klæder" (1837; "The Emperor's New Clothes"), and "Den lille Havfrue" (1837; "The Little Mermaid"), which were originally published in the various volumes of *Eventyr, Fortalte for Børn* (1835-42; *Fairy Tales for Children*), have become known worldwide, and have been translated into numerous languages. In all, Andersen wrote more than 150 fairy tales, primarily between 1835 and 1874. Andersen is credited with revitalizing and expanding the genre by merging the traditional folk tale with the more sophisticated literary tale. To this end he employed conversational language suitable for children, often provided sad rather than happy endings, combined an adult sensibility with a child-like simplicity, and blended into his tales aspects of his own personal life. One major trend in Andersen criticism has involved psychoanalytic studies seeking to draw connections between the suffering depicted in Andersen's stories and the troubles of Andersen's own life, including his various emotional problems and incidences of unrequited love. Throughout his life, critics and biographers have noted, Andersen was ashamed of his working-class background, and many scholars have posited that Andersen sought to overcome this sense of shame and inferiority through fantasy, in stories that feature protagonists triumphing over evil, persecution, poverty, and scorn.

As fairy tales accumulated on the literary landscape, other nineteenth-century British writers incorporated existing fairy-tale motifs into their stories, sometimes following the conventional tale, sometimes changing character types or deviating from the traditional narrative patterns. Even with such deviations, the narrative structure of fairy tales and psychological elements of fairy-tale characters shaped the fiction. Critics have observed how Charles Dickens' early novels follow the typical fairy-tale narrative pattern of a villain pitted against a small child who, with assistance, eventually triumphs over the villain. Dickens sometimes strayed from the classic fairy godmother as the means of intervention. In *Nicholas Nickleby* (1839), for example, intervention comes in the form of the Cheeryble brothers, a type described by one critic as a fairy godfather. In Dickens' novels after *David Copperfield* (1850), the central character, no longer relying on intervention from others, becomes responsible, hard-working, and unselfish. Throughout his oeuvre, Dickens blends realism with these embedded fairy-tale motifs and their deviations. The melding of these elements enriches Dickens' exploration and commentary on contemporary issues in novels such as *Dombey and Son* (1848) and *The Old Curiosity Shop* (1841), both of which examine capitalism and socio-economic forces.

Women writers also drew inspiration from fairy tales and their heroines. Before the eighteenth century, fairy-tale heroines in the oral tradition actively faced their adversaries. With the arrival of the print culture in the eighteenth century, passive fairy-tale heroines waited for a man to rescue them. By the nineteenth century, many women novelists used fairy tales and their female protagonists to challenge societal attitudes toward idealized womanhood, gender inequality, and class inequality. Several critics have studied how these stories function in their work. One critic argued that George Sand in her novels *Mauprat* (1837) and *François le Champi* (1847) appropriated "Beauty and the Beast" to call for marriage as a union of equals. In both novels Sand reversed the fairy-tale vision of a man saving the passive heroine to the vision of the heroine actively saving an uncivilized man whom she educates and eventually mar-

ries once he meets her standards. Jane Austen, like Sand, challenged societal conventions, particularly in *Persuasion* (1818). Austen revisited and reversed the "Cinderella" story through the marriage of her heroine to a man who is her social inferior, thus suggesting that society embrace a more liberal view of class and marriage. Other critics have noted a more subtle function of the fairy tale in nineteenth-century literature. Frances Hodgson Burnett's exploration of the upper- and lower-class spheres of British domestic life led one critic to conclude that, in Burnett's view, the maid can never transcend her position because housework always needs to be done; thus all characters do not have a fairy-tale ending. *Jane Eyre* (1847) has been lauded by many critics for its portrayal of contemporary life and its rich characterization. An interpretation of the novel that viewed Jane's character and fate under the lens of "Bluebeard" and "Cinderella" argued that the marriage Jane knowingly enters into holds no better future for her than it had for her husband's first wife.

While fairy tales entertain and offer moral lessons for children, the genre further serves as an effective means through which writers can express their views on contemporary issues as well.

REPRESENTATIVE WORKS

Hans Christian Andersen

Eventyr, Fortalte for Børn [*Fairy Tales Told for Children*] (fairy tales) 1835-42

Nye Eventyr [*New Fairy Tales*] (fairy tales) 1844-48

Eventyr [*Fairy Tales*] (fairy tales) 1850

Historier [*Stories*] (fairy tales) 1852-55

Nye Eventyr og Historier [*New Fairy Tales and Stories*] (fairy tales) 1858-60

Nye Eventyr og Historier [*New Fairy Tales and Stories*] (fairy tales) 1861-66

The Complete Andersen [translated by Jean Hersholt] (fairy tales) 1949

The Complete Fairy Tales and Stories [translated by Erik Christian Haugaard] (fairy tales) 1974

Fairy Tales. 4 vols. [translated by R. P. Keigwin] (fairy tales) 1986

Fairy Tales [translated by Tiina Nunnally] (fairy tales) 2004

Jane Austen

Pride and Prejudice. 3 vols. (novel) 1813

Mansfield Park. 3 vols. (novel) 1814

Northanger Abbey and Persuasion. 4 vols. (novels) 1818

Charlotte Brontë

Jane Eyre: An Autobiography. 3 vols. [as Currer Bell] (novel) 1847

Frances Hodgson Burnett

Little Lord Fauntleroy (juvenile novel) 1886

Sara Crewe; or, What Happened at Miss Minchin's (juvenile fiction) 1888

A Little Princess: Being the Whole Story of Sara Crewe, Now Told for the First Time (juvenile novel) 1905

Marie-Catherine d-Aulnoy

Les Contes de fees. 4 vols. [*Tales of the Fairies*] (fairy tales) 1697-98

Charles Dickens

*Posthumous Papers of the Pickwick Club [as Boz] (novel) 1837

*The Life and Adventures of Nicholas Nickleby (novel) 1839

*The Old Curiosity Shop (novel) 1841

A Christmas Carol in Prose (short story) 1843

The Chimes: A Goblin Story of Some Bells That Rang an Old Year Out and a New Year In (short story) 1844

*The Life and Adventures of Martin Chuzzlewit (novel) 1844

The Cricket on the Hearth: A Fairy Tale of Home (short story) 1845

The Battle of Life: A Love Story (short story) 1846

*Dealings with the Firm of Dombey and Son (novel) 1848

The Haunted Man, and The Ghost's Bargain (short stories) 1848

*The Personal History of David Copperfield (novel) 1850

*Bleak House (novel) 1853

*Little Dorrit (novel) 1857

*A Tale of Two Cities (novel) 1859

*Great Expectations (novel) 1861

*Our Mutual Friend (novel) 1865

Jakob and Wilhelm Grimm

Kinder- und Hausmärchen [*German Popular Stories*] (fairy tales) 1812-15; also published as *Grimm's Fairy Tales,* 1872; *Fairy Tales,* 1900, and *Household Tales,* 1906

Charles Perrault

†*Histoires, ou Contes du temps passé avec des moralitez* [*Histories or Tales of Past Times*] (fairy tales) 1697; also published as *Fairy Tales or Histories of Past Times, with Morals,* 1794

George Sand

Mauprat (novel) 1837

La Mare au diable [*The Haunted Marsh*] (novel) 1846

François le champi [*The Country Waif*] (novel) 1848

Oscar Wilde

‡*The Happy Prince and Other Tales* (fairy tales) 1888

§*A House of Pomegranates* (fairy tales) 1891

*All of Dickens' novels were first published serially in magazines, usually over a period of one to two years.

†This collection includes the fairy tale "Bluebeard."

‡This collection includes the fairy tales "The Happy Prince," "The Nightingale and the Rose," "The Selfish Giant," "The Devoted Friend," and "The Remarkable Rocket."

§This collection includes the fairy tale "The Star Child."

OVERVIEW

Michael C. Kotzin (essay date 1972)

SOURCE: Kotzin, Michael C. "The Fairy Tale." In *Dickens and the Fairy Tale,* pp. 7-31. Bowling Green, Ohio: Bowling Green University Popular Press, 1972.

[*In the following essay, Kotzin delineates the roots of fairy tales and their role in nineteenth-century life and literature.*]

Fairy tales are perhaps more easily recognized than defined. Folklorists group them with other kinds of folktales, such as animal stories, jests, and fables. They are a type of narrative which has traditionally been told aloud by peoples throughout the world, and although some of the fairy tales in oral traditions have literary sources and many literary versions of the tales have been written, the popular, primitive origins of the fairy-tale genre are often thought of as having determined its character.

The tales get their name from their inclusion of "fairy," but that is a word with more than one meaning. Thomas Keightley speculated that the root of the word "fairy" was the Latin *fatum.* This led to the Latin verb *fatare* (to enchant) which in French became *faer,* from which was made the substantive *faerie,* "illusion, enchantment, the meaning of which was afterwards extended, particularly after it had been adopted into the English language." According to Keightley, then, the first meaning of "faerie" was illusion; the second the land of illusions; the third the inhabitants of that land; and the fourth an individual inhabitant.[1] J. R. R. Tolkien insists that the fairy tale gets its name from reference to the second of those meanings. He says: "Fairy-stories are not in normal English usage stories *about* fairies or elves, but stories about Fairy, that is *Faërie,* the realm or state in which fairies have their being."[2]

Particular qualities of the world of "Fairie" include the presence there of magical acts, the animation of non-living things, the transformation of one thing or person into another, and an unnaturally quick or unnaturally slow passage of time. Fairy tales are recognized by the recurrence in them of this subject matter, and by the recurrence of certain narrative patterns or combinations of them. The typical fairy tale has a central character, usually an isolated, virtuous young man or woman who is often a youngest child. This hero confronts a villain, such as a cruel stepmother or a supernatural figure such as a giant, ogre, or witch. He may receive help from a supernatural being, such as some sort of good fairy. He usually is victorious over his adversary, achieves comfort and happiness, and sometimes gets married.

Two other forms of narrative, myths and legends, share some of this content, but fairy tales frequently are distinguished from them, as they were by James Frazer. He defined myths as "mistaken explanations of phenomena, whether of human life or of external nature"; legends as "traditions, whether oral or written, which relate the fortunes of real people in the past, or which describe events, not necessarily human, that are said to have occurred at real places"; and he describes folktales as "narratives which, though they profess to describe actual occurrences, are in fact purely imaginary, having no other aim than the entertainment of the hearer and making no real claim on his credulity."[3] In other words, the subjects of myths are prehistorical, of legends historical, and of folktales ahistorical.

The lines dividing these categories are faint and overlapping, though, and fairy tales and legends are often particularly difficult to separate, especially in the English narrative tradition. The distinction between fairy tales and myths is easier. It can be made in various ways, one of which Frazer hints at: not only by content, but by function (myths, he says, explain; folktales entertain). A similar contrast of function was discovered by Bronislaw Malinowski among stories told on the Trobriand Islands. The mythology which Malinowski found on the Islands "expresses, enhances, and codifies beliefs; . . . safeguards and enforces morality; . . . vouches for the efficiency of ritual and contains practical rules for the guidance of man,"[4] and can be thought of as duplicating the function of Christian mythology in Victorian England. Similarly, the major function of folktales on the Islands, to provide amusement, was one of the major functions of fairy tales in Victorian England; but there was also another declared function: to have a moral effect. The first of these is perhaps the more "natural" function of fairy tales, but before amusement could be accepted as an official justification for allowing children to read fairy tales in England they had to be seen as fulfilling the second function too, and that did not happen until the nineteenth century. During the previous century the influence of didacticism and ratio-

nalism on the printing of children's books had helped bring fairy tales near extinction. But the few native fairy tales which had survived earlier hazards and a considerable supply of imported ones were given a new lease on life when, during the early Victorian period, certain Romantic ideas took hold. This history deserves to be told in some detail.

By the nineteenth century or sooner, most of the native fairy tales once available, and drawn upon by Shakespeare, Spenser, Peele, and Jonson, had become "scarce and fragmentary in England."[5] In 1822 Wilhelm Grimm speculated that "it is probable that the greater part of the stories known in Germany are indigenous in Great Britain also," but after citing a few of the types of stories found in both countries, he had to add that "little, however, has as yet been collected or communicated. This department of literature has been filled up by translations from the French." Grimm then summarized and discussed three "characteristic and genuine English stories" which had been printed by Benjamin Tabart earlier in the century: "Jack the Giant-Killer," "Tom Thumb," and "Jack and the Beanstalk."[6] The truth, as discovered by later folklorists, appears to be that by that time there were few other "characteristic and genuine English stories" to collect—not much more than "Tom Tit Tot" (a kind of "Rumpelstiltskin"—AT 500) and "Dick Whittington and his Cat" (which can just barely be considered a fairy tale—AT 1651). Richard M. Dorson says: "The fact had become painfully evident, by the close of Victoria's reign, that the treasure trove of fairy tales unearthed for nearly every European country, in replica of the Grimms' discovery in Germany, would not be found in England. . . . Why had a blight struck Merry England? No one has yet produced a satisfactory answer."[7]

One theory is that French and German tales drove out the native ones,[8] but it seems to me that the most satisfactory answer to the problem was advanced by Edwin Sidney Hartland, who observed that whereas there are few English fairy tales, there is a considerable body of folktale material of the legend type, such as the Robin Hood tales. Hartland's theory was that Puritanism was responsible: the English Nonconformists of the sixteenth, seventeenth, and eighteenth centuries objected to the fantastic, obviously untrue stories and killed off much of the earlier native tradition;[9] the tales from France would then have been filling a vacuum. Whether or not that was the process, the result was that the imported tales became common. They were resisted for a long time by forces similar to the ones which perhaps had been responsible for a shortage of tales in the first place—by latter-day Puritans, the earnest Evangelicals, who objected to the frivolousness of the stories (despite the self-proclaimed moral intentions of some of them); by the newly-cultured, who objected to their primitiveness; and by the rationalists, who objected to their falseness. However, though the resistance temporarily prevented the tales from becoming accepted as children's literature, it could not prevent them from being translated and published, from appearing in chapbooks, and thence from entering the oral folk corpus.

Among the first fairy tales to be translated into English in the eighteenth century were those found in the *Thousand and One Nights,* also known as the *Arabian Nights Entertainment.* First collected in about 1550, the Arabic stories in that volume were translated into French by Antoine Galland in 1704, and from French to English by 1708 (and possibly as early as 1704[10]). In 1707 and 1716 there were separate translations of the courtly, literary *Les Contes des Fées* of Marie Catherine d'Aulnoy, which had appeared in France in about 1700, and in 1729 Robert Samber translated eight fairy tales which had been published in one volume in France in 1697 with the inscription *Contes de ma mère l'Oye.* Probably quite close to folk sources but beautifully polished by Charles Perrault or his son, the stories included "Sleeping Beauty," "Little Red-Riding Hood," "Bluebeard," "Puss-in-Boots," and "Cinderella," and in England became ascribed to "Mother Goose."[11]

All of these collections were reprinted during the eighteenth century, in part or in full, and so were translations of selections from other collections of fairy tales, including the forty-one volume *Le Cabinet des Fées* (1785-89), which held "Beauty and the Beast." The forces of enlightenment could not keep these stories out of the country. But they could keep them from entering whatever "recommended" lists there might have been for children. When John Newbery, the first publisher of children's books, entered the trade in the mid-'forties, he became known not for imaginative fairy tales, but for moral, instructive tales, which were to be the dominant acceptable children's fare for the rest of the century and the beginning of the next. When the fairy-type stories were printed by the official presses, they usually were made heavily didactic. And Newbery's followers were even more oppressively moral and insistently rational than he had been. He was interested in entertaining the child as well as educating him. (It was he, in fact, who attached the name of Mother Goose to nursery rhymes.) But those who next influenced children's reading had more limited goals. Mostly women, such as Anna Laetitia Barbauld and Sarah Trimmer, they advocated a predominantly didactic and factual literature for children and resisted irrational flights of imagination. In Mrs. Trimmer's aptly-named magazine, *The Guardian of Education* (1802-06), *Mother Bunch's Fairy Tales,* a collection of re-told d'Aulnoy stories which Newbery had found suitable enough to publish, was reviewed in this way: "Partial, as we confess ourselves to be, to most of the books of the old school, we cannot approve of those which are only fit to fill the heads of children with confused notions of wonderful and supernatural events, brought about by the agency of imaginary be-

ings. Mother Bunch's Tales are of this description." A review of the Mother Goose tales said: "Though we will remember the interest with which, in our childish days, when books of amusement for children were scarce, we read, or listened to the history of 'Little Red Riding Hood,' and 'Blue Beard,' & c. we do not wish to have such sensations awakened in the hearts of our grandchildren, by the same means; for the terrific images, which tales of this nature present to the imagination, usually make deep impressions, and injure the tender minds of children, by exciting unreasonable and groundless fear. Neither do the generality of tales of this kind supply any moral instruction level to the infantine capacity."[12] An unidentified correspondent, who impressed Mrs. Trimmer as being "so good a judge of what children *ought* and *ought not* to read," shows the extreme of the state of affairs which prevailed at the beginning of the century. Referring to the most popular fairy tale in the world, she said that "Cinderella" "is perhaps one of the most exceptionable books that was ever written for children. . . . It paints some of the worst passions that can enter into the human breast, and of which little children should, if possible, be totally ignorant; such as envy, jealousy, a dislike to mothers-in-law and half-sisters, vanity, a love of dress, & c. & c."[13]

Some fairy tales, meanwhile, had survived in the *Arabian Nights,* which benefited from the Orientalism it stimulated, and which was imitated in English by the Rev. James Ridley's *Tales of the Genii.*[14] Some which came from France survived in another way. These stories were kept alive primarily thanks to chapbooks and the folk that the chapbooks brought them to. The chapbook, mostly a seventeenth, eighteenth, and early nineteenth-century phenomenon, was a cheap, illustrated form of popular entertainment which contained everything from riddles and jokes to Bible stories. An 1847 reviewer of fairy tales recalled "the days of their former popularity; when their fascinations were usually comprised within some half dozen greyish-white pages, displaying a curious combination of large and small type—the proportion varying according as a story of greater or less length had to be compressed within the same inexorable limits; and adorned with woodcuts, which, as some scribes would say, 'may be imagined better than described.'" In this format many sorts of stories with fairy-tale affinities—ones from the *Arabian Nights* and Perrault, chivalric romances reduced in length, native folktales—came to be associated. Though chapbooks were not printed specially for him, through them the English child as well as the folk could meet such figures as Aladdin, Bluebeard, St. George, Jack the Giant-Killer, and Tom Thumb.[15] The chapbook brought the imported, printed stories into the native, oral and sub-literary traditions. Lower-class and country-dwelling children heard the stories from their elders and, if they could, read them in chapbooks. Wealthier and urban children heard them from their lower-class and country nurses and, if they could, also read them in chapbooks. In these ways the stories were available to the Romantics who, applying their beliefs in the primacy of the child and the value of imagination, came to the defense of the tales and attacked the official children's reading.

In a letter to [Samuel Taylor] Coleridge dated October 23, 1802, Charles Lamb strongly attacked the anti-fairy tale educators, saying:

> I am glad the snuff and Pi-pos's Books please. "Goody Two Shoes" is almost out of print. Mrs. Barbauld's stuff has banished all the old classics of the nursery; and the shopman at Newbery's hardly deigned to reach them off an old exploded corner of a shelf, when Mary asked for them. Mrs. B.'s and Mrs. Trimmer's nonsense lay in piles about. Knowledge insignificant and vapid as Mrs. B.'s books convey, it seems, must come to a child in the *shape of knowledge,* and his empty noddle must be turned with conceit of his own powers when he has learnt that a Horse is an animal, and Billy is better than a Horse, and such like; instead of that beautiful Interest in wild tales which made the child a man, while all the time he suspected himself to be no bigger than a child. Science has succeeded to Poetry no less in the little walks of children than with men. Is there no possibility of averting this sore evil? Think what you would have been now, if instead of being fed with Tales and old wives' fables in childhood, you had been crammed with geography and natural history?
>
> Damn them!—I mean that cursed Barbauld Crew, those Blights and Blasts of all that is Human in man and child.[16]

Coleridge himself as a child had passionately read his father's copy of the *Arabian Nights,* and had read chapbook versions of "Jack the Giant-Killer," *The Seven Champions of Christendom,* and other stories. Later he had defended fairy tales for children, basing his judgment on his own experiences. On October 16, 1797, he wrote Thomas Poole how

> from my early reading of fairy tales and genii, etc., etc., my mind had been habituated *to the Vast,* and I never regarded *my senses* in any way as the criteria of my belief. I regulated all my creeds by my conceptions, not by my *sight,* even at that age. Should children be permitted to read romances, and relations of giants and magicians and genii? I know all that has been said against it; but I have formed my faith in the affirmative. I know no other way of giving the mind a love of the Great and the Whole.[17]

Wordsworth also read and defended fairy tales. In *The Prelude* he remembered being "a Child not nine years old," and seeing "the shining streams / Of Fairy land, the Forests of Romance, (Book Five, ll. 474-77), and said that he "had a precious treasure at that time / A little, yellow canvas-cover'd Book, / A slender abstract of the Arabian Tales" (ll. 482-84). Earlier in the poem he criticized the current system of education by portray-

ing a knowledgeable product of it (". . . 'tis a Child, no Child, / But a dwarf Man"—ll. 294-95), and then said:

> Meanwhile old Grandame Earth is grieved to find
> The playthings, which her love design'd for him,
> Unthought of: in their woodland beds the flowers
> Weep, and the river sides are all forlorn.
>
> (ll. 346-49)
>
> . . . . .
>
> Oh! give us once again the Wishing-Cap
> Of Fortunatus, and the invisible Coat
> Of Jack the Giant-killer, Robin Hood,
> And Sabra in the forest with St. George!
> The child, whose love is here, at least, doth reap
> One precious gain, that he forgets himself.[18]
>
> (ll. 364-69)

For Wordsworth, Nature is the best educator; next best, it would seem, or at least better than what was taught in the schools, are fairy tales.

Despite the Romantics (whose writings about the fairy tale frequently were private), children's reading continued to be "enlightened" early in the nineteenth century, and the fairy tale was threatened even in its underground form as folk and chapbook literature. But there were signs of change. The chapbook stories were given a new popular form as they began to be drawn upon for the plots of entertaining pantomimes put on in the theaters at Christmas time;[19] and a legitimate book publisher brought out a volume of fairy tales. He was Sir Richard Phillips who, in 1809, under the name of Benjamin Tabart, published some of the stories from Mother Goose, Countess d'Aulnoy, and the *Arabian Nights,* the three native tales cited by Grimm, and other legends and romances, under the title *Popular Fairy Tales; or, a Liliputian* [sic] *Library.* In a preface Phillips claimed that earlier English versions of the stories, presumably chapbook ones in particular, had been "obsolete in their style, . . . gross in their morals, and . . . vulgar in their details." His intention was "to elevate the language and sentiments to a level with the refined manners of the present age": to save the tales from the chapbooks. Though his intention of making the tales respectable in style and content was not based on didactic justification (on the contrary; he believed that he had produced "one of the most entertaining volumes in any language"[20]), didacticism still plays an obvious part in the versions of the stories he used. "Beauty and the Beast" is presented as an exemplum, and Jack of "Jack and the Beanstalk," his behavior explained by footnotes, is a good boy who is avenging his father's death and recovering stolen property. Still, this volume was a milestone.

But other publishers did not follow Phillips' lead. They did not yet publish semi-authentic fairy tales for the entertainment of children. When a second printing of the

Tabart collection appeared in 1818, it evoked an important article from the pen of Francis Cohen, later Francis Palgrave and the father of Francis Turner Palgrave, which describes the current situation. In the article Cohen claims that nursery stories have changed, that children's literature no longer is imaginative because fanciful stories are considered "too childish." The forces of enlightenment had done their job well. And what is more, Cohen maintains, the core of adult popular reading material has also changed: nurses no longer read fairy tales, so do not know them as well as they used to themselves, and are less able to tell them to children. "Scarcely any of the *chap books* which were formerly sold to the country people at fairs and markets have been able to maintain their ancient popularity; and we have almost witnessed the extinction of this branch of our national literature": Gothic romances are read instead of legends, newspapers instead of broadside ballads.[21]

Cohen, who regrets the disappearance of the old nursery stories, defends their value and spends most of his time noting the sharing by many peoples of similar stories. He, like [Sir Walter] Scott, is an example of the descendants of eighteenth-century antiquarians who accompanied or followed the brothers Grimm (to whom he refers with the highest praise) into the field of folklore. The German Grimms—themselves working in a tradition which had been strongly influenced by English forces, particularly by Ossian and by Percy, who had had a great effect on Herder—had more to do with the fate of the fairy tale in England than did any of their English Romantic contemporaries. Their most influential works were the *Kinder-und Hausmärchen,* that great collection of folktales recorded by them and published in Germany in 1812 and 1815; a scholarly study of the origins and diffusion of the tales attached in 1822 to an 1819 edition of them; and the *Deutsche Mythologie* (1835). The Grimms's method of collecting tales was in some ways duplicated by Thomas Crofton Croker for his *Fairy Legends and Traditions of the South of Ireland* (1825), though, as the title suggests and Richard M. Dorson points out, the content is "not *Märchen* or fictional fairy tales, but traditional stories about demonic beings."[22] Their kind of scholarly approach to tales was followed by Thomas Keightley in *The Fairy Mythology* (1828). And they were a specific influence on the third volume of Croker's work (1828), on an enlargement of Keightley's (1850), and on many other folklore studies from then on, such as Thomas Wright's *Essays on Subjects Connected with the Literature, Popular Superstitions, and History of England in the Middle Ages* (1846), and the studies of William John Thoms, coiner of the term "Folk-Lore" in the August 22, 1846, issue of the *Athenaeum* and founder in 1849 of *Notes and Queries.*

The Grimms were not only a major influence on folktale scholarship; they were also a major influence on the printing of fairy tales, for children as well as scholars. Tabart's earlier collection had less of an effect than the *Kinder-und Hausmärchen* in bringing fairy tales to the child. As Cohen notes in his article, chapbooks were dying out; but the printing of fairy stories was soon to be made respectable. As he also notes, the folk were losing the tales; but children were gaining (or regaining) them.

In 1821, two years after Cohen's article appeared, Edgar Taylor published an article on "German Popular and Traditionary Literature" in which he said:

> There exists, at present, a very large and increasing class of readers, for whom the scattered fragments of olden time, as preserved in popular and traditionary tales, possess a powerful attraction. The taste for this species of literature has particularly manifested itself of late; the stories which had gone out of fashion during the prevalence of the prudery and artificial taste of the last century, began, at its close, to re-assert every where their ancient empire over the mind. Our literati had fancied themselves, and persuaded the world to think itself, too wise for such amusements—they considered themselves as come to man's estate, and determined, on a sudden, to put away childish things. The curious mementos of simple and primitive society, the precious glimmerings of historic light, which these invaluable relics have preserved, were rejected as beneath the dignity to which these philosophers aspired; and even children began to be fed with a stronger diet.
>
> A better taste, say the patrons of these blossoms of nature and fancy, is now springing up. Our scholars busy themselves in tracing out the genealogy and mythological connexions of Tom Thumb and Jack the Giant Killer; and surely if the grave and learned embark in these speculations, we are justified in expecting to be able to welcome the æra when our children shall be allowed once more to regale themselves with that mild food which will enliven their imaginations, and tempt them on through the thorny paths of education;—when the gay dreams of fairy innocence shall again hover around them, and scientific compendiums, lisping botanics, and leading-string mechanics, shall be postponed to the Delights of Valentine and Orson, the beautiful Magalona, or Fair Rosamond.[23]

In 1823, two years after he wrote this article, Taylor presented the first English translation of Grimm, called *German Popular Stories* and illustrated by George Cruikshank. In his preface Taylor indicated that folklore interests were among the reasons prompting him to publish the stories, but he also thought it important that the tales be made available to English children. Echoing his earlier statement, he said:

> The popular tales of England have been too much neglected. They are nearly discarded from the libraries of childhood. Philosophy is made the companion of the nursery: we have lisping chemists and leading-string

mathematicians: this is the age of reason, not of imagination; and the loveliest dreams of fairy innocence are considered as vain and frivolous. Much might be urged against this rigid and philosophic (or rather unphilosophic) exclusion of works of fancy and fiction. Our imagination is surely as susceptible of improvement by exercise, as our judgement or our memory; and so long as such fictions only are presented to the young mind as do not interfere with the important department of moral education, a beneficial effect must be produced by the pleasurable employment of a faculty in which so much of our happiness in every period of life consists.[24]

After Taylor's translation (and greatly because of it), ideas similar to those expressed earlier by the English Romantics began to be voiced more frequently. On January 16, 1823, Sir Walter Scott wrote Taylor a letter to thank him for his translation and to praise it. He said of the tales that "there is . . . a sort of wild fairy interest in them which makes me think them fully better adapted to awaken the imagination and soften the heart of childhood than the good-boy stories which have been in later years composed for them. . . . Our old wild fictions like our own simple music will have more effect in awakening the fancy & elevating the disposition than the colder and more elevated compositions of more clever authors & composers."[25] Several of the reviewers of Taylor's edition dealt with its antiquarian folklore qualities, but many also approached the collection as children's literature. A common reaction of a reviewer was that the tales reminded him of those he knew during his childhood, and that he felt it good that they were available to children again. Such was the position of the reviewer in *Gentleman's Magazine,* who recommended the book for children and adults, and of the one in *London Magazine,* who praised the stories as "delightful food for a child's imagination" and said: "It is the vice of parents now-a-days to load their children's minds with useful books. . . . Why should little children have grown-up minds?—Why should the dawning imagination be clouded and destroyed in its first trembling light? Is the imagination a thing given to be destroyed?—Oh no!"[26]

The response to Taylor's Grimm prompted a second volume in 1826, a time when Englishmen were being exposed to a related product of the German Romantic movement (some examples of which were in this second volume of Grimm), the *Kunstmärchen,* folk tales transformed into fantasy literature for adults. Johann August Musäus had been adapting folk tales for sophisticated adults as early as 1782, and Goethe used folklore motifs in his complex "Mährchen" of 1795. Then, with "Der blonde Eckbert" of 1797, Ludwig Tieck established the most common form the *Kunstmärchen* would take, in other stories of his and in works by Wackenroder, Novalis, Brentano, la Motte Fouqué, Cha-

misso, and E. T. A. Hoffmann. Musäus' collection of tales was translated by William Beckford and published as *Popular Tales of the Germans* in 1791. But England knew little about these writings until the appearance of Madame de Staël's *De l'Allemagne* of 1813, and even then, though la Motte Fouqué's *Undine* was translated in 1818, extensive translation awaited the stimulus of Taylor's translation of Grimm. It was followed by a flood.

Some of the most important translations of this time were: *Popular Tales of the Northern Nations* (1823—it included the first English translation of Tieck); Chamisso's *Peter Schlemihl* (1824); Thomas Roscoe's four volume translation *The German Novelists* (1826); and above all, Thomas Carlyle's four volume *German Romance: Specimens of its chief authors, with biographical and critical notes* (1827). Publication of such stories continued through the Victorian period, as their popularity increased, so that Tieck, for example, achieved his "banner year" in 1845, a year in which J. A. Froude, Julius Hare, and others translated a collection of his.[27]

By the 1830's, British writers were imitating the German tales, particularly in the magazines. *Peter Schlemihl* gave rise to "The Man Without a Shadow. Tale from the German" (*Pocket Magazine,* 1830) and to James Roscoe's "My After-Dinner Adventures with Peter Schlemihl" (*Blackwood's* and *Mirror of Literature,* 1839). Otmar's "Peter Claus" was imitated in "Dorf Juystein" (*Fraser's Magazine,* 1832). It had earlier been imitated by the American Washington Irving in "Rip Van Winkle" (1820), and Irving also imitated a Musäus story, in "The Legend of Sleepy Hollow" (1820). Two other American short story writers, who started out in the 'thirties, Edgar Allan Poe and Nathaniel Hawthorne, have been seen as if not influenced by, at least in the lines of, Hoffmann and Tieck.[28] In England the German Romantic fairy tale (especially Goethe's "Mährchen," which he had translated in 1825 and interpreted, as a "phantasmagory," in 1832) was one of the influences on Carlyle's *Sartor Resartus* in the 1830's and the Germans later inspired George MacDonald to write *Phantastes: A Faerie Romance for Men and Women* (1858).[29] But the major Victorian novelists were mostly to use fairy tales in more realistic ways, as we shall see.

During the same decade which saw the beginnings of extensive translation from and some imitations of German folktales, the English were putting native, French, and Arabian Nights tales to greater use as the bases of gay Christmas-time pantomimes. On December 26, 1825, according to the *Times* of that date, the child and his parents who sat through an ordinary play could then have seen *Harlequin and the Magic Rose; or, Beauty and the Beast* at Covent Garden, and at the Adelphi something called *The Three Golden Lamps; or, Harlequin and the Wizard Dwarf.* A decade later he could have seen *Whittington and his Cat* at Drury Lane, *Harlequin Jack and his Eleven Brothers* at the Victoria, and at the Adelphi both *The Elfin Queen* and *The Battle of the Fairies.* By the end of the 'thirties J. R. Planché had established himself as the master at this sort of thing, writing almost annually a clever extravaganza, full of horseplay, puns, and clever rhymes, and usually based on a story from Madam d'Aulnoy.

Finally, with fairy tales recognized as the subject of serious study by scholars, appreciated as the source of some popular adult literature, and enjoyed as holiday entertainment, in the late 1830's and the 1840's, the Romantic ideas about fairy tales were accorded a public acceptance, and the tales were widely praised as good children's literature, worth publishing. In two articles in 1842 and 1844 Elizabeth Eastlake pointed out that a recognition of the need for children's books had not necessarily resulted in appropriate books for children. She said that although children now had libraries, which their greatgrandmothers did not have, the books provided for them in those libraries are not necessarily better than the "fairy tales and marvellous histories" and "little tales of a moral tendency" which the ancestors had been able to obtain. Books today, she argued, do not separate entertainment and instruction, and fail to achieve either purpose. She reviewed those books which she considered bad, and she then listed examples of the kinds of books she considered good, including "Beauty and the Beast," "Jack and the Beanstalk," Grimm, and the *Arabian Nights* among those works which are good for entertainment.[30] The kinds of books she wanted were being published increasingly frequently even as she wrote. From that time on, English bookshelves were filled more and more with translations of foreign folktales, with new collections of the few native stories that could be found, which early reviewers of Taylor's Grimm had called for, and even with newly-composed fairy stories. The battle of the children's books continued, but fairy tales at last gained a recognition and availability they had lacked before.

The increased publication included new translations of Grimm in 1839, 1846, 1853, 1855, and frequently thereafter. There also were many reprintings, and a reviewer of one of the later editions of Edgar Taylor's translation of Grimm indicates the popularity the tales had reached by 1847. He says that Taylor's earlier claim that the tales were "out of fashion" is no longer true: "the more elegant guise in which our old friends present themselves, radiant in their gay bindings, and red and black title pages, would rather intimate that they are becoming very much the fashion."[31]

The new taste was encouraged by Robert Southey, who held an interest in folklore and included in *The doctor, & c.* (1837) as a chapter "for the nursery" a version of a popular tale, "The Story of the Three Bears."[32] The new fashion was also notably marked by translations of older collections of stories, such as the *Arabian Nights* in 1839-40 (by Edwin Lane) and Basile's *Pentamerone* of 1634-36 in 1848, and by the publication of anthologies which contained versions of stories from such standards as Mother Goose, Madame d'Aulnoy, and the Grimms, from other foreign sources, and from the native stock. These collections include Felix Summerly's (Henry Cole's) *Home Treasury,* 1841-49 (in one volume of which, *Beauty and the Beast,* the editor objected to other "modern English versions" which "are filled with moralizings on education, marriage, & c., futile attempts to grind everything as much as possible into dull logical probability. . . . I have thought it no sin . . . to attempt to re-write the legend more as a fairy tale than a lecture"); Ambrose Merton's (William John Thoms's) *The Old Story Books of England,* 1845, reprinted in 1846 as *Gammer Gurton's Pleasant Stories* and *Gammer Gurton's Famous Histories* (whose introductions said: "Their design is to cultivate the heart, to enrich the fancy, to stir up kindly feelings, to encourage a taste for the BEAUTIFUL, and to accomplish this by taking advantage of the youthful longing for amusement"); and Anthony Montalba's *Fairy Tales from All Nations,* 1849 (the preface of which declared that England had "cast off that pedantic folly" of condemning fairy tales "as merely idle things, or as pernicious occupations for faculties that should be always directed to serious and profitable concerns").[33] And there also was C. B. Burkhardt's *Fairy Tales and Legends of Many Nations,* 1849, J. R. Planché's translation of *Four and Twenty [French] Fairy Tales,* 1858, and Dinah Maria Mulock Craik's *The Fairy Book,* 1863.

Writers did not limit themselves to revising and reprinting old stories: they also began to write original ones which used fairy-tale motifs and patterns. Though such stories usually had moral implications, their authors also usually showed respect for their sources and acceptance of, even delight in, fantasy. The earliest was Catherine Sinclair's humorous "Uncle David's Nonsensical Story about Giants and Fairies" (in *Holiday House,* 1839). Then in 1841 John Ruskin wrote *The King of the Golden River,* more like a folktale and, as he said, "a fairly good imitation of Grimm and Dickens, mixed with a little true Alpine feeling of my own,"[34] which was not published until 1850. Another type of fairy tale was written by F. E. Paget in *The Hope of the Katzeko-*

pfs (1844). This book begins as a burlesque of Court fairy tales which open with christenings and uninvited guests (e.g., AT 410), then becomes a serious version of the type, full of magic. But the full development of original fairy tales for children in England awaited another leader, and once again an influence came from abroad. This time it was the Danish Hans Christian Andersen, whose first collection of fairy stories appeared in 1835, and who was first translated into English in 1846. F. J. H. Darton says: "The fairytale had at last come into its own. The story of its struggle without the aid of originality like Andersen's had culminated in such versions as Tabart's and in the immediate success of *Grimm*. But now there was added the recognition that it was lawful, and even praiseworthy, to invent and release fantasy, and to circulate folk-lore itself."[35]

Among the many original children's fairy tales which followed until 1870, the year of Dickens' death, there was the rare *Alice Learmont* (1852) by Mrs. Craik, a sensitive, serious book which, like Ruskin's, seems especially close to the folk traditions. But more of the stories of the period followed Catherine Sinclair's in seeming to be presented for the entertainment of modern children (not as being true folktales), sometimes followed Paget's (and French ones) in adapting Court motifs, sometimes followed both in portraying visits to Fairyland—and often followed both, and Andersen's stories, in being freely fantastic. These stories included Thackeray's *The Rose and the Ring* (1854); Frances Browne's *Granny's Wonderful Chair and its Tales of Fairy Times* (1856); Harriet Parr's *Legends from Fairy Land* (1860) and its sequels; Charles Kingsley's *The Water Babies: A Fairy Tale for a Land Baby* (1863); Annie Keary's rather condescending *Little Wanderlin and other Fairy Tales* (1865); George MacDonald's several more serious works, with their debts to the Germans—"The Fairy Fleet: an English Mährchen" (1866), *Dealings with the Fairies* (1867, though parts of it appeared in 1864), and *At the Back of the North Wind* (serialized 1868-70); Jean Ingelow's *Mopsa the Fairy* (1869); and "Amelia and the Dwarfs" in Juliana Horatia Ewing's *The Brownies and other Tales* (1870).

Major "adult" authors were not only trying their hands at writing these children's stories, but also joined the ranks of their defenders. Thackeray, who showed his appreciation of fairy tales in two reviews, wrote the following in one of the brief interpolated essays in *Vanity Fair* (1847-48):

> Some time after this interview, it happened that Mr. Cuff, on a sunshiny afternoon, was in the neighbourhood of poor William Dobbin, who was lying under a tree in the play-ground, spelling over a favourite copy of the Arabian Nights which he had—apart from the rest of the school, who were persuing their various sports—quite lonely, and almost happy. If people would but leave children to themselves; if teachers would cease to bully them; if parents would not insist upon directing their thoughts, and dominating their feelings—those feelings and thoughts which are a mystery to all (for how much do you and I know of each other, of our children, of our fathers, of our neighbour, and how far more beautiful and sacred are the thoughts of the poor lad or girl whom you govern likely to be, than those of the dull and world-corrupted person who rules him?)—if, I say, parents and masters would leave their children alone a little more,—small harm would accrue, although a less quantity of *as in præsenti* might be acquired.

(ch. 5)[36]

During the 1850's Dickens' journal *Household Words* presented articles which defended fairy tales more specifically and extensively than Thackeray's statement did, including ones by the poet and essayist R. H. Horne and the educator and literary scholar Henry Morley, who later was to publish several collections of original fairy tales.

Horne's article, "A Witch in the Nursery," objected to stories which contain excessive descriptions of death and violence, calling them immoral, but it defended as an alternative not directly didactic stories but others, ones such as Andersen's, which "indirectly" ("through the heart and the imagination") instill "the purest moral principles."[37] Morley's article, "The School of the Fairies," is a review of J. R. Planché's translation of Countess d'Aulnoy. It says that fairy tales have educational values: they teach children about different nationalities and they provide them with moral values such as sympathy for others. Morley says: "The mind has its own natural way of growing, as the body has, and at each stage of growth it asks for its own class of food. We injure minds or bodies by denying either. . . . Fairy tales . . . make the mind active, and indisposed for other work that does not give it enough exercise." He looks at d'Aulnoy's French tales, and sees what their traits are, and what values they can teach. And then he says that he

> would have them . . . set in their places among others, read in their turn with the legends gathered by the brothers Grimm, with choice tales from Musæus, and such more spiritual freaks of fancy as the fairy tales of Tieck and Goethe furnish; with the wild stories of Hoffmann; of course, with our own Red Riding Hood, and others of its class; with the Irish fairy legends; the story of King Arthur and his Round Table; with the Seven Champions of Christendom, and all the legends of the days of chivalry;—farther back still, with all the good fables ever written, up to Æsop, and up farther, to Pilpay; with the Arabian Nights; Greek and Roman leg-

ends; with choice gold of the fancy coined of old in Persia, China, Hindostan. The ways through which a happy child to guide, "in this delightful land of Faery,"

> Are so exceeding spacious and wide,
> And sprinkled with such sweet variety,

that we desire to claim for children right of way through all of them, with privilege to pick the flowers on all sides.[38]

In 1850 *The Prelude* was published, making public the ideas of the recently-deceased poet laureate. And at this time, while their ideas were being accepted, other Romantics were being cited. In 1853 the *Athenaeum*'s reviewer of a new translation of Grimm preceded a citation of Scott's 1823 letter to Edgar Taylor by saying:

> We are also inclined to think, that a considerable *per contra* to any aspect of triviality is to be found in the superior moral tendency (as it appears to us) of these tales to that of *professedly* moral fictions. The former are less selfish and worldly-wise than the latter,—more truly good, and more spontaneous in their goodness. The one class aims at making us "respectable members of society,"—the other seeks to mould us into thoroughly kind, just, and considerate human beings.[39]

In 1860 the anonymous author of a *London Quarterly Review* article on "Children's Literature" quoted Coleridge on the fairy tale, agreed with him, and went on to say: "After all, it is a great point in education to awaken the curiosity, and feed the fancy, because we thus give a child a sense of the greatness of the universe in which he has come to live." Later, echoing Dickens' image in *Hard Times* of the children in M'Choakumchild's school being vessels waiting to be filled with facts, and anticipating "progressive" modern educators, he said:

> On the whole, we may conclude that the great purpose of children's books is not so much to impart instruction, as to promote growth. We must not think of a child's mind as of a vessel, which it is for us to fill, but as a wonderfully organized instrument, which it is for us to develop and to set in motion. He will be well or ill educated, not according to the accuracy with which he retains the notions which have been impressed upon him from without, but according to the power which he puts forth from within, and to the activity and regularity with which the several feelers or *tentacula* of his nature lay hold on all that is to be seen and thought and known around him.

The writer suggests that the following question should be asked of good children's literature: "Above all, does it make the eye glisten and the cheek glow, and the limbs of the little one move with delight?" Of fairy tales he answers, yes.[40]

A mid-Victorian culmination in the acceptance of the fairy tale occurred in 1868, when the Edgar Taylor translation of Grimm was reprinted in one volume, complete with the Cruikshank illustrations, and with a new introduction by no less a figure than John Ruskin. Ruskin, asserting that fairy tales are the best kind of literature for children, described the well-raised, well-educated child and said:

> Children so trained have no need of moral fairy tales; but they will find in the apparently vain and fitful courses of any tradition of old time, honestly delivered to them, a teaching for which no other can be substituted, and of which the power cannot be measured; animating for them the material world with inextinguishable life, fortifying them against the glacial cold of selfish science, and preparing them submissively, and with no bitterness of astonishment, to behold, in later years, the mystery—divinely appointed to remain such to all human thought—of the fates that happen alike to the evil and the good.[41]

The cause for which the Romantics spoke came to have greater urgency as the conditions which provoked them to defend the fairy tale intensified during the Victorian period. Earnest, artless, middle-class Evangelicalism increased its influence; the educational theories of the Enlightenment were succeeded by those of its even less imaginative descendant. Utilitarianism; and the age of the city, industrialism, and science came fully into being. These conditions of England were objected to by Carlyle and by such followers and admirers of his as Ruskin and Kingsley. In discussing the fairy tale these men followed the Romantics by stressing its imaginative value in the new world. But they also reverted a bit to the position of the enemy: the educational values they pointed to in the tales, while not usually as simply and exclusively instructional as those the Enlightenment advocated, are more conventionally moral than those which had been defended by Wordsworth and Coleridge. With their statements in defense of the fairy tale (made more publicly than those of the Romantics had been), the Victorian men of letters probably contributed to its new status. In those statements and elsewhere, they reveal the synthesis of appreciation of the imagination and moral posture which characterizes the Victorian acceptance of the fairy tale.

Carlyle represents the two aspects of the position: he spoke for the powers of the imagination and helped bring the *Kunstmarchen* to England, and he was intensely moralistic. In his essay, Ruskin calls for the reading of authentic, fanciful fairy tales; but he also points to the moral values of such tales, and he used his own imaginative fairy tale to teach a moral lesson—how sympathy for a dog is rewarded, and how an "inheritance, which had been lost by cruelty, was regained by love."[42] Kingsley's fanciful *Water Babies,* in which there is playful defense of the existence of fairies and support of the fairy tale itself, is even more pointedly moral. To "little books" about "little people" the hero prefers "a jolly good fairy tale, about Jack the Giant-killer or Beauty and the Beast, which taught him something that he didn't know already" (ch. 8). From his experiences this hero learns about kindness, cleanliness, and self-sacrifice, among other things, and a "Moral" follows the "parable" to drive some of the lessons home for readers.[43] Even Thackeray, who could not write his fairy tale without making it in part a mock-fairy tale and who rejected the simple morality of virtue rewarded, imbued *The Rose and the Ring* with both delightful fantasy and the moral that "misfortune" is a useful and perhaps necessary condition for the molding of character.

Children's writers were even more inclined to reflect the view that fantasy is good for the child, and to conceive of moral purposes for their fantasies. Many followed the technique of Catherine Sinclair and made their fairy tales allegories. Hers is about Master Nobook, the fairy Do-nothing who lives in Castle Needless, the fairy Teach-all, and so on. F. E. Paget's is about a child named "Eigenwilling," which he translates for us, and its ending resembles *Pilgrim's Progress*; his purpose in writing it was to see whether children's "hearts can be moved to noble and chivalrous feelings, and to shake off the hard, cold, calculating, worldly, selfish temper of the times, by being brought into more immediate contact with the ideal, the imaginary, and the romantic, than has been the fashion of late years."[44] Even in the stories which seem closest to folktales, such as *Alice Learmont* and some of the stories in *Granny's Wonderful Chair*, there usually is an unobtrusive moral thrust, one which, as Katharine M. Briggs says of Miss Browne's and some other stories, resembles the morality of many folktales, in which "generosity and a merry heart are the prime virtues."[45]

One should not think that all versions of fairy tales had only a tempered morality. There still were many original tales like Margaret Gatty's "The Fairy Godmother" (1851), not much of a fairy tale but heavily moral, and there still could be versions of traditional tales like the four presented by George Cruikshank in a Fairy Library (1853-54, 1864), stories insistently instructive, primarily in the virtues of temperance (in them giants and ogres are repeatedly overcome because they are drunk). The association of fairy tales with morality was so strong that a writer like Lewis Carroll, a man far from committed to didacticism, when writing about fairies ended up teaching a lesson (of the need to work before playing—"Bruno's Revenge," 1867). And George Mac-Donald, despite his flights of fantasy and his ability to usually keep the preacher in him under control, could burden *At the Back of the North Wind* with an ever-present didacticism. Still, the period saw, alongside of its morality, a real appreciation of fairy tales and of the kind of imagination which can create and respond to them.

The Victorian pater-familias, who was only recently persuaded of the Romantic claim that children were special and deserved special literature,[46] found that fairy tales filled the requirement best. Accepting their claimed morality and approving of their playfulness, he let them in to his child's nursery. He must have been reassured by their rather domestic nature (even the Grimms ascribe them to the nursery and the home), and their portrayal of love and marriage without sex. And he might have been attracted to them himself, for these reasons, for their sympathetic renderings of children, and for other reasons as well.

Beset by a changing world, the Victorian could find stability in the ordered, formulary structure of fairy tales. He could be called from his time and place to a soothing other world by the faintly blowing horns of Elfland. He could be taken from the corruptions of adulthood back to the innocence of childhood; from the ugly, competitive city to beautiful, sympathetic nature; from complex morality to the simple issue of good versus evil; from a difficult reality to a comforting world of imagination. The author of an 1855 article on "German Story-Books" says that he pleads "guilty to a very childlike love of story-books. . . . Although the days of our childhood are over and gone, we are by no means insensible to the charms of Cinderella." He admires the German appreciation of fairy tales, and goes on to say: "The *Volksmährchen* form the wonder-land, ever bright, and beautiful, and grand, into which the popular mind escapes from the dull and dusty paths of a toil-worn existence."[47] His speculation on the value of fairy tales for German peasants is suggestively appropriate for Victorian Englishmen, and the attraction was not only for the "popular mind."

The 1853 *Athenaeum* reviewer of Grimm, discussing this attraction of the tales, said:

> Another reason for the pleasure which imaginative men find in an occasional visit to infantine fairy-land, is probably to be found in the complete contrast which that land presents to the realities of life. . . . One of the great charms of a child's fairy tale is, in the utter absence of all reference to passion. . . . We hear, it is true, of love, and hate, and revenge; but in forms so different from those of the actual world, that our own feelings are untouched, and we are not tossed into the conflict of sympathy and antipathy. We behold all things as we beheld them in childhood—through the transparent medium of simple faith. Our intellect is not harassed, as we read, by being obliged to combat for or against any set of principles. We are no longer in the lists fighting for a dogma or a system. We have ceased for the nonce to be politicians, or sectarians, or casuists. The gates are shut upon the outer world,—shut even against ourselves, as we ordinarily appear. The fight of existence is excluded, and, for a little space, disbelieved in. We only know that there is the earth all around us, and the conscious Heavens everywhere above us,—and noble, undiscovered regions in the dis-

tance, which we feel to be full of wonder, and magnificence, and mystery, and adventures without end.[48]

The youthful Tennyson, associating fairy tales with beauty, enchantment, stillness, and sleep, expressed their escapist attraction in such early poems of his as "Recollections of the Arabian Nights" (1830) and "The Sleeping Beauty" (1830). In a final enlargement of the latter poem ("The Day-Dream," 1842), he indicates another function for fairy tales. This version of the poem presents a daydreaming lover who imagines the fairy-tale prince achieving something which is denied to himself in his own waking life: the fulfillment of love (he says his beloved "sleeps a dreamless sleep to me; / A sleep by kisses undissolved"[49]). In other ways other Victorians, through identification of themselves with the heroes of fairy tales, could achieve a fulfillment of wishes, often of ones denied to them in their own lives. They could imagine themselves having their true worth recognized and attaining material wealth and happiness, with or without effort. And they could fulfill wishes they were less consciously aware of.

The author of the remarkable 1860 *London Quarterly Review* article on "Children's Literature" said: "Pictures and gay colors and romances do not give us literal truth, nor indeed truth in an objective sense at all; but they are true subjectively. They interpret our dreams and fancies to ourselves, and keep the imaginative power in healthy exercise, by employing it upon some object of external interest, when otherwise it would brood painfully and unhealthily upon itself."[50] Modern psychoanalysts have elaborated on some of these insights. Ernest Kris says that fairy tales enable children to work out their psychic fantasies vicariously, in a harmless way approved by society. As Kate Friedlaender puts it: "One reason, therefore, for the child's love of the fairy-tale is that he finds in it his own instinctual situation and meets again his own fantasies which explains the pleasure in reading or listening to fairy-stories [sic]; moreover, the fairy-tale's particular solutions for these conflicts appear to be a means for alleviating anxiety in the child."[51]

It is not only children who can find their psychic fantasies in fairy tales: adults can too, and that, psychoanalysts say, is because fairy tales seem to share a set of symbols with dreams, and therefore can function like them. C. G. Jung claims that "in myths and fairytales, as in dreams, the psyche tells its own story, and the interplay of the archetypes is revealed in its natural setting as 'formation, transformation / the eternal Mind's eternal recreation.'"[52] For Jung, in fairy tales as in dreams the archetypes are confronted in a concrete form and enable man to gain a particular insight into the world and himself. Freud, who is more concerned than Jung with the fulfillment of wishes through particular symbols, says: "This symbolism is not peculiar to dreams, but is characteristic of unconscious ideation, in

particular among the people, and is to be found in folk-lore, and in popular myths, legends, linguistic idioms, proverbial wisdom and current jokes, to a more complete extent than in dreams."[53] Without going in to the sometimes forced, sometimes contradictory interpretations that followers of these men have given specific tales, we can agree with them that fairy tales often seem dream-like and that they have a symbolic texture (which was also responded to by nineteenth-century solar mythologists, who interpreted the tales as describing the conflict between the sun and night);[54] and we can observe that the Victorians are notorious for having repressed certain basic urges, including ones which are acted out in fairy tales. These include the expression of violent impulses (the good as well as the evil in the tales have few inhibitions on this count) and of revolt against authority. Thus, while coming to him in the guise of innocent children's stories which he might have felt did not affect his feelings, fairy tales could on the one hand provide the troubled Victorian with an escape into a happy, ordered world, and on the other help him work out an urge for violent self-assertion against people he unknowingly felt aggressive towards, including his social betters.

And, finally, the fairy tale was not only moral entertainment, escape, and wish fulfillment. Psychoanalysts claim that the fairy tale is a symbolically realistic image of the urges of the psyche, and it in other ways too returned to the Victorian an image of himself. Its optimism was duplicated in an age in which fortunes were made and men flew up the ladder of success, and in which progress was speeded magically by "the fairy tales of science."[55] And it reflected reality in its darker parts, too. For fairy tales, before they reach their happy endings, have the nature not only of daydream but of nightmare too. In that age of anxiety, even when trying to escape, the Victorian might confront the nature of his own existence. There was no escape if, unlike the *Athenaeum* reviewer quoted above, one emotionally submitted himself to the tales. And no one submitted himself more thoroughly than Charles Dickens, for whom fairy tales were not just an occasional attraction, but a lifelong fascination.

Notes

1. *The Fairy Mythology* (London, 1850), pp. 5-10. The *OED* entry for "fairy" is more or less similar. Katharine M. Briggs defines the term as the "late, though general, name for the whole race. Originally Fay, from *Fatae,* the Fates. Faërie was first used for enchantment." *The Fairies in Tradition and Literature* (London, 1967), p. 217.

2. "On Fairy Stories," *Tree and Leaf,* in *The Tolkien Reader* (New York, 1966), p. 9. As Tolkien points out (p. 4), the *OED* Supplement omits this meaning from its definitions of "fairy tale."

3. *Apollodorus: The Library* (London, 1921), I, xxvii-xxix.

4. "Myth in Primitive Psychology," *Magic, Science and Religion* (Garden City, N. Y., 1954), p. 101.

5. Katharine M. Briggs, Introduction, *Folktales of England,* ed. Briggs and Ruth L. Tongue (London, 1965), pp. xxiii-xxvi. And see her "English Fairy Tales," *Internationaler Kongress der Volkserzählungsforscher in Kiel und Kopenhagen,* ed. Kurt Ranke (Berlin, 1961), pp. 38-43.

6. Notes, *Grimm's Household Tales,* trans. and ed. Margaret Hunt (London, 1884), II, 501.

7. Foreword, *Folktales of England,* ed. Briggs, p. vi.

8. See Joseph Jacobs, *English Fairy Tales* (London, 1898), p. 229.

9. *English Fairy and Other Folktales* (London, [1890]), pp. xii-xxi.

10. See "Notes on Sales," *Times Literary Supplement,* April 10, 1930, 324. The periodical will hereafter be called *TLS.*

11. On the controversy over authorship and for bibliographical information see: Andrew Lang, Introduction, *Perrault's Popular Tales,* ed. Lang (Oxford, 1888), pp. xxiv-xxxii; Percy Muir, *English Children's Books, 1600-1900* (London, 1954), pp. 45-51; Geoffrey Brereton, Introduction, *The Fairy Tales of Charles Perrault* (Harmondsworth, 1957), pp. xvii-xxii; and Marc Soriano, *Les Contes de Perrault* (Paris, 1968).

12. *The Guardian of Education,* II (1803), 185-86.

13. *Ibid.,* 448.

14. This popular collection of stories, frequently reprinted, was presented by Ridley in 1764 under the name of Sir Charles Morell, who supposedly heard them from their Eastern author, called Horam. Both the "Editor" and Horam claim moral purposes for the tales—but Horam ironically admits that the prince he made them up for actually became vicious. By 1808, the publishers made the claim of didacticism even stronger; they added a preface which identified Ridley as the author and praised his "manner of inculcating morality." *Tales of the Genii* (London, 1808), p. x.

On the book (and Dickens' connections with it) see Jane W. Stedman, "Good Spirits: Dickens's Childhood Reading," *Dickensian,* LXI (1965), 150-54.

15. The quotation is from a review in the *British Quarterly Review,* VI (1847), 189.

The affinities of courtly romance and fairy tale are discussed by Erich Auerbach in ch. 6 of *Mimesis* (New York, 1957). They can be seen in such English romances as *Sir Gawain and the Green Knight* and the *Faerie Queene.* Edgar Osborne mentions the chapbook versions of romances as reposits of fairy-tale material in "Children's Books to 1800," *Junior Bookshelf,* IV (1939), 18-19. And see Florence V. Barry, *A Century of Children's Books* (London, 1922), pp. 14-16. On the chapbook see John Ashton, *Chapbooks of the Eighteenth Century* (London, 1882), and F. J. Harvey Darton, *Children's Books in England* (Cambridge, 1958), ch. 5. John Livingston Lowes said: "A book of surpassing interest could (and should) be written on the neglected influence of these enormously popular books of the folk." *The Road to Xanadu* (Boston, 1927), p. 461.

16. *The Letters of Charles and Mary Lamb,* ed. E. V. Lucas (London, 1935), I, 326.

17. *Letters of Samuel Taylor Coleridge,* ed. Ernest Hartley Coleridge (London, 1895), I, 16. And see 11-12, letter to Poole of October 9, 1797, and note on lecture of 1811; and Coleridge, *The Friend* (London, 1818), I, 252.

18. *The Prelude,* ed. Ernest de Selincourt (London, 1926), p. 160, pp. 150-54 (text of 1805-06).

19. See Allardyce Nicoll, *A History of Early Nineteenth Century Drama, 1800-1850* (Cambridge, 1955), pp. 152-54, and V. C. Clinton-Baddeley, *All Right on the Night* (London, 1954), ch. 8, "Traditions of the Pantomime," pp. 203-34.

20. *Popular Fairy Tales* (London, 1818), pp. iii-iv.

21. "Antiquities of Nursery Literature," *Quarterly Review,* XXI (1819), 91-92.

22. Richard M. Dorson, *The British Folklorists: A History* (London, 1968), p. 45. The work is a source for much of my information on this subject. And see also Katharine M. Briggs, "The Influence of the Brothers Grimm in England," *Hessische Blätter Für Volkskunde,* LIV (1963), 511-24.

23. "German Popular and Traditionary Literature," *New Monthly Magazine,* II (1821), 146-47.

24. Preface to the Original Edition, *German Popular Stories* (London, 1869), p. xvi.

25. *Letters,* VII, 312.

26. *Gentleman's Magazine,* XCII, 2 (1822), 620-22; "Grimm's German Popular Stories," *London Magazine,* VII (1823), 91.

27. Edwin H. Zeydel, *Ludwig Tieck and England: A Study in the Literary Relations of Germany and England During the Early Nineteenth Century* (Princeton, 1931), p. 71. On all of the translations

see: Violet A. Stockley, *German Literature as Known in England, 1750-1830* (London, 1929); Bayard Quincy Morgan, *A Critical Bibliography of German Literature in English Translation, 1481-1927* (Stanford, 1938); and Max Batt, "The German Story in England About 1826," *Modern Philology,* V (1907), 167-76. And on the *Kunstmärchen* itself see Marianne Thalmann, *The Romantic Fairy Tale: Seeds of Surrealism,* trans. Mary B. Corcoran (Ann Arbor, 1964).

28. See Henry A. Pochmann, *German Culture in America: Philosophical and Literary Influences, 1600-1900* (Madison, 1961); Palmer Cobb, *The Influence of E. T. A. Hoffmann on the Tales of Edgar Allan Poe* (Chapel Hill, 1908); Dorothy Scarborough, *The Supernatural in Modern English Fiction* (New York, 1917), pp. 56-59; and Eberhard Alsen, "Hawthorne: A Puritan Tieck," unpubl. diss. (Indiana, 1967). On its subject I benefitted from the use of Alsen's unpublished MS. "The 'German Tale' in the British Magazines, 1790-1840."

29. Note to "The Tale by Goethe," *Fraser's Magazine,* VI (1832), 258. See G. B. Tennyson, *Sartor Called Resartus: The Genesis, Structure, and Style of Thomas Carlyle's First Major Work* (Princeton, 1965), esp. pp. 189-93; and Robert Lee Wolff, *The Golden Key: A Study of the Fiction of George MacDonald* (New Haven, 1961).

30. "Books for Children," *Quarterly Review,* LXXI (1842), 55; "Children's Books," *Quarterly Review,* LXXIV (1844), 1-26.

31. *British Quarterly Review,* VI (1847), 189.

32. Folklorists now believe that this was not an original story. See Dorson, *The British Folklorists,* p. 95, and Briggs, *The Fairies,* p. 169, and especially her "The Three Bears," *International Congress for Folk-Narrative Research in Athens,* IV, ed. Georgios A. Megas (Athens, 1965), pp. 53-57.

33. Cole, *Beauty and the Beast* (London, 1843), p. iv; Thomas, Note to Reader, *The Old Story Books of England* (Westminster, 1845), no p., and *Gammer Gurton's Pleasant Stories* and *Gammer Gurton's Famous Histories* (Westminster, 1846), no p.; Montalba, *Fairy Tales from All Nations* (London, 1849), no p.

34. *Præterita,* in *The Complete Works of John Ruskin,* ed. E. T. Cook and Alexander Wedderburn (London, 1903), XXXV, 304. The story revolves around Motif Q2, "kind and unkind," and resembles, e.g., AT 431.

35. Darton, *Children's Books,* p. 247. See Elias Bredsdorff, *Danish Literature in English Translation,* with a special Hans Christian Andersen Supplement: A Bibliography (Copenhagen, 1950).

36. *Vanity Fair,* ed. Geoffrey and Kathleen Tillotson (Boston, 1963). The reviews are: "Christmas Books—No. 2," *Morning Chronicle,* December 26, 1845, in *Thackeray's Contributions to the Morning Chronicle,* ed. Gordon N. Ray (Urbana, 1955), pp. 93-100 (on a new translation of Grimm); and "On Some Illustrated Children's Books," *Fraser's Magazine,* XXXIII (1846), 495-502 (greatly on Cole's and Thoms's collections).

37. "A Witch in the Nursery," *Household Words,* September 20, 1851, 608. Hereafter I will abbreviate the title of the journal as *HW.*

38. "The School of the Fairies," *HW,* June 30, 1855, 509-13. Morley had made similar points allegorically in "The Two Guides of the Child," *HW,* September 7, 1850, 560-61.

39. *Athenaeum,* 1323 (1853), 284.

40. "Children's Literature," *London Quarterly Review,* XIII (1860), 482, 486-87.

41. Introduction, *German Popular Stories,* p. ix.

42. *The King of the Golden River, Works,* I, 347.

43. *The Water Babies* (London, 1882).

44. *The Hope of the Katzekopfs* (London, 1846), pp. xvi-xvii.

45. *The Fairies,* p. 186.

46. See Peter Coveney, *The Image of Childhood* (Baltimore, 1967), which covers some of the same ground as I do, with different concerns.

47. "German Story Books," *Chambers's Journal,* XXIV (1855), 316-17

48. *Athenaeum,* 284.

49. "The Day-Dream," L'Envoi, ll. 50-51, *The Works of Tennyson,* ed Hallam, Lord Tennyson (London, 1913), p. 108.

The same fairy tale (AT 410) provided the subject for escapist work in several media by the Pre-Raphaelite artist Edward Burne-Jones.

50. "Children's Literature," 480. The final sentence echoes Wordsworth's claim that "the child, whose love is here, at least, doth reap / One precious gain, that he forgets himself" (*Prelude,* ll. 368-69).

51. Kris, *Psychoanalytic Explorations in Art* (New York, 1952), p. 42; Friedlaender, "Children's Books and Their Function in Latency and Prepuberty," *American Imago,* III (1942), 129.

52. "The Phenomenology of the Spirit in Fairytales," *The Archetypes and the Collective Unconscious, The Collected Works,* trans. R. F. C. Hall (London, 1969), Vol. IX, part 1, 217.

53. *The Interpretation of Dreams,* trans. and ed. James Strachey (New York, 1965), p. 386.

54. Some specific interpretations can be compared. The Jungian Joseph Campbell considers the frog in "The Frog-King" (AT 440) to be "the representative of that unconscious deep . . . wherein are hoarded all of the rejected, unadmitted, unrecognized, unknown, or undeveloped factors, laws and elements of existence." The Freudian Ernest Jones says: "The frog is in the unconscious a constant symbol of the male organ when viewed with disgust." Max Müller, leader of the solar-mythologist school, claimed that "frog was used as a name of the sun" and so the frog in the story really is the sun. Modern folklorist-anthropologists commonly reject these approaches. My point is not that the interpretations necessarily are valid, but that they represent an understandable type of response to the "flat," unreal, dream-like tales. One modern folklorist who agrees is Max Lüthi, who says: "It is indisputable that the *Märchen* plainly invites symbolic interpretation." He adds the necessary warning: "But in the interpretation of special traits opinions can differ, and arbitrary judgment easily slips in." "Aspects of the *Märchen* and the Legend," trans. Barbara Flynn, *Genre,* II (1969), 169. The quotations above are from Campbell, *The Hero With a Thousand Faces* (Cleveland, 1956), p. 52; Jones, "Psychoanalysis and Folklore," *Jubilee Congress of the Folklore Society: Papers and Transactions* (London, 1930), p. 233; and Müller, "Tales of the West Highlands" (1861), in *Chips from a German Workshop* (London, 1867), II, 247. The same three interpretations are compared by Richard M. Dorson, in an article in which he presents a standard folklorist critique of them. See "Theories of Myth and the Folklorist," *Myth and Mythmaking,* ed. Henry A. Murray (New York, 1960), pp. 76-89.

55. Tennyson, "Locksley Hall" (1842), l. 12, *Works,* p. 98.

Bibliography

Alsen, Eberhard. "Hawthorne: A Puritan Tieck: A Comparative Analysis of the Tales of Hawthorne and the *Märchen* of Tieck." Unpublished Ph.D. dissertation. Indiana University, 1967.

Ashton, John. *Chapbooks of the Eighteenth Century.* London, 1882.

Auerbach, Erich. *Mimesis: The Representation of Reality in Western Literature.* New York, 1957.

Barry, Florence V. *A Century of Children's Books.* London, 1922.

Batt, Max. "The German Story in England About 1826," *Modern Philology,* V (1907), 167-76.

Bredsdorff, Elias. *Hans Andersen and Charles Dickens: A Friendship and Its Dissolution.* Copenhagen, 1956.

Brereton, Geoffrey. Introduction to *The Fairy Tales of Charles Perrault.* Harmondsworth, 1957. Pp. ix-xli.

Briggs, Katharine M. "English Fairy Tales." *Internationaler Kongress der Volkserzählungsforscher in Kiel und Kopenhagen.* Ed. Kurt Ranke. Berlin, 1961. Pp. 38-43.

——. *The Fairies in Tradition and Literature.* London, 1967.

——. "The Folklore of Charles Dickens," *Journal of the Folklore Institute,* VII (1970), 3-20.

——, and Ruth L. Tongue, eds. *Folktales of England.* London, 1965.

——. "The Influence of the Brothers Grimm in England," *Hessische Blätter Für Volkskunde,* LIV (1963), 511-24.

——. "The Three Bears." *International Congress for Folk-Narrative Research in Athens,* IV. Ed. Georgios A. Megas. Athens, 1965. Pp. 53-57.

Campbell, Joseph. *The Hero with a Thousand Faces.* Cleveland, 1956.

Clinton-Baddeley, V. C. *All Right on the Night.* London, 1954.

Coveney, Peter. *The Image of Childhood: The Individual and Society: A Study of the Theme in English Literature.* Baltimore, 1967.

Darton, F. J. Harvey. *Children's Books in England.* Cambridge, 1958.

Dorson, Richard M. "Current Folklore Theories," *Current Anthropology,* IV (1963), 93-112.

——. *The British Folklorists: A History.* London, 1968.

Frazer, James. Introduction to *Apollodorus: The Library.* 2 vols. London, 1921.

Freud, Sigmund. *Collected Papers.* Trans. under supervision of Joan Riviere. 5 vols. London, 1946.

——. *The Interpretation of Dreams.* Trans. and ed. James Strachey. New York, 1965.

Friedlaender, Kate. "Children's Books and Their Function in Latency and Prepuberty," *American Imago,* III (1942), 129-50.

Hartland, Edwin Sidney. *English Fairy and Other Folktales.* London, [1890].

Jacobs, Joseph. *English Fairy Tales.* London, 1898.

———. *More English Fairy Tales.* New York, 1922.

Jones, Ernest. "Psychoanalysis and Folklore." *Jubilee Congress of The Folklore Society: Papers and Transactions.* London, 1930. Pp. 220-37.

Jung, C. G. *The Collected Works.* Ed. Herbert Read et al. Trans. R. F. C. Hall. 17 vols. London, 1957-69.

Keightley, Thomas. *The Fairy Mythology.* London, 1850.

Lang, Andrew. Introduction to *Perrault's Popular Tales.* Oxford, 1888. Pp. vii-cxv.

Lowes, John Livingston. *The Road to Xanadu: A Study in the Ways of the Imagination.* Boston, 1927.

Lüthi, Max. "Aspects of the *Märchen* and the Legend," trans. Barbara Flynn, *Genre,* II (1969), 162-78.

———. "Parallel Themes in Folk Narrative and in Art Literature," trans. Paul and Millicent Furrer, *Journal of the Folklore Institute,* IV (1967), 3-16.

Malinowski, Bronislaw. *Magic, Science and Religion.* Garden City, N. Y., 1954.

Müller, Max. *Chips From a German Workshop.* 4 vols. London, 1867-75.

Muir, Percy. *English Children's Books, 1600-1900.* London, 1954.

Murray, Henry A., ed. *Myth and Mythmaking.* New York, 1960. Esp. Richard M. Dorson, "Theories of Myth and The Folklorist," pp. 76-89; Harry Levin, "Some Meanings of Myth," pp. 103-14.

Nicoll, Allardyce. *A History of Early Nineteenth Century Drama, 1800-1850.* Cambridge, 1955.

Osborne, Edgar. "Children's Books in the Nineteenth Century," *Junior Bookshelf,* II (1937), 62-67.

———. "Children's Books to 1800," *Junior Bookshelf,* IV (1939), 15-22.

Pochmann, Henry A. *German Culture in America: Philosophical and Literary Influences, 1600-1900.* Madison, 1961.

Scarborough, Dorothy. *The Supernatural in Modern English Fiction.* New York, 1917.

Soriano, Marc. *Les Contes de Perrault: Culture savante et traditions populaires.* Paris, 1968.

Stedman, Jane W. "Good Spirits: Dickens's Childhood Reading," *Dickensian,* LXI (1965), 150-54.

Stockley, Violet A. *German Literature as Known in England, 1750-1830.* London, 1929.

Tennyson, G. B. *Sartor Called Resartus: The Genesis, Structure, and Style of Thomas Carlyle's First Major Work.* Princeton, 1965.

Thalmann, Marianne. *The Romantic Fairy Tale: Seeds of Surrealism.* Trans. Mary B. Corcoran. Ann Arbor, 1964.

Tolkien, J. R. R. *The Tolkien Reader.* New York, 1966.

Wolff, Robert Lee. *The Golden Key: A Study of the Fiction of George MacDonald.* New Haven, 1961.

Zeydel, Edwin H. *Ludwig Tieck and England: A Study in the Literary Relations of Germany and England During the Early Nineteenth Century.* Princeton, 1931.

———. *Ludwig Tieck, The German Romanticist.* Princeton, 1935.

Abbreviations

Antti Aarne and Stith Thompson, *The Types of the Folktale* (Helsinki, 1961). Type numbers, which sometimes appear in the text, are preceded by the letters AT. References are to Stith Thompson's *Motif-Index of Folk-Literature* (Copenhagen, 1955-58), 6 vols.

THE BROTHERS GRIMM

David Blamires (essay date autumn 1989)

SOURCE: Blamires, David. "The Early Reception of the Grimms' *Kinder- und Hausmärchen* in England." In *The Translation of Children's Literature: A Reader,* edited by Gillian Lathey, pp. 163-74. Clevedon, England: Multilingual Matters, 2006.

[*In the following essay, which was originally published in* Bulletin of the John Rylands Library *in autumn, 1989, Blamires provides contextual information regarding how English Romantic sensibilities and other factors determined the translation of the Grimm brothers' fairy tales into English, and the reception of these tales by English-language readers.*]

When the two volumes of what turned out to be the first edition of Jacob and Wilhelm Grimms' *Kinder-und Hausmärchen* (KHM) were published by the Realschulbuchhandlung in Berlin in 1812 and 1815, the two brothers can hardly have suspected that the product of their scholarly collecting would turn out to be the most widely disseminated and translated work of German literature.[1] In the English language alone the *British Library Catalogue of Works Printed up to 1975* lists over 300 separate publications (excluding adaptations) ranging from translations of the complete collection to printings of a single story. Even that is not a complete account of everything that was printed during the period.

The Grimms, it is well known, embarked on their collecting of *Märchen* in the wake of Arnim and Brentano's *Des Knaben Wunderhorn* (Heidelberg: Mohr und Zimmer, 1806-08). Their sources were many and various. Originally they had wanted to confine themselves to contemporary oral versions, but in order to make their collection comprehensive, they eventually extended their interest to older, printed tales and even made adaptations from medieval Latin poems. They scoured recent publications of *Märchen* in Germany, but were largely dismissive of what they found, though they mentioned them in the preface to their 1812 volume. Fairy tales were far from unknown to German readers of the previous half-century, but they were diverse in mood and form and were more self-consciously literary than the Grimms wanted. [. . .][2]

The *Kinder- und Hausmärchen,* therefore, need to be seen in a fourfold context: (1) the transmission of fashionable fairy tales from France ([Charles] Perrault and Mme [Marie Catherine] d'Aulnoy) and the Middle East (via Antoine Galland's *Mille et une Nuits*); (2) the development of a narrative literature for children, which includes the occasional adaptation of traditional oral tales such as Otmar's *Volcks-Sagen* (Bremen, 1800) and Johann Gustav Gottlieb Büsching's *Volks-Sagen, Märchen und Legenden* (Leipzig, 1812); (3) the antiquarian and scholarly collection of traditional tales and songs, represented by such works as Macpherson's *Ossian* (1760-63), Percy's *Reliques of Ancient English Poetry* (1765), Herder's *Volkslieder* (1778-79), and Arnim and Brentano's *Des Knaben Wunderhorn* (1806-08); (4) the imaginative use of fairy tale themes and structure in contemporary literature, for example Goethe's 'Das Märchen' in *Unterhaltung deutscher Ausgewanderten* (1795). Alongside all this there was a political dimension to the Grimms' enterprise: the recording of folktales, folksongs and folk traditions proved to be a powerful element in the development of national consciousness. This can be seen not only in a fragmented Germany seeking to free itself from the shackles of France, but also later in Norway and Ireland, for example.

The Grimms worked at the KHM from about 1806 right through to the end of their lives, the seventh edition of 1857 being the final product of Wilhelm's continual reshaping and (as he saw it) improvement of the collection. When people nowadays talk of the KHM, it is the 1857 edition that they usually mean, with its deliberately numbered 200 items, plus the ten *Kinderlegenden*. However, it is important to remember that each of the seven editions of the KHM differs in some measure, smaller or greater, from the rest. Tales were added and subtracted, texts were altered as new versions flowed in, and stylistic changes were made all the time, sometimes for reasons that were entirely subjective and cannot be accounted for by the normal criteria of scholar-

ship. The first edition was published in two volumes, dated 1812 and 1815, with 86 and 70 items respectively in each volume, making a total of 156. A second edition appeared in two volumes in 1819, with a third volume consisting of notes in 1822. This made drastic changes in every respect to the first edition. Much smaller alterations were made between the succeeding editions—the third in 1837, the fourth in 1840, the fifth in 1843, the sixth in 1850 and the seventh in 1857.

The first translation of the KHM into English appeared in 1823 with the title *German Popular Stories, translated from the Kinder und Haus Märchen, collected by M. M. Grimm, from Oral Tradition* (London: C. Baldwyn). The first copies of this volume omitted the umlaut sign from 'Märchen'. It was reprinted in 1823, 1824, and 1825. Its success led to a second volume, published in 1826, but with different publishers—James Robins & Co., London, and Joseph Robins Jr and Co., Dublin—though the format was identical. This second volume was reprinted in 1827 with no date on the title-page.[3] The anonymous translators were Edgar Taylor (1793-1839) and, presumably, others in his immediate circle of family and acquaintances. Edgar Taylor had set up, in 1817, the firm of Taylor and Roscoe, solicitors, in partnership with Robert Roscoe,[4] for whom as a boy the famous children's book *The Butterfly's Ball* (London: J. Harris, 1807) had been written by his father, the highly successful and cultivated Liverpool merchant and MP, William Roscoe.[5] Edgar Taylor's interests were not confined to children's literature. He deserves considerable credit for his pioneering efforts to introduce medieval German lyric poetry to the English public, in his translations entitled *Lays of the Minnesingers* (London: Longman, Hurst, Rees, Orme, Brown and Green, 1825). Taylor's translations, as represented by these two books, should be seen as part of the growing English interest in German literature and culture.[6]

Over the previous 30 or so years a considerable number of contemporary works of German literature had been translated into English. Goethe's *Werther* had appeared even earlier, in 1779, though it is symptomatic of English unfamiliarity with the German language that it was translated from the French; new translations directly from the German came from 1801 onwards. [. . .] Among children's books J. D. Wyss's *Der schweizerische Robinson,* first published in Zürich in 1812-13, made its debut in English as *The Family Robinson Crusoe* in 1814, a second edition following in 1818, when it received its better-known title *The Swiss Family Robinson.* [. . .] But what was the situation with regard to fairy tales? Perrault and Madame d'Aulnoy had long been made available in English, and individual tales by them circulated, usually anonymously, in chapbook form for children. The latest reprint of Madame d'Aulnoy was the 1817 *Fairy Tales and Novels* (London: Walker and Edwards). Sections of the *Arabian Nights* had circulated in English throughout the 18th century,[7] but in 1811 Jonathan Scott produced a new six-volume edition based mainly on Galland. There were also chapbooks of English fairy tales such as 'Tom Thumb' and 'Whittington and his Cat'. In 1804 Benjamin Tabart brought out a *Collection of Popular Stories for the Nursery* in four volumes, containing some thirty-four stories taken from French, Italian, and English writers. This included tales from Perrault, Madame d'Aulnoy, and the English chapbooks, but also others such as 'Fortunatus', 'Griselda', and 'The Children in the Wood'. The material all came from printed sources, but it is probably the nearest thing to the KHM existing in England at the time, and the Grimms refer to it in their notes.[8] [. . .] The systematic collection of English fairy tales, however, did not come until towards the end of the 19th century.

This, then, was the context for Edgar Taylor's translation of the KHM into English. Despite the fact that it was made long before the KHM reached its final form and despite its various inadequacies from the scholarly point of view, the time was certainly ripe. It has been constantly reprinted in some shape or form ever since it was first published. A vital factor in this was George Cruikshank's engravings, to which I shall return later. The text and illustrations were republished as a Puffin Book by Penguin Books in 1948, and this edition is, I believe, still in print. A facsimile of the original two volumes of 1823 and 1826 was published by Scolar Press in 1977 and reprinted in 1979. With all its faults, Taylor's translation has achieved a sort of classic status of its own. If modern readers were aware that it is a period piece, that would not much matter, but most do not realize just how skewed a picture of the Grimms' collection they get through reading Taylor. Not that Taylor attempted to camouflage what he was doing in adapting, combining and expurgating his originals—on the contrary, he signalled his changes very frankly in the notes he appended to the tales. But what he presents is not what a modern reader would be entitled to expect.

Let us look first at the contents of the two volumes. Taylor's principal source, the 1819 edition of the KHM, contains 161 fairy tales and 19 *Kinder-Legenden,* from which Taylor took 57 plus one further tale ('The Nose') that he extracted from the notes in the third volume of 1822. That is about a third of the total then available. Most of these correspond to single tales in the translation, but he combined '*Das Lumpengesindel*', '*Herr Korbes*' and '*Von dem Tod des Hühnchens*' into the one story 'Chanticleer and Partlet' (incidentally taking the names from Chaucer), and '*Der junge Riese*' and '*Das tapfere Schneiderlein*' were joined to make 'The Young Giant and the Tailor'. Similarly, '*Das kluge Grethel*', '*Der gescheidte Hans*', and '*Die faule Spinnerin*' were turned into 'Hans and his Wife', while '*Vom Fundevogel*', '*Der Liebste Roland*', and 'Hänsel und

Grethel' were transformed into the one story 'Roland and Maybird'. The first volume contained 'The Grateful Beasts', a translation of a story that retained its place in the KHM up to the sixth edition of 1850, but was then relegated to the appendix as no. 18 in the 1857 edition. In the same volume only one of the three tales that form '*Die Wichtelmänner*' is retained in 'The Elves and the Shoemaker'.

The second volume is distinguished from the first in that it contains four tales that do not belong to the Grimms' collection at all. Two of these were taken from Johann Büsching's *Volks-Sagen, Märchen und Legenden* (Leipzig, 1812), namely, 'Pee-wit' ('*Kibitz*') and 'Cherry, or the Frog-bride' ('*Das Märchen von der Padde*'). 'Peter and the Goatherd' is taken from Otmar's *Volcks-Sagen* (Bremen, 1800), probably prompted by the recent publication of Washington Irving's *Rip van Winkle* (1819), which Taylor refers to in his notes and which is a version of the same tale-type. Finally, with 'The Elfin-Grove' Taylor provided a much abridged adaptation of Ludwig Tieck's *Die Elfen*.

It is noticeable that Taylor zealously avoided using any of the tales with a religious dimension, so there is no '*Marienkind*', no '*Der Schneider im Himmel*', no '*Der Gevatter Tod*', no '*Bruder Lustig*'—the list could be extended. The prevalence of the Devil in the German tales caused Taylor worry, so these tales also were omitted, or the Devil was converted into a giant, as in 'The Giant with the Three Golden Hairs'. '*Von dem Fischer und siine Fru*' (The Fisherman and his Wife), one of the two Low German tales submitted by Philipp Otto Runge to the Grimms, had to be slightly modified in the end. Where the fisherman's wife declares finally that she wants to be '*as de lewe Gott*' (like our dear God), Taylor 'soften[ed] the boldness of the lady's ambition'[9] by saying that she wants to be 'lord of the sun and moon'.

Taylor tended also to avoid stories that contained too much of a frightening character, so there is no '*Märchen von einem, der auszog, das Fürchten zu lernen*' (The man who set out to learn fear), and '*Der singende Knochen*' (The singing bone) with its sorrowful ending probably did not commend itself to him for that very reason. It is surprising that he actually included 'The Robber Bridegroom' in his selection, though he eliminated the cannibalistic intentions of the robbers, their deliberate murder of the captured maiden, and their chopping off of her finger. These horrifying details are some of the most memorable features of the KHM, and similar ones are to be found in several other tales. '*Aschenputtel*' (Cinderella), for example, ends with the doves picking out the eyes of the wicked stepsisters as the heroine goes to her wedding, but this final paragraph of the German version is excised from Taylor's translation so that the story ends on a happier note. His second volume ends with 'The Juniper Tree', the Low German '*Van den Machandel-Boom*', the second of Runge's tales. Taylor translated this rather freely, perhaps because the Low German was difficult for him, but again he cut out the cannibalistic episode in which the father is served up the flesh of his murdered son in a stew. Taylor simply has the father given 'a large dish of black soup' with no implication as to its content. Furthermore, he had then to alter the second line of the famous song of the bird—the song that Gretchen sings in Goethe's *Faust*—so that instead of

> *Min Moder de mi slacht't*
> *Min Vader de mi att*
> (My mother slew me, my father ate me)

we have the much milder

> My mother slew her little son
> My father thought me lost and gone.

There is still plenty of violence left in the tale, especially at the end where the bird drops the millstone on the stepmother's head and crushes her to pieces, but it is clear that Taylor took pains to reduce the elements of terror and cruelty that he found in the KHM.

This first of the translators of the Grimms into English is very concerned about the impact of the stories on his readers. In his introduction he alludes to 'many stories of great merit, and tending highly to the elucidation of ancient mythology, customs and opinions, which the scrupulous fastidiousness of modern taste, especially in works likely to attract the attention of youth, warned [the translators] to pass by.' This 'scrupulous fastidiousness of modern taste', an expression which may be linked with the growth of Evangelicism and of prudery that is characteristic of the end of the 18th and beginning of the 19th century, accounts for Taylor's alterations of religious and other features mentioned earlier, but there are a few others that should be noted too. The original of 'The Fisherman and his Wife' has the couple initially living in a 'Pispott', which Taylor changed to a 'ditch', while in his 1839 revision of the text (which I shall come to in due course) he altered it again to a 'pig-stye'.

But there were other places where sexuality was the issue. 'Rapunzel', with its unavoidable implication that the girl and the prince have made love in the tower, was not translated at all. Then there was the 'Frog-Prince', the ending of which Taylor drastically altered. Exceptionally here, Taylor was translating from the 1812 text of the story, not the 1819 edition that was the source for all his other tales. This is the opening tale in all seven editions of the KHM, and it seems likely that Taylor first encountered the Grimms' collection in the first edition and made at that time a translation of the

first tale. When he later got down to serious work on the tales, he then followed the more recent second edition.

In the German original the frog is supposed to sleep with the princess in her bed, but she cannot bring herself to do this, despite the king's insistence that she must fulfil her promise to the frog:

> *Es half nichts, si musste tun, wie ihr Vater wollte, aber sie war bitterböse in ihrem Herzen. Sie packte den Frosch mit zwei Fingern und trug ihn hinaus in ihre Kammer, legte sich ins Bett und statt ihn neben sich zu legen, warf sie ihn bratsch! an die Wand; 'da, nun wirst du mich in Ruh lassen, du garstiger Frosch!'*
>
> *Aber der Frosch fiel nicht tot herunter, sondern wie er herab auf das Bett kam, da war's ein schöner junger Prinz. Der war nun ihr lieber Geselle, und sie hielt ihn wert, wie sie versprochen hatte, und sie schliefen vergnügt zusammen ein.*

> (It was no good, she had to do what her father wanted, but there was bitter anger in her heart . . . She took hold of the frog with two fingers and carried him to her room where she got into bed but, instead of placing him next to her, she threw him thump! against the wall 'There, now you'll leave me alone you nasty frog!'
>
> But the frog did not fall down dead; when he came down onto the bed he was a handsome young prince. He was now her dear companion and she admired him as she had promised and they fell happily asleep together.)

> [Literal translation by Gillian Lathey, editor of *The Translation of Children's Literature*]

Taylor's version—it cannot be called a translation—tells a different set of events:

> . . . the princess took him up in her hand and put him upon the pillow of her own little bed, where he slept all night long. As soon as it was light he jumped up, hopped down stairs, and went out of the house. 'Now', thought the princess, 'he is gone, and I shall be troubled with him no more.'
>
> But she was mistaken; for when night came again, she heard the same tapping at the door, and when she opened it, the frog came in and slept upon her pillow as before till the morning broke; and the third night he did the same: but when the princess awoke on the following morning, she was astonished to see, instead of the frog, a handsome prince gazing on her with the most beautiful eyes that ever were seen, and standing at the head of her bed.
>
> He told her that he had been enchanted by a malicious fairy, who had changed him into the form of a frog, in which he was fated to remain till some princess should take him out of the spring and let him sleep upon her bed for three nights.

There is nothing in Taylor's adaptation of the prince and princess sleeping together in human form, though he allows the frog to sleep on the princess's pillow for three nights running. He obviously cannot countenance the princess's attempt to kill the frog by hurling it against the wall. The transformation takes place as it were unconsciously, while the princess is asleep. The transformed frog is not in her bed, as one might have expected from its lying on her pillow, but is 'standing at the head of the bed'. One detail Taylor may have taken from the 1819 text of the story, and that is the emphasis on the fact that the prince has the 'most beautiful eyes that ever were seen'. The 1812 edition has no comparable comment here, but the 1819 version says: '*Was aber herunterfiel, war nicht ein todter Frosch, sondern ein lebendiger, junger Königssohn mit schönen und freundlichen Augen*' (but what fell down was not a dead frog, but a living, young prince with beautiful, friendly eyes). In making his alterations Taylor has rendered the princess passive and obedient to her father's commands and thus deprived her of taking her own initiative and responsibility for what follows. In the German original she confronts her own distaste and causes, however unwittingly, the prince's transformation; she does not simply submit to male authority as embodied in the king, her father.

Taylor was an inveterate softener of harsh details that he found in the Grimms' tales. In the story of '*Rumpelstilzchen*' the 1819 edition has a disturbing conclusion:

> '*Das hat dir der Teufel gesagt! Das hat dir der Teufel gesagt!*' *schrie das Männlein und stiess mit dem rechten Fuss vor Zorn so tief in die Erde, dass es bis an den Leib hineinfuhr, dann packet es in einer Wuth den linken Fuss mit beiden Händen und riss sich mitten entzwei.*

> ('The devil told you that! The devil told you that!' shouted the little man and in his fury stamped his right foot and leg into the ground right up to his crotch, then in a rage he took hold of his left leg with both hands and tore himself in two.)

> [Editor Gillian Lathey's translation with advice from Anthea Bell.]

With Taylor it has become a childish temper tantrum, whereas the German ending can be seen as an act of self-destruction that removes the threat of Rumpelstilzchen for ever from the queen's life.

Taylor's interferences with the German texts are too extensive to deal with *in toto* here, but they can be characterized as tending to make the stories more reassuring and less disturbing to the children whom he envisaged as readers. This first English translation thus has a markedly different tone from that of the Grimms' text. Yet we must remember that this is a commonplace occurrence in the transmission of fairy tales, whether oral or in printed form. Every storyteller puts his or her own mark on the tale told. There is no perfect, uncontaminated process, as a comparison of the summaries in

their manuscript collection with the printed forms of the seven editions readily demonstrates. Where they used printed texts from the 16th to the early 19th centuries, the same kind of adaptation and homogenisation is also to be seen.

Of crucial consequence for the popularity of Taylor's translation is the fact that he secured the collaboration of the greatest illustrator of the day to provide twelve etchings for the first volume and a further ten for the second volume. George Cruikshank (1792-1878) was an extraordinarily prolific artist and caricaturist, and his illustrations have elicited the highest praise. John Ruskin declared that the original etchings done for *German Popular Stories* were 'unrivalled in masterfulness of touch since Rembrandt; (in some qualities of delineation unrivalled even by him).'[10]

In addition to frontispieces depicting scenes of listening to stories round a fire, Cruikshank provided illustrations for the following tales: 'Hans in Luck', 'The Travelling Musicians, or the Waits of Bremen', 'The Golden Bird', 'Jorinda and Jorindel', 'The Waggish Musician', 'The Elves and the Shoemaker', 'The Turnip', 'The Jew in the Bush', 'The King of the Golden Mountain', 'The Golden Goose', and 'Rumpel-stilts-kin' (volume 1); 'The Goose Girl', 'The Blue Light', 'Pee-wit', 'Cherry, or the Frog-Bride', 'The Elfin-Grove', and 'The Nose'. Cruikshank's delight in the comic and the grotesque has proved enduringly attractive to English-speaking readers, though the Germans tend to prefer the more gentle, somewhat sentimental approach of their own 19th-century artists.

The immediate success of Taylor's translation in terms of the new impressions during the 1820s has already been noted. [. . .]More than a dozen years elapsed before Edgar Taylor's translation, together with preface and notes, made a second appearance in 1839 with the new title *Gammer Grethel; or German Fairy Tales, and Popular Stories, from the collection of MM. Grimm, and Other Sources* (London: John Green). This was quite a new book, as the translation was heavily revised and recast and contained a lot of additions in the nature of asides specifically addressed to a child audience. A number of the originally anonymous protagonists of the stories were given names, and some of the titles of the stories were changed. 'The Grateful Beasts', for example, becomes 'Fritz and his Friends', while Otmar's 'Peter the Goatherd' is renamed 'Karl Katz'. Eighteen of the originally translated stories were omitted, and one new one was added—'The Bear and the Skrattel'. [. . .] The tales in *Gammer Grethel* were arranged in a completely different sequence from *German Popular Stories* and designed to be read over a dozen evenings, with three or four tales per evening. Cruikshank's etchings were replaced by wood-engravings by John Byfield after Cruikshank's designs. The revised text was reprinted in 1849 (Bohn's Illustrated Library), 1888 and 1897 (George Bell and Sons) and possibly at other times as well.

Meanwhile, the original translation continued to be reprinted. It appeared with stereotype reproductions of Cruikshank's illustrations, issued by John Camden Hotten in 1869, the original two volumes being printed together as one. This contained a ten-page introduction by John Ruskin. Chatto and Windus, who purchased Hotten's business on his death in 1873,[11] did another edition in 1884. Taylor's original translation continued to be used for a large number of subsequent editions, right into the 20th century, though almost always without any indication of his name. The translation is, however, easily recognizable by the occurrence of certain characteristic titles of individual tales, for example, 'Rose-bud' ('*Dornröschen*'), 'Snow-drop' ('*Sneewittchen*'), 'Roland and Maybird' ('*Der Liebste Roland*', '*Fundevogel*', and '*Hänsel und Grethel*' combined), and by the presence of the four tales not from the KHM.

Edgar Taylor's translation was made in the early stages of the development of the KHM, before it had reached its full growth. The second English translation had the advantage of some additional growth to the collection, though it was still not complete. In 1846 John Edward Taylor published a translation of an additional selection of tales under the title of *The Fairy Ring: A New Collection of Tales, translated from the German of Jacob and Wilhelm Grimm* (London: John Murray). It contained twelve illustrations by the up-and-coming artist Richard Doyle (1824-83). Doyle later illustrated Ruskin's *King of the Golden River* (London: Smith, Elder and Co., 1851). John Edward Taylor used the Grimms' fifth edition of 1843 for his translation, including a number of tales that made their first appearance in print in that edition, namely, 'The Nix in the Millpond', 'The Hedgehog and the Hare', 'The Goosegirl at the Well', 'The Spindle, the Shuttle and the Needle', 'The Drummer', 'The True Bride', and 'The Giant and the Tailor'. He made the first translation of 'Rapunzel', though he gave the heroine the name Violet, with the consequent alteration in the type of plant that the pregnant mother longs for.

John Edward Taylor referred to Edgar Taylor in the introduction to *The Fairy Ring* as being his kinsman (Taylor, 1846: iv), and he was indeed a cousin. He was a printer in Little Queen Street, London, and he is credited in the *British Library Catalogue* with eight other translations over the period 1840-55. Most important in the context of *The Fairy Ring* is the fact that he translated thirty tales from Basile's *Pentamerone*, first published in 1848, a couple of years after Felix Liebrecht had made the first German translation. *The Fairy Ring* proved popular, a third edition being published in Philadelphia in 1854, while Murray in London produced a new edition in 1857.

At this point in the mid-century new editions began to pour from various publishing houses. The two Taylors had established the Grimms as a favourite with the reading public, and it was now possible to produce a much more comprehensive translation of the KHM. In this the new two-volume edition entitled *Household Stories*, published by Addey and Co. in 1853, led the way. Despite the fact that it provided translations of 191 tales and five children's legends and was thus much more wide-ranging than anything previously attempted, it still found it prudent to omit a certain number. These were '*Der Schneider im Himmel*', '*Des Teufels russiger Bruder*', '*Das eigensinnige Kind*', '*Das junggeglühte Männlein*', '*Das Herrn und des Teufels Getier*', '*Das Bürle im Himmel*', '*Die ungleichen Kinder Evas*', '*Die Brosamen auf dem Tisch*' and five of the *Kinderlegenden* '*Die zwölf Apostel*', '*Gottes Speise*', '*Muttergottesgläschen*', '*Die himmlische Hochzeit*', and '*Die Haselrute*'. They are all religious tales. Yet it was not the religious element as such that caused any given tale to be excluded, since five children's legends are incorporated in the translation. It seems to be the element of religious superstition or perceived contravention of Biblical teaching that leads to the omission. The preface in fact states quite baldly: 'The mixture of sacred subjects with profane, though frequent in Germany, would not meet with favour in an English book.'

In 1853 the preface to Addey and Co.'s edition could refer quite simply to KHM as 'a world-renowned book', though it was somewhat prematurely hyperbolic in claiming that 'hundreds of Artists have illustrated' the fairy tales. Their edition contained 240 pictures by Edward H. Wehnert, of which 36 were full-page illustrations. These are agreeable period pieces and typical of the Victorian predilection for sentimentality and reassurance. With the addition of colour-printing they reappeared in later collections of the tales published by George Routledge & Co.

Addey and Co.'s edition was translated from the Grimms' sixth edition of 1850, still not quite the final form of the KHM. Nonetheless, it is so markedly different from the selections of the two Taylors that it is no longer part of the pioneering world that they represent. The first complete translation of the KHM only came with Margaret Hunt in 1884, published by Bohn and with an introduction by the eminent folklorist Andrew Lang. Every few years since then has seen new editions of the Grimms' fairy tales in English. Publishers, translators and especially illustrators have collaborated in presenting the tales afresh to every generation of children. The most remarkable feature in this never-ending enterprise has been the durability of Edgar Taylor's translation, usually, but not always, accompanied by Cruikshank's illustrations. The product of the English Romantic fascination with German folktales and folklore is still with us.

Notes

1. Heinz Rölleke (ed.) (1982) *Brüder Grimm, Kinder- und Hausmärchen; Nach der zweiten vermehrten und verbesserten Auflage von 1819, textkritisch revidiert und mit einer Biographie der Grimmschen Märchen versehen* (pp. 523-4) (2 vols). Köln: Diederichs.

2. [. . .] indicates points where David Blamires' original article has been edited. [See David Blamires (1989) The early reception of the Grimms' *Kinder- und Hausmärchen* in England. *Bulletin John Rylands Library* 3, 63-77. Reprinted by permission of the author and the John Rylands Library.]

3. Percy Muir (1979) *English Children's Books, 1600-1900* (p. 51). London: Batsford, 1979, 51.

4. *Dictionary of National Biography.*

5. See F. J. Harvey Darton (1958) *Children's Books in England* (pp. 205-6). Cambridge: Cambridge University Press.

6. For a literary-historical and folklore background, see Katharine M. Briggs (1963) The influence of the Brothers Grimm in England. In Gerhard Heilfurth, Ludwig Denecke and Ina-Maria Greverus (eds) *Brüder Grimm Gedenken* (pp. 511-24). Marburg: Elwert.

7. See Harvey Darton (1982) *Children's Books in England*, 90.

8. See Rölleke, KHM: Ausgabe letzter Hand, iii (326-7).

9. *German Popular Stories*, i, 221 (notes).

10. Edgar Taylor (ed.) (1869) *German Popular Stories, with Illustrations after the Original Designs of George Cruikshank*. Introduction by John Ruskin. London: John Camden Hotten.

11. The Osborne Collection. See *The Osborne Collection of Early Children's Books: A Catalogue* (1958-75). Prepared by Judith St John. Toronto: Toronto Public Library, 479.

G. Ronald Murphy (essay date 2000)

SOURCE: Murphy, G. Ronald. "The Roots of Spiritual Stories." In *The Owl, the Raven, and the Dove: The Religious Meaning of the Grimms' Magic Fairy Tales*, pp. 3-15. Oxford, England: Oxford University Press, 2000.

[*In the following essay, Murphy explores the multifaceted spirituality of the Grimm brothers and how this informed their re-telling of folk tales.*]

The brothers Grimm thought of fairy tales as remnants of ancient faith expressed in poetry. Through all the revisions of their collections of tales, their preface always begins with a description of gleaning, a biblical image recalling the command that the poor are not to be prevented from gathering the remnants that survive the harvest or the storm, nor the grain that has grown unnoticed by the hedgerow or the roadside.[1] The brothers, and especially Wilhelm, who continually revised the tales over a period of forty years, found those untouched grains of wheat still surviving on the margins of religious and poetic consciousness in traditional figures of speech, common superstitions, and, above all, in old stories. Wilhelm was a gleaner, he believed, of remnants of ancestral Germanic religious faith surviving on the margins of culture in popular poetic tales. The gleaner, however, was also a kneader and blender of other ancient stories embodying religious faith. He collected and reexpressed the religious faith found in the poetic tales primarily of three ancient traditions: Classical Greco-Roman, Norse-Germanic, and Biblical. In all three he was at home as a fluent reader, student, and storyteller, and in one of them, Christianity, he was a devout believer. His personal style of Johannine spirituality with its emphasis on love as the divine and life-giving form of faith, enabled him to have a serene reverence for pre-Christian, pagan religious awareness in Germanic and Greek forms, especially insofar as they too spoke of the primacy of love and the tragic and violent nature of its violation. To do justice to Wilhelm Grimm's retelling of the tales it is not enough to treat them as narratives that ignore the spiritual feelings of the past and integrate only the middle-class morals of the nineteenth century as some scholars seem to maintain.[2]

Through many editions over the years the preface to the brother's collection of fairy tales always ends with a religious thought parallel to that at the beginning: the tales enable a blessing. The brothers stated that their book consists of stories which are precious crumbs of ancient faith, gleaned wheat, made into bread, and that they wished to place it only into benevolent hands which have the power to bless, hoping that these "breadcrumbs of poetry" will never come to the attention of those who would withhold them from the poor.[3]

My first acquaintance with the work of the brothers Grimm made an unforgettable impression. It was a long time ago when I first saw *Snow White* in Walt Disney's film version of the Grimms' story. To tell stories as affecting as that, I thought as a child, is a great human achievement. I am aware that since then Disney has been criticized for his alterations to the story, especially for his naming of the seven dwarfs, and so when I was almost finished with this book, after the lapse of many years I saw the movie again. Disney did well. His rendition of the ending with the sleeping Snow White surrounded by the kneeling dwarfs, a candle placed on either side of her glass casket, music changed to solemnly religious, and the slowly paced entry of the prince into what is unmistakably a church atmosphere, captures well Wilhelm Grimm's religious spirit. It occurs to no one viewing the film to think that Germanic elves are out of place amidst the candles and organ music of Christian piety, and that is the style and achievement of the brothers Grimm, well depicted by Disney. When the princess is awakened from death with the kiss of the king's son, the prince and Snow White leave, going hand in hand up the hillside toward his father's castle. Disney then has the father's castle appear in the distance, not on the horizon as one might expect in a Disney film, but high above and ahead of the prince and his bride, radiant in the sky, shinning like a golden city made of sunlight. My mother, eighty years old at the time, turned to me and asked quietly, "Is she dead?" That question in its astonishing clarity shows how effectively Disney perceived and presented the Grimms' style in his *Snow White*.

The curious and inclusive religious richness of German Romanticism came to its most classical and effective expression in the fairy tales of the brothers Grimm. Not in all 210 of them, to be sure, but most tellingly, even in their own day, in certain stories that were recognized as their *Zaubermärchen,* "magic fairy tales." Five of those have become so beloved throughout the English-speaking world that they constitute our most well known and familiar works of German literature, so familiar to us and to our newspapers as often to be thought of as our own. Our own they have become. The Grimms and their tales have also become controversial. Some maintain that the Grimms' stories are really French tales retold in German (and now English) translation; this claim we will examine in each case. Some feel that they are neither religiously inspired nor inspiring and much too violent to be of spiritual value—notwithstanding the bible's own faithful accounts of cannibalism in besieged cities, royal adultery, and murder, not to mention mockery and crucifixion. There is also the criticism that the Grimms thoroughly reworked the tales while at the same time publicly maintaining that they were faithfully retelling ancient stories transmitted to them orally by folk storytellers. This criticism is very important. There is truth on both sides of the fence in this argument, and the religious nature of the tales, especially as perceived by Wilhelm, is pivotal in resolving the issue.

The Grimms were professors and librarians whose great area of interest was the literature of the Middle Ages, philology, the history of stories, words, and languages. They enjoyed uncovering the hidden verbal connections of the past to the present. Jacob's concentration was on law and linguistics, Wilhelm's was on stories and literature, and both followed the historical method first introduced to them by Karl von Savigny, co-founder of the

historical school of the interpretation of law, which they did as much by their personal inclination as by his instruction. Together the brothers initiated publication in 1854 of what has become the great historical dictionary of the German language, the *Deutsches Wörterbuch.* In this they most likely inspired the English Philological Society to begin their great project three years later, in 1857, of a dictionary "to begin at the beginning," with dictionary entries to use quotations from "all the great English writers of all ages, and from all writers whatever before the sixteenth century," in order to give an account of the "meaning, origin, and history of English words now in general use."[4] This is an exact description of the procedure of the Grimms' *Deutsches Wörterbuch,* then well under way. The Philological Society's dictionary has now come to be called the *Oxford English Dictionary,* but its original title when it first appeared in 1888, *A New English Dictionary on Historical Principles,* pointed to its source of inspiration.

On his trip to Paris to work for and with Savigny, Jacob continually attempted to collect and save all the fragments of medieval German literature and law that he could. I say this only to emphasize the curious fact that the oldest known piece of secular German literature, the *Hildebrandslied,* was published by the brothers Grimm without alteration or addition, much less any attempt to supply an ending to make this single-page fragment an effective piece of literature. When it came to the remnants of ancient religious stories however, which the Grimms believed the fairy tales to be, they often reworked the material extensively and for effect. Why?

The answer may lie partially in their observation and criticism of the uneven quality of many of the variants created in oral and written transmission, but it lies also in Wilhelm Grimm's concept of the fairy tales as being remnants of belief, in his affective approach to belief, and, in the concrete, in his intense liking of German medieval models of effective transcultural religious storytelling. This is true of the many epics which he taught and read, but especially of *Parzival* and the *Heliand,* in which Christianity reexpressed itself in Northern, Germanic forms, reimagining the Christian story and accepting "pagan" religious values. At the time when the Grimms' fairy tales were first published, their curious pagan-Christian nature was noted immediately by an English reviewer and was republished with obvious approval in the second edition of the *Kinder- und Hausmärchen* (*Grimms' Fairy Tales*): "Among the most venerable remains of ancient Teutonic literature we should rank the abundant stores of popular legends and traditions, which often preserve most curious illustrations of heathen mythology and still more frequently exhibit it in a most incongruous combination with the Christian faith."[5]

Christian faith was so important a subject for the Grimms that, even though they were evidently not theologians, the entry in the seventh volume of their German dictionary covering *Glaube* (faith, belief) extends from page 7777 to page 7847! Significantly, the entry begins with the Greek word *pistis* and the Latin *fides,* and it goes on to note the relationship of the word to its medieval Low German equivalent, *gelof,* a form not entirely distant from the English "love." The word is directly related to medieval English *leaf* meaning "dear" or "esteemed." The Grimms briefly note Aquinas's definition—"faith is an act of the intellect moved by the will" (fides est actus intellectus secundum quod a voluntate movetur)—and then extensively and affirmatively cite Luther's counter to that definition:

> Against this there is Luther's rejection of any definition of belief as essentially something of the intellect: "this sort of faith is more a kind of science. . . . They (the papists) define faith as accepting all the things which they have heard and keep from Christ as true, but the devils believe the same things and that doesn't make them any more holy. . . . [True faith] is not just a type of acknowledgment in which I hold everything which God has revealed to us in his word to be true, but it is also a trust that comes from the heart which the Holy Spirit works up in me through the gospel. . . . Faith is a firm, unwavering, unshaking position taken by the heart. . . . Faith is always belief in a person."

> (dagegen Luthers ablehnung einer wesentlichen intellectuellen bewertung: "diszer glaub ist mehr eyn wissenschafft . . . sie (die papisten) heiszen das glauben, das sie von Christo gehört haben und halten, es sey alles war, wie denn auch die teuffel auch glauben und werden dennoch nicht frum da durch. . . . [warer glaub] ist nicht allein eine gewisse erkandtnusz, dardurch ich alles für war halte was uns gott in seinem wort hat offenbaret: sondern auch ein hertzliches vertrauen, solches der heilige geist durchs evangelium in mir würket . . . der glaub ist und sol auch sein ein standfest des hertzens, der nicht wancket, wackelt. . . . Der glaub geht allezeit auf eine person.")

To further bolster this definition, the Grimms give five individual citations from German antiquity's unique version of the gospel story, the *Heliand,* including "hluttro habas thu an thinan herron gilobon" (You should have transparent trust in your Lord). The Grimms therefore saw faith as effective only if it moves the heart of the reader of the gospel to trust. "The devils hear and know all the same things and it does them no good, because they are not moved." This Luther-inspired insight on the nature of faith is important if the Grimms regarded the fragments of religious poetry, the fairy tales, as documents of faith. Such documents would then do the reader no good if the reader were not moved by them in his heart. Wilhelm said as much when he wrote that the reason for telling fairy tales was to awaken the thoughts and feelings of the heart. The theology of the Reformed church in which the brothers were raised would have said much the same thing on the importance of faith as a felt movement of the heart. Calvin in his *Institutes of the Christian Faith* would perhaps go even further than the gospel story and say that the purpose of the sacraments themselves, of Baptism and Communion, is to strengthen the faith of the recipient and the congregation, since it is through their feeling of the emotion of belief that they know that they are saved. Arousing such feelings of the heart is the very purpose of the Reformed preacher whose office Wilhelm so admired as a vocation when he mused in the little church in Steinau where his grandfather had been the preacher and pastor. The purpose of the preacher and the purpose of telling fairy tales coincided for Wilhelm Grimm, and if the tales were only fragments, and as such had become incapable of arousing the religious feelings of the heart, then Wilhelm would and did restore them to religious life, giving them back their ancient ability to move the spirit. In sum, to leave a secular fragment as it is and publish it meticulously as it is, a possibly ineffective remnant of a story, is to do no injury to it. To publish a fragment of a poem of belief in the same manner would be to publish it not for what it is, but rather for its value as information, effective perhaps as a secular document, ineffective as a story of faith, a fragment without its heart. A religious poem requires resuscitation in order to be published as what it is. The challenge which Wilhelm faced was how to revive the religious feelings in fragmented ancient pagan stories in such a way that they would elicit a religious reaction of the heart of Christian contemporaries.

EARLY MODELS OF RELIGIOUS STORYTELLING

Over the years from 1808 to 1857 the brothers, and especially Wilhelm Grimm, had many medieval models for effective transcultural religious storytelling at their fingertips. The *Heliand* was first written c. 830 and first published, with the help and encouragement of Grimm scholarship, in 1830 by a printing press. In Northern Europe and England in the early Middle Ages the *Heliand* had been a well-known religious epic poem. When I went to Berlin to see the copy that had been in Jacob's library, I was quite astonished by the stark brevity of the two-word dedication of the work printed by Schmeller, the publisher, in inch-high letters: *Iacobo Grimmio,* "to Jacob Grimm." Nothing could have been more appropriate. The *Heliand* would have amazed the English reviewer mentioned above, who was taken aback by the juxtaposition of the pagan and Christian in the *Grimms' Fairy Tales.* The entire story of Jesus is recast in pagan Germanic terms. There are no trolls or dwarfs, but the Holy Spirit does land and perch on the shoulder of Jesus, following the iconography of Woden. The prophets Simeon and Anna are "soothsayers," Jesus is the "chieftain" of mankind, and his most dangerous enemy is not Satan but "the workings of fate." Jacob did note in his realism, however, on the rear flyleaf of his copy of the *Heliand,* that the jackass which carried

Jesus into Jerusalem on Palm Sunday had been omitted from the story. That absence was probably a deliberate adaptation, to avoid inappropriate Germanic laughter.

Wilhelm also had his own copy of the *Heliand,* now in the Hessian state archives in Marburg. In it I found his notation of the fact that the preface is parallel to the Caedmon story in Bede. There is an *arbor vitae* sprig marking Song 32 in which Christ is not thrown over the cliff at Nazareth because it is not yet his fated time, and a second marker at the story of the birth of John the Baptist. The latter story is one whose beginning has a very familiar parallel in the fairy tales: it begins with a childless couple who are promised an infant. The author of the *Heliand* is also quite concerned at this point to find a proper role for pagan fate within the Christian gospel:

> [The angel is speaking in the temple to priest Zachary.] My name is Gabriel, I always stand before God, I am always in the presence of the All-Ruler, except when He wishes to send me off on His affairs. Now He has sent me on this journey and told me to let you know that a child will be born to you—from your elderly wife a child will be granted to you in this world—and he will be wise in words. Never in his lifetime will he drink hard cider or wine in this world: this is the way the workings of fate made him, time formed him, and the power of God as well. . . .

> Soon thereafter the power of God, His mighty strength, was felt: the wife [Elizabeth], a woman in her old age, became pregnant—soon the husband, that godly man, would have an heir, an infant boy born in the hill-fort.

> The woman awaited the workings of fate. The winter skidded by and the year measured its way past. John came to the light of mankind. His body was beautiful and his skin was fair, as were his hair and fingernails, and his cheeks shone![6]

The *Heliand* provides a unique example for the attempt to weave pagan piety into the gospel story itself. The unknown author's method is to allow God the ultimate power to bring things and people into existence, but fate and time play their ancient roles as well. Fate and time determine the physical characteristics of the baby, the length of pregnancy, and assign the time and hour of death. Even winter is woven into the tale of John the Baptist's birth. The religious tone and pagan-Christian compositional style of Wilhelm's revision of the tales are here, including the beauty of the child, the passing of winter, the combined decrees of fate and the power of God, worked into a Christian narrative. And, if the *Heliand* depicts Jesus as a chieftain, might not the Grimms have felt it appropriate to see him as a prince?

Wilhelm Grimm's other model may well have been the knight Wolfram von Eschenbach's early thirteenth-century *Parzival.* In that sweeping, medieval crusader's epic, faith is reimagined as a knightly quest for the grail. Belief as acceptance of Jesus is changed, reimagined as arriving at feelings, arriving at loving interest in the suffering of Anfortas who is in pain caused by a mysterious bleeding lance (Crucifixion story) and by the zenith of the planet Saturn (Roman god of time). The surprising thing about Wolfram's story of salvation is that it is ecumenical. At the end of the epic, when Parzival the Christian knight is engaged in a last desperate fight with a pagan knight, Feirefiz, who is disconcertingly his equal in swordsmanship, Parzival's sword shatters. Though Parzival is helpless, his pagan enemy, a character created by the author in order to make his point, refuses to kill Parzival because there would be no glory in killing an unarmed man. The two equally chivalrous and exhausted knights sit down on the ground among the flowers and gradually recognize each other as sons of the same father, Gahmuret of Anjou. They are brothers biologically and also religiously, since, as they talk on, they agree that Christian and Moslem, and all human beings, have only one Father who created them. The crusader then realizes that this makes killing a Moslem an act of fratricide—which means the central activity of the Crusades must be divinely forbidden. This religious epic of the thirteenth century, which so acknowledges the spirituality of the chivalry of knights of other religions because it is rooted in feelings of belief and love, even has a passage at the end in which the Moslem decides to be baptized because of love—he has fallen in love with Parzival's aunt, a Christian woman. Before anything can happen, Parzival notices that tears of love are streaming down the face of his pagan brother and realizes further that those flowing waters of human love are a kind of baptism.

This surpassing masterpiece of pagan-Christian harmony within the love of the one Father is one of the works which Wilhelm Grimm taught at the University of Marburg. His copy of the text is still there in the Hessian state archives in Marburg, and it still has his underlining and marginal notes on difficult expression requiring explanation during class. When I went through it, looking at his notes in his precise and minute handwriting, I realized how close its world of human and religious feelings was to the world of the Grimms' fairy tales.

The most important lines of *Parzival* noted by Wilhelm in this regard may be the following realization, which the hero of the tale arrives at after finally feeling enough interest in his uncle's suffering to break the rules of decorum to ask Anfortas what is troubling him. (It is marked with a vertical line alongside the text and one verse is underlined.) As he rides along, Parzival is filled with happiness over Anfortas's healing from the spear wound in his genitals and from his years of lying poisoned in his bed made of the skin of a snake. The scene thus alludes sexually to the results of the Fall in the

Garden of Eden, with the effect of the "poisoned apple" and the original sin being human weakness, a possible meaning of "An-fortas." Parzival has cured An-fortas by bringing compassionate interest to the snake-skin bed of "human weakness" simply by asking his uncle what the problem is. Parzival has become a spontaneously goodhearted person, he now feels great happiness for Anfortas's sake. He is thinking out loud: "God has enormous greatness. Who ever sat in council to give him advice? Or who knows any limit of his strength? All the companies of angels could never get to the bottom of it." (797,23ff). The next three lines are the ones noted by Wilhelm:

> Got ist mensch unt sins vater wort
> got ist vater unde suon,
> sin geist mac groze helfe tuon.
>
> (797, 28-30)

> (God is human, and also the father's word,
> *God is father and son:*
> this spirit of God can be of great help.)

The Divinity itself gives an example of how two religiously separate persons are one: God is the Father and the Son, Christ is both human and the divine Word. The crusader is being prepared to see himself and the Moslem as brothers, united by the baptism of love. The Holy Spirit is in the passage because it is by the waters of baptism that the effects of the Fall are taken away, and this very passage is repeated by the priest at the moment of the baptism of Feirefiz. The second occurrence of this passage was underlined as above and also marked by Wilhelm with a double line in the margin, and is therefore of importance to him. The "Spirit" who as the dove is everywhere in the fairy tales is seen here in its transcendent identity as the divine spirit of love and unifying harmony. In his revised fairy tales, Wilhelm has the dove play this role in *Hansel and Gretel* and in *Cinderella*—in the one case leading the children home when the bread crumbs cannot, and in the other creating a transcendent unity between the belief-filled daughter and her dead mother. The dove in *Parzival* is ubiquitous because it is the insignia of the knights of the Holy Grail, but also because it unites heaven and earth by bringing down the communion wafer to rest on the stone of the Grail. As in the fairy tales, therefore, the dove is the manifestation of the harmonizing and communicating function of the Holy Spirit.

Wilhelm also underlined the simple question asked about Christ by the gray knight. He is speaking to Parzival, who is oblivious that it is Good Friday, "Do you mean God to whom the virgin gave birth?" ("meint ir got den diu magt gebar?" 449, 29). Wilhelm underscored the passage about the shield brought to Parzival painted inside and out with the pierced man (42, 28) and the reference to weeping and providence in the

blessing said to Gawain: "May He whose hand salted the sea give you support in your trouble" ("des hant dez mer gesalzen hat, der geb iu für kumber rat" 514, 15).

Passages of feelings of love are marked everywhere. After describing the lips of two daughters of the gray knight in the Good Friday passage as red, hot, and thick, Wilhelm put a double line in the margin next to the comment that follows in the text, "however, the lips were not held sensuously, in accordance with nature of the day" (449. 29-30), and wrote in the margin "Vor scham bewegt wie am Karfreitag" (moved by shame as on Good Friday). For Wilhelm it seems that shame, in good medieval style, is a very good thing because it shows that the hero has a sense of religious honor; he is capable of feeling ashamed of himself, especially in comparing his own demeanor to the modesty exhibited by the two young women in honor of Good Friday. Love as the force that leads the good knight on to chivalry by putting the capability of feeling shame in his heart is also able to "conduct" high feelings into his heart. This passage is marked with an "X" in the margin:

> die minne condwierte
> in sin manlich herze hohon muot,
> als sie noch heute dem minne gernden tuot.
>
> (736, 6-8)

> (Love led
> exalted feelings into his manly heart,
> as she still does to lovers today.)

"Love leads the way" is also the name of the woman whom Parzival loves, "Condwiramurs," lightly disguised by using a French form. The same disguised form is used for the place of the Grail to which Parzival is destined and being led by her (but where he initially fails the test for lack of loving interest). It is called "Munsalvaesche," probably from *mons salvationis,* "Mount Salvation." Wilhelm's "little house deep in the forest" serves as the parallel destined place of testing and eventual rescue or salvation, to which the dove leads Hansel and Gretel and Little Red Riding Hood and Snow White.

On the front flyleaf of his *Parzival,* Wilhelm wrote in very minute script, "Gawain findet auf dem weg eine haarflechte . . . drei blutstropfen im schnee, die ihn an seine geliebte erinnern" (Gawain finds a braid of hair on the road . . . three drops of blood in the snow which remind him of the woman he loves). Granted the many variants on this image in the fairy tale tradition of *Snow White,* it is obvious that the *three* drops in *Parzival* made the brothers change the manuscript version, "*a couple of* drops" to "*three*" drops, trusting to the authenticity of the medieval text to show the oldest Germanic tradition. The same is true for the snow. In alternate versions of *Snow White* the blood falls on cheese, or even on milk. The Grimms would consider only "snow" appropriate, because of the light snow on the ground in the parallel scenes with Parzival and Gawain in the thirteenth-century epic.

Wilhelm placed a double vertical line alongside another passage referring to love: "Parzival's radiance [beauty] would be good as a set of tongs, it holds his faithfulness fast." He also marked Wolfram's complaint that love makes his head spin and takes his sense away (287, 11-18), which follows on the passage in which Parzival is supposed to be defending himself in combat, but is utterly entranced by the image of three drops of blood in the snow and the memory they bring of his beloved. The blood comes from a bird just downed by a hawk, the common medieval symbol of the amorous, searching heart. Wilhelm underlined the word "jewel" in the passage marked with a vertical line (371, 27-30) in which love promises to grant the power which she possesses to make her servitor unsurpassable and invincible. "I will take pains to prepare my *jewel* for you. Whenever you wear it, in fame no one will ever be able to surpass you" (371, 27-30). The tone of *amor vincit omnia* is heard in all these passages and finds its echo in the Grimms' version of the ending of *Sleeping Beauty.*

There are two mentions of fairy tales in the margins of the *Parzival* text, the one noted above with regard to the drops of blood in the snow, and another next to the curious passage with the analogy of the short cow's tail and infidelity, "his faithfulness has such a short tail that even the third bite doesn't make it swat, he just runs off with the horseflies into the woods" (2, 21). Wilhelm's comment is interesting: "refers to an unknown fable, cf. *Grimms' Fairy Tales* 2, 101—" (Wilhelm's reference is to the persevering fidelity of a promised bride to her wildman-like husband). The interesting thing is that Wilhelm was clearly attempting to establish connections to the Grimms' fairy tales, and making reference to them even on obscure or unclear matters, while reading *Parzival.* In another passage he seems again to have been fascinated by an apparent allusion to a story that he is unfamiliar with. He wrote "unknown reference" next to "then he made a thrust with the knife through the hand." (310, 10) Several vertical lines appear next to remarks about the importance of stories' never lying and always telling the truth "It would be better if a lying story ("maere") were left outside in the snow for its mouth to freeze" (338, 17-21); for Wilhelm, apparently it was equally important for a fairy tale (*maerchen*) to tell the truth, the ultimate truth. His conviction that fairy tales could and should do this was, I think, the principle that guided (*condwirte*) his retelling of them as stories of the spirit.

Finally, Wilhelm noted three texts on the passage of time which may bear on the fairy tales. At the very end of *Parzival* he underlined the two lines which mention

casually that there are many people in Brabant who may still know about the happy couple (826, 10). Wilhelm trusted that stories were handed down over time, even if with distortions imposed by the imperfection of human memory. The second passage is one of a more haunting memory. "*It is still for him as it was then,* when the people after the tournament were all in the windows" (*im ist noch wirs dan, end die gent / nach porte alda die venster stent*) (171, 5-6). The knight is aging, and this is at the beginning of the story, and already he sees his present reality through the eyes of the way it once was. He is conscious of an audience that once was there. This moving half-line almost betrays the whole way in which Wilhelm Grimm and many of the German Romantics felt about human consciousness of the world and the concomitant passage of time. One has only to look at the touching passage in his autobiography about his visit to his hometown of Steinau, many years after his parents had died, and his experience there of the past coming back to him in the church, and his experience outside his childhood house in which he almost thought he could see his mother moving across the field toward him as she once did, clothes blowing in the wind. "It is still for him as it was then." There is no wonder that he found it moving to discover this short and compassionate line written 700 years before him, and perhaps no wonder that he had such reverence for the Germanic religion which felt that memory was a divine attribute, a spiritual raven on the shoulder of Woden.

The last text which we will consider in the *Parzival* epic is one that Wilhelm noted as special by putting double lines alongside it both on the left and on the right side. It reads "hiest der aventiur wurf gespilt, / und ir begin ist gezilt" ("here the dice of the story has been rolled, and its beginning has been set") (112, 9-10). Parzival is fatherless at birth; Gahmuret is fourteen days in the grave as he is born. The ending of the story has been set, aimed at, too, since the death prevents father and brothers from knowing each other from the beginning, and all paths will lead to the two brothers, sons of a father they will never find, into recognizing each other in the midst of a religious fight. They will realize late that they are spiritual brothers as well, because of having another Father, and it all happened this way because the story began with such a curious cast of the dice. The thread of the narrative is determined from the first, just as the Greeks felt in the myth of the three spinners, the parcae, that the narrative of each life was set and predetermined. Greek myth is also a root of Indo-European heritage, and it too finds its way into Wilhelm's artistic efforts at bringing the old fragments of tales back to life.

Among the most important spiritual roots of the Grimms' tales are Wilhelm Grimm's own Christian spirituality. Instead of relying on his membership in the

Reformed church to be the guide as to what his religious feelings must have been, I searched in the little town of Haldensleben and in Berlin at the Prussian State Library and in the adjacent Humboldt University Library for more concrete evidence. Wilhelm Grimm's New Testament, in the original Greek, was in Berlin, and his German Bible was in Haldensleben. The results of examining the numerous critical passages which he underlined and annotated are in their own chapter in this book. The results are gratifying. Wilhelm has been made out to be a moralizing type, he was, rather, more of a private, mystic soul. His biblical Christian devotion seems to have centered on three mysteries: the Holy Spirit as the divine awareness of human events, the Resurrection of Christ, and the two great commandments, love for God and for neighbor. The influence of this spirituality will be examined in each of the five fairy tales that follow.

In the following chapters I will first review some of the work of scholars who have dealt with the question of religion in the Grimms' tales. I will then detail the results of studying Wilhelm Grimm's markings in his choice of Scripture and consider five of the better-known stories from the point of view of his spirituality as found therein, looking at the stories in their earliest manuscript form, contrasting them with Perrault and Basile's version to show the difference in tone and intent, and this will lead to the interpretation of the Grimms' final version of the five tales. I have appended the rarely seen first version of *Red Riding Hood* and an essay on that most revered of Germanic, pagan-Christian symbols, the Christmas tree.

It should surprise no one that the Grimms thought of religious belief in diachronic, or historical, terms. As they thought of words in terms of their historical roots, they thought in the same manner of the persistence of little spiritual stories as stemming from ancient roots in human faith, hope, and love. They thought of faith as a diachronic phenomenon. Thus, if asked to explain the theological importance of "fairy tale," they might begin in verbal chronological order as they did in what they called "witnesses" to fairy tales: the Greeks called them myths, the Romans called them fables, the Germans call them little stories, the English and French have come to call them fairy tales. The stories express changing forms of religious awareness over the course of time. The fables and myths express a feeling that nature is aware of us. We in turn are afraid of the passing of time and aging, the fates. Religious wisdom is to be conscious that nature is aware of us, and to be in awe of the parcae: the owl of Athena. Another form of religious awareness is to feel reverence for human thought and memory as divine phenomena, like twin birds perched on the shoulders: the ravens of Woden. Another

form of religious consciousness is to be touched by the phenomenon of love when it occurs between us, or hovers between us and the world of nature: the dove from heaven.

The form of the bird has changed over time. For Wilhelm Grimm's storytelling that would be merely the effect of time passing. What always remains is the patient alertness of the bird's eye, the human feeling of faithful love, and the curious ability which both of these give the heart to awaken and fly.

Notes

1. Brüder Grimm, *Kinder- und Hausmärchen, Ausgabe letzter Hand mit den Originalanmerkungen der Brüder Grimm*, (*Jubiläumsausgabe*), hrsg. Heinz Rölleke (Stuttgart: Reclam, 1993), I, p. 15.

2. See, for example, Marina Warner, *From the Beast to the Blonde, On Fairy Tales and Their Tellers* (New York: Farrar, Straus and Giroux, 1994), p. 211.

3. Rölleke, *Jubiläumsausgabe*, I, p. 24.

4. *A New English Dictionary on Historical Principles*, ed. James A. H. Murray, M.A. Oxon., Ph.D. Freiburg im Breisgau (Oxford: Clarendon, 1888), I, pp. iii-iv. It is significant that Murray's doctorate was taken in Germany where the historical method of the Grimms and Kluge would have been a strong influence on him.

5. *The New Monthly Magazine*, no. VIII (August), London, 1821, p. 148. Cited in Rölleke, *Jubiläumsausgabe*, III, p. 293.

6. *The Heliand, The Saxon Gospel*, trans. G. Ronald Murphy, S. J. (New York: Oxford University Press, 1992), pp. 7-10.

Select Bibliography

PRIMARY SOURCES

Kinder- und Hausmärchen, gesammelt durch die Brüder Grimm. Bd.1, 1812; Bd. 2, 1815. Berlin: in der Realschulbuchhandlung [Reimer]. [contains first brief source information and comment given by the brothers; at the Beineke Library, Yale]

Kinder- und Hausmärchen, 2. Auflage, Bd. 1 & 2, 1819; Bd. 3, 1822. Berlin: Reimer. [vol. 3 contains expanded annotations and Wilhelm's essay on the nature of fairy tales; at the Firestone Library, Princeton University]

Novum Testamentum Graece, ed. Schott. Leipzig: 1811. [at the Humboldt University Library, Berlin]

SECONDARY LITERATURE

Brüder Grimm. Kinder- und Hausmärchen (*Jubiläumsausgabe*), *Ausgabe letzter Hand mit den*

Original Anmerkungen der Brüder Grimm, I-III, hrsg. Heinz Rölleke. Stuttgart: Reclam, 1993.

Complete Fairy Tales of the Brothers Grimm, trans. and with an introduction by Jack Zipes. New York: Bantam Books, 1992. [contains brief source notes for each tale]

Complete Grimm's Fairy Tales, trans. Margaret Hunt, revised by James Stern, with an introduction by Padraic Colum, and a folkloristic commentary by Joseph Campbell. New York: Random House, Pantheon Books, 1972.

Deneke, Ludwig, und Irmgard Teitge. *Die Bibliothek der Brüder Grimm, Annotiertes Verzeichnis des festgestellten Bestandes,* hrsg. Friedhilde Krause. Weimar: Hermann Böhlaus Nachfolger, 1989. [an indispensable aid for locating the scattered books of the Grimms' personal libraries]

Deutsches Wörterbuch, Jacob Grimm und Wilhelm Grimm. Leipzig: Hinzel, 1873.

Flint, Valerie I. J. *The Rise of Magic in Early Medieval Europe.* Princeton: Princeton University Press, 1991. [an excellent interpretation of the early mutual accommodation of European pagan and Christian religious practice and ritual]

Graves, Robert. *The Greek Myths,* 2 vols. New York: Penguin Books USA Inc., 1990.

Grimm, Jacob. *Selbstbiographie,* hrsg. Ulrich Wyss. München: DTV, 1984.

Grimm, Wilhelm. "Über das Wesen der Märchen." *Jacob und Wilhelm Grimm Werke, Abteilung II, Die Werke Wilhelms,* Bd. 31, hrsg. Otfried Ehrismann. Hildesheim, Zürich, New York: Olms—Weidmann, 1992.

Grimm, Wilhelm. *Selbstbiographie* in Jacob Grimm und Wilhelm Grimm Werke, hrsg. Ludwig Erich Schmitt. Hildesheim, Zürich, New York: Olms—Weidmann, 1992.

Jacob Grimm und Wilhelm Grimm Werke, Forschungsausgabe, hrsg. Ludwig Erich Schmitt. Hildesheim, Zürich, New York: Olms—Weidmann, 1992. [contains the autobiographies and Wilhelm's essay on the nature of fairy tales]

Kamenetsky, Christa. *The Brothers Grimm and their Critics, Folktales and the Quest for Meaning.* Athens, Ohio: Ohio University Press, 1992.

Lange, Günter. "Grimms Märchen aus der Sicht eines Religionspädagogen." *Hanau, 1986-1986, 200 Jahre Brüder Grimm.* Hanau: Stadt Hanau, 1986. [sees the fairy tales' religious use, with some misgivings, as, at best, propaedeutic to faith]

Murphy, G. Ronald. "Yggdrasil, the Cross and the Christmas Tree." *America,* Vol. 175, No. 19 (Dec. 14, 1996). New York: America Press, 1996.

———. *The Heliand, The Saxon Gospel.* New York: Oxford University Press, 1992.

———. "From Germanic Warrior to Christian Knight: the Heliand Transformation." *Arthurian Literature and Christianity: Notes from the Twentieth Century.* New York: Garland, 1999.

———. "Magic in the Heliand." *Monatshefte,* 83, No. 4 (1991), 386-97.

———. *The Saxon Savior, The Germanic Transformation of the Gospel in the Ninth-Century Heliand.* New York: Oxford University Press, 1989.

New English Dictionary on Historical Principles, A, ed. James A. H. Murray. Oxford: Clarendon, 1888.

New Greek-English Interlinear New Testament, trans. Robert Brown and Philip Comfort, ed. J. D. Douglas. Wheaton, Ill.: Tyndale House Publishers, Inc., 1993. [uses the Kurt Aland text of the 26th edition, Novum Testamentum Graece, from the Institute for New Testament Textual Research, Münster, Westfalen.]

Peppard, Murray B. *Paths Through the Forest, A Biography of the Brothers Grimm.* New York: Holt, Rinehart, Winston, 1971. [a very good and sensitive biography]

Reception of the Grimms' Fairy Tales, Responses, Reactions, Revisions, ed. Donald Haase. Detroit: Wayne State University Press, 1993.

Rölleke, Heinz. *Wo das Wünschen noch geholfen hat: Gesammelte Aufsätze zu den Kinder- und Hausmärchen der Brüder Grimm.* Wuppertaler Schriftenreihe Literatur, 23. Bonn: Bouvier, 1985.

———. "Die 'stockhessischen' Märchen der 'alten Marie': das Ende eines Mythos um die frühesten KHM-Aufzeichnungen der Brüder Grimm." *Germanisch-Romanische Monatsschrift,* n.s. 25 (1975), 74-86.

———. "New Research on Grimms' Fairy Tales." *The Brothers Grimm and Folktale,* ed. James M. McGlathery. [Urbana: University of Illinois Press, 1988.]

Russell, James C. *The Germanization of Early Medieval Christianity, A Sociohistorical Approach to Religious Transformation.* New York: Oxford University Press, 1994.

Ryan, Judith. "Hybrid Forms in German Romanticism." *Prosimetrum, Crosscultural Perspectives on Narrative in Prose and Verse,* ed. Joseph Harris and Karl Reichl. Cambridge: D. S. Brewer, 1997.

Stone, Kay. "Three Transformations of Snow White." *The Brothers Grimm and Folktale,* ed. James M. McGlathery.

Ward, Donald. "New Misconceptions about Old Folktales: The Brothers Grimm." *The Brothers Grimm and Folktale,* ed. James M. McGlathery.

Warner, Marina. *From the Beast to the Blonde, On Fairy Tales and their Tellers.* New York: Farrar, Straus and Giroux, 1995.

Wolfram von Eschenbach. *Parzival, (Studienausgabe) mittlehochdeutscher Text nach der 6. Ausgabe von Karl Lachmann.* Berlin: Walter de Gruyter, 1998.

Wolfram von Eschenbach. *Parzival,* trans. Helen Mustard and Charles Passage. New York: Vintage Books, 1961.

David Blamires (essay date 2003)

SOURCE: Blamires, David. "A Workshop of Editorial Practice: The Grimms' *Kinder- und Hausmärchen.*" In *A Companion to the Fairy Tale,* edited by Hilda Ellis Davidson and Anna Chaudhri, pp. 71-83. Cambridge, England: D. S. Brewer, 2003.

[*In the following essay, Blamires offers insight into the scholarly concerns that profoundly affected the Grimm brothers' choices regarding the editing, inclusion, and treatment of their works in their* Kinder- und Hausmärchen.]

The most famous collection of fairy tales the world over is that made by Jacob and Wilhelm Grimm (1785-1863 and 1786-1859) and published under the title *Kinder-* und *Hausmärchen,* 'Children's and Household Tales' (hereafter *KHM*). The first edition appeared in two volumes dated 1812 and 1815, and six more editions, each different from the others, followed during their lifetime: 1819-22 (second), 1837 (third), 1840 (fourth), 1843 (fifth), 1850 (sixth) and 1857 (seventh). The seventh edition is the basis of virtually all subsequent printings of the tales in German. Here the tales are numbered 1-200, but with an additional item, 151*; no. 38, 'Die Hochzeit der Frau Füchsin' ('The Wedding of Mrs Fox'), consists of two separate items, while no. 39, 'Die Wichtelmänner' ('The Goblins') and no. 105, 'Märchen von der Unke' ('Tales about the Toad') are both divided into three parts. At the end of the collection ten *Kinderlegenden* (pious tales for children) are added. This makes for a total of 216 items. But in the forty-five-year-long process of editing many more tales were collected. Some of them were new; others were alternative versions of already known tales, while thirty-four items printed in the 1812 volume were removed from subsequent editions. The mass of material thus published is very extensive. The numbering of the tales up to 200 clearly had some sort of symbolic significance for Wilhelm Grimm, who was responsible for editing the collection from 1819 onwards. It was not until 1850 that the collection amounted to two hundred items, exactly twice the number of tales in Boccaccio's *Decameron,* that most influential late medieval collec-

tion of popular story material. Also in that same year of 1850, Friedrich Heinrich von der Hagen (1780-1856), appointed first Professor of German at the newly founded University of Berlin in 1810, published a collection of one hundred medieval German tales entitled *Gesammtabenteuer,* clearly emulating Boccaccio. Wilhelm Grimm and von der Hagen were elected members of the Prussian Academy of Sciences in Berlin in 1840 and 1841 respectively, so one can perhaps infer that Grimm was aiming to outdo his colleague.

Both Boccaccio and von der Hagen were writing or collecting material designed for an adult readership. The Grimms, on the other hand, were concerned with traditional tales for children, a form of literature hitherto neglected or looked down upon by intellectuals in Germany and circulating, so they believed, chiefly in oral form. Initially they were not aiming at producing a book for children but rather at rescuing from oblivion stories that were part of a rapidly disappearing popular tradition. Their scholarly enterprise was all of a piece with their preoccupation with medieval literature, language and mythology. Indeed, the annotations that they made to the tales they collected frequently drew attention to parallels between fairy-tale motifs and aspects of mythology.

The Grimms were pioneers in the scholarly study and collection of what they referred to in the preface to the first edition of *KHM* as 'these innocent household tales' (Rölleke 1986: I, vi). That is what made them different from their literary predecessors and contemporaries who also published versions of the same kind of traditional material. (I shall come back to the question of definitions in due course.) The late eighteenth and early nineteenth century in Germany was not short of books presenting *Märchen* in a variety of formats to the middle-class reader, but these books were decidedly literary, rather than scholarly, in character. Foremost among them was J. K. A. Musäus's *Volksmährchen der Deutschen* ('Popular Tales of the Germans') published in Gotha in five volumes between 1782-6 (Musäus 1977), in which the author retold in a discursive, ironic and linguistically ambitious style some fourteen tales that were not wholly German by origin nor all traditional tales. Musäus himself makes the point, in a prefatory letter to a friend, that he was writing for adults (Musäus 1977: 12):

> Popular tales, however, aren't children's tales either, for a nation doesn't consist of children, but mainly of grown-ups, and in ordinary life one usually speaks differently with them than one does with children. It would therefore be a mad idea if you supposed that all *Märchen* ought to be told in the tone that Mother Goose uses for children.

Many other writers of the time shared Musäus's view that fairy tales were not specifically designed for children and Goethe, Wieland and the Romantics followed him in composing *Märchen* for adults. Benedicte Naubert followed up Musäus's popularity by producing *Neue Volksmährchen der Deutschen* ('New Popular Tales of the Germans') published in four volumes between 1789-93 in Leipzig (Zipes 2000: 335-6).

Individual *Märchen* for children, however, were included in a number of eighteenth- and early-nineteenth-century collections.[1] Several of these collections were mentioned, mainly dismissively, by the Brothers Grimm in the preface to the first volume of the first edition of the *KHM* (Rölleke 1986: I, xviii-xix). The Grimms do not spell out the precise grounds for their objections, but one can fairly assume that they had to do with expansive or elaborate treatments of the plots and with the invention of superfluous detail. That, however, was the style of the time and can be seen in other countries too, as, for example, in Thomas Crofton Croker's *Fairy Legends and Traditions of the South of Ireland* (1825-8). The Grimms were breaking new ground by concentrating on simplicity of expression and clarity of structure.

The fascinating thing about the Grimms' enterprise of producing the *KHM* is that we are able to follow the whole process from their initial impetus and researches right through to the definitive edition of 1857. With most other editors of fairy tales, by contrast, we have simply a final printed edition, so their methods of working are less transparent. The two brothers were indefatigable letter-writers, so often personal documentation of details about particular tales and informants can be found in their correspondence. They sent their manuscript collection of tales in October 1810 to their friend, the Romantic poet Clemens Brentano (1778-1842), who was interested in using them for a project of his own which, however, never came to fruition. Prudently, the Grimms had made a copy for themselves, which was used for printing the first edition of the *KHM* and then destroyed. Brentano never returned the original and, decades later, it was found among his posthumous papers and has been edited at least twice (Lefftz 1927; Rölleke 1975). This gives the earliest documentation for some forty-six items, not all of which got into print. In addition to this, there is extant Wilhelm Grimm's personal copy of the two volumes of the first edition of the *KHM,* which contains his autograph notes and emendations of the text for the second edition (Brüder Grimm-Museum, Kassel). This wealth of material allows us an unparalleled insight into the brothers' working methods.

Jacob Grimm was a student at the University of Marburg from 1802 to 1805, Wilhelm following him from 1803 to 1806. There they became acquainted with Brentano and his sister, Bettina and subsequently with Brentano's friend, Achim vom Arnim (1781-1831). Although the Grimms studied law at Marburg with Friedrich Karl von Savigny (1779-1861), they were both passionately involved in reading and rediscovering older German literature. It was in this capacity that they were drawn into contributing material to Arnim and Brentano's influential 1806-8 collection of popular songs, *Des Knaben Wunderhorn* ('The Boy's Magic Horn'). The first volume of that work concluded with an essay by Arnim, in which he declared the aim of collecting and publishing 'the faith and knowledge of the people, what accompanies them in pleasure and death, songs, legends, sayings, stories, prophecies and melodies' (Rölleke 1987: I, 413). Encouraged by both Arnim and Brentano, the brothers embarked on collecting stories and legends from 1807 onwards, though with no clearly formulated idea of publication. They were happy to let Brentano have the fruits of their labours in the manuscripts that they sent him in October 1810, but in March 1811, when he had failed to do anything about them, they set about working on the material with a view to publishing a volume of their own (Rölleke 1985: 1160).

The 1810 manuscript, sometimes known as the Ölenberg manuscript from the abbey of Ölenberg in Alsace, where Brentano's posthumous papers came to rest (it is now in the Fondation Martin Bodmer, Cologny, Geneva), represents the earliest stage of the Grimms' collection. This heteregeneous assemblage of material gives the lie to the popular conception of the two brothers busily going round Hessian villages taking down fairy tales from elderly peasant men and women. The first thing to strike home is the proportion of items taken from literary sources—thirteen out of forty-six. These go back as far as Martin Montanus's *Wegkhürtzer* (1557), but include material as recent as Albert Ludwig Grimm's *Kindermährchen* (1809). There is a preponderance of items from the period from 1790 onwards. Three are derived directly or indirectly from French material: 'Von der Nachtigall und der Blindschleiche' ('The Nightingale and the Slowworm'), no. 38, 'Der Drache' ('The Dragon'), no. 20, 'Murmelthier' ('Marmot'), no. 37, while 'Der Mond und seine Mutter' ('The Moon and his Mother'), no. 36, goes back to a German translation of a passage from Plutarch. Thus already the Grimms make plain their interests in both the historical and comparative aspects of the fairy tale. Though their focus was on German material, it was far from exclusive. Perhaps this is why the word *Deutsch* does not figure in the title of their book. The notes they added to the printed texts from the first volume of the first edition onwards indicate their continuing concern to place what they collected from oral sources within as comprehensive a framework as possible.

As to the orally collected tales in the manuscript, the Grimms' informants were not of peasant stock, but chiefly educated middle-class young women from the Grimms' own social circle. The largest number of tales came from the Wild family in Kassel—Dorothea Catharina (Frau Wild, 1752-1813), Lisette (1782-1858),

Gretchen (1787-1819), Dortchen (1793-1867), who became Wilhelm Grimm's wife in 1825, and Mie (1794-1867). Herr Wild was an apothecary and both he and his wife came from Swiss families. Then there were the three Hassenpflug sisters, Marie (1788-1856), Jeanette (1791-1860) and Amalie (1800-71), whose parents had moved from Hanau to Kassel in 1798-9. Their mother was of Huguenot stock and there was a strong tradition of speaking French in the family (Rölleke 1975: 391). A few other tales came from Friederike Mannel (1783-1833), the daughter of a pastor from Hilmes, near Hersfeld. It is possible that another tale came from the Ramus sisters, Julia (1792-1862) and Charlotte (1793-1858), daughters of the French pastor in Kassel. So much for the manuscript and core of the first volume of the first edition.

As far as the second volume is concerned, we have to contend with the figure of Frau Dorothea Viehmann, described in the preface to that volume as 'a peasant woman from the village of Zwehrn near Kassel, through whom we received a considerable portion of the tales communicated here, which are thus genuinely Hessian, along with several additions to the first volume'. However, research has shown that Frau Viehmann was also of Huguenot descent. As John M. Ellis, summarising the results of Georg Textor's investigations of 1955, puts it (1983: 32):

> Dorothea Viehmann's first language was French, not German, and she was a member of the large community of Huguenots who had settled in the area, in which the language of church and school was still French. She was not a peasant but a thoroughly middle-class woman; she was not an untutored transmitter of folk tradition but, on the contrary, a literate woman who knew her Perrault; she was not a German but of French stock.

It is impossible to account for the discrepancy between the Grimms' claim in their preface and the facts that Textor uncovered. Some scholars, like Ellis, regard the Grimms as disingenuous or even duplicitous not only in regard to Frau Viehmann's background, but also in their claims about methodology.

The French connections have been emphasised a good deal recently, undermining the common opinion that the Grimms' collection is peculiarly German and free from any foreign influence. We need to remember, however, that Perrault composed only eleven fairy tales, eight in prose and three in verse. Only two items in the Grimms' manuscript—'Dornröschen' ('Thorn Rose'), no. 19, and 'Prinzessin Mäusehaut' ('Princess Mouseskin'), no. 35—betray a strong resemblance to tales by Perrault ('La Belle au bois dormant' and 'Peau d'âne' respectively). Similarly, out of the twenty-five items supplied by Frau Viehmann only two—'Der arme Müllerbursch und das Kätzchen' ('The Poor Miller's

Son and the Cat') and 'Sechse kommen durch die ganze Welt' ('Six travel through the whole World') have clear parallels in Madame d'Aulnoy's 'La Chatte blanche' and 'Belle-Belle ou le chevalier fortuné'. The 1812 volume also included 'Der gestiefelte Kater' ('Puss-in-Boots') and 'Blaubart' ('Bluebeard'), both provided by the Hassenpflugs, but they were eliminated from subsequent editions because of their close correspondence to Perrault's 'Le Chat botté' and 'La Barbe bleue'. This helps to put in perspective the French contribution to the Grimms' collection. The only remaining problem case is perhaps 'Rothkäppchen' ('Little Red Riding-Hood'), which appears to be a conflation of Perrault's 'Le Petit Chaperon rouge' with 'Der Wolf mit den sieben jungen Geißlein' ('The Wolf with the Seven Little Kids').

To return to the Grimms' manuscript, Heinz Rölleke has shown that the collection sent to Brentano must have consisted of fifty-three items (Rölleke 1975: 15). These can be broken down into the broad categories of the Aarne-Thompson classification of folktale types as follows: eight animal tales, thirty-seven tales of magic, one tale of the stupid ogre, two novellas, one cumulative tale and four tales that do not fit the classification. This last group includes one aetiological tale, 'Der Mond und seine Mutter' ('The Moon and his Mother'), one that might fit somewhere among AT 275-99, 'Blutwurst', and two religious tales similar to those collected later as *Kinderlegenden,* namely 'Armes Mädchen' ('Poor Girl') and 'Von dem gestohlenen Heller' ('The Stolen Penny').

Overwhelmingly, therefore, the emphasis in this *ur-*collection lies on tales of magic, that is, fairy tales in the narrower sense of the term. Approximately seven tenths of the tales are fairy tales. It is interesting to compare this with the 1857 edition of the *KHM,* where the proportion of fairy tales in this sense is about half. Already the *ur-*collection contains versions of such famous fairy tales as 'Allerleirauh' ('All Kinds of Fur'), 'Die zwölf Brüder' ('The Twelve Brothers'), 'Brüderchen und Schwesterchen' ('Little Brother and Little Sister'), 'Hänsel und Gretel' ('Hansel and Gretel'), 'Der Froschkönig' ('The Frog Prince'), 'Fundevogel', 'Die goldene Gans' ('The Golden Goose'), 'Rumpelstilzchen' ('Rumpelstiltskin'), 'Sneewittchen' ('Snow White'), 'Aschenputtel' ('Cinderella') and 'Der goldene Vogel' ('The Golden Bird'). What we must remember, though, with regard to these manuscript versions is that they are not verbatim records of an orally performed tale, but more like plot summaries. Some are very brief indeed; others needed very little editorial treatment before being printed in the 1812 volume. In this initial collaboration, Jacob seems to have played the leading role: some twenty-nine tales were collected by him in comparison with Wilhelm's eighteen. Friederike Mannel and Jeanette Hassenpflug wrote down one tale each, while the origin of four others is not clear.

Not all this manuscript material was used for the first edition. It represents only the first stage of the Grimms' collection, since they continued their work after sending this preliminary material to Brentano. By the time they were ready to move towards their own publication they had amassed many more tales, including some that they considered better versions of tales they already had. So seven items (nos. 13, 20, 22, 29, 32, 36 and 46) found a place only in the notes to the 1812 volume, supplementing these better versions. Three tales were not published at all (nos. 23, 31 and *vor* 48). The first two had been excerpted from printed sources, while the third, 'Vom König von England' ('The King of England'), was probably eliminated because of its close similarity to the story of 'The Three Sisters' from the *Thousand and One Nights*. The Grimms did not want to include tales that they ultimately considered literary in presentation and style. They were looking for material, whether in printed sources or in contemporary oral form, that was simple and unpretentious and could be regarded as reflecting the ideas, tastes and aspirations of ordinary people.

The preface to the 1812 volume of the *KHM* begins with a comparison from the world of nature. The persistence of fairy tales (in the broader sense) among the peasantry is seen as analogous to that of ears of corn that escape the destructiveness of storms and flourish by hedgerows and on the edge of fields, where they are carefully gathered by 'poor, pious hands', taken home and provide nourishment through the winter.

> Seats by the stove, the kitchen range, attic stairs, holidays still celebrated, pastures and forests in their quietness, above all the unsullied imagination, these were the hedges that kept them safe and passed them on from one era to another.

The Grimms make high claims about their presentation of the tales:

> We have taken pains to present these tales in as pure a manner as was possible. In many one will find the narrative interrupted by rhymes and verses that sometimes even alliterate, but are never sung while the story is being told, and these very tales are the oldest and best. No detail has been added or embellished and altered, for we should have been afraid of enlarging stories that are so rich in themselves with analogies or reminiscences taken from them; they are not to be fabricated.

The latter part of this claim has proved very contentious, since the comparison of printed tale with manuscript format has shown that, in a number of instances, the Grimms did alter and embellish not merely unimportant or trivial details but also critical events or aspects of a tale. We shall need to take our consideration of changes as far as the second edition (1819), since the issues are not entirely straightforward. Let us turn now to some examples.

'The Frog Prince or Iron Henry', placed first in the collection from 1812 onwards, derives from a manuscript summary by Wilhelm Grimm headed 'Die Königstochter und der verzauberte Prinz, Froschkönig' ('The King's Daughter and the Enchanted Prince, Frog King'), which he expands to about twice that length. The manuscript starts by referring to the protagonist as the youngest daughter of the king, while the printed texts make the fact known only through the frog's appeal to her in what is printed in verse format: 'King's daughter, youngest one, open up for me, don't you know what you said to me yesterday by the cool water of the fountain? King's daughter, youngest one, open up for me.' But in neither manuscript nor printed text is there any allusion to other sisters.

In the 1812 text the princess offers 'everything, my clothes, my jewels, my pearls and everything in the world' for the return of her lost golden ball, while the manuscript says nothing. The manuscript has the frog offering to fetch it 'if you will take me home with you'. This the 1812 text expands to: 'but if you will take me as your companion and I sit next to you at table and eat from your little golden plate and sleep in your little bed and you respect and love me'. The 1819 version is even more specific: 'if you will take me as your *friend and* companion, I shall sit at your table *at your right side,* eat *with you* from your little golden plate, *drink from your little goblet* and sleep in your little bed' (my italics).

Th climax of the tale comes when the princess flings the frog at the wall, which the manuscript presents as: 'However, when he hit the wall, he fell down into the bed and lay in it as a young, handsome prince, and the princess lay down with him.' The 1812 text is slightly different: 'But the frog did not fall down dead, but when it came on to the bed it was a handsome young prince. He was now her dear companion, and she respected him as she had promised, and they fell contentedly asleep together.' The 1819 version is again more specific: 'But what fell down was not a dead frog, but an alive young king's son with beautiful and kind eyes. He was now, rightfully and according to her father's will, her dear companion and spouse. Then they fell contentedly asleep together.' The sequence of changes made between the manuscript and the 1819 text make ever clearer the nature of the marriage contract and the father's role in determining his daughter's future. In the manuscript it is the frog that takes the initiative and states his conditions for fetching the golden ball for the disconsolate princess, while in the 1812 text, it is the princess who weeps and laments and declares what she will give in order to get her ball back.

Some of these changes Wilhelm Grimm must have made quite consciously, but possibly not all of them. It is only when we know about them that we can properly assess the significance of the final text of 1857, which is not so very different from that of 1819. All of the German texts are content with the prince falling into the princess's bed and the two going to sleep together, but the first English version of the tale, by Edgar Taylor (1823), could not cope with it and changed the ending completely. Taylor has the frog sleep on the princess's pillow for three nights, 'but when the princess awoke on the following morning, she was astonished to see, instead of the frog, a handsome prince gazing on her with the most beautiful eyes that ever were seen, and standing at the head of her bed'. There is no flinging against the wall and no prince and princess sleeping together in bed. The English reading public would have thought it immoral (Blamires 1989; Sutton 1990), but it caused no problems in Germany.

A fairy tale that did cause problems in its first printed state was 'Rapunzel'. This derives from a story by Friedrich Schultz included in his *Kleine Romane,* which in its turn goes back to the fairy tale 'Persinette' by Mademoiselle de la Force (Rölleke 1980: III, 447). 'Rapunzel' is now mainly known in a version in which the heroine incriminates herself by asking her godmother why the latter is so much heavier to pull up into the tower than the young prince who is up in a moment. This poorly motivated incident features in all the editions of Grimm from 1819 onwards, but the 1812 text is much more convincing. There, after the prince has been visiting for some time, Rapunzel asks her godmother why her clothes have become so tight and don't fit any more. This allusion to premarital pregnancy was severely criticised, so Wilhelm Grimm removed it from subsequent editions. The fact of pregnancy remains in the story, since Rapunzel gives birth to twins while the prince, blinded from his fall from the tower, wanders around miserably in the forest; but it is not talked about.

Another fairy tale that undergoes far-reaching changes between manuscript and printed text is 'Snow White'. Not until the 1819 edition do we get the figure of the wicked stepmother; up to that point it was Snow White's own mother who was her jealous persecutor. In the manuscript she takes her daughter into the forest to pick red roses and abandons her, hoping wild animals will eat her. In the 1812 text she orders a hunter to kill Snow White and bring back lung and liver as proof. In the manuscript it is Snow White's own father who finds her supposed corpse in the glass coffin when he returns from abroad. The doctors in his entourage bring her back to life, she is taken home and married to a handsome prince. But already in the 1812 text, Snow White in her coffin is given to a prince who has fallen in love with her beauty, and she comes back to life when an irritated servant knocks the body and dislodges the poisonous piece of apple from her throat. This latter motif is removed from the 1819 text, so that the apple is dislodged as a result of servants merely stumbling while carrying Snow White. In every version Snow White is a passive victim whose only activity is keeping house for the seven dwarves. The main interest of the tale lies in the figure of the wicked (step)mother, and it is noteworthy that the Grimms' predecessor, Musäus, in his version of this fairy tale, concentrated virtually all his attention on the stepmother and made her name, Richilde, the title of his complex ironic story.

The changes in textual form do not depend solely on Wilhelm Grimm's whim, but on new variants of the tale with which he had become acquainted. The manuscript version came from the Hassenpflugs, while the altered ending given in 1812 derives from Ferdinand Siebert, a young theologian and student of German philology, who provided the Grimms with several tales. The further change to Snow White's restoration to consciousness in the 1819 text comes from a variant provided by Heinrich Leopold Stein (Rölleke 1980: III, 465). The change of mother to stepmother, however, seems to be Wilhelm Grimm's own and to reflect a peculiarly protective and idealised view of the mother figure.

As the Grimms continued collecting tales, principally from oral sources and from people outside their own immediate circle, they constantly encountered variant versions of tales that they already knew and thus had to make some judgement about how to treat them. What they did was to follow the practice then employed in editing medieval texts. Scholars attempted to reconstruct the original form of a work on the basis of a comparison of extant versions varying in date, dialect, substance, vocabulary, aesthetic skill and so on. In this way a 'critical' text could be established. When the Grimms had variants of fairy tales they tended to construct composite texts. They would choose a variant with the most coherent plot structure as the basis, but modify or amplify it with details taken from other variants. Because they were also interested in things like proverbs, traditional verses and folk customs, they often included them, where appropriate, in particular tales. As they became more familiar with the structural features of fairy tales, they tended to standardise patterns such as threefold repetitions of actions or the protagonist being the youngest of three siblings of the same sex. Often the reason for editorial changes in the form of a particular tale from, say, the first edition to a later one, was that the brothers had been provided with a new variant which they considered better than what they previously possessed. The rejected variant was often, but not invariably, relegated to the notes that the Grimms appended to their texts from the first edition on. By the time of the second edition they had so much material that the notes formed a separate volume published in 1822. A third edition of the notes, greatly expanded, was published in 1856. It is thus possible, in some cases, to locate discarded versions of a tale in these notes.[2]

A particularly striking instance of the substitution of a new text occurs with 'Der Eisenhans' ('Iron John'), a composite standard German text that replaced, as late as 1850, the Low German 'De wilde Mann' ('The Wild Man'), which had reached the Grimms via the Haxthausen family from Paderborn and been included in the *KHM* from the 1815 volume of the first edition up to 1843. The Low German text, which is simpler, rougher and only about half the length, but more difficult of access owing to its dialect form, was completely supplanted; it was not included in the 1856 edition of the Grimms' notes. The new version is more literary and, in the complexity of its plot moves, somewhat akin to an abbreviated *Volksbuch*. This new text has recently attracted considerable attention through Robert Bly's interpretation in *Iron John: A Book about Men* (1990).

Another tale that underwent a similar process of substitution is 'Der Räuberbräutigam' ('The Robber Bridegroom'), a disturbing tale analogous to the English 'Mister Fox'. The manuscript version, written by Jacob and taken from Marie Hassenpflug, is basically a plot summary mixing past and present tenses and has a princess and a prince as its key figures. The 1812 text expands the narrative, which it gives entirely in the past tense, increases the mood of fear and gives the supposed dream sequence in full. The atmosphere of suspense is very striking. However, the version printed in 1819 is quite different and compounded of two other variants from Hessen, contaminated with some details from the 1812 text. We now have a miller's daughter and a would-be bridegroom of unspecified background, though supposed to be wealthy. The latter marks his bride's path through the forest with ashes, whereas the prince had tied ribbons to the trees. On arrival at the lonely forest house, the miller's daughter is warned of danger by the voice of a bird in a cage, not simply by the old woman housekeeper. This is the only non-realistic element in the story. In the manuscript and the 1812 text, the robbers murder the princess's grandmother, while in the 1819 version, they murder 'another young woman', first making her drunk with white, red and yellow wine, before hacking her body into pieces and salting it. The horror is intensified through this clearer alignment of the robbers' victim with the protagonist of the story. Presumably also Wilhelm Grimm preferred a miller's daughter to a princess because it fitted better with the belief in the popular origins of the fairy tale. Further, mainly stylistic alterations were made to the story for the 1837 edition.

Several other tales show comparable kinds of changes in textual form from the manuscript or the first edition onwards, among them 'Rumpelstilzchen', 'Das Mädchen ohne Hände' ('The Girl without Hands') and 'Der Jude im Dorn' ('The Jew in the Brambles'). With the majority of the remaining tales, however, the changes tend to be verbal or stylistic rather than centring on content. The main criticisms that had been levelled at the 1812 volume when it first appeared focused on style and presentation, which were felt to be rough and unpolished. Both Brentano and A. L. Grimm mentioned Runge as a model that ought to have been followed (Rölleke 1985: 1162-3). Philipp Otto Runge (1777-1810), a leading Romantic artist, had provided the Grimms with two Low German tales—'Van den Fischer un siine Fru' ('The Fisherman and his Wife') and 'Van den Machandel-Boom' ('The Juniper Tree')—that were printed in the 1812 volume and quickly achieved great popularity. Oddly enough, these texts were also subjected to verbal and orthographical changes from the fifth edition (1843) onwards, as Wilhelm Grimm tried to iron out variations that went back to two different versions that Runge himself had made (Rölleke 1980: III, 449-50). A Low German dialect form was nonetheless retained, and indeed the 1857 edition contains twenty-one tales in a variety of dialects. Runge's two tales were narrated in a simple, straightforward manner but certain episodes were made more immediate through the use of dialogue and lines of verse. 'The Juniper Tree', for example, is famous for the song that Goethe included in *Faust,* in which the murdered boy, in the form of a bird, recounts what has happened:

> Min Moder de mi slacht't,
> min Vader de mi att,
> min Swester de Marleeniken
> söcht alle mine Beeniken,
> un bindt se in een siden Dook,
> legts unner den Machandelboom;
> kywitt, kywitt! Ach watt een schön Vagel bin ick!

> My mother slew me,
> My father ate me,
> My sister Marleeniken
> Sought all my bones
> And bound them in a silken cloth,
> Put them under the juniper tree;
> Kywitt, kywitt, what a beautiful bird I am!

The inclusion of verse material is something that we find in about a quarter of all the tales (53 items) in the 1857 edition.

The 1812 volume was experimental. The Grimms were trying out the material they had collected and it presents a considerable variety of kinds of tale as well as modes of narration. When it came to revising the collection for the second edition of 1819-22, a great deal was altered. Nineteen texts were entirely eliminated, while fourteen were removed to the notes. From the 1815 volume five were eliminated, and two removed to the notes. The differences in the changes made to the two volumes demonstrate how much the brothers had learnt between 1812 and 1815. They had realised from their own continued collecting, as well as from the reactions of friends and critics, that some of their tales could be replaced with better versions, while some were more appropriately removed altogether. Among the latter perhaps the most striking excision affected the two versions of 'Wie Kinder Schlachtens miteinander gespielt haben' ('How Children Played at Butcher Together'), a gruesome tale of children playing at butcher, in the course of which one little boy has his throat slit. Both versions have literary sources that go back to the sixteenth and seventeenth centuries respectively, though Wilhelm Grimm claimed he had heard it from his mother as a child (Rölleke 1980: III, 520-1). Other tales, such as 'Der gestiefelte Kater' ('Puss-in-Boots'), 'Blaubart' ('Bluebeard') and 'Die drei Schwestern' ('The Three Sisters'), were excluded because of their closeness to Perrault's 'Le Chat botté' and 'La Barbe bleue' and Musäus's 'Die Bücher der Chronika der drei Schwestern'. The fifth edition (1843) included a story entitled 'Die Erbsenprobe' ('The Pea Ordeal'), which was removed from subsequent editions because of its dependence on Andersen's 'The Princess on the Pea'. A few other tales were omitted because they were more like legends than fairy tales. All this omitted material is of interest, but it is accessible only in the first edition or in the appendix to a modern scholarly edition such as Rölleke's 1980 edition or in the English translation by Ruth Michaelis-Jena and Arthur Ratcliff (Grimm 1956/1960).

The biggest change in the presentation of the *KHM* occurred between the first and the second edition, but further smaller changes took place all the way through to the seventh edition of 1857. New tales were added, better versions were substituted, and stylistic improvements and other verbal alterations were made. These changes, beginning already in 1819, turned the collection increasingly into a work calculated to appeal to a child readership, while at the same time maintaining an ambitious basis in the production of 'better' texts of individual tales and the provision of a scholarly commentary. Through the removal of morally questionable elements from certain stories and their alignment with the values and feelings of the middle class, including their attitudes towards religion and gender roles, the Grimms created a work of immense appeal. While the complete collection was perhaps dauntingly long, a selection of fifty tales, attractively illustrated by their younger brother, Ludwig Emil Grimm, created a more accessible 'small edition' that went through ten editions from 1825 to 1859, the year of Wilhelm Grimm's death, and had reached thirty-six editions by 1887 (Gerstner 1982: 351).

Many people referring to the *KHM* today are unaware of the textual history of the collection and are apt to make pronouncements on the basis of slender or fragmentary acquaintance with the material. If they rely on translations the situation is increasingly fraught, as many translators have made modifications of their own to their chosen text. There is also a tendency among some writers to judge the Grimms with the hindsight of 150 or more years of critical experience and then to blame them for not occupying the critical positions of today. But the Grimms were men of their own era and reflected, consciously or unconsciously, the accepted social, moral and religious standards of their day. Maria Tatar and Ruth Bottigheimer have skilfully laid these standards bare, particularly in respect of the Grimms' understanding of gender roles. The fact that the brothers imposed their own ideas and views on the material they published is no different from what happens with storytellers of any period. Scholars may construct what they believe to be the 'original' or base-text of a particular tale, but each storyteller, whether in speech or in print, creates his or her own narrative. Only with printed texts do we approach standardised forms. But anyone who examines different translations of the same base-text will see that changes occur here too. Moreover, even with one and the same text, we can see how different illustrations can create varying interpretations and reader reactions.

There is in fact no form of a fairy tale that can be regarded as normative, since the storytelling tradition is a process in which tales are constantly reinvented. We may imagine that in going back to the earliest examples we are getting closer to a hypothetical 'original', but we have no means of knowing what may have preceded those earliest extant examples in oral tradition. In recording in print different versions of orally current tales, usually through intermediaries, the Grimms were, as it were, making snapshots of a living, developing tradition (though, ironically, they thought it was actually dying). They themselves contributed to this living tradition through the work they published in the seven editions of the *KHM*. It thus seems fruitful to regard these editions as a workshop of editorial practice, the progressive shaping of contemporary and historical folktale material so as to make it simultaneously available to child readers of their day and the world of scholars too.

Notes

1. Schummel, J. G. (1776-8) *Kinderspiele und Gespräche* ('Children's Games and Conversations') 3 vols. Leipzig. Günther, C. W. (1787) *Kindermährchen aus mündlichen Erzählungen gesammelt* ('Children's Tales collected from Oral Narratives'). Erfurt. The anonymous (1791-2) *Ammenmärchen* ('Nurses' Tales'). Weimar. Münch, J. G. (1799) Das *Mährleinbuch für meine Nachbarsleute* ('The Book of Little Tales for my Neighbours'. Leipzig. The anonymous (1801)

Feen-Mährchen ('Tales of the Fairies'). Braunschweig. Grimm, A. L. (1809) *Kindermährchen* ('Children's Tales'). Heidelberg.

2. Rölleke reprinted the 1856 edition in his three-volume Reclam edition of 1980.

References

Aarne, A., and Thompson, S. (1981), *The Types of the Folktale. A Classification and Biography.* FFC 184. Helsinki.

Blamires, D. (1989), 'The Early Reception of the Grimms' *Kinder- und Hausmärchen* in England', *Bulletin of the John Rylands University Library of Manchester,* 71.3, 63-77.

Bly, R. (1990), *Iron John: A Book about Men.* Reading, MA.

Bottigheimer, R. B. (1987), *Grimms' Bad Girls and Bold Boys: The Moral and Social Vision of the Tales.* New Haven/London.

Ellis, J. M. (1983), *One Fairy Story Too Many: The Brothers Grimm and Their Tales.* Chicago/London.

Gerstner H. (1982) ed., *Grimms Märchen: die kleine Ausgabe aus dem Jahr 1825.* Dortmund.

Grimm, J. and W. (1956/1960), *New Tales from Grimm,* trans. R. Michaelis-Jena and A. Ratcliff. Edinburgh/London. (First published as *Grimms' Other Tales.* London.)

Lefftz, J. (1927) ed., *Märchen der Brüder Grimm: Urfassung nach der Originalhandschrift der Abtei Ölenberg im Elsaß.* Heidelberg.

Musäus, J. K. A. (1977), *Volksmärchen der Deutschen.* Munich.

Rölleke, H. (1975) ed., *Die älteste Märchensammlung der Brüder Grimm.* Cologny/Geneva.

———, (1980) ed., *Brüder Grimm, Kinder- und Hausmärchen: Ausgabe letzter Hand mit den Originalanmerkungen der Brüder Grimm.* 3 vols. Stuttgart.

———, (1982) ed., *Brüder Grimm, Kinder- und Hausmärchen: nach der zweiten vermehrten und verbesserten Auflage von 1819.* 2 vols. Cologne.

———, (1985) ed., *Kinder- und Hausmärchen gesammelt durch die Brüder Grimm: vollständige Ausgabe auf der Grundlage der dritten Auflage (1837).* Frankfurt.

———, (1986) ed., *Kinder- und Hausmärchen gesammelt durch die Brüder Grimm: vergrößerter Nachdruck der zweibändigen Erstausgabe von 1812 und 1815.* 2 vols. Göttingen.

———, (1987), *Des Knaben Wunderhorn: alte deutsche Lieder gesammelt von Achim von Arnim und Clemens Brentano.* 3 vols. Stuttgart.

Sutton, M. (1990), 'A Prince Transformed: The Grimms' "Froschkönig" in English', *Seminar* 24.2, 119-37.

Tatar, M. (1987), *The Hard Facts of the Grimms' Fairy Tales.* Princeton.

Taylor, E. (1979) trans., *Grimms' Fairy Tales,* illustrated by George Cruikshank, reproduced in facsimile from first English edn. 2 vols. London.

Zipes, J. (2000) ed., *The Oxford Companion to Fairy Tales.* Oxford.

Abbreviations

AT Aarne-Thompson

KHM Grimms' *Kinder- und Hausmärchen*

CHARLES DICKENS

Shirley Grob (essay date winter 1964)

SOURCE: Grob, Shirley. "Dickens and Some Motifs of the Fairy Tale." *Texas Studies in Literature and Language* 5, no. 4 (winter 1964): 567-79.

[*In the following essay, Grob surveys Dickens's various uses of fairy-tale plots and imagery in his works.*]

Dickens' confession in an 1853 issue of *Household Words* that he entertained "a very great tenderness for the fairy literature" of his childhood is not likely to come as much of a surprise to his readers.[1] Casual references to this literature—particularly to the Arabian Nights—brighten the pages of almost every novel and testify concretely to his belief that in "an utilitarian age, of all other times, it is a matter of grave importance that fairy tales should be respected."[2] More importantly, both character and plot in Dickens owe something to this primitive form of fiction. Critics unresponsive to the magic of "story" and interested only in clinical reactions describe Dickens' good and bad characters as "monsters"[3] of virtue and villainy, but countless readers have happily recognized that Mr. Pickwick, as he sets out "walking to the end of the world,"[4] or Little Nell, as she makes her way "untouched and unstained"[5] through the perils of the enchanted wood, retain some likeness to the prince and princess of the fairy tale. Dickens deliberately generates the greatest amount of external conflict possible by following the simple fairy-tale formula of pitting the smallest boy against the greatest giant or the gentlest girl against the wickedest witch. Similarly, his plots are ordered with a felicity and completeness found only in the fairy world. Just as the grateful fox who was spared by the kind young hero reappears at the end of the fairy tale to assist the hero in delivering the castle from an evil spell, so the seemingly unrelated elements in Dickens' plots eventually come together in the way most likely to please the reader.

This kind of hidden relatedness is also characteristic of the plot of many eighteenth-century novels and Elizabethan plays and romances, but Dickens' novels are particularly close to the spirit of the fairy tale in their concern for the underdog. In the fairy tale it is always the younger brother who wins the fortune, the ugly duckling who becomes the swan, and the poor goose girl who marries the prince and lives happily ever after. To Dickens these victories against impossible odds are always moral victories, and in his article on the fairy tale in *Household Words* he claims that

> It would be hard to estimate the amount of Gentleness and Mercy that has made its way among us through these slight channels. Forbearance, Courtesy, Consideration for the Poor and Aged, Kind Treatment of Animals, Love of Nature, Abhorrence of Tyranny and Brute Force—many such good things have been first nourished in the child's heart by this powerful aid.[6]

This is undeniably a somewhat idealized impression of the fairy tale, as any adult who returns to them for the first time since childhood can affirm, but it is central to an understanding of Dickens' use of this material to recognize that this *is* his impression. Actually the same fairy tale is likely to contain elements from savage tribes, barbaric civilizations, and Christian societies; so that shockingly cruel customs, Eastern magic, and Christian virtues may be inextricably intertwined. Thus the underdog hero of the fairy tale may succeed, as Dickens suggests, by virtue of his moral superiority; but he may also succeed by luck, magic, physical strength, or even by cunning (as in the Puss-in-Boots cycle where the hero obtains riches by fraud and lying).

At any rate, Dickens particularly delights in such morally edifying fairy-tale favorites as "the ill-treated child," "the wicked step-parent," "the proud princess," and "the good bear," but the type which I should like to consider in the most detail is that of the man or woman who has some of the attributes and performs some of the functions of the benevolent fairy godmother. Such characters are present in Dickens all the way from *The Pickwick Papers* to *Our Mutual Friend,* but Dickens is not, of course, a static artist and the use he makes of this type changes correspondingly as his vision darkens and his methods mature. Moreover, the "fairy godmothers" are related to the running conflict in Dickens between self-responsible work and elective grace as the

most desirable means of fulfilling "great expectations";[7] but they have not been discussed in any very systematic way or with much attention to their fairy-tale ancestry. I have no "expectations" of arriving at any very original conclusions regarding Dickens' changing beliefs, but I should like to suggest the "fairy godmother" as one convenient, and sometimes illuminating, perspective from which to view these changes. And in *Our Mutual Friend* we shall see how Dickens' partial return to his earliest manner in the handling of fairy-tale motifs contributes to the lack of intellectual and artistic unity in the novel.

The Good Rich Man who cheers his corner of the world by the simple expedient of distributing gold at the end of the novel is primarily a phenomenon of Dickens' early optimistic period. This generous *deus ex machina,* represented by such figures as Pickwick, the Cheerybles, old Chuzzlewit, and Scrooge, is compositely described by Orwell as a "superhumanly kindhearted old gentleman who 'trots' to and fro, raising his employees' wages, patting children on the head, getting debtors out of jail, and, in general, acting the fairy godmother."[8] "Acting the fairy godmother" is an accurate description of the function of such characters, but Dickens has not yet begun to make much use of their fairy-tale associations. Indeed, old Martin Chuzzlewit is reminiscent of the "crusty old man with heart of gold" common in Eighteenth century novels.

It is not until *David Copperfield* that Dickens begins to exploit the fairy tale. "The ill-treated child who runs away from his stepmother" (fairy-tale fathers invariably make appalling mistakes in choosing their second wives) and "the young man who seeks his fortune" are two basic fairy-tale situations which are often fused in the novel, particularly in the so-called novel of education. David Copperfield then has some resemblance to all the sensitive young men who, as Trilling has put it, inevitably go through a "Tunnel of Horrors" in early life but, almost as inevitably, "come out safely at the other end."[9] But David's story is more closely related to the fairy tale than to the usual *Bildungsroman,* for young David sees the world as a place of ogres and good fairies, and, more importantly, he has a private fairy godmother who helps him out of the "tunnel."

Dickens is particularly skillful at giving a sense of the way the world looks to a child. One of his devices is the repeated use of fairy-tale imagery to suggest the intensity of childhood impressions. Children seldom see people as commonplace, so that somewhat uncommon persons become in their eyes exaggeratedly so. David consoles himself, while living under the Murdstone tyranny, by "impersonating" his favorite adventure story and fairy-tale characters and by "putting Mr. and Miss Murdstone into all the bad ones."[10] David himself is generally Tom Jones, Roderick Random, or Captain

Somebody, but he sees the people he loves and hates as fairy-tale figures. Mr. and Miss Murdstone are obviously the "ogres" of the piece, the schoolmaster is a "giant in a story-book," (89) Rose Dartle is a "cruel princess," (667) Uriah Heep is an "ugly and rebellious genie," (747) and Mrs. Heep is an "ill-looking enchantress." (571) Little Emily, Dora, and Agnes are all fairies or good spirits. Although the fairy-tale imagery decreases as David grows older (Agnes, for example, comes more and more to be his "good Angel"), (367) it reappears abundantly, even tiresomely, in connection with David's infatuation for the incurably childish Dora. Dora is an enchanting "Fairy," (390) being in love with Dora is like being "in Fairyland," (396) and speaking seriously to Dora makes one either "Blue Beard," (636) or a "Monster who had got into a Fairy's bower." (543)

The description of David's birth on the first page of the novel immediately introduces the themes of luck and enchantment. The baby is born at a late hour of a Friday night, an hour which augurs that he may be unlucky in life but that he will be privileged to see spirits; while, on the other hand, he is born with a lucky caul. The grown-up David claims to have seen no actual spirits, but he admits that his great-aunt, Miss Betsy Trotwood, reminds him of "one of those super-natural beings whom it was popularly supposed I was entitled to see." (12) The suddenness of Miss Betsy's first appearance, the imperiousness of her manner, and the abruptness of her departure are unmistakable signs of Miss Betsy's kinship with the fairy people. David's mother sits weeping before the fire like Cinderella at the hearth when, lifting her eyes, she sees through the window a strange lady who is touched by the glow of the setting sun. (4) With all the quaint unpredictability of such creatures, Miss Betsy peers in at the window before entering, makes the odd request that David's mother take off her cap so that she can see her, and announces that she intends to be the new baby girl's godmother. The new baby is a boy, and Miss Betsy silently puts on her bonnet and walks out of the house never to return, vanishing "like a discontented fairy." (12) Miss Betsy is certainly discontented, but she is not revengeful like the uninvited fairy in "Sleeping Beauty," who makes a wish that the infant Princess "shall prick herself with a distaff in her fifteenth year and fall down dead." Indeed there is a hint, in the best story-book manner, that Miss Betsy is very likely to turn out to be the good fairy. As David's mother sits hanging her head and weeping during the visit, she has "a fancy that she felt Miss Betsy touch her hair, and that with no ungentle hand; but looking at her, in her timid hope, she found that lady sitting with the skirt of her dress tucked up, her hands folded on one knee, and her feet upon the fender, frowning at the fire." (5) Later in the novel it is this "fancy," of which his mother had told him, that gives some faint encouragement to David in his desperate resolve to run away from the countinghouse of Murdstone and Grinby.

The ragged runaway has no sooner been put to rest on his aunt's sofa than there is a reception of this kind of moment:

> It might have been a dream, originating in the fancy which had occupied my mind so long, but I woke with the impression that my aunt had come and bent over me, and had put my hair away from my face, and laid my head more comfortably, and had then stood looking at me. The words, "Pretty fellow," or "Poor Fellow," seemed to be in my ears, too; but certainly there was nothing else, when I awoke, to lead me to believe that they had been uttered by my aunt, who sat in the bow-window gazing at the sea.
>
> (196)

It is an almost symbolic touch—the blessing of the good spirit, the wand of the fairy godmother. David remains anxious about what will be done with him, but it is all over for the reader, who knows quite well that Aunt Betsy is going to use her powers (which are really the resources of a good heart) to vanquish the wicked step-parents of the ill-treated child. The Murdstones loom gigantic to a frightened child, but when they appear in Miss Betsy's parlor "their physical strength, their awful visages, their hypocritical assumptions of respectability, are no match for the goodness and directness of one brave frail old woman."[11]

Later in the novel David's aunt temporarily loses her money, but by this point David is no longer an ill-treated child. If he is a fairy-tale figure at all, he is the young man who must perform impossible tasks for the hand of his fairy princess. On being faced with the necessity for earning money, David thinks of himself rather romantically as setting out to clear his way through the "forest of difficulty," (520) cutting down trees one by one until he shall come to Dora. The difficulties of shorthand become one "gnarled oak" (545) in the forest. The prince and princess do not quite live "happily ever after," but Dora obligingly leaves David to Agnes, with whom he does live happily. Indeed the only fully ironic play on the conventions of the fairy tale occurs when Miss Mowcher, skeptical of the disinterestedness of Steerforth's criticisms of Emily's suitor, answers slyly, "Quite a long story. Ought to end 'and they lived happily ever afterward,' oughtn't it?" (334)

With the exception of *Our Mutual Friend,* Dickens' tendency after *David Copperfield* is toward an increasingly ironic use of the fairy tale. Esther Summerson, for example, begins her narrative in *Bleak House* with the comment that she had been brought up "like some of the princesses in the fairy stories" (15) by her godmother; but this godmother, far from sending Esther to the ball in a golden coach, keeps her home from the birthday parties of other children with the comment "It would have been far better, little Esther, that you had had no birthday; that you had never been born." (17)

But at least the discovery of her disgrace—the illegitimacy of her birth—liberates her, as J. Hillis Miller points out, from false expectations and "forces her to assume full responsibility for her own life."[12]

Jarndyce is in some ways like the good rich man of the earlier novels, but he prefers helping his young charges into congenial professions to rescuing them from the necessity of earning a living. More importantly, if they persist in clinging to flimsy expectations, he is powerless to help them. Richard Carstone restlessly abandons surgery, the law, and the army, one after another, because "his blood is infected" (492) by the prospect of easy money from the settlement of "Jarndyce versus Jarndyce." Dickens is satirizing Chancery, of course, but he does not exonerate Richard from lack of self-discipline. Martin Chuzzlewit, it will be remembered, had also "been bred up from childhood with great expectations," (93) and, like Richard, is unable to make a go of his profession; but as soon as he learns a lesson in unselfishness, he is rescued and rewarded by the rich old man who has been anxiously watching over him. The biographical basis of *David Copperfield* makes one hesitate to call this novel the turning point in Dickens' attitude toward self-responsible work versus elective grace (good rich men, fairy godmothers, wills, etc.) as the most desirable means of getting money, but there is some change in the latter part of the novel, for the grown-up David lectures on the value of "steady, plain, hard-working qualities" (606) while his aunt commends him for coming out of their trial "persevering, self-reliant and self-denying." (776) Richard's trial, on the other hand, ends only with his death, and his whole career is a depressing process of mental and physical deterioration.

Great Expectations is both Dickens' most serious exploration of the theme of "expectations" and his most ironic (and sophisticated) use of the conventions of the fairy tale. Modern commentators have justly praised the discipline which Dickens exercises in this novel in subordinating everything to the central theme of innocence, false expectations, selfishness, disillusionment, and redemptive suffering. Similarly, in his use of fairy-tale material, Dickens exercises rigorous selection, and one of the minor ways he reworks some of the materials of *David Copperfield* is to eliminate all merely decorative or incidental fairy-tale images. The three or four fairy-tale references in *Great Expectations* are carefully selected to provide highly ironic commentary on the theme of "expectations."

Young Pip soothes his wounded feelings and thwarts the vulgar curiosity of his sister and uncle by telling extravagant lies about his visit to Satis House, but he has seen for himself that Miss Havisham has some mysterious connection with death. Although his first impression was of richness and splendor, he had seen, after a moment, that everything in the room was faded and withered, "that everything had stopped, like the watch and the clock, a long time ago." (55) Pip finds Miss Havisham "perfectly incomprehensible"; (61) but, on his second visit, when he is taken to see the cobwebby bridal cake inhabited by splotchy spiders, he finds a name for her out of the fairy-tale books. He calls her "the Witch of the place." (79) Pip can not yet know the accuracy of his designation, for Miss Havisham's neurotic desire to mold a heartless beauty who will break the hearts of the men who love her is only a refinement of the traditional witch practice of bewitching children in order to eat their hearts; but at least he recognizes that she is bad. After Pip acquires his "expectations," his moral values deteriorate so that he is not able, or does not want to be able, to tell good from bad. On his way to London to take up his new station in life, Pip stops at Satis House to say good-by to Miss Havisham. She is again leaning on her crutch-stick, but this time Pip sees it, not as the stick of a witch, but as the wand of a fairy godmother. In painful contrast to his restrained parting from Joe and Biddy, Pip goes down on his knees to kiss Miss Havisham's hand:

> She stretched out her hand, and I went down on my knee and put it to my lips. . . . She looked at Sarah Pocket with triumph in her weird eyes, and so I left my fairy godmother, with both her hands on her crutch stick, standing in the midst of the dimly lighted room.
>
> (149)

A comparison of Betsy Trotwood and Miss Havisham as fairy godmothers is a good measure of Dickens' tighter control over his materials and his greater interest in theme. Miss Betsy has a past, but it is not very important to her role as a fairy godmother (except in so far as we would *not* expect her to help David). It is not very important in explaining her character, for it may have bearing on her outward abruptness of manner but surely has no connection with her other eccentricities like her fear of fire or her objection to donkeys. Indeed, Miss Betsy's past does not come to light until she has ceased to be important as a character, and it is used primarily as an illustration of the theme of the "undisciplined heart" (661) which dominates the latter part of the novel. Miss Havisham, fantastic as she may be, is all of a piece, for every detail of her character takes its meaning from the most shattering event of her past. She is half-mad, but her madness has made her an artist, for in fashioning Estella into a breaker of hearts and in making her own life into an unrelieved "reproach"[13] to the man who jilted her, she is an inspired creator and a brilliantly false fairy godmother.

But the deepest irony of the novel comes not from the false fairy godmother, but from the true one. Miss Havisham, judged as a fairy godmother, simply reverses the fairy tale by seeking to frustrate the wishes of others;

but Abel Magwitch, as a socially unacceptable "fairy godmother" creates a problem foreign to fairy-tale literature.[14] In this primitive form of fiction the swineherd of natural nobility may become king by a stroke of good fortune with no questions asked. In "The Golden Goose," for a typical example, a mistreated youngest son shares his cake and wine with a little old gray man he meets in the wood. As a consequence of his good deed, he receives a golden goose, which eventually enables him to marry the king's daughter and inherit the kingdom. The old man's identity is not important. Pip, on the other hand, loses his natural goodness when he moves up in society, and he is snobbishly horrified when he learns that his "golden goose" was sent to him by a crude convict in gratitude for some wine and a pork pie. It is not, of course, until Pip learns to love the convict, accept the limitations of his place in society, and assume full responsibility for his own life that he becomes a gentleman in the true sense.

Our Mutual Friend I should like to consider in somewhat more detail, for the full extent of Dickens' use of fairy-tale motifs in this novel has not, I think, been commented on. The novel has been described both as Dickens' Wasteland and as his Indian summer, as the "darkest and bitterest"[15] of his novels and as a return to his "merrier and more normal manner."[16] Surely it is something of both, for the characters who compose the two main lines of plot—(1) Bella Wilfer-John Harmon-Noddy Boffin, and (2) Lizzie Hexam-Eugene Wrayburn-Bradley Headstone—are denizens of two different and really irreconcilable worlds. The theme of materialism, brought out most clearly perhaps in a third group of characters who bear the brunt of the social satire (Mr. Podsnap, Lady Tippins, Fledgeby, the Lammles, the Veneerings), is common to both strands of plot, but the treatment and implications are quite unlike. Recent critics tend to emphasize the darker side of the novel, the vision of vulturism. Society, from the slimy scavengers of the Thames underworld to the parasites of high society, is a swamp of "crawling, creeping, fluttering and buzzing creatures, attracted by the gold dust" (209) of the Harmon mounds. But muddy water does not trickle through all the pages of the novel, and the Bella-John-Boffin story is treated, with a surprising absence of irony, in the manner of the fairy story. Thus, elements from both Dickens' early and his late visions of society and the world are present in the novel, but I can not see that there is what has been called an intellectual and artistic "synthesis of his developing insight throughout a lifetime."[17]

Noddy Boffin does not perhaps look much like a fairy godmother, but as the agent responsible for raising Bella from "rags to riches," he fulfills something of this function. He might, of course, be called a final example of the Good Rich Man who appeared in some of the earlier novels, but, although he does not seem to be based on a specific fairy-tale figure (both he and Bella are composite types), the plot lines, the stock incidents, and the imagery suggest that he is of fairy-tale ancestry. Boffin's title immediately suggests the gold motif common to the fairy tale, but the "Golden Dustman" is no descendant of King Midas, for he knows too well the difference between the tarnished gold of misers and the "true golden gold" (773) of the generous heart. Mr. and Mrs. Boffin formulate two plans for doing good with their inheritance. They will adopt an orphan child (they have wished for a child "like the Kings and Queens in the Fairy Tales," (103) and they will try to bring true the "wishes" (112) of the girl who was disappointed of her riches.

Bella is often praised by commentators as a refreshing change from such monsters of virtue as Florence Dombey, Agnes Wickfield, and Esther Summerson, and so she is; but her portrait does not seem to me to have the psychological depth which distinguishes Bradley Headstone as a change from the usual monster of villainy. Her greediness is a "given" of the story which is as easily rooted out as the flaw in the character of any beautiful fairy-tale princess. Her initial selfishness has been intensified by her position in the will of old John Harmon, but her greediness is seldom put in a social context and she does not really impress one as trying "to keep up with" the Podsnaps, the Lammles, and the Veneerings. She longs for "money, money, money" (460) but the few times her longings take concrete form they are of an exotic nature—as when she thinks of sailing along coral reefs in the company of an Indian prince who has emeralds blazing on his turban. (319) The unmistakable fairy-tale touch, however, is Bella's tendency to ask questions of her looking glass like the proud queen in "Snow White and the Seven Dwarfs," who asks her magic mirror "Looking glass upon the wall / Who is the fairest of us all?"

Certainly there is a strong element of the incredible in the stratagem devised by Mr. Boffin and John Harmon for curing Bella of her greediness. Posing as a "regular brown bear" or "grisly old growler," (773) Mr. Boffin is somewhat reminiscent of all the tales like "Beauty and the Beast" or "Snow-White and Rose-Red" in which the hero is freed of his beast- or bear-covering when the heroine exhibits the requisite virtue. John, who has been posing all along as a poor man in order to test whether Bella can love him for himself, is more closely related to such stories as "The Swineherd" or "King Thrushbeard." In the latter, for example, the father of a haughty, but beautiful, princess, who scorns all her suitors, decides that his daughter shall marry the next beggar who knocks at the door. The beggar, who is really one of her old suitors in disguise, forces her to do the dirty work of the kitchen and to sell crockery in the marketplace. When the princess learns to regret her old pride and haughtiness, the beggar reveals himself as

King Thrushbeard and explains, "for love of you I disguised myself . . . all this I did to bend your proud spirit and to punish you for the haughtiness with which you mocked me." The princess now feels she is not worthy to be his wife, but the King answers, "Be Happy! Those evil days are over. Now we will celebrate our wedding." Surely it is in such a spirit that we must read Bella's story if we are to believe that Bella does not mind having been deceived by her husband during her courtship, engagement, and the entire first year of her marriage, or that she does not mind having been subjected to an elaborate character test. Indeed, the whole episode of Bella's married life savors of the mysterious marriage tabus of primitive societies which have been preserved in fairy tales. Bella, for example, does not know her husband's real name and must never ask the reason of anything he does. One of the most famous of the fairy tales based on a primitive tabu, this time the religious tabu of the sacred enclosure, is "Bluebeard," and John admits that he does have a "secret chamber" (745) but that Bella must demonstrate perfect faith in him.

Moreover, the fairy-tale atmosphere of the Bella-John-Boffin story is reinforced by a quantity of fairy-tale imagery almost as great as in *David Copperfield,* where it is used to suggest the child's viewpoint. The little engagement supper celebrated by Bella, John, and Mr. Wilfer in the countinghouse of Chicksey, Veneering, and Stobbles is described three times as a supper of "three nursery hobgoblins at their house in the forest." (609) The wedding party, on the other hand, is somewhat more exotic with golden drinks from the Golden Age and fish from the *Arabian Nights.* (668) And, appropriately, the only anxiety of the wedding party had been the thought that perhaps Bella's mother might suddenly appear "like the spiteful Fairy at the christening of the Princesses, to do something dreadful to the marriage service." (665) But Bella's marriage is not jinxed and she assures John that his tender regard means as much to her "as the wishes in the fairy story that were all fulfilled as soon as spoken." (680) Even concrete objects, in keeping with the general atmosphere, hint delicately of the fairy tale—the rich dresses left behind when Bella flees down Boffin's great staircase, (601-602) the shoes that are a full size too large for Bella's little feet, (681) the lock of hair given to her father. (662)

But perhaps the most telling distinction between the atmosphere of Bella's romance and the atmosphere of Lizzie Hexam's romance is the more romantic handling of social status. Bella is raised *up* by the Boffins but it is hard to say what she has been raised up to. Mr. Boffin considers Henrietta Boffin to be a "high-flyer at Fashion" (55) and Lady Tippins leaves a card, but it requires quite an act of the imagination to think of the Boffins as really belonging to any social class. Even

John Harmon's social status is not as clear as that of Eugene Wrayburn and it is reckoned in golden coins and sparkling jewels rather than family and visiting cards. Lizzie, of course, is raised from a much lower position than Bella to a higher one; but, as she has a kind of natural nobility, this in no way precludes a more romantic treatment of her story. She is, however, treated realistically. As the uneducated Cinderella of an unidealized world, she finds it somewhat painful to leap from class to class. She is eventually married to Eugene and in the final distribution of nosegays receives even the blessing of Eugene's "Reverend Father," but there is certainly considerable indication, as Boll points out in an article on the plotting of the novel,[18] that Dickens has geared the story for an unhappy ending with the death of Eugene. At any rate, love cannot silence the voice of Society, stupid as that voice may be, and Eugene has to become something of a hero, resolutely turning his back on the idea of taking his wife out to the colonies to escape the sneers of Podsnap and Lady Tippins.

The conclusion of the novel shows Dickens at his least responsible, for he does not seem able to resist showering riches on everyone in sight. Bella has been primarily the haughty princess who loses her false values and repudiates the golden coach of the Golden Dustman to walk with the muddy street sweeper, (599) but Dickens has been eagerly waiting to make her Cinderella again. Compared to Esther's new cottage at the end of *Bleak House,* Bella's new house is Aladdin's palace. Indeed there are echoes of the *Arabian Nights* in the description of the ivory casket of jewels on Bella's toilette table or the "charming aviary, in which a number of tropical birds, more gorgeous in color than the flowers, were flying about; and among those birds were gold and silver fish, and mosses and water-lilies, and a fountain, and all manner of wonders." (767) John, far from being a street sweeper (or a secretary or a China House employee for that matter), is again a rich man through the generosity of Mr. Boffin. The money seems rightfully his, of course, but the delight Dickens takes in dissolving the China House forever is an indication of the way Dickens appears, in this strand of the novel, to have returned full circle to his earliest position on the related matters of work, money, and expectations. But the passage which seems almost like self-parody on Dickens' part is the one in which John and Bella, having taken over the fortune from Mr. Boffin, play at being fairy godmothers themselves and bestow money on every underdog remotely associated with them:

> In tracing out affairs for which John's fictitious death was to be considered in any way responsible, they used a very broad and free construction; regarding, for instance, the dolls' dressmaker as having a claim on their protection, because of her association with Mrs. Eugene Wrayburn, and because of Mrs. Eugene's old association, in her turn, with the dark side of the story. It

followed that the old man, Riah, as a good and service-able friend to both, was not to be disclaimed. Nor even Mr. Inspector, as having been trepanned into an indus-trious hunt on a false scent.

(803)

There is, however, one place in the novel where the grim world of the Thames waterside and the golden world of the fairy tale make contact, for there is yet a third "Cinderella" in the person of Miss Jenny Wren. The little dolls' dressmaker does not look at first glance like Cinderella, for she is a queer little person of inde-terminate age with a deformed body and a drunken fa-ther. Moreover, she is not an angel of patience, and Dickens does not shrink from revealing the bitterness and sharpness which the circumstances of her life have created in her. But Jenny has another side which these realities have not been able to crush completely, a side represented visually by her long golden hair, and men-tally by her shining visions of a better world where children are never chilled, anxious, ragged, or in pain. In his working notebook for *Our Mutual Friend,* Dick-ens sums up these two sides of the dolls' dressmaker as "her earthy side and her imaginative side."[19] Jenny does not escape from this life. She works incessantly and meets her responsibilities with all the resources of her deformed body, but the secret of her endurance, of her ability to cope with the grimness of her life, is her "imaginative side." One of the first things we learn about her is that her real name is Fanny Cleaver but that "she had long ago chosen to bestow upon herself the appellation of Miss Jenny Wren." (234) Similarly, she chooses to think of herself as her father's parent rather than as his neglected child, because in choosing the situation and accepting the responsibility for it, she can live with it. As Miller points out, the act of chang-ing a situation into "an imaginative version of itself is a way of dealing with it."[20]

It is some such consolation and encouragement which Jenny and the gentle Jew, Riah, derive from referring to each other as "Cinderella" and "fairy godmother," a ritual which prevents their best selves from being to-tally submerged in their material environment. The fairy tale, Dickens claims in *Household Words,* helps "keep us, in some sense, ever young, by preserving through our worldly ways one slender track not overgrown with weeds."[21] *Our Mutual Friend* lacks artistic unity be-cause it tries to fuse two worlds which are governed by different laws, but the pleasure which Jenny takes in re-garding her crutch-stick (the sign of her infirmity) as the wand of her fairy godmother (434) suggests that Dickens has not lost sight of the value of the type of novel which he began his career by writing. It is, of course, a more limited kind of literature than the dark complex novels of Dickens' last phase, but there is something eternally refreshing to the human spirit in the ritual fairy-tale triumph of the hero and heroine over the forces of darkness.

Notes

1. Charles Dickens, "Frauds on the Fairies," *House-hold Words,* VIII (October, 1853), p. 97.

2. *Ibid.*

3. Eugene Goodheart, "Dickens' Method of Charac-terization," *The Dickensian,* LIV (1958), p. 35.

4. G. K. Chesterton, *Charles Dickens: The Last of the Great Men* (New York, 1942), p. 67.

5. Edgar Johnson, *Charles Dickens: His Tragedy and Triumph* (New York, 1952), I, 325.

6. "Frauds on the Fairies," *Household Words,* p. 97.

7. The fullest and most recent discussion of this topic may be found in J. Hillis Miller, *Charles Dickens: The World of his Novels* (Cambridge, 1959).

8. George Orwell, "Charles Dickens," *A Collection of Essays by George Orwell* (New York, 1954), p. 59.

9. Lionel Trilling, *E. M. Forster* (Norfolk, 1943), p. 79.

10. *David Copperfield,* p. 56. All quotations from the novels are from *The New Oxford Illustrated Dick-ens* (London, n.d.).

11. E. K. Browne, "David Copperfield," *Yale Review,* XXXVII (June, 1948), p. 659.

12. Miller, *Charles Dickens: The World of His Novels,* p. 332.

13. *Ibid.,* p. 258.

14. Harry Stone, in an admirable analysis of the mythical elements of "Fire, Hand, and Gate in *Great Expectations," The Kenyon Review,* XXIV (1962), pp. 676-677, suggests that Magwitch ful-fills not only the role of fairy godmother but that of the beast in "Beauty and the Beast."

15. Johnson, *Charles Dickens: His Tragedy and Tri-umphs,* II, 1043.

16. Chesterton, *Charles Dickens: The Last of the Great Men,* p. 168.

17. Johnson, *Charles Dickens: His Tragedy and Tri-umph,* II, 1041.

18. Ernest Boll, "The Plotting of *Our Mutual Friend," Modern Philology,* XLII (1944), p. 101.

19. *Ibid.,* p. 107.

20. Miller, *Charles Dickens: The World of His Novels,* p. 308.

21. "Frauds on the Fairies," *Household Words,* p. 97.

Harry Stone (essay date 1966)

SOURCE: Stone, Harry. "The Novel as Fairy Tale: Dickens' *Dombey and Son*." *English Studies* 47, no. 1 (1966): 1-27.

[In the following essay, Stone analyzes the elements of fairy-tale sensibility and imagery in Dickens's novel, Dombey and Son.]

If one reads Dickens' novels chronologically, one is astonished, upon beginning *Dombey and Son* (1847-48), to find that Dickens has achieved a totally new mastery. The first half of *Dombey* is almost perfect in conception and execution; each scene connects with the next, each throws light on what has come before and what is yet to come. Dickens calls up intricate themes and images, develops them, sustains them, and finally merges them with one another. He introduces experimental techniques—the child's point of view, the microcosmic world of servants and tradesmen as chorus—and does so with great assurance. But most important, he masters a new structural method which fuses autobiography, psychology, symbolism, and fairy-tale fancy.

This startling mastery, hardly hinted at in his six earlier novels, was advanced by a variety of circumstances. The two-year hiatus in novel writing which occurred between the completion of *Martin Chuzzlewit* (1843-44) and the beginning of *Dombey*—for Dickens an unprecedented pause—gave him his first real chance for leisurely observation and stocktaking since he had begun to write. He found that both he and his age were in a period of transition. What he now saw was the new iron era with its *sui generis* miseries, dislocations, and diminishments, a state of disorder paralleled by disturbing changes going on within himself. He was beginning to grow disenchanted with the fruits of success, and he had already begun to anatomize his mounting restlessness and unhappiness. He was also gaining a new objectivity and cosmopolitanism. He lived on the continent for almost half the four years between the completion of *Chuzzlewit* and the completion of *Dombey*. The vantage point of Italy and Switzerland enabled him to view the new English society—the commercial-industrial society about which he would now write—with a critical detachment.

But above all, the years between *Chuzzlewit* and the completion of *Dombey* provided him with unique opportunities for literary experimentation. In the Christmas books he wrote during that interval (*A Christmas Carol* [1843], *The Chimes* [1845], *The Cricket on the Hearth* [1846], *The Battle of Life* [1847], and *The Haunted Man* [1848]—the last conceived and partly written in the interval, but not finished until *Dombey* was completed) he had five opportunities to experiment with structure, symbol, and subject matter, to manipulate in exceptionally fluid and foreshortened form old elements which had troubled him, and new elements he had not yet used or mastered. The Christmas books, as I have demonstrated elsewhere, profoundly altered his artistic methods. And when he came to write his first post-Christmas-book novel, he adapted the techniques that had served him so well in the Christmas books. That he did so is not surprising. The first chapters of *Dombey* were written in Switzerland in the midst of planning and writing *The Battle of Life* and formulating *The Haunted Man*. As he worked on *Dombey,* therefore, his mind was preoccupied with devices and patterns, primarily cohesive in nature, which were helping him integrate the Christmas books. His problem in *Dombey* was almost identical. For in *Dombey,* as in the Christmas books, he self-consciously set out to blend autobiography, social criticism, story-telling, and fairy tales; as he put it, he was taking fairy tales and 'giving them a higher form'.

Dickens was using the term fairy tales in an idiosyncratic way; he was giving a convenient label to his special fusion of fairy story, fantasy, myth, magic, and folklore. He had created this blend out of materials familiar to him from childhood, out of the Gothic novel, the ghost story, the melodrama, the pantomime, the 'Ancient Mariner' type of ballad, the Bunyanesque allegory, and the moral tract, as well as the fairy tale. But for Dickens all these elements were aspects of his suprarational view of life; he found such elements congenial because they touched his imagination, an imagination formed and sensitized by the logic and fancy of fairy tales. Following Dickens' authority, therefore, the term fairy tale may be used (and it will be so used in this essay) to designate this crucial confluence in his writings.

To see how fundamentally the fairy tale shapes *Dombey and Son,* one must keep in mind its central plot, and then isolate its deftly integrated social, autobiographical, psychological, and fairy-tale strands; and one must also remember that Dickens, buttressed by his Christmas-book experiments, set out to do something he had never attempted before in a novel: to write a realistic story on the most up-to-date subject matter, a story which would be a detailed social and psychological analysis of the Victorian businessman, and yet, at the same time, be a magical fable of contemporary life.

Dombey and Son centers about the relationship of Mr. Dombey and his unloved daughter, Florence. Mr. Dombey is a cold, proud, self-centered business baron. He is not a bad man, but wealth and authority have made him arrogant, and his single passion is to see the great shipping and trading firm of Dombey and Son perpetuated once more by a male heir. Mr. Dombey is certain that money can buy everything—everything, that is, but perhaps a son—and when six years after

Florence's birth his wife dies in giving birth to a son, Mr. Dombey's thoughts cluster obsessively about his infant heir. The book opens with the birth of Paul and the death of Mrs. Dombey, and the huge novel which follows is designed to explore Mr. Dombey's parental sin and to humble him and shatter his money ethic. Mr. Dombey's sin is his rejection of the freely offered love of his daughter; he must come to realize that what Florence yearns to give him is a gift more valuable than anything money can buy. He must also learn that love can never be bought; that to be loved, one must love, and one must allow oneself to be loved. This theme, fresh in Dickens' day, has become hackneyed through much imitation (one recalls nineteenth-century examples such as George Eliot's *Silas Marner* or twentieth-century examples such as D. H. Lawrence's 'The Rocking-Horse Winner'), but Dickens' exploration of the theme, even after a century of recapitulations, is moving and illuminating.

Mr. Dombey's harrowing is thorough. At first he merely neglects timid Florence, but gradually he grows envious of her, then jealous of the love she inspires in others, and finally baffled and guilty, he hates her as the symbol of his own failure to inspire love. Dickens sets forth the father-daughter relationship at great length and with great subtlety. Mr. Dombey emerges from the book, in spite of a number of scenes which are unbearably painful, not as a villain, but as a helpless victim of his personality and the new times, as a lonely, bewildered, money-centered man, to be pitied rather than hated.

The humbling of Mr. Dombey is pointed up by a series of key episodes. The first inkling Mr. Dombey has that his money ethic may be wanting occurs when tiny Paul asks him (as Paul in 'The Rocking-Horse Winner' asks his mother) what money is and what it can do. Mr. Dombey (again like the mother in 'The Rocking-Horse Winner') is nonplussed by the question—he himself had always thought of money and its value as beyond examination—and he answers Paul in terms of his faith. 'Money, Paul', he says, 'can do anything.' 'Why', then asks Paul, 'didn't money save my mamma?' The question is not sentimental, and it echoes through the remainder of the book. For Paul, with his strange fairy-tale prescience, intuitively perceives what his father must learn through disappointment and suffering; and when the little boy unwittingly emphasizes that money cannot buy life, he is foreshadowing his own death a few years later. That death is the first crushing lesson in Mr. Dombey's painful education, but it brings him no closer to Florence. Paul had lavished all his love on his sister, and Paul's death intensifies Mr. Dombey's jealousy of that love and his resentment that his unwanted daughter lives while his son and the plans he had centered upon him perish.

But Mr. Dombey having failed to buy life seeks to buy love and thereby a new son. He buys Edith, a beautiful, accomplished woman who knows she is being bought, despises the marriage contract she enters into, yet accepts it as a fair bargain freely and openly arrived at. Edith is Mr. Dombey's female counterpart; she is proud, but she is not deluded by her pride as is Mr. Dombey, and it irritates him that she makes no pretence that their marriage is anything other than a commercial arrangement. Dickens lavishes much attention on this business courtship and marriage; he shows Mr. Dombey inquiring about the widowed Edith's fertility, testing her ability as an artist and a musician, and displaying his power to command her to perform and obey. The marriage soon degenerates into a humiliating contest of wills, and Mr. Dombey watches in growing frustration as Edith, like Paul, gives Florence the love she withholds from him. Mr. Dombey, in his pride, still cannot comprehend why this is so, and Florence's shy but still-offered love is now rejected as the cause of his misery. Florence, as he had dreaded many years before, has at last become hateful to him. He now looks upon her as a nemesis, a reminder of the insufficiency of his money and his mastery. Florence, in turn, feels guilty because her father rejects her. She has been a stranger to him since childhood, has long since become timid and inarticulate in his presence, yearns to discover the magic formula which will make him love her, and upbraids herself for not having won his love. Edith's position in the household at last becomes unbearable, and she agrees to run off with Carker, Mr. Dombey's trusted business manager. When the scandal of Edith's flight descends bolt-like upon Mr. Dombey, Florence rushes to him, her timidity overcome by love and pity, but he strikes her; and alienated at last, she flees from the house.

Mr. Dombey's proud world of money and power is now fast crumbling. Money has not saved his son, restrained his manager, bound his wife, or secured his daughter. When the neglected firm of Dombey and Son fails also, the world wags on with clucking tongue, the showy vanities of Mr. Dombey's wealth are auctioned off as an ironic reminder of what money can and cannot do, and his bought servants march out of his house in self-righteous indignation. Mr. Dombey can no longer delude himself; stripped of every defense, he must see himself as he really is. What he does see horrifies him, and tortured by the perversity of personality and values which have brought ruin to himself and those closest to him, he decides to kill himself. He is saved by the return of Florence, and after a long illness (symbolic of the death of the old Dombey and the birth of a new chastened Dombey) he is shown briefly in the humbled twilight of his life.

But *Dombey* is much more than a domestic novel. The full title of the book is *Dealings with the Firm of Dombey and Son, Wholesale, Retail and for Exportation*. The title, even when interpreted ironically as intended, emphasizes the centrality of the social or business aspects of the story. These aspects are not limited to tracing the bankruptcy of Mr. Dombey's money ethic, important as this feature is. Dickens wished to underscore the deleterious tendencies in the new industrial order, and by depicting those tendencies in their multiplicity—in relation to machines, methods, persons—show their danger and their destructiveness. The real villain of *Dombey and Son* is the soullessness of the new business world; the most condensed emblem of that world is the manager Carker—clever, compulsive, ruthless, amoral—a representative of the new anonymous power breed.

The business theme, as we shall see, is wedded in Christmas-book fashion to the fairy-tale and autobiographical aspects of the story. And like these other aspects, the business theme is developed by contrast. Sol Gills' nautical instrument shop is a perfect counterpart to the great Dombey firm, for Sol's business, like Dombey's, takes its living from the sea. But while Dombey's firm prospers, Sol sits forlornly amid his instruments, watching the tide of commerce sweep by his door. Sol's business is beyond repair (he is saved at the end by investments which, in fairy-tale fashion, suddenly pour gold into his pocket), but his shop is a place of healing refuge where the simple, the good, and the uncorrupted can congregate and take strength from one another. To it come Captain Cuttle, Toots, and Susan Nipper, and finally Florence and Walter.

Dombey's empire is flourishing, but Dickens, again using parallel construction to underline and integrate his themes, makes Dombey's business, in contrast to Gills', a source of infection. Walter (in his role as originally planned), Carker's brother, Rob the Grinder, and other characters illustrate this blighting influence. Two segments of the business theme—the Toodles (a group of minor characters), and the railroad—will demonstrate how carefully Dickens was now elaborating his Christmas-book method, and how skilfully he was using it to integrate social, symbolic, and fanciful themes.

Rob the Grinder, for instance, is a Toodle gone wrong, a Toodle touched by the Dombeian business infection. But there are many other Toodles, and they also elucidate *Dombey*'s business fable. The Toodles are the new proletariat, clothed in the garb of their calling (Mr. Toodle is covered by the dirt and cinders of his railroad occupation even as Rob is branded by his Grinder uniform), taking their sustenance from the new world of business, but also contributing to that world and essential to it. Mr. Dombey in his pride refuses to recognize the latter fact; he only acknowledges the Toodles' dependency and servitude. It is one of the defects of the new business world (and an element in Mr. Dombey's harrowing) that this relationship—in effect the relationship between capital and labor—has not been humanely established.

How Mr. Dombey regards this relationship is apparent in the domestic as well as the industrial focus of the story. At the beginning of the book, Mr. Dombey hires Rob's mother, Polly Toodle, to nurse motherless Paul. Paul, symbolically, must take his sustenance from lower-class Polly, his very life depends upon her bounty and good will; the milk which turns into his blood and sinews emphasizes the commonalty of rich and poor, their symbiotic relationship. But for Mr. Dombey, placing Paul at Polly's breast is a degrading necessity, and in order to blur this necessity, he seeks to make the arrangement a mere matter of business. He emphasizes to Polly that her milk is only a commodity; he warns her against forming any attachments to Paul; and he even buys her name—replacing the plebian 'Toodle' with the businesslike 'Richards'.

But Mr. Dombey cannot entirely free his mind from the thought that Polly's Toodlish milk is contaminating his young son, and he has wild fears that this mixing process will go even farther, that Polly may substitute her own infant for his son. And a modern redaction of a fairy-tale changeling scene, a scene which emphasizes Mr. Dombey's money-centered obtuseness, does in fact occur. Paul is taken by Polly from his great rich nursery in Portland Place, Bryanstone Square, to Staggs' Gardens, the cindery slum where the Toodles live. The slum—and here Dickens begins to work intricate counterpoint on the Toodles, the railroads, and their many larger ramifications in the story—the slum is a wasteland, a landscape made hell-like by the new railroad which is being built in its environs.

The railroad landscape is doubly appropriate; it is an emblem of the new industrial order (and, as we shall see, of death) and the source of Mr. Toodle's livelihood. Paul, then, in being brought to the nether depths of the industrial world, is brought to the original source of his sustenance, an equivalence which is enforced whether one looks at that journey in terms of Polly's breast or of the new industrialism which undergirds his father's wealth. When Polly arrives home and sees her infant son in her sister's arms, she rushes forward and instantly exchanges him with Paul. She clutches her son to her breast, and the exchange Dombey feared occurs for the paradoxical reason that the lure of Dombeian wealth and advantage is not sufficient to make Polly forgo her motherhood. The exchange also emphasizes the essential equality of the infants, and by implication, despite the distance and outward distinction between Portland Place and Staggs' Gardens, and despite the fact that Polly is later dismissed for this lapse, the equality of all Dombeys and Toodles.

In the remainder of the book the Toodles reinforce the lessons of their earlier appearances. Dickens continues to show that an unfeeling ruling class sows the seeds of its own destruction. Whelplike Rob eventually becomes

Carker's tool and helps Carker run off with Edith. Rob's Dombey-engendered delinquency thus plays a part in Dombey's own ruin. Dombey's ruin comes at the end of the book, and when it comes we acknowledge its justice. For Dombey rebuffs every attempt to reach his humanity. On the industrial level of the story there are several such attempts. These attempts parallel Florence's strivings on the domestic level; they show that the businesslike aridity which withers Dombey's personal life, also withers all his other relationships, and ultimately (since Dombey is representative of the new ruling class) endangers the whole structure of Victorian society. This message is made very clear by scenes which further interweave Dombey, the Toodles, and the railroad, with Dickens' theme.

After Paul's death, when Dombey is waiting at the railway station for the train which will take him and Major Bagstock to Birmingham, he is approached by Mr. Toodle, the stoker of the train. Dombey fails to recognize him, then treats him with frosty haughtiness, and finally assumes that Toodle has approached him for money. Dombey can understand such an approach, but he cannot understand Toodle's real motivation. When Dombey discovers Toodle has come to commiserate with him, and wears mourning crepe, not for the death of one of his own children (Toodle assures Dombey they are flourishing in their usual apple-cheeked manner), but for Paul, Mr. Dombey is humiliated. Mr. Toodle's act of brotherhood, which again asserts the interdependence of Dombeys and Toodles and reawakens memories of Paul's nursing at Polly Toodle's breast, is intolerable to Mr. Dombey. He believes his money and position make him superior to Mr. Toodle; sonless Dombey never stops to think that Mr. Toodle possesses something which neither his money nor his position can buy. As a matter of fact, Mr. Dombey's train journey will emphasize this Dombeian obtuseness, for it will result in his meeting Edith, which in turn will lead to his disastrous attempt to buy her, and through her a son.

The symbolism here becomes extraordinarily rich. For after his colloquy with Mr. Toodle, Mr. Dombey is hurried toward his ruin on a train stoked by Mr. Toodle. Dombey's dependence on the Toodles and the new industrialism is absolute; ultimately, in generic terms, it is Toodle labor and machine power which insure Dombey's position and money. The train is an ambiguous industrial servant, rushing Dombey toward his desire, but since his industrial ethic is distorted, his desire is self-wounding, and the train hastens him toward his destruction: toward Edith and a money marriage, toward friction, scandal, and bankruptcy. For Toodle the railroad and the new industrialism mean salvation: the railroad gives him a livelihood and leads to advancement (he becomes an engineer, sends his children to school, learns to read, and so on).

As we have seen, this dual thesis, that an industrial society is symbiotic and that an individual reaps what he sows, has already been elaborated in the nursing and changeling episodes of the novel, but it is simultaneously elaborated by the railroad imagery—imagery which enters the novel and undergirds the business theme in three major integrating episodes. First we see the railroads being built and watch them change the face of the land. Here is the new Dombeian business world constructing its vital arteries and nerves:

> Everywhere were bridges that led nowhere; thoroughfares that were wholly impassable; Babel towers of chimneys, wanting half their height; temporary wooden houses and enclosures, in the most unlikely situations; carcases of ragged tenements, and fragments of unfinished walls and arches, and piles of scaffolding, and wildernesses of bricks, and giant forms of cranes, and tripods straddling above nothing. There were a hundred thousand shapes and substances of incompleteness.

This description of dislocation becomes more expressionistic as it goes on, until Dickens turns it into an image of hell: 'Hot springs and fiery eruptions . . . lent their contributions of confusion to the scene. Boiling water hissed and heaved within dilapidated walls; whence, also, the glare and roar of flames came issuing forth; and mounds of ashes blocked up rights of way, and wholly changed the law and custom of the neighbourhood.'

But if the railroad building is hell, the railroad built is death. In the next great railroad episode, the one in which Mr. Dombey converses with Mr. Toodle and then travels to Edith, Dickens makes this death identification explicit. The train forces 'itself upon its iron way—its own—defiant of all paths and roads, piercing through the heart of every obstacle, and dragging living creatures of all classes, ages, and degrees behind it . . . a type of the triumphant monster, Death.' The latter phrase, in Christmas-book fashion, is repeated with slight variations four times in the course of a two-page impressionistic description of a rapid rail journey, and becomes (along with imagery of the flowing seabound river—an ever more persistent death image in *Dombey*) the ominous motif of Mr. Dombey's headlong journey. Yet it is Dombey and what he stands for, not the railroad itself, which is the villain. Dickens emphasizes that 'as Mr. Dombey looks out of his carriage window, it is never in his thoughts that the monster who has brought him there has let the light of day in on these things [blight and misery]: not made or caused them.'

The symbolism is heightened and completed in the last great railroad episode of the book. This episode climaxes the magnificent flight chapter in which Carker, pursued by Dombey, flees through France to England, where he waits for the train which will take him to safety. The phantasmagoric flight has been punctuated—

again in Christmas-book fashion—by the reiterated leit-motif of 'bells and wheels, and horses feet, and no rest', and now Carker, dazed and sick with weariness, shudders each time the ground trembles and a great train, dropping glowing coals and exhaling a deathlike breath, goes shrieking by. Confused by lack of sleep, bewildered by unearthly railroad noises, Carker suddenly sees Dombey emerge through the station door. He staggers back, loses his footing, and topples in front of a train. The wheels which rolled endlessly through his dreamlike flight now coalesce into the great avenging wheel of the locomotive 'that spun him round and round and struck him limb from limb, and licked his stream of life up with its fiery heat.' The death is appropriate. For Carker the manager, the new industrial man par excellence, is destroyed by the iron idol, that 'type of the triumphant monster, Death', he had so inhumanly served. Dombey, for his part, goes from this scene of judgment to face his own imminent ruin, while Toodle and his apple-cheeked brood roll blithely forward.

Though the Toodles and railroads are subordinate elements in Dickens' larger design, they subserve major ends. For Dickens' design now dominates the detail as well as the grand sweep of the novel, and even minor or specialized elements (in this case primarily social or industrial elements) blend with—are actually a part of—his central conception. The blending is much richer than is suggested here, for it is compounded of the imagery of plants, plumages, clocks, jewels, rivers, and staircases, as well as railroads; it embraces characters such as Dombey, Edith, Paul, Florence, Mrs. Skewton, and Major Bagstock as well as the lowly Toodles; and it works through leitmotifs more persistent and all-embracing than the wheel leitmotif of the flight chapter. All these interrelated and endlessly refracting aspects of plot, theme, image, and symbol give *Dombey and Son* an organic unity no previous Dickens novel had had. What he had done here was to elaborate and combine Christmas-book patterns and Christmas-book techniques with the basic organizing idea of the micro-macrocosmic novel, the novel which consciously depicts a whole society through a unified and manageable fragment thereof. In *Dombey* the fragment is the new business world, 'Wholesale, Retail, and for Exportation': in later works it is the legal world (*Bleak House*), or the prison world—the phrase taken in its metaphorical and psychological as well as literal meaning—(*Little Dorrit*). *Bleak House* has been cited by Edmund Wilson and others as the commencement of this micro-macrocosmic organization in Dickens, but in *Dombey*, six years before *Bleak House*, Dickens had introduced the fundamental form and attendant techniques of this powerful type of novel. The first appearance of this important innovation has been overlooked because the structure of *Dombey* falls below that of *Bleak House* and *Little Dorrit* and obscures Dickens' intent. The second half of *Dombey*, like the ending of the Christmas books, is in-

ferior to the earlier portions; indeed the latter portions at times belie what Dickens set out to do. The micro-macrocosmic form and the Christmas-book method are present in *Dombey* nevertheless, and the reasons for *Dombey*'s initial superiority and subsequent falling off—very different from the reasons for the falling off of the Christmas books—throw light on how Dickens adapted the Christmas-book method to his new type of novel and the difficulties he encountered when pursuing that method at length for the first time.

Paradoxically, the fact that Dickens planned *Dombey* with greater care than any previous novel contributes to its falling off. In his earlier works improvisation was a central part of his method and led to some of his happiest effects. In intricately constructed *Dombey*, improvisation carried with it the danger that carefully planned groundwork would be left incomplete, or worse, would be completed by incongruous extensions. This is what actually occurred. Dickens, for instance, had originally intended that Edith commit adultery with Carker and then be killed, but at the last minute, at the urging of his close friend, John Forster, he decided to turn the episode into 'an inverted *Maid's Tragedy*', have Edith run away from Dombey, meet Carker by prearrangement in a Dijon hotel suite, humble him by refusing to become his mistress, humiliate Dombey by letting the world think she had eloped with Carker and spent a night with him, and then flee into a lifetime of seclusion. The change weakened the novel, not merely because Dickens placed middle-class moral sensibilities above everyday probabilities, but because the Edith-Carker-Dombey denouement overthrew what he had carefully built into the novel earlier and what, as a consequence, the aesthetic structure of the story now required.

Carker, for example, is often projected through cat and snake imagery, Edith through bird and plumage imagery, and Dombey through gold imagery—imagery which forms and guides our expectations. Such imagery gives ominous meaning to Dombey's breakfast at Carker's residence (throughout the meal Carker's brightly plumed parrot—a symbol of Edith—plays in its symbolic cage and swings precariously on its great golden wedding-ring hoop), and such imagery gives terrible significance to the frantic scene with Carker in which Edith tears the decorative plumage from her wrist and rains it on the ground. These and similar imagistic foreshadowings are perverted by Edith's melodramatic escape. The escape is false not only to a web of imagery (for the bird imagery is reinforced by the imagery of Edith's magically sympathetic jewels, and by Carker's sinister catlike and snakelike stalking), but to the central thesis of the story. For the humbling of Dombey and all that Dickens attaches thereto demands that no mere appearance of disgrace be substituted for the irrevocable act; and Carker, for his part, should not be thwarted by a wilful woman (he should degrade her as he degrades everything he touches), but should be quelled solely by his idol, by the implacable wheels of industry. Furthermore, Dickens had designed Edith's money marriage and her relationship to her mother, Mrs. Skewton, to parallel the prostitution of Alice and her relationship to her mother, Good Mrs. Brown. His whole purpose was to demonstrate that the sale of one's body and one's accomplishments is prostitution no matter how exalted the contractors or how sanctified by marriage vows the contract. To imprison, transport, debauch, and kill Alice, and then cause Edith to escape her preordained adultery and death, is to overturn that demonstration.

The same damaging reversal also occurs with Walter. As Dickens' letters and avowals to Forster show, Walter was to have ended a wastrel, another sacrifice to Dombey methods and Dombey business. His degeneration was to have been accentuated by the *Cinderella* and *Dick Whittington* dreams of Sol Gills, Captain Cuttle, and himself—dreams to the effect that he was favored by Mr. Dombey, would rise to the top of the firm, marry Florence, and be rich and happy. The success imagery which surrounds Walter and Florence in the opening portions of the book was to have been ironic, it was to have served at the climax of the book to underline the blighting effect of the new business ethic—an underlining turned upside down by the revised ending.

These weakening changes were compounded by Dickens' decision in the midst of *Dombey* to abandon the business theme, a decision forced upon him by his mode of writing and publishing. Unable to go back and modify the monthly parts already published, unable to extend the monthly parts yet to be written, he found himself, now that the ending was looming before him, impossibly cramped. The detailed psychological analysis of the Dombey-Florence-Carker relationship—a type of analysis he had never attempted before—was taking an immense amount of room. Popular comic characters such as Captain Cuttle, Susan Nipper, Mrs. MacStinger, and Toots had to be paraded periodically and given scenes in which to display their talents. And the overriding requirements of the culminating plot and its abundance of melodramatic climaxes (Edith's spurning of Carker, Carker's flight and death, Walter's homecoming, Alice's death, Florence's return to her father, and Florence's last interview with Edith) could neither be eliminated nor postponed. As a result the world of business and all that revolved about it had to be severely attenuated in the second half. The complex initial unity of the domestic and commercial strands is perpetuated only by the reader's memory of Dickens' careful introductory weaving, and by a few major plot culminations

planned from the first—the crash of the Dombey business, the symbolic railroad death of Carker, and the proliferation and staying power of the advancing Toodles.

But *Dombey,* though it fails to live up to the promise of its opening numbers, is a great achievement nevertheless. That achievement is made all the more auspicious by the departures it marks for Dickens—by its new emphasis on realism, psychology, and contemporary life, and by the successful transfer from Christmas book to novel of such mechanisms as leitmotif, symbolism, significant imagery, and fairy-tale episode and structure. It may seem strange that fairy-tale elements should wax strong when Dickens is emphasizing a new realism, but this is so, and *Dombey,* as we shall now see in greater detail, owes much of its special effectiveness to the fairy tale.

The central design of *Dombey,* for example, works changes on the *Cinderella* theme, and this familiar theme and the fears and fulfillments it embodies gives *Dombey* a part of its emotional appeal. The opening paragraph of *Cinderella* recalls the central situation of Dickens' business novel: 'Once there was a gentleman who married, for his second wife, the proudest and most haughty woman that was ever seen . . . He had . . . by another wife, a young daughter, but of unparalleled goodness and sweetness of temper, which she took from her mother, who was the best creature in the world.'

Dombey, of course, contains much more. For instance, Dickens also reworks the *Cinderella* theme—more subtly and psychologically than with Florence and Walter—through Florence and her father. Florence is the dispossessed, the cinder girl, the princess in disguise, the treasure whom Dombey must learn to recognize and appreciate. Dombey combines the roles of the wicked stepmother, the proud vain stepsisters, and the searching prince: he neglects and humiliates his princess daughter, leaves her home when he goes off to the balls and fetes of the world, and persecutes her for his own failings. Dickens gives this *Cinderella* (and poor-little-rich-girl) theme a mythlike power and fascination, but he also maintains the story's realism, and infuses his fairy tale with autobiographical passion.

That passion stems from the waif theme; it grows out of the fact that Dickens was able to project into Mr. Dombey's rejection of Florence, his own sense of parental abandonment. Florence, like Dickens (and like Oliver, Little Nell, Pip, and many other Dickens characters) is an orphan. But Florence is the most pitiful kind of orphan—and here Dickens' sense of his own abandonment makes the Florence-Dickens identification most intense—she is an orphan whose father is still alive. The scene in which Dickens gives this notion explicit form is accompanied by great waves of emotion and by an unusual richness of complementary imagery (imagery notably of falling flowers and flowing water) and is followed by an interpolated exemplum, a reverse father-daughter story which accentuates Dickens' horror at the rejection he is depicting. The term orphan is no critical subtlety, for Dickens himself applies the metaphor to Florence: 'The flowers were scattered on the ground like dust; the empty hands were spread upon the face; and orphaned Florence, shrinking down upon the ground, wept long and bitterly.' The sense of being orphaned, of being a lonely waif in a great unfeeling city, runs through all of *Dombey*, though usually by implication or dramatic demonstration rather than direct statement. Its first strong enunciation occurs when Florence, as a child is lost in the city of London, a scene which recalls Dickens' similar childhood experience, but which also mirrors his more general childhood response to London. This crucial scene sets the pattern for what is to follow, for the orphan label or the lost-child symbolism reappears at climactic moments throughout the story. The predictability with which Dickens sounds this chord at such moments testifies to its profound meaning for him. When Dombey strikes Florence, Dickens writes, 'She saw she had no father upon earth, and ran out, orphaned, from his house.' And when she is running through the streets, he has her think: 'Where to go? . . . She thought of the only other time she had been lost in the wide wilderness of London—though not lost as now—and went that way.' Loss and abandonment become intertwined with rejection, and significantly (in view of Dickens' own experiences), when Florence feels Walter also rejects her, she summons up her childhood days, again remembers the trauma of her symbolic city experience, and recalls 'when she was a lost child in the staring streets'.

In such recurrent nightmare scenes fairy tale and autobiography coalesce. And by the same token (for it is the essence of Dickens' Christmas-book method to fuse fact and fairy-tale fancy into a more profound form of truth) the *Cinderella* structure of the Florence-Walter episodes carries with it suggestive autobiographical overtones. The Florence-Walter love relationship is treated through much of the book as a brother-sister relationship. It thus parallels the other central love relationship of the novel, the brother-sister relationship of Paul and Florence. Dickens counterpoises the love which exists between Paul and Florence to the love which is lacking between Florence and her father. The sisterly-brotherly love becomes for Florence (and for Paul) a substitute for the outgoing parental love Dombey is incapable of giving.

These relationships are similar to Dickens' early closeness to his sister Fanny and his turning to her for love in the face of what he took to be parental neglect and rejection. The importance of the brother-sister relation-

ship is accentuated when Dickens insists upon making the Florence-Walter conjunction (despite its sexual and *Cinderella* aspects) a brother-sister situation. In a most curious way, the sibling quality of that relationship is emphasized at the same time that the possibility of sexual love and marriage is also underscored. In this respect, Dickens is perpetuating through Walter and Florence, little Paul's equally curious yearning. "'I mean'", said Paul, "to put my money all together in one bank, never try to get any more, go away into the country with my darling Florence, have a beautiful garden, fields, and woods, and live there with her all my life!'" And when Paul dies, and the Captain Cuttle—Sol Gills circle views Walter's marriage to Florence and his accession to the head of Dombey and Son as certain, Dickens goes out of his way to make Walter a surrogate of Paul, and to give the brother-sister relationship of Walter and Florence an almost legal status. The day before Walter voyages into shipwreck on the *Son and Heir*, Florence visits him and says, 'If you'll be a brother to me, Walter, now that he [Paul] is gone and I have none on earth I'll be your sister all my life, and think of you like one wherever we may be!' Walter accepts the offer, the clock strikes, Florence gets into a waiting coach, says 'You are my brother, dear!' and the coach drives off. But Walter is to be Florence's husband, not her brother, and years later when he returns and realizes that he loves her sexually, the pledge of brotherhood becomes a torment to him, forces him to avoid her, and is dissolved only when Florence confesses her unsisterly love for him.

This strange brother-sister-husband-wife conjunction which Dickens idealizes in *Dombey* is similar to the one he strove to achieve in his own life. His sister Fanny, his parent substitute in childhood, who became the object of his love and then, so Dickens thought, betrayed him (even as his mother had earlier), was later, along with his mother and his first love, the equally unsteadfast Maria Beadnell, made his image of womanhood, an image which shaped his attitude toward love and his wife. What Dickens sought was a wife who would be a companion, a sexual partner, a bearer of children, but at the same time (and unlike his unforgiven mother or the inconstant Maria) be steadfast and innocent, untouched and untouchable, the matured and idealized image of his childhood sister. The very terms of his desire made it unattainable; for to find the paragon wife was to destroy the sister, and to preserve the immature sister, was to have no wife at all. Hence Dickens' curious domestic compromise, his anomalous household which from shortly after his marriage contained not only his wife, but his wife's sixteen-year-old sister, Mary Hogarth. And when adored Mary died in his arms at the age of seventeen (still budlike and perfect, still, in the words he wrote for her tombstone, 'young, beautiful, and good,' and thus forever so) he was able to convince himself that he had rediscovered, though again in fleeting form, the all-loving sister he had apotheosized in childhood. Now more than ever, therefore, he sought to give actual form to his dream of a sister-wife fusion. Five years later, he brought fifteen-year-old Georgina, another Hogarth sister, into his household. And there Georgina remained, unmarried and sisterly, sisterly even after her sister, Dickens' wife, moved out of his home, sisterly until his death, clinging to that portion of her brother-in-law which had need of a worshiping sister surrogate such as she. Yet what Dickens really wanted was not two women in his house, a wife and an aging sister substitute, but one woman who would be both wife and ever-young ever-adoring sister. His makeshift attempts to give his dream reality by means of resident sisters-in-law, infatuations with teenage girls (such as Christiana Weller), and finally, in his forties, by a liaison with an eighteen-year-old actress—these attempts and the will-o'-the-wisp dream which prompted them had much to do with his growing restlessness, his increasingly unsatisfactory marriage, and his latter-day unhappiness.

His need and the dream which embodied it also led to a host of female characters into whom he projected (and through whom he partly vicariously realized) the confused sister-wife ideal of his emotional yearning. In the early works the projection is usually an idealized blending of Fanny Dickens and Mary Hogarth, a combination of the perfect but vanished childhood sister companion and the doomed sister substitute: a figure who is most notably represented by Little Nell. Or more commonly, such female characters are sister-wife figures who are depicted both as perfect sisters and perfect wives. (One usually gets the feeling that the sister role is the important one, that happy wifehood is a vague status which comes late in the novel as a reward for loyal sisterhood.) In the typical case, the dutiful, loving sister, having proved her boundless devotion, is allowed to marry an impeccable but bloodless spouse: Rose Fleming, the foster-sister of Oliver (and his aunt, as it turns out), marries Harry Maylie (whose foster-sister—to compound the pattern—is the very same Rose); Kate Nickleby, the sister of Nicholas, marries Frank Cheeryble; Ruth Pinch, the sister of Tom, marries John Westlock. In each case the marriage occurs at the end of the book, and it is the sister relationship, not the lover relationship, which is important. Sometimes, as with Ruth Pinch, the sister perpetuates the brother-sister relationship after marriage by bringing the brother into (or next to) her new household; and in some cases, the sister never marries, but as with Harriet Carker, sacrifices her chance for marriage and happiness (nobly and fittingly as Dickens makes clear) in loyalty to her brother.

In later works the brother-sister relationship is more complex and usually reflects Dickens' feelings with greater insight. In *A Tale of Two Cities,* through Sydney

Carton and Charles Darnay (two projections of Dickens, as Dickens himself recognized) he was again able to depict a love which combined sexual and brother-sister qualities. The pale married love of Lucie and Charles represents Dickens' ideal husband-wife relationship; the emotional Lucie-Sydney conjunction represents (as Chapter XIII of Book II makes clear) a forbidden sexual love which is repressed and finally sublimated into a precarious brotherly love. At the end of the book this brotherly love is purged of its remaining sexual taint when Sydney forgoes the possibility of marrying a widowed Lucie and saves Lucie's lawful sexual partner by sacrificing himself.

In *David Copperfield* the bifurcation of *A Tale of Two Cities* is reversed. David has two loves, one Dora, a provocative but immature lover and an unsatisfactory wife, the other, Agnes, a sister figure whom he finally recognizes, after Dora's death, as his proper spouse. In *Copperfield* Dickens came close to consciously understanding his dilemma and the impossibility of resolving it; for though David at last marries Agnes, he does so in a curiously asexual way, realizing that her love, no matter how deep, lacks something which his first love possessed. As Dickens later partly confessed, Agnes is a recrudescence of the sisterly Fanny-Mary-Georgina figure, while Dora is compounded of Maria and his wife, Catherine, that is, of his early sexual love and disillusionment.

Pip and Estella in *Great Expectations,* to cite only one more instance of this repeated pattern, also have an odd brother-sister-lover relationship. The brother-sister aspects of their relationship, built up by years of childhood association, make Pip a confidant, a person singled out for favorable treatment, a charmed being who is supposedly safe from a destructive sexual love for Estella. Yet his presumed immunity proves to be his curse, for his favored position causes him to love Estella all the more. He loves her as sister, as wife, and as ideal (as Estella, the star); he loves her though he knows he cannot, and for his well-being should not, attain her. But knowledge, reason, conscience are powerless to restrain him; he pursues her, and thus he pursues his own misery.

Dickens was probably only vaguely aware of the exact relationship between the loves he was depicting fictionally and his own emotional situation; yet his great urge to give creative objectivity to what he was feeling assured that the shaping pressures of the life would be projected into his fiction. His self-analysis therefore was partly unconscious and partly calculated. It was emotional and dramatic, not systematic. But is was not naive, and it was not static. *Copperfield* and *Great Expectations* examine the brother-sister-wife conjunction with a depth and sophistication that is beyond *Dombey* and the earlier novels.

Yet fittingly, as Dickens' first psychological novel, *Dombey* is also the first novel to deal with this node of his life with anything more than the idealized and impossible brother, sister, and wife figures of his early works. And *Dombey*'s fairy-tale structure helped give aesthetic form to the psychological complexities of the Florence-Walter, Florence-Paul, Florence-Dombey relationships—all of which body forth central aspects of his emotional life.

Mary Hogarth's death in Dickens' arms is a case in point. That death is projected into *Dombey* more than once, but with modifications important both autobiographically (in terms of the death's larger meaning to him) and aesthetically (in terms of his new care in constructing his novels). When Paul lies dying he recalls that his mother held Florence in her arms as she was dying, and therefore must have loved Florence much better than her father, 'for even he, her brother, who had such dear love for her, could have no greater wish than that.' Accordingly Dickens has Paul in his last moments (in the Dickens-Mary Hogarth manner), clasp Florence to his breast: 'Sister and brother wound their arms around each other, and the golden light came streaming in, and fell upon them, locked together. Again the parent is excluded from this final gesture of love (a fact which makes Mr. Dombey jealous and helps turn him against his daughter), and the love of the sister is made to compensate for the inadequate love of the parent. That Dickens connected the brother-sister love of Paul and Florence with his love for Mary Hogarth, and Mary's death with Paul's, is made even clearer a few pages earlier. In the earlier scene, Paul, already in his prescient final illness, watches Florence, and thinks how 'young, and good, and beautiful' she is—the words Dickens placed on Mary Hogarth's tombstone.

Although these parallels are not always true to the outward events of Dickens' experiences, they are true to the emotions of his experiences; and the parallels are subordinated to the larger demands of the novel—a new feature in Dickens' writing. The emotion-charged autobiographical relationships he projects into *Dombey* are modified, sometimes to accord with his wish-fulfilling desires, but more often to blend with his fictional purposes (though the two are not mutually exclusive). Similarly, the fairy-tale structures which carry his thesis, and the specific fairy-tale borrowings themselves, are also subordinated to the artistic whole. If Walter, owing to Dickens' change in plans, fulfills the *Cinderella* myth, Mr. Dombey in his *Cinderella* role can only enjoy his tardily recognized princess in diminished form—a switch from the old method which would have turned the converted Mr. Dombey into a fairy godmother and caused him to shower golden blessings on the elect.

Dickens' use of the fairy tale has changed. The fairy tale has become a more important force in his writings, but it has also become a more humanized, flexible, inte-

grated force. This shift may be seen not only in *Dombey*'s complex double-tiered *Cinderella* framework, but in other areas. A portion of the plot is worked out through quasi-supernatural means, through the prophecy, special knowledge, portentous interference, and ultimately the astonishing blood relationship of Good Mrs. Brown, a realistic hag who is also a witch out of folklore and fairy literature. And the plot is unified by devices which for Dickens are allied to fairy tales, devices such as repeated phrases, leitmotifs, allegorical symbolism, and so on.

The Dombey mansion, for example, owes its mythlike potency to fairy-tale origins. The supernatural atmosphere of the mansion broods over the entire novel, but the scenes which wed the house most directly to the story's fairy-tale nimbus begin with the opening words of Chapter XXIII: 'Florence lived alone in the great dreary house, and day succeeded day and still she lived alone; and the blank walls looked down upon her with a vacant stare, as if they had a Gorgon-like mind to stare her youth and beauty into stone.' This introduction, with its repetition and its supernatural and fable elements (later, the whole sentence becomes a refrain repeated throughout the chapter) reminds one of Dickens' Christmas-book technique, a similarity strengthened when Dickens goes on in the next sentences to introduce a host of fairy-tale allusions. 'No magic dwelling-place in magic story, shut up in the heart of a thick wood, was ever more solitary and deserted to the fancy, than was her father's mansion in its grim reality.' Although there were not 'two dragon sentries keeping ward before the gate of this abode, as in magic legend are usually found on duty over the wronged innocence imprisoned', there was a 'monstrous fantasy of rusty iron'; and though there were 'no talismanic characters engraven on the portal', neighborhood boys had chalked the neglected railings and pavements with ghosts. The decaying mansion is bewitched: 'The spell upon it was more wasting than the spell that used to set enchanted houses sleeping once upon a time, but left their waking freshness unimpaired.' The allusion is to *Sleeping Beauty*; but the spell on Dombey's mansion is far different from that on Sleeping Beauty's enchanted castle. In the Dombey mansion, curtains droop, mirrors grow dim, boards creak and shake, keys rust, fungus proliferates, and spiders, moths, black beetles, and rats multiply in frightening multitudes. Dickens makes the decaying house and its spell-like isolation mark the passage of time, underscore Dombey's neglect of Cinderella-Sleeping-Beauty Florence, and dramatize her magical transformation into lovely womanhood. The interlude (like the interlude in Virginia Woolf's *To the Lighthouse* which describes a similar scene and achieves an identical effect) goes on for several pages without slackening in tautness or evocativeness. The house is now boldly termed 'an enchanted abode', and in this supernatural mansion, Florence 'bloomed . . . like the king's fair daughter in the story'. The interlude continues, associating the staircase, flower, and lost-child imagery with the fairy-tale atmosphere, and after further allusions to the 'circle' which enabled Florence to live on while 'nothing harmed her', and references to 'an enchanted vision', and 'a haunted house', and after an intricate juxtaposition of the mansion with Florence's solitary life and frustrated will to love, Dickens concludes by repeating the Gorgon refrain for a third time.

This synthesis of prosaic detail, suprarealistic atmosphere, and fairy-tale point of view is not confined to interpolated interludes. Mrs. Pipchin, for example, the dour and redoubtable teacher of little Paul, and his later overseer and nurse, combines meticulous realism with the most artful supernaturalism. Mrs. Pipchin is the old fairy-tale ogre-witch, but so thoroughly transformed that she bears little relationship to the one-dimensional witches and godmothers of Dickens' early writings. For Mrs. Pipchin's diablerie is more than Gothic trimming, it is a reflection of Paul's view of her. Mrs. Pipchin was modeled on two real persons, a Mrs. Roylance, a hard and unresponsive lady who took Dickens in to board during a portion of his blacking-warehouse days, and another woman, probably the keeper of a dame school he attended briefly several years earlier; but his childhood sufferings (especially those of his blacking-warehouse days) caused him to transform his flesh-and-blood models into a flesh-and-blood witch. Mrs. Pipchin is a young child's image of evil—it is noteworthy that Dickens in his self-pity makes Paul younger than he himself was—and her representation accentuates the child's view of the world that Dickens is depicting in this portion of the book.

Mrs. Pipchin is a 'marvellous ill-favoured, ill-conditioned old lady' with a 'stooping figure', 'mottled face', 'hook nose', and 'hard grey eye'. Her witchlike appearance is accentuated by her 'black bombazeen' clothing of a 'lustreless, deep, dead, sombre shade', and by the fact that her presence is always a 'quencher'. Dickens then goes on to describe the hostilely animistic contents of the 'Castle of this ogress and child-queller'. Paul's first conversation with Mrs. Pipchin adds still other touches to the frightening fairy-tale atmosphere:

> 'Well, sir', said Mrs. Pipchin to Paul, 'how do you think you shall like me?'
>
> 'I don't think I shall like you at all', replied Paul. 'I want to go away. This isn't my house.'
>
> 'No. It's mine', retorted Mrs. Pipchin.
>
> 'It's a very nasty one', said Paul.
>
> 'There's a worse place in it than this though', said Mrs. Pipchin, 'where we shut up our bad boys.'

This 'worse place', an empty apartment at the back devoted to correctional purposes, Dickens calls the 'Castle Dungeon'. Paul's predicament, in his childish view, is

catastrophic. He is trapped in a horrible fairy-tale castle presided over by a merciless witch. Words such as 'ogress', 'castle', 'black', and 'dungeon' reverberate through the remainder of the passage, and harmonize with Mrs. Pipchin's 'black teapot', 'coiled' black cat, and 'hard grey eye'.

Paul, who is not lacking in supernatural qualities himself, is fascinated by this horrific old lady, even as Dickens was fascinated by his own lady mentors and nursemaids and their terrifying folklore stories. Soon a strange fairy-tale rapport develops between Paul and Mrs. Pipchin. The two would sit before the fire and Paul would stare at his keeper 'until he sometimes quite confounded . . . [her], ogress as she was.' The atmosphere of the scene, despite its foundation of realism, becomes charged with an ever-increasing supernaturalism. 'The good old lady', writes Dickens, 'might have been—not to record it disrespectfully—a witch, and Paul and the cat her two familiars, as they all sat by the fire together. It would have been quite in keeping with the appearance of the party if they had all sprung up the chimney in a high wind one night, and never been heard of any more.'

'This', continues Dickens in the next sentence, 'never came to pass', and with that remark (though the supernatural atmosphere continues to hover over the chapter) the emphasis shifts from the fairy-tale level to the realistic. The passage is a good example of Dickens' method of combining the realistic and the fantastic, and the passage illustrates what he gained thereby: a suggestive atmosphere, an evocative point of view, a flexible suprarealism, and a unity of vision.

Dickens puts this synthesis to work throughout the novel. Another, even more important, case in point is the Walter-Florence-Good-Mrs.-Brown conjunction, a conjunction which appears mystifyingly vexing and unorganic until viewed from its fairy-tale conception. So viewed, the conjunction emerges as one of the chief symbolic nodes of the story, a node at which the *Cinderella,* lost child, business world, witch, and enchantment themes meet and intermingle. Florence had accompanied Polly Toodle and Susan Nipper on Paul's fateful visit to Staggs' Gardens, but in a moment of confusion on the way home, had become separated from them. An old woman hobbles up to Florence, grasps her by the wrist, and promises to bring her back to her friends. The old woman has 'red rims round her eyes, . . . a mouth that mumbled and chattered of itself', and a 'shrivelled yellow face and throat' that went through 'all sorts of contortions'. When the old woman seeks to soothe Florence and lead her away, Florence asks, 'What's your name?' 'Mrs. Brown', answers the old woman, 'Good Mrs. Brown.'

Good Mrs. Brown leads Florence through dirty lanes and muddy roads to a 'shabby' 'closely shut up' house.

She unlocks the door, and pushes the child into a room with black walls, black ceiling, and no furniture. On the floor there is 'a great heap of rags of different colours, . . . a heap of bones, and a heap of sifted dust or cinders.' 'Sit upon the rags', says Good Mrs. Brown. And then Good Mrs. Brown, taking her own seat on the bones, warns, 'Don't vex me. If you don't . . . I won't hurt you. But if you do, I'll kill you. I could have you killed at any time even if you was in your own bed at home.'

So little Cinderella sits near her heap of identifying cinders and confronts her own Mrs. Pipchin, a witch and child-queller infinitely more terrifying than Paul's. But the episode and its symbolic implications have only begun. Good Mrs. Brown (who all through the episode, and elsewhere in the novel, in addition to being a witch, is also a realistic Victorian rag and bone scavenger) now commands Florence to take off her clothes. The command and its consequences are deeply emblematic, for in *Sartor Resartus* fashion, Florence's garments, like Rob the Grinder's, Mr. Toodle's, Mr. Toots', and those of other characters in *Dombey*, proclaim and conceal identity. Florence trembles and obeys. Off come her costly frock, bonnet, petticoats, and shoes; on (taken from the heap of rags) go two wretched substitutes for shoes, an old worn girl's cloak, and the 'crushed remains of a bonnet that had probably been picked up from some ditch or dunghill.' Florence is now clothed in an outfit which correctly represents her outcast state. Then, suddenly, in a frightening scene, she almost undergoes a more crippling transformation. In putting on her filthy substitute bonnet, she had entangled it in her 'luxuriantly' beautiful hair, and Good Mrs. Brown, watching like a great black spider, falls into a strange fit of excitement. Trembling with desire, the old woman 'whip[s] out a large pair of scissors', ruffles Florence's very saleable curls 'with a furious pleasure', and prepares to cut them off. But then, remembering her distant daughter's long hair, she pauses, finally stops, and at last gives way to a 'wild tossing up of her lean arms' and a passionate parental grief that 'thrilled to the heart' of the unloved Florence. The old woman tells Florence to hide her curls under her bonnet and 'let no trace of them escape.'

Mrs. Brown's passionate daughter, Alice, tossing her wild hair, will later appear in the story, a transmutation of the innocent Florence, and a foil to upper-class Edith (just as Good Mrs. Brown is a foil to Edith's mother, Mrs. Skewton); and Alice and her mother will also serve as one more study of a blighting parent-child relationship. But the talismanic hair episode, with its frightening despoliation implications, and its many fairy-tale and legendary analogues, is more than a clue to a character who must appear much later. It is part of the terrifying fairy-tale evil which hovers about the immature Florence, and it is part of the enchanted atmosphere of the entire story. For the whole episode is a way of objectifying in a magical and exceptionally evocative manner—and also, from a child's point of view, in a brilliantly appropriate manner—the mortal peril which encompasses innocent Florence. And it follows that Florence's brief sojourn in the hell-like charnel house (a house which is identical, emotionally to her bleak palace home) epitomizes the hellishness of her daily life. The symbolic significance of the episode is carried forward when Good Mrs. Brown returns with Florence to the London streets.

The two leave the black room of cinders, rags, and bones, but only after Mrs. Brown has insisted that Florence not go home but find her way 'to her father's office in the City'. Mrs. Brown accompanies this injunction with terrifying threats, and enjoins Florence to wait at the street corner 'until the clock [strikes] three'. Florence waits in fear and bewilderment. She looks back to see 'the head of Good Mrs. Brown peeping out of a low wooden passage . . . likewise the fist of Good Mrs. Brown shaking towards her', but at last the witch disappears, London's many clocks toll the magic number three, and Florence ventures into the London thoroughfare, seeking her father's offices. Of the offices she knows fittingly and ironically only 'that they belonged to Dombey and Son'.

Lost and in rags, Florence goes through the commercial heart of the city asking the way to Dombey and Son. Symbolically, Florence has begun the great pilgrimage of her life—she is seeking the way to her father's heart, the way into the cold commercial citadel which is her father's life. At last, she comes to a dock where Dombey's name is known. Walter, Dombey's office boy is nearby, and when she hears that he is from Dombey and Son, she runs eagerly up to him, leaving one of the slipshod shoes upon the ground. 'I am lost', she cries, bursting into tears. At the same time her bonnet falls off, her hair comes 'tumbling down about her face', and Walter, moved to 'speechless admiration' by this magical sign, falls into a worshipful daze of love. But he is not too dazed to champion Florence and guide her through the city labyrinth. His first act is to pick up the shoe 'and put it on the little foot as the Prince in the story might have fitted Cinderella's slipper on.' This done, they walk arm-in-arm through the London streets, Walter neat and prosperous and Florence dirty and neglected, in a reversal of their social roles but in accordance with their spiritual status—and also in ironic reversal of the planned degeneration of Walter and the apotheosis of Florence.

Walter brings her to Uncle Sol's nautical instrument shop (the refuge she will again come to when she flees her father's house and once more hurries dispossessed through London streets), and he calls out to his uncle, 'Here's Mr. Dombey's daughter lost in the streets, and robbed of her clothes by an old witch.' After dinner, Florence falls asleep and Walter goes off to tell Mr. Dombey what he has found. Sol remains by Florence's side, 'building a great many airy castles of the most fantastic architecture; and looking, in the dim shade, and in the close vicinity of all the instruments, like a magician . . . who held the child in an enchanted sleep.'

Walter returns with Susan, Florence's maid, and with fresh clothing. Florence once more takes off her garments, again dons her usual clothes, and reassumes her former appearance. Walter and Florence exchange a kiss, Florence gets into the waiting coach, and the coach carries her off to her father's palace. 'The entrance of the lost child', comments Dickens, made 'a slight sensation, but not much', for Mr. Dombey 'had never found her'.

This remarkable episode, so striking in its fairy-tale analogues, so momentous in its symbolism and foreshadowing, encompasses in foreshortened form much of what Dickens was trying to do in *Dombey*. The groundwork is here laid for the intricate interaction of many of *Dombey's* central characters: for the interaction of Florence, Walter, Mr. Dombey, Uncle Sol, Good Mrs. Brown, and Carker Junior; and for the interaction of characters who have not yet appeared or who have not yet been entangled in the enchanted web—Edith, Mrs. Skewton, Alice, Harriet Carker, and Carker himself. But Dickens has also succeeded in casting a penumbra of magic, myth, and fairy lore over this scene. The events and characters take on an overwhelming significance; and for Dickens they had such a significance, for they embodied crucial engrams of his experience—the waif or lost child (especially in city streets), the inadequate parent, the witchlike child-queller, the fairy-tale refuge, and the magical transformation. The real and the supernatural mingle and strengthen one another, and the union helps produce Dickens' special vision of life.

That vision enhances reality. For Dickens' re-creation of his everyday world, even when he records it with hypnotic exactitude, possesses a fairy-tale essence which is projected and works upon the reader even when the reader has no clear notion of what he is responding to. Like *Gulliver's Travels, Moby-Dick,* and similar works of literature, *Dombey* and the later Dickens novels can be read pleasurably on the most superficial level. Readers accustomed to thinking of Dickens as a popular author, and remembering their youthful introduction to him, do not often look in him for the hidden meanings, ambiguities, and wordplays they have been taught to search for in Joyce. Joyce demands such attention. Portions of *A Portrait of the Artist as a Young Man,* much of *Ulysses,* and all of *Finnegans Wake* are unintelligible without precise exegesis. But *Dombey* is

more like *Dubliners,* for *Dombey* can be read meaningfully, and to all appearances, satisfactorily, on a casual perusal. This universal availability is a virtue and a trap: it enables the work to speak unencumbered to a huge differentiated audience, but it also leads to misinterpretation. For if a reader responds to elements of a work of art without knowing they are there or why he is responding, he may respond erratically and incompletely. If the symbolism, the fairy-tale core, the recurring themes of *Dombey* are missed, the book's meaning is attenuated, and the novel's impact is lessened. One can see this very quickly if one follows Good Mrs. Brown through the rest of *Dombey*. For the fairy-tale filaments which knot momentarily in the opening Good Mrs. Brown scene, float in thousands of threadlike spinnings through the rest of the book, knotting again here and there, until they form an intricate web which binds together one whole movement of the novel. Good Mrs. Brown retains her witchlike nature throughout the novel; indeed her role is scarcely intelligible unless one constantly views her as a double image: as an evocation of a miserable London scavenger, and as a full-fledged necromancer.

The scene in which Good Mrs. Brown's magical associations are projected with the greatest force occurs halfway through the book. The episode takes place in Leamington. Dombey is courting Edith, testing her accomplishments, and displaying her to Carker whom he has called down from London. Carker, like most of the important characters in *Dombey,* has his share of fairy-tale qualities. He is the folklore devil who often appears disguised as an animal—in *Dombey* he is described most frequently as a cat, but notably also as a wolf and a snake. Carker, the sinister stalking cat or hypnotizing snake, affects Florence, Edith, Rob the Grinder, Diogenes the dog, and others, in supernatural ways. Florence shudders whenever he comes near, and almost faints when he fixes his serpent's eyes upon her; Diogenes growls and barks ferociously when he appears; and Rob is so terrorized and hypnotized by him that he follows him trance-like through the London streets, his eyes never wavering from Carker. Carker often imposes his silent will upon others and speaks to them without articulating. In his passionate interviews with Edith, his malignancy, magnified by the surrounding supernatural symbolism, creates truly terrifying effects. In one interview, he looks at her, and Dickens writes, 'He saw the soft down tremble once again, and he saw her lay the plumage of the beautiful bird against her bosom for a moment; and he unfolded one more ring of the coil into which he had gathered himself.' The horror condensed into these words is difficult to convey, for the terror of the scene accumulates from associations which have been building around Carker from the first. This aura of terror always clings to Carker. It is with him in the Leamington scene, and it adds its special appropriateness to the meaning and effect of that scene.

The scene occurs before breakfast in the countryside. Carker has strolled beyond the town, and on his return he goes by way of a 'deep shade of leafy trees'. Once in this grove, he begins a strange serpentine ritual: 'Mr. Carker threaded the great boles of the trees, and went passing in and out, before this one and behind that, weaving a chain of footsteps on the dewy ground.' As he softly glides round the trunk of one large tree 'on which the obdurate bark was knotted and overlapped like the hide of a rhinoceros or some kindred monster of the ancient days before the Flood,' he sees a figure sitting on a nearby bench 'about which, in another moment, he would have wound the chain he was making'. The figure is that of a beautiful, elegantly dressed lady who is struggling with herself. The lovely lady in distress is Edith, whom Carker has not yet met. But even as he looks at her from behind his antediluvian tree, a 'very ugly old woman scrambled up from the ground— out of it, it almost appeared—and stood in the way.' The old woman—who is Good Mrs. Brown, although never so identified in this scene—disturbs Edith with her demands for silver and her threats to call out her fortune. Edith, frightened, rushes toward the hidden Carker, who snakelike is 'slinking against his tree', and who seizes this moment to cross her path and assume her defense. But Good Mrs. Brown is not put down. 'Give me something', she tells Carker, 'or I'll call it after *you*!' Carker throws her a piece of silver, and Good Mrs. Brown, in Shakespearian image, 'munching', Dickens writes, 'like that sailor's wife of yore who had chestnuts in her lap, and scowling like the witch who asked for some in vain', picks up the coin, crouches 'on the veinous root of an old tree', and utters the following gnomic spell: 'One child dead, and one child living; one wife dead, and one wife coming. Go and meet her!' Carker, in spite of himself, is startled by the prescience of the old hag's utterance, and turns to look at her. Munching and mumbling, she 'pointed with her finger in the direction he was going, and laughed.' Carker pauses, but then hurries on. As he leaves the wood, however, he looks over his shoulder 'at the root of the old tree'. 'He could yet see the finger pointing before him, and thought he heard the woman screaming, "Go and meet her!"'

The scene is penetrated with suggestion and foreshadowing. The enchanted grove, the chain of fate, the forbidden antediluvian, Biblical tree, the serpent in the garden, the piece of silver, the gnomic prophecy, the finger pointing the way to adultery and destruction—all these signs heighten the events which are to come, underline their inevitability, and give the episode a cosmic significance.

That significance and the fairy-tale contributions to it are forged bit by bit. For example, much of the irony and tension of a scene which occurs several pages later are lost if the implications of the episode in the magic woods are missed. The new scene takes place after breakfast on the day of the meeting in the enchanted grove. The Dombey party is exploring the neighborhood of Warwick Castle, and Dombey is again testing and displaying Edith, now by requesting her to sketch for him. She asks him negligently what he would like her to sketch, and Dombey chooses a nearby view. The view is portentous: 'There happened to be in the foreground, at some little distance, a grove of trees, not unlike that in which Mr. Carker had made his chain of footsteps in the morning, and with a seat under one tree, greatly resembling, in the general character of its situation, the point where his chain had broken.' Carker suggests that it is 'an interesting—almost a curious— point of view'. His statement, meaningful only to Edith, is the beginning of the skillful psychological process whereby he forces upon her a peculiarly personal and secret relationship. 'Will you like that?' Edith asks Mr. Dombey. 'I shall be charmed,' is Dombey's unwitting reply. 'Therefore', continues Dickens, 'the carriage was driven to the spot where Mr. Dombey was to be charmed'; and a few moments later Carker, watching Edith sketch, commends her 'extraordinary skill—especially in trees'.

Such ironies and directives, underlined and extended by *Dombey*'s fairy-tale structure, save scene after scene from having only melodramatic or coincidental significance, for episodes which would be impossibly contrived in a purely realistic novel become acceptable and meaningful in so expressionistic a work as *Dombey*. Good Mrs. Brown's integrating supernatural-realistic role continues through the remainder of the book: through the Dombey wedding, the return of Alice, and the threatening of Rob. As the book progresses we begin to understand Good Mrs. Brown's unforgivable sin and its relationship to Dickens' fundamental purpose. Her sin is avarice, a willingness to sacrifice everything—she has already so sacrificed her daughter—for money. A money ethic has turned her into a veritable witch; yet her sin is identical with Mrs. Skewton's and Mr. Dombey's sin (and one might add, with Dickens' conception of his parents' sin—especially his mother's—in the blacking-warehouse days). Good Mrs. Brown is therefore another permutation of *Dombey*'s central fable; she is a character who forces the reader to see that placing money before human values is witch-like and disastrous. That these characters are part of the central fable and exhibit the same sin is made explicit through a confrontation scene, with strong supernatural overtones, involving Good Mrs. Brown, Alice, Mrs. Skewton, and Edith, and by the revelation at the end of the book, in fairy-tale fashion, that Alice is Good Mrs. Brown's illegitimate daughter by Edith's father's brother, so that Edith and Alice—whose physical as well as emotional and moral resemblances have been pointed up throughout the novel—are first cousins. Finally, parallelism, poetic justice, and fairy-tale coincidence are additionally served by Good Mrs. Brown's thaumaturgic part in the destruction of Edith, Carker, and Mr. Dombey.

This intricate interdependence and compensation, like that developed in the industrial and domestic levels of the story, points Dickens' theme of the essential unity of society. The coincidences serve Dickens' moral purpose, but they are more than mere happenstance and moral juggling, for the atmosphere of myth and fairy tale he blends with them gives them a poetic appropriateness which helps universalize the novel.

As the novel progresses, Dickens develops other fairy-tale characters and themes. The original *Cinderella* conjunction of Florence and Walter (associated from its outset with Good Mrs. Brown's fairy-tale abduction of Florence) is elaborated by many subsequent *Cinderella* touches. Walter preserves Florence's slipshod shoes and enshrines them in his room. This act, and Dickens' later references to it, keep our memory of the *Cinderella* meeting alive and prepare us for what is to come. But Walter's action also reflects his personality, and his romantic gesture links the realistic and fairy-tale levels of the story. Dickens tells us that Walter has a 'strong infusion' of the 'spice of romance and love of the marvellous' in his nature, and attributes to this trait Walter's 'uncommon and delightful interest' in the adventures of Florence with Good Mrs. Brown. Walter, then, is attracted to Florence by a fairy-tale episode, but he exemplifies in his own relationship to her another fairy tale. He not only preserves the *Cinderella* shoes, he dreams fairy-tale dreams. He will go to sea, come back an admiral with epaulettes of 'insupportable brightness', and bear Florence off to the 'blue shores of somewhere or other triumphantly'. And when Walter does go to sea, sent there for very unromantic reasons by Mr. Dombey, he takes with him Florence's slipshod shoes.

But the *Cinderella* atmosphere does not evaporate with Walter's nautical exile. Just before he leaves for his ship, Florence comes to Sol Gills' shop in a coach. This visitation casts a fairy-tale aura over Walter's departure and holds his future in suspense. In depicting the atmosphere of the scene, Dickens speaks specifically of a 'fairy influence', and that influence, which clings to Walter and shapes our lasting impression of him (for he now disappears from the book for hundreds of pages), hovers about Florence in all her subsequent relations with the Sol Gills-Captain Cuttle world.

Much later, for example, when Florence seeks sanctuary in Sol Gills' shop (now in charge of Captain Cuttle, owing to Sol's wandering search for the missing Walter), Dickens uses *Sleeping Beauty* and *Beauty and the Beast* imagery to maintain the reader's sense of the marvellous and to intensify Florence's aura of fairy-tale enchantment. Florence has fled her father's house, hurried once more through the frightening streets, and come at last to the nautical instrument shop. She is led through the shop to a high upstairs room and there falls asleep on a couch. The beautiful girl, slumbering on a couch, isolated from the bustling world, is a Sleeping Beauty who has come to an enchanted sanctuary and who waits for the wakening kiss of her absent prince. She even has her magical warders. Her dog, Diogenes, miraculously follows her and becomes a protective dragon who keeps guard by her side (Sleeping Beauty also had a dog who slumbered by her side); and good Captain Cuttle, sensing her fairy lineage, goes softly into her room and gazes upon the sleeping girl 'with a perfect awe of her youth and beauty'.

When the action is resumed (for Dickens used the above scene to conclude a monthly part), the fairy-tale atmosphere is maintained, but now primarily in *Beauty and the Beast* imagery. Dickens contrasts Florence's 'youth and beauty' (echoing the *Sleeping Beauty* words of the month before) with Captain Cuttle's 'knobby face', 'great broad weather-beaten person', and 'gruff voice'. The situation, Dickens remarks, was 'an odd sort of romance, perfectly unimaginative, yet perfectly unreal'. And a few lines farther on he tells the reader that 'a wandering princess and a good monster in a story-book might have sat by the fireside, and talked as Captain Cuttle and poor Florence thought—and not have looked very much unlike them.' This conjunction of the real, the grotesque and the fanciful, bound together and made viable by a fairy-tale essence, shapes the remaining adventures of Florence in her castle sanctuary. High up in that sanctuary, in her magical chambers, Florence lives on, safe at last from the cruelities of the commercial streets. It is while in her new home, an enchanted castle under a different and more benign spell than that which grips her father's house, that Florence finally receives and returns the love of the resurrected Walter. The imagery surrounding their castle trysts and the rapturous emotion Dickens lavishes on their romance meetings maintain the fable atmosphere: 'Florence never left her high rooms but to steal downstairs to wait for him when it was his time to come, or, sheltered by his proud encircling arm, to bear him company to the door again and sometimes peep into the street.'

The wedding which finally unites Florence and Walter rounds out one major fairy-tale motif. The wedding is symbolic and magical: it exorcises the childhood trauma of the London streets (Florence had only dared 'peep' into the streets, even though in the castle sanctuary and encircled by Walter's protective arm), and it unites Cinderella with her Prince Charming. 'It is very early,

Walter', says Florence on her marriage morning, 'and the streets are almost empty yet. Let us walk.' Walter asks if walking to church will not tire her, but Florence answers, 'Oh no! I was very tired the first time that we ever walked together, but I shall not be so to-day.' And so 'Florence and Walter, on their bridal morning, walk through the streets together.' 'Not even in that childish walk of long ago', Dickens reminds the reader, 'were they so far removed from all the world about them as to-day. The childish feet of long ago, did not tread such enchanted ground as theirs do now.' And with this cyclical ritual, in which the symbolic and unsatisfactory walk to Dombey and Son is replaced by the equally symbolic but satisfactory walk to church, one great tension of the novel is resolved.

Dickens weaves this complex *Cinderella* imagery and action, like his other fairy-tale elements—his witches, child-quellers, enchanted abodes spells, sacred groves, and magic circles—into functional patterns. Taken together, experienced concurrently as they actually appear, buttressed by the other fairy-tale episodes of the book, aided by hundreds of additional fairy-tale touches ranging from isolated words to recurrent symbolic motifs, and blended with the other major strands of the story—with the industrial, psychological, and autobiographical strands—these fairy-tale elements become a central foundation of *Dombey*'s method and meaning.

That fact is momentous. In *Dombey*, for the first time in a Dickens novel, fairy-tale juggling—the arbitrary interposition of supernatural agencies—becomes far less significant than subtle and pervasive fairy-tale enhancement. Dickens had learned the lessons of the Christmas books well. He had found a congenial means of organizing and enriching his writings, and he had successfully adapted that method to the novel. All his subsequent works would be fairy tales raised to 'a higher form'. He would fuse the magic, the suggestiveness, and the patterned order of fairy tales into the heart of his writings, endowing his mature masterpieces with the power and harmony of myth.

Richard Hannaford (essay date summer 1974)

SOURCE: Hannaford, Richard. "Fairy-Tale Fantasy in *Nicholas Nickleby*." *Criticism* 16, no. 3 (summer 1974): 247-59.

[*In the following essay, Hannaford asserts that "[i]n* Nicholas Nickleby *both design and purpose spring from Dickens's use of fairy-tale motifs in diction, plot, and characterization."*]

Recent studies continue to stress how Dickens's novels are derived from fairy tales; Toby Olshin identifies "The Yellow Dwarf" as the likely source for *The Old Curios-*

ity Shop, and Michael Kotzin summarizes the nineteenth century interest in fairy tales, points out allusions scattered throughout Dickens's novels, and reiterates that the novels often follow fairy-tale, narrative patterns.[1] However, most studies of fairy tales in Dickens's fiction have been primarily descriptive, relying upon the commonplace assertions that Dickens sophisticates the more simple style of fairy stories or shifts them to the city;[2] there has been little scrutiny of how fairy-tale motifs function in one of Dickens's novels. In *Nicholas Nickleby* both design and purpose spring from Dickens's use of fairy-tale motifs in diction, plot, and characterization.

In *Nickleby* there are references to Gog and Magog (legendary giants guarding London) and to Cormoran and Blunderbore (giants in "Jack the Giant Killer"); charms, spells, talismans, magic circles, old nursery tales, the Cock-lane Ghost, enchanted gardens, princesses, goblins, witches and dragons color the imagery in the novel. This is not to say that all allusions in the novel have their source in fairy-tale fantasy; at the close of the novel Dickens refers to Newman Noggs as a "master of the revels," (lxv,831)[3] a character found in pantomime. Other qualities in the book seem to depend more upon melodrama than fairy tales. Therefore, in order to appreciate how fairy tales especially contribute to the novel's structure and theme, it is necessary to make some distinctions between these popular forms of entertainment.

In the Crummles's section of the novel the infant phenomenon acts out a pantomime, "The Fairy Porcupine," similar to those acted in many theaters during the eighteen-thirties. Dickens enthusiastically enjoyed such performances, describing his fascination in "The Pantomime of Life," [*Bentley's Miscellany*. I(1837)] and praising the stage master's capacity to brandish his wand and to transform immediately setting and characters. When the excited and jealous Mr. Lenville is defeated by Nicholas on the stage at Portsmouth, the episode reflects the antics of Pantaloon and his cohorts, and when Newman Noggs grimaces or shadow punches the imagined nose of Ralph Nickleby, Dickens is again drawing upon the pantomime tradition. In an appraisal of the theatrical influence upon Dickens, William Axton describes in detail the many characteristics of pantomime and its derivatives in extravaganza and burlesque. All three often begin with a fairy story or old children's tale, but these stories merely initiate the comic action upon the stage. "In short, pantomime as Dickens knew it was a curious amalgam of fantasy, realism, topicality, anachronism, grotesquerie, burlesque, spectacle, music, verse, dance, and a serious story."[4] For the most part then, the pantomime serves Dickens as a source for much of his broad comedy and farce.

When Oliver leaves Sowerberry to seek his fortune in *Oliver Twist,* he portrays an archetypal, fairy-tale underdog and not just any orphan (like poor Dick) at the mercy of parish authorities or just any London boy (like Charley Bates); we never expect Oliver to become corrupted by his experiences although Nancy and Fagin's boys do. Nicholas is a similar kind of hero in *Nickleby* who seeks his fortune and whose evil uncle attempts to thwart his progress. But in the course of his adventures, it becomes obvious that Nicholas is also very much a stock figure out of melodrama as Dickens saw it performed in Victorian theaters. For example, in the critical episode in chapter fifty-four, Ralph Nickleby and Arthur Gride have attempted to coerce Madeline Bray into a fulsome marriage, and only the sudden death of her father saves her. Nicholas responds at this point with a splendid example of melodramatic rhetoric: "'Stand off!' cried Nicholas, letting loose all the passion he had restrained till now, 'if this is what I scarcely dare to hope it is, you are caught, villains, in your own toils.'" (718) Like so many characters in the book, Nicholas betrays his melodramatic origin through gesture and speech; even his "story" seems conventional and little more than a version of one of Mr. Crummles's presentations in which "the sympathies of the audience" are stimulated by setting up "a little man contending against a big one." (xxii,280) But as Axton has noted, melodrama like pantomime tends "to appropriate historical, legendary, and folklore materials."[5] The plot action in both pantomime and melodrama, then, is often derived from a fairy-tale source, pantomime adapting it for farce and melodrama for emotional extravagance. This exaggerated, emotional appeal is the most distinguishing trait of melodrama, but as Northrup Frye points out, the apparent ferocity of the emotions aroused is checked by *play* (that is, play-acting); a "protecting wall of play" keeps the reader *from taking seriously* the action and turmoil of the melodramatic mode.[6] On the whole, Dickens's readers have long responded to this formula for making 'em "laugh shudder, and cry."[7]

Fairy tales are not play. In the first place, more than simply stories about younger brothers, stolen princesses, cats in top boots, or ugly ducklings, fairy tales concern what John Buchan calls the very "soul of man"; he asserts that they have their origin in "the most distant deeps of human experience and human fancy," that they are the result of "an eternal impulse in human nature to enliven the actual working life by the invention of tales of another kind of life."[8] These tales disclose a secondary world which possesses its own inner consistency of reality, and, in contrast to a "bewildering and unpredictable everyday world," it is "simple, orderly, and just."[9] In one sense, melodrama is closely allied to this quality of fairy tales; Michael R. Booth explains that "melo-

drama is a dream world, inhabited by dream people and dream justice, offering audiences the fulfillment and satisfaction found only in dreams."[10] But in Faërie the secondary world "obeys its own laws and decorum" and truth is never to be mistaken for the wish-fulfillment of dream; on the contrary, in fairyland the power exists to make "immediately effective by the will the visions of 'fantasy.'"[11] An article in *Household Words* reveals, in part, Dickens's sympathies with fairy-tale fantasy: "There is in all literature nothing that can be produced which shall represent the essential spirit of a man or of a people so completely as a legend or a fairy tale."[12] And in his own fragmentary autobiography Dickens records how the shame and drabness of his boyhood experiences in London forced him to take refuge in a fictitious world. He tells how he would meet at London Bridge the little servant girl engaged by his family which was then lodged in debtor's prison. While waiting for the prison gates to be opened, he filled the time "by telling her quite astonishing fictions about the wharves and tower. 'But I hope I believed them "myself," he would say.'"[13]

Secondly, fairy tales are not merely an art of extravaganza or gesture; they possess a distinctive narrative mode. Northrop Frye has identified three kinds of narrative design: one extreme is *myth* ("an art of implicit metaphor") and the other extreme is *naturalism* ("an art of verisimilitude"). Between the two lies *romance,* the tendency "to displace myth in a human direction and yet, in contrast to 'realism,' to conventionalize content in an idealized direction."[14] Fairy tales comprise this romance mode. When a fairy story begins, an initial low-mimetic emphasis establishes a certain degree of reality, but as the story continues, verisimilitude gradually becomes displaced by an increasing idealization and tendency toward metaphor. Thus, it is the tendency of fairy tales to embrace yet to transcend ordinary experience. In the first chapter of *Nickleby* Dickens describes a world that is bewildering, unjust, and corrupt, and even though Mr. Godfrey Nickleby risks marrying "out of mere attachment," the London world is indifferent to his affectionate nature. The novel begins, then, with a realistic, satirical portrayal of a cash-nexus society filled with financiers who cheat stockholders, parents who abandon children, husbands who ruin wives, and wives who desert husbands. But if people are callously indifferent to values like integrity, generosity, and compassion, this vision of a harsh, realistic world will be transcended in *Nickleby* by another vision of a fairy-tale world where human values are respected.

Dickens relies fundamentally upon fairy-tale plotting to establish the narrative pattern in *Nickleby*. Jerome Meckier shows how "the quest" provides primary thematic and structural unity in the novel.[15] This quest motif represents one of the essential staples of the familiar success story (plot-of-fortune) which is the basis for the narrative formula of fairy stories. This formula involves the instinctively generous but ingenuous protagonist who gains a fortune against seemingly impossible odds. The plot-of-fortune in *Nickleby* is illustrated on the one hand by Nicholas's adventures in Yorkshire and in the evil London world, adventures similar to those endured by all fairy-tale heroes who confront a "Tunnel of Horrors."[16]

Early in the novel Nicholas undertakes his quest for fame and fortune; he has "a thousand visionary ideas" (iii,27) about his future and he enthusiastically encounters the perils of the wide world for he is as bold and free "as any knight that ever set lance in rest." (xvi,202) Although initially deceived by his evil uncle, obstacles and setbacks do not discourage Nicholas and he tells Smike, "I shall surface many thousand times yet, and the harder the thrust that pushes me down, the more quickly I shall rebound." (xxxv,442) This is the nature of the hero as determined by the plot-of-fortune, and it is this buoyancy that ultimately frustrates all of Ralph's cunning and power. Yet if Nicholas is essentially successful against the evil forces that dwell in the dark forest, he does not really learn how to deal with this world. In the plot-of-fortune the hero is not an "innocent" who must learn through agonizing trials to see and act judiciously. Thus, Nicholas is not a prototype for David Copperfield who is "blind" because he acts foolishly. For the most part Nicholas is the typically passive, fairy-tale hero who, acted upon by the evil forces in the world, relies on others' benevolent intervention for his success. When Ralph ultimately fails to destroy Nicholas, he angrily sputters, "There is some spell about that boy. . . . Circumstances conspire to help him. Talk of fortune's favours! What is even money to such Devil's luck as this!" (xliv,569) Ralph pinpoints an essential ingredient of Nicholas's quest and even of the plot-of-fortune itself. Evil may for a time effectively dominate the good, but it cannot extinguish it. It is the hero's task to "hold on."

A further extension of the plot-of-fortune in the novel is Madeline Bray's story. Madeline like Nicholas is a victim of selfish, tyrannical behavior, and she is forced to confront a harsh world (her own "Tunnel of Horrors"). Madeline lives in a hostile world where, as Ralph Nickleby says, there are "'well off; good, rich, substantial men; who would gladly give their daughters, and their own ears with them, to that very man yonder, ape and mummy as he looks.'" (liv,714) Isolated and alone she seems a vulnerable prey to Arthur Gride's lust and Ralph Nickleby's covetousness. These villains are threatening ogres that typically must be overcome in fairy tales; Ralph is "a dragon," (li,676) Gride is "a goblin," (xlvii,623) and Peg Sliderskew is "half a witch." (xi,671) Although faced with such ogres, Nicholas tries to persuade Madeline to reconsider her imminent marriage to Gride, and he vaguely implies that some hidden fortune awaits her if only she can temporarily put off the ceremony. She replies, "No, no, no! It is impossible; it is a child's tale." (liii, 700) Unknowingly, Madeline accurately describes the nature of the plot action, and her fate will depend upon one of the standard narrative devices in the fairy-tale plot-of-fortune, *peripetea*—an unlooked-for reversal. Her father's death illustrates this sudden turn, and Madeline thereby escapes Ralph's trap.

Distinct from pantomime or melodrama, *peripetea* in fairy tales represents what J. R. R. Tolkien calls "sudden and miraculous grace: never to be counted on to recur. It does not deny the existence . . . of sorrow and failure [Smike, for example, dies]: the possibility of these is necessary to the joy of deliverance; it denies (in the face of much evidence, if you will) universal final defeat and in so far is *evangelium,* giving a fleeting glimpse of Joy, Joy beyond the wall of the world, poignant as grief."[17] A fairy wand may happily transform a scene in pantomime; a sudden turn may satisfy a sentimental wishfulfillment in melodrama. But fairy tales posit a secondary world which every so often impinges upon an otherwise quotidian reality. *Peripetea* therefore has a particular poignancy because of our recognition that some of the qualities and even details in this fairy world are similar to normal existence, that the "laws and decorum" experienced in fairyland also operate to a degree in reality, and that joy experienced in Faërie can also exist in our world. As Tolkien states, the joyful ending is "a brief vision that . . . may be a far-off gleam or echo of *evangelium* in the real world."[18]

Besides the search for fortune by a wandering protagonist and the reversal-of-fortune motif, the fairy-tale plot in *Nickleby* also incorporates another standard ingredient—the active intervention by a fairy godfather (the Cheeryble brothers). In fairy tales, protagonists are for the most part child-like or innocent and neither expected nor required to assume adult responsibilities; fairy godfathers accept the responsibility for resolving conflict and creating the possibility for the inevitable "and they lived happily ever after." An early reviewer of Dickens's novels notes precisely this quality in Dickens's fiction: "One is tempted to make in favour of Dickens's fictitious children the wish which in our own childhood we fondly expressed in reference to kittens and lambs; namely, that they might never grow up into cats and sheep respectively."[19] It is Nicholas's role to await the Cheeryble's help and their commands; their benevolent but serious comment, "you must do as you are bid," accurately defines both their own and Nicholas's role in the plot.

The Cheerybles appear exactly when Ralph has determined to inflict upon Nicholas the full knowledge that wealth possesses power. As intervening fairy-godfathers they immediately enter the action against Ralph and commit themselves to protect Nicholas: "'Nobody [brother Charles is speaking] belonging to you shall be wronged. They shall not hurt a hair of your head, or the boy's head, or your mother's head or your sister's head. I have said it, brother Ned has said it, Tim Linkinwater has said it. We have all said it, and we'll all do it.'" (xlvi,596-97) From the beginning description of Charles Cheeryble, Dickens emphasizes the lively energy radiating through and outward from him: "there were so many little lights hovering about the corners of his mouth and eyes, that it was not a mere amusement, but a positive pleasure and delight to look at him." (xxxv, 449) Both Cheerybles possess "restless excitement," and, whenever they rub their hands in satisfied delight (which they do constantly) over some good works presented for their action, they perform like Aladdin's genie who is summoned by rubbing the lamp. Nursery rhyme allusion also accentuates their fairy-tale nature; their speech is softly modulated as if "they had, in collecting the plums from Fortune's choicest pudding, retained a few for present use, and kept them in their mouths." (xxxv,453) As fairy godfathers (who illustrate the virtue of hearty and selfless benevolence) the Cheerybles belong at the very heart of the joyful community, and a vision of festivity and good cheer concludes the novel as the Cheerybles invite the worthy to a feast, the like of which has not been seen "since the world began." This feast inaugurates a new Eden, and it is through the plot-of-fortune and a fairy-tale mode that the Cheeryble world is offered as a substitute vision for reality.

II

In *Nickleby* the world of Faërie is contrasted with a dull and ugly commercial world. London seethes with activity, and Dickens indicates that because Newgate prison lies "at the very heart" of the city, the source and lifeblood of this activity are contaminated. Crowds mill around vendors in the street, and "giant currents of life . . . flow ceaselessly" by the prison, but the lonely men sentenced to die look out upon masses of white faces which lack any "impress of pity or compassion." (iv,29-30) The city of London is thus a great wasteland devoid of beauty and greenness. In chapter two Ralph Nickleby closes a large account book and then gazes abstractedly through a dirty window: "Some London houses have a melancholy little plot of ground behind them, usually fenced in by four high whitewashed walls, and frowned upon by stacks of chimneys. . . . People sometimes call these dark yards 'gardens': it is not supposed that they were ever planted, but rather that they are pieces of unreclaimed land, with the withered vegetation of the original brick-field. No man thinks of walking in this desolate place, or of turning it to any account." (ii,8) Chapter four heightens the sense of desolation with the description of Snow Hill, and the following Dotheboys Hall chapters reveal that the world outside London is equally bleak and brutal. The insert story, "The Five Sisters of York," also contributes to the wasteland imagery; the narrator of the story realizes that men could indeed build a heaven on earth if men had hearts as pure as children: "But, the faint image of Eden which is stamped upon them in childhood, chafes and rubs in our rough struggles with the world, and soon wears away: too often to leave nothing but a mournful blank remaining."[20] This faded and tarnished image of a Garden of Eden recalls the blighted garden Ralph gazed at earlier; both contrast the new Eden to be created by the Cheerybles at the conclusion to the novel. But in the early portions of the book, the fallen Eden re-emphasizes how reality is a wilderness in which men lead lonely lives: London is "as complete a solitude as the plains of Syria;" (xx, 246) Nicholas faces "the wilderness of London;" (xxxv,450) Smike fears to return to the city "so great was his apprehension of traversing the streets alone"; (xl,510) and Kate reminds her mother how she has "seen all the misery and desolation that death can bring, and known the lonesome feeling of being solitary and alone in crowds." (xliii,563) Throughout the novel, then, Dickens portrays a society of the lonely and dispossessed.

Nicholas's quest is ultimately a search for a solution to such catastrophe, and despite the brutalizing forces at work in society, Dickens seems to suggest in the first half of *Nickleby* that something might yet be done to change social conditions. Although the characters who flash by in the novel appear as grotesque as the dismal chimneys leaning crazily in the "tumble-down street" where the Kenwigs live, yet Miss La Creevy, a typical representative of the dispossessed, still has a heart big enough for Gog and Magog, and Dickens asserts that "there are many warm hearts in the same solitary guise as poor little Miss La Creevy's." (xx,246) The business of the novel is to assure us that this inherent affection and good will need not be further diminished, that a society can develop where men are decent to one another. But on a low-mimetic level where protagonists have the same "power of action" as ordinary mortals,[21] rational attempts to survive and to inaugurate this new society fail. Nicholas's "opportunity" in Squeers's school is illusory; forced to attempt some new method for supporting himself and his family, he reasonably applies to the unemployment office only to encounter a society filled with stupidity, lust and self-aggrandisement. Kate also seeks employment but meets with similar disillusion both at the Mantalini's and Wititterly's. Frustrated in all attempts, Nicholas suddenly meets Charles Cheeryble, and as the fairy-tale plot assumes its predominance in the story, it becomes clear that Dickens has not discovered any means whereby society might be realistically regenerated.

Only in a fairy tale can Dickens make "immediately effective by the will" the values of the heart, good cheer, and fellow-feeling which he so enthusiastically embraces in the novel. Although Bernard Bergonzi concludes that Dickens's solutions to dilemmas based upon fairy-tale idealism "could only have been presented . . . by a writer who was not yet thinking in social terms,"[22] E. L. Woodward has noted in *The Age of Reform, 1815-1870* (Oxford, 1938) that in the early Victorian period "the fund of skill and experience at the service of society was limited, and . . . the treatment of social and economic questions was more haphazard and empirical than Englishmen were ready to acknowledge." (p. 15) By superimposing the fairy tale upon a low-mimetic mode in *Nickleby,* Dickens dramatizes emphatically this lack of "skill and experience at the service of society." As a result, *Nickleby* must rely upon good cheer and benevolence which exist outside ordinary experience in a realm of Faërie. The fairy-tale mode in the novel becomes an appeal to men's hearts, an appeal to reject sordid reality in favor of an imaginatively conceived, ideal community created by the Cheeryble brothers.

III

On the whole, Dickens's use of fairy tale in *Nickleby* is in keeping with his essential "Carol philosophy" and belief in the desirability of infusing the most ordinary life with fantasy.[23] Nevertheless, although fantasy establishes the primary mode in the novel, the low-mimetic insistently intrudes. Even after Nicholas and Kate have fulfilled their quests and communed at the Cheerybles's apocalyptic feast, they cannot fully escape reality. In the next to the last chapter, the two of them lose their way in London's "labyrinth of streets" and encounter the hypocritical Mantalini and the scold with whom he is now living. The novel seems to have returned full-cycle to where it began, and Nicholas, himself, observes how "everything looked as if he had seen it but yesterday, and not even a flake of the white crust on the roofs had melted away." (822) Indeed, underlying Dickens's art in *Nickleby* is an unresolved dichotomy between the claims of fantasy and realism. One episode especially (dealing with the mad, old gentleman who courts Mrs. Nickleby), reveals how Dickens's comic sense seems almost unwittingly to be challenging the validity of the fairy-tale vision as a viable alternative to real life.

At one time a "covetous," "selfish," and "guzzling" scoundrel who spurned wife, daughters and sons, the old gentleman represents another of the villains like Squeers, Ralph, and Gride who sneak through the pages of *Nicholas Nickleby.* Other characters in the novel know the man has gone mad, his speech being incomprehensible and nonsensical: "'Why is it that beauty is always obdurate. . . . Is it . . . in consequence of the

statue at Charing Cross having been lately seen on the Stock Exchange at midnight, walking arm-in-arm with the Pump from Aldgate, in a riding habit?'" (xli,533-34) Mrs. Nickleby immediately understands her neighbor and assumes that he is courting her in good faith, but then throughout the book Mrs. Nickleby apparently triumphs over the facts of real life; her breezy vivacity continually shrinks looming portents of evil and petty viciousness to inconsequential dimensions, allowing her to spend her time cheerfully pursuing her own interests and dreams. In this episode she "naturally understands" the gentleman because like him she speaks through inflated metaphor. For example, speaking of Smike's behavior, she says at one point,

> "I hope . . . that this unaccountable conduct may not be the beginning of his taking to his bed and living there all his life, like the Thirsty Woman of Tutbury, or the Cock-lane Ghost, or some of those extraordinary creatures. . . . Miss La Creevy, you know, of course. Which was it that didn't mind what the clergyman said?"
>
> "The Cock-lane Ghost, I believe."
>
> "Then I have no doubt . . . that it was with him by great-grandfather went to school; for I know the master of his school was a dissenter, and that would, in a great measure, account for the Cock-lane Ghost's behaving in such an improper manner to the clergyman when he grew up. Ah! Train up a Ghost—child, I mean. . . ."
>
> (xlix,641-42)

The gentleman courts Mrs. Nickleby, punctuating his speeches with references from fairy tale and romance; yet it is on the whole Mrs. Nickleby's perception of the man's behavior and diction which maintains the illusion of the courtship. The whole episode in fact depends upon Mrs. Nickleby's imagination and metaphoric power to alter reality to fit her conception of how it ought to be.

Mrs. Nickleby's gentleman caller professes his love in the fairest terms. "'Queen of my soul . . . this goblet sip!'" (xli,533) He believes the Nickleby garden "'an enchanted spot, where the most divine charms . . . waft mellifluousness over the neighbor's gardens.'" (xli,534) Addressing her as "fairest creature," the man wishes to know if Mrs. Nickleby is "a princess" and he asserts that "'beings like you can never grow old. . . . So be mine, be mine . . . Gog and Magog, Gog and Magog.'" (xli,536-37) Blacking the sky with a shower of vegetable tribute and plunging down the chimney intoning "'Is she then failed in her truth, the beautiful maid I adore!'", (xlix,644) the man performs the tasks a fairy-tale hero undertakes to woo his princess. This behavior is credible to Mrs. Nickleby because she considers herself a worthy princess and therefore recognizes that the poor man places "'himself in such a dreadful situation on my account.'" (xlix,647)

When the passionate lover, invoking the aid of "Cormoran and Blunderbore," spurns Mrs. Nickleby and unexpectedly lays siege to Miss La Creevy's heart, Mrs. Nickleby's power to triumph over adversity is brilliantly revealed. Earlier, the mad gentleman had wished to know if Mrs. Nickleby was the "niece to the commissioners of Paving." (xli,535) Attempting to redirect the gentleman's attention from Miss La Creevy to herself, Mrs. Nickleby reminds her gallant that she, indeed, is the one he had earlier mistaken for the "niece to the Council of Paving Stones." (xlix,649) The slight alteration "to the Council of Paving Stones" underscores Mrs. Nickleby's metaphoric exuberance, extravagance, and comic absurdity, and when the man's insistently fickle behavior ("Avaunt! Cat!") apparently compels Mrs. Nickleby to confront at last her deluded perception of the world, her astonishing power to transcend the obvious reaches its peak. "'I shall never forgive myself, Kate . . . never! That gentleman has lost his senses, and *I* am the unhappy cause.'" (xlix,650) Having warned Nicholas and Kate not to treat the matter lightly and at peace in her virtuous heart, Mrs. Nickleby washes her hands of responsibility and turns immediately to new concerns, effectively dismissing any unpleasantness which the scene might have reasonably created.

Yet, upon consideration, one is aware that Mrs. Nickleby is not particularly admirable: she slights Miss La Creevy; she misconstrues the characters and motives of Pyke and Pluck; she makes Kate's life especially trying. Only fleetingly does she ever sense what the reader is forced to contemplate uncomfortably: "Mrs. Nickleby began to have a glimmering that she had been rather thoughtless now and then, and was conscious of something like self-reproach as she embraced her daughter." (xliii,564) In the characterization of Mrs. Nickleby as contrasted with that of the Cheerybles, Dickens illustrates the fine line between the latter's creative imagination which makes the possible true and the former's unhealthy, shabby, sentimental state of mind which is satisfied by dream-like escapism. In this sense one may see in Mrs. Nickleby a prototype for Sairy Gamp, a character Dickens later condemns for trying to manipulate the world to satisfy pointedly selfish ends. But in *Nicholas Nickleby* where Dickens has relied heavily upon a fairy-tale fantasy to create an alternative to a world peopled with vicious, self-seeking individuals, it is disconcerting to find Dickens insisting that Mrs. Nickleby's "prophetic anticipations" are at last realized.

Jerome Meckier suggests that in *Nicholas Nickleby* Dickens strives "for an unattainable inclusiveness that combines romance, melodrama, tragedy, Bible, and the different moods associated with each."[24] But despite the conflicting modes of pantomime, sentimental romance, comic gothicism, melodrama, and fairy-tale fantasy, a documentation of the fairy-tale motifs central to Dickens's conception clarifies the design and thematic unity of *Nicholas Nickleby.* The novel begins with Ralph Nickleby rich and powerful sitting at his desk, his head sprinkled with powder in an unsuccessful attempt to conceal his meanness; it concludes with a joyous picture of Tim Linkinwater, his head "powdered like a twelfth cake." If reality never fully disappears in the novel, the low-mimetic never intrudes enough to subvert completely the book's fairy-tale vision, and motifs from fairy tale lead consistently toward the novel's resolution. The dingy house Ralph provided for Kate and Mrs. Nickleby, symbolic of decrepit shabbiness and the blight which infests the real world, is ultimately transformed into the comfortable retreat in Devonshire.

Notes

1. "'The Yellow Dwarf' and *The Old Curiosity Shop,*" *NCF* [*Nineteenth-Century Fiction*], 25(1970), 96-99; *Dickens and the Fairy Tale* (Bowling Green: Bowling Green State University Press, 1972).

2. Russell M. Goldfarb, review of *Dickens and the Fairy Tale,* by Michael Kotzin, *DSN* [*Dickens Studies Newsletter*], 3(1972), 112.

3. References to *Nicholas Nickleby* are to The Oxford Illustrated Dickens (London: Oxford University Press, 1966); chapter and page numbers are included when appropriate.

4. *Circle of Fire* (Lexington: University of Kentucky Press, 1966), p. 20.

5. *Ibid.,* p. 25.

6. *Anatomy of Criticism* (Princeton: Princeton University Press, 1957), p. 47.

7. George H. Ford, *Dickens and His Readers* (New York: Norton, 1965), p. 38.

8. *The Novel and the Fairy Tale,* The English Association Pamphlet, No. 79 (Oxford: Oxford University Press, 1931), pp. 6-7.

9. Alfed David and Mary Elizabeth David, eds., *The Twelve Dancing Princesses* (New York: New American Library, 1964), p. xii.

10. *English Melodrama* (London: H. Jenkins, 1965), p. 14.

11. J. R. R. Tolkien, "On Fairy-Stories," *The Tolkien Reader* (New York: Ballantine Books, 1966), 22.

12. "The School of the Fairies," *Household Words,* 11(1855), 546.

13. John Forster, The Life of Charles Dickens, 2 vols., n. d., with Notes and an Index by A. J. Hoppé (1872); rpt. London: Dent, 1966, I, 27.

14. Frye, p. 137.

15. "The Faint Image of Eden: The Many Worlds of *Nicholas Nickleby*," *Dickens Studies Annual*, 1(1970), 129-146.

16. Lionel Trilling, *E. M. Forster* (Norfolk: New Directions Books, 1943), p. 79.

17. Tolkien, p. 68.

18. *Ibid.*, p. 71.

19. "Charles Dickens and *David Copperfield*," review article, *Fraser's Magazine* (Dec., 1850), 75.

20. On the whole, of course, the insert tales in *Nickleby*, "The Five Sisters of York" (sentimental romance) and "The Baron of Grogzwig" (comic gothicism), maintain an essentially fanciful tone, another example of Dickens drawing on genres somewhat related to fairy-tale fantasy in that both tales reinforce the value of fancy in men's lives and deal pointedly with characters who have tried to deny this value. In their respective stories the oppressive monk and the Baroness fail to stifle in Alice or the Baron von Koëldwethout an enthusiasm of being alive, but shortly after this Nicholas will discover how Squeers has effectively destroyed all hope in the boys at Dotheboys Hall so that their only respite lies in fleeting dreams, "the bright creatures of poem and legend," and even these are too quickly dispelled by "grim care and stern reality." (xiii, 146) Yet Dickens was always opposed to what he would eventually define as a Gradgrind philosophy, and these insert tales in *Nickleby* emphasize that "relaxation and diversion, 'flowers' and 'colour' . . . were for Dickens self-justifying." P. A. W. Collins, "Queen Mab's Chariot Among the Steam Engines: Dickens and 'Fancy,'" *EST* [*English Studies Today,*] 42(1961), 81.

21. Frye, p. 33.

22. "*Nicholas Nickleby*," in *Dickens and the Twentieth Century*, ed. John Gross and Gabriel Pearson (1962; rpt. Toronto: University of Toronto Press, 1966), 76.

23. Collins, p. 78.

24. Meckier, p. 145.

Ella Westland (essay date June 1991)

SOURCE: Westland, Ella. "Little Nell and the Marchioness: Some Functions of Fairy Tale in *The Old Curiosity Shop*." *Dickens Quarterly* 8, no. 2 (June 1991): 68-75.

[In the following essay, Westland maintains that Dickens used fairy-tale motifs in The Old Curiosity Shop *to advance his own rather radical critique of the capitalist system.]*

> The Ring, with all its gods and giants and dwarfs, its water-maidens and Valkyries, its wishing-cap, magic ring, enchanted sword, and miraculous treasure, is a drama of today, and not of a remote and fabulous antiquity. It could not have been written before the second half of the nineteenth century, because it deals with events which were only then consummating themselves.
>
> George Bernard Shaw, *The Perfect Wagnerite* (167)

Readers likely to fall under the spell of that arch-magician, Charles Dickens, would do well to keep this warning of Shaw in mind when they are debating Dickens's uses of fairy tale. Shaw insisted that *The Ring* was not a timeless work of myth, but inevitably a work of its own place and time—a product of Europe at the height of nineteenth-century capitalism. In this essay, I proceed on the basis that *The Old Curiosity Shop,* with its sweet doomed maiden, its gold-laden dwarf, its rags-to-riches princess, and its feckless folk hero, is a fiction of England in 1840, and not of a distant and fairytale past. I find in its old fairytale motifs new meanings about Britain's burgeoning capitalist system; ultimately I suggest that Dickens's political thinking, though often contradictory, is sometimes more radical than recent critics have come to believe.

The *Old Curiosity Shop* is a novel of many modes, and its fairytale structures function in a variety of ways. Little Nell's story, which works through the inversion of the storybook paradigm, can be interpreted as a closed allegory, a pessimistic rendering of the early Victorian economic process. In light relief to Nell's somber story, the comic transformation of a kitchen slavey into a "Marchioness" invokes an alternative fairytale form, and opens up unexpectedly optimistic possibilities for a capitalist future.

When Dickens revised the serial version of his novel, he added to an early chapter the explicit comment that Nell "seemed to exist in a kind of allegory" (56; ch. 1), so signalling to his readers that they should ponder the deeper "real" meaning of this fairytale world of ugly dwarfs and sleeping beauties. In the following pages, I argue that Nell's story is dominated by the villainous Quilp, a brilliant incarnation of the forces of early nineteenth-century capitalism; Nell comes to stand for capitalism's many victims, and above all for the threatened economic life of the countryside. The Marchioness's tale, by contrast, offers the seductive hypothesis that the poorest people of the cities may yet survive and thrive under the new economic system. Dick Swiveller, who plays the necessary part of the Prince in the servant's story, also has the important role of channelling the reader's potential skepticism away from the Marchioness, enabling her to hold out some hope for a capitalist future beyond the end of the novel and the death of Little Nell.

If we hold Little Nell's narrative against the fairytale template produced by Vladimir Propp, we can account for some of the most powerful and painful effects of her story. According to Propp's classic paradigm—which would have been immediately recognizable to Dickens's readers—the heroine's happy home is targeted for destruction by the villain, who goes off in chase when she attempts to escape. But though Nell and Quilp play their archetypal roles to perfection in the opening chapters, raising the reader's expectations of a traditional confrontation and dénouement, the pattern gradually begins to fall apart. There is no successful rescue to follow the villain's pursuit, and although there is a struggle with the villain ending in Quilp's death, Nell plays no part in the victory. Instead of a triumphant return and a wedding, we read of Nell's gradual decline and death. As the fairytale possibility of a happy resolution is drawn out at agonizing length, the tension between the two patterns increases, and the alternative Proppian conclusion foregrounds both the failure of Nell's quest for peace and security, and the ultimate victory of the evil forces represented by Quilp.[1]

When Quilp enters the curiosity shop with his bag of gold, his supernatural presence introduces into the story one of its most potent symbols for the capitalist economy. Ancient storybook dwarf though he seems, it is Quilp who incarnates the principles of the modern capitalist world. (Dickens can be at his most socially relevant when he is furthest away from realism.) The villain quickly reveals himself as a shape-changing creature of many forms—Rumpelstiltskin and ogre, bad angel and stepfather, usurer and landlord, husband and rapist. He gives an impression of being ubiquitous and indestructible, inhabiting several abodes in the city, materialising unexpectedly in the provinces in pursuit of the escaping travellers, and returning home when everyone believes him dead. Like the demon of industrial capitalism described in Thomas Carlyle's 1839 essay on "Chartism" (which Dickens seems to have read while writing the *Curiosity Shop*), the dwarf is capable of "changing his *shape* like a very Proteus" (Carlyle 174). His strange powers of mobility and metamorphosis are like those of capital, which converts itself from coin to paper, from sterling to marks, from commodities to land, from shipping to machinery. Quilp is not a seedy example of a minor capitalist; he stands for capital itself.

It is a lust for power, not wealth, that drives Quilp. He likes to own people's dwellings (and by extension their inhabitants), to force them to work for him, to control their lives and their freedom. In his counting-house he tortures a huge wooden sailor, symbolizing his terrible design of denying people their humanity and subjecting them to his cruel whims. The possession of people, of labor, is a central principle of capitalism. The surreal potency of this priapic creature is another weapon in his

war of humiliation and domination. And the insistent sexual metaphor is developed further in Quilp's cannibalistic traits, as he hangs in his counting-house hammock like a spider in the center of a web, waiting to feed off his helpless prey (470; ch. 50).[2] The vampire analogy takes this line of thinking further. A stake is to be thrust through Quilp's heart at burial, under the pretext of his being a suicide (665; ch. 73), but this rationalization does not obscure the stake's folk significance: Quilp is a vampire, lusting for blood and endlessly reviving, whose resurrections can be ended only by this violent ritual. So the dwarf manifests capital's "vampire thirst for the living blood of labour" (Marx 1: 259),[3] and Little Nell becomes the vampire's prey, growing weaker and weaker as he keeps up his pursuit. She dies with the vitality leeched out of her by that oppressor of the people from whom there is no hiding-place in the length and breadth of England, the capitalist system.

Recognizing Nell as the representative of capitalism's victims, particularly the exploited children of the industrial towns, is now a longstanding critical position (e.g., Schwarzbach 70-77). But in my reading Nell stands for the country rather than the city, and dies because the countryside is dying. Of course the English village was not totally dead in 1840 (or in 1990); nevertheless, it was slowly and quietly declining. The land, so overwhelmingly important throughout history, was by 1840 becoming economically subordinate to commerce, finance and industry. The forces that were crowding the population into towns were also sapping the strength of the rural communities—and unnatural demographic movement which Thomas Hardy later bitterly compared to "the tendency of water to flow uphill when forced by machinery" (*Tess,* 395; ch. 51). Nell cannot survive in an urban environment and tries to reverse the trend in the hope of returning to society's rural roots, but the villages offer no refuge from the gathering momentum of economic change. Her quest takes her back to a crumbling medieval ruin, where she fades away into a distant feudal past.

The marred fairytale plot provides the underlying structure that carries the novel's anti-pastoral theme. The predictable Proppian story-line that points towards Nell's ultimate rescue and triumph turns out to be as misleading as the "broken finger-post" (248; ch. 24) which points to a succession of half-deserted villages. From the beginning of the book, there is a build-up of resistance to the folktale rhythm. The heroine's early death is heard in her name ("knell"); the talk of death and cemeteries that starts in the opening pages grows into a strong earthward pull as Nell looks down into grave and crypt and pit. The victim drifts further away from the villain and has no share in his defeat. The seeker's suffering, and the reader's, mimics the pain of a whole dying culture.

So there was no way of saving Nell, any more than there was a way of saving the old villages, and Dickens only pretended that he could have protected his heroine. He tried to prevaricate about the necessity of her death (letters and friends tell us), but he could not go against its inevitability. John Ruskin accused Dickens of sending Nell like a lamb to the slaughter for the sake of his sentimental market (34: 275), but an inveterate city-hater like Ruskin should have read Dickens better. Nell was indeed murdered, but by the economic events around her that no-one was able to impede. It was Dickens's sense of historical determinism that sapped the energies of Nell and her narrative, and rendered the author powerless to save his heroine as the plot unwound towards its predestined end.

If my interpretation of Little Nell's narrative seems valid to other readers, this will partly be due to the support it receives from other structures in the text. My reading of Quilp, for example, invites a connection with other images and associations. As John Lucas has recognised (86-87), there are marked correspondences between the dynamic dwarf and the diabolical Midlands furnaces that encourage the attribution of socio-economic significance to the nature and narrative of Quilp. Similarly, my case for an allegorical parallel between Nell and the declining village is reinforced within the text by Dickens's insistent use of the literary image of the lost village green, that communal meeting place of Goldsmith's "Deserted Village" and Blake's "Songs of Innocence" which echoes through the writing of the industrial revolution. When Nell reaches the hamlet she is to die in, the old clergyman wishes that he could see her "dancing on the green" rather than "sitting in the shadow of our mouldering arches" (486; ch. 52).[4] But Nell's life is bound up with the fate of the village greens, and the time for dancing is over.

Vladimir Propp would have deeply disliked such a reading of Little Nell's story. In an essay on "Folklore and Reality" (1963), he attacks such crude class interpretations of Russian tales, where the wolf is seen as an "oppressor of the people" and Baba Jaga as "a real exploiter" of her animal servants. However, in the same paper he makes another vital point that will help to support my interpretation of the Marchioness's tale, when he claims that folk literature has the important function of "represent[ing] the *aspirations* of a particular period" (16-17; emphasis added). This statement opens up a large literary debate about romance and realism—debate which the genre of fairy tale concentrates in a peculiarly intense way. And it is by following this lead that we will gain some valuable insights into the purpose of *The Old Curiosity Shop*'s rags-to-riches plot.

One meaning of the Marchioness's story emerges from its mirroring of Nell's narrative. Like the old folk tales that follow the fate of brothers as they leave home and go their different ways, *The Old Curiosity Shop* presents Nell and the Marchioness as two "sisters" with divergent destinies. Sophronia is Nell's urban double: the girls are the same age, both small and overworked, one an orphan and the other illegitimate. But the Marchioness, shut into a cagelike kitchen in the heart of this urban complex of cages, can use her native wit to escape. And when challenged to gamble, she becomes an avid student in the art of winning sixpences, happy to establish her right to take part in the economic game around her. Nell, gentle and innocent, cannot cope with London's competitiveness and corruption; the Marchioness, resilient and streetwise, can survive and succeed. Nell is the spiritual child of the declining countryside; but the Marchioness is the child of the growing city—the Gretel who escapes from the cage and boils the witch, living proof that the evils of Quilpish capitalism can be overcome by the same people who seem destined to be its victims.

The Marchioness looks at first less like a resourceful heroine than a passive Cinderella awaiting a fairy godmother. She is relegated to the kitchen by her wicked stepmother (or locked in a dungeon by a she-dragon), with Dick playing the role of Buttons and risking his employers' wrath to entertain her. But as the fairytale plot thickens, her role changes (to use Propp's terms) from "victim" to "seeker-hero": she defies her captors, outwits them with her magical key, and flies after Dick to save him. In a marvellous parody of the sleeping princess being awakened by her prince, Dick is roused from his delirium to find the Marchioness in his bachelor rooms. He persists in believing that he has woken up in an enchanted palace in the presence of the Princess of China: "'Arabian Night, certainly,' thought Mr. Swiveller; 'they always clap their hands instead of ringing the bell. Now for the two thousand black slaves with jars of jewels on their heads'" (582; ch. 64). But it turns out that Dick's princess is the kitchen urchin herself, who is transformed over the years into a lovely young woman. From being a nameless child she wins a plethora of names: Marchioness, Sophronia Sphynx, Sophronia Swiveller. She marries her middle-class prince and takes a huge step up in the social hierarchy, symbolized by the courtesy title of Marchioness that her husband has bestowed on her.

For the novel to prioritize the most fantastic kind of fairy tale in this way is a bold strategic move. The Marchioness's story gives the urban poor some hope of escape from the trap of economic exploitation, demonstrating that action can be taken by the smallest servant girls to bring about a dramatic improvement in their daily lot. Admittedly, the Marchioness does not herald anything as revolutionary as the end of industrial capitalism. She may win in the capitalist city, but she does so on capitalist terms: her childlike cardplaying is a way of rehearsing her part for the real guilty gambling that constitutes the economic system. Dickens, in the furthest reaches of his imagination, never fantasized about the abolition of capitalism. But he dared to envisage its transformation, creating here a radical vision of the rise of the oppressed. This is a plot, to stress Propp's crucial point, that can represent the *aspirations* rather than the actualities of a period of great social turmoil and distress.

Many readers and theorists have come to believe in the fairy tale's aspirational function, its essential liberating power. In any new situation it tends to be subversive rather than subservient, retaining what some historians see as its original function as an expression of hope among people whose practical scope for changing their social situation was small. As Jack Zipes has put it,

> Folk and fairy tales have always spread word through their fantastic images about the feasibility of utopian alternatives, and this is exactly why the dominant social classes have been vexed by them. Beginning with the period of the Enlightenment, folk and fairy tales were regarded as useless for the bourgeois rationalization process.
>
> (3)[5]

But it would be naive to think that, in the hands of a middle-class writer producing sophisticated fiction for a mixed but predominantly middle-class audience, fairy tales perform the same functions as oral folk tales in rural societies. And this is where Dick Swiveller comes crucially into the total picture of *The Old Curiosity Shop,* allowing us to explore the more dubious bourgeois functions of fairy tale without jeopardizing the radical message of the Marchioness.

For we must accept that Dickens's passionate post-Romantic faith in fairy tale is a key context for understanding his small servant's victory. Since he believed in the power of storytelling to nurture the imagination and bring magic into the dreariest lives, protecting the fairy tale for the children and adults of Victorian England became for Dickens a crusade against the creeping advance of utilitarianism.[6] But this presents us with the strong possibility that the utopian promise of the Marchioness's story might be mere escapism, a harmless diversion to comfort the culturally underprivileged. Dickens was later to claim in the opening issue of *Household Words* that he desired to teach

> the hardest workers at this whirling wheel of toil, that their lot is not necessarily a moody, brutal fact, excluded from the sympathies and graces of imagination . . . [for] in all familiar things, even in those which are repellant on the surface, there is Romance enough, if we will find it out.
>
> (30 March 1850; quoted in Stone, *Uncollected Writings* 1:13)

This is hardly radical rhetoric. It does not take a Chartist to see that distracting workers from their whirling wheel of toil is likely to prevent them fighting the bru-

tal facts of their oppression. If any mistreated servants did read the serial numbers of *The Old Curiosity Shop,* it was unlikely to lead them to seize the keys of their own kitchens. Such an ideology of the imagination also allowed more privileged Victorians to believe that the distress on their doorsteps could be alleviated without any further effort or material intervention on their part. Dickens's middle-class readers could therefore feel that some kind of poetic justice was being done in the novel to a whole oppressed class, who would otherwise remain on the collective conscience of the enlightened bourgeoisie.

However, the novel itself confronts this concern about the abuses of fairy tale through the role of Dick Swiveller. On the one hand, as several critics have convincingly pointed out, Dick represents the kind of creativity that Dickens himself believed in (e.g., Schlicke 135). He is a kind of folktale figure, a self-baptized Dick Whittington; he is also an endless fount of fantastic and delightful ideas, which can transfigure the unglamorous post of clerk and distract even a Sally Brass from her deskbound toil:

> Mr. Swiveller burst in full freshness as something new and hitherto undreamed of [upon the Brasses' legal establishment], lighting up the office with scraps of song and merriment, conjuring with inkstands and boxes of wafers, catching three oranges in one hand, balancing stools upon his chin and penknives on his nose, and constantly performing a hundred other feats of equal ingenuity. . . .
>
> (348-49; ch. 36)

Small wonder that Dick ends with a modest annuity that will allow him to leave his office stool for life, and exchange his single rented room for love in an idyllic semi-rural cottage. He is an expression of his author's brave belief in the uses of enchantment, and the plot brings him his due rewards.

But, on the other hand, the fate of Dick Swiveller is also nicely calculated to show the limits of his powers. He does indeed receive a small fortune, but it is commensurate with his social station and modest enough to be within the bounds of possibility. Although he is rewarded for keeping Fancy alive, making the conspiracies of the Quilp-ites seem somehow irrelevant to the possible joys of living, he has no power to confront and defeat the villain. It is instead the little Marchioness who holds the keys to the master plot. She not only frees herself and saves Dick; she is instrumental, through her intelligent spying on the Brasses, in the release of Kit Nubbles, the resumption of the search for Nell, and the death of the arch-enemy Quilp. By counterpointing the stories of Dick Swiveller and the Marchioness, the novel thus raises questions within the text about the philosophy of fairy tale and the validity of its utopian promise.

I cannot adjudicate in the debate on the production of fairy tale between the romantic radicals who uphold its continuing potency for subversion, and the skeptics who reveal its frequent role in repression. I would argue that every case must be examined in its specific ideological context. In the instance of the Marchioness's tale, however, I would strongly claim that the emancipatory potential of the fairy tale is fulfilled, releasing what Zipes has called the "hope of self-transformation and a better world" (ix). It is here that the novel moves onto different territory, signalling its own attempt to find a way out of the predetermining social forces—and literary forms—that threaten to hedge in its vision. Through the fairy tales of Nell and the Marchioness, Dickens acknowledges both the determining power of socio-economic forces and the possibility of escape. *The Old Curiosity Shop* responsibly allegorizes the workings of early Victorian capitalism, and bravely aspires to find a way out.

Notes

1. The revelant "functions" set out in Propp's *Morphology* trace the opening gambits of the villain (Functions IV-VIII); the departure and adventures of the victim-hero/ine (IX-XV); the pursuit and rescue of the hero/ine (XXI-XXII); the struggle with the villain, ending in his death (XVI, XVIII & XXX); the "transfiguration" (XXIX)—e.g., "A maiden suddenly awakens . . . in a marvelous palace" (63); and the hero's return and wedding (XX & XXXI). Kotzin is ready to entertain an alternative Babes-in-the-Wood model for Nell, but he points out that Dickens's own fairytale paradigm normally involved a happy conclusion: "after Little Nell he refused to strike down a prince or princess at the end" (73).

2. See also 65-6; ch. 3, 82; ch. 4, 223; ch. 21, 242-43; ch. 23, 614; ch. 67, 618; ch. 67, and the illustration that labels Quilp as "man and beast" (549; ch. 60).

3. See also Moretti, especially 91-92.

4. See also 248; ch. 24, 260; ch. 25, 261; ch. 26, 505; ch. 54.

5. See also Bloch and Jameson. For a brilliant attack on commercialized fairy tale, and on naive defenses of fairy tale's radicalism, see Dorfman.

6. See Stone, *Dickens and the Invisible World* (2-5), on Dickens's explicit statements of the 1850s, which culminated in the writing of *Hard Times*. Dickens's feelings had remained constant on this matter from the beginning of his career.

Works Cited

Bloch, Ernst. "The Fairy Tale Moves on in Its Own Time." 1930. Reprinted in Zipes (133-35).

Carlyle, Thomas. *Selected Writings*. Harmondsworth: Penguin, 174.

Dickens, Charles. *The Old Curiosity Shop*. 1841. Harmondsworth: Penguin, 1972.

Dorfman, Ariel, and Armand Mattelart. *How To Read Donald Duck: Imperialist Ideology in the Disney Comic*. 1971. Trans. David Kunzle. 2nd ed. Hungary: International General, 1984.

Hardy, Thomas. *Tess of the d'Urbervilles*. 1891. Paperback edition. London: Macmillan, 1965.

Jameson, Frederic. "Magical Narratives." *The Political Unconscious*. London: Methuen, 1981.

Kotzin, Michael. *Dickens and the Fairy Tale*. Bowling Green: Bowling Green University Popular Press, 1972.

Lucas, John. *The Melancholy Man*. London: Methuen, 1970.

Marx, Karl. *Capital*. 1867. Everyman edition. London: Dent, 1930.

Moretti, Franco. "Dialectic of Fear." *Signs Taken for Wonders*. Trans. Susan Fischer et al. London: Verso, 1983.

Propp, Vladimir. *Morphology of the Folktale*. 1928. Austin: U of Texas P, 1968.

———. "Folklore and Reality." *Theory and History of Folklore*. Manchester: Manchester UP, 1984.

Ruskin, John. Vol. 34 of *The Works of John Ruskin*. London: George Allen, 1908.

Schlicke, Paul. *Dickens and Popular Entertainment*. London: Allen & Unwin, 1985.

Schwarzbach, F. S. *Dickens and the City*. London: Athlone Press, 1979.

Shaw, George Bernard. "The Perfect Wagnerite." 1898. *Major Critical Essays*. London: Constable, 1932.

Stone, Harry. *Dickens and the Invisible World*. London: Macmillan, 1980.

———. Vol. 1 of *The Uncollected Writings of Charles Dickens*. London: Allen Lane, 1969.

Zipes, Jack. *Breaking the Magic Spell: Radical Theories of Folk and Fairy Tales*. London: Heinemann, 1979.

OSCAR WILDE

Michael C. Kotzin (essay date fall 1979)

SOURCE: Kotzin, Michael C. "'The Selfish Giant' as Literary Fairy Tale." *Studies in Short Fiction* 16, no. 4 (fall 1979): 301-09.

[*In the following essay, Kotzin interprets Wilde's "The Selfish Giant" as a "nineteenth-century literary fairy tale," a distinct genre with conventions that distinguish the stories from traditional retellings of folk tales in significant ways.*]

The stories in Oscar Wilde's *The Happy Prince and Other Tales* have delighted children and adults alike since the collection first appeared in 1888, and "The Selfish Giant" has been a particular favorite for many readers. Soon after the book appeared Walter Pater wrote Wilde to tell him "how delightful" he had found the Happy Prince "and his companions." He continued: "I hardly know whether to admire more the wise wit of 'The Wonderful [Remarkable] Rocket,' or the beauty and tenderness of 'The Selfish Giant': the latter certainly is perfect in its kind." Yeats has described the collection as "charming and amusing," and Auden fairly recently singled it out as an example of Wilde's nondramatic prose which "we can still read . . . with great pleasure."[1] But despite the continued exposure and prestigious acclaim that the stories have received, they have been granted little critical attention ("The Selfish Giant," very little), and when criticism has appeared it usually has been in the form of comments relating the stories to broader concerns about Wilde's writings in general.[2] It is time, then, for "The Selfish Giant" to be approached more fully and more directly than it yet has been, as can be done with particular profit if it is looked at as an instance of its "kind," that is, a nineteenth-century literary fairy tale.

The literary fairy tale can be defined as an "original" story similar but not necessarily identical to the anonymous traditional fairy tales of folk culture. The author of a literary fairy tale is aware of the conventions which make the traditional fairy tale a very characteristic type of story. He often reveals considerable self-consciousness in his use of those conventions. Yet he is not bound by them. His purpose is usually not to create a new fairy tale which one might mistake for a folk tale. Rather, he wants to produce a work with clear ties to the fairy-tale tradition but which also has an apparent artfullness; thus the German Romantics, who to a certain extent invented the form, called it the *"Kunstmärchen."* (There is no such standard term in English, and of the alternatives I prefer "literary fairy tale"; "art fairy tale" has other connotations, I think.[3]) Furthermore, the author of the literary fairy tale is not as much of a "mere" storyteller as was the teller of folk fairy tales. He usually also has a purpose in mind which he wants to use the tale to accomplish, and this is so whether the tale is clearly aimed at an adult audience or whether it is ostensibly a "children's" story. The fairy tale thus becomes a vehicle for the investigation of human psychology, the criticism of social behavior, the portrayal of a Christian doctrine, the teaching of a moral lesson, or the expression of an aspect of Romantic philosophy. Though there were literary treatments of fairy tales before the Romantic period, the coming of Romanticism notably stimulated the development of the literary fairy tale. The Romantic respectful appreciation of folk fairy tales drew men of letters toward them, and Romantic tastes led authors to want to create literature which in some ways resembled fairy tales. Then, following the early Romantics, a long list of nineteenth-century writers throughout Europe, including England, produced a series of instances of the literary fairy tale. And Oscar Wilde was one of them.

Of all the conventions of traditional folk fairy tales, two aspects of the tales stand out as most central in characterizing them: they follow typical sorts of narrative patterns in which typical character types participate (thus structuralists find them a particularly rich field for study); and they move in a characteristic unreal world, defined by the presence of a special kind of magic (and it is this aspect of them which is especially emphasized and appreciated by J. R. R. Tolkien[4]). "The Selfish Giant" is built around the kind of narrative structure typical of fairy tales and it is rich in fairy-tale fantasy. In it a group of children, playing the part usually filled by one or two children, face the opposition of a fairy-tale villain, a giant who deprives them of happiness by driving them out of his garden, where they had played during the seven years he was away visiting an ogre. In describing the effects of this expulsion Wilde makes use of animism, a device found in traditional fairy tales which was highly favored by Hans Christian Andersen, Wilde's major precursor as a writer of literary fairy tales, and which was also used by Wilde's personal mentor John Ruskin in his lone instance of the genre, "The King of the Golden River."[5] Like Andersen and Ruskin, Wilde personifies objects in nature, giving them human feelings and describing them as acting in accordance with those feelings. It was spring elsewhere, but

> in the garden of the Selfish Giant it was still winter. The birds did not care to sing in it as there were no children, and the trees forgot to blossom. Once a beautiful flower put its head out from the grass, but when it saw the notice-board [forbidding trespassing] it was so sorry for the children that it slipped back into the ground again, and went off to sleep. The only people who were pleased were the Snow and the Frost. . . . The Snow covered up the grass with her great white cloak, and the Frost painted all the trees silver. Then they invited the North Wind to stay with them, and he came. He was wrapped in furs, and he roared all day about the garden, and blew the chimney-pots down. "This is a delightful spot," he said, "we must ask the Hail on a visit." So the Hail came. Every day for three hours he rattled on the roof of the castle till he broke most of the slates, and then he ran round and round the garden as fast as he could go. He was dressed in grey, and his breath was like ice.[6]

As in most fairy tales, the fortunes of the children ultimately undergo a radical change for the better. A year later, the children creep into the garden through a hole in the wall. The giant, looking out of his bedroom window, sees them in its trees and he sees that the spring too has returned, except in one corner of the garden where there stands a crying boy too small to reach the branches of the tree near him. Again objects in nature are personified: "The poor tree was still quite covered with frost and snow, and the North Wind was blowing and roaring above it. 'Climb up! little boy,' said the Tree, and it bent its branches down as low as it could; but the boy was too tiny." And then the turning point in the story comes, marked by a simple metaphoric touch which is indeed, to use Pater's words, beautiful, tender, and perfect. "And the Giant's heart melted as he looked out" at the boy, Wilde writes, endowing a cliché with new power in this story about a year-long winter which suddenly thaws. "'How selfish I have been!'" says the giant, who now changes his ways as well as his attitudes. He comes down into the garden to put the boy into the tree and to knock down the wall and open the garden to the children "'for ever and ever.'" At first the children are frightened by him and run away, but when they see how kind he is to the little boy they come "running back, and with them [comes] the Spring." The giant is no longer a threat and the children's permanent happiness is assured.

In the remaining part of the story we discover that the children, like the central characters of many fairy tales, achieved their final happiness thanks to outside, supernatural assistance. However, by the time we make that discovery the focus of the story has shifted from the children to the giant. The giant, who plays in the garden with the children, becomes sad because the little boy never returns with the others and they don't know where he is. A note of pathetic sentimentality is sounded, reminiscent of the tone of some of Andersen's stories, as the giant's feelings of loss are described. Years pass and at last, as the moment of his death approaches, the giant is reunited with the child. Magic pervades the scene. Though it is winter, "in the farthest corner of the garden was a tree quite covered with lovely white blossoms. Its branches were golden, and silver fruit hung down from them, and underneath it stood the little boy." He has "the prints of two nails" on his hands and his feet and he tells the giant that they "'are the wounds of Love.'" "'Who art thou?'" asks the giant, who is moved to feel "a strange awe" by these revelations and kneels. The child answers that "'You let me play once in your garden, to-day you shall come with me to my garden, which is Paradise.'" The child, we realize, is Christ, who came as a child and later was crucified. In stimulating the giant's heart to melt, Christ the child had not only helped the innocent children to remain in the garden, thus aiding them the way a good fairy might help children in a fairy tale; he also had served the giant, making him worthy of gaining happiness in the garden during the balance of his life and in heaven after his death, which now comes. "When the

children ran in [to the garden] that afternoon, they found the Giant lying dead under the tree, all covered with white blossoms." The child's wounds are the wounds of Love in that he allowed himself to suffer them because he loved sinners like the giant, and so that through love of him such men could be saved. "The Selfish Giant" is not just a fairy tale about the children's victory over the giant. It is also a Christian parable about the salvation of the giant, salvation which he gains by loving Christ.

It is not altogether rare for a fairy tale to have a Christian dimension, and Iona and Peter Opie point out that "a curious parallel to the Christ story is apparent" particularly in fairy tales which describe spells and releases from them. "The man of perfect heart, living in the guise of a poor carpenter's son [in our case as a weak child], has to be accepted in his lowly state. . . . Had Christ been shown in his full glory, recognition of his virtues, whether by pauper or by prince, would have been valueless. On the face of it the message of the fairy tales is that transformation to a state of bliss is effected not by magic, but by the perfect love of one person for another."[7] In the stories discussed by the Opies, such as "Beauty and the Beast," the Christ-like figure is helped and loved and then, transformed, he reveals his true identity and the glory that is his, and brings happiness to his helper. Similarly, Wilde's child, helped and loved by the giant, reappears to reveal himself as not only wounded but also with magical powers and the ability to bring the giant to Paradise.

In Wilde's story, as we have noticed, the Christian meaning is not submerged the way that it is in most of those traditional folk fairy tales where it can be found. Here the Christian meaning is quite explicit, as it is in many literary fairy tales and particularly in ones by Andersen and by George MacDonald, a British Victorian writer who, along with Andersen and Ruskin, was a possible influence on Wilde as an author of fairy tales. Famous stories like Andersen's "The Little Mermaid" and "The Red Shoes" and MacDonald's *At the Back of the North Wind* are obvious exempla for Christian sermons. Like "The Selfish Giant" they are versions of the Everyman story in which it is shown that the reward for proper Christian behavior is a happiness which comes after death. In these and in other, similar stories by Andersen and MacDonald the introduction of such meaning can strike one as the injection of an alien element into the fairy-tale context. Characters no longer dwell in the timeless realm of fairy tales. Instead, they live in a world of time where time is worthless in reference to eternity. Happiness is not available to them in fairyland or on earth but only in heaven. Despite his Christian meanings, Wilde is able to keep his story closer to the fairy-tale context than Andersen and MacDonald do. He does that by making it, in effect, two stories: the "pure" fairy tale about the children whose final status in the garden is intended to last "for ever and ever" (and indeed, we never hear about their growing old), and the fairy tale with obvious Christian implications about the giant who does grow "very old and feeble" and finally dies and goes to heaven. The ending of the children's story, which we had been prepared to respond to as though it were something final, thus also becomes but one stage in the giant's story, which has its own major climax later. This introduces a structural awkwardness which I think deprives the story as a whole of the perfection which Pater claimed for it. But nevertheless Wilde here is quite successful in having things both ways, for despite the presence of the Christian elements the story remains dominated by its fairy-tale ambience, thanks to the presence within it of the children's "pure" fairy tale and of the fairy-tale elements in the giant's story, particularly the workings of its plot.

As fairy tale the giant's story has parallels with tales of the "Toads and Diamonds" type in which a person confronts a strange creature who often is later discovered to have supernatural powers: if the person responds to the creature in a selfish way then he is punished, as is the sister from whose mouth toads fall, but if he is generous and kind then he gains a reward, as does the other sister, who produces diamonds. This motif, repeated, provides the major narrative pattern of Ruskin's "The King of the Golden River." In its first chapter a strange man is treated cruelly by Hans and Schwartz, two "black brothers" who refuse to share shelter or food with him on a stormy night. As a result the man, who really is the Southwest wind, punishes them by blowing off the roof of their house and inundating it with water, and by turning their fertile valley into a wasteland. A third brother, Gluck, had responded to the man differently from them. His "heart [had] melted" and he had wanted to help him, but his brothers had interfered. He therefore is spared some of the direct suffering brought by the Southwest wind the night of the storm and he gets a full reward later in the story. His kindness was witnessed by the King of the Golden River who, because of enchantment, was in the form of a mug and who, when freed from enchantment, provides Gluck with the secret of how to turn into gold the river which he has high on a mountain. He also helps Gluck fulfill this task after the boy, on his way up to the river, once again in contrast to his brothers shows further kindness and generosity toward an old man, a child, and a dog (who reveals himself to be the King, as perhaps the others were too). Instead of becoming actual gold for Gluck though, the river instead is rechanneled so that it flows into the valley, which is revived: "the Treasure Valley became a garden again," and Gluck's reward is a good Victorian Puritan one, requiring him to continue to work.[8]

In Wilde's version of this type of fairy tale the giant's selfish expulsion of the children from his garden brings it perpetual winter and then, after his heart has melted and he has acted kindly toward one child, the garden is rejuvenated and he is rewarded. However, "The Selfish Giant" differs from standard fairy tales of this type because the giant in effect plays the part of all of the brothers, both the selfish ones who are punished and the kind one who is rewarded. In fairy tales a person who would perform a good action will do so every chance that he has to, whereas a person who acts wrongly, as the giant does, is simply punished, even destroyed. As the Opies put it: "In fairy tales there is no saving of the wicked in heart. Their fate is to have inflicted on them the evil they would inflict on others."[9] Gluck's two brothers try before he does to fulfill the task and be rewarded by the river, but they have learned nothing from their earlier experience, continue to be cruel and selfish, and end up transformed into the black stones which they metaphorically resemble. The giant, unlike them and unlike the conventional villains of fairy tales whom he resembles by being the enemy of the children in the first part of the story, is not destroyed but converted.

Though it does not deal with outright villains, there is one kind of fairy tale which does portray a character's conversion to virtue, and it is to it that we can turn for further parallels with "The Selfish Giant." In stories of the "King Thrushbeard" type proud princesses are humbled and learn to love the seemingly-poor men they have been forced to marry, who are really wealthy royalty. MacDonald's "The Light Princess" is a variant on this type of tale. In it a princess suffers from the curse of being light physically and of not being able to take anything seriously; by falling in love with a prince who, Christ-like, is sacrificing himself to save her and the community she is able to acquire physical gravity and to learn about the importance of being earnest. The giant, then, can be regarded as similar to these princesses who must replace false values with true ones; he does so after being deprived (cf. "King Thrushbeard") and after feeling love for a Christ figure (cf. "The Light Princess").

Most traditional fairy tales have at least a moral thrust, but the types of fairy tales which we have seen the giant's story most closely resemble are ones with very obvious didactic implications. Indeed, the potential didacticism of fairy tales provided one of the main bases for their acceptance as suitable children's literature during the Victorian period and was exploited by most of the period's authors of original fairy tales, and Wilde, albeit a spokesman of the doctrine of "art for art's sake," was no exception. Ruskin underlines the lesson of his story by saying that "the inheritance, which had been lost by cruelty, was regained by love,"[10] and Wilde makes his rather similar lesson equally explicit in "The Selfish Giant," drawing a reader's attention to it even in the title of the story. Selfishness, the vice attacked by the story, is exemplified by the giant, who says "'My own garden is my own garden'" when he drives the children out. "He was a very selfish Giant," we are told. Then we are shown how he is punished for his selfishness. Neither spring, summer, nor fruit-bearing autumn come to his garden. "'He is too selfish,'" says autumn. Finally, discovering the sad little boy among the happy other children in his garden, the giant, moved to sympathy, recognizes the error of his ways. "'How selfish I have been!' he said; 'now I know why the Spring would not come here. I will put that poor little boy on the top of the tree, and then I will knock down the wall, and my garden shall be the children's playground for ever and ever.' He was really very sorry for what he had done." Properly motivated, he now acts properly as well, and just as his vice was punished so his virtue is rewarded; in acting to make the child happy he brings himself happiness too, temporal and, ultimately, eternal.

The ending of the story can leave us with a final speculation about it, strengthened by the observation that fairy tales, saturated by fantasy, can lend themselves to the expression of their authors' dreams (and so "The Ugly Duckling," for example, can be seen in the light of Andersen's biography), and additionally provoked by the fact that we inevitably come to all of Wilde's writings with his life in mind more than for almost any other writer. "The Selfish Giant" turns out to be about a sinner who is forgiven, as Wilde the sinner hoped that he himself would be. Richard Ellmann points out that Wilde provided this happy fate for many of his characters. "In self-abasement they are usually rescued with fairy-tale speed and indulgence. Wilde cancelled his nightmare of being found out with light-hearted dreams of pardon and transfiguration. . . . The fairy tale was a natural form for him to choose to write in, and perhaps all his creative work belongs to this genre."[11] Wilde may have identified himself with the giant particularly strongly, since he himself was a person of considerable size; in fact, after claiming that Wilde's mother was the victim of a disease that made her hands and feet abnormally large, Shaw said: "I have always maintained that Oscar was a giant in the pathological sense."[12] The forgiveness which Wilde dreamed of for himself is thus dramatically rendered in his portrayal of the selfish giant achieving salvation. But, ironically, the giant qualified for salvation thanks to his act of love toward a boy, a "little boy [who] stretched out his two arms and flung them round the Giant's neck, and kissed him" and whom "the Giant loved . . . the best [of all the children] because he had kissed him." As elsewhere, Wilde wants to eat his cake and have it too. The giant's act of expiation, his loving and being kissed by the boy, resembles the very "sin" that Wilde would want to be forgiven for committing in his life, which tragically would not imitate all of the developments in his art.[13] Even the crucified Christ, whom the giant loves and who loves the giant, appears in the form of a boy, and though he and the giant were separated in life they are reunited

for eternity as Wilde ends his fairy tale with what can be regarded as his version of the marriage of the redeemer and the redeemed.

Like "The Nightingale and the Rose," of which Wilde said "I like to fancy that there may be many meanings in the tale, for in writing it I did not start with an idea and clothe it in form, but began with a form and strove to make it beautiful enough to have many secrets and many answers," "The Selfish Giant" resonates with "many meanings, . . . many secrets and many answers." Soon after he published *The Happy Prince* Wilde wrote Ruskin that "there is in you something of prophet, of priest, and of poet,"[14] naming the roles that he himself had been filling in addition to that of storyteller as he composed works like the literary fairy tale "The Selfish Giant," which is at once a children's story, a Christian allegory, a moral exemplum, and a personal dream.

Notes

1. Pater's letter is quoted in *The Letters of Oscar Wilde,* edited by Rupert Hart-Davis (New York: Harcourt, 1962), p. 219. Yeats' remark. from the Introduction to volume iii of *The Complete Works of Oscar Wilde* (New York: Doubleday, 1923), is taken from *Oscar Wilde: The Critical Heritage,* edited by Karl Beckson (London: Routledge & Kegan, 1970), p. 397. The Auden passage, from "An Improbable Life," first appeared in *The New Yorker,* 39:3 (March 9, 1963); it is quoted from *Oscar Wilde: A Collection of Critical Essays,* edited by Richard Ellmann (Englewood Cliffs, N. J.: Prentice-Hall, 1969), p. 135.

2. In two recent studies the tales have begun to get the attention they deserve. In "The Literary Fairy-Tale: A Study of Oscar Wilde's 'The Happy Prince' and 'The Star-Child'" David M. Monaghan examines those two stories from *The Happy Prince* "in relation to the typical stylistic and structural elements established by Axel Olric and Vladimir Propp respectively" and to "Joseph Campbell's structuralist study of myth"—but he has nothing to say about "The Selfish Giant" (*Canadian Review of Comparative Literature,* 1 [1974], 156-166). In *Into the Demon Universe: A Literary Exploration of Oscar Wilde* (New Haven: Yale University Press, 1974) Christopher S. Nassaar does include "The Selfish Giant" in his extended treatment of Wilde's fairy tales. However, in his attempt to make the story illustrate the general pattern of a "fall from the world of innocence and subsequent attainment of a higher innocence" which he claims is "the governing principle of Wilde's fairy tales" (p. 20) Nassaar introduces some very questionable interpretations and even commits some errors of fact. To give just one ex-

ample: Nassaar implies that before the giant expels the children from his garden he is an innocent occupant of its "beautiful private world" when we know no such thing but rather only that he returns to the garden after a seven-year visit with an ogre (p. 22).

3. Marianne Thalmann rejects *"Kunstmärchen"* even in reference to the stories written by the German Romantics, preferring to call them *"Märchen der Romantik." (Das Märchen und die Moderne: Zum Begriff der Surrealität im Märchen der Romantik* [Stuttgart, 1961], translated as *The Romantic Fairy Tale: Seeds of Surrealism* [Ann Arbor: University of Michigan Press, 1964].) Another label, "modern fairy tale," is used by Roger Lancelyn Green in a collection which includes "The Selfish Giant" and stories by Ruskin, MacDonald, and other English writers *(Modern Fairy Tales* [London: J. M. Dent, 1955]).

4. J. R. R. Tolkien, "On Fairy-Stories," *Tree and Leaf,* in *The Tolkien Reader* (New York: Houghton Mifflin, 1966), pp. 3-84.

5. Similarities to Andersen were noticed even by the earliest reviewers of *The Happy Prince.* One of them said that the stories in the volume "are not unworthy to compare with Hans Andersen," and another, Alexander Galt Ross, cited Andersen as a writer "whom Mr. Wilde's literary manner so constantly recalls to us." *Athenaeum,* September 1, 1888, p. 286; [Alexander Galt Ross,] *Saturday Review,* 66 (October 20, 1888), 472. The passages are quoted from *The Critical Heritage,* p. 60 and p. 61.

When *The Happy Prince* was published Wilde sent a copy of it to Ruskin and wrote him two letters which indicate the great esteem in which he then held the older man, who, however, apparently never acknowledged receipt of the volume. See *Letters,* pp. 217-218, 221. Ruskin's story appeared in 1850.

6. All quotations from "The Selfish Giant" are from *Complete Works of Oscar Wilde* (London: Collins, 1966), pp. 297-300.

7. *The Classic Fairy Tales* (London: Oxford University Press, 1974), p. 14.

Tolkien sees fairy tales as having another kind of Christian value. He says that their happy endings give readers "a fleeting glimpse of Joy, Joy beyond the walls of the world," and he regards this joy as a verification of the Christian belief in redemption. ("On Fairy-Stories," pp. 68-73.) In Wilde's story the giant's happy ending *is* his being redeemed.

8. *The Complete Works of John Ruskin,* edited by E. T. Cook and Alexander Wedderburn (London:

Allen, 1903), I, 309-348. The story known as "Diamonds and Toads" appeared as "The Fairies" in Charles Perrault's *Tales of Mother Goose* (1697).

9. *The Classic Fairy Tales,* p. 14. Cf. George MacDonald's story "The Giant's Heart," in which children fail to convert a villainous giant and have to kill him to save themselves. In *The Light Princess and Other Tales* (London, Victor Gollancz, 1973), pp. 64-86. This story and "The Light Princess" were first published in 1864, when Wilde was ten.

10. Ruskin, 347.

11. Introduction to Oscar Wilde, *Selected Writings* (London: Oxford University Press, 1961), p. xii.

12. Shaw's remark, from Frank Harris, *Oscar Wilde: His Life and Confessions* (New York: Covici, 1930), can be found in "My Memories of Oscar Wilde," in *Oscar Wilde: A Collection of Critical Essays,* ed. Ellmann, pp. 97-98.

13. There is a related irony in the fact that the giant's act of love toward the child (his putting him into the tree) somewhat resembles the crucifixion.

14. For both quotations from Wilde see *Letters,* p. 218.

Elizabeth Goodenough (essay date September 1999)

SOURCE: Goodenough, Elizabeth. "Oscar Wilde, Victorian Fairy Tales, and the Meanings of Atonement." *Lion and the Unicorn* 23, no. 3 (September 1999): 336-54.

[*In the following essay, Goodenough focuses on Wilde's treatment of the themes of atonement and redemption in his Christian-themed children's stories.*]

> What the age needs is not a genius but a martyr.
>
> (Søren Kierkegaard, 1813-1855)

> But it was not only each epoch that found its reflection in Jesus; each individual created Him in accordance with his own character.
>
> (Albert Schweitzer, 1875-1965)

In 1889 W. B. Yeats was invited to the Wildes's house at Chelsea. The young poet, whose *Fairy and Folk Tales of the Irish Peasantry* (1888) was reviewed that year by Wilde, was asked by Oscar to tell his son a fairy tale. Yeats got as far as "Once upon a time there was a giant," when the little boy ran screaming out of the room. "Wilde looked grave and I was plunged into the shame of clumsiness," the poet recalled in his autobiography (91). This act of storytelling seduction that backfired dramatizes how the verbal formulas of adults can pale before the authorial divinity of the very young. Even as they conjure ghosts of the punitive father, such sensitive listeners seem to determine the fate of adult words at their moment of utterance. As William Blake's *Songs* suggest, the literal-minded innocent can be a creative visionary as well. "Children are never earnest in the way that adults are," Dusinberre states, which is why they became Wilde's most explosive weapon in attacking Victorian earnestness (261). The self-authorizing world of children, like the self-referential work of art, embodied Wilde's esthetic credo that "[i]t is the spectator, and not life, that art really mirrors" (17) and that self-realization is the aim of life.

Yeats was mortified as a storyteller, but his fairy-tale incantation worked like a charm in making the hidden bogeys of childhood visible. Like the inner tyrant of retributive justice, the terrors of a grown-up, a semi-divine monster moving on legs, is well-known to small children and their nightmares. During the last decades of the nineteenth century, an intellectual fascination with the irrational and unconscious mind catalyzed a variety of linguistic rituals, esoteric doctrines, and literary alchemies. As Alex Owen has shown, the suggestive power of magic, like the supersensual, paranormal, and occult phenomena attractive to Wilde's circle, anticipated psychoanalysis as an avant garde mode of self-realization and the "inward-looking spirituality" of C. G. Jung. In 1892 Yeats, who like Wilde's wife was a member of the Hermetic Order of the Golden Door, declared in a letter to John O'Leary that "[i]f I had not made magic my constant study I could not have written a single word" (211). For Wilde, another verbal wizard, magic was not the art of covering things up but the act of embodying secrets of the self. Feminist criticism has examined the way women writers of the nineteenth century (Mary Shelley, Charlotte Brontë, Charlotte Perkins Gilman) used Gothic elements to express subversive female feelings (rage, sexual desire, reproductive dread). Less attention has been paid to the way Victorian fairy tales blend sensual imagery, physical abandon, and corporeal suffering to explore the mysteries of atonement.

John Ruskin, William Makepeace Thackeray, A. E. Housman, E. Nesbit, and Kenneth Grahame all wrote magical tales, just as Charles Dickens, Benjamin Disraeli, T. S. Eliot, Alfred Lord Tennyson, and Robert Browning invoked, in a variety of genres, the figure of Christ. But oral wonder tales by George MacDonald, Christina Rossetti, and Oscar Wilde recast the gendered and generational stereotypes of religious authority in the Victorian period. Unlike the lengthy German "liberal lives" of Jesus, which proliferated from scholarly presses of the 1860s, these works were brief and spoke directly to the need to find a new human Christ implicit in Mary Arnold Ward's enormously popular *Robert Elsmere* (1888). In the widespread speculation of Victori-

ans about the personality and divinity of Jesus may be glimpsed tensions inherent in Christology since the pre-Nicene church regarding the problem of post-baptismal sin. Whether the body of Christ was conceived as the bestower of all divine good or the supreme sacrifice for our sins, opposing views of his efficacy developed early in church history and spawned competing, though sometimes overlapping, meanings of atonement: repentance as change of life or the work of penance.[1] How the lapsed could find salvation—by changing their mind or that of God, by meritorious works, or by grace, faith, love, friendship, prayer, suffering, or art—became for Rossetti, MacDonald, and Wilde an intense inner question that inspired their fantasy. Tapping realities that could not be approached through the logic of a sermon or a novel, archetypal fairy tales by these three writers revitalized Christianity with energies of the body suppressed in the dominant culture. In an immaterial space somewhere between Calvinism, Catholicism, and the Church of England, a Scots "stickit" minister without a pulpit, a woman poet who rejected the call of the cloister, and the Irish nephew of three clergymen who aspired to write "the Epic of the Cross" established unorthodox ministries through radical fairy tales that have now transcended their communal meaning.

At the end of the twentieth century these works of narrative fantasy endure not only as popular children's texts but as tales of transformation for adults who seek through mainstream churches, identity politics, and New Age therapies to connect the creative spirit of the inner Child and feminist and gay liberation with religious faith. In the case of Wilde, this appropriation is especially striking since a century ago his Salome, the "Ur-nymphet" or "paedophile's femme fatale" of recent criticism, created such a stir in London with Sarah Bernhardt in the title role that the play was banned for portraying biblical characters on stage (Hutcheon 19). The 1998 *Anglican Digest,* however, recommends as "gems of Christian literature" the "children's stories" of Oscar Wilde, "one of the most fascinating figures of the nineteenth century"—"a must, not only for your children or grandchildren" (10). Wilde's once iconoclastic creeds now undergird a wide body of literature connecting faith with fiction in conservative and mainstream religious circles that look to the arts to "incarnate our experience of mystery, wonder and awe" and to "aid us to encounter the holy or sacred" in "the original vision" of embodied childhood (3). While writers like Woolf and Hemingway undermined a Godlike authorship in their fiction, contemporary novelists like Tim O'Brien in "The Lives of the Dead" (1990)[2] and Frederick Buechner in *The Wizard's Tide* (1987) illustrate how telling stories for a child within—oneself or an imagined other—can save us. As Buechner explains in his 1991 memoir, retelling the tale of his father's suicide "in language a child could understand" and reliving it "for that child and as that child" released him from the spiritual dungeon of his fifties (34).

The Romantic revaluation of childhood epitomized in William Wordsworth's paradox that "The Child is father of the Man" prefigures the sacred privilege of juvenile readers in the Victorian period, the Jungian archetypes of Christ and the child, MacDonald's reverence for the Childlike, and Rossetti's seductive nursery lyrics. Like Dickens's angelic girls, Wilde's injured boys and helpless "wee folk" have become a powerful trope of "post-traumatic culture," suggesting how homeless and fatally abused children in the media indict a ruthless economic system (Kirby 132). At the same time Wilde, who wore a crucifix on his chest as he died, struggled to define something about himself through claiming the godlike inspiration of a first-century Jew. How Wilde identified with the prophet who came as a child, melted people's hearts, and was reviled and crucified illustrates, like Yeats's anecdote, the profit and peril of traipsing backwards to that distant uncharted borderland where words are first beginning to establish meaning on the tongue.

"The mind of a child is a great mystery . . . who shall divine it, or bring it its own peculiar delights?" Wilde remarked to Richard Le Gallienne about fairy tales. Before it "You humbly spread . . . the treasures of your imagination, and they are as dross" (252). Sanctifying and flirting with this impressionable subject beyond the generation gap, he embraced the Shavian irony that youth is wasted on the young. A flagrant cross-writer, he ignored conventional boundaries between juvenile and adult literature when he spun out two volumes of literary fairy tales in the 1880s and early 1890s, persuading many like Swinburne that turn-of-the-century writing for children—works like Graham's *The Golden Age* (1895) and E. Nesbit's Bastable stories—provided the best reading for adults. But when asked by a reviewer about the "suitability" for the young of *A House of Pomegranates* (1891), Wilde remarked in a letter to the *Pall Mall Gazette,* "I had about as much intention of pleasing the British child as I had of pleasing the British public" (301).

Less catechetical than casuistical, Oscar Wilde claimed at his trial that "I rarely think that anything I write is true." Although slighted until gay studies reenergized Wilde criticism, his nine fairy tales, written while he wrote *The Portrait of Dorian Gray* (1890) and tasted both fatherhood and homosexual experience for the first time, are pivotal in understanding the consistency of Wilde's moral and aesthetic philosophy. Just as the ironic wit of *The Decay of Lying* rehabilitated fiction, the beautiful boy and the enchanted but "safe" turf of children's fantasy articulated Wilde's vision of pain as the redemptive heart of life. The doctrine of physical

anguish and self-giving developed in "The Nightingale and the Rose," "The Happy Prince," "The Young King," "The Fisherman and His Soul," and "The Star Child" prefigures his later ennoblement of suffering as "the supreme emotion" in *De Profundis* and "The Ballad of Reading Gaol."

Wilde's unorthodox mingling of spirituality and sensuality, framed in moral guise, turned the Evangelical on its head in a darker, more disturbing way than MacDonald and Rossetti had done. Celebrating self-discovery and transformation over self-denial and obedience, he pro-claimed in "Phrases and Philosophies for the Use of the Young" that "[t]he first duty in life is to be as artificial as possible" (1205). Blending biblical language with homoerotic imagery and Protestant discourses of heroic martyrdom, subverting the Victorian pathos of broken hearts and the cult of dying children, his tales are strikingly sad and graphic portrayals of expiation and renunciation, failure and death. Motifs of nakedness, penetration, piercing and wounding illuminate the perception of his own later extremity of hurt as a Tiger of Experience. Like childhood's "moments of being" that Virginia Woolf claimed as the basis of her creative life, the terrible shocks received in prison were ultimately viewed by Wilde as Blakean auguries, moments of searing revelation and visionary intensity. The face of the trooper Woolridge, hanged in Reading Gaol, Wilde said, would "haunt me till I die" (Ellman 533). Although they may be read like Rossetti's and MacDonald's tales as an alternative religious discourse, or what Ellman calls "sacraments of a lost faith" (299), Wilde's fairy tales also reveal why the child embodied the creative spring of his tragic sense of life. From this imaginative construct, he drew not only his flamboyant style and fatal boyish lover, but also his figure of Christ and the social conscience that compelled him to write on behalf of incarcerated juveniles. The Wildean child finally explains the mythologizing of his own public shaming and affliction in prison as a discovery of his Soul. "Praise makes me humble," he said, "but when I am abused I know I have touched the stars" (Redman 249).

"At every single moment of one's life one is what one is going to be," Wilde wrote in *De Profundis* (922). Not surprisingly, the sadness and grief of the fairy tales, which launched his great years of creative production, have been read as allegories of homosexual oppression. Why, for example, does "The Star Child" end on such a gratuitously melancholy note: "Yet ruled he not long, so great had been his suffering, and so bitter the fire of his testing, for after the space of three years he died. And he who came after him ruled evilly" (284). "Was some deep tragic and prophetic instinct urging Oscar to anticipate the mere three years he himself was to live after his 'bitter' testing in prison?" Gary Schmidgall asks in *The Stranger Wilde* (148). Elucidating the tales as tragic idylls of the Love that dare not speak its name or wish fulfillment fantasies of gay liberation (158) thus provides a compelling reading of Wilde's spiritual self-portrait of multiple selves. Wilde inscribed *The Happy Prince* to a special American friend, eleven years his junior: "Faery-stories for one who lives in Faery-Land" (Schmidgall 154). Presupposing the author's inner circle of gay male readers illuminates the existential estrangement pervading these wintry tales as well as the warm valedictory kisses that liberate and transform such odd couples as the happy prince and swallow, the fisherman and his mermaid. But while the homosexual subtext in Wilde's other experiments in popular subgenres crackles with insouciant drawing room wit and urbane double entendres, the tension between child and adult reader and the presence of the child as auditor or observer in the fairy tales lend gravity to these works that deepen their resonance beyond the recovery of erotic messages from London's *fin de siècle* gay subculture.

Moreover, modern conceptions and analyses of sexuality, usually framed in secular contexts, may overlook why intense identification, or at-one-ment, with another person is so compellingly embodied in Wilde. Accused at his 1895 trial of "acts of gross indecency with another male person" (Hyde, *Trials* 1179), he eloquently defended the "deep, spiritual affection" between an elder and a younger man as the noblest of human attachments, "such as Plato made the very basis of his philosophy, and such as you find in the sonnets of Michaelangelo and Shakespeare." Wilde's brilliance in reviving the "idiom of Greek ideality" does not just signify, as Linda Dowling points out, a triumph of Victorian Hellenism and the seizing of a new vocabulary for "an epistemological space that would soon enough . . . be reconquered in the name of new clinical or psychiatric languages of sexual pathology" (3). Wilde, Ellman argues, was convicted for sexual acts that Douglas actually committed. His passionate apology for same-sex love while on trial was based on the enlargement of human capacities flowing not just from Oxbridge classical ideals and the one-on-one tutorial system but also from the Christian doctrine of atonement and a romanticized Jesus.

Combining these energies steadily undermined the idea of "effeminacy" as corrupt, "vain, luxurious, and selfish," and therefore dangerous as this master term had been used in British civic discourse over the previous two centuries. As Dowling points out, the "protean figure" of the *effeminatus* in classical republican theory relied not on the gender oppositions of today but on a conception of "aimless and self-regarding egoism" undermining the rights of full citizenship as these were thought to derive in ancient times from the willingness of a single warrior to die "in the name of a community not present on the field of battle" (7). Styling the aesthete as the champion of "purer" Platonic love and male

procreancy, Wilde proclaimed at the end of "The Soul of Man Under Socialism" that "the new Individualism is the new Hellenism" (1104) and resolved in his prison cell, where he read the Gospels in Greek, that his next work would be a study of Jesus as precursor of the Romantic movement. The prophet of individualism, Christ according to Wilde felt sympathy for mankind in ways that led him to realize "his perfection through pain" (1103).

Comparing miraculous scenes of feeding and corporal rescue in MacDonald and of healing embrace and bodily recovery in Rossetti with scenes of heterodox encounter and isolate injury in Wilde suggests how variously the fairy tale has served a faith whose murdered messiah has never lost his symbolic identity as a child. Nevertheless the choice of this traditional mode with pagan roots as an alternative religious discourse may seem an odd conjoining. Fiction was disdained in the Scots Calvinist ethos where George MacDonald grew up, and in more liberal environments where children's fairy tales still competed with the primer and the moral tale, educated adults influenced by German historical criticism had come to regard Christianity itself anthropologically. Matthew Arnold in his Preface to *God and the Bible* wrote in 1875, "For us, the God of popular religion is a legend, a fairy tale; learned theology has simply taken the fairy tale and dressed it metaphysically." In retrospect, however, it is the empirical and rationalizing trend of nineteenth-century thought—the positivist tendency to make science sacred—that makes fairy stories an attractive form in which to articulate a sacramental world view.

Not only did the use of a presumably less serious and traditional form generate a "willing suspension of disbelief," but this tolerant and looser genre was well-suited to writers reluctant to interpret their own works. In fact MacDonald, Rossetti, and Wilde each seems to have adopted this mode from a need to express a larger, more personal understanding of his or her own gendered spirituality than was available through conventional discourses. Christina Rossetti, for example, was excluded from the pre-Raphaelite brotherhood that her brother founded. When William Holman Hunt used her as a model for "The Light of the World," the painter was reviled by Thomas Carlyle for making Christ "a puir, weak, girl-faced nonentity, bedecked in a fine silken sort of gown" (Zemka 103). A lifelong spinster, she dedicated her life to Anglo-Catholicism and the writing of poetry, much of it devotional, in the Tractarian mode. Working with her sister, an Anglican nun, with prostitutes at the St. Mary Magdalene Home, Rossetti dramatized in "Goblin Market" (1862) the psychological effects of succumbing to temptation. D. M. R. Bentley has conjectured that "Goblin Market" was read, or was written to be read, aloud by the author to an audience of Anglican sisters and fallen women at the

House of Charity where Rossetti worked (58). As U. C. Knoepflmacher points out, it is possible to read this work as "an Anglican tract, a lesbian allegory, a feminist manifesto" as well as "a children's book attractive to such major illustrators as Laurence Houseman (1893), Arthur Rackham (1933), and Martin Ware (1980)" (321). As Lorraine Janzen Kooistra's study of "Goblin Market" as a "cross-audienced poem" suggests, the work cut through many boundaries from the outset: "it was written for adults; it used the form of the children's fairy tale; and it was about sex" (183). Yet Rossetti claimed that the title work of her first collection, *Goblin Market and Other Poems* (1862), which established her reputation in literary London, was simply a fairy tale. In 1904 when her brother William glossed this point, he only maintained that its "incidents are such as to be at any rate suggestive, and different minds may be likely to read different messages into them" (459).

George MacDonald, who said he wrote for "the childlike, whether of five, or fifty, or seventy-five," went further in explaining the spiritual value of tales like *The Light Princess* (1864) which can't have one meaning. Called a *jeu d'esprit* by his son Greville (324), this light, even satiric work parodies Sleeping Beauty and anticipates *The Waste Land* in using the Percival legend to portray the sterility of never connecting with other people. Along with *The Golden Key* (1867), *At the Back of the North Wind* (1871), and *The Princess and the Goblin* (1872), *The Light Princess* has gained today what Jonathan Cott has called a "pop Scriptural status" for a Congregational minister forced to resign his pulpit because of his unorthodox beliefs about salvation. To account for the ongoing appeal of *The Light Princess* and other tales in 1904, Greville MacDonald recurred to the catechistic method of his father in "The Fantastic Imagination" where the process of "calling up" forgotten materials in writer and reader into "new forms" is given an extra-literary sanction: "When such forms are new embodiments of old truths we call them the product of the Imagination; when they are mere invention, however lovely, I should call them the work of the Fancy." Sanctifying the mind of the maker as well as the "germinal power" of early life enabled the author not to dogmatize his writing. Instead he invited his auditors and readers to awaken and reverence the play of their own minds when he concluded "your meaning may be superior to mine" (317).

Wilde developed this creed of the redemptive power of Imagination by deifying and embodying Art, likening self-realization to at-onement. The experience of Russell Hoban, himself a children's writer, might exemplify Wilde's ideal reader. Hoban's memory of the look and feel of *A House of Pomegranates,* which he discovered at age eight or nine in the family library, exemplifies Terry Eagleton's assertion that "aesthetics is born as a discourse of the body" (13): "a small orange volume with the author's signature stamped in black on the cover . . . came off the shelf into my hand like magic," Hoban recalls, in a distant space where sunlight flooded his reading on a rose and gold Orientalish carpet (23). He credits "the Wildeness of the prose" in this volume bursting upon him "in widescreen glorious colour" with setting him on the writing road (29). "Enthralled by the language and the brilliance of the images," he responded not only to the sadness of "The Fisherman and his Soul" but also to "the dark stillness and lethal clarity of the mirror in which the dwarf sees himself for the first time in 'The Birthday of the Infanta.' That mirror took me to a place I'd never known before, a place that has stayed with me ever since" (23). This child, a sensory explorer converted to art at the same time that he falls into Experience through the mirror of literature, fulfills Wilde's ultimate agenda: the only way a critic can interpret the personality and work of others is "by an intensification of his own personality": he must treat Art "not as a riddling Sphinx, whose shallow secret may be guessed . . . but as a goddess whose mystery it is his province to intensify." Indeed the little boy's "wild" response to Yeats's hackneyed beginning is an exemplum of Wildean art, for Wilde celebrated interpretations that are in their own way "more creative than creation," likening the highest criticism to "the purest form of personal impression."

Developing his own embodied psychology of faerie, J. R. R. Tolkien, a Catholic whose orcs descended from "the goblin tradition" of MacDonald (178), suggested that children's books "like their clothes should allow for growth" and indeed encourage it. But he argued there is no natural connection between the minds of children and fairy stories, and he saw these tales as essentially Christian or as an archetypal version of the Christian (hi)story: among the marvels of the Gospels is "the greatest and most complete conceivable eucatastrophe." For Tolkien, fantasy is "the most nearly pure . . . and so (when achieved) the most potent" form of Art (69), the one that helps us recover what age takes away: the capacity to "be startled anew" (77). The criminal prosecution in which Christ suffered unto blood may be counted a "good catastrophe" only in the "otherworld" setting the fairy tale provides: "a sudden and miraculous grace: never to be counted on to recur" (86). Evangelists, Tolkien argued, are no more the authors of the story of the Resurrection and how it becomes the eucatastrophe of the story of Incarnation than children are the sole or natural audience of these works of fantasy. Establishing the Child as a trope for the soul, Rossetti and MacDonald make happy endings of growing Childlike, bearing children, and the "sense of belonging" intrinsic to early oral tales (Zipes 2), but Wilde depicts the "terrible beauty" of human potential with darker irony, "on that imaginative plane of art where Love can indeed find in Death its rich fulfillment" (1045). Or as in "The Remarkable Rocket," "The Birthday of the Infanta," and "The Devoted Friend," he shows how the self can be destroyed, its capacity for growth wasted, thwarted, or blighted by egoism or the sadism of others.

Alice in Wonderland (1865), which was given by Charles Dodgson to his friend MacDonald in manuscript to try out on his children, was dubbed by Harvey Darton "the spiritual volcano of children's books" (quoted in Dusinberre 37). But the "directness of such work," inspired by Carroll's eros for little girls, did not encompass in its "liberty of thought" their own carnality. "Goblin Market" and *The Light Princess*—also tales of fallen females—showed several years before Lewis Carroll's secularizing text the spiritual implications of the female eros. In these tales a young hero and two heroines are saved—not by a magic wand or a prince galloping in or by awakening from a dream—but by the utterly real self-sacrifice of a peer. Yet unlike in Wilde's tales, each case of atonement involves scenes of eucharistic tasting. Unusual sexual overtones arise in these intense moments of bonding and conjure the agony of the addicted. "Curious Laura" regenders Francesco Petrarca's "disastrous passion" as Rossetti described it in *The Imperial Dictionary of Universal Biography* (1857-1863): the poet-lover became a "veritable slave of love," "harassed" by "temptations of the flesh" from the moment he "first beheld that incomparable golden-haired Laura" (164). After seeing the Goblin Men, Laura "sucked and sucked and sucked the more / Fruits which that unknown orchard bore, / She sucked until her lips were sore; / Then flung the emptied rines away." Gnashing her teeth "in a passionate yearning," "weeping as if her heart would break," Laura is then tortured by cravings for exotic fruits but is never able to hear the goblin men hawking their wares a second time. Her sister Lizzie, who brings back the fruit as medicine for Laura, defies the goblins, refusing to eat in a violent and graphic scene suggesting rape. But with the syrup running down her face, the pulp smashed to her lips, she rushes back to Laura crying,

> Hug me, kiss me, suck my juices
> Squeeezed from goblin fruits for you,
> Goblin pulp and goblin dew.
> Eat me, drink me, love me:
> Laura, make much of me:
> For your sake I have braved the glen
> And had to do with goblin men.

After a hideously painful convalescence in which the antidote acts like poison on Laura, the poem celebrates the power of sisterhood:

> For there is no friend like a sister
> In calm or stormy weather
> To cheer one on the tedious way
> To fetch one if one goes astray
> To lift one if one totters down
> To strengthen whilst one stands.

In *The Light Princess* a baby cursed by a bad fairy at her christening is deprived of her gravity. The child sails laughingly above the heads of adults, unable to touch ground or feel anything but giddy delight. Even spectacles of human suffering give her "violent hysterics." At seventeen, however, she discovers ecstasy in swimming, especially with the help of a young prince who jumps off cliffs into a lake with the light princess in his arms. The two share a passion for plunging into the warm water and floating together on moonlit nights until the lake begins to dry up—a drought caused by the killjoy wicked fairy. The prince, who has "fallen" for the weightless princess, offers to staunch the flow of the lake with his own body since only a voluntary human sacrifice can reverse the curse. The princess, who just cares about swimming in her lake, falls asleep in a boat while the young prince awaits death by drowning. At his request, she offers him biscuit, wine, and then a "long, sweet, cold kiss" before he goes under. But as the bubbles of his last breath break on the water, she "gives a shriek," springs into the lake and risks her own life to save him. Only the next morning, when the young prince revives, does she finally burst into tears and regain gravity, as the rain falls throughout the land.

Traditionally fairy-tale characters are destined to be orphaned, exposed, and abandoned so they can go on perilous quests, be empowered by magic, and eventually transformed into sparkling adults. In Rossetti's and MacDonald's fairylands, however, the misogynist myth of Eve's frailty and biblical pattern of fall and redemption are framed as sexual maturation, a process occurring in an interpersonal context where acts of intercession diminish individual achievement and autonomy. Alone, each heroine is completely lost were it not for the intervention of a Christ-like friend. In "Goblin Market" "sweet-tooth" delight is prelude to enthrallment and death, while in MacDonald's work, bodily pleasure leads to authentic recovery and flowering fertility. But both fairylands offer a world apart to explore how a riot of sexual yearning leads to a recognition of self-giving as the ultimate human value. Such an accommodating space was not available in the realistic novel of the period. Nor presumably in juvenile literature—even if such writing, because children were deemed innocent, generally went uncensored. Although Wordsworth suggested in "We Are Seven" that children could not conceive of death, Rossetti and MacDonald portray the prospect of dying young without sentimental piety or reverence for the ideal of progress implicit in the *bildungsroman*. The spiritual awakening of both heroines is manifested by their growing young at the end: Laura wakes laughing "in the old innocent way . . . her gleaming locks showed not thread of grey," and the light princess finds herself lying on the floor like a baby who must learn to walk.

After administering last rites, the princess jumps into the lake to save the prince, a reversal no less surprising than Lizzie's rescue of Laura from the harassment of stunted animal men. The triumph of virginity and heroic resistance, the womanly eucharist and Rossetti's pun on cloistered "sisters" together suggest the relevance of this text for feminist theology. MacDonald also revived the Motherhood of God from medieval mysticism in images of female plenitude and power that resonate with Dante Gabriel Rossetti's portraits. North Wind, for example, has a streaming mane of hair that blends with the night: the darkness of Diamond's hayloft looked "as if it were made of her hair." Her numinous presence and that of MacDonald's other magical grandmother and goddess figures, wise old women and earth sprites, communicate Juliana of Norwich's insight that at the core of life all will be well. Cultivating a language to express the interiority of things when seen from the vantage point of spiritual enlightenment, he asked,

> Why should I not speculate in the only direction in which things worthy of speculation appear likely to lie? There is a wide *may be* around us and every speculation widens the probability of changing the *may be* into the *is*.

In their complex and haunting symbolism developed with Pre-Raphaelite visual intensity, MacDonald and Rossetti defamiliarize the ordinary as Wilde does—whether it be voluptuous goblin fruit or tears that fall like jewels of rain, or a marvelous rose, crimson as a ruby at the heart. These puzzling images, ellipses and reversals, oppositional language and symbolist techniques reclaim the creative and mythmaking power for the religious sensibility. Like Blake's "Auguries of Innocence," these fairy tales work to regenerate ways of seeing the human body and to stimulate a palpable understanding of their parabolic meanings.

"Evangelicalism at its best is an offensive religion," Mark Noll argues, and Ruskin found scenes of a girl's maturing sexuality and loss of restraint in *The Light Princess* salacious. But MacDonald's wish to awaken the emotional imagination is grounded in his sense of how body and spirit are interconnected in the mutual dependence of male and female development. The hungry female kisses that exorcise Laura's "poison in the blood" become a distant memory at the end of "Goblin Market" when both sisters become wives "with children of their own," and Laura weaves cautionary tales of "her early prime." That Lizzie "stood in deadly peril to do her good" acts as a warning of forbidden pleasures, for few Victorian parents would advocate careers culminating in martyrdom. (Wilde's mother was an exception.) The assault on Lizzie suggests Stephen's grisly fate, described with agonizing traits in Acts. Yet writers who would make Christ's love real, that is, relevant and contemporary, cannot leave the Cross as a dogmatic abstraction: they must reconcile a criminally executed Jew with a divine Savior. When Paul developed the classic theory of atonement that in Christ God is Man and Man is God (2 Cor. 5:19), he also gave rise to the notion of the church as the body of Christ (1 Cor.12:27), an entity later enlisted by the penance tradition as an essential mediator of forgiveness. Preaching the widest, simplest basis for salvation—identification of "Christ as the source of Life"—and distancing himself from the doctrine of vicarious atonement and the punitive God it implied became a critical issue in MacDonald's search for a parish after losing his first (and only) pastorate at Arundel.[3] Discarding the Calvinist notion of infant depravity, he drew on a christology of the child that developed in early Christianity as well as the ancient tradition in which the newly baptized or converted were considered as newborn or small children (Bovon 20). Embodying the mind of a beginner in the flesh of a child, he celebrated the abandonment of *a priori* modes of thought. To rouse trust, that "indescribable vague intelligence" that enables progress through Experience, he placed at the heart of *The Golden Key* (1865), "in the secret of the earth and all its ways," the oldest man of all who can help everybody—a naked child "who had no smile, but the love in his large grey eyes was deep as the center" (61). In *Phantastes*, which C. S. Lewis claimed had "baptized his imagination," MacDonald's narrator states:

> It is no use trying to account for things in fairy land; and one who travels there soon learns to forget the whole idea of doing so, and takes everything as it comes; like a child, who being in a chronic state of wonder, is surprised by nothing.

Wilde's sexuality and utopian orientation toward Individualism radicalized the socializing mission of the literary fairy tale in starker ways than Rossetti and MacDonald. While the latter emphasize the miraculous change of life that standing in another's place can bring, Wilde is closer to the penance tradition in his vision of Christ as the Man of Sorrows and his emphasis on feeling others' pain as prelude to self-sacrifice. Rossetti's idyll of sisterly love is set in an elfin glen where wares luscious as budding sexuality are hawked morning and night; MacDonald's Fairyland offers journeys to mystic awareness. But Wilde's settings are detailed like Blake's visionary and satiric *Songs* to depict the brutal injustice and crass conformity of contemporary society. Whatever sacred moments of sacrificial love arise amid the world's wanton cruelty thus come as fleeting miracles. No feeding ritual makes self and other "one body." Instead neglect of the poor is expiated by the Star-Child in beatings by a Magician who "set before him an empty trencher, and said, 'Eat,' and an empty cup and said, 'Drink'" (199). At the end of "The Happy Prince," an Angel brings God the Prince's leaden heart and the dead bird from a trash heap: their suffering is sanctified as "the two most precious things in the city" (291).

While the Grimms rarely eliminated violence from *Nursery and Household Tales* (1817), lurid depictions of murder, cannibalism, and mutilation were muted in fairy tales written during Victoria's reign. Self-inflicted injury or the sight of a horrifying and alien face in the mirror were not part of this complacent agenda. But the practice of reading the body of a dying child for signs of God's presence had shaped the earliest tradition of writing for juveniles in the seventeenth century and had mutated into the most sentimental scenes of Victorian novels. Literary representations of the spiritual precocity of dying children, like scenes of execution in John Foxe's *Book of Martyrs,* shaped the enduring ideal of protestant heroism. Wilde's description of Guido Reni's St. Sebastian recalls these Marian martyrs who affirm their identity as true Christians by gestures like clapping their hands in the flames.

When Wilde wrote in 1886, "I would go to the stake for a sensation and be a sceptic to the last," he added that one infinite fascination remained for him, "the mystery of moods." His fairy tales, he said, were "Studies in prose . . . meant partly for children, and partly for those who have kept the childike faculties of wonder and joy, and who find in simplicity a subtle strangeness" (*Letters* 219). The poignant and satiric tonalities of the tales, which verge on religious mysticism as they expound a Christian socialism, sound a dual audience. They invert the logic of Janeway's premature little adults and the Victorian morbidity of gazing on childish pain by registering a childlike responsiveness to the feelings of others, a compelling lyric to which adults are tone deaf. The prosperous Miller's youngest son in "The Devoted Friend," for example, hears of little Hans the gardener having troubles, and wants to invite little Hans into their home, saying, "I will give him half my porridge, and show him my white rabbits." At this he is rebuked by his father with a hearty sermon:

> What a silly boy you are! . . . I really don't know what is the use of sending you to school. You seem not to learn anything. Why if Little Hans came up here, and saw our warm fire, and good supper, and our great cask of red wine, he might get envious, and envy is a most terrible thing, and would spoil anybody's nature. I certainly will not allow Hans's nature to be spoiled. I am his best friend, and I will always watch over him, and see that he is not led into any temptations.
>
> (303)

"When friends are in trouble, they should be left alone," the Miller righteously declares. Opposed to this paternalistic exploitation of the poor, which institutionalizes pain through schooling, church, and state, is Wilde's representation of childhood as fraught with passionate personal experience. Although feelings of being lost, confused, vulnerable, and small are aroused, Wilde avoids what Marina Warner calls "the Oxfam Syndrome"—which makes the oppression of children "look like endemic, perennial hopelessness" (47)—by drawing on energies of creatures like "the little people" of Irish folklore. The small boy in "The Selfish Giant" and the Star-Child are christlike beings who emanate new life; they function in the narrative like Jungian archetypes to pave "the way for a future change in personality" (83). The Giant who has built a wall around his garden so children can't trespass has a change of heart when he sees a boy "so small he could not reach up to the branches of the tree . . . wandering all around it and crying bitterly" (298). After he has kissed the boy, opened his garden to all the children, and grown old, his special little friend reappears with wounds on his hands and feet. His longing for the Christ child prefigures the salvation that awaits the Giant in death, as he leaves his body to join the boy in Paradise. That we do not see this child receive stigmata after the conversion of the Giant is characteristic of the way Wilde represents suffering as unseen theatrical.

Gaston Bachelard observed that "the nest image is generally childish. . . . Physically, the creature endowed with a sense of refuge huddles up to itself, takes cover, hides away, lies snug, is concealed" (93). Within these intricately framed tales are nested multiple narratives that converge on or circle round some secret or unregarded pain at their heart. Culminating moments of misery, public spectacles or private exhibitions of pain, strike contradictory responses in bystanders—the romantic, the pragmatist, and the cynic parody Victorian community in their solipsistic points of view. Only to the statue of the Happy Prince comes the revelation in his blindness that "[t]here is no Mystery so great as Misery" (290). Only the Charity School children recognize the Prince as an Angel like the one they have seen in their dreams. To the Mayor and the Town Councillors—the philistine, utilitarian, and worldy—the statue divested of gold looks shabby, "[l]ittle better than a beggar" (291). When Wilde asked in prison if his hair must be cut, he added with tears in his eyes, "You don't know what it means to me." The hair was cut. "The horror of Prison life," he later wrote, "is the contrast between the grotesqueness of one's aspect, and the tragedy in one's soul" (Ellman 496). Such oppositions that privilege suffering on a private stage form the crux of Wilde's tales.

In "The Nightingale and the Rose," for example, a little bird leaves her nest in the oak tree to enact the highest form of sympathy. To help a student in the agonies of unrequited love, the nightingale impales herself on a thorn to create a red rose for the youth to give to his beloved. Moving from spectatorship to identification and finally to self-abandonment and hurt, the nightingale herself proves to be the true lover and artist. Wilde wrote his own name into the poetry describing the fierce pang that shot through her at the last: "Bitter, bitter was the pain, and wilder and wilder grew her song, for she sang of the Love that is perfected by Death, of the Love that dies not in the tomb." Yet the nightingale's sacrifice is callously ignored and misunderstood: when the girl rejects his red rose, the student throws this token of the nightingale into the gutter where a cart wheels over it. Nevertheless, the personal injures that inscribe Wilde's modes of self-realization gesture toward a transfigured realm. At the little bird's "last burst of music,"

> [t]he white Moon . . . forgot the dawn, and lingered on in the sky. The red rose heard it, and it trembled all over with ecstacy, and opened its petals to the cold morning air. Echo bore it to her purple cavern in the hills, and woke the sleeping shepherds from their dreams. It floated through the reeds of the river and they carried its message out to sea.
>
> (295)

Of Jesus, Wilde said, "one always thinks of him . . . as a lover for whose love the whole world was too small" (925). The too small world of partial and partisan vision depicted in these narratives ultimately conjures a God-suffused reaction. Crucifixion, the highest mode of perfection in a hostile world, can only be seen as sublime in a realm that cannot be figured. Wilde's use of Christian metaphor anticipates Tolkien's claim that the fairy tale "does not deny the existence of . . . sorrow and failure" but gives "a fleeting glimpse of Joy, Joy beyond the walls of the world, poignant as grief" (86).

Notes

1. Contending with apostates in mid-third-century Rome, Cyprian used Paul's notion of the church as the body of Christ to establish an ecclesiastical centralized hierarchy in which bishops had authority to approve penance for the lapsed and to forgive those who had made sacrifices to the emperor. See Daniel Goodenough, "Repentance of Life vs. The Work of Penance," unpublished manuscript, 1975, p. 53.

2. Brian Attebery suggests "postmodernism is a return to story-telling in the belief that we can be sure of nothing but story" (40). O'Brien opens, "But this too is true: stories can save us" (255).

3. "For as we have many members in one body, but all the members do not have the same function, so we, being many, are one body in Christ, and individually members of one another." (1 Rom 12:4, 5). See *The Letters of George MacDonald*: "I believe in the perfect and full atonement of Jesus Christ—that he has, as it were, saved all men already, if by unbelief they did not put themselves out of his salvation" (24). His belief that animals have souls and the Heathen might be saved in the afterlife were deemed heretical at Arundel (Greville MacDonald, 180).

Works Cited

Allen, Charlotte. *The Human Christ: The Search for the Historical Jesus*. New York: Simon and Schuster, 1998.

The Anglican Digest. "SPEAKing of the Arts: Oscar Wilde's Children's Stories." 40.6 (Michaelmas 1998):10.

Attebery, Brian. *Strategies of Fantasy*. Bloomington, IN: U of Indiana P, 1992.

Bachelard, Gaston. *The Poetics of Space*. Boston: Beacon Press, 1969.

Bentley, D. M. R. "The Meretricious and the Meritorious in *Goblin Market*: A Conjecture and an Analysis." In *The Achievement of Christian Rossetti*, ed. David A. Kent. Ithaca: Cornell UP, 1987.

Bovon, Francois. "The Child and the Beast." *Harvard Divinity Bulletin* 27.4 (1998): 16-21.

Buechner, Frederick. *Telling Secrets*. San Francisco: HarperCollins, 1991.

Cott, Jonathan, ed. *Beyond the Looking Glass: Extraordinary Works of Fairy Tale and Fantasy*. Intro. Leslie Fiedler. Woodstock, NY: Overlook Press, 1973.

Dowling, Linda. *Hellenism and Homosexuality in Victorian Oxford*. Ithaca: Cornell UP, 1994.

Dusinberre, Juliette. *Alice to the Lighthouse: Children's Books and Radical Experiments in Art*. London: Macmillan, 1987.

Eagleton, Terry. *The Ideology of the Aesthetic*. Oxford: Blackwell Publishers, 1990.

Ellman, Richard. *Oscar Wilde*. New York: Knopf, 1988.

Farrell, Kirby. *Post-Traumatic Culture: Injury and Interpretation in the Nineties*. Baltimore: Johns Hopkins UP, 1998.

Hoban, Russell. "Wilde Pomegranates." *Children's Literature in Education* 28.1 (1997): 19-29.

Hutcheon, Linda and Michael. "'Here's Lookin' at You, Kid': The Empowering Gaze in *Salome*." *MLA Profession* (1998): 11-22.

Hyde, H. Montgomery. *The Trials of Oscar Wilde*. London: William Hodge, 1948.

Jung, C. G., and C. Kerenyi. *Essays on a Science of Mythology*. Bollingen Series 22. Princeton: Princeton UP, 1973.

Knoepflmacher, U. C. *Ventures into Childland*. Chicago: U of Chicago P, 1998.

Kooistra, Lorraine Janzen. "*Goblin Market* as a Cross-Audienced Poem." *Children's Literature* 25 (1997): 181-204.

Le Gallienne, Richard. *The Romantic 90s*. New York: Putnam, 1925.

MacDonald, George. *The Complete Fairy Tales*. New York: Schocken, 1997.

———. *An Expression of Character: The Letters of George MacDonald*. Ed. Glenn Edward Sadler. Grand Rapids, MI: Wm. B. Eerdmans, 1994.

———. "The Fantastic Imagination." *A Dish of Orts: Chiefly Papers on the Imagination and Shakespeare*. London: Edwin Dalton, 1908.

MacDonald, Greville. *George MacDonald and His Wife*. New York: Dial Press, 1924.

Noll, Mark A. "Evangelicalism at Its Best." *Harvard Divinity Bulletin* 27.2/3 (1998): 8-12.

O'Brien, Tim. *The Things They Carried*. New York: Penguin, 1990.

Owen, Alex. "Magic and the Ambiguities of Modernity." Unpublished paper presented at the University of Michigan, March, 1999.

Robinson, Edward. *The Original Vision of Childhood: A Study of the Religious Experience of Childhood*. New York: Seabury Press, 1983.

Rossetti, Christina. *The Complete Poems of Christina Rossetti*. Ed. R. W. Crump. Variorum ed. Vol. 1. Baton Rouge: Louisiana State UP, 1979.

———. *Selected Prose of Christina Rossetti*. Ed. David A. Kent and P. G. Stanwood. New York: St. Martin's, 1998.

Rossetti, William M., ed. "Notes by W. M. Rossetti." In *The Poetical Works of Christina Georgina Rossetti*. London: Macmillan, 1904.

Schmidgall, Gary. *The Stranger Wilde*. New York: Dutton, 1994.

Tolkien, J. R. R. "Tree and Leaf." *The Tolkien Reader*. New York: Ballantine. 1966.

Warner, Maria. *Six Myths of Our Time*. New York: Random House, 1994.

Wilde, Oscar. *The Complete Works of Oscar Wilde*. New York: Harper & Row, 1989.

———. *The Wit and Humor of Oscar Wilde*. Ed. Alvin Redman. New York: Dover, 1959.

Woolf, Virginia. *Moments of Being: Unpublished Autobiographical Writings*. Ed. Jeanne Schulkind. New York: Harcourt, 1976.

Yeats, William Butler. *Autobiography*. New York: Macmillan, 1965.

———. *Letters*. Ed. Allan Wade. New York: Macmillan, 1955.

Zemka, Sue. *Victorian Testaments*. Stanford, CA: Stanford UP, 1997.

Zipes, Jack. *When Dreams Came True*. New York: Routledge, 1999.

Jarlath Killeen (essay date 2007)

SOURCE: Killeen, Jarlath. Introduction to *The Fairy Tales of Oscar Wilde,* pp. 1-17. Aldershot, England: Ashgate, 2007.

[*In the following essay, an introduction to his full-length study of Wilde's* The Happy Prince and Other Tales *and* A House of Pomegranates, *Killeen "examine[s] the critical history of the fairy tales and attempt[s] to explain why they have received relatively little attention."*]

> Is *A House of Pomegranates* intended for a child's book? We confess that we do not exactly know. . . .
>
> *Pall Mall Gazette,* 30 November 1891[1]

[*The Fairy Tales of Oscar Wilde*] is the first full-length study of Oscar Wilde's two collections of children's literature, *The Happy Prince and other tales* (1888) and *A House of Pomegranates* (1891). Although the tales which comprise these collections have received some important critical attention they remain marginal in Wilde Studies, simply because most critics are unsure what to make of them. Wilde is collectively understood, and written about, as a subversive writer, an amoral aesthete and an enemy of Victorian social and sexual values, a judgement based on the corpus of works that generally engage interpreters' critical faculties, *The Picture of Dorian Gray* (1891), the critical essays, and the five major plays. In a strange way the two collections of fairy tales he wrote appear somehow anomalous, tangential, if not entirely unrelated to his canon and attempts to incorporate them have been, while often significant, few and far between. This is partly because children's literature in general is considered a didactic and conservative form by many of the best writers on Wilde, and due to this there has seemed little to gain in looking at such theoretically conformist work when trying to put forward a case for Wilde as a social subversive. This book will attempt to explain the 'mystery' of the fairy tales through a close textual and contextual analysis, arguing that they should be read as containing both conservative and subversive energies, and that they allow us to see Wilde himself as displaying the qualities of a conservative as well as a radical writer. I contend that the fairy tales should be read in relation to the field of force from which Wilde drew much of his creative energies—Ireland—and that when placed in this context the strange, often disturbing, qualities of the stories begin to make sense. In re-situating these fairy tales in the complex nexus of theological, political, social and national concerns of late nineteenth-century Ireland, some of the difficulties critics have encountered in interpreting them will, hopefully, be removed and their relation to the Wildean canon will become clearer. This Introduction will examine the critical history of the fairy tales and attempt to explain why they have received relatively little attention.

In May 1888 Oscar Wilde published a collection of stories entitled *The Happy Prince and other tales* and, in doing so, confounded his critics. He compounded this over three years later in November 1891 when *A House of Pomegranates* appeared. What confused his contemporaries was that their understanding of Oscar Wilde, the 'Professor of Aesthetics', sometimes seemed far removed from the constructions to which he was putting his name. A series of ostensibly orthodox fairy tales jarred with his shocking collection of *Poems,* which had received so much adverse publicity in 1887. This confusion has not really dissipated, and many commentators on Wilde now prefer to ignore the fairy tales entirely rather than work out how exactly they fit into the interpretation of Wilde at which they have arrived. Richard Pine has posed the vital question: 'Why . . . do the stories remain a mystery?' (165). The puzzle, in the 1890s as now, is in how they relate to Wilde's other writings. It seems to me, however, that the problem arises from, firstly, the academic approach to Wilde and, secondly, the attitude of some Wilde critics to children's literature itself.

The dominant interpretation of Wilde as a 'subversive' writer is central to the problem of the fairy tales. Jonathan Dollimore and Eve Kosofsky Sedgwick, the two critics at the forefront of the 're-evaluation' of Wilde's *oeuvre,* have tended to ignore the early tales and concentrate on the 'major' works, especially *The Picture of Dorian Gray* and *The Importance of Being Earnest* (performed 1895, published 1899). This avoidance has taken place despite the fact that, for example, both *Intentions* and *Dorian Gray* were published in book form in 1891, and were thus being written synchronously with both *The Happy Prince and other tales* and *A House of Pomegranates.* The erasure of the fairy tales from the critical canon is matched by the discomfort some critics experience when confronted with *De Profundis* (1905) and *The Ballad of Reading Gaol* (1898). Dollimore, for example, worries that Wilde had effectively renounced his 'transgressive aesthetic' with the writing of his great prison letter, broken by the penal system and hard labour (95-8). However, the thesis that it was his horrific experiences in prison which led him to recant his subversive agenda is harder to maintain when the 'conservative' fairy tales are taken into account, as they were written at the height of Wilde's creative powers. A large number of major Wilde critics have simply erased the fairy tales from their account of Wilde, including Lawrence Danson, Julia Prewitt

Brown, Bruce Bashford, Alan Sinfield, Linda Dowling and Jeffrey Nunokawa. While I completely accept that it is simply not possible to deal comprehensively with the entire oeuvre of a particular writer in any one study, it is surely strange that the absence of the children's literature is one of the few things that these critics have in common.

Those critics who *have* engaged with the tales have often attempted to negotiate them into the dominant interpretation, one prominent instance of which is the endeavour to deny that the term 'fairy tale' applies to Wilde's stories at all. Many critics have insisted that Wilde never wrote fairy tales but was, in fact, a writer of folk tales. Critics have claimed that while fairy tales are designed to socialise children, to 'educate' them into a pre-existing adult world, folk tales are counter-hegemonic challenges to the 'adult' aristocrats by 'childlike' peasants who desire some kind of social upheaval. The best example of this in Wilde criticism is Richard Pine who argues forcefully that:

> A fairy-story is an allegory designed to give children a picture of the real, adult, world, and to enable them, by understanding its constituent parts, to negotiate a satisfactory path in the real world. A folk-tale is more vicious, a parable: it is a tale for adults who have lost their way among the signposts and have experienced some of the disruption related in the tale . . . Wilde's stories belong to the folk genre.
>
> (165)

Fairy tales are ideologically conformative; folk tales are primitively subversive; Wilde is subversive so his stories *must* be folk-tales.

Such an analysis operates with the critical vocabulary mapped out by many historians of both folk and fairy tales. Oral folk tales have existed time-out-of-mind, probably from at least the Neolithic, and were passed from generation to generation through figures whose primary function was the preservation of these tales in memory. One important fact about such tales is their relatively fluid character; the storyteller would invariably change the tale to suit the audience, although this elasticity must not be exaggerated since it is probable that an audience would demand that certain elements remained the same in each re-telling. Some time in the medieval period, although where and when exactly this occurred is unknown for certain, the narrative elements which link the oral wonder tale and the folk tale to the literary fairy tale began to appear in Europe and these tales began to be written down, first in Latin and then, gradually, in the vernacular and the form of the fairy tale established certain relatively stable features and conventions. The key change from the oral folk tale to the literary fairy tale appears to have been the audience: whereas the folk tale emerged from and was composed for the 'folk', the peasants of feudal Europe, the literary fairy tale was written initially by and for the aristocracy and then by and for the middle classes and excluded the lower orders of society. What we effectively witness in this transition is the appropriation by the higher social orders of the tales of the peasantry; in this appropriation many elements were altered even though some of the conventions and beliefs of the oral tale were incorporated into the literary tradition.

In his classic study *The Morphology of the Folktale* (English translation, 1958), Vladimir Propp identified 31 basic motifs and conventions common to both the folk and fairy tale. As Propp outlines the plot involves a protagonist who transgresses a prohibition for which he is banished. To overcome this banishment he must solve a problem and this will define his character. In the problem-solving task the protagonist will meet either enemies or friends, or sometimes both, and usually acquires a mysterious instrument or tool to help in the task, which he eventually succeeds in completing. There is normally a sudden setback for the protagonist, which is overcome miraculously, and he is rewarded with marriage or money or position or indeed all of the above. Propp's study indicates that these conventions are the stable factors uniting oral and literary tales and probably evolved to usefully allow for easy recall for oral storytellers. Wilde himself, as many commentators have pointed out, certainly did stick closely to the conventions as outlined by Propp. In a close study of two of Wilde's fairy tales David M. Monaghan concludes that they follow Propp's conventions very closely (156-7). Critics often point out that these conventions allow for radical change and the transformation of the poor protagonist and his rise in status. Despite the fact that the stories may have been told with ideologically conservative motives in different communities, for many historians of the genre this conservatism is overcome by the emphasis on transformation: it suggests the liberatory possibilities of social movement. Jack Zipes, an important historian of the folk and fairy tale, has argued that although the ideology of the tale depended 'on the position that the narrator assumed with regard to developments in his or her community' (*When Dreams Came True* 6), ultimately the folk tale articulated a utopian desire by the peasantry for a better life, a life free from the oppressive elements of hunger, poverty and fear. Marina Warner's analysis supports this position since she argues that the oral tale was largely, though not exclusively, in the control of women and therefore largely reflected a feminine perspective on the universe (*From the Beast to the Blonde* passim).

What happened when these oral transformative stories were written down and appropriated by the aristocracy and the middle class was that this radical potential was muted if not completely eradicated. According to Zipes, the upper classes had always been suspicious of the oral folk tale with its promise of sudden and total social transformation. When writers such as Charles Perrault (*Histoires ou Contes du Temps Passé* [1697]), Jacob and Wilhelm Grimm (*Kinder- und Hausmärchen* [1812]), and, especially, Hans Christian Anderson (*Eventyr, fortale for børn* [1832-42]), appropriated these folk tales they changed their ideological focus and effectively made them stories to socialise middle-class children rather than stories to offer hope to folk communities. While these writers did indeed (to some extent—a radically truncated one in Anderson's case) gather tales from authentic folk populations they changed them to suit their own ideological purposes and it is these new versions which formed the basis for the fairy tale traditions of the West. The fairy tale was considered a useful instrument in countering the atomising effect of modernity on middle-class individuals and families; it was believed that through escapism the fairy tale could make life in a capitalist society easier to bear (Zipes, *Breaking the Magic Spell* 4-16). Moreover, the middle classes found that the new fairy tales had an additional use in that, when given to working-class children, they educated them in the values important to the middle classes and thus helped to reconcile them to their subordinate position in society. Fairy tales and the middle class emerged simultaneously, they perpetuated middle-class morality and functioned to keep the middle class in power.

The purported ideological difference between the folk and fairy tale is crucial to understand why it may be that many critics are uncomfortable with Wilde's stories. While a psychoanalyst like Bruno Bettelheim in *The Uses of Enchantment* (1976) plays down the difference between the two genres and argues that both represent basic truths about the human condition which are crucial for a child to learn in order to cope with the world, Jack Zipes is equally certain that the fairy tale distorts the much more attractive folk tradition whose 'radical' vales he finds personally more attractive. Thus, Zipes contends that folk tales incline towards subversive tactics to a larger degree than fairy-tale. In *Fairy Tales and the Art of Subversion* he argues that 'Since the imaginative motifs and symbolical elements of class conflict and rebellion in the pre-capitalist folk tales ran counter to the principles of rationalism and utilitarianism developed by a bourgeois class, they had to be suppressed', and that 'the fairy-tale discourse was controlled by the same socio-political tendencies which contributed towards strengthening bourgeois domination of the public sphere in the first half of the nineteenth century' (24, 98). Zipes's overarching argument is that as folk tales were changed into fairy tales by emerging capitalist societies, the dominant culture attempted to repress the subversive potential in the utopianism of the oral tradition, with varying success. Thus, the 'fairy tale' has, for Zipes, a split identity: it is used by commercial and institutional interests to convey the ideology of the culture industry and make its readers passive but, in so far as it utilises the feudal utopianism of the underground, it disrupts this primary purpose. Indeed, he accepts that some fairy tale writers, including Wilde, did tap into the subversive aspects of fairy tales more than emphasising their conservative elements (*Fairy Tales and the Art of Subversion* 111-21). It is, however, the genre's conservatism that has been intensely focused on by many fairy tale critics and historians (Stone; Lieberman; Dworkin).

A similar process of bourgeois appropriation of folk traditions took place in nineteenth-century Ireland to that which had occurred earlier in Continental Europe, a process in which the Wilde family played a large part. This process was driven by the Protestant Ascendancy who began, in the late eighteenth century, to investigate and embrace aspects of native Irish culture through the study of, initially, antiquities and then of archaeology, mythology and folklore. These Protestants were descendents of those who had arrived in Ireland from England and Scotland during the Plantations of the sixteenth and seventeenth centuries and were ethnically, politically and religiously divided from the native inhabitants. Their antiquarian and archaeological work helped wed the Irish Protestant community to Ireland in a period when they had become alienated from their 'homeland'—England. Traditionally, the Protestants of Ireland had been reluctant to accept the ethnic marker of Irish and preferred to think of themselves as simply Englishmen and women who happened to live in Ireland. The eighteenth century, however, witnessed a long process whereby England effectively abandoned the Protestants in Ireland to their own devices and also insisted that these Protestants were indeed Irish and had to accept this nationality. This caused a difficulty as native Irish culture was suffused with Catholicism, an aspect of Irish identity Protestants could clearly not appropriate. In the search for a basis for a common culture many Irish Protestants looked to the pre-Christian period and its remnants in contemporary Ireland as a means of bringing the different ethnicities together. Ancient Ireland and the folk-survivals of that period were thus doubly attractive to Irish Protestants (Canny).

Antiquarians and folklorists produced a large amount of important work in the eighteenth and nineteenth centuries. This included General Charles Vallancey's *Collectanea de rebus Hibernicis* (1770-1804), a multi-volume work on Irish folk customs, Charlotte Brooke's collection *Reliques of Irish Poetry* (1789), which included folk songs and myths, Edward Bunting's *A General Collection of the Ancient Music of Ireland* (1796) and the writings of Thomas Crofton Croker. Croker corresponded with the Grimms and published two important and influential collections of folklore: *Researches in the South of Ireland, Illustrative of the Scenery, Architectural Remains and the Manners and Superstitions of the Peasantry* (1824) and *Fairy Legends and Traditions of*

the South of Ireland (1925). These collections are indicative of both intense attraction for the Irish peasantry and yet discomfort with their 'primitive' and superstitious condition. Because of the theological transformation of middle-class Catholicism in the nineteenth century (during which many 'folkloric' beliefs and rituals were discarded in an attempt to purify Catholicism of its 'pagan' past), many Catholics had become increasingly embarrassed by what were now considered 'superstitious' beliefs in fairies, witches, ghosts and practices such as patterns and wakes, although many still retained their investment in these traditions. Intellectually such degraded beliefs and practices became almost the sole interest and preserve of Irish Protestants who found them both distasteful yet profoundly attractive, both what they admired about the natives and what they hated (Bourke, 'Baby and Bathwater' 80-1). Croker is paradigmatic of this Protestant ambivalence.

It is, of course, crucial to realise that fairylore and superstition were not really pagan or primitive alternatives to Catholicism for the Irish peasantry as many Irish Protestant antiquarians and folklore collectors maintained in their attempts to divest 'essential' Irish culture of the stain of Catholicism. The religion of Irish people up to the nineteenth century was a version of folk-Catholicism, an eclectic mixture of the theologically heterodox and the orthodox, common among communities which were relatively untouched by the modernising projects of church and state. In most communities 'folk belief' and Catholic orthodoxy lived side by side in people's minds without any clashing or difficulty (see Ó Giolláin, 'The Fairy Belief' 199), and those who believed in, for example, fairies did not consider themselves less than Catholic because of that belief. This changed during the nineteenth century as a new group of intensely Tridentine priests and religious set out to purify Irish Catholicism of its folkloric past, but it was a slow transformation.

Wilde's own parents contributed significantly to the tradition of Irish Protestant investigation of native religious conventions (see Pulido). His father Sir William Wilde was a noted folklorist, whose collection *Irish Popular Superstitions* (1852) was composed of stories and traditions he picked up in his time in the West of Ireland, both as a child in County Roscommon and also while staying at his holiday homes in Moytura House and Illaunroe Cottage, both in County Mayo. There he travelled to the cottages of the peasantry, offering medical help in exchange for stories (see Markey for a judicious study of Wilde's knowledge of folklore). After his death his wife, Lady 'Speranza' Wilde, collected his notes and compiled two collections out of them: *Ancient Legends* (1882) and *Irish Charms* (1890). The key point to make about these three collections is that they conform to Zipes' ideological cartography of the transition from oral folklore to literary fairylore: they exhibit both attraction to and unease with the traditions they are theoretically transcribing faithfully. Sir William Wilde was well aware of this duality. In *Irish Popular Superstitions,* he laments the passing of the folk traditions due to emigration, the Irish Famine (1845-1850), the loss of the Irish language, and urbanisation, but also notes that his own publications are part of this process of destruction:

> . . . these legendary Tales and Popular Superstitions have now become the history of the past—a portion of the traits and characteristics of other days. Will their recital revive their practice? No! Nothing contributes more to uproot superstitious rites and forms than to print them; to make them known to the many instead of leaving them hidden among, and secretly practised by the few.
>
> (6-7)

Sir William here acknowledges the damaging aspect to both folklore collection and fairy tale writing. Both undermine the very group, the peasantry, they depend on.

Of course, in writing fairy tales Wilde may be as much reacting to, as well as fulfilling Matthew Arnold's description of the Irish as a race which revolted against, and was revolted by, the despotism of fact ('On the Study of Celtic Literature' 344). This would make his writing of such fugitive pieces an act of literary nationalism, an attempt, like his parents', to identify with the West of Ireland peasants who told him versions of these stories in the first place. Jerusha McCormack believes that the fairy tales are 'dangerous' since they 'drew their inspiration from a degraded culture, driven underground—whether that of the "little people", fairies or children, or of the emerging gay subculture of the 1890s' (102). However, in making such associations it is important to accept that Wilde must bear some responsibility for the endangering of such traditions by writing them down, a danger he knew of from his father's warnings about the clash between the literary and the oral.

Most of Wilde's critics do not want to associate him directly with this destruction of folk traditions and instead try to see him almost completely within a liberatory folk history rather than a middle-class conformist fairy tale mode. Such attempts to make Wilde into a peasant in aristocratic drag are not completely convincing. Richard Pine makes the argument that Wilde is a folk-tale teller rather than a fairy-tale writer on the basis of 'something apocryphal [in the stories], something existing before its composition . . . ; Wilde's storytelling [is] a form of self-identification with a Homeric and primitive society' (165). This resonance of the primitive is found in the repeated motifs of Irish folklore in the stories: the changeling in 'The Young King' and 'The Star-Child'; the obvious use of Famine legends in 'The Young King'; the raiding of his mother's *Ancient Leg-*

ends of Ireland necessary for the composition of 'The Fisherman and his Soul'; the haunt of *Tír-na-nÓg* floating over both collections (177-83; see also Cohen 73-6; Edwards, 'Impressions' 52-60). Undue recognition of these elements is, argues Pine, the cause of the critical 'mystery' surrounding the tales.

Moreover, so the argument goes, the stories in the two collections originate in performance, and Wilde is often configured as a kind of reverse-colonising *seanachaí,* deconstructing the literary culture of England through the most oral culture in Europe. André Gide insisted that 'Wilde did not converse: he narrated' (2), and W. B. Yeats believed that Wilde was 'the greatest talker of his time. I have never and shall never meet conversation that could match his' (*Autobiographies* 172). W. Graham Robertson termed Wilde 'a born *raconteur*' and recalled how 'his stories seemed to grow naturally out of the general conversation and not to interrupt it; their length was not perceptible and his hearers did not realise how long they had been silent' (in Mikhail, vol. 1, 208). The 'orality' of Wilde's project has been a recurrent theme in much recent criticism, especially in the stimulating work of Deirdre Toomey (see also Pine 161; McCormack 97-103). The oral 'intention' of the tales, combined with the recurrent motifs of Irish legends, transforms Wilde, the middle-class writer of fairy tales, into the *seanachaí* providing parables of amoral liberation to the working classes.

However, Wilde is not so different to others whose status as fairy-tale writers is not in doubt, including the Grimms. He probably accompanied his father into the homes of the peasantry and there picked up the basic plots and motifs he would use in his fairy tales (although see Markey for the argument that Wilde may not have followed his father into the West of Ireland cottages). In other words, like the Grimms, he collected folk material and then transformed that material for his own ends. After all, the use of folk motifs does not definitively make him a *seanachaí* since all fairy tales assimilate aspects of folk culture, often merely for 'authentic' window dressing, though more habitually to situate the fairy tale in a particular cultural *milieu.* The folk-motif argument is not, therefore, very convincing.

The differences between the genres really indicate that with Wilde we are dealing with a fairy-tale writer and not a folk tale teller: folk tales are oral and custom-related; they are traditional in form and transmission retaining a fixed plot structure; they are anonymous; they exist in different variants (Brunvand 12, 15). Working with this reading of folklore, it is clear that Wilde's collections cannot be incorporated. These texts are fixed. Claims of Wilde's orality work better in relation to his prose poems most of which he never wrote down, than with his collected stories. Deirdre Toomey argues that anonymity was important to Wilde in that he did not assert proprietorship over his oral tales. She cites as evidence the story of Wilde's meeting with the young W. B. Maxwell who confessed to him that he had used one of his stories he had heard in a conversation. Wilde reportedly told him that 'stealing my story was the act of a gentleman, but not telling me you had stolen it was to ignore the claims of friendship', and asked him not to appropriate the oral story of Dorian Gray (Toomey 26). What this demonstrates is Wilde's demarcation of the oral (folk) and the literary (fairy) genres: it was perfectly appropriate for an oral tale to continue being passed around, but he claims authorship (ownership) of a narrative he is about to *write*.

Indeed, many of his acquaintances noted a marked difference between the stories-as-spoken and the stories-as-written. Yeats claimed that 'the further Wilde goes from the method of speech, from improvisation, from sympathy with some especial audience, the less original he is, the less accomplished' (*Prefaces and Introductions* 137). Likewise, Robertson contended that 'when committed to paper, his tales lost much of their charm' (Mikhail, vol. 1, 211). For his friends and acquaintances the oral tales were more vividly alive than the written stories; this indicates that to a middle-class constituency the oral stories smacked more of folk authenticity than the two collections. This division, in fact, follows Zipes' formula very well: the oral tale is transformative, but in its transfer to a written culture the motifs lose their original agency and are muffled in the logocentric discourses of the 'civilised' world. Wilde himself, in a letter to John Ruskin in July 1888 distinctly refers to the *The Happy Prince and other tales* as 'a little book of fairy stories', not folk tales (*Letters* 355).

Neil Sammells argues that claiming that Wilde is really a figure of orality rather than literacy is a means of absolving his decadence, dissolving his relation to a literature of fragmentation, in favour of a culture of authenticity and organicism (233), and he favours seeing Wilde's texts as a hybrid form of oral-literate culture. Wilde is caught between two worlds and uses each to interrogate the other. This has been supported by Paul K. Saint-Amour who believes that a hankering after authenticity haunts most designations of Wilde as a practitioner of primal orality. He argues instead that Wilde's work recognises that primary orality:

> is in part a construction by literate culture of its Other, and therefore not revivable in practice. Instead, Wilde's more forcibly transgressive writings, and his career generally, suggest that to import the forms of primary orality into typographical England does less to ventilate literate culture than to translate orality into terms that literacy can recognise . . . Rather than naively imagine orality as a tonic to writing, as nature to writing's artifice . . . Wilde recognised that the longing for orality as origin, nature and authentic prehistory may be the most characteristic thing about print culture, which

thrives by manufacturing origins and measuring its distance from them in order, alternately, to wound or worship itself.

> (64)

Writing fairy tales may be a means of ending rural life, but also a means of identification with it; in neither case, however, does it make the writer one of the 'people'.

It is in relation to the subversive agenda, of course, that critics have attempted to deny that the two collections are to be considered fairy tales or indeed, and bizarrely, even children's literature, as it is still a critical commonplace that the literature written for, and approved of as being good for, children is predominantly conservative (code word for patriarchal, Eurocentric and logocentric). Karin Lesnik-Oberstein argues that most literary critics still assume (rightly) that children's literature is a highly politicised genre rather than a value-free carrier of oral home culture (an innocent text) (24; for the politics of children's literature, see also Tease; Zimet; Leeson; Bratton; Stephens). It is pertinent to point out that children's literature became a subject of major academic interest in the 1970s and 1980s. The excavation of the reactionary and conservative nature of children's literature happened to coincide with a re-emergence of the interest by radical critics in Wilde's writings. The two projects seemed mutually exclusive. A large number of articles and books charting and examining the development of writing for children in the late nineteenth century emphasised how it, explicitly or implicitly, inculcates the dogmas of patriarchy, empire and capitalism into young minds (see Bristow; Dunae; Fox; Applebee). To assert that Wilde was a major contributor to the burgeoning market for this genre was to risk labelling *him* orthodox. Of course, some critics have accepted this interpretation of Wilde as an orthodox children's writer. John Allen Quintus claims that Wilde's moral affirmations in his stories 'in simple terms . . . propose decency and generosity in human relations' (710), while Kimberly Reynolds posits that while in general Wilde was a writer who set out to deconstruct social values, 'in writing which was intended to include children in its audience, even Oscar Wilde felt it necessary to provide instruction' (21). The 'even Oscar Wilde' is particularly illuminating. Reynolds is prepared to accept the critical orthodoxy of Wildean amorality but finds the fairy tales the exception that proves the rule. Regenia Gagnier claims that the fairy tales 'reek of middle-class virtue and sentimentality' (63), while Vincent O' Sullivan, a friend of Wilde's, believed that such morality is everywhere in his work in general and that 'one is struck by the facility with which he runs into moralising—indirect moralising, it is true' (207).

A terror of the moral appears to have convinced many to go to great lengths to remove Wilde from the community of writers for children. Critics contend that Wilde effectively disguised his collections as children-oriented in order to ensure that his work reached the Victorian *parents,* arguing that Wilde was writing, 'not for nursery children . . . but for adult-children' (Pine 165), and appeal to Wilde's letters to support such a claim. Declan Kiberd, in a very carefully phrased sentence, suggests that 'Wilde's fairytales are intended, perhaps mainly, for adults—but for children too' (*Irish Classics* 326). A recent article by Michelle Ruggaber insists that while *The Happy Prince and other tales* may have been for children, *A House of Pomegranates* certainly was not and that the stories in that collection, 'while they can still be enjoyed by children, are meant to challenge and destabilise the expectations of adults' (142). Rodney Shewan's *Art and Egotism* is a brilliant examination of Wilde's work in the round, but his discomfort with the category 'children's literature' provokes him to extreme measures to absolve Wilde. He states that 'with one exception, all of his recorded remarks about the tales make it clear that they were not primarily children's stories' (36). This 'one exception' is Wilde's letter to William Gladstone in June 1888, to whom he explicitly professes that the stories in *The Happy Prince and other tales* are 'really meant for children' (*Letters* 350). We know, however, that Wilde initially intended the stories to entertain his own children and, although definitions of 'children's literature' are problematic, it would be perverse to exclude texts explicitly conceived *for* children and this means that Wilde's tales should be included. Vyvyan Holland recalled that Wilde told all the stories in the volumes to himself and his brother (53-4) and Wilde remarked to one friend that:

> It is the duty of every father . . . to write fairy tales for his children. But the mind of a child is a great mystery. It is incalculable, and who shall divine it, or bring to it his own peculiar delights? You humbly spread before it the treasures of your imagination, and they are as dross.
>
> (Le Gallienne 252)

Like George MacDonald and C. S. Lewis, Wilde saw himself as writing for the 'child-like' rather than simply 'children', but this certainly does not exclude the young (*Letters* 388). In a letter to a fellow writer G. H. Kersley, Wilde states that the tales are 'meant partly for children, and partly for those who have kept the child-like faculties of wonder and joy' (ibid 352). This indicates a more divided audience, but the adults he incorporates are those who have not yet lost a child-like perspective. Wilde himself was child-like, a fact noted by many of his contemporaries. Max Beerbohm, for example, called him 'a huge overgrown schoolboy' (286) and in a letter to Leonard Smithers in May 1898 he claimed he possessed a 'childlike simple nature' (*Letters* 1073). Ian Small is, I think, correct in his argument that

the 'constancy of Wilde's affection towards his children . . . goes some way towards explaining that initial decision to write fairy stories' ('Introduction' xv).

Rodney Shewan is uncomfortable with the designation 'children's literature' because it seems too slight to hold the philosophy he thinks defines the stories: nihilism. He insists that, far from potentially didactic tales set up to educate the young into a form of morality, 'Wilde's characteristic morals are anti-morals', obsessively pessimistic and destructive of all moral opportunity (38). Shewan is explicit in his belief that sophisticated philosophy cannot be aimed at the young and considers this the vital issue in determining audience. Recent analysts of children's literature, however, have pointed out that children's books are certainly not different from their adult-oriented counterparts in terms of subject matter, tone or emotional complexity. According to Natalie Babbitt, there are few, if any, differences in content between adult and children's fiction (157). This lack of difference between the contents of children's and adults' books is crucial to this study as a whole, because a complaint may be raised that the readings offered here are 'far beyond' either children's capacity for understanding or their general knowledge.

I contend, however, that not only is there no real difference between the issues tackled by children's and adults' books, or the relative complexity of their treatment, but that it is not necessary to think that the contemporary children's audience 'picked up' on the references or understood the contexts I posit as essential to analysing the tales. Wilde himself appears to have been committed to a theory of Gnosticism whereby knowledge is transmitted from the initiated to acolytes through codes and symbols and he also believed that such codes and symbols often operated in some mysterious and magical fashion on the human mind. This may seem strange but such Gnostic beliefs were hardly alien to the literary culture of the 1890s. It is well known that W. B. Yeats believed in the existence of secret knowledge that could only be reached through the use of symbols and that he considered the Irish peasantry to be in possession of a repository of such symbols as encoded into their myths, legends and folklore. Wilde's father believed similar things about the Irish peasantry when he worried that printing folk beliefs would unfortunately lead to 'make them known to the many instead of leaving them hidden among, and secretly practised by, the few'. As a Freemason, Sir William saw his intimate contact with the Irish peasantry as a privileged access to a hidden and encrypted form of knowledge. While it is well-known that Oscar Wilde was also a Freemason, having joined while at Oxford, it is not so widely known that his wife Constance was a member of the Order of the Golden Dawn, perhaps the most important Theosophical society in the British Isles in this period. She had joined the Order in 1888 after being previously involved with both spiritualism and the Theosophical Society. She would not have been lonely there as Wilde's brother Willie was also a member. Wilde himself was present at some Theosophical meetings and also associated with some groups at the periphery of the theosophical movement (Owen, *Enchantment* 62-3, 108).

The Order of the Golden Dawn was designed to appeal to those, like Wilde, attracted by Freemasonry and was in fact set up by Freemasons. In Oxford Wilde had advanced very quickly upwards in the Freemasons, a training for occult knowledge which prepared him well for the theosophists. Masonic imagery pervades his writing. As Marie Mulvey-Roberts points out, the symbol of the Rose-Cross is important in Masonic iconography as a symbol of female sexuality combined with the phallus (140), which goes some way to explaining the importance of the rose in 'The Nightingale and the Rose'. For Irish Protestants there was a link between their interest in native Irish culture and their attraction towards occultism. The apparently mystical and magical beliefs of the Irish peasantry were seen by many Protestant nationalists as versions of occult and secret theologies and Wilde's childhood initiation into the mysteries of the religion of the Irish peasantry would have laid the foundation for his later occult development.

The naming of *A House of Pomegranates* is significant in this context. The Greek myths tell the story of Persephone, the daughter of Zeus and Demeter, who was kidnapped by Hades, the god of the underworld. In protest at the kidnap of her daughter Demeter refused to let the crops grow and Hades was forced to return Persephone to her parents. After her return, however, they discovered that while in the underworld she had eaten the seeds of a pomegranate, and as the pomegranate is a symbol of fertility, by eating it Persephone had effectively consummated her relationship with Hades. Demeter agreed to let Persephone go back to Hades for three months of every year, during which time Winter descends and no crops grew. The fertility symbol Wilde met with in Greek mythology would have resonated with the fertility symbols and rituals he encountered in the West of Ireland and in his parents' folklore and which we will have occasion to return to again. The image of the pomegranate represents a fertile but dangerous descent into the occult underground required by both Theosophy and folk and fairy lore, and opens up onto a vast repository of myth and symbology never made explicit in Wilde's stories. The tales in these two collections are built out of such symbols and resonate with Irish and folk-Catholic meanings.

Wilde's refusal to make such connections explicit is crucial in understanding the tales. Although many mystics and occultists believed that access to hidden (or forbidden) knowledge needed to be kept to an elite few who would gain in occult wisdom as the Mason moves through rites of initiation, others felt that the signifiers of this knowledge, particularly certain symbols, should be dispersed through works that would be read and experienced by larger numbers. In his 1896 essay on 'William Blake and his Illustrations to the *Divine Comedy*' for example, Yeats wrote that 'A symbol is indeed the only possible expression of some invisible essence, a transparent lamp about a spiritual flame' (*Essays and Introductions* 116). Symbols were the active articulators of a world beyond this one, and could put those who encountered them into contact with transcendent reality, even if they were completely unaware of this process. Wilde, indeed, did not expect his child reader to grasp in a conscious fashion the issues being raised or the symbols being used in the fairy tales, but rather hoped that they would operate mysteriously on both parent and child. This means that the fairy tales are multilayered and operate with a high level of both occult symbolism and allegorical inflection.

This kind of hermeneutic intensity is not unusual in Irish writing which has often been read as deeply attracted to allegorical coding and doubleness (Donoghue, 3-18, 148-52). Jerusha McCormack has argued that 'doublespeak' is a characteristic of Wilde's writing in general, a doublespeak characteristic of the occult imagination (97). Indeed, the occult and Irish context of these stories could explain why Wilde took different approaches to the publication of the collections: while *The Happy Prince and other tales* was published to appeal to a large and popular market, *A House of Pomegranates* was a much more expensive volume and was clearly designed to only tempt connoisseurs. The failure of the symbolic structure of the first volume to transform the Victorian public may have led Wilde to use even more arcane discourses which could only be understood by a self-elected elite who could afford a collector's book and read it to their children. Wilde may have felt that some audiences would understand him better than others. He was, after all, a member of an Irish elite (the Ascendancy), many of whom would have readily understood the esoteric codes he was employing. In his essay on 'Protestant Magic', Roy Foster has ably demonstrated how attracted to and involved in occult and theosophical societies and rituals were a large percentage of the Protestant Ascendancy. Of course, allegory, codes and hidden knowledge were widely used in Ireland more generally; agrarian culture was deeply invested in secret societies, folkloric beliefs and quasi-mystical religion and this 'doubleness' may be linked to the colonial situation. It is widely accepted that allegory is a teleological mode of writing as it points to a future possibility, a way of life that is better than that being lived now, and so is attractive to societies undergoing historical trauma. The most obvious example of this allegorising is the book of Revelation, composed by a people undergoing exile and persecution, and which depends on past models for its allegory to work (including the Garden of Eden, city of God, New Jerusalem, sheep and goats, beast, whore of Babylon), but points forward to a future of hope in the new Garden of Eden and the new city of God. As Laurence Coupe has written in his important study of Myth, 'all myths presuppose a previous narrative, and in turn form the model for future narratives. Strictly speaking, the pattern of promise and fulfilment need never end' (108). In Ireland, the use of myth during the period called the Celtic Revival worked in exactly this way in that the patterns of the Fianna and Cuchulain myths were seen, not as a way of closing off history and bringing interpretation to an end, but of opening up new hope and possibility in an historical situation that seemed full of doubt and despair (especially after the death of the great nationalist leader Charles Stewart Parnell). Fairy tales work like this too. Wilde 'rewrites' models he takes from both the literary tradition of Hans Christian Anderson, and the oral folk traditions of the peasants of the West of Ireland, and in his allegory attempts to create a tentative history of the future as well as a diagnosis of the past.

At least one critic has argued that the unconscious influence of symbols and archetypes in Wilde's fairy tales is one reason why they remain popular today. Clifton Snider has claimed that 'those literary fairy tales which have endured have done so precisely because they appeal to the collective unconscious' (1). Placing these texts in this occult and historical context also explains the political and intellectual sophistication of the ideas encoded within them in symbols. For a true believer, contact with these symbols will eventually transform the children who read the stories, give them access to a world of hidden knowledge and thus change the world.

Occultism is often as conservative as it is liberatory and linking Wilde with this movement may not ease the anxiety of some critics who see in children's literature a sinister space for socialising of the vulnerable into oppressive ideologies. Although both Alison Lurie and Juliet Dusinberre have argued that children's literature is actually subversive rather than conservative, it is fair to say that the general critical consensus is that a strict morality is inherent in most writing for children (Lesnik-Oberstein, *Children's Literature* 4). Placing Wilde's collections into the realm of children's literature seems unavoidable and didacticism *is* the most pervasive note in such writing. As Kimberley Reynolds argues, 'no literature is neutral, but children's literature is more concerned with shaping its readers' attitudes than most' (ix). Marina Warner broadly agrees and accepts that 'fairy tale is essentially a moralising form' (*From the Beast to the Blonde* 24). Quite simply, children's literature has always been a crucial repository of authoritarian ideology. Ellen Terry recognised this didactic quality in Wilde's stories when she wrote to him stating:

They are quite beautiful, dear Oscar, and I thank you for them from the best bit of my heart . . . I should like to read one of them some day to NICE people—or even NOT nice people, and MAKE 'em nice.

(quoted in Murray 9)

Critics of Wilde do not like to see him as a moralist and even his best commentators are wary of designating the tales 'children's literature' for this reason. For example, Jerusha McCormack is concerned about the claim that Wilde was a children's writer. She insists that as readers we must become as subversive and radical as the stories themselves, and that we too must alter our perspectives, from being subjects of the patriarchal order to being its objects: 'It is from the margins of society, from the perspective of the poor, the colonised, the disreputable and dispossessed, that these stories must be read' (102). Our current perspectives assign us within the dominant order, but this blinds us to the power of the tales which are rubrics against personal property but advocates of social freedom, socialist and permissive, and engaged in actively conscribing boundaries and limits to personal expression to the past. She castigates those who see the tales as directed at children as engaging in a 'stupefied reading' (105). However, I believe that the volumes were designed to be contributions to debates on contemporary moral and political issues as well as didactic texts for children's instructions and, in avoiding this, critics are being unnecessarily elusive.

Much of this critical work has come from those who wish to definitively shift Wilde to the political left and repudiate the view of Friedrich Engels that he was merely a sedan-chair socialist. The idea of Wilde as a moralistic, conservative writer of middle-class fairy tales for children does not fit comfortably with a 'socialist' and transgressive view of him. However, it is perfectly possible to be a conservative moraliser and a subversive critic; it is possible to write didactic children's literature and simultaneously preach the overthrow of oppressive social, political and religious structures. In other words, Wilde can be both subversive and conservative, both a didactic children's writer and a social radical—indeed, I would contend that most writers of children's literature are precisely that. It is possible to reconcile the views of Wilde critics that he was radically transgressive with the possibility that he was also a conservative moralist.

The main problem is with setting unworkable dichotomies: if subversive, not conservative; if written for children then unsophisticated and hegemonic; if fairy tale, then repressively conservative. With this type of framework in place, and with the radical architecture already erected around Wilde, critics are faced with a dilemma when interpreting the two collections. It is illustrative to reflect that this same dilemma, or 'mystery', confronted the original reviewers of the stories: radical or conservative? Morally dangerous or morally edifying? This is aptly demonstrated in the anonymous review in the *Pall Mall Gazette,* 30 November 1891, which admitted a confusion in the provenance and intended audience of *A House of Pomegranates*: 'Is [the collection] intended for a child's book? We confess we do not exactly know . . .'. Most reviewers thought that they were the best things that Wilde had written and were a relief after the subtle and not-so-subtle decadence of *Poems.* The *Universal Review* of June 1888 stated that the volume *The Happy Prince and other tales* 'shows Mr. Oscar Wilde's genius at its best', while an unsigned note in *Athenaeum* claimed that 'the gift of writing fairy tales is rare, and Mr. Oscar Wilde shows he possesses it in a rare degree'. The September 1888 edition of the *Athenaeum* compared the stories to those of Hans Christian Anderson whose work has come in for much criticism from left-wing critics. In contrast, the brother of Robert Ross in the *Saturday Review,* 20 October 1888, detected in the tales 'a bitter satire differing widely from that of Hans Anderson'. The *Pall Mall Gazette* was divided on the matter. It thought that:

> the stories are somewhat after the manner of Hans Andersen—and have pretty poetic and imaginative flights like his; but then again they wander off too often into something between a "Sinburnian" ecstasy and the catalogue of a high art furniture dealer.

> (all found in full in Beckson 6-7, 60, 61, 113)

What we may be detecting in the critical reception of the fairy tales is a conceptual confusion: commentators seem unable to accept the possibility that the stories may be simultaneously subversive *and* conservative; that they may at once attack and criticise the dominant contemporary social and moral order and yet concurrently resurrect another conservatism to take its place. However, such a technique is not alien to the genre of fairy tales. We should remember Zipes' conception of the split identity of the fairy tale: it is used to convey interests and ideologies that may be considered conservative, but insofar as it utilises the feudal utopianism of the underground, it remains subversive. Wilde's two collections *are* subversive in that they undercut the morality of late Victorian England and yet they are conservative as they serve to legitimate the moral claims of another orthodoxy: that of folk-Catholicism. It will be this latter explanation that will be put forward in this book as a possible solution to the 'mystery' of the fairy tales.

After all, the history of the fairy tale is not one of straight-forward appropriation. Jack Zipes does argue that 'subversive' writers could put the usually conservative form of the fairy tale to good use, and he includes Wilde, L. Frank Baum and even George MacDonald in a group of such subversive writers (*Art of Subversion* 97-133). Zipes holds that in the appropriation of folk tales by the middle-class writers of fairy tales many subversive elements were contained and modified (purposely) to rob them of their emancipatory power, but that this does not mean that the fairy tale is by definition conservative, firstly because the attempt to regulate subversive elements was not a complete success, and secondly because the subversive material is still there ready to be set free if the right author comes along. We must never accept the utterly conservative reading of the fairy tale implicit in many commentaries and should instead remember, with Ernst Bloch, that the fairy tale can also be read as a means of disrupting the monological tendencies of the epic as well as the rationalist and realist orientation of the novel. As Zipes says of the fairy tale, 'the once upon a time is not a past designation but futuristic: the timelessness of the tale and lack of geographical specificity endow it with utopian connotations' (*When Dreams Came True* 4). This allows some writers to use the fairy tale form as a means of reflecting a radically different future for a hegemonic society.

Fairy tales are in the dubious (or perhaps beneficial) position of having thus come under attack from both the political left (which see in them the usual patriarchal, misogynist, elitist, conservative ideology we have all been fed for the past few millennia) and the political right (which see them as dangerously distracting, immoral, violent, sexual, unreal, the kind of stuff that lefties like). A writer like Wilde, caught between these ideological poles, would have seen in this form the perfect means of articulating his view of the world. The fairy tale is also usefully refracted through the form of the short story which originated in part in mythic narratives and Old Testament tales such as the stories of Noah's flood and Joseph in Genesis and is also connected to the fables of Æsop and the parables of Jesus. Indeed, along with myth, the short narrative may be the prototypical Hebraic and Western literary form. Wilde saw the Bible as an anthology of such narratives and told one friend: 'Do you know, the Bible is a wonderful book. How beautifully artistic the little stories are!' (Gide 7). He may have seen his own collections as emulations of, and perhaps even versions of, these biblical stories. He had once famously complained that 'when I think of all the harm that book [the Bible] has done, I despair of ever writing anything to equal it' (quoted in Pearson 165).

Many anthropologists and literary critics have argued that the short story operates on the borders of the sacred and the profane; it is not necessarily a religious form but it is implicated in ways that the secular novel is not with versions of a sacred past. Just as the mystical experiences of ancient communities came in brief episodes, fragments of the divine, so the short narrative was viewed by many as an effective formal device to express such momentary revelations. In some ways the short story as a form is deeply implicated in the sacred which may be why Joyce used it as a means of articulating 'epiphany' in the narrative methodology of *Dubliners* (1914). As Mary Rohrberger writes:

> The metaphysical view that there is more to the world than that which can be apprehended through the senses provides the rationale for the short story which is a vehicle for the author's probing of the nature of the real. As in the metaphysical view, reality lies beyond the ordinary world of appearances, so in the short story, meaning lies beneath the surface of the narrative'.

(141; see also May 1-5; Wheelwright 148-153)

Many have noticed the religious accent that dominates the short story form, an accent which links well with the view of J. R. R. Tolkein that fairy tales 'have now a mythical or total (unanalysable) effect . . . they open a door on Other time, and if we pass through, though only for a moment, we stand outside our own time, outside Time itself maybe' (128-9). The door Tolkien believes fairy tales open may allow what Rudolf Otto calls the '*mysterium temendum*' to enter and be experienced again by modern readers. But that experience of Great Otherness is always mediated through a particular historical moment and the structures of meaning available at that moment—and this is where nineteenth-century Irish folk-Catholicism comes in for Wilde, as it is how he allows the numinous to comment on the world he lives in.

This scared history also helps to explain the attraction of the short story to writers from societies whose entry into modernity was problematised by disruptions such as those caused by colonisation. Frank O' Connor called such societies 'submerged population groups' (18); they are places where the transition into secular time was delayed or never fully realised and which exist on the edges of the supposedly 'civilised' world. Declan Kiberd notes that 'the short story is particularly appropriate to a society in which revolutionary upheavals have shattered the very idea of normality' (*Irish Writer and the World* 43-4). Taking this view allows us to pull together the universalising understanding of fairy tales put forward by the likes of Bruno Bettelheim and in the context of Wilde Studies by Clifton Snider and the more historicised interpretation given by Jack Zipes and Richard Pine. Fairy tales tap into basic narrative structures and patterns which have been around since the Neolithic and which articulate what Mircea Eliade calls 'an ahistorical, archetypal behaviour pattern of the human psyche' especially as it relates to the relations between humans and the sacred (*Myth and Reality* 196), but they do so in a way deeply inscribed by historical context and local influences, in a different way in different places at different times. Wilde stands somewhere between what Angela Bourke calls the 'marginal

verbal art' of Irish fairylore and the sophisticated constructions of literary fairy tales ('Virtual Reality' 7). Fairy tales, which have strong connections to the oral and literary worlds, are also means of tracing the boundaries between these two conditions, as well as between the worlds of the sacred and the profane, the Irish and the English, colonised and coloniser, children and adults, tradition and modernity; they belong uneasily to both and yet to neither. Telling fairy tales may also have been a means by which Wilde could feel connected with the rural Irish emigrants in London for fairylore is, as Angela Bourke points out, 'a shared intellectual resource' (ibid 17).

Wilde articulated his position in these forms which are essentially linked to versions of the sacred. As Ellis Hanson notes, 'like Christ, he spoke in proverbs and parables of a sort' (231). This essentially religious and national context for the fairy tales has been rather ignored by most critics. Those who have looked at the fairy tales have tended to do so from a sexual perspective searching for evidence of Wilde's sexual practices and politics in them. Gary Schmidgall has argued that 'the sense of estrangement felt by a late-Victorian homosexual . . . helps to explain the subtle strangeness in several of the most moving tales' (152), while John-Charles Duffy believes that 'once one becomes familiar with the various ways in which Wilde and his contemporaries conceptualised male love, one can begin to see how these conceptualisations make their way into the fairy tales' (329). Naomi Wood supports this reading arguing that 'Wilde's choice of the fairy tale was part of his own pederastic mentorship of youths into aesthetic fulfilment' (81). Likewise, though less positively, Christopher S. Nassaar argues that 'the movement . . . through *The Happy Prince and other tales* to the tales of *A House of Pomegranates* is toward an increasing awareness of the demonic [homosexual] and a corresponding inability to control or contain it' (*Into the Demon Universe* 31).

I perhaps here need to stress that this book in no way wants to negate such analyses. I have learned a great deal about the stories from previous critics, especially those who have elucidated the sexual-textual relations within them. I hope that far from negating or contradicting, my attempt to situate the tales in a religious and national context will build on and complement the body of critical work that already exists. Reading the tales against both Irish history and Wilde's theological engagements (primarily Catholic since this was the Christian denomination Wilde was most interested in) merely opens them up to further research. The chapters which follow look at each of the stories in the two collections individually. Each chapter follows roughly the same pattern, starting with a brief synopsis of previous critical readings, before setting out my own interpretation which will supplement these readings. I am suggesting that recognising the Irishness of these tales and their folk-Catholic elements helps to banish some of the critical mystery that has adhered to them. Wilde encountered the fairy tale and folklore traditions he uses through an Irish lens first and while this certainly does not mean that he was not influenced by other sources, it does mean that it is important to take serious account of this Irish material. The other sources for Wilde's creative genius have been (and are still being) brilliantly examined by other scholars—here I am just trying to add an Irish layer, and not seeking to cancel out other approaches. Throughout, the connections between Ireland, the Gnostic, the folk-Catholic and Wilde should become clearer and a new, and even more interesting Wilde, should emerge from 'once upon a time'.

Notes

1. A generous selection of the contemporary reviews of both *The Happy Prince and Other Tales* and *A House of Pomegranates* can be found in Beckson (ed.), pp. 59-62 and 113-18.

Bibliography

Anderson, Hans Christian (1983), *The Complete Fairy Tales and Stories,* Erik Christian Haugaard (trans.), New York: Anchor.

Applebee, Arthur (1978), *The Child's Concept of Story,* Chicago: University of Chicago Press.

Aquinas, St. Thomas (1989), *Summa Theologica: A Concise Translation,* Timothy McDermott (ed.), Texas: Allen.

Arnold, Matthew (1962), 'On the Study of Celtic Literature', in *The Complete Prose Works of Matthew Arnold,* vol. 3, *Lectures and Essays in Criticism,* R. H. Super (ed.) with the assistance of Sister Marion Hoctor, Ann Arbor: University of Michigan Press, pp. 291-386.

Babbitt, Natalie (1973), 'Happy Endings? Of course, and also joy', in Haviland, V. (ed.), *Children and Literature: Views and Reviews,* London: Bodley Head.

Bashford, Bruce (1999), *Oscar Wilde: The Critic as Humanist,* Cranbury, NJ: Associated University Presses.

Baum, L. Frank, (1997), *The Wonderful Wizard of Oz,* Susan Wolstenholme (ed.), Oxford: Oxford World's Classics.

Beckson, Karl (ed.) (1970), *Oscar Wilde: The Critical Heritage,* London: Routledge and Kegan Paul.

Beerbohm, Max (1964), *Letters to Reggie Turner,* Rupert Hart-Davis (ed.), London: Richard Clay and Company.

Bettelheim, Bruno (1976), *The Uses of Enchantment,* New York: A. A. Knopf.

Bloch, Ernest (1995), *The Principle of Hope,* Neville Plaice, Stephen Plaice and Paul Knight (trans.), Cambridge, Massachusetts: MIT Press. 3 Vols.

Bourke, Angela (1996), 'The Virtual Reality of Irish Fairy Legend', *Éire-Ireland* 31 (1-2), 7-25.

——— (1998), 'The Baby and the Bathwater: Cultural Loss in Nineteenth Century Ireland', in Foley, Tadhg and Sean Ryder (eds), *Ideology and Ireland in the Nineteenth Century,* Dublin: Four Courts Press, pp. 79-92.

Bratton, J. S. (1981), *The Impact of Victorian Children's Fiction,* London: Croom Helm.

Briggs, Asa (1963), *Victorian Cities,* London: Odhams Press.

Bristow, Joseph (1991), *Empire Boys: Adventures in a Man's World,* London: Unwin Hyman.

Broadbent, D. E. (1958), *Perception and Communication,* Oxford: Pergamon.

Brooke, Charlotte (1970), *Reliques of Irish Poetry,* Gainesville: Scholars' Facsimiles & Reprints.

Brown, Julia Prewitt (1997), *Cosmopolitan Criticism: Oscar Wilde's Philosophy of Art,* Charlottsville: University of Virginia Press.

Brunvand, Jans Harold (1998), *The Study of American Folklore: An Introduction,* New York-London: W. W. Norton and Company.

Bunting, Edward (1983), *Bunting's ancient music of Ireland,* edited from the original manuscripts by Donal O'Sullivan with Mícheál Ó Súilleabháin, Cork: Cork University Press.

Canny, Nicholas (1987), 'Identity Formation in Ireland: the Emergence of the Anglo-Irish', in Canny, Nicholas and Anthony Pagden (eds), *Colonial Identity in the Atlantic World, 1500-1800,* Princeton: Princeton University Press, pp. 159-212.

Cohen, Philip K. (1978), *The Moral Vision of Oscar Wilde,* London: Associated University Presses.

Coupe, Laurence (1997), *Myth,* London and New York: Routledge.

Croker, Thomas Crofton (1969), *Researches in the South of Ireland, Illustrative of the Scenery, Architectural Remains and the Manners and Superstitions of the Peasantry,* introduction by Kevin Danaher, Shannon: Irish University Press.

——— (1998), *Fairy Legends and Traditions of the South of Ireland,* introduction by Francesca Diano, Cork: Collins Press.

Danson, Lawrence (1997), *Wilde's Intentions: the Artist in His Criticism,* Oxford: Clarendon Press.

Dollimore, Jonathan (1991), *Sexual Dissidence: Augustine to Wilde, Freud to Foucault,* Oxford: Clarendon Press.

Donoghue, Denis (1986), *We Irish: The Selected Essays of Denis Donoghue,* Brighton: The Harvester Press.

Dowling, Linda (1994), *Hellenism and Homosexuality in Victorian Oxford,* Ithaca and London: Cornell University Press.

Duffy, John Charles (2001), 'Gay Related Themes in the Fairy Tales of Oscar Wilde', *Victorian Literature and Culture,* 327-49.

Dunae, Patrick A. (1980), 'Boy's Literature and the Idea of Empire, 1870-1914', *Victorian Studies,* 24 (1), 105-122.

Dusinberre, Juliet (1987), *Alice to the Lighthouse: Children's Books and Radical Experiments in Art,* Basingstoke: Macmillan.

Dworkin, Andrea (1974), *Woman Hating,* New York: Plume.

Edwards, Owen Dudley (1989), *The Fireworks of Oscar Wilde,* London: Barrie and Jenkins.

———(1998), 'Impressions of an Irish Sphinx', in McCormack, Jerusha (ed), *Wilde the Irishman,* New Haven-London: Yale University Press, pp. 52-60.

Eliade, Mircea (1963), *Myth and Reality,* Williard R. Trask (trans.), New York: Harper Torchbooks.

——— (1998), *Patterns in Comparative Religion,* Rosemary Sheed (trans.), John Clifford Holt (intro.), Lincoln and London: Bison Books.

Ellmann, Richard (1987), *Oscar Wilde,* London: Penguin.

Engels, Frederich (1985), *The Origin of the Family,* Michèle Barrett (ed.), London: Penguin.

Foster, Roy (1993), 'Protestant Magic: W. B. Yeats and the Spell of History', in *Paddy and Mr. Punch: Connections in Irish and English History,* London: Penguin, pp. 212-32.

Fox, Carol (1993), *At the Very Edge of the Forest: The Influence of Literature on Storytelling by Children,* London: Cassell.

Gagnier, Regina (1987), *Idylls of the Marketplace: Oscar Wilde and the Victorian Public,* Aldershot: Scolar Press.

Gide, André (1949), *Oscar Wilde: In Memoriam (Reminiscences): De Profundis,* Bernard Frecthman (trans.), New York: Philosophical Library.

Grimm, Jacob and Wilhelm (1987), *The Complete Fairy tales of the Brother's Grimm,* Jack Zipes (trans.), New York: Bantam.

Hanson, Ellis (1997), *Decadence and Catholicism,* Cambridge, Massachusetts: Harvard University Press.

Holland, Merlin and Rupert Hart-Davis (eds) (2000), *The Complete Letters of Oscar Wilde,* London: Fourth Estate.

Holland, Vyvyan (1988), *Son of Oscar Wilde,* foreword by Merlin Holland, Oxford-New York: Oxford University Press.

Kiberd, Declan (1996), *Inventing Ireland: The Literature of the Modern Nation,* London: Vintage.

——— (1997), 'Oscar Wilde: The Resurgence of Lying', in Raby, Peter (ed.), *The Cambridge Companion to Oscar Wilde,* Cambridge: Cambridge University Press, pp. 276-94.

——— (2000), *Irish Classics,* London: Granta.

——— (2005), *The Irish Writer and the World,* Cambridge: Cambridge University Press.

Killeen, Jarlath (2005), *The Faiths of Oscar Wilde: Catholicism, Folklore and Ireland,* London: Palgrave-Macmillan.

Leeson, Roger (1977), *Children's Books and Class Society,* London: Writers and Readers Publishing Cooperative.

Le Gallienne, Richard (1925), *The Romantic '90s,* New York: Doubleday.

Lesnik-Oberstein, Karin (1994), *Children's Literature: Criticism and the Fictional Child,* Oxford: Clarendon Press.

——— (1996), 'Defining Children's Literature and Childhood', in Hunt, Peter (ed.), *The International Companion Encyclopaedia of Children's Literature,* London-New York: Routledge, pp. 17-31.

Lieberman, Marcia (1972), '"Some Day My Prince Will Come": Female Acculturation Through the Fairy Tale', *College English,* 34, 383-395.

Lurie, Alison (1990), *Don't Tell the Grown-ups: Subversive Children's Literature,* London: Bloomsbury.

MacDonald, George (1976), *The Princess and Curdie,* London: Puffin.

——— (1996), *The Princess and the Goblin,* London: Puffin.

Markey, Anne (2006), 'Oscar Wilde and Folklore', unpublished PhD thesis, Trinity College Dublin.

May, Charles E. (1995), *The Short Story: the Reality of Artifice,* New York: Simon and Schuster Macmillan.

McCormack, Jerusha (1997), 'Wilde's fiction(s)', in Raby, Peter (ed.), *The Cambridge Companion to Oscar Wilde,* Cambridge: Cambridge University Press, pp. 96-118.

Mikhail, E. H. (ed.) (1979), *Oscar Wilde: Interviews and Recollections,* London: Macmillan, 2 Vols.

Monaghan, David M. (1974), 'The Literary Fairy Tale: A Study of Oscar Wilde's "The Happy Prince" and "The Star-Child"', *Canadian Study of Comparative Literature,* 1, 156-66.

Murray, Isobel (1998), 'Introduction', Oscar Wilde, *Complete Short Fiction,* Oxford: Oxford World's Classics, pp. 1-17.

Nassaar, Christopher S. (1974), *Into The Demon Universe: A Literary Exploration of Oscar Wilde,* New Haven-London: Yale University Press.

——— (1995), 'Anderson's "The Shadow" and Wilde's "The Fisherman and His Soul": A Case of Influence', *Nineteenth-Century Literature,* 50 (2), 217-24.

——— (1997), 'Anderson's "The Ugly Duckling" and Wilde's "The Birthday of the Infanta"', *The Explicator,* 55 (2), 83-5.

——— (2002), 'Wilde's *The Happy Prince and Other Tales* and *A House of Pomegranates',* *The Explicator,* 60 (3), 142-5.

Nunokawa, Jeff (2003), *Tame Passions of Wilde: The Styles of Manageable Desire,* Princeton: Princeton University Press.

Ó Giolláin, Diarmuid (1991), 'The Fairy Belief and Official Religion in Ireland', in Narváez, P. (ed.), *The Good People: New Fairylore Essays,* New York: Garland, pp. 199-214.

——— (2000), *Locating Irish Folklore: Tradition, Modernity, Identity,* Cork: Cork University Press.

O'Connor, Frank (1963), *The Lonely Voice: A Study of the Short Story,* London: Macmillan and Co.

O'Sullivan, Vincent (1936), *Aspects of Wilde,* London: Constable.

Otto, Rudolf (1959), *The Idea of the Holy: An Inquiry into the Non-Rational Factors in the Idea of the Divine and its Relation to the Rational,* John W. Harvey (trans.), London.

Owen, Alex (1989), *The Darkened Room: Women, Power, and Spiritualism in Late Victorian England,* London: Virago.

——— (2004), *The Place of Enchantment: British Occultism and the Culture of the Modern,* Chicago and London: University of Chicago Press.

Pearson, Hesketh (1954), *The Life of Oscar Wilde,* London: Metheun.

Perrault, Charles (1993), *The Complete Fairy Tales,* Neil Philip and Nicoletta Simborowski (trans.), New York: Clarion Books.

Pine, Richard (1995), *The Thief of Reason: Oscar Wilde and Modern Ireland,* Dublin: Gill and Macmillan.

Propp, Vladimir (1971), *The Morphology of the Folktale,* Laurence Scott (trans.), Svatava Pirova-Jakobson (intro.), Louis A. Wagner (ed.), new intro. by Alan Dundes, Austin: University of Texas Press for the American Folklore Society, Inc. and the Indiana Research Centre for the Language Sciences.

Pulido, Maria Pilar (1998), 'The Incursion of the Wildes into Tír-na-nÓg', in Stewart, Bruce (ed.), *That Other World: The Supernatural and the Fantastic in Irish Literature and its Contexts,* Gerrards Cross: Colin Smythe, vol. 2, pp. 219-27.

Quintus, John Allen (1977), 'The Moral Prerogative of Oscar Wilde: A Look at the Fairy Tales', *The Virginia Quarterly Review,* 53 (4), 708-717.

Reynolds, Kimberley (1994), *Children's Literature in the 1890s and 1990s,* Plymouth: Northcote House in association with the British Council.

Roberts, Marie Mulvey (1997), 'The Importance of being a Freemason: The Trials of Oscar Wilde', in Hill, Tracey (ed.), *Decadence and Danger: Writing, History and the Fin de Siecle,* Bath: Sulis Press, pp. 138-49.

Rohrberger, Mary (1966), *Hawthorne and the Modern Short Story: A Study in Genre,* The Hague: Mouton.

Ruggaber, Michelle (2003), 'Wilde's *The Happy Prince* and *A House of Pomegranates*: Bedtime Stories for Grown-Ups', *English Literature in Transition,* 46 (2), 141-54.

Saint-Amour, Paul K. (2000), 'Oscar Wilde: Orality, Literary Property, and Crimes of Writing', *Nineteenth-Century Literature,* 55 (1), 59-91.

Schmidgall, Gary (1994), *The Stranger Wilde: Interpreting Oscar,* London: Abacus.

Sedgwick, Eve Kosofsky (1994), *Epistemology of the Closet,* London: Penguin.

Shaw, George Bernard (1989), 'My Memories of Oscar Wilde', *Oscar Wilde* by Frank Harris, New York: Dorset Press, pp. 329-46.

Shewan, Rodney (1977), *Oscar Wilde: Art and Egotism,* London: Macmillan.

Sinfield, Alan (1994), *The Wilde Century: Effeminacy, Oscar Wilde, and the Queer Movement,* London: Cassell.

Small, Ian (1994), 'Introduction', *Oscar Wilde, Complete Short Fiction,* Ian Small (ed.), London: Penguin, pp. vii-xxviii.

——— (2000), *Oscar Wilde: Recent Research, A Supplement to 'Oscar Wilde Revalued',* North California: ELT Press.

Snider, Clifton (1993), 'Eros and Logos in Some Fairy Tales by Oscar Wilde: A Jungian Interpretation', *The Victorian Newsletter,* 84, 1-8.

Stephens, John (1992), *Language and Ideology in Children's Fiction,* Harlow: Longman.

Stone, Kay (1975), 'Things Walt Disney Never Told Us', in Farrer, Clare R. (ed.), *Woman and Folklore,* Austin: University of Texas Press, pp. 42-45.

Tease, Geoffrey (1964), *Tales out of School,* London: Heinemann.

Tolkien, J. R. R. (1997), 'On Fairy Stories', in *The Monsters and the Critics and Other Essays,* London: HarperCollins, pp. 109-61.

Toomey, Deirdre (1998), 'The Story-Teller at Fault: Oscar Wilde and Irish Orality', in McCormack, Jerusha (ed.), *Wilde the Irishman,* New Haven-London: Yale University Press, pp. 24-35.

Vallancey, General Charles (1770-1804), *Collectanea de rebus Hibernicis,* Dublin: Luke White.

Warner, Marina (1979), *Alone of all her Sex: The Myth and the Cult of the Virgin Mary,* New York: Vintage Books.

—— (1994), *From the Beast to the Blonde: On Fairytales and their Tellers,* London: Chatto and Windus.

—— (2000), *No Go the Bogeyman: Scaring, Lulling and Making Mock,* London: Vintage.

Wheelwright, Philip (1968), *The Burning Fountain,* Bloomington: Indiana University Press.

Wilde, Oscar (1993), *The Collected Works of Oscar Wilde,* Robert Ross (ed.), London: Routledge, 15 vols.

—— (1999), *Collins Complete Works of Oscar Wilde,* Merlin Holland (ed.), London: Harper Collins.

Wilde, Lady Jane (1864), *Poems by Speranza,* Dublin: James Duffy.

—— (1887), *Ancient Legends, Mystic Charms, and Superstitions of Ireland; with Sketches of the Irish Past, to which is appended a chapter on 'the ancient races of Ireland', by the late Sir William Wilde,* London: Ward and Downey.

—— (1890), *Ancient Cures, Charms and Usages of Ireland: Contributions to Irish Lore,* London: Ward and Downey.

—— (1891), *Notes on Men, Women and Books: Selected Essays,* London: Ward and Downey.

Wilde, Sir William (1979), *Irish Popular Superstitions* (1852); Dublin: Irish Academic Press.

Wood, Naomi (2004), 'A Child's Garden of Decadence: Paterian Aesthetics, Pederasty, and Oscar Wilde's Fairy Tales', *Litterazia Pragensia,* 14 (27), 74-92.

Yeats, W. B. (1927), *Autobiographies: Reveries over Childhood and Youth and The Trembling of the Veil,* New York: Macmillan.

—— (1961), *Essays and Introductions,* London: Macmillan.

—— (1988), *Prefaces and Introductions: Uncollected Prefaces and Introductions by Yeats to Works by Other Authors and Anthologies edited by Yeats,* William H. O'Donnell (ed.), London: Macmillan.

Zimet, S. G. (1976), *Print and Prejudice,* Seven Oaks: Hodder and Stoughton.

Zipes, Jack (1979), *Breaking the Magic Spell: Radical Theories of Folk and Fairy Tales,* London: Heinemann.

—— (1983), *Fairy Tales and the Art of Subversion: The Classical Genre for Children and the Process of Civilisation,* New York: Heinemann.

—— (1987), 'Introduction', *Victorian Fairy Tales: The Revolt of the Fairies and Elves,* Jack Zipes (ed.), New York-London: Methuen, pp. xiii-xxix.

—— (1997), *Happy Ever After: Fairy Tales, Children, and the Culture Industry,* New York-London: Routledge.

—— (1999), *When Dreams Came True: Classical Fairy Tales and Their Tradition,* New York-London: Routledge.

—— (2000), 'Introduction', *The Oxford Companion to Fairy Tales,* Jack Zipes (ed.), Oxford: Oxford University Press, pp. xv-xxxii.

WOMEN AUTHORS

Annabelle Rea (essay date fall 1979)

SOURCE: Rea, Annabelle. "Maternity and Marriage: Sand's Use of Fairy Tale and Myth." *Studies in the Literary Imagination* 12, no. 2 (fall 1979): 37-47.

[*In the following essay, Rea highlights George Sand's use of fairy tales and myths to promote feminist ideas in her works* Mauprat *and* François le Champi.]

Until recent years only the life of George Sand was generally deemed worthy of scholarly attention. Neglect of her works drew its source partially from their romantic exaggerations, melodramatic effects and incredible coincidences as well as from the didactic tone of Sand's evangelical socialism. Some, perhaps following the lead of Marcel Proust, even thought of Sand as primarily a children's writer because of the simplicity of certain of her stories. However, the very simplicity of the tales, the familiarity of their motifs, increased the chance of their acceptability to her broad readership; we must not forget that Sand was an enormously successful writer in her time, second only to Victor Hugo in popularity. Her "mission of sentiment and love" (*Mare,* 30) led her to want to touch as many readers as possible, not to speak of her need to sell her works to support herself and an extended household.

A closer study of some of Sand's apparently simple stories allows us to note the presence of a number of elements from fairy tales, myths, legends or other archetypal patterns. We can find parallels with the tale of Beauty and the Beast as written in the eighteenth century by Madame de Beaumont or of Erich Neumann's "The Lady of the Beasts" who domesticates the male.[1] We discover Sand's version of Pygmalion and Galatea as well as her interpretation of the mystical union of the androgyne, also treated by her contemporary, Balzac. It is this complex of references which I propose to analyze in two of Sand's works, through a study of her treatment of maternity and marriage, to show that under the surface simplicity lie some highly significant feminist ideas.

A brief look at Sand's life will provide us with necessary background material for this discussion of *Mauprat* and *François le Champi.* We know from *Histoire de ma vie*[2] of the "délices" (I, 618, 629, 630) she experienced in listening to myths and fairy tales or in contemplating their illustrations "with interest and admiration" (I, 540) before learning to read, and of her learning to read through these tales. Nothing can compare, said Sand, with the "first joys of the imagination" (I, 618). We know that this delight continued via the stories she invented as a child and later through Berry folk tales and religious stories.

Her life also provided important raw materials in the matters of marriage and maternity. Her own unfortunate marriage to a man far from her intellectual and cultural equal was to make the issue of marriage one of Sand's most vital crusades starting with her first novel, *Indiana.* Extremely rich in Sand's background, the question of maternity merits much further exploration. Sand gives a very broad definition to the term: it signifies for her many things, including nurturing, caring, and educating, and ranges from her childhood "true maternal affection" (I, 734) for some of her dolls, her "maternal passion" for small children, her caring in the convent dormitory for smaller, ill children, to her adulthood "strange illusion" while writing *Histoire de ma vie* that she was her young father's mother,[3] and "maternal solicitude" (I, 1025) for her dying grandmother. Germaine Brée has spoken and written of the "happy triangle"[4] of Aurore and her two mothers, the one, "the unique ob-

ject of my love" (I, 643), who shared her daughter's world as a child, and the other, the educator who strove to form her granddaughter's taste and judgment. Sand's biological maternity as well as her maternal concern for several young, weaker lovers contribute to this leitmotiv of her life.

Adoption too played an important role in Sand's life. During her convent years, because of her "need to venerate someone" (I, 925), she asked Mother Alicia to serve as her adoptive mother. One might say, for instance, that she "adopted" Frédéric Chopin as her third child or that Augustine Brault was also for some time an adopted child. Adoption, very broadly defined (for example, Fadette and Landry and their children "adopt" all of the poor children of the neighborhood; Indiana and Ralph "adopt" poor, ailing slaves), is a most important theme in the Sand novels. It plays a much greater role than does any biological mother-child relationship except that between an adoring, widowed mother and her grown son.[5] Helene Deutsch's term "rescue fantasy" is most appropriate to the Sand mission.[6]

Deutsch, despite her rigid categorization of traditional passivity as "normal" in women, provides other fruitful concepts for our understanding of Sand in her chapter on adoption. She sees adoption as a means for a woman, "the androgynous woman," to separate sexuality from the nurturing aspects of motherhood. It also avoids, according to her, the narcissistic or Oedipal associations with motherhood. Sand's treatment of adoption enters much more specifically and more frequently into her novels written after age forty. This may serve in some measure to explain the apparent contradiction between the 1834 comment: "but a love without the union of bodies is mystical and incomplete"[7] and the much later, "If I had my life to begin again, I would be chaste."[8]

The two works in which I have chosen to study the elements of fairy tale and myth, *Mauprat* and *François le Champi,* might be replaced by a number of others which will come to the minds of those who know Sand well; these patterns are widely represented in her works. However, *Mauprat,* because the savage Bernard comes from a truly bestial milieu, and *François le Champi,* because the themes of maternity and marriage so neatly telescope into one, seem to me the most fruitful choices. Published ten years apart (*Mauprat,* 1837; *François le Champi,* 1847), both are typical of Sand's love stories. In the first, the heroine is alone in a world of men, except for the minor character, Mademoiselle Leblanc, her unattractive maid, while in the second, several other women characters serve as contrasts or comparisons with the heroine who has only one man and two male children around her. The first tells of nobles in a rural setting, and the second, of the lower classes of the country. Despite the many differences, the similar patterns emerge clearly.

The young Bernard de Mauprat is variously treated as a beast, specifically a wolf, guided by instinct or by chance; a barbarian, a brute, and a savage. He lives in a castle "shrouded in perpetual darkness"[9] with his all-male family of outlaws whose debauchery, pillaging, torturing, and general feudal brutality evoke Blue Beard, the thief Cartouche, the Ogre, and Croquemitaine. Bernard, though not as totally corrupt as his grandfather and uncles and who resists the life he leads, is arrogant and often drunk. His only culture comes from a few tales of chivalry, for his mother had died after giving him only "good notions" (p. 28), just enough for him to resist full participation in the activities of La Roche-Mauprat. Women for him existed as two types: "insolent prostitutes" or "stupid victims" (p. 71). For the Mauprats they were objects of scorn and/or animal desire. Edmée appears and incarnates for Bernard the rescuing fairy of one of his legends of chivalry (p. 71). He desires her because of her beauty. For him only the simple formula held: "She is beautiful, therefore I am in love."

Edmée de Mauprat, Bernard's second cousin, possesses not only great beauty, but extraordinary moral strength, energy, courage, pride and personal ambition. Devoted to her father, she is also tender and consoling to all who need her: the ill, the poor. Her exemplary charity, her reputation and her goodness are not widely known; she has no desire for a brilliant reputation in the outside world. Her closeness to nature is revealed by the flowers and birds that populate her room. Impetuous physical activity, particularly on horseback, is balanced by the passions of intellectual activity. Rousseau instills in the essentially self-educated woman her theory of absolute equality among human beings; Tasso is a favorite among poets; her letter writing style is virile in its precision (p. 259). However, with her father's old age, she sacrifices her need for physical and intellectual activity to remain at his side, taking up needlework which she terms, with other "feminine occupations," "amusements of captivity" (p. 291). Although she possesses many "virile" qualities, Edmée has moments of weakness, "like the true woman" she is (p. 187).

While Edmée feels immediate sensual attraction to her cousin, she protects her "honor" as the fiancée of another man, and defends her theories on the difference between desire and love through the knife she carries at all times in the early stages of Bernard's presence. A Freudian interpretation would identify the knife with the penis, giving Edmée equality with the male. Even after Bernard has attained a high level of education, has proven himself in war, the "volcano" (p. 353) of his passion erupts one final time. His bestial side endangers Edmée's honor once again and this time it is her riding whip that serves to tame him. Bernard is punished for this final breakdown by his trial for attempted murder. Edmée's reason has controlled her senses; only when

Bernard has attained the same civilized stage will he marry Edmée. Through this parable Sand clearly reveals what Germaine Brée has termed her "gloriously pre-Freudian" characteristics (p. 440). However, Sand's fantasies do not all typify those Freudian attributes to women but cross Freud's sexual lines to reveal rather a "person's" fantasies.

Edmée's power over Bernard—she orders him, she defies him—in its early stages backed by the knife, is transferred to the education she arranges for him. Sand stresses her belief that people may be corrected through love, that even one's flaws may be directed toward good ends. The transformation process is termed "giving birth" to a new destiny (p. 182) and sculpting from stone (p. 123, "tailler ce quartier de roc"); both expressions are highly pertinent to our analysis. The process is painful for Bernard, the brutally uncultured young man, who has entered an incomprehensible world of tenderness and affection between family members, of cordial relations between nobles and peasants, of love of nature, of prayer, of generosity, modesty and liberty. He understands the language of this new world but cannot speak it. During his time at the castle of Sainte Sévère, Bernard begins the essential task of knowing himself, and also learns quickly the matters presented to him. He hears from Edmée that women are not the crafty liars he once thought but rather the weak victims of oppressors whose use of violence and tyranny makes ruse women's only salvation (p. 161). Edmée becomes for Bernard a Madonna, his "dame," as he moves off to six years of new trials in the American War of Independence and the law court of Bourges before finally attaining his goal of marriage with Edmée. She has molded a husband of whom she will not be ashamed, now worthy of herself; Bernard has raised himself to her level in intelligence and wisdom as well as in the qualities of the heart. As Edmée says: "Est-ce ta faute, malheureux enfant, si depuis sept ans, je te cache le secret de mon affection, si j'ai voulu attendre pour te le dire que tu fusses le premier des hommes par la sagesse et l'intelligence, comme tu en es le premier par le coeur?" (p. 447).[10] Because Bernard serves as the narrator of the story and because modesty is now one of his qualities, we do not learn in detail of the qualities of the reformed beast.

Thus, marriage is a serious commitment which must be carefully considered so it will not become an "enchained future" (p. 318). Perfect equality in marriage, as on the larger scale of society, will ensure the end of slavery. During their long years of harmonious marriage, Bernard "abandons" (p. 469) his life to Edmée's guidance. Her logic and rectitude lead him to defend the Republic against its enemies and, again on her orders, to return home where she has remained, after the defeat of the Republic. Both extraordinary individuals, husband and wife, enjoy high respect in the region.

Bernard's rescuing of Edmée from La Roche-Mauprat, and, reciprocally, Edmée's rescuing Bernard from his bestiality makes the story an example of the Beauty and the Beast motif although the heroine has not accepted bestiality as Beauty does. Edmée has refused the erotic, the violent, in favor of the civilized man. Adoption also appears, although less importantly than marriage. In the most literal sense, the chevalier Hubert, Edmée's father, has requested, twice before the story began, permission to adopt the child Bernard and bring him up as his heir and the intended husband of his only child. He does "adopt" Bernard, but only after the escape of the young man from La Roche-Mauprat. More importantly, Edmée in a sense also adopts Bernard as her child. Her caress recalls to him his mother's final kiss. She carries out her correction of his bad qualities with tenderness; she serves as a mother to him in sending him away from her and receives him with maternal pride on his return. The rescue motif does link the transformation of the beast and the adoption of the "poor child." (Edmée uses this term for Bernard as late as the trial [p. 446]).

Sand uses the same link with the hero of *François le Champi*. The novel's title introduces a dirty, ragged and feverish foundling, stronger and larger than his age, who knows nothing, although he seems to understand what is said to him, who can express nothing and who thus appears to all a perfect simpleton. His eyes express his goodness; he knows to help others, but expresses no reaction to being helped himself, neither astonishment nor pleasure. As a foundling, a "child of sorrow" in the terms of Helene Deutsch (p. 394), François is a beast in the eyes of the rigidly prejudiced society represented by the heroine's mother-in-law: ". . . je suis sûre qu'il est déjà voleur. Tous les champis le sont de naissance, et c'est une folie que de compter sur ces canailles-là."[11]

Madeleine Blanchet's welcoming of the seemingly slow-witted François typifies her generosity, her charitable and democratic acceptance of all persons, and her selflessness. Sand's portraits of others in the novel intensify the heroine's goodness. Her miserly and brutal husband drinks heavily, gambles, and keeps a mistress. Although she has no love of this man to whom she "let herself be married at sixteen," she makes a patient effort to respect him. Other women characters also serve as contrast as do Beauty's Sisters in Mme. de Beaumont's tale: the jealous, greedy and revengeful mother-in-law; the husband's wickedly self-centered, pleasure-seeking mistress whose control over her lover almost ruins his family; the heroine's frivolous, spoiled and self-centered fifteen-year-old sister-in-law; and the foster mother of François, who, while not a bad woman, thinks first of her own survival. Of the women characters only Jeannette, the daughter of the man for whom François works, has certain similarities to Madeleine.

Like Edmée and many others of Sand's heroines, Madeleine Blanchet is physically weak but morally strong. She stands up to her husband, giving him orders and marching off "like a soldier to battle" (p. 247) when her conscience tells her she must. In order to do what she considers right, she is willing to cover up the truth of her actions, to "lie" and "steal" from her miserly husband to feed the needy. She works long, hard hours for others, sleeping and eating little, charitably active as are Edmée and other Sand heroines. She typifies the Sandian nurturer and caretaker[12] as she cares selflessly for the ill, even her husband and mother-in-law. Madeleine's education puts her into a superior category in her milieu; she reads, she writes, possessing the power with words that characterizes so many Sand heroines.[13] Although outstanding compared with others of her world, Madeleine has done nothing to seek this reputation; she is modest. She is not her husband's rival but complements him, winning his respect despite his undisciplined ways. Because of her difference, however, she feels herself alone; only her duty to her son, Jeannie, counterbalances her dreams of suicide.

Madeleine transforms the foundling child from an outcast and simpleton into a strong, intelligent and articulate, caring man, to whom all the younger women in the book are attracted. As his master, Jean Vertaud, says of him: "Car ce qui me plaît de toi, c'est que tu as le coeur aussi bon que la tête et la main . . ." (p. 307).[14] Unlike the biological son who remains essentially a shadow throughout the book, the adopted son takes over as the central figure in the final pages. Madeleine's nourishment of François has been physical through the "stealing" of food from her household; it has been both intellectual and emotional through her instruction in reading and writing and through her maternal love which enabled François to learn about his feelings and to express them, at first only to her. Finally, her nurture has been moral; her self-sacrifice, her uncomplaining caring, her tenderness and consolation have served as models for the foundling child.

With considerable money, transmitted by a priest from his biological mother of whom he knows nothing, François is able to return to rescue the woman who once rescued him. As Madeleine did at the beginning of the book, François now works into the night, cares for her tenderly during her illness, lies, plots and spies according to his pure conscience in order to save her. So much has the strong young man taken on "feminine" characteristics that he is asked by Madeleine's sister-in-law why he does not wear women's clothes and he is teased that soon he will take up spinning and sewing.

Sand has set up a series of parallels to show the equality of François and Madeleine by the end of the book. François was cured of his early fever by Madeleine whom he cures of her illness at the end. Madeleine saves François from his situation as a foundling, even offering to "buy" him from La Zabelle who planned to return him to the orphanage. François buys back the property of Madeleine which had fallen into the hands of the evil mistress of her husband. The reciprocity of many actions underlines their exceptional qualities and their complementary nature. At the time of their decision to marry, the androgynous couple appear almost asexual, except for a slight pressure of François hands:

> mais comme tout en tremblant elle voulait aller du côté où étaient Jeannie et Jeannette, il la retint comme de force et la fit retourner avec lui. Et Madeleine, sentant comme sa volonté le rendait hardi de résister à la sienne, comprit mieux que par des paroles que ce n'était plus son enfant le champi, mais son amoureux François qui se promenait à son côté.
>
> (p. 402)[15]

Before turning to the conclusions that may be drawn from the two novels, it is necessary to answer two questions about Sand's writing that may be raised concerning *Mauprat* and *François le champi*. Sand has published many love stories where love is the purified union of souls. As we know from Simone de Beauvoir's *Le Deuxième Sexe,* love has traditionally been woman's primary occupation. Are these novels, then, "feminine" novels? According to Simone de Beauvoir, the woman in love traditionally waits for her lover to come rescue her; in Sand it is the woman who rescues the man and actively transforms him according to her standards. De Beauvoir also speaks of the woman's activity in daydreaming. Could one not suggest that Sand's novels represent her personal quest for the ideal man and her creation of an imaginary substitute for the often disappointing reality? This transformation of personal fantasies into artistic creations is discussed by Freud in "Creative Writers and Day-Dreaming": "The motive forces of phantasies are unsatisfied wishes, and every single phantasy is the fulfillment of a wish, a correction of an unsatisfactory reality."[16] Albert Thibaudet has resolved the question for us, enabling us to deny that Sand's works represent the "feminine novel," by defining "the true novel" as "an autobiography of the possible."[17]

Other writers have suggested that Sand's life is of far greater importance than her works because of her connections to all the cultural, political and philosophical movements of the day, and because of her living essentially as did men at the time. Samuel Edwards states: "Her life is significant a century after her death, far more because of her accomplishments as a woman than for her books and plays."[18] Even Simone de Beauvoir in *Le Deuxième Sexe* talks about little more than Sand's life. Although Carolyn Heilbrun emphasizes British and American literature in *Toward a Recognition of Androgyny,* she does mention Sand, saying that she "evidences the passionate pull toward androgyny far more in her life than in her works, which rather record the disabilities of womankind."[19] Our study of Edmée de

Mauprat and Madeleine Blanchet has not shown us only the "disabilities" of women. Rather, we have seen superior women, as defined in *Mauprat* by Bernard's "brother at arms" in the American War of Independence: "Les hommes s'imaginent que la femme n'a point d'existence par elle-même et qu'elle doit toujours s'absorber en eux, et pourtant ils n'aiment fortement que la femme qui paraît s'élever, par son caractère, au dessus de la faiblesse et de l'inertie de son sexe." (p. 261)[20]

Edmée de Mauprat and Madeleine Blanchet, with their androgynous natures, are representative of Sand's heroines. These are physically active women, morally strong, intuitively intelligent, and often more educated than others of their milieu. Hiding their superiority, they concentrate their efforts on educating those around them, especially men, to elevate them to their level. Maternal always, they spend much of their time and energy not only educating but also nurturing the ill and the needy through quietly charitable acts. From time to time Sand speaks of her heroines as having "virile" characteristics, as in the case of Edmée's virile style of writing. Critics have noticed the androgynous nature of certain of Sand's heroines; for example, in his introduction to *La Mare au Diable* Pierre Reboul states: "Jeune Marie, si aimante, si maternelle, mais si virile, si forte—gracieux androgyne!" (p. 19)[21]

Less often noticed, however, and perhaps of greater significance is the androgynous nature of Sand's men, as they have been created by her women. As [Henry] James so wisely commented in *Notes on Novelists*: ". . . the moral of George Sand's tale, the beauty of what she does for us . . . is not the extension she gives to feminine nature, but the richness she adds to the masculine" (Barry, p. 384). The need for education to change women's situation has been much discussed and Sand did criticize the traditional education given to women, but her originality lies in her proposal that it is even more necessary to revise men's education. Bernard and François are men who practice tenderness and compassion, sensitivity and affection. Bernard retains some of the hardness of his past, is perfectly "virile" enough to battle in war and to father six children, but he abandons himself to his wife's judgment to guide his future. François cares tenderly for the ailing Madeleine while performing clever business manipulations. Both men are in adoration, painted in religious and chivalric terms, before their women, but these women in no measure represent the romantic muse passively posed upon a pedestal.[22]

Neither heroine has rejected the traditional nineteenth-century role of wife and mother but both have themselves finally come to control the conditions of those traditional occupations through their creation of the ideal companion. As Barry states so well: "Over a century of time has brought a certain political equality, but it has yet to bring that equality in life, in marriage, in the family, in the one-to-one relationship of a man and a woman, which, essentially, is what George Sand's life and work are all about" (p. 290). These are women, not passively waiting for a man, not willing to accept man's bestiality, but actively educating, civilizing a future husband. The husband is not a narcissistic choice representing, as Freud believed, "what (women) would have liked to become"[23] but that husband is made by them to become what they will him to be. In our title, maternity—and we continue to refer to maternity through adoption—precedes marriage. Sand's treatment of maternity serves almost as a synonym for education because it is the "rescue" through education that leads to marriage in these works of Sand. Always tailored to the individual, education as we have seen in *Mauprat,* bears the synonyms: "giving birth" and "sculpting." The romantic demiurge, here a woman "sculptor" in rivalry with the gods, creates from an adopted male a future husband. We clearly see the coming together of the complex of Beauty and the Beast, Pygmalion, and the myth of the androgyne. Adrienne Rich indicts the patriarchal system whereby the relationship of a woman and her child has been "manipulated and mutilated."[24] She says, "For me, poetry was where I lived as no one's mother, where I existed as myself." By constructing their own ideal marital situations these heroines of Sand do not have the "disabilities" cited by Heilbrun as much as does Andrienne Rich. Sand's symbol of the patriarchal society attacked by Rich might be La Roche-Mauprat, the all-male society enshrouded in darkness, destroyed during the novel.

The civilizing motif, the taming of the beast in man, and the rescue motif of adoption become one in both novels but more obviously in *François le champi.* Edmée de Mauprat and Madeleine Blanchet have, like Beauty, wed a former Beast. However, they have not accepted and agreed to love man's bestiality, as Beauty did. Both have, like Pygmalion, created the ideal companion but, unlike Pygmalion, they have not created only exterior perfection nor have they received any supernatural aid. These women have, by dint of hard work, suffering, long years of patience, and good example, educated the perfect companion. A close look at Sand's novels shows that she has indeed taken elements from familiar tales but she has transformed these elements so that they serve to illustrate her original ideas.

In these seemingly simple love stories, using the familiar elements of fairy tale and myth, Sand, the eternal optimist, was calling for social change through her ideas on marriage as a union of equals, of a woman and a man who complement each other, both sharing traditionally masculine and feminine qualities; her thoughts on the freedom to love without regard to age or class; her criticism of the male's use of violence and tyranny;

her protest for the dignity of women. As she wrote to Flaubert, the close friend of her old age, 1872: "If our advice is sound, if the mirror we hold up to society is accurate enough for man to recognize his reflection, and little by little persuade him to change his image, then we will not have written in vain . . ." (Edwards, p. 257). She was of her century in calling for social reform but very much of ours in demanding the kinds of change she called for: "I will lift up woman from her abjection in my person and in my writing."[25] In her *Histoire de ma vie* she writes about her own memories in order to encourage her readers to call forth and know theirs (p. 938). Perhaps this is her ultimate message: woman must first know herself and then rescue herself by developing her own androgynous qualities and demanding them of her male companions.

Notes

1. Erich Neumann, *The Great Mother: An Analysis of the Archetype,* trans. Ralph Manheim (Princeton: Princeton Univ. Press, 1955).

2. George Sand, *Oeuvres autobiographiques,* ed. Georges Lubin (Paris: Gallimard, 1970).

3. Passage eliminated from the final text, given on page 1344.

4. Germaine Brée, "George Sand and the Fictions of Autobiography," Proc. of the George Sand Colloquium, Amherst College, February, 1976, *Nineteenth Century French Studies,* IV (1976), 438-49.

5. In the Sand works I have been able to read, of all the heroines only Marié of *La Mare au Diable* has a living, present mother,

6. Helene Deutsch, *The Psychology of Women: A Psychoanalytic Interpretation* (New York: Grune and Stratton, 1945), II, 416. Chapter 11, Adoptive Mothers, pp. 393-433.

7. George Sand, *Journal Intime,* Vol. II, Pleiade, 22 November, 1834, p. 966. Quoted in Francine Mallet, *George Sand* (Paris: Grasset, 1976), p. 163.

8. Joseph A. Barry, *Infamous Woman: The Life of George Sand* (Garden City, N.Y.: Doubleday, 1976), p. 359.

9. George Sand, *Mauprat* (Paris: Nelson/Calmann-Lévy, n.d.), p. 9.

10. "Is it your fault, poor child, if I've hidden the secret of my affection from you for seven years? I wanted to wait to tell you until you became the first among men in wisdom and intelligence as you are the first by your heart." (All translations by A. Rea).

11. "I'm sure he's already a thief. All foundling children are from birth and it's madness to count on

those scoundrels." George Sand, *François le champi* (Paris: Garnier, 1960), p. 240.

12. For a discussion of this general subject see Ehrenreich, Barbara and Deirdre English, *Witches, Midwives and Nurses: A History of Women Healers* (Old Westbury, N.Y.: The Feminist Press, 1973).

13. For example, Consuelo sings, Fadette speaks beautifully of her dreams and meditations, Caroline of *Le Marquis de Villemer* inspires by her oral interpretation, Edmée's reading makes difficult works become clear for Bernard.

14. "For what pleases me about you is that you have as good a heart as your head and your hands."

15. But since, trembling all the while, she wanted to go over near Jeannie and Jeannette, he held her back as if by force and made her stay with him. And Madeleine, sensing that his will made him bold enough to resist hers, understood better than through words that no longer was it her child the foundling but her love François who was walking at her side.

16. Sigmund Freud, *Standard Edition,* Strachey, James and Anna Freud, eds. (London: Hogarth Press, 1968-74), 9, 146.

17. Albert Thibaudet, "Réflexions sur le roman," *NRF,* ler août 1912, *Le Roman depuis la Révolution,* Michael Raimond, ed. (New York, St. Louis, San Francisco: McGraw-Hill/Armand Colin, 1967), p. 288.

18. Noël Bertrand Gerson (Samuel Edwards, pseud.), *George Sand: A Biography of the First Modern, Liberated Woman* (New York: D. McKay, 1972), p. 8.

19. Carolyn Heilbrun, *Toward a Recognition of Androgyny* (New York: Knopf, 1973), p. 87.

20. Men think that woman has no existence of her own and that she must always absorb herself in them, and yet they only love passionately the woman who seems, through the force of her character, to raise herself above the weakness and inertia of her sex.

21. Young Marie, so loving, so maternal, but yet so virile, so strong—graceful representative of androgyny.

22. For example, Bernard guards his relics, Edmée's letter and ring, in a gold scapulary during his stay in North America (p. 250). François weeps with joy at the "paradise" he has attained through Madeleine's maternal kiss (p. 257). Sand suggests in *Mauprat* that the only true conversion comes through love; Jean de Mauprat as a Trappist monk casts a highly suspicious shadow on religious conversion.

23. Julia A. Sherman, *On the Psychology of Women: A Survey of Empirical Studies* (Springfield, Illinois: Charles C. Thomas, 1971), p. 58.

24. Adrienne Rich, *Of Woman Born: Motherhood as Experience and Institution* (New York: Norton, 1976), p. 31.

25. Mallet, p. 178, also in Barry, p. 226.

Eileen Connell (essay date 1995)

SOURCE: Connell, Eileen. "Playing House: Frances Hodgson Burnett's Victorian Fairy Tale." In *Keeping the Victorian House: A Collection of Essays,* edited by Vanessa D. Dickerson, pp. 149-71. New York: Garland, 1995.

[*In the following essay, Connell studies both the overt and covert subversive commentary on nineteenth-century middle-class life presented in Frances Hodgson Burnett's* A Little Princess.]

In *Sara Crewe, Or What Happened at Miss Minchin's?* (1888), Frances Hodgson Burnett re-imagines the Cinderella story for children and adults who were still enchanted with her first romantic, rags-to-riches tale, *Little Lord Fauntleroy* (1886). English and American audiences so enjoyed *Sara Crewe* and its theatrical adaptations that Burnett expanded it, and this longer version, *A Little Princess* (1905), remains popular today.[1] Burnett modeled *Sara Crewe* on the fairy tales about princesses that were first widely read in the nineteenth century.[2] In such tales, a wicked queen or stepmother figure punishes her rival and tries to prevent her from assuming her royal station. Despite an enforced slumber that lasts one hundred years or a childhood spent sweeping cinders, the adolescent girl preserves her princess's soul and, in the end, she escapes to a castle with maid service. The torture or the trial the heroine endures often involves housekeeping. Cinderella sweeps her step family's fireplaces; Sleeping Beauty pricks her finger on a spindle and falls asleep; the miller's daughter in "Rumpelstiltskin" must spin straw into gold or lose her life; and Snow White survives her stepmother's wrath by keeping house for seven dwarfs.

These tales of the horrors of housework would seem to disenchant the middle-class home life that Victorian culture made the locus of personal happiness and fulfillment.[3] Considered in isolation from the rest of the narrative, the representation of Cinderella sweeping fireplaces while the rest of the family frolics exposes what other sentimental representations of domestic life obscure: The British home may need a virtuous woman's care and supervision, but it also requires the physical labor of several servants who are excluded from the middle-class domestic comfort they manufacture. The subversive origins of such fairy tales as "Cinderella" are lost, however, in modern translations that engage in the most direct form of mystification.[4] While the tales mentioned above represent real social problems and describe some of their concrete ramifications, each invokes magic to make them disappear. Everything that gets in the way of the happy ending is attributed to mysterious causes, and everything that brings it about, to felicitous magic. In the case of the princess in rags, housekeeping becomes imaginative play that transforms the unpleasant realities of the work intended to punish her into magical keys to an enchanted, leisured life. For example, Cinderella's rats and garden vegetables turn into the elegant coach that takes her away from her garret; and the miller's daughter not only manages to spin straw into gold but captures a king in the process. The vision of "happily ever after" domestic bliss the fairy tale offers so enchants readers that they forget that while powerful household magic saves the princess from the less than romantic aspects of housekeeping, somewhere in the margins of the story there is a maid who must keep the castle clean. Fairy tales also banish to untold regions the far away, exploited lands that supply the castle's wealth.

Because Burnett represents classes and races that are usually omitted from the fairy tale domestic narrative, one can more readily discern the exotic "dark-faced . . . man-servant" and the "ugly" maid hard at work in the corners of the idyllic British home.[5] Located within an ancient tradition of fairy tales about the horrors and delights of housekeeping, *Sara Crewe* contributes to our understanding of the "domestic woman" recent studies of the domestic novel have helped to make a rising star of feminist literary scholarship. More clearly than such novels as *Pamela* or *Jane Eyre, Sara Crewe* shows that the production and maintenance of English domestic life depends upon the hierarchies of class and race domestic discourse ostensibly critiques. Like "Cinderella," Burnett's representation of a princess who is forced to be a maid both reveals and conceals the physical, dirty work swept under the rug in most fictions about household romances.[6] Burnett includes more details about Sara's domestic life in *A Little Princess,* explaining: "Between the lines of every story there is another story. . . . When I wrote *Sara Crewe* I guessed that a great deal more had happened at Miss Minchin's than I had time to find out just then."[7] Stories told "between the lines" of *Sara Crewe* and elaborated more fully in *A Little Princess* show that the housework would-be princesses perform can be torture that produces only an "ugly" house with a "severe varnished look." But for a privileged few, love and imaginative labor make housekeeping an effortless game of turning tissue-paper into "golden platters."[8] In a backwards game of hide and seek, the story uncovers the social and racial oppression within the domestic sphere and

then hides it with a little magic, some otherworldly glamour, and a home-made love potion. In *A Little Princess* the objects of this game are Ram Dass the Indian servant and Becky the un-princess-like scullery maid.

"IF SARA HAD BEEN A BOY AND LIVED A CENTURY AGO. . . ."

Ram Dass and Becky are two of the "things and people who had been left out," or merely sketched into, *Sara Crewe.*[9] *A Little Princess* also includes other stories and characters only alluded to in *Sara Crewe,* but in each version of the story the main events of the plot are the same. As the story begins, Sara, who strives always to behave "like a princess," arrives in "strange" London from India, where she has lived all her seven years with her devoted young father, a wealthy officer in the British regiment. Because her mother died after her birth, she is his "little Missus." Sara's fondest wish is to return to India and "keep the house for her father": "to ride with him, and sit at the head of the table when he had dinner parties; to talk to him and read his books—that would be what she would like most in the world, and if one must go away to . . . England to attain it, she must make up her mind to go."[10] Captain Crewe buys his seven-year-old a doll and a lavish wardrobe and regretfully leaves her at Miss Minchin's Select Seminary for Young Ladies, where a greedy Miss Minchin pampers her wealthiest and most select young lady. When Sara is eleven, Captain Crewe dies after losing his entire fortune, and she becomes Miss Minchin's "little drudge and an outcast."[11] Days spent running errands for the cook, mending, and learning "to dust a room well and to set things in order" teach Sara a much different form of "keeping house" than the one she imagined when she first arrived at the school.[12] Through it all, she remains "a princess in rags and tatters" who escapes her household drudgery by constructing detailed fantasies of a domestic comfort that appears magically. Her virtue and imaginative effort are rewarded when her neighbor and his Indian servant furnish her comfortless attic. This neighbor, Mr. Carrisford, turns out to be the friend who supposedly lost Captain Crewe's fortune, and Sara, now wealthier than ever, moves next door to keep house for him and to live happily ever after.

Sara Crewe repeats the theme of Burnett's runaway bestseller *Little Lord Fauntleroy* (1886), which by 1888 had launched in England and America a Fauntleroy fad that outlasted the generation of boys who were cajoled into wearing velvet and lace Fauntleroy suits.[13] Both books overtly preach that boy "frogs" and girl "Cinderellas" can become princes and princesses because nobility and virtue are interior qualities rather than matters of title, fortune, or rank. Like most children's literature of the period, however, Burnett's two stories differ in significant ways because each reproduces the dominant late Victorian narratives of gender identity. In *Sara Crewe,* Burnett teaches female children the rewards of discovering, after enduring domestic hardships, whether they are really "nice" or "horrid" girls. The reward for surviving the torture of household toil is the realization of the heroine's domestic daydreams and the fulfillment of her childhood desire to "keep the house for her father."[14] Sara becomes a "little Missus" of a substitute father and of a house that requires only her virtuous presence to be a home. *Little Lord Fauntleroy*'s triumphant Cedric, on the other hand, has many adventures before he becomes, despite his unmanly velvet breeches, the future "master of everything" in his earldom.[15] Cedric has stereotypically feminine characteristics as well as clothes and Sara is far more intelligent and well read than most story book girls, but both stories clearly reinforce the familiar message that it is "natural" for men to take action to reach their goals and for women to take a more indirect route through the realm of emotion and imagination. In *Sara Crewe,* for instance, Sara imagines how her attic could be made comfortable and beautiful, and Mr. Carrisford and his Indian servant make it so.[16]

Burnett's tale about a "little princess" who is rescued from one form of housekeeping and transported to a higher one does more, though, than remind us that traditional gender roles are drummed into children's heads from the moment they can follow a story. As *A Little Princess*'s representation of Becky suggests, nineteenth-century culture's association of femininity with a powerful interiority encodes class as well as gender difference. Born and bred scullery maids were excluded from the ideology of Victorian "true womanhood" that reified feminine morality and self-restraint and turned the physical work of housekeeping into a spiritual endeavor.[17] As several recent critics of nineteenth-century fiction have argued, these two related domestic ideologies both enforced women's subordination to men and extended the power and influence of middle-class women in the home and in the public sphere. The way in which Sara passively endures her indentured servitude calls attention to the limitations of a "feminine" inner power, but the lower-class female characters who inhabit the margins of Burnett's story have not even the ability to imagine and to dream their way out of the kitchen.

IF THE SHOE FITS . . .

Like "Cinderella," Burnett's story depicts an adolescent heroine who closely resembles the domestic woman Nancy Armstrong argues emerged about the time of [Samuel] Richardson's *Pamela, or Virtue Rewarded* (1740). Although Burnett's Sara Crewe is eleven when her trials begin and is tortured by a greedy woman rather than a lustful man, she can be usefully compared to Richardson's slightly older adolescent domestic

woman. Armstrong reads *Pamela* to describe how in the modern period an ideology that elevated a sexually pure and morally superior middle-class woman above her aristocratic counterpart helped to construct the modern, privatized self, as well as to bolster the ideology of separate spheres and to authorize middle-class hegemony.[18] She shows how Richardson's Pamela epitomizes the woman who is valued for her moral virtue, which is evidence of an interior subjectivity, rather than for her sexual attributes, appearance, or economic status."[19] In *Pamela* as in many eighteenth- and nineteenth-century novels, the romantic love plot often works to manage and to displace "the more politically volatile issue of class."[20] In other words, such novels as *Pamela* appear to argue for the equality of all individuals and to maintain that virtue endows even a servant girl with an upwardly mobile status, but the political content of this argument is counteracted by romance plots in which gender difference emerges as a magical solution to the economic, class, and other differences represented.

In *Sara Crewe,* on the other hand, the minimal romantic love interest of the story concerns a girl and her father, and the father figure who replaces him. Both "fathers" are of the same economic class as Sara herself. Thus, when Sara finally achieves domestic bliss, the social inequities the story represents are not formally resolved as they are in *Pamela* or in "Cinderella." Burnett instead attempts to make the fellowship and affection that characterizes Sara's relations with Becky and the male Indian servant Ram Dass perform the magic that marriage does in other domestic narratives. Compared to a romantic love potion that can displace one form of difference with another though, platonic love is a weak form of magic that barely conceals the story's more potent celebration of hierarchy.

Throughout most of *A Little Princess* Sara and Becky perform the same sort of domestic chores and inhabit adjoining attic "cells," but Sara possesses imaginative powers that Becky does not. These powers are paradoxical, given the social disenfranchisement of women and the domestic incarceration of Sara herself. But to the reader, Sara's vivid imagination is a sign that although she no longer has an extravagant, womanly wardrobe and must spend her days cleaning, she retains the essence, if not the status, of the princess she was when she "gobbled" books, told exotic stories to herself and to others, and provided for the other girls in the school an example of "perfect" manners and morality. Like Richardson's Pamela, Sara never deviates from her commitment to virtue, she daydreams constantly, and only the most extreme kind of physical stress causes her to lose self-control. Becky is as consistently kind and generous as Sara, but she lacks the other "royal" attributes that make Sara a princess whether she wears rags or silk gowns.

In both "Cinderella" and *Sara Crewe,* a princess must have access to both an interior nobility and a royal wardrobe. A perfectly sized "glass slipper" that signifies wealth and external beauty may not be all it takes to transform a girl into a princess, but it does contribute to and symbolize her unique powers. As I have suggested, recent interpretations of the domestic novel maintain that the Cinderella-like heroine signifies the end of the reign of the aristocratic woman and the ascendancy of the middle-class housekeeper who, unlike her predecessor, does not wear flamboyant, costly clothing to display her husband's income but rather imparts her inner virtues to the household.[21] This argument suggests that in a capitalist culture any virtuous woman can attain the democratic "authority" of the domestic woman, whether or not she has the money necessary to buy clothing that signifies a privileged class position. Fairy tales reveal, however, that this is wishful thinking. While Sara's internal virtues constitute an essential worth that does not alter when she becomes a shabby maid, in the beginning of the story, her possessions add another dimension to her value. Just as her "odd" expression signals her internal singularity, her "extraordinary wardrobe" of dresses of "silk and velvet and India cashmere" causes people to speculate about her father's status: "That odd little girl with the big, solemn eyes must be at least some foreign princess—perhaps the daughter of an Indian rajah."[22] Dressed-up, she serves the same purpose as does the female aristocrat the domestic woman supposedly replaces: she displays the wealth of the man who heads the household and "authorize[s] a political system that made sumptuary display the ultimate aim of production."[23] In 1888, the political system Sara's "much too grand" wardrobe authorizes is British Imperialism. Burnett represents the "business" of the British occupation of India as something mysteriously removed from life in London. The diamond mines are, as Sara puts it in *A Little Princess,* like something from "'Arabian Nights,'" and she imagines that "strange, dark men" dig for the diamonds."[24] Dressed in her exotic, "ridiculous" clothing, she embodies the most important "product" of the British Indian venture, the enigma of India itself.[25]

This adolescent domestic woman also epitomizes characteristics of the undecorated, vigilant, and unseen housekeeper Armstrong says authorizes "the power of the middle classes."[26] Although as a student and as a maid, Sara has little authority over the household, her ability to regulate her desire and to observe others gives her a moral authority that helps her to control her own fate. In one of the most memorable scenes in the story, a ravenous Sara gives a starving street child five of the six buns she bought with a six pence she found in the mud. Sara can also control her anger. When Miss Minchin subjects her to verbal or physical abuse, she retaliates in the same way Richardson's Pamela does; she withholds the interiority the abuser strives to vio-

late: "When people are insulting you, there is nothing so good for them as not to say a word—just look at them and *think*. Miss Minchin turns pale with rage when I do it."[27] In her unobtrusive rags, Sara does what she can to empower herself. Once her finery is gone, "nobody took any notice of her except when they ordered her about," or they notice "her odd little habit of fixing her eyes upon them and staring them out of countenance."[28] Just as Cinderella's tiny feet symbolize the moral worth that makes her suitable for the prince, the haunting eyes staring out of Sara's thin face distinguish her from Becky and signal an indestructible interior value. The inner spirit no punishment can crush reveals itself in an expression that makes even Miss Minchin wonder, "What is the child made of?"[29]

> "IF YOU KEEP HOUSE FOR US, COOK, MAKE THE
> BEDS, WASH, SEW, AND KNIT, IF YOU'LL KEEP
> EVERYTHING NEAT AND ORDERLY, YOU CAN STAY
> WITH US, AND WE WILL PROVIDE YOU WITH
> EVERYTHING YOU NEED."[30]

Because Sara is made of the qualities that constitute idealized Victorian womanhood, she never becomes like Becky and the other "machines who carried coal scuttles and made fires."[31] When Sara loses both her money and her father, Miss Minchin offers her a housekeeping contract that is far less good-hearted than the one that the seven dwarfs offer the orphaned Snow White. Moments after Sara learns of her father's death, Miss Minchin tells her: "If you work hard and prepare to make yourself useful in a few years, I shall let you stay here."[32] Since Sara is "a sharp child," Miss Minchin plans to use her as a housemaid only until she is old enough to save the school the cost of a real teacher's salary. Although Burnett implies that Sara's reversal of fortune bridges the distance between Becky and Sara, this addendum to the housekeeping contract alone indicates that Sara is not, as Miss Minchin cruelly puts it, "like Becky" now. The maid's work the "princess in rags" performs does not alter her essential identity as an "exceptional girl," but Becky has no identity apart from her work. A "machine," "not a little girl," Becky does not possess the "feminine" attributes Victorian culture most prizes because that culture defines her as a lower-class worker rather than as a woman. Without these attributes, she has little chance of even imaginatively escaping her life of blacking boots and grates, scrubbing floors, and cleaning windows. Burnett gives Sara everything a character in a fairy tale needs to survive her banishment to the kitchen and to become a princess again, but Becky is not the type of character who can be taken for a fairy tale princess: ". . . [Becky] was in a deep sleep as if she had been, like the Sleeping Beauty, slumbering for a hundred years. But she did not look—poor Becky!—like a Sleeping Beauty at all. She looked only like an ugly, stunted, worn-out little scullery drudge. Sara seemed as much unlike her as if she were a creature from another world."[33]

When Sara first meets Becky, she is still the wealthiest child in the school, but she insists that she and Becky "are just the same" and begins to give her the lessons in genteel femininity that would make them more alike. After Sara loses her princess's wealth, her ability to tell stories, to remain self-controlled before Miss Minchin, and to be kind continues to provide Becky with an example of princess-like behavior. These lessons do not transform Becky's prosaic thoughts into imaginative ones or cure her tendency to respond to Miss Minchin's abuse with wild tears, but they do teach her the "feminine" preference for spiritual rather than material comfort, an important precept of the Victorian ideology of womanhood. Although Becky is always hungry, she soon learns to enjoy the stories Sara tells her more than the food she offers: "The mere seeing of Miss Sara (in her sitting room) would have been enough without meat-pies." Even when Sara becomes a maid too and has nothing but stories to offer, Becky needs only to listen to them and to serve "Miss Sara" to endure her miserable life. Unlike the beggar Sara encounters, a "little ravening savage" on the lowest rung of the social ladder, Becky has mental capabilities that distinguish her from "a poor wild animal." But while the beggar may not know enough to thank Sara, her "wolfish" behavior does get her food. Becky's cultivation of a spiritual nature merely teaches her to be an ascetic and obedient servant who resigns herself not to "mind *how* heavy the coal-boxes was—or *what* the cook done."[34] Sara, on the other hand, frequently likens her own stoicism to that of a soldier in battle or of a prisoner of the French Revolution. She invents a reason for her suffering, inwardly rebels against the injustice of that reason, and convinces herself that she will be rewarded and empowered if she serves her temporary sentence bravely.

Burnett's "ugly" Sleeping Beauty cannot impart such meaning to her suffering, nor can she become "like" "Princess Sara," who insists that "it's just an accident" that Becky is not the princess. Indeed, the rest of the narrative undermines the tentative suggestion that the qualities the culture attributes to upper- and middle-class women can be attained and exploited by all women. In fact, the dynamic of the two girls' friendship indicates that these qualities may help to construct and to maintain class divisions between women rather than work to dissolve them. Sara's condescending desire to "scatter largess to the populace" motivates her to befriend and to educate Becky who, in turn, expresses her gratitude by worshipping and "wait[ing] on" Sara. Becky gives Sara a homemade pincushion that inspires Sara to exclaim, "I love you Becky!" but neither love nor loss of wealth alters the hierarchical positions of "Miss Sara" and Becky. They remain creatures from different worlds, because even when they inhabit the same world in the attic, Sara's mental skills raise her to an immaculate palace far above Becky and her coal scuttle. While Sara can learn to "dust a room well and set things in order,"[35] Becky cannot learn to pretend.

As Sara carries out her chores, she plays house. She imagines, for instance, that the attic, "almost like a nest in a tree," is "really a beautiful little room," and she tries to "guess something about . . . people" by imagining how furniture reveals personalities. In *A Little Princess,* the scene in which Sara plays her most elaborate game of house illustrates the ways in which the story as a whole shores up class differences as it reproduces the class-specific identity of the Victorian woman who presides over and sanctifies the household. Just before the climatic transformation of the attic, Sara's friend Ermengarde, the only school girl who has not redefined the erstwhile school "princess" as an inconsequential "under servant," offers to sneak up to the attic with some food. Becoming her own fairy godmother, Sara decides to turn her dismal room into a grand banquet hall. Becky and Ermengarde join in her game. Although Sara is "pretending" that they are the princess and the "maids of honor" of a fairy land castle, each of the three girls imitates the role of one of the members of an English middle-class household. Like the male provider, Ermengarde goes off to get the food for the meal. Meanwhile, Sara "devote[s] herself to "the wifely" effort of accomplishing an end so much to be desired," the transformation of the attic into a play house, and Becky carries out "Miss Sara's" polite orders. Sara pretends that odds and ends from her attic room are golden plates, garlands, and embroidered napkins for the "royal feast." She instructs Becky to "pretend" along with her as well as to fetch a soap dish, but Becky's attempt to pretend only underlines, and naturalizes, the difference between the two girls. "Pretending" comes easily to Sara, but for Becky "it takes a lot o' stren'th" to even "almost" "see it like [Sara] does." Obediently, Becky undertakes the challenge, "twisting her face in strange, convulsive contortions, her hands hanging stiffly clenched at her sides." After this effort, Becky returns with relief to her usual task of following more concrete instructions and allows Sara to do the pretending for both of them. In this way, Becky plays along, but while she can "view the splendors" Sara describes, she does not have the ability to create them herself. Although she sits at the same table with Sara and Ermengarde as a "maid of honour," she is transformed again into an "impudent creature" when Miss Minchin comes in and breaks the spell Sara has cast.[36]

RAM DASS THE MAGICIAN

Sara's attempt to create a fairy tale household provokes Miss Minchin to make Sara's life at the boarding house more miserable than ever, but the reward for her efforts outweighs the punishment. In both *Sara Crewe,* which does not include the scene in which Sara and her friends play house, and *A Little Princess,* the "magical" transformation of Sara's attic into a miniature domestic paradise follows the heroine's most memorable displays of her unique morality and exceptional imaginative power.[37] In *Sara Crewe,* Sara's reward of "magical surroundings" and abundant food follows her gift of buns to a beggar child who cannot, as she herself can, imagine that one bun is more than a whole meal. The game of house that in *A Little Princess* precedes the arrival of "the magic" indicates that Sara is rewarded not just for being virtuous in a general sense, but for mimicking the task of the ideal Victorian housewife. As I have suggested, the nineteenth-century image of domestic life as a realm separate from an alienating market place depended upon the displacement of the physical household labor lower-class women were paid to perform with the imaginative household labor women of the upper classes did supposedly free of charge. The idealization of domesticity and the magic of the fairy tale plot depend upon this displacement. Although Miss Minchin interrupts Sara's imaginative labor to punish her with additional housekeeping chores, *A Little Princess* ends with a celebration of enchanted domestic life. Sara falls asleep without dreading these chores because she dreams again of an attic that does not require labor or commodities to be homey: "Suppose there was a bright fire in the grate. . . . Suppose there was a comfortable chair before it. . . ."[38]

When Sara awakens to find that a "magician" has decorated her attic to correspond to her vision, she exclaims that "it is bewitched!" The narrator tells us that "the little, cold, miserable room seemed changed into Fairyland."[39] This "Fairyland" is merely an attic room furnished with the simple comforts of middle-class Victorian domestic life: a brass kettle on the hob, a blazing fire, books, a rug, a chair, and a table spread with a meal. Burnett's rendering of a comfortable room also transports readers to a "Fairyland" they imagine, with Sara, was created by "something glittering and strange—not at all like a real person, but bearing resemblance to a sort of Eastern magician, with long robes and a wand."[40] Just as readers of *Peter Pan* (1904) enjoy Peter and Wendy's flight from a mundane English nursery to Never Never Land, the moment when an aura of exoticism enters Sara's attic has always captivated fans of *Sara Crewe.* Although Sara remains in "dull" London, India makes her private part of the city "like something fairy come true."[41]

India's contribution to nineteenth-century domestic life helps to explain the "rapturous awe" in the narrative that accompanies the appearance of terrestrial chairs, decorations, and food. Ram Dass, who at his English master's request secretly brings the "magic" to Sara's dreary attic, does bear a "resemblance to a sort of Eastern magician." Although he does not have long robes and a wand, he does have a turban, a monkey, and a

"picturesque, white-swathed form."[42] Like many Western representations of Eastern men, this one is feminized.[43] Burnett aligns Ram Dass with female, disenfranchised identities: "There was a head and part of a body emerging from the skylight, but it was not the head or body of a little girl or a housemaid; it was the . . . dark-faced, gleaming-eyed, white-turbaned head of a native Indian man-servant."[44] This "Lascar" who embodies the India of Sara's past gives the story much of its magic and romance. Even before "the magic," the arrival of the Anglo-Indian gentleman, his servant, and his "rich," "Oriental" furniture enliven Miss Minchin's "big, dull brick house."[45] Like other discourses of this period, the story represents India as the locus of the exotic. In doing so, Burnett obscures the reality that the imperialist exploitation of India contributed significantly to the economic expansion in nineteenth-century Great Britain that both produced and upheld the ideology of separate spheres informing British domestic life. In *Sara Crewe* this unpleasant reality is contained in several ways, but the most interesting is the reversal of the positions of the imperialist invader and of the native implied when the Lascar enters Sara's home in order to bring her the comforts of civilization.

As many scholars have pointed out, in the mid-nineteenth century, Great Britain successfully disguised the economic and political motivations of its exploitation of India by mobilizing the rhetoric of domestic ideology.[46] In political, social, and literary discourses of the period England is habitually constructed as a mother figure who benevolently undertakes the task of providing uncivilized, child-like Indians with moral guidance and material domestic comfort. The British "parent" also justifies its control over India by representing the East as the locus of the mysterious, the wayward, and the irresponsible. Toward the end of the century, as resistance at home and abroad to the British venture in India increased, the domestic narrative became a less effective means of masking the racism and avarice behind imperialism. Burnett's revision of these dated narratives symbolically resolves the tension surrounding Great Britain's exploitative relation to India.

Instead of representing an Indian who gratefully receives the fruits of English civilization, Burnett constructs an Indian who gives Sara the services and commodities representing his subjugation to a country that robs his own country of its resources. The first morning after Ram Dass visits the attic Sara receives simple, typically English elements of household comfort, but on the second morning she awakens to the superfluous "odd and luxurious things" that make the room "like a fairy story come true." These decorations are Indian exports: "odd materials of rich colors," "brilliant fans," "large cushions," "a curious wadded silk robe." Just as India finances the British economy that makes the idealization of domestic life and its female superintendent possible, Ram Dass and the Indian commodities he provides turn a mundane domestic setting into a magical "fairy story." Sara's notion that she "might wish for anything—diamonds or bags of gold—and they would appear" reveals what the audience already knows: the source behind the magic is the return of the Indian diamond mines her father had lost. Mr. Carrisford, Ram Dass's master and Sara's neighbor, is in fact the friend who mistakenly was said to have "robbed" Sara's father. To distract himself from his obsessive search for the daughter of Captain Crewe, heiress of the diamond mines, Mr. Carrisford undertakes Ram Dass's plan to make the "visions" of the "maid" next door "real things."[47]

This far-fetched scenario would be less entertaining if the narrative exposed and censured the political realities behind the diamond mines that supply Sara and Mr. Carrisford with their wealth. In A Little Princess, however, any suspicion that Ram Dass is unhappy in his servitude, or that he is coerced into performing his "magic" for Sara, disappears when he explains to Mr. Carrisford's English secretary why he suggested the "plan" to his master: "It is true that the first thought was mine, Sahib. . . . I am fond of this child; we are both lonely. . . . Being sad one night, I lay close to the open skylight and listened. The vision she related told what this miserable room might be if it had comforts in it." When Becky and Sara play house, Becky follows Sara's instructions, and in this game, Ram Dass follows his master's. The home he makes with treasures from his country belongs to Sara and to Mr. Carrisford, and his imaginative housekeeping does not magically transform his own class position. As Sara's claim that she and Becky are "just the same" is refuted, so is Ram Dass's more qualified suggestion that he and Sara are alike. When Sara meets Ram Dass, they are both domestic servants, yet when she returns his monkey he thanks her with "grateful obeisance," "as if he were speaking to the little daughter of a rajah." The English secretary's interpretation of the scheme to help Sara also emphasizes Ram Dass's radical difference from the little housemaid he watches with such empathy and affection: "It will be like a story from 'Arabian Nights' . . . Only an Oriental could have planned [the transformation of Sara's attic]. It does not belong to London fogs."[48]

The rhetorical construction of Ram Dass and his "magic" as utterly different from, yet benevolently sympathetic to, his English master and mistress lifts the "London fogs," beautifies Miss Minchin's "respectable and well furnished" but "ugly" house, and allows Mr. Carrisford to claim this alien magic as his household property. After Sara ascends to her position as a "little Missus" of Mr. Carrisford's household and ceases to be "little drudge," Ram Dass becomes "her devoted slave," and Mr. Carrisford becomes her "magician."[49] This division of household labor resembles the one between Sara, who keeps Mr. Carrisford "amused and interested," and Becky, one of the many servants who cares for the house in which Mr. Carrisford and his "princess" live."[50]

AND THEY ALL LIVED HAPPILY EVER AFTER. . . .

As all fairy tales do, A Little Princess ends with the comforting implication that "they all lived happily ever after." In tales that create a magic circle around a royal couple, this sudden gesture of inclusion, "all," casts out any problems the story has not already resolved. Stepping outside the enchanted circle, however, one wonders: Will Becky live happily ever after as Sara's "delighted attendant"? Is Ram Dass's life as Sara's "devoted slave" as fulfilling as Sara's life as a "princess" who "can give buns and bread to the populace"?[51] Can these household servants ever become household spirits who hover over a castle that maintains itself without agency? Like many domestic novels and fairy tales, Burnett's romantic story transports its readers to a land where such questions do not seem to matter. Poverty and injustice evaporate once the protagonist reaches her goal. The magic along the way, disenchanted, is merely the comfort of home, and one of the magic's most insidious messages is that even the most clever and bookish adolescent girl should above all things desire to keep the house for the man who loves her. Yet for over one hundred years the story has enchanted readers and has encouraged them to desire the particular form of gratification and power Burnett conjures up for Sara. Like other fairy tales, A Little Princess's magic appears to be available to all who wish for it hard enough, but it visits only the princess, and not the lower-class "ugly Sleeping Beauty" in the "adjoining cell."[52]

The book ends with an event designed to put the class issues it raises behind closed doors. In the last chapter of both versions, Sara returns to the bakery where she once saw the beggar girl in order to give the baker money to feed other hungry children. Anne, the beggar, no longer sits outside in the gutter but stands "clean and neatly clothed" behind the counter of the bakery that is now her home. Unlike Miss Minchin, the owner of the bakery bases her domestic arrangement with the destitute girl on affection: "I told [Anne] to come here when she was hungry, and when she'd come I'd give her odd jobs to do, an' . . . she was willing, an' somehow I got to like her; an' the end of it was I've given her a place an' a home, an' she helps me."[53] Ironically, Sara's punishment resembles Anne's reward. Like Becky, Anne attains a happy ending that involves little change in fortune or in class position, but merely a more pleasant life of domestic servitude. And like Becky, Anne will do some of the physical work required to realize Sara's imaginative schemes. Since

Sara wishes to "give bread and buns to the populace," she asks the no longer "savage" Anne to distribute the food for which she once begged.[54] This final unglamorous transformation of a "wolfish" beggar to a cherished bakery worker is hardly the stuff of a "fairy story come true," but it does help to keep the spell *Sara Crewe* casts over readers from breaking. In the story, class differences are not symbolically managed in a marriage union, but rather naturalized and contained in friendly, well-managed households. Becky, Ram Dass, and Anne cannot play house along with Sara because they are too busy keeping house for her, but in this fairy tale, they do not seem to mind.

Everyone should be able to experience the fun of playing house, but current middle-class domestic ideologies show that many versions of the game are as exclusive as they were a century ago. The lasting appeal of a story based upon one of the most enduring and popular stories of all should encourage us not to recognize in it an "essential truth" about social organization, but to consider more carefully the various, historically specific messages of each variation of the Cinderella plot. *A Little Princess* remains a well-loved, charming story because even grown-up twentieth-century readers try in their own lives to transform domestic drudgery into domestic joy. Playing house can be a harmless and pleasurable pursuit as long as, like Goldilocks, we invade and examine the home when the family is away and the dirty dishes are on the table.

Notes

1. Frances Hodgson Burnett, *Sara Crewe, Or What Happened at Miss Minchin's?* (New York: Scribner's, 1888) and *A Little Princess* (New York: Scribner's, 1905). In this essay, I refer to both published versions of the story to support my argument. On the differences between the two versions of Burnett's story, as well as a brief discussion of the story's many stage productions, see Marion E. Brown, "Three Versions of *A Little Princess*: How the Story Developed," *Children's Literature in Education* 19, 4 (1988): 199-210.

2. The publication in 1823 of an English translation of the brothers Grimm tales popularized fairy tales in England and in America. *German Popular Stories* included "Snow-Drop" (Snow White) and "Hansel and Gretel." English translations of Frenchman Charles Perrault's versions of "Cinderella" and "Sleeping Beauty" also became available in the nineteenth century. See Iona and Peter Opie, *The Classic Fairy Tales* (London: Oxford University Press, 1974),1-26; and Maria Tartar, *Off With Their Heads!: Fairy Tales and the Culture of Childhood* (Princeton: Princeton University Press, 1992). Tartar notes that the "myth of folk tales as sacred, 'natural' texts was deftly propa-

gated by Charles Dickens" who "praised the tales as powerful instruments of socialization" (17). For a discussion of Burnett's literary relation to fairy tale and popular children's literature traditions, see Phyllis Bixler, "The Oral-Formulaic Training of a Popular Fiction Writer: Frances Hodgson Burnett," *Journal of Popular Culture* 15, 4 (1982): 42-52; and Phyllis Bixler Koppes, "Tradition and the Individual Talent of Frances Hodgson Burnett: A Generic Analysis of *Little Lord Fauntleroy, A Little Princess,* and *The Secret Garden,*" *Children's Literature* 7 (1979):191-207.

3. As nineteenth-century domestic novels so clearly show, Victorian England's industrial, capitalist economy came to depend upon an ideology of separate spheres, the gender-based division of private and public spaces which held that a "true" woman, as the weaker and intellectually inferior but morally superior sex, should remain enshrined in a home she could make a refuge for a man weary of the world of public affairs. There have been several studies in the past two decades of the ways in which nineteenth-century domestic novels and domestic ideology represent and help to construct the female subjectivity that was a crucial part of the organization of nineteenth-century consumer culture. These critical and historical works provide an important background and context for my argument. Some argue that many nineteenth-century domestic and sentimental novels written by women were a literary reaction against and subversion of an ideology of separate spheres. Others suggest that the majority of these novels offered romantic, conservative responses to domestic ideology, in part because the women who wrote them wanted their work to be marketable. See, for instance, Monica Correa Fryckstedt, "Defining the Domestic Genre: English Women Novelists of the 1850's," *Tulsa Studies in Women's Literature* 6, 1 (1987): 9-23; Helen Papishvilly, *All the Happy Endings* (New York: Harper's, 1966); Nancy Armstrong, *Desire and Domestic Fiction: A Political History of the Novel* (New York: Oxford University Press, 1987); Mary Poovey, *Uneven Developments: The Ideological Work of Gender in Mid-Victorian England* (Chicago: University of Chicago Press, 1988).

4. For an extended analysis of this aspect of the fairy tale genre, as well as a suggestion about how "fairy tales can still be told . . . so that they challenge and resist, rather than simply reproduce, the constraints of a culture," see Tartar, *Off with Their Heads!* 229-38.

5. Burnett, *A Little Princess,* 51, 141.

6. In her analysis of eighteenth- and nineteenth-century British texts, Armstrong proposes that "the

power of the middle classes had everything to do with the power of middle class love" (*Desire and Domestic Fiction,* 4). She argues as well that novels that enclose class conflict within a domestic sphere "demonstrate that despite the vast inequities of the age virtually anyone could find gratification within this private framework" (38). Because Armstrong limits her discussion, for the most part, to representations of relatively powerful, middle-class domestic women, her study neglects the laboring classes who were excluded from this particular "gratification."

7. Burnett, *A Little Princess,* v.

8. Burnett, *A Little Princess,* 7, 202.

9. Burnett, *A Little Princess,* vii.

10. Burnett, *A Little Princess,* 6. The suggestion of father-daughter incest pervades fairy tales. In one of the oldest versions of Cinderella, for example, a widower is bound by a spell not to marry until he finds a woman who is as beautiful as his dead wife and can also wear her ring. The only woman who fits this description is his own daughter. She runs away when he tries to force her to marry him (Opie, *Classic Fairy Tales,* 13). For a feminist interpretation of such tales, see Tartar, *Off with Their Heads!* 120-40.

11. Burnett, *Sara Crewe,* 17.

12. Burnett, *Sara Crewe,* 19; *A Little Princess,* 100.

13. According to Ann Thwaite, *Waiting for the Party: The Life of Frances Hodgson Burnett, 1849-1924* (London: Secker and Warburg, 1974), *Little Lord Fauntleroy* has sold well over a million copies in English and has been translated into a dozen languages (94). For years after the book's publication, representations of the sweet, virtuous, fantastically dressed Cedric proliferated in America and in England. Plays adapted from the novel were produced successfully as late as 1911, and in 1924 Mary Pickford starred as both Cedric and his mother in a film version (231, 118). *Little Lord Fauntleroy* inspired Victorian mothers to dress unwilling boys in velvet and lace "Fauntleroy suits" which remained faddish until the early years of the twentieth century.

14. Burnett, *A Little Princess,* 35, 6.

15. Frances Hodgson Burnett, *Little Lord Fauntleroy* (New York: Scribner's, 1914), 281.

16. An advertisement in the back of the original edition of *Sara Crewe* synopsizes these fundamental Victorian gender roles. In a single advertisement, Scribner's offers a "handybook" for girls subtitled "how to amuse yourself and others," and a "handy-book" for boys subtitled "what to do and how to do it." A reviewer quoted in the advertisement writes of the girl's book: "It is an invaluable aid in making a home attractive, comfortable, artistic, and refined. The book preaches the gospel of cheerfulness, industry, economy, and comfort." Another reviewer makes the boy's book sound much more exciting: "It tells boys how to make all kinds of things—boats, traps, toys, puzzles, aquariums, fishing tackle . . . how to rear wild birds, to train dogs, and do the thousand and one things that boys take delight in." For further instructions about these two distinct types of fun, consult Lina and Adelia B. Beard, *The American Girl's Handybook; Or, How to Amuse Yourself and Others* (New York: Scribner's, 1888); and Daniel C. Beard, *The American Boy's Handybook; Or, What to Do and How to Do It* (New York: Scribner's, 1888).

17. In addition to Armstrong's study of the ideology of domestic womanhood, see, for example, Martha Vicinus, ed., *A Widening Sphere: Changing Roles for Victorian Women* (Bloomington: Indiana University Press, 1977); and Carol Smith-Rosenberg, "In Search of Woman's Nature, 1850-1920," *Feminist Studies* 3,1/2 (1975): 141-54. See also Barbara Welter's study of the Englishwoman's American counterpart, "The Cult of True Womanhood: 1800-1860," in *Dimity Convictions: The American Woman in the Nineteenth Century,* ed. Barbara Welter (Athens: Ohio University Press, 1976).

18. The story of "Cinderella," which is at least one thousand years old, indicates that the construction of the domestic woman began long before the age of eighteenth- and nineteenth-century English domestic novels (Opie, *Classic Fairy Tales,* 12).

19. Armstrong, *Desire and Domestic Fiction,* 108-34.

20. Armstong, *Desire and Domestic Fiction,* 18.

21. For example, see Armstrong, *Desire and Domestic Fiction,* 86.

22. Burnett, *Sara Crewe,* 10-11; *A Little Princess,* 10.

23. Armstrong, *Desire and Domestic Fiction,* 73.

24. Burnett, *A Little Princess,* 58.

25. For an extended analysis of the English relation to the Orient, see Edward Said, *Orientalism* (New York: Pantheon Books, 1978). Said argues that "Europe . . . articulates the Orient": "This articulation is the prerogative, not of a puppet-master, but of a genuine creator, whose life-giving power represents, animates, constitutes the otherwise silent and dangerous space beyond familiar boundaries" (17).

26. Armstrong, *Desire and Domestic Fiction,* 4. In Armstrong's archeology, as discourse rather than physical force becomes the primary practice through which subjects are constituted, the cultural meaning the publicly displayed female body carries is displaced by the signifying power of a feminine interiority (*Desire and Domestic Fiction,* 73-82). What modern capitalism needs is "not a woman who attracts the gaze as she did in an earlier culture, but one who fulfills her role by disappearing into the woodwork to watch over the household." Situated in the woodwork, this nearly invisible housekeeper wields power by supervising the household. Like the surveyors Foucault describes in *Discipline and Punish* (New York: Pantheon Books, 1977), the domestic woman subjects herself as well as her surroundings to disciplinary practices: "The domestic woman executes her role in the household by regulating her own desire . . . self-regulation became a form of labor that was superior to labor. Self-regulation alone gave a woman authority over the field of domestic objects and personnel where her supervision constituted a form of value in its own right and was therefore capable of enhancing the value of other people and things" (81).

27. Burnett, *Sara Crewe,* 21.

28. Burnett, *Sara Crewe,* 19-20.

29. Burnett, *A Little Princess,* 217.

30. Jacob and Wilhelm Grimm, "Snow White and the Seven Dwarves," in *The Complete Fairy Tales of the Brother's Grimm,* trans., Jack Zipes (Toronto: Bantam, 1987), 199.

31. Burnett, *A Little Princess,* 74.

32. Burnett, *Sara Crewe,* 17.

33. Burnett, *A Little Princess,* 51.

34. Burnett, *A Little Princess,* 67, 170, 57.

35. Burnett, *A Little Princess,* 57, 88, 100.

36. Burnett, *A Little Princess,* "a beautiful little room": 112-16; "something about . . . people": 135; "wifely effort," "royal feast": 199; "see it like [Sara] does": 200; "clenched at her sides": 200; "impudent creature": 204.

37. When *Sara Crewe* was produced for the stage as *A Little Princess,* New York and London audiences were treated to an expanded representation of the scenes in which the attic is transformed (Brown, "Three Versions of *A Little Princess,*" 206).

38. Burnett, *A Little Princess,* 207.

39. Burnett, *Sara Crewe,* 53; *A Little Princess,* 221.

40. Burnett, *Sara Crewe,* 55.

41. Burnett, *A Little Princess,* 221.

42. Burnett, *Sara Crewe,* 55; *A Little Princess,* 141.

43. See, for example, Said's *Orientalism.* Said argues that the "'threatening otherness' [of India and other Eastern countries] is often gendered 'feminine' and sexually available, so that it can be penetrated, catalogued, and therefore contained by the 'superior' rationality of the Western mind" (56).

44. Burnett, *A Little Princess,* 141.

45. Burnett, *Sara Crewe,* 6.

46. For example, in "A Housewifely Woman: The Social Construction of Florence Nightingale," Poovey discusses how England's late nineteenth-century imperial campaigns "appropriated the terms of the domestic ideology that underwrote the separation of spheres, male identity, and female nature, and by which Nightingale masked her own territorial ambitions" (*Uneven Developments,* 194-95).

47. Burnett, *A Little Princess,* "fairy story come true": 221, 222; "odd materials . . . silk robe": *Sara Crewe,* 1, 56-57; *A Little Princess,* 209, 221; ". . . they would appear": *A Little Princess,* 221; "real things": *A Little Princess,* 179.

48. Burnett, *A Little Princess,* 179, 144, 180.

49. Burnett, *A Little Princess,* 153; *Sara Crewe,* 74.

50. Burnett, *A Little Princess,* 260, 262.

51. Burnett, *A Little Princess,* 263, 262.

52. Burnett, *A Little Princess,* 51, 109.

53. Burnett, *Sara Crewe,* 82; *A Little Princess,* 265.

54. Burnett, *Sara Crewe,* 82; *A Little Princess,* 265, 264.

Select Bibliography

Armstong, Nancy. *Desire and Domestic Fiction: A Political History of the Novel.* New York: Oxford University Press, 1987.

Beard, Daniel C. *The American Boy's Handybook; Or, What to Do and How to Do It.* New York: Scribner's, 1888.

Beard, Lina and Adelia B. *The American Girl's Handybook; Or, How to Amuse Yourself and Others.* New York: Scribner's, 1888.

Bixler, Phyllis. (See also Koppes, Phyllis Bixler.) "The Oral Formulaic Training of a Popular Fiction Writer:

Frances Hodgson Burnett." *Journal of Popular Culture* 15, no. 4 (1982): 42-52.

Brown, Marion E. "Three Versions of *A Little Princess*: How the Story Developed." *Children's Literature in Education* 19, no. 4 (1988): 199-210.

Burnett, Frances Hodgson. *A Little Princess.* New York: Scribner's, 1905.

———. *Little Lord Fauntleroy.* New York: Scribner's, 1914.

———. *Sara Crewe, Or What Happened at Miss Minchin's?* New York: Scribner's, 1888.

Foucault, Michel. *Discipline and Punish: The Birth of the Prison.* Translated by Alan Sheridan. New York: Pantheon Books, 1977.

Fryckstedt, Monica Correa. "Defining the Domestic Genre: English Women Novelists of the 1850's." *Tulsa Studies in Women's Literature* 6, no. 1 (1987): 9-23.

Grimm, Jacob and Wilhelm. *The Complete Fairy Tales of the Brothers Grimm.* Translated by Jack Zipes. Toronto: Bantam, 1987.

Koppes, Phyllis Bixler. "Tradition and the Individual Talent of Frances Hodgson Burnett: A Generic Analysis of *Little Lord Fauntleroy, A Little Princess,* and *The Secret Garden.*" *Children's Literature* 7 (1979): 191-207.

Opie, Peter and Iona Opie. *The Classic Fairy Tales.* London: Oxford University Press, 1974.

Papishvilly, Helen. *All the Happy Endings.* New York: Harper's, 1966.

Poovey, Mary. *Uneven Developments: The Ideological Work of Gender in Mid-Victorian England.* Chicago: University of Chicago Press, 1988.

Said, Edward. *Orientalism.* New York. Pantheon Books. 1978.

Smith-Rosenberg, Carroll. *Disorderly Conduct: Visions of Gender in Victorian America.* New York: Oxford University Press, 1985.

———. "The Female World of Love and Ritual: Relations Between Women in Nineteenth-Century America." *Signs* 1 (1975): 1-29.

———. "In Search of Woman's Nature, 1850-1920." *Feminist Studies* 3 (1975): 141-54.

Tartar, Maria. *Off With Their Heads!: Fairy Tales and the Culture of Childhood.* Princeton: Princeton University Press, 1992.

Thwaite, Ann. *Waiting for the Party: The Life of Frances Hodgson Burnett, 1849-1924.* London: Secker and Warburg, 1974.

Vicinus, Martha. *Independent Women: Work and Community for Single Women, 1850-1920.* London: Virago, 1985.

———, ed. *A Widening Sphere: Changing Roles for Victorian Women.* Bloomington: Indiana University Press, 1977.

———, ed. *Suffer and Be Still: Women in the Victorian Age.* Bloomington: Indiana University Press, 1972.

Welter, Barbara. "The Cult of True Womanhood: 1800-1860." In *Dimity Convictions: The American Woman in the Nineteenth Century,* edited by Barbara Welter. Athens: Ohio University Press, 1976.

Victoria Anderson (essay date 2007)

SOURCE: Anderson, Victoria. "Investigating the Third Story: 'Bluebeard' and 'Cinderella' in *Jane Eyre.*" In *Horrifying Sex: Essays on Sexual Difference in Gothic Literature,* edited by Ruth Bienstock Anolik, pp. 111-21. Jefferson, N.C.: McFarland, 2007.

[*In the following essay, Anderson examines Charlotte Brontë's use of the "Bluebeard" and "Cinderella" folk tales in her novel* Jane Eyre.]

> I, by dint of groping, found the outlet from the attic, and proceeded to descend the narrow garret staircase. I lingered in the long passage to which this led, separating the front and back rooms of the third story—narrow, low and dim, with only one little window at the far end, and looking, with its two rows of small black doors all shut, like a corridor in some Bluebeard's castle.
>
> —Charlotte Brontë, *Jane Eyre*

"Among its other distinctions," writes John Sutherland, "*Jane Eyre* can claim to be the first adult, non-burlesque treatment of the Bluebeard theme in English Literature" (314). Quite so. Wives incarcerated in secret rooms in the bowels of rambling mansions are precisely the stuff of "Bluebeard," of which breed of men Edward Fairfax Rochester proves himself a fine specimen. In fact, there can be no denying the close correlation between "Bluebeard" and the general trajectory of the Gothic novel, from *The Mysteries of Udolpho* to *The Turn of the Screw* and beyond.

The eighteenth century marked a decisive shift from oral to print culture, whereupon print was suddenly distributed to a mass audience—not just as novels, but in chapbooks, as well. Chapbooks contained "real-life" stories not dissimilar from our contemporary tabloids and scandal sheets, but also English (Scottish, Irish) ballads, fairy tales (often derived from literary versions which chiefly originated in aristocratic France) and, by the latter half of the century, much-abridged popular novels. Thus the enormous distinction which our contemporary culture makes between novels and fairy tales (which we identify as simple children's tales on a par with nonsense rhymes) was not present in eighteenth century Britain, when oral tradition was still in existence, diminishing, certainly, with the onward march of print, but alive nonetheless. Furthermore, despite our twenty-first century conception of fairy tales as being profoundly unfeminist, it was only when fairy tales began to be widely disseminated in print that the heroines became uniformly vapid. Tales that preceded and, in remote communities, eluded print domination (which tales were, fortunately, to some degree preserved by nineteenth century folklorists), more often than not present a female protagonist as actively combating obstacles and assailants, rather than waiting passively to be saved by a man. Since the passive femininity with which we often associate fairy tales is typically confined to its printed manifestations, when British women began to write novels in the eighteenth century, the only model for female heroics upon which they could reasonably draw was that of fairy tale and oral culture.[1]

The tale that we know as "Bluebeard" was written by Charles Perrault and included in his 1695 collection of Mother Goose Tales: *Histoires ou Contes de Temps Passé*. The story runs thus: a young woman is courted by an ugly man with a blue beard; his wealth induces her to accept his proposal. One day he forbids her to enter one particular chamber; as soon as he has left the house she tries the door and finds, to her horror, a bloody chamber full of the corpses of women. On Bluebeard's return he is enraged by her transgression and prepares to kill her; she asks for a moment or two to say her prayers, and in the time gained her brothers fortuitously turn up and save her.

Versions of similar tales long pre-existed Perrault's, circulating orally.[2] Although the tales vary, there is almost always a "forbidden chamber" sequence; if there is no specific chamber in which dead bodies are sequestered, the girl spies on the murderer from a concealed spot and establishes his criminal intent. In fact, all the conjoined props that would come to be identified as Gothic (the mansion, the secret chamber, the murderous patriarch, our goodly heroine) pre-existed the Gothic in tales of the "Bluebeard" type. Through all the variations of the basic story, the defining feature is a murderous husband or fiancé who keeps the corpses of his previous victims sequestered in his large house.

So for example, [Jacob and Wilhelm] Grimm collected a tale called "Fitcher's Bird," which details a wizard who abducts one of three sisters, and takes her to be his bride. He forbids her access to one room only; however, she disobeys this injunction, discovers the bloody chamber and drops the key in the blood. The key will not come clean, so her transgression is visible; she is dispatched and her blood and limbs wind up in the chamber also. Then the next sister is abducted and meets the same fate; the third sister is also abducted, but when

she investigates the chamber she has the presence of mind to put the key away first; thus her transgression passes unnoticed. The balance of power now shifted, she then magically revivifies her sisters and burns the whole house down, wizard and all. (We should take note of this house-burning, which prefigures the burnings in *Jane Eyre, Rebecca* and *Wide Sargasso Sea*.) "The Robber Bridegroom," a related story, is also collected by the Grimms. In the Grimm version, a young woman is betrothed by her father to a suitor whom she finds unaccountably sinister. Her fiancé invites her to come to his house on a particular day, and she accepts the invitation warily. When she gets there she is warned to turn back by a caged bird: "Turn back, turn back, young maiden dear, / 'Tis a murderer's house you enter here" (Grimm and Grimm 201). Inside she moves about the house but finds no one until she comes to the cellar. There she finds an old woman who tells her she is betrothed to a murderer who will kill and eat her. She then hides the girl behind a hogshead, and as soon as she has done so the groom and "his godless crew" return, dragging a girl with them; they drug, strip and dismember her, before eating her. A ring belonging to the dead girl flies up and lands in the hidden girl's lap; the old woman distracts the robbers from looking for it, thus saving her. When the robbers are asleep, both girl and old woman escape; the girl runs home and tells her father what she has seen. Subsequently the groom comes to a great dinner at the girl's house. She relates what she saw at his house as if she has dreamt it, before revealing the ring, still attached to the dead girl's finger, as proof of the deed; the bridegroom and his crew are then executed.

It should be noted that continental European tales such as "Fitcher's Bird" and the Italian tale "How the Devil Came to Marry Three Sisters" figure a supernatural instead of a human male villain. This villain also abducts his victims in a manner of bride capture rather than courting their attentions legitimately. On the other hand, the Grimms' "The Robber Bridegroom" is grounded in realism, featuring a girl whose betrothal is led by her father, against her own better judgment. The parallels between this type of plotting and the Gothic—*The Mysteries of Udolpho,* for example—are evident, for in both the heroine is posited as representing male property, the object of exchange and violent dispatch. In fact, [Ann] Radcliffe's *oeuvre* typically tracks the root of supernatural fears to a living man rather than a specter. [Jane] Austen too engages in this process in *Northanger Abbey,* where the fear is tragicomically severed from a supernatural origin, or even an exoticized Italianate context, and re-established within a mundane, non-spectral, English environment.

In the examples mentioned thus far, the villain is *not* the heroine's lover, even if he contrives to have her as his bride. Rather he is a predatory male for whom the heroine holds no sympathy, only fear and loathing. However, what we see in novels in the Gothic mode, certainly during the nineteenth century—possibly inaugurated by [Mary] Wollstonecraft's *Maria, or The Wrongs of Woman*—is the scenario in which the villain is not only human and non-supernatural, he is actually the woman's husband or lover. Here we should backstep to look at the folkloric antecedents for this development. Among the oldest varieties of this folkloric schema is the old English tale "Mr. Fox"; this fascinating tale is unusual since the heroine's murderous lover is hers by choice rather than betrothal or abduction. However, she discovers his secret before the marriage and ultimately has the villain slain. In that sense it differs from all European versions of any of these grouped-together "sister" tales, since in other versions of the tale the suitor is either outright repellent but rich ("Bluebeard"), indecipherably sinister ("The Robber Bridegroom"), or an abductor ("Fitcher's Bird"). Only in "Mr. Fox" is the female protagonist in love with her charmingly murderous suitor.[3] What we see in novelistic representations of these character relationships is that prior to *Jane Eyre,* the male villain/protagonist tends to be one of either the "Mr. Fox" or "Fitcher's Bird" variety: either a seemingly attractive suitor whose reptilian underbelly is exposed, or a clearly rapacious abductor. In *Jane Eyre,* however, Bluebeard's secret is exposed, excused and altogether palliated when Jane marries Rochester. Yet, we do not forget (even if Jane does) that a woman who has been incarcerated for years in a secret room now lies dead.

The idea that it is the human husband, rather than a rapacious and inhuman villain, who is at fault reveals a connection to Middle Eastern folk tales; in fact, both "Bluebeard" and *Jane Eyre* share distinctly Asian aspects. Brontë was herself responsible for those to be discerned in *Jane Eyre,* but Perrault was quite innocent of the posthumous "ameliorations" made to his story. For example, in Sir Arthur Quiller-Couch's 1912 retelling of Perrault's "Bluebeard," the story is set somewhere near Baghdad, and Bluebeard gorges his new wife, Fatima, on "eastern" delicacies (Perrault and Quiller-Couch 33). Winfried Menninghaus observes that there existed a "(pseudo) orientalizing vogue for *Märchen* [German folk tales] in the eighteenth century." Following Perrault (who, as we know, did not add eastern flavor to his rendition), the tales of the celebrated fairy-tale writer Madame [Marie-Catherine] d'Aulnoye (whose tales, such as "The Blue Bird," were also extremely popular in England) "and the first translation of the *Tales of 1001 Nights* by Antoine Galland [in 1704]," it became the case that "the fairytale-like" was identified "with the Oriental and vice versa" (Menninghaus 72-3). In other words, since the vogue for fairy tales coincided temporally with the eighteenth century fad for Orientalia, the two became conflated.

During the eighteenth century England relied on France for cultural guidance; literary fashions were watched from across the Channel and followed obsessively (Conant 238). Perrault's collected *Contes* were not translated into English until 1729, owing, Martha Pike Conant suggests, to the French specificity of the tales that did not immediately lend itself to the English imagination. Thus the English translations of *The Thousand and One Nights* preceded the arrival in England of Perrault, allowing the *Contes* to settle down into an arabesque nest that, to the English, seemed ready-made. Both came from fashionable France to an insular England (Conant 234), where the *Mother Goose Tales* were suddenly exotic by association. But it was not only *The Arabian Nights* that stirred the French and English imaginations—a flurry of oriental and, as Conant terms it, "pseudo-oriental" literary outpourings flooded the scene; in England, she tells us, the "pseudo" tales were derived from French arabesques (Conant vii).

Though fairy tales and Arabian tales may well have been conflated during the eighteenth century, by the mid-nineteenth century only "Bluebeard" retained its oriental associations. It is unclear at what point "Bluebeard" became particularly associated with oriental themes, but by the nineteenth century all British illustrations accompanying versions of the tale showed orientalized characters[4] and in many cases the text was altered to include such oriental ameliorations as setting the tale in Baghdad. Hand-colored engravings from an 1804 edition of *Tabart's Popular Stories for the Nursery* show contemporary European settings for all the tales but Bluebeard's; he wears an ornate turban as he prepares to decapitate his wife. Such depictions continued as the norm throughout the nineteenth century and into the twentieth, finely wrought by the likes of Aubrey Beardsley, Arthur Rackham, W. Heath Robinson and Edmund Dulac.[5] Menninghaus observes that the conjunction between oriental themes and fairy tales "made it possible later for the disquietingly violent aspects of fairy tales—such as the serial murder of women—to be blamed on its oriental pedigree" (Menninghaus 73), thus displaying the strategy of cultural and geographic distancing common in the Gothic. But in fact it was Bluebeard alone who continued to carry that particular train of associations long after the eighteenth century Arabian vogue had peaked and waned. Since "the East" had in any case become, to some considerable extent, a metonym for "fabulous wealth or excessive tyranny" (Conant 234), as well as a world that, as Edward Said demonstrates, "exuded dangerous sex" and "perverse morality" (*Orientalism* 166-7), it ought not to surprise us that the so-called "oriental" world came to carry a particular association with "Bluebeard," in which all these elements are present in quantity.

Suggestions of orientalism are overt within Brontë's text. As Joyce Zonana notes, *Jane Eyre*'s "diffusely orientalist background has long been recognized" (Zonana 595).[6] Zonana lists the numerous instances of orientalism in the novel, from the framing of *Rasselas* (Brontë 87) to Jane's objections to *suttee*, but pays particular attention to the "harem as a metaphor for aspects of Western life" (Zonana 598), since in the novel Rochester is frequently cast as a despotic (and polygamous) sultan and Jane his slave. Zonana argues that the orientalism within *Jane Eyre* is primarily "a rhetorical strategy (and a form of thought) by which a speaker or writer neutralizes the threat inherent in feminist demands and makes them palatable to an audience that wishes to affirm its occidental superiority" (Zonana 594). While this may be true (and an example of Gothic distancing), in fact the orientalism within *Jane Eyre* is also a clearly identifiable link to the orientalism of "Bluebeard." The Bluebeard associations and the harem metaphor both indicate marital despotism that may, moreover, be differentiated from the antifeminist violence presented in the tales themselves. In fact, even in Perrault's "Bluebeard" the wife is complicit to some degree with her husband's illegal acts. Shifting the action to an oriental setting revisits and amplifies the implication that such marital despotism is *not* in opposition to the law and, indeed, is sanctioned by the law of the land, if not actually promoted and enforced by that law. Therefore, although in one sense one could accuse Brontë of transparent Eurocentricism in her use of oriental metaphors, at the same time she is indicting an Englishman, Rochester, in terms usually reserved for Arabian despots. Brontë thus suggests that this despotism is *not* something that only exists abroad, thereby reversing conventional Gothic distancing in her novel. Indeed, the fact that the concealed wife is actually from the slave colonies of the Caribbean is a frightful, truly shocking reminder (albeit one not fully explored by the novel, which leaves that task to Jean Rhys) that overseas is not necessarily all that far away, and that Elsewhere, with all its attendant horrors, can still be Here.

"Bluebeard" is certainly not the only folk tale that resonates in *Jane Eyre*. Over the years a number of critics have identified Brontë's novel as following a "Cinderella" patterning (Burkhart; Moglen; Clarke; Sullivan). In his introduction to Marian Roalfe Cox's exhaustive volume on the tale-type, Andrew Lang describes "the fundamental idea of Cinderella" as "a person in a mean or obscure position, by means of supernatural assistance" who "makes a good marriage" (vii). By a "good marriage" we are, of course, given to understand a marriage that raises the protagonist from poverty. This does not completely apply to Jane, as she is independently rich before she finally marries Rochester. However, the narrative certainly adheres to some sort of "Cinderella" plot up until the first marriage sequence, when Jane is still poor as she stands at the altar, and Mason exposes Rochester as a would-be bigamist. It is worth noting here that the marriage sequence strongly echoes what

Cox designates the "false bride" motif that is evident in many "Cinderella"-type stories, including the Grimms' "Aschenpüttel."[7]

In Brontë's novel, Jane is propelled into flight after Rochester tries to induce her to become his mistress. In fact, Jane's ascent from "poor, obscure, plain and little" (281) beginnings is not linear; she ascends twice. Her first ascent takes her up to the failed wedding, where it is she herself (or then again, Rochester) who assumes the "false bride" position usually assigned to one of the horrid stepsisters. Following this she descends back into meanness, once again "the poor orphan child" (54); again she rises and ultimately weds Rochester without incident. This extended fairy tale format follows more closely the structure outlined by [Vladimir] Propp in his study of the more elaborate Russian fairy tale, but in terms of its second phase alone is structured almost to the letter in terms of a "Catskin-Cinderella."

"Catskin" is the British variant of a tale also made famous by Perrault, and called "Peau D'Ane." There are many echoes of the "Catskin" story in *Jane Eyre*. In the fairy tales, the endangered princess seeks counsel from a fairy godmother-type character. Ironically, Rochester plays this role when he assumes the disguise of a gypsy fortune-teller. In *Jane Eyre* it is ultimately the moon that fulfils the magical maternal function (Rich 102), advising Jane to flee, like the fairy tale princess who escapes unseen. The Lang version ("Donkeyskin") says that the princess slips away "without being seen by anyone" (Lang 7); in the Grimm version, "Allerleirauh," the title character runs away from the castle at dead of night, taking only a few magical belongings. Alone in the world, our heroine "walked on a long, long way, trying to find someone who would take her in, and let her work for them; but though the cottagers, whose houses she passed, gave her food from charity, the ass's skin was so dirty they would not allow her to enter their houses" (Lang 7). In the corresponding section in *Jane Eyre*, Jane leaves what little money she has in the carriage, begs door-to-door for employment, then charity, though she is repelled by most on account of her impoverished appearance. Hannah, the Rivers' housekeeper, agrees to give her a piece of bread but then turns her out: "'You are not what you ought to be, or you wouldn't make such a noise. Move off'" (361). In the folk tales the refugee finally secures menial work, as does Jane, who is quick to announce that she "felt degraded" by her work in the schoolroom (385).

The "Catskin" stories, "practically worldwide in distribution" (Briggs 424), are according to Cox part of the "Cinderella" family. But there is one important motif that distinguishes them: the "unnatural father,"[8] the father who wishes to marry his daughter. Many "Catskin" tales in the British tradition have had this particular element edited out of them, but it is present in Perrault's

"Peau D'Ane," the Irish tale "The Princess in the Catskins," and the Grimm tale "Allerleirauh." This motif too resurfaces in *Jane Eyre.* Paula Sullivan draws attention to Rochester's paternal function, pointing out the several occasions within the text when the "twenty-year difference in their ages is called into question"; she also points out that "Rochester's blindness and subsequent partial recovery of vision correspond to Mr Patrick Brontë's near-blindness and partial recovery due to a cataract operation." Nevertheless, Sullivan continues, "Rochester figures primarily as a lover rather than a surrogate parent" (Sullivan 67). This notwithstanding, Rochester's paternalist role as Jane's master is further underscored by Mrs. Fairfax's observation that "'He might almost be your father.'" Jane refutes this statement with an uncharacteristic pique that reveals her discomfort: "'No, indeed, Mrs Fairfax!' I exclaimed, nettled; 'he is nothing like my father! No-one, who saw us together, would suppose it for an instant. Mr Rochester looks as young, and is as young, as some men at five-and-twenty'" (293). Yet when at the local pub she later hears her own story recited back to her, she discovers that it is not only Mrs. Fairfax who sees her relationship with Mr. Rochester in this light: "'She was a little, small thing, they say, almost like a child. . . . Mr Rochester was about forty, and this governess not twenty. . . . Well, he would marry her" (452). Rochester himself observes that he "should entertain none but fatherly feelings" (460) for Jane; moreover, as Sullivan observes, Jane sits on Rochester's knee in a daughterly fashion (67).

Thus in casting Rochester in a paternal relationship with Jane, Brontë reminds us that he is the "unnatural father" of the fairy tales, hoping to marry his daughter, just as she suggests that he is Bluebeard, the "unnatural husband." In referencing the fairy tales, Brontë encodes her message regarding the dangers posed by Mr. Rochester to Jane and to her reader: he is not merely the dangerously powerful Victorian husband, legally authorized to lock up his insane wife; he is the preternaturally dangerous husband and father of the folk tale. Thus while it may seem puzzling to note the conjunction of seemingly opposite tale-types—one that directs itself towards the blissful union of marriage; the other predicated upon the murderous reality of marriage—in fact, in the "Catskin-Cinderella," as in "Bluebeard," it is a man who is the source of terror. In layering the two tales, Brontë reminds her readers that husbands and fathers are both preternaturally dangerous.

This encoded, but nevertheless clear, message amplifies a troubling aspect of *Jane Eyre,* the masochism of the protagonist who refuses to heed the encoded warning and who accepts the terms of her problematic marriage, eventually returning to the man who has attempted bigamy and who has—directly or indirectly—killed his wife, having incarcerated her in a garret. The explana-

tion for Jane's wilful disregard of the textual warnings, too, may be found in the fairy tale sources of her story. Significantly, in Perrault's "La Barbe-Bleue," the wife's ambivalent complicity with the terms of her marriage hinges on scopic terms; it is a matter of *seeing or not seeing* that determines her choices. For instance, her paramour's blue beard makes him frightful to women; however, after he showers her with expensive gifts and shows her his expansive mansion (most of it, at least) she decides that his beard is not so blue after all. When she looks inside the secret chamber, she does not see straight away: "at first she saw nothing, since the windows were closed; after some moments she began to see that the floor was covered in clotted blood, and that in this blood were reflected the corpses of several women hung from the walls" (Perrault 63). And as we know, even at that point *she does not attempt to escape,* but rather tries to pretend she has *seen nothing.* The denouement returns to the question of sight. While waiting for the arrival of her brother, the protagonist asks Sister Anne up on the tower if she sees them coming: "Anne, ma soeur Anne, ne vois-tu rien venir?" ("Anne, Sister Anne, do you see nothing coming?") This famous phrase is repeated three times, while Anne replies: "Je ne vois rien que."⁹ Sister Anne sees *nothing*; even when she sees *something,* it is cast as *nothing,* since it is not the approach of the two phallic brothers: "Je ne vois rien que le soleil qui poudroie et l'herbe qui verdoie." ("I see nothing but the dappled sunlight and the rippling grass.")

The sightlessness with which Perrault's "Bluebeard" is infused seems to travel to *Jane Eyre.* Jane is wilfully blind in ignoring Rochester's flaws. The physical blindness with which Rochester is ultimately blighted is the price he pays for rendering Jane figuratively blind. And yet, as the folk tale suggests, Jane herself is to blame for her blindness. Thus, if Mr. Rochester's blindness appears to put Jane and him on an equal footing, in fact it merely enables Jane to accept her own sightlessness without acknowledging it. Meanwhile, a house is burned and a woman is dead, as if she never existed; and the future promises nothing better for Jane, who refuses to learn from the all-too-visible examples of all her predecessors.

Notes

1. It is important that we recognize the extremely close connections between the fairy tale and the early novel. Indeed, the inception of the European novel occurred in the salons of seventeenth century France, where novels and fairy tales were written and created in tandem, as noted by DeJean and Seifert.

2. The Aarne-Thompson folklore classification system differentiates schematically between three essentially similar tale-types: type 312, wherein the

endangered woman's brothers rescue her from the murderous man; 311, where she is typically the last of three sisters to be abducted by a wizard or devil, and saves herself and her sisters through trickery (the Grimms' "Fitcher's Bird" is of this type); and type 955, known as "Robber Bridegroom" tales, wherein a suitor is foiled in his murderous/cannibalistic aims by the girl who discovers his plot and exposes him, often using riddles to expose the murderer in a public space.

3. This scenario is exploited to perfection by Beatrix Potter, whose Jemima Puddleduck became positively enamoured of "the foxy gentleman" who showed her to his wood-shed: "quite full of feathers—it was almost suffocating; but it was comfortable and very soft." Indeed, "Jemima thought him mighty civil and handsome" (Potter 164).

4. French illustrations, it should be noted, do not seem to follow this trend to a significant degree; woodcut illustrations from the eighteenth century show contemporary settings.

5. The association between Bluebeard and "the oriental" existed too in Germany, since, as Menninghaus notes, in 1797 Ludwig Tieck published his *The Seven Wives of Bluebeard,* which featured the "bibliographic mystification" of presenting the publication details as "'Istanbul by Heraklius Murusi, Court Bookseller of High Gate; in the Year of Hedschrach 1212'" (Menninghaus 71).

6. One explanation of this is the larger context provided by Edward Said: "everywhere in nineteenth and early twentieth century British and French culture we find allusions to the facts of empire, but perhaps nowhere with more regularity and frequency than in the British novel" (Culture and Imperialism 73).

7. In tales of this type, the prince, having only the mystery woman's shoe by which to recognize her, goes about the land having all the women try the shoe for size. Cinderella's stepmother has one of the stepsisters mutilate her foot by slicing off toe or heel so that it may fit the shoe; the prince is fooled and a wedding arranged with the false bride. However, the false bride is exposed as she walks up the aisle, usually by a bird who draws attention to the bleeding foot with a rhyming song.

8. The opening pattern of all these tales runs thus: The queen on her deathbed bids the king promise that he will marry no one who is not as wise and beautiful as she. After the queen's death, the heartbroken king has the land scoured for just such a woman and finds not a one who can in any way compare with his dead wife. Finally his eye lights upon his daughter and he sees that only she is as beautiful and wise as her mother; he wants to marry her. The daughter, understandably, is appalled by the suggestion, but the king will not be put off.

9. "Anne, ma soeur Anne" rhymes with "rien"—indeed, this may be the only reason why Anne comes into it at all, since she has figured in the tale neither by name nor reference prior to her sudden appearance on the tower.

Works Cited

Aarne, Antti. *The Types of the Folktale: A Classification and Bibliography.* Trans. Stith Thompson. 2nd ed. Helsinki: Suomalainen Tiedeakatemia, Academia Scientiarum Fennica, 1961.

Briggs, Katharine M. *A Dictionary of British Folk Tales in the English Language.* Vol. 1. London: Routledge and Kegan Paul, 1970.

Brontë, Charlotte. *Jane Eyre,* ed. Q. D. Leavis. Harmondsworth: Penguin, 1988.

Burkhart, Charles. *Charlotte Bronte: A Psychosexual Study of Her Novels.* London: Gollancz, 1973.

Clarke, Micael M. "Brontë's *Jane Eyre* and the Grimms' 'Cinderella.'" *Studies in English Literature 1500-1900* 40.4 (2000): 695-710.

Conant, Martha Pike. *The Oriental Tale in England in the Eighteenth Century.* London: Frank Cass, 1966.

Cox, Marian Roalfe. *Cinderella: Three Hundred and Forty-Five Variants of Cinderella, Catskin, and Cap O'Rushes.* London: David Nutt, 1893.

DeJean, Joan. *Tender Geographies: Women and the Origins of the Novel in France.* New York: Columbia University Press, 1991.

Grimm, Jacob, and Wilhelm Grimm. *The Complete Fairy Tales.* Ware: Wordsworth, 1997.

Lang, Andrew. *The Grey Fairy Book.* New York: Dover, 1967.

Menninghaus, Winfried. *In Praise of Nonsense: Kant and Bluebeard.* Stanford, Calif.: Stanford University Press, 1999.

Moglen, Helene. *Charlotte Brontë: The Self Conceived.* New York: Norton, 1978.

Perrault, Charles. *Contes,* ed. Marc Soriano. Paris: Flammarion, 1991.

Perrault, Charles, and Sir Arthur Quiller-Couch. *Perrault's Fairy Tales.* London: Folio, 2001.

Potter, Beatrix. "Jemima Puddleduck." In *The Complete Tales,* 161-72. London: Frederick Warne, 2002.

Propp. Vladimir. *Morphology of the Folktale,* edited with an introduction by Svatava Pirkova-Jakobson, translated by Laurence Scott. Bloomington, Ind.: Research Center, Indiana University, 1958. Rich, Adrienne. *On Lies, Secrets and Silence: Selected Prose, 1966-1978.* New York: Norton, 1995.

Said, Edward. *Culture and Imperialism.* London: Chatto and Windus, 1993.

———. *Orientalism.* London: Routledge, 1978.

Seifert, Lewis Carl. *Fairy Tales, Sexuality, and Gender in France, 1690-1715.* Cambridge: Cambridge University Press, 1996.

Sullivan, Paula. "Fairy Tale Elements in Jane Eyre." *Journal of Popular Culture* 12.1 (1978): 61-74.

Sutherland, John. *The Literary Detective: 100 Puzzles in Classic Fiction.* New York: Oxford University Press, 2000.

Zonana, Joyce. "The Sultan and the Slave: Feminist Orientalism and the Structure of Jane Eyre." *Signs* 18.3 (1993): 592-617.

FURTHER READING

Criticism

Bredsdorff, Elias. "The Range of Andersen's Tales." In *Hans Christian Andersen: The Story of His Life and Work, 1805-75,* pp. 308-32. London: Phaidon, 1975.

> Discusses the sources of some of Hans Christian Andersen's fairy tales and proposes a system for grouping them.

Chinitz, Lisa G. "Fairy Tale Turned Ghost Story: James's *The Turn of the Screw.*" *Henry James Review* 15, no. 3 (October 1994): 264-85.

> Argues that "our response to *The Turn of the Screw* is carefully orchestrated by [Henry] James's deliberate genre confusion: by twisting a fairy tale into a ghost story, the turns (and returns) of the narrative create in the reader's experience a crisis in reality testing that is nothing less than uncanny."

Dolle-Weinkauff, Bernd. "Nineteenth-Century Fairy Tale Debates and the Development of Children's Literature Criticism in Germany." *Children's Literature Association Quarterly* 24, no. 4 (January 1999): 166-73.

> Surveys critical and scholarly discussion of fairy tales and folk tales during the nineteenth and twentieth centuries in Germany, and how this informed the conception of children's literature.

Eitelgeorge, Janice S. and Nancy A. Anderson. "The Work of Hans Christian Andersen: More than Just Fairy Tales." *Bookbird* 42, no. 3 (July 2004): 37-44.

> Examines how Andersen's works depart from the thematic and narrative models of traditional folktales and fairy tales.

Ewers, Hans-Heino. "H. C. Andersen as Seen by Critics of German Children's Literature since the Beginning of the Twentieth Century." *Marvels & Tales* 20, no. 2 (2006): 142, 208-23.

> Surveys the widespread critical opinion that Hans Christian Andersen's works are inappropriate for children, and contends that Andersen originated a new type of literature for children that wasn't adopted by later writers until the latter half of the twentieth century.

Griffith, John. "Personal Fantasy in Andersen's Fairy Tales." *Kansas Quarterly* 16, no. 3 (summer 1984): 81-8.

> Contends that Andersen depicted death as a welcome escape for the innocent from the terrors of sexuality.

Hovet, Theodore R. "'Once upon a Time': Sarah Orne Jewett's 'A White Heron' as a Fairy Tale." *Studies in Short Fiction* 15, no. 1 (winter 1978): 63-8.

> Interprets the structure of Sarah Orne Jewett's "A White Heron" as that of a classic fairy tale.

Ingwesern, Niels. "'I Have Come to Despise You': Andersen and His Relationship to His Audience." *Fabula: Zeitschrift für Erzählforschung/Journal of Folktale Studies/Revue d'Etudes sur le Conte Populaire* 46, no. 1-2 (2005): 17-28.

> Focuses upon Hans Christian Andersen's "complicated relationship" with his readers, and how the author portrayed his audience in his works.

Kleiman, E. "The Wizardry of Nathaniel Hawthorne: *Seven Gables* as Fairy Tale and Parable." *English Studies in Canada* 4, no. 3 (fall 1978): 289-304.

> Discusses Hawthorne's *House of the Seven Gables* as "a parable dressed up as a fairy tale."

Kudszus, W. G. *Terrors of Childhood in Grimms' Fairy Terrors.* New York: Peter Lang, 2005, 149 p.

> Book-length linguistic analysis of the Grimm brothers' fairy tales as expressions of childhood fears.

Martin, Robert K. "Oscar Wilde and the Fairy Tale: 'The Happy Prince' as Self-Dramatization." *Studies in Short Fiction* 16, no. 1 (winter 1979): 74-7.

> Interprets Wilde's "The Happy Prince" as a tale of the transformative power of love.

Martin, W. R. "The Use of the Fairy-Tale: A Note on the Structure of *The Bostonians.*" *English Studies in Africa* 2, no. 1 (March 1959): 98-109.

> Traces the influence of fairy tales on Henry James's novel, *The Bostonians.*

Paradiž, Valerie. *Clever Maids: The Secret History of the Grimm Fairy Tales.* New York: Basic, 2005, 240 p.

> Book-length study devoted to the women who related the folk tales to the Grimm brothers.

Robbins, Hollis. "The Emperor's New Critique." *New Literary History* 34, no. 4 (October 2003): 659-75.

> Illustrates the narrative complexity of Hans Christian Andersen's "The Emperor's New Clothes," reading the story as a literary, social, and political commentary.

Rowen, Norma. "Reinscribing Cinderella: Jane Austen and the Fairy Tale." In *Functions of the Fantastic: Selected Essays from the Thirteenth International Conference on the Fantastic in the Arts,* edited by Joe Sanders, pp. 29-36. Westport, Conn.: Greenwood, 1995.

> Centers on Jane Austen's realistic interpretation of the Cinderella theme in her novels *Pride and Prejudice, Mansfield Park,* and *Persuasion.*

Sweeney, Gerard M. "Melville's Hawthornian Bell-Tower: A Fairy-Tale Source." *American Literature* 45, no. 2 (May 1973): 279-85.

> Argues that Herman Melville's "The Bell-Tower" was strongly influenced by "The Minotaur," Nathaniel Hawthorne's re-telling of the Theseus myth.

Physiognomy in Nineteenth-Century Literature

The following entry provides critical commentary on physiognomy in nineteenth-century literature.

INTRODUCTION

Physiognomy—the study of the supposed correlations between facial features and bodily characteristics and human personality and behavior—was discussed and practiced starting in classical antiquity. It was Johann Caspar Lavater, however, a Protestant minister in Switzerland, who revived the prestige of physiognomy in a series of works published in the 1770s, most notably the *Physiognomische Fragmente* (1775-78; *Essays on Physiognomy*). Seeking to combat the traditional associations of physiognomy with divination and the occult, Lavater asserted that his physiognomic system was completely new, based on reason and empirical observation. He held out the promise that modern scientific physiognomy would provide a comprehensive explanation of human behavior, a promise that fascinated many people at all levels of society. To Lavater, not only facial features and expressions, but hair, hand placement, clothing, and tone of voice could reveal much about individuals' characters. Lavater's physiognomic theory aroused heated controversy: many intellectuals and literary authors praised it, while others attacked it as overly subjective and laden with emotionally charged Christian rhetoric. Physiognomy also became a popular fad, inspiring parlor games in social gatherings where partygoers vied to read each other's faces. Lavater's works were soon translated from German into English, French, and other European languages, doing much to spread the popularity of physiognomy throughout much of the Western hemisphere.

Lavater's physiognomic theory was ambiguous about key points, which actually contributed to its popularity. On one hand, he identified physical attractiveness with innate intelligence and virtue, and ugliness or deformity with innate stupidity and viciousness. On the other hand, he averred that individuals' life experiences can imprint themselves on their faces, and moreover suggested that persons who consciously practice virtue can become more attractive in appearance. He asserted that everyone judges other creatures based on their looks, even if they prefer to pretend otherwise, and promised he could help everyone learn how to read other people's faces and bodies more accurately. At the same time he insisted that some people are more naturally talented at making proper physiognomic judgments, and that physiognomic skill depends on intuition and experience and cannot be reduced to formulas.

Even in the eighteenth century and before, many literary authors paid careful attention to describing the appearance of their characters. Indeed, Lavater and other physiognomists drew upon descriptions of fictional characters to provide evidence for their theories. However, after 1800, novelists tended to make greater use of character description, showing how facial features and bodily gestures express their characters' inner lives. Character description began serving as a structural element within novels, suggesting the passage of time and changes within characters' personalities, and enriching the texture of literary works by allowing readers to compare differing descriptions of the same characters. Many authors portrayed characters who were avid observers of personal appearance, illustrating how their worldly inexperience or psychological faults often lead them to assess other people erroneously. Physiognomy became a cultural code through which novelists could convey expectations and judgments to perceptive readers about the behavior and morality of their characters. Critic Jeanne Fahnestock details how Victorian British novelists classified and assessed the heroines of their books according to the size and shape of their chins, mouths and lips, noses, and foreheads. Physically unattractive traits indicated qualities regarded as morally undesirable in women; for instance, prominent chins were associated with strong willpower, and large and rounded mouths with sexual desire.

Lavater believed that modern physiognomics would promote Christian goodwill and social harmony, helping usher in a utopian future. He insisted, however, that most humans' character and capacities are fixed from birth, and that different races and nationalities have distinctive physiognomies. Lavater, along with many of his successors, maintained that what they perceived as the mental and cultural superiority of light-skinned northern Europeans, and the corresponding inferiority of most of the world's other peoples—as well as the superiority of men over women in general—was plainly written on their faces. During the nineteenth century and beyond, physiognomy was often applied to support ethnocentric and racist prejudices. Critics such as Shearer West have discussed ways in which novelists, dramatists, and graphic artists—as well as scientists, reformers, and journalists—used physiognomy to classify Jews as racially distinct from white Europeans and reinforce traditional anti-Semitic stereotypes, while commentators such as Jennifer Jones have described how popular physiognomy informed the portrayals of villains in stage melodramas as dark-skinned foreigners.

While the influence of physiognomy on nineteenth-century Western literature is clear, critics vary in assessing how pervasive this influence was and when it began. Commentators tend to agree that even if certain authors consciously drew upon the concepts of Lavater and other physiognomists, they adapted them flexibly to fit their own artistic visions. Even writers who used elaborate character descriptions might have been simply following the example of previous authors rather than applying the precepts of a particular physiognomist. Indeed, some novelists, such as George Eliot and Gustave Flaubert, openly attacked the habit of physiognomic stereotyping, making a point of creating heroes and heroines with undistinguished appearances that would contradict physiognomists' identification of outward beauty with inner character. Critic Graeme Tytler has suggested that many nineteenth-century novelists, including those who criticized physiognomic theories and avoided making direct physiognomic correlations, nonetheless described their characters in distinctive ways that expressed their artistic standpoints and demonstrated a familiarity with the tenets of physiognomy.

REPRESENTATIVE WORKS

Jane Austen
Emma. 3 vols. (novel) 1816

Honoré de Balzac
Eugénie Grandet [*Eugenia Grandet; or, The Miser's Daughter: A Tale of Everyday Life in the Nineteenth Century*] (novel) 1834; published in *Études de moeurs du XIXe siècle*

Charlotte Brontë
Jane Eyre: An Autobiography. 3 vols. [as Currer Bell] (novel) 1847
Villette. 3 vols. [as Currer Bell] (novel) 1853
The Professor: A Tale. 2 vols. [as Currer Bell] (novel) 1857

Emily Brontë
Wuthering Heights. 2 vols. [as Ellis Bell] (novel) 1847

Champfleury
Les Bourgeois de Molinchart [*The Molinchart Bourgeois*] (novel) 1855

Wilkie Collins
The Woman in White. 3 vols. (novel) 1860

Charles Dickens
Oliver Twist (novel) 1838
Great Expectations (novel) 1861

George Du Maurier
Trilby (novel) 1894

George Eliot
Adam Bede (novel) 1859
The Mill on the Floss (novel) 1860

Gustave Flaubert
Madame Bovary: mouers de province. 2 vols. [*Madame Bovary: A Tale of Provincial Life*] (novel) 1857

Karl Leberecht Immermann
Die Epigonen: Familienmemoiren in neun Büchern. 3 vols. (novel) 1836

Julia Kavanagh
Queen Mab: A Novel. 3 vols. (novel) 1864

Gottfried Keller
Der Grüne Heinrich. 4 vols. [*Green Henry*] (novel) 1854-55

Charles Kingsley
Alton Locke, Tailor and Poet: An Autobiography. 2 vols. (novel) 1850

Johann Caspar Lavater
Von der Physiognomik. 2 vols. [*On Physiognomics*] (nonfiction) 1772
Physiognomische Fragmente zur Beförderung der Menschenkenntniss und Menschenliebe. 4 vols. [*Essays on Physiognomy; Designed to Promote the Knowledge and the Love of Mankind*] (nonfiction) 1775-78

Stuart Ogilvie
Hypatia [adaptor; from the novel by Charles Kingsley] (play) 1894

Emilia Pardo Bazán
Obras Completas. 3 vols. [edited by Federico Carlos Sáinz de Robles] (novels, novellas, short stories, and criticism) 1956-73
Cuentas Completos. 4 vols. [*Complete Stories*] (short stories) 1990

Jane Porter
Thaddeus of Warsaw. 4 vols. (novel) 1845

Ludwig Raabe
Chronik der Sperlingsgasse [as Jakob Corvinus; *The Chronicle of Sparrow Alley*] (novel) 1857

George Sand
Mauprat (novel) 1837

Sir Walter Scott

The Heart of Midlothian. 4 vols. (novel) 1818

Friedrich Spielhagen

Problematische Naturen. 4 vols. [*Problematic Characters*] (novel) 1861

Stendhal

Le Rouge et le Noir [*The Red and the Black*] (novel) 1831

Adalbert Stifter

Der Nachsommer: Eine Erzählung. 3 vols. [*Indian Summer*] (novel) 1857

Thomas Russell Sullivan

Dr. Jekyll and Mr. Hyde [adaptor; from the novel by Robert Louis Stevenson] (play) 1887

Ludwig Tieck

Vittoria Accorombona: Ein Roman in fünf Büchern. 2 vols. [*The Roman Matron; or, Vittoria Accorombona: A Novel*] (novel) 1840

Anthony Trollope

Can You Forgive Her? 2 vols. (novel) 1864

OVERVIEWS

Jeanne Fahnestock (essay date spring 1981)

SOURCE: Fahnestock, Jeanne. "The Heroine of Irregular Features: Physiognomy and Conventions of Heroine Description." *Victorian Studies* 24, no. 3 (spring 1981): 325-50.

[*In the following essay, Fahnestock explores how the detailed representations of heroines' physical features in nineteenth-century novels relates to the widely-held belief in physiognomics.*]

When Sir Walter Scott Presented Edith Bellenden, The Heroine Of *Old Mortality* (1816), to his reader's imagination, he simply noted her "cast of features, soft and feminine, yet not without a certain expression of playful archness."[1] Almost fifty years later when Charlotte Mary Yonge introduced her heroine Rachel Curtis in *The Clever Woman of the Family* (1865) she took an inventory of a "set of features of an irregular, characteristic cast," the broad low brow, nose *retroussé*, sensitive nostrils, round cheeks and full pouting lips.[2] In 1816

Scott's brief, vague description was typical, and in 1865 Yonge's fuller depiction was common. In fifty years the heroine came out of the shadows and into focus.

Why did the conventions of heroine description change over half a century, minute detail replacing vague generalities? One answer has to do with economy and efficiency of means. Nineteenth-century novelists often wanted to tell readers about a character before showing that character in action. They could always digress in the narrator's voice and summarize a character's personality, but they could also achieve something of the same effect more dramatically and concisely if they gave instead details of physical description which stood for character traits. Of course this substitution only worked if writers and readers shared a system of meaning, a code for translating descriptive terminology into aspects of personality. Readers from the 1850s through the 1870s could be relied on to understand something of the code of *physiognomy,* the "science" of reading character in the face.

Novelists have always been physiognomists in the broadest sense, maintaining a certain fitness between a character's outward and inward being. But in the mid-nineteenth century they were often physiognomists in a precise sense, and, what is most interesting, they began to give particular descriptions of the heroine as well as of male and minor characters, endowing her at the same time with more character and more importance in the novel. The pressure to idealize female character was strong for the mid-Victorian novelist, reflecting the stake contemporary society had in an ideal of gentle, innocent, truthful womanhood, no matter how far from reality.[3] And while it is true that the splendid gallery of these authors' heroines contains such complex and varied exceptions as Jane Eyre, Becky Sharpe, Maggie Tulliver, and Lizzie Eustace, the Edith Millbanks, Mary Bartons, and Madeline Staveleys are far more typical. It was particularly difficult for a novelist to break from the stereotype with any outright declaration of a heroine's imperfections. But the physiognomical description was a way of suggesting without proclaiming, of imputing intelligence, caprice, and even sexuality to heroines without indecorous explicitness. Thus although physiognomy can be a key to the description of any character, the physiognomical descriptions of heroines are especially revealing. This essay looks at the evolution of heroine description, traces the contemporary surge of interest in physiognomy, and decodes the meanings of some of the most frequently described feminine features.

In the early nineteenth-century novel the heroine is not often described in any particular detail. Take as a common instance Jane Porter's description of her heroine, Mary, from the once very popular *Thaddeus of Warsaw,* first published in 1803:

> Though a large Turkish shawl involved her fine person, a modest grace was observable in its every turn. Her exquisitely moulded arm, [was] rather veiled than concealed by the muslin sleeve that covered it. . . . Her lucid eyes shone with a sincere benevolence, and her lips seemed to breathe balm while she spoke. His [Thaddeus's] soul startled within itself as if by some strange recognition that agitated him, and drew him inexplicably towards its object. It was not the beauty he beheld, not the words she uttered, but he did not withdraw his fixed gaze until it encountered an accidental turn of her eyes, which instantly retreated with a deep blush mantling her face and neck.[4]

The reader learns nothing about the color of Mary's eyes or hair, the shape of her nose or chin, or her size, but is left with the one irreducible impression that Mary must be very beautiful. Jane Porter is not concerned with physical details but rather with spiritual ones—Mary's "modest grace," "sincere benevolence," and breath of "balm." For Mary is a morally superior being, and a contemporary reader would accept the union of physical and moral perfection and rest content without a detailed verbal portrait.

Jane Porter is actually quite generous with space about Mary. Often in an early nineteenth-century novel only a word or phrase is devoted to the heroine's appearance. Susan Ferrier's Edith, the heroine of *Destiny,* is "reckoned the prettiest girl in the county,"[5] and in remarks scattered over hundreds of pages other characters acknowledge that the heroine of Maria Edgeworth's *Belinda* is "pretty," "lovely," or "handsome."[6]

Admittedly some early nineteenth-century novelists are a bit more generous with descriptive details, and invariably the first detail added is color—hair color and eye color. Sir Walter Scott's Rose Bradwardine in *Waverly* has "a profusion of hair of paley gold, and a skin like the snow of her own mountains in whiteness," while Flora MacIvor has "jetty ringlets."[7] Lucy Ashton of *The Bride of Lammermoor* also has locks of "shadowy gold,"[8] while Diana Vernon of *Rob Roy* has long black hair crowning her "uncommonly fine face and person."[9] Scott pays attention to coloring in part because he wishes to create antithetical pairs of heroines, to play off the striking Rebecca-and-Rowena differences of light and dark. But even when heroines are not being paired the only detail usually added in novels at this time is color. Mrs. Gore's Frederica in *Pin Money* (1831) has tears in her hazel eyes, and the necessary heroine in Frederick Marryat's *Mr. Midshipman Easy* (1836) is a splendid brunette. Except for such spots of color, the portraiture from hair line to neck line is vague.

William Dean Howells noticed the lack of precise heroine description in the early English novel. In 1901 he published a pleasant excursion through the novel called *Heroines of Fiction.*[10] When he came to *The Vicar of*

Wakefield he complained about the vague descriptions of Olivia and Sophia and made some suggestions about how they might look (I, 7). What is interesting is that he thought he could infer each girl's appearance from her character. When Howells looked back on Jane Austen's work, he appointed her first in the personal description of heroines: "Almost to her time the appearance of the different characters was left to the reader's imagination; it is only in the modern novel that the author seems to feel it his duty to tell how his people look" (I, 57). But Jane Austen was not as innovative as Howells would have had her.[11] The essential difference in her novels is that the generalized descriptions of the heroine are not romantically heightened.[12] They are therefore more comfortably human, but still have nothing like the detail we find in heroine description later in the century. Howells's characterization of the change in conventions of heroine description is nevertheless generally correct.

In an essay of "Criticism on Female Beauty" written in 1825, Leigh Hunt approved of the then dominant technique of not describing the heroine in detail. "It has been observed justly," he says, "that heroines are best painted in general terms, as in Paradise Lost. *Grace was in all her steps, heaven in her eye, & c.* or by some striking instance of the effects of their beauty. . . . Particular description divides the opinion of readers, and may offend some of them."[13] Hunt's is surely the best available aesthetic justification of descriptive vagueness. When the image of the heroine is left blank, readers can fill it in according to their own tastes.

From 1830 to 1860 more and more detail gradually replaces vague description until finally in the 1860s the reader is often given a virtual inventory of the heroine's features. There is no simple dividing line, no single date between novels with and without full descriptions; Thomas Love Peacock's *Crochet Castle* in 1831 has an itemized accounting of its heroine, though this is unusual. In the early decades of the century novelists were not especially interested in giving any exact impression of the heroine's appearance. By the 1860s, despite the survival of vague description, many of them were very interested indeed. The following passage from Charles Kingsley's *Alton Locke* seems to show the change in the descriptive conventions taking place. Alton, the hero-narrator, is in a gallery standing before a St. Sebastian, himself about to be shafted by beauty. He hears a conversation behind him:

> I looked round, yet not at the speaker. My eyes, before they could meet hers, were caught by an apparition the most beautiful I had ever yet beheld. And what—what—have I seen equal to her since? Strange, that I should love to talk of her. Strange, that I fret at myself now because I cannot set down on paper line by line, and hue by hue, that wonderful loveliness of which— But no matter. Had I but such an imagination as Pe-

trarch, or rather, perhaps, had I his deliberate cold self-consciousness, what volumes of similes and conceits I might pour out, connecting that peerless face and figure with all lovely things which heaven and earth contain. As it is, because I cannot say all, I will say nothing, but repeat to the end again and again, Beautiful, beautiful, beautiful, beyond all statue, picture, or poet's dream.[14]

Here is a descriptive passage much like that in *Thaddeus of Warsaw* forty-seven years earlier. But Alton likes to contradict himself as well as repeat himself, and after vowing to say nothing he immediately continues the description in quite a different mode:

> Seventeen—slight but rounded, a masque and features delicate and regular, as if fresh from the chisel of Praxiteles—I must try to describe after all, you see—a skin of alabaster (privet-flowers, Horace and Ariosto would have said, more true to Nature), stained with the faintest flush; auburn hair, with that peculiar crisped wave seen in the old Italian pictures, and the warm, dark hazel eyes which so often accompany it; lips like a thread of vermilion, somewhat too thin, perhaps—but I thought little of that then; with such perfect finish and grace in every line and hue of her features and her dress, down to the little fingers and nails which showed through her thin gloves. . .
>
> (p. 101)

A more detailed description surfaces to replace the description of Lilian's effect in this passage. And something else is worth noticing. Though she is perfect and—the key word—"regular" in every other detail, Lilian's lips are too thin. Some imperfection in one or more of the heroine's features is a common consequence of detailed description. The minutely described heroine has a much harder time being perfectly beautiful; she is often a heroine of irregular features instead. In 1858 Walter Bagehot complained about this new "atrocious species of plain heroines" in the midst of an appreciation of the Waverley novels. "Possibly none of the frauds which are now so much the topic of common remark are so irritating, as that to which the purchaser of a novel is a victim on finding that he has only to peruse a narrative of the conduct and sentiments of an ugly lady. 'Two-and-sixpence to know the heart which has high cheekbones!' Was there ever such an imposition?"[15]

Irregular features must deviate from some standard of feminine beauty, and in the early and mid-nineteenth-century that standard was predominantly a classical one. Of Harold Skimpole's three daughters in *Bleak House,* Beauty, Sentiment, and Comedy, Beauty quite appropriately wears her hair "in the classic manner."[16] One of the authorities behind this standard was the great German art historian and aesthetician Johann Winckelmann, whose name is a touchstone in works on physiognomy. Winckelmann's prescription was clear: "it is impossible to conceive of beauty without propor-

tion."[17] He gave elaborate instructions for composing the perfect face—three noses long and two noses wide. Subtle proportions based on this division into three regulate the size and position of all the features; the distance between the eyes must, for example, be one-half of one-third the length of the face. The general idea is that perfect beauty is invariable symmetry, a harmony of just proportion. Obviously no novelist describes a heroine by saying that her nose is exactly one third the length of her face or that the distance from her upper lip to her nostril is a certain fraction of the distance from her nostril to her chin (Winckelmann, pp. 377-378). But the words "Grecian," "perfect," and "regular," so often used in the description of the Victorian heroine's face, suggest conformity to this standard.

When novelists begin to create irregularly featured heroines who deviate from the standard of beauty, what happens to the female characters behind the faces? The characters are allowed imperfection, too. The face remains an accurate mirror of the character, for the heroine of irregular features is capable of irregular conduct.[18] She can act, make mistakes, learn from them, and grow, exercising a privilege usually only the hero's. Twentieth-century readers will perhaps evaluate the active and erring heroines of the mid-Victorian novel more positively than nineteenth-century readers did, but unquestionably the appearance of the heroine of irregular features adds to the evidence that the depiction of womanly character was changing in the mid-nineteenth-century novel.[19]

Anthony Trollope often described his heroines fully, and many of them are not perfect. Alice Vavasor from *Can You Forgive Her?* (1865) is typical:

> In person she was tall and well made, rather large in her neck and shoulders, as were all the Vavasors, but by no means fat. Her hair was brown, but very dark, and she wore it rather lower upon her forehead than is customary at the present day. Her eyes, too, were dark, though they were not black, and her complexion, though not quite that of a brunette, was far away from being fair. Her nose was somewhat broad, and retroussée too, but to my thinking it was a charming nose, full of character, and giving to her face at times a look of pleasant humour, which it would otherwise have lacked. Her mouth was large, and full of character, and her chin oval, dimpled, and finely chiselled. . . .[20]

Two of Alice's features in this inventory are out of proportion, and the phrase "full of character" follows the description of her nose and mouth as though these imperfect features tell us something important about the character behind them. That is of course just what they do.

Alton Locke's Lilian turns out to be no worthy object for the hero's love. She is incapable of appreciating his fine mind and overlooking his poverty, unattractiveness, and low birth; she makes a merely satisfactory marriage for position. Trollope's Alice Vavasor is temporarily mistaken about the worth of John Grey, a sign of her deeper uncertainty about what her function in life should be, for she fears a retired domestic life and longs to be near the centers of political activity. When she can accept John Grey, she is rewarded with the fulfillment of her desires. Rachel Curtis, the clever woman of Charlotte Yonge's novel, makes essentially the same mistake as Alice; she does not think the domestic, maternal sphere is for her. But her mistake has far more serious consequences (as do most mistakes in Yonge's novels). Rachel patronizes a clergyman of Low-Church sympathies who opens a school for the daughters of distressed lacemakers. The school is shamefully run, and one of the girls dies of scarlet fever. When Rachel renounces her intellectual pretensions, she too is rewarded with marriage and maternity. These confused heroines with their irregular features should be compared with lovely ones like Eleanor Bold, Lucy Feverel, or Agnes Wickfield, who know a woman's proper place and duty.

A good sign that a convention is taking hold is its misuse by a novelist whose work is as much imitation as creation. An example of such an imperfect reflex of the heroine of irregular features occurs in the description of the heroine of *Queen Mab* (1863) by Julia Kavanagh:

> Mab was neither beautiful nor pretty, she was that something beyond both, for which there is no name. She had golden hair and a radiant face. Brightness was her prevailing aspect. Life, light, and joy played and moved around her. Few could see her and not smile with pleasurable emotion. She had fine grey eyes, and a pure complexion, but her features, though not unpleasing, were irregular . . .[21]

This description is almost as vague and heightened as the one from *Thaddeus of Warsaw,* but the author has thrown in with the account of the heroine's effect the gratuitous assertion that she is not pretty and has irregular features. The word "irregular" is a knell of doom. The author never reveals exactly which features of Mab's face are out of proportion, but after such a description a contemporary reader would expect the heroine to be guilty of some irregular conduct. That expectation is fulfilled, for Mab commits the impropriety of revealing a repressed love and entering briefly into a second engagement while the old love is off in Australia. After years of good deeds and self-sacrifice, Mab lives this error down, and she and the hero are finally reunited in advanced middle age. The heroines of Julia Kavanagh's *Dora* (1868) and *Sybil's Second Love* (1867) are not described as irregularly featured, but then these two, who suffer the impediments of money problems and wicked people, never do anything wrong themselves.

How did the novel audience react to the loss of the perfectly beautiful heroine? The answer is that in a way they did not really lose her. For even though they have freckles instead of snow-white skin, turned-up instead of delicate noses, low brows or broad chins, the irregular heroines are still beautiful. In fact the author of an article on "Women's Faces" in *Once a Week* declared a new aesthetic of the imperfect, conveniently in time to justify these new heroines:

> Men no longer sigh for the perfectly beautiful woman. Regularity of the most faultless kind in physical form is held to be of lesser account than those variations which are supposed, rightly or wrongly, to indicate special emotional or intellectual characteristics [a reference to physiognomy]. When a man thinks over the beautiful women whom he knows—that is to say, the women whose profile is correct, whose head and figure are admirably in accordance with artistic types—does he not invariably find that the handsomest women are also the dullest? Does he not in trying to decide which is really the most beautiful woman of his acquaintance, choose out her whose irregularities of feature are lost in the movement and light of the face, in the glow and colour of the eyes, in preference to the woman of cold and formal accuracy of outline?[22]

Thus the imperfections of the irregular heroine do not detract from her overall beauty just as her mistakes in conduct do not completely compromise her moral character. Rachel, Alice, and Mab are all attractive women who come to happy conclusions.

I

A gradual change in the permissible depiction of womanly character does not, however, necessarily entail a change in descriptive conventions. The question of why the change came about has yet to be satisfactorily answered. One possible answer depends on how the novel—or any other mass-entertainment form, for that matter—evolves. From 1830 to 1860 the novel-reading habit burgeoned, and the number of novels published increased to keep pace with the habit. Author after author created the mandatory heroine while searching for at least slightly new devices to capture attention in a competitive market. Thus the detailed description of heroines may have had selective advantage in the marketplace.

To say that something changes because it "evolves," however, looks suspiciously like begging the question. Fortunately another explanation can be added to the "evolutionary" model, one which also gives a reason for the choice of certain descriptive tags. From 1840 to 1870, over the same period of time that descriptive conventions changed, the Victorian reading public rediscovered physiognomy. Any claim that interest in physiognomy was the sole cause of the change in the description of heroines would be an exaggeration, but physiognomy was an important contributing factor.

Physiognomy is an ancient science. The first treatise on it, *De Physiognoma,* is attributed to Aristotle, and this work begins by examining earlier, unrecorded systems.

De Physiognoma is in part based on the rather circular process of reading human character in animal analogies which are themselves projections of human character. (To have a low forehead, for example, is to be like a swine, because a swine has a low forehead—though whatever is swinish about a swine is certainly in the eye of the human beholder.) In the middle ages physiognomy was one of the arts of divination; in fact until 1824 fortunetelling by physiognomy was punishable as vagrancy.[23] In the sixteenth century a number of authors took up the subject seriously again, though in the seventeenth and early eighteenth centuries it languished once more.[24]

An eighteenth-century Swiss pastor, Johann Kaspar Lavater, gave physiognomy its greatest impetus. Lavater was a friend of Goethe and the author of many pious works, both literary and practical. But the passion of his life was physiognomy. Though he had no knowledge of physiology, Lavater saw the possibility of transforming physiognomy into an exact science if only the correspondences between parts of the body, especially features of the face, and traits of personality could be systematized. Between 1775 and 1778, Lavater published four volumes of his first thoughts, bolstered by copious corroborating extracts, in *Physiognomische Fragmente zur Beförderung der Menschenkenntnis und Menschenliebe.*

Lavater's essays on physiognomy were well known on the continent and in England in the late eighteenth and early nineteenth centuries. The English novelist and dramatist Thomas Holcroft produced a translation that was in print, both in a full and an abridged version, from the 1790s through the 1860s. But even though Lavater's theories were known, physiognomy as a nascent science received less attention in the early nineteenth century than its closely allied rival phrenology, the reading of character from the shape and bumps of the skull. Lavater had emphasized the importance of the skull, but he had never claimed its sufficiency as an index of character.

Although physiognomy and phrenology were respectable studies in the late eighteenth and early nineteenth century, they had no immediate impact on the descriptive techniques of contemporary novelists. Holcroft translated Lavater, yet with a single, obviously experimental exception, *The Memoris of Bryan Perdue* (1805) he did not give physiognomical descriptions of his characters. And although physiognomy as character reading is discussed in Henry Brooke's *A Fool of Quality* (1776-80) and acknowledged in Henry Mackenzie's *The Man of Feeling* (1771), these references are not accompanied by any detailed description of faces. Perhaps an idea like that of the connection between certain physical features and personality traits must grow for decades and be very familiar indeed before it can become part of the conventional repertoire of the popular novelist.

Phrenology was better known than physiognomy early in the nineteenth century; more books were written about it, a journal was devoted to it, and polemics and public interest were aroused over it, especially in the United States, where it created far more of a sensation than it ever did in England.[25] But phrenology could not lend itself to the novelist's uses as easily as physiognomy. Aside from an occasional mention of a "bump of ideality," or the like, a detailed description of cranial contours would seem ludicrously out of place in a novel, and a visit to a phrenologist too artificial a scene to repeat often. But the face is open to all observers.

Although the popular mind may have compounded phrenology and physiognomy, apologists of the 1860s wished to disentangle the two. Citing the anatomical fact that the shape of the skull does not correspond to the underlying contours of the brain, the author of the *Dublin University Magazine* article "Phases of Physiognomy" declared emphatically, "Phrenology must therefore be acknowledged to be an illusory science."[26] And Eneas Sweetland Dallas wrote in a two-part article on physiognomy in the *Cornhill* in 1864, "at last phrenology is confessed to be a failure and a mock science. . . . The phrenological structure has fallen into ruin, and we now ask ourselves whether it be not possible to rear a more stable fabric on a broader foundation."[27]

Lavater knew that his own work on physiognomy was incomplete; he hoped that careful workers would come after him to perfect and refine his theories, and they did. Even during the decades of physiognomy's eclipse by phrenology many French and English works on physiognomy appeared.[28] Although several independent systems flourished, they all shared the same methodology. Some association or analogy linked the feature to a quality—the forehead to intellect, the mouth to taste, the chin to amativeness, and so on. Perfection of an individual feature was a sign of perfection in the quality, and any exaggeration of size or deformity of shape indicated a corresponding aberration in the character trait.

One of the first English writers to take up Lavater's challenge seriously was Alexander Walker, at one time a lecturer on anatomy and physiology at Edinburgh, who published his *Physiognomy founded on Physiology* in 1834. Walker's system is certainly more precise and detailed than Lavater's. Furthermore, he attempts to explain why a particular feature indicates a certain trait. He reasons, for example, that since the lips are sensitive to touch and associated with the tongue, they are indicators of taste and the "passions which are dependent upon it."[29] Narrow lips indicate less taste or desire, thick lips more. Similarly, he explains that the Greek nose is the highest form possible because it gives easiest access for the nerves from the nose to the brain. An even more precise and indeed ludicrously detailed system of physiognomy was formulated by an American physician, Dr. James W. Redfield, whose *Outline of a New System of Physiognomy* appeared in 1849. Redfield found 184 different faculties indicated in the face. According to his minute analysis, the faculties of discovery, combination, and analysis are encoded for in the septum of the nose alone. Needless to say, Redfield offers no support for his whimsical analogies; his system is interesting as an example of the kind of extreme systematization physiognomy could lead to.

No doubt the early, infrequent works on physiognomy, like Walker's, had few readers. But their influence was gradually extended by the journals until "physiognomy" became a catchword. In 1851, for example, the *Quarterly Review* printed a lengthy notice of three works, only one of which was unambiguously on physiognomy.[30] The term "physiognomy" was nevertheless used as the running title of the review, which, characteristically paying little attention to the works noticed, propounded its own synthesis of the meaning of the features. By books and reviews, and certainly by word of mouth, the general idea of physiognomy, of reading character in the face, had become thoroughly familiar and even respectable by mid-century.

We have an index of the change in two reviews of physiognomical works. An 1820 *Blackwood's* review of Taylor Cooke's *A Practical and Familiar View of the Science of Physiognomy* called it a defense of a "disputed but interesting science."[31] But by 1853 an *Athenaeum* reviewer, Edwin Lankester, could only complain of yet another physiognomical work, Thomas Woolnoth's *Facts and Faces; or, the Mutual Connexion between Linear and Mental Portraiture morally considered* (1853):

> Unfortunately for Mr. Woolnoth, this is not an age in which a dissertation on so very prosaic and well-worn a fact as the connexion between face and character is likely to be studied. Even the science of nasology which undertakes to register a man's mental peculiarities from the shape of his nose and palmology which does the same thing from the shape of the hand, are too positive, too conclusive, for our would-be philosophers.[32]

After its treatment in the prestigious reviews, physiognomy filtered into the polite shilling monthlies of the 1860s. The important critic E. S. Dallas wrote two essays ("On Physiognomy" and "The First Principle of Physiognomy") in William Makepeace Thackeray's *Cornhill* in 1861; *Temple Bar* published a little piece on "Noses: a Chapter out of Lavater" in 1862; the *Dublin University Magazine* had a very thorough review, "Phases of Physiognomy," in 1866; and *Once a Week* had an article on "Women's Faces" in 1868.[33] Thus the greatest concentration of articles on physiognomy came just in the years when we find novelists' descriptive conventions altered.

No doubt physiognomy appealed to the scientific spirit of the age by promising to bring a Linnaean orderliness to the moral types of humanity on the basis of careful measurement and analysis of signs in the features. That the physiological basis of physiognomy was undetermined posed no real obstacle to its scientific pretensions; in fact, unlike phrenology, it was all the more difficult to refute because of this vagueness. Even the new notion of natural selection, which seemed to promise a reason for every morphological detail in a living creature, may have rejuvenated the promise of physiognomy.

Perhaps a technological innovation also encouraged the renewed interest in physiognomy in the middle of the century. Lavater and other early physiognomists had to depend largely on paintings, etchings, and even statues in their attempts to systematize the correspondences between faces and characters. Such representations were not dependable for tracing small differences from feature to feature; the lips of one portrait could not be accurately compared with those of another. And even in a telling likeness some smoothing and conforming to an ideal had taken place. Mechanical drawing aids like the *camera lucida* or the physiontrace could produce portraits that were at least accurate in outline, but they did not help the user assess the contours of a face. By the 1850s, however, the Victorians believed they had a medium which never idealized a lip or eyebrow, never smoothed over an irregularity: photography. To Dallas in the *Cornhill* article "On Physiognomy," a new era was beginning:

> As the science of chemistry was nothing until a perfect balance was invented, and as the science of physiology was really unknown until the microscope was improved, so it may be that the faithful register of the camera supplying us with countless numbers of accurate observations, will now render that an actual science which has hitherto been only a possible one. We shall get a great variety of heads, and be able to classify them according to each separate feature, and according to each leading trait of character . . . These are facts which we have only now for the first time the means of getting in sufficient number.[34]

After the flurry of interest in the 1860s physiognomy shared the fate of phrenology in the last decades of the century; it degenerated from science to fad, finally reaching a popular handbook stage when works like *Noses and what they indicate* (1892) and *The ABC of Physiognomy: How to Tell Your Neighbour's Character* (1901) were published.

II

When novelists in mid-century described the shape of any of a heroine's features they gave their readers a clue to her character. The meanings conveyed were not as precise as those detailed in physiognomy books; they were simply the broad indications of an opening sketch. A large, mobile mouth was a sign of sensuality, delicate nostrils of sensitivity, a high forehead of intelligence, bright eyes of quick perceptions, and so on. The following is a short analysis of the predominant types of features and the meanings clustered around them.

The chin has two dimensions, width and projection, which combine to give it its characteristic shape. Physiognomists found two meanings in the chin: will or determination in the projection and amativeness, the desire to love, in the roundness. In his *New Physiognomy*, Samuel Wells catalogues five chin shapes, each with a corresponding faculty of love. The grammar of Wells's system is simply this: the wider the chin, the greater the ability to love. A broad square chin reveals a character susceptible to violent love and its attendant miseries, lovesickness and jealousy. The broad round chin is a sign of ardent love and great devotion to a married partner.[35]

When the heroine's chin is described at all, its breadth and roundness are often noticed. Thackeray's Beatrix Esmond has unsymmetrical features, and, in particular, "her mouth and chin, they said, were too large and full, and so they might be for a goddess in marble, but not for a woman whose eyes were fire, whose look was love . . ."[36] Margaret Hale of Mrs. Gaskell's *North and South* has a "round, massive, upturned chin."[37] The physiognomical message of these chins is that their owners are ardent and amorous. That is obviously true of Beatrix Esmond, who tends to wantonness, though it is at first surprising to think of Margaret Hale as amative. Margaret does, however, commit the great impropriety of throwing herself on the hero, Thornton, to protect him from the stones of his striking workmen. When he offers to marry her the next day she haughtily refuses him, throwing her head back, and therefore her chin forward, as a sign of will; but she is at war with one part of her nature, that expressed by the roundness of her chin. Obviously the careful details in such descriptions and scenes tell more than the twentieth-century reader often realizes.

Excessive will was not a desirable feminine attribute in the nineteenth century, and the strong chin which indicates it is a deviation from beauty. Miss Cains of Julia Kavanagh's *Sybil's Second Love* has a "square chin, which somewhat marred the beauty of her countenance, [and] gave it the meaning of strength and will associated with the development of that feature."[38] Miss Cains, however, is not really the heroine; she is the first love of the heroine's second love, whom she abandons for the heroine's wealthier father. Magdalen Vanstone of Wilkie Collins's *No Name* has a "chin too square and massive for her sex and age" but appropriate for the daring heroine who will marry a fool and pretend to be a housemaid for the sake of regaining her inheritance.[39]

Collins deviates from the norm in making so forceful a girl his heroine. Too much determination is not appropriate for a heroine, but then neither is too little, a fault which shows up in the chin. When Walter Hartright describes his beloved Laura Fairlie in Collins's *The Woman in White,* he lingers over her hair and is enthralled by her eyes, but he eventually admits that "the lower part of the face is too delicately refined away towards the chin to be in full and fair proportion with the upper part."[40] Several paragraphs of rapture later, Hartright admits to second impressions and second thoughts:

> At one time it seemed like something wanting in *her*; at another, like something wanting in myself, which hindered me from understanding her as I ought. The impression was always strongest, in the most contradictory manner, *when she looked at me* [italics mine]; or, in other words, when I was most conscious of the harmony and charm of her face, and yet, at the same time, most troubled by the sense of an incompleteness which it was impossible to discover. Something wanting, something wanting—and where it was, and what it was, I could not say.
>
> (I, 78)

Of course Hartright senses, though he cannot specifically recall, the resemblance between Laura and the woman in white. But the emphasis on a lack of something, coming after the description as it does, also reminds the reader who understands some physiognomy that what is missing is sufficient chin and therefore sufficient force of character. In the description of Laura Fairlie, Collins gently foreshadows the fate of his heroine, who becomes quite childlike and silly as the victim of the machinations of villains like Count Fosco and Sir Percival Glyde. What Laura lacks is found in her magnificently ugly half sister, Marian Halcombe, who has a "large, firm, masculine mouth and jaw" (I, 47) and enough decision and energy to crouch on a window ledge in the rain to overhear the villains plotting. Fortunate Walter Hartright does not have to forfeit character for beauty by the end of the novel. He marries Laura, but Marian promises to live with the happy couple for the rest of her life.

Of all the physiognomical meanings in the features, those of the mouth are the most familiar to a twentieth-century reader. Since the mouth is associated with taste and appetite, it is "the organ therefore of animal passion and propensity" (Walker, p. 247). When physiognomists simplified the incredible human variety found in the mouth in order to systematize, they considered two variable dimensions, width and thickness, as signs of two aspects of the "animal propensities." "The horizontal width of the lips indicates the permanence of these functions; their vertical extent, the intensity" (Walker, p. 247).

The perfect feminine mouth is the rosebud, "small" and "delicate" as it is so often described. The rosebud compresses passion into fastidiousness; it is the mouth of the flitting, infantine heroine, and this "rosy little mouth" appears more often in the incomplete descriptions of perfect heroines than in the inventories of irregular ones.

When the small, finely formed mouth disappears, so does perfect beauty, as the novelists themselves acknowledge. "Her mouth," says Trollope of Fanny Wyndham, "was large, too large for beauty, and therefore she was not a regular beauty."[41] Mrs. Gaskell is even more outspoken in her description of Margaret Hale:

> Sometimes people wondered that parents so handsome should have a daughter who was so far from regularly beautiful; not beautiful at all, was occasionally said. Her mouth was wide; no rosebud that could only open just enough to let out a "yes" and "no," and "an't please you sir." But the wide mouth was one soft curve of rich red lips. . . .
>
> (I, 20)

Quite a number of heroines in the 1860s have large mouths which bring a tinge of sensuality to their characterizations.[42] Large-mouthed Clara Amedroz from Trollope's *The Belton Estate* (1866), for example, is kissed in an uncommonly passionate way. Trollope seems to be anticipating the shocking scenes and heroines of Rhoda Broughton's early novels. The heroine of her *Cometh Up as a Flower* (1867) has a wide mouth, and Kate Chester of *Not Wisely but Too Well* (1867) has a mouth which is "wide, full-lipped, smiling . . . with an immensity of latent, undeveloped passion in some of the curves it fell into."[43] Kate Chester was perhaps as far as taste could go at the time. When Geraldine Jewsbury reviewed *Not Wisely* for the *Athenaeum* pretending it was by the author of *Guy Livingstone,* she complained about its disgusting immodesty.[44] But it sold.

The meaning of thin lips is obvious—restraint and lack of feeling, as in *Alton Locke*'s Lilian. Far more interesting are the lips which do not match because one is shorter or thinner than the other. The more systematic physiognomists find separate traits in the separate lips. They reason that since the upper lip moves less than the lower, it indicates passive enjoyment. The lower lip on the hinged jaw moves more and therefore indicates active enjoyment, the determination to enjoy, even the desire for gratification and passion.

If both lips are very well developed, so that both are everted, the physiognomists all agree that voluptuousness is indicated. But a happy compromise is a mouth with one lip voluptuous and one a bit more restrained, like the girl in Sir John Suckling's poem whose bottom lip looks as though a bee had stung it. These uneven lips are best described in G. A. Lawrence's *Guy Livingstone.* The dark heroine's upper lip is "just defined by a pencilling of down, the lower one full and pouting—

[glistening] with the brilliant smoothness of a pomegranate flower where the dew is clinging."[45] Perhaps this uneven mouth is the most sensual of all, for following the physiognomical interpretation, it promises to give more enjoyment than it demands in return.

Lavater considered the nose the "foundation, or abutement, of the brain." He gave a careful description of the perfect nose from many points of view and claimed that such a nose was worth more than a kingdom.[46] The author of an article in *Temple Bar* on noses in 1862 was as extravagant in his claims: "And if we are to look in the face for the strongest, highest, and most perfect expression of character, even in the face of a beast, there must be some feature of the face on which it is preeminently written. That feature, to keep the reader in suspense no longer, is The Nose!"[47] The feature so lauded received the special attention of nineteenth-century physiognomists. One book was written solely about the nose: *Nasology; or, Hints towards a Classification of Noses.*[48] By George Jabet under the pseudonym Eden Warwick, it first appeared in 1848 and was republished as *Notes on Noses* in 1852 and again in the 1860s.

Jabet identified six prominent nose types which he admitted were "well known" and "long established" (Warwick, pp. 9-11). The Roman or acquiline nose was a sign of energy and firmness; the Greek or straight nose indicated a refined character, one who preferred to act indirectly; and the hawk nose was a sign of shrewdness or insight. These nose types were identified in profile, but one type was seen straight on: the cogitative or wide-nostrilled nose. Always combined with some characteristic profile, the cogitative nose indicated strong powers of thought. Two more nose types, the snub and the celestial or turned-up, indicated weakness. These are the meanings for men; those for women are somewhat different.

The nose is not often featured in heroine description. Even when we begin to get descriptive details in Benjamin Disraeli or E. R. Bulwer Lytton, the nose is usually passed over for the eyes or the mouth, and its symmetry is taken for granted amid the "regular and delicate lineaments" or the "finely molded features." Jabet's chapter on "Feminine Noses" contains the pre-Freudian explanation of this absence of female noses:

> The energies and tastes of women are generally less intense than those of men; hence their characters appear less developed and exhibit greater uniformity. That their passions are stronger is undeniable, but these do not constitute character, nor are exhibited in the Nose. Their indexes [sic] are the eyes and mouth.
>
> (Warwick, p. 108)

In short, we might amend Alexander Pope's line, quoted by Jabet, "Most women have no characters at all," into "Most heroines have no noses at all." Even when feminine description breaks into the novel, the eyes and mouth receive more attention as indicators of feminine nature. Thus when the heroine's nose is described the reader is being told something very important.

Valeria Macallan, the heroine of Wilkie Collins's *The Law and the Lady,* looks in a mirror in the beginning of that novel and describes her own appearance objectively. "Her nose just inclines toward the acquiline bend, and is considered a little too large by persons difficult to please in the matter of noses."[49] The acquiline nose is a sign of energy and determination for men and women and is therefore as clear an indication of Valeria's character as her Roman name. Though she is repeatedly warned not to act, Valeria persisits in uncovering her husband's past. He has been accused of murdering his first wife, and Valeria finds the evidence to prove him innocent and overturn the disgraceful Scottish verdict of "Not Proven."

Another nose which merits descriptive attention is the *nez retroussé.* It is the feminine version of the celestial nose, an unfortunate shape for a man's nose but an admired one for a woman's. The turned-up nose was proper for the *soubrette,* the vivacious lady's maid of the stage ("Noses: A Chapter out of Lavater," p. 525). It is not so short as a snub or pug nose; no heroine could ever have a pug nose.[50] The *nez retroussé* is the nose of the flawed heroines Rachel Curtis, Alice Vavasor, and Gwendolen Harleth. While they are neither vivacious nor amusing, they are certainly wayward and unpredictable. They all follow their inclinations, or their noses, into misfortune: Rachel into her school, Alice into a second engagement with her cousin George, and Gwendolen into gambling and marriage with Grandcourt. Fortunately, their other features save them.

The physiognomists went as high as the forehead, and the phrenologists crept down over the skull to it. They may have disputed some of the finer meanings, but both agreed that the forehead was that part of the face, or of the cranium, which indicated the faculties of intelligence. When physiognomists talked about the forehead, they took three variables into account: height, width, and arch—that is, how much or at what angle the forehead sloped backward. Physiognomists measured the slope of the forehead and, at the same time, they thought, the capacity of the cranium, by the so-called facial line or angle of Camper. The facial angle was calculated by drawing a straight line from under the nose to under the ear (this can only be done precisely on a skull). From this base line, an oblique line was raised touching the sockets of the front teeth and the most prominent part of the forehead. The more acute the angle formed between the base and raised lines, the more sloped the forehead. To obtain classical grandeur, the facial angle had to be ninety degrees, and in some classical statues the angle was actually found to exceed ninety degrees.

Since the physiognomists always reasoned that the size of a feature was an indication of the degree of the characteristic it represented, the higher and broader the forehead, the more intelligent the owner. Heroes are often admired for their lofty foreheads, but heroines are not. The physiognomists' theories and the novelists' descriptions tell us some of the current notions about women's intellect, or rather lack of it, for one and all the physiognomists prefer low foreheads and little intellect in women. Taylor Cooke in *A Practical and Familiar View of the Science of Physiognomy* says that a high straight forehead indicates profundity in a man, but "in women, cannot indicate a quality they neither have nor need."[51] Alexander Walker is even more outspoken in his book on female beauty. Any development of the intellectual system must be, he feels, at the expense of the vital or procreative system and therefore "less proper to women."[52] Walker, a physiologist at Edinburgh, literally believed that the female brain was soft, that its tissue was looser and more mucoid than the brain tissue of men (Walker, *Beauty,* p. 237).

Novelists who include descriptive details about the forehead follow the high-low code faithfully. Take again G. A. Lawrence's very popular *Guy Livingstone* (1857), a novel to which *The Mill on the Floss* is oddly in debt. The hero is posed between two women, one dark and sensual and the other light and spiritual. The dark one, Flora, whom the narrator calls "Lust of the Eye incarnate," has a "forehead rather low" (p. 65); the high-souled, poetic one has a "forehead too high" (p. 178). The hero is to marry the high forehead, but she discovers him kissing the low forehead (not on the forehead) and goes off to die of consumption. As Alexander Walker could have warned the hero, no woman with too high a forehead could have the physical stamina to make a suitable wife.

Since the forehead has more than one dimension, a novelist who wants to abandon height for fashion and yet not diminish the sign of intellect can extend the forehead laterally and call it "broad." The witty Diana Warwick, in George Meredith's *Diana of the Crossways* (1885) has a broad forehead. So does Mrs. Eiloart's Grace Roslyn of *From Thistles—Grapes?* (1871), a "girl of genius" who spends a great deal of time reading and conversing with learned old men until she drowns in a pool running away from, as she thinks, a would-be rapist.

To say that width is as much an indication of intellect as height is to oversimplify a bit. Actually the physiognomists found two separate meanings in the two dimensions of the forehead. As Alexander Walker put it in his *Physiognomy founded on Physiology,* "on the lenght of the cerebral organs depends the intensity of their function, and on the breadth of these organs the permanence of their function" (Walker, p. 41). There is then a moral difference between the two dimensions. A forehead which is high without being broad indicates a quick, sharp mind, but one without the nobler quality of wisdom. Mdlle. Reuter in *The Professor,* Madame Beck in *Villette* (two versions of the same shrewd but deceptive maîtresse), and Lady Mason, the forger from Trollope's *Orley Farm,* have the high, narrow foreheads of perspicacity without the breadth of moral knowledge.

III

The novelists themselves give direct evidence of the influence of physiognomy. Trollope provided a facial inventory of the heroine of his second novel, *The Kellys and the O'Kellys.* This heroine, Fanny Wyndham, looks remarkably like Alice Vavasor—not a surprising resemblance, since she commits the same error of temporarily breaking an engagement with the right man. The description of Fanny actually seems a bit too meaningful and a bit too full for an 1847 novel—until one of the characters looks in Fanny's face and says, "I'm sure you must have ambition. I have studied Lavater well enough to know that such a head and face as yours never belonged to a mind that could satisfy itself with worsted-work" (p. 315). In Trollope's second novel, then, we find the authority for his very precise use of descriptive detail to reveal character. As he wrote after his description of Hetty Carbury in *The Way We Live Now* (1875), "her face was a true index of her character."[53]

It would be difficult to overestimate the importance of reading character in faces in the novels of Charlotte Brontë. In her earliest novel, *The Professor* (first published in 1857), the hero-narrator, William Crimsworth, peers through his shortsighted eyes at the faces of everyone he meets and gives pages of character analyses based on feature reading. As a teacher in Belgium, he passes very severe judgments on the continental pupils in his English class, whose faces, he says, convict them of "precocious impurity" and "mental depravity." "Suspicion," he says of one, "sullen ill-temper were on her forehead, vicious propensities in her eye, envy and panther-like deceit about her mouth."[54] One of the four other teachers in the school flits at first on the periphery of his attention, "but of her I never had more than a passing glimpse . . . consequently I had no opportunity of studying her character" (I, 205). When he finally does study the face and therefore the nature of Frances Henry, he finds at last an "ample forehead" he can admire and love.

In the famous scene of face reading in *Jane Eyre* (1847), Rochester, disguised as an old gypsy, rejects Jane's palm in favor of reading her character physiognomically. "Ah now," says Jane, "you are coming to reality."[55] And Rochester's reading of Jane Eyre's character and destiny is accurate. The eye and mouth are favorable, but the forehead says, "Reason sits firm . . ." (II, 101).

M. Paul is the physiognomist in *Villette.* Madame Beck consults him on the evening of Lucy's chance arrival at the pensionnat: "'I want your opinion. We know your skill in physiognomy; use it now. Read that countenance.'"[56] M. Paul achieves no overwhelming feat of interpretation; he finds both good and bad in Lucy's face, and yet recommends that his cousin engage her. But much later his continued scrutiny of Lucy yields a meaning. In the days of their growing affection for one another he tells her of the physiognomical basis of the sympathy between them:

> I was conscious of rapport between you and myself. You are patient, and I am choleric; you are quiet and pale, and I am tanned and fiery; you are a strict Protestant, and I am a sort of lay Jesuit: but we are alike—there is affinity between us. Do you see it mademoiselle? Do you observe that your forehead is shaped like mine—that your eyes are cut like mine? Do you hear that you have some of my tones of voice? Do you know that you have many of my looks?
>
> (III, 90)

Like Jane Eyre and William Crimsworth, Lucy Snowe is a narrator who judges character behind faces. She sees that Madame Beck's forehead is "high, but narrow," expressing "capacity and some benevolence, but no expanse," (I, 135) and that Zélie de St. Pierre, the Parisian teacher, is a "cold, callous epicure" with "lips like a thread" and a "large, prominent chin" (I, 247). Even of Miss Marchmont's heir, who passes through the novel in only a few lines, the telltale signs of miserliness are noted: a "pinched nose and narrow temples" (I, 77). Readers are sometimes repelled by the harsh, quick judgments that Lucy Snowe, Jane Eyre, and William Crimsworth make of the characters they watch from quiet corners. These judgments, however, are not made from natural animus or excessive self-assurance, but from a conviction of the fixed principles of correspondence between the face and character.

George Eliot's attack on the validity of physiognomy in *Adam Bede* (1859) is more evidence of the current connection between face reading and character description. Though an antiphysiognomy theme runs through the authorial commentary in the novel, the central physiognomical problem in *Adam Bede* is of course Hetty, whose loveliness masks a lack of feeling as a peach hides a stone.[57] In the long chapter describing Hetty primping in her bedroom before her shilling glass, George Eliot imagines the feelings of the envied man who marries a sweet bride like Hetty: "Every man under such circumstances is conscious of being a great physiognomist. . . . Nature has written out his bride's character for him in those exquisite lines of cheek and lip and chin. . . . How she will dote on her children!" (I, 283-284). Given that Hetty murders her child, the irony is very heavy here. George Eliot's common sense tells her that any invariable correspondence between face and character is implausible, but she cannot quite give it up. So when the narrator "places" the physiognomical misinterpretation of Hetty in the reader's world, she leaves a little escape hatch, the same one that many of the more skeptical writers on physiognomy left: perhaps not enough is known yet.

> After all, I believe the wisest of us must be beguiled in this way sometimes, and must think both better and worse of people than they deserve. Nature has her language, and she is not unveracious; but we don't know all the intricacies of her syntax just yet, and in a hasty reading we may happen to extract the very opposite of her real meaning. Long dark eyelashes, now: what can be more exquisite? I find it impossible not to expect some depth of soul behind a deep grey eye with a long dark eyelash, in spite of an experience which has shown me that they may go along with deceit, peculation, and stupidity. But if, in the reaction of disgust, I have betaken myself to a fishy eye, there has been a surprising similarity of result. One begins to suspect at length that there is no direct correlation between eyelashes and morals; or else, that the eyelashes express the disposition of the fair one's grandmother, which is on the whole less important to us.
>
> (I, 286)

George Eliot's questioning of physiognomy in *Adam Bede* may have been a response to one of its proponents who was well known to her. In 1854 Herbert Spencer wrote two articles on "Personal Beauty" in the *Leader.*[58] A true physiognomist who held to the Greek ideal of beauty as well, Spencer concluded that "mental and facial perfection are fundamentally connected" ("Haythorne Papers, No. IX," p. 452). Surely it is not too farfetched to say that when George Eliot conjectured "there is no connection between morals and eyelashes" she was answering him.

Altogether, George Eliot's use of descriptive details to aid characterization is just as wavering as her opinion of phrenology and physiognomy.[59] She uses physiognomical detail in the portraits of Dinah Morris, Romola, and Gwendolen Harleth; for each of these three, specific features are described, though complete inventories are lacking. But she gives little information about Dorothea Brooke, Maggie Tulliver, or Esther Lyon. That scarcity is probably surprising, for most readers of *Middlemarch* and *The Mill on the Floss* have images of Dorothea and Maggie in their memories. But those images can only be accurate about coloring. There is, for example, much testimony about Dorothea's beauty, but aside from red lips, dark hair, and hazel eyes, no precise description, perhaps because that description would have told too much. When George Eliot does give a trait, however, whether for a heroine or any other character, it has accurate physiognomical significance.

Throughout the nineteenth century, physiognomy was "about to be" made into an exact science. It never was. While all the efforts of physiognomical speculators went into ever more accurate observations and measurements of the face, the other half of the physiognomical equation, the character traits that were supposedly being indicated, remained hopelessly inaccessible to systematization. But though nature's grammar of the human face may be unreadable, the descriptive grammar of the mid-Victorian novelists is another thing entirely, and with the help of the physiognomists it can be deciphered.

Notes

1. Sir Walter Scott, *Old Mortality,* in *Tales of My Landlord, Collected and Arranged by Jedediah Cleishbothom,* 4 vols. (Edinburgh: John Murray, 1816), I, 95.

2. Charlotte Mary Yonge, *The Clever Woman of the Family,* 2 vols. (London: Macmillan & Co., 1865), I, 2-3.

3. Alexander Welsh, "The Allegory of Truth in English Fiction," *Victorian Studies,* 9 (1965), 8.

4. Jane Porter, *Thaddeus of Warsaw,* 4 vols. (London: George Virtue, 1845), I, 280.

5. Susan Ferrier, *Destiny; or, the Chief's Daughter,* 3 vols. (London: Whittaker & Co., 1831), I, 296.

6. Maria Edgeworth, *Belinda,* 3 vols. (London: J. Johnson, 1801). See, for example: I, 2, 244; II, 152.

7. Sir Walter Scott, *Waverly; or, 'Tis Sixty Years Since,* 3 vols. (Edinburgh: James Ballantyne and Co., 1814), I, 126, 317.

8. Sir Walter Scott, *The Bride of Lammermoor* in *Tales of My Landlord, Collected and Arranged by Jedediah Cleishbotham,* (Edinburgh: Constable, 1819), I, 69.

9. Sir Walter Scott, *Rob Roy,* 3d ed., 3 vols. (Edinburgh: Constable, 1818), I, 95.

10. William Dean Howells, *Heroines of Fiction,* 2 vols. (London and New York: Harper Bros., 1901).

11. Henry Fielding and Tobias Smollett did describe their heroines in greater detail, but the descriptions do not match what character their women show. Samuel Richardson's practice of not describing his heroines' faces seems to have had greater influence on the late eighteenth- and early nineteenth-century novel.

12. Catherine Morland, Howell's example of particularity, does have at ten "a thin, awkward figure, a sallow skin without colour, dark lank hair, and strong features"; at fifteen "her features [are] softened by plumpness and colour, her eyes [have] gained more animation, and her figure more consequence" (Jane Austen, *Northanger Abbey and*

Persuasion, 4 vols. [London: John Murray, 1818], I, 2, 6). And at seventeen, just before she goes to Bath, she is "pleasing, and, when in good looks, pretty" (p. 12). The reader is given nothing very tangible in this progression; in fact the closer Catherine comes to heroine age the vaguer the description. Emma would have been a better example for Howells; in her dark hair, hazel eyes, and lovely features we have the limits of Jane Austen's particularity.

13. [Leigh Hunt], ["Criticism on Female Beauty"] *New Monthly Magazine and Literary Journal,* 14, pt. 2 (1825), 72.

14. Charles Kingsley, *Alton Locke, Tailor and Poet: An Autobiography,* 2 vols. (London: Chapman and Hall, 1850), I, 101.

15. Walter Bagehot, "The Waverley Novels," *Literary Studies,* ed. Richard Holt Hutton, 2 vols. (London: Longmans, Green & Co., 1910), II, 107-108. This essay first appeared in the *National Review* in October 1858.

16. Charles Dickens, *Bleak House* (London: Bradbury & Evans, 1852-53), p. 422.

17. John [Johann] Winckelmann, *The History of Ancient Art,* trans. G. Henry Lodge, 2 vols. (Boston: James R. Osgood & Co., 1880), I, 371. Winckelmann's *Reflections on the Painting and Sculpture of the Greeks* was translated by J. H. Fuseli in 1765. Lodge's translation of the *History* first appeared in 1849 and was reprinted in 1856, 1871, 1872, and 1880.

18. Both Anthony Trollope and George Meredith explicitly connect perfection of the features and a heroic cast of character, and likewise imperfection of appearance and behavior. See *The Eustace Diamonds* (1873), and *Diana of the Crossways* (1885). Meredith specifically speaks of the "featureless" heroine of romance and the heroine of reality who is a mixture of good and bad with "features to some excess." (George Meredith, *Diana of the Crossways* [London: Chapman & Hall, 1885], III, 134-135).

19. Other scholars have of course marked this change. Patricia Thomson (*The Victorian Heroine: A Changing Ideal, 1837-1873* [London: Oxford University Press, 1956]), while carefully resisting overgeneralization, nevertheless finds that heroines show certain "advanced qualities" at the end of her period, among them "physical well-being rather than actual beauty" (p. 167). And Elaine Showalter (*A Literature of Their Own* [Princeton, New Jersey: Princeton University Press, 1977]) traces a change in feminine characterization to the women sensation novelists: "Readers were introduced to a new kind of heroine, one who could put her hostility toward men into violent action" (p. 160).

20. Anthony Trollope, *Can You Forgive Her?,* 2 vols. (London: Chapman and Hall, 1864), I, 6.

21. Julia Kavanagh, *Queen Mab: A Novels,* 3 vols. (London: Hurst & Blackett, 1864), I, 238.

22. "Women's Faces," *Once a Week,* 26 December 1868, p. 531. The writer here is simply rediscovering the aesthetic principle fundamentally opposed to the classical tradition of perfect proportion. Sir Francis Bacon put this principle forward in his "Essay on Beauty": "There is no Excellent Beauty that hath not some strangeness in the proportion."

23. No doubt this law remained on the books as a convenient pretext to move the gypsies along; we ought to be reminded of Rochester as gypsy crone in *Jane Eyre,* reading character in the face and liable to the magistrates' action. Perhaps this residual association of physiognomy with the disreputable explains in part the lag between Johann Kaspar Lavater's work and the recognition of physiognomy as a respectable study in the mid-nineteenth century.

24. The classical works on physiognomy were rediscovered and printed in the sixteenth century and the study carried on in a number of new works, the most important of which was Giambattista della Porta's *De Humana Physiognoma* (1584). An English adaptation of some of the Italian works on physiognomy, Thomas Hill's *The Contemplation of Mankynde, containing a singular Discourse after the Art of Physiognomie,* appeared in 1571.

25. See John D. Davies, *Phrenology, Fad and Science: A Nineteenth-Century American Crusade* (New Haven, Connecticut: Yale University Press, 1955), p. 6.

26. "Phases of Physiognomy," *Dublin University Magazine,* 68 (October 1866), 472.

27. [E. S. Dallas], "On Physiognomy," *Cornhill Magazine,* 4 (October 1861), 476.

28. P. Camper's *Dissertation sur les Variètés Naturelles qui caracterisent la Physiognomie des Hommes* (1791); J. J. Sue's *Essai sur la Physiognomie des Corps Vivans* (1797); R. Brown's *An Essay on the Truth of Physiognomy, and its application to medicine* (1807); P. J. Blanchen's *Essai sur la Physiognomie* (1815); E. Walmsley's *Physiognomical Portraits* (1824); J. Varley's *A Treatise on Zodiacal Physiognomy* (1828); T. Thore's *Dictionnaire de Phrénologie et de Physiognomie* (1836); L. Bourdon's *La Physiognomie* (1830);

and N. J. Ottin's *Précis analytique et raisonne des principes de Lavater sur les signes physiognomoniques* (1834).

29. Alexander Walker, *Physiognomy founded on Physiology* (London: Smith, Elder & Co., 1834), pp. 246-247.

30. [Elizabeth Eastlake], "Physiognomy," *Quarterly Review,* 90 (December 1851), 62-91. The books reviewed were Eden Warwick's *Nasology* (1848), (truly a physiognomical work), G. Schadow's *Polycet, oder von den Massen des Menschen, u.s.w.* (1835), and Sir Charles Bell's *The Anatomy and Philosophy of Expression, as connected with the Fine Arts* (1847).

31. "On the Science of Physiognomy," *Blackwood's Magazine,* 6 (March 1820), 650-655.

32. [Edwin Lankester], "Our Library Table," *Athenaeum* (1853), p. 888. This review was put in the "Our Library Table" section as the *Athenaeum*'s way of disposing of the reviews of less important books. Since Thomas Woolnoth was engraver to the Queen, however, the book had to be more than simply listed. The reviewer, Edwin Lankester, was at the time lecturer in anatomy and physiology at Grosvenor Place School of Medicine; his assessment of physiognomy therefore has authority.

33. I cite in the text only those articles solely on physiognomy. Other related articles touch on the interpretation of character in the face: C. A. Collins's "On the Expression of the Eye," *Macmillan's,* 14 (September 1866), 357-363; H. Calderwood's "The Expression of Emotions on the Human Countenance," *International Review,* 6 (1878), 195-204; Daniel H. Tuke's "How the Feelings Affect the Hair," *Popular Science Monthly,* 2 (1872), 158-161; "On Beauty and Other Conditions of the Face," *London Magazine,* 7 (May 1823), 526-532 (an early article: the author declares himself not a physiognomist); Francis Gerry Fairfield's "Beautiful Women," *Appleton's Journal,* 16 (1876), 328-332; and "Good Looks," *Cornhill Magazine,* 14 (September 1866), 334-341.

34. See Dallas, "On Physiognomy," p. 475. The author of "Phases of Physiognomy" in the *Dublin University Magazine* makes the same optimistic forecast of aid from "the improvements of photographic apparatus and processes" (68 [October 1866], 480).

35. Samuel R. Wells, *New Physiognomy; or, Signs of Character, as manifested through Temperament and External Forms, and especially in 'The Human Face Divine'* (London: L. N. Fowler & Co., 1866), pp. 154-156.

36. William Makepeace Thackeray, *The History of Henry Esmond, Esq.,* 3 vols. (London: Smith, Elder & Co., 1852), II, 115-116.

37. Elizabeth Gaskell, *North and South,* 2 vols. (London: Chapman and Hall, 1855), I, 92.

38. Julia Kavanagh, *Sybil's Second Love,* 3 vols. (London: Hurst and Blackett, 1867), I, 188.

39. Wilkie Collins, *No Name,* 3 vols. (London: Sampson Low, Son & Co., 1863), I, 12-13.

40. Wilkie Collins, *The Woman in White,* 3 vols. (London: Sampson Low, Son & Co., 1860), I, 75-76.

41. Anthony Trollope, *The Kellys and the O'Kellys; or, Landlords and Tenants, a Tale of Irish Life,* (London: Chapman and Hall, 1867), p. 111.

42. See also Lucy Morris in *The Eustace Diamonds* (1873), Magdalen Vanstone in *No Name* (1863), Mrs. Hurtle in Anthony Trollope's *The Way We Live Now* (1875), and Car Eversfield in Elizabeth Grey's *Passages in the Life of a Fast Young Lady* (1862).

43. Rhoda Broughton, *Not Wisely but Too Well* (London: Richard Bentley and Son, 1879), p. 11.

44. [Geraldine Jewsbury], review of *Not Wisely but Too Well, Athenaeum* (1867), p. 569. Jewsbury knew the true author of the book because she had read it for Bentley in her capacity as publisher's reader.

45. G. A. Lawrence, *Guy Livingstone; or, 'Thorough'* (London: J. W. Parker & Son, 1857), p. 65.

46. John Casper [Johann Kaspar] Lavater, *Essays on Physiognomy; for the Promotion of the Knowledge and Love of Mankind,* trans. Thomas Holcroft, 2d ed., 3 vols. (London: C. Whittingham, 1804), III, 185-186.

47. "Noses, a Chapter out of Lavater," *Temple Bar,* 5 (July 1862), 523.

48. Eden Warwick [George Jabet], *Nasology; or, Hints towards a Classification of Noses* (London: Bentley, 1848).

49. Wilkie Collins, *The Law and the Lady* (New York: Harper & Brothers, 1893), p. 12.

50. Mrs. Oakes Smith, who wrote an article on this disgraceful nose in *Godey's Lady's Magazine,* 41 (August 1850), 101-102, said of the pug-nosed, "There is no dignity in such a face, and, of course, none in the character."

51. Taylor Cooke, quoted in "On the Science of Physiognomy," *Blackwood's Magazine,* 6 (March 1820), 654.

52. Alexander Walker, *Beauty: Illustrated by an Analysis and Classification of Beauty in Woman, with a Critical View of the Hypotheses of Hume, Hogarth, Burke, Knight, Alison, etc. and of The Hypotheses of Beauty in Sculpture and Painting, by Leonardo da Vinci, Winckelmann, Mangs, Bossi, etc.* (London: Henry G. Bohn, 1852), p. 235.

53. Anthony Trollope, *The Way We Live Now* (London: Chapman and Hall, 1875), p. 14.

54. Currer Bell [Charlotte Brontë], *The Professor: A Tale,* 2 vols. (London: Smith, Elder & Co., 1857), I, 197.

55. Currer Bell [Charlotte Brontë], *Jane Eyre: An Autobiography,* 3 vols. (London: Smith, Elder & Co., 1847), II, 94.

56. Currer Bell [Charlotte Brontë], *Villette,* 3 vols. (London: Smith, Elder & Co., 1853), I, 125.

57. George Eliot, *Adam Bede* (London: William Blackwood and Sons, 1859). The narrator defends a Dutch painting she admires in which a broad-faced bride dances "while elderly and middle-aged friends look on, with very irregular noses and lips. . . ." "But, bless us," she says, "things may be lovable that are not altogether handsome, I hope?" (II, 6). The narrator has known mothers who were never lovely and who yet received love letters, heroes "of middle stature and feeble beards" who find themselves content with a wife who waddles (II, 7), and poor singers of "splendid physiognomy" (II, 48). See also the description of Hetty's face as seeming to mean more than it actually does (II, 213-214).

58. Herbert Spencer, "The Haythorne Papers. No. VIII. Personal Beauty," *Leader,* 5 (15 April 1854), 356-357; and "The Haythorne Papers. No. IX. Personal Beauty, Part II," *Leader,* 5 (13 May 1854), 452.

59. George Eliot was introduced to phrenology by Caroline and Charles Bray and came to know one of its chief proponents, George Combe. See Gordon S. Haight, *George Eliot: A Biography* (Oxford: Oxford University Press, 1968), p. 51.

Graeme Tytler (essay date 1982)

SOURCE: Tytler, Graeme. "Physiognomical Awareness in the Nineteenth-Century European Novel." In *Physiognomy in the European Novel: Faces and Fortunes,* pp. 260-315. Princeton, N.J.: Princeton University Press, 1982.

[In the following essay, Tytler offers a detailed study of the history of physiognomy and its impact on nineteenth-century literature and culture, and on the novel in particular.]

Studies of physiognomy in the nineteenth-century European novel have tended to be prompted by the discovery of specific references to Lavater and Gall, physiognomy and phrenology, in contexts of literary portraiture.[1] Such references have also been thought a useful means not only of gauging the intensity and duration of the Lavaterian physiognomical climate but also of substantiating arguments put forward about the influence of these sciences on the novel. This would be hardly less true of a number of long-forgotten literary works, especially satires, farces, and extravaganzas, in which one or other science constitutes the main theme, and Lavater or Gall is occasionally portrayed as hero.[2] Moreover, those concerned with drawing parallels between Lavater's theories and say, the treatment of character description in the English novel down to the mid-nineteenth century might somewhat propitiate their readers in advance by pointing out, for instance, that a play about Lavater and his physiognomical skills was staged in London as late as 1867, and was even attended by Ruskin and Lewis Carroll.[3]

But whatever the uses or limitations of such historical material for purposes of persuasion, the literary critic is ultimately bound to have to consider what aesthetic value, if any, is to be attached to these extrinsic elements, or, at least, how far their presence in literature deserves his attention. That physiognomy and phrenology should have been thought admirable subject matter for comedies and melodramas scarcely needs to be elaborated here: both sciences were the cause of much fierce controversy and, inevitably, aroused tensions which, as playwrights have wisely shown, are often best released in the theater. Yet the very topicality of the subject matter that originally guaranteed the success of these comedies also doomed them to eventual oblivion; and however admirable still their dialogues or skillful their plots, such works now seem to possess greater interest for the historian than for the literary critic. The same is also true of a number of novels or short stories in which physiognomy and phrenology are of prime importance for the plot.[4] Topical references are, of course, prominent enough even in the best fiction of the period, which is a reminder of the extent to which some novelists, particularly the realists, regarded it as their function to be historians of contemporary manners: we need only think of Balzac, Stendhal, Dickens, and George Eliot. This historical function is nowhere more evident than in contexts of character description, where the merest mention of physiognomy or phrenology, whether in serious or in comic vein, sometimes gives the impression that the author is eager to assure his reader that he is up to date with the latest thinking, if not to suggest that both are participating in a familiar ritual.[5]

Although the presence of physiognomy and phrenology in the novel may point up the aesthetic shortcomings of the genre during that period, it would be mistaken to suppose that documentary elements necessarily vitiate a novel as a work of art, just as it would be to declare that the purest aesthetic treatment of an idea has no documentary interest at all. On the other hand, when it is a question of evaluating the uses of physiognomy and phrenology in the novel, certain distinctions can, and should, be made at the outset. Thus, there is a sense in which, by virtue of its having always been intrinsic to human observation in the novel, physiognomy may be rightly said—*pace* Lavater—to be ahistorical, whereas every reference to phrenology can only be properly understood in terms of the history of that science from Gall onward. Moreover, the fact that phrenology is usually subordinated to physiognomy in studies on literature portraiture, and that no such study has hitherto been made in the light of phrenology alone, is enough to suggest the limitations of the science as an object of literary criticism. Nevertheless, in view of its very close association with physiognomy, it would be fitting at this point to consider briefly the uses of phrenology in nineteenth-century literature and, more particularly, to estimate how far phrenology in the novel may be said to retain an aesthetic interest for the present-day reader.

First of all, there can be no question that phrenology had an important enough influence on nineteenth-century cultural life to have attracted the attention of scholars in several disciplines, much research on the science having been concerned so far with its relevance to anthropology, sociology, criminology, and political theory as well as the occult sciences.[6] Literary critics, too, have pointed to the different ways in which phrenology affected the language and thinking of poets and novelists such as Vigny, Marryat, Poe, Baudelaire, Whitman, Melville, Emerson, Hawthorne, and Mark Twain.[7] One critic has recently shown that three tenets of Romanticism—evolutionism, individualism, and perpetual striving—had their roots partly in phrenological theory.[8] This preoccupation with the influence of phrenology is conspicuous in studies on American writers, some of whom might be described as having been veritably smitten by the science. Indeed, it has been shown, for example, how much Whitman drew on phrenology for some of the central ideas in *Leaves of Grass*.[9] Phrenology also permeates Poe's writings, where his ambivalent attitude to the science is illustrated by the different narratorial stances he adopts. Thus, in a study of the author it has been suggested that, whereas Poe is utterly serious about phrenology in *The Murders of the Rue Morgue, The Fall of the House of Usher,* and *Ligeia,* he was just as ready to see its humorous side in sketches such as "The System of Dr. Tarr and Professor Fether," "Diddling Considered as One of the Exact Sciences," and "Some Words with an Enemy," the satire in each case being directed less at phrenology than the pretensions of phrenologists.[10]

References and allusions to phrenology are also evident in the European novel throughout the nineteenth century, and it is interesting to discover a fictional reference to Gall as late as 1898, in Svevo's admirable *Senilità*.[11] Something of the essence of the phrenological atmosphere has been caught in much of the minor fiction of the period—in Arnim's *Gräfin Dolores* (1810), Mary Russell Mitford's *Our Village* (1824-32), Willibald Alexis' *Ruhe ist die erste Bürgerpflicht* (1852), Meredith's *Ordeal of Richard Feverel* (1859), Henry Kingsley's *Recollections of Geoffrey Hamlyn* (1859), and Oliver Wendell Holmes' *Elsie Venner* (1861), to mention but a few. Phrenological correlations are, as stated earlier, common enough in literary portraits: in Dickens and Thackeray, for example, such correlations are always ironic; in Balzac, Charlotte Brontë, and George Sand, rarely so. But whatever their aesthetic function, there can be little doubt that most such references now seem curiously dated, all the more as the reader is conscious of phrenology's historical failure as a science. Perhaps this may explain why an essentially humorous treatment of phrenology, such as we see in, say, Peacock's *Headlong Hall* (1816) or in Oliver Wendell Holmes' delightful *Breakfast-Table* fictions (1858-72), still has a certain appeal. There is a similar appeal, too, in Dickens' and Flaubert's treatment of phrenology, even though the humor, which is always thematically integrated, is utterly satirical. Thus, Dickens implies that the cult of phrenology is quite as stupid as are many other Victorian cults he attacks in his novels. This is amply suggested in *Edwin Drood,* where a satirical thrust at phrenology occurs, appropriately enough, in the context of a dig at one of the author's pet aversions: philanthropy. Flaubert's debunking of phrenology, too, has a distinctly thematic function in that it exemplifies his distaste for the naive optimism underlying the inveterate tendency of his contemporaries to confuse metaphysics with science. We see this not only in *Bouvard et Pécuchet,* where the premises of phrenology and its educational uses are called into question, but also in *Madame Bovary,* in which Charles Bovary's medical incompetence is subtly underlined by three references to a phrenological skull in his possession.

Flaubert's skeptical attitude toward phrenology reminds us of his exasperation with the physiognomical obsessions of his era, as evident, for instance, in Homais' disquisition on temperaments and national types in *Madame Bovary* and, again, in the *Dictionnaire des idées reçues,* where, for example, *blondes* are defined as "plus chaudes que les brunes," [more hot-blooded than brunettes] and vice-versa; *embonpoint* as "signe de richesse et de fainéantise" [a sign of affluence and indolence]; *front* as "large et chauve, signe de génie et d'aplomb" [wide and bald, a sign of genius and poise]; and *visage* as "miroir de l'âme. Alors il y a des gens qui ont l'air bien laide." [the mirror of the soul. That means there are some very ugly people.] Flaubert was, of course, not the first to treat physiognomy banteringly any more than he was the only novelist of his time to do so. Indeed, the idea of the physiognomist as an eccentric or a fool lingered on in the novel well into the nineteenth century, colored as it was now and again by allusions to the controversies aroused by physiognomy in everyday life. There is a good example of this in *Der Grüne Heinrich* when the narrator compares a quarrel that has started among a group of intellectuals, who are railing at someone for his reactionary outlook, to a heated argument between "die doktrinärsten Physiognomisten."[12] Keller's dig here at the adherents of Lavater and his successors has the same ironic quality with which some of his contemporaries portray their fictional physiognomists. Two novelists who mention Lavater's name in their fiction, Bulwer Lytton and Champfleury, show up the comicality of physiognomical judgments in *Pelham* and *Les Bourgeois de Molinchart*, respectively, and Dickens, who, as we saw earlier, ridicules the typical Lavaterian disciple in *Our Mutual Friend*, pokes fun at the earnestness with which some of his minor characters, say, a landlord in *Little Dorrit* or Magwitch in *Great Expectations*, take their physiognomical skills.[13] Charlotte Brontë, too, has humorous episodes about physiognomical readings both in *Jane Eyre*, as when Rochester, disguised as a gypsy fortuneteller, reads the heroine's destiny in her face, and in *Villette*, as when Lucy Snowe, having just arrived at Madame Beck's *pension*, is informed by the latter that her teaching appointment is contingent upon the result of a physiognomical reading to be made by one of the staff, M. Paul Emanuel The humor of the episode is admirably conveyed in the ensuing dialogue between Madame Beck and M. Paul, whose "judgement," the narrator tells us, "when it at last came, was as indefinite as what had gone before it."[14]

The comicality of a physiognomical reading, as suggested in the foregoing, derives in part from the idea of the apparent undemonstrability of physiognomy as a science. In the case of a phrenological reading, the comicality seems to be scarcely different in kind. But whereas the comicality of a phrenological reading is to be understood almost entirely in terms of the scientific fallibility of phrenology, that of a physiognomical reading may be, and has often been, expressive of the moral or intellectual limitations of the physiognomist himself. This concept of the physiognomist is, as we saw in [one of chapters I-VI of *Physiognomy in the European Novel*], fairly prevalent in the novel before 1800. On the other hand, just as a physiognomical reading may bespeak the shortcomings of the physiognomist himself, so it may, by the same token, bespeak his moral depth and intelligence, his perspicacity and his sensitivity; and it was, in fact, this latter concept that was to find favor with nineteenth-century novelists. Even Flaubert, for all his impatience with the banalities of physiognomical generalizations and phrenological claims, could

hardly have denied that, in this respect at least, physiognomy offered far greater aesthetic possibilities than phrenology. In fact, there is evidence that, despite his famous quest for scientific truth and objectivity, he regarded the art of narrative as a fundamentally physiognomical activity. It would be enough here to recall not only the famous advice he gave to Maupassant, but also a letter to Sainte-Beuve (23-24 December 1862), in which he declared that all his descriptions have a definite function in respect to character and action.[15] To be sure, one should not expect to find physiognomy and phrenology in Flaubert as one does in, say, Balzac; in fact, Flaubert eschews all phrenological correlations in his portraits, and where he describes facial and bodily features, he prefers to suggest rather than to specify their physiognomical significance. Nevertheless, it is by studying Flaubert's novels against the historical background discussed in [chapters 1-6 of *Physiognomy in the European Novel*] that we come to realize that character descriptions in his novels, whatever they may tell us about the persons described, often tell us something about the person (or viewing agent) through whose eyes the description is given. The fact that this particular treatment of physiognomy obtains in much other nineteenth-century fiction would, moreover, suggest that character descriptions should be analyzed not merely for their morphological development or the extrinsic influences they betray but also, more particularly, as manifestations of a certain point of view, be it understood in the Jamesian sense of the term or not. This point of view, which may otherwise be designated as "physiognomical awareness," will now be discussed in some detail in respect to the narrator's function.

Few methods of literary criticism could be more instructive than to study the development of the fictional treatment of human observation against the background of Lavaterian physiognomy. The traditional fictional medium of observation is, of course, the narrator himself, whose existence in the modern novel can be traced back partly to those highly observant narrators we find in the picaresque and realist novels of the seventeenth and eighteenth centuries. Influenced by the descriptive techniques used in "charactery" and the "moral weeklies," as well as by the fine arts, these narrators are commonly portrayed as intelligent, perspicacious beings, whose capacity to reveal the psychological or pictorial essence of someone's appearance we assume to be the fruits of worldly experience. Yet despite differences of character, sex, and way of life, there is very little to distinguish them from one another in respect to descriptive approach; nor does their gift for observation necessarily tell the reader much about their particular individuality. Moreover, what observational powers they possess are generally confined to seizing the essence of a character once and for all and presenting him in a single portrait in the manner of the French moralists.

The physiognomical restrictions of pre-1800 fictional narrators become most evident once we begin to compare the latter with their nineteenth-century counterparts; indeed, there is no question that the nineteenth-century narrator not only displays a virtually new sensibility in his methods of observation but is also endowed with a far wider range of physiognomical skills than ever possessed by his predecessors. It is true that he still makes occasional use of the cool, detached approach to literary portraiture typical of earlier fiction; but his analyses of appearances are often marked by a profound interest in faces for their own sakes as well as a sensitivity that sometimes causes him to react quite physically when attracted or repelled by the outward man. Such a narrator is especially common in minor fiction, Bulwer Lytton's *Pelham* being a notable case in point: no fictional first-person narrator could, indeed, be more inclined to physiognomical observation than the hero of this novel, with his tendency to describe in scrupulous detail every character introduced, his ability to recognize someone by his features (usually at a single glance), and his gift for striking analogies and metaphors, all of which testify to a new physiognomical atmosphere. What also marks the nineteenth-century first-person narrator as observer is his essentially contemplative approach to character description. This approach added a delightful lyrical dimension to narrative art, as we can see, for example, in Raabe's *Chronik der Sperlingsgasse* (1859), whose lyricism derives partly from the way in which characters both living and dead are evoked not so much in portraits as in references to significant physical features. The narrator's physiognomical outlook is already suggested in an early passage, which occurs, significantly for us, shortly after he has related how, in order to dispel a melancholy mood, he has looked through a collection of Chodowiecki engravings:

> Schaue ich auf aus meinen Träumen, so sehe ich zwar dasselbe Lächeln, dasselbe Schmerzenszucken auf den Menschengesichtern um mich her, wie vor langen, blühendern Jahren, aber wenn auch Freud und Leid dieselben sind auf der alten Mutter Erde: die Gesichter selbst sind mir fremd—ich bin allein! Allein—und doch nicht allein. Aus der dämmerigen Nacht des Vergessens taucht es auf und klingt es: Gestalten, Töne, Stimmen, die ich kannte, die ich vernahm, die ich einst gern sah und hörte in vergangenen bösen und guten Tagen, werden wieder wach und lebendig. . . .[16]

> [If I gaze up out of my dreams, I can certainly see the same smiles, the same agonized looks on people's faces around me as I could in halcyon days long ago. But if the joys and sorrows are still the same on old mother earth, the faces themselves are foreign to me—I am alone—alone—and yet not alone. Out of the twilight of oblivion I hear a singing and a ringing—figures, sounds, voices that I used to know and hear in good and bad days of yore reawake and come to life again.]

In Raabe's novel, physiognomical contemplation is essentially an expression of love, as it is in *Dominique* and, as we shall see, in *Der Grüne Heinrich.*

It would not be too much, then, to say that the nineteenth-century first-person narrator sometimes reflects Lavater's concept of physiognomy as an act of love and understanding. Moreover, the narrator's physiognomical disposition is often a manifestation of the particular moral values he or she represents. We see this most clearly in *Villette,* whose heroine, Lucy Snowe, is one of the most gifted and "objective" of all nineteenth-century first-person narrators and, with her neo-Platonic views on the relationship between character and appearance, one of the most understanding. But what is remarkable is the way her moral development goes hand in hand with her development as a physiognomist, just as her almost excessive predilection for observation seems to be essential to her role as a spectator of life rather than a participant in it.

The idea of the physiognomical narrator as essentially a spectator of life also appears to underlie the presentation of the two main narrators of *Wuthering Heights,* Lockwood and Nelly Dean. Nelly Dean's physiognomical disposition and Lavaterian ideas have been discussed in [chapter 6 of *Physiognomy in the European Novel*]; and there are many parts of her narrative where we note how acutely, even painfully, sensitive she is to the facial expressions she describes. What is especially appropriate about her presentation as a physiognomist is not merely that as a servant she is bound to be a spectator of events rather than a participant in them but also that her dependence on physiognomy underlines her frequent lack of communication with the main characters, not to say her virtual incapacity to help them in their plight. Indeed, it is through Nelly Dean's powers of observation that the author succeeds in ironically marking out the inevitable course of the action.

Lockwood, too, is portrayed with a certain gift for physiognomical observation, but his gift serves an altogether different ironic function. Like Nelly Dean, he is prone to describing appearances in all parts of his narrative; and, like her, he has a keen eye for momentary states of mind or psychological development as suggested by a facial expression. His propensity for physiognomical analysis is, no doubt, essential to his presentation as an aesthete, who prefers to observe life rather than live it to the full; it is also an aspect of his inveterate curiosity, which, besides enhancing the dramatic interest of the opening chapters, constitutes the motive for the narration of the story. We note already in the first two chapters that Lockwood shows a certain familiarity with physiognomical theory, possibly Lavaterian theory (for the date heading the first diary entry is 1801), as he speaks in two separate contexts of the "language" of appearances. We may also refer to his use of the word *physiognomy* on two occasions, and that in the sense of "general appearance." More interesting, however, is his tendency to make physiognomical judgments, for they throw considerable light on his character. Thus, although in an attempt to ingratiate himself with Catherine Heathcliff in Chapter II (just before he asks her to tell him the way back to Thrushcross Grange) he flatters her by saying that "with that face" he is sure that she "cannot help being goodhearted,"[17] later in the novel he bids himself "beware the fascination that lurks in [Catherine Heathcliff's] eyes," adding that "I should be in a curious taking if I surrendered my heart to that young person, and the daughter turned out a second edition of the mother!" This cautionary remark is directly related to an earlier physiognomical comment in his diary which tells how, on being shown a portrait of Edgar Linton, he "marvelled how he [Edgar] with a mind to correspond to his person could fancy [Lockwood's] idea of Catherine Earnshaw." The particular interest of these physiognomical judgments is that they confirm as much as anything else his extraordinary fear of human relationships—a fear already evident in the first chapter when he relates how he spurned the affections of a young lady at a seaside resort, even though, as he adds, "the merest idiot might have guessed I was over head and ears."[18] Indeed, the more we study Lockwood as an observer of man, the more we realize how much his gift for observation is a manifestation of his profound misanthropy as well as his inability to experience that passionate love which Heathcliff, misanthropist as he is in a different way, is so capable of experiencing. Hence the sterility of Lockwood's life.

The fact that physiognomy in the nineteenth-century novel is sometimes significant for what it tells us about the observer no less than about the observed would appear to be linked with a tendency to reduce the importance of the narrator's viewpoint and, as we noted in Chapter V [of *Physiognomy in the European Novel*], to present portraits from the angle of a non-narratorial observing character, even in such novels as *Eugénie Grandet, Vanity Fair, Les Bourgeois de Molinchart, Les Mystères de Paris, Doctor Thorne, Vittoria Accorombona,* and *Die Epigonen,* with their prominent and occasionally Lavaterian third-person narrators. In some third-person novels we find literary portraiture used as a pretext for the author to display the physiognomical skills of several characters. In order to give some idea of this, let us consider Scott's *Heart of Midlothian.*

One of the most signal effects of physiognomy on this novel is the way in which both major and minor characters are given to observing and analyzing one another's appearances. Thus apart from the observant Reuben Butler, through whose eyes we get the description of George Staunton already referred to, and that of the jail-bird Ratcliffe at Staunton's trial ("Butler's eyes were instantly fixed on the person whose examination was at present proceeding"),[19] the heroine, Jeanie Deans, is presented in a number of situations in which she shows certain physiognomical reactions. For example, there is one occasion when the heroine, on her way down to London to get a reprieve for her sister Effie (who, because of Jeanie's truthful testimony in court, has been sentenced to death for killing her illegitimate baby), falls into the hands of the highwayman Levitt, and encounters Meg Wildfire and her insane daughter Madge. However, the following morning Jeanie and Madge manage to escape while the others are still asleep, and, as it is a Sunday, attend a church service. Impressed by the officiating clergyman, "an aged gentleman, of a dignified appearance and deportment, who read the service with an undisturbed and decent gravity," Jeanie decides to go to him for help because, as she has been warned by Madge, Meg Wildfire intends to obstruct her journey. While Jeanie waits in the anteroom of the vicarage in order to see the vicar, a Reverend Mr. Staunton (who, by ironic coincidence, turns out to be the father of Effie's lover), the narrator tells of her reflecting as follows: "and from whom could she hope for assistance if not from Mr. Staunton? His whole appearance and demeanour encouraged her hopes. His features were handsome, though marked with a deep cast of melancholy; tone and language were gentle and encouraging."[20] Nor, indeed, is she disappointed.

Once arrived in London, Jeannie succeeds in getting an interview with the Duke of Argyle, who, on the morning after her first visit to him, calls for her at her London inn and takes her in his carriage to Richmond Park. On this occasion Jeanie pays particular attention to his attire: "She remarked that the Duke's dress, though still such as indicated rank and fashion (for it was not the custom of men of quality to dress themselves like their own coachman or groom), was nevertheless plainer than that in which she had seen him upon a former occasion."[21] Jeanie also has an opportunity at Richmond Park to get a close view of Queen Caroline and Lady Suffolk, who are both described in great detail. Noteworthy is the way in which the description begins: "As they advanced slowly, Jeanie had time to study their features and appearances."[22] When, toward the end of the novel, Effie turns up in Scotland, we learn that, as Lady Staunton, she has led an aristocratic life of late, which in turn has had its influence on her general appearance: "Her manner was easy, dignified and commanding, and seemed to evince high birth, and the habits of elevated society." Ironically, however, Jeanie does not immediately recognize her sister, though the physiognomist in her becomes active at the same time:

> There was something about the whole of the stranger's address, and tone, and manner which acted upon Jeanie's feelings like the illusions of a dream, that tease us with a puzzling approach to reality. Something there was of her sister in the gait and manner of the stranger,

as well as in the sound of her voice, and something also, when, lifting her veil, she showed features in which, changed as they were in expression and complexion, she could not but attach many remembrances.[23]

In this connection, it is interesting to note that, shortly before Effie's arrival in Scotland, the Duke of Argyle himself pays a visit to Jeanie (now Mrs. Reuben Butler) and tells of his meeting a Lady Staunton of Wellingham. The reason he mentions this person, he explains to Jeanie, is "because she has something in the sound of her voice and cast of her countenance that reminded me of you. . . ." Furthermore, the Duke's observation of Effie suggests how sensitive a physiognomist *he* is: "Amidst her noble and elegant manners, there is now and then a little touch of bashfulness and conventual rusticity, if I may call it so, that makes her quite enchanting. You see at once the rose that had bloomed untouched amid the chaste precincts of the cloister, Mrs. Butler."[24]

Nor is the Duke of Argyle the only minor character with a physiognomical eye. For example, at the London inn where Jeanie puts up, there is a hostess whose interest in royal and aristocratic persons is so stimulated by the thought of Jeanie's outing with the Duke of Argyle that she gives the heroine a description of an aristocratic lady, a Mrs. Dably, which is presented in *style indirect libre*: "She used sometimes afterwards to draw a parallel betwixt her [Mrs. Dably] and the Queen, in which she observed, that Mrs. Dably was dressed twice as grand, and was twice as big, and spoke twice as loud, and twice as muckle, as the Queen did, but she hadna the same goss-hawk glance that makes the skin creep and the knee bend. . . ."[25] No less observant is David Deans, Jeanie's father, as we can tell, for example, when he notices how marriage has transformed the general appearance of Dumbiedikes, the somewhat gauche Scottish landowner and formerly unsuccessful suitor of Jeanie:

> There was a change also, David did not very well know of what nature, about the exterior of the proprietor—an improvement in the shape of his garments, a spruceness in the air with which they were put on, that were both novelties. Even the old hat looked smarter; the cock had been newly painted, the lace had been refreshed, and instead of slouching backwards and forwards on the laird's head as it happened to be thrown on, it was adjusted with a knowing inclination over one eye.[26]

It is evident that Scott's treatment of the physiognomical disposition of his characters, though useful for the construction of the plot, is too self-conscious to have any true aesthetic interest for us today; indeed, it is difficult to escape the impression that, despite the obvious anachronisms, he is concerned here largely to pay homage to the physiognomical climate of his day for its own sake. Much the same might be said of Immer-

mann's *Epigonen,* in which the *Herzogin*'s remarkable eye for family physiognomies is used as a means of thickening the plot concerning Hermann's aristocratic heredity. Nevertheless, such instances of physiognomical awareness were important signs of a new moral and intellectual climate in which the capacity to use one's eyes with sensitivity and understanding had evidently become an important means of sympathetic characterization. It is perhaps no accident that a physiognomical gift of one kind or another had by now become practically a moral attribute of many a non-narratorial hero and heroine. We note, for example, in *Die Epigonen* that the hero Hermann, through whose eyes many characters are described, is presented as one of those "welche durch eine Physiognomie, durch den Klang einer Stimme bis in das Innerste zu verwunden sind." [who are terribly sensitive to a person's physiognomy, to the sound of a voice.][27] Much the same words could be applied to some heroines of third-person novels, such as the heroine of *Vittoria Accorombona* and Madame de Rênal in *Le Rouge et le Noir.* Part of Madame de Rênal's charm for the reader lies in her physiognomical sensitivity, which is evident in her tendency to be shocked by the harsh tones of voice of unsympathetic characters, as well as in her appreciation of Julien Sorel's physical beauty. Mathilde de la Mole is similarly sensitive, as we note when, at the height of her passion for Julien, she draws a profile of him with a speaking likeness. And in *The Mill on the Floss,* Philip Wakem, too, is inspired by love for Maggie Tulliver to draw a portrait of her face, whose peculiar qualities he understands better than do the other characters in the novel. We could also point to other love relationships, such as that between Resli and Anne Mareili in *Geld und Geist* and between Julien Donquières and Louise Creton in *Les Bourgeois de Molinchart,* where the lover's physiognomical appreciation of the beloved plays a prominent part. Sometimes even a minor character is used to indicate the importance of physiognomy in a love relationship, as we note, for example, in Trollope's *Doctor Thorne* when Squire Gresham's approval of his son's choice of Mary Thorne as a wife stems from his suddenly becoming aware of the peculiar appeal of her appearance.

Perhaps the finest treatment of physiognomy in the delineation of a love relationship is given in *Villette,* a novel in which the attitudes of the literary world to physiognomy may be said to have been compendiously embodied in the very presentation of Paul Emanuel in so far as his steady rise to full sympathetic stature is marked essentially by his development from an essentially caricatural figure to one of great moral depth and vision, with an extraordinary capacity to love. And yet of all love relationships in fiction none, it seems, could begin more inauspiciously than between Lucy Snowe and Paul Emanuel, as we note how, during that strange first physiognomical reading, the heroine is made forcibly conscious of the latter's eccentric manner and for-bidding appearance. Gradually, however, Lucy learns not merely to discover depth of character behind the eccentricity but also to discern positive qualities in the forbidding exterior, qualities which, ironically enough, remain hidden to the beautiful but shallow Ginevra Fanshawe, who considers him "hideously plain," and even to the handsome Graham Bretton, who on one occasion refers to him as "savage looking."[28] The development of the relationship between Lucy Snowe and Paul Emanuel from antagonism to mutual love is one of the most remarkable achievements of this novel; and we see how skillfully this is shown not only through Lucy's increasingly mature physiognomical approach to M. Paul but also in the latter's eventual transformation from the comical physiognomist we find at the beginning of the novel into a poetic one, whose following analysis of Lucy's face must be surely one of the most lyrical expressions of love in all nineteenth-century fiction:

> . . . you are a strict Protestant, and I am a sort of lay Jesuit; but we are alike—there is affinity between us. Do you see it, mademoiselle, when you look in the glass? Do you observe that your forehead is shaped like mine? Do you hear that you have some of my tones of voice? Do you know that you have many of my looks? I perceive all this, and believe that you were born under my star. Yes, you were born under my star! Tremble! for where that is the case with mortals, the threads of their destinies are difficult to disentangle; knottings and catchings occur—and sudden breaks leave damages in the web. But these "impressions," as you say, with English caution. I, too, have had my "impressions."[29]

The idea that two people should share the same destiny by virtue of their physiognomical resemblance is one that would no doubt have appealed to Lavater. But there is also a poignant irony in this lyrical physiognomical judgment in the way it foreshadows, particularly with the words "sudden breaks leave damages in the web," the tragic death of Paul Emanuel on the high seas. Lucy's fate is to be deprived of the happiness almost within her reach—a happiness which the more fortunate Graham Bretton and Polly Home will find together in marriage. Yet, as the heroine sums up her friendship with Paul Emanuel before she hears the tragic news, we see how much she has matured in her attitude to the eccentric "lay Jesuit." And in the following words of one whose observant eye has been responsible for a remarkable number of analytical and almost excessively physiognomical character descriptions in the novel, it becomes clear to the reader that Lucy's experience of M. Paul has enriched not only her life but also her physiognomical vision:

> He deemed me born under his star; he seemed to have spread over me its beam like a banner. Once—unknown, and unloved, I held him harsh and strange;

the low stature, the wiry make, the angles, the darkness, the manner, displeased me. Now, penetrated with his influence, and living by his affection, having his worth by intellect, and his goodness by heart—I preferred him before all humanity.[30]

The extent to which relationships between main characters in nineteenth-century fiction may be described as physiognomical is again well illustrated in *Madame Bovary*. First of all, we note Charles Bovary's fascination with Emma's appearance and, in particular, the attention he gives to specific physiognomical characteristics. Here, for instance, is how he observes her hands on his first visit to the Rouault farm:

> Charles fut surpris de la blancheur de ses ongles. Ils étaient brillants, fins du bout, plus nettoyés que les ivoires de Dieppe, et taillés en amande. Sa main pourtant n'était pas belle, point assez pâle, et un peu seche aux phalanges; elle était trop longue aussi et sans molies inflexions de lignes sur les contours.[31]

> [Charles was surprised at the whiteness of her fingernails. They were shining, tapering, and smoother than Dieppe ivories, and almond-shaped. Yet it was not a lovely hand, it was not white enough, and the skin was rather dry round the knuckles; it was also too long, and lacked a gentleness of contour round the edges.]

In a later passage Charles is shown being aware of the way in which Emma's eyes change color according to the time of day. Such physiognomical sensitivity may strike the reader as incompatible with the generally doltish figure Charles cuts in the novel, and it would suggest that he is as incurably a Romantic as the heroine herself. But the chief function of Charles' analyses is to underline the lack of communication between him and Emma, in much the same way as does the heroine's revulsion for Charles' physical appearance, one instance of which, as we saw earlier, is evident when, having renewed her love affair with Rodolphe, Emma becomes more conscious than usual of Charles' squarish fingers and vulgarity of manner. Another instance of Emma's revulsion occurs when she gets a back view of Charles at the loom factory which they are being taken round by Homais:

> Il avait sa casquette enfoncée sur les sourcils, et ses deux grosses lèvres tremblotaient, ce qui ajoutait à son visage quelque chose de stupide; son dos même, son dos tranquille était irritant à voir, et elle y trouvait étalée sur la redingote toute la platitude du personnage.[32]

> [He had his cap pulled down over his eyes, and his fleshy lips were trembling, which lent his face a certain look of stupidity; even his back, his placid back, was irritating to look at, and she could see spread all over his frock coat the utter mediocrity of his character.]

That this passage has unquestionable physiognomical significance may be seen if we compare it with an excerpt from a letter (25 February 1800) which Lavater wrote to his friend L. H. Nicolay (1737-1820):

Der Mensch . . . kann sich in keinem einzigen Punkte seines Wesens verläugnen. Besonders hab'ich die Menschen auch vom Rücken her zu beobachten gesucht—und sehr oft—äussert entscheidende Merkmale der Weisheit und Dummheit, ja wahrlich, der Tugend und des Lasters bemerkt.[33]

[People give away their character in the most trivial details. In particular, I have tried to observe people from behind—and I have very often noticed extraordinarily distinctive characteristics of intelligence and stupidity, even of vice and virtue.]

Emma's physiognomical reactions to Charles are, of course, utterly characteristic; and it is precisely through her constantly disillusioning visual experiences—disillusioning because they are ever set against the ideal world created by the excesses of her imagination—that Flaubert partly expresses the pessimism and nihilism that permeate his novel.

It was most particularly in the English novel of our period that physiognomy came to play a decisive role in the treatment of love and hate. We note, for example, in *Wuthering Heights* (a novel in which relations between the main characters are largely determined by their acute consciousness of one another's appearances) how Heathcliff's vicious attitude toward the Earnshaws and the Lintons is maintained throughout the novel partly because, with their characteristic physiognomical features, they are each of them a poignant reminder not only of the memory of Cathy but also of the part they have played in depriving him of her love. We might even go so far as to say that Heathcliff's tragedy is essentially a physiognomical one, foreshadowed already in his childhood in those snobbish reactions to his gypsy appearance and in his own boyish awareness of the stark contrast between himself and the other characters, with their Anglo-Saxon physiognomies.

But whereas in *Wuthering Heights* criticism of the undue importance attached to appearances is implicit, in *The Mill on the Floss* it is utterly explicit. To be sure, George Eliot's novel is hardly less physiognomical than any other nineteenth-century novel in respect to literary portraiture; and despite the author's evident dislike of the *Fragmente,* it is remarkable how often her prominent non-participating first-person narrator makes use of Lavaterian ideas, notably that of family physiognomies. Nevertheless, physiognomist as she is herself indirectly, the author is mainly concerned here with the dangers of certain physiognomical attitudes in the provincial English society she portrays, whether these be clannish, even racial assumptions about the advantages of the Anglo-Saxon physiognomy or the bigotry and narrowmindedness underlying physiognomical opinions and judgments. This concern is quite evident in the narrator's essayistic digressions on the subject, as, for example, when she jibes at the idea (which Lavater himself puts forward in the *Fragmente*) that the appearance of the adult may be predicted by a study of his physiognomy as a child. Thus the narrator describes Tom Tulliver as possessing

a physiognomy in which it seems impossible to discern anything but the general character of boyhood; as different as possible from poor Maggie's phiz, which Nature seemed to have moulded and coloured with the most decided intention. But that same Nature has the deep cunning which hides itself under the appearance of openness, so that simple people think they can see through her quite well, and the while she is secretly preparing a refutation of their confident prophecies. Under these average boyish physiognomies that she seems to turn off by the gross, she conceals some of her most rigid, inflexible purposes, some of her most unmodifiable characters; and the dark-eyed, demonstrative, rebellious girl may after all turn out to be a passive being compared with this pink-and-white bit of masculinity with the indeterminate features.[34]

George Eliot sees the habit of prejudiced physiognomical judgments taking root in childhood; and notwithstanding Lavater's claim that children make excellent physiognomists, she shows them to be no less subjective and biased in their reactions than adults. We note this particularly when the narrator comments with gentle irony on Tom and Maggie Tulliver's childish physiognomical reactions to, say, the blond Mrs. Clegg or the red-haired Bob Jakin. More serious in the narrator's eyes, however, is Tom Tulliver's physiognomical attitude to the hump-backed Philip Wakem: "An anatomist—even a mere physiognomist—would have seen that the deformity of Philip's spine was not a congenital hump, but the result of an accident in infancy; but you do not expect from Tom any acquaintance with such distinctions: to him Philip was simply a humpback."[35] Tom's inveterate revulsion for Philip's appearance is, of course, one of the ironic motifs in the novel, and it plays an important part in undermining Maggie's relationship with the latter.

Interesting, too, is the narrator's intervention in the episode concerning Mr. Tulliver's conflict with Philip Wakem's father. Thus when Mrs. Tulliver visits the latter at his office in an attempt to effect a reconciliation between the two men, the narrator alludes to Tulliver's earlier physiognomical judgment of Wakem as "a hook-nosed glib fellow."[36] In ironic vein the narrator then assumes that the reader is "possibly wondering whether [Wakem] was really as eminent a rascal . . . as he is represented to be in that eidolon or portrait of him we have seen to exist in the miller's mind," and then goes on to discourse upon the habit of judging people on first impressions:

But it is really impossible to decide this question by a glance at his person: the lines and lights of the human countenance are like other symbols—not always easy to read without a key. On an *a priori* view of Wakem's aquiline nose, which offended Mr. Tulliver, there was not more rascality than in the shape of his stiff shirt-collar, though this, too, along with his nose, might have become fraught with damnatory meaning when once the reality was ascertained.[37]

Although *The Mill on the Floss* may be considered to be the one novel of George Eliot's in which she is at her most antiphysiognomical, a study of her narrators in, say, *Adam Bede* or *Middlemarch,* with their poetic disquisitions on the beauty or hereditary significance of the human face, shows her to have been quite as deeply imbued with physiognomical thought as any of her contemporaries. In any event, no novel better reflects the controversies of the Lavaterian physiognomical era than *The Mill on the Floss*; and there is little doubt that in her brilliant structural use of physiognomy as a means of showing up the limitations of second-hand thinking, and, occasionally, as in the case of the Tullivers, its harmful consequences, she belongs very clearly to the moralistic tradition of Fielding, and, as we shall see at the end of this [essay], to that of Jane Austen.

Having given a general idea of what we mean by physiognomical awareness in nineteenth-century fiction, we shall now go on to confirm our argument by considering a number of major and minor novels, including some that have received little or no attention hitherto. Let us start by discussing three major novels, narrated in first or third person, in which the hero is presented as a physiognomical observer. Our first hero is Julien Sorel in *Le Rouge et le Noir.*

It is interesting to see the extent to which the literary portraits in this novel are presented from the hero's viewpoint, at the same time as his physiognomical reactions play an essential part in his characterization. First of all, we note early in the novel his appreciation of specific characteristics of Madame de Rênal's beauty. At the rendezvous in the garden at Verrières, on the eve of the departure for three days' leave of absence, he anticipates seeing her thus: "il songeait à sa main si jolie" [he thought of her lovely hand]; and when he is with her at the rendezvous, we read: "il admirait ces bras si beaux qu'un châle jeté à la hâte laissait apercevoir." [he admired those lovely arms, which a hastily cast-off shawl made it possible for him to see.] For Julien, Madame de Rênal's beauty is of true aesthetic interest: "Cette beauté modeste et touchante, et cependant pleine de pensées que l'on ne trouve point dans les classes inférieures, semblait révéler à Julien une faculté de son âme qu'il n'avait jamais sentie."[38] [This modest, fascinating beauty—a beauty full of those inner qualities not to be found in the lower classes—seemed to rouse feelings in Julien that he had never had before.] There is a similar aesthetic reaction in Julien when he sees Madame de Rênal's children on returning to the Rênal household after a short absence. Part of this reaction is conditioned, no doubt, by his recent tedious experience as guest of the Valenods and his meeting with other bourgeois provincials: "Il était étonné de la douceur de leur voix, de la simplicité et de la noblesse de leurs petites façons; il avait besoin de laver son imagination de toutes les façons d'agir vulgaires, de toutes les pensées désagréables au milieu desquelles il respirait à Verrières."[39] [He was astonished at their gentle voices, their simple, noble way of doing things; he felt an urge to cleanse his imagination of all vulgar forms of behavior, all the unpleasant thoughts he had been immersed in at Verrières.]

Julian's first impressions of people are usually quite definite, even if they sometimes have to be corrected later. When he is first introduced to the marquise de la Mole, we read that he "luitrouva l'air impertinent" [thought she was stuck-up];[40] and this impression is subsequently confirmed as he becomes better acquainted with her. His first impression of M. de la Mole, whom he sees on the occasion of the king's visit to Verrières, is also unfavorable: "Il lui trouva l'air hautain et même violent."[41] [He thought him haughty, even vicious looking.] But when the abbé Pirard introduces him to the marquis in Paris, we are told that Julien "eut beaucoup de peine à le reconnaître." [found it hard to recognize him.] Indeed, he finds a certain incongruity about the marquis: "Le descendant de l'ami de Henri III lui parut d'abord avoir une tournure assez mesquine."[42] [The descendant of Henri III's companion seemed to have a rather puny figure.] Ironically enough, however, the marquis turns out to be an excellent friend to Julien. The hero also reacts unfavorably to Mathilde at first sight: "Elle ne lui plut point . . ." [He didn't like her]; but at least he takes time at the dinner table to analyze her eyes: "cependant en la regardant attentivement, il pensa qu'il n'avait jamais vu des yeux aussi beaux; mais ils annonçaient une froideur d'âme" [yet as he gazed at her more attentively, he realized that he had never before seen such lovely eyes, even though they bespoke a cold heart], and he proceeds to compare them with Madame de Rênal's to the advantage of the latter.[43] It is, therefore, no small irony that Mathilde's physical appearance is what eventually decides Julien that he is in love with her: "C'était après s'être perdu en rêveries sur l'élégance de la taille de Mlle. de la Mole, sur l'excellent goût de sa toilette, sur la blancheur de sa main, sur la beauté de son bras, sur la *disinvoltura* de tous ses mouvements, qu'il se trouvait amoureux."[44] [It was after being absorbed in dreams about the elegance of Mademoiselle de la Mole's figure, her excellent taste in clothes, the whiteness of her hands, the beauty of her arms, the nonchalance of all her movements, that he realized he was in love with her.]

Sometimes, however, Julien can be physically overwhelmed by a first impression. Thus, after having been admitted into the Besançon seminary by a hideous-looking hall-porter, whose face he analyzes very physiognomically, Julien faints in the abbé Pirard's study. Pirard's retort to Julien's excuse that he had passed out because "la figure du portier m'avait glacé" [the janitor's face had transfixed him] is that Julien is merely used to "visages riants, véritables théâtres de mensonge."[45] [laughing faces, veritable theaters of deceit.] This remark in some way foreshadows the occasion when Julien compares Pirard's appearance with that of the various guests in Mathide's salon. Irritated by Mathide's remark on the abbé's ugliness, even though he cannot disagree with her judgment, he is nevertheless convinced that Pirard is "le plus honnête homme du salon," which then leads him to question the validity of physiognomical theory: "Croyez après cela aux physionomies, pensa Julien, c'est dans le moment où la délicatesse de l'abbé Pirard se reproche quelque peccadile, qu'il a l'air atroce; tandis que sur la figure de ce Napier, espion connu de tous, on lit un bonheur pur et tranquille."[46] ["Who'd believe in physiognomy after that!" thought Julien. "It's at the very moment the abbé Pirard's conscience reproaches him for some peccadillo that he looks evil, whereas on that notorious spy Napier's face you can read utter self-satisfaction."]

Julien's allusion to physiognomy reminds us that he is something of an amateur physiognomist himself, though this may seem strange in one who has obviously read the adverse comments on Lavater and Gall made by his idol Napoleon in the *Mémorial de Sainte-Hélène*. It is true that he is sometimes comically wrong in his judgments, as, for example, when he mistakes the young bishop of Agde for his secretary or for some lackey, or when he challenges the comte de Beauvoisis' coachman to a duel (on account of an insult) because he assumes the latter to be an aristocrat. On one occasion Julien actually resorts to physiognomy in order to extricate himself from a difficult situation. This happens when, after receiving three letters from Mathilde urging him to come to her room one night, he suspects that a trap is being laid for him; and so he is particularly watchful one evening in the dining room: "Il regardait tous ces domestiques en grande livrée Il étudiait leur physionomie. Quels sont ceux qu'on a choisis pour l'expédition de cette nuit? . . . Il regarda Mlle. de la Mole pour lire dans ses yeux les projets de sa famille. . . ."[47] [He looked at all the lackeys in their grand liveries; he studied their physiognomies. Which of them have been chosen for tonight's expedition? . . . He looked at Mademoiselle de la Mole to see if he could read the family plans in her eyes.] Of course, his anxiety proves later to have been misplaced. Another example of Julien's propensity for physiognomical observation is to be noted on the occasion he attends the secret political meeting with M. de la Mole, and carefully studies each of the participants as they arrive one by one. Let us quote three statements made by the narrator to this effect: (1)

"Julien lui trouva la physionomie et l'éloquence d'un homme qui digère" [Julien thought he had the physiognomy and eloquence of a man with good digestion]; (2) ". . . pour juger le nouveau venu, Julien on fut réduit à ce que pouvaient lui apprendre ses traits et sa tournure" [in order to size up the new arrival Julien was reduced to finding out what he could learn from his face and his figure]; and (3) "Julien fut vivement interrompu dans ses observations physionomiques par la voix de M. de la Mole."[48] [Julien was interrupted in his physiognomical observations by M. de la Mole's voice.]

Stendhal's presentation of Julien as constantly observing, watching, or analyzing people's appearances is, of course, an important aspect of his characterization of the hero as an ambitious young upstart bent on conquering society. And yet this treatment of Julien as a physiognomist, so to speak, is essentially ironic; for though it is true that he can be extremely perceptive in his physiognomical judgments, we see how often envy and admiration, combined with his youthfulness and lack of worldly experience, lead him into comically erroneous assessments of people. Moreover, Stendhal seems to suggest that Julien's extreme sensitivity to outward appearances also has its negative side in so far as it partly prevents him from coming to terms with himself and the world of reality.

Let us now discuss Pip as physiognomical narrator of *Great Expectations*. From his earliest years Pip is shown as being very sensitive to people around him. His physiognomical awareness is so intense that as a small boy he can actually conjure up images of his parents, whom he never knew, simply by reading the inscriptions on their graves:

> The shape of the letters on my father's gave me an odd idea that he was a square, stout, dark man, with curly black hair. From the character and turn of the inscription, "Also Georgiana Wife of the Above," I drew a childish conclusion that my mother was freckled and sickly.[49]

One aspect of Pip's powers of observation is his tendency not so much to describe a person in detail as to concentrate on one salient characteristic, whether it be a physical feature, a gesture, or a mannerism. For example, we do not see Mrs. Gargery as a physical entity so much as a series of physiognomical aspects. Thus apart from her eternal apron and her strange way of cutting bread already referred to, Pip notices one memorable detail: "Mrs. Joe . . . had such a prevailing redness of skin, that I sometimes used to wonder whether it was possible she washed herself with a nutmeg-grater instead of soap."[50] In one passage where he describes Magwitch eating the stolen pie, he shows a physiognomist's flair for noting analogies between man and beast: "I have often watched a large dog of ours eating his food; and now I noticed a decided similarity between the dog's way of eating and the man's. The man took strong sharp sudden bites, just like the dog."[51] In his vivid description of Mr. Wopsle, Pip draws attention to the latter's voice, which is particularly noticeable in church, where "he punished the Amens tremendously."[52] But it is Wopsle's nose that becomes a special source of irritation for the hero during the Christmas dinner, and also a starting point for a discussion of Roman noses: "I think the Romans must have aggravated one another very much, with their noses. Perhaps, they became the restless people they were in consequence. Anyhow, Mr. Wopsle's Roman nose so aggravated me, during the recital of my dismeanours, that I should have liked to pull it until he howled."[53] We might also refer to Pip's ability to use appropriate figurative language as a means of conveying the peculiarity of a person's appearance. An example of this is best seen in part of his description of Wemmick:

> Casting my eyes on Mr. Wemmick as we went along, to see what he was like in the light of day, I found him to be a dry man, rather short in stature, with a square wooden face, whose expression seemed to have been imperfectly chipped out with a dull-edged chisel. There were some marks in it that might have been dimples, if the material had been softer and the instrument finer, but which, as it were, were only dints. The chisel had made three or four attempts at embellishments over his nose, but had given them up without an effort to smooth them off.[54]

Pip's sensitivity to appearances may be seen as essential for the growth of his snobbery. Thus in his description of Biddy ("an orphan like myself") he writes: "She was most noticeable, I thought, in respect of her extremities; for her hair always wanted brushing, her hands always wanted washing, and her shoes always wanted mending, and pulling up at the heel."[55] Later, but only after he has come to know Estella, he notices an improvement in Biddy's appearance: "Imperceptibly I became conscious of a change in Biddy, however. Her shoes came up at heel, her hair grew bright and neat, her hands were always clean." But his snobbishness comes out again in the next sentence: "She was not beautiful—she was common, and could not be like Estella—but she was pleasant and wholesome and sweet-tempered." These references to Biddy's character are then ironically confirmed when he discovers one evening her "curiously thoughtful and attentive eyes; eyes that were very pretty and very good."[56] Through this favorable physiognomical analysis of Biddy's eyes, Pip becomes fully aware of her inherent good nature; but, sadly, he cannot forget Estella's cruel remarks to him about his "coarse hands" and "thick boots," just as he is unable to resist her beauty. As he says to Biddy: ". . . she's more beautiful than anybody ever was, and I admire her dreadfully, and I want to be a gentleman on her account."[57] Part of Pip's tragedy, then, is that he almost willfully refuses to be guided by his observa-

tional powers for his own good in so far as he rejects Biddy for Estella.

There are occasions in the novel when we see something of the physiognomist proper in Pip. The first occurs when he analyzes the general appearance of Herbert Pocket, who is now trying to make his living as a young man in London: "There was something wonderfully hopeful about his general air, and something that at the same time whispered to me that he would never be successful or rich. I don't know how this was. I became imbued with the notion on that first occasion before we sat down to dinner, but I cannot define by what means."[58] Pip's physiognomical interpretation, however, turns out at the end of the novel to have been ill-founded, for he discovers that, whereas he himself has failed to make his mark in London, Herbert has become fairly prosperous. In fact, after joining Herbert's firm, Pip soon realizes what a good businessman Herbert is. Thus he writes: "We owed so much to Herbert's ever cheerful industry and readiness, that I often wondered how I had conceived that old idea about his ineptitude."[59] Clearly, Pip has forgotten that his initial misjudgment of Herbert's capacity was made at a time when he was still cherishing snobbish illusions about future successes of his own.

The other occasion Pip makes a physiognomical reading is when, as a guest to dinner at Jaggers' house, he suddenly becomes aware that the housekeeper, whom Jaggers has rescued from the clutches of the law, is actually Estella's long-lost mother. It is noteworthy that Pip arrives at this conclusion after paying careful attention to specific physiognomical features: "I looked at those hands, I looked at those eyes, I looked at that flowing hair; and I compared them with other hands, other eyes, other hair, that I knew of, and with what these might be after twenty years of a brutal husband and a stormy life. . . . And I felt absolutely certainly that this woman was Estella's mother."[60] This dramatic revelation has the ironic effect of immediately shattering Pip's illusions about Estella's aristocratic origins, thereby bringing him closer still to the realities of life, from which he has been largely shielded but which he is destined to have to face in the end.

From these few excerpts, as well as from others discussed in [chapters I-VI of *Physiognomy in the European Novel*], we can see that Pip has a fairly wide range of physiognomical skills. Part of this is, of course, due to the fact that Dickens has placed the burden of character description almost entirely on the hero's shoulders. And though it is true that Pip makes little use of physiognomical correlations or the analytical procedures that typify many a nineteenth-century composite portrait, there is little doubt that his ability to fasten on a characteristic feature, his ingenious use of metaphors and analogies, and his gift for conveying the essence of a person without a concatenation of details all bespeak the talented physiognomist that Dickens was in all his novels. At the same time, however, it is to Dickens' credit that, by using Pip as a vehicle for his character description, he gives us to understand that the hero's physiognomical outlook is an essential aspect of his character. Thus, on the one hand, we see how, for example, Pip's concentration on the absurdities or oddities of the human appearance, his obsession with Estella's beauty, and his mistaken judgment of Herbert are each in their way expressive of his snobbishness; on the other hand, Pip's physiognomical awareness of Biddy's good nature, as well as his ability to trace Estella's mother through an analysis of her physical features, seem to be manifestations of that positive side of his nature which is tragically smothered until, perhaps too late, he comes to full self-realization at the end of the novel.

Der Nachsommer, like *Great Expectations,* tells the story of the moral and spiritual development of a young man, but with the difference that Heinrich Drendorf's takes place mostly in a sheltered environment where he undergoes a number of educative experiences in preparation for an ideal life of happiness. One significant aspect of his steady growth to maturity is the way in which he learns to observe people and things with a keener and more sensitive vision. At the beginning of the novel we learn that Heinrich has had a relatively pious upbringing, but also, in so far as he has not yet gone into the deeper issues of life, a narrow and conventional one. This is especially noticeable on the first occasion he comes down to the *Rosenhaus.* He is convinced that there is going to be a storm, and there is something overweening not only in the way he argues with the master of the house, Risach, who assures him (correctly, as it turns out) that there will be no storm, but also in his reaction to the general appearance of Risach, whom he initially mistakes for a servant: "Ich sah, dass es ein Mann mit schneeweissen Haaren war, die er nicht bedeckt hatte. Sonst war er unscheinbar und hatte eine Art Hausjacke an, oder wie man das Ding nennen soll, das ihm überall enge anlag und fast bis auf die Knie herabreichte."[61] [What I saw was a man with snow-white hair and without headgear. Otherwise he was insignificant looking and wore a kind of house-jacket, or whatever you might call it, which was very tight fitting and reached almost down to his knees.] And on the morning after his first night at the *Rosenhaus,* he again notices Risach still wearing the same strange outfit: "Sein Anzug war heute wieder sonderbar."[62] [His outfit was again a strange sight that day.] Heinrich spends a few more days at the house, where he witnesses the remarkable routine and efficient organization which Risach has established for himself and for the servants and workers under him; but he still cannot reconcile Risach's methodical approach to everyday life, his profound knowledge of the laws of nature (we have

seen what a good meteorologist he is), and his appreciation of art with his curious attire: "Ich bewunderte den Mann, der, da er so redete, in einem sonderbaren, ja abgeschmackten Kleide ging."[63] [I was puzzled by this man, who, as he uttered these words, walked along in his strange, even tasteless attire.] Heinrich is, indeed, still a long way from understanding that simplicity of being which is of paramount importance for Risach. But if Heinrich finds Risach's jacket distasteful, he nevertheless has an eye for its details:

> Die Jacke war weisslich, hatte jedoch über die Brust und den Rücken hinab einen rötlichen Streifen, der fast einen halben Fuss breit war, als wäre die Jacke aus zwei Stoffen verfertigt worden, einem weissen und einem roten. Beide Stoffe aber zeigten ein hohes Alter; denn das Weiss war gelblichbraun und das Rot zu purpurbraun geworden.[64]

> [The jacket was whitish, but across the chest and down the back was a red stripe which was about six inches wide, as though the jacket had been made out of two materials, one white and the other red. But both materials looked very old, for the white had turned a yellowy brown, and the red a purplish brown.]

On another occasion he finds it strange that Risach and the boy Gustav should wear no headgear in the strong sun: "Ich wusste nicht, kamen mir die beiden ohne Kopfbedeckung sonderbar vor, oder ich neben ihnen mit meinem Reisehute auf dem Haupt."[65] [I didn't know which seemed more curious to me: the two of them without any headgear or myself with my traveling-hat on my head.] This latter reference amply suggests that, although Heinrich is reasonably observant, his vision is still conditioned by his conventional attitudes. Indeed, it is clear that his social background has prevented him from seeing the world around him with anything more than a superficial gaze.

It is noteworthy that, by contrast, Risach is presented at the outset as a man of true physiognomical vision. This is first hinted at when he asks Heinrich a question which foreshadows the appearance of Mathilde:

> Habt ihr denn nie eine jener alten Frauen gesehen, . . . die in ihrer Jugend sehr schön gewesen waren und sich lange kräftig erhalten haben? Sie gleichen diesen Rosen. Wenn sie selbst schon unzählige kleine Falten in ihrem Angesichte haben, so ist doch noch zwischen ihnen die Anmut herrschend und eine sehr schöne liebe Farbe.[66]

> [have you ever observed one of those elderly women . . . who, having been beautiful in their youth, are still well preserved? They are like the roses. And though these women now have countless wrinkles in their faces, there is, nevertheless, a certain grace and beauty of color between the wrinkles which continues to prevail.]

As is to be expected at this stage, Heinrich then adds: "Ich antwortete, dass ich das noch nie beobachtet hätte. . . ." [I replied that I had not noticed them before.] Evidence of Risach's physiognomical outlook is shown on two other occasions: first, when, by a judgment of Heinrich's appearance, he foresees that the latter will make great progress once he has chosen to pursue a particular path of life; and, secondly, when, having philosophized about the way in which clothes take on the shape and structure of the wearer, he goes on to say: "Wie es mit dem Gewande ist, ist es auch mit dem Leibe, der das Gewand der Seele ist, welchen der Künstler durch das Bild und Gleichnis des Leibes darstellt."[67] [As with the attire, so with the body, which is the inner man's attire, which the artist represents through the image and symbol of the body.] But, as we can already see, Risach is no ordinary physiognomist. Indeed, in the second half of the novel, we learn that he has a profound love of classical sculpture as well as a wide knowledge and understanding of art. Particularly interesting is Risach's virtually Lavaterian concern with homogeneity in art, and his admiration for the old masters because they copied nature more faithfully than the moderns. And so it seems that, through his presentation of Risach as one who has learnt to use his eyes with aesthetic feeling, Stifter is drawing attention to the importance of true physiognomical vision as constituting an integral part of the completely mature human being.

Heinrich's spiritual development, then, consists partly in his learning to appreciate the human appearance with a more aesthetic eye. His early days at the *Rosenhaus* already show that he is in the right atmosphere for such a development. But the turning point in his physiognomical progress comes after he has noticed a girl (who later turns out to be Natalie) weeping with great emotion at a performance of *King Lear*: "Das Angesicht war von Tränen übergossen, und ich richtete meinen Blick unverwandt auf sie."[68] [Tears were streaming down her face, and I kept my eyes incessantly fixed on her.] This experience has such an overwhelming effect on the hero that afterward, when he returns to his own home, he begins to consider the human face as the finest subject for drawing, and proceeds to study it: ". . . ich suchte mir Kenntnisse über das menschliche Antlitz zu verschaffen."[69] [I tried to acquire some knowledge about the human face.] Furthermore, he finds it curious that he has never before thought of seeing whether his sister's facial features were worth drawing. Later, Heinrich discovers that drawing people helps him to understand them better, an idea we find also expressed by Lavater. When he returns to the *Rosenhaus,* he seems to be much more observant than he was on his first visit. He describes the appearance of the gardener and his wife; he also observes changes in Gustav, and at table becomes aware of another aspect of Risach's appearance: "Da ich so, da die Speisen erschienen, meinem alten Gastfreunde gegenüber sass, fiel mir plötzlich auf, was der Mann für schöne Zähne habe. Sehr dicht, weiss, klein und mit einem Schmelze überzogen sassen sie in dem Munde, und kein einziger fehlte."[70] [As I sat oppo-

site my host at dinner, I suddenly noticed what a fine set of teeth he had. They were very compact, white, small, and enameled, and there was not one missing.] Indeed, Heinrich's way of looking at people has by now taken a distinctly positive turn. This is especially emphasized by the change in his attitude to Risach's general appearance:

> Seine seltsame Kleidung und seine Gewohnheit, immer barhäuptig zu gehen, welch beides mir anfangs aufgefallen war, beirrte mich endlich gar nicht mehr, ja es stimmte eigentlich zu der Umgebung sowohl seiner Zimmer als der immer um ihn herum wohnenden Bevölkerung, von der er sich nicht als etwas Vornehmes abhob, der er vielmehr gleich war, und von der er sich doch wieder als etwas Selbständiges unterschied.[71]

> [His strange attire and his habit of going about bareheaded, which I had noticed at the beginning, no longer bothered me after a while; indeed, I thought it toned in both with the rooms in the house and the household staff, whom he did not stand out from as a superior, but, rather, was equal with, while retaining a distinct individuality.]

Another example of Heinrich's new physiognomical awareness (which was discussed in the [chapter VI of *Physiognomy in the European Novel*]) is shown when, on seeing Mathilde and Natalie for the second time, he notes a family resemblance between them and Gustav. He also refers from time to time to his artistic pursuits: "Ich malte die Hände oder Büsten verschiedener Leute, die sich in dem Rosenhause oder in dem Meierhofe befanden."[72] [I painted the hands and busts of people living at the *Rosenhaus* and the farmhouse.] He describes, too, the joy of constantly improving his draftsmanship:

> Besondere Freude machte es mir, dass ich nach und nach die Feinheiten des menschlichen Angesichtes immer besser behandeln lernte, besonders, was mir früher so schwer war, wenn der leichte Duft der Farbe über die Wangen schöner Mädchen ging, die sich sanft rundeten, schier keine Abwechslung zeigten und doch so mannigfaltig waren. Mir waren die Versuche am angenehmsten, das Liebliche, Sittige, Schelmische, das sich an manchem jungen Land-oder Gebirgsmädchen darstellte, auf der Leinwand nachzuahmen.[73]

> [It was especially gratifying for me to learn to understand the subtleties of the human face better and better and, above all, to be able to do something I had previously found so difficult, that is, to catch that slight aura which could be noted on the cheeks of fair damsels—cheeks which, though gently curving, and seeming to lack variety of contour, were, nevertheless, so full of character. But what I enjoyed doing most of all was to try and reproduce that peculiar mixture of demureness, charm, and roguishness you could see in the faces of many a country girl or mountain lass.]

Thanks to his father, who possesses a number of paintings, the hero is also able to study the work of such masters as Titian and Veronese and to read books about art, just as he takes the opportunity to look at the sculptures in his native city.

As Heinrich acquires a more thorough knowledge of the fine arts, he develops more and more into a sensitive observer of the human appearance. This is shown particularly in his attitude to the beauty of older women:

> Seit ich Mathilden kannte . . . war ich auf die Angesichter ältlicher und alter Frauen aufmerksam geworden. Man tut sehr unrecht, und ich bin mir bewusst, dass ich es auch getan habe, und gewiss handeln andere Leute ebenfalls so, wenn man die Angesichter von Frauen und Mädchen, sobald sie ein gewisses Alter erreicht haben, sofort beseitigt und sie für etwas hält, das die Betrachtung nicht mehr lohnt. Ich fing jetzt zu denken an, dass es anders sei.[74]

> [Since coming to know Mathilde . . . I had become interested in the faces of old and elderly women. It is quite mistaken—and I realize I have been no less guilty in this respect than others—to dismiss the faces of women and girls once they have reached a certain age, and to consider them no longer worth looking at. I began to see now that it was quite otherwise.]

And each time he sees Mathilde, he is able to discover more evidence of her beauty, but, as he adds: "Und mehr als diese Schönheit war es, wie ich wohl jetzt erkannte, da ich so viele Angesichter so genau betrachtet hatte, um sie nachzubilden, die Seele, welche gütig und abgeschlossen sich darstellte und auf die Menschen, die ihr nahten, wirkte."[75] [And having made such a careful study of faces in order to copy them, I now realized that it was [Mathilde's] inner being rather than her physical beauty, a demure, beneficent beauty, that had such an effect on people in her presence.] (Here we are reminded of a remark made by Lavater: "Echter, reiner physiognomischer Sinn in Ansehung des weiblichen Geschlechtes ist die beste Würze und Stärkung des menschlichen Lebens—und das allerwürksamste Verwahrungsmittel vor Erniedrigungen seiner selbst und anderer."[76] [To have a genuine physiognomical sense when gazing at the fair sex is the best spice and tonic of life—and the most effective preventive against debasing oneself and others.] The refinement of Heinrich's physiognomical outlook is again confirmed when he compares Gustav's healthy appearance with the somewhat jaded facial features of youths living in the city.

The high point in his descriptions is the long portrait of Natalie, which culminates a series of observations he has made of her since first he saw her at the theater. Noteworthy is the way he compares her with antique sculpture:

> Ich erkannte erst jetzt, warum sie mir immer so merkwürdig gewesen ist, ich erkannte es, seit ich die geschnittenen Steine meines Vaters gesehen hatte. Mir erschien es, Natalie sehe einem der Angesichter ähnlich, welche ich auf den Steinen erblickt hatte, oder vielmehr in ihren Zügen war das nämliche, was in den Zügen auf den Angesichtern der geschnittenen Steine ist. . . .

> Natalie stammte also gleichsam aus einem Geschlechte, das vergangen war und das anders und selbständiger war als das jetzige.[77]

> [Only then did I realize what I had found so remarkable about her, and I realized it when I had seen my father's sculptures. It seemed to me that Natalie looked like the faces I had seen in those sculptures, or rather her features had the essence of the facial features of the sculptures. . . . Natalie was, then, the symbol of a race which had vanished, which was different, more independent than the present race.]

For Heinrich, Natalie is, indeed, not merely someone to be compared with sculptural forms, but an actual physical embodiment of classical beauty and simplicity, just as she is also a symbolic expression of a certain humanistic ideal, to a knowledge and understanding of which the hero's *Bildung* is mainly directed. At this stage, then, we see how much the hero has benefited by his increasingly physiognomical appreciation of the human appearance, by his study of paintings and sculpture, and by his own artistic activities. In fact, if we consider Heinrich's character from this point of view, we may say that he has, so to speak, acquired many of the aptitudes which Lavater requires the ideal physiognomist to possess. But the peculiar merit of Stifter's treatment of Heinrich as a physiognomist lies in the skillful way in which he incorporates it in the story of Heinrich's inner moral development while relating it as well to the other ethical and aesthetic themes of the novel.

One of the most significant aspects of the nineteenth-century novel is the widespread and varied structural use of character description, such as we rarely find in the novel before 1800. Not content with the single composite portrait, the novelists of our period delight in describing their characters again and again, according to the demands of their narratives. In many cases we find that with each successive description we become more and more familiar with the inner essence of the characters. Character description is also used as an effective means of suggesting the passage of time, and is particularly helpful in showing, amongst other things, the development from childhood to adulthood of such characters as Tom and Maggie Tulliver and Bob Jakin in *The Mill on the Floss*, Graham Bretton and Polly Home in *Villette*, Heathcliff in *Wuthering Heights*, Charles Bovary in *Madame Bovary*, and Olivier d'Orsel in *Dominique*. Sometimes character description goes hand in hand with the development of the action. For instance, a series of misfortunes or tragic events may with time bring about a noticeable decline or deterioration in a character's physical appearance. This is true of Captain Brown in *Cranford*, Signora Accorombona and Torquato Tasso in *Vittoria Accorombona*, Baron Rothsattel, Veitel Itzig, Hirsch Ehrenthal, Schröter, and Schmeie Tinkeles in *Soll und Haben*, Old Osborne in *Vanity Fair*, Julie in *Dominique*, Miss Haversham in *Great Expectations*, and Professor Berger, Xenobie, and Baroness Grenwitz in *Problematische Naturen.* On the other hand, a positive inner development usually leads to a pleasing maturity in the appearance, as we see in Joe Gargery and Biddy in *Great Expectations,* Amelia and Dobbin in *Vanity Fair,* the heroine of *Eugénie Grandet,* Frank Gresham in *Doctor Thorne,* Anton and Lenore in *Soll und Haben,* Judith in *Der Grüne Heinrich,* and Augustin in *Dominique.* That all this is in itself ample testimony to the physiognomical awareness of novelists themselves is self-evident. But apart from adding to our understanding and appreciation of the characters, the tendency to describe them at various stages in the narrative bespeaks a fine use of physiognomy in the novel. First of all, as far as the first-person narrator is concerned, there is a certain physiognomical validity in presenting characters in a drawn-out portrait. Thus by not restricting himself to a single description, the narrator is free to choose significant moments for referring to particular features or noting facial expressions or describing physical changes. Moreover, in so far as the narrator avoids the Olympian practice of observing everything en bloc, the drawn-out portrait is, of course, much more realistic, as well as dramatically more interesting. Indeed, the drawn-out portrait may be regarded in some sense as an aesthetic expression of Lavater's injunction to physiognomists to make repeated observations of their subjects.

Notes

A key to the abbreviations of frequently cited sources can be [found in the Select Bibliography.] Other works listed in the Bibliography are cited here by author and short title only.

1. Lavater is referred to in Sénancour's *Oberman* (1804), Anna Maria Porter's *Hungarian Brothers* (1807), Vigny's *Cinq Mars* (1826), Stendhal's *Lucien Leuwen* (posth. 1896), George Sand's *Mauprat* (1847), Melville's *Moby Dick* (1851) and *Pierre* (1852), Borrow's *Lavengro* (1851), Champfleury's *Bourgeois de Molinchart* (1857), Spielhagen's *Problematische Naturen* (1860-61), Raabe's *Gänse von Butzow* (1865) and *Wunnigel* (1876), and Barbey d'Aurevilly's *Les Diaboliques* (1874), not to mention fiction discussed in [chapters I-VI of *Physiognomy in the European Novel.*] Lavater's name was also commonly coupled with Gall's, and sometimes so in a rather patronizing manner. Thus Wilhelm Wundt writes: "Die vier Folianten des phrenologischen Hauptwerkes verhalten sich in der That zu Lavaters Fragmenten ungefähr ebenso, wie ein trockenes anatomisches Compendium zu einer Predigtsammlung." (The four tomes of [Gall's] main phrenological study more or less go together with Lavater's *Fragmente* as a dry-as-dust anatomical compendium does with

a collection of sermons.) "Über den Ausdruck der Gemüthsbewegungen," p. 124.

2. Among several comic novels inspired by phrenology, we may refer in particular to August Langbein's *Thomas von Pampel* (1806), Giovanni Battista Balscopo's *Travels in Phrenologasto* (London, 1829), and [Anon.], *The Phrenologist's Daughter* (London, 1854). Of theatrical satires may be mentioned François Llaunet's *Docteur Gall,* a one-act vaudeville (n.d.) and Alexandre Duval's *Monsieur Tête ou la cranomanie* (Paris, 1803?). In England there were farces or burlettas such as [Anon.], *The Phrenologist,* first performed at Edinburgh on 4 April 1825; Thomas Wade's *Phrenologists,* first performed on 30 November 1829; Joseph Coyne's *Phrenologist,* first performed at Dublin on 3 June 1835; [Anon.], *The Organ of Order,* first performed on 23 June 1839; John Faucit's *Bump of Benevolence,* first performed on 1 September 1841; and S. Roxby's *Shifts of Genius; or, Phrenological Philanthropy,* first performed at Manchester on 14 December 1843. One of the most famous satires on Gall was Kotzebue's *Organe des Gehirns* (1806), which has been described by Rabany, *Kotzebue,* as "une des meilleures comédies et des plus amusantes de l'auteur" (one of the author's best and funniest comedies), p. 306. In this connection, Champfleury, referring to the lampooning of Gall by cartoonists, writes: "Indifférent au blâme ou à la louange, Gall n'éprouvait aucune meurtrissure des ridicules dont ses adversaires voulaient le couvrir. A Berlin il était le premier à la représentation d'une comédie satirique de Kotzebuë, La Craniologie. . . ." (Indifferent to praise or blame, Gall was not at all offended by the ridicule which his enemies wanted to heap on him. In Berlin he was the first to attend Kotzebue's satirical comedy, *Craniology.*) *Histoire de la caricature sous la république,* p. 338. Kotzebue's play was translated into English by A. Capadose in 1838 as *The Organs of the Brain.* (For all this information, I am grateful partly to François Jost and partly to Allardyce Nicoll, *A History of English Drama 1660-1900,* Vols. IV-VI [Cambridge, 1955-59]). As for French satires on physiognomy, we may mention *La Physionomanie,* a one-act comic opera by Alexandre Piccini to a libretto by Razy and Ferrière, first performed at the Théâtre des Troubadours on 17 January 1801, and *Avis au public, ou le physionomiste en défaut,* a two-act comic opera by Piccini to a libretto by Émile Désaugiers, first performed at the Théâtre Feydeau on 22 November 1806. We may also refer to three other dramas, each of them entitled *Lavater:* a one-act comedy by Armand Séguier (Paris, 1809); a five-act prose drama by Joseph Mathurin Brisset, first performed

at the Comédie Française on 14 September 1835; and a two-act vaudeville by Philippe Dumanoir and Louis Clairville, first performed at the Théâtre Dramatique on 10 January 1848. In England Lavater was satirized in the farce *False Colours* (1783) and Azile d'Arcy's *Prejudice; or Physiognomy* (London, 1817), and in Germany in Christoph Bretzner's *Karl und Sophie; oder, die Physiognomie* (Leipzig, 1780). One Austrian satire to mention is the anonymous *Der Talisman oder: Trau, Schau, Wem? Neuestes, Scherzhafftes . . . Nimm mich mit. Nach Grundsätzen des J. C. Lavaters* (Graz, 1847).

3. Ruskin, *The Diaries,* II, 612-13. The editor of Ruskin's diaries, Joan Evans, assumes the entry *Lavater* to be J. R. Planché's play *Not a Bad Judge,* which was first performed at the Lyceum Theatre, London, on 2 March 1848, and was given 42 performances, being the fifth most popular play of the season. Cf. Charles Dickens, Jr, *The Life of Charles James Mathews* (London, 1879), p. 322. According to a diary entry of Lewis Carroll's, however, this play was entitled *Lavater the Liar,* being, in fact, an adaptation of a Samuel Foote comedy by Charles Mathews, who himself played the hero as he had done in the Planché play. Cf. *The Diaries of Lewis Carroll,* ed. Roger Lancelyn Green (London, 1953), I, 253. Allardyce Nicoll (V, 784) ascribes a play called *Lavater* to H. C. Coape, which seems plausible in so far as the latter dedicated his three-volume theatrical novel *What Will People Say* (1880) to Mathews.

4. We may refer here to Dickens' short story *Hunted Down* (1859), whose action is motivated by the narrator's firm belief in physiognomy.

5. In this connection, it was not unusual for men of letters to show an open preference for one or other of the two sciences, usually physiognomy. Godwin, for example, writes: "There is a distinction, not unworthy to be attached to, that is here to be made between Lavater's system of physiognomy, and Gall's craniology, which is much in favour of the former." *Thoughts on Man* (London, 1831), p. 371. Moreover, the question was sometimes raised in articles as to whether physiognomy revealed the inner man better than phrenology, or vice-versa. Thus a minor German philosopher writes: "Das Antlitz, das bewegliche Mienenspiel, die Physiognomie überhaupt, ist ein adäquaterer Spiegel des Geistes, als die Hirnschale." (The face, the mobile features, in short, the physiognomy, is a more adequate mirror of the soul than the skull.) J. H. Fichte, "Anthropologie und Psychologie," p. 278. On the other hand, an anonymous writer, having referred to physiognomy as being less "deep" than phrenology, goes on to say: "Let any

man read the books of our same doctors [Gall and Spurzheim], and those of Lavater: and he will see that the two modes cannot bear comparison." *Foreign Quarterly Review,* II (1828), p. 37.

6. Apart from articles on phrenology referred to in Chapter III [of *Physiognomy in the European Novel*], we may mention Robert E. Riegel, "The Introduction of Phrenology to the United States," *American Historical Review,* XXXIX (1933): 73-78; Anthony A. Walsh, "Phrenology and the Boston Medical Community in the 1830's," *Bulletin of the History of Medicine,* L, 2 (1976): 261-73; Madeleine B. Stern, *Heads and Headlines: The Phrenological Fowlers* (Norman, Oklahoma, 1971); "Mathew B. Brady and the Rationale of Crime. A Discovery in Daguerreotypes," *The Quarterly Journal of the Library of Congress,* XXXI 1974): 127-35; "Mathew Brady Again," *The Quarterly Journal of the Library of Congress,* XXXV (1978): 242-43.

7. Of several academic writings concerned with the influence of phrenology on literature may be mentioned Hungerford, "Poe and Phrenology"; idem, "Walt Whitman and his Chart of Bumps"; G. T. Clapton, "Lavater, Gall and Baudelaire," *Revue de Littérature Comparée,* XIII (1933): 259-98 & 429-56; A. L. Cooke, "Whitman's Indebtedness to the Scientific Thought of his Day," *University of Texas Studies in English,* XVI (1936): 115-24; H. O. Lokensgard, "Oliver Wendell Holmes's 'Phrenological Character,'" *New England Quarterly,* XIII (1940): 711-18; Carroll D. Laverty, "Science and Pseudo-Science in the Writings of E. A. Poe" (Diss., Duke University, 1951); Tyrus Hillway, "Melville's Use of Two Pseudo-Sciences," *Modern Language Notes,* LXIV (1949), 149-50; Irving Massey, "The Contribution of Neurology to the Scepticism of Alfred de Vigny," *Journal of the History of Medicine,* IX (1954): 329-48; Stanley M. Vogel, *German Literary Influences on the American Transcendentalists* (New Haven, 1955); J. B. Wilson, "Phrenology and the Transcendentalists," *American Literature,* XXVIII (1956): 220-25; T. L. Brasher, "Whitman's Conversion to Phrenology," *Walt Whitman Newsletter,* IV (1958): 95-97; W. V. McDonald, Jr., "Scottish Phrenologists and Scott's Novels," *Notes and Queries,* IX (1962): 415-17; Stephen S. Conroy, "Emerson and Phrenology," *American Quarterly,* XVI (1964): 215-17; Kuno Schuhmann, "Phrenologie und Idealogie: Frederick Marryat's *Mr. Midshipman Easy,*" *Die Neueren Sprachen,* XIII (1964): 567-73; Harold Aspiz, "Educating the Kosmos: 'There was a Child went forth,'" *American Quarterly,* XVIII (1966): 655-66; idem, "Phrenologizing the Whale," *Nineteenth-Century Fiction,* XXIII (1968): 18-27; N. N. Feltes, "Phrenology: From

Lewes to George Eliot," *Studies in the Literary Imagination,* I (1966): 13-22; Madeleine B. Stern, "Poe: 'The Mental Temperament' for Phrenologists," *American Literature,* XL (1968): 155-63; idem, "Mark Twain Had His Head Examined," *American Literature,* XLI (1969): 207-18; Alan Gribben, "Mark Twain, Phrenology, and the 'Temperaments': A Study of Pseudoscientific Influences," *American Quarterly,* XXIV (1972): [45]-68; Jason T. Hall, "Gall's Phrenology: A Romantic Psychology," *Studies in Romanticism,* XVI (1977): 305-17.

8. Cf. Hall, "Gall's Phrenology," passim.

9. Cf. Hungerford, "Walt Whitman and His Chart of Bumps," pp. 366-84.

10. Cf. Hungerford, "Poe and Phrenology," passim.

11. Italo Svevo, *Senilità* (Milan, 1927), p. 45.

12. *GH,* p. 339.

13. Bulwer Lytton, *Pelham,* p. 204; *BM,* p. 18; Dickens, *Little Dorrit,* p. 129; *GE,* p. 310.

14. Charlotte Brontë, *Jane Eyre,* pp. 225-34, and *V,* p. 47.

15. Quoted in Stephen Heath, *The Nouveau Roman: A Study in the Practice of Writing* (London, 1972), p. 127n.

16. Raabe, *Werke,* I, 12.

17. *WH,* pp. 8, 16, & 112.

18. *WH,* pp. 19, 188, 82, & 7.

19. *HM,* p. 163.

20. *HM,* pp. 367 & 380.

21. *HM,* p. 428.

22. *HM,* p. 432.

23. *HM,* pp. 557 & 559.

24. *HM,* p. 545.

25. *HM,* p. 456.

26. *HM,* p. 490.

27. Immermann, *Werke,* III, 23.

28. *V,* pp. 94 & 165.

29. *V,* p. 275.

30. *V,* p. 369.

31. *MB,* p. 14.

32. *MB,* p. 95.

33. Quoted in Heier, "J. C. Lavater und der russische Zarenhof," p. 844.

34. *MF,* pp. 27-28.

35. *MF,* p. 150.

36. *MF,* p. 147.

37. *MF,* p. 230.

38. *RN,* p. 69.

39. *RN,* p. 143.

40. *RN,* p. 242.

41. *RN,* p. 108.

42. *RN,* pp. 238-39.

43. *RN,* p. 242.

44. *RN,* p. 318.

45. *RN,* p. 173.

46. *RN,* p. 257.

47. *RN,* p. 335.

48. *RN,* pp. 371-74.

49. *GE,* p. 1.

50. *GE,* p. 5.

51. *GE,* p. 16.

52. *GE,* p. 21.

53. *GE,* p. 24.

54. *GE,* pp. 158-59.

55. *GE,* p. 40.

56. *GE,* p. 116.

57. *GE,* p. 119.

58. *GE,* p. 165.

59. *GE,* p. 450.

60. *GE,* pp. 364-65.

61. *DN,* p. 44.

62. *DN,* p. 81.

63. *DN,* p. 115.

64. *DN,* p. 81.

65. *DN,* p. 143.

66. *DN,* p. 57.

67. *DN,* p. 412.

68. *DN,* p. 423.

69. *DN,* p. 207.

70. *DN,* p. 223.

71. *DN,* p. 237.

72. *DN,* p. 391.

73. *DN,* p. 394.

74. *DN,* p. 494.

75. *DN,* p. 523.

76. *PF,* III, 290.

77. *DN,* p. 529.

Select Bibliography

A. A LIST OF FREQUENTLY CITED PRIMARY
AND SECONDARY SOURCES, WITH
ABBREVIATIONS

BM Champfleury. *Les Bourgeois de Molinchart.* Paris, 1859.

DN Stifter, Adalbert. *Der Nachsommer.* Leipzig, 1925.

E Austen, Jane. *Emma.* London, Toronto, & New York, 1922.

EG Balzac, Honoré de. *Eugénie Grandet,* ed. H. J. Hunt. Oxford, 1967.

GE Dickens, Charles. *Great Expectations.* London, 1947.

GG Gotthelf, Jeremias. *Geld und Geist, oder die Versöhnung.* Zurich & Stuttgart, 1962.

GH Keller, Gottfried. *Der Grüne Heinrich,* Originalausgabe. Stuttgart, 1957.

HM Scott, Walter. *The Heart of Midlothian.* Oxford, 1912.

M Sand, George. *Mauprat.* Paris, 1857.

MB Flaubert, Gustave. *Madame Bovary,* ed. Édouard Mayniel. Paris, 1958.

MF Eliot, George. *The Mill on the Floss.* London, 1964.

PF Lavater, Johann Caspar. *Physiognomische Fragmente zur Beförderung der Menschenkenntniss und Menschenliebe,* 4 vols. Leipzig & Winterthur, 1775-78.

PN Spielhagen, Friedrich. *Problematische Naturen,* 2 vols. Leipzig, 1902.

RN Stendhal. *Le Rouge et le Noir,* ed. Henri Martineau. Paris, 1960.

V Brontë, Charlotte. *Villette.* London, 1947.

WH Brontë, Emily. *Wuthering Heights,* ed. Ian Jack & Hilda Marsden. Oxford, 1976.

B. OTHER PRIMARY SOURCES

Borrow, George. *Lavengro.* London, 1970.

Brontë, Charlotte. *Jane Eyre,* ed. Q. D. Leavis. Harmondsworth, 1971.

Bulwer Lytton, Edward. *Pelham.* London, n.d.

Dickens, Charles. *Little Dorrit.* Oxford, 1953.

———. *The Mystery of Edwin Drood.* Oxford, 1956.

———. *Our Mutual Friend.* Oxford, 1952.

Flaubert, Gustave. *Dictionnaire des idées reçues.* Paris, 1951.

Gaskell, Elizabeth. *Cranford.* London, 1913.

Immermann, Karl Leberecht. *Werke,* 4 vols., ed. Harry Maync. Leipzig, 1906.

Meredith, George. *The Ordeal of Richard Feverel.* London, 1878.

Mitford, Mary Russell. *Our Village. Sketches of Rural Character and Scenery.* London, 1907.

Raabe, Wilhelm. *Werke,* vol. I, ed. Karl Hoppe. Munich, 1964.

Ruskin, John. *The Diaries,* vol. II, ed. Joan Evans, Oxford, 1958.

Spielhagen, Friedrich. *Problematische Naturen,* 2 vols. Leipzig, 1902.

Stifter, Adalbert. *Der Nachsommer.* Leipzig, 1925.

Tieck, Ludwig. *Werke,* 4 vols., ed. Marianne Thalmann. Munich, 1966.

C. SECONDARY SOURCES

Fichte, J. H. "Der bisherige Zustand der Anthropologie und Psychologie." *Zeitschrift für Philosophie und spekulative Theologie,* XII (1844): 66-105; 243-78.

Heier, Edmund. "J. C. Lavater und der russische Zarenhof." *Schweizer Monatshefte,* XLV (1965): 831-50.

Wundt, Wilhelm. "Über den Ausdruck der Gemüthsbewegungen." *Deutsche Rundschau,* XI (1877): 120-33.

Lee Fontanella (essay date 1987)

SOURCE: Fontanella, Lee. "Physiognomics in Romantic Spain." In *From Dante to García Márquez: Studies in Romance Literatures and Linguistics,* edited by Gene H. Bell-Villada, Antonio Giménez, and George Pistorius, pp. 100-13. Williamstown, Mass.: Williams College, 1987.

[In the following essay, Fontanella examines the use of human stereotypes in nineteenth-century Spanish literature and the extent of the influence of physiognomy on Spanish authors.]

Thirty years ago, Professor Piper was completing the preparation of an ingenious little text, *¡Así es la vida!,* which he would use as a reader in his Beginning Spanish classes. I'll bet that he never dreamed that his book was going to outlive his career, by virtue of its eight printings. I'll wager, also, that the young man who wrote the brochure which introduced Piper's text never imagined that he would someday become president and chairman of the board of Norton Publishers, the firm which had the vision to publish this book. More astonishingly, I could never have suspected that *¡Así es la vida!*, that little reader with the commonplace title, the first book I ever read in the Spanish language, would signal the beginning of my professional activity.

Today, thirty years after my marvelous introduction to the Spanish language, I would like to celebrate the thematics of that reader. I am not sure that don Anson could rightfully imagine that his book would become my point of departure, my object of celebration, as opposed to—let us say—an unforgettable, insightful article of his, on the Spanish classic, *Lazarillo de Tormes,* or one of his own favorites, concerning José de Ribera's painting of the sleeping Jacob, which was published in 1963, the year I graduated from Williams.[1] But I do so in all seriousness, and apart from any personal affinity to the little book. For quite coincidentally, the cultural tradition from which *¡Así es la vida!* derives is part and parcel of the broad cultural context which I customarily study: the para-literary phenomena of the eighteenth and nineteenth centuries.

¡Así es la vida! is a series of physiognomic vignettes, in which imaginary characters of the Hispanic world are typed according to their "brethren" (we should not say "counterparts") in the animal world. These vignettes are much simpler to read now, as I look them over again, but all of them still ring a bell, just as vignettes and their human types should do, loud and clear, if they are to fulfill their ultimate purpose. Since they do pertain to the related traditions of the literature of human types and fabular literature, many of these vignettes are pleasingly moralistic.

The squirrel-man, that hoarder who lived by choice in a poor section of Madrid, although he did not have to, had amassed enough *pesetas* to afford himself a glorious funeral and a sumptuous tomb; but no one ever visited it. That assiduous traveler, the swallow-man, devoted his existence to planning his family's vacation; but after the vacation was spent, they were unable to improve the quality of their lives under their own roof. The lion-man, for all his ostentatious nudity, wound up with a bad cold, unable to show it off. The owl-man suffers from an ingenuous philosophical remove from practical experience. The rabbit-man is afraid of his shadow, and the sheep-man can follow well, but make no decisions. Similar to the squirrel-man, the foxy type has become a land-baron in lucrative Buenos Aires, to which he came to make his fortune; but he is despised by all his tenants. The magpie-man experiences the im-

possibility of intelligible conversation, because he talks and interrupts compulsively. The ostrich-man is the consummate disbeliever, although he ironically believes in the figural predication of Biblical tales. Oddly, too, the turtle-man heads up an alarm-clock business, but he cannot drag himself out of bed. The whimsicality of the butterfly-man results in such a serious lack of *Sitzfleisch* that he achieves nothing. The only possibility of love remaining to the peacock-man, for all his egocentricity, is between him and his sports-car. The chameleon-man, an opportunist, destroys his political candidacy when he foolishly tries to play friendly first-cousins off against each other, in an attempt to profit from the denigration of each.

There can be no doubt about it: don Anson was attempting to make ideal Williams graduates of us all, even as he taught us the skills of the Castilian language. Now, that making of literature the anticipatory representation of what ideally would be in fact, whether morally or artistically, is the stuff of fabular literature. Unfortunately, we know these things best in retrospect, but I prefer to think that by the subtle wiles of fabular moralizing, we all grew up a bit then, in the process of reading *¡Así es la vida!*—all but a couple of dozers, I guess, who probably did not even catch the moral of that turtle-man who was in an alarm-clock business which did him no practical good. In the course of reading this sly and beguiling, but apparently innocent little book, we who went on with Hispanic Studies also got a glimpse of what was to constitute portions of our future academic concerns. In history, Pelayo and the Glorious Revolution of 1868; in geography, cities of Latin America and Spain; and in literature and philosophy, Fray Luis de León, Cervantes, Ortega y Gasset, Unamuno, Larra, and Galdós. And speaking of these last two names—Larra and Galdós—don Anson mentions them as if to say that he knows exactly the literary tradition from which *¡Así es la vida!* has sprung. (These two names appear in the last chapter, about the eagle-man.)

Before my final remarks about *¡Así es la vida!*, I would like to state in unequivocal terms where I am heading with this preamble. It is in the direction of cultural-historical and literary-theoretical questions, concerning the literature of types and the psychology behind the application of the type in Spain's modern period, which I assume to date from the eighteenth century. Professor Piper had the basics of the question in mind when in the final chapter, he, as author, meets up with the eagle-man, Federico Ulloa. Piper constructs, here, a sort of dialogue with himself as author; Ulloa is the alter-ego. The variety of possible human types is great, if not limitless, observes Ulloa. But of most concern is the dialogue concerning the legitimacy of emphasizing a single character trait above all others, for the sake of moral criticism. This amounts to running the risk of overgeneralization, Ulloa notes. "But other writers have done so," argues the author. The resolution to the question appears to be that too high a degree of generalization is, in effect, caricature. No matter; ¡Así es la vida! has already been written, and the reader has already been affected by its linguistic and moral lessons.

I suppose I wondered as a student, why that eagle-man chapter was there, tacked on as an overview of other animal-men, and as a speculation about the parameters of typification. Nevertheless, those musings about the limits of generalization amounted to more than self-indulgent remarks about one's own text. They were, instead, hints—very subtle ones, to be sure, in a primer like this—about the limits of scientific observation, and they implied notions about how we prefer to view human personality in different historical periods; or, at least, how our psyche at a given historical point is *able* to perceive personality. All literary examples lead us to know that man has never perceived human nature in exactly the same way in all places at all times. The perception of character has never been entirely willy-nilly, and don Anson's eagle-man chapter prompts us to consider why not. These are highfalutin claims, in the light of the apparent levity of ¡Así es la vida!; nor do I mean at all to turn Professor Piper's book into something it does not pretend to be.

Truth be told, we can approach definitions of the different views of human character which man has held in different periods. Ivy McClelland has remarked that especially in the eighteenth century, there was a psychological need for the type, but that that need diminished later on in the nineteenth.[2] McClelland, a noteworthy commentator on Enlightenment and Romantic Spain, may have said, more insistently, more discriminatingly, that that psychological need actually changed substantially in the course of the nineteenth century. It is pretty safe to take such observations as remarks pertinent to most, if not all, countries of the modern Western world at the time. My main, but not sole, focus is Spain, one of those countries which sensed itself a ripe candidate for entry into the new, analytical mode of thought. This new mode of thought derived from the rationalism which had flourished in European intellectual circles since the early seventeenth century; however, the ancestral relation of the new intellectual mode to rationalism was, in a way, ironic, since the new intellectual mode would eventually turn against itself, undoing, not reconfirming, that which gave it life. Just how technological Spain was at the turn of the eighteenth century is questionable, but that does not imply, necessarily, a lack of impetus for the fresh, empirical scientific view, which is in fact at the root of our philosophical considerations as regards the topic at hand.

This new impetus for analytical observation was to affect the way in which man viewed his fellows. For the literary artist, at least, it led to the utter refusal, if not to the perceptual inability, to type the human being. (I say this, even taking into account the dozens of highly significant titles and the hundreds of character sketches registered or implicit in the unforgettable study by Margarita Ucelay DaCal, on the literature of types in Spain's nineteenth century.)[3] Seen in the reverse, the new impetus for analytical observation was opposed to any former universalizing view, since it sought diversity in the particularities of individual character, even as it struggled to retain a vision of the traditional type. In this, precisely, rests the great drama of the coming of the new vision in the early nineteenth century. Both opposing visions—typification and particularization—have prompted several of Arthur O. Lovejoy's most memorable essays, and they are reflected in a single expression by George Boas, as he attempted to delineate what he called the "limits of reason":

> This philosophical assumption of the regularity of nature, of the possibility of always discovering some unity beneath or behind or above the apparent diversity, is the source of all science. But it will be observed that whatever unity is found is always found following one of the prepositions in question. It cannot be expressed in literal terms and the words "beneath," "behind," and "above" are all metaphorical. The unity is what we are looking for, the diversity is what we encounter.[4]

If we apply these "limits of reason" to a traditional, then to a more modern scientific view of the parameters of human character, we find that the former aligns itself with Boas's "source of all science." But as the nineteenth century attempted to retain the perception of the type, it found the type increasingly in need of qualification. Although the nineteenth century began by looking for the unity, it encountered the diversity, in words of Boas. This became, truly, a philosophical and perceptual problem.

Professor Piper, in his effort to teach a moral lesson by the slow uncovering of human nature, resorted to that "source of all science"; for practical purposes, he was obliged to assume the unity of character. But Federico Ulloa, the eagle-man and another facet still of Anson Piper, was by comparison the philosophic skeptic, unable to accept the facile typification of human nature, so he thought that the professor's depictions of character were in need of further qualification and diversification. Professor Piper's final chapter may have seemed at first glance "out of character" with the rest of his book, self-indulgent, or gratuitous. On the contrary: when we recognize that Federico Ulloa is the alter-ego of the author, the eagle-man chapter comes to imply the limits of reason as Boas described them.

What is more, author and Ulloa imply the full circle of deductive and inductive reasoning, faith as opposed to science, Platonism and Aristotelianism—and a gamut of polar opposites representative of the passing from the eighteenth to the nineteenth century. Naturally, Larra, the immediate heir to the eighteenth-century mentality, found it perceptually simpler, more philosophically justifiable, to typify the *castellano viejo* than did Galdós when he depicted Benina in *Misericordia,* to name the two examples cited by the authorial voice in the final chapter. (The fictional author in the eagle-man chapter, unwittingly or not, mentions both of these examples as two modes of typification, not necessarily alike.) If don Anson appears in the end to be more akin to Larra in *¡Así es la vida!,* that is likely because he *wished* to resort to the more unified vision of human character that makes the *castellano viejo* more easily memorable than Galdós' Benina.

What was a psychological necessity for the eighteenth-century mind constitutes the fundamental effectiveness of *¡Así es la vida!*. That is, the vision of the world as essentially unchanging is a useful moralistic and mnemonic device. We remember these types, because we may presume their constancy. I, for example, remember these types not in the context of their every circumstance, undertaking, and adventure, but rather, for what they were most likely to do, granted their animal "brethren." It is in this respect that the skeptic, Ulloa, grows too critical: these human types are not caricaturesque exaggerations, as he supposes, but rather universal constants, if we the offspring of scientific empiricism (well tempered by relativism) can accept that as a functional part of the reading game that *¡Así es la vida!* requires. Professor Piper's confidence regarding this fine distinction was probably what moved him to expose his alterego in the final chapter. He knew that he was the generalist dealing in articles of faith, and that if this was what it took to create the pedagogical device, then he could accept Ulloa's criticism when Ulloa warned of the close approximation to caricature.

The main difference between the vast majority of Galdós's characters and those of Larra is not solely that Galdós's develop over lengthier narrative time. It is, instead, that they develop . . . period. No age became more keenly aware of the phenomenon of character development than did Romanticism—egocentric as it was—and in Spain, this awareness hit in the mid-1820's, just at the time of the reinstatement of non-constitutional despotism in Spain. How strange that while politics was moving one way (in the direction of undue centralism and singlemindedness), the art of character definition was moving in another (in the direction of analytical particularism)! No one knew this better than Carlos Ernesto Cook, an Englishman and political emigré, preoccupied with the physical and biological sciences, and one of the editors and contributors to the extraordinary Spanish Romantic periodical, *El Europeo* (Barcelona, 1823-24).[5] In a remarkably telling article on

the subject of man's "character in general and in particular," Cook writes the following:

> *El hombre es un ser tan complicado, que el conocimiento de sus particulares virtudes o vicios, considerados aisladamente, no nos presenta todavía su verdadero carácter:* pues se hallan tan combinados entre sí, que muchas de las acciones que se cometen, consideradas cada una por sí sola, parecen enteramente agenas a la virtud o al vicio. Es menester contemplar el *todo,* y cada individuo debe ser delineado paso a paso, a fin de poder decir: aquí está el hombre . . . Para hacer investigaciones sobre el carácter del hombre, es necesario estudiar por estenso la naturaleza humana, y las anomalías particulares que pertenecen a ella. Sin su conocimiento, es imposible estudiar un individuo. Para delinear un carácter, es menester seguir todas las huellas que se apartan de la armonía general de la naturaleza. Por lo mismo debemos saber en primer lugar, *cuáles son las particularidades esclusivas en cada hombre, o en cada clase de hombres.*[6]

The meaning of the quotation by Cook is profound. The insistence on seeing the whole being, and the simultaneous obsession with the particular qualities of the whole being, place Cook right on the line between the need to type character and the naturally consequent need to undo that synthetic unity in an analytic, discriminatory, individualizing, particularistic act. The latter intellectual procedure was that which was taking the stronger hold in Spain. And it is important to note, also, that *El Europeo,* Cook's vehicle, was a fundamental periodical with the force of manifesto for the new mentality; so Cook's message probably was well heard.

Without the ability to appreciate the philosophical and perceptual attitude so well expressed by Cook in 1824, we cannot get at the traditional novel of character of the nineteenth century: a daring claim, but one which also has its roots in a singular fact of literary history. I refer specifically to a "novel" by the known writer of character sketches and *costumbrista* scenes, Antonio Flores, surely one of the most unsung of nineteenth-century Spain's ingenious writers; *Doce españoles de brocha gorda, que no pudiéndose pintar a sí mismos, me han encargado a mí, Antonio Flores, sus retratos* (1846). Actually, the review of the second edition (1848) of the novel gives away its key role in the history of literature.[7] The reviewer (very possibly Flores himself) states that what started out by being a "gallery of heterogeneous portraits" ended up being a novel whose characters each possess an individuality. This novel, the first Spanish novel to deny critically the faith in and the feasibility of strict physiognomic typing—even at the hand of an artist of literary sketches!—is central to any lengthy study on this topic. For the 1848 reviewer, these characters somehow grew out of the unifying mode. They escaped the limitations implicit in universalistic thought and developed according to the non-prescriptiveness of particularistic empiricism—which was just what Cook had recommended to his readership a quarter century before.

The instances which I am citing are not freakish; they were indicative, even while they were not yet the norm in 1846, and much less so in 1824. They were just a couple of facets of a general tendency to view the world at the time, in its parts (particles!); and this new view was the reason why new technologies for the written word *had* to be invented, such as the relatively inexpensive periodical press (established for Spain in April 1836, by Ramón de Mesonero Romanos). Mesonero Romanos, a writer of sketches himself, required the periodical as an incorporative vehicle for expressing a world which he thought had grown fractionalized and difficult to control, perceptually. He saw the world as divided experience, and he devoted his periodical *Semanario Pintoresco Español* to expressing it. His sketches, on the other hand, must have satisfied his more traditionalist bent—or, if you will, the other side of the coin of scientific understanding—which yearned for the unified, synthetic vision.

It ought to be evident by now that the most facile sort of physiognomic vision had no chance of survival within the context of the perceptual norms that were on the rise in the nineteenth century. That explains why the "physiognomic fallacies", which were prompted by Johann Caspar Lavater in the 1770's as scientific method for the observation of character, would be discredited as hogwash a century and a half later. By 1960, when E. H. Gombrich wrote his brilliant study "On Physiognomic Perception," Lavater was almost laughable—a far remove from the scientific creditability which he enjoyed in his own time.[8] Gombrich cannot put much stock in the initial physiognomic response, but he recognizes its value as discreetly synthetical. The important thing to note is that Gombrich is right alongside Boas; his summary statement is the analogue in physiognomics to Boas's comment in the philosophy of scientific reason. Gombrich says:

> What should emerge from this discussion is both the value and the fallibility of physiognomic intuition. Without its initial response we could never arrive at a hypothesis which we could subsequently modify and adjust to the evidence provided by life or by history. But we destroy the value of this instrument if we overrate that initial groping, our first move in the effort to make sense.
>
> (50)

In Spain's Romantic period (somewhere between Larra and Galdós, as pertains to character study), "the evidence provided by life or history" (Gombrich) acquired

heightened creditability, so that physiognomics were tempered, resulting in a para-science, even a pseudo-science. John Graham, who in our time has studied Lavater relentlessly, has shown us that indeed Lavater influenced prose characterization.[9] In Spain, too, Lavater must have been influential, although Spain's imaginative prose had not been enjoying the quantity or quality of the prose literature that was being produced in a country such as England; Antonio Alcalá Galiano made that painfully clear from his viewpoint as an exile in England.[10] In Spain, in fact, just between the first two editions of Flores' *Doce españoles* . . . , Antonio Rotondo (eventually known for his history and description of El Escorial) prepared *La fisnomía, o sea El arte de conocer a sus semejantes por las formas exteriores; extractado de las mejores obras de Lavater.*[11]

Probably no vehicle in Spain could better spread notice of the physiognomic sciences than the *Semanario Pintoresco Español*. In its twenty-one years of existence, frequent mention of physiognomics (and later, of its offspring, phrenology) appeared in the periodical. Often, these took the form of visual amusements; at other times they were articles in their own right. Right after the periodical began, there appeared an article on Napoleon's visage, a perennial favorite in physiognomics.[12] Napoleon, a favorite amid the gallery of *planches physiologiques* which boasted such rogues as Louis XI and Richelieu, also appeared alongside such luminaries as Milton, Voltaire, and Mirabeau in serious treatises such as those by J. Ottin, published in Castilian, in Barcelona, in 1845.[13] Ottin did not limit his investigations to Lavater; rather, he also studied Doctor Gall's craneoscopy and animal magnetism. The physiognomic value of the nose was the topic under consideration not long after the *Semanario*'s mention of Napoleon's visage, and in the same periodical.[14] A "natural history" feature showed how the features of man could descend gradually into those of a brute, and vice-versa, how the features of the animal can approach those of a man.[15] This sort of visual-evolution game became, almost, a shibboleth of physiognomic articles, while it also predicated Darwinian concerns.

In fact, these man-to-animal series sketches came to Spain straight from Grandville, as one example (of man-to-fish) from the *Semanario* admitted.[16] Grandville had introduced his humanized animals into Spain in 1841 (*Escenas de la vida privada y pública de los animales*), and these physiognomic and Darwinian relatives, heirs to the eighteenth-century Giambattista Casti (Parliament of Beasts) tradition, flourished.[17] Again, with Grandville in mind, the *Semanario* published a "physiognomy of the cat," wherein the reviewer told how Grandville had observed seventy-five different expressions of the cat, which correspond to the signs of human "passions."[18]

The article is a telling one. Grandville, according to the report, might have subdivided and recombined further, had his pen not simply come to an astonished halt before the "infinite variety" of feline expressions. In so saying, he was the victim of the new diversitarian vision. Yet in a more traditional vein, Grandville believed that the physiognomic principle that the face mirrors the soul held true to a point for animals. *The Museo de las Familias,* another tremendously successful periodical of mid-century, could not drop the topic either, and it published a physiognomic article on dogs and their masters.[19]

By mid-century, the public had become so accustomed to physiognomics that they actually could be given physiognomic puzzles in the *Semanario.*[20] On this occasion, the reader was given six facial expressions and asked what they represented, as if there were one correct answer per outward expression. What incalculable implications these instances must have held for the then modern science of theatrical gesture! This puzzle may seem lighthearted and simplistic, but it is exactly the sort of signal we need in order to be able to view the physiognomic trajectory up as far, historically, as Darwin's *The Expression of the Emotions in Man and Animals* (London: John Murray, 1872), for which the photographer Oscar G. Rejlander made the images of facial expressions which are so important in photohistory today. The puzzle in the *Semanario* signals, as well, famed publications such as that by the Italian physician, Cesare Lombroso, in which he treats of criminal man (1876). Moreover, it indicates a level of sophistication in the reading public which would apply nearly as well to character descriptions in novelistic prose at the time. These unimposing periodical features, taken as a group, can be one gauge by which to measure the degree to which physiognomics might have affected novelistic prose—*and* its interpretation—at mid-century.

It is my opinion—although it is a fact seldom, if ever, mentioned, probably because of the more obvious influence of Lavater on physiognomics—that the genre "physiology of the passions" also greatly influenced the cultivation of literary physiognomics. Also, it was the physiology of the passions which abetted the scientistic schematics that defined the studies by the famous Doctor Gall, father of phrenological sciences, which also had a tremendous influence on art. Various physiologies of passions were published in Spain especially from the 1830's on, beginning, I believe, with the translation of J. L. Alibert: *Fisiología de las pasiones, o Nueva doctrina de los afectos morales* (Madrid: Imp. de D. M. de Burgos, enero de 1831); trans. Lucas de Tornos. Later, none other than Pedro Felipe Monlau translated *La medicina de las pasiones, o Las pasiones consideradas con respecto a las enfermedades, las leyes y a la re-*

ligión (Barcelona: Imp. y Lib. de Pablo Riera, 1857; 2nd ed.). Still later (n.d.), A. Abella translated the *Fisiología de las pasiones* of Ch. Letourneau (Barcelona: Jané Hmnos.). The data in these publications are always set forth schematically, scientistically, and their message is basic: *nosce te ipsum*; then, by implication, you can know your fellow by his outward manifestations.

It was Gall who carried the message too far, in the opinion of many. However, Gall fascinated Spain, possibly because of the immediate link between his phrenological sciences and animal magnetism, or mesmerism. His phrenology was popularized by at least as many articles in the *Semanario Pintoresco Español* as those on physiognomics, and Mariano Cubí y Soler wrote his highly successful *Elementos de frenología, fisonomía y magnetismo humano, en completa armonía con la espiritualidad, libertad e inmortalidad del alma* (Barcelona: Imp. Hispana, 1849). Cubí, extensively studied by Ramón Carnicer, was the George Combe of Spain, in effect: promoter of the "science" of Gall and popularizer of the layman's facile approach to the understanding of human character.[21] (F. Soulié's *Le Magnétiseur* was translated into Castilian in 1845, and was just one of many such examples that foretold George DuMaurier's Svengali character [in *Trilby*] at the end of the century.)

It is crucial to recognize, in consonance with our prefatory citations by Boas, Gombrich, and Cook, that physiognomics as a science implied the *constancy* of human nature, indeed of Nature in general: a certain outward aspect was a sign for a certain inner characteristic, which, for all intents and purposes, was incontrovertible and unchangeable. This was the simpler side to the story; the one which eighteenth-century rationalism might have chosen to have exist, unencumbered by variants. But variants there were, of course, and that is *part* of the message of our three cited guideposts, above: the more we look, the more we see. It is the optimistic reverse of the terribly cynical "plus ça change . . ." saying. It concerned Piper's Ulloa so much that he started an argument with his own Maker!

The *Semanario Pintoresco Español* and the *Museo de las Familias* were often preoccupied with the theory of "character" (namely, the *variability* of character); yet they often published articles on literary types which, by implication, presume that a notion of character is linked to philosophical constants and uniformitarianism (to use a phrase of Lovejoy). Nevertheless, the *Museo* gave away its true convictions, I think, in a half-page visual, accompanied by scanty text.[22] "Las amistades de salón. La palabra y el pensamiento" depicts two women, each unfolded in triplicate, facing each other, thinking to each other uncomplimentary (catty!) thoughts about the other. The faces seem to say one thing; the text belies what the faces seem to express. The sketch indicates in a flash the subtlety and deceptive expression which make eighteenth-century epistolary novels curious, and the levels of meaning which become possible in the prosaic observation of character in later nineteenth-century novels. "Amistades" and the physiognomic puzzle are the sort of popular touch, almost unwitting, that foretells the philosophical preoccupations to which Piper made us privy in his eagle-man chapter.

Anson Piper was in sound literary-critical company when he conceived that chapter. In a stunning article which couples the history of ideas and literary matters, Peter Demetz unwound a long-standing confusion between the "romantic" (traditional) concept of the type and the "realistic" (scientific) concept of the type.[23] His focus was Balzac:

> I think Balzac was aware of a divergence: traditional types as defined by romantic writers embody myths, ideas, essences, principles, tendencies, forces, and powers and greatly strain the narrow human form in which they are forced to fit. These traditional types symbolize supra-human, overpowering forces of existence, while a scientific type (as suggested by the methodological traditions of zoology and comparative anatomy) summarizes recurrent human characteristics in a model reminiscent of many individual lives. Traditional, or romantic, types incarnate ontological energies of fate and failure; the new, or scientific, type is concerned with the representation of the many by the one.
>
> (408)

"Platonism tempered by laboratory experience" is what Demetz said about the method to which the scientists ascribed (404):

> I would suggest that the two concepts differ in at least five elements: the traditional type (often defined by the Romantics) strikes me as "selective," intuitively conceived, symbolic of supra-human forces and energies, largely a-historical, and suggesting the grand and distant; Balzac's scientific type emerges as concerned with "pluralities," composed in a sober process of analysis and synthesis, representative of many human individuals of the analogous kind, basically historical, and suggesting the modest and humble.
>
> (417)

All of Demetz's considerations in this unforgettable article smack of those philosophical foundations which underlay the pieces by Boas, and Gombrich, Cook, and Lovejoy, too. All of these pieces hint not only that the observational, scientific departure from Romantic Platonism was on the rise among prose artists in the nineteenth century. They hint, also, that there is another side

to that coin, which will always be operative even in our most discriminating observation of reality. Curiously enough, this other side of the coin, which is non-scientific and rather intuitive, in itself represents a constant of rational thought. For this was the lesson of Boas.

The eagle-man and the fictional author of *¡Así es la vida!* were the two sides of that same coin. Let us not be fooled: what obliged the fictional author to converse with Ulloa in that final chapter was not Ulloa himself. Better said, don Anson was, at that compositional moment, the product of 175 years of fluctuating modes of physiognomic perception, understood in one way; understood in another, don Anson had grown into the uncomfortable skeptic, disquieted by centuries (since Theophrastus, perhaps) of varying concepts of the type. The eagle-man chapter is necessary and ingenious, because it attempts to resolve these divergent views—at least to lay them out again for those who accept types at face value to see. By doubting himself, Professor Piper let us students save a bit of face after we had been accused in the course of reading his primer. For surely, each of us was at least *one* of those animal types.

(I confess to having been a couple.)

Notes

1. "The 'Breadly Paradise' of Lazarillo de Tormes," *Hispania,* XLIV (1961); "Ribera's 'Jacob' and the Tragic Sense of Life," *Hispania,* XLVI (1963).

2. "Biblioteca de Autores Españoles: 1846-1946," *Bulletin of Hispanic Studies,* XXIII, no. 92 (Oct. 1946), 244.

3. *Los españoles pintados por sí mismos* (*1843-1844*) (México: Colegio de México, 1951).

4. *The Limits of Reason* (New York: Harper and Bros., 1961), 19-20. The Lovejoy article which best exemplifies my philosophical reference here is "Romanticism and the Principle of Plenitude," in *The Great Chain of Being: A Study of the History of an Idea* (New York: Harper and Row, 1960; orig. 1936), 288-314.

5. See Luis Garner, *El Europeo* (*Barcelona, 1823-1824*) (Madrid: CSIC, 1954), xxi.

6. "Filosofía práctica. Estudio del corazón del hombre, o de su carácter en general y en particular," *El Europeo,* no. 4 (Jan. 31, 1824), 103-104.

7. In *Semanario Pintoresco Español,* 4th Series, III, no. 41 (Oct. 8, 1848), 324-325.

8. In *Meditations on a Hobby Horse and Other Essays on the Theory of Art* (London: Phaidon, 1965;

2nd ed.); originally a contribution to *The Visual Arts Today* (1960).

9. "Character Description and Meaning in the Romantic Novel," *Studies in Romanticism,* V, no. 4 (summer 1966), 208-218. See, also, Graham's *Lavater's Essays on Physiognomy: A Study in the History of Ideas* (Berne: Peter Lang, 1979).

10. "Literature of the Nineteenth Century. Spain," *The Athenaeum,* nos. 338, 340, 342, 344, 346 (April 19, May 3, 17, 31, June 14, 1834), 290-295, 329-333, 370-374, 411-414, 450-454; see especially no. 340.

11. Madrid: Mellado, 1847. Ref. Graham, "Lavater's *Physiognomy*: A Checklist," *The Papers of the Bibliographical Society of America,* LV, no. 4 (Oct.-Dec., 1961), 308.

12. I, no. 9 (May 29, 1836), 78-80.

13. *Sistema de Lavater sobre los signos fisiognomónicos* [sic], *o Medio de penetrar las disposiciones de los hombres, sus inclinaciones, sus aptitudes, su género de talento, su grado de cultura y de madurez, por la observación de sus hábitos exteriores y principalmente por el examen de las formas de la cabeza, de su capacidad y de las facciones de su rostro*; and *Sistema del Doctor Gall sobre las facultades del hombre y funciones del cerebro, vulgarmente llamado frenología o craneoscopia*; both published by the Agencia Médica Catalana (Botica del Doctor don José Martí y Artigas).

14. "Fisonomía: La nariz," in I, no. 20 (Aug. 14, 1836), 163-165.

15. "El hombre desciende hacia el bruto; el animal se eleva hacia el hombre," in 3rd Ser., I, no. 33 (Aug. 13, 1843), 260-261.

16. "Lo que puede parecer un rostro," in 3rd Ser., II, no. 42 (Oct. 20, 1844), 336.

17. Reviewed in *El Gabinete de Lectura,* no. 2 (Nov. 10, 1841), 16. José Feliu y Godina did a deluxe-edition translation for the Barcelona publisher, Celestino Verdaguer, in 1850, and this was recently reissued (1984) in facsimile by José J. de Olañeta.

18. "Miscelánea. Fisionomía del gato," in 3rd Ser., II, no. 58 (Sept. 22, 1844) and no. 59 (Sept. 30, 1844), 300-301 and 310-311.

19. "Los perros y sus amos," in XVIII (1860), 239-240.

20. "Problema fisonómico [sic]," no. 19 (May 7, 1854), 152; the solution two issues later, p. 168.

21. *Entre la ciencia y la magia: Mariano Cubí (En torno al siglo XIX español)* (Barcelona: Seix Barral, 1969). Combe, *The Constitution of Man considered in relation to external objects . . . with an additional chapter on the harmony between phrenology and revelation by Joseph A. Warne* (Boston: William D. Ticknor, 1835; 4th American from the 2nd English ed.); also, Combe, *A System of Phrenology* (New York: William H. Colyer, 1842; from the 4th Edinburgh ed.).

22. *Museo de las Familias,* XII (Oct. 1854), 240.

23. "Balzac and the Zoologists: A Concept of the Type," in *The Disciplines of Criticism: Essays in Literary Theory, Interpretation, and History,* eds. Demetz, Green, Nelson (New Haven; London: Yale Univ. Press, 1968), 399-418.

Richard T. Gray (essay date 2004)

SOURCE: Gray, Richard T. "Physiognomic 'Surface Hermeneutics' and the Ideological Context of German Modernism." In *About Face: German Physiognomic Thought from Lavater to Auschwitz,* pp. xxix-lvi. Detroit, Mich.: Wayne State University Press, 2004.

[*In the following essay, Gray investigates the cultural, intellectual, and aesthetic context surrounding the popularity of physiognomy in Germany.*]

False consciousness is simultaneously correct; internal and external existence are torn asunder.

Theodor W. Adorno ("Zum Verhältnis von Soziologie und Psychologie" 45)

Physiognomics, the knowledge of and acquaintance with the relationship of the external with the internal, of the visible surface with the invisible content, of what is *visible* and perceptibly *animated* with what is *invisible* and imperceptibly *animates,* of the visible effect to the invisible force.

Johann Caspar Lavater (*Physiognomische Fragmente* 1: 13)

PHYSIOGNOMICS AND GERMAN CIVIL SOCIETY

The years 1770 to 1780 can with certain justification be designated the physiognomic decade of German intellectual and cultural history. To be sure, the study of the human physiognomy as symptomatic of character, fate, and talents of the individual subject was no eighteenth-century invention. Indeed, as an intellectual discipline, physiognomics has venerable roots that are commonly traced back as far as the Greek philosopher Aristotle (384-322 B.C.), to whom an early Greek physiognomic treatise, entitled *Physiognomica,* is often attributed. But traditional physiognomics received revolutionary new impulses and was substantially revitalized by the physiognomic theories of the Swiss pastor Johann Caspar Lavater (1741-1801) in what I designate as the physiognomic decade of German intellectual-cultural history. Lavater sought to dissociate physiognomics from such prophetic avocations as chiromancy, the guise it took in the ancient tradition carried on by Antonius Polemo (88-145) and Adamantius (184-253), elevating it to the status of a positivistic empirical science. As such, physiognomics was considered capable of supplying valid and accurate information about the supersensual character of the human "soul" based on interpretive conclusions drawn from its sensual manifestations.

While from today's perspective it is perhaps tempting merely to decry Lavater as a quack and shake our heads over the apparent naiveté and simplicity of his physiognomic notions, such responses fail to come to grips with the tremendous appeal the man and his theories held for his contemporaries. Beyond being generally accepted as a legitimate academic-scientific discipline, physiognomics also assumed the character of one of the first widely dispersed movements of modern popular culture. During this period the interpretive "reading" of the facial features of one's social contacts acquired the status of a parlor game that was de rigueur in the social circles of emergent German civil society,[1] and the exchange of character-revealing silhouettes as a sign of intimacy and friendship became a veritable fad. These (pseudo-)intellectual physiognomic crazes proliferated among the representatives of civil society not only in German-speaking lands, but throughout Europe. By 1810, less than forty years after the publication of Lavater's magnum opus, the *Physiognomische Fragmente, zur Beförderung der Menschenkenntniß und Menschenliebe* (Physiognomic fragments for the promotion of human understanding and human love; 1775-1778), no fewer than sixteen German, fifteen French, and twenty English editions had appeared, and even two Russian, one Dutch, and one Italian translation had been published (Herrmann 27). In his *Physiognomische Reisen* (Physiognomic travels), first published in 1778-1779, Johann Karl August Musäus (1735-1787) both documents and scathingly satirizes the prominence that physiognomic practices had assumed in the social intercourse of European civil society in the wake of Lavater's reception.[2]

Lavater unleashed and fueled this physiognomic vogue with the publication of a series of treatises between the years 1772 and 1778. The first of these, an essay entitled "Von der Physiognomik" (On physiognomics), represents the script of a lecture Lavater read before the Scientific Society of Zurich. It is one of the ironies of the history of physiognomics that Lavater himself apparently did not at first sense that the time was especially auspicious for the propagation of his theories. Indeed, he cannot be credited with initiating the publication of these first reflections on physiognomics. This honor falls to his friend and mentor, the physician and cultural dilettante Johann Georg Zimmermann (1728-1795), who published Lavater's essay anonymously and without the consent of its author in the *Hannoverisches Magazin* of February 1772. When Lavater reissued—in book form and under his own name—this disquisition that sought to establish the positivistic foundations of physiognomy, he appended to it an outline of the various subfields into which he imagined this new "scientific" discipline could be divided.[3] But it was ultimately the four costly, profusely illustrated folio volumes of the *Physiognomische Fragmente,* which appeared from 1775 to 1778, with which Lavater placed his stamp on the intellectual physiognomy of this decade.

The popular reception of the *Physiognomische Fragmente* stands in a relationship of ironic paradox with Lavater's own stated intentions for these volumes. Already in the preface to the first volume he openly asserts: "It [this volume] is not written for the large mass of common people. It is costly in its very nature . . . ; and anyway, different people can pitch in, buy it together, and own it as a group" (1: "Vorrede" [unpaginated]). Although it was not expressly written for the masses, the *Fragmente*'s receptive history is marked above all by its mass circulation. To be sure, Lavater perhaps piqued the interest of the general readership by asserting the very distinction of these volumes and their readers: who would not want to number themselves among those distinguished few for whose eyes these richly illustrated volumes were composed?

The innovative distribution method of this work also contributed to its dissemination. It was among the first in Germany to be published based on the principle of subscription; indeed, the first volume contains a list of two hundred sixty-nine subscribers, for a total of more than three hundred volumes, that includes the names of many prominent aristocrats and the principal representatives of German civil society. The tactic of subscription allowed Lavater and his publisher to leverage the exorbitant cost of the volumes up-front, thereby guaranteeing from the outset the financial success of this publishing venture. Moreover, Lavater proved to be an enormously effective salesman: he persuaded many individuals to subscribe by requesting that they send him a portrait or silhouette, in return for which he promised to analyze the contributor's physiognomy in a future volume (Swoboda 93). By playing on the vanity-driven desires of individuals who might attain a certain public stardom by being featured in the *Fragmente,* Lavater found a shrewd way of insuring the success of this grandly conceived project. This ploy of requesting portraits or silhouettes from his contemporaries was so well orchestrated that Lavater ultimately assembled a collection of more than twenty-two thousand images.[4] It is symptomatic of Lavater's shrewd sense of commodity value and of his belief in his own self-worth that he added value to these images by adorning them with hand-written titles and interpretive comments. By means of this practice Lavater transformed these simple images into Baroque-like *emblemata* (Rauchensteiner and Swoboda 112). And by presenting them to friends and supporters as gifts, he consciously developed a clever marketing strategy for his physiognomic theories and interpretations (see Siegrist, "Nachwort" 379). These physiognomic *emblemata* ultimately acquired the status of highly regarded cultural artifacts that circulated among the German cultural elite, who collected and displayed them with pride. Lavater thereby instituted a subtle and highly successful marketing campaign that both fueled and played off of the emerging discourse of fashion and the nascent consumerism it promoted.[5] In this sense Lavater brilliantly exploited the mechanism and the media of the public sphere in order to underwrite the dissemination of his physiognomic theories and practices.

One further element related to the marketing and reception of the *Fragmente* is relevant here: the community-building function of these volumes, hinted at by Lavater's comment that people might pool their money to purchase these works as a group. As Isabel Hull notes, reading societies were among the major institutions of late eighteenth-century German civil society, and Lavater's remark would seem to be directed at these societies. In fact, the *Physiognomische Fragmente* were often purchased by reading groups, which then met not only for communal reading but also to practice their interpretive physiognomic skills.[6] As Ingrid Goritschnig has shown ("Faszination des Porträts" 138), the *Physiognomische Fragmente* called forth a true cult of personality; people began to meet, in the fashion of the modern social game, for communal "Lavaterizing," seeking to characterize individuals on the basis of their images or silhouettes. In a very concrete sense, then, Lavater's rich and expensive volumes came to be regarded as cult objects that formed the focal point of small, self-sustaining communities. These societies modeled in microcosm the larger community-building function, the definition of social-physiognomic insiders and outsiders, that physiognomic theory and practice sought to institute on a wider scale.

The inherent vitality of any upstart intellectual movement is perhaps best measured by the significance and vehemence of the critical opposition it evokes, rather than by its ability to attain broad appeal. Measured by this standard as well, Lavaterian physiognomics truly represented a thriving intellectual phenomenon. Indeed,

it acquired the status of a scholarly event that the erudite of the day simply could not ignore. the claim that Lavater's theories divided the bourgeois intelligentsia into two camps, physiognomists and supporters of Lavater on the one side, antiphysiognomists and more circumspect critics of his theories on the other (Siegrist, "Nachwort" 387-88), is no exaggeration. A great deal was at stake in the controversy over physiognomy that raged in these years, as is best demonstrated by the vociferousness of Lavater's most zealous critic, the Göttingen physicist Georg Christoph Lichtenberg (1742-1800). In the caustically satirical treatise "Über Physiognomik; wider die Physiognomen. Zu Beförderung der Menschenliebe und Menschenkenntnis" (On physiognomics; against the physiognomists. For the promotion of human love and human understanding; 1778),[7] Lichtenberg initiated a crusade against the popularization of Lavater's physiognomic hermeneutics. He later ridiculed Lavater's interpretive practices in the parodistic piece "Fragment von Schwänzen: Ein Beitrag zu den Physiognomischen Fragmenten" (Fragment on tails: A contribution to the Physiognomic Fragments; 1783),[8] in which the purported character traits of pigs are derived from interpretations of the kinks in their tails. Yet despite the wittiness of these attacks, in the final analysis physiognomics was no laughing matter, even for Lichtenberg, and Lavater and his disciples went to great lengths to refute his objections.[9]

In literary and cultural histories the phenomenon of physiognomics is commonly reduced to this high-pitched dispute between Lichtenberg and Lavater. Their exchange is somewhat simplistically interpreted as a confrontation between the rationality of the physicist Lichtenberg and the irrational eruptions of the Storm-and-Stress "genius" Lavater—a conflict, moreover, in which the Enlightenment dragon-killer successfully if viciously subdues the beast of prejudice and unreason.[10] This reductive understanding ignores the fact that Lavater himself conceived physiognomics all too rationally as a positivistic, empirical science in the Enlightenment tradition (see Pestalozzi, "Physionomische Methodik" 137-53). Moreover, it fails to register both the breadth and complexity of Lavater's physiognomic project, as well as the degree to which it is interwoven with the ideological fabric of German civil society. Indeed, what constitutes physiognomics as a significant historico-cultural "event" is precisely the fact that it managed to gather into a single unitary economy the diverse intellectual currencies in circulation at the time.

It is well known that physiognomics found substantial support among the chief "enthusiasts" of the so-called "genius" generation: Johann Wolfgang von Goethe (1749-1832), Johann Gottfried Herder (1744-1803), and Johann Michael Reinhold Lenz (1751-1792) all defended Lavaterian physiognomics and even contributed actively to the composition of the *Physiognomische*

Fragmente.[11] But even such leading critical spirits of the German Enlightenment as Moses Mendelssohn (1729-1786) and Friedrich Nicolai (1733-1811) could not resist the seductive power that emanated from Lavater's theories. To be sure, Nicolai assailed Lavater's zealotry, but only because to his mind it threatened to undercut the scientific basis of physiognomics, in which, by his own admission, he firmly believed.[12] Nicolai even contributed to the institutionalization of physiognomics as a serious intellectual discipline by assigning it a separate disciplinary heading in his *Allgemeine Deutsche Bibliothek,* the central scholarly publishing organ of Enlightenment culture in Germany, thereby implicitly setting it equal to such traditional disciplinary classifications as the fine arts and mathematics. Even Lichtenberg could not stop short of admitting his own proclivity to interpret character out of people's faces (see "Über Physiognomik" 260); while he denied the validity of Lavater's physiognomic readings, he refused to question the essential readability of physical creation ("Über Physiognomik" 265).

The emergence and popular reception of physiognomics in the 1770s and beyond was intimately connected with the ideological substance of German civil society. If, as Hull has argued, the private/public split generated "a powerful symbol system used to bring order to emerging posttraditional relations" (5), then the power of physiognomic discourse in this period stemmed in large part from the fact that it was ideally suited to inhabiting a theoretical space at the interstice of the public and the private. Indeed, the revelatory thrust of physiognomic practice can be conceived as a disclosure of the private, its "publication," or making-public through the physiognomist's interpretive practices. The very ardor with which individuals sought to turn themselves and their graven images over to public viewing and interpretation in the volumes of Lavater's *Physiognomische Fragmente* indicates the perverse pleasure associated with this revelatory hermeneutic. We must imagine the practitioners of civil society as moral "flashers," individuals who experience titillation at the exposure of their private selves to the unobstructed view of the public. To be sure, the discourse of revelation and authenticity associated with the belief that physiognomic interpretation uncovers the genuine core of the individual actually disguises the fundamentally constructivist principle at work in physiognomic theory and practice: rather than *uncovering* the self hidden behind the public façade, physiognomic interpretation in fact participates in the *construction* of this private self.

One of the commonplaces among scholars studying the history of modern physiognomics is the recognition that it thrives in particular during times of social and political disorientation.[13] The transition from the absolutist state to civil society marked a period of particular disorientation with regard to the self-understanding and

self-definition of the individual. As Helmut König has pointed out (59), absolutist society had no conception of the individual as individual; instead, each person was the representative of a trans-individual system of reference that detected personal essence not in terms of psychological or physiological traits, but rather on the basis of external identifiers such as clothes, hairstyle, manner of speech, gestures, and general habitus.

This situation changed radically with the emergence of civil society in the last half of the eighteenth century in Germany. Now the individual steps out of the social fabric woven by the order of estates. Instead of identifying itself by means of an affiliation with a social group, it seeks these identifying traits in its own self. Because outward appearance no longer gives a clear indication of whom one is dealing with, the order of visibility that had previously permitted sure orientation in everyday interactions disappears. One consequence of this is that the equality of civil society is not automatically accompanied by new, freer social contacts; it can also culminate in uncertainty and lack of orientation. Where previously a system of visible coordinates ensured the existence of transparency and order, confusion and uncertainty are now the rule. One can no longer clearly distinguish people from one another (König 60).

Given this collapse of the previously valid system of visibility, physiognomics emerges as an attempt to ordain a new system of visibility in line with the ideological mechanisms underpinning the new order of civil society. As Daniel Purdy has shown for the case of German civil society, the demise of sumptuary laws dictating the attire appropriate to a given estate goes hand in hand with the consumerism that powers the mercantile economy and the discourse of fashion that identifies clothes not with class representation, but as indicators of the vital internal self (79). As a manner of redefining the relationship between the human body and personal identify, fashion contributes to the production of the civil subject. This civil subject is the reflex not of the larger social group, but of an individually defined *style*. Indeed, under the hegemony of fashion it is not so much the case that clothes make the (wo)man, as that he or she is a function of a personally choreographed *style*.[14] This distinction is important, because style is attached not simply to external adornments; it penetrates to the internal essence of the self. In this sense, the discourse of physiognomics plays a role that is complementary to that of fashion: both operate toward the production of different aspects of the civil subject, fashion constructing its external, physiognomics its internal substance.

The relationship between physiognomics and fashion is particularly complex, for this element of complementarity only captures one aspect of their interaction. Viewed from another perspective, physiognomics can also be interpreted as a countermeasure against the stylistic flourishes of fashion. Here again physiognomics relies on its greater authority as the arbiter of personal authenticity, predicated above all on the dialectic of surface and depth that defines its ideological crux. Several considerations come into play here. One is that fashion is largely, although by no means exclusively, addressed to and carried by women, whereas physiognomics is a distinctly male discipline—practiced by males, and for the most part applied to males. If Hull is correct in her judgment that the most significant sociological observation about this period is that Enlightenment discourse was produced exclusively by and for men (207), then this also helps explain the obsessiveness with which physiognomic theory—not merely in the eighteenth century, but throughout its modern history—concentrates on men, glosses over questions of gender, and marginalizes examinations of and observations about women.[15] To be sure, Lavater dedicated one small section of *Physiognomische Fragmente* to the study of women (3: 239-330), but instead of generating criteria for the differentiation of individuality, his observations there reduce women to the prejudices and stereotypes typical of the time and hence simply reinforce the prevalent societal consensus about women (Lachs, "Frauenbild" 152-54). In its general exclusion and marginalization of women, then, the discipline of physiognomics repeats that more concrete act of exclusion typical of the institutions of civil society, its lodges, associations, and reading societies (see Hull 211-12). By the same token, this did not prevent women from subscribing to the tenets of physiognomics and engaging in its practices; indeed, Lavater and his works enjoyed particular popularity among women (Lachs, "Frauenbild" 160). But the general suppression of gender matters in the discourse of modern physiognomics explains why such questions go unaddressed in the present historical examination.

The relationship between physiognomics and the ideology of consumption is just as paradoxical as that between this hermeneutics of the body and fashion. Hull has convincingly made the case that civil society replaced an ethic of abstention that previously governed the self-understanding of the non-aristocratic classes with an ethic of production and consumption (4). This is the place, of course, at which economic issues impinge directly on the evolution and ideology of civil society. But once again the relationship between physiognomics and the drive for production and consumption seems problematic. As a primer for the recognition and cultivation of an "essential self" untouched by the artifacts of emergent consumerism, physiognomics appears as a potential antidote to the ideology of consumption. It would not be surprising if the reversal in the evaluation of luxury, once considered a sin but in the context of civil society now viewed as the useful motor behind a developing economy, called forth a bad conscience in those who began to embrace this new, more positive

evaluation. Physiognomics could be interpreted as the expression of this bad conscience to the extent that it can be read as a neutralization of the relationship between consumption, acquisition, and personal style: it preaches, in a word, the virtues of abstention in the service of an ideology of authenticity. On the other hand, as we have seen, Lavater cleverly manipulated the mechanisms and the mentality of consumer culture to promote his physiognomic project and disseminate his theories. He might be regarded as an incipient televangelist, someone who exploited the consumer market as a vehicle for propagating a Christian anti-consumerist, essentialist ideology that identified moral substance as its structural cornerstone.

If the major practitioners of civil society were an intelligentsia who produced and mediated meaning (Hull 216), then the discipline of physiognomics was central to the ideological self-constitution of civil society insofar as it invoked and reinforced the two pillars on which this new sociopolitical formation rested: morality and rationality. Lavater's reliance on the methods and discourse of enlightened science will be the subject of the next chapter and need not be developed here. More important than this scientific dimension is the role of physiognomic discourse in generating and buttressing not only a set of clearly defined moral values—honesty, empathy, intelligence, ingenuousness, constancy, sensitivity, grace, and so on—but also a *language* capable of transmitting and manifesting this new moral substance. A further reason for the tremendous popularity of Lavater's writings on physiognomics was their engagement of the new language of sentimentalism, emotion, and intimacy. As Purdy has astutely observed, the empathy that formed the core of this ideology of sentimentalism presumed the existence of a universal moral psychology (41-42). To physiognomics fell the significant task of producing the tenets of this universal moral psychology and disseminating them among the populace in the form not simply of a body of knowledge, but as a set of practices that could be employed to identify those individuals with whom one shared this palette of characterological virtues. The body became the vehicle for projections of and about that individual private core that constituted communal identity beyond all individual difference.

Although ostensibly glorifying the human body by conceiving it as the sensual concretization of divine significance, Lavaterian physiognomics in fact pursues a strategic program for the negation of the body, the repression of its sensual being in the very process by which it is lent "significance." As such, physiognomics as discipline manifests one of the significant ideological drives of civil society, what Michel Foucault has termed the "docility" of the body (*Discipline and Punish* 135-69). Similarly, Herbert Marcuse has argued that the hypostatization of the "soul" as the supersensual essence that escapes the structures of a reifying socioeconomic practice represents the fundamental reflex in what he terms the "affirmative" culture of modernism (78). While the obsession with the ethereality of this inner-worldly spiritual domain must be considered, as Foucault so clearly demonstrates, to be a critical response to the waxing oppression of the subject in emerging civil society, it simultaneously "affirms" these concrete structures of alienation insofar as it, at the very least, passes over them in silence. Instead of intervening in the conditions responsible for its physical coercion, the civil subject reacts by denying the significance of the physical, empirical sphere, substituting for it the fantasy of the all-important life of the soul. This internal domain is hypostatized as the sphere of the "private" self that must be set apart and shielded from the public domain. The irony of physiognomic theory and practice is that in order to *identify* this isolated kernel that is the passport to acceptance in civil society, it must explode the barrier between private and public life and expose the private core to the public eye. The keen *empirical* observation on which this hypostatization of the metaphysical soul and its revelation is based ultimately turns into a form of omnipresent surveillance, a universalized panopticism in which the social subject is coerced into compliance with a certain set of norms. In the words of Michel Foucault:

> Our society is one not of spectacle, but of surveillance; under the surface of images, one invests bodies in depth; . . . the play of signs defines the anchorages of power; it is not that the beautiful totality of the individual is amputated, repressed, altered by our social order, it is rather that the individual is carefully fabricated in it, according to a whole technique of forces and bodies. . . . We are neither in the amphitheatre, nor on the stage, but in the panoptic machine, invested by its effects of power, which we bring to ourselves since we are part of its mechanism.

> (*Discipline and Punish* 217)

Physiognomics became one of the primary tools deployed by civil society for this fabrication of the individual according to preordained ethical, characterological, national, or racial definitions. Its prominence throughout the modern epoch is tied to the fact that, as instrument both for the promulgation of ideological values and the coercive policing of their implementation, it represents an impressively efficient disciplinary mechanism. As Richard Sennett persuasively argues, "[w]hen everyone has each other under surveillance, sociability decreases, silence being the only form of protection" (15). Paradoxically, then, physiognomics, which styles itself as a strategy for increased intimacy, actually increases the isolation of the individual by subjecting it to a totalizing regime of visibility. But whereas Sennett views the open-floor office plan as the culmination of this paradox of visibility and isolation, modern physiognomics, as systematized scrutiny of the social Other, is

certainly the most effective and insidious—because least obvious—manifestation of this paradox.

The ideological program for the tactical segregation of the "soul" from all empirical, sociopolitical facticity is paradigmatically manifest in Gottfried Wilhelm Leibniz's (1646-1716) conceptualization of the human subject as a "windowless monad": "Monads do not have any windows through which things can enter or exit. . . . Thus neither external substance nor external accident can ever have any influence on a monad," he unequivocally asserts in the *Monadologie* (440). This absolute self-containment of the monad constitutes its autonomy, its total isolation from all impulses that derive from the physical world of the senses. Lavater's physiognomic theories operate from this Leibnizian presumption of the civil subject as a windowless monad upon whose entelechy external forces, be they of historical, sociological, or merely of accidental nature, can by definition have no impact. Lavater sets himself the somewhat paradoxical task of extending this monadic quality to the human body itself, thereby liberating it from all worldly conjunctures. This belief will resurface, of course, in the racial theories of the late-nineteenth and early-twentieth centuries as an argument against environmental influences on the human individual and the thesis of the absolute genetic predetermination of every human being. But what makes Lavater's physiognomic project especially noteworthy is that it goes about this autonomization of the body as reflection of the monadic "soul" by drawing specifically on *semiotic* arguments. This suggests that Lavater's physiognomics is particularly well suited for an analysis of the role of emergent semiotic theory in the ideological program of self-mastery endemic of civil society.

Physiognomics operates by semioticizing the body, by transforming it into a discursive system composed explicitly of *natural* signs, which, according to the semiotic understanding current in Lavater's day, are utterly transparent and hence vanish behind their (spiritual) signifieds. This insistence on the requisite transparency of signs, which dominated semiotic thought in Germany in this period (Wellbery 7-8), is appropriated in Lavaterian physiognomics as a tactic for the desubstantialization of the body, the sublation of its sensual being by means of its "en-signment," its reduction to the transitory token of the supersensual "essence." It is important not to confuse this semiotic transparency with a doctrine of immanence, which would hold that things—in this case the body—have meaning in and of themselves. This error is committed, for example, by Hans-Georg von Arburg, who views physiognomic traces as hieroglyphs rather than as signs (49), as well as by Claudia Schmölders (*Der exzentrische Blick* 16), who claims that physiognomics treats the body as simple embodiment (*Inbegriff*) of transsensual Being.

Modern physiognomics always assumes—if with reluctance and a wistful nostalgia for the immediacy of immanence—a fundamental split between transsensual essence and bodily appearance. This forces it to divide the body into distinct "texts" that operate according to their own codes and read these texts as representational signs, with all their attendant advantages and disadvantages. The necessary corollary of this semiotics of somatic representation—body parts as *signifiers* that point to transsensual signifieds—is the demand that these somatic signifiers be decoded according to a systematic hermeneutic, the organized and disciplinarily codified interpretive methodology that informs physiognomic practice.

With this broader historico-cultural context in mind I have coined the phrase "surface hermeneutics," in conscious allusion to the concept of depth hermeneutics associated with Freudian psychoanalysis, to describe the interpretive practice Lavater, as the founder of modern physiognomics, pursued in his analyses. A comparison of the Lavaterian and Freudian interpretive projects, which mark the historical inception and culmination of cultural modernism, as well as a look at the relation between physiognomics and Edmund Husserl's (1859-1938) phenomenology, will allow us to throw into relief certain continuities and discontinuities in this intellectual-historical formation. We must keep in mind, of course, that Lavaterian physiognomics is no isolated phenomenon in the history of modern German culture. But perhaps the persistence with which the star of physiognomics reappears on the cultural horizon of German-speaking Europe during the modern age testifies more convincingly than anything else to the manner in which it is fundamentally interwoven into the fabric of German civil society.

LAVATER'S PHYSIOGNOMIC PROJECT

The aim of Lavaterian physiognomics was to develop a unifying theory of the human subject, one able to establish an ineluctable interconnection between body and soul, between the entelechy of the spirit and the external existence of the empirical being subject to natural, sociopolitical, economic, and other laws. What distinguishes Lavater's undertaking as a peculiarly modern enterprise was his desire to conceive the human physiognomy specifically in terms of a *language* whose seemingly inscrutable signs can ultimately be deciphered.[16] In the early essay "Von der Physiognomik" he explicitly invokes the linguistic nature of this physiognomic idiom when he ends his defense of the aesthetic harmony of the human body with the assertion: "From this one can incontrovertibly conclude, in my opinion, that everything about the human body, small and large, is significant, that nature possesses a tenthousandfold language in which it speaks to us simultaneously, that it principally speaks in a very comprehensible, very un-

equivocal manner, and that it is not nature's fault, but our own, if we fail to understand it or if we understand it incorrectly" (160). Especially significant is Lavater's insistence on the absolute unequivocality of this natural language of the body, which leads him to the corollary that all physiognomic misunderstandings are simply misreadings attributable to the hermeneutic deficiencies of human beings. As a corrective to this interpretive inadequacy, physiognomics takes on the specific character of a hermeneutics of the body—a "surface hermeneutics," as I have chosen to call it—which Lavater defines as *"the facility for being able to recognize the inner nature of a human being on the basis of his or her external qualities,* the ability to perceive what does not immediately appear to the senses by means of some natural form of expression" (*Physiognomische Fragmente* 1: 13).

Lavater recognizes that the elaboration of such an infallible hermeneutic practice invariably depends on the identification of a semiotic theory that governs the constitution of the natural signs that make the sensual body "significant," that is, that cause it to signify. In order to provide physiognomics with an adequate theory of bodily signs Lavater appeals to semiotic conceptions widely disseminated in the German Enlightenment. In particular he invokes the discipline of medical semiotics, which concerns itself with the localization of specific physical symptoms as the index of particular illnesses, expanding its "symptomatic" theory of the interconnection between external sign and internal signified to encompass the moral, characterological, and intellectual spheres as well (see Pestalozzi, "Physiognomische Methodik" 140-42). "Are we not able to demonstrate on the basis of reason alone that consumption, due to its very nature, modifies our face in such and such a way; that excreted gall must color the eyes in such and such a manner; that a more violent seething of the blood calls forth this specific color? Are these purely arbitrary signs, or signs that are founded in nature, in the immediate connection of the external and the internal?" ("Von der Physiognomik" 151-52).

As this passage makes amply clear, Lavater's contention that the language of the human physiognomy is wholly unequivocal leads him necessarily to the claim that its signs are not *arbitrary*; they are explicitly *natural* or *motivated*—that is, the connection between signifier and its signified is grounded in a relation of cause and effect. He thus adopts in toto the semiotic principles propagated by Enlightenment philosophy in an attempt to legitimate "scientifically" the reading strategies of his physiognomic surface hermeneutics. In his physiognomic theories Lavater "en-signs" the human body by grafting this semiotic doctrine onto his understanding of its "significant" sensual features. He thereby establishes the secondariness and transparency of the body, in its status as signifying medium, to an underlying, meaning-producing human "spirit": "One should never forget," he asserts in the *Physiognomische Fragmente,* "that external expression *exists precisely for the purpose* of making the internal recognizable by means of it!" (1: 165; emphasis added). The only purpose of the body, it would seem, is to serve as a sensual manifestation of the soul; the body becomes a text whose decoding is the business of physiognomic hermeneutics. In chapter 1 [of *About Face*], I will examine in detail the relevant tenets of Enlightenment semiotics and the aporias into which the adoption of these principles leads Lavater's physiognomic theory and practice.

The ideological dialectic of Lavater's physiognomics crystallizes around an all-out war against the principles of (semiotic) arbitrariness that constitute the condition of possibility of the enlightened episteme.[17] This arbitrary relation is Lavater's nemesis, and he envisions its eradication as the ultimate aim of all culture ("Von der Physiognomik" 150; *Physiognomische Fragmente* 1: 47). The *Natursprache,* or language of nature "spoken" by the human physiognomy, represents for Lavater the paradigm of a non-arbitrary code in which sensually discernible features function as natural signs for supersensual characteristics. But clearly Lavater cannot designate *all* external bodily features as symptoms of genuine internal traits; indeed, he admits that dissimulation and mimicry, "the capacity to imitate everything by applying reason, arbitrariness, and choice" (*Physiognomische Fragmente* 2: 30), are fundamental to human nature. This recognition leads him to voice a critique of the fascination with superficialities he senses among his contemporaries, an assault on the alienated state of enlightened culture that rings similar to the typical denunciations articulated by the generation of Storm-and-Stress poets. "The great mass of human beings constantly feast on and satiate themselves with words without meaning, externalities without energy, bodies without spirit, structure and form without animating essence—. . . and yet this is the most universally valid assertion . . . : *it is the spirit that breathes life into these things, the flesh is good for nothing*" (*Physiognomische Fragmente* 1: 144-45). The sociocultural context that Lavater invokes is marked by a widening breach between semblance and essence, surface and depth, external sign and internal significance. Symptomatic of this cultural phenomenon is the vigorous proliferation of arbitrary, dissimulative signs; there is a near-pathological obsession with such empty externalities.

It is against this backdrop that Lavater formulates his physiognomic theories, conceiving them as an antidote to the cultural malaise of emergent civil society. A preoccupation with the sensuality of the body is indicative for him of this degenerate cultural state, and his critique culminates with ideological necessity in a typically Christian condemnation of the flesh.[18] The attempt to establish the human physiognomy as, strictly speaking, *significant* leads Lavater to theorize the body as a malleable shell that is shaped and animated—in effect *created*—by the spirit that occupies it. Thus he defines physiognomics as "the acquaintance with the relationship of the external with the internal, of the visible surface with the invisible content, of what is *visible* and perceptibly *animated* with what is *invisible* and imperceptibly *animates*" (*Physiognomische Fragmente* 1: 13). Taking this organic unity of body and soul as his point of departure, Lavater's aim is the generation of a hermeneutic science that cannot be misled by the dissimulations of arbitrary signs; physiognomics represents for him a hermeneutics to end all hermeneutics in the sense that it performs the interpretive acid test capable of infallibly segregating genuineness and authenticity from falsehood and dissemblance. Physiognomics, as a surface hermeneutics that decodes the natural traces the supersensual essence engraves upon the sensual body, circumscribes a discipline in which one can pursue metaphysics as an *empirical* science. This tension between transrational metaphysical faith and scientist rationality lends Lavaterian physiognomics its fundamentally paradoxical character. This curious blend of scientific self-understanding with a metaphysical, sometimes even mystical line of thought is one of the defining features of modern, post-Lavaterian physiognomics.

It is no coincidence that the attack Georg Wilhelm Friedrich Hegel (1770-1831) launched against Lavater in the section entitled "Physiognomik und Schädellehre" (Physiognomics and phrenology) in his *Phänomenologie des Geistes* (Phenomenology of mind) takes aim specifically at the semiotic underpinnings of physiognomics. Indeed, Hegel undercuts Lavater's theory precisely by asserting the absolute arbitrariness of the semiotic relationship on whose non-contingency Lavater insisted (*Phänomenologie des Geistes* 236). Hegel's critique is aimed primarily at Lavater's contention that physiognomic significance expresses itself involuntarily, employing the body as a purely passive medium. Lavater's dogmatic insistence that only those expressions not subject to the arbitrariness of human intentionality constitute determinate signs of supersensual "spirit" opened up physiognomics to the charge that it amounted to nothing but a theory of human determinism. For Hegel, by contrast, the a priori givens of *stable* character in no way reflect the essence of the individual; rather, this essence is *self*-created in the very process by which the human being externalizes and transmutes its physical givenness in intentional acts such as speech and labor (*Phänomenologie des Geistes* 235). In stark contrast to the essentialist and conservationist position of Lavater, which locates individuality in a transsensual and a priori Being called the "soul," Hegel argues that individuality arises only when this Being, in its givenness, is sacrificed to a process of becoming that manifests itself externally in words and deeds. According to

Hegel, these externalizations are the only noncontingent, nonarbitrary signs of authentic character because they are inherently bound up with it in a dialectical process of reciprocal self-determination. Moreover, Hegel stresses that the physiognomic conception of a given and stable physical being that is tailored by a soul so as to serve as its sensual sign is not only far more arbitrary than Lavater is willing to concede; it further robs the physical body of its *actuality,* transforming it merely into the passive index of this supersensual other. Thus Hegel recognizes that to conceive the body as *sign* is to deny it any Being-in-itself, demoting it to the incidental status of a being-(sign)-for-something-other. In other words, Lavater's en-signment of the body is tantamount to a monumental act of repression in which the sensuality, freedom, and creativity of the human being as individual are fundamentally negated.

LAVATER, FREUD, HUSSERL

It may at first glance strike one as an exaggeration or oversimplification to situate Lavater's physiognomic surface hermeneutics in a single intellectual-historical continuum with Freud's psychoanalytical depth hermeneutics and Husserl's phenomenology. By the same token, the possibility that physiognomics and psychoanalysis exhibit a certain historical interwovenness is suggested by the fact that the same Carl Gustav Carus (1789-1869) who attempted to rehabilitate physiognomics in the nineteenth century also composed a significant psychological treatise, which in many respects anticipates Freud's central theories, including his conceptions of the unconscious and the preconscious.[19] The natural affinities between physiognomics and empirical psychology can also be witnessed in their close imbrication in the characterology of Ludwig Klages (1872-1956). Now, although it is obvious, to be sure, that Lavater's wholly non-dynamic conception of human character knows none of the complexity and conflict characteristic of the modern Freudian view of the psyche, there is at least one important respect in which Lavaterian physiognomics resembles Freud's psychoanalytic project: the common force behind these theories is the irrepressible urge to uncover a genuine, authentic level of expression and internal Being that exists *beyond* the active will and conscious intentions of the human subject. Lavater's crusade against all that is arbitrary (*willkürlich*) is inadequately comprehended if this concept is limited to the connotation of semiotic arbitrariness; indeed, Lavater understood this word to signify quite literally that which is *will-kürlich,* that is, to describe whatever is subject to the discretion (*küren*) of the human will (*Wille*). This fundamental distrust of human intentionality, a distrust that we perhaps take for granted in the post-Freudian era, strikes one as particularly paradoxical in a figure such as Lavater, who is otherwise steeped in the joyous optimism of a Christian anthropology. Yet his interest in physiognomy as an au-

thentic, super-intentional expression of the genuine, "true" sentiments of the human subject represents but one variation on a theme that forms a persistent leitmotif in the thought of his contemporaries and is omnipresent throughout German modernism in general. The fascination with gesture, mime, and other forms of nonverbal communication at the end of the eighteenth century is only one of the symptoms of this obsession with authentic expression,[20] as is the valorization of the "naive" over whatever is deliberate and reflective.[21] Freud is the modern heir to this strain of thought that seeks ideologically to reconcile the external and internal dimensions of human subjectivity, to rejoin those two halves of the integral being that modern life praxis tears asunder. Only in a life world in which interpersonal obligation and interhuman trust have ceased to be dependable intersubjective bonds, a world whose mechanisms are concealed behind the playful if illusory simulacra of arbitrary signs, can such a fixation on modes of verity, untouched by intention, will, reflection, or consciousness, take hold. According to Sennett, this belief in the involuntary disclosure of the emotions and the self was one of the principal developments of the nineteenth century, leading to a blurring of the lines between the public and the private spheres (24-25). Ironically, this blurring made the creation of such hermeneutic tools as physiognomics all the more necessary, which in turn sought to expose the private life to ever greater public scrutiny, thereby further erasing the line that separated these two domains.

Physiognomy as theorized by Lavater can be understood as a kind of *Fehlleistung,* an unintentional "slip" in the Freudian sense: it circumscribes the domain of human self-expression in which the individual is not master in his or her own house. Lavaterian physiognomy and Freudian psycho-theory have this involuntaristic, deterministic element in common—with the noteworthy difference, of course, that the authoritative voice that Lavater's "transcendental ventriloquism" (Lichtenberg, "Über Physiognomik" 257) projects into a *meta*physical beyond, Freud's "psychological ventriloquism," if we may call it that, locates in an *intra*physical, an intra*psychical* agency, namely in the unconscious. Physiognomics as the science of this super-intentional language is a surface hermeneutics that resembles in kind the dream analyses on which Freud's depth hermeneutics is predicated: both seek to reconstitute the noncontingent, uncensored "text" of authentic human character. Lichtenberg, the enlightened crusader against the prophetic quality of physiognomy, unwittingly becomes a prophet in his own right when he observes in one of his notebooks: "If people would honestly relate their dreams, we could surmise their character better from this than from the interpretation of their face" (*Sudelbücher* 447).

Lichtenberg obviously could not know that this sarcastic remark, which belittles physiognomics by comparing it disfavorably with oneiromancy, anticipates what Freud would argue little over a century later in his groundbreaking study *Die Traumdeutung* (The interpretation of dreams). And in fact what Lavater attempted in the four volumes of his *Physiognomische Fragmente* has—relatively speaking, of course—further rather astonishing parallels to Freud's psychoanalytic program. Like Freud, Lavater was concerned with the systematization of a symbolic language, with the ascertainment of its semantics or semiotics, and with the determination of its syntax. To be sure, whereas Lavater modestly promises only to provide a few letters of the physiognomic alphabet (*Physiognomische Fragmente* 1: "Vorrede" [unpaginated]), Freud seeks to reconstruct the language of the unconscious in its entirety by pinpointing the laws that govern its deep structure. Moreover, both sought to rehabilitate interpretive disciplines traditionally disparaged as groundless prophetics, and each pursued this aim by appropriating the methodological procedures and empirical credibility of positivistic sciences. Both Lavaterian physiognomics and Freudian psychoanalysis thereby succumb to that scientistic self-misunderstanding that, according to Jürgen Habermas, is endemic to the human sciences in the modern epoch (see *Erkenntnis und Interesse* 88-233).

Despite these similarities we cannot fail to note that Lavater and Freud could scarcely be farther apart where their conceptions of sensuality and the body are concerned. For Freud, of course, it is precisely the repressed sensual needs and desires of the body that authorize the super-intentional language of the unconscious, which thereby functions as the custodian of repressed sensuality. For Lavater, on the other hand, the en-signment of the body signals precisely the repressive moment inherent in "Protestant ethics," in which sensuality is strategically reduced to a negligible epiphenomenon of the "soul."[22] Whereas for Lavater the body is nothing but the sensual sign of a supersensual signified, Freud reverses the roles of sign and signified in this semiotic equation: the super- or intrasensual psychic "text" constitutes the sign that marks the place once held by negated, absent sensuality. Insofar as Freud's hermeneutics attempts to liberate the sensual from this chain of repressive denial, of which physiognomics is but one prominent link, its thrust is directed decidedly against one of the mainstays of modern ideology. On the other hand, it simultaneously replicates the structure of false consciousness in that it seeks to purchase the liberation of sensuality at the price of disregarding the sociopolitical and economic structures that triggered this repressive self-mastery in the first place. In Freudian depth hermeneutics this moment of ideological self-deception is marked by the masking of sociopolitical coercion behind the interpersonal demands of the patriarchal family.[23]

Lavaterian surface hermeneutics and Freudian depth hermeneutics share the overriding paradox that while they are initially conceived as neutralizers of the ideological cleavage between internal and external existence in modern life praxis, each ultimately reveals itself to be the agent of a repression that serves to buttress this rift. Lavaterian physiognomics as surface hermeneutics writes the body large, paradoxically, only so as to be able better to erase it by means of its reduction to transparent signs: it trans-scribes the body, so to speak, in invisible ink. By contrast, Freudian depth hermeneutics attempts to rescue the script of that sensuality that Lavater would expunge. We can perhaps best throw this mechanism into relief by borrowing from Freud the image of the "magic writing pad" that he employed in the late essay "Notiz über den 'Wunderblock'" (Note on the magic writing pad) in order to illustrate the operation of the psyche. The *Wunderblock* is a simple apparatus consisting of a dark wax pad covered by a transparent cellophane sheet. Under the pressure of a stylus the wax sublayer leaves traces on the surface sheet that can be erased simply by separating it from this backing (363-64). Taking this magic pad as a metaphor for the body-soul dichotomy of the human subject, Lavaterian physiognomics can be imagined writing the text of the body on this transparent cellophane surface only in order better to wipe away its traces in a flurry of hermeneutic activity. Lavater overlooks, however, that this writing leaves a permanent inscription on the underlying wax pad. Psychoanalytic hermeneutics concerns itself with this inscription as the return of the repressed, the indelible remainder and reminder of an act of self-coercion that suppresses human sensuality. In this sense we can view Lavater's physiognomic surface hermeneutics as one of the ideological-historical conditions of possibility constitutive of psychoanalytic depth hermeneutics. On the other hand, however, Freud's attempted intervention in the ideology of the civil subject, much like Lavater's, amounts to a mystification that ultimately contributes to the perpetuation of that ideological self-deceit it aims to dismantle. This self-abrogating dialectic is the most profound trait shared by physiognomic surface hermeneutics and psychoanalytic depth hermeneutics. This deep-structural commonality points to the resilience and continuity-constitutive power of ideology in the intellectual-historical conglomerate we designate as cultural modernism.

Husserlian phenomenology, which, along with Freudian psychoanalysis, represents one of the major intellectual-historical contributions of twentieth-century German thought, has close affinities with both physiognomics and psychology. However, while Husserl openly acknowledges what he calls "the intimate connection between phenomenology and psychology" (*Ideen I* 177), the proximity of phenomenology to the physiognomic tradition remains largely unarticulated. The major point of overlap is, of course, the conception of the human being as an entity in which body and soul, external and internal being, form an inherent unity. Thus in the second book of his *Ideen zu einer reinen Phänomenologie und phänomenologischen Philosophie* (Ideas for a pure phenomenology and phenomenological philosophy), which focuses on the constitution of materiality, Husserl stresses that the ego "encompasses the 'entire' human being, body and soul" (94). Moreover, like physiognomics, phenomenology understands the soul as an active, animating power, and the body as the more or less passive medium of its expressions. Indeed, the material body, for Husserl, is the condition of possibility for the objective manifestation of the psychic domain as such: "In order to be experienced objectively," he asserts in *Ideen II,* "spirit must be animation of a material body" (96). The human body, then, as a living entity, is always a body animated by the psyche, the soul, or the internal, non-perceptible essence. Husserl employs the German word *Leib* to designate this animate body, which he distinguishes from *Körper* as purely material, inanimate body. Hence *Leib,* as the animate, animated body, always manifests the expressions of the internal spirit. "The animate body is not just a thing, but rather the expression of spirit," Husserl insists, and he goes on to maintain in absolute terms that *"everything* about the animate body can assume psychic significance" (*Ideen II* 96). The body thus becomes the sole indicator of the psychic life, and as such it is the vehicle by means of which we gain access to this internal domain. Indeed, for Husserl intersubjective experience would be impossible without a hermeneutics of the body that uncovers or projects psychic meanings on the basis of bodily expressions (see *Ideen II* 95).

Phenomenology's understanding of the expressive connection between soul and body, psyche and the realm of physicality, reads like the foundations for a theoretical physiognomics. Moreover, Husserl, like Lavater, even draws a comparison between the psychic expressions of the body and language, claiming that there is a certain "analogy between this sign system for the 'expression' of psychic events . . . and the sign system of language for the expression of thoughts" (*Ideen II* 166). Yet whereas he suggests that one ought to be able to "systematically study the 'expression' of the psychic life" and "establish the grammar of this expression" (*Ideen II* 166), Husserl himself never embarks upon such a project; if he had, he would have produced a practical physiognomics. As we will see, this move from phenomenological theory to physiognomic practice was reserved for one of Husserl's students, Ludwig Ferdinand Clauss (1892-1974), who consciously sought to develop a pragmatic physiognomics based on the theory and methodology of Husserlian phenomenology. More important, perhaps, is that, in contrast to Lavater, who stressed the significance of the firm and unchanging features of the body, for Husserl it is the body in mo-

tion, the animate, animated body, that manifests psychic significance. Like Lavater's two critics Lichtenberg and Hegel, Husserl will take sides with pathognomics, which ascribes significance solely to the motive, dynamic body.

Husserl's lack of practical application and systematization for his theory of the animate body as expressive medium of the psyche and the stress he places on pathognomic expression over the meaning of stable bodily form comprise two features that distinguish phenomenology from Lavaterian physiognomics. A third difference can be found in the self-understanding of phenomenological theory vis-à-vis the positivism of the natural sciences. Whereas Lavater sought to appropriate the methods and the discourse of the empirical sciences in order to lend scientific validity to his physiognomic interpretations, Husserl explicitly distances himself from the natural sciences. If science is concerned with empirical "facts," phenomenology, according to Husserl, concentrates on the discernment of "essences" (*Ideen I* 6). Taking up Wilhelm Dilthey's (1833-1911) distinction between the human sciences (*Geisteswissenschaften*; literally: "sciences of spirit or mind") from the natural sciences (*Naturwissenschaften),* Husserl explicitly locates phenomenology in the realm of the human sciences (*Ideen II* 191). As such, phenomenology does not rely on empirical data, as do the natural sciences, but depends instead on intuition, or *Anschauung.* This German term is key to phenomenological theory. Derived from the German verb *schauen,* meaning to see or to view, *Anschauung* has both the concrete meaning of "visual perception" and the more figurative significance of "intuition." The fusion of these two meanings in the word *Anschauung* is essential to phenomenological practice. Indeed, one could argue that the marriage of concrete and abstract meanings in this central term parallels the fusion of concrete body and supersensual psyche in the phenomenological understanding of the human body. Just as the psyche only makes itself manifest through the medium of the body, intuition of transsensual essence—what Husserl calls *Wesensanschauung* or *Wesenserschauung*—can only transpire as a corollary to visual perception. Sight, seeing, vision, and their metaphors become the key terms of phenomenological discourse. Husserl acknowledges the prominence of this transsensual seeing when he writes: "*Immediate 'seeing,'* not merely sensual, experiential seeing, but *seeing as such as an originary dative consciousness of any sort whatever,* is the ultimate source of grounding for all reasonable assertions" (*Ideen I* 43). For phenomenology as for physiognomics, "vision" implies both concrete visual perception and intuitive discernment. Indeed, for both the physiognomist and the phenomenologist every act of empirical seeing simultaneously entails a moment of supersensual intuition. Thus phenomenology rejects the positivistic, natural-scientific impulse of modern physiognomics only in order to highlight more emphatically the intuitive dimension that is always inherent in physiognomic practice.

When we recognize the intermediary position physiognomics assumes between Freudian psychoanalysis and Husserlian phenomenology we can begin to appreciate its significance as an intellectual-historical phenomenon in the fabric of German modernist thought. Physiognomics is wedded so closely with the emergence and development of modern culture in Germany that the issues around which it turns help to spawn some of the most notable positions of modern German intellectuals. Clearly, there is more at stake in the phenomenon of physiognomics, especially given its persistence in modern German thought, than just the interpretation of character out of the face. Physiognomics is about more than just the face. The chapters that follow will attempt to explore some of the many dimensions of physiognomics and physiognomic theory in German thought from Lavater through to the racist physiognomics of the Weimar Republic and National Socialism.

Notes

1. Throughout this examination I follow historians such as Isabel Hull in employing the more inclusive and ideologically neutral term "civil society" to designate the sociopolitical formation that emerged in late-eighteenth century Germany with the dissolution of the absolutist state and its social order of well defined estates. As Hull has argued (201-4), the tendency of social critics, following the lead of Jürgen Habermas, to narrowly identify German *bürgerliche Gesellschaft* with the middle class and with capitalist economic practices is both anachronistic and reductionist when applied to the situation of German-speaking Europe at the end of the eighteenth century and beyond. The phrase "civil society" indicates that the practitioners of these new forms of social and political interaction were more diverse than has often been assumed, encompassing hordes of state and city officials, the German *Bildungsbürgertum* composed of scholars, educators, doctors, lawyers, and other professionals, and finally, as just one subgroup, the economically productive bourgeoisie involved in commerce, manufacturing, and finance.

2. Musäus's *Physiognomische Reisen,* which were published anonymously, enjoyed enough popularity to warrant reissues in 1781, 1788, and 1803.

3. See especially pp. 1-40 in the second volume of Lavater's *Von der Physiognomik.*

4. Excerpts from this so-called "physiognomic cabinet," which is currently held in large part at the Portrait Collection of the Austrian National Library in Vienna, have recently been made available by Gerda Mraz and Uwe Schlögl in *Das Kunstkabinett des Johann Caspar Lavater,* the catalogue to the first exhibition of Lavater's private physiognomic collection. On the substance and nature of this collection, see Mraz and Schlögl's introduction (7-9).

5. On the emergence of the fashion system and the mentality of consumerism in German-speaking Europe in the final decades of the eighteenth century, see Purdy (esp. 1-73).

6. Musäus parodies this tendency toward the formation of societies centered around the study of Lavater's treatises when he has one of the characters of his *Physiognomische Reisen* form a physiognomic academy in his native village (1: 59).

7. Lichtenberg's treatise was first published in the *Göttingischer Taschen-Kalender für 1778* and later appeared as an independent pamphlet.

8. This parody first appeared in the *Neues Magazin für Ärzte* 5 (1783): 3-11.

9. Lavater himself gives an extended reply to Lichtenberg's critique in the fourth volume of the *Physiognomische Fragmente* (3-38). These remarks are reprinted with an introduction by Zimmermann in the *Deutsches Museum* (1778, 2: 289-317). Among Lavater's most ardent supporters, the poet Johann Michael Reinhold Lenz counterattacked Lichtenberg in his "Nachruf zu der im Göttingschen Almanach Jahrs 1778 an das Publikum gehaltenen Rede über Physiognomik" (Answer to the public address on physiognomics presented in the Göttingen Almanac of 1778), which was first published in Christoph Martin Wieland's *Teutscher Merkur* (1777, 4: 106-19). Zimmermann assaulted Lichtenberg with a barrage of ad hominem attacks in various submissions to the journal *Deutsches Museum* of 1778.

10. The persistence of this oversimplified understanding of the controversy between Lavater and Lichtenberg is repeated even in the most recent scholarship on this debate. See especially Gurisatti and Huizing, who, pursuing a Foucauldian archaeological analysis, invert the traditional hierarchy and valorize Lavater as the representative of a prerational sensibility that is mercilessly eradicated by the intolerance of enlightened reason. This transvaluation implicitly accepts the conventionalized terms in which this debate has been un-

derstood and overlooks the fact that Lavater himself appropriated the discourse of enlightened rationality in order to legitimate his physiognomic project.

11. See Eduard von der Hellen, *Goethes Anteil an Lavaters Physiognomischen Fragmenten*; Reinhold Steig gives a survey of Herder's relations to Lavater's physiognomics; Fr[iedrich] Waldmann summarizes Lenz's contributions.

12. Nicolai affirms his fundamental belief in the scientific basis of physiognomics in a letter to Lichtenberg dated 15 April 1778, published in Lichtenberg's *Briefwechsel* 1: 815-17. See also Nicolai's reviews of Lavater's physiognomic writings in his *Allgemeine Deutsche Bibliothek* 23 (1775): 313-46; 29 (1776): 349-414; and the supplement to volumes 25-36, pp. 1251-73.

13. On the connection of physiognomics to periods of sociopolitical disorientation see, for example, Arburg (42), Mattenklott (*Der übersinnliche Leib* 17-18), Schmölders (*Der exzentrische Blick* 12-13).

14. For an examination of the reflexes in style and fashion that contribute to the production of the civil subject, see Halpern (32).

15. Regarding the focus of physiognomics on the male and its general disinterest in issues of gender and women, see Regener ("Frauen," esp. 90-91).

16. I principally disagree with Andreas Käuser's view ("Die Physiognomik des 18. Jahrhunderts als Ursprung der modernen Geisteswissenschaft" 136) that the development from physiognomics to psychoanalysis is marked by a rupture or discontinuity characterized by a turn away from bodily to linguistic expression. Although the medium that reveals the "unconscious" does change from physical gesture to dream and linguistic slippage, the *metaphor* of language for conceiving the systematic, revelatory aspect of the unconscious remains constant.

17. For a definition of the epistemic structure of the enlightened world, see Foucault (*Order of Things* 50-63).

18. This motif is present throughout the *Fragmente*; see, for example, 3: 9-10; 3: 229.

19. On Carus as a precursor of Freud's theory, see Buser (68-79).

20. On this obsession with natural, "primordial" languages in this period, especially in the domain of art, see Herrmann (71-78).

21. The proximity of the "naive" to a trans-intentional unconscious is brought out best in Moses Mendelssohn's "Ueber das Erhabene und Naive in den schönen Wissenschaften" (esp. 240-42).

22. On the role of "Protestant" self-discipline in the constitution of modern socioeconomic practices, see Max Weber, "Die protestantische Ethik und der Geist des Kapitalismus" (esp. 47-48; 135-36; 187).

23. Stallybrass and White (149-70) have made especially persuasive arguments about this displacement of socioeconomic considerations by familial relationships in Freudian theory.

Select Bibliography

Arburg, Hans-Georg von. "Johann Caspar Lavaters Physiognomik: Geschichte—Methodik—Wirkung." In Mraz and Schögl. 40-59.

Aristotle [Pseudo-Aristotle]. *Physiognomica*. Trans. T. Loveday and E. S. Forster. *Aristotle: Complete Works*. Ed. Jonathan Barnes. Princeton: Princeton University Press, 1984. 1: 1237-50.

Buser, Remo. *Ausdruckspsychologie: Problemgeschichte, Methodik und Systematik der Ausdruckswissenschaft*. Munich and Basel: Ernst Reinhardt, 1973.

Foucault, Michel. *Discipline and Punish: The Birth of the Prison*. Trans. Alan Sheridan. New York: Vintage, 1979.

———. *The Order of Things: An Archaeology of the Human Sciences*. New York: Vintage, 1973.

Freud, Sigmund. "Notiz über den 'Wunderblock.'" *Freud Studienausgabe*. Ed. Alexander Mitscherlich et al. Frankfurt am Main: Fischer, 1967-1979. 3: 363-69.

Goritschnig, Ingrid. "Faszination des Porträts." In Mraz and Schögl. 138-51.

Habermas, Jürgen. *Erkenntnis und Interesse*. Frankfurt am Main: Suhrkamp, 1968.

Hegel, Georg Wilhelm Friedrich. *Phänomenologie des Geistes*. Vol. 3 of *Theorie-Werkausgabe*. Eds. Eva Moldenhauer and Karl Markus Michel. Frankfurt am Main: Suhrkamp, 1970.

Herrmann, Sabine. *Die natürliche Sprache in der Kunst um 1800: Praxis und Theorie der Physiognomik bei Füssli und Lavater*. Frankfurt am Main: Fischer, 1994.

Hull, Isabel. *Sexuality, State, and Civil Society in Germany*. Ithaca: Cornell University Press, 1996.

Husserl, Edmund. *Ideen zu einer reinen Phänomenologie und phänomenologischen Philosophie*. First Book.

Vol. 3 of *Gesammelte Werke*. Ed. Karl Schumann. The Hague: Nijhoff, 1976.

———. *Ideen zu einer reinen Phänomenologie und phänomenologischen Philosophie*. Second Book. Vol. 4 of *Gesammelte Werke*. Ed. Marly Biemel. The Hague: Nijhoff, 1952.

Käuser, Andreas. "Die Physiognomik des 18. Jahrhunderts als Ursprung der modernen Geisteswissenschaften." *Germanish-Romanische Monatsschrift* 41 (1991): 129-44.

König, Helmut. *Zivilisation und Leidenschaft: Die Masse im bürgerlichen Zeitalter*. Reinbek: Rowohlt, 1992.

Lachs, Daniela. "Lavaters Frauenbild—Lavaters Frauenbilder." In Mraz and Schögl. 152-61.

Lavater, Johann Caspar. *Physiognomische Fragmente zur Beförderung der Menschenkenntniß und Menschenliebe*. 4 vols. Leipzig and Winterthur: Weidmanns Erben & Reich, 1775-1778.

———. "Von der Physiognomik." *Hannoverisches Magazin* (1772): columns 145-92.

———. *Von der Physiognomik*. 2 vols. Leipzig: Weidmanns Erben & Reich, 1772.

Leibniz, Gottfried Wilhelm. *Les principes de la philosophie ou la Monadologie*. Vol. 1 of *Philosophische Schriften*. Ed. Hanz Heinz Holz. Darmstadt: Wissenschaftliche Buchgesellschaft, 1965.

Lenz, Johann Michael Reinhold. "Nachruf zu der im Göttingschen Almanach Jahrs 1778 an das Publikum gehaltenen Rede über Physiognomie." *Werke und Briefe*. Ed. Sigrid Damm. 3 vols. Munich: Hanser, 1987. 2: 761-68.

Lichtenberg, Georg Christoph. "Fragment von Schwänzen: Ein Beitrag zu den *Physiognomischen Fragmenten*." *Schriften und Briefe*. 3: 533-38.

———. "Über Physiognomik; wider die Physiognomen: Zu Beförderung der Menschenliebe und Menschenkenntnis." *Schriften und Briefe*. 3: 256-95.

Marcuse, Herbert. "Über den affirmativen Charakter der Kultur." *Kultur und Gesellschaft I*. Frankfurt am Main: Suhrkamp, 1965. 56-101.

Mattenklott, Gert. *Der übersinnliche Leib: Beiträge zur Metaphysik des Körpers*. Reinbek: Rowohlt, 1982.

Mendelssohn, Moses. "Ueber das Erhabene und Naive in den schönen Wissenschaften." *Ästhetische Schriften in Auswahl*. Ed. Otto F. Best. Darmstadt: Wissenschaftliche Buchgesellschaft, 1974. 207-46.

Mraz, Gerda, and Uwe Schögl, eds. *Das Kunstkabinett des Johann Caspar Lavater*. Vienna: Böhlau, 1999.

Musäus, Johann Karl August. *Physiognomische Reisen*. 4 vols. Altenberg: Richtersche Buchhandlung, 1778-1779.

Nicolai, Friedrich. Letter to Georg Christoph Lichtenberg dated 15 April 1778. In Lichtenberg, *Briefwechsel*. 1: 815-16.

[Nicolai, Friedrich]. Review of Lavater's *Physiognomische Fragmente*. *Allgemeine deutsche Bibliothek* 29 (1776): 379-414; and supplement to vols. 25-36: 1251-73.

[Nicolai, Friedrich]. Review of Lavater's *Von der Physiognomik*. *Allgemeine deutsche Bibliothek* 23 (1775): 313-46.

Pestalozzi, Karl. "Physiognomische Methodik." *Germanistik aus interkultureller Perspektive*. Eds. Adrien Finck and Gertrud Gréciano. Strasbourg: Université des Sciences Humaines, 1988. 137-53.

Purdy, Daniel L. *The Tyranny of Elegance: Consumer Cosmopolitanism in the Era of Goethe*. Baltimore: Johns Hopkins University Press, 1998.

Rauchensteiner, Meinhard, and Gudrun Swoboda. "Physiognomische Rhetorik I." In Mraz and Schögl. 110-17.

Regener, Susanne. "Frauen, Phantome und Hellseher: Zur Geschichte der Physiognomik des Weiblichen." In Schmölders, *Der exzentrische Blick*. 187-212.

Schmölders, Claudia, ed. *Der exzentrische Blick: Gespräch über Physiognomik*. Berlin: Akademie Verlag, 1996.

Sennett, Richard. *The Fall of Public Man*. Cambridge: Cambridge University Press, 1976.

Siegrist, Christoph. "Nachwort" to Lavater's *Physiognomische Fragmente*. Stuttgart: Reclam, 1984. 377-94.

Stallybrass, Peter, and Allon White. *The Politics and Poetics of Transgression*. Ithaca: Cornell University Press, 1986.

Steig, Reinhold. "Herders Verhältnis zu Lavaters *Physiognomischen Fragmenten*." *Euphorion* 1 (1894): 540-57.

Swoboda, Gudrun. "Die Sammlung Johann Caspar Lavater in Wien." In Mraz and Schögl. 74-95.

Waldmann, Friedrich. "Lenz' Stellung zu Lavaters Physiognomik." *Baltische Monatsschrift* 40 (1893): 419-36; 482-97; 516-33.

Weber, Max. "Die protestantische Ethik und der Geist des Kapitalismus." *Die protestantische Ethik I*. Ed. Johannes Winkelmann. Gütersloh: Verlagshaus Mohn, 1984. 27-317.

Wellbery, David. *Lessing's Laokoön: Semiotics and Aesthetics in the Age of Reason.* Cambridge: Cambridge University Press, 1984.

[Zimmermann, Johann Georg]. "Über einige Einwürfe gegen die Physiognomik, und vorzüglich gegen die von Herrn Lavater behauptete Harmonie zwischen Schönheit und Tugend." *Deutsches Museum* (1778) 1: 193-98.

Kevin Berland (essay date 2005)

SOURCE: Berland, Kevin. "Inborn Character and Free Will in the History of Physiognomy." In *Physiognomy in Profile: Lavater's Impact on European Culture,* edited by Melissa Percival and Graeme Tytler, pp. 25-38. Newark, Del.: University of Delaware Press, 2005.

[*In the following essay, Berland surveys general physiognomic thought in relation to philosophy regarding human nature, emphasizing Johann Caspar Lavater's physiognomy in particular.*]

> Est igitur Physiognomia scientia passionum animae naturalium, corporisque accidentium, habitum vicissim permutantium utriusque.[1]
>
> By Physiognomy then I mean, the talent of discovering the interior of Man by his exterior—of perceiving by certain natural signs, what does not immediately strike the senses. . . . Physiognomy would accordingly be, the Science of discovering the relation between the exterior and the interior—between the visible surface and the invisible spirit which it covers—between the animated, perceptible matter, and the imperceptible principle which impresses the character of life upon it— between the apparent effect, and the concealed cause which produces it.[2]

Physiognomy has traditionally combined moral philosophy with the observation of human character. How does the inner "invisible spirit" produce action? People act on impulse or deliberate choice; they are also affected by internal factors of which they are not always aware: emotional, temperamental, and cognitive predispositions. Physiognomists seek signs of the inner person marked on the outside, backtracking from effect to cause to show how inclination leads to action.

Are individuals determined by such signs? The language of some physiognomists suggests they are. Cocles, for instance, stated in 1556: "The foreheade verye great, declareth that man to be slowe and a heauy goer on the earth, a dullard and folysh, compared to the Oxe."[3] Corporeal structure corresponds with character. He will act the way he looks, and he looks that way because the shape of his forehead conforms with his innate constitution. But Cocles stops short of fatalism, assuring his readers that "reason and grace may handle nature or turn the prouocacions thereof unto goodnes."[4]

During the late Middle Ages and the early modern era, the church condemned divination—oneirology, chiromancy, physiognomy, metoposcopy, fortune-telling, and judicial astrology. Divination is sacrilegious because it attempts to foresee the future, which is God's to dispose of as he sees fit. It also fails to acknowledge the power of grace to effect moral change. Early modern physiognomists usually advance counterarguments like that proffered by Cocles: reason and grace may alter innate tendencies. Christian and classical physiognomists share the notion that visible marks of character indicate possibility, not necessity.

Lavater's physiognomy was a means of promoting Christian benevolence; his work was meant to help his readers know and love human nature. Although his *Physiognomische Fragmente* were influential from the first, his work was soon disengaged from its original purpose. Holcroft's English translation, for instance, excised the Protestant apologetics informing the original; still, Lavater's compassionate position opposing necessity remains.

There are continuities in the history of physiognomy from its earliest foundations in classical antiquity up to Lavater. This essay outlines some essential ideas put forward by early physiognomists, then examines ways in which Lavater's work reflects a greater similarity to historical "authorities" than is usually recognized.[5]

I. Signs

Partiality for reading character in outward appearance may be among the oldest effects of human curiosity. Classical poets and historians practiced characterization through physical description *(prosopographia, effictio, mimesis).*[6] The face registers transitory emotions; in time, physiognomy came to consider both fleeting expression and more permanent features. The pseudo-Aristotelian *Physiognomonica* furnishes the conceptual foundation for physiognomy: "Mental character is not independent of and unaffected by bodily process, but is conditioned by the state of the body. . . . And contrariwise the body is evidently influenced by the affections of the soul—by the emotions of love and fear, and by states of pleasure and pain." A natural accord exists between mind and body: "There never was an animal with the form of one kind and the mental character of another: the soul and body appropriate to the same kind always go together, and this shows that a specific body involves a specific mental character."[7]

The *Physiognomonica* articulates three modes of discovery. First, if a "peculiar mental character" belongs to a certain kind of animal, then human resemblance to that animal must be significant.[8] Second is the physiognomy of racial difference, the most stubbornly deterministic approach. Racist categories are fixed; the occult physiognomist "Acandam" typically pronounces that natural "complexion" (physical constitution) may be conjectured from skin color, "for naturally black men are fearefull." Yellow men are malicious, pale men are slow, red-faced men lose their wits.[9] Such accounts settle the race of the writer (white, European) as normative and fix instances of the Other in a zone defined by such words as "deformed."[10] Finally, the third mode develops a vocabulary of visible signs in facial expression and structure.

Another internal influence on character was the balance, or *krasis,* of the four humors.[11] The right blend of the humors, the four material qualities (warmth, cold, dryness, moisture), and the four elements produce well-being.[12] The balance or imbalance of humors generates character types, each bearing typical marks. Trained observers read external signs of inward disposition. Early modern medical texts and physiognomical manuals often share a common admixture of Galen, Hippocrates, and the Pseudo-Aristotle.[13]

In the late sixteenth century Porta absorbed the treatises of the Pseudo-Aristotle, Polemon, and Adamantius, providing illustrative examples from poets together with striking engraved images of paired human and animal faces. His work is best known as a system of theriological physiognomy, but his attention to other issues, especially humoral physiology, and his encyclopedic knowledge of the physiognomic tradition, are remarkable.[14]

In the seventeenth century Charles Le Brun studied facial expression from a Cartesian viewpoint. Pursuit of the good and aversion to the harmful generates passions in the mind. The brain is adjacent to the face, allowing a direct line between the mental site of passion and the locus of expression. Moral conduct is initially produced by impulses, which the face expresses. Thus the study of facial expression has a moral dimension. Le Brun did not write a systematic treatise on physiognomy, so we cannot ascertain his position on free will or on the individual's power to temper or transcend disposition.[15]

Each of these physiognomic systems, the humoral, the theriological, and the Cartesian, introduces processes that influence human character. Generally they agree that we may understand, and thus transcend, these powerful influences.

II. Beauty as an Outward Sign of an Inward Condition?

Is beauty a reliable outward sign of an inward moral condition, as the influential Platonic notion of *kalakogatheia* contends? Plato considers the "correspondence of a beautiful disposition in the soul and corresponding and harmonious beauties of the same type in the bodily form" the fairest of spectacles.[16] Galen defined beauty as "the functional perfection of bodily parts."[17] Similarly, the best facial structure is perfected physical form; teleologically, the beautiful face reflects a beautiful soul, itself the moral perfection of human nature.

Kalakogatheia becomes a commonplace among early modern writers. For example, Castiglione asserts that beauty comes from God, and cannot exist without goodness:

> Whereupon doth very seldom an ill soule dwelle in a beautifull bodie. And therefore is the outwarde beautie a true signe of the inwarde goodnesse, and in bodies this comelines is imprinted more and lesse (as it were) for a marke of the soule, whereby she is outwardly knowne: as in trees, in which the beautie of the buddes giveth a testimonie of the goodnesse of the fruite. And the very same happeneth in bodies.[18]

The converse is also true. The foul, "darke, uglesome, unpleasant" is usually evil. Castiglione's confident declaration includes a small but significant qualification: "very seldom"—words that perforce rule out "never."

Still, the harmony of beauty and virtue was widely accepted. A popular early modern *topos* found in collections of wise sayings, emblem books, and handbooks of manners and morality illustrates the importance of understanding outward beauty as a matter of *potential*. In his *English Gentleman,* Richard Brathwait tells of a philosopher who kept a mirror for his students. He told the beautiful to suit comeliness of face to the beauty of a virtuous mind, the ugly to adorn their minds with virtue.[19] This emblematic narrative indicates the widespread view that facial features do not guarantee character.

III. The Problem of Dissonance

Lucy Hartley explains physiognomic practice as "a classificatory act which functions in a profoundly normative manner," taking particular expressions as an instance of a character type, and in turn describing individual character as typical of that category.[20] Normativity imparts coherence to confusing human phenomena by referring to an explicatory scheme of natural knowledge.

But systems elicit close inspection by skeptical critics, who ask difficult questions. Must a person born with certain physical characteristics perform according to the way they look? Not every beautiful person is good, not every leonine man is courageous, not every crabbed and ugly face belongs to a person of deformed moral character. Physiognomists must confront the problem of dissonance, the apparent discrepancy between the evidence of an individual's face and reliable knowledge of that individual's character.[21]

The visual testimony of ancient portraiture, George Herbert suggested, could help physiognomists understand the limitations of their science. The expectation of what the great men of the past *ought* to have looked like clashes with the way they actually looked. Diogenes had narrow eyes "and no very advantageous looks," Cicero's head was very small, supported by a long, slender neck, and Socrates was bald, snubnosed, and ugly as Silenus.[22] The countenance mirrors the soul, and generally we are fixed in our passions by innate disposition. Still, Herbert admits dissonance. An inveterate sinner may have a promising countenance, probably because innate virtue was perverted by "some other external, adventitious Cause and Corruption; such as neglect of Education, early and religious Principles and Institution, Want, Poverty, and above all the evil Examples of the Age, and Conversation with others so tainted" (293). The face of a good man may bear marks of depravity, probably because he was born vicious, but education and philosophy has effected a change, or Christianity a cure (293). The "Signatures" which the physiognomist observes in the face indicate disposition, not necessity (338), and Herbert sustains free will.

Cicero first articulates the problem in *De Fato* as he measures free will against fate. His test case is Socrates:

> Again, do we not read how Socrates was stigmatized by the "physiognomist" Zopyrus, who professed to discover entire characters and natures from their body, eyes, face and brow? He said that Socrates was stupid and thick-witted because he had not got hollows in the neck above the collarbone . . . He also added that he was addicted to women—at which Alcibiades is said to have given a loud guffaw![23]

A tendency to vice may be inborn, but, as Cicero insists, such natural inclinations are reversible with effort, education, and strength of will. Socrates admitted Zopyrus had diagnosed him correctly, "saying that he was naturally inclined to the vices named, but had cast them out of him by the help of reason."[24] Character, Cicero explains, is not fixed at birth, though some people will lean more heavily in the direction of one vice or another. The key to overcoming leanings is the rational control of the passions.

Early modern medical writers considered all this relevant to their professional concerns. In a sixteenth-century treatise Guglielmo Gratarolo explains that physiologically induced facial signs indicate character, and he again introduces Socrates to exemplify the contrast between inner and outer character.[25] Working through his inventory of facial signs, Gratarolo reads Socrates in some detail, focusing especially on ugly features that may mislead the observer. But, as he insists, a discerning eye may note subtle counterindications, such as bright, pellucid eyes signifying justice, meekness, foresight, and admonition (117).

Physiognomists advocate the practical uses of their discipline in daily life, but they use examples drawn from the past, especially when referring to dissonance. That classically based physiognomy is not deterministic may be seen in the way Cicero's physiognomic story recurs

across the ages whenever a writer wishes a counter-argument to fatalism. For instance, William Alley employs the tale of Zopyrus (mistakenly substituting the name of Plato for that of his master) in his own argument against predestination. Alley moves from Biblical testimonies to patristic accounts of men who with reason, will, and grace overcame an innately vicious disposition, and then from Christian to classical precedents:

> If to heauen with prayer man lift vp his voyce,
> Agaynst destenie he shall triumphe and reioyce,
> Authorities agaynst destenie we neede no moe,
> But yet let vs bring an example or two.
> A certayne man beholding Plato his face
> Did him much dispraise and greatly disgrace,
> And iudged him to be a corrupter of youth,
> A lyar, a dissembler, no teller of truth,
> To whom Plato aunswered making relation
> That he had ouercome the planetes inclination
> By knowledge, and learning, and wise gouernment,
> And by godly vertues dayly intertainement.[26]

The argument that innate disposition may be overcome was always an important part of physiognomical system-making. Dissonance is not a sign of failed praxis, but an opening for the operation of free will in individual development. Indeed, this is precisely why physiognomy has so often been taken up by writers of moral philosophy. John Hartcliffe writes of the importance of testing our natural inclinations and learning how a middle way may be achieved:

> But there is no Man, that hath his Faculties so equally balanc'd, of his Affections so justly poised, as that he doth not incline to one of the extremes of *Virtue* more than to the other: Whosoever then would walk in the middle path of a *good* life, must take particular care to avoid that Rock, on which he is most apt to fall.[27]

He then draws on the familiar Ciceronian tale of Zopyrus's diagnosis; Socrates corrected his vicious inclinations "by *assiduous cares* and *pains.*" From this example Hartcliffe concludes, "so much the more industrious ought we to be in watching o'er our own natural Dispositions."[28]

The question of how free will may be constrained by innate disposition and how this constraint may be transcended pervades the history of physiognomy. According to Lavater, the physiognomist perceives within his fellow creatures "the noblest dispositions, at least the germs of them, which will perhaps be completely unfolded till the world to come. He distinguishes in characters what is original from what is the effect of habit, and what is habitual from that which is accidental: thus he judges Man only by himself" (1:77). Lavater's physiognomist specializes in transcendence.

Lavater is capable of a degree of contradictoriness. While it is true that he sometimes insists that certain physical structures fix character, he more often positions himself as a supporter of Christian free will, made effective by grace, manifest in the human ability to overcome innate dispositions. This stance is implicit in his distinction between physiognomy and pathognomy.[29] Pathognomy studies plastic features that register change, physiognomy fixed features that register proclivities established from birth. Lavater uses an apt financial metaphor: "Physiognomy points out the fund of the human faculties, and Pathognomy the interest or revenue which it produces."[30]

Expression itself produces change. "What passes in the mind is expressed in the face," and repeated facial expressions "at length produce a lasting impression on the flexible parts of the face." Repetition becomes propensity, "propensities become habits, and the passions are their offspring" (1:132-35). By "passions" Lavater means the momentary responsive emotions that produce facial expression (not to be confused with the notion of "passions" as deeply ingrained emotional tendencies, primary, irrational, and needing moderation by reason). In succumbing to these tendencies, individuals initiate patterns of conduct that become set components of daily life. Aristotle defines virtue and vice as acquired habits of the soul. Habituation involves either succumbing to or overcoming innate disposition. Habitual response to stimulus produces impulses that translate into facial expressions, leaving legible marks discernible by trained physiognomists. Lavater, like earlier physiognomists, insists that physiognomy is neither deterministic nor divinatory. It studies both innate potential and the motivations and tendencies that change or confirm this potential.

IV. LAVATER'S SENSIBILITY

In the "History of the Author's Physiognomical Knowledge" that opens his *magnum opus,* Lavater outlines the methodology of the true physiognomist, who relies upon a finely tuned sensibility capable of recognizing natural correspondences. "Lavater," the narrative persona of the book, models this sensibility, just as he models the Christian compassion he preaches. Lavater's presentation is mediated through a discourse of sensibility that kindles the reader's own curiosity and enthusiasm. He tells of the impressionistic beginning of his project: "Sometimes . . . at first sight of certain faces, I felt an emotion which did not subside for a few moments after the object was removed; but I did not know the cause" (1:7). Lavater never parts from these fundamental intuitions—"instinctive judgements, which the impression of the moment dictated" (1:7)—though it took him years to rely on the truth of such moments. Then he began to attempt to understand rationally what he had already perceived intuitively. He modestly states that he never intended to become an expert in physiognomy. Truth sought him out; he had no choice but to follow its promptings. Eventually he decided to investigate what had been written about the face as a register of character:

Oftener than once I began to study the Authors who have written of Physiognomy, but was soon disgusted with their verbose jargon; and I discovered that most of them only pilfered from *Aristotle*; I then gave up books. . . .

(1:11)

He gave up books to pursue observation, "to discover the beautiful, the noble, the perfect; to define them, to familiarize them to my eye, and to give fresh energy to the sensations which they excited" (1:12). Lavater calls his method "the study of Nature herself. . . . Everything in Man that can be known, is discovered solely through the medium of the Senses" (1:14). This admixture of observation and feeling might be called sentimental quasiempiricism: during the course of observation, the test of truth is always the responsive *sensation* of the trained observer. Lavater's use of the language of induction suggests an empirical collection of data, but in practice Lavater moves deductively from physiognomic principle to illuminate specific cases, often brilliantly. He tests particulars against truth intuitively recognized.

Therefore, because physiognomy depends upon intuitive perception—a gift for noticing truth in natural language—Lavater cannot rely on authorities. His method rejects scholastic tradition, like the best "*nulla in verba*" new scientists, but he replaces words not with things themselves, but impressions of things. Lavater calls his antecedents tedious, verbose, and unoriginal, and yet the authorities are still present through much of his work. In the third volume he discusses the authors a pupil of physiognomy should read: "The number of those who can be mentioned with approbation is small," he declares; "a fortnight is sufficient to run over all of them, and even their most sensible observations have still need to be closely examined." That is, none of them can be trusted and must be checked against what is intuitively known. At one point he attempts to contain the authorities within the boundaries of their own Fragment. Those not ready for full intuitive practice may benefit from the "easier" way of consulting historical accounts. "Authority has more weight with the multitude than reason" (1:44). By "reason" Lavater means not analysis or logic, but the refined intuitive practice he has developed:

> Physiognomy is a source of delicate and sublime sensations; it is a new eye which perceives in the creation a thousand traces of the Divine Wisdom and Goodness. . . . With secret ecstasy the benevolent physiognomist penetrates into the interior of his fellow creatures and perceives the noblest dispositions.

(1:77)

Lavater regularly asserts the primacy of intuition:

> Physiognomy is a poetic feeling, which perceives causes in effects. Most men appreciate a poem as they do a picture: in both they look for beauties, resemblances, caricaturas.

(2:443)

Authorities are superfluous to a method based on ec-static, penetrating insight; their rules and tables of marks cannot deliver the thrilling, responsive sensation he calls "Physiognomical Discernment" (1:93).

Lavater revisits the standard problems and issues. "I am neither a Teacher of Necromancy, nor the inventor of a secret of difficult investigation" (1:83); here he rejects the charge that physiognomy is an occult or divinatory art. He also discusses the modes of analysis outlined by the Pseudo-Aristotle—passages on animal-human corre-spondences, on racial character, and on humoral physi-ology.[31]

Two problems that have beset physiognomists concern Lavater. First, he is an ardent supporter of the doctrine of *kalokagatheia.* In the Fragment "Of the Harmony Between Moral Beauty and Physical Beauty," he takes on the question whether there is "a real disagreement between moral beauty and physical deformity; between moral deformity and corporal beauty" (1:128). He uses affective rhetoric—exclamation, assertion and rhetorical questions—to support his appealing personal presenta-tion of an a priori argument. Since human beings are "the workmanship of sovereign Wisdom, is it not in the first place highly probable, that there exists a harmony between moral and physical beauty?" (1:129). After several pages of such questions, defying sensible read-ers to deny or confute his assertions, Lavater produces the keystone of his argument:

> Beauty and ugliness have a strict connection with the moral constitution of Man. In proportion as he is mor-ally good, he is handsome; and ugly, in proportion as he is morally bad.

> (1:135)

Anticipating a "host of objections . . . like an impetu-ous torrent rushing down the precipice" threatening to overwhelm him, Lavater explains his view of disso-nance. It is common enough to encounter beautiful, vi-cious men and homely, virtuous men, but the physiog-nomist "with eyes somewhat experienced" will readily discern subtle signs of the true original disposition, as well as the distance traveled toward vice and virtue (1:139). Virtue is not the only cause of beauty, nor vice of ugliness (1:135), but virtue and vice have transfor-mative power:

> Every species of immorality less or more affects the body; alters, enervates and degrades it: on the contrary, moral energy and activity prevent this degradation, and dispose all that is excellent and honorable, and conse-quently create also the expression of beauty of every species.

Moral degradation changes the body, producing "carica-turas" of the original, while true goodness confers "last-ing charms" on the exterior (1:142). The face and body become an archive of experience and transformation; virtue improves and vice debilitates the external appear-ance.

In a word, there is not in Man any one species of physi-cal beauty—nor any one member of the body—which may not receive from virtue and from vice, taken in the most general sense, a good or a bad impression.

> (1:148)

Lavater recognizes dissonance in the case of a beautiful person who bears the marks of vice, "the faithful ex-pression of the impure passions, which polluted, and had taken root in his soul." Conversely, the true physi-ognomist may see in an ugly, good man an overlay of virtuous marks softening the hard structure of his innate disposition to vice (1:140). In the firm structures and forms of the face are seen innate dispositions to virtue and vice. The physiological constitution, hunger, dis-ease, heredity, health and happiness all affect the char-acter and alter the face. Likewise, volitional change, ac-quiring virtuous habits, and practicing moderation all leave their marks in the softer structures and forms of the face.

There is always evidence for a discerning physiogno-mist to intuit a complex blend of characteristics. Thus, in his analysis of the central test case of dissonance, Lavater accepts the claim that Socrates was inclined to stupidity, lechery, and other vices, since some of the hard facial structures so indicate. But instead of "aston-ishment at finding no harmony between the exterior and interior" (1:168), Lavater goes on to demonstrate how many marks of change may be observed. The problem of dissonance is resolved by emphasizing that change for the better is possible, good news for those who, like the author, Lavater says disarmingly, are dissatisfied with their manifest defects (1:150).[32]

Despite critical objections, Lavater remained committed to the doctrine of *kalokagatheia.*[33] This commitment gives rise to one or two astonishing statements, as when he asserts that the handsomest painters have gained the greatest eminence in their art, and only those with a "good figure" will be fit to discern physiognomical truth:

> Physiognomists the most highly favoured with respect to their exterior, will ever become the most intelligent. As the virtuous Man is best qualified to judge of virtue . . . so persons who have the most beautiful faces are most capable of pronouncing on the beauty and dignity of Physiognomies, and of discovering, at the same time, what is faulty and defective.

> (1:117)

Lavater can say this seriously because he knows he is not beautiful, and he is not (yet) a physiognomist.[34] This passage is consonant with Lavater's belief that the most benevolent, virtuous observer of humanity must show the effects of his good nature in his outward appear-ance, and is thus perfectly consistent with his progres-sive version of *kalokagatheia,* outlined above. In some passages, as we have seen, he acknowledges the problem of dissonance, but in practice he denies the objection outright, arguing that there always must remain sufficient evidence for a discerning and tutored eye, even in a face that appears to bear signs that contradict the known character.

What Lavater has done is to deny history at the same time as he appropriates it. I am not suggesting that this appropriation and revision is gratuitous, however. Although Lavater might have gleaned a great deal of value from the work of his predecessors, his dedication to the physiognomics of sensibility precluded him from building explicitly on the precepts and arguments of the past. The art he proposed could not be learned by rule and rote. Rather, he wrote in a manner designed to affect his readers, to inundate them with heightened emotion, to encourage empathy, and to coerce them into intuitive discernment. Lavater shows his readers a picture and invites them to judge—no, he interrupts himself, "no, there is no need of judgement—only give way to natural feeling" (1:187). On another similar occasion, he states, "It is certain that every reasonable man, unless he formally contradict his internal feeling, will acknowledge in the form of that face, in the contour of the parts, and the relation they have to one another—the superior man" (1:257).

Lavater often speaks of physiognomy as a science based on an empirical survey of forms, contours, and relations. But, in fact, he relies on assertion, not demonstration, and his method of persuasion is not induction but an affective discourse that kindles in the reader a kind of enthusiasm implicitly linked to the internal, felt discernment Lavater places at the heart of the physiognomical project. Lavater steers his readers to intuition-based recognition, sometimes planting evidence, sometimes planting conclusions. That both evidence and conclusions parallel the findings of some of the ancients may be a coincidence, a matter of finding out similar truths by different paths, or it may not. There is still much work to be done.

Notes

The author would like to thank the William P. McDowell Endowment at Penn State Shenango, and the Penn State Commonwealth College for research and travel support.

1. "Thus physiognomy is the science of the natural passions of the soul and the contingencies of the body, which both exchange their characteristics in turn." Bartolommeo della Rocca Cocles, *Barptolomaei Coclitis Bononiensi, naturalis Philosophiae ac Medicinae Doctoris, Physiognomiae & Chiromantiae Compendium,* trans. Thomas Hill (Argentorati: Apud Gregorium Machaeropoeum, 1556), sig. A2v.

2. Lavater, *Essays on Physiognomy,* 3 vols., ed. T. Holloway, trans. H. Hunter (London: J. Murray, 1789-98), 1:20. Further references appear in the text.

3. Cocles, *A briefe and most pleasant epitomye of the whole art of physiognomie,* trans. Thomas Hyll (London: by Iohn Wayland, 1556), sig. [A. v.] v.

4. Cocles, preface to *A briefe and most pleasaunt epitomye,* n.p.

5. Primary texts are collected in R. Förster, *Scriptores Physiognomonici* (Leipzig, 1893). The essential study of classical physiognomy is Elizabeth C. Evans, "Physiognomics in the Ancient World," *Transactions of the American Philosophical Society,* n.s. 59/5 (1969). See also Tamsyn Barton, *Power and Knowledge: Astrology, Physiognomics and Medicine under the Roman Empire* (Ann Arbor: University of Michigan Press, 1994). For Early Modern European physiognomy, see Jean-Jacques Courtine and Claudine Haroche, *Histoire du visage: exprimer et taire ses émotions, XVIème-début XIXème siècles* (Paris: Rivages, 1988); Melissa Percival, *The Appearance of Character: Physiognomy and Facial Expression in Eighteenth-Century France* (Leeds: W. S. Maney & Sons for the Modern Humanities Research Association, 1999); and the first chapter of Lucy Hartley, *Physiognomy and the Meaning of Expression in Nineteenth-Century Culture* (Cambridge: Cambridge University Press, 2001).

6. See Evans, "Ancient World," 47-74. Evans considers such descriptions antecedent to physiognomy.

7. *Physiognomonica,* 805a; *The Complete Works of Aristotle,* ed. Jonathan Barnes, trans. T. Loveday and E. S. Forster, Bollingen Series 71, 2 (Princeton: Princeton University Press, 1984), 1:1237.

8. Later writers who took up this mode include Polemon and Adamantius in the second century AD, Giovanni Battista della Porta in the sixteenth, and Charles Le Brun in the seventeenth. George Herbert discusses "Theriologic Physiognomy" in *A Discourse of Medals, Antient and Modern* (London: for Benj. Tooke, 1697), 296.

9. [Richard Roussat], *The Most Excellent, Profitable, and Pleasant Booke of the famous Doctor, and expert Astrologian, Arcandam, or Alcandrin, to finde the fatall destiny, constellation, complexion, and naturall inclination of euery man and child by his birth: With an addition of Phisiognomie, very pleasant to reade,* trans. William Warde (London: by Felix Kyngston, 1626), fol. J3v.

10. On race-based physiognomy, see Kay Flavell, "Mapping Faces: National Physiognomies as Cul-

tural Prediction," *Eighteenth-Century Life* 18 (November 1994): 8-22. See Miriam Claude Meijer, *Race and Aesthetics in the Anthropology of Petrus Camper, 1722-1789* (Amsterdam: Rodopi, 1999) for a discussion of the appropriation of early anthropological measurement ("facial angle") to justify racist ethnology.

11. See W. Thiessen, "An Outline of the Development of Concepts of Humoral Medicine," *Medical Life* 39 (1934): 3-19; Ian Maclean, *Logic, Signs, and Nature in the Renaissance: The Case of Learned Medicine* (Cambridge: Cambridge University Press, 2002).

12. On the relation between physiognomy and ancient humoral medicine, see Evans, "Ancient World," 17-28.

13. On Galen, see Margaret Tallmadge May's introduction to her translation, *On the Usefulness of the Parts of the Body* (Ithaca: Cornell University Press, 1968), 44-64. On Galen's physiognomy, see Evans, "Ancient World," 24-26.

14. Giovanni Battista della Porta, *De humana physiognomonia* (Vici Aequensis, apud I. Cacchius, 1586).

15. On Le Brun's Cartesianism, see Percival, *Appearance of Character,* 41-63, and Hartley, *Meaning of Expression,* 19-26.

16. Plato, *The Republic,* 402d, in *The Collected Dialogues of Plato,* ed. Edith Hamilton and Huntington Cairns, trans. Paul Shorey, Bollingen Series 71 (Princeton: Princeton University Press, 1963), 646. On Lavater's *kalakogatheia,* see Robert E. Norton, *The Beautiful Soul: Aesthetic Morality in the Eighteenth Century* (Ithaca: Cornell University Press, 1995), especially chap. 5.

17. Galen, "On the Usefulness of the Parts," 79. Galen here credits Socrates, in Xenophon, *Symposium,* 5, Loeb Classical Library (Cambridge: Harvard University Press, 1923), 598-603.

18. Baldassare Castiglione, *The Book of the Courtier* [*Il Libro del Cortegiano,* 1528; trans. Sir Thomas Hoby, 1591], Everyman's Library, 807 (London: Dent, 1928), 308-9.

19. Richard Brathwait, *The English Gentleman,* 2d ed. (London: by Felix Kyngston, 1633), 18-19. The philosopher in question is most often Socrates; see Diogenes Laertius, *Lives of the Eminent Philosophers,* trans. R. D. Hicks, Loeb Classical Library (Cambridge: Harvard University Press, 1931), 2:33.

20. Hartley, *Meaning of Expression,* 2.

21. Lavater quotes Gellert in Fragment Seventh, "Authorities": "If it be true, that a mind replete with mildness and serenity is frequently veiled by a sad and gloomy exterior; and that a haughty and boisterous look sometimes disguises an amiable character; this *dissonance* may arise from having contracted bad habits, or from the imitation of bad examples. Perhaps this offensive exterior may be the effect of some constitution vice; or, it may be a man's own workmanship, the consequence of a long train of self-indulgence, which he has now overcome." Lavater, *Essays,* 1:54 [emphasis added].

22. Herbert, *Discourse of Medals,* 319, 339. Further references appear in the text.

23. Marcus Tullius Cicero, *De Fato,* vol. 10, trans. J. E. King, Loeb Classical Library (Cambridge: Harvard University Press, 1948), 203-5.

24. *Tusculan Disputations,* IV.xxxvii.80; trans. J. E. King, Loeb Classical Library (Cambridge: Harvard University Press, 1927), 419.

25. Guglielmo Gratarolo, *Artium & medicinæ doctoris opuscula* (Basileæ, apud Nicolaum Episcopium iunidem, 1554), 8. Further references appear in the text.

26. William Alley, ΠΤΩΧΟΜΥΣΕΙΟΝ, *The poore mans librarie* (London: by John Day, 1565), 2:fols. 31v-35v.

27. John Hartcliffe, *A Treatise of Moral and Intellectual Virtues* (London: for C. Harper, 1691), 42-43.

28. Ibid., 43.

29. On Buffon's distinction between physiognomy and pathognomy, see Percival, *Appearance of Character,* 28-37; on Lavater, idem, 177. In adopting this distinction Lavater follows Lichtenberg's suggestion; see Lavater, *Essays,* 1:235. On Lichtenberg's impact, see Siegfried Frey, "Lavater, Lichtenberg, and the Suggestive Power of the Human Face," in *The Faces of Physiognomy: Interdisciplinary Approaches to Johann Caspar Lavater,* ed. Ellis Shookman (Columbia, SC: Camden House, 1993), 73-83; Norton, *The Beautiful Soul,* 196-200; and Kevin Berland, "'The Air of a Porter': Lichtenberg and Lavater Test Physiognomy by Looking at Johnson," *The Age of Johnson* 10 (1999): 219-30.

30. Lavater, *Essays,* 1:78.

31. Not having studied animals, Lavater refers the task to "the Buffons and Campers of the age," but offers an extended set of general observations, comments on the Pseudo-Aristotle's reading of animals, animal skulls and character, human-animal resemblance, Porta's illustrations, animal heads and character. See Lavater, *Essays,* 2:96-144. Lavater posits a "natural sentiment of the

beautiful" which only cultural factors, "the tyranny of an ancient national and hereditary prejudice could have extinguished or altered." The examples he cites of such deviance from the norm of beauty include an unnamed tribe that admires wens, and Africans who admire African features: "none except Negros admire a flat nose" (Lavater outlines a humoral physiognomy based on the four qualities of the body (humidity, dryness, heat, cold) which have as their basis earth, air, fire, and water, producing the temperaments, melancholic, sanguine, choleric, and phlegmatic. He cites no ancient authorities, connects some notions of contemporary chemistry with the four elements, and shows no sign of recognizing that humoral physiology had long been exploded. In concluding, he pronounces that the first question that should be answered is whether natural temperament may be subdued (Lavater, *Essays,* 3:93-94, 128).

32. On Lavater's analysis of Socrates, see K. J. H. Berland, "Reading Character in the Face: Lavater, Socrates, and Physiognomy," *Word and Image* 9/3 (1993): 252-69.

33. On contemporary objections, see Norton, *The Beautiful Soul,* 196-206.

34. "It is not false modesty, it is thorough conviction, which constrains me to acknowledge, that I am very far from being a Physiognomist. I am but the Fragment of one; just as the Work I present to the Public contains not a complete Treatise, but merely Fragments of Physiognomy" (Lavater, *Essays,* 1:127).

WOMEN AUTHORS

Graeme Tytler (essay date 1994)

SOURCE: Tytler, Graeme. "Physiognomy in *Wuthering Heights.*" *Brontë Society Transactions* 21, part 4 (1994): 137-48.

[*In the following essay, Tytler explores the influence of physiognomic concepts on Emily Brontë's* Wuthering Heights.]

The study of physiognomy in the novel has in recent years become a fairly well established domain of literary criticism.[1] Some of this scholarship has been concerned with the novels of the Brontë sisters; and though physiognomy is hardly as conspicuous in *Wuthering Heights* as it is in Charlotte Brontë's novels, which abound in physiognomical (and phrenological) refer-

ences and descriptions, it is, nevertheless, important enough to deserve critical discussion.[2] Broadly speaking, physiognomy in fiction has to do not only with the moral significance of facial and bodily features, gestures, gait, handwriting, laughter, clothes, national, regional or family characteristics, resemblances between human beings and animals, the effects of inner and external influences on the appearance, and so on, but also with the presentation of narrators and characters as more or less skilled observers of the human appearance; that is to say, elements in fiction which have usually been examined in the light of the physiognomic theories of Johann Caspar Lavater (1741-1801) and against the background of their diffusion in Europe from the late eighteenth century onwards. There is, however, no evidence that Emily read Lavater or any other physiognomists, or took any particular interest in physiognomic theory; but it would be hard to imagine her not having become as familiar with popular physiognomy as Charlotte appears to have been, especially during the nine months of 1843 when they were both teaching at M. Heger's school in Brussels, that city which, incidentally, had brought out at least five French editions of Lavater's physiognomic essays in the 1820s and 1830s.[3] In any case, by the time Emily began to write *Wuthering Heights,* Lavater's historic work had already appeared in several English translations and editions, and been the main impetus behind a number of British publications on physiognomy, including Alexander Walker's *Physiognomy founded on Physiology* (1834), a copy of which is known to have been housed in the Keighley Mechanics' Institute in 1841, being one of several books to which the Brontë family had access at that time.[4]

Whatever Emily Brontë's knowledge of physiognomy, her treatment of personal appearances in *Wuthering Heights* is very much in line with that of her immediate predecessors, Ann Radcliffe and Walter Scott in particular, whose detailed descriptions of fictional characters sometimes include references to physiognomy and physiognomists, and even to Lavater himself.[5] In this connection, it is noteworthy that Emily's two main narrators, Lockwood and Nelly Dean, are presented as acute observers, with a sensitivity to faces one might have readily attributed to the numerous disciples of Lavater who flourished in late eighteenth-century Europe and beyond.[6] Certainly it would be surprising if, with his dilettante disposition, Lockwood had not heard of, or even dipped into, at least one of the English editions of Lavater's essays that had appeared in Britain by 1801, the year heading his first diary entry.[7] Lockwood's familiarity with physiognomy is suggested, for example, when, seeing Heathcliff give Catherine Linton 'a look of hatred', he qualifies this judgment by adding 'unless he has a set of facial muscles that will not, like those of other people, interpret the language of the soul' (16) and, earlier, when referring to his encounter with a young lady at the seaside, he remarks that 'if looks have language, the merest idiot might have guessed I was over head and ears' (7), as it is also hinted at through his physiognomical judgments of Heathcliff's voice (15), Catherine Linton's face (19) and Edgar's portrait (82), as well as his use of the word 'physiognomy' in two contexts (8 & 112).[8] Yet for all that Lockwood purports to be a physiognomist in his propensity for reading and analysing faces, it would appear that physiognomy itself has at best encouraged in him a tendency not only to categorise people into types rather than to see them as individuals, but also to keep them at arm's length; indeed, far from teaching him to come to know and love his fellow men, as Lavater would have it, physiognomy may have even enhanced Lockwood's aestheticism and, hence, fostered his preference to remain a detached spectator of life.[9]

A similar predilection for observation may be noted in Nelly—no doubt as the effect of a life lived mainly through those she has served as nursemaid or housekeeper—and, like Lockwood, she seems to be quite familiar with physiognomic theory. For example, Lavater's sundry comments about the influence of virtue or vice on the development of beauty or ugliness, as well as other factors determining the facial appearance, have a certain bearing on the occasion when, having wished that, like Edgar, he had 'light hair and a fair skin' as a means of becoming 'decent' and 'good', Heathcliff is taken by Nelly to a looking-glass, shown his morose facial features in all their grim detail, and then, rather than wish for his rival's physiognomy, is advised, instead, to 'wish and learn away the surly wrinkles, to raise [his] lids frankly and change the fiends to confident, innocent angels . . .' (72). Realising presently, however, that Heathcliff has drawn a false conclusion from her physiognomic premise in assuming she meant him to wish for Edgar's 'great blue eyes and even forehead' (72), Nelly retorts: 'A good heart will help you to a bonny face, my lad, . . . if you were a regular black, and a bad one will turn the bonniest into something worse than ugly' (72).[10] Characteristic as that aphoristic utterance is of Nelly's tendency to live her life according to fixed principles, it is, nevertheless, borne out to some extent by her observations of Hareton Earnshaw. Thus, despite being aware of a certain loutishness in his general appearance at the age of sixteen, Nelly describes him as 'a well-made athletic youth, good-looking in features', in whose 'physiognomy', as she puts it, she can detect 'a mind owning better qualities than his father ever possessed' (240f)—a judgment which, apart from bespeaking Hareton's intelligence and good nature, foreshadows that moment when Nelly will describe how Catherine's educative influence has affected his outward appearance: 'His brightening mind brightened his features and added spirit and nobility to their aspect—I could hardly fancy it the same indi-

vidual I had beheld on the day I discovered my little lady at Wuthering Heights, after her expedition to the Crags' (391).[11]

Another aspect of physiognomy used by Nelly, and one to which Lavater was practically the first physiognomist to draw attention, is the human appearance in death or in a moribund state. For example, when he speaks of a certain refinement in one's appearance shortly before death, and even for several hours afterwards, whereby the facial features become 'visibly ennobled', we are forcibly reminded of Nelly's final descriptions of Cathy. Thus, having described the physical effects of the heroine's 'brain fever' with phrases such as 'ghastly countenance', 'strange exaggerated manner' and 'wasted face', and underlined the physiognomic interest of her illness by mentioning the alarm and horror with which she and Edgar have reacted to her haggard looks and changing facial expressions, Nelly inevitably becomes aware of a significant alteration in her appearance on the eve of her death, whereby, conscious of 'unearthly beauty in the change', she recalls that 'the flash of her eyes had been succeeded by a dreamy and melancholy softness' so that they 'appeared always to gaze beyond, and far beyond—you would have said out of this world—' (192).[12] No less 'Lavaterian', it might be said, is Nelly's following description of Cathy shortly after her death:

> Her brow smooth, her lids closed, her lips wearing the expression of a smile, no angel in heaven could be more beautiful than she appeared, and I partook of the infinite calm in which she lay. My mind was never in a holier frame than while I gazed on that untroubled image of Divine rest.
>
> (201f)[13]

Furthermore, since Lavater's observations on the dying and the dead are an expression of the Christian theology underlying his physiognomic thinking, they have a particular relevance to the way in which, despite having just remarked on the heroine's 'wayward and impatient existence' (202), Nelly is, ironically enough, so heartened by the sight of the latter's corpse 'asserting its own tranquillity' (202) as to re-affirm her simple-hearted, not to say naïve, belief in a heavenly afterlife.

But perhaps the most important aspect of physiognomy in *Wuthering Heights* is the family physiognomy, not least because Emily Brontë's treatment of it entails a remarkably dramatic use of the observational skills of some of her main characters. It is interesting, first of all, to note the way in which the differences between the Earnshaws and the Lintons in character and temperament are already suggested by specific references to personal appearance. The fact that, for example, the Earnshaws have dark eyes and brown hair (Cathy's 'brown ringlets' (65) are mentioned, as are Hareton's 'thick brown curls' (14) and 'brown locks' (372)), and the Lintons, blue eyes and fair hair, seems to make physiognomic sense if we accept Lavater's view that '*blue* eyes announce more weakness, a character softer and more effeminate than *hazel* or *black* eyes'; and, again, his statement, made amid vague and, sometimes, unfavourable assessments of dark hair, that 'flaxen hair', to which he assigns the epithet '*noble*', generally announces 'a delicate and sanguino-phlegmatic temperament'.[14] Furthermore, since references to family features are rare in physical character description before 1790, and then usually perfunctory, our comparison here between *Wuthering Heights* and the *Essays on Physiognomy* may be deemed justifiable, all the more because, apart from making simple comments on heredity that were by no means commonplace in the late eighteenth century, Lavater found that none of the great physiognomists before him had said much on the subject of the family physiognomy.[15] And though by 1847 Emily might have come to know of the sophisticated scientific theories of heredity propounded by Comte, Lamarck and others, there can be little doubt that her elaborate treatment of family resemblances and differences, which is virtually unprecedented in the English novel, is a sort of homage to Lavater's categorical claim that 'family physiognomy is as undeniable as national [physiognomy]'.[16]

Family physiognomy plays an important part in relations between the Earnshaws and the Lintons on the one hand, and in the conflict between the Lintons and Heathcliff, on the other. Let us first consider the Linton physiognomy, which is treated in two ways: first, the 'light hair' and 'fair skin' of Edgar Linton are associated, it seems, with social privilege and cultural refinement; secondly, they imply a certain decadence, which becomes evident in the child of Heathcliff and Isabella Linton. By marrying Isabella, Heathcliff has sought to avenge himself both on Cathy and on the Lintons. But fate answers this quest for vengeance with an act of counter-vengeance, for Heathcliff's son proves not only to bear no physical resemblance to himself, but to possess a sickly version of that Linton physiognomy which his father had once so coveted as a boy, and which, to judge by the latter's condemnation of Isabella in front of Cathy for 'that mawkish, waxen face' and for her blue eyes inasmuch as they 'detestably resemble Linton's' (131), he has by now come to hate and despise. The irony of this is made plain when Nelly Dean notes Linton Heathcliff's resemblance to his uncle: 'A pale, delicate, effeminate boy, who might have been taken for my master's younger brother, so strong was the resemblance, but there was a sickly peevishness in his aspect that Edgar Linton never had' (245). Pathos is then added to irony in Nelly Dean's dialogue with Linton Heathcliff, who learns to his dismay that he is physically quite different from his father with the 'black hair and eyes' (252), and then again in the boy's own aware-

ness of this difference as expressed in a letter to his uncle Edgar: 'I believe an interview would convince you that my father's character is not mine, he affirms I am more your nephew than his son, . . .' (314f). Disappointed for obvious reasons by the physical appearance of his son, Heathcliff resolves, nevertheless, to have him well looked after in order to use him later for purposes of revenge; though, as time passes, his dislike of the boy becomes more and more apparent, being typified, for instance, by his 'antipathy to the sound of his voice' (258). However, his plan to win a vicarious triumph over the Lintons by having his descendant 'lord of [the Lintons'] estates' and 'hiring their children, to till their fathers' land for wages—' (255) is thwarted; for, though Heathcliff forces Catherine Linton to marry his son, the latter dies an invalid's death shortly afterwards.

The fair hair and blue eyes of the Lintons are also contrasted with the Earnshaws' brown hair and dark eyes, which, in the person of Catherine Earnshaw, represent that boisterous vitality which is lacking in the Lintons. Moreover, the fundamental incompatibility between Cathy and Edgar is suggested to some extent by their being physically quite unalike—an incompatibility which is made symbolically manifest in the mixture of sensitivity and discontent we so often see in the child of their tragic union. Nevertheless, as Nelly Dean implies in her first detailed description of Catherine Linton, the child has clearly inherited the best of both parents:

> She was the most winning thing that ever brought sunshine into a desolate house—a real beauty in face—with the Earnshaws' handsome dark eyes, but the Lintons' fair skin, and small features, and yellow curling hair. Her spirit was high, though not rough, and qualified by a heart sensitive and lively to excess in its affections. That capacity for intense attachments reminded me of her mother; still she did not resemble her; for she could be soft and mild as a dove, and she had a gentle voice, and pensive expression:. . .
>
> (232)[17]

Catherine's heredity becomes the basis for her role in the novel. Thus with her Earnshaw vitality and Linton sensitivity, she not only offers resistance, however ineffective, to Heathcliff's tyranny, but manages after a long period of conflict with Hareton Earnshaw (for which her inherited snobbishness is largely to blame) to draw the latter out and, as we saw earlier, to educate him. Not the least interesting thing about this relationship is the cousins' growing resemblance to each other through mutual spiritual and emotional influences, all the more as Lavater observes:

> I have found the progress of resemblance most remarkable when two persons, the one richly communicative, the other apt to receive, have lived a considerable time

together, without foreign interventions; when he who gave had given all, or he who received could receive no more, physiognomical resemblance, if I so dare say, had attained its *punctum saturationis*. It was incapable of further increase.[18]

But however 'Lavaterian' Catherine's resemblance to Hareton may be, it serves an unmistakable structural function, for, as we shall see presently, its effect on Heathcliff is such as to mark the final turning point of the action.

The idea that Heathcliff should be profoundly affected by this family resemblance need not surprise us here if we remember the account of his visit to the Lintons in Chapter VI, where, despite his naïve assumptions about physiognomy in Chapter VII mentioned above, his reference to the 'vacant blue eyes of the Lintons' gazing 'full of stupid admiration' at Cathy's 'own enchanting face' (63), already bespeaks that gift for observation which Lavater found so often in children.[19] In any case, it may be supposed that Heathcliff's physiognomic sensitivity has already taken root in that moment when, in order to reassure his wife in her terror of the boy, Mr Linton falls back on the following age-old physiognomic half-truth: 'Don't be afraid, it is but a boy—yet the villain scowls so plainly in his face, would it not be a kindness to the country to hang him at once, before he shows his nature in acts, as well as features?' (61). Indeed, it needs only the reference to Mrs Linton's raising her hands 'in horror' and Isabella's suggesting that he be put down in the cellar because he looks 'exactly like the son of the fortune-teller, that stole [her] tame pheasant' (61) for the reader to imagine the essence of Heathcliff's self-consciousness about his personal appearance. All such details, together with several (mainly) derogatory references to Heathcliff as a gipsy and Nelly's constant, and sometimes nervous, awareness of his 'black eyes' and 'black hair' are, no doubt, satirical comments on physiognomic prejudice, not to say outright Anglo-Saxon racism, as manifest most patently in Mr Linton's contemptuous designation of Heathcliff as 'a little Lascar, or an American or Spanish castaway' (62). And though it is true that later in the novel Heathcliff's physicality has, as a consequence of his three-year absence, become strong and refined enough to impress Nelly, Cathy and Edgar, and even to cause the fastidious Isabella to become infatuated with him, it is one of the remarkable ironies of the novel that a man of such impressive physical characteristics should have failed to pass them on to his off spring. Furthermore, it would be hard to find anywhere in fiction a more admirable treatment of physiognomy than that which Emily Brontë provides us through her presentation of Heathcliff. For just as Heathcliff enters the world of Gimmerton a physiognomic outsider, so he departs it, as it were, a physiognomic wreck, defeated at first by the Linton physiognomy, as we have already seen, and,

then, as we shall see presently, overcome in the end by the Earnshaw physiognomy.

The earliest significant reference to the Earnshaw physiognomy from Heathcliff's standpoint occurs in Isabella's letter to Nelly Dean, in which Hareton is described as having 'a look of Catherine in his eyes and about his mouth' (167), and Hindley's eyes are likened to 'a ghostly Catherine's, with all their beauty annihilated' (168). Such references are, of course, to be expected of the very observant Isabella, though their function here is to adumbrate the moment when, in her brave attempt to intervene on Hindley's behalf against Heathcliff, she will address the latter as follows: 'Now that [Cathy's] dead, I see her in Hindley; Hindley has exactly her eyes, if you had not tried to gouge them out, and make them black and red, . . .' (223). That these words should have an ironically painful effect on Heathcliff is only later made apparent; but through them the reader comes to suppose that Heathcliff's inveterate brutality to Hindley may have been much more than a matter of settling a childhood score. Heathcliff's ill-treatment of Catherine Linton can also be similarly explained: some psychologists might even describe it as an expression of inverted love. For example, in one of her many acts of defiance towards Heathcliff, she is described with her 'black eyes flashing with passion and resolution' (328). This description prefigures a moment in their conflict when, just after Catherine has demanded the key of the door, Heathcliff is described by Nelly Dean thus: 'He looked up, seized with a sort of surprise at her boldness, or, possibly, reminded by her voice and glance, of the person from whom she inherited it' (328).

With each reminder of Cathy's physiognomy, Heathcliff undergoes a kind of psychological jolt, every one of which marks a stage in his gradual spiritual decline. This is first suggested when, just after Hareton has burnt his books out of spite, Lockwood overhears Heathcliff talking to himself about how, in his attempt to discover Hareton's resemblance to his father, he can only detect his uncanny likeness to Cathy—a likeness so painful for him that he 'can hardly bear to see him' (367). Another tormenting reminder of Cathy occurs when Hareton and Catherine are behaving frivolously at the breakfast table. On this occasion Nelly Dean describes how, after having 'rapidly surveyed [their] faces', and then been 'abhorred' by Catherine's 'accustomed look of nervousness and yet defiance' (386), Heathcliff addresses the latter as follows: 'What fiend possesses you to stare back at me, continually, with those infernal eyes? Down with them! and don't remind me of your existence again' (386f). Such, indeed, is the impact of this physiognomic resemblance on him that, a few minutes later, when Heathcliff has seized hold of Catherine for refusing to leave the kitchen and, as Nelly Dean observes, seems 'ready to tear [her] to pieces' (389), he suddenly relaxes his grip on her while gazing 'intently in her face' (390). And as he draws his hand 'over his eyes' (390), and then threatens to kill her should she provoke him again, the hero's spiritual decline is further confirmed.

It is, then, little wonder that, with his essentially superstitious nature, Heathcliff should show signs of 'monomania' (394) by the time he has become vividly aware of the cousins' mutual resemblance, especially since Cathy's haunting of him is now at its most intense.[20] Thus Nelly Dean relates how, on returning home unexpectedly from one of his daily rambles, Heathcliff finds Hareton and Catherine reading together by the fire, their faces 'animated with the eager interest of children' (392). The narrative then continues as follows:

> They lifted their eyes together, to encounter Mr Heathcliff—perhaps you have never remarked that their eyes are precisely similar, and they are those of Catherine Earnshaw. The present Catherine has no other likeness to her, except a breadth of forehead, and a certain arch of the nostril that makes her appear rather haughty, whether she will or not. With Hareton the resemblance is carried farther: it is significant at all times—then, it was particularly striking: because his senses were alert, and his mental faculties wakened to unwonted activity.
>
> I suppose the resemblance disarmed Mr Heathcliff: he walked to the hearth in evident agitation, but it quickly subsided, as he looked at the young man; or I should say, altered its character, for it was there yet.
>
> (392)

Nelly Dean's physiognomic interpretation of Heathcliff's agitation proves to be correct, for, once the cousins have left the room, he feels impelled to confide in her about his sufferings. That his 'monomania' is now at its very worst is also evident when he refers to Hareton and Catherine as 'the only objects which retain a distinct material appearance to [him]' (393). This 'appearance', moreover, causes him, as he confesses, 'pain, amounting to agony' (393): through Catherine, he is reminded of her mother, while, through Hareton, he undergoes a kind of *déjà vu* boyhood experience. And having, as he has just said, now 'lost the faculty of enjoying their destruction' and feeling the need to 'turn [his mind] over to another' (393), Heathcliff regains much of the sympathy which we felt for him in his physiognomic dialogue with Nelly Dean in Chapter VII, and which we feel perhaps more strongly through his following confession to her:

> Five minutes ago, Hareton seemed a personification of my youth, not a human being—I felt to him in such a variety of ways, that it would have been impossible to have accosted him rationally.
>
> In the first place, his startling likeness to Catherine connected him fearfully with her—That, however, which you may suppose the most potent to arrest my imagination, is actually the least—for what is not connected with her to me? and what does not recall her? I

cannot look down to this floor, but her features are shaped on the flags! In every cloud, in every tree—filling the air at night, and caught by glimpses in every object by day, I am surrounded with her image! The most ordinary faces of men and women—my own features—mock me with a resemblance. The entire world is a dreadful collection of memoranda that she did exist, and that I have lost her!

> (393f)

With these words, the mystery of Heathcliff's earlier reactions to the Earnshaw physiognomy is at last unravelled that is to say; they suggest that every single reference to a resemblance to Cathy has constituted part of the ironic leitmotif of her haunting of him. Thus we discover that the heroine's constant presence in the novel, far from being that of some vague apparition, has throughout been an utterly physiognomic phenomenon. It is, moreover, in this penultimate chapter that Emily Brontë shows how skilfully she has used physiognomy in the treatment of her central themes: for just as Heathcliff's downfall, as manifest in the mental deterioration he betrays in this long confession, may be said to be in part the consequence of his physiognomic sensitivity, not to mention his failure to survive physiognomically in his 'descendant', so the resolution of the conflict between the Earnshaws and the Lintons, and hence the establishing of peace and harmony at the end of the novel, which was already foreshadowed in the description of Catherine Linton's physiognomic make-up, may be said to have been symbolically sealed by the growing mutual resemblance of the two cousins as brought about by their love for each other.

Notes

1. For a recent bibliography of such studies, see Graeme Tytler, 'Lavater and the nineteenth-century English novel' in Ellis Shookman, ed., *The Faces of Physiognomy: Interdisciplinary Approaches to Johann Caspar Lavater* (Columbia, SC: Camden House, 1993): pp. 222n-4n.

2. For physiognomy in Charlotte Brontë's fiction, see Wilfred M. Senseman, 'Charlotte Brontë's use of physiognomy and phrenology', *Papers of the Michigan Academy of Sciences, Arts and Letters,* 38: pp. 475-83: (1953); Ian Jack, 'Physiognomy, phrenology and characterisation in the novels of Charlotte Brontë', *Brontë Society Transactions,* 15: pp. 377-91: (1970); Graeme Tytler, 'Character description and physiognomy in the European novel (1800-1860) in relation to J. C. Lavater's *Physiognomische Fragmente*' (Diss. University of Illinois, Urbana, 1970): pp. 143f, 229n, 242-4, 254-5, 321-2: *idem, Physiognomy in the European Novel: Faces and Fortunes* (Princeton, NJ: Princeton University Press, 1982): pp. 190-2, 236-8, 275-7. For physiognomy in *Wuthering Heights,* see Tytler, 'Character description and

physiognomy': pp. 234, 250-1, 258-61: *idem, Physiognomy in the European Novel*: pp. 227-9, 242-53, 256-9, 278f.

3. For details, see John Graham, *Lavater's Essays on Physiognomy. A Study in the History of Ideas* (Bern: Peter Lang, 1979): p. 92f.

4. For a bibliography of nineteenth-century British publications on physiognomy, see Tytler, *Physiognomy in the European Novel*: p. 348f. For the reference to Walker, see Clifford Whone, 'Where the Brontës borrowed books', *Brontë Society Transactions,* 60: 358 (1950). Walker devotes a few paragraphs to Lavater's physiognomic essays; and though he dismisses them as scientifically inadequate, he acknowledges them to be 'the most valuable work which has appeared on physiognomical science'. See Alexander Walker, *Physiognomy founded on Physiology* (London: A. K. Newman, 1834): p. 216f.

5. For details, see Tytler, 'Lavater and the English novel': p. 225f.

6. For an account of the Lavaterian physiognomic culture in Europe, see Graham, *Lavater's Essays on Physiognomy: passim,* and Tytler, *Physiognomy in the European Novel*: pp. 82-119.

7. Two of the best-known English translations are John Caspar Lavater, *Essays on Physiognomy for the Promotion of the Knowledge and the Love of Mankind,* tr. Thomas Holcroft, 3 vols. (London: G. G. J. & J. Robinson, 1789) and *idem, Essays on Physiognomy calculated to extend the Knowledge and the Love of Mankind,* tr. C. Moore, 3rd ed., 3 vols. (London: H. D. Symonds, 1797). Since Holcroft's translation of the original *Physiognomische Fragmente* (Leipzig & Winterthur, 1775-1778) contains details that are not to be found in Moore's translation of Lavater's original French edition, *Essai sur la physionomie* (Paris, 1781-1803), and vice-versa, reference will be made to both texts in our discussion here. For a list of English editions and versions of Lavater, see Graham, *Lavater's Essays on Physiognomy*: pp. 87-90.

8. For the increasing use of the term 'physiognomy', and the widening of its meaning, in European literature after the 1790s, see Tytler, *Physiognomy in the European Novel*: pp. 117f, 364.

All quotations from the novel are taken from Emily Brontë, *Wuthering Heights,* ed. Ian Jack & Hilda Marsden (Oxford: Clarendon Press, 1976).

9. For Lavater's concept of physiognomy as an act of neighbourly love, see *Essays on Physiognomy,* tr. Moore, Vol. II, pp. 41-5.

10. Lavater's numerous comments on the relationship between virtue and vice, and beauty and ugliness, are central to his physiognomic outlook. See especially the section 'Of the Harmony of Moral and Corporeal Beauty' in Lavater, *Essays on Physiognomy,* tr. Holcroft, Vol. I, pp. 175-208.

11. For the influence of education and other factors on the human appearance, see especially, Lavater, *Essays on Physiognomy,* tr. Holcroft, Vol. I, p. 184.

12. For Lavater's experience of the physiognomy of the dying, see *Essays on Physiognomy,* tr. Moore, Vol. III, p. 150.

13. Lavater, *Essays on Physiognomy,* tr. Moore, writes:

> As often as I have seen dead persons, so often have I made an observation which has never deceived me: that after a short interval of sixteen or twenty-four hours, sometimes even sooner, according to the malady which preceded death, the design of the physiognomy comes out more, and the features become infinitely more beautiful than they had been during life: they acquire more precision and proportion, you may perceive in them more harmony and homogeneity, they appear more noble and sublime.

(Vol. III, p. 149)

14. Lavater, *Essays on Physiognomy,* tr. Moore, Vol. III, p. 323f.

15. Lavater, *Essays on Physiognomy,* tr. Holcroft, writes: 'Striking and frequent as the resemblance between parents and children is, yet have the relations between the character and countenances of families never been enquired into. No one has, to my knowledge, made any regular observations on this subject' (Vol. III, p. 128f). For Lavater's comments on the family physiognomy and heredity, see *Essays on Physiognomy,* tr. Holcroft, Vol. I, p. 196f & Vol. III, pp. 128-47.

16. Lavater, *Essays on Physiognomy,* tr. Holcroft, Vol. III, p. 128.

17. Of particular interest for Brontë's treatment of the Earnshaw eyes is Lavater's following comment: 'If the eyes of the mother have any extraordinary vivacity, there is almost a certainty that these eyes will become hereditary'. *Essays on Physiognomy,* tr. Holcroft, Vol. III, p. 132.

18. Lavater, *Essays on Physiognomy,* tr. Holcroft, Vol. III, p. 148.

19. See Tytler, *Physiognomy in the European Novel*: p. 64.

20. See Graeme Tytler, 'Heathcliff's Monomania: an Anachronism in *Wuthering Heights*', *Brontë Society Transactions,* 20: pp. 331-43 (1992).

Ronald J. Quirk (essay date 2002)

SOURCE: Quirk, Ronald J. "Physiognomy in Pardo Bazán's Portrayal of the Human Body." *Anales Galdosianos* 37 (2002): 125-33.

[*In the following essay, Quirk studies Emilia Pardo Bazán's emphasis on descriptions of her characters' eyes and how this narrative is informed by physiognomy.*]

Emilia Pardo Bazán's narrative strategies and literary techniques have long been a topic of interest to scholars and continue to attract ever more perceptive analyses.[1] Yet one of Pardo Bazán's descriptive methods-the physical representation of her fictional creations—is in need of further investigation. Specifically, Doña Emilia's recurrent attention to the eyes of her characters warrants examination and offers a key to her assimilation of physiognomy and that theory's influence in her literary works.

Pardo Bazán's creation of a wide variety of strong and submissive, stereotypical and idiosyncratic, pious and worldly figures in her volumes of novels and short stories is so extensive as to elicit a "Censo de personajes" for them.[2] Descriptions of individuals constitute a proportionately sizable and artistically significant part of Doña Emilia's works. In these descriptions the frequency with which she describes the eyes of her characters is noteworthy. From her first novel, *Pascual López,* of 1879, through her major novels and short stories of the late nineteenth and early twentieth centuries, Pardo Bazán is insistent in her focus on that part of the human body.

The theory that eyes, eyebrows, and other facial features reveal personality and character is called "physiognomy": "the widely accepted and ancient art or science of judging an interior reality by the external appearance" (Graham 35). This theory was first articulated by Aristotle, was accepted by many subsequent philosophers, and was promoted by the famous sixteenth- and seventeenth-century scholar and scientist, Francis Bacon.[3] A revived interest in physiognomy in the eighteenth century is credited to Johann Caspar Lavater, a Swiss philosopher, Protestant theologian, and friend of Goethe. Lavater's *Essays on Physiognomy* (1775-1778) popularized the idea that temperament and character can be ascertained by careful analysis of outward appearance, especially facial features. Lavater's *Essays* circulated widely and exerted considerable international influence in the late eighteenth and early nineteenth centuries: "there were by 1810 at least sixteen German, fifteen French, two American, two Russian, one Dutch, one Italian, and twenty English versions in five different translations [. . .] in less than forty years" (Graham 77).

Nineteenth-century Spain felt the influence of Lavater somewhat later. In three editions between 1842 and 1848 Antonio Rotondo published *La fisonomía, o sea El arte de conocer a sus semejantes por las formas exteriores; extractado de las mejores obras de Lavater.* Mariano Aguirre de Venero, another ardent follower of Lavater, dedicated to his Swiss mentor his *Primer sistema del lenguaje universal, fisiognomónico de los ojos: Nuevo arte de conocer a los hombres.* Aguirre's book, published in 1865, is a compendium of human characteristics and the supposed manifestations of those traits by the size, colour, movement, and expression of eyes and eyebrows. The work includes an application of the theory to fifty-seven well-known figures from history, the Bible, science, literature, and art. In his introduction "Al lector," Aguirre uses the same words that Pardo Bazán would later employ as he calls eyes the "*espejo del alma*" (xii, emphasis is author's) and he singles out their prime importance for his theory of physiognomy: "en mi sentir representan el más importante papel en la expresión fisonómica del hombre" (xii). Near the end of his treatise, Aguirre reiterates the pre-eminence of eyes in his system: "Ellos [los ojos] pertenecen al alma, sin que otro órgano pueda competir con ellos en paralelo; siendo indudable que ellos la tocan y la siguen en todos sus movimientos. La inteligencia, el sentimiento del espíritu, las emociones dulces o tumultuosas, el fuego del alma, y la acción de la vida, todo está en los *ojos*" (334).

Lee Fontanella (107) has examined the role of physiognomy in Spanish Romanticism and indicates that the theory's waning persuasiveness still commanded attention and some adherence late in the nineteenth century. The ideas of the physiognomists were part of the intellectual atmosphere that surrounded Emilia Pardo Bazán in the early years of her formation, and Carmen Bravo-Villasante reports that in her youth Emilia became acquainted with the illustrations of the *Fragmentos fisiognómicos* of Lavater (Bravo-Villasante 15). Her literary works would later show reflections of this childhood reading of Lavater.

Emilia Pardo Bazán's literary use of eyes ranges from the casual, almost superficial, to a more purposeful treatment, related to underlying beliefs. Her simplest references are stereotypical and offer a good point at which to begin an analysis. She generally depicts the peoples of southern Europe as having dark eyes that reveal warmth and passion. Three examples will illustrate her customary practice. She calls the eyes of Rita Pardo, who appears in several novels, "voluptuosos ojos negros" and "bellos ojos meridionales" (1: 489, 490),[4] where the adjective "meridionales" openly asserts the connection between eyes and nationality. The Sicilian Giacinto in *Misterio* has "ojos negrisimos, aterciopelados" (2: 859 and 863). And in *Dulce Dueño,* José María Mascareñas, an Andalusian who is designated as a "tipo clásico," has black eyes "espléndidamente lucientes y sombríos, árabes legítimos" (2: 982). In contrast, she describes British and Americans as having blue, light-coloured, yellowish, or even colourless eyes that often betoken lack of emotion and a cold absence of sympathy. The livestock dealer of "Cuesta abajo" is an "inglesote de azules ojos" (2: 1289). The English Protestant catechist, Ezmite (Smith), has "azules ojos" (2: 160). The Scottish maid, Maggie, of *Dulce Dueño* is "de ojos incoloros" (2: 998). The American Ricardo Stoddard, in the short story, "Entre razas," has "ojos incoloros y fríos;" "pupilas descoloridas y aceradas" (1: 1533, 1534). The American woman of "Vengadora" is portrayed with "ojos amarillentos" and, lest there be any doubt of the relation between physical appearance and nationality, the author introduces this description with the words "anglosajona, saltaba a la vista: la marca étnica no podía desmentirse" (1: 1515). Other nationalities, too, are characterized by their eyes. The sea captain in *Misterio* has "verdes ojos célticos" (2: 803), and the Asians of the short story, "El templo," are described as "los indianos del Himalaya, de negros ojos de gacela y dorada piel; los siberianos, de azules pupilas" (1: 1530). Such stereotypical depiction of eyes does not diminish from the early novel, *La tribuna*, of 1883 (2: 160) to the late novels, *Misterio,* of 1903 (2: 813), *La sirena negra,* of 1908 (2: 914, 920), and the descriptions we have seen in *Dulce Dueño* of 1911.

Eyes, however, do not only symbolize nationality. The eyes of Pardo Bazán's characters also reflect the life experiences through which they have passed and the style of life to which the are accustomed. The female convict who awaits execution in *La piedra angular* has "ojos grandes, oscuros y de mirada dura" (2: 335). María Vicenta, the seamstress, whose child has died in "Consuelos," has "hinchados y extraviados ojos" (2: 1284). The eyes of the shy intellectual, Hilario Aparicio, are "miopes, indecisos" (2: 974). At times, Pardo Bazán accompanies these anatomical descriptions with explicit declarations of their connection to the life and personality of the character being portrayed. Thus, the Jesuit priest, Urtazu, has eyes that are "levemente bizcos, como son los de las personas hechas a concentrar y sujetar la mirada" (1: 71), and the elderly "señorita Merry [es] de ojos azules, descoloridos como violetas marchitas; de fatigados párpados, como tienen las personas que han llorado mucho" (2: 1326). Doña Emilia takes particular care in characterizing Gabriel Pardo de la Lage at the beginning of *La madre Naturaleza* before she reveals his name. She describes his eyes as "garzos y grandes, de párpado marchito y enrojecido, como suelen tenerlo las personas que leen mucho o viven aprisa" (1: 301), and she adds "su mirada, intensa, dulce, miope, tenía esa concentración propia de las personas muy inteligentes, bien avenidas con los libros, inclinadas a la reflexión y aun al ensueño" (1: 303).

Eyes are, thus, a testimony to one's life experiences and style of life. But for Pardo Bazán, they are even more. Doña Emilia posits in human eyes a key to understanding, and to depicting, a person's personality and character. She calls eyes "aquel espejo de los movimientos del alma" (1: 527). This declaration is significant for it verbalizes the connection she saw between physical appearance—the body—and character. Previous writers had, of course, often linked eyes to the soul. Typical is Guillaume Du Bartas of the sixteenth century, who, in his *Divine Weeks and Works,* called eyes "these lovely lamps, [. . .] these windows of the soul" (Du Bartas 1: 277). For Pardo Bazán, however, eyes are not merely the windows through which the soul gazes on external reality and life, but rather the mirrors that reflect, and reveal, the soul. This correspondence between appearance and inner being calls for a closer examination in her writings.

A salient feature of characterization in Pardo Bazán's fiction is the frequency with which particular types of eyes coincide with particular types of people. Sinister figures, especially those given to violence, have very dark and small eyes. Primitivo Suárez, the incarnation of barbarism who plots to kill the priest, Julián Álvarez, in *Los pazos de Ulloa,* has "ojuelos negros" (1: 170, 181). Natolia, the ominous old witch of "Ofrecido" in *Cuentos de la tierra,* also has eyes of which the darkness and smallness are emphasized: "los dos toques de azabache de los ojuelos" (2: 1529). Other fearsome characters who have small eyes are the "cazador furtivo [. . .] Bico de Rato" (1: 245) and the Philippine chieftain of "La exangüe" (1: 1521). Cruel Tío Clodio of "Las medias rojas" has "ojos pequeños" (2: 1474), and the usurious Cipriano Lourido of *El tesoro de Gastón* features "rasgos de incomparable astucia y disimulo en los diminutos y recelosos ojuelos" that are also called "sagaces ojillos" and "ratoniles ojillos" (2: 547, 553, 567). The young gunsmith's son, Cartucho, in *La piedra angular* has "ojuelos maliciosos y bizcos" (2: 284). Large black eyes, on the other hand, are not linked to a sinister heart. Thus, Manolita and her mother, with their "ojazos negros," are admired in *La madre Naturaleza* (1: 322, 332), and Concha of *La piedra angular,* who has "fogosos ojazos," is a "buena moza" (2: 291). Dark eyes that are neither particularly large nor small may manifest beauty, as do those of Manuelita in "Un parecido" (1: 1142) or have a less favourable connotation, as do the "ojos negros y duros" of Paquín in *La Quimera* (1: 848). What is more constant is the use of blackness in connection with resolute, vigorous personalities like Silvestre Moreno and Carmiña Aldao of *Una cristiana* (1: 564, 567) and, particularly, the aged Sor Aparición of the tale named after her, whose eyes have special significance: "Lo singular de aquella cara espectral [. . .] eran los ojos. Desafiando a la edad, conservaban, por caso extraño, su fuego, su intenso negror, y una violenta expresión apasionada y dramática" (1: 1163).

Black is not the only colour used in conjunction with small eyes to portray frightful characters. In *Los pazos de Ulloa* and other stories that share its cast and locale, Barbacana and "el Tuerto de Castrodorna" are savage criminals who terrorize rural Galicia. While Barbacana does have typical black eyes (1: 266), the single eye of el Tuerto is an "ojuelo verde" or "verdoso" (1: 267). Pardo Bazán uses the colour green with various connotations in her descriptions of eyes. It can signify beauty, as with Margarita Elviña of *Cuentos de Marineda* (1: 1102), or intelligence, as in the depiction of the learned St. Catherine of Alexandria (2: 943). But, as we have seen with "el Tuerto," green can denote a menacing or fear-inspiring interior. This is the case in the portrait of Martín, the old visionary of *Misterio,* with his "dos ojos verdes, gatunos, fatidicos," which are later called "verdes ojos de brujo" (2: 736, 741). Occasionally the greenness of the eyes of a character establishes such a deep connection with nature that the character becomes almost an emanation of the countryside: Maripepiña de Norla of *Cuentos de la tierra* has "ojos verdes, del color de los pámpanos de la vid" (2: 1484), and in Maripepa of *Bucólica* "un alma inculta [. . .] se asomó a unos ojos del color del follaje, ojos que parecían espejos de la Naturaleza agreste" (1: 939). In *Morriña* the green eyes of the protagonist evoke the freshness of spring and the nature of Galicia for which she pines: "Sus interesantes ojos verdes, con reflejos amarillentos, acentuaba[n] el carácter primaveral y tierno de la hermosura de Esclavitud, asemejando su faz a un valle regado por dos cristalinos arroyos" (1: 498). Finally, the frequently ambiguous significance of green eyes is shown by Sidoriña of *Cuentos del terruño* "con sus ojos verdes, enigmáticos" (2: 1313).

Brown eyes are relatively infrequent in Pardo Bazán's creations, but they do appear in some of her characters who have lively or passionate, romantic imaginations. Thus, Clara Ayamonte of *La Quimera* has "ojos pardos" (1: 740), and Jorge Viodal of *El saludo de las brujas* and María Silveria, the young "aldeana ruda" of "La hoz," have "ojos castaños" (2: 659, 1550). Lina Mascareñas, the protagonist of *Dulce Dueño,* is portrayed with "ojos color de café" (2: 962), as is Leonor of "El fantasma" (1: 1136).

Félix O'Narr, the strange professor of chemistry in *Pascual López,* has "los ojos grises, más penetrantes, inquisidores y claros del mundo," (2: 36, 52). The grey eyes of Camila in *La sirena negra* are also "penetrantes" (2: 892), but those of the physician, Pelayo Moragas, in *La piedra angular* (2: 320), and the "ojos grises, incoloros" of the withered, old Andrea in *La madre Naturaleza* (1: 347) appear insignificant.

In many of Pardo Bazán's other creations, passivity, submissiveness, or weakness are distinguishing traits. These persons are given blue eyes. The priest, Julián

Álvarez, is such an individual. Characters in which beauty, or even seductiveness, dominates also frequently have blue eyes. Indeed, in her personification of love Pardo Bazán depicts Amor as having "azules pupilas" (1: 1123). Beautiful women with blue eyes in her works include Lucía González of *Un viaje de novios* (1: 95), Nieves Comba of *El cisne de Vilamorta* (2: 228), Silvestriña of "Dios castiga" (2: 1560), María Vega of "Desquite" (1: 1130), Micaeliña of "Viernes Santo" (1: 1347), and Dalinda from the story with the same name (2: 1290). Great attention is given to the eyes of the temptress, Sabel, in *Los pazos de Ulloa;* they are "ojos azules, húmedos y sumisos" (1: 172), and their significance is reinforced with the phrase "la melosa ternura y sensualidad de sus ojos azules" (1: 230). Age and degeneracy take their toll on Sabel's appearance, and in *La madre Naturaleza* the reader learns that "el azul de sus pupilas, antes tan claro y puro, amarilleaba" (1: 333). Other figures, too, are depicted with blue eyes; among them are two amorous suitors, the hesitant Hilario Aparicio of *Dulce Dueño* (2: 974) and the forward Diego Pacheco of *Insolación* (1: 467), and the young boy, Perucho, of *Los pazos de Ulloa.* Interestingly, the eyes of both Perucho and Diego Pacheco darken when they become angry (1: 387, 467). The blue of Perucho's eyes also shows his genetic inheritance from his mother, a resemblance the author makes explicit: "parecíase a Sabel, y aun se le aventajaba en la claridad y alegría de sus ojos celestes" (1: 173). Likewise, Manuela's dark eyes in *La madre Naturaleza* recall those of her mother (1: 384).

Pardo Bazán regularly uses blue eyes to signify the candour, freshness, and innocence of youth. The beautiful daughter of la Corpana in *Cuentos de la tierra* and the young hero, Angelito, of "El catecismo" both have blues eyes (2: 1480; 1: 1518), and those of Concha in *La dama joven* are "garzos y candorosos todavía" (1: 907). The connection between youth, innocence, and blue eyes is so well established that the Marqués de Solar de Fierro is described as having "ojos azules, limpios como los de los niños" (1: 801). As with green, blue is also employed to compare, and even to identify, a character with nature. Thus, for Minia of "Un destripador de antaño": "[le] brillaban los ojos con un toque celeste, como el azul que a veces se entrevé al través de las brumas del montañés celaje" (1: 1307), and the eyes of the Breton, Juan Vilain, have the "color del agua del mar que bate los escollos de la costa bretona" (2: 824).

Eyes, with all their attributes of colour, size, and expression, are not the full extent of Pardo Bazán's ocular characterization. She also portrays eyelashes and eyebrows to complete this portion of her facial portraits. Afra Reyes, the title character of one of the *Cuentos de amor,* has "ojos verdes, coronados por cejas negrísimas, casi juntas, que les prestaban una severidad singular" (1: 1172). Mariña of *Cuentos de la tierra* has "pestañas densas [. . .] [l]as cejas, sombrías, pobladas y juntas, imprimían cierta dureza a la fisonomía" (2: 1493). Grotesque María la Sabia of *Los pazos de Ulloa* and *La madre naturaleza* has "cejas hirsutas [. . .] canas" (1: 182, 356). Vicente Prado, the Church canon in *Pascual López,* has "pobladas cejas [. . .] cejas anchas (2: 17, 18). In the face of the cruel Tío Clodio of "Las medias rojas" one sees "ojos pequeños, engarzados en duros párpados, bajo cejas hirsutas" (2: 1474). The hermit, Trifón, of *Dulce Dueño* has "peludas cejas que le comían los párpados rugosos" (2: 935), and the stern but good vicar in "El baile del Querubín" dispels "chispas por sus ojuelos, enterrados entre el párpado y emboscados tras la ceja tupida e hirsuta" (2: 1463).

Emilia Pardo Bazán's many portrayals of eyes and their proximate facial features show a significant adherence to the tenets of physiognomy. Perhaps the most easily noticeable correspondence between the postulates of Lavater and the practices of Pardo Bazán are in Doña Emilia's treatment of characters who have been imprinted by their deeds and experiences. The Swiss physiognomist maintained that there is a close parallel between one's life experiences and one's physical appearance (Lavater 1: 153-58). We have already observed such a connection in Pardo Bazán's depiction of the convict in *La piedra angular* with a "mirada dura," as a result of her hard life; in her representation of María Vicenta in "Consuelos" with "hinchados y extraviados ojos," filled with grief for her dead child; and in her portrayal of the intellectual, Gabriel Pardo, with his "mirada, intensa, dulce, miope." We might also cite the physical manifestation of the ravages of dissolute living on Pedro Moscoso: "Para los cincuenta y pico en que debía frisar, parecíale muy atropellado y desfigurado el marqués [. . .]. El abandono de la persona, [. . .] el exceso, en suma, de vida animal habían arruinado rápidamente la torre de aquella un tiempo robustísima y arrogante persona" (1: 329). Lavater had drawn direct connections between idleness and debauchery and their physical effects over time (1: 153-58).

Although it is not clear whether Pardo Bazán was familiar with the work of Lavater's disciple, Mariano Aguirre, this Spanish physiognomist's theory and his emphasis on eyes are also in striking concert with many descriptions in her novels and stories. Aguirre's "Clasificación de los Colores de los Ojos" asserts: "ojos negros indican firmeza, vigor y voluntad" (339). The eyes of strong-willed Silvestre Moreno and Carmiña Aldao are black, and Pardo Bazán calls particular attention to the blackness of the eyes of the determined Sor Aparición. Aguirre says that "ojos negros, pequeños [son] intrigantes y de engaño" (339), and Pardo Bazán's sinister characters (Primitivo Suárez, Natolia, the Philippine chieftain, and others) have just such small, black eyes.

"Ojos verdes," according to Aguirre, "dicen poco y son para todo confusos" (339). We have shown that Pardo Bazán uses green for a variety of connotations, ranging from fearsomeness, ominous mystery, and enigma to beauty, intelligence, and unity with nature.

Aguirre's classifications declare that "ojos azules son siempre indicio de pereza, flojera," but "ojo azul muy claro=concepción, sensibilidad, e inventiva" (339). Pardo Bazán's blue-eyed characters at times exhibit passivity (Julián Álvarez and Hilario Aparicio), but often beauty (Lucía González, Nieves Comba, and many others), and also sensuality (Sabel).

Aguirre de Venero treats eyebrows also, and Pardo Bazán's descriptions bear an affinity to his axioms on the significance of various forms, thickness, and the closeness of eyebrows to each other and to eyes. Aguirre says that "cejas juntas" indicate "mal carácter" (342), and Pardo Bazán's Afra Reyes, with just such eyebrows, has a mysterious and perhaps violent past (1: 1173-74). Likewise, Mariña, who also has close brows, is rumoured to have poisoned her husband (2: 1494). According to Aguirre, "cejas bajas que ocultan los ojos" are a sign of "maldad, perversidad" (342), and Clodio, with his small eyes under hard lids and thick brows, mercilessly beats his daughter in "Las medias rojas" (2: 1475). Aguirre maintains that "cejas gruesas" reveal "energía, genio, vivacidad" (342). These qualities are present in Trifón, the hermit, "muy renombrado a causa de sus penitencias aterradoras," who converts and baptizes Catherine of Alexandria (2: 934), and in the vicar of "El baile del Querubín," both of whom have thick eyebrows (2: 1461). Similarly, the "cejas pobladas, anchas" of Canon Vicente Prado are prominent characterizing features of this "hombre de vigorosos miembros y recias proporciones" who recalls warrior prelates of the past (2: 17). The hirsute, white eyebrows of María la Sabia are part of her "imponente [. . .] fealdad de [. . .] bruja" (1: 182).

Physiognomists frequently compared the variety of human visages to animals. Aguirre devotes a section of his treatise (297-323) to delineating the supposed correspondence between the eyes of different animals and their nature. Pardo Bazán's animal comparisons sometimes serve merely as similes or metaphors to convey an image to her readers. Thus, Nils Limsoe "tiene unos ojos verdes, que relucen como los de un gato" (1: 858), and in *Morriña,* when Esclavitud heard the name of her beloved "patria chica," her eyes "fulguraron en la oscuridad, como los de los gatos" (1: 514). Often, though, Doña Emilia's animal comparisons have a deeper intention of revealing the interior of her characters. The "temible cacique," Trampeta, has "ojos, vivos, ratoniles" (1: 300, 301); the solitary eye of the equally sinister Tuerto de Castrodorna "relucía felinamente" (1: 267); the rapacious Primitivo Suárez has "fascinadores ojuelos de víbora" (1: 275); the humble peasants, Julián and Cibrao, feature "ojillos enfosados, inquietos, como de ave cautiva" (1: 1332); the handsome "Gallo" displays eyes "como los del sultán del corral" (1: 329); but the innocent Manuela has "ojos de novilla virgen" (1: 345).

The many examples we have cited demonstrate that Emilia Pardo Bazán's descriptions of eyes often coincide with physiognomic theory. Does this conformity arise from a belief in physiognomy held by the author? We recall her declaration, quoted earlier, that eyes are the "espejo de los movimientos del alma." In several of her novels she refers to eyes as "espejos del corazón," and a "reflejo" of interior states or of "la honradez del alma," and she speaks of "la mirada" as "la ventana que abre sobre el alma."[5] A further, and perhaps better, indication of the philosophical basis of Pardo Bazán's physical descriptions is given by her statements that include a wider frame of reference to the human body. In *La sirena negra* she depicts Trini in terms that link intelligence with the form of her face: "corta de entenderas, corta de cara, carirredonda ¡Malo!" (2: 881). In the same novel, she is quite explicit in joining the mind and physical appearance of Desiderio Solís: "la frente huye hacia el occipital-señal de desequilibrio" (2: 905). Years before, in *Un viaje de novios,* Doña Emilia had already made that connection in her presentation of Ignacio Artegui with his "padecimiento moral, o mejor dicho, intelectual, que sólo hunde algo la ojera, labra la frente, empalidece las sienes y condensa la mirada" (1: 93).

Nevertheless, Emilia Pardo Bazán is not constantly an adherent of physiognomy in her depiction of eyes. Her works reveal a more eclectic spirit that was influenced by the theory of physiognomy but not circumscribed by it. The descriptions we have quoted are testimony to the wide variety of allusions, connotations, and intentions that are present in her portrayals. Pardo Bazán at times presents eyes as stereotypical signs of nationality. At other times, she uses eyes to illustrate the biological inheritance from parent to child or to represent the candour and innocence of youth. In symbolic, poetic departures from realism, she employs eyes with the verdant hue of nature or the radiant blue of the sky or sea in order to link characters with their physical surroundings. In addition, Mariano Baquero Goyanes (54) has shown that some of Doña Emilia's portrayals of eyes have their inspiration in great works of art to which she refers. An illustration of this is Argos, whose "inmensos ojazos negros" in *Doña Milagros* are part of her depiction as "una Dolorosa," which is then further qualified: "el lienzo de 'Doña Juana la Loca' de Pradilla puede dar idea del semblante y expresión" (2: 383). Sometimes an adjective pointedly evokes the artistic source that underlies the portrait, as in the figure of Sor Margarita of *La Quimera* with her "dos ojos negros, murillescos, melados" (1: 880).

Some of Pardo Bazán's other descriptions are also simply unrelated to physiognomy, as we have seen in the case of grey eyes. For brown eyes as well, she establishes a connection not prescribed by physiognomists. Aguirre says "ojos pardos" are simply "vulgares" (339), but Doña Emilia's brown-eyed characters manifest transforming passion. Clara Ayamonte is a romantic who experiences a religious conversion; Lina Mascareñas searches for her "dulce Dueño"; Jorge Viodal appears reinvigorated by the love of a younger woman; Leonor of "El fantasma" is "pálida, nerviosa, romántica, perseguidora del ideal" (1: 1136); and at the end of "La hoz" the passionate, brown-eyed María Silveria is poised to kill her former lover with the sickle that gives its name to that short story.

Not infrequently, a character's eyes belie the physiognomic correspondences of Lavater and his followers. For example, Feíta Neira of *Doña Milagros* has "diminutos ojuelos verdes, que destellaban atención e inteligencia" (2: 427). The "ojuelos negros y chicos" of Leocadia Otero of *El cisne de Vilamorta* function as part of the portrayal of that conspicuously ugly character, rather than as a physiognomic sign of deceit and evil (2: 201). The blue eyes of the title character of "Saletita" and those of the old villager of "De polizón" also contradict physiognomy, for the innocent eyes of Saletita conceal her secret plot, while the old man of "De polizón" has blue eyes that, by the author's statement, express craftiness and sagacity (1: 1376, 1370).

In the final balance, nevertheless, the examination of Emilia Pardo Bazán's manner of portraying eyes in the depiction of her characters demonstrates that she was significantly influenced by physiognomy in her literary creation. Her frequent physiognomic treatment of eyes means that many "realistic" descriptions in her writings are not simply creative representations of observed reality but rather a view of reality filtered, as always, by the scientific and philosophical tenets of that age. But Pardo Bazán's portrayal of eyes throughout her lengthy literary career is also evidence of the lack of any complete dominance over her by physiognomy. Her vision was too wide to be totally encompassed by a theory that, as Fontanella has pointed out, was ultimately inimical to the character individualization and development essential to the novel.

Notes

1. The earliest examinations of Pardo Bazán's narrative style were by her contemporaries, including Clarín and Juan Valera. In more modern times, Benito Varela Jácome has conducted an extensive study of the narrative techniques of her novels. Current critical investigation is summarized and evaluated in recent volumes of *The Year's Work in Modern Language Studies,* particularly years 1993 and 1996.

2. As early as 1964 Robert E. Osborne (64) called for a catalogue of Pardo Bazán's characters. At the end of his exhaustive four-volume *Cuentos completos,* Juan Paredes Núñez includes a 45-page "Censo de personajes" of Pardo Bazán's short stories.

3. Book XXXI of Aristotle's *Problemata* deals exclusively with eyes, and the *Physiognómica* expounds his theory of bodily representation of mental character. Ross questions the Aristotelian authorship of these texts (Aristotle, Prefaces to *Problemata* and to *Physiognomonica*). The French essayist, Montaigne, and the Italian Giovanni Battista della Porta, both of the sixteenth century, are examples of later physiognomists. Bacon specifically claimed for physiognomy the capacity to reveal the soul: "physiognomia, quae per corporis lineamenta animi indicat propensiones" (Bacon 2: 343-44).

4. All our references to Pardo Bazán's works, noted parenthetically, are to the Aguilar edition of her *Obras completas.*

5. In *El cisne de Vilamorta* Pardo Bazán calls eyes "el claro reflejo de [. . .] pureza candorosa" and speaks of the "concentrada e indefinable expresión que constituye una mirada de persona grande" (2: 259); in *La piedra angular* she says that the eyes of Telmo Rojo "eran dos espejos del corazón del muchacho" (2: 282); and in *Doña Milagros* she has Benicio Neira say that his eyes reflect "la honradez de mi alma" (2:361). The final reference is from *El niño de Guzmán* (2: 605).

Works Cited

Aguirre de Venero, Mariano. *Primer Sistema del Lenguaje Universal, Fisiognómico de los Ojos.* New York: John F. Trow, 1865,

Aristotle. *The Works of Aristotle.* Ed. W. D. Ross. Vol. 9: *Ethica Nicomachea.* Oxford: Clarendon Press, 1964.

Bacon, Francis. *The Works of Lord Bacon.* 2 vols. London: William Ball, 1838.

Baquero Goyanes, Mariano. *La novela naturalista española: Emilia Pardo Bazán.* Murcia: Univ. de Murcia, 1986.

Bravo-Villasante, Carmen. *Vida y obra de Emilia Pardo Bazán.* Madrid: Revista de Occidente, 1962.

Du Bartas, Guillaume de Saluste, Sieur. *The Divine Weeks and Works.* Ed. Susan Snyder. Tr. Josuah Sylvester. 2 vols. Oxford: Clarendon Press, 1979.

Fontanella, Lee. "Physiognomics in Romantic Spain." *From Dante to García Márquez.* Eds. Gene H. Bell-Villada, Antonio Giménez, and George Pistorius. Williamstown, Massachusetts: Williams College, 1987. 100-13.

Graham, John. *Lavater's Essays on Physiognomy: A Study in the History of Ideas.* Berne: Peter Lang, 1979.

Lavater, John Caspar. *Essays on Physiognomy.* Tr. Henry Hunter, 3 vols. London: John Murray, 1789.

Osborne, Robert E. *Emilia Pardo Bazán: su vida y sus obras.* Mexico: Ediciones de Andrea, 1964.

Pardo Bazán, Emilia. *Cuentos completos.* Ed. Juan Paredes Núñez. 4 vols. La Coruña: Fundación Pedro Barrie de la Maza Conde de Fenosa, 1990.

———. *Obras completas.* 3 vols. Madrid: Aguilar, 1956-1973.

Varela Jácome, Benito. *Estructuras novelísticas de Emilia Pardo Bazán.* Santiago de Compostela: Instituto P. Sarmiento, 1973.

THEATER

Shearer West (essay date summer 1993)

SOURCE: West, Shearer. "The Construction of Racial Type: Caricature, Ethnography, and Jewish Physiognomy in Fin-de-Siècle Melodrama." *Nineteenth Century Theatre* 21, no. 1 (summer 1993): 5-40.

[*In the following essay, West discusses physiognomic thought as part of a larger discussion of the context surrounding the portrayal of Jewish characters in nineteenth-century melodrama.*]

Of all the attributes of nineteenth-century melodrama, the notion of character type is perhaps the most ubiquitous. The character types of melodrama could be recognized as soon as they walked on the stage by their dress, gait, accent, name, or demeanor; their affiliation on the side of good or evil within this ethical fantasy world was clearly defined. The critic William Archer recognized the importance of the stage type, not just for melodrama, but for theatre in general, as well as for the other arts:

> The dramatist (and I might add the novelist and the painter, were not the drama our immediate theme) by placing an observed type before us under circumstances which force us to concentrate our attention upon it, stimulates our memory, formulates our observations for

us, and makes us fully and intelligently conscious of experiences which have lain vague and inarticulate in the limbo of semi-consciousness.[1]

As Archer suggested, the character type could be a manifestation of Victorian ideologies, but it was also a complex mediator between audience expectation and contemporary social concerns. In order to understand how the character type functioned in Victorian melodrama, it is essential to consider the historical context, the relationship with art,[2] and the critical reception of the plays themselves.[3]

One of the ubiquitous stock characters in nineteenth-century melodrama was the Jew, whose association with popular drama reaches back to the Middle Ages.[4] Although some theatre historians, such as M. J. Landa, have insisted that the story of the stage Jew is merely one long saga of anti-Semitism, a closer examination of the history and circumstances of the Jewish type on the nineteenth-century stage reveals a more diverse picture. Not all Jewish characters were usurious Shylocks or criminal Fagins, and their frequent role as the *deus ex machina* often gave them a mythical quality which enhanced the more fantastical aspects of the melodramas themselves. The Jewish type was constructed and perpetuated by the tensions between xenophobia and religious toleration which characterized British liberal thinking until the beginning of the twentieth century. The expectations about what a Jew should look like and how he[5] should act were determined by scientific assumptions about race, polemics on immigration, and artistic representation, including caricature. These elements fed the public imagination throughout the nineteenth century, but they came together in the 1890s, when melodrama itself was suffering from the barbed attacks of the more "progressive" critics. In order to understand the stage Jews of the 1890s, it is first necessary to examine the layers of race theory, artistic representation, and theatrical performance which comprised the Jewish type in the culture of nineteenth-century England.

RACIAL TYPOLOGY

The idea that different Jews had common physical and mental characteristics dominated popular opinion during the Victorian period, leading Charles Salaman in his defensive *Jews As they Are* to complain: "It is noticeable that many Christian orators and writers, when referring to Jews in general, persist in designating them 'The Jews'; thus mingling in one heterogeneous mass, and placing on the same social level human beings wholly dissimilar in character and condition."[6] Salaman's argument had particular poignancy, as the very phrase "Jew" had pejorative connotations until the ad-

vent of Zionism in the late 1890s.[7] But Jews were not only seen as a contemporary type; the characteristics of their type were considered to have been inherited from their primitive ancestors. The Lamarckian idea that inherited mental and physical characteristics prevailed through centuries (or even millennia) was a familiar assertion of Victorian Science. In 1854, for example, J. C. Nott and George Gliddon's *Types of Mankind* defined a "type" as "those primitive original forms which are independent of Climatic or other Physical influences," and they claimed that the Jews "have maintained their own type, from the epoch assigned to Abraham, down to the present day."[8] Such positivist classifications saw human beings as little more than variant species of animal, with "type" a barely disguised synonym for "race."

Jews were particularly prone to racial classification, despite the religious nature of their community. Although many Jews denied that their racial heritage was as important as their religious one,[9] even they often argued their case on the racial agenda set up by their adversaries. Thus Salaman, although claiming Jews were as diverse as Christians, later went on to declare, "There is a remarkable buoyancy in the racial spirit of Jews! . . . Jews in general are observant, discerning, ambitious and energetic" (11). However, anti-Semites such as Goldwin Smith paraded their assumptions more often and more publicly. "Israel," according to Smith, "is not a sect but a tribe and . . . the difficulty with which they have to deal arises not merely from difference of opinion . . . but from consecrated exclusiveness of race" ("The Jewish Question" 513). The construction of Jews as "tribal" was a nineteenth-century commonplace: not only were they accused of maintaining their "primitive" religion, but rituals such as circumcision were seen to be a "tribal" mark of "racial distinction" (Mantegazza, *Sexual Relations* 98-99). In the imperialist discourse of the mid-Victorian period, such references to "tribes" and "race" conveyed echoes of the African societies which were beginning to be subjected to Western scientific study. Such studies, including those of Darwin and his followers, used cranial and other physical evidence to "prove" the intellectual superiority of the white Europeans and the inferiority of the "other" race. When the Italian anthropologist Paolo Mantegazza visualized different races of men in terms of branches on a tree, he represented Aryans and Semites as nearly equal in intellectual, aesthetic, and "morphological" development (*Physiognomy and Expression* 29). However, while Mantegazza classified Jews as Caucasian, others admitted the possibility that the Jews could be associated with "Negroes" in their personality and in their physical characteristics. John Beddoe's *Races of Britain* postulated that color was a more important racial characteristic than brain size, and he calculated an "Index of Nigrescence" on which the Jews scored over 100 per cent (5, 224). His comments about the mental characteristics of fair and dark races did not point specifically to the Jews, but they echoed other contemporary stereotypes about submissive and home-loving aspects of the Jewish character:

> It may be said that, with a few notable exceptions, conquering and ruling races have always been fair, while the vanquished and submissive races have been dark. . . . If anything can be confidently predicated as to the two principal complexions, it is that the fair goes more usually with active courage and a roving adventurous disposition, the dark with patient industry and attachment to local and family ties—the one with the sanguine, the other with the melancholic temperament.

(218-19)

Another race theorist, Robert Knox, claimed that a swarthy Jewish face could have "an African look" (196-97), and the Italian criminologist Cesare Lombroso suggested that climatic and geographical conditions could actually alter certain racial characteristics, so that the essentially Caucasian Jews could possess Negroid features in hot climates (107-8). Whether relying on clear statement or innuendo, these scientific race theories found the means to separate and marginalize Jews from the "superior" Caucasians.

The terms of Knox's and Lombroso's arguments were, broadly speaking, physiognomic—that is, they used facial characteristics as a code for mental and emotional qualities. The continuing importance of the pseudoscience of physiognomy, and its offspring, phrenology, has received much attention in recent years.[10] Its terms were used freely by scientists and race theorists in the nineteenth century as a way of pinpointing and classifying distinctions between racial types. Jews figure prominently within physiognomic studies, so that "the Jewish physiognomy" became as commonplace an idea as "the Jew":

> How indelible is the image of a *type* once impressed on the mind's eye. When, for example, the word "Jew" is pronounced, a type is instantly brought up by memory, which could not be so described to another person as to present to his mind a faithful portrait.

(Nott and Gliddon 412)

Attempts to describe facial features often led to a combination of literary narrative and character judgment which could reinforce popular prejudice. Novelettish descriptions of Jews appeared even in serious studies, such as Beatrice Potter's account of the poor East London Jews in Charles Booth's muckraking examination of London poverty, *Life and Labour of the People of London* (580-81), but they also dominated popular physiognomic manuals. For example, John Taylor's *Noses, and What They Indicate* distinguishes the Roman, Greek, and Jewish noses: the first, a sign of conquering energy; the second, a manifestation of culture; the third, evidence of commercial acumen (8-10). An illustration of "Acquisitiveness" from Gustavus Cohen's physiognomic manual, *The Modern Self-Instructor,* visually associated the Jews with this character trait through the agent of a hooked nose. Mantegazza went so far as to isolate a race-specific facial expression: he claimed that a "grotesque or simian expression" is characteristic of Negroes, an "intelligent expression" of Europeans, whereas "the Jews in all Europe have an embarrassed and timid expression" (*Physiognomy and Expression* 232, 242).

The combination of physiognomic and race theories drew a composite picture of Jewish character that was neither consistent nor verifiable. Jews were described by various sources as rich, poor, sober, dirty, home-loving, intelligent, anarchist, unpatriotic, patriotic, non-agricultural, sensual, religious, exploitative, timid, respectful, and determined.[11] Their appearance, with some variation, was seen in more consistent terms, with dark eyes, heavy beard, and hooked nose being isolated as recurrent features. Despite the contradictions inherent in statements about Jewish character, people could still refer to this heterogeneous group as if it were a homogeneous entity by focusing on one set of character stereotypes at a time and referring to a limited set of physical features. The emphasis on physical features as a shorthand for specific aspects of character was reinforced by the representation of Jews in art—specifically, painting and engraving with an ethnographic purpose, and caricature.

The Jew in Victorian Popular Art

The idea that Jews could provide some sort of ethnographic interest for artists was fuelled by the writings and paintings of the Pre-Raphaelite William Holman Hunt, who travelled extensively in the Holy Land in 1854-55. Hunt's insistence that he was seeking "truth" was belied by his account of his travels, which exposed his barely disguised prejudices and imperialist attitude. He claimed to have a genuine interest in the history and ceremonies of the Jews, and he visited Jewish families and witnessed holy day ceremonies in the synagogues. However, his continued efforts to coax the reluctant Jerusalem Jews to model for his *Finding of the Saviour in the Temple* (1854-60) and his eventual plea to Sir Moses Montefiore to intervene with them on his behalf indicate that he neither understood nor sympathized with the community that he was painting.[12] The popularity of Biblical subjects and the archaeological concerns of such "Olympians" as Lawrence Alma-Tadema,

Edwin Long, and Edward Poynter later in the century consolidated this ethnographic approach to the culture and religion of the Holy Land, but in doing so, further aestheticized the Jewish type.[13]

This ethnographic exploration of Jewish life was also characteristic of contemporary journals, such as *The Graphic* and the *Illustrated London News,* in which illustrations of Jews were juxtaposed with long descriptions of their way of life, religious observances, and character. Both periodicals ran a series of illustrated articles on Judaism: *The Graphic* (1889) focused on the East End of London and the *Illustrated London News* (1891) on Eastern Europe. The combination of word and image served to reinforce the "otherness" of Jews through exploitation of physiognomic assumptions. By presenting Jews within such an ostensibly documentary context, illustrations could serve to reinforce popular stereotypes. Although Lucien Wolf's articles in *The Graphic* offered a sensitive account of London Jews, Joseph Pennell's series in the *Illustrated London News* was soured by his dismissive racial judgments. For example, Pennell described a Jew in Carlsbad as "a miserable, weak, consumptive-looking specimen of humanity, a greasy corkscrew ringlet over each ear" ("The Jew at Home, I—Austria and Hungary" 732). Such comments were accompanied by ostensibly accurate illustrations of Jewish life which added a documentary flavor to racist assertion.

Indeed, it was often a very short step from such ethnographic treatment to the exaggerated representation of Jews in caricature. Late eighteenth- and nineteenth-century caricature revealed changes in the depiction of Jews: the use of "attributes" such as pigs and gold sacks were abandoned in favor of a reliance on facial features to identify the racial type.[14] By the middle of the nineteenth century, magazines such as *Punch* could use a standard visual icon to represent the whole Jewish race, and, more importantly, as a shorthand for perceived aspects of Jewish character.[15] Jewish caricatures in *Punch* intensified during Disraeli's ministership, for despite his renunciation of his Jewish heritage, satirists found it a convenient device with which to attack him. Disraeli's vacillations about Jewish emancipation were a particular target for caricaturists, and in one issue (9 Nov. 1867) Disraeli is represented as the treacherous Fagin after his sudden decision to support the Reform Bill. Other uses of a Jewish type in *Punch* make the allusion less obvious and rely more fully on the features of the caricature itself. For example, *Punch* (13 Dec. 1890) attacked the scandalous "sweating" industry, the growth of which was attributed to the influx of Jewish immigrants from Eastern Europe (see below). Although the cartoon was labelled "Punch to the Sweating Shylock," and the features of the "sweater" included a hooked

nose, there was no mention of Jews in the accompanying poem. In another cartoon, "Sir George and the Dragon of Usury", the dragon has a dark beard and a hooked nose, but there is no other indication that he is meant to be a Jew. Even the attacks on Russian persecution of Jews in the 1890s relied on a stereotype of the Jew, based on both costume and feature, and other illustrated satires of contemporary life used the same preconceptions about Jewish character and appearance for their effect.[16] The proliferation of Jewish characters in the popular novels by Trollope and Thackeray and the use of illustration in such novels served as further reinforcement for these visual referents.

THE JEW IN VICTORIAN MELODRAMA

The visual impact of the created Jewish type reinforced both racial and physiognomic assumptions, which were highlighted by the translation into English of Wagner's vicious diatribe on the Jews in 1894. Wagner insisted that Jews were "unfitted for artistic treatment," but despite the enthusiastic reception of his writings in England, English art and theatre did not reject the Jewish type, as Wagner did, nor did they necessarily present the Jew as evil or reprehensible.[17] However, in melodrama particularly, the Jewish type was endowed with the elements of fantasy and foreignness isolated by Wagner, and these qualities were fed by the prevalence of visual satire and physiognomic theory. The role of the stage Jew could be altered to suit the melodrama concerned, but the visual representation and the underlying racial typology remained remarkably consistent until the 1890s, when stage representation was complicated by both theatrical changes and changes in attitude towards the Jews.

Indeed, there was a direct relationship between more popular forms of art, such as caricature and journal illustration, and the presentation of Jews on the stage in mid-Victorian melodrama. William Archer pinpointed this alliance in one of his attacks on the pictorial concerns of theatre managers in the 1890s:

> Illustration, as some one pointed out the other day, has of late become enormously popular. The demand for picture-books and picture-papers seems to increase every day; and a similar tendency, I believe, is apparent in the melodramatic theatres. People do not care how slight a setting of text is provided, so long as the "plates" are numerous and highly coloured.
>
> (*Theatrical World of 1895* 264-5)

The melodramas which Archer so derided were seen to perpetuate an easily accessible visual image of the world which destroyed ambiguity and allowed no room for more subtle character development.

The relationship between popular illustration and popular theatre was highlighted in 1878 when a melodramatic version of Dickens's *Oliver Twist* was produced at the Olympic Theatre. *Nancy Sykes* was one of several adaptations of *Oliver Twist* in the nineteenth and early twentieth century, each of which focused upon the caricatural aspects of Dickens's tale and drew heavily on George Cruikshank's illustrations, which were published with the text in *Bentley's Miscellany* in 1837.[18] Cruikshank later claimed to have invented the character of Fagin, and at least one critic noticed the resemblance between an actor performing the melodramatic Jewish villain and Cruikshank's illustrations.[19] Dickens himself was forced to defend his decision to make his criminal a Jew. His explanation (given in a letter to a Jewish correspondent, Eliza Davis), was presented in terms of the Victorian racial discourse discussed above:

> Fagin, in *Oliver Twist,* is a Jew, because it unfortunately was true of the time to which the story refers, that that class of criminal almost invariably *was* a Jew. But surely no sensible man or woman of your persuasion can fail to observe—firstly, that all the rest of the wicked dramatis personae are Christians; and secondly, that he is called "The Jew," not because of his religion, but because of his race. If I were to write a story, in which I pursued a Frenchman, or Spaniard, as "the Roman Catholic," I should do a very indecent and unjustifiable thing; but I make mention of Fagin as the Jew, because he is one of the Jewish people, and because it conveys that kind of idea of him, which I should give my readers of a Chinaman by calling him Chinese.

(Dickens and Hogarth, eds. 2: 204)

Indeed, the prominence of Fagin in the nineteenth century seems to indicate that the Jew's role in melodrama was that of villain, rather than hero—a conception that was reinforced by a continued interest in the character of Shylock. Shylock continued to be a synonym for both "Jew" and "usurer," despite the sympathetic interpretations of such actors as Henry Irving, Nutcombe Gould, and Beerbohm Tree. Neither Irving's "picturesque and refined Italianized Jew" nor Gould's "prophet from the Sistine Chapel" answered the preconceptions of the soulless usurer, but popular caricature continued to use Shylock as a synonym for monetary corruption.[20] Not only did *Punch*'s satires on sweating and usury often allude to the *Merchant of Venice,* but popular pamphlets on Jews evoked the ghost of Shylock in attacking or defending Jewish character, while in other countries, such as France, Shylock became a code word used by anti-Semites to deride the Jewish race.[21]

Although Fagin and Shylock were the most prominent stage Jews of the nineteenth century, the real role of Jews in melodrama was somewhat more complicated than these models suggest. Certainly there were Jewish characters in melodrama who conformed to the villainous type by possessing an excess of those qualities felt to be racially characteristic of Jews. For example, Dion Boucicault's *After Dark* (Princess's, 12 August 1868) included a sinister Jewish gaming house keeper called Dicey Morris. In a penny novel version of the play, the description of Morris coincided with widely held racial and physiognomic stereotypes of wealthy Jews:

> His curly black hair was lustrous with oil; and so were his whiskers, which almost came round to his nose—a nose that revealed the Israelites a mile off, though Mr. Dicey Morris has the impudence to deny he was born one of "the Peoplesh."[22]

However, like early stage representations of Shylock, the character of Dicey Morris was inevitably performed as the "comic man," rather than the tragic villain.

A similarly caricatural treatment of Jews was apparent in Tom Taylor's *Helping Hands* (Adelphi, 20 June 1855), a play based upon a lost Stradivarius. The Jewish broker Isaac Wolff and his assistant Lazarus Solomon were costumed in "eccentric Jew's dress," and they were given the fabricated Yiddish accent often associated with Jews on the stage.[23] The extent to which Wolff and Solomon were exaggerated was noticed by a critic of the *Athenaeum,* who referred to the eager way with which they anticipated a bargain as "revoltingly characteristic," and he went on to extend a visual metaphor: "Indeed, all these persons are broadly painted; and the play is indebted for its extraordinary length to the prominence bestowed on such individual portraitures" (23 June 1855). The relationship between melodramatic characters and the graphic art of caricature was not lost on contemporary observers, and much of the Jew's significance in the plot rested upon widely held assumptions about their race and appearance which were fed by caricature.

Even in plays in which the Jew did not take on the exaggerated features of the stage type, the usual association of Jewishness and money was inevitably invoked. Such was the case in Tom Taylor's *Payable on Demand* (Olympic, 11 July 1859), reportedly based on a legend of the Rothschild family.[24] Although *Payable on Demand* was not a melodrama, Taylor did introduce Jews in several melodramas: these include a villainous forger in *Ticket-of-Leave Man* (Olympic, 27 May 1863), and heartless bailiffs in *Going to the Bad* (Olympic, 5 June 1858). The extent to which Jews in melodrama were exaggerated and subject to racial assumptions was noticed by a critic of Andrew Halliday's *The Great City* (Drury Lane, 27 April 1867) who was appalled by the Jewish villain Mendez: "The sentiments he is enforced to utter are likely to keep alive popular prejudices which should long since have been consigned to oblivion" (*Era* 18 Apr. 1867).

Jews did not always take on the role of villain or comic man, however; they could also hold the position of moral rectitude in nineteenth-century melodrama. In such cases, the Jewish type was hardly altered in visual or behavioral terms, but these qualities were construed as picturesque, rather than repellent. The several adaptations of Eugène Scribe's *La Juive* which appeared on the London stage in the 1830s (e.g., Drury Lane, 16 November 1835) were intended to have this picturesque attribute, and some sympathy was evoked in C. H. Hazlewood's "romantic drama" *The Stolen Jewess* (Britannia, 1 April 1872), in which the Jew Tomaso and his wife Miriam are the innocent victims of persecution at the very beginning of the play. The production of such works during years in which the question of Jewish emancipation was being debated in Parliament gave these Jewish subtexts a sensitive referent. When a new version of Salomon Mosenthal's *Deborah,* called *Leah,* was performed at the Grecian Theatre (15 February 1864), one critic claimed that "every sentence in favour of religious toleration was loudly applauded."[25]

Such plays as *The Jew* and *The Stolen Jewess* relied upon exotic settings and frenetic incident, and the Jewish characters thus became merely one more element in the picturesque unity of the melodrama, despite the apparent sympathy with which they were depicted. In other plays, the realism of the Jewish characters was further eroded when they retained their familiar attributes, but were located in uncharacteristic settings or situations. Charles Reade's *Gold* (Drury Lane, 10 January 1853), for example, places the friendly Jewish money-lender, Isaac Levi, in the middle of a farming community, despite the stereotype which denied Jews any agricultural heritage. Levi's benevolence is tempered, however, by other, more mythical attributes. He delivers his speeches in pseudo-Biblical language which is nevertheless concerned with money and value: "Lo, I will lend you monies for your rent," he says to a beleaguered farmer, but then "(*sharply*) upon fair interest" (17). In plays such as this, the Jew becomes the agent of moral probity, but he does not lose his Jewish features or his interest in money. The Polish Jew in Leopold Lewis's *The Bells* serves this function most obviously. In the interpretation made famous by Henry Irving, the Jew who has been killed by Mathias for his thirty thousand francs (an allusion to the Biblical thirty pieces of silver) is seen only in a tableau vivant, but here he becomes the harbinger of justice and retribution. The allegorical qualities of the ghostly Jew are underlined by the fact that Mathias's potential son-in-law is called Christian.

The consistency with which Jews were depicted in terms of their appearance and character gave them a mythical role within the moral world of melodrama: they were not represented as individuals, but as agents of either good or evil. However, the role of Jews within melodrama's self-contained moral world was not as clear-cut as that of some non-Jewish melodramatic types, and the issue became further complicated by changes in attitudes to Jews in the 1880s and the 1890s.

REGENERATION AND ASSIMILATION: THE JEW IN FIN-DE-SIÈCLE MELODRAMA

A commentator in the *Illustrated London News* of 3 May 1890 reported, "It is marvellous to me how many Jews of different types and idiosyncrasies can be seen on the stage," and another critic of 1893 reflected more acerbically that "*Cherchez le Juif* may, for a session or two, supersede the older *Cherchez la femme*."[26] Both authors were recognizing that the Jew had moved from a minor stock character in melodrama to a position at center stage. The reasons for these changes are complex, but they reveal a new interest in Jewish issues which resulted at least in part from a more public debate about the "Jewish question." At a time when melodrama itself was dissipated by other dramatic forms, the issue of Jewish immigration was prominent in the public mind. The significance of the immigration issue to the representation of stage Jews in the 1890s indicates tensions between toleration and anti-Semitism, and reveals other hidden anxieties about the role of Jews in modern Britain. Discourses of race, physiognomy, caricature, and ethnography, as well as the heritage of the stage Jew both before and during the nineteenth century, were expressed in the representation of Jews in melodramas of the 1890s. By the end of the century, the grotesque caricatural Jewish villain had been transformed into a gentle comic figure at a time when anti-Jewish feeling in Britain was at its height.

The immigration of large numbers of Polish and Russian Jews from 1881 onwards was due primarily to the anti-Jewish pogroms in Russia initiated after the assassination of Tsar Alexander II. Fleeing from persecution and poverty in the East, hundreds of thousands of Jews swept across Europe, and many went to America. Although figures vary, the Jewish population in Britain increased from approximately 65,000 in 1880 to 260,000 by 1914; many of these immigrants settled in the East End of London.[27] Despite the care and attention of Jewish charities such as the Board of Guardians, the unhappy state of many immigrants and their sheer number inspired a great deal of fear and prejudice—particularly among the English working classes. This prejudice intensified when more and more immigrants established themselves rapidly in jobs and positions that English workers felt were not their due. Furthermore, the association of Polish Jews with sweating, costermongering, pawn-broking, and other forms of disreputable trade fuelled the prejudice already created by their increasing presence in the country. Although there were Parliamentary enquiries into sweating (1888) and immigration (1888 and 1902-03), there were no laws restricting immigration until the Aliens Act of 1905.

This delayed legislation led to massive public debate in which many voices spoke against unchecked immigration. However, Britain's long-standing reputation as a tolerant nation stifled overt anti-Semitism, which emerged in various covert or disguised forms. The claim of some writers in the 1880s and 1890s that racial anti-Semitism did not exist in Britain must be tempered by the knowledge that liberal thinking did not allow the sort of virulent public *Judenhetze* characteristic of other European countries. Racist assertions were, therefore, often displaced or redirected.[28] During the 1890s, the over-scientific statements characteristic of mid-Victorian race theories were transformed into more sociologically and psychologically based ideas of racial degeneration. The term "degeneration" was rife with contemporary significance, as it indicated a physical and mental atavism at one time associated with insane individuals, but by the 1890s was used to refer to the regressive aspects of society at large.[29] In much writing about Jewish immigrants, the idea that Eastern European Jews were themselves a "degenerating" race and were somehow responsible for dilution and degeneration of the British race was frequently mentioned. The intent was clear: the influx of Jews into Britain was seen as a symptom of the collapse of civilized society.

Despite these dramatic changes in public awareness, the stage was free of impoverished Jews or Jewish sweaters, costermongers, or money-lenders. Jewish characters did, however, receive more serious press and public attention during the 1890s, although underlying the ostensible sympathy of this treatment were the remnants of racial stereotyping, laced with a new ambivalence about the large presence of Jewish immigrants and the increasing respectability and assimilationist tendencies of the Jewish middle class. In melodrama both the ethnographic and caricatural aspects of Jews continued to predominate and, indeed, intensified, while the pictorial emphasis on physiognomy was enhanced through the performance of at least one prominent actor, Herbert Beerbohm Tree.

Ethnography was the basis of the immediate popularity of such historical plays as Stuart Ogilvie's *Hypatia* and Wilson Barrett's *The Daughters of Babylon,* which used the techniques of *The Graphic* and the *Illustrated London News* to give an ostensibly "historical" view of Jewish character. The emphasis on stage effect, pictorialism, and historical accuracy diverted attention from the racial features of the Jewish characters, but the reception of these works indicates that the significance of the Jews was prominent in the minds of those who witnessed the performances. Ogilvie's *Hypatia,* based on Charles Kingsley's novel, premiered at the Haymarket on 2 January 1893. The stage adaptation omitted or replaced several of Kingsley's characters; the most notable change was the introduction of the clever, conspiratorial Jew, Issachar, in place of Kingsley's less

conspicuous Miriam. The character of Issachar attracted a great deal of comment from both Jewish and non-Jewish critics, and the distinctiveness of the character was enhanced by Herbert Beerbohm Tree's use of gesture and make-up to emphasize Issachar's visual presence.

Tree had publicly expressed a desire to bring a strong Jewish character to the stage in a speech given to the Jewish Maccabaean Society on 10 December 1892 in which he indicated his great respect for the Jewish contribution to contemporary theatre.[30] With the success of *Hypatia,* a number of reviewers commended Tree on his performance, and at least one referred to the promise made in his earlier speech (*Daily Telegraph* 3 Jan. 1893). But the most significant response came from the Jewish community itself. *The Jewish Chronicle* condemned the novelist Kingsley for his "strange inability to form anything like a true conception of the Jewish character and ideals," but praised and even defended the character of Issachar, who

> is an original conception, and adds an altogether new figure to the small repertory of stage-Jews. Issachar scarcely deserves the hard epithets that have been flung at his head during the past week. He is ambitious and able, he plots and counterplots but there is no suspicion or meanness in his nature.

This unusually sympathetic view was accompanied by a denial that Issachar had racial traits particularly characteristic of Jews, and, following this, an assertion that he was the "least conventional and least offensive of recent stage Jews" (6 Jan. 1893). As an organ of the affluent middle classes, the *Jewish Chronicle* evinced enthusiasm for any artistic representation of Jews which avoided the crass stereotyping of earlier Victorian theatre, literature, and art. But the *Journal* failed—perhaps deliberately—to comment on the essentially racial preconceptions which informed both Tree's physical creation of Issachar and the audience's response to the character.

Tree's careful development of the visual impact of his character was the subject of much attention: several commentators referred to Issachar as "pictorial" or "picturesque," and some claimed that his introduction in the play was to the ruination of an otherwise balanced plot.[31] The use of stage designs by the Royal Academician Lawrence Alma-Tadema enhanced this pictorial emphasis, which distracted attention from the undercurrents present in the plot, including the significance of Issachar's own appearance and behavior. One of the most striking aspects of Issachar's appearance—and one which drew almost universal comment in non-Jewish papers—was the color of his skin. Issachar's coloring was described variously as "tanned," "dark-brown," and, in one instance, "as black as Othello."[32] Tree's decision to blacken the features of Issachar may have been based on the traditional representation of Jews as "southern," but it actually served the additional purpose of equating the Jewish character with African, rather than Asian, races. In the wake of Victorian race theories, such an equation would have served to debase the Jews by associating them with "primitive" or "atavistic" characteristics. By presenting Issachar as black, Tree was implicitly portraying him as inferior to both the Christians and the pagans in the play.

A second undercurrent in *Hypatia* was the religious emphasis of the plot itself, which concerned the conflict between Christianity and paganism in Early Christian Alexandria. Again, there is a strong tension in the critical literature between the ostensible liberalism of the play's message and the actual narrowness of its subtexts. The "tolerant" and "open-minded" approach to diverse religions was indicated in a number of reviews of the play: praise was extended to Ogilvie for the even-handed treatment of pagans, Christians, and Jews, and the largely Christian audience was commended for its calm acceptance of the wickedness of the Christian characters.[33] This air of toleration, however, masked other, less evident, implications. Changes made to the prompt copy of *Hypatia* (Bristol University Theatre Collection, HBT 29) reveal that Tree was not convinced of his audience's open-mindedness; in a number of passages, references to "God," "the Church," "the Lord," and "the Book" are either scored through or rephrased. The religious aspects of the play were thus downplayed in favor of the pictorial qualities, which relegated religion to a purely decorative or archaeological role.

With religious controversy subsumed beneath picturesque trappings, the real function of Issachar could also be obscured. Issachar manipulates the Christian and pagan parties against each other, and this conspiratorial nature is identified as an aspect of the Jewish character by Cyril, Bishop of Alexandria, who rails, "The Jews! The Jews! They publicly support the Caesar's throne, which is the Christian cause, but secretly they plot against us" (11). His fears are justified by Issachar himself, whose sycophantic attitude toward the weak Orestes is belied by his own stage asides. In one such aside, presented in the form of a prayer, Issachar makes his aim clear: he wants to be "A second Moses to my People's weal; / And bid them back to power, as was foretold, / Should be the portion of the chosen race" (50); and in an earlier passage, after Orestes exits, Issachar had expressed his contempt for Christian gullibility:

> Another silly snake whose head beats time
> Unto the charmer's piping. Thus we Jews
> Are well content to stand aside and watch
> In patient ambush while our hands, unseen
> Still slyly shape the Gentile's history.

(31)

The persecution which Issachar and his daughter suffer in the play is undercut by his own Machiavellian behavior: although the Jew is given an ostensibly sympathetic role in this Christian/pagan world, he is seen to be one of the agents of that world's corruption. Fear of conspiracy, stereotyped aspects of Jewish racial character, and a strong visual emphasis combined to echo public expectations about the role of Jews in modern society.

The ethnographic detail provided in the set designs and costumes of *Hypatia* were carried further in Barrett's *Daughters of Babylon* (Lyric, 6 Feb. 1897), which had, not one, but many Jewish characters. William Archer referred to it acidly as "melodrama of the second or third order" and was not impressed by the play's pictorialism (*Theatrical World of 1897* 29). *The Souvenir of "The Daughters of Babylon,"* which was published at the time of the production, was really a history of the Babylonian Captivity, complete with details about the "tribal" existence of the Israelites, and it included a number of photographs of actresses in the role of Jewish women in the play—wearing "Biblical" dress, standing next to wells, and carrying vases of water. These posed photographs bear a conspicuous resemblance to the Biblical paintings of William Holman Hunt and the Olympians.

The advantages of such melodramas as *Hypatia* and *The Daughters of Babylon* lay in the fact that this historical and pictorial emphasis served to distance the plays from the daily lives of the audience and thereby allowed a freer exploration of controversial, or even dangerous, contemporary issues. A similar sort of distancing could also be achieved through fantasy and caricature, which was the basis of the most famous Jewish character on the London stage in the 1890s, Tree's portrayal of Svengali in *Trilby*. Although separated by time and place from the East London Jews of the same period, Svengali was invested with the typological qualities frequently associated with them in both polemical literature and caricature. The novelist, George Du Maurier, based many of the fictional characters in *Trilby* on people he had known in Paris during the 1850s, but Svengali seems to have been an invention of the author.[34] Du Maurier's illustrations which accompanied the novel served to fix this *outré* character in the public mind, and later stage adaptations sought to remind the audience of the images, as much as the text of the book. Paul Potter's stage version of *Trilby* (Boston, 4 Mar. 1895) redirected Du Maurier's emphasis from the character of Trilby to her seducer, the Polish Jew Svengali. The most exaggerated character in the book became the primary focus of the melodrama.

Du Maurier's description of Svengali in the novel matches contemporary analyses of the physiognomy and dress of Jewish immigrants by writers such as Beatrice Potter and Joseph Pennell. Svengali is a tall, bony individual of any age between thirty and forty-five, of Jewish aspect, well-featured but sinister. He was very shabby and dirty, and wore a red *béret* and a large velveteen cloak, with a big metal clasp at the collar. His thick, heavy, languid, lustreless black hair fell down behind his ears on to his shoulders, in that musician-like way that is so offensive to the normal Englishman. He had bold, brilliant black eyes, with long heavy lids, and thick, sallow face, and a beard of burnt-up black, which grew almost from under his eyelids; and over it his moustache, a shade lighter, fell in two long spiral twists.[35]

These physical features are borne out not only by Du Maurier's illustrations, but by photographs and descriptions of Beerbohm Tree's performance of the character. The *Times* commented on Tree's facility with make-up, referring to "the stage Svengali, with his long, matted black hair and beard, his hooked nose, his unwholesome, sallow face, his piercing eye, and his long octopus-like limbs" (31 Oct. 1895). Few descriptions avoided Svengali's physical appearance, and many more were tinged with pejorative or anti-Semitic sentiments, in more than one case referring to the "unwashed Hebrew" or making explicit comparisons between Svengali and Russian Jewish Immigrants.[36] The focus on the physical features of Svengali was enhanced by Tree's particular skills as an actor. His ability to use make-up, as well as his predilection for "weird," "eccentric," and "bizarre" characters, gave his interpretation this special grotesque quality.[37] Some of the more prominent theatre critics related Svengali's features to caricature and denied that Svengali was anything other than a fantasy figure.[38]

The caricatural aspects of Svengali were descended directly from the mythical Jewish types present in earlier Victorian melodramas, but Tree's mannerisms were original and may have been based on his observations of behavior among Jewish immigrants in London. Tree's use of excessive and fussy stage business, as well as his frequent, unusual, and somewhat manic gestures, are apparent from both the promptbooks of *Trilby* and the 1914 film version of the play.[39] These caricatural qualities were stressed in descriptions of the character as an insect or animal, rather than a human being. Du Maurier's engraving of Svengali as a spider in the novel was evoked in the stage production through the use of a web which appeared upstage while Svengali hypnotized Trilby. Reviewers frequently referred to Svengali as a "human spider,"[40] and this attribute had a previous association with Jewish usury through at least one famous *Punch* cartoon. The dehumanization of the Jewish character was part of a long caricatural tradition; from the Renaissance, physiognomic theories, such as G. B. della Porta's *De humana physiognomonia* (1586), insisted that there was a direct equation between the human face and the physical and characteristic qualities of animals. Jews were frequently subjected to this species of carica-

tural debasement, the most bitter example of which was the representation of Alfred Dreyfus as a scapegoat, based on Holman Hunt's famous painting (*Punch* 29 Jan. 1898).

The disgust with which many critics referred to the character of Svengali combined a distaste for his physical aspect with anger at his exploitation of the vivacious Trilby—another quality which the audience could have associated with his Jewishness.[41] Svengali's evil nature was reflected in his use of mesmerism, which would have had immediate associations for the audience of the play. Although by the 1890s mesmerism had been discredited in favor of hypnotism, the two forms of suggestion were inevitably related, and the latter seen to be a development of the former. Du Maurier's ideas about mesmerism were based on his own youthful experiments, but by the 1890s new debates in France about the benefits and disadvantages of hypnotism were bringing the whole question of subconscious suggestion into the public forum. The controversy in France involved a disagreement between two eminent psychologists, J.-M. Charcot of Paris and Hippolyte Bernheim of Nancy.[42] The former held that only insane people could be hypnotized and that hypnotism was therefore not a public danger, whereas Bernheim and his followers believed that anyone was prone to suggestion—and that hypnosis could therefore be used for criminal purposes.

The Charcot/Bernheim debate was well known in England and was referred to in the *Times* review of *Trilby*.[43] At least two controversial events involving Jews formed part of this debate. First of all, the accusation of ritual murder in the Hungarian village of Tisza-Esslar (1882) was levelled against the Jewish community by a young Jew, Moritz, whom many believed was "confessing" under the hypnotic suggestion of a severe anti-Semitic judge. More interestingly, a Jewish dentist in Rouen was arrested in 1878 for hypnotizing his patient and then persuading her to have sex with him on the dentist chair.[44] In this case, the Jew is seen as a potential exploiter and manipulator of the power of hypnotism, and conspiracy theorists generally expressed fear about the potential abuse of hypnotism by such marginal groups as working-class anarchists, criminals, and Jews. Svengali's use of mesmerism for manipulation and public exhibitionism associated him firmly with this debate by placing him on the side of the manipulator. The *Manchester Courier* made this association explicit: "In . . . watching the marvelous power Svengali is able to exercise over Trilby . . . [one must ask] why, if such wonders can be performed by means of hypnotism, the power is not exerted in other and more important directions? What if such a power were possessed by an Anarchist, or by a thief?"[45] Although there was no direct allusion to contemporary immigrants in the character of Svengali, such understated referents exhibited widely-held fears about the power of the growing Jewish population in England. Conspiracy theories, racialist subtexts, and unease about immigration were all exposed in an American publication of 1897, Alfred Welch's *Extracts from the Diary of Moritz Svengali*, which used Svengali's fictional diary to attribute all his evil practices to the religious persecution that drove him out of Poland.[46]

Tree's subsequent Jewish characters dissolved further into caricature, as their relationship with real Jews became increasingly tenuous. The figure of Isidore Izard in Sydney Grundy's *Business is Business* (Her Majesty's, 13 May 1905) was never classified as Jewish, but his physical features and association with money led audiences to make this assumption. Tree came perilously close to lapsing into mid-Victorian melodramatic stereotypes in his portrayal of Fagin in Comyns Carr's version of *Oliver Twist* (Her Majesty's, 10 July 1905). Despite the late date, critics still hinted that public expectation of the character of Fagin was formed by Cruikshank's plates for Dickens's novel, and several newspaper illustrations show Tree crouched in the famous pose of Fagin in the condemned cell.[47] Critics further considered the extent to which Tree's representation embodied the Jewish character. A long diatribe against representations of Jews on the stage in the *Jewish Journal* praised Tree's Fagin, but concluded, "There is nothing . . . in Mr. Tree's 'Fagin' to which a Jew ought to take exception or feel any injury to his Jewish feelings. 'Fagin,' as presented by Mr. Tree, is no more a type of Jew than Bill Sikes [sic] and the Artful Dodger are types of Englishmen."[48] Another reviewer compared Tree's portrayal to anti-Jewish propaganda placards in Russia, thus drawing attention to the thin line between exaggeration and condemnation in the representation of Fagin's character (*Sketch* 19 July 1905). But these dark hints about the anti-Semitic nature of Fagin's characterization are deflated in other reviews, which construed Tree's interpretation as more humorous than horrible; Fagin was "no longer the Fagin of our juvenile nightmares, but Mr. Tree, being extraordinarily clever . . . with a queer nose and an uncanny shuffle" (*Theatre* 11 July 1905). The strong racial association that Dickens had made between Fagin's character and his Jewishness was replaced in late melodrama by an exaggeration which neutralized the significance of the racial referents. The attributes of Jewish characters were magnified to the point where it was no longer possible to accept the modicum of reality that melodrama pretended to represent.

As such extreme caricatural aspects of stage Jews became increasingly prominent, so the Jewish characters themselves were more frequently associated with comedy and with dramatic sketches for music halls and vaudeville performances.[49] These caricatural qualities allowed audiences to laugh safely at Jewish characters and, through laughter, to dissipate their own anxieties about the role of Jews in modern society. Indeed, although Jewish characters did not disappear from melodrama, as the 1890s progressed they became more commonly associated with comedy. A transitional figure appeared in the character of Julius Sterne in Sydney Grundy's comedy *An Old Jew* (Garrick, 6 January 1894). On the one hand, Julius Sterne represents the legacy of the melodramatic stereotyped Jew: he wears "patriarchal garb," is full of "curious smiles," and appears everywhere in the play where money can solve the problems of his estranged family. However, Sterne is neither a villain nor a convincing comic figure; he stands strangely apart from the satirical tone of the play itself and becomes virtually a mythical embodiment of Jewish racial characteristics. This is evident when he tells the story of his life to his children and invokes the very racial stereotypes used to attack Jews throughout the century:

> I had a wife. But a cloud came between us. I was a man of business. Type of my race. I was too much a man of business. Type of my race. . . . My wife betrayed me. What was I to do? I could not live with her; my love was dead. I could not publish her disgrace. It would have been her ruin; it would have been my children's. I went away. I went out into the wilderness. Type of my race! I had no ties—no interest—no occupation—save to make money. I made it. Type of my race! I became rich, richer and richer, till one day, I said to myself, what do riches mean? Not happiness, not even peace of mind. I loathed the riches; but the riches grew, as though to mock me with their vanity. Then I bethought myself, I had a son and a daughter, growing up somewhere, hating me. Soon I could think of nothing else; and I came back to England—only to see them, only to speak to them, only to touch them. And now in England, here I am—alone—rich beyond avarice—courted, yet scorned—flattered, yet feared—but striving still to do some little good with my great wealth. Type of my race!
>
> (49)

Sterne represents an uneasy compromise between the Jew of melodrama and the Jew of comedy, but here the racial characteristics are self-consciously labored in an attempt to milk the humor out of a familiar melodramatic character type.

The transformation of the Jew from melodramatic villain to comic character was made complete by the work of a Jewish playwright, Israel Zangwill, whose stage version of his novel, *Children of the Ghetto* (Adelphi, 11 December 1899), focused for the first time on poor London Jews. Zangwill was a Zionist and the son of an immigrant, but his interpretations of Jewish characters are often as exaggerated as those of his non-Jewish contemporaries. In the tradition of *Trilby*, his *King of the Schnorrers* (significantly subtitled *Grotesques and Fantasies*) included illustrations by Phil May, George

Hutchinson, and F. H. Townsend which highlighted the more caricatural aspects of the Jewish protagonists, just as his text emphasized the humorous aspects of their lives. The stage versions of Zangwill's works were equally dogged by a caricatural approach. A critic of *Children of the Ghetto* isolated this racial typing:

> Concerning the fidelity of Mr. Zangwill's types we have nothing to say. His Jews, shabby or comic, are not, however, an attractive people. . . . The Hebrew poet, Melchitsedek Pinchas, as rendered by Mr. William Norris, displayed an intensity that made him only the more repulsive. There was much in the character reminding us of Svengali.
>
> (*Athenaeum* 114 [16 Dec. 1899] 844)

The reference to Svengali shows that the Jewish villain was rarely far from people's minds, even when watching a comic play written by a Jew. However, the displacement of the Jewish stage character from minor villain to comic caricature removed him from accusations of villainy at a time when anti-Semitism was becoming a political force in many European countries. The melodramatic villain persisted in early films, but the Jewish type of the early twentieth century appeared more prominently in vaudeville and music hall performance, as well as in a thriving Yiddish theatre which sought to foster Jewish themes. The racial stereotyping of the nineteenth century persisted, however, even while the invidious associations of Jews with conspiracy, manipulation, greed, and revenge were divorced from the self-contained moral landscape of stage melodrama and transposed into the morally ambiguous world of comedy.[50]

Notes

1. Archer, *About the Theatre* 334. For character types, see Jerome and Booth.

2. The best overview of the relationship between Victorian art and theatre is Meisel, but see also West, "Painting and Theatre."

3. In this essay I use the term "melodrama" in its broadest sense, referring not only to plays which were classed as such in the nineteenth century, but also to those which had some elements of the melodramatic good/evil polarity and character typologies. For a sophisticated assessment of the discourse of melodrama, see Brooks, who considers melodrama a "mode of conception and expression" (xiii).

4. For the use of Jewish characters in specifically popular (as opposed to high) drama, see Coleman 39.

5. Throughout this essay I use the pronoun "he" rather than "he or she" because the Jewish stereotype—whether in art, theatre, or popular polemic—was primarily a male one. The association of Jews with public economic issues fostered a conception of the Jewish type as male.

6. Salaman 6. For a general discussion of racial stereotyping, see Gilman.

7. See, for example, White's examination of the term in *The Modern Jew* 3.

8. Nott and Gliddon 81, 112; for the Lamarckian argument see 96.

9. See, for example, the sermons of Hermann Adler, including "Jew and Gentile" (1895), "The Jews During the Victorian Era" (1897), and "Religious Versus Political Zionism" (1898), all published in *The North London Pulpit.*

10. See, for example, Cowling, Grilli, Wechsler, and Tytler. For the eighteenth-century background and the relationship between physiognomic theories in art and theatre, see West, *Image of the Actor* and West, "Polemic and the Passions."

11. See Dyche: "I cannot think of these accusations without being struck with the curious fact that all that is said against us in England is just the contrary to what we are accused of in Russia" (37). For other statements on Jewish character, see, for example, White, *The Modern Jew*; "A Typical Alien Immigrant" (answering Dyche); Banister; Pennell; *Regeneration*; Smith, "Can Jews be Patriots?"; "The Jewish Question"; Adler, "Jews and Judaism"; Russell and Lewis; and Drumont for a comparative example.

12. Hunt 1: chapters XIV-XVIII; 2: chapters I-III. For a study of Hunt's attitudes to the "other" races of the Holy Land, see Pointon.

13. Surprisingly little has been written on Jewish themes in the art of the "Olympians"; most scholars concentrate on the classical subject matter. See Kestner, and, for a complete contrast, Jenkyns. For the theatre, see Mayer. Mayer's sensible definition of "toga play" embraces the religious pluralism characteristic of these works. Jewish themes and types were also used by the Jewish artist Simeon Solomon. See *Solomon, a Family of Painters*; and Reynolds. For a comparative example of the Jewish subject in French art, see Ockman.

14. Fuchs 160-61. Fuchs's unusual compilation is the only work of its kind, but it is colored by a Marxist anti-Semitism. He refers to "dieses spezifisch judische Rassenmerkel" when discussing the hooked nose, and he claims that Jewish emancipation was one symptom of the intensifying capitalism in nineteenth-century Europe.

15. The Jews were obviously not the only group who were on the sharp end of such physiognomic satire; cf. Perry Curtis.

16. See, for example, *Punch* 9 Aug. 1890: 66-7; 20 Dec. 1890: 290-91; and 16 May 1891: 234-5; cf. Mayhew.

17. Wagner 3: 82-4. For Wagner's reception in England see Large and Weber.

18. On Dickens and Cruikshank see Evans and Evans, Miller and Borowitz, and Kitton.

19. "Mr. Anson played the Jew cleverly enough, modelling the character very closely after Cruikshank's famous portrait, and he, too, cannot be said to have exceeded the lines laid down for him either by author or artist" (*Times* 11 July 1878).

20. For a comprehensive overview of the character of Shylock, see Gross. For Irving, see Fitzgerald 131; for Gould, see Archer, *Theatrical World of 1897* 154, and for Tree's similarly sympathetic rendering see Maud Tree's assessment in Beerbohm 149.

21. For examples, see *Punch* 2 April 1898: 146: "A Matter of interest: Modern Shylock (leaving Money-lending Committee)"; Salaman 20, and his chapter "Shylock from a Jewish Point of View"; Hawkins; Dyche; and, for a context, see Glassman. For France see, for example, Drumont, "Sous le membre du Jockey-Club, Shylock se retrouve aussi repace que sous la souquenille safranée" (93).

22. Boucicault, *After Dark*, 2. See reviews in the *Athenaeum* 52 (15 Aug. 1868) 218-19, and *Theatre* n.s. 18 (1891) 279-80. For another Jewish caricature in Boucicault's plays, see *Flying Scud* in Clark.

23. Taylor's caricatural conception of Jews may have been influenced by his knowledge of art. For his role as art critic, see West, "Tom Taylor." For a discussion of the stage Jewish accent, see Landa 119-20. In addition to the accent, stage Jews were often given a prominent lisp—a convention that began in the eighteenth century but was not always indicated by the published texts of plays (Coleman xiv). Landa identifies the origin of the lisp as a corruption of the Sephardic pronunciation of Hebrew, but he vilifies its use well into the twentieth century as a racial stamp of low comic and villainous Jews (207). The lisp was even used by Jewish playwrights such as Israel Zangwill and in "naturalistic" Jewish plays such as Herman Heijermans's *The Ghetto* (*Comedy,* 9 Sept. 1899; see *The Times* 11 Sept. 1899). As the lisp was an aural, rather than a visual, idiosyncrasy, it was particularly characteristic of the theatre and theatrically-inspired novels by Thackeray and Dickens. Race theorists did not refer to it, and artists obviously could not make use of it.

24. Taylor, *Payable on Demand* 38. For a discussion of the play's source see *Athenaeum* 34 (16 July 1859) 89.

25. *Athenaeum* 43 (20 Feb. 1864) 271. For another example of toleration see J. P. Wooler's *The Branded Race, or The Fatal Secret,* which premiered at the Surrey in 1858—the year Leonard Rothschild was allowed to sit in the House of Commons. The play is discussed in Foulkes, *The Calverts* 31.

26. The latter quotation was plagiarized from a speech made by Herbert Beerbohm Tree (see note 30).

27. These figures are taken from Black 4; but see also Callotti, Pollins, Lipman, and Holmes.

28. For oblique anti-Semitism, see White, *The Modern Jew; The Problems of a Great City*; Wilkins, *The Immigration of Destitute Foreigners*; The *Alien Invasion*; Banister; Cunningham; and Wolf, "A Jewish View."

29. The most famous contemporary source is Nordau, and see West, *Fin de Siècle,* chapter 2, which discusses the issue of degeneration. For references to the degeneration of Russian and Polish Jews, see White, *The Modern Jew* 12; Russell and Lewis 178-79; Smith, "Can Jews Be Patriots?" 876; and Pennell 3: 840.

30. For versions of the text of his speech, see the *Standard* (11 Dec. 1892), *Morning Post* (16 Nov. 1892), *Era* (11 Nov. 1892), and *St. James's Gazette* (11 Nov. 1892).

31. See *The Times* (3 Jan. 1893); *Theatre,* n.s., 21 (1893) 105-6; *Punch* (24 Sept. 1894) 139; *Daily News* (3 Jan. 1893); *Graphic* (Jan. 1893); *Daily Graphic* (3 Jan. 1893); and Archer, *Theatrical World for 1893* 16.

32. See the *Chronicle* (3 Jan. 1893); *Weekly Sun* (8 Jan. 1893); and *Sunday Chronicle* (8 Jan. 1893).

33. See especially *Era* (7 Jan. 1893), and *Star* (3 Jan. 1893).

34. For the source of Du Maurier's characters, see Ormond. See also *Trilbyana,* and Alexander, 22-3, who argues somewhat unconvincingly that Svengali too was modelled on a real-life prototype.

35. Du Maurier 12. Cf. Potter: "For the most part they [Jewish immigrants] are men between 20 and 40 years of age, of slight and stooping stature, of shallow and pinched countenance, with low foreheads, high cheekbones and protruding lips. They wear uncouth and dirt-bespattered garments" (580).

36. See, for example, *Punch* (16 Nov. 1895) 232; *Star* (31 Oct. 1895), and *Woman* (13 Nov. 1895).

37. See the commentaries of various observers in Beerbohm, including that of Desmond MacCarthy (22), Gilbert Parker (228), and W. L. Courteney (256).

38. Especially Scott, 2: 380, and Archer, *Theatrical World of 1895* 330.

39. The *Trilby* Promptbooks (Bristol University Theatre Collection, HBT 9) are riddled with stage directions for Tree, and the 1914 film with Tree shows the odd, mannered effect of these gestures, which separate Svengali strikingly from the other characters in the play. I am grateful to the National Film Theatre for the screening of Harold Shaw's 1914 film of *Trilby,* which allowed me to make these observations.

40. See, for instance, *Daily Graphic (1 June 1903), and Globe* (1 June 1903).

41. Taylor, in Foulkes, ed.

42. The best discussion of this controversy is Harris. For contemporary English references to the Charcot/Bernheim debate, see, for example, Crisfield.

43. "Mr. Tree performs feats which, we suspect, even the 'Nancy school' would repudiate" (*Times* 31 Oct. 1895).

44. See Bernheim's assessment of the Tisza-Esslar case; see also *The Graphic* (11 Aug. 1883), and Wright. For a general account of the history of ritual murder, see Dundes. The Rouen dentist is discussed in Harris 186.

45. *Manchester Courier* (9 Sept. 1895). The suspicious British public often linked Jews with anarchists; see Holmes 43.

46. It is interesting to note that Svengali's first name is the same as the Hungarian Jewish boy who alleged the Jewish conspiracy at Tisza-Esslar.

47. See *Daily Express* (11 July 1905), *Evening Standard* (11 July 1905), and *Daily Mirror* (5 Sept. 1905).

48. *Jewish Journal* (8 Sept. 1905); typescript translation from the Hebrew (dated 10 Sept. 1895) in the Bristol University Theatre Collection, TB33.

49. An early example of this is John "Jew" Lawson's dramatic sketch, *Humanity (in Eighteen Minutes),* which combined a dramatic scenario involving a Jewish-Gentile confrontation with a song about Jewishness—"Only a Jew." I am grateful to David Mayer for bringing this to my attention and for his suggestion that such sketches may have contributed to the representation of the Jew in early cinema.

50. A version of this essay was delivered at the conference on melodrama at the British Film Institute in July 1992. I would like to thank Christopher Robinson of the University of Bristol Theatre Collection. I owe special thanks to David Mayer and Richard Foulkes for welcome suggestions and encouragement.

Works Cited

Adler, Hermann. "Jews and Judaism: a Rejoinder." *Nineteenth Century* 4 (1878): 133-50. *The North London Pulpit.* London: Alfred J. Isaacs & Sons, 1895-98.

Alexander, Peter, ed. *Svengali: George Du Maurier's Trilby.* London: W. H. Allen, 1983.

Archer, William. *About the Theatre.* London: T. Fisher Unwin, 1886. *The Theatrical World for 1893.* London: Walter Scott, 1894. *The Theatrical World of 1895.* London: Walter Scott, 1896. *The Theatrical World of 1897.* London: Walter Scott, 1898.

Athenaeum.

Banister, Joseph. *England Under the Jews.* London: Joseph Banister, 1901.

Beerbohm, Max, ed. *Herbert Beerbohm Tree.* London: Hutchinson, [1921].

Beddoe, John. *The Races of Britain.* Bristol: J. W. Arrowsmith, 1885.

Bernheim, Hippolyte. *De la suggestion et ses applications.* Paris: Octave Doin, 1886.

Black, Eugene. *The Social Politics of Anglo-Jewry 1880-1920.* Oxford: Basil Blackwell, 1988.

Booth, Michael R. *English Melodrama.* London: H. Jenkins, 1965.

Boucicault, Dion. *After Dark.* London: Edward Ashman, 1880. *Flying Scud. Favorite American Plays of the Nineteenth Century.* Ed. Barrett H. Clark. Princeton: Princeton UP, 1943.

Brooks, Peter. *The Melodramatic Imagination: Balzac, Henry James, Melodrama and the Mode of Excess.* New Haven: Yale UP, 1976.

Callotti, Enzo. "Nationalism, Anti-Semitism, Socialism and Political Catholicism as Expressions of Mass Politics in the Twentieth Century." *Fin de Siècle and its Legacy.* Ed. Mikûlás Teich and Roy Porter. Cambridge: Cambridge UP, 1990. 80-97.

Chronicle.

Cohen, Gustavus. *The Modern Self-Instructor in Phrenology, Physiology and Physiognomy.* London: Gustavus Cohen, 1884.

Coleman, Edward. *The Jew in English Drama: An Annotated Bibliography.* New York: New York Public Library, 1968.

Cowen, Anne, and Roger Cowen. *Victorian Jews Through British Eyes.* Oxford: Oxford UP, 1986.

Cowling, Mary. *The Artist as Anthropologist: The Representation of Type and Character in Victorian Art.* Cambridge: Cambridge UP, 1989.

Crisfield, Thomas. *The Value of Hypnotism.* London, 1893.

Cunningham, W. *Alien Immigrants to England.* London: Swan Sonnenschein, 1897.

Curtis, L. Perry. *Apes and Angels: the Irishman in Victorian Caricature.* Newton Abbot: David and Charles, 1971.

Daily Express.

Daily Graphic.

Daily Mirror.

Daily News.

Daily Telegraph.

Dickens, Mamie, and Georgina Hogarth, eds. *The Letters of Charles Dickens.* 3 vols. London: Chapman and Hall, 1880-82.

Drumont, Edouard. *La France juive devant l'opinion.* Paris: C. Marpon and E. Flammarion, 1886.

Du Maurier, George. *Trilby.* London: Osgood, McIlvaine, 1895.

Dundes, Alan, ed. *The Blood Libel Legend: a Casebook in Anti-Semitic Folklore.* Madison: U of Wisconsin P, 1992.

Dyche, John. "The Jewish Workman." *Contemporary Review* 73 (1898): 35-50.

Era.

Evans, Hilary, and Mary Evans. *The Man Who Drew the Drunkard's Daughter: The Life and Art of George Cruikshank 1792-1878.* London: Frederick Muller, 1978.

Evening Standard.

Fitzgerald, Percy. *Henry Irving: a Record of Twenty Years at the Lyceum.* London: Chapman and Hall, 1893.

Foulkes, Richard, ed. *British Theatre in the 1890s: Essays on Drama and the Stage.* Cambridge: Cambridge UP, 1992. *The Calverts: Actors of Some Importance.* London: Society for Theatre Research, 1992.

Fuchs, Eduard. *Die Juden in der Karikatur.* Munich: A. Langen, 1921.

Gilman, Sander. *Difference and Pathology: Stereotypes of Sexuality, Race and Madness.* Ithaca: Cornell UP, 1985.

Glassman, Bernard. *Anti-Semitic Stereotypes Without Jews: Images of the Jews in England 1290-1700.* Detroit: Wayne State UP, 1975.

Globe.

The Graphic.

Grilli, Stephanie. "Pre-Raphaelitism and Phrenology." *Pre-Raphaelite Papers.* Ed. Leslie Parris. London: Tate Gallery, 1984.

Gross, John. *Shylock: Four Hundred Years in the Life of a Legend.* London: Chatto & Windus, 1992.

Grundy, Sydney. *A Son of Israel.* London: J. Miles, 1896.

Harris, Ruth. *Murders and Madness: Medicine, Law and Society in the Fin de Siècle.* Oxford: Oxford UP, 1989.

Hawkins, Frederick. "Shylock and Other Stage Jews." *Theatre* (1 Nov. 1879): 191-98.

Hazlewood, Colin Henry. *The Stolen Jewess.* Lacy's Acting Editions, no. 492. London: Thomas H. Lacy, n.d.

Holmes, Colin. *Anti-Semitism in British Society 1876-1939.* London: Edward Arnold, 1979.

Hunt, William Holman. *Pre-Raphaelitism and the Pre-Raphaelite Brotherhood.* 2 vols. London: Macmillan, 1905. Vol. 1: chapters XIV-XVIII; vol. 2: chapters I-III.

Hypatia Promptbooks. Bristol University Theatre Collection, HBT 29.

Illustrated London News.

Jenkyns, Richard. *Dignity and Decadence: Victorian Art and the Classical Inheritance.* London: Harper Collins, 1992.

Jerome, Jerome K. *Stage Land.* London: Chatto & Windus, 1890.

Jewish Chronicle.

Jewish Journal.

Kestner, Joseph. *Mythology and Misogyny: the Social Discourse of Nineteenth-Century British Classical Subject Painting.* Madison: U of Wisconsin P, 1989.

Kitton, Frederick. *Dickens and His Illustrators.* London: George Redway, 1899.

Knox, Robert. *The Races of Men: A Philosophical Enquiry into the Influence of Race Over the Destinies of Nations.* 2nd ed. London: Henry Renshaw, 1862.

Landa, M. J. *The Jew in Drama*. London: P. S. King & Son, 1926.

Large, David C., and William Weber, eds. *Wagnerism in European Culture and Politics*. Ithaca: Cornell UP, 1984.

Lipman, V. D. *Social History of the Jews in England 1850-1950*. London: Watts, 1954.

Lombroso, Cesare. *L'uomo bianco e l'uomo di colore*. Padua: F. Sacchetto, 1871.

Mayhew, Henry. *London Characters*. London: Chatto & Windus, 1874.

Manchester Courier.

Mantegazza, Paolo. *Physiognomy and Expression*. London: Walter Scott, 1890. *The Sexual Relations of Mankind*. New York: Eugenics, 1935 [translation of *Gli amori degli uomini* (1885)].

Mayer, David. "Toga Plays." In Foulkes, ed., 71-92.

Meisel, Martin. *Realizations: Narrative, Pictorial, and Theatrical Arts in Nineteenth-Century England*. Princeton: Princeton UP, 1983.

Miller, J. Hillis, and David Borowitz. *Charles Dickens and George Cruikshank*. Los Angeles: William Andrews Clark Memorial Library, 1971.

Morning Post.

Nordau, Max. *Degeneration*. London: William Heinemann, 1895.

Nott, J. C., and George Gliddon. *Types of Mankind*. Philadelphia: Trübner, 1854.

Ockman, Carol. "'Two Large Eyebrows à l'Orientale': Ethnic Stereotyping in Ingres's *Baronne de Rothschild.*" *Art History* 14 (1991): 521-39.

Ogilvie, Stuart. *Hypatia*. London: Heinemann, 1894.

Ormond, Leonée. *George Du Maurier*. London: Routledge & Kegan Paul, 1969.

Pennell, Joseph. "The Jew at Home, I—In Austria and Hungary: II—In Austrian Poland; III—In Russia." *Illustrated London News* 5 Dec. 1891: 732-34; 12 Dec. 1891: 765-66; 26 Dec. 1891: 840.

Pointon, Marcia. "The Artist as Ethnographer: Holman Hunt and the Holy Land." In *The Pre-Raphaelites Reviewed*. Ed. Marcia Pointon. Manchester: Manchester UP, 1989. 22-44.

Pollins, Harold. *Economic History of the Jews in England*. East Brunswick: Associated UPs, 1982.

Potter, Beatrice. "The Jewish Community." *Life and Labour of the People of London*. Ed. Charles Booth. Vol. I: East London. London: Williams and Norgate, 1889. 564-90.

Punch.

Reade, Charles. *Gold*. Lacy's Acting Editions, no. 152. London: Thomas H. Lacy, n.d.

Regeneration: A Reply to Max Nordau. London: Archibald Constable, 1895.

Reynolds, Simon. *The Vision of Simeon Solomon*. Stroud: Catalpa, 1985.

Russell, C., and H. S. Lewis. *The Jew in London: a Study of Racial Character and Present-Day Conditions*. London: T. Fisher Unwin, 1900.

St. James's Gazette.

Salaman, Charles Kensington. *Jews as They Are*. London: Simkin, Marshall, 1882.

Scott, Clement. *The Drama of Yesterday and Today*. 2 vols. London: Macmillan, 1899.

Sketch.

Smith, Goldwin. "Can Jews be Patriots?" *Nineteenth Century* 3 (1878): 875-87. "The Jewish Question." *Nineteenth Century* 10 (1881): 494-515.

Solomon, A Family of Painters. Exhibition Catalogue. London: Geffreye Museum, 1985.

Souvenir of The Daughters of Babylon. London, 1897.

Souvenir of Trilby. London, 30 Oct. 1895.

Standard.

Star.

Sunday Chronicle.

Taylor, John William. *Noses, and What They Indicate*. London, 1892.

Taylor, George. "Svengali: Mesmerist and Aesthete." In Foulkes, ed., 93-110.

Taylor, Tom. *Payable on Demand*. Lacy's Acting Editions, no. 614. London: Thomas H. Lacy, n.d.

The Times.

Theatre.

Trilby Promptbooks. Bristol University Theatre Collection, HBT 9.

Trilbyana: The Rise and Progress of a Popular Novel. New York: The Critic, 1895.

Tytler, Graeme. *Physiognomy and the European Novel: Faces and Fortunes*. Princeton: Princeton UP, 1982.

Wagner, Richard. "Judaism in Music." *Richard Wagner's Prose Works*. Trans. William Ashton Ellis. 8 vols. London: Trench, Trübner, 1892. 3: 79-122.

Wechsler, Judith. *A Human Comedy: Physiognomy and Caricature in Nineteenth-Century Paris.* Chicago: U of Chicago P, 1982.

Welch, Alfred. *Extracts from the Diary of Moritz Svengali.* New York: Henry Holt, 1897.

Weekly Sun.

West, Shearer. *Fin de Siècle: Art and Society in an Age of Uncertainty.* London: Bloomsbury, 1993. *The Image of the Actor: Verbal and Visual Representation in the Age of Garrick and Kemble.* London: Pinter, 1991. "Painting and Theatre in the 1890s." In Foulkes, ed., 93-110. "Polemic and the Passions: Dr. James Parsons's Human Physiognomy Explained and Hogarth's Desire for British History Painting." *British Journal for Eighteenth Century Studies* 13 (1990): 73-89. "Tom Taylor, William Powell Frith and the British School of Art." *Victorian Studies* 33 (1990): 307-26.

White, Arnold. *The Modern Jew.* London: Heinemann, 1899. *The Problems of a Great City.* London: Remington, 1886. "A Typical Alien Immigrant." *Contemporary Review* 73 (1898): 241-50.

Wilkins, W. H. *The Alien Invasion.* London: Methuen, 1892. *The Immigration of Destitute Foreigners.* London: P. S. King & Son, 1891.

Wolf, Lucien. "A Jewish View of the Anti-Jewish Agitation." *Nineteenth Century* 9 (1881): 338-57. "The Jews in London." *The Graphic* (16 Nov. 1889).

Woman.

Wright, Rev. Charles H. H. "The Jews and the Malicious Charge of Human Sacrifice." *Nineteenth Century* 14 (1883): 753-78.

Zangwill, Israel. *The King of the Schnorrers: Grotesques and Fantasies.* London: William Heinemann, 1894.

Jennifer Jones (essay date 1996)

SOURCE: Jones, Jennifer. "The Face of Villainy on the Victorian Stage." *Theatre Notebook* 50, no. 2 (1996): 95-108.

[*In the following essay, Jones "examines how the popular physiognomic sciences of the nineteenth century interacted with the conventions of melodramatic villainy to circulate and authenticate the 'foreign face of villainy' in Victorian England."*]

> Is it not marvelous to be able, at the sight of a mere portrait of a man, to tell what are his virtues, his vices, his talents or his tastes?
>
> *Not a Bad Judge; or Lavater the Physiognomist* by J. R. Planché (Olympic Theatre, London 1848)

Pliny the Elder tells us that in ancient rome, wax impressions, or *imagines,* were taken from corpses, incorporated into terra-cotta busts and proudly displayed by family members as a testament to the character of the deceased.[1] Physiognomy, or the art of reading people's character and personality in the features of their faces, is as strong an impulse today as it was thousands of years ago, and despite proverbial warnings to the contrary, we are still judging books by their covers. Today we often attribute our reactions to instinct, but in the eighteenth and nineteenth centuries the "science" of Physiognomy attempted to codify and document a methodical equation between a person's facial features and his dominant character traits.

In the second half of the eighteenth-century, Johann Caspar Lavater, a Swiss pastor and teacher, started a vogue for reading character in portrait silhouettes. Lavater's book, *Essays on Physiognomy,* illustrated with his own drawings and translated into many languages, became a best seller throughout Europe. So it is safe to say that in *Not a Bad Judge; or Lavater the Physiognomist* (produced at London's Olympic Theatre in 1848) J. R. Planché was depicting a figure well known to British audiences. In this precursor to the "detective drama", Lavater unmasks an Italian bandit, Mariano Mariani, who is masquerading as a French count. Lavater instantly recognizes criminal traits in the Italian's features, and in doing so saves an innocent young lady from a terrible marriage, thereby convincing a doubting public of the legitimacy of his "science". Though he proves correct in the end, Lavater cautions that a clever criminal can easily change his outward appearance to fool the non-trained eye. He censures the local Burgomaster for doubting that the elegant "Count" could ever be a bandit.

BURGOMASTER:

> He doesn't give me the least notion of Mariani.

LAVATER:

> Because, Mr. Burgomaster you are one of those who fancy every brigand must wear a ferocious beard and carry a cocked pistol . . . a villain can too often look like an honest man.[2]

Though Planché's Lavater may have believed this to be true, in the Victorian theatre audiences preferred a man who wore his villainy plainly on his face. Two nineteenth-century actors, N. T. "Bravo" Hicks and Mr. O. Smith (Richard Jonathan Smith), specialized in just such villains, and images of the players in costume show surly characters, with dark hair, dark moustaches, bushy eyebrows, deep lined faces . . . and, oh yes, cocked pistols.

The meaning we derive from the face and figure of another person is subject to our participation in the conventions of our own culture, and we may assume that nineteenth-century theatrical conventions correlated in some degree to the spectators' world. When the stage villain entered, the audience saw something they collectively recognized as villainous in his appearance. What qualities, cocked pistols aside, identified actors like Bravo Hicks or O. Smith as criminals? Particularly, what facial qualities? As one starts to look (with the help of sketches, character descriptions and contemporary accounts) at the dark face of villainy, recognized by Victorian theatre goers, one thing becomes clear: it is quite unlike the English faces in the audience. This article examines how the popular physiognomic sciences of the nineteenth-century interacted with the conventions of melodramatic villainy to circulate and authenticate the "foreign face of villainy" in Victorian England.

Lavater declared that his system was based on common sense and that he merely "systematized what for centuries philosophers had taken for granted".[3] The guide books written by eighteenth- and nineteenth-century physiognomists attempted to create an objective science which would codify character traits revealed in facial structure. The methodology of these "pseudo-scientists" reveals a strong ethnocentric bias. Physiognomic guide books offered portraits of "the great men of Western civilization", and in these faces would locate and categorize noble qualities. Correlating negative qualities would be represented by roughly drawn portraits of "an idiot" or "a gorilla" or "an African girl". Physiognomists formulated their semiotic categories from within the dominant belief systems of their culture, making of these subjective classification an unproblematized science which prioritized the physiognomy of their own race. In these treatises, moral worth was exclusively assigned to those who possessed a Caucasian physiognomy. In 1889, Joseph Simms published a treatise on physiognomy entitled *Physiognomy Illustrated, or Nature's Revelations of Character,* in which he wrote a chapter on "The Colours of Races and What They Indicate".

> The Guinea negro being the darkest of all races, is the most impure and imperfect; but the negroes in America are far removed from the Guinea type; while, in contrast with these, the white races move in the highest plane of social life, and are foremost in the march of civilization.[4]

Lavater insisted that his system was "designed to promote knowledge and the Love of Mankind",[5] but inevitably the "science" of physiognomy was used for less humanitarian purposes. Cesare Lombroso, an Italian professor of psychiatry in the late nineteenth century, concluded that the criminal was an evolutionary throwback to primitive man, a being several steps lower on the evolutionary ladder. Through Lombroso's work, the school of positivist criminology evolved, espousing the belief that the criminal could be identified through spe-

cific and categorizable physical attributes. Like the work of earlier British, Swiss and American physiognomists, Lombroso's list of identifying criminal characteristics reveals strong racial prejudices. He wrote in *Criminal Man* (1870) of the flattened nose "common to criminals and apes" and went on to identify a list of ethnocentric criminal characteristics that included "squinty or slanted eyes; twisted or flattened nose with a Negroid character; fleshy, swollen and protruding lips as in negroes; and dark hair and bushy eyebrows that meet across the nose".[6]

A thorough discussion of Lombroso's work deserves a volume of its own, but I include excerpts from his theories here in order to examine their resonances with the representation of criminals on the nineteenth-century stage. Evidence of make-up practices is scarce in the nineteenth century, but by examining character descriptions, contemporary accounts, and theatrical prints, we can draw a partial picture of the signs of villainy on the Victorian stage. In *Crime and the Drama,* an account of nineteenth-century crime plays, H. Chance Newton includes photographs of several actors who specialized in villain roles in the latter part of the century—they are all dark haired, most are moustached and their faces are deeply lined.[7] Lombroso had identified a heavily wrinked face or lined face as a clear indication of criminal physiognomy and another nineteenth-century physiognomist, Samuel Wells, agreed that:

> Perplexed, deeply indented wrinkles of the forehead, in opposition to each other are always a certain sign of a harsh, perplexed and difficult to manage character . . . rude, harsh, indelicately suspicious, vain-glorious, ambitious are all those upon whose foreheads are formed strong, confused, oblique wrinkles.[8]

In Watts Phillips' farce, *Ticket of Leave* (1862), the nervous Mr. Quiver, suspicious of his servant, declares, "What a farce—there's a criminal in every wrinkle, and it's full of them!"[9] Nicola Helmer's *Actor's Make-up Book,* a manual published in New York in 1888, has a long section instructing actors on the proper application of wrinkles to the face and neck. The manual says of wrinkles that "these distinguishing traits are as plain to the observer as the printed characters of an open book. They are generally located around the mouth and are angular and vertical about the sides and corners of the mouth to denote a sullen character".[10] Wrinkles at first may seem a strange characteristic for a villain, but they were thought to be the traces left on a face that was perpetually fixed in the expression of anger or hatred. In 1824 a French critic, describing the character of the villain, wrote:

> In hatred the forehead is wrinkled, the eyebrows are lowered and frowning . . . the nostrils are flaring, more pronounced than usual, drawn back, which makes wrinkles appear in the cheeks.[11]

A swarthy, dark complexion was a standard attribute of the stage villain. It was not uncommon to hear evil characters referred to as "villains of the deepest dye", and dark coloring, produced by burnt cork or India ink, was considered an essential sign of villainy. A character in W. E. Suter's *The Felon's Bond* (1859), an actor specializing in villain roles, says, "I play all the villains. I look fierce you know; the amount of burnt cork I use is really something awful".[12] According to Helmer's make-up guide, burnt cork was applied in the following manner, "A suitable quantity is moistened in the hands like soap, and rubbed over the face, ears and hands". The actor is then instructed to rub the palms of the hands clean, "to avoid blackening everything which occasion requires to be touched".[13]

One of the most useful sources for information on the make-up practices of actors portraying villains in the Victorian theatre comes from Twynihoe William Erle, a nineteenth-century scene-painter whose book, *Letters from a Theatrical Scene-Painter* (1880), contains several accounts of villains he saw at the Royal Victoria and the Royal Effingham theatres in the early 1860's. Erle wrote that there were two kinds of villains, the black and the white, and whereas the white villain was rather mousy and ineffective,

> The black is a strong minded and bold villain. A personage of this class is *corked up to such a pitch* that his face rivals in blackness that of a metropolitan statue, or a Hyde Park sheep's, or the looks of a quarrelsome gentleman when you put him out. His forehead is ploughed with such *prodigious wrinkles,* indicative of his haggard mind, that it resembles the leather of a pair of bellows or the creases in a fat gentleman's waistcoat. His countenance is steeped in gloom.[14] (my italics).

In a later passage, Erle describes the darkened colouring of the villain in humorous detail. He describes the villain Rob in *Destiny*; or the *Broken Heart* performed at the Royal Victoria (1860):

> Rob's face is coloured up with ruddle to the orthodox murky tint by which the R. V. [Royal Victoria] marks its ruffians of the more rugged and violent class. The hue is the same as that of the unpleasant mixture of blood and brick-dust of which London-made "chocolate" is composed.[15]

Erle describes a band of villains from a production of *Adelbert the Deserter; or, The Robbers of the Black Forest* performed at the Royal Effingham.[16] I quote his portrait at length because it provides a rare detailed contemporary description of the villain's make-up and hairstyle.

> The make-up of the several accomplices forms each a tableau in itself. The management of the R. E. [Royal Effingham] obviously enjoys the advantage of a complete practical acquaintance with all the attributes of

ruffianism in their most minute details. One of the villains displays the results of a guilty mind by *such dark furrows across his brow,* that he looks as if his forehead had been subjected to the action of a dirty rake. Another betokens the *deep stains upon his conscience by so wholesale an outlay of burnt cork* upon his face, that his features are almost as black as those of a Christy minstrel, or of a maid-of-all-work at a lodging-house, who usually, poor thing, would seem from her appearance to avail herself of the coal-scuttle as pillow. Even his hands are blackened also! so that the beholder is naturally enough impressed with the conviction that the gentleman must have contemplated turning Ethiopian serenader . . . And the consumption of Berlin wool, required to form the *long sable locks* of the whole party taken together, must have been such as to have imparted a feverish impulse to the worsted trade.[17] (my italics)

Aside from darkened skin and "prodigious" wrinkles, a third identifying characteristic of the Victorian stage villain was dark hair and often a dark moustache and beard. Lombroso had identified dark hair and bushy eyebrows as criminal characteristics and Victorian actors and audiences agreed. Gilbert B. Cross writes in *Next Week, East Lynne: Domestic Drama in Performance 1820-1874*, "When F. A. Scudamore tried to play a villain with flaxen locks, the audience would have none of it, considering this novelty to be a dangerous innovation leading to unnecessary complexities of character".[18] Actor Jerome K. Jerome acknowledged the physiognomists when he wrote that because of his light coloring, without make-up he could not possibly portray a villain. "It was outraging every law of Lavater . . . but with a black beard, I felt fit for any amount of crime".[19] John Coleman describes his first meeting with Samuel Phelps, on the day Phelps opened Sadler's Wells. "Having only seen him on the stage made up to represent villains and old men, I was astonished to find him with a smooth, beardless face, almost colourless eyes and an abundance of light brown hair".[20] Another account comes from playwright Tom Robertson who describes an actor making-up for a "heavy" role in nautical melodrama:

> With black wig, black whiskers, black moustaches, black eyebrows, and a broad black line under each eye, intended to represent black eyelashes, every trace of good-humor of his face has vanished, and his mouth looks fit only for treasons, stratagems and spoils.[21]

Character descriptions in many scripts confirm that the villain often sported long black hair and a black moustache. The villain in *Formosa; or, the Road to Ruin* (1869) is described as having "long black moustache, hair rather long and straggling down on forehead; eyebrows shaped to indicate determination".[22] Helmer's make up guide indicates that the villain's wig was to be set low on his brow, because a high forehead indicated intelligence and breeding.

> If an actor has to play the part of a villain, he cannot very well do it in a wig with a high, lofty forehead, but

must wear a forbidding, low-browed one, indicating the assumed character at a glance.[23]

The eyebrows were also an important physiognomic clue to character. Lombroso wrote that bushy, dark eyebrows—especially those which met across the bridge of the nose—denoted a criminal temperament. Robertson's description of the "heavy man" indicates that the actor applied black eyebrows, and Helmer gives us some indication of how this was done.

> To paste a piece in, so as to make the brows meet, adds to the sternness and gives an expression of low cunning to the countenance. To paste a long, heavy and bushy strip low on, or under, the eyebrows, will give a forbidding expression to the eyes: an effect, together with that of the brows meeting, to be especially studied by artists who would like to represent villains effectively.[24]

Though crepe hair was the recommended material for creating moustaches and beards, some actors resorted to burnt cork to create the illusion of dark facial hair. Olive Logan writes in *Before the Footlights and Behind the Scenes* (1870) that it was a common habit for actors to make whiskers and moustaches with burnt cork, a method she considered to be "an idle, filthy mode—involving too, the danger of transferring your lip ornaments to the cheek of a lady if it be necessary in the scene to salute her".[25]

Criminal physiognomists and actors seemed to agree on at least three signs of criminality: dark coloring, dark hair and moustache, and a heavily lined face. Even when the same actor was cast as both villain and hero, as Henry Irving was in *The Lyons Mail* (1877), the necessary minor changes in make-up seem still to have resulted in darker coloring and more "wrinkles". In a sketch by Branbsy Williams one can see this clearly in the superimposed images of Irving as Dubosc and as Lesurques.[26] Can we assume that the actor's make-up conventions were influenced by Lombroso and the other physiognomists? It is tempting to think so, but before establishing a correlation between the two, it is important to remember that British actors had codified their signs of villainy years before Lombroso was even born. "Gentleman" William Smith (1730-1819), a leading man at both Covent Garden and Drury Lane, included among his proudest accomplishments the fact that "he had never blacked his face",[27] and Mr. O. Smith, the actor who made his career playing villains of the "deepest dye", had been dead for twenty years when Lombroso wrote his first treatise on criminal physiognomy. Under these circumstances, one is left to ponder whether the criminologists may have been drawing their physiognomic conclusions from the well established conventions of the theatre.

Obviously I do not posit a direct correlation, but it seems clear that through the circulation and recirculation of criminal "characteristics" between scientists, actors, and the public, a common understanding of what was "suspicious" and villainous in the culture was formed and reaffirmed. Through instruction, experience and observation, Victorians learned to recognize the darker, read "foreign", face of villainy. Though some of the Victorian villains were undoubtedly English, many like Mariano Mariani, the bandit unmasked by Lavater, were unmistakably aliens. Though this essay has focused on the male villain, it is interesting to note that Jerome K. Jerome in *Stage-Land: Curious Habits and Customs of its Inhabitants,* humorously describes the Adventuress as "generally of foreign extraction. They do not make bad women in England, the article is entirely of continental manufacture, and has to be imported".[28]

The strange case of *Dr. Jekyll and Mr. Hyde* marks the shifting boundaries between the theatrical and nontheatrical understanding of villainy as manifested in the physiognomy of the criminal. Richard Mansfield's production of *Dr. Jekyll and Mr. Hyde* opened in London on 4 August 1888 to very positive reviews; the British audiences were thrilled and horrified by Mansfield's seemingly impossible on-stage transformations from the outstanding doctor into the hideously evil Hyde. According to contemporaneous reports, men screamed and women were carried fainting from the theatre. Mansfield's biographer Paul Wilstach writes:

> Everyone speculated on the secret of the transformations which they saw yet could not believe. He was accused of using acids, phosphorus, all manner of chemicals . . . some declared it perfectly simple—he uses a rubber suit which he inflates and exhausts at pleasure. Mansfield told the simple fact that his only change was in the muscles of his face and the tones of his yielding voice, and the posture of his body.[29]

Here the actor had learned to subvert physiognomy and exploit it at the same time. He relied on the ugliness of Hyde to bespeak his evil character but he also showed that Hyde's was the very same face and body of the respectable Doctor Jekyll. On one level the sign "appearance" was recognizable and stable but on a deeper level it became volatile and unreadable. How could one trust appearance if a man could make the image of a person other than himself materialize before the eyes of ordinary people without aid of makeup or costume change? The notion that the criminal impulses, or nature, of a man might be concealed under a perfectly "normal" exterior, subverted the whole notion of Lombrosian criminology, though Planché's Lavater had warned of such a phenomenon.

Three weeks into Mansfield's run, Mary Ann Nichols, the first victim of Jack the Ripper was found in Whitechapel. One week later a second victim, Annie Chapman, was found mutilated in a bricked-in Whitechapel yard. Suddenly, London "walked in terror".[30] The Ripper's invisibility, and almost miraculous ability to escape detection led to wild speculation on the part of the public and the police at Scotland Yard. One of the first people to come under suspicion was Mansfield, the actor who could seemingly transform himself at will. Harry Geduld writes:

> The sudden bloodbath galvanized London. The police were deluged with names of suspects, and high on the list was Richard Mansfield . . . [one of] Mansfield's anonymous accusers claimed that no man could disguise himself so well and that, since Mansfield worked himself up into such a frenzy on-stage, he probably did the real life murders too.[31]

Although the public was suspicious, it is not clear if Mansfield was ever questioned by the police; however authorities did entertain the theory that the murderer had been inspired by the actor's performance. Police began to refer to the Ripper as a "real life Jekyll and Hyde", and though it will never be known whether the killer ever saw the play, the Jekyll and Hyde story and the Ripper case quickly became inextricably confused in the popular imagination.[32] This conflation of fact and fiction has been perpetuated by twentieth century film versions of the story which make Hyde an abuser and killer of prostitutes—Stevenson's original story has no women in it.[33]

In deference to public opinion Richard Mansfield withdrew his production of *Dr. Jekyll and Mr. Hyde* from the Lyceum in October after a run of only ten weeks. The *Daily Telegraph* wrote: "Mr. Richard Mansfield has determined to abandon the 'creepy drama' evidently beloved in America, in favour of a wholesome comedy . . . Experience has taught this clever young actor that there is no taste in London just now for horrors on the stage. There is quite sufficient to make us shudder out of doors".[34]

The figure of Jack the Ripper embodies the nationalist prejudice in Victorian criminology as well as the unstable boundaries between the theatrical and non-theatrical conceptions of villainy. Historian Tom Cullen interviewed Whitechapel residents seventy years after the Ripper murders, and he found that the perception of Jack the Ripper which East Londoners retained "is straight out of Victorian melodrama—he is the waxen-moustached villain of *Maria Marten*".[35] The image that lingers today is the same image Londoners had of the Ripper in 1888 when residents believed the killer was a dark and swarthy foreigner, probably from the Mediterranean countries.[36] They held this belief despite the fact that the only eyewitness identification considered reliable by the police—a man seen clearly with the fourth victim ten minutes before her body was found—described the killer as a man about thirty years of age with a fair complexion and a small fair moustache.[37]

George Hutchinson, a retired night watchman, claimed to have seen the Ripper with his fifth victim at about two o'clock in the morning, just a few hours before her mutilated body was discovered in her lodgings. Hutchinson said the man was wearing "a long dark coat trimmed with astrakhan, a white collar and a black necktie, in which was fixed a horseshoe pin . . . he also wore a massive gold watch chain from which hung a seal with a red stone". Hutchinson further described the Ripper as a man about thirty-five years old, five feet, six inches tall, with a dark complexion, bushy eyebrows and a moustache that curled up at the ends. He added that the man definitely looked like a foreigner.[38] This might just as well have been a description of the Victorian stage villain.

Undoubtedly the press contributed to the conflation of the stage villain with Jack the Ripper. One broadsheet, hoping to beat its competitors to the street, actually illustrated its report of the double murder (the third and fourth victims were killed on the same night) with a stock woodcut from a melodrama which showed a villain about to strike a prostrate woman lying at his feet.[39] It is not surprising that the public, unable to fix a face to the criminal among them, fixated on the type of face they had learned to recognize as villainous. They saw this face in the theatre, in the newspapers, and in the popular physiognomic treatises of their day; it circulated throughout the culture, authenticating itself with every repetition.

Elizabeth Burns, writing in 1972, observed that "Actors model social conventions in use at a specific time and in a specific place or milieu" and that their conventions "suggest a total and external code of values and norms of conduct from which the speech and action of the play are drawn". This external code of values, culturally negotiated and understood, functions to "authenticate the play".[40] In turn, I would argue that the stage conventions of the nineteenth-century served to authenticate an external code of values, reinscribing the notion that criminality, and murderous impulses were the natural character traits of the dark skinned foreigner. *Dr. Jekyll and Mr. Hyde,* which metaphorically suggested the possibility that unconscious psychological motives might compel an otherwise "respectable" man to commit a heinous crime, was withdrawn after ten weeks on the London stage. Perhaps the public was not ready to accept the idea that the seeds of criminality may be present in everyone.

One final image from the Ripper saga seems to exemplify the strange fusion of crime on and off the nineteenth-century stage. Two days after the last victim was found, a man stood on the corner of Wentworth and Commercial Street shouting "I am Jack the Ripper!" He had blackened his face with burnt cork, the standard make-up for Victorian stage villains, and drawn rings of white around his eyes. Police arrested him, but he was soon released. Three weeks later his body was pulled from the Thames, the black burnt cork "hideously evident" on his decomposing features.[41]

Notes

1. Michael G. Ketcham, "The Arts of Gesture: The *Spectator* and Its Relationship to Physiognomy, Painting and the Theater", *Modern Language Quarterly,* June 1981, 42 (2), 115.

2. J. R. Planché, *Not a Bad Judge; or Lavater the Physiognomist,* London, 1848, 30.

3. Michael Shortland, "The Power of a Thousand Eyes: Johann Caspar Lavater's Science of Physiognomical Perception", *Criticism,* 1986, 28 (4), 388.

4. Joseph Simms, *Physiognomy Illustrated, or, Natures Revelations of Character,* New York, 1889, 265

5. Shortland, 383.

6. Cesare Lombroso, *Criminal Man: According to the Classification of Cesare Lombroso,* New York, 1911, 8.

7. Chance Newton, *Crime and the Drama, or, Dark Deeds Dramatized,* London, 1927, 96.

8. Samuel Wells, *The New Physiognomy, or, Signs of Character,* New York, 1887, 38.

9. Watts Phillips, *Ticket of Leave,* London, 1862, 12.

10. Nicola Helmer, *Actor's Make Up Book,* New York, 1888, 46.

11. Louis Dubroca, *L'Art de lire à haute voix* (Paris, 1824) quoted in "Idealization of Characters and Specialization of Acting in Eighteenth Century Tragedy: The Villain" by Jeanette Massy-Westropp, in *Theatre Research International,* 9 (2), Summer 1984, 121.

12. W. E. Suter, *The Felon's Bond,* London, 1859, 27.

13. Helmer, 63.

14. Twynihoe William Erle, *Letters from a Theatrical Scene-Painter,* London, 1880, 48.

15. Ibid., 93-94.

16. There is no record of a play by this name in Nicoll. It is quite possible that Erle was referring to W. E. Suter's *The Robber of the Pyrenees* that opened at the Royal Effingham on 22 September, 1862.

17. Erle, 12.

18. Gilbert B. Cross, *Next Week, East Lynne: Domestic Drama in performance 1820-1874,* London, 1977, 118.

19. Jerome K. Jerome, *On the Stage and Off: The Brief Career of a Would-be-Actor,* 1885, reprinted Wolfeboro Falls, USA, and Stroud, Gloucestershire, 1991, 3.

20. John Coleman, *Fifty Years of an Actor's Life,* London, 1904, 114.

21. Tom Robertson, "Theatrical Types. No. X: Heavy Men and Character Parts", *Illustrated Times,* 26 June 1864.

22. James C. Burge, *Lines of Business: Casting Practice and Policy in the American Theatre 1752-1899,* New York, 1986, 102.

23. Helmer, 11.

24. Ibid., 35-36.

25. Olive Logan, *Before the Footlights and Behind the Scenes: A Book About "The Show Business" in all its Branches,* Philadelphia, 1870, 87.

26. Denis Salter, "Henry Irving, the 'Dr. Freud' of Melodrama", in *Themes in Drama, Number 14: Melodrama,* edited by James Redmond, Cambridge, 1992, 173.

27. *The Concise Oxford Companion to the Theatre,* Entry on William Smith, 472.

28. Jerome K. Jerome, *Stage-Land: Curious Habits and Customs of the Inhabitants,* New York, 1890, 71.

29. Paul Wilstach, *Richard Mansfield: The Man and Actor,* (1908) quoted in The *Definitive Dr. Jekyll and Mr. Hyde Companion,* edited by Harry Geduld, New York, 1983, 161.

30. Tom A. Cullen, *When London Walked in Terror,* Boston, 1965.

31. Geduld, 6.

32. Ibid., 7.

33. Except for a young match girl who is trampled by Hyde as he crosses the street.

34. Cullen, 104.

35. Ibid., 8.

36. Ibid., 235.

37. Ibid., 241.

38. Ibid., 202.

39. Ibid., photo opposite 147.

40. Elizabeth Burns, *Theatricality,* New York, 1972, 32.

41. Cullen, 207.

FURTHER READING

Criticism

Hollington, Michael. "Dickens, 'Phiz' and Physiognomy." In *Imagination on a Long Rein: English Literature Illustrated*, edited by Joachim Möller, pp. 125-35. Marburg, Germany: Jonas, 1988.

> "[Shows] the potential value, as an aid to the reading of the intersections of text and illustration in Dickens's novels, of an awareness of physiognomy and its tradition, in particular its development from the theories of Lavater into one of the popular sciences of the nineteenth century."

————. "Monstrous Faces: Physiognomy in *Barnaby Rudge*." *Dickens Quarterly* 8, no. 1 (March 1991): 6-15.

> Centers on the "grotesque or monstrous faces and surfaces" in Barnaby Rudge to illustrate the impact of physiognomy on the novel.

————. "Physiognomy in *Hard Times*." *Dickens Quarterly* 9, no. 2 (June 1992): 58-66.

> "[Explores] the extent and significance of the attention paid to the external appearance of people and things in Hard Times."

————. "The Live Hieroglyphic: *Physiologie* and Physiognomy in *Martin Chuzzlewit*." *Dickens Quarterly* 10, no. 1 (March 1993): 57-68.

> Traces Dickens's thoughts on and treatment of physiognomy and other popular "scientific" theories of the nineteenth century as evidenced in Dickens's novel Martin Chuzzlewit.

Shookman, Ellis, ed., *The Faces of Physiognomy: Interdisciplinary Approaches to Johann Caspar Lavater*. Columbia, S.C.: Camden House, 1993, 192 p.

> Collection of essays on Johann Caspar Lavater's physiognomic theories, and the influence of Lavater's physiognomy on the works of nineteenth-century authors and artists.

Stoehr, Taylor. "Physiognomy and Phrenology in Hawthorne." *Huntington Library Quarterly* 37, no. 4 (August 1974): 355-400.

> Surveys references to phrenology and physiognomy in Nathaniel Hawthorne's works.

Tytler, Graeme. "Physiognomy in Stendhal's Novels: 'La Science de Lavater' or 'Croyez après cela aux physionomies'?" *Studia Romanica et Anglica Zagrabiensia* 39 (1994): 59-76.

> Scholarly analysis of Stendhal's interpretation of the physiognomic theories of Johann Caspar Lavater and of Stendhal's narrative emphasis upon his characters' perceptions of one another.

How to Use This Index

The main references

> **Calvino, Italo**
> 1923-1985 .... CLC 5, 8, 11, 22, 33, 39,
> 73; SSC 3, 48

list all author entries in the following Gale Literary Criticism series:

AAL = *Asian American Literature*
BG = *The Beat Generation: A Gale Critical Companion*
BLC = *Black Literature Criticism*
BLCS = *Black Literature Criticism Supplement*
CLC = *Contemporary Literary Criticism*
CLR = *Children's Literature Review*
CMLC = *Classical and Medieval Literature Criticism*
DC = *Drama Criticism*
FL = *Feminism in Literature: A Gale Critical Companion*
GL = *Gothic Literature: A Gale Critical Companion*
HLC = *Hispanic Literature Criticism*
HLCS = *Hispanic Literature Criticism Supplement*
HR = *Harlem Renaissance: A Gale Critical Companion*
LC = *Literature Criticism from 1400 to 1800*
NCLC = *Nineteenth-Century Literature Criticism*
NNAL = *Native North American Literature*
PC = *Poetry Criticism*
SSC = *Short Story Criticism*
TCLC = *Twentieth-Century Literary Criticism*
WLC = *World Literature Criticism, 1500 to the Present*
WLCS = *World Literature Criticism Supplement*

The cross-references

> See also CA 85-88, 116; CANR 23, 61;
> DAM NOV; DLB 196; EW 13; MTCW 1, 2;
> RGSF 2; RGWL 2; SFW 4; SSFS 12

list all author entries in the following Gale biographical and literary sources:

AAYA = *Authors & Artists for Young Adults*
AFAW = *African American Writers*
AFW = *African Writers*
AITN = *Authors in the News*
AMW = *American Writers*
AMWR = *American Writers Retrospective Supplement*
AMWS = *American Writers Supplement*
ANW = *American Nature Writers*
AW = *Ancient Writers*
BEST = *Bestsellers*
BPFB = *Beacham's Encyclopedia of Popular Fiction: Biography and Resources*
BRW = *British Writers*
BRWS = *British Writers Supplement*
BW = *Black Writers*
BYA = *Beacham's Guide to Literature for Young Adults*
CA = *Contemporary Authors*
CAAS = *Contemporary Authors Autobiography Series*
CABS = *Contemporary Authors Bibliographical Series*
CAD = *Contemporary American Dramatists*
CANR = *Contemporary Authors New Revision Series*
CAP = *Contemporary Authors Permanent Series*
CBD = *Contemporary British Dramatists*
CCA = *Contemporary Canadian Authors*
CD = *Contemporary Dramatists*
CDALB = *Concise Dictionary of American Literary Biography*

CDALBS = *Concise Dictionary of American Literary Biography Supplement*
CDBLB = *Concise Dictionary of British Literary Biography*
CMW = *St. James Guide to Crime & Mystery Writers*
CN = *Contemporary Novelists*
CP = *Contemporary Poets*
CPW = *Contemporary Popular Writers*
CSW = *Contemporary Southern Writers*
CWD = *Contemporary Women Dramatists*
CWP = *Contemporary Women Poets*
CWRI = *St. James Guide to Children's Writers*
CWW = *Contemporary World Writers*
DA = *DISCovering Authors*
DA3 = *DISCovering Authors 3.0*
DAB = *DISCovering Authors: British Edition*
DAC = *DISCovering Authors: Canadian Edition*
DAM = *DISCovering Authors: Modules*
    DRAM: *Dramatists Module;* **MST:** *Most-studied Authors Module;*
    MULT: *Multicultural Authors Module;* **NOV:** *Novelists Module;*
    POET: *Poets Module;* **POP:** *Popular Fiction and Genre Authors Module*
DFS = *Drama for Students*
DLB = *Dictionary of Literary Biography*
DLBD = *Dictionary of Literary Biography Documentary Series*
DLBY = *Dictionary of Literary Biography Yearbook*
DNFS = *Literature of Developing Nations for Students*
EFS = *Epics for Students*
EW = *European Writers*
EWL = *Encyclopedia of World Literature in the 20th Century*
EXPN = *Exploring Novels*
EXPP = *Exploring Poetry*
EXPS = *Exploring Short Stories*
FANT = *St. James Guide to Fantasy Writers*
FW = *Feminist Writers*
GFL = *Guide to French Literature,* Beginnings to 1789, 1798 to the Present
GLL = *Gay and Lesbian Literature*
HGG = *St. James Guide to Horror, Ghost & Gothic Writers*
HW = *Hispanic Writers*
IDFW = *International Dictionary of Films and Filmmakers: Writers and Production Artists*
IDTP = *International Dictionary of Theatre: Playwrights*
LAIT = *Literature and Its Times*
LAW = *Latin American Writers*
JRDA = *Junior DISCovering Authors*
MAICYA = *Major Authors and Illustrators for Children and Young Adults*
MAICYAS = *Major Authors and Illustrators for Children and Young Adults Supplement*
MAWW = *Modern American Women Writers*
MJW = *Modern Japanese Writers*
MTCW = *Major 20th-Century Writers*
NCFS = *Nonfiction Classics for Students*
NFS = *Novels for Students*
PAB = *Poets: American and British*
PFS = *Poetry for Students*
RGAL = *Reference Guide to American Literature*
RGEL = *Reference Guide to English Literature*
RGSF = *Reference Guide to Short Fiction*
RGWL = *Reference Guide to World Literature*
RHW = *Twentieth-Century Romance and Historical Writers*
SAAS = *Something about the Author Autobiography Series*
SATA = *Something about the Author*
SFW = *St. James Guide to Science Fiction Writers*
SSFS = *Short Stories for Students*
TCWW = *Twentieth-Century Western Writers*
WLIT = *World Literature and Its Times*
WP = *World Poets*
YABC = *Yesterday's Authors of Books for Children*
YAW = *St. James Guide to Young Adult Writers*

Literary Criticism Series
Cumulative Author Index

Alexander, Barbara
    See Ehrenreich, Barbara
Alexander, Lloyd 1924-2007 .... **CLC 35**
    See also AAYA 1, 27; BPFB 1; BYA 5, 6,
    7, 9, 10, 11; CA 1-4R; 260; CANR 1, 24,
    38, 55, 113; CLR 1, 5, 48; CWRI 5; DLB
    52; FANT; JRDA; MAICYA 1, 2; MAIC-
    YAS 1; MTCW 1; SAAS 19; SATA 3, 49,
    81, 129, 135; SATA-Obit 182; SUFW;
    TUS; WYA; YAW
Alexander, Lloyd Chudley
    See Alexander, Lloyd
Alexander, Meena 1951- .... **CLC 121**
    See also CA 115; CANR 38, 70, 146; CP 5,
    6, 7; CWP; DLB 323; FW
Alexander, Rae Pace
    See Alexander, Raymond Pace
Alexander, Raymond Pace
    1898-1974 .... **SSC 62**
    See also CA 97-100; SATA 22; SSFS 4
Alexander, Samuel 1859-1938 .... **TCLC 77**
Alexeiev, Konstantin
    See Stanislavsky, Constantin
Alexeyev, Constantin Sergeivich
    See Stanislavsky, Constantin
Alexeyev, Konstantin Sergeyevich
    See Stanislavsky, Constantin
Alexie, Sherman 1966- .... **CLC 96, 154;**
    NNAL; PC 53; SSC 107
    See also AAYA 28; BYA 15; CA 138;
    CANR 65, 95, 133, 174; CN 7; DA3;
    DAM MULT; DLB 175, 206, 278; LATS
    1:2; MTCW 2; MTFW 2005; NFS 17;
    SSFS 18
Alexie, Sherman Joseph, Jr.
    See Alexie, Sherman
al-Farabi 870(?)-950 .... **CMLC 58**
    See also DLB 115
Alfau, Felipe 1902-1999 .... **CLC 66**
    See also CA 137
Alfieri, Vittorio 1749-1803 .... **NCLC 101**
    See also EW 4; RGWL 2, 3; WLIT 7
Alfonso X 1221-1284 .... **CMLC 78**
Alfred, Jean Gaston
    See Ponge, Francis
Alger, Horatio, Jr. 1832-1899 .... **NCLC 8, 83**
    See also CLR 87; DLB 42; LAIT 2; RGAL
    4; SATA 16; TUS
Al-Ghazali, Muhammad ibn Muhammad
    1058-1111 .... **CMLC 50**
    See also DLB 115
Algren, Nelson 1909-1981 ..... **CLC 4, 10, 33;**
    SSC 33
    See also AMWS 9; BPFB 1; CA 13-16R;
    103; CANR 20, 61; CDALB 1941-1968;
    CN 1, 2; DLB 9; DLBY 1981, 1982,
    2000; EWL 3; MAL 5; MTCW 1, 2;
    MTFW 2005; RGAL 4; RGSF 2
al-Hamadhani 967-1007 .... **CMLC 93**
    See also WLIT 6
al-Hariri, al-Qasim ibn 'Ali Abu
    Muhammad al-Basri
    1054-1122 .... **CMLC 63**
    See also RGWL 3
Ali, Ahmed 1908-1998 .... **CLC 69**
    See also CA 25-28R; CANR 15, 34; CN 1,
    2, 3, 4, 5; DLB 323; EWL 3
Ali, Tariq 1943- .... **CLC 173**
    See also CA 25-28R; CANR 10, 99, 161
Alighieri, Dante
    See Dante
al-Kindi, Abu Yusuf Ya'qub ibn Ishaq c.
    801-c. 873 .... **CMLC 80**
Allan, John B.
    See Westlake, Donald E.
Allan, Sidney
    See Hartmann, Sadakichi
Allan, Sydney
    See Hartmann, Sadakichi

Allard, Janet .... **CLC 59**
Allen, Betsy
    See Harrison, Elizabeth (Allen) Cavanna
Allen, Edward 1948- .... **CLC 59**
Allen, Fred 1894-1956 .... **TCLC 87**
Allen, Paula Gunn 1939-2008 . **CLC 84, 202;**
    NNAL
    See also AMWS 4; CA 112; 143; 272;
    CANR 63, 130; CWP; DA3; DAM
    MULT; DLB 175; FW; MTCW 2; MTFW
    2005; RGAL 4; TCWW 2
Allen, Roland
    See Ayckbourn, Alan
Allen, Sarah A.
    See Hopkins, Pauline Elizabeth
Allen, Sidney H.
    See Hartmann, Sadakichi
Allen, Woody 1935- .... **CLC 16, 52, 195**
    See also AAYA 10, 51; AMWS 15; CA 33-
    36R; CANR 27, 38, 63, 128, 172; DAM
    POP; DLB 44; MTCW 1; SSFS 21
Allende, Isabel 1942- ... **CLC 39, 57, 97, 170,**
    264; HLC 1; SSC 65; WLCS
    See also AAYA 18, 70; CA 125; 130; CANR
    51, 74, 129, 165; CDWLB 3; CLR 99;
    CWW 2; DA3; DAM MULT; NOV; DLB
    145; DNFS 1; EWL 3; FL 1:5; FW; HW
    1, 2; INT CA-130; LAIT 5; LAWS 1;
    LMFS 2; MTCW 1, 2; MTFW 2005;
    NCFS 1; NFS 6, 18, 29; RGSF 2; RGWL
    3; SATA 163; SSFS 11, 16; WLIT 1
Alleyn, Ellen
    See Rossetti, Christina
Alleyne, Carla D. .... **CLC 65**
Allingham, Margery (Louise)
    1904-1966 .... **CLC 19**
    See also CA 5-8R; 25-28R; CANR 4, 58;
    CMW 4; DLB 77; MSW; MTCW 1, 2
Allingham, William 1824-1889 ...... **NCLC 25**
    See also DLB 35; RGEL 2
Allison, Dorothy E. 1949- .... **CLC 78, 153**
    See also AAYA 53; CA 140; CANR 66, 107;
    CN 7; CSW; DA3; FW; MTCW 2; MTFW
    2005; NFS 11; RGAL 4
Alloula, Malek .... **CLC 65**
Allston, Washington 1779-1843 .... **NCLC 2**
    See also DLB 1, 235
Almedingen, E. M.
    See Almedingen, Martha Edith von
Almedingen, Martha Edith von
    1898-1971 .... **CLC 12**
    See also CA 1-4R; CANR 1; SATA 3
Almodovar, Pedro 1949(?)- .... **CLC 114, 229;**
    HLCS 1
    See also CA 133; CANR 72, 151; HW 2
Almqvist, Carl Jonas Love
    1793-1866 .... **NCLC 42**
al-Mutanabbi, Ahmad ibn al-Husayn Abu
    al-Tayyib al-Jufi al-Kindi
    915-965 .... **CMLC 66**
    See also RGWL 3; WLIT 6
Alonso, Damaso 1898-1990 .... **CLC 14**
    See also CA 110; 131; 130; CANR 72; DLB
    108; EWL 3; HW 1, 2
Alov
    See Gogol, Nikolai (Vasilyevich)
al'Sadaawi, Nawal
    See El Saadawi, Nawal
al-Shaykh, Hanan 1945- .... **CLC 218**
    See also CA 135; CANR 111; CWW 2;
    DLB 346; EWL 3; WLIT 6
Al Siddik
    See Rolfe, Frederick (William Serafino Aus-
    tin Lewis Mary)
Alta 1942- .... **CLC 19**
    See also CA 57-60
Alter, Robert B. 1935- .... **CLC 34**
    See also CA 49-52; CANR 1, 47, 100, 160

Alter, Robert Bernard
    See Alter, Robert B.
Alther, Lisa 1944- .... **CLC 7, 41**
    See also BPFB 1; CA 65-68; CAAS 30;
    CANR 12, 30, 51, 180; CN 4, 5, 6, 7;
    CSW; GLL 2; MTCW 1
Althusser, L.
    See Althusser, Louis
Althusser, Louis 1918-1990 .... **CLC 106**
    See also CA 131; 132; CANR 102; DLB
    242
Altman, Robert 1925-2006 .... **CLC 16, 116,**
    242
    See also CA 73-76; 254; CANR 43
Alurista
    See Urista (Heredia), Alberto (Baltazar)
Alvarez, A. 1929- .... **CLC 5, 13**
    See also CA 1-4R; CANR 3, 33, 63, 101,
    134; CN 3, 4, 5, 6; CP 1, 2, 3, 4, 5, 6, 7;
    DLB 14, 40; MTFW 2005
Alvarez, Alejandro Rodriguez
    1903-1965 . **CLC 49; DC 32; TCLC 199**
    See also CA 131; 93-96; EWL 3; HW 1
Alvarez, Julia 1950- .. **CLC 93, 274; HLCS 1**
    See also AAYA 25; AMWS 7; CA 147;
    CANR 69, 101, 133, 166; DA3; DLB 282;
    LATS 1:2; LLW; MTCW 2; MTFW 2005;
    NFS 5, 9; SATA 129; SSFS 27; WLIT 1
Alvaro, Corrado 1896-1956 .... **TCLC 60**
    See also CA 163; DLB 264; EWL 3
Amado, Jorge 1912-2001 ... **CLC 13, 40, 106,**
    232; HLC 1
    See also CA 77-80; 201; CANR 35, 74, 135;
    CWW 2; DAM MULT; NOV; DLB 113,
    307; EWL 3; HW 2; LAW; LAWS 1;
    MTCW 1, 2; MTFW 2005; RGWL 2, 3;
    TWA; WLIT 1
Ambler, Eric 1909-1998 .... **CLC 4, 6, 9**
    See also BRWS 4; CA 9-12R; 171; CANR
    7, 38, 74; CMW 4; CN 1, 2, 3, 4, 5, 6;
    DLB 77; MSW; MTCW 1, 2; TEA
Ambrose c. 339-c. 397 .... **CMLC 103**
Ambrose, Stephen E. 1936-2002 .... **CLC 145**
    See also AAYA 44; CA 1-4R; 209; CANR
    3, 43, 57, 83, 105; MTFW 2005; NCFS 2;
    SATA 40, 138
Amichai, Yehuda 1924-2000 .. **CLC 9, 22, 57,**
    116; PC 38
    See also CA 85-88; 189; CANR 46, 60, 99,
    132; CWW 2; EWL 3; MTCW 1, 2;
    MTFW 2005; PFS 24; RGHL; WLIT 6
Amichai, Yehudah
    See Amichai, Yehuda
Amiel, Henri Frederic 1821-1881 .... **NCLC 4**
    See also DLB 217
Amis, Kingsley 1922-1995 . **CLC 1, 2, 3, 5, 8,**
    13, 40, 44, 129
    See also AAYA 77; AITN 2; BPFB 1;
    BRWS 2; CA 9-12R; 150; CANR 8, 28,
    54; CDBLB 1945-1960; CN 1, 2, 3, 4, 5,
    6; CP 1, 2, 3, 4; DA; DA3; DAB; DAC;
    DAM MST, NOV; DLB 15, 27, 100, 139,
    326; DLBY 1996; EWL 3; HGG; INT
    CANR-8; MTCW 1, 2; MTFW 2005;
    RGEL 2; RGSF 2; SFW 4
Amis, Martin 1949- ... **CLC 4, 9, 38, 62, 101,**
    213; SSC 112
    See also BEST 90:3; BRWS 4; CA 65-68;
    CANR 8, 27, 54, 73, 95, 132, 166; CN 5,
    6, 7; DA3; DLB 14, 194; EWL 3; INT
    CANR-27; MTCW 2; MTFW 2005
Amis, Martin Louis
    See Amis, Martin
Ammianus Marcellinus c. 330-c.
    395 .... **CMLC 60**
    See also AW 2; DLB 211

Ammons, A.R. 1926-2001 .. **CLC 2, 3, 5, 8, 9, 25, 57, 108; PC 16**
See also AITN 1; AMWS 7; CA 9-12R; 193; CANR 6, 36, 51, 73, 107, 156; CP 1, 2, 3, 4, 5, 6, 7; CSW; DAM POET; DLB 5, 165, 342; EWL 3; MAL 5; MTCW 1, 2; PFS 19; RGAL 4; TCLE 1:1

Ammons, Archie Randolph
See Ammons, A.R.

Amo, Tauraatua i
See Adams, Henry (Brooks)

Amory, Thomas 1691(?)-1788 .... **LC 48**
See also DLB 39

Anand, Mulk Raj 1905-2004 ..... **CLC 23, 93, 237**
See also CA 65-68; 231; CANR 32, 64; CN 1, 2, 3, 4, 5, 6, 7; DAM NOV; DLB 323; EWL 3; MTCW 1, 2; MTFW 2005; RGSF 2

Anatol
See Schnitzler, Arthur

Anaximander c. 611B.C.-c. 546B.C. .... **CMLC 22**

Anaya, Rudolfo A. 1937- . **CLC 23, 148, 255; HLC 1**
See also AAYA 20; BYA 13; CA 45-48; CAAS 4; CANR 1, 32, 51, 124, 169; CLR 129; CN 4, 5, 6, 7; DAM MULT, NOV; DLB 82, 206, 278; HW 1; LAIT 4; LLW; MAL 5; MTCW 1, 2; MTFW 2005; NFS 12; RGAL 4; RGSF 2; TCWW 2; WLIT 1

Anaya, Rudolpho Alfonso
See Anaya, Rudolfo A.

Andersen, Hans Christian 1805-1875 .... **NCLC 7, 79; SSC 6, 56; WLC 1**
See also AAYA 57; CLR 6, 113; DA; DA3; DAB; DAC; DAM MST, POP; EW 6; MAICYA 1, 2; RGSF 2; RGWL 2, 3; SATA 100; TWA; WCH; YABC 1

Anderson, C. Farley
See Mencken, H(enry) L(ouis); Nathan, George Jean

Anderson, Jessica (Margaret) Queale 1916- .... **CLC 37**
See also CA 9-12R; CANR 4, 62; CN 4, 5, 6, 7; DLB 325

Anderson, Jon (Victor) 1940- .... **CLC 9**
See also CA 25-28R; CANR 20; CP 1, 3, 4, 5; DAM POET

Anderson, Lindsay (Gordon) 1923-1994 .... **CLC 20**
See also CA 125; 128; 146; CANR 77

Anderson, Maxwell 1888-1959 .... **TCLC 2, 144**
See also CA 105; 152; DAM DRAM; DFS 16, 20; DLB 7, 228; MAL 5; MTCW 2; MTFW 2005; RGAL 4

Anderson, Poul 1926-2001 .... **CLC 15**
See also AAYA 5, 34; BPFB 1; BYA 6, 8, 9; CA 1-4R, 181; 199; CAAE 181; CAAS 2; CANR 2, 15, 34, 64, 110; CLR 58; DLB 8; FANT; INT CANR-15; MTCW 1, 2; MTFW 2005; SATA 90; SATA-Brief 39; SATA-Essay 106; SCFW 1, 2; SFW 4; SUFW 1, 2

Anderson, Robert 1917-2009 .... **CLC 23**
See also AITN 1; CA 21-24R; CANR 32; CD 6; DAM DRAM; DLB 7; LAIT 5

Anderson, Robert Woodruff
See Anderson, Robert

Anderson, Roberta Joan
See Mitchell, Joni

Anderson, Sherwood 1876-1941 ... **SSC 1, 46, 91; TCLC 1, 10, 24, 123; WLC 1**
See also AAYA 30; AMW; AMWC 2; BPFB 1; CA 104; 121; CANR 61; CDALB 1917-1929; DA; DA3; DAB; DAC; DAM MST, NOV; DLB 4, 9, 86; DLBD 1; EWL

3; EXPS; GLL 2; MAL 5; MTCW 1, 2; MTFW 2005; NFS 4; RGAL 4; RGSF 2; SSFS 4, 10, 11; TUS

Anderson, Wes 1969- .... **CLC 227**
See also CA 214

Andier, Pierre
See Desnos, Robert

Andouard
See Giraudoux, Jean(-Hippolyte)

Andrade, Carlos Drummond de
See Drummond de Andrade, Carlos

Andrade, Mario de
See de Andrade, Mario

Andreae, Johann V(alentin) 1586-1654 .... **LC 32**
See also DLB 164

Andreas Capellanus fl. c. 1185- .... **CMLC 45**
See also DLB 208

Andreas-Salome, Lou 1861-1937 ... **TCLC 56**
See also CA 178; DLB 66

Andreev, Leonid
See Andreyev, Leonid (Nikolaevich)

Andress, Lesley
See Sanders, Lawrence

Andrew, Joseph Maree
See Occomy, Marita (Odette) Bonner

Andrewes, Lancelot 1555-1626 .... **LC 5**
See also DLB 151, 172

Andrews, Cicily Fairfield
See West, Rebecca

Andrews, Elton V.
See Pohl, Frederik

Andrews, Peter
See Soderbergh, Steven

Andrews, Raymond 1934-1991 .... **BLC 2:1**
See also BW 2; CA 81-84; 136; CANR 15, 42

Andreyev, Leonid (Nikolaevich) 1871-1919 .... **TCLC 3**
See also CA 104; 185; DLB 295; EWL 3

Andrezel, Pierre
See Blixen, Karen (Christentze Dinesen)

Andric, Ivo 1892-1975 .... **CLC 8; SSC 36; TCLC 135**
See also CA 81-84; 57-60; CANR 43, 60; CDWLB 4; DLB 147, 329; EW 11; EWL 3; MTCW 1; RGSF 2; RGWL 2, 3

Androvar
See Prado (Calvo), Pedro

Angela of Foligno 1248(?)-1309 .... **CMLC 76**

Angelique, Pierre
See Bataille, Georges

Angell, Judie
See Angell, Judie

Angell, Judie 1937- .... **CLC 30**
See also AAYA 11, 71; BYA 6; CA 77-80; CANR 49; CLR 33; JRDA; SATA 22, 78; WYA; YAW

Angell, Roger 1920- .... **CLC 26**
See also CA 57-60; CANR 13, 44, 70, 144; DLB 171, 185

Angelou, Maya 1928- ...... **BLC 1:1; CLC 12, 35, 64, 77, 155; PC 32; WLCS**
See also AAYA 7, 20; AMWS 4; BPFB 1; BW 2, 3; BYA 2; CA 65-68; CANR 19, 42, 65, 111, 133; CDALBS; CLR 53; CP 4, 5, 6, 7; CPW; CSW; CWP; DA; DA3; DAB; DAC; DAM MST, MULT, POET, POP; DLB 38; EWL 3; EXPN; EXPP; FL 1:5; LAIT 4; MAICYA 2; MAICYAS 1; MAL 5; MBL; MTCW 1, 2; MTFW 2005; NCFS 2; NFS 2; PFS 2, 3; RGAL 4; SATA 49, 136; TCLE 1:1; WYA; YAW

Angouleme, Marguerite d'
See de Navarre, Marguerite

Anna Comnena 1083-1153 .... **CMLC 25**

Annensky, Innokentii Fedorovich
See Annensky, Innokenty (Fyodorovich)

Annensky, Innokenty (Fyodorovich) 1856-1909 .... **TCLC 14**
See also CA 110; 155; DLB 295; EWL 3

Annunzio, Gabriele d'
See D'Annunzio, Gabriele

Anodos
See Coleridge, Mary E(lizabeth)

Anon, Charles Robert
See Pessoa, Fernando

Anouilh, Jean 1910-1987 ..... **CLC 1, 3, 8, 13, 40, 50; DC 8, 21; TCLC 195**
See also AAYA 67; CA 17-20R; 123; CANR 32; DAM DRAM; DFS 9, 10, 19; DLB 321; EW 13; EWL 3; GFL 1789 to the Present; MTCW 1, 2; MTFW 2005; RGWL 2, 3; TWA

Ansa, Tina McElroy 1949- .... **BLC 2:1**
See also BW 2; CA 142; CANR 143; CSW

Anselm of Canterbury 1033(?)-1109 .... **CMLC 67**
See also DLB 115

Anthony, Florence
See Ai

Anthony, John
See Ciardi, John (Anthony)

Anthony, Peter
See Shaffer, Anthony; Shaffer, Peter

Anthony, Piers 1934- .... **CLC 35**
See also AAYA 11, 48; BYA 7; CA 200; CAAE 200; CANR 28, 56, 73, 102, 133; CLR 118; CPW; DAM POP; DLB 8; FANT; MAICYA 2; MAICYAS 1; MTCW 1, 2; MTFW 2005; SAAS 22; SATA 84, 129; SATA-Essay 129; SFW 4; SUFW 1, 2; YAW

Anthony, Susan B(rownell) 1820-1906 .... **TCLC 84**
See also CA 211; FW

Antiphon c. 480B.C.-c. 411B.C. .... **CMLC 55**

Antoine, Marc
See Proust, (Valentin-Louis-George-Eugene) Marcel

Antoninus, Brother
See Everson, William (Oliver)

Antonioni, Michelangelo 1912-2007 .... **CLC 20, 144, 259**
See also CA 73-76; 262; CANR 45, 77

Antschel, Paul 1920-1970 .... **CLC 10, 19, 53, 82; PC 10**
See also CA 85-88; CANR 33, 61; CDWLB 2; DLB 69; EWL 3; MTCW 1; PFS 21; RGHL; RGWL 2, 3

Anwar, Chairil 1922-1949 .... **TCLC 22**
See also CA 121; 219; EWL 3; RGWL 3

Anyidoho, Kofi 1947- .... **BLC 2:1**
See also BW 3; CA 178; CP 5, 6, 7; DLB 157; EWL 3

Anzaldua, Gloria (Evanjelina) 1942-2004 .... **CLC 200; HLCS 1**
See also CA 175; 227; CSW; CWP; DLB 122; FW; LLW; RGAL 4; SATA-Obit 154

Apess, William 1798-1839(?) .... **NCLC 73; NNAL**
See also DAM MULT; DLB 175, 243

Apollinaire, Guillaume 1880-1918 .... **PC 7; TCLC 3, 8, 51**
See also CA 104; 152; DAM POET; DLB 258, 321; EW 9; EWL 3; GFL 1789 to the Present; MTCW 2; PFS 24; RGWL 2, 3; TWA; WP

Apollonius of Rhodes
See Apollonius Rhodius

Apollonius Rhodius c. 300B.C.-c. 220B.C. .... **CMLC 28**
See also AW 1; DLB 176; RGWL 2, 3

Bacon, Francis 1561-1626 ..... **LC 18, 32, 131**
See also BRW 1; CDBLB Before 1660;
DLB 151, 236, 252; RGEL 2; TEA

Bacon, Roger 1214(?)-1294 ... **CMLC 14, 108**
See also DLB 115

Bacovia, George 1881-1957 .... **TCLC 24**
See also CA 123; 189; CDWLB 4; DLB
220; EWL 3

Badanes, Jerome 1937-1995 .... **CLC 59**
See also CA 234

Bage, Robert 1728-1801 .... **NCLC 182**
See also DLB 39; RGEL 2

Bagehot, Walter 1826-1877 .... **NCLC 10**
See also DLB 55

Bagnold, Enid 1889-1981 .... **CLC 25**
See also AAYA 75; BYA 2; CA 5-8R; 103;
CANR 5, 40; CBD; CN 2; CWD; CWRI
5; DAM DRAM; DLB 13, 160, 191, 245;
FW; MAICYA 1, 2; RGEL 2; SATA 1, 25

Bagritsky, Eduard
See Dzyubin, Eduard Georgievich

Bagritsky, Edvard
See Dzyubin, Eduard Georgievich

Bagrjana, Elisaveta
See Belcheva, Elisaveta Lyubomirova

Bagryana, Elisaveta
See Belcheva, Elisaveta Lyubomirova

Bailey, Paul 1937- .... **CLC 45**
See also CA 21-24R; CANR 16, 62, 124;
CN 1, 2, 3, 4, 5, 6, 7; DLB 14, 271; GLL
2

Baillie, Joanna 1762-1851 ...... **NCLC 71, 151**
See also DLB 93, 344; GL 2; RGEL 2

Bainbridge, Beryl 1934- ...... **CLC 4, 5, 8, 10,
14, 18, 22, 62, 130**
See also BRWS 6; CA 21-24R; CANR 24,
55, 75, 88, 128; CN 2, 3, 4, 5, 6, 7; DAM
NOV; DLB 14, 231; EWL 3; MTCW 1,
2; MTFW 2005

Baker, Carlos (Heard)
1909-1987 .... **TCLC 119**
See also CA 5-8R; 122; CANR 3, 63; DLB
103

Baker, Elliott 1922-2007 .... **CLC 8**
See also CA 45-48; 257; CANR 2, 63; CN
1, 2, 3, 4, 5, 6, 7

Baker, Elliott Joseph
See Baker, Elliott

Baker, Jean H.
See Russell, George William

Baker, Nicholson 1957- .... **CLC 61, 165**
See also AMWS 13; CA 135; CANR 63,
120, 138; CN 6; CPW; DA3; DAM POP;
DLB 227; MTFW 2005

Baker, Ray Stannard 1870-1946 .... **TCLC 47**
See also CA 118; DLB 345

Baker, Russell 1925- .... **CLC 31**
See also BEST 89:4; CA 57-60; CANR 11,
41, 59, 137; MTCW 1, 2; MTFW 2005

Bakhtin, M.
See Bakhtin, Mikhail Mikhailovich

Bakhtin, M. M.
See Bakhtin, Mikhail Mikhailovich

Bakhtin, Mikhail
See Bakhtin, Mikhail Mikhailovich

Bakhtin, Mikhail Mikhailovich
1895-1975 .... **CLC 83; TCLC 160**
See also CA 128; 113; DLB 242; EWL 3

Bakshi, Ralph 1938(?)- .... **CLC 26**
See also CA 112; 138; IDFW 3

Bakunin, Mikhail (Alexandrovich)
1814-1876 .... **NCLC 25, 58**
See also DLB 277

Bal, Mieke (Maria Gertrudis)
1946- .... **CLC 252**
See also CA 156; CANR 99

Baldwin, James 1924-1987 ...... **BLC 1:1, 2:1;
CLC 1, 2, 3, 4, 5, 8, 13, 15, 17, 42, 50,
67, 90, 127; DC 1; SSC 10, 33, 98;
WLC 1**
See also AAYA 4, 34; AFAW 1, 2; AMWR
2; AMWS 1; BPFB 1; BW 1; CA 1-4R;
124; CABS 1; CAD; CANR 3, 24;
CDALB 1941-1968; CN 1, 2, 3, 4; CPW;
DA; DA3; DAB; DAC; DAM MST,
MULT, NOV, POP; DFS 11, 15; DLB 2,
7, 33, 249, 278; DLBY 1987; EWL 3;
EXPS; LAIT 5; MAL 5; MTCW 1, 2;
MTFW 2005; NCFS 4; NFS 4; RGAL 4;
RGSF 2; SATA 9; SATA-Obit 54; SSFS
2, 18; TUS

Baldwin, William c. 1515-1563 .... **LC 113**
See also DLB 132

Bale, John 1495-1563 .... **LC 62**
See also DLB 132; RGEL 2; TEA

Ball, Hugo 1886-1927 .... **TCLC 104**

Ballard, J.G. 1930-2009 ..... **CLC 3, 6, 14, 36,
137; SSC 1, 53**
See also AAYA 3, 52; BRWS 5; CA 5-8R;
CANR 15, 39, 65, 107, 133; CN 1, 2, 3,
4, 5, 6, 7; DA3; DAM NOV, POP; DLB
14, 207, 261, 319; EWL 3; HGG; MTCW
1, 2; MTFW 2005; NFS 8; RGEL 2;
RGSF 2; SATA 93; SCFW 1, 2; SFW 4

Balmont, Konstantin (Dmitriyevich)
1867-1943 .... **TCLC 11**
See also CA 109; 155; DLB 295; EWL 3

Baltausis, Vincas 1847-1910
See Mikszath, Kalman

Balzac, Guez de (?)-
See Balzac, Jean-Louis Guez de

Balzac, Honore de 1799-1850 ... **NCLC 5, 35,
53, 153; SSC 5, 59, 102; WLC 1**
See also DA; DA3; DAB; DAC; DAM
MST, NOV; DLB 119; EW 5; GFL 1789
to the Present; LMFS 1; RGSF 2; RGWL
2, 3; SSFS 10; SUFW; TWA

Balzac, Jean-Louis Guez de
1597-1654 .... **LC 162**
See also DLB 268; GFL Beginnings to 1789

Bambara, Toni Cade 1939-1995 ..... **BLC 1:1,
2:1; CLC 19, 88; SSC 35, 107; TCLC
116; WLCS**
See also AAYA 5, 49; AFAW 2; AMWS 11;
BW 2, 3; BYA 12, 14; CA 29-32R; 150;
CANR 24, 49, 81; CDALBS; DA; DA3;
DAC; DAM MST, MULT; DLB 38, 218;
EXPS; MAL 5; MTCW 1, 2; MTFW
2005; RGAL 4; RGSF 2; SATA 112; SSFS
4, 7, 12, 21

Bamdad, A.
See Shamlu, Ahmad

Bamdad, Alef
See Shamlu, Ahmad

Banat, D. R.
See Bradbury, Ray

Bancroft, Laura
See Baum, L(yman) Frank

Banim, John 1798-1842 .... **NCLC 13**
See also DLB 116, 158, 159; RGEL 2

Banim, Michael 1796-1874 .... **NCLC 13**
See also DLB 158, 159

Banjo, The
See Paterson, A(ndrew) B(arton)

Banks, Iain 1954- .... **CLC 34**
See also BRWS 11; CA 123; 128; CANR
61, 106, 180; DLB 194, 261; EWL 3;
HGG; INT CA-128; MTFW 2005; SFW 4

Banks, Iain M.
See Banks, Iain

Banks, Iain Menzies
See Banks, Iain

Banks, Lynne Reid
See Reid Banks, Lynne

Banks, Russell 1940- . **CLC 37, 72, 187; SSC
42**
See also AAYA 45; AMWS 5; CA 65-68;
CAAS 15; CANR 19, 52, 73, 118; CN 4,
5, 6, 7; DLB 130, 278; EWL 3; MAL 5;
MTCW 2; MTFW 2005; NFS 13

Banks, Russell Earl
See Banks, Russell

Banville, John 1945- .... **CLC 46, 118, 224**
See also CA 117; 128; CANR 104, 150,
176; CN 4, 5, 6, 7; DLB 14, 271, 326;
INT CA-128

Banville, Theodore (Faullain) de
1832-1891 .... **NCLC 9**
See also DLB 217; GFL 1789 to the Present

Baraka, Amiri 1934- .. **BLC 1:1, 2:1; CLC 1,
2, 3, 5, 10, 14, 33, 115, 213; DC 6; PC
4; WLCS**
See also AAYA 63; AFAW 1, 2; AMWS 2;
BW 2, 3; CA 21-24R; CABS 3; CAD;
CANR 27, 38, 61, 133, 172; CD 3, 5, 6;
CDALB 1941-1968; CN 1, 2; CP 1, 2, 3,
4, 5, 6, 7; CPW; DA; DA3; DAC; DAM
MST, MULT, POET, POP; DFS 3, 11, 16;
DLB 5, 7, 16, 38; DLBD 8; EWL 3; MAL
5; MTCW 1, 2; MTFW 2005; PFS 9;
RGAL 4; TCLE 1:1; TUS; WP

Baratynsky, Evgenii Abramovich
1800-1844 .... **NCLC 103**
See also DLB 205

Barbauld, Anna Laetitia
1743-1825 .... **NCLC 50, 185**
See also DLB 107, 109, 142, 158, 336;
RGEL 2

Barbellion, W. N. P.
See Cummings, Bruce F(rederick)

Barber, Benjamin R. 1939- .... **CLC 141**
See also CA 29-32R; CANR 12, 32, 64, 119

Barbera, Jack (Vincent) 1945- .... **CLC 44**
See also CA 110; CANR 45

Barbey d'Aurevilly, Jules-Amedee
1808-1889 .... **NCLC 1; SSC 17**
See also DLB 119; GFL 1789 to the Present

Barbour, John c. 1316-1395 .... **CMLC 33**
See also DLB 146

Barbusse, Henri 1873-1935 .... **TCLC 5**
See also CA 105; 154; DLB 65; EWL 3;
RGWL 2, 3

Barclay, Alexander c. 1475-1552 .... **LC 109**
See also DLB 132

Barclay, Bill
See Moorcock, Michael

Barclay, William Ewert
See Moorcock, Michael

Barea, Arturo 1897-1957 .... **TCLC 14**
See also CA 111; 201

Barfoot, Joan 1946- .... **CLC 18**
See also CA 105; CANR 141, 179

Barham, Richard Harris
1788-1845 .... **NCLC 77**
See also DLB 159

Baring, Maurice 1874-1945 .... **TCLC 8**
See also CA 105; 168; DLB 34; HGG

Baring-Gould, Sabine 1834-1924 ... **TCLC 88**
See also DLB 156, 190

Barker, Clive 1952- .... **CLC 52, 205; SSC 53**
See also AAYA 10, 54; BEST 90:3; BPFB
1; CA 121; 129; CANR 71, 111, 133, 187;
CPW; DA3; DAM POP; DLB 261; HGG;
INT CA-129; MTCW 1, 2; MTFW 2005;
SUFW 2

Barker, George Granville
1913-1991 .... **CLC 8, 48; PC 77**
See also CA 9-12R; 135; CANR 7, 38; CP
1, 2, 3, 4, 5; DAM POET; DLB 20; EWL
3; MTCW 1

Barker, Harley Granville
See Granville-Barker, Harley

Barker, Howard 1946- .... **CLC 37**
See also CA 102; CBD; CD 5, 6; DLB 13, 233

Barker, Jane 1652-1732 .... **LC 42, 82; PC 91**
See also DLB 39, 131

Barker, Pat 1943- .... **CLC 32, 94, 146**
See also BRWS 4; CA 117; 122; CANR 50, 101, 148; CN 6, 7; DLB 271, 326; INT CA-122

Barker, Patricia
See Barker, Pat

Barlach, Ernst (Heinrich)
1870-1938 .... **TCLC 84**
See also CA 178; DLB 56, 118; EWL 3

Barlow, Joel 1754-1812 .... **NCLC 23**
See also AMWS 2; DLB 37; RGAL 4

Barnard, Mary (Ethel) 1909- .... **CLC 48**
See also CA 21-22; CAP 2; CP 1

Barnes, Djuna 1892-1982 .... **CLC 3, 4, 8, 11, 29, 127; SSC 3; TCLC 212**
See also AMWS 3; CA 9-12R; 107; CAD; CANR 16, 55; CN 1, 2, 3; CWD; DLB 4, 9, 45; EWL 3; GLL 1; MAL 5; MTCW 1, 2; MTFW 2005; RGAL 4; TCLE 1:1; TUS

Barnes, Jim 1933- .... **NNAL**
See also CA 108, 175, 272; CAAE 175, 272; CAAS 28; DLB 175

Barnes, Julian 1946- .... **CLC 42, 141**
See also BRWS 4; CA 102; CANR 19, 54, 115, 137; CN 4, 5, 6, 7; DAB; DLB 194; DLBY 1993; EWL 3; MTCW 2; MTFW 2005; SSFS 24

Barnes, Julian Patrick
See Barnes, Julian

Barnes, Peter 1931-2004 .... **CLC 5, 56**
See also CA 65-68; 230; CAAS 12; CANR 33, 34, 64, 113; CBD; CD 5, 6; DFS 6; DLB 13, 233; MTCW 1

Barnes, William 1801-1886 .... **NCLC 75**
See also DLB 32

Baroja, Pio 1872-1956 .... **HLC 1; SSC 112; TCLC 8**
See also CA 104; 247; EW 9

Baroja y Nessi, Pio
See Baroja, Pio

Baron, David
See Pinter, Harold

Baron Corvo
See Rolfe, Frederick (William Serafino Austin Lewis Mary)

Barondess, Sue K(aufman)
1926-1977 .... **CLC 3, 8**
See also CA 1-4R; 69-72; CANR 1

Baron de Teive
See Pessoa, Fernando

Baroness Von S.
See Zangwill, Israel

Barres, (Auguste-)Maurice
1862-1923 .... **TCLC 47**
See also CA 164; DLB 123; GFL 1789 to the Present

Barreto, Afonso Henrique de Lima
See Lima Barreto, Afonso Henrique de

Barrett, Andrea 1954- .... **CLC 150**
See also CA 156; CANR 92, 186; CN 7; DLB 335; SSFS 24

Barrett, Michele
See Barrett, Michele

Barrett, Michele 1949- .... **CLC 65**
See also CA 280

Barrett, (Roger) Syd 1946-2006 .... **CLC 35**

Barrett, William (Christopher)
1913-1992 .... **CLC 27**
See also CA 13-16R; 139; CANR 11, 67; INT CANR-11

Barrett Browning, Elizabeth
1806-1861 ...... **NCLC 1, 16, 61, 66, 170; PC 6, 62; WLC 1**
See also AAYA 63; BRW 4; CDBLB 1832-1890; DA; DA3; DAB; DAC; DAM MST, POET; DLB 32, 199; EXPP; FL 1:2; PAB; PFS 2, 16, 23; TEA; WLIT 4; WP

Barrie, J(ames) M(atthew)
1860-1937 .... **TCLC 2, 164**
See also BRWS 3; BYA 4, 5; CA 104; 136; CANR 77; CDBLB 1890-1914; CLR 16, 124; CWRI 5; DA3; DAB; DAM DRAM; DFS 7; DLB 10, 141, 156; EWL 3; FANT; MAICYA 1, 2; MTCW 2; MTFW 2005; SATA 100; SUFW; WCH; WLIT 4; YABC 1

Barrington, Michael
See Moorcock, Michael

Barrol, Grady
See Bograd, Larry

Barry, Mike
See Malzberg, Barry N(athaniel)

Barry, Philip 1896-1949 .... **TCLC 11**
See also CA 109; 199; DFS 9; DLB 7, 228; MAL 5; RGAL 4

Bart, Andre Schwarz
See Schwarz-Bart, Andre

Barth, John (Simmons) 1930- ... **CLC 1, 2, 3, 5, 7, 9, 10, 14, 27, 51, 89, 214; SSC 10, 89**
See also AITN 1, 2; AMW; BPFB 1; CA 1-4R; CABS 1; CANR 5, 23, 49, 64, 113; CN 1, 2, 3, 4, 5, 6, 7; DAM NOV; DLB 2, 227; EWL 3; FANT; MAL 5; MTCW 1; RGAL 4; RGSF 2; RHW; SSFS 6; TUS

Barthelme, Donald 1931-1989 ... **CLC 1, 2, 3, 5, 6, 8, 13, 23, 46, 59, 115; SSC 2, 55**
See also AMWS 4; BPFB 1; CA 21-24R; 129; CANR 20, 58, 188; CN 1, 2, 3, 4; DA3; DAM NOV; DLB 2, 234; DLBY 1980, 1989; EWL 3; FANT; LMFS 2; MAL 5; MTCW 1, 2; MTFW 2005; RGAL 4; RGSF 2; SATA 7; SATA-Obit 62; SSFS 17

Barthelme, Frederick 1943- ...... **CLC 36, 117**
See also AMWS 11; CA 114; 122; CANR 77; CN 4, 5, 6, 7; CSW; DLB 244; DLBY 1985; EWL 3; INT CA-122

Barthes, Roland (Gerard)
1915-1980 .... **CLC 24, 83; TCLC 135**
See also CA 130; 97-100; CANR 66; DLB 296; EW 13; EWL 3; GFL 1789 to the Present; MTCW 1, 2; TWA

Bartram, William 1739-1823 .... **NCLC 145**
See also ANW; DLB 37

Barzun, Jacques (Martin) 1907- ..... **CLC 51, 145**
See also CA 61-64; CANR 22, 95

Bashevis, Isaac
See Singer, Isaac Bashevis

Bashevis, Yitskhok
See Singer, Isaac Bashevis

Bashkirtseff, Marie 1859-1884 .... **NCLC 27**

Basho, Matsuo
See Matsuo Basho

Basil of Caesaria c. 330-379 .... **CMLC 35**

Basket, Raney
See Edgerton, Clyde (Carlyle)

Bass, Kingsley B., Jr.
See Bullins, Ed

Bass, Rick 1958- .... **CLC 79, 143; SSC 60**
See also AMWS 16; ANW; CA 126; CANR 53, 93, 145, 183; CSW; DLB 212, 275

Bassani, Giorgio 1916-2000 .... **CLC 9**
See also CA 65-68; 190; CANR 33; CWW 2; DLB 128, 177, 299; EWL 3; MTCW 1; RGHL; RGWL 2, 3

Bassine, Helen
See Yglesias, Helen

Bastian, Ann .... **CLC 70**

Bastos, Augusto Roa
See Roa Bastos, Augusto

Bataille, Georges 1897-1962 .... **CLC 29; TCLC 155**
See also CA 101; 89-92; EWL 3

Bates, H(erbert) E(rnest)
1905-1974 .... **CLC 46; SSC 10**
See also CA 93-96; 45-48; CANR 34; CN 1; DA3; DAB; DAM POP; DLB 162, 191; EWL 3; EXPS; MTCW 1, 2; RGSF 2; SSFS 7

Bauchart
See Camus, Albert

Baudelaire, Charles 1821-1867 . **NCLC 6, 29, 55, 155; PC 1; SSC 18; WLC 1**
See also DA; DA3; DAB; DAC; DAM MST, POET; DLB 217; EW 7; GFL 1789 to the Present; LMFS 2; PFS 21; RGWL 2, 3; TWA

Baudouin, Marcel
See Peguy, Charles (Pierre)

Baudouin, Pierre
See Peguy, Charles (Pierre)

Baudrillard, Jean 1929-2007 .... **CLC 60**
See also CA 252; 258; DLB 296

Baum, L(yman) Frank 1856-1919 .. **TCLC 7, 132**
See also AAYA 46; BYA 16; CA 108; 133; CLR 15, 107; CWRI 5; DLB 22; FANT; JRDA; MAICYA 1, 2; MTCW 1, 2; NFS 13; RGAL 4; SATA 18, 100; WCH

Baum, Louis F.
See Baum, L(yman) Frank

Baumbach, Jonathan 1933- .... **CLC 6, 23**
See also CA 13-16R; CAAS 5; CANR 12, 66, 140; CN 3, 4, 5, 6, 7; DLBY 1980; INT CANR-12; MTCW 1

Bausch, Richard 1945- .... **CLC 51**
See also AMWS 7; CA 101; CAAS 14; CANR 43, 61, 87, 164; CN 7; CSW; DLB 130; MAL 5

Bausch, Richard Carl
See Bausch, Richard

Baxter, Charles 1947- .... **CLC 45, 78**
See also AMWS 17; CA 57-60; CANR 40, 64, 104, 133, 188; CPW; DAM POP; DLB 130; MAL 5; MTCW 2; MTFW 2005; TCLE 1:1

Baxter, Charles Morley
See Baxter, Charles

Baxter, George Owen
See Faust, Frederick (Schiller)

Baxter, James K(eir) 1926-1972 .... **CLC 14**
See also CA 77-80; CP 1; EWL 3

Baxter, John
See Hunt, E. Howard

Bayer, Sylvia
See Glassco, John

Bayle, Pierre 1647-1706 .... **LC 126**
See also DLB 268, 313; GFL Beginnings to 1789

Baynton, Barbara 1857-1929 . **TCLC 57, 211**
See also DLB 230; RGSF 2

Beagle, Peter S. 1939- .... **CLC 7, 104**
See also AAYA 47; BPFB 1; BYA 9, 10, 16; CA 9-12R; CANR 4, 51, 73, 110; DA3; DLBY 1980; FANT; INT CANR-4; MTCW 2; MTFW 2005; SATA 60, 130; SUFW 1, 2; YAW

Beagle, Peter Soyer
See Beagle, Peter S.

Bean, Normal
See Burroughs, Edgar Rice

Beard, Charles A(ustin)
1874-1948 .... **TCLC 15**
See also CA 115; 189; DLB 17; SATA 18

Beardsley, Aubrey 1872-1898 .... **NCLC 6**

Beattie, Ann 1947- ..... **CLC 8, 13, 18, 40, 63, 146; SSC 11**
See also AMWS 5; BEST 90:2; BPFB 1; CA 81-84; CANR 53, 73, 128; CN 4, 5, 6, 7; CPW; DA3; DAM NOV, POP; DLB 218, 278; DLBY 1982; EWL 3; MAL 5; MTCW 1, 2; MTFW 2005; RGAL 4; RGSF 2; SSFS 9; TUS

Beattie, James 1735-1803 .... **NCLC 25**
See also DLB 109

Beauchamp, Kathleen Mansfield 1888-1923 . **SSC 9, 23, 38, 81; TCLC 2, 8, 39, 164; WLC 4**
See also BPFB 2; BRW 7; CA 104; 134; DA; DA3; DAB; DAC; DAM MST; DLB 162; EWL 3; EXPS; FW; GLL 1; MTCW 2; RGEL 2; RGSF 2; SSFS 2, 8, 10, 11; TEA; WWE 1

Beaumarchais, Pierre-Augustin Caron de 1732-1799 .... **DC 4; LC 61**
See also DAM DRAM; DFS 14, 16; DLB 313; EW 4; GFL Beginnings to 1789; RGWL 2, 3

Beaumont, Francis 1584(?)-1616 .. **DC 6; LC 33**
See also BRW 2; CDBLB Before 1660; DLB 58; TEA

Beauvoir, Simone de 1908-1986 .... **CLC 1, 2, 4, 8, 14, 31, 44, 50, 71, 124; SSC 35; WLC 1**
See also BPFB 1; CA 9-12R; 118; CANR 28, 61; DA; DA3; DAB; DAC; DAM MST, NOV; DLB 72; DLBY 1986; EW 12; EWL 3; FL 1:5; FW; GFL 1789 to the Present; LMFS 2; MTCW 1, 2; MTFW 2005; RGSF 2; RGWL 2, 3; TWA

Beauvoir, Simone Lucie Ernestine Marie Bertrand de
See Beauvoir, Simone de

Becker, Carl (Lotus) 1873-1945 ..... **TCLC 63**
See also CA 157; DLB 17

Becker, Jurek 1937-1997 .... **CLC 7, 19**
See also CA 85-88; 157; CANR 60, 117; CWW 2; DLB 75, 299; EWL 3; RGHL

Becker, Walter 1950- .... **CLC 26**

Becket, Thomas a 1118(?)-1170 .... **CMLC 83**

Beckett, Samuel 1906-1989 ... **CLC 1, 2, 3, 4, 6, 9, 10, 11, 14, 18, 29, 57, 59, 83; DC 22; SSC 16, 74; TCLC 145; WLC 1**
See also BRWC 2; BRWR 1; BRWS 1; CA 5-8R; 130; CANR 33, 61; CBD; CDBLB 1945-1960; CN 1, 2, 3, 4; CP 1, 2, 3, 4; DA; DA3; DAB; DAC; DAM DRAM, MST, NOV; DFS 2, 7, 18; DLB 13, 15, 233, 319, 321, 329; DLBY 1990; EWL 3; GFL 1789 to the Present; LATS 1:2; LMFS 2; MTCW 1, 2; MTFW 2005; RGSF 2; RGWL 2, 3; SSFS 15; TEA; WLIT 4

Beckford, William 1760-1844 .... **NCLC 16**
See also BRW 3; DLB 39, 213; GL 2; HGG; LMFS 1; SUFW

Beckham, Barry (Earl) 1944- .... **BLC 1:1**
See also BW 1; CA 29-32R; CANR 26, 62; CN 1, 2, 3, 4, 5, 6; DAM MULT; DLB 33

Beckman, Gunnel 1910- .... **CLC 26**
See also CA 33-36R; CANR 15, 114; CLR 25; MAICYA 1, 2; SAAS 9; SATA 6

Becque, Henri 1837-1899 .... **DC 21; NCLC 3**
See also DLB 192; GFL 1789 to the Present

Becquer, Gustavo Adolfo 1836-1870 .... **HLCS 1; NCLC 106**
See also DAM MULT

Beddoes, Thomas Lovell 1803-1849 .. **DC 15; NCLC 3, 154**
See also BRWS 11; DLB 96

Bede c. 673-735 .... **CMLC 20**
See also DLB 146; TEA

Bedford, Denton R. 1907-(?) .... **NNAL**

Bedford, Donald F.
See Fearing, Kenneth (Flexner)

Beecher, Catharine Esther 1800-1878 .... **NCLC 30**
See also DLB 1, 243

Beecher, John 1904-1980 .... **CLC 6**
See also AITN 1; CA 5-8R; 105; CANR 8; CP 1, 2, 3

Beer, Johann 1655-1700 .... **LC 5**
See also DLB 168

Beer, Patricia 1924- .... **CLC 58**
See also BRWS 14; CA 61-64; 183; CANR 13, 46; CP 1, 2, 3, 4, 5, 6; CWP; DLB 40; FW

Beerbohm, Max
See Beerbohm, (Henry) Max(imilian)

Beerbohm, (Henry) Max(imilian) 1872-1956 .... **TCLC 1, 24**
See also BRWS 2; CA 104; 154; CANR 79; DLB 34, 100; FANT; MTCW 2

Beer-Hofmann, Richard 1866-1945 .... **TCLC 60**
See also CA 160; DLB 81

Beg, Shemus
See Stephens, James

Begiebing, Robert J(ohn) 1946- .... **CLC 70**
See also CA 122; CANR 40, 88

Begley, Louis 1933- .... **CLC 197**
See also CA 140; CANR 98, 176; DLB 299; RGHL; TCLE 1:1

Behan, Brendan (Francis) 1923-1964 .... **CLC 1, 8, 11, 15, 79**
See also BRWS 2; CA 73-76; CANR 33, 121; CBD; CDBLB 1945-1960; DAM DRAM; DFS 7; DLB 13, 233; EWL 3; MTCW 1, 2

Behn, Aphra 1640(?)-1689 .. **DC 4; LC 1, 30, 42, 135; PC 13, 88; WLC 1**
See also BRWS 3; DA; DA3; DAB; DAC; DAM DRAM, MST, NOV, POET; DFS 16, 24; DLB 39, 80, 131; FW; TEA; WLIT 3

Behrman, S(amuel) N(athaniel) 1893-1973 .... **CLC 40**
See also CA 13-16; 45-48; CAD; CAP 1; DLB 7, 44; IDFW 3; MAL 5; RGAL 4

Bekederemo, J. P. Clark
See Clark Bekederemo, J.P.

Belasco, David 1853-1931 .... **TCLC 3**
See also CA 104; 168; DLB 7; MAL 5; RGAL 4

Belcheva, Elisaveta Lyubomirova 1893-1991 .... **CLC 10**
See also CA 178; CDWLB 4; DLB 147; EWL 3

Beldone, Phil "Cheech"
See Ellison, Harlan

Beleno
See Azuela, Mariano

Belinski, Vissarion Grigoryevich 1811-1848 .... **NCLC 5**
See also DLB 198

Belitt, Ben 1911- .... **CLC 22**
See also CA 13-16R; CAAS 4; CANR 7, 77; CP 1, 2, 3, 4, 5, 6; DLB 5

Belknap, Jeremy 1744-1798 .... **LC 115**
See also DLB 30, 37

Bell, Gertrude (Margaret Lowthian) 1868-1926 .... **TCLC 67**
See also CA 167; CANR 110; DLB 174

Bell, J. Freeman
See Zangwill, Israel

Bell, James Madison 1826-1902 ..... **BLC 1:1; TCLC 43**
See also BW 1; CA 122; 124; DAM MULT; DLB 50

Bell, Madison Smartt 1957- ..... **CLC 41, 102, 223**
See also AMWS 10; BPFB 1; CA 111, 183; CAAE 183; CANR 28, 54, 73, 134, 176; CN 5, 6, 7; CSW; DLB 218, 278; MTCW 2; MTFW 2005

Bell, Marvin (Hartley) 1937- ...... **CLC 8, 31; PC 79**
See also CA 21-24R; CAAS 14; CANR 59, 102; CP 1, 2, 3, 4, 5, 6, 7; DAM POET; DLB 5; MAL 5; MTCW 1; PFS 25

Bell, W. L. D.
See Mencken, H(enry) L(ouis)

Bellamy, Atwood C.
See Mencken, H(enry) L(ouis)

Bellamy, Edward 1850-1898 ..... **NCLC 4, 86, 147**
See also DLB 12; NFS 15; RGAL 4; SFW 4

Belli, Gioconda 1948- .... **HLCS 1**
See also CA 152; CANR 143; CWW 2; DLB 290; EWL 3; RGWL 3

Bellin, Edward J.
See Kuttner, Henry

Bello, Andres 1781-1865 .... **NCLC 131**
See also LAW

Belloc, (Joseph) Hilaire (Pierre Sebastien Rene Swanton) 1870-1953 .... **PC 24; TCLC 7, 18**
See also CA 106; 152; CLR 102; CWRI 5; DAM POET; DLB 19, 100, 141, 174; EWL 3; MTCW 2; MTFW 2005; SATA 112; WCH; YABC 1

Belloc, Joseph Peter Rene Hilaire
See Belloc, (Joseph) Hilaire (Pierre Sebastien Rene Swanton)

Belloc, Joseph Pierre Hilaire
See Belloc, (Joseph) Hilaire (Pierre Sebastien Rene Swanton)

Belloc, M. A.
See Lowndes, Marie Adelaide (Belloc)

Belloc-Lowndes, Mrs.
See Lowndes, Marie Adelaide (Belloc)

Bellow, Saul 1915-2005 ...... **CLC 1, 2, 3, 6, 8, 10, 13, 15, 25, 33, 34, 63, 79, 190, 200; SSC 14, 101; WLC 1**
See also AITN 2; AMW; AMWC 2; AMWR 2; BEST 89:3; BPFB 1; CA 5-8R; 238; CABS 1; CANR 29, 53, 95, 132; CDALB 1941-1968; CN 1, 2, 3, 4, 5, 6, 7; DA; DA3; DAB; DAC; DAM MST, NOV, POP; DLB 2, 28, 299, 329; DLBD 3; DLBY 1982; EWL 3; MAL 5; MTCW 1, 2; MTFW 2005; NFS 4, 14, 26; RGAL 4; RGHL; RGSF 2; SSFS 12, 22; TUS

Belser, Reimond Karel Maria de 1929- .... **CLC 14**
See also CA 152

Bely, Andrey
See Bugayev, Boris Nikolayevich

Belyi, Andrei
See Bugayev, Boris Nikolayevich

Bembo, Pietro 1470-1547 .... **LC 79**
See also RGWL 2, 3

Benary, Margot
See Benary-Isbert, Margot

Benary-Isbert, Margot 1889-1979 .... **CLC 12**
See also CA 5-8R; 89-92; CANR 4, 72; CLR 12; MAICYA 1, 2; SATA 2; SATA-Obit 21

Benavente (y Martinez), Jacinto 1866-1954 .... **DC 26; HLCS 1; TCLC 3**
See also CA 106; 131; CANR 81; DAM DRAM, MULT; DLB 329; EWL 3; GLL 2; HW 1, 2; MTCW 1, 2

Berry, Wendell 1934- .... **CLC 4, 6, 8, 27, 46; PC 28**
See also AITN 1; AMWS 10; ANW; CA 73-76; CANR 50, 73, 101, 132, 174; CP 1, 2, 3, 4, 5, 6, 7; CSW; DAM POET; DLB 5, 6, 234, 275, 342; MTCW 2; MTFW 2005; PFS 30; TCLE 1:1

Berryman, John 1914-1972 ... **CLC 1, 2, 3, 4, 6, 8, 10, 13, 25, 62; PC 64**
See also AMW; CA 13-16; 33-36R; CABS 2; CANR 35; CAP 1; CDALB 1941-1968; CP 1; DAM POET; DLB 48; EWL 3; MAL 5; MTCW 1, 2; MTFW 2005; PAB; PFS 27; RGAL 4; WP

Bertolucci, Bernardo 1940- ...... **CLC 16, 157**
See also CA 106; CANR 125

Berton, Pierre (Francis de Marigny) 1920-2004 .... **CLC 104**
See also CA 1-4R; 233; CANR 2, 56, 144; CPW; DLB 68; SATA 99; SATA-Obit 158

Bertrand, Aloysius 1807-1841 .... **NCLC 31**
See also DLB 217

Bertrand, Louis oAloysiusc
See Bertrand, Aloysius

Bertran de Born c. 1140-1215 .... **CMLC 5**

Besant, Annie (Wood) 1847-1933 ..... **TCLC 9**
See also CA 105; 185

Bessie, Alvah 1904-1985 .... **CLC 23**
See also CA 5-8R; 116; CANR 2, 80; DLB 26

Bestuzhev, Aleksandr Aleksandrovich 1797-1837 .... **NCLC 131**
See also DLB 198

Bethlen, T.D.
See Silverberg, Robert

Beti, Mongo
See Biyidi, Alexandre

Betjeman, John 1906-1984 ...... **CLC 2, 6, 10, 34, 43; PC 75**
See also BRW 7; CA 9-12R; 112; CANR 33, 56; CDBLB 1945-1960; CP 1, 2, 3; DA3; DAB; DAM MST, POET; DLB 20; DLBY 1984; EWL 3; MTCW 1, 2

Bettelheim, Bruno 1903-1990 .... **CLC 79; TCLC 143**
See also CA 81-84; 131; CANR 23, 61; DA3; MTCW 1, 2; RGHL

Betti, Ugo 1892-1953 .... **TCLC 5**
See also CA 104; 155; EWL 3; RGWL 2, 3

Betts, Doris (Waugh) 1932- ..... **CLC 3, 6, 28; SSC 45**
See also CA 13-16R; CANR 9, 66, 77; CN 6, 7; CSW; DLB 218; DLBY 1982; INT CANR-9; RGAL 4

Bevan, Alistair
See Roberts, Keith (John Kingston)

Bey, Pilaff
See Douglas, (George) Norman

Beyala, Calixthe 1961- .... **BLC 2:1**
See also EWL 3

Beynon, John
See Harris, John (Wyndham Parkes Lucas) Beynon

Bialik, Chaim Nachman 1873-1934 .... **TCLC 25, 201**
See also CA 170; EWL 3; WLIT 6

Bialik, Hayyim Nahman
See Bialik, Chaim Nachman

Bickerstaff, Isaac
See Swift, Jonathan

Bidart, Frank 1939- .... **CLC 33**
See also AMWS 15; CA 140; CANR 106; CP 5, 6, 7; PFS 26

Bienek, Horst 1930- .... **CLC 7, 11**
See also CA 73-76; DLB 75

Bierce, Ambrose (Gwinett) 1842-1914(?) . **SSC 9, 72, 124; TCLC 1, 7, 44; WLC 1**
See also AAYA 55; AMW; BYA 11; CA 104; 139; CANR 78; CDALB 1865-1917; DA; DA3; DAC; DAM MST; DLB 11, 12, 23, 71, 74, 186; EWL 3; EXPS; HGG; LAIT 2; MAL 5; RGAL 4; RGSF 2; SSFS 9, 27; SUFW 1

Biggers, Earl Derr 1884-1933 .... **TCLC 65**
See also CA 108; 153; DLB 306

Billiken, Bud
See Motley, Willard (Francis)

Billings, Josh
See Shaw, Henry Wheeler

Billington, (Lady) Rachel (Mary) 1942- .... **CLC 43**
See also AITN 2; CA 33-36R; CANR 44; CN 4, 5, 6, 7

Binchy, Maeve 1940- .... **CLC 153**
See also BEST 90:1; BPFB 1; CA 127; 134; CANR 50, 96, 134; CN 5, 6, 7; CPW; DA3; DAM POP; DLB 319; INT CA-134; MTCW 2; MTFW 2005; RHW

Binyon, T(imothy) J(ohn) 1936-2004 .... **CLC 34**
See also CA 111; 232; CANR 28, 140

Bion 335B.C.-245B.C. .... **CMLC 39**

Bioy Casares, Adolfo 1914-1999 ... **CLC 4, 8, 13, 88; HLC 1; SSC 17, 102**
See also CA 29-32R; 177; CANR 19, 43, 66; CWW 2; DAM MULT; DLB 113; EWL 3; HW 1, 2; LAW; MTCW 1, 2; MTFW 2005; RGSF 2

Birch, Allison .... **CLC 65**

Bird, Cordwainer
See Ellison, Harlan

Bird, Robert Montgomery 1806-1854 .... **NCLC 1, 197**
See also DLB 202; RGAL 4

Birdwell, Cleo
See DeLillo, Don

Birkerts, Sven 1951- .... **CLC 116**
See also CA 128; 133, 176; CAAE 176; CAAS 29; CANR 151; INT CA-133

Birney, (Alfred) Earle 1904-1995 .. **CLC 1, 4, 6, 11; PC 52**
See also CA 1-4R; CANR 5, 20; CN 1, 2, 3, 4; CP 1, 2, 3, 4, 5, 6; DAC; DAM MST, POET; DLB 88; MTCW 1; PFS 8; RGEL 2

Biruni, al 973-1048(?) .... **CMLC 28**

Bishop, Elizabeth 1911-1979 ... **CLC 1, 4, 9, 13, 15, 32; PC 3, 34; TCLC 121**
See also AMWR 2; AMWS 1; CA 5-8R; 89-92; CABS 2; CANR 26, 61, 108; CDALB 1968-1988; CP 1, 2, 3; DA; DA3; DAC; DAM MST, POET; DLB 5, 169; EWL 3; GLL 2; MAL 5; MBL; MTCW 1, 2; PAB; PFS 6, 12, 27; RGAL 4; SATA-Obit 24; TUS; WP

Bishop, George Archibald
See Crowley, Edward Alexander

Bishop, John 1935- .... **CLC 10**
See also CA 105

Bishop, John Peale 1892-1944 ..... **TCLC 103**
See also CA 107; 155; DLB 4, 9, 45; MAL 5; RGAL 4

Bissett, Bill 1939- .... **CLC 18; PC 14**
See also CA 69-72; CAAS 19; CANR 15; CCA 1; CP 1, 2, 3, 4, 5, 6, 7; DLB 53; MTCW 1

Bissoondath, Neil 1955- .... **CLC 120**
See also CA 136; CANR 123, 165; CN 6, 7; DAC

Bissoondath, Neil Devindra
See Bissoondath, Neil

Bitov, Andrei (Georgievich) 1937- ... **CLC 57**
See also CA 142; DLB 302

Biyidi, Alexandre 1932- ... **BLC 1:1; CLC 27**
See also AFW; BW 1, 3; CA 114; 124; CANR 81; DA3; DAM MULT; EWL 3; MTCW 1, 2

Bjarme, Brynjolf
See Ibsen, Henrik (Johan)

Bjoernson, Bjoernstjerne (Martinius) 1832-1910 .... **TCLC 7, 37**
See also CA 104

Black, Benjamin
See Banville, John

Black, Robert
See Holdstock, Robert

Blackburn, Paul 1926-1971 .... **CLC 9, 43**
See also BG 1:2; CA 81-84; 33-36R; CANR 34; CP 1; DLB 16; DLBY 1981

Black Elk 1863-1950 .... **NNAL; TCLC 33**
See also CA 144; DAM MULT; MTCW 2; MTFW 2005; WP

Black Hawk 1767-1838 .... **NNAL**

Black Hobart
See Sanders, (James) Ed(ward)

Blacklin, Malcolm
See Chambers, Aidan

Blackmore, R(ichard) D(oddridge) 1825-1900 .... **TCLC 27**
See also CA 120; DLB 18; RGEL 2

Blackmur, R(ichard) P(almer) 1904-1965 .... **CLC 2, 24**
See also AMWS 2; CA 11-12; 25-28R; CANR 71; CAP 1; DLB 63; EWL 3; MAL 5

Black Tarantula
See Acker, Kathy

Blackwood, Algernon 1869-1951 .... **SSC 107; TCLC 5**
See also AAYA 78; CA 105; 150; CANR 169; DLB 153, 156, 178; HGG; SUFW 1

Blackwood, Algernon Henry
See Blackwood, Algernon

Blackwood, Caroline (Maureen) 1931-1996 .... **CLC 6, 9, 100**
See also BRWS 9; CA 85-88; 151; CANR 32, 61, 65; CN 3, 4, 5, 6; DLB 14, 207; HGG; MTCW 1

Blade, Alexander
See Hamilton, Edmond; Silverberg, Robert

Blaga, Lucian 1895-1961 .... **CLC 75**
See also CA 157; DLB 220; EWL 3

Blair, Eric (Arthur) 1903-1950 .... **SSC 68; TCLC 2, 6, 15, 31, 51, 123, 128, 129; WLC 1**
See also BPFB 3; BRW 7; BYA 5; CA 104; 132; CDBLB 1945-1960; CLR 68; DA; DA3; DAB; DAC; DAM MST, NOV; DLB 15, 98, 195, 255; EWL 3; EXPN; LAIT 4, 5; LATS 1:1; MTCW 1, 2; MTFW 2005; NFS 3, 7; RGEL 2; SATA 29; SCFW 1, 2; SFW 4; SSFS 4; TEA; WLIT 4; YAW X

Blair, Hugh 1718-1800 .... **NCLC 75**

Blais, Marie-Claire 1939- .... **CLC 2, 4, 6, 13, 22**
See also CA 21-24R; CAAS 4; CANR 38, 75, 93; CWW 2; DAC; DAM MST; DLB 53; EWL 3; FW; MTCW 1, 2; MTFW 2005; TWA

Blaise, Clark 1940- .... **CLC 29, 261**
See also AITN 2; CA 53-56, 231; CAAE 231; CAAS 3; CANR 5, 66, 106; CN 4, 5, 6, 7; DLB 53; RGSF 2

Blake, Fairley
See De Voto, Bernard (Augustine)

Blake, Nicholas
See Day Lewis, C(ecil)

Blake, Sterling
See Benford, Gregory

Boot, William
See Stoppard, Tom
Booth, Irwin
See Hoch, Edward D.
Booth, Martin 1944-2004 .... **CLC 13**
See also CA 93-96, 188; 223; CAAE 188; CAAS 2; CANR 92; CP 1, 2, 3, 4
Booth, Philip 1925-2007 .... **CLC 23**
See also CA 5-8R; 262; CANR 5, 88; CP 1, 2, 3, 4, 5, 6, 7; DLBY 1982
Booth, Philip Edmund
See Booth, Philip
Booth, Wayne C. 1921-2005 .... **CLC 24**
See also CA 1-4R; 244; CAAS 5; CANR 3, 43, 117; DLB 67
Booth, Wayne Clayson
See Booth, Wayne C.
Borchert, Wolfgang 1921-1947 .... **TCLC 5**
See also CA 104; 188; DLB 69, 124; EWL 3
Borel, Petrus 1809-1859 .... **NCLC 41**
See also DLB 119; GFL 1789 to the Present
Borges, Jorge Luis 1899-1986 ... **CLC 1, 2, 3, 4, 6, 8, 9, 10, 13, 19, 44, 48, 83; HLC 1; PC 22, 32; SSC 4, 41, 100; TCLC 109; WLC 1**
See also AAYA 26; BPFB 1; CA 21-24R; CANR 19, 33, 75, 105, 133; CDWLB 3; DA; DA3; DAB; DAC; DAM MST, MULT; DLB 113, 283; DLBY 1986; DNFS 1, 2; EWL 3; HW 1, 2; LAW; LMFS 2; MSW; MTCW 1, 2; MTFW 2005; PFS 27; RGHL; RGSF 2; RGWL 2, 3; SFW 4; SSFS 17; TWA; WLIT 1
Borne, Ludwig 1786-1837 .... **NCLC 193**
See also DLB 90
Borowski, Tadeusz 1922-1951 .... **SSC 48; TCLC 9**
See also CA 106; 154; CDWLB 4; DLB 215; EWL 3; RGHL; RGSF 2; RGWL 3; SSFS 13
Borrow, George (Henry)
1803-1881 .... **NCLC 9**
See also BRWS 12; DLB 21, 55, 166
Bosch (Gavino), Juan 1909-2001 ..... **HLCS 1**
See also CA 151; 204; DAM MST, MULT; DLB 145; HW 1, 2
Bosman, Herman Charles
1905-1951 .... **TCLC 49**
See also CA 160; DLB 225; RGSF 2
Bosschere, Jean de 1878(?)-1953 ... **TCLC 19**
See also CA 115; 186
Boswell, James 1740-1795 ... **LC 4, 50; WLC 1**
See also BRW 3; CDBLB 1660-1789; DA; DAB; DAC; DAM MST; DLB 104, 142; TEA; WLIT 3
Boto, Eza
See Biyidi, Alexandre
Bottomley, Gordon 1874-1948 ..... **TCLC 107**
See also CA 120; 192; DLB 10
Bottoms, David 1949- .... **CLC 53**
See also CA 105; CANR 22; CSW; DLB 120; DLBY 1983
Boucicault, Dion 1820-1890 .... **NCLC 41**
See also DLB 344
Boucolon, Maryse
See Conde, Maryse
Bourcicault, Dion
See Boucicault, Dion
Bourdieu, Pierre 1930-2002 .... **CLC 198**
See also CA 130; 204
Bourget, Paul (Charles Joseph)
1852-1935 .... **TCLC 12**
See also CA 107; 196; DLB 123; GFL 1789 to the Present

Bourjaily, Vance (Nye) 1922- .... **CLC 8, 62**
See also CA 1-4R; CAAS 1; CANR 2, 72; CN 1, 2, 3, 4, 5, 6, 7; DLB 2, 143; MAL 5
Bourne, Randolph S(illiman)
1886-1918 .... **TCLC 16**
See also AMW; CA 117; 155; DLB 63; MAL 5
Boursiquot, Dionysius
See Boucicault, Dion
Bova, Ben 1932- .... **CLC 45**
See also AAYA 16; CA 5-8R; CAAS 18; CANR 11, 56, 94, 111, 157; CLR 3, 96; DLBY 1981; INT CANR-11; MAICYA 1, 2; MTCW 1; SATA 6, 68, 133; SFW 4
Bova, Benjamin William
See Bova, Ben
Bowen, Elizabeth (Dorothea Cole)
1899-1973 . **CLC 1, 3, 6, 11, 15, 22, 118; SSC 3, 28, 66; TCLC 148**
See also BRWS 2; CA 17-18; 41-44R; CANR 35, 105; CAP 2; CDBLB 1945-1960; CN 1; DA3; DAM NOV; DLB 15, 162; EWL 3; EXPS; FW; HGG; MTCW 1, 2; MTFW 2005; NFS 13; RGSF 2; SSFS 5, 22; SUFW 1; TEA; WLIT 4
Bowering, George 1935- .... **CLC 15, 47**
See also CA 21-24R; CAAS 16; CANR 10; CN 7; CP 1, 2, 3, 4, 5, 6, 7; DLB 53
Bowering, Marilyn R(uthe) 1949- .... **CLC 32**
See also CA 101; CANR 49; CP 4, 5, 6, 7; CWP; DLB 334
Bowers, Edgar 1924-2000 .... **CLC 9**
See also CA 5-8R; 188; CANR 24; CP 1, 2, 3, 4, 5, 6, 7; CSW; DLB 5
Bowers, Mrs. J. Milton 1842-1914
See Bierce, Ambrose (Gwinett)
Bowie, David
See Jones, David Robert
Bowles, Jane (Sydney) 1917-1973 ..... **CLC 3, 68**
See also CA 19-20; 41-44R; CAP 2; CN 1; EWL 3; MAL 5
Bowles, Jane Auer
See Bowles, Jane (Sydney)
Bowles, Paul 1910-1999 ..... **CLC 1, 2, 19, 53; SSC 3, 98; TCLC 209**
See also AMWS 4; CA 1-4R; 186; CAAS 1; CANR 1, 19, 50, 75; CN 1, 2, 3, 4, 5, 6; DA3; DLB 5, 6, 218; EWL 3; MAL 5; MTCW 1, 2; MTFW 2005; RGAL 4; SSFS 17
Bowles, William Lisle 1762-1850 . **NCLC 103**
See also DLB 93
Box, Edgar
See Vidal, Gore
Boyd, James 1888-1944 .... **TCLC 115**
See also CA 186; DLB 9; DLBD 16; RGAL 4; RHW
Boyd, Nancy
See Millay, Edna St. Vincent
Boyd, Thomas (Alexander)
1898-1935 .... **TCLC 111**
See also CA 111; 183; DLB 9; DLBD 16, 316
Boyd, William 1952- .... **CLC 28, 53, 70**
See also CA 114; 120; CANR 51, 71, 131, 174; CN 4, 5, 6, 7; DLB 231
Boyesen, Hjalmar Hjorth
1848-1895 .... **NCLC 135**
See also DLB 12, 71; DLBD 13; RGAL 4
Boyle, Kay 1902-1992 .... **CLC 1, 5, 19, 58, 121; SSC 5, 102**
See also CA 13-16R; 140; CAAS 1; CANR 29, 61, 110; CN 1, 2, 3, 4, 5; CP 1, 2, 3, 4, 5; DLB 4, 9, 48, 86; DLBY 1993; EWL 3; MAL 5; MTCW 1, 2; MTFW 2005; RGAL 4; RGSF 2; SSFS 10, 13, 14

Boyle, Mark
See Kienzle, William X.
Boyle, Patrick 1905-1982 .... **CLC 19**
See also CA 127
Boyle, T. C.
See Boyle, T. Coraghessan
Boyle, T. Coraghessan 1948- ..... **CLC 36, 55, 90; SSC 16**
See also AAYA 47; AMWS 8; BEST 90:4; BPFB 1; CA 120; CANR 44, 76, 89, 132; CN 6, 7; CPW; DA3; DAM POP; DLB 218, 278; DLBY 1986; EWL 3; MAL 5; MTCW 2; MTFW 2005; SSFS 13, 19
Boz
See Dickens, Charles (John Huffam)
Brackenridge, Hugh Henry
1748-1816 .... **NCLC 7**
See also DLB 11, 37; RGAL 4
Bradbury, Edward P.
See Moorcock, Michael
Bradbury, Malcolm (Stanley)
1932-2000 .... **CLC 32, 61**
See also CA 1-4R; CANR 1, 33, 91, 98, 137; CN 1, 2, 3, 4, 5, 6; CP 1; DA3; DAM NOV; DLB 14, 207; EWL 3; MTCW 1, 2; MTFW 2005
Bradbury, Ray 1920- ... **CLC 1, 3, 10, 15, 42, 98, 235; SSC 29, 53; WLC 1**
See also AAYA 15; AITN 1, 2; AMWS 4; BPFB 1; BYA 4, 5, 11; CA 1-4R; CANR 2, 30, 75, 125, 186; CDALB 1968-1988; CN 1, 2, 3, 4, 5, 6, 7; CPW; DA; DA3; DAB; DAC; DAM MST, NOV, POP; DLB 2, 8; EXPN; EXPS; HGG; LAIT 3, 5; LATS 1:2; LMFS 2; MAL 5; MTCW 1, 2; MTFW 2005; NFS 1, 22, 29; RGAL 4; RGSF 2; SATA 11, 64, 123; SCFW 1, 2; SFW 4; SSFS 1, 20; SUFW 1, 2; TUS; YAW
Bradbury, Ray Douglas
See Bradbury, Ray
Braddon, Mary Elizabeth
1837-1915 .... **TCLC 111**
See also BRWS 8; CA 108; 179; CMW 4; DLB 18, 70, 156; HGG
Bradfield, Scott 1955- .... **SSC 65**
See also CA 147; CANR 90; HGG; SUFW 2
Bradfield, Scott Michael
See Bradfield, Scott
Bradford, Gamaliel 1863-1932 .... **TCLC 36**
See also CA 160; DLB 17
Bradford, William 1590-1657 .... **LC 64**
See also DLB 24, 30; RGAL 4
Bradley, David, Jr. 1950- ...... **BLC 1:1; CLC 23, 118**
See also BW 1, 3; CA 104; CANR 26, 81; CN 4, 5, 6, 7; DAM MULT; DLB 33
Bradley, David Henry, Jr.
See Bradley, David, Jr.
Bradley, John Ed 1958- .... **CLC 55**
See also CA 139; CANR 99; CN 6, 7; CSW
Bradley, John Edmund, Jr.
See Bradley, John Ed
Bradley, Marion Zimmer
1930-1999 .... **CLC 30**
See also AAYA 40; BPFB 1; CA 57-60; 185; CAAS 10; CANR 7, 31, 51, 75, 107; CPW; DA3; DAM POP; DLB 8; FANT; FW; GLL 1; MTCW 1, 2; MTFW 2005; SATA 90, 139; SATA-Obit 116; SFW 4; SUFW 2; YAW
Bradshaw, John 1933- .... **CLC 70**
See also CA 138; CANR 61
Bradstreet, Anne 1612(?)-1672 .... **LC 4, 30, 130; PC 10**
See also AMWS 1; CDALB 1640-1865; DA; DA3; DAC; DAM MST, POET; DLB 24; EXPP; FW; PFS 6; RGAL 4; TUS; WP

Brady, Joan 1939- .... **CLC 86**
See also CA 141

Bragg, Melvyn 1939- .... **CLC 10**
See also BEST 89:3; CA 57-60; CANR 10,
48, 89, 158; CN 1, 2, 3, 4, 5, 6, 7; DLB
14, 271; RHW

Brahe, Tycho 1546-1601 .... **LC 45**
See also DLB 300

Braine, John (Gerard) 1922-1986 . **CLC 1, 3,
41**
See also CA 1-4R; 120; CANR 1, 33; CD-
BLB 1945-1960; CN 1, 2, 3, 4; DLB 15;
DLBY 1986; EWL 3; MTCW 1

Braithwaite, William Stanley (Beaumont)
1878-1962 ...... **BLC 1:1; HR 1:2; PC 52**
See also BW 1; CA 125; DAM MULT; DLB
50, 54; MAL 5

Bramah, Ernest 1868-1942 .... **TCLC 72**
See also CA 156; CMW 4; DLB 70; FANT

Brammer, Billy Lee
See Brammer, William

Brammer, William 1929-1978 .... **CLC 31**
See also CA 235; 77-80

Brancati, Vitaliano 1907-1954 .... **TCLC 12**
See also CA 109; DLB 264; EWL 3

Brancato, Robin F(idler) 1936- .... **CLC 35**
See also AAYA 9, 68; BYA 6; CA 69-72;
CANR 11, 45; CLR 32; JRDA; MAICYA
2; MAICYAS 1; SAAS 9; SATA 97;
WYA; YAW

Brand, Dionne 1953- .... **CLC 192**
See also BW 2; CA 143; CANR 143; CWP;
DLB 334

Brand, Max
See Faust, Frederick (Schiller)

Brand, Millen 1906-1980 .... **CLC 7**
See also CA 21-24R; 97-100; CANR 72

Branden, Barbara 1929- .... **CLC 44**
See also CA 148

Brandes, Georg (Morris Cohen)
1842-1927 .... **TCLC 10**
See also CA 105; 189; DLB 300

Brandys, Kazimierz 1916-2000 .... **CLC 62**
See also CA 239; EWL 3

Branley, Franklyn M(ansfield)
1915-2002 .... **CLC 21**
See also CA 33-36R; 207; CANR 14, 39;
CLR 13; MAICYA 1, 2; SAAS 16; SATA
4, 68, 136

Brant, Beth (E.) 1941- .... **NNAL**
See also CA 144; FW

Brant, Sebastian 1457-1521 .... **LC 112**
See also DLB 179; RGWL 2, 3

Brathwaite, Edward Kamau
1930- ..... **BLC 2:1; BLCS; CLC 11; PC
56**
See also BRWS 12; BW 2, 3; CA 25-28R;
CANR 11, 26, 47, 107; CDWLB 3; CP 1,
2, 3, 4, 5, 6, 7; DAM POET; DLB 125;
EWL 3

Brathwaite, Kamau
See Brathwaite, Edward Kamau

Brautigan, Richard (Gary)
1935-1984 .... **CLC 1, 3, 5, 9, 12, 34, 42;
PC 94; TCLC 133**
See also BPFB 1; CA 53-56; 113; CANR
34; CN 1, 2, 3; CP 1, 2, 3, 4; DA3; DAM
NOV; DLB 2, 5, 206; DLBY 1980, 1984;
FANT; MAL 5; MTCW 1; RGAL 4;
SATA 56

Brave Bird, Mary
See Crow Dog, Mary

Braverman, Kate 1950- .... **CLC 67**
See also CA 89-92; CANR 141; DLB 335

Brecht, (Eugen) Bertolt (Friedrich)
1898-1956 ..... **DC 3; TCLC 1, 6, 13, 35,
169; WLC 1**
See also CA 104; 133; CANR 62; CDWLB
2; DA; DA3; DAB; DAC; DAM DRAM,
MST; DFS 4, 5, 9; DLB 56, 124; EW 11;
EWL 3; IDTP; MTCW 1, 2; MTFW 2005;
RGHL; RGWL 2, 3; TWA

Brecht, Eugen Berthold Friedrich
See Brecht, (Eugen) Bertolt (Friedrich)

Bremer, Fredrika 1801-1865 .... **NCLC 11**
See also DLB 254

Brennan, Christopher John
1870-1932 .... **TCLC 17**
See also CA 117; 188; DLB 230; EWL 3

Brennan, Maeve 1917-1993 ... **CLC 5; TCLC
124**
See also CA 81-84; CANR 72, 100

Brenner, Jozef 1887-1919 .... **TCLC 13**
See also CA 111; 240

Brent, Linda
See Jacobs, Harriet A(nn)

Brentano, Clemens (Maria)
1778-1842 .... **NCLC 1, 191; SSC 115**
See also DLB 90; RGWL 2, 3

Brent of Bin Bin
See Franklin, (Stella Maria Sarah) Miles
(Lampe)

Brenton, Howard 1942- .... **CLC 31**
See also CA 69-72; CANR 33, 67; CBD;
CD 5, 6; DLB 13; MTCW 1

Breslin, James
See Breslin, Jimmy

Breslin, Jimmy 1930- .... **CLC 4, 43**
See also CA 73-76; CANR 31, 75, 139, 187;
DAM NOV; DLB 185; MTCW 2; MTFW
2005

Bresson, Robert 1901(?)-1999 .... **CLC 16**
See also CA 110; 187; CANR 49

Breton, Andre 1896-1966 .. **CLC 2, 9, 15, 54;
PC 15**
See also CA 19-20; 25-28R; CANR 40, 60;
CAP 2; DLB 65, 258; EW 11; EWL 3;
GFL 1789 to the Present; LMFS 2;
MTCW 1, 2; MTFW 2005; RGWL 2, 3;
TWA; WP

Breton, Nicholas c. 1554-c. 1626 .... **LC 133**
See also DLB 136

Breytenbach, Breyten 1939(?)- .. **CLC 23, 37,
126**
See also CA 113; 129; CANR 61, 122;
CWW 2; DAM POET; DLB 225; EWL 3

Bridgers, Sue Ellen 1942- .... **CLC 26**
See also AAYA 8, 49; BYA 7, 8; CA 65-68;
CANR 11, 36; CLR 18; DLB 52; JRDA;
MAICYA 1, 2; SAAS 1; SATA 22, 90;
SATA-Essay 109; WYA; YAW

Bridges, Robert (Seymour)
1844-1930 .... **PC 28; TCLC 1**
See also BRW 6; CA 104; 152; CDBLB
1890-1914; DAM POET; DLB 19, 98

Bridie, James
See Mavor, Osborne Henry

Brin, David 1950- .... **CLC 34**
See also AAYA 21; CA 102; CANR 24, 70,
125, 127; INT CANR-24; SATA 65;
SCFW 2; SFW 4

Brink, Andre 1935- .... **CLC 18, 36, 106**
See also AFW; BRWS 6; CA 104; CANR
39, 62, 109, 133, 182; CN 4, 5, 6, 7; DLB
225; EWL 3; INT CA-103; LATS 1:2;
MTCW 1, 2; MTFW 2005; WLIT 2

Brinsmead, H. F.
See Brinsmead, H(esba) F(ay)

Brinsmead, H. F(ay)
See Brinsmead, H(esba) F(ay)

Brinsmead, H(esba) F(ay) 1922- ...... **CLC 21**
See also CA 21-24R; CANR 10; CLR 47;
CWRI 5; MAICYA 1, 2; SAAS 5; SATA
18, 78

Brittain, Vera (Mary) 1893(?)-1970 . **CLC 23**
See also BRWS 10; CA 13-16; 25-28R;
CANR 58; CAP 1; DLB 191; FW; MTCW
1, 2

Broch, Hermann 1886-1951 ... **TCLC 20, 204**
See also CA 117; 211; CDWLB 2; DLB 85,
124; EW 10; EWL 3; RGWL 2, 3

Brock, Rose
See Hansen, Joseph

Brod, Max 1884-1968 .... **TCLC 115**
See also CA 5-8R; 25-28R; CANR 7; DLB
81; EWL 3

Brodkey, Harold (Roy) 1930-1996 .. **CLC 56;
TCLC 123**
See also CA 111; 151; CANR 71; CN 4, 5,
6; DLB 130

Brodsky, Iosif Alexandrovich 1940-1996
See Brodsky, Joseph
See also AAYA 71; AITN 1; AMWS 8; CA
41-44R; 151; CANR 37, 106; CWW 2;
DA3; DAM POET; DLB 285, 329; EWL
3; MTCW 1, 2; MTFW 2005; RGWL 2, 3

Brodsky, Joseph . **CLC 4, 6, 13, 36, 100; PC
9; TCLC 219**
See Brodsky, Iosif Alexandrovich

Brodsky, Michael 1948- .... **CLC 19**
See also CA 102; CANR 18, 41, 58, 147;
DLB 244

Brodsky, Michael Mark
See Brodsky, Michael

Brodzki, Bella .... **CLC 65**

Brome, Richard 1590(?)-1652 .... **LC 61**
See also BRWS 10; DLB 58

Bromell, Henry 1947- .... **CLC 5**
See also CA 53-56; CANR 9, 115, 116

Bromfield, Louis (Brucker)
1896-1956 .... **TCLC 11**
See also CA 107; 155; DLB 4, 9, 86; RGAL
4; RHW

Broner, E(sther) M(asserman)
1930- .... **CLC 19**
See also CA 17-20R; CANR 8, 25, 72; CN
4, 5, 6; DLB 28

Bronk, William (M.) 1918-1999 .... **CLC 10**
See also CA 89-92; 177; CANR 23; CP 3,
4, 5, 6, 7; DLB 165

Bronstein, Lev Davidovich
See Trotsky, Leon

Bronte, Anne
See Bronte, Anne

Bronte, Anne 1820-1849 ..... **NCLC 4, 71, 102**
See also BRW 5; BRWR 1; DA3; DLB 21,
199, 340; NFS 26; TEA

Bronte, (Patrick) Branwell
1817-1848 .... **NCLC 109**
See also DLB 340

Bronte, Charlotte
See Bronte, Charlotte

Bronte, Charlotte 1816-1855 ...... **NCLC 3, 8,
33, 58, 105, 155; WLC 1**
See also AAYA 17; BRW 5; BRWC 2;
BRWR 1; BYA 2; CDBLB 1832-1890;
DA; DA3; DAB; DAC; DAM MST, NOV;
DLB 21, 159, 199, 340; EXPN; FL 1:2;
GL 2; LAIT 2; NFS 4; TEA; WLIT 4

Bronte, Emily
See Bronte, Emily (Jane)

Bronte, Emily (Jane) 1818-1848 ... **NCLC 16,
35, 165; PC 8; WLC 1**
See also AAYA 17; BPFB 1; BRW 5;
BRWC 1; BRWR 3; CDBLB
1832-1890; DA; DA3; DAB; DAC; DAM
MST, NOV, POET; DLB 21, 32, 199, 340;
EXPN; FL 1:2; GL 2; LAIT 1; TEA;
WLIT 3

Brontes
See Bronte, Anne; Bronte, (Patrick) Branwell; Bronte, Charlotte; Bronte, Emily (Jane)

Brooke, Frances 1724-1789 .... **LC 6, 48**
See also DLB 39, 99

Brooke, Henry 1703(?)-1783 .... **LC 1**
See also DLB 39

Brooke, Rupert (Chawner)
1887-1915 .. **PC 24; TCLC 2, 7; WLC 1**
See also BRWS 3; CA 104; 132; CANR 61; CDBLB 1914-1945; DA; DAB; DAC; DAM MST, POET; DLB 19, 216; EXPP; GLL 2; MTCW 1, 2; MTFW 2005; PFS 7; TEA

Brooke-Haven, P.
See Wodehouse, P(elham) G(renville)

Brooke-Rose, Christine 1923(?)- ..... **CLC 40, 184**
See also BRWS 4; CA 13-16R; CANR 58, 118, 183; CN 1, 2, 3, 4, 5, 6, 7; DLB 14, 231; EWL 3; SFW 4

Brookner, Anita 1928- . **CLC 32, 34, 51, 136, 237**
See also BRWS 4; CA 114; 120; CANR 37, 56, 87, 130; CN 4, 5, 6, 7; CPW; DA3; DAB; DAM POP; DLB 194, 326; DLBY 1987; EWL 3; MTCW 1, 2; MTFW 2005; NFS 23; TEA

Brooks, Cleanth 1906-1994 . **CLC 24, 86, 110**
See also AMWS 14; CA 17-20R; 145; CANR 33, 35; CSW; DLB 63; DLBY 1994; EWL 3; INT CANR-35; MAL 5; MTCW 1, 2; MTFW 2005

Brooks, George
See Baum, L(yman) Frank

Brooks, Gwendolyn 1917-2000 .... **BLC 1:1, 2:1; CLC 1, 2, 4, 5, 15, 49, 125; PC 7; WLC 1**
See also AAYA 20; AFAW 1, 2; AITN 1; AMWS 3; BW 2, 3; CA 1-4R; 190; CANR 1, 27, 52, 75, 132; CDALB 1941-1968; CLR 27; CP 1, 2, 3, 4, 5, 6, 7; CWP; DA; DA3; DAC; DAM MST, MULT, POET; DLB 5, 76, 165; EWL 3; EXPP; FL 1:5; MAL 5; MBL; MTCW 1, 2; MTFW 2005; PFS 1, 2, 4, 6; RGAL 4; SATA 6; SATA-Obit 123; TUS; WP

Brooks, Mel 1926-
See Kaminsky, Melvin
See also CA 65-68; CANR 16; DFS 21

Brooks, Peter 1938- .... **CLC 34**
See also CA 45-48; CANR 1, 107, 182

Brooks, Peter Preston
See Brooks, Peter

Brooks, Van Wyck 1886-1963 .... **CLC 29**
See also AMW; CA 1-4R; CANR 6; DLB 45, 63, 103; MAL 5; TUS

Brophy, Brigid (Antonia)
1929-1995 .... **CLC 6, 11, 29, 105**
See also CA 5-8R; 149; CAAS 4; CANR 25, 53; CBD; CN 1, 2, 3, 4, 5, 6; CWD; DA3; DLB 14, 271; EWL 3; MTCW 1, 2

Brosman, Catharine Savage 1934- ..... **CLC 9**
See also CA 61-64; CANR 21, 46, 149

Brossard, Nicole 1943- .... **CLC 115, 169; PC 80**
See also CA 122; CAAS 16; CANR 140; CCA 1; CWP; CWW 2; DLB 53; EWL 3; FW; GLL 2; RGWL 3

Brother Antoninus
See Everson, William (Oliver)

Brothers Grimm
See Grimm, Jacob Ludwig Karl; Grimm, Wilhelm Karl

The Brothers Quay
See Quay, Stephen; Quay, Timothy

Broughton, T(homas) Alan 1936- ..... **CLC 19**
See also CA 45-48; CANR 2, 23, 48, 111

Broumas, Olga 1949- .... **CLC 10, 73**
See also CA 85-88; CANR 20, 69, 110; CP 5, 6, 7; CWP; GLL 2

Broun, Heywood 1888-1939 .... **TCLC 104**
See also DLB 29, 171

Brown, Alan 1950- .... **CLC 99**
See also CA 156

Brown, Charles Brockden
1771-1810 .... **NCLC 22, 74, 122**
See also AMWS 1; CDALB 1640-1865; DLB 37, 59, 73; FW; GL 2; HGG; LMFS 1; RGAL 4; TUS

Brown, Christy 1932-1981 .... **CLC 63**
See also BYA 13; CA 105; 104; CANR 72; DLB 14

Brown, Claude 1937-2002 ..... **BLC 1:1; CLC 30**
See also AAYA 7; BW 1, 3; CA 73-76; 205; CANR 81; DAM MULT

Brown, Dan 1964- .... **CLC 209**
See also AAYA 55; CA 217; MTFW 2005

Brown, Dee 1908-2002 .... **CLC 18, 47**
See also AAYA 30; CA 13-16R; 212; CAAS 6; CANR 11, 45, 60, 150; CPW; CSW; DA3; DAM POP; DLBY 1980; LAIT 2; MTCW 1, 2; MTFW 2005; NCFS 5; SATA 5, 110; SATA-Obit 141; TCWW 1, 2

Brown, Dee Alexander
See Brown, Dee

Brown, George
See Wertmueller, Lina

Brown, George Douglas
1869-1902 .... **TCLC 28**
See also CA 162; RGEL 2

Brown, George Mackay 1921-1996 ... **CLC 5, 48, 100**
See also BRWS 6; CA 21-24R; 151; CAAS 6; CANR 12, 37, 67; CN 1, 2, 3, 4, 5, 6; CP 1, 2, 3, 4, 5, 6; DLB 14, 27, 139, 271; MTCW 1; RGSF 2; SATA 35

Brown, James Willie
See Komunyakaa, Yusef

Brown, James Willie, Jr.
See Komunyakaa, Yusef

Brown, Larry 1951-2004 .... **CLC 73**
See also CA 130; 134; 233; CANR 117, 145; CSW; DLB 234; INT CA-134

Brown, Moses
See Barrett, William (Christopher)

Brown, Rita Mae 1944- .... **CLC 18, 43, 79, 259**
See also BPFB 1; CA 45-48; CANR 2, 11, 35, 62, 95, 138, 183; CN 5, 6, 7; CPW; CSW; DA3; DAM NOV, POP; FW; INT CANR-11; MAL 5; MTCW 1, 2; MTFW 2005; NFS 9; RGAL 4; TUS

Brown, Roderick (Langmere) Haig-
See Haig-Brown, Roderick (Langmere)

Brown, Rosellen 1939- .... **CLC 32, 170**
See also CA 77-80; CAAS 10; CANR 14, 44, 98; CN 6, 7

Brown, Sterling Allen 1901-1989 ...... **BLC 1; CLC 1, 23, 59; HR 1:2; PC 55**
See also AFAW 1, 2; BW 1, 3; CA 85-88; 127; CANR 26; CP 3, 4; DA3; DAM MULT, POET; DLB 48, 51, 63; MAL 5; MTCW 1, 2; MTFW 2005; RGAL 4; WP

Brown, Will
See Ainsworth, William Harrison

Brown, William Hill 1765-1793 .... **LC 93**
See also DLB 37

Brown, William Larry
See Brown, Larry

Brown, William Wells 1815-1884 ... **BLC 1:1; DC 1; NCLC 2, 89**
See also DAM MULT; DLB 3, 50, 183, 248; RGAL 4

Browne, Clyde Jackson
See Browne, Jackson

Browne, Jackson 1948(?)- .... **CLC 21**
See also CA 120

Browne, Sir Thomas 1605-1682 .... **LC 111**
See also BRW 2; DLB 151

Browning, Robert 1812-1889 . **NCLC 19, 79; PC 2, 61, 97; WLCS**
See also BRW 4; BRWC 2; BRWR 2; CD-BLB 1832-1890; CLR 97; DA; DA3; DAB; DAC; DAM MST, POET; DLB 32, 163; EXPP; LATS 1:1; PAB; PFS 1, 15; RGEL 2; TEA; WLIT 4; WP; YABC 1

Browning, Tod 1882-1962 .... **CLC 16**
See also CA 141; 117

Brownmiller, Susan 1935- .... **CLC 159**
See also CA 103; CANR 35, 75, 137; DAM NOV; FW; MTCW 1, 2; MTFW 2005

Brownson, Orestes Augustus
1803-1876 .... **NCLC 50**
See also DLB 1, 59, 73, 243

Bruccoli, Matthew J. 1931-2008 .... **CLC 34**
See also CA 9-12R; 274; CANR 7, 87; DLB 103

Bruccoli, Matthew Joseph
See Bruccoli, Matthew J.

Bruce, Lenny
See Schneider, Leonard Alfred

Bruchac, Joseph 1942- .... **NNAL**
See also AAYA 19; CA 33-36R, 256; CAAE 256; CANR 13, 47, 75, 94, 137, 161; CLR 46; CWRI 5; DAM MULT; DLB 342; JRDA; MAICYA 2; MAICYAS 1; MTCW 2; MTFW 2005; SATA 42, 89, 131, 176; SATA-Essay 176

Bruin, John
See Brutus, Dennis

Brulard, Henri
See Stendhal

Brulls, Christian
See Simenon, Georges (Jacques Christian)

Brunetto Latini c. 1220-1294 .... **CMLC 73**

Brunner, John (Kilian Houston)
1934-1995 .... **CLC 8, 10**
See also CA 1-4R; 149; CAAS 8; CANR 2, 37; CPW; DAM POP; DLB 261; MTCW 1, 2; SCFW 1, 2; SFW 4

Bruno, Giordano 1548-1600 .... **LC 27, 167**
See also RGWL 2, 3

Brutus, Dennis 1924- ...... **BLC 1:1; CLC 43; PC 24**
See also AFW; BW 2, 3; CA 49-52; CAAS 14; CANR 2, 27, 42, 81; CDWLB 3; CP 1, 2, 3, 4, 5, 6, 7; DAM MULT, POET; DLB 117, 225; EWL 3

Bryan, C(ourtlandt) D(ixon) B(arnes)
1936- .... **CLC 29**
See also CA 73-76; CANR 13, 68; DLB 185; INT CANR-13

Bryan, Michael
See Moore, Brian

Bryan, William Jennings
1860-1925 .... **TCLC 99**
See also DLB 303

Bryant, William Cullen 1794-1878 . **NCLC 6, 46; PC 20**
See also AMWS 1; CDALB 1640-1865; DA; DAB; DAC; DAM MST, POET; DLB 3, 43, 59, 189, 250; EXPP; PAB; PFS 30; RGAL 4; TUS

Bryusov, Valery Yakovlevich
1873-1924 .... **TCLC 10**
See also CA 107; 155; EWL 3; SFW 4

Buchan, John 1875-1940 .... **TCLC 41**
See also CA 108; 145; CMW 4; DAB; DAM POP; DLB 34, 70, 156; HGG; MSW; MTCW 2; RGEL 2; RHW; YABC 2

Butler, Samuel 1835-1902 .... **TCLC 1, 33; WLC 1**
See also BRWS 2; CA 143; CDBLB 1890-1914; DA; DA3; DAB; DAC; DAM MST, NOV; DLB 18, 57, 174; RGEL 2; SFW 4; TEA

Butler, Walter C.
See Faust, Frederick (Schiller)

Butor, Michel (Marie Francois)
1926- .... **CLC 1, 3, 8, 11, 15, 161**
See also CA 9-12R; CANR 33, 66; CWW 2; DLB 83; EW 13; EWL 3; GFL 1789 to the Present; MTCW 1, 2; MTFW 2005

Butts, Mary 1890(?)-1937 ... **SSC 124; TCLC 77**
See also CA 148; DLB 240

Buxton, Ralph
See Silverstein, Alvin; Silverstein, Virginia B(arbara Opshelor)

Buzo, Alex
See Buzo, Alexander (John)

Buzo, Alexander (John) 1944- .... **CLC 61**
See also CA 97-100; CANR 17, 39, 69; CD 5, 6; DLB 289

Buzzati, Dino 1906-1972 .... **CLC 36**
See also CA 160; 33-36R; DLB 177; RGWL 2, 3; SFW 4

Byars, Betsy 1928- .... **CLC 35**
See also AAYA 19; BYA 3; CA 33-36R, 183; CAAE 183; CANR 18, 36, 57, 102, 148; CLR 1, 16, 72; DLB 52; INT CANR-18; JRDA; MAICYA 1, 2; MAICYAS 1; MTCW 1; SAAS 1; SATA 4, 46, 80, 163; SATA-Essay 108; WYA; YAW

Byars, Betsy Cromer
See Byars, Betsy

Byatt, Antonia Susan Drabble
See Byatt, A.S.

Byatt, A.S. 1936- .... **CLC 19, 65, 136, 223; SSC 91**
See also BPFB 1; BRWC 2; BRWS 4; CA 13-16R; CANR 13, 33, 50, 75, 96, 133; CN 1, 2, 3, 4, 5, 6; DA3; DAM NOV, POP; DLB 14, 194, 319, 326; EWL 3; MTCW 1, 2; MTFW 2005; RGSF 2; RHW; SSFS 26; TEA

Byrd, William II 1674-1744 .... **LC 112**
See also DLB 24, 140; RGAL 4

Byrne, David 1952- .... **CLC 26**
See also CA 127

Byrne, John Keyes 1926-2009 .... **CLC 19**
See also CA 102; CANR 78, 140; CBD; CD 5, 6; DFS 13, 24; DLB 13; INT CA-102

Byron, George Gordon (Noel)
1788-1824 ..... **DC 24; NCLC 2, 12, 109, 149; PC 16, 95; WLC 1**
See also AAYA 64; BRW 4; BRWC 2; CD-BLB 1789-1832; DA; DA3; DAB; DAC; DAM MST, POET; DLB 96, 110; EXPP; LMFS 1; PAB; PFS 1, 14, 29; RGEL 2; TEA; WLIT 3; WP

Byron, Robert 1905-1941 .... **TCLC 67**
See also CA 160; DLB 195

C. 3. 3.
See Wilde, Oscar

Caballero, Fernan 1796-1877 .... **NCLC 10**

Cabell, Branch
See Cabell, James Branch

Cabell, James Branch 1879-1958 .... **TCLC 6**
See also CA 105; 152; DLB 9, 78; FANT; MAL 5; MTCW 2; RGAL 4; SUFW 1

Cabeza de Vaca, Alvar Nunez
1490-1557(?) .... **LC 61**

Cable, George Washington
1844-1925 .... **SSC 4; TCLC 4**
See also CA 104; 155; DLB 12, 74; DLBD 13; RGAL 4; TUS

Cabral de Melo Neto, Joao
1920-1999 .... **CLC 76**
See also CA 151; CWW 2; DAM MULT; DLB 307; EWL 3; LAW; LAWS 1

Cabrera Infante, G. 1929-2005 ... **CLC 5, 25, 45, 120; HLC 1; SSC 39**
See also CA 85-88; 236; CANR 29, 65, 110; CDWLB 3; CWW 2; DA3; DAM MULT; DLB 113; EWL 3; HW 1, 2; LAW; LAWS 1; MTCW 1, 2; MTFW 2005; RGSF 2; WLIT 1

Cabrera Infante, Guillermo
See Cabrera Infante, G.

Cade, Toni
See Bambara, Toni Cade

Cadmus and Harmonia
See Buchan, John

Caedmon fl. 658-680 .... **CMLC 7**
See also DLB 146

Caeiro, Alberto
See Pessoa, Fernando

Caesar, Julius
See Julius Caesar

Cage, John (Milton), (Jr.)
1912-1992 .... **CLC 41; PC 58**
See also CA 13-16R; 169; CANR 9, 78; DLB 193; INT CANR-9; TCLE 1:1

Cahan, Abraham 1860-1951 .... **TCLC 71**
See also CA 108; 154; DLB 9, 25, 28; MAL 5; RGAL 4

Cain, Christopher
See Fleming, Thomas

Cain, G.
See Cabrera Infante, G.

Cain, Guillermo
See Cabrera Infante, G.

Cain, James M(allahan) 1892-1977 .. **CLC 3, 11, 28**
See also AITN 1; BPFB 1; CA 17-20R; 73-76; CANR 8, 34, 61; CMW 4; CN 1, 2; DLB 226; EWL 3; MAL 5; MSW; MTCW 1; RGAL 4

Caine, Hall 1853-1931 .... **TCLC 97**
See also RHW

Caine, Mark
See Raphael, Frederic (Michael)

Calasso, Roberto 1941- .... **CLC 81**
See also CA 143; CANR 89

Calderon de la Barca, Pedro
1600-1681 . **DC 3; HLCS 1; LC 23, 136**
See also DFS 23; EW 2; RGWL 2, 3; TWA

Caldwell, Erskine 1903-1987 ... **CLC 1, 8, 14, 50, 60; SSC 19; TCLC 117**
See also AITN 1; AMW; BPFB 1; CA 1-4R; 121; CAAS 1; CANR 2, 33; CN 1, 2, 3, 4; DA3; DAM NOV; DLB 9, 86; EWL 3; MAL 5; MTCW 1, 2; MTFW 2005; RGAL 4; RGSF 2; TUS

Caldwell, (Janet Miriam) Taylor (Holland)
1900-1985 .... **CLC 2, 28, 39**
See also BPFB 1; CA 5-8R; 116; CANR 5; DA3; DAM NOV, POP; DLBD 17; MTCW 2; RHW

Calhoun, John Caldwell
1782-1850 .... **NCLC 15**
See also DLB 3, 248

Calisher, Hortense 1911-2009 .... **CLC 2, 4, 8, 38, 134; SSC 15**
See also CA 1-4R; CANR 1, 22, 117; CN 1, 2, 3, 4, 5, 6, 7; DA3; DAM NOV; DLB 2, 218; INT CANR-22; MAL 5; MTCW 1, 2; MTFW 2005; RGAL 4; RGSF 2

Callaghan, Morley Edward
1903-1990 ..... **CLC 3, 14, 41, 65; TCLC 145**
See also CA 9-12R; 132; CANR 33, 73; CN 1, 2, 3, 4; DAC; DAM MST; DLB 68; EWL 3; MTCW 1, 2; MTFW 2005; RGEL 2; RGSF 2; SSFS 19

Callimachus c. 305B.C.-c.
240B.C. .... **CMLC 18**
See also AW 1; DLB 176; RGWL 2, 3

Calvin, Jean
See Calvin, John

Calvin, John 1509-1564 .... **LC 37**
See also DLB 327; GFL Beginnings to 1789

Calvino, Italo 1923-1985 .... **CLC 5, 8, 11, 22, 33, 39, 73; SSC 3, 48; TCLC 183**
See also AAYA 58; CA 85-88; 116; CANR 23, 61, 132; DAM NOV; DLB 196; EW 13; EWL 3; MTCW 1, 2; MTFW 2005; RGHL; RGSF 2; RGWL 2, 3; SFW 4; SSFS 12; WLIT 7

Camara Laye
See Laye, Camara

Cambridge, A Gentleman of the University of
See Crowley, Edward Alexander

Camden, William 1551-1623 .... **LC 77**
See also DLB 172

Cameron, Carey 1952- .... **CLC 59**
See also CA 135

Cameron, Peter 1959- .... **CLC 44**
See also AMWS 12; CA 125; CANR 50, 117, 188; DLB 234; GLL 2

Camoens, Luis Vaz de 1524(?)-1580
See Camoes, Luis de

Camoes, Luis de 1524(?)-1580 . **HLCS 1; LC 62; PC 31**
See also DLB 287; EW 2; RGWL 2, 3

Camp, Madeleine L'Engle
See L'Engle, Madeleine

Campana, Dino 1885-1932 .... **TCLC 20**
See also CA 117; 246; DLB 114; EWL 3

Campanella, Tommaso 1568-1639 .... **LC 32**
See also RGWL 2, 3

Campbell, Bebe Moore 1950-2006 . **BLC 2:1; CLC 246**
See also AAYA 26; BW 2, 3; CA 139; 254; CANR 81, 134; DLB 227; MTCW 2; MTFW 2005

Campbell, John Ramsey
See Campbell, Ramsey

Campbell, John W(ood, Jr.)
1910-1971 .... **CLC 32**
See also CA 21-22; 29-32R; CANR 34; CAP 2; DLB 8; MTCW 1; SCFW 1, 2; SFW 4

Campbell, Joseph 1904-1987 .... **CLC 69; TCLC 140**
See also AAYA 3, 66; BEST 89:2; CA 1-4R; 124; CANR 3, 28, 61, 107; DA3; MTCW 1, 2

Campbell, Maria 1940- .... **CLC 85; NNAL**
See also CA 102; CANR 54; CCA 1; DAC

Campbell, Ramsey 1946- ... **CLC 42; SSC 19**
See also AAYA 51; CA 57-60, 228; CAAE 228; CANR 7, 102, 171; DLB 261; HGG; INT CANR-7; SUFW 1, 2

Campbell, (Ignatius) Roy (Dunnachie)
1901-1957 .... **TCLC 5**
See also AFW; CA 104; 155; DLB 20, 225; EWL 3; MTCW 2; RGEL 2

Campbell, Thomas 1777-1844 .... **NCLC 19**
See also DLB 93, 144; RGEL 2

Campbell, Wilfred
See Campbell, William

Campbell, William 1858(?)-1918 ..... **TCLC 9**
See also CA 106; DLB 92

Campbell, William Edward March
1893-1954 .... **TCLC 96**
See also CA 108; 216; DLB 9, 86, 316; MAL 5

Campion, Jane 1954- .... **CLC 95, 229**
See also AAYA 33; CA 138; CANR 87

Campion, Thomas 1567-1620 . **LC 78; PC 87**
See also CDBLB Before 1660; DAM POET; DLB 58, 172; RGEL 2

Camus, Albert 1913-1960 ...... **CLC 1, 2, 4, 9, 11, 14, 32, 63, 69, 124; DC 2; SSC 9, 76; WLC 1**
See also AAYA 36; AFW; BPFB 1; CA 89-92; CANR 131; DA; DA3; DAB; DAC; DAM DRAM, MST, NOV; DLB 72, 321, 329; EW 13; EWL 3; EXPN; EXPS; GFL 1789 to the Present; LATS 1:2; LMFS 2; MTCW 1, 2; MTFW 2005; NFS 6, 16; RGHL; RGSF 2; RGWL 2, 3; SSFS 4; TWA

Canby, Vincent 1924-2000 .... **CLC 13**
See also CA 81-84; 191

Cancale
See Desnos, Robert

Canetti, Elias 1905-1994 .. **CLC 3, 14, 25, 75, 86; TCLC 157**
See also CA 21-24R; 146; CANR 23, 61, 79; CDWLB 2; CWW 2; DA3; DLB 85, 124, 329; EW 12; EWL 3; MTCW 1, 2; MTFW 2005; RGWL 2, 3; TWA

Canfield, Dorothea F.
See Fisher, Dorothy (Frances) Canfield

Canfield, Dorothea Frances
See Fisher, Dorothy (Frances) Canfield

Canfield, Dorothy
See Fisher, Dorothy (Frances) Canfield

Canin, Ethan 1960- .... **CLC 55; SSC 70**
See also CA 131; 135; DLB 335; MAL 5

Cankar, Ivan 1876-1918 .... **TCLC 105**
See also CDWLB 4; DLB 147; EWL 3

Cannon, Curt
See Hunter, Evan

Cao, Lan 1961- .... **CLC 109**
See also CA 165

Cape, Judith
See Page, P(atricia) K(athleen)

Capek, Karel 1890-1938 .... **DC 1; SSC 36; TCLC 6, 37, 192; WLC 1**
See also CA 104; 140; CDWLB 4; DA; DA3; DAB; DAC; DAM DRAM, MST, NOV; DFS 7, 11; DLB 215; EW 10; EWL 3; MTCW 2; MTFW 2005; RGSF 2; RGWL 2, 3; SCFW 1, 2; SFW 4

Capella, Martianus fl. 4th cent. - .. **CMLC 84**

Capote, Truman 1924-1984 . **CLC 1, 3, 8, 13, 19, 34, 38, 58; SSC 2, 47, 93; TCLC 164; WLC 1**
See also AAYA 61; AMWS 3; BPFB 1; CA 5-8R; 113; CANR 18, 62; CDALB 1941-1968; CN 1, 2, 3; CPW; DA; DA3; DAB; DAC; DAM MST, NOV, POP; DLB 2, 185, 227; DLBY 1980, 1984; EWL 3; EXPS; GLL 1; LAIT 3; MAL 5; MTCW 1, 2; MTFW 2005; NCFS 2; RGAL 4; RGSF 2; SATA 91; SSFS 2; TUS

Capra, Frank 1897-1991 .... **CLC 16**
See also AAYA 52; CA 61-64; 135

Caputo, Philip 1941- .... **CLC 32**
See also AAYA 60; CA 73-76; CANR 40, 135; YAW

Caragiale, Ion Luca 1852-1912 ...... **TCLC 76**
See also CA 157

Card, Orson Scott 1951- .... **CLC 44, 47, 50**
See also AAYA 11, 42; BPFB 1; BYA 5, 8; CA 102; CANR 27, 47, 73, 102, 106, 133, 184; CLR 116; CPW; DA3; DAM POP; FANT; INT CANR-27; MTCW 1, 2; MTFW 2005; NFS 5; SATA 83, 127; SCFW 2; SFW 4; SUFW 2; YAW

Cardenal, Ernesto 1925- .... **CLC 31, 161; HLC 1; PC 22**
See also CA 49-52; CANR 2, 32, 66, 138; CWW 2; DAM MULT, POET; DLB 290; EWL 3; HW 1, 2; LAWS 1; MTCW 1, 2; MTFW 2005; RGWL 2, 3

Cardinal, Marie 1929-2001 .... **CLC 189**
See also CA 177; CWW 2; DLB 83; FW

Cardozo, Benjamin N(athan) 1870-1938 .... **TCLC 65**
See also CA 117; 164

Carducci, Giosue (Alessandro Giuseppe) 1835-1907 .... **PC 46; TCLC 32**
See also CA 163; DLB 329; EW 7; RGWL 2, 3

Carew, Thomas 1595(?)-1640 ..... **LC 13, 159; PC 29**
See also BRW 2; DLB 126; PAB; RGEL 2

Carey, Ernestine Gilbreth 1908-2006 .... **CLC 17**
See also CA 5-8R; 254; CANR 71; SATA 2; SATA-Obit 177

Carey, Peter 1943- .... **CLC 40, 55, 96, 183**
See also BRWS 12; CA 123; 127; CANR 53, 76, 117, 157, 185; CN 4, 5, 6, 7; DLB 289; EWL 3; INT CA-127; MTCW 1, 2; MTFW 2005; RGSF 2; SATA 94

Carey, Peter Philip
See Carey, Peter

Carleton, William 1794-1869 ... **NCLC 3, 199**
See also DLB 159; RGEL 2; RGSF 2

Carlisle, Henry (Coffin) 1926- .... **CLC 33**
See also CA 13-16R; CANR 15, 85

Carlsen, Chris
See Holdstock, Robert

Carlson, Ron 1947- .... **CLC 54**
See also CA 105, 189; CAAE 189; CANR 27, 155; DLB 244

Carlson, Ronald F.
See Carlson, Ron

Carlyle, Jane Welsh 1801-1866 ... **NCLC 181**
See also DLB 55

Carlyle, Thomas 1795-1881 ..... **NCLC 22, 70**
See also BRW 4; CDBLB 1789-1832; DA; DAB; DAC; DAM MST; DLB 55, 144, 254, 338; RGEL 2; TEA

Carman, (William) Bliss 1861-1929 ... **PC 34; TCLC 7**
See also CA 104; 152; DAC; DLB 92; RGEL 2

Carnegie, Dale 1888-1955 .... **TCLC 53**
See also CA 218

Carossa, Hans 1878-1956 .... **TCLC 48**
See also CA 170; DLB 66; EWL 3

Carpenter, Don(ald Richard) 1931-1995 .... **CLC 41**
See also CA 45-48; 149; CANR 1, 71

Carpenter, Edward 1844-1929 .... **TCLC 88**
See also BRWS 13; CA 163; GLL 1

Carpenter, John (Howard) 1948- ... **CLC 161**
See also AAYA 2, 73; CA 134; SATA 58

Carpenter, Johnny
See Carpenter, John (Howard)

Carpentier (y Valmont), Alejo 1904-1980 . **CLC 8, 11, 38, 110; HLC 1; SSC 35; TCLC 201**
See also CA 65-68; 97-100; CANR 11, 70; CDWLB 3; DAM MULT; DLB 113; EWL 3; HW 1, 2; LAW; LMFS 2; RGSF 2; RGWL 2, 3; WLIT 1

Carr, Caleb 1955- .... **CLC 86**
See also CA 147; CANR 73, 134; DA3

Carr, Emily 1871-1945 .... **TCLC 32**
See also CA 159; DLB 68; FW; GLL 2

Carr, H. D.
See Crowley, Edward Alexander

Carr, John Dickson 1906-1977 .... **CLC 3**
See also CA 49-52; 69-72; CANR 3, 33, 60; CMW 4; DLB 306; MSW; MTCW 1, 2

Carr, Philippa
See Hibbert, Eleanor Alice Burford

Carr, Virginia Spencer 1929- .... **CLC 34**
See also CA 61-64; CANR 175; DLB 111

Carrere, Emmanuel 1957- .... **CLC 89**
See also CA 200

Carrier, Roch 1937- .... **CLC 13, 78**
See also CA 130; CANR 61, 152; CCA 1; DAC; DAM MST; DLB 53; SATA 105, 166

Carroll, James Dennis
See Carroll, Jim

Carroll, James P. 1943(?)- .... **CLC 38**
See also CA 81-84; CANR 73, 139; MTCW 2; MTFW 2005

Carroll, Jim 1951- .... **CLC 35, 143**
See also AAYA 17; CA 45-48; CANR 42, 115; NCFS 5

Carroll, Lewis 1832-1898 . **NCLC 2, 53, 139; PC 18, 74; WLC 1**
See also AAYA 39; BRW 5; BYA 5, 13; CD-BLB 1832-1890; CLR 18, 108; DA; DA3; DAB; DAC; DAM MST, NOV, POET; DLB 18, 163, 178; DLBY 1998; EXPN; EXPP; FANT; JRDA; LAIT 1; MAICYA 1, 2; NFS 27; PFS 11, 30; RGEL 2; SATA 100; SUFW 1; TEA; WCH; YABC 2

Carroll, Paul Vincent 1900-1968 ...... **CLC 10**
See also CA 9-12R; 25-28R; DLB 10; EWL 3; RGEL 2

Carruth, Hayden 1921-2008 .... **CLC 4, 7, 10, 18, 84; PC 10**
See also AMWS 16; CA 9-12R; 277; CANR 4, 38, 59, 110, 174; CP 1, 2, 3, 4, 5, 6, 7; DLB 5, 165; INT CANR-4; MTCW 1, 2; MTFW 2005; PFS 26; SATA 47; SATA-Obit 197

Carson, Anne 1950- .... **CLC 185; PC 64**
See also AMWS 12; CA 203; CP 7; DLB 193; PFS 18; TCLE 1:1

Carson, Ciaran 1948- .... **CLC 201**
See also BRWS 13; CA 112; 153; CANR 113, 189; CP 6, 7; PFS 26

Carson, Rachel
See Carson, Rachel Louise

Carson, Rachel Louise 1907-1964 .... **CLC 71**
See also AAYA 49; AMWS 9; ANW; CA 77-80; CANR 35; DA3; DAM POP; DLB 275; FW; LAIT 4; MAL 5; MTCW 1, 2; MTFW 2005; NCFS 1; SATA 23

Cartagena, Teresa de 1425(?)- .... **LC 155**
See also DLB 286

Carter, Angela 1940-1992 ...... **CLC 5, 41, 76; SSC 13, 85; TCLC 139**
See also BRWS 3; CA 53-56; 136; CANR 12, 36, 61, 106; CN 3, 4, 5; DA3; DLB 14, 207, 261, 319; EXPS; FANT; FW; GL 2; MTCW 1, 2; MTFW 2005; RGSF 2; SATA 66; SATA-Obit 70; SFW 4; SSFS 4, 12; SUFW 2; WLIT 4

Carter, Angela Olive
See Carter, Angela

Carter, Martin (Wylde) 1927- .... **BLC 2:1**
See also BW 2; CA 102; CANR 42; CD-WLB 3; CP 1, 2, 3, 4, 5, 6; DLB 117; EWL 3

Carter, Nick
See Smith, Martin Cruz

Carter, Nick
See Smith, Martin Cruz

Carver, Raymond 1938-1988 ..... **CLC 22, 36, 53, 55, 126; PC 54; SSC 8, 51, 104**
See also AAYA 44; AMWS 3; BPFB 1; CA 33-36R; 126; CANR 17, 34, 61, 103; CN 4; CPW; DA3; DAM NOV; DLB 130; DLBY 1984, 1988; EWL 3; MAL 5; MTCW 1, 2; MTFW 2005; PFS 17; RGAL 4; RGSF 2; SSFS 3, 6, 12, 13, 23; TCLE 1:1; TCWW 2; TUS

Cary, Elizabeth, Lady Falkland 1585-1639 .... **LC 30, 141**

Cary, (Arthur) Joyce (Lunel) 1888-1957 .... **TCLC 1, 29, 196**
See also BRW 7; CA 104; 164; CDBLB 1914-1945; DLB 15, 100; EWL 3; MTCW 2; RGEL 2; TEA

Casal, Julian del 1863-1893 .... **NCLC 131**
See also DLB 283; LAW

Casanova, Giacomo
See Casanova de Seingalt, Giovanni Jacopo

Casanova, Giovanni Giacomo
See Casanova de Seingalt, Giovanni Jacopo

Casanova de Seingalt, Giovanni Jacopo
1725-1798 .... **LC 13, 151**
See also WLIT 7

Casares, Adolfo Bioy
See Bioy Casares, Adolfo

Casas, Bartolome de las 1474-1566
See Las Casas, Bartolome de

Case, John
See Hougan, Carolyn

Casely-Hayford, J(oseph) E(phraim)
1866-1903 .... **BLC 1:1; TCLC 24**
See also BW 2; CA 123; 152; DAM MULT

Casey, John (Dudley) 1939- .... **CLC 59**
See also BEST 90:2; CA 69-72; CANR 23, 100

Casey, Michael 1947- .... **CLC 2**
See also CA 65-68; CANR 109; CP 2, 3; DLB 5

Casey, Patrick
See Thurman, Wallace (Henry)

Casey, Warren (Peter) 1935-1988 .... **CLC 12**
See also CA 101; 127; INT CA-101

Casona, Alejandro
See Alvarez, Alejandro Rodriguez

Cassavetes, John 1929-1989 .... **CLC 20**
See also CA 85-88; 127; CANR 82

Cassian, Nina 1924- .... **PC 17**
See also CWP; CWW 2

Cassill, R(onald) V(erlin)
1919-2002 .... **CLC 4, 23**
See also CA 9-12R; 208; CAAS 1; CANR 7, 45; CN 1, 2, 3, 4, 5, 6, 7; DLB 6, 218; DLBY 2002

Cassiodorus, Flavius Magnus c. 490(?)-c.
583(?) .... **CMLC 43**

Cassirer, Ernst 1874-1945 .... **TCLC 61**
See also CA 157

Cassity, (Allen) Turner 1929- .... **CLC 6, 42**
See also CA 17-20R; 223; CAAE 223; CAAS 8; CANR 11; CSW; DLB 105

Cassius Dio c. 155-c. 229 .... **CMLC 99**
See also DLB 176

Castaneda, Carlos (Cesar Aranha)
1931(?)-1998 .... **CLC 12, 119**
See also CA 25-28R; CANR 32, 66, 105; DNFS 1; HW 1; MTCW 1

Castedo, Elena 1937- .... **CLC 65**
See also CA 132

Castedo-Ellerman, Elena
See Castedo, Elena

Castellanos, Rosario 1925-1974 .... **CLC 66; HLC 1; SSC 39, 68**
See also CA 131; 53-56; CANR 58; CD-WLB 3; DAM MULT; DLB 113, 290; EWL 3; FW; HW 1; LAW; MTCW 2; MTFW 2005; RGSF 2; RGWL 2, 3

Castelvetro, Lodovico 1505-1571 .... **LC 12**

Castiglione, Baldassare 1478-1529 ..... **LC 12, 165**
See also EW 2; LMFS 1; RGWL 2, 3; WLIT 7

Castiglione, Baldesar
See Castiglione, Baldassare

Castillo, Ana 1953- .... **CLC 151**
See also AAYA 42; CA 131; CANR 51, 86, 128, 172; CWP; DLB 122, 227; DNFS 2; FW; HW 1; LLW; PFS 21

Castillo, Ana Hernandez Del
See Castillo, Ana

Castle, Robert
See Hamilton, Edmond

Castro (Ruz), Fidel 1926(?)- .... **HLC 1**
See also CA 110; 129; CANR 81; DAM MULT; HW 2

Castro, Guillen de 1569-1631 .... **LC 19**

Castro, Rosalia de 1837-1885 ... **NCLC 3, 78; PC 41**
See also DAM MULT

Castro Alves, Antonio de
1847-1871 .... **NCLC 205**
See also DLB 307; LAW

Cather, Willa (Sibert) 1873-1947 . **SSC 2, 50, 114; TCLC 1, 11, 31, 99, 132, 152; WLC 1**
See also AAYA 24; AMW; AMWC 1; AMWR 1; BPFB 1; CA 104; 128; CDALB 1865-1917; CLR 98; DA; DA3; DAB; DAC; DAM MST, NOV; DLB 9, 54, 78, 256; DLBD 1; EWL 3; EXPN; EXPS; FL 1:5; LAIT 3; LATS 1:1; MAL 5; MBL; MTCW 1, 2; MTFW 2005; NFS 2, 19; RGAL 4; RGSF 2; RHW; SATA 30; SSFS 2, 7, 16, 27; TCWW 1, 2; TUS

Catherine II
See Catherine the Great

Catherine, Saint 1347-1380 .... **CMLC 27**

Catherine the Great 1729-1796 .... **LC 69**
See also DLB 150

Cato, Marcus Porcius
234B.C.-149B.C. .... **CMLC 21**
See also DLB 211

Cato, Marcus Porcius, the Elder
See Cato, Marcus Porcius

Cato the Elder
See Cato, Marcus Porcius

Catton, (Charles) Bruce 1899-1978 . **CLC 35**
See also AITN 1; CA 5-8R; 81-84; CANR 7, 74; DLB 17; MTCW 2; MTFW 2005; SATA 2; SATA-Obit 24

Catullus c. 84B.C.-54B.C. .... **CMLC 18**
See also AW 2; CDWLB 1; DLB 211; RGWL 2, 3; WLIT 8

Cauldwell, Frank
See King, Francis (Henry)

Caunitz, William J. 1933-1996 .... **CLC 34**
See also BEST 89:3; CA 125; 130; 152; CANR 73; INT CA-130

Causley, Charles (Stanley)
1917-2003 .... **CLC 7**
See also CA 9-12R; 223; CANR 5, 35, 94; CLR 30; CP 1, 2, 3, 4, 5; CWRI 5; DLB 27; MTCW 1; SATA 3, 66; SATA-Obit 149

Caute, (John) David 1936- .... **CLC 29**
See also CA 1-4R; CAAS 4; CANR 1, 33, 64, 120; CBD; CD 5, 6; CN 1, 2, 3, 4, 5, 6, 7; DAM NOV; DLB 14, 231

Cavafy, C. P.
See Kavafis, Konstantinos Petrou

Cavafy, Constantine Peter
See Kavafis, Konstantinos Petrou

Cavalcanti, Guido c. 1250-c.
1300 .... **CMLC 54**
See also RGWL 2, 3; WLIT 7

Cavallo, Evelyn
See Spark, Muriel

Cavanna, Betty
See Harrison, Elizabeth (Allen) Cavanna

Cavanna, Elizabeth
See Harrison, Elizabeth (Allen) Cavanna

Cavanna, Elizabeth Allen
See Harrison, Elizabeth (Allen) Cavanna

Cavendish, Margaret Lucas
1623-1673 .... **LC 30, 132**
See also DLB 131, 252, 281; RGEL 2

Caxton, William 1421(?)-1491(?) .... **LC 17**
See also DLB 170

Cayer, D. M.
See Duffy, Maureen (Patricia)

Cayrol, Jean 1911-2005 .... **CLC 11**
See also CA 89-92; 236; DLB 83; EWL 3

Cela (y Trulock), Camilo Jose
See Cela, Camilo Jose

Cela, Camilo Jose 1916-2002 .... **CLC 4, 13, 59, 122; HLC 1; SSC 71**
See also BEST 90:2; CA 21-24R; 206; CAAS 10; CANR 21, 32, 76, 139; CWW 2; DAM MULT; DLB 1989; EW 13; EWL 3; HW 1; MTCW 1, 2; MTFW 2005; RGSF 2; RGWL 2, 3

Celan, Paul
See Antschel, Paul

Celine, Louis-Ferdinand
See Destouches, Louis-Ferdinand

Cellini, Benvenuto 1500-1571 .... **LC 7**
See also WLIT 7

Cendrars, Blaise
See Sauser-Hall, Frederic

Centlivre, Susanna 1669(?)-1723 .... **DC 25; LC 65**
See also DLB 84; RGEL 2

Cernuda (y Bidon), Luis
1902-1963 .... **CLC 54; PC 62**
See also CA 131; 89-92; DAM POET; DLB 134; EWL 3; GLL 1; HW 1; RGWL 2, 3

Cervantes, Lorna Dee 1954- ..... **HLCS 1; PC 35**
See also CA 131; CANR 80; CP 7; CWP; DLB 82; EXPP; HW 1; LLW; PFS 30

Cervantes (Saavedra), Miguel de
1547-1616 .... **HLCS; LC 6, 23, 93; SSC 12, 108; WLC 1**
See also AAYA 56; BYA 1, 14; DA; DAB; DAC; DAM MST, NOV; EW 2; LAIT 1; LATS 1:1; LMFS 1; NFS 8; RGSF 2; RGWL 2, 3; TWA

Cesaire, Aime
See Cesaire, Aime

Cesaire, Aime 1913-2008 .... **BLC 1:1; CLC 19, 32, 112; DC 22; PC 25**
See also BW 2, 3; CA 65-68; 271; CANR 24, 43, 81; CWW 2; DA3; DAM MULT, POET; DLB 321; EWL 3; GFL 1789 to the Present; MTCW 1, 2; MTFW 2005; WP

Cesaire, Aime Fernand
See Cesaire, Aime

Chaadaev, Petr Iakovlevich
1794-1856 .... **NCLC 197**
See also DLB 198

Chabon, Michael 1963- ... **CLC 55, 149, 265; SSC 59**
See also AAYA 45; AMWS 11; CA 139; CANR 57, 96, 127, 138; DLB 278; MAL 5; MTFW 2005; NFS 25; SATA 145

Chabrol, Claude 1930- .... **CLC 16**
See also CA 110

Chairil Anwar
See Anwar, Chairil

Challans, Mary 1905-1983 ...... **CLC 3, 11, 17**
See also BPFB 3; BYA 2; CA 81-84; 111; CANR 74; CN 1, 2, 3; DA3; DLBY 1983; EWL 3; GLL 1; LAIT 1; MTCW 2; MTFW 2005; RGEL 2; RHW; SATA 23; SATA-Obit 36; TEA

Challis, George
See Faust, Frederick (Schiller)

Chambers, Aidan 1934- .... **CLC 35**
See also AAYA 27; CA 25-28R; CANR 12, 31, 58, 116; JRDA; MAICYA 1, 2; SAAS 12; SATA 1, 69, 108, 171; WYA; YAW

Chambers, James 1948- .... **CLC 21**
See also CA 124; 199

Chambers, Jessie
See Lawrence, D(avid) H(erbert Richards)

Corso, Gregory 1930-2001 .... **CLC 1, 11; PC 33**
See also AMWS 12; BG 1:2; CA 5-8R; 193; CANR 41, 76, 132; CP 1, 2, 3, 4, 5, 6, 7; DA3; DLB 5, 16, 237; LMFS 2; MAL 5; MTCW 1, 2; MTFW 2005; WP

Cortazar, Julio 1914-1984 ... **CLC 2, 3, 5, 10, 13, 15, 33, 34, 92; HLC 1; SSC 7, 76**
See also BPFB 1; CA 21-24R; CANR 12, 32, 81; CDWLB 3; DA3; DAM MULT, NOV; DLB 113; EWL 3; EXPS; HW 1, 2; LAW; MTCW 1, 2; MTFW 2005; RGSF 2; RGWL 2, 3; SSFS 3, 20; TWA; WLIT 1

Cortes, Hernan 1485-1547 .... **LC 31**

Cortez, Jayne 1936- .... **BLC 2:1**
See also BW 2, 3; CA 73-76; CANR 13, 31, 68, 126; CWP; DLB 41; EWL 3

Corvinus, Jakob
See Raabe, Wilhelm (Karl)

Corwin, Cecil
See Kornbluth, C(yril) M.

Cosic, Dobrica 1921- .... **CLC 14**
See also CA 122; 138; CDWLB 4; CWW 2; DLB 181; EWL 3

Costain, Thomas B(ertram) 1885-1965 .... **CLC 30**
See also BYA 3; CA 5-8R; 25-28R; DLB 9; RHW

Costantini, Humberto 1924(?)-1987 . **CLC 49**
See also CA 131; 122; EWL 3; HW 1

Costello, Elvis 1954- .... **CLC 21**
See also CA 204

Costenoble, Philostene
See Ghelderode, Michel de

Cotes, Cecil V.
See Duncan, Sara Jeannette

Cotter, Joseph Seamon Sr. 1861-1949 .... **BLC 1:1; TCLC 28**
See also BW 1; CA 124; DAM MULT; DLB 50

Couch, Arthur Thomas Quiller
See Quiller-Couch, Sir Arthur (Thomas)

Coulton, James
See Hansen, Joseph

Couperus, Louis (Marie Anne) 1863-1923 .... **TCLC 15**
See also CA 115; EWL 3; RGWL 2, 3

Coupland, Douglas 1961- .... **CLC 85, 133**
See also AAYA 34; CA 142; CANR 57, 90, 130, 172; CCA 1; CN 7; CPW; DAC; DAM POP; DLB 334

Coupland, Douglas Campbell
See Coupland, Douglas

Court, Wesli
See Turco, Lewis

Courtenay, Bryce 1933- .... **CLC 59**
See also CA 138; CPW

Courtney, Robert
See Ellison, Harlan

Cousteau, Jacques-Yves 1910-1997 .. **CLC 30**
See also CA 65-68; 159; CANR 15, 67; MTCW 1; SATA 38, 98

Coventry, Francis 1725-1754 .... **LC 46**
See also DLB 39

Coverdale, Miles c. 1487-1569 .... **LC 77**
See also DLB 167

Cowan, Peter (Walkinshaw) 1914-2002 .... **SSC 28**
See also CA 21-24R; CANR 9, 25, 50, 83; CN 1, 2, 3, 4, 5, 6, 7; DLB 260; RGSF 2

Coward, Noel (Peirce) 1899-1973 . **CLC 1, 9, 29, 51**
See also AITN 1; BRWS 2; CA 17-18; 41-44R; CANR 35, 132; CAP 2; CBD; CD-BLB 1914-1945; DA3; DAM DRAM; DFS 3, 6; DLB 10, 245; EWL 3; IDFW 3, 4; MTCW 1, 2; MTFW 2005; RGEL 2; TEA

Cowley, Abraham 1618-1667 .. **LC 43; PC 90**
See also BRW 2; DLB 131, 151; PAB; RGEL 2

Cowley, Malcolm 1898-1989 .... **CLC 39**
See also AMWS 2; CA 5-8R; 128; CANR 3, 55; CP 1, 2, 3, 4; DLB 4, 48; DLBY 1981, 1989; EWL 3; MAL 5; MTCW 1, 2; MTFW 2005

Cowper, William 1731-1800 ..... **NCLC 8, 94; PC 40**
See also BRW 3; DA3; DAM POET; DLB 104, 109; RGEL 2

Cox, William Trevor
See Trevor, William

Coyne, P. J.
See Masters, Hilary

Coyne, P.J.
See Masters, Hilary

Cozzens, James Gould 1903-1978 . **CLC 1, 4, 11, 92**
See also AMW; BPFB 1; CA 9-12R; 81-84; CANR 19; CDALB 1941-1968; CN 1, 2; DLB 9, 294; DLBD 2; DLBY 1984, 1997; EWL 3; MAL 5; MTCW 1, 2; MTFW 2005; RGAL 4

Crabbe, George 1754-1832 ... **NCLC 26, 121; PC 97**
See also BRW 3; DLB 93; RGEL 2

Crace, Jim 1946- .... **CLC 157; SSC 61**
See also BRWS 14; CA 128; 135; CANR 55, 70, 123, 180; CN 5, 6, 7; DLB 231; INT CA-135

Craddock, Charles Egbert
See Murfree, Mary Noailles

Craig, A. A.
See Anderson, Poul

Craik, Mrs.
See Craik, Dinah Maria (Mulock)

Craik, Dinah Maria (Mulock) 1826-1887 .... **NCLC 38**
See also DLB 35, 163; MAICYA 1, 2; RGEL 2; SATA 34

Cram, Ralph Adams 1863-1942 ..... **TCLC 45**
See also CA 160

Cranch, Christopher Pearse 1813-1892 .... **NCLC 115**
See also DLB 1, 42, 243

Crane, (Harold) Hart 1899-1932 .... **PC 3; TCLC 2, 5, 80; WLC 2**
See also AMW; AMWR 2; CA 104; 127; CDALB 1917-1929; DA; DA3; DAB; DAC; DAM MST, POET; DLB 4, 48; EWL 3; MAL 5; MTCW 1, 2; MTFW 2005; RGAL 4; TUS

Crane, R(onald) S(almon) 1886-1967 .... **CLC 27**
See also CA 85-88; DLB 63

Crane, Stephen (Townley) 1871-1900 .... **PC 80; SSC 7, 56, 70; TCLC 11, 17, 32, 216; WLC 2**
See also AAYA 21; AMW; AMWC 1; BPFB 1; BYA 3; CA 109; 140; CANR 84; CDALB 1865-1917; CLR 132; DA; DA3; DAB; DAC; DAM MST, NOV, POET; DLB 12, 54, 78; EXPN; EXPS; LAIT 2; LMFS 2; MAL 5; NFS 4, 20; PFS 9; RGAL 4; RGSF 2; SSFS 4; TUS; WYA; YABC 2

Cranmer, Thomas 1489-1556 .... **LC 95**
See also DLB 132, 213

Cranshaw, Stanley
See Fisher, Dorothy (Frances) Canfield

Crase, Douglas 1944- .... **CLC 58**
See also CA 106

Crashaw, Richard 1612(?)-1649 .. **LC 24; PC 84**
See also BRW 2; DLB 126; PAB; RGEL 2

Cratinus c. 519B.C.-c. 422B.C. ..... **CMLC 54**
See also LMFS 1

Craven, Margaret 1901-1980 .... **CLC 17**
See also BYA 2; CA 103; CCA 1; DAC; LAIT 5

Crawford, F(rancis) Marion 1854-1909 .... **TCLC 10**
See also CA 107; 168; DLB 71; HGG; RGAL 4; SUFW 1

Crawford, Isabella Valancy 1850-1887 .... **NCLC 12, 127**
See also DLB 92; RGEL 2

Crayon, Geoffrey
See Irving, Washington

Creasey, John 1908-1973 .... **CLC 11**
See also CA 5-8R; 41-44R; CANR 8, 59; CMW 4; DLB 77; MTCW 1

Crebillon, Claude Prosper Jolyot de (fils) 1707-1777 .... **LC 1, 28**
See also DLB 313; GFL Beginnings to 1789

Credo
See Creasey, John

Credo, Alvaro J. de
See Prado (Calvo), Pedro

Creeley, Robert 1926-2005 .... **CLC 1, 2, 4, 8, 11, 15, 36, 78, 266; PC 73**
See also AMWS 4; CA 1-4R; 237; CAAS 10; CANR 23, 43, 89, 137; CP 1, 2, 3, 4, 5, 6, 7; DA3; DAM POET; DLB 5, 16, 169; DLBD 17; EWL 3; MAL 5; MTCW 1, 2; MTFW 2005; PFS 21; RGAL 4; WP

Creeley, Robert White
See Creeley, Robert

Crenne, Helisenne de 1510-1560 .... **LC 113**
See also DLB 327

Crevecoeur, Hector St. John de
See Crevecoeur, Michel Guillaume Jean de

Crevecoeur, Michel Guillaume Jean de 1735-1813 .... **NCLC 105**
See also AMWS 1; ANW; DLB 37

Crevel, Rene 1900-1935 .... **TCLC 112**
See also GLL 2

Crews, Harry 1935- .... **CLC 6, 23, 49**
See also AITN 1; AMWS 11; BPFB 1; CA 25-28R; CANR 20, 57; CN 3, 4, 5, 6, 7; CSW; DA3; DLB 6, 143, 185; MTCW 1, 2; MTFW 2005; RGAL 4

Crichton, John Michael
See Crichton, Michael

Crichton, Michael 1942-2008 .. **CLC 2, 6, 54, 90, 242**
See also AAYA 10, 49; AITN 2; BPFB 1; CA 25-28R; 279; CANR 13, 40, 54, 76, 127, 179; CMW 4; CN 2, 3, 6, 7; CPW; DA3; DAM NOV, POP; DLB 292; DLBY 1981; INT CANR-13; JRDA; MTCW 1, 2; MTFW 2005; SATA 9, 88; SATA-Obit 199; SFW 4; YAW

Crispin, Edmund
See Montgomery, (Robert) Bruce

Cristina of Sweden 1626-1689 .... **LC 124**

Cristofer, Michael 1945(?)- .... **CLC 28**
See also CA 110; 152; CAD; CANR 150; CD 5, 6; DAM DRAM; DFS 15; DLB 7

Cristofer, Michael Ivan
See Cristofer, Michael

Criton
See Alain

Croce, Benedetto 1866-1952 .... **TCLC 37**
See also CA 120; 155; EW 8; EWL 3; WLIT 7

Crockett, David 1786-1836 .... **NCLC 8**
See also DLB 3, 11, 183, 248

Crockett, Davy
See Crockett, David

Crofts, Freeman Wills 1879-1957 .. **TCLC 55**
See also CA 115; 195; CMW 4; DLB 77; MSW

Croker, John Wilson 1780-1857 .... **NCLC 10**
See also DLB 110

Crommelynck, Fernand 1885-1970 .. **CLC 75**
See also CA 189; 89-92; EWL 3
Cromwell, Oliver 1599-1658 .... **LC 43**
Cronenberg, David 1943- .... **CLC 143**
See also CA 138; CCA 1
Cronin, A(rchibald) J(oseph)
1896-1981 .... **CLC 32**
See also BPFB 1; CA 1-4R; 102; CANR 5;
CN 2; DLB 191; SATA 47; SATA-Obit 25
Cross, Amanda
See Heilbrun, Carolyn G(old)
Crothers, Rachel 1878-1958 .... **TCLC 19**
See also CA 113; 194; CAD; CWD; DLB
7, 266; RGAL 4
Croves, Hal
See Traven, B.
Crow Dog, Mary (?)- .... **CLC 93; NNAL**
See also CA 154
Crowfield, Christopher
See Stowe, Harriet (Elizabeth) Beecher
Crowley, Aleister
See Crowley, Edward Alexander
Crowley, Edward Alexander
1875-1947 .... **TCLC 7**
See also CA 104; GLL 1; HGG
Crowley, John 1942- .... **CLC 57**
See also AAYA 57; BPFB 1; CA 61-64;
CANR 43, 98, 138, 177; DLBY 1982;
FANT; MTFW 2005; SATA 65, 140; SFW
4; SUFW 2
Crowne, John 1641-1712 .... **LC 104**
See also DLB 80; RGEL 2
Crud
See Crumb, R.
Crumarums
See Crumb, R.
Crumb, R. 1943- .... **CLC 17**
See also CA 106; CANR 107, 150
Crumb, Robert
See Crumb, R.
Crumbum
See Crumb, R.
Crumski
See Crumb, R.
Crum the Bum
See Crumb, R.
Crunk
See Crumb, R.
Crustt
See Crumb, R.
Crutchfield, Les
See Trumbo, Dalton
Cruz, Victor Hernandez 1949- ... **HLC 1; PC
37**
See also BW 2; CA 65-68, 271; CAAE 271;
CAAS 17; CANR 14, 32, 74, 132; CP 1,
2, 3, 4, 5, 6, 7; DAM MULT, POET; DLB
41; DNFS 1; EXPP; HW 1, 2; LLW;
MTCW 2; MTFW 2005; PFS 16; WP
Cryer, Gretchen (Kiger) 1935- .... **CLC 21**
See also CA 114; 123
Csath, Geza
See Brenner, Jozef
Cudlip, David R(ockwell) 1933- .... **CLC 34**
See also CA 177
Cullen, Countee 1903-1946 ..... **BLC 1:1; HR
1:2; PC 20; TCLC 4, 37, 220; WLCS**
See also AAYA 78; AFAW 2; AMWS 4; BW
1; CA 108; 124; CDALB 1917-1929; DA;
DA3; DAC; DAM MST, MULT, POET;
DLB 4, 48, 51; EWL 3; EXPP; LMFS 2;
MAL 5; MTCW 1, 2; MTFW 2005; PFS
3; RGAL 4; SATA 18; WP
Culleton, Beatrice 1949- .... **NNAL**
See also CA 120; CANR 83; DAC
Culver, Timothy J.
See Westlake, Donald E.

Culver, Timothy J.
See Westlake, Donald E.
Cum, R.
See Crumb, R.
Cumberland, Richard
1732-1811 .... **NCLC 167**
See also DLB 89; RGEL 2
Cummings, Bruce F(rederick)
1889-1919 .... **TCLC 24**
See also CA 123
Cummings, E(dward) E(stlin)
1894-1962 .. **CLC 1, 3, 8, 12, 15, 68; PC
5; TCLC 137; WLC 2**
See also AAYA 41; AMW; CA 73-76;
CANR 31; CDALB 1929-1941; DA;
DA3; DAB; DAC; DAM MST, POET;
DLB 4, 48; EWL 3; EXPP; MAL 5;
MTCW 1, 2; MTFW 2005; PAB; PFS 1,
3, 12, 13, 19, 30; RGAL 4; TUS; WP
Cummins, Maria Susanna
1827-1866 .... **NCLC 139**
See also DLB 42; YABC 1
Cunha, Euclides (Rodrigues Pimenta) da
1866-1909 .... **TCLC 24**
See also CA 123; 219; DLB 307; LAW;
WLIT 1
Cunningham, E. V.
See Fast, Howard
Cunningham, J. Morgan
See Westlake, Donald E.
Cunningham, J(ames) V(incent)
1911-1985 .... **CLC 3, 31; PC 92**
See also CA 1-4R; 115; CANR 1, 72; CP 1,
2, 3, 4; DLB 5
Cunningham, Julia (Woolfolk)
1916- .... **CLC 12**
See also CA 9-12R; CANR 4, 19, 36; CWRI
5; JRDA; MAICYA 1, 2; SAAS 2; SATA
1, 26, 132
Cunningham, Michael 1952- .... **CLC 34, 243**
See also AMWS 15; CA 136; CANR 96,
160; CN 7; DLB 292; GLL 2; MTFW
2005; NFS 23
Cunninghame Graham, R. B.
See Cunninghame Graham, Robert
(Gallnigad) Bontine
**Cunninghame Graham, Robert (Gallnigad)
Bontine** 1852-1936 .... **TCLC 19**
See also CA 119; 184; DLB 98, 135, 174;
RGEL 2; RGSF 2
Curnow, (Thomas) Allen (Monro)
1911-2001 .... **PC 48**
See also CA 69-72; 202; CANR 48, 99; CP
1, 2, 3, 4, 5, 6, 7; EWL 3; RGEL 2
Currie, Ellen 19(?)- .... **CLC 44**
Curtin, Philip
See Lowndes, Marie Adelaide (Belloc)
Curtin, Phillip
See Lowndes, Marie Adelaide (Belloc)
Curtis, Price
See Ellison, Harlan
Cusanus, Nicolaus 1401-1464
See Nicholas of Cusa
Cutrate, Joe
See Spiegelman, Art
Cynewulf c. 770- .... **CMLC 23**
See also DLB 146; RGEL 2
Cyrano de Bergerac, Savinien de
1619-1655 .... **LC 65**
See also DLB 268; GFL Beginnings to
1789; RGWL 2, 3
Cyril of Alexandria c. 375-c. 430 . **CMLC 59**
Czaczkes, Shmuel Yosef Halevi
See Agnon, S.Y.
Dabrowska, Maria (Szumska)
1889-1965 .... **CLC 15**
See also CA 106; CDWLB 4; DLB 215;
EWL 3

Dabydeen, David 1955- .... **CLC 34**
See also BW 1; CA 125; CANR 56, 92; CN
6, 7; CP 5, 6, 7; DLB 347
Dacey, Philip 1939- .... **CLC 51**
See also CA 37-40R, 231; CAAE 231;
CAAS 17; CANR 14, 32, 64; CP 4, 5, 6,
7; DLB 105
Dacre, Charlotte c. 1772-1825(?) . **NCLC 151**
Dafydd ap Gwilym c. 1320-c. 1380 ..... **PC 56**
Dagerman, Stig (Halvard)
1923-1954 .... **TCLC 17**
See also CA 117; 155; DLB 259; EWL 3
D'Aguiar, Fred 1960- ..... **BLC 2:1; CLC 145**
See also CA 148; CANR 83, 101; CN 7;
CP 5, 6, 7; DLB 157; EWL 3
Dahl, Roald 1916-1990 ...... **CLC 1, 6, 18, 79;
TCLC 173**
See also AAYA 15; BPFB 1; BRWS 4; BYA
5; CA 1-4R; 133; CANR 6, 32, 37, 62;
CLR 1, 7, 41, 111; CN 1, 2, 3, 4; CPW;
DA3; DAB; DAC; DAM MST, NOV,
POP; DLB 139, 255; HGG; JRDA; MAI-
CYA 1, 2; MTCW 1, 2; MTFW 2005;
RGSF 2; SATA 1, 26, 73; SATA-Obit 65;
SSFS 4; TEA; YAW
Dahlberg, Edward 1900-1977 . **CLC 1, 7, 14;
TCLC 208**
See also CA 9-12R; 69-72; CANR 31, 62;
CN 1, 2; DLB 48; MAL 5; MTCW 1;
RGAL 4
Daitch, Susan 1954- .... **CLC 103**
See also CA 161
Dale, Colin
See Lawrence, T(homas) E(dward)
Dale, George E.
See Asimov, Isaac
d'Alembert, Jean Le Rond
1717-1783 .... **LC 126**
Dalton, Roque 1935-1975(?) ..... **HLCS 1; PC
36**
See also CA 176; DLB 283; HW 2
Daly, Elizabeth 1878-1967 .... **CLC 52**
See also CA 23-24; 25-28R; CANR 60;
CAP 2; CMW 4
Daly, Mary 1928- .... **CLC 173**
See also CA 25-28R; CANR 30, 62, 166;
FW; GLL 1; MTCW 1
Daly, Maureen 1921-2006 .... **CLC 17**
See also AAYA 5, 58; BYA 6; CA 253;
CANR 37, 83, 108; CLR 96; JRDA; MAI-
CYA 1, 2; SAAS 1; SATA 2, 129; SATA-
Obit 176; WYA; YAW
Damas, Leon-Gontran 1912-1978 ... **CLC 84;
TCLC 204**
See also BW 1; CA 125; 73-76; EWL 3
Dana, Richard Henry Sr.
1787-1879 .... **NCLC 53**
Dangarembga, Tsitsi 1959- .... **BLC 2:1**
See also BW 3; CA 163; NFS 28; WLIT 2
Daniel, Samuel 1562(?)-1619 .... **LC 24**
See also DLB 62; RGEL 2
Daniels, Brett
See Adler, Renata
Dannay, Frederic 1905-1982 .... **CLC 3, 11**
See also BPFB 3; CA 1-4R; 107; CANR 1,
39; CMW 4; DAM POP; DLB 137; MSW;
MTCW 1; RGAL 4
D'Annunzio, Gabriele 1863-1938 ... **TCLC 6,
40, 215**
See also CA 104; 155; EW 8; EWL 3;
RGWL 2, 3; TWA; WLIT 7
Danois, N. le
See Gourmont, Remy(-Marie-Charles) de
Dante 1265-1321 .... **CMLC 3, 18, 39, 70; PC
21; WLCS**
See also DA; DA3; DAB; DAC; DAM
MST, POET; EFS 1; EW 1; LAIT 1;
RGWL 2, 3; TWA; WLIT 7; WP

Deighton, Leonard Cyril 1929- ..... **CLC 4, 7, 22, 46**
 See also AAYA 57, 6; BEST 89:2; BPFB 1; CA 9-12R; CANR 19, 33, 68; CDBLB 1960- Present; CMW 4; CN 1, 2, 3, 4, 5, 6, 7; CPW; DA3; DAM NOV, POP; DLB 87; MTCW 1, 2; MTFW 2005

Dekker, Thomas 1572(?)-1632 ..... **DC 12; LC 22, 159**
 See also CDBLB Before 1660; DAM DRAM; DLB 62, 172; LMFS 1; RGEL 2

de Laclos, Pierre Ambroise Franois
 See Laclos, Pierre-Ambroise Francois

Delacroix, (Ferdinand-Victor-)Eugene 1798-1863 .... **NCLC 133**
 See also EW 5

Delafield, E. M.
 See Dashwood, Edmee Elizabeth Monica de la Pasture

de la Mare, Walter (John) 1873-1956 ..... **PC 77; SSC 14; TCLC 4, 53; WLC 2**
 See also CA 163; CDBLB 1914-1945; CLR 23; CWRI 5; DA3; DAB; DAC; DAM MST, POET; DLB 19, 153, 162, 255, 284; EWL 3; EXPP; HGG; MAICYA 1, 2; MTCW 2; MTFW 2005; RGEL 2; RGSF 2; SATA 16; SUFW 1; TEA; WCH

de Lamartine, Alphonse (Marie Louis Prat)
 See Lamartine, Alphonse (Marie Louis Prat) de

Delaney, Franey
 See O'Hara, John (Henry)

Delaney, Shelagh 1939- .... **CLC 29**
 See also CA 17-20R; CANR 30, 67; CBD; CD 5, 6; CDBLB 1960 to Present; CWD; DAM DRAM; DFS 7; DLB 13; MTCW 1

Delany, Martin Robison 1812-1885 .... **NCLC 93**
 See also DLB 50; RGAL 4

Delany, Mary (Granville Pendarves) 1700-1788 .... **LC 12**

Delany, Samuel R., Jr. 1942- .... **BLC 1:1; CLC 8, 14, 38, 141**
 See also AAYA 24; AFAW 2; BPFB 1; BW 2, 3; CA 81-84; CANR 27, 43, 116, 172; CN 2, 3, 4, 5, 6, 7; DAM MULT; DLB 8, 33; FANT; MAL 5; MTCW 1, 2; RGAL 4; SATA 92; SCFW 1, 2; SFW 4; SUFW 2

Delany, Samuel Ray
 See Delany, Samuel R., Jr.

de la Parra, (Ana) Teresa (Sonojo) 1890(?)-1936 .... **HLCS 2; TCLC 185**
 See also CA 178; HW 2; LAW

Delaporte, Theophile
 See Green, Julien (Hartridge)

De La Ramee, Marie Louise 1839-1908 .... **TCLC 43**
 See also CA 204; DLB 18, 156; RGEL 2; SATA 20

de la Roche, Mazo 1879-1961 .... **CLC 14**
 See also CA 85-88; CANR 30; DLB 68; RGEL 2; RHW; SATA 64

De La Salle, Innocent
 See Hartmann, Sadakichi

de Laureamont, Comte
 See Lautreamont

Delbanco, Nicholas 1942- ..... **CLC 6, 13, 167**
 See also CA 17-20R, 189; CAAE 189; CAAS 2; CANR 29, 55, 116, 150; CN 7; DLB 6, 234

Delbanco, Nicholas Franklin
 See Delbanco, Nicholas

del Castillo, Michel 1933- .... **CLC 38**
 See also CA 109; CANR 77

Deledda, Grazia (Cosima) 1875(?)-1936 .... **TCLC 23**
 See also CA 123; 205; DLB 264, 329; EWL 3; RGWL 2, 3; WLIT 7

Deleuze, Gilles 1925-1995 .... **TCLC 116**
 See also DLB 296

Delgado, Abelardo (Lalo) B(arrientos) 1930-2004 .... **HLC 1**
 See also CA 131; 230; CAAS 15; CANR 90; DAM MST, MULT; DLB 82; HW 1, 2

Delibes, Miguel
 See Delibes Setien, Miguel

Delibes Setien, Miguel 1920- .... **CLC 8, 18**
 See also CA 45-48; CANR 1, 32; CWW 2; DLB 322; EWL 3; HW 1; MTCW 1

DeLillo, Don 1936- ..... **CLC 8, 10, 13, 27, 39, 54, 76, 143, 210, 213**
 See also AMWC 2; AMWS 6; BEST 89:1; BPFB 1; CA 81-84; CANR 21, 76, 92, 133, 173; CN 3, 4, 5, 6, 7; CPW; DA3; DAM NOV, POP; DLB 6, 173; EWL 3; MAL 5; MTCW 1, 2; MTFW 2005; NFS 28; RGAL 4; TUS

de Lisser, H. G.
 See De Lisser, H(erbert) G(eorge)

De Lisser, H(erbert) G(eorge) 1878-1944 .... **TCLC 12**
 See also BW 2; CA 109; 152; DLB 117

Deloire, Pierre
 See Peguy, Charles (Pierre)

Deloney, Thomas 1543(?)-1600 .... **LC 41; PC 79**
 See also DLB 167; RGEL 2

Deloria, Ella (Cara) 1889-1971(?) ..... **NNAL**
 See also CA 152; DAM MULT; DLB 175

Deloria, Vine, Jr. 1933-2005 .... **CLC 21, 122; NNAL**
 See also CA 53-56; 245; CANR 5, 20, 48, 98; DAM MULT; DLB 175; MTCW 1; SATA 21; SATA-Obit 171

Deloria, Vine Victor, Jr.
 See Deloria, Vine, Jr.

del Valle-Inclan, Ramon (Maria)
 See Valle-Inclan, Ramon (Maria) del

Del Vecchio, John M(ichael) 1947- .. **CLC 29**
 See also CA 110; DLBD 9

de Man, Paul (Adolph Michel) 1919-1983 .... **CLC 55**
 See also CA 128; 111; CANR 61; DLB 67; MTCW 1, 2

de Mandiargues, Andre Pieyre
 See Pieyre de Mandiargues, Andre

DeMarinis, Rick 1934- .... **CLC 54**
 See also CA 57-60, 184; CAAE 184; CAAS 24; CANR 9, 25, 50, 160; DLB 218; TCWW 2

de Maupassant, (Henri Rene Albert) Guy
 See Maupassant, (Henri Rene Albert) Guy de

Dembry, R. Emmet
 See Murfree, Mary Noailles

Demby, William 1922- ...... **BLC 1:1; CLC 53**
 See also BW 1, 3; CA 81-84; CANR 81; DAM MULT; DLB 33

de Menton, Francisco
 See Chin, Frank (Chew, Jr.)

Demetrius of Phalerum c. 307B.C.- .... **CMLC 34**

Demijohn, Thom
 See Disch, Thomas M.

De Mille, James 1833-1880 .... **NCLC 123**
 See also DLB 99, 251

Democritus c. 460B.C.-c. 370B.C. . **CMLC 47**

de Montaigne, Michel (Eyquem)
 See Montaigne, Michel (Eyquem) de

de Montherlant, Henry (Milon)
 See Montherlant, Henry (Milon) de

Demosthenes 384B.C.-322B.C. ...... **CMLC 13**
 See also AW 1; DLB 176; RGWL 2, 3; WLIT 8

de Musset, (Louis Charles) Alfred
 See Musset, Alfred de

de Natale, Francine
 See Malzberg, Barry N(athaniel)

de Navarre, Marguerite 1492-1549 .... **LC 61, 167; SSC 85**
 See also DLB 327; GFL Beginnings to 1789; RGWL 2, 3

Denby, Edwin (Orr) 1903-1983 .... **CLC 48**
 See also CA 138; 110; CP 1

de Nerval, Gerard
 See Nerval, Gerard de

Denham, John 1615-1669 .... **LC 73**
 See also DLB 58, 126; RGEL 2

Denis, Julio
 See Cortazar, Julio

Denmark, Harrison
 See Zelazny, Roger

Dennis, John 1658-1734 .... **LC 11, 154**
 See also DLB 101; RGEL 2

Dennis, Nigel (Forbes) 1912-1989 ...... **CLC 8**
 See also CA 25-28R; 129; CN 1, 2, 3, 4; DLB 13, 15, 233; EWL 3; MTCW 1

Dent, Lester 1904-1959 .... **TCLC 72**
 See also CA 112; 161; CMW 4; DLB 306; SFW 4

Dentinger, Stephen
 See Hoch, Edward D.

De Palma, Brian 1940- .... **CLC 20, 247**
 See also CA 109

De Palma, Brian Russell
 See De Palma, Brian

de Pizan, Christine
 See Christine de Pizan

De Quincey, Thomas 1785-1859 ..... **NCLC 4, 87, 198**
 See also BRW 4; CDBLB 1789-1832; DLB 110, 144; RGEL 2

De Ray, Jill
 See Moore, Alan

Deren, Eleanora 1908(?)-1961 .. **CLC 16, 102**
 See also CA 192; 111

Deren, Maya
 See Deren, Eleanora

Derleth, August (William) 1909-1971 .... **CLC 31**
 See also BPFB 1; BYA 9, 10; CA 1-4R; 29-32R; CANR 4; CMW 4; CN 1; DLB 9; DLBD 17; HGG; SATA 5; SUFW 1

Der Nister 1884-1950 .... **TCLC 56**
 See also DLB 333; EWL 3

de Routisie, Albert
 See Aragon, Louis

Derrida, Jacques 1930-2004 ...... **CLC 24, 87, 225**
 See also CA 124; 127; 232; CANR 76, 98, 133; DLB 242; EWL 3; LMFS 2; MTCW 2; TWA

Derry Down Derry
 See Lear, Edward

Dersonnes, Jacques
 See Simenon, Georges (Jacques Christian)

Der Stricker c. 1190-c. 1250 .... **CMLC 75**
 See also DLB 138

Desai, Anita 1937- . **CLC 19, 37, 97, 175, 271**
 See also BRWS 5; CA 81-84; CANR 33, 53, 95, 133; CN 1, 2, 3, 4, 5, 6, 7; CWRI 5; DA3; DAB; DAM NOV; DLB 271, 323; DNFS 2; EWL 3; FW; MTCW 1, 2; MTFW 2005; SATA 63, 126

Desai, Kiran 1971- .... **CLC 119**
 See also BYA 16; CA 171; CANR 127; NFS 28

de Saint-Luc, Jean
 See Glassco, John

EWL 3; LAIT 3; MAL 5; MTCW 1, 2; MTFW 2005; NFS 6; RGAL 4; RGHL; RHW; SSFS 27; TCLE 1:1; TCWW 1, 2; TUS

Dodgson, Charles Lutwidge
See Carroll, Lewis

Dodsley, Robert 1703-1764 .... **LC 97**
See also DLB 95; RGEL 2

Dodson, Owen (Vincent)
1914-1983 .... **BLC 1:1; CLC 79**
See also BW 1; CA 65-68; 110; CANR 24; DAM MULT; DLB 76

Doeblin, Alfred 1878-1957 .... **TCLC 13**
See also CA 110; 141; CDWLB 2; DLB 66; EWL 3; RGWL 2, 3

Doerr, Harriet 1910-2002 .... **CLC 34**
See also CA 117; 122; 213; CANR 47; INT CA-122; LATS 1:2

Domecq, H(onorio) Bustos
See Bioy Casares, Adolfo; Borges, Jorge Luis

Domini, Rey
See Lorde, Audre

Dominic, R. B.
See Hennissart, Martha

Dominique
See Proust, (Valentin-Louis-George-Eugene) Marcel

Don, A
See Stephen, Sir Leslie

Donaldson, Stephen R. 1947- ... **CLC 46, 138**
See also AAYA 36; BPFB 1; CA 89-92; CANR 13, 55, 99; CPW; DAM POP; FANT; INT CANR-13; SATA 121; SFW 4; SUFW 1, 2

Donleavy, J(ames) P(atrick) 1926- .... **CLC 1, 4, 6, 10, 45**
See also AITN 2; BPFB 1; CA 9-12R; CANR 24, 49, 62, 80, 124; CBD; CD 5, 6; CN 1, 2, 3, 4, 5, 6, 7; DLB 6, 173; INT CANR-24; MAL 5; MTCW 1, 2; MTFW 2005; RGAL 4

Donnadieu, Marguerite
See Duras, Marguerite

Donne, John 1572-1631 ... **LC 10, 24, 91; PC 1, 43; WLC 2**
See also AAYA 67; BRW 1; BRWC 1; BRWR 2; CDBLB Before 1660; DA; DAB; DAC; DAM MST, POET; DLB 121, 151; EXPP; PAB; PFS 2, 11; RGEL 3; TEA; WLIT 3; WP

Donnell, David 1939(?)- .... **CLC 34**
See also CA 197

Donoghue, Denis 1928- .... **CLC 209**
See also CA 17-20R; CANR 16, 102

Donoghue, Emma 1969- .... **CLC 239**
See also CA 155; CANR 103, 152; DLB 267; GLL 2; SATA 101

Donoghue, P.S.
See Hunt, E. Howard

Donoso (Yanez), Jose 1924-1996 ... **CLC 4, 8, 11, 32, 99; HLC 1; SSC 34; TCLC 133**
See also CA 81-84; 155; CANR 32, 73; CD-WLB 3; CWW 2; DAM MULT; DLB 113; EWL 3; HW 1, 2; LAW; LAWS 1; MTCW 1, 2; MTFW 2005; RGSF 2; WLIT 1

Donovan, John 1928-1992 .... **CLC 35**
See also AAYA 20; CA 97-100; 137; CLR 3; MAICYA 1, 2; SATA 72; SATA-Brief 29; YAW

Don Roberto
See Cunninghame Graham, Robert (Gallnigad) Bontine

Doolittle, Hilda 1886-1961 . **CLC 3, 8, 14, 31, 34, 73; PC 5; WLC 3**
See also AAYA 66; AMWS 1; CA 97-100; CANR 35, 131; DA; DAC; DAM MST, POET; DLB 4, 45; EWL 3; FL 1:5; FW; GLL 1; LMFS 2; MAL 5; MBL; MTCW 1, 2; MTFW 2005; PFS 6, 28; RGAL 4

Doppo
See Kunikida Doppo

Doppo, Kunikida
See Kunikida Doppo

Dorfman, Ariel 1942- .... **CLC 48, 77, 189; HLC 1**
See also CA 124; 130; CANR 67, 70, 135; CWW 2; DAM MULT; DFS 4; EWL 3; HW 1, 2; INT CA-130; WLIT 1

Dorn, Edward (Merton)
1929-1999 .... **CLC 10, 18**
See also CA 93-96; 187; CANR 42, 79; CP 1, 2, 3, 4, 5, 6, 7; DLB 5; INT CA-93-96; WP

Dor-Ner, Zvi .... **CLC 70**

Dorris, Michael 1945-1997 .... **CLC 109; NNAL**
See also AAYA 20; BEST 90:1; BYA 12; CA 102; 157; CANR 19, 46, 75; CLR 58; DA3; DAM MULT, NOV; DLB 175; LAIT 5; MTCW 2; MTFW 2005; NFS 3; RGAL 4; SATA 75; SATA-Obit 94; TCWW 2; YAW

Dorris, Michael A.
See Dorris, Michael

Dorsan, Luc
See Simenon, Georges (Jacques Christian)

Dorsange, Jean
See Simenon, Georges (Jacques Christian)

Dorset
See Sackville, Thomas

Dos Passos, John (Roderigo)
1896-1970 ... **CLC 1, 4, 8, 11, 15, 25, 34, 82; WLC 2**
See also AMW; BPFB 1; CA 1-4R; 29-32R; CANR 3; CDALB 1929-1941; DA; DA3; DAB; DAC; DAM MST, NOV; DLB 4, 9, 274, 316; DLBD 1, 15; DLBY 1996; EWL 3; MAL 5; MTCW 1, 2; MTFW 2005; NFS 14; RGAL 4; TUS

Dossage, Jean
See Simenon, Georges (Jacques Christian)

Dostoevsky, Fedor Mikhailovich
1821-1881 .. **NCLC 2, 7, 21, 33, 43, 119, 167, 202; SSC 2, 33, 44; WLC 2**
See also AAYA 40; DA; DA3; DAB; DAC; DAM MST, NOV; DLB 238; EW 7; EXPN; LATS 1:1; LMFS 1, 2; NFS 28; RGSF 2; RGWL 2, 3; SSFS 8; TWA

Dostoevsky, Fyodor
See Dostoevsky, Fedor Mikhailovich

Doty, Mark 1953(?)- .... **CLC 176; PC 53**
See also AMWS 11; CA 161, 183; CAAE 183; CANR 110, 173; CP 7; PFS 28

Doty, Mark A.
See Doty, Mark

Doty, Mark Alan
See Doty, Mark

Doty, M.R.
See Doty, Mark

Doughty, Charles M(ontagu)
1843-1926 .... **TCLC 27**
See also CA 115; 178; DLB 19, 57, 174

Douglas, Ellen 1921- .... **CLC 73**
See also CA 115; CANR 41, 83; CN 5, 6, 7; CSW; DLB 292

Douglas, Gavin 1475(?)-1522 .... **LC 20**
See also DLB 132; RGEL 2

Douglas, George
See Brown, George Douglas

Douglas, Keith (Castellain)
1920-1944 .... **TCLC 40**
See also BRW 7; CA 160; DLB 27; EWL 3; PAB; RGEL 2

Douglas, Leonard
See Bradbury, Ray

Douglas, Michael
See Crichton, Michael

Douglas, Michael
See Crichton, Michael

Douglas, (George) Norman
1868-1952 .... **TCLC 68**
See also BRW 6; CA 119; 157; DLB 34, 195; RGEL 2

Douglas, William
See Brown, George Douglas

Douglass, Frederick 1817(?)-1895 .. **BLC 1:1; NCLC 7, 55, 141; WLC 2**
See also AAYA 48; AFAW 1, 2; AMWC 1; AMWS 3; CDALB 1640-1865; DA; DA3; DAC; DAM MST, MULT; DLB 1, 43, 50, 79, 243; FW; LAIT 2; NCFS 2; RGAL 4; SATA 29

Dourado, (Waldomiro Freitas) Autran
1926- .... **CLC 23, 60**
See also CA 25-28R; 179; CANR 34, 81; DLB 145, 307; HW 2

Dourado, Waldomiro Freitas Autran
See Dourado, (Waldomiro Freitas) Autran

Dove, Rita 1952- . **BLC 2:1; BLCS; CLC 50, 81; PC 6**
See also AAYA 46; AMWS 4; BW 2; CA 109; CAAS 19; CANR 27, 42, 68, 76, 97, 132; CDALBS; CP 5, 6, 7; CSW; CWP; DA3; DAM MULT, POET; DLB 120; EWL 3; EXPP; MAL 5; MTCW 2; MTFW 2005; PFS 1, 15; RGAL 4

Dove, Rita Frances
See Dove, Rita

Doveglion
See Villa, Jose Garcia

Dowell, Coleman 1925-1985 .... **CLC 60**
See also CA 25-28R; 117; CANR 10; DLB 130; GLL 2

Downing, Major Jack
See Smith, Seba

Dowson, Ernest (Christopher)
1867-1900 .... **TCLC 4**
See also CA 105; 150; DLB 19, 135; RGEL 2

Doyle, A. Conan
See Doyle, Sir Arthur Conan

Doyle, Sir Arthur Conan
1859-1930 ..... **SSC 12, 83, 95; TCLC 7; WLC 2**
See also AAYA 14; BPFB 1; BRWS 2; BYA 4, 5, 11; CA 104; 122; CANR 131; CD-BLB 1890-1914; CLR 106; CMW 4; DA; DA3; DAB; DAC; DAM MST, NOV; DLB 18, 70, 156, 178; EXPS; HGG; LAIT 2; MSW; MTCW 1, 2; MTFW 2005; NFS 28; RGEL 2; RGSF 2; RHW; SATA 24; SCFW 1, 2; SFW 4; SSFS 2; TEA; WCH; WLIT 4; WYA; YAW

Doyle, Conan
See Doyle, Sir Arthur Conan

Doyle, John
See Graves, Robert

Doyle, Roddy 1958- .... **CLC 81, 178**
See also AAYA 14; BRWS 5; CA 143; CANR 73, 128, 168; CN 6, 7; DA3; DLB 194, 326; MTCW 2; MTFW 2005

Doyle, Sir A. Conan
See Doyle, Sir Arthur Conan

Dr. A
See Asimov, Isaac; Silverstein, Alvin; Silverstein, Virginia B(arbara Opshelor)

Drabble, Margaret 1939- ...... **CLC 2, 3, 5, 8, 10, 22, 53, 129**
See also BRWS 4; CA 13-16R; CANR 18, 35, 63, 112, 131, 174; CDBLB 1960 to Present; CN 1, 2, 3, 4, 5, 6, 7; CPW; DA3; DAB; DAC; DAM MST, NOV, POP; DLB 14, 155, 231; EWL 3; FW; MTCW 1, 2; MTFW 2005; RGEL 2; SATA 48; TEA

Drakulic, Slavenka 1949- .... **CLC 173**
See also CA 144; CANR 92

Duong, Thu Huong 1947- .... **CLC 273**
   See also CA 152; CANR 106, 166; DLB
     348; NFS 23
Duong Thu Huong
   See Duong, Thu Huong
du Perry, Jean
   See Simenon, Georges (Jacques Christian)
Durang, Christopher 1949- .... **CLC 27, 38**
   See also CA 105; CAD; CANR 50, 76, 130;
     CD 5, 6; MTCW 2; MTFW 2005
Durang, Christopher Ferdinand
   See Durang, Christopher
Duras, Claire de 1777-1832 .... **NCLC 154**
Duras, Marguerite 1914-1996 . **CLC 3, 6, 11,**
   20, 34, 40, 68, 100; SSC 40
   See also BPFB 1; CA 25-28R; 151; CANR
     50; CWW 2; DFS 21; DLB 83, 321; EWL
     3; FL 1:5; GFL 1789 to the Present; IDFW
     4; MTCW 1, 2; RGWL 2, 3; TWA
Durban, (Rosa) Pam 1947- .... **CLC 39**
   See also CA 123; CANR 98; CSW
Durcan, Paul 1944- .... **CLC 43, 70**
   See also CA 134; CANR 123; CP 1, 5, 6, 7;
     DAM POET; EWL 3
d'Urfe, Honore
   See Urfe, Honore d'
Durfey, Thomas 1653-1723 .... **LC 94**
   See also DLB 80; RGEL 2
Durkheim, Emile 1858-1917 .... **TCLC 55**
   See also CA 249
Durrell, Lawrence (George)
   1912-1990 ..... **CLC 1, 4, 6, 8, 13, 27, 41**
   See also BPFB 1; BRWS 1; CA 9-12R; 132;
     CANR 40, 77; CDBLB 1945-1960; CN 1,
     2, 3, 4; CP 1, 2, 3, 4, 5; DAM NOV; DLB
     15, 27, 204; DLBY 1990; EWL 3; MTCW
     1, 2; RGEL 2; SFW 4; TEA
Durrenmatt, Friedrich
   See Duerrenmatt, Friedrich
Dutt, Michael Madhusudan
   1824-1873 .... **NCLC 118**
Dutt, Toru 1856-1877 .... **NCLC 29**
   See also DLB 240
Dwight, Timothy 1752-1817 .... **NCLC 13**
   See also DLB 37; RGAL 4
Dworkin, Andrea 1946-2005 ..... **CLC 43, 123**
   See also CA 77-80; 238; CAAS 21; CANR
     16, 39, 76, 96; FL 1:5; FW; GLL 1; INT
     CANR-16; MTCW 1, 2; MTFW 2005
Dwyer, Deanna
   See Koontz, Dean R.
Dwyer, K.R.
   See Koontz, Dean R.
Dybek, Stuart 1942- .... **CLC 114; SSC 55**
   See also CA 97-100; CANR 39; DLB 130;
     SSFS 23
Dye, Richard
   See De Voto, Bernard (Augustine)
Dyer, Geoff 1958- .... **CLC 149**
   See also CA 125; CANR 88
Dyer, George 1755-1841 .... **NCLC 129**
   See also DLB 93
Dylan, Bob 1941- .... **CLC 3, 4, 6, 12, 77; PC**
   37
   See also AMWS 18; CA 41-44R; CANR
     108; CP 1, 2, 3, 4, 5, 6, 7; DLB 16
Dyson, John 1943- .... **CLC 70**
   See also CA 144
Dzyubin, Eduard Georgievich
   1895-1934 .... **TCLC 60**
   See also CA 170; EWL 3
E. V. L.
   See Lucas, E(dward) V(errall)
Eagleton, Terence (Francis) 1943- .. **CLC 63,**
   132
   See also CA 57-60; CANR 7, 23, 68, 115;
     DLB 242; LMFS 2; MTCW 1, 2; MTFW
     2005

Eagleton, Terry
   See Eagleton, Terence (Francis)
Early, Jack
   See Scoppettone, Sandra
East, Michael
   See West, Morris L(anglo)
Eastaway, Edward
   See Thomas, (Philip) Edward
Eastlake, William (Derry)
   1917-1997 .... **CLC 8**
   See also CA 5-8R; 158; CAAS 1; CANR 5,
     63; CN 1, 2, 3, 4, 5, 6; DLB 6, 206; INT
     CANR-5; MAL 5; TCWW 1, 2
Eastman, Charles A(lexander)
   1858-1939 .... **NNAL; TCLC 55**
   See also CA 179; CANR 91; DAM MULT;
     DLB 175; YABC 1
Eaton, Edith Maude 1865-1914 .... **AAL**
   See also CA 154; DLB 221, 312; FW
Eaton, (Lillie) Winnifred 1875-1954 .... **AAL**
   See also CA 217; DLB 221, 312; RGAL 4
Eberhart, Richard 1904-2005 ...... **CLC 3, 11,**
   19, 56; PC 76
   See also AMW; CA 1-4R; 240; CANR 2,
     125; CDALB 1941-1968; CP 1, 2, 3, 4, 5,
     6, 7; DAM POET; DLB 48; MAL 5;
     MTCW 1; RGAL 4
Eberhart, Richard Ghormley
   See Eberhart, Richard
Eberstadt, Fernanda 1960- .... **CLC 39**
   See also CA 136; CANR 69, 128
Ebner, Margaret c. 1291-1351 ...... **CMLC 98**
Echegaray (y Eizaguirre), Jose (Maria
   Waldo) 1832-1916 .... **HLCS 1; TCLC 4**
   See also CA 104; CANR 32; DLB 329;
     EWL 3; HW 1; MTCW 1
Echeverria, (Jose) Esteban (Antonino)
   1805-1851 .... **NCLC 18**
   See also LAW
Echo
   See Proust, (Valentin-Louis-George-Eugene)
     Marcel
Eckert, Allan W. 1931- .... **CLC 17**
   See also AAYA 18; BYA 2; CA 13-16R;
     CANR 14, 45; INT CANR-14; MAICYA
     2; MAICYAS 1; SAAS 21; SATA 29, 91;
     SATA-Brief 27
Eckhart, Meister 1260(?)-1327(?) .. **CMLC 9,**
   80
   See also DLB 115; LMFS 1
Eckmar, F. R.
   See de Hartog, Jan
Eco, Umberto 1932- .... **CLC 28, 60, 142, 248**
   See also BEST 90:1; BPFB 1; CA 77-80;
     CANR 12, 33, 55, 110, 131; CPW; CWW
     2; DA3; DAM NOV, POP; DLB 196, 242;
     EWL 3; MSW; MTCW 1, 2; MTFW
     2005; NFS 22; RGWL 3; WLIT 7
Eddison, E(ric) R(ucker)
   1882-1945 .... **TCLC 15**
   See also CA 109; 156; DLB 255; FANT;
     SFW 4; SUFW 1
Eddy, Mary (Ann Morse) Baker
   1821-1910 .... **TCLC 71**
   See also CA 113; 174
Edel, (Joseph) Leon 1907-1997 .. **CLC 29, 34**
   See also CA 1-4R; 161; CANR 1, 22, 112;
     DLB 103; INT CANR-22
Eden, Emily 1797-1869 .... **NCLC 10**
Edgar, David 1948- .... **CLC 42**
   See also CA 57-60; CANR 12, 61, 112;
     CBD; CD 5, 6; DAM DRAM; DFS 15;
     DLB 13, 233; MTCW 1
Edgerton, Clyde (Carlyle) 1944- ...... **CLC 39**
   See also AAYA 17; CA 118; 134; CANR
     64, 125; CN 7; CSW; DLB 278; INT CA-
     134; TCLE 1:1; YAW

Edgeworth, Maria 1768-1849 ... **NCLC 1, 51,**
   158; SSC 86
   See also BRWS 3; DLB 116, 159, 163; FL
     1:3; FW; RGEL 2; SATA 21; TEA; WLIT
     3
Edmonds, Paul
   See Kuttner, Henry
Edmonds, Walter D(umaux)
   1903-1998 .... **CLC 35**
   See also BYA 2; CA 5-8R; CANR 2; CWRI
     5; DLB 9; LAIT 1; MAICYA 1, 2; MAL
     5; RHW; SAAS 4; SATA 1, 27; SATA-
     Obit 99
Edmondson, Wallace
   See Ellison, Harlan
Edson, Margaret 1961- ...... **CLC 199; DC 24**
   See also AMWS 18; CA 190; DFS 13; DLB
     266
Edson, Russell 1935- .... **CLC 13**
   See also CA 33-36R; CANR 115; CP 2, 3,
     4, 5, 6, 7; DLB 244; WP
Edwards, Bronwen Elizabeth
   See Rose, Wendy
Edwards, Eli
   See McKay, Festus Claudius
Edwards, G(erald) B(asil)
   1899-1976 .... **CLC 25**
   See also CA 201; 110
Edwards, Gus 1939- .... **CLC 43**
   See also CA 108; INT CA-108
Edwards, Jonathan 1703-1758 .... **LC 7, 54**
   See also AMW; DA; DAC; DAM MST;
     DLB 24, 270; RGAL 4; TUS
Edwards, Sarah Pierpont 1710-1758 .. **LC 87**
   See also DLB 200
Efron, Marina Ivanovna Tsvetaeva
   See Tsvetaeva (Efron), Marina (Ivanovna)
Egeria fl. 4th cent. - .... **CMLC 70**
Eggers, Dave 1970- .... **CLC 241**
   See also AAYA 56; CA 198; CANR 138;
     MTFW 2005
Egoyan, Atom 1960- .... **CLC 151**
   See also AAYA 63; CA 157; CANR 151
Ehle, John (Marsden, Jr.) 1925- ...... **CLC 27**
   See also CA 9-12R; CSW
Ehrenbourg, Ilya (Grigoryevich)
   See Ehrenburg, Ilya (Grigoryevich)
Ehrenburg, Ilya (Grigoryevich)
   1891-1967 .... **CLC 18, 34, 62**
   See Erenburg, Ilya (Grigoryevich)
   See also CA 102; 25-28R; EWL 3
Ehrenburg, Ilyo (Grigoryevich)
   See Ehrenburg, Ilya (Grigoryevich)
Ehrenreich, Barbara 1941- ...... **CLC 110, 267**
   See also BEST 90:4; CA 73-76; CANR 16,
     37, 62, 117, 167; DLB 246; FW; MTCW
     1, 2; MTFW 2005
Ehrlich, Gretel 1946- .... **CLC 249**
   See also ANW; CA 140; CANR 74, 146;
     DLB 212, 275; TCWW 2
Eich, Gunter
   See Eich, Gunter
Eich, Gunter 1907-1972 .... **CLC 15**
   See also CA 111; 93-96; DLB 69, 124;
     EWL 3; RGWL 2, 3
Eichendorff, Joseph 1788-1857 .... **NCLC 8**
   See also DLB 90; RGWL 2, 3
Eigner, Larry
   See Eigner, Laurence (Joel)
Eigner, Laurence (Joel) 1927-1996 ..... **CLC 9**
   See also CA 9-12R; 151; CAAS 23; CANR
     6, 84; CP 1, 2, 3, 4, 5, 6, 7; DLB 5; WP
Eilhart von Oberge c. 1140-c.
   1195 .... **CMLC 67**
   See also DLB 148
Einhard c. 770-840 .... **CMLC 50**
   See also DLB 148

Engelhardt, Frederick
See Hubbard, L. Ron
Engels, Friedrich 1820-1895 .. **NCLC 85, 114**
See also DLB 129; LATS 1:1
Enquist, Per Olov 1934- .... **CLC 257**
See also CA 109; 193; CANR 155; CWW
2; DLB 257; EWL 3
Enright, D(ennis) J(oseph)
1920-2002 .... **CLC 4, 8, 31; PC 93**
See also CA 1-4R; 211; CANR 1, 42, 83;
CN 1, 2; CP 1, 2, 3, 4, 5, 6, 7; DLB 27;
EWL 3; SATA 25; SATA-Obit 140
Ensler, Eve 1953- .... **CLC 212**
See also CA 172; CANR 126, 163; DFS 23
Enzensberger, Hans Magnus
1929- .... **CLC 43; PC 28**
See also CA 116; 119; CANR 103; CWW
2; EWL 3
Ephron, Nora 1941- .... **CLC 17, 31**
See also AAYA 35; AITN 2; CA 65-68;
CANR 12, 39, 83, 161; DFS 22
Epicurus 341B.C.-270B.C. .... **CMLC 21**
See also DLB 176
Epinay, Louise d' 1726-1783 .... **LC 138**
See also DLB 313
Epsilon
See Betjeman, John
Epstein, Daniel Mark 1948- .... **CLC 7**
See also CA 49-52; CANR 2, 53, 90
Epstein, Jacob 1956- .... **CLC 19**
See also CA 114
Epstein, Jean 1897-1953 .... **TCLC 92**
Epstein, Joseph 1937- .... **CLC 39, 204**
See also AMWS 14; CA 112; 119; CANR
50, 65, 117, 164
Epstein, Leslie 1938- .... **CLC 27**
See also AMWS 12; CA 73-76, 215; CAAE
215; CAAS 12; CANR 23, 69, 162; DLB
299; RGHL
Equiano, Olaudah 1745(?)-1797 ..... **BLC 1:2;**
LC 16, 143
See also AFAW 1, 2; CDWLB 3; DAM
MULT; DLB 37, 50; WLIT 2
Erasmus, Desiderius 1469(?)-1536 ..... **LC 16,**
93
See also DLB 136; EW 2; LMFS 1; RGWL
2, 3; TWA
Erdman, Paul E. 1932-2007 .... **CLC 25**
See also AITN 1; CA 61-64; 259; CANR
13, 43, 84
Erdman, Paul Emil
See Erdman, Paul E.
Erdrich, Karen Louise
See Erdrich, Louise
Erdrich, Louise 1954- .... **CLC 39, 54, 120,**
176; NNAL; PC 52; SSC 121
See also AAYA 10, 47; AMWS 4; BEST
89:1; BPFB 1; CA 114; CANR 41, 62,
118, 138; CDALBS; CN 5, 6, 7; CP 6, 7;
CPW; CWP; DA3; DAM MULT, NOV,
POP; DLB 152, 175, 206; EWL 3; EXPP;
FL 1:5; LAIT 5; LATS 1:2; MAL 5;
MTCW 1, 2; MTFW 2005; NFS 5; PFS
14; RGAL 4; SATA 94, 141; SSFS 14,
22; TCWW 2
Erenburg, Ilya (Grigoryevich)
See Ehrenburg, Ilya (Grigoryevich)
See also DLB 272
Erickson, Stephen Michael
See Erickson, Steve
Erickson, Steve 1950- .... **CLC 64**
See also CA 129; CANR 60, 68, 136;
MTFW 2005; SFW 4; SUFW 2
Erickson, Walter
See Fast, Howard
Ericson, Walter
See Fast, Howard
Eriksson, Buntel
See Bergman, Ingmar

Eriugena, John Scottus c.
810-877 .... **CMLC 65**
See also DLB 115
Ernaux, Annie 1940- .... **CLC 88, 184**
See also CA 147; CANR 93; MTFW 2005;
NCFS 3, 5
Erskine, John 1879-1951 .... **TCLC 84**
See also CA 112; 159; DLB 9, 102; FANT
Erwin, Will
See Eisner, Will
Eschenbach, Wolfram von
See von Eschenbach, Wolfram
Eseki, Bruno
See Mphahlele, Es'kia
Esekie, Bruno
See Mphahlele, Es'kia
Esenin, S.A.
See Esenin, Sergei
Esenin, Sergei 1895-1925 .... **TCLC 4**
See also CA 104; EWL 3; RGWL 2, 3
Esenin, Sergei Aleksandrovich
See Esenin, Sergei
Eshleman, Clayton 1935- .... **CLC 7**
See also CA 33-36R, 212; CAAE 212;
CAAS 6; CANR 93; CP 1, 2, 3, 4, 5, 6,
7; DLB 5
Espada, Martin 1957- .... **PC 74**
See also CA 159; CANR 80; CP 7; EXPP;
LLW; MAL 5; PFS 13, 16
Espriella, Don Manuel Alvarez
See Southey, Robert
Espriu, Salvador 1913-1985 .... **CLC 9**
See also CA 154; 115; DLB 134; EWL 3
Espronceda, Jose de 1808-1842 ..... **NCLC 39**
Esquivel, Laura 1950(?)- ... **CLC 141; HLCS**
1
See also AAYA 29; CA 143; CANR 68, 113,
161; DA3; DNFS 2; LAIT 3; LMFS 2;
MTCW 2; MTFW 2005; NFS 5; WLIT 1
Esse, James
See Stephens, James
Esterbrook, Tom
See Hubbard, L. Ron
Esterhazy, Peter 1950- .... **CLC 251**
See also CA 140; CANR 137; CDWLB 4;
CWW 2; DLB 232; EWL 3; RGWL 3
Estleman, Loren D. 1952- .... **CLC 48**
See also AAYA 27; CA 85-88; CANR 27,
74, 139, 177; CMW 4; CPW; DA3; DAM
NOV, POP; DLB 226; INT CANR-27;
MTCW 1, 2; MTFW 2005; TCWW 1, 2
Etherege, Sir George 1636-1692 . **DC 23; LC**
78
See also BRW 2; DAM DRAM; DLB 80;
PAB; RGEL 2
Euclid 306B.C.-283B.C. .... **CMLC 25**
Eugenides, Jeffrey 1960- .... **CLC 81, 212**
See also AAYA 51; CA 144; CANR 120;
MTFW 2005; NFS 24
Euripides c. 484B.C.-406B.C. .... **CMLC 23,**
51; DC 4; WLCS
See also AW 1; CDWLB 1; DA; DA3;
DAB; DAC; DAM DRAM, MST; DFS 1,
4, 6, 25; DLB 176; LAIT 1; LMFS 1;
RGWL 2, 3; WLIT 8
Eusebius c. 263-c. 339 .... **CMLC 103**
Evan, Evin
See Faust, Frederick (Schiller)
Evans, Caradoc 1878-1945 ... **SSC 43; TCLC**
85
See also DLB 162
Evans, Evan
See Faust, Frederick (Schiller)
Evans, Marian
See Eliot, George
Evans, Mary Ann
See Eliot, George

Evarts, Esther
See Benson, Sally
Evelyn, John 1620-1706 .... **LC 144**
See also BRW 2; RGEL 2
Everett, Percival 1956- .... **CLC 57**
See Everett, Percival L.
See also AMWS 18; BW 2; CA 129; CANR
94, 134, 179; CN 7; MTFW 2005
Everett, Percival L.
See Everett, Percival
See also CSW
Everson, R(onald) G(ilmour)
1903-1992 .... **CLC 27**
See also CA 17-20R; CP 1, 2, 3, 4; DLB 88
Everson, William (Oliver)
1912-1994 .... **CLC 1, 5, 14**
See also BG 1:2; CA 9-12R; 145; CANR
20; CP 1; DLB 5, 16, 212; MTCW 1
Evtushenko, Evgenii Aleksandrovich
See Yevtushenko, Yevgeny (Alexandrovich)
Ewart, Gavin (Buchanan)
1916-1995 .... **CLC 13, 46**
See also BRWS 7; CA 89-92; 150; CANR
17, 46; CP 1, 2, 3, 4, 5, 6; DLB 40;
MTCW 1
Ewers, Hanns Heinz 1871-1943 ..... **TCLC 12**
See also CA 109; 149
Ewing, Frederick R.
See Sturgeon, Theodore (Hamilton)
Exley, Frederick (Earl) 1929-1992 .... **CLC 6,**
11
See also AITN 2; BPFB 1; CA 81-84; 138;
CANR 117; DLB 143; DLBY 1981
Eynhardt, Guillermo
See Quiroga, Horacio (Sylvestre)
Ezekiel, Nissim (Moses) 1924-2004 .. **CLC 61**
See also CA 61-64; 223; CP 1, 2, 3, 4, 5, 6,
7; DLB 323; EWL 3
Ezekiel, Tish O'Dowd 1943- .... **CLC 34**
See also CA 129
Fadeev, Aleksandr Aleksandrovich
See Bulgya, Alexander Alexandrovich
Fadeev, Alexandr Alexandrovich
See Bulgya, Alexander Alexandrovich
Fadeyev, A.
See Bulgya, Alexander Alexandrovich
Fadeyev, Alexander
See Bulgya, Alexander Alexandrovich
Fagen, Donald 1948- .... **CLC 26**
Fainzil'berg, Il'ia Arnol'dovich
See Fainzilberg, Ilya Arnoldovich
Fainzilberg, Ilya Arnoldovich
1897-1937 .... **TCLC 21**
See also CA 120; 165; DLB 272; EWL 3
Fair, Ronald L. 1932- .... **CLC 18**
See also BW 1; CA 69-72; CANR 25; DLB
33
Fairbairn, Roger
See Carr, John Dickson
Fairbairns, Zoe (Ann) 1948- .... **CLC 32**
See also CA 103; CANR 21, 85; CN 4, 5,
6, 7
Fairfield, Flora
See Alcott, Louisa May
Falco, Gian
See Papini, Giovanni
Falconer, James
See Kirkup, James
Falconer, Kenneth
See Kornbluth, C(yril) M.
Falkland, Samuel
See Heijermans, Herman
Fallaci, Oriana 1930-2006 .... **CLC 11, 110**
See also CA 77-80; 253; CANR 15, 58, 134;
FW; MTCW 1
Faludi, Susan 1959- .... **CLC 140**
See also CA 138; CANR 126; FW; MTCW
2; MTFW 2005; NCFS 3

Fraser, Antonia 1932- .... **CLC 32, 107**
See also AAYA 57; CA 85-88; CANR 44, 65, 119, 164; CMW; DLB 276; MTCW 1, 2; MTFW 2005; SATA-Brief 32

Fraser, George MacDonald
1925-2008 .... **CLC 7**
See also AAYA 48; CA 45-48, 180; 268; CAAE 180; CANR 2, 48, 74; MTCW 2; RHW

Fraser, Sylvia 1935- .... **CLC 64**
See also CA 45-48; CANR 1, 16, 60; CCA 1

Frater Perdurabo
See Crowley, Edward Alexander

Frayn, Michael 1933- .... **CLC 3, 7, 31, 47, 176; DC 27**
See also AAYA 69; BRWC 2; BRWS 7; CA 5-8R; CANR 30, 69, 114, 133, 166; CBD; CD 5, 6; CN 1, 2, 3, 4, 5, 6, 7; DAM DRAM, NOV; DFS 22; DLB 13, 14, 194, 245; FANT; MTCW 1, 2; MTFW 2005; SFW 4

Fraze, Candida (Merrill) 1945- .... **CLC 50**
See also CA 126

Frazer, Andrew
See Marlowe, Stephen

Frazer, J(ames) G(eorge)
1854-1941 .... **TCLC 32**
See also BRWS 3; CA 118; NCFS 5

Frazer, Robert Caine
See Creasey, John

Frazer, Sir James George
See Frazer, J(ames) G(eorge)

Frazier, Charles 1950- .... **CLC 109, 224**
See also AAYA 34; CA 161; CANR 126, 170; CSW; DLB 292; MTFW 2005; NFS 25

Frazier, Charles R.
See Frazier, Charles

Frazier, Charles Robinson
See Frazier, Charles

Frazier, Ian 1951- .... **CLC 46**
See also CA 130; CANR 54, 93

Frederic, Harold 1856-1898 ... **NCLC 10, 175**
See also AMW; DLB 12, 23; DLBD 13; MAL 5; NFS 22; RGAL 4

Frederick, John
See Faust, Frederick (Schiller)

Frederick the Great 1712-1786 .... **LC 14**

Fredro, Aleksander 1793-1876 .... **NCLC 8**

Freeling, Nicolas 1927-2003 .... **CLC 38**
See also CA 49-52; 218; CAAS 12; CANR 1, 17, 50, 84; CMW 4; CN 1, 2, 3, 4, 5, 6; DLB 87

Freeman, Douglas Southall
1886-1953 .... **TCLC 11**
See also CA 109; 195; DLB 17; DLBD 17

Freeman, Judith 1946- .... **CLC 55**
See also CA 148; CANR 120, 179; DLB 256

Freeman, Mary E(leanor) Wilkins
1852-1930 .... **SSC 1, 47, 113; TCLC 9**
See also CA 106; 177; DLB 12, 78, 221; EXPS; FW; HGG; MBL; RGAL 4; RGSF 2; SSFS 4, 8, 26; SUFW 1; TUS

Freeman, R(ichard) Austin
1862-1943 .... **TCLC 21**
See also CA 113; CANR 84; CMW 4; DLB 70

French, Albert 1943- .... **CLC 86**
See also BW 3; CA 167

French, Antonia
See Kureishi, Hanif

French, Marilyn 1929- .. **CLC 10, 18, 60, 177**
See also BPFB 1; CA 69-72; CANR 3, 31, 134, 163; CN 5, 6, 7; CPW; DAM DRAM, NOV, POP; FL 1:5; FW; INT CANR-31; MTCW 1, 2; MTFW 2005

French, Paul
See Asimov, Isaac

Freneau, Philip Morin 1752-1832 .. **NCLC 1, 111**
See also AMWS 2; DLB 37, 43; RGAL 4

Freud, Sigmund 1856-1939 .... **TCLC 52**
See also CA 115; 133; CANR 69; DLB 296; EW 8; EWL 3; LATS 1:1; MTCW 1, 2; MTFW 2005; NCFS 3; TWA

Freytag, Gustav 1816-1895 .... **NCLC 109**
See also DLB 129

Friedan, Betty 1921-2006 .... **CLC 74**
See also CA 65-68; 248; CANR 18, 45, 74; DLB 246; FW; MTCW 1, 2; MTFW 2005; NCFS 5

Friedan, Betty Naomi
See Friedan, Betty

Friedlander, Saul 1932- .... **CLC 90**
See also CA 117; 130; CANR 72; RGHL

Friedman, B(ernard) H(arper)
1926- .... **CLC 7**
See also CA 1-4R; CANR 3, 48

Friedman, Bruce Jay 1930- ...... **CLC 3, 5, 56**
See also CA 9-12R; CAD; CANR 25, 52, 101; CD 5, 6; CN 1, 2, 3, 4, 5, 6, 7; DLB 2, 28, 244; INT CANR-25; MAL 5; SSFS 18

Friel, Brian 1929- .. **CLC 5, 42, 59, 115, 253; DC 8; SSC 76**
See also BRWS 5; CA 21-24R; CANR 33, 69, 131; CBD; CD 5, 6; DFS 11; DLB 13, 319; EWL 3; MTCW 1; RGEL 2; TEA

Friis-Baastad, Babbis Ellinor
1921-1970 .... **CLC 12**
See also CA 17-20R; 134; SATA 7

Frisch, Max 1911-1991 ...... **CLC 3, 9, 14, 18, 32, 44; TCLC 121**
See also CA 85-88; 134; CANR 32, 74; CD-WLB 2; DAM DRAM, NOV; DFS 25; DLB 69, 124; EW 13; EWL 3; MTCW 1, 2; MTFW 2005; RGHL; RGWL 2, 3

Fromentin, Eugene (Samuel Auguste)
1820-1876 .... **NCLC 10, 125**
See also DLB 123; GFL 1789 to the Present

Frost, Frederick
See Faust, Frederick (Schiller)

Frost, Robert 1874-1963 . **CLC 1, 3, 4, 9, 10, 13, 15, 26, 34, 44; PC 1, 39, 71; WLC 2**
See also AAYA 21; AMW; AMWR 1; CA 89-92; CANR 33; CDALB 1917-1929; CLR 67; DA; DA3; DAB; DAC; DAM MST, POET; DLB 54, 284, 342; DLBD 7; EWL 3; EXPP; MAL 5; MTCW 1, 2; MTFW 2005; PAB; PFS 1, 2, 3, 4, 5, 6, 7, 10, 13; RGAL 4; SATA 14; TUS; WP; WYA

Frost, Robert Lee
See Frost, Robert

Froude, James Anthony
1818-1894 .... **NCLC 43**
See also DLB 18, 57, 144

Froy, Herald
See Waterhouse, Keith (Spencer)

Fry, Christopher 1907-2005 ... **CLC 2, 10, 14**
See also BRWS 3; CA 17-20R; 240; CAAS 23; CANR 9, 30, 74, 132; CBD; CD 5, 6; CP 1, 2, 3, 4, 5, 6, 7; DAM DRAM; DLB 13; EWL 3; MTCW 1, 2; MTFW 2005; RGEL 2; SATA 66; TEA

Frye, (Herman) Northrop
1912-1991 .... **CLC 24, 70; TCLC 165**
See also CA 5-8R; 133; CANR 8, 37; DLB 67, 68, 246; EWL 3; MTCW 1, 2; MTFW 2005; RGAL 4; TWA

Fuchs, Daniel 1909-1993 .... **CLC 8, 22**
See also CA 81-84; 142; CAAS 5; CANR 40; CN 1, 2, 3, 4, 5; DLB 9, 26, 28; DLBY 1993; MAL 5

Fuchs, Daniel 1934- .... **CLC 34**
See also CA 37-40R; CANR 14, 48

Fuentes, Carlos 1928- .. **CLC 3, 8, 10, 13, 22, 41, 60, 113; HLC 1; SSC 24; WLC 2**
See also AAYA 4, 45; AITN 2; BPFB 1; CA 69-72; CANR 10, 32, 68, 104, 138; CDWLB 3; CWW 2; DA; DA3; DAB; DAC; DAM MST, MULT, NOV; DLB 113; DNFS 2; EWL 3; HW 1, 2; LAIT 3; LATS 1:2; LAW; LAWS 1; LMFS 2; MTCW 1, 2; MTFW 2005; NFS 8; RGSF 2; RGWL 2, 3; TWA; WLIT 1

Fuentes, Gregorio Lopez y
See Lopez y Fuentes, Gregorio

Fuertes, Gloria 1918-1998 .... **PC 27**
See also CA 178; 180; DLB 108; HW 2; SATA 115

Fugard, (Harold) Athol 1932- . **CLC 5, 9, 14, 25, 40, 80, 211; DC 3**
See also AAYA 17; AFW; CA 85-88; CANR 32, 54, 118; CD 5, 6; DAM DRAM; DFS 3, 6, 10, 24; DLB 225; DNFS 1, 2; EWL 3; LATS 1:2; MTCW 1; MTFW 2005; RGEL 2; WLIT 2

Fugard, Sheila 1932- .... **CLC 48**
See also CA 125

Fujiwara no Teika 1162-1241 .... **CMLC 73**
See also DLB 203

Fukuyama, Francis 1952- .... **CLC 131**
See also CA 140; CANR 72, 125, 170

Fuller, Charles (H.), (Jr.) 1939- ..... **BLC 1:2; CLC 25; DC 1**
See also BW 2; CA 108; 112; CAD; CANR 87; CD 5, 6; DAM DRAM, MULT; DFS 8; DLB 38, 266; EWL 3; INT CA-112; MAL 5; MTCW 1

Fuller, Henry Blake 1857-1929 .... **TCLC 103**
See also CA 108; 177; DLB 12; RGAL 4

Fuller, John (Leopold) 1937- .... **CLC 62**
See also CA 21-24R; CANR 9, 44; CP 1, 2, 3, 4, 5, 6, 7; DLB 40

Fuller, Margaret
See Ossoli, Sarah Margaret (Fuller)

Fuller, Roy (Broadbent) 1912-1991 ... **CLC 4, 28**
See also BRWS 7; CA 5-8R; 135; CAAS 10; CANR 53, 83; CN 1, 2, 3, 4, 5; CP 1, 2, 3, 4, 5; DLB 15, 20; EWL 3; CWRI 5; RGEL 2; SATA 87

Fuller, Sarah Margaret
See Ossoli, Sarah Margaret (Fuller)

Fuller, Thomas 1608-1661 .... **LC 111**
See also DLB 151

Fulton, Alice 1952- .... **CLC 52**
See also CA 116; CANR 57, 88; CP 5, 6, 7; CWP; DLB 193; PFS 25

Furey, Michael
See Ward, Arthur Henry Sarsfield

Furphy, Joseph 1843-1912 .... **TCLC 25**
See also CA 163; DLB 230; EWL 3; RGEL 2

Furst, Alan 1941- .... **CLC 255**
See also CA 69-72; CANR 12, 34, 59, 102, 159; DLBY 01

Fuson, Robert H(enderson) 1927- .... **CLC 70**
See also CA 89-92; CANR 103

Fussell, Paul 1924- .... **CLC 74**
See also BEST 90:1; CA 17-20R; CANR 8, 21, 35, 69, 135; INT CANR-21; MTCW 1, 2; MTFW 2005

Futabatei, Shimei 1864-1909 .... **TCLC 44**
See also CA 162; DLB 180; EWL 3; MJW

Futabatei Shimei
See Futabatei, Shimei

Futrelle, Jacques 1875-1912 .... **TCLC 19**
See also CA 113; 155; CMW 4

GAB
See Russell, George William

Gaberman, Judie Angell
See Angell, Judie

Gaboriau, Emile 1835-1873 .... **NCLC 14**
See also CMW 4; MSW

Gadda, Carlo Emilio 1893-1973 ...... **CLC 11;**
TCLC 144
See also CA 89-92; DLB 177; EWL 3;
WLIT 7

Gaddis, William 1922-1998 ... **CLC 1, 3, 6, 8,**
10, 19, 43, 86
See also AMWS 4; BPFB 1; CA 17-20R;
172; CANR 21, 48, 148; CN 1, 2, 3, 4, 5,
6; DLB 2, 278; EWL 3; MAL 5; MTCW
1, 2; MTFW 2005; RGAL 4

Gage, Walter
See Inge, William (Motter)

Gaiman, Neil 1960- .... **CLC 195**
See also AAYA 19, 42; CA 133; CANR 81,
129, 188; CLR 109; DLB 261; HGG;
MTFW 2005; SATA 85, 146, 197; SFW
4; SUFW 2

Gaiman, Neil Richard
See Gaiman, Neil

Gaines, Ernest J. 1933- ..... **BLC 1:2; CLC 3,**
11, 18, 86, 181; SSC 68
See also AAYA 18; AFAW 1, 2; AITN 1;
BPFB 2; BW 2, 3; BYA 6; CA 9-12R;
CANR 6, 24, 42, 75, 126; CDALB 1968-
1988; CLR 62; CN 1, 2, 3, 4, 5, 6, 7;
CSW; DA3; DAM MULT; DLB 2, 33,
152; DLBY 1980; EWL 3; EXPN; LAIT
5; LATS 1:2; MAL 5; MTCW 1, 2;
MTFW 2005; NFS 5, 7, 16; RGAL 4;
RGSF 2; RHW; SATA 86; SSFS 5; YAW

Gaitskill, Mary 1954- .... **CLC 69**
See also CA 128; CANR 61, 152; DLB 244;
TCLE 1:1

Gaitskill, Mary Lawrence
See Gaitskill, Mary

Gaius Suetonius Tranquillus
See Suetonius

Galdos, Benito Perez
See Perez Galdos, Benito

Gale, Zona 1874-1938 .... **DC 30; TCLC 7**
See also CA 105; 153; CANR 84; DAM
DRAM; DFS 17; DLB 9, 78, 228; RGAL
4

Galeano, Eduardo 1940- ... **CLC 72; HLCS 1**
See also CA 29-32R; CANR 13, 32, 100,
163; HW 1

Galeano, Eduardo Hughes
See Galeano, Eduardo

Galiano, Juan Valera y Alcala
See Valera y Alcala-Galiano, Juan

Galilei, Galileo 1564-1642 .... **LC 45**

Gallagher, Tess 1943- .... **CLC 18, 63; PC 9**
See also CA 106; CP 3, 4, 5, 6, 7; CWP;
DAM POET; DLB 120, 212, 244; PFS 16

Gallant, Mavis 1922- ..... **CLC 7, 18, 38, 172;**
SSC 5, 78
See also CA 69-72; CANR 29, 69, 117;
CCA 1; CN 1, 2, 3, 4, 5, 6, 7; DAC; DAM
MST; DLB 53; EWL 3; MTCW 1, 2;
MTFW 2005; RGEL 2; RGSF 2

Gallant, Roy A(rthur) 1924- .... **CLC 17**
See also CA 5-8R; CANR 4, 29, 54, 117;
CLR 30; MAICYA 1, 2; SATA 4, 68, 110

Gallico, Paul (William) 1897-1976 ..... **CLC 2**
See also AITN 1; CA 5-8R; 69-72; CANR
23; CN 1, 2; DLB 9, 171; FANT; MAI-
CYA 1, 2; SATA 13

Gallo, Max Louis 1932- .... **CLC 95**
See also CA 85-88

Gallois, Lucien
See Desnos, Robert

Gallup, Ralph
See Whitemore, Hugh (John)

Galsworthy, John 1867-1933 .... **SSC 22;**
TCLC 1, 45; WLC 2
See also BRW 6; CA 104; 141; CANR 75;
CDBLB 1890-1914; DA; DA3; DAB;
DAC; DAM DRAM, MST, NOV; DLB
10, 34, 98, 162, 330; DLBD 16; EWL 3;
MTCW 2; RGEL 2; SSFS 3; TEA

Galt, John 1779-1839 .... **NCLC 1, 110**
See also DLB 99, 116, 159; RGEL 2; RGSF
2

Galvin, James 1951- .... **CLC 38**
See also CA 108; CANR 26

Gamboa, Federico 1864-1939 .... **TCLC 36**
See also CA 167; HW 2; LAW

Gandhi, M. K.
See Gandhi, Mohandas Karamchand

Gandhi, Mahatma
See Gandhi, Mohandas Karamchand

Gandhi, Mohandas Karamchand
1869-1948 .... **TCLC 59**
See also CA 121; 132; DA3; DAM MULT;
DLB 323; MTCW 1, 2

Gann, Ernest Kellogg 1910-1991 ..... **CLC 23**
See also AITN 1; BPFB 2; CA 1-4R; 136;
CANR 1, 83; RHW

Gao Xingjian 1940-
See Xingjian, Gao

Garber, Eric 1943(?)- .... **CLC 38**
See also CA 144; CANR 89, 162; GLL 1

Garber, Esther
See Lee, Tanith

Garcia, Cristina 1958- .... **CLC 76**
See also AMWS 11; CA 141; CANR 73,
130, 172; CN 7; DLB 292; DNFS 1; EWL
3; HW 2; LLW; MTFW 2005

Garcia Lorca, Federico 1898-1936 ...... **DC 2;**
HLC 2; PC 3; TCLC 1, 7, 49, 181,
197; WLC 2
See also AAYA 46; CA 104; 131; CANR
81; DA; DA3; DAB; DAC; DAM DRAM,
MST, MULT, POET; DFS 4; DLB 108;
EW 11; EWL 3; HW 1, 2; LATS 1:2;
MTCW 1, 2; MTFW 2005; PFS 20;
RGWL 2, 3; TWA; WP

Garcia Marquez, Gabriel 1928- .... **CLC 2, 3,**
8, 10, 15, 27, 47, 55, 68, 170, 254; HLC
1; SSC 8, 83; WLC 3
See also AAYA 3, 33; BEST 89:1, 90:4;
BPFB 2; BYA 12, 16; CA 33-36R; CANR
10, 28, 50, 75, 82, 128; CDWLB 3; CPW;
CWW 2; DA; DA3; DAB; DAC; DAM
MST, MULT, NOV, POP; DLB 113, 330;
DNFS 1, 2; EWL 3; EXPN; EXPS; HW
1, 2; LAIT 2; LATS 1:2; LAW; LAWS 1;
LMFS 2; MTCW 1, 2; MTFW 2005;
NCFS 3; NFS 1, 5, 10; RGSF 2; RGWL
2, 3; SSFS 1, 6, 16, 21; TWA; WLIT 1

Garcia Marquez, Gabriel Jose
See Garcia Marquez, Gabriel

Garcilaso de la Vega, El Inca
1539-1616 .... **HLCS 1; LC 127**
See also DLB 318; LAW

Gard, Janice
See Latham, Jean Lee

Gard, Roger Martin du
See Martin du Gard, Roger

Gardam, Jane 1928- .... **CLC 43**
See also CA 49-52; CANR 2, 18, 33, 54,
106, 167; CLR 12; DLB 14, 161, 231;
MAICYA 1; MTCW 1; SAAS 9; SATA
39, 76, 130; SATA-Brief 28; YAW

Gardam, Jane Mary
See Gardam, Jane

Gardner, Herb(ert George)
1934-2003 .... **CLC 44**
See also CA 149; 220; CAD; CANR 119;
CD 5, 6; DFS 18, 20

Gardner, John, Jr. 1933-1982 ... **CLC 2, 3, 5,**
7, 8, 10, 18, 28, 34; SSC 7; TCLC 195
See also AAYA 45; AITN 1; AMWS 6;
BPFB 2; CA 65-68; 107; CANR 33, 73;
CDALBS; CN 2, 3; CPW; DA3; DAM
NOV, POP; DLB 2; DLBY 1982; EWL 3;
FANT; LATS 1:2; MAL 5; MTCW 1, 2;
MTFW 2005; NFS 3; RGAL 4; RGSF 2;
SATA 40; SATA-Obit 31; SSFS 8

Gardner, John 1926-2007 .... **CLC 30**
See also CA 103; 263; CANR 15, 69, 127,
183; CMW 4; CPW; DAM POP; MTCW
1

Gardner, John Edmund
See Gardner, John

Gardner, Miriam
See Bradley, Marion Zimmer

Gardner, Noel
See Kuttner, Henry

Gardons, S.S.
See Snodgrass, W. D.

Garfield, Leon 1921-1996 .... **CLC 12**
See also AAYA 8, 69; BYA 1, 3; CA 17-
20R; 152; CANR 38, 41, 78; CLR 21;
DLB 161; JRDA; MAICYA 1, 2; MAIC-
YAS 1; SATA 1, 32, 76; SATA-Obit 90;
TEA; WYA; YAW

Garland, (Hannibal) Hamlin
1860-1940 .... **SSC 18, 117; TCLC 3**
See also CA 104; DLB 12, 71, 78, 186;
MAL 5; RGAL 4; RGSF 2; TCWW 1, 2

Garneau, (Hector de) Saint-Denys
1912-1943 .... **TCLC 13**
See also CA 111; DLB 88

Garner, Alan 1934- .... **CLC 17**
See also AAYA 18; BYA 3, 5; CA 73-76,
178; CAAE 178; CANR 15, 64, 134; CLR
20, 130; CPW; DAB; DAM POP; DLB
161, 261; FANT; MAICYA 1, 2; MTCW
1, 2; MTFW 2005; SATA 18, 69; SATA-
Essay 108; SUFW 1, 2; YAW

Garner, Hugh 1913-1979 .... **CLC 13**
See also CA 69-72; CANR 31; CCA 1; CN
1, 2; DLB 68

Garnett, David 1892-1981 .... **CLC 3**
See also CA 5-8R; 103; CANR 17, 79; CN
1, 2; DLB 34; FANT; MTCW 2; RGEL 2;
SFW 4; SUFW 1

Garnier, Robert c. 1545-1590 .... **LC 119**
See also DLB 327; GFL Beginnings to 1789

Garrett, George 1929-2008 ... **CLC 3, 11, 51;**
SSC 30
See also AMWS 7; BPFB 2; CA 1-4R; 202;
272; CAAE 202; CAAS 5; CANR 1, 42,
67, 109; CN 1, 2, 3, 4, 5, 6, 7; CP 1, 2, 3,
4, 5, 6, 7; CSW; DLB 2, 5, 130, 152;
DLBY 1983

Garrett, George P.
See Garrett, George

Garrett, George Palmer
See Garrett, George

Garrett, George Palmer, Jr.
See Garrett, George

Garrick, David 1717-1779 .... **LC 15, 156**
See also DAM DRAM; DLB 84, 213;
RGEL 2

Garrigue, Jean 1914-1972 .... **CLC 2, 8**
See also CA 5-8R; 37-40R; CANR 20; CP
1; MAL 5

Garrison, Frederick
See Sinclair, Upton

Garrison, William Lloyd
1805-1879 .... **NCLC 149**
See also CDALB 1640-1865; DLB 1, 43,
235

Garro, Elena 1920(?)-1998 .. **HLCS 1; TCLC**
153
See also CA 131; 169; CWW 2; DLB 145;
EWL 3; HW 1; LAWS 1; WLIT 1

Griffin, Gerald 1803-1840 .... **NCLC 7**
See also DLB 159; RGEL 2
Griffin, John Howard 1920-1980 ..... **CLC 68**
See also AITN 1; CA 1-4R; 101; CANR 2
Griffin, Peter 1942- .... **CLC 39**
See also CA 136
Griffith, David Lewelyn Wark
See Griffith, D.W.
Griffith, D.W. 1875(?)-1948 .... **TCLC 68**
See also AAYA 78; CA 119; 150; CANR 80
Griffith, Lawrence
See Griffith, D.W.
Griffiths, Trevor 1935- .... **CLC 13, 52**
See also CA 97-100; CANR 45; CBD; CD
5, 6; DLB 13, 245
Griggs, Sutton (Elbert)
1872-1930 .... **TCLC 77**
See also CA 123; 186; DLB 50
Grigson, Geoffrey (Edward Harvey)
1905-1985 .... **CLC 7, 39**
See also CA 25-28R; 118; CANR 20, 33;
CP 1, 2, 3, 4; DLB 27; MTCW 1, 2
Grile, Dod
See Bierce, Ambrose (Gwinett)
Grillparzer, Franz 1791-1872 .... **DC 14;**
NCLC 1, 102; SSC 37
See also CDWLB 2; DLB 133; EW 5;
RGWL 2, 3; TWA
Grimble, Reverend Charles James
See Eliot, T(homas) S(tearns)
Grimke, Angelina (Emily) Weld
1880-1958 .... **HR 1:2**
See also BW 1; CA 124; DAM POET; DLB
50, 54; FW
Grimke, Charlotte L(ottie) Forten
1837(?)-1914 .... **BLC 1:2; TCLC 16**
See also BW 1; CA 117; 124; DAM MULT,
POET; DLB 50, 239
Grimm, Jacob Ludwig Karl
1785-1863 .... **NCLC 3, 77; SSC 36, 88**
See also CLR 112; DLB 90; MAICYA 1, 2;
RGSF 2; RGWL 2, 3; SATA 22; WCH
Grimm, Wilhelm Karl 1786-1859 .. **NCLC 3,**
77; SSC 36
See also CDWLB 2; CLR 112; DLB 90;
MAICYA 1, 2; RGSF 2; RGWL 2, 3;
SATA 22; WCH
Grimm and Grim
See Grimm, Jacob Ludwig Karl; Grimm,
Wilhelm Karl
Grimm Brothers
See Grimm, Jacob Ludwig Karl; Grimm,
Wilhelm Karl
Grimmelshausen, Hans Jakob Christoffel
von
See Grimmelshausen, Johann Jakob Christ-
offel von
Grimmelshausen, Johann Jakob Christoffel
von 1621-1676 .... **LC 6**
See also CDWLB 2; DLB 168; RGWL 2, 3
Grindel, Eugene 1895-1952 .... **PC 38; TCLC**
7, 41
See also CA 104; 193; EWL 3; GFL 1789
to the Present; LMFS 2; RGWL 2, 3
Grisham, John 1955- .... **CLC 84, 273**
See also AAYA 14, 47; BPFB 2; CA 138;
CANR 47, 69, 114, 133; CMW 4; CN 6,
7; CPW; CSW; DA3; DAM POP; MSW;
MTCW 2; MTFW 2005
Grosseteste, Robert 1175(?)-1253 . **CMLC 62**
See also DLB 115
Grossman, David 1954- .... **CLC 67, 231**
See also CA 138; CANR 114, 175; CWW
2; DLB 299; EWL 3; RGHL; WLIT 6
Grossman, Vasilii Semenovich
See Grossman, Vasily (Semenovich)

Grossman, Vasily (Semenovich)
1905-1964 .... **CLC 41**
See also CA 124; 130; DLB 272; MTCW 1;
RGHL
Grove, Frederick Philip
See Greve, Felix Paul (Berthold Friedrich)
Grubb
See Crumb, R.
Grumbach, Doris 1918- .... **CLC 13, 22, 64**
See also CA 5-8R; CAAS 2; CANR 9, 42,
70, 127; CN 6, 7; INT CANR-9; MTCW
2; MTFW 2005
Grundtvig, Nikolai Frederik Severin
1783-1872 .... **NCLC 1, 158**
See also DLB 300
Grunge
See Crumb, R.
Grunwald, Lisa 1959- .... **CLC 44**
See also CA 120; CANR 148
Gryphius, Andreas 1616-1664 .... **LC 89**
See also CDWLB 2; DLB 164; RGWL 2, 3
Guare, John 1938- .... **CLC 8, 14, 29, 67; DC**
20
See also CA 73-76; CAD; CANR 21, 69,
118; CD 5, 6; DAM DRAM; DFS 8, 13;
DLB 7, 249; EWL 3; MAL 5; MTCW 1,
2; RGAL 4
Guarini, Battista 1538-1612 .... **LC 102**
See also DLB 339
Gubar, Susan 1944- .... **CLC 145**
See also CA 108; CANR 45, 70, 139, 179;
FW; MTCW 1; RGAL 4
Gubar, Susan David
See Gubar, Susan
Gudjonsson, Halldor Kiljan
1902-1998 .... **CLC 25**
See also CA 103; 164; CWW 2; DLB 293,
331; EW 12; EWL 3; RGWL 2, 3
Guedes, Vincente
See Pessoa, Fernando
Guenter, Erich
See Eich, Gunter
Guest, Barbara 1920-2006 ... **CLC 34; PC 55**
See also BG 1:2; CA 25-28R; 248; CANR
11, 44, 84; CP 1, 2, 3, 4, 5, 6, 7; CWP;
DLB 5, 193
Guest, Edgar A(lbert) 1881-1959 ... **TCLC 95**
See also CA 112; 168
Guest, Judith 1936- .... **CLC 8, 30**
See also AAYA 7, 66; CA 77-80; CANR
15, 75, 138; DA3; DAM NOV, POP;
EXPN; INT CANR-15; LAIT 5; MTCW
1, 2; MTFW 2005; NFS 1
Guevara, Che
See Guevara (Serna), Ernesto
Guevara (Serna), Ernesto
1928-1967 .... **CLC 87; HLC 1**
See also CA 127; 111; CANR 56; DAM
MULT; HW 1
Guicciardini, Francesco 1483-1540 ..... **LC 49**
Guido delle Colonne c. 1215-c.
1290 .... **CMLC 90**
Guild, Nicholas M. 1944- .... **CLC 33**
See also CA 93-96
Guillemin, Jacques
See Sartre, Jean-Paul
Guillen, Jorge 1893-1984 . **CLC 11; HLCS 1;**
PC 35
See also CA 89-92; 112; DAM MULT,
POET; DLB 108; EWL 3; HW 1; RGWL
2, 3
Guillen, Nicolas (Cristobal)
1902-1989 .... **BLC 1:2; CLC 48, 79;**
HLC 1; PC 23
See also BW 2; CA 116; 125; 129; CANR
84; DAM MST, MULT, POET; DLB 283;
EWL 3; HW 1; LAW; RGWL 2, 3; WP
Guillen y Alvarez, Jorge
See Guillen, Jorge

Guillevic, (Eugene) 1907-1997 .... **CLC 33**
See also CA 93-96; CWW 2
Guillois
See Desnos, Robert
Guillois, Valentin
See Desnos, Robert
Guimaraes Rosa, Joao 1908-1967 ... **CLC 23;**
HLCS 1
See also CA 175; 89-92; DLB 113, 307;
EWL 3; LAW; RGSF 2; RGWL 2, 3;
WLIT 1
Guiney, Louise Imogen
1861-1920 .... **TCLC 41**
See also CA 160; DLB 54; RGAL 4
Guinizelli, Guido c. 1230-1276 ...... **CMLC 49**
See also WLIT 7
Guinizzelli, Guido
See Guinizelli, Guido
Guiraldes, Ricardo (Guillermo)
1886-1927 .... **TCLC 39**
See also CA 131; EWL 3; HW 1; LAW;
MTCW 1
Gumilev, Nikolai (Stepanovich)
1886-1921 .... **TCLC 60**
See also CA 165; DLB 295; EWL 3
Gumilyov, Nikolay Stepanovich
See Gumilev, Nikolai (Stepanovich)
Gump, P. Q.
See Card, Orson Scott
Gump, P.Q.
See Card, Orson Scott
Gunesekera, Romesh 1954- .... **CLC 91**
See also BRWS 10; CA 159; CANR 140,
172; CN 6, 7; DLB 267, 323
Gunn, Bill
See Gunn, William Harrison
Gunn, Thom(son William)
1929-2004 . **CLC 3, 6, 18, 32, 81; PC 26**
See also BRWS 4; CA 17-20R; 227; CANR
9, 33, 116; CDBLB 1960 to Present; CP
1, 2, 3, 4, 5, 6, 7; DAM POET; DLB 27;
INT CANR-33; MTCW 1; PFS 9; RGEL
2
Gunn, William Harrison
1934(?)-1989 .... **CLC 5**
See also AITN 1; BW 1, 3; CA 13-16R;
128; CANR 12, 25, 76; DLB 38
Gunn Allen, Paula
See Allen, Paula Gunn
Gunnars, Kristjana 1948- .... **CLC 69**
See also CA 113; CCA 1; CP 6, 7; CWP;
DLB 60
Gunter, Erich
See Eich, Gunter
Gurdjieff, G(eorgei) I(vanovich)
1877(?)-1949 .... **TCLC 71**
See also CA 157
Gurganus, Allan 1947- .... **CLC 70**
See also BEST 90:1; CA 135; CANR 114;
CN 6, 7; CPW; CSW; DAM POP; GLL 1
Gurney, A. R.
See Gurney, A(lbert) R(amsdell), Jr.
Gurney, A(lbert) R(amsdell), Jr.
1930- .... **CLC 32, 50, 54**
See also AMWS 5; CA 77-80; CAD; CANR
32, 64, 121; CD 5, 6; DAM DRAM; DLB
266; EWL 3
Gurney, Ivor (Bertie) 1890-1937 ... **TCLC 33**
See also BRW 6; CA 167; DLBY 2002;
PAB; RGEL 2
Gurney, Peter
See Gurney, A(lbert) R(amsdell), Jr.
Guro, Elena (Genrikhovna)
1877-1913 .... **TCLC 56**
See also DLB 295
Gustafson, James M(oody) 1925- ... **CLC 100**
See also CA 25-28R; CANR 37

Hogarth, Charles
See Creasey, John

Hogarth, Emmett
See Polonsky, Abraham (Lincoln)

Hogarth, William 1697-1764 .... **LC 112**
See also AAYA 56

Hogg, James 1770-1835 .... **NCLC 4, 109**
See also BRWS 10; DLB 93, 116, 159; GL
2; HGG; RGEL 2; SUFW 1

Holbach, Paul-Henri Thiry
1723-1789 .... **LC 14**
See also DLB 313

Holberg, Ludvig 1684-1754 .... **LC 6**
See also DLB 300; RGWL 2, 3

Holbrook, John
See Vance, Jack

Holcroft, Thomas 1745-1809 .... **NCLC 85**
See also DLB 39, 89, 158; RGEL 2

Holden, Ursula 1921- .... **CLC 18**
See also CA 101; CAAS 8; CANR 22

Holderlin, (Johann Christian) Friedrich
1770-1843 .... **NCLC 16, 187; PC 4**
See also CDWLB 2; DLB 90; EW 5; RGWL
2, 3

Holdstock, Robert 1948- .... **CLC 39**
See also CA 131; CANR 81; DLB 261;
FANT; HGG; SFW 4; SUFW 2

Holdstock, Robert P.
See Holdstock, Robert

Holinshed, Raphael fl. 1580- .... **LC 69**
See also DLB 167; RGEL 2

Holland, Isabelle (Christian)
1920-2002 .... **CLC 21**
See also AAYA 11, 64; CA 21-24R; 205;
CAAE 181; CANR 10, 25, 47; CLR 57;
CWRI 5; JRDA; LAIT 4; MAICYA 1, 2;
SATA 8, 70; SATA-Essay 103; SATA-Obit
132; WYA

Holland, Marcus
See Caldwell, (Janet Miriam) Taylor
(Holland)

Hollander, John 1929- .... **CLC 2, 5, 8, 14**
See also CA 1-4R; CANR 1, 52, 136; CP 1,
2, 3, 4, 5, 6, 7; DLB 5; MAL 5; SATA 13

Hollander, Paul
See Silverberg, Robert

Holleran, Andrew
See Garber, Eric

Holley, Marietta 1836(?)-1926 .... **TCLC 99**
See also CA 118; DLB 11; FL 1:3

Hollinghurst, Alan 1954- .... **CLC 55, 91**
See also BRWS 10; CA 114; CN 5, 6, 7;
DLB 207, 326; GLL 1

Hollis, Jim
See Summers, Hollis (Spurgeon, Jr.)

Holly, Buddy 1936-1959 .... **TCLC 65**
See also CA 213

Holmes, Gordon
See Shiel, M(atthew) P(hipps)

Holmes, John
See Souster, (Holmes) Raymond

Holmes, John Clellon 1926-1988 ...... **CLC 56**
See also BG 1:2; CA 9-12R; 125; CANR 4;
CN 1, 2, 3, 4; DLB 16, 237

Holmes, Oliver Wendell, Jr.
1841-1935 .... **TCLC 77**
See also CA 114; 186

Holmes, Oliver Wendell
1809-1894 .... **NCLC 14, 81; PC 71**
See also AMWS 1; CDALB 1640-1865;
DLB 1, 189, 235; EXPP; PFS 24; RGAL
4; SATA 34

Holmes, Raymond
See Souster, (Holmes) Raymond

Holt, Samuel
See Westlake, Donald E.

Holt, Victoria
See Hibbert, Eleanor Alice Burford

Holub, Miroslav 1923-1998 .... **CLC 4**
See also CA 21-24R; 169; CANR 10; CD-
WLB 4; CWW 2; DLB 232; EWL 3;
RGWL 3

Holz, Detlev
See Benjamin, Walter

Homer c. 8th cent. B.C.- .... **CMLC 1, 16, 61;
PC 23; WLCS**
See also AW 1; CDWLB 1; DA; DA3;
DAB; DAC; DAM MST, POET; DLB
176; EFS 1; LAIT 1; LMFS 1; RGWL 2,
3; TWA; WLIT 8; WP

Hong, Maxine Ting Ting
See Kingston, Maxine Hong

Hongo, Garrett Kaoru 1951- .... **PC 23**
See also CA 133; CAAS 22; CP 5, 6, 7;
DLB 120, 312; EWL 3; EXPP; PFS 25;
RGAL 4

Honig, Edwin 1919- .... **CLC 33**
See also CA 5-8R; CAAS 8; CANR 4, 45,
144; CP 1, 2, 3, 4, 5, 6, 7; DLB 5

Hood, Hugh (John Blagdon) 1928- . **CLC 15,
28, 273; SSC 42**
See also CA 49-52; CAAS 17; CANR 1,
33, 87; CN 1, 2, 3, 4, 5, 6, 7; DLB 53;
RGSF 2

Hood, Thomas 1799-1845 . **NCLC 16; PC 93**
See also BRW 4; DLB 96; RGEL 2

Hooker, (Peter) Jeremy 1941- .... **CLC 43**
See also CA 77-80; CANR 22; CP 2, 3, 4,
5, 6, 7; DLB 40

Hooker, Richard 1554-1600 .... **LC 95**
See also BRW 1; DLB 132; RGEL 2

Hooker, Thomas 1586-1647 .... **LC 137**
See also DLB 24

hooks, bell 1952(?)- .... **BLCS; CLC 94**
See also BW 2; CA 143; CANR 87, 126;
DLB 246; MTCW 2; MTFW 2005; SATA
115, 170

Hooper, Johnson Jones
1815-1862 .... **NCLC 177**
See also DLB 3, 11, 248; RGAL 4

Hope, A(lec) D(erwent) 1907-2000 .... **CLC 3,
51; PC 56**
See also BRWS 7; CA 21-24R; 188; CANR
33, 74; CP 1, 2, 3, 4, 5; DLB 289; EWL
3; MTCW 1, 2; MTFW 2005; PFS 8;
RGEL 2

Hope, Anthony 1863-1933 .... **TCLC 83**
See also CA 157; DLB 153, 156; RGEL 2;
RHW

Hope, Brian
See Creasey, John

Hope, Christopher 1944- .... **CLC 52**
See also AFW; CA 106; CANR 47, 101,
177; CN 4, 5, 6, 7; DLB 225; SATA 62

Hope, Christopher David Tully
See Hope, Christopher

Hopkins, Gerard Manley
1844-1889 .... **NCLC 17, 189; PC 15;
WLC 3**
See also BRW 5; BRWR 2; CDBLB 1890-
1914; DA; DA3; DAB; DAC; DAM MST,
POET; DLB 35, 57; EXPP; PAB; PFS 26;
RGEL 2; TEA; WP

Hopkins, John (Richard) 1931-1998 .. **CLC 4**
See also CA 85-88; 169; CBD; CD 5, 6

Hopkins, Pauline Elizabeth
1859-1930 .... **BLC 1:2; TCLC 28**
See also AFAW 2; BW 2, 3; CA 141; CANR
82; DAM MULT; DLB 50

Hopkinson, Francis 1737-1791 .... **LC 25**
See also DLB 31; RGAL 4

Hopley, George
See Hopley-Woolrich, Cornell George

Hopley-Woolrich, Cornell George
1903-1968 .... **CLC 77**
See also CA 13-14; CANR 58, 156; CAP 1;
CMW 4; DLB 226; MSW; MTCW 2

Horace 65B.C.-8B.C. .... **CMLC 39; PC 46**
See also AW 2; CDWLB 1; DLB 211;
RGWL 2, 3; WLIT 8

Horatio
See Proust, (Valentin-Louis-George-Eugene)
Marcel

**Horgan, Paul (George Vincent
O'Shaughnessy)** 1903-1995 .. **CLC 9, 53**
See also BPFB 2; CA 13-16R; 147; CANR
9, 35; CN 1, 2, 3, 4, 5; DAM NOV; DLB
102, 212; DLBY 1985; INT CANR-9;
MTCW 1, 2; MTFW 2005; SATA 13;
SATA-Obit 84; TCWW 1, 2

Horkheimer, Max 1895-1973 .... **TCLC 132**
See also CA 216; 41-44R; DLB 296

Horn, Peter
See Kuttner, Henry

Hornby, Nick 1957(?)- .... **CLC 243**
See also AAYA 74; CA 151; CANR 104,
151; CN 7; DLB 207

Horne, Frank (Smith) 1899-1974 ...... **HR 1:2**
See also BW 1; CA 125; 53-56; DLB 51;
WP

Horne, Richard Henry Hengist
1802(?)-1884 .... **NCLC 127**
See also DLB 32; SATA 29

Hornem, Horace Esq.
See Byron, George Gordon (Noel)

Horne Tooke, John 1736-1812 ..... **NCLC 195**

**Horney, Karen (Clementine Theodore
Danielsen)** 1885-1952 .... **TCLC 71**
See also CA 114; 165; DLB 246; FW

Hornung, E(rnest) W(illiam)
1866-1921 .... **TCLC 59**
See also CA 108; 160; CMW 4; DLB 70

Horovitz, Israel 1939- .... **CLC 56**
See also CA 33-36R; CAD; CANR 46, 59;
CD 5, 6; DAM DRAM; DLB 7, 341;
MAL 5

Horton, George Moses
1797(?)-1883(?) .... **NCLC 87**
See also DLB 50

Horvath, odon von 1901-1938
See von Horvath, Odon
See also EWL 3

Horvath, Oedoen von -1938
See von Horvath, Odon

Horwitz, Julius 1920-1986 .... **CLC 14**
See also CA 9-12R; 119; CANR 12

Horwitz, Ronald
See Harwood, Ronald

Hospital, Janette Turner 1942- .... **CLC 42,
145**
See also CA 108; CANR 48, 166; CN 5, 6,
7; DLB 325; DLBY 2002; RGSF 2

Hosseini, Khaled 1965- .... **CLC 254**
See also CA 225; SATA 156

Hostos, E. M. de
See Hostos (y Bonilla), Eugenio Maria de

Hostos, Eugenio M. de
See Hostos (y Bonilla), Eugenio Maria de

Hostos, Eugenio Maria
See Hostos (y Bonilla), Eugenio Maria de

Hostos (y Bonilla), Eugenio Maria de
1839-1903 .... **TCLC 24**
See also CA 123; 131; HW 1

Houdini
See Lovecraft, H. P.

Houellebecq, Michel 1958- .... **CLC 179**
See also CA 185; CANR 140; MTFW 2005

Hougan, Carolyn 1943-2007 .... **CLC 34**
See also CA 139; 257

Household, Geoffrey (Edward West)
1900-1988 .... **CLC 11**
See also CA 77-80; 126; CANR 58; CMW
4; CN 1, 2, 3, 4; DLB 87; SATA 14;
SATA-Obit 59

Kandinsky, Wassily 1866-1944 .... **TCLC 92**
See also AAYA 64; CA 118; 155
Kane, Francis
See Robbins, Harold
Kane, Paul
See Simon, Paul
Kane, Sarah 1971-1999 .... **DC 31**
See also BRWS 8; CA 190; CD 5, 6; DLB 310
Kanin, Garson 1912-1999 .... **CLC 22**
See also AITN 1; CA 5-8R; 177; CAD; CANR 7, 78; DLB 7; IDFW 3, 4
Kaniuk, Yoram 1930- .... **CLC 19**
See also CA 134; DLB 299; RGHL
Kant, Immanuel 1724-1804 ..... **NCLC 27, 67**
See also DLB 94
Kantor, MacKinlay 1904-1977 .... **CLC 7**
See also CA 61-64; 73-76; CANR 60, 63; CN 1, 2; DLB 9, 102; MAL 5; MTCW 2; RHW; TCWW 1, 2
Kanze Motokiyo
See Zeami
Kaplan, David Michael 1946- .... **CLC 50**
See also CA 187
Kaplan, James 1951- .... **CLC 59**
See also CA 135; CANR 121
Karadzic, Vuk Stefanovic
1787-1864 .... **NCLC 115**
See also CDWLB 4; DLB 147
Karageorge, Michael
See Anderson, Poul
Karamzin, Nikolai Mikhailovich
1766-1826 .... **NCLC 3, 173**
See also DLB 150; RGSF 2
Karapanou, Margarita 1946- .... **CLC 13**
See also CA 101
Karinthy, Frigyes 1887-1938 .... **TCLC 47**
See also CA 170; DLB 215; EWL 3
Karl, Frederick R(obert)
1927-2004 .... **CLC 34**
See also CA 5-8R; 226; CANR 3, 44, 143
Karr, Mary 1955- .... **CLC 188**
See also AMWS 11; CA 151; CANR 100; MTFW 2005; NCFS 5
Kastel, Warren
See Silverberg, Robert
Kataev, Evgeny Petrovich
1903-1942 .... **TCLC 21**
See also CA 120; DLB 272
Kataphusin
See Ruskin, John
Katz, Steve 1935- .... **CLC 47**
See also CA 25-28R; CAAS 14, 64; CANR 12; CN 4, 5, 6, 7; DLBY 1983
Kauffman, Janet 1945- .... **CLC 42**
See also CA 117; CANR 43, 84; DLB 218; DLBY 1986
Kaufman, Bob (Garnell)
1925-1986 .... **CLC 49; PC 74**
See also BG 1:3; BW 1; CA 41-44R; 118; CANR 22; CP 1; DLB 16, 41
Kaufman, George S. 1889-1961 ...... **CLC 38; DC 17**
See also CA 108; 93-96; DAM DRAM; DFS 1, 10; DLB 7; INT CA-108; MTCW 2; MTFW 2005; RGAL 4; TUS
Kaufman, Moises 1964- .... **DC 26**
See also CA 211; DFS 22; MTFW 2005
Kaufman, Sue
See Barondess, Sue K(aufman)
Kavafis, Konstantinos Petrou
1863-1933 .... **PC 36; TCLC 2, 7**
See also CA 104; 148; DA3; DAM POET; EW 8; EWL 3; MTCW 2; PFS 19; RGWL 2, 3; WP
Kavan, Anna 1901-1968 .... **CLC 5, 13, 82**
See also BRWS 7; CA 5-8R; CANR 6, 57; DLB 255; MTCW 1; RGEL 2; SFW 4

Kavanagh, Dan
See Barnes, Julian
Kavanagh, Julie 1952- .... **CLC 119**
See also CA 163; CANR 186
Kavanagh, Patrick (Joseph)
1904-1967 .... **CLC 22; PC 33**
See also BRWS 7; CA 123; 25-28R; DLB 15, 20; EWL 3; MTCW 1; RGEL 2
Kawabata, Yasunari 1899-1972 ..... **CLC 2, 5, 9, 18, 107; SSC 17**
See also CA 93-96; 33-36R; CANR 88; DAM MULT; DLB 180, 330; EWL 3; MJW; MTCW 2; MTFW 2005; RGSF 2; RGWL 2, 3
Kawabata Yasunari
See Kawabata, Yasunari
Kaye, Mary Margaret
See Kaye, M.M.
Kaye, M.M. 1908-2004 .... **CLC 28**
See also CA 89-92; 223; CANR 24, 60, 102, 142; MTCW 1, 2; MTFW 2005; RHW; SATA 62; SATA-Obit 152
Kaye, Mollie
See Kaye, M.M.
Kaye-Smith, Sheila 1887-1956 .... **TCLC 20**
See also CA 118; 203; DLB 36
Kaymor, Patrice Maguilene
See Senghor, Leopold Sedar
Kazakov, Iurii Pavlovich
See Kazakov, Yuri Pavlovich
Kazakov, Yuri Pavlovich 1927-1982 . **SSC 43**
See also CA 5-8R; CANR 36; DLB 302; EWL 3; MTCW 1; RGSF 2
Kazakov, Yury
See Kazakov, Yuri Pavlovich
Kazan, Elia 1909-2003 .... **CLC 6, 16, 63**
See also CA 21-24R; 220; CANR 32, 78
Kazantzakis, Nikos 1883(?)-1957 .... **TCLC 2, 5, 33, 181**
See also BPFB 2; CA 105; 132; DA3; EW 9; EWL 3; MTCW 1, 2; MTFW 2005; RGWL 2, 3
Kazin, Alfred 1915-1998 ..... **CLC 34, 38, 119**
See also AMWS 8; CA 1-4R; CAAS 7; CANR 1, 45, 79; DLB 67; EWL 3
Keane, Mary Nesta (Skrine)
1904-1996 .... **CLC 31**
See also CA 108; 114; 151; CN 5, 6; INT CA-114; RHW; TCLE 1:1
Keane, Molly
See Keane, Mary Nesta (Skrine)
Keates, Jonathan 1946(?)- .... **CLC 34**
See also CA 163; CANR 126
Keaton, Buster 1895-1966 .... **CLC 20**
See also AAYA 79; CA 194
Keats, John 1795-1821 ...... **NCLC 8, 73, 121; PC 1, 96; WLC 3**
See also AAYA 58; BRW 4; BRWR 1; CD-BLB 1789-1832; DA; DA3; DAB; DAC; DAM MST, POET; DLB 96, 110; EXPP; LMFS 1; PAB; PFS 1, 2, 3, 9, 17; RGEL 2; TEA; WLIT 3; WP
Keble, John 1792-1866 .... **NCLC 87**
See also DLB 32, 55; RGEL 2
Keene, Donald 1922- .... **CLC 34**
See also CA 1-4R; CANR 5, 119
Keillor, Garrison 1942- ..... **CLC 40, 115, 222**
See also AAYA 2, 62; AMWS 16; BEST 89:3; BPFB 2; CA 111; 117; CANR 36, 59, 124, 180; CPW; DA3; DAM POP; DLBY 1987; EWL 3; MTCW 1, 2; MTFW 2005; SATA 58; TUS
Keith, Carlos
See Lewton, Val
Keith, Michael
See Hubbard, L. Ron
Kell, Joseph
See Burgess, Anthony

Keller, Gottfried 1819-1890 .... **NCLC 2; SSC 26, 107**
See also CDWLB 2; DLB 129; EW; RGSF 2; RGWL 2, 3
Keller, Nora Okja 1965- .... **CLC 109**
See also CA 187
Kellerman, Jonathan 1949- .... **CLC 44**
See also AAYA 35; BEST 90:1; CA 106; CANR 29, 51, 150, 183; CMW 4; CPW; DA3; DAM POP; INT CANR-29
Kelley, William Melvin 1937- .... **BLC 2:2; CLC 22**
See also BW 1; CA 77-80; CANR 27, 83; CN 1, 2, 3, 4, 5, 6, 7; DLB 33; EWL 3
Kellock, Archibald P.
See Mavor, Osborne Henry
Kellogg, Marjorie 1922-2005 .... **CLC 2**
See also CA 81-84; 246
Kellow, Kathleen
See Hibbert, Eleanor Alice Burford
Kelly, Lauren
See Oates, Joyce Carol
Kelly, M(ilton) T(errence) 1947- ...... **CLC 55**
See also CA 97-100; CAAS 22; CANR 19, 43, 84; CN 6
Kelly, Robert 1935- .... **SSC 50**
See also CA 17-20R; CAAS 19; CANR 47; CP 1, 2, 3, 4, 5, 6, 7; DLB 5, 130, 165
Kelman, James 1946- .... **CLC 58, 86**
See also BRWS 5; CA 148; CANR 85, 130; CN 5, 6, 7; DLB 194, 319, 326; RGSF 2; WLIT 4
Kemal, Yasar
See Kemal, Yashar
Kemal, Yashar 1923(?)- .... **CLC 14, 29**
See also CA 89-92; CANR 44; CWW 2; EWL 3; WLIT 6
Kemble, Fanny 1809-1893 .... **NCLC 18**
See also DLB 32
Kemelman, Harry 1908-1996 .... **CLC 2**
See also AITN 1; BPFB 2; CA 9-12R; 155; CANR 6, 71; CMW 4; DLB 28
Kempe, Margery 1373(?)-1440(?) ... **LC 6, 56**
See also BRWS 12; DLB 146; FL 1:1; RGEL 2
Kempis, Thomas a 1380-1471 .... **LC 11**
Kenan, Randall (G.) 1963- .... **BLC 2:2**
See also BW 2, 3; CA 142; CANR 86; CN 7; CSW; DLB 292; GLL 1
Kendall, Henry 1839-1882 .... **NCLC 12**
See also DLB 230
Keneally, Thomas 1935- .... **CLC 5, 8, 10, 14, 19, 27, 43, 117**
See also BRWS 4; CA 85-88; CANR 10, 50, 74, 130, 165; CN 1, 2, 3, 4, 5, 6, 7; CPW; DA3; DAM NOV; DLB 289, 299, 326; EWL 3; MTCW 1, 2; MTFW 2005; NFS 17; RGEL 2; RGHL; RHW
Keneally, Thomas Michael
See Keneally, Thomas
Kennedy, A. L. 1965- .... **CLC 188**
See also CA 168, 213; CAAE 213; CANR 108; CD 5, 6; CN 6, 7; DLB 271; RGSF 2
Kennedy, Adrienne (Lita) 1931- .... **BLC 1:2; CLC 66; DC 5**
See also AFAW 2; BW 2, 3; CA 103; CAAS 20; CABS 3; CAD; CANR 26, 53, 82; CD 5, 6; DAM MULT; DFS 9; DLB 38, 341; FW; MAL 5
Kennedy, Alison Louise
See Kennedy, A. L.
Kennedy, John Pendleton
1795-1870 .... **NCLC 2**
See also DLB 3, 248, 254; RGAL 4

La Fontaine, Jean de 1621-1695 .... **LC 50**
See also DLB 268; EW 3; GFL Beginnings to 1789; MAICYA 1, 2; RGWL 2, 3; SATA 18

LaForet, Carmen 1921-2004 .... **CLC 219**
See also CA 246; CWW 2; DLB 322; EWL 3

LaForet Diaz, Carmen
See LaForet, Carmen

Laforgue, Jules 1860-1887 . **NCLC 5, 53; PC 14; SSC 20**
See also DLB 217; EW 7; GFL 1789 to the Present; RGWL 2, 3

Lagerkvist, Paer (Fabian) 1891-1974 .. **CLC 7, 10, 13, 54; SSC 12; TCLC 144**
See also CA 85-88; 49-52; DA3; DAM DRAM, NOV; DLB 259, 331; EW 10; EWL 3; MTCW 1, 2; MTFW 2005; RGSF 2; RGWL 2, 3; TWA

Lagerkvist, Par
See Lagerkvist, Paer (Fabian)

Lagerloef, Selma (Ottiliana Lovisa)
See Lagerlof, Selma (Ottiliana Lovisa)

Lagerlof, Selma (Ottiliana Lovisa) 1858-1940 .... **TCLC 4, 36**
See also CA 108; 188; CLR 7; DLB 259, 331; MTCW 2; RGWL 2, 3; SATA 15; SSFS 18

La Guma, Alex 1925-1985 .. **BLCS; CLC 19; TCLC 140**
See also AFW; BW 1, 3; CA 49-52; 118; CANR 25, 81; CDWLB 3; CN 1, 2, 3; CP 1; DAM NOV; DLB 117, 225; EWL 3; MTCW 1, 2; MTFW 2005; WLIT 2; WWE 1

Lahiri, Jhumpa 1967- .... **SSC 96**
See also AAYA 56; CA 193; CANR 134, 184; DLB 323; MTFW 2005; SSFS 19, 27

Laidlaw, A. K.
See Grieve, C(hristopher) M(urray)

Lainez, Manuel Mujica
See Mujica Lainez, Manuel

Laing, R(onald) D(avid) 1927-1989 . **CLC 95**
See also CA 107; 129; CANR 34; MTCW 1

Laishley, Alex
See Booth, Martin

Lamartine, Alphonse (Marie Louis Prat) de 1790-1869 .... **NCLC 11, 190; PC 16**
See also DAM POET; DLB 217; GFL 1789 to the Present; RGWL 2, 3

Lamb, Charles 1775-1834 ..... **NCLC 10, 113; SSC 112; WLC 3**
See also BRW 4; CDBLB 1789-1832; DA; DAB; DAC; DAM MST; DLB 93, 107, 163; RGEL 2; SATA 17; TEA

Lamb, Lady Caroline 1785-1828 ... **NCLC 38**
See also DLB 116

Lamb, Mary Ann 1764-1847 ...... **NCLC 125; SSC 112**
See also DLB 163; SATA 17

Lame Deer 1903(?)-1976 .... **NNAL**
See also CA 69-72

Lamming, George (William) 1927- . **BLC 1:2, 2:2; CLC 2, 4, 66, 144**
See also BW 2, 3; CA 85-88; CANR 26, 76; CDWLB 3; CN 1, 2, 3, 4, 5, 6, 7; CP 1; DAM MULT; DLB 125; EWL 3; MTCW 1, 2; MTFW 2005; NFS 15; RGEL 2

L'Amour, Louis 1908-1988 .... **CLC 25, 55**
See also AAYA 16; AITN 2; BEST 89:2; BPFB 2; CA 1-4R; 125; CANR 3, 25, 40; CPW; DA3; DAM NOV, POP; DLB 206; DLBY 1980; MTCW 1, 2; MTFW 2005; RGAL 4; TCWW 1, 2

Lampedusa, Giuseppe (Tomasi) di
See Tomasi di Lampedusa, Giuseppe

Lampman, Archibald 1861-1899 .. **NCLC 25, 194**
See also DLB 92; RGEL 2; TWA

Lancaster, Bruce 1896-1963 .... **CLC 36**
See also CA 9-10; CANR 70; CAP 1; SATA 9

Lanchester, John 1962- .... **CLC 99**
See also CA 194; DLB 267

Landau, Mark Alexandrovich
See Aldanov, Mark (Alexandrovich)

Landau-Aldanov, Mark Alexandrovich
See Aldanov, Mark (Alexandrovich)

Landis, Jerry
See Simon, Paul

Landis, John 1950- .... **CLC 26**
See also CA 112; 122; CANR 128

Landolfi, Tommaso 1908-1979 .... **CLC 11, 49**
See also CA 127; 117; DLB 177; EWL 3

Landon, Letitia Elizabeth 1802-1838 .... **NCLC 15**
See also DLB 96

Landor, Walter Savage 1775-1864 .... **NCLC 14**
See also BRW 4; DLB 93, 107; RGEL 2

Landwirth, Heinz
See Lind, Jakov

Lane, Patrick 1939- .... **CLC 25**
See also CA 97-100; CANR 54; CP 3, 4, 5, 6, 7; DAM POET; DLB 53; INT CA-97-100

Lane, Rose Wilder 1887-1968 ...... **TCLC 177**
See also CA 102; CANR 63; SATA 29; SATA-Brief 28; TCWW 2

Lang, Andrew 1844-1912 .... **TCLC 16**
See also CA 114; 137; CANR 85; CLR 101; DLB 98, 141, 184; FANT; MAICYA 1, 2; RGEL 2; SATA 16; WCH

Lang, Fritz 1890-1976 .... **CLC 20, 103**
See also AAYA 65; CA 77-80; 69-72; CANR 30

Lange, John
See Crichton, Michael

Langer, Elinor 1939- .... **CLC 34**
See also CA 121

Langland, William 1332(?)-1400(?) .... **LC 19, 120**
See also BRW 1; DA; DAB; DAC; DAM MST, POET; DLB 146; RGEL 2; TEA; WLIT 3

Langstaff, Launcelot
See Irving, Washington

Lanier, Sidney 1842-1881 . **NCLC 6, 118; PC 50**
See also AMWS 1; DAM POET; DLB 64; DLBD 13; EXPP; MAICYA 1; PFS 14; RGAL 4; SATA 18

Lanyer, Aemilia 1569-1645 .... **LC 10, 30, 83; PC 60**
See also DLB 121

Lao-Tzu
See Lao Tzu

Lao Tzu c. 6th cent. B.C.-3rd cent. B.C. .... **CMLC 7**

Lapine, James (Elliot) 1949- .... **CLC 39**
See also CA 123; 130; CANR 54, 128; DFS 25; DLB 341; INT CA-130

Larbaud, Valery (Nicolas) 1881-1957 .... **TCLC 9**
See also CA 106; 152; EWL 3; GFL 1789 to the Present

Larcom, Lucy 1824-1893 .... **NCLC 179**
See also AMWS 13; DLB 221, 243

Lardner, Ring
See Lardner, Ring(gold) W(ilmer)

Lardner, Ring W., Jr.
See Lardner, Ring(gold) W(ilmer)

Lardner, Ring(gold) W(ilmer) 1885-1933 ..... **SSC 32, 118; TCLC 2, 14**
See also AMW; BPFB 2; CA 104; 131; CDALB 1917-1929; DLB 11, 25, 86, 171; DLBD 16; MAL 5; MTCW 1, 2; MTFW 2005; RGAL 4; RGSF 2; TUS

Laredo, Betty
See Codrescu, Andrei

Larkin, Maia
See Wojciechowska, Maia (Teresa)

Larkin, Philip (Arthur) 1922-1985 ... **CLC 3, 5, 8, 9, 13, 18, 33, 39, 64; PC 21**
See also BRWS 1; CA 5-8R; 117; CANR 24, 62; CDBLB 1960 to Present; CP 1, 2, 3, 4; DA3; DAB; DAM MST, POET; DLB 27; EWL 3; MTCW 1, 2; MTFW 2005; PFS 3, 4, 12; RGEL 2

La Roche, Sophie von 1730-1807 .... **NCLC 121**
See also DLB 94

La Rochefoucauld, Francois 1613-1680 .... **LC 108**
See also DLB 268; EW 3; GFL Beginnings to 1789; RGWL 2, 3

Larra (y Sanchez de Castro), Mariano Jose de 1809-1837 .... **NCLC 17, 130**

Larsen, Eric 1941- .... **CLC 55**
See also CA 132

Larsen, Nella 1893(?)-1963 ... **BLC 1:2; CLC 37; HR 1:3; TCLC 200**
See also AFAW 1, 2; AMWS 18; BW 1; CA 125; CANR 83; DAM MULT; DLB 51; FW; LATS 1:1; LMFS 2

Larson, Charles R(aymond) 1938- ... **CLC 31**
See also CA 53-56; CANR 4, 121

Larson, Jonathan 1960-1996 .... **CLC 99**
See also AAYA 28; CA 156; DFS 23; MTFW 2005

La Sale, Antoine de c. 1386-1460(?) . **LC 104**
See also DLB 208

Las Casas, Bartolome de 1474-1566 .... **HLCS; LC 31**
See also DLB 318; LAW; WLIT 1

Lasch, Christopher 1932-1994 .... **CLC 102**
See also CA 73-76; 144; CANR 25, 118; DLB 246; MTCW 1, 2; MTFW 2005

Lasker-Schueler, Else 1869-1945 ... **TCLC 57**
See also CA 183; DLB 66, 124; EWL 3

Lasker-Schuler, Else
See Lasker-Schueler, Else

Laski, Harold J(oseph) 1893-1950 . **TCLC 79**
See also CA 188

Latham, Jean Lee 1902-1995 .... **CLC 12**
See also AITN 1; BYA 1; CA 5-8R; CANR 7, 84; CLR 50; MAICYA 1, 2; SATA 2, 68; YAW

Latham, Mavis
See Clark, Mavis Thorpe

Lathen, Emma
See Hennissart, Martha

Lathrop, Francis
See Leiber, Fritz (Reuter, Jr.)

Lattany, Kristin
See Lattany, Kristin (Elaine Eggleston) Hunter

Lattany, Kristin (Elaine Eggleston) Hunter 1931- .... **CLC 35**
See also AITN 1; BW 1; BYA 1; CA 13-16R; CANR 13, 108; CLR 3; CN 1, 2, 3, 4, 5, 6; DLB 33; INT CANR-13; MAICYA 1, 2; SAAS 10; SATA 12, 132; YAW

Lattimore, Richmond (Alexander) 1906-1984 .... **CLC 3**
See also CA 1-4R; 112; CANR 1; CP 1, 2, 3; MAL 5

Laughlin, James 1914-1997 .... **CLC 49**
See also CA 21-24R; 162; CAAS 22; CANR 9, 47; CP 1, 2, 3, 4, 5, 6; DLB 48; DLBY 1996, 1997

Leger, Alexis
See Leger, (Marie-Rene Auguste) Alexis Saint-Leger

Leger, (Marie-Rene Auguste) Alexis Saint-Leger 1887-1975 .. **CLC 4, 11, 46; PC 23**
See also CA 13-16R; 61-64; CANR 43; DAM POET; DLB 258, 331; EW 10; EWL 3; GFL 1789 to the Present; MTCW 1; RGWL 2, 3

Leger, Saintleger
See Leger, (Marie-Rene Auguste) Alexis Saint-Leger

Le Guin, Ursula K. 1929- ...... **CLC 8, 13, 22, 45, 71, 136; SSC 12, 69**
See also AAYA 9, 27; AITN 1; BPFB 2; BYA 5, 8, 11, 14; CA 21-24R; CANR 9, 32, 52, 74, 132; CDALB 1968-1988; CLR 3, 28, 91; CN 2, 3, 4, 5, 6, 7; CPW; DA3; DAB; DAC; DAM MST, POP; DLB 8, 52, 256, 275; EXPS; FANT; FW; INT CANR-32; JRDA; LAIT 5; MAICYA 1, 2; MAL 5; MTCW 1, 2; MTFW 2005; NFS 6, 9; SATA 4, 52, 99, 149, 194; SCFW 1, 2; SFW 4; SSFS 2; SUFW 1, 2; WYA; YAW

Lehmann, Rosamond (Nina) 1901-1990 .... **CLC 5**
See also CA 77-80; 131; CANR 8, 73; CN 1, 2, 3, 4; DLB 15; MTCW 2; RGEL 2; RHW

Leiber, Fritz (Reuter, Jr.) 1910-1992 .... **CLC 25**
See also AAYA 65; BPFB 2; CA 45-48; 139; CANR 2, 40, 86; CN 2, 3, 4, 5; DLB 8; FANT; HGG; MTCW 1, 2; MTFW 2005; SATA 45; SATA-Obit 73; SCFW 1, 2; SFW 4; SUFW 1, 2

Leibniz, Gottfried Wilhelm von 1646-1716 .... **LC 35**
See also DLB 168

Leino, Eino
See Lonnbohm, Armas Eino Leopold

Leiris, Michel (Julien) 1901-1990 ..... **CLC 61**
See also CA 119; 128; 132; EWL 3; GFL 1789 to the Present

Leithauser, Brad 1953- .... **CLC 27**
See also CA 107; CANR 27, 81, 171; CP 5, 6, 7; DLB 120, 282

le Jars de Gournay, Marie
See de Gournay, Marie le Jars

Lelchuk, Alan 1938- .... **CLC 5**
See also CA 45-48; CAAS 20; CANR 1, 70, 152; CN 3, 4, 5, 6, 7

Lem, Stanislaw 1921-2006 ..... **CLC 8, 15, 40, 149**
See also AAYA 75; CA 105; 249; CAAS 1; CANR 32; CWW 2; MTCW 1; SCFW 1, 2; SFW 4

Lemann, Nancy (Elise) 1956- .... **CLC 39**
See also CA 118; 136; CANR 121

Lemonnier, (Antoine Louis) Camille 1844-1913 .... **TCLC 22**
See also CA 121

Lenau, Nikolaus 1802-1850 .... **NCLC 16**

L'Engle, Madeleine 1918-2007 .... **CLC 12**
See also AAYA 28; AITN 2; BPFB 2; BYA 2, 4, 5, 7; CA 1-4R; 264; CANR 3, 21, 39, 66, 107; CLR 1, 14, 57; CPW; CWRI 5; DA3; DAM POP; DLB 52; JRDA; MAICYA 1, 2; MTCW 1, 2; MTFW 2005; SAAS 15; SATA 1, 27, 75, 128; SATA-Obit 186; SFW 4; WYA; YAW

L'Engle, Madeleine Camp Franklin
See L'Engle, Madeleine

Lengyel, Jozsef 1896-1975 .... **CLC 7**
See also CA 85-88; 57-60; CANR 71; RGSF 2

Lenin 1870-1924 .... **TCLC 67**
See also CA 121; 168

Lenin, N.
See Lenin

Lenin, Nikolai
See Lenin

Lenin, V. I.
See Lenin

Lenin, Vladimir I.
See Lenin

Lenin, Vladimir Ilyich
See Lenin

Lennon, John (Ono) 1940-1980 .. **CLC 12, 35**
See also CA 102; SATA 114

Lennox, Charlotte Ramsay 1729(?)-1804 .... **NCLC 23, 134**
See also DLB 39; RGEL 2

Lentricchia, Frank, Jr.
See Lentricchia, Frank

Lentricchia, Frank 1940- .... **CLC 34**
See also CA 25-28R; CANR 19, 106, 148; DLB 246

Lenz, Gunter .... **CLC 65**

Lenz, Jakob Michael Reinhold 1751-1792 .... **LC 100**
See also DLB 94; RGWL 2, 3

Lenz, Siegfried 1926- .... **CLC 27; SSC 33**
See also CA 89-92; CANR 80, 149; CWW 2; DLB 75; EWL 3; RGSF 2; RGWL 2, 3

Leon, David
See Jacob, (Cyprien-)Max

Leonard, Dutch
See Leonard, Elmore

Leonard, Elmore 1925- .... **CLC 28, 34, 71, 120, 222**
See also AAYA 22, 59; AITN 1; BEST 89:1, 90:4; BPFB 2; CA 81-84; CANR 12, 28, 53, 76, 96, 133, 176; CMW 4; CN 5, 6, 7; CPW; DA3; DAM POP; DLB 173, 226; INT CANR-28; MSW; MTCW 1, 2; MTFW 2005; RGAL 4; SATA 163; TCWW 1, 2

Leonard, Elmore John, Jr.
See Leonard, Elmore

Leonard, Hugh
See Byrne, John Keyes

Leonov, Leonid (Maximovich) 1899-1994 .... **CLC 92**
See also CA 129; CANR 76; DAM NOV; DLB 272; EWL 3; MTCW 1, 2; MTFW 2005

Leonov, Leonid Maksimovich
See Leonov, Leonid (Maximovich)

Leopardi, (Conte) Giacomo 1798-1837 .... **NCLC 22, 129; PC 37**
See also EW 5; RGWL 2, 3; WLIT 7; WP

Le Reveler
See Artaud, Antonin (Marie Joseph)

Lerman, Eleanor 1952- .... **CLC 9**
See also CA 85-88; CANR 69, 124, 184

Lerman, Rhoda 1936- .... **CLC 56**
See also CA 49-52; CANR 70

Lermontov, Mikhail Iur'evich
See Lermontov, Mikhail Yuryevich

Lermontov, Mikhail Yuryevich 1814-1841 .... **NCLC 5, 47, 126; PC 18**
See also DLB 205; EW 6; RGWL 2, 3; TWA

Leroux, Gaston 1868-1927 .... **TCLC 25**
See also CA 108; 136; CANR 69; CMW 4; MTFW 2005; NFS 20; SATA 65

Lesage, Alain-Rene 1668-1747 .... **LC 2, 28**
See also DLB 313; EW 3; GFL Beginnings to 1789; RGWL 2, 3

Leskov, N(ikolai) S(emenovich) 1831-1895
See Leskov, Nikolai (Semyonovich)

Leskov, Nikolai (Semyonovich) 1831-1895 .. **NCLC 25, 174; SSC 34, 96**
See also DLB 238

Leskov, Nikolai Semenovich
See Leskov, Nikolai (Semyonovich)

Lesser, Milton
See Marlowe, Stephen

Lessing, Doris 1919- .. **CLC 1, 2, 3, 6, 10, 15, 22, 40, 94, 170, 254; SSC 6, 61; WLCS**
See also AAYA 57; AFW; BRWS 1; CA 9-12R; CAAS 14; CANR 33, 54, 76, 122, 179; CBD; CD 5, 6; CDBLB 1960 to Present; CN 1, 2, 3, 4, 5, 6, 7; CWD; DA; DA3; DAB; DAC; DAM MST, NOV; DFS 20; DLB 15, 139; DLBY 1985; EWL 3; EXPS; FL 1:6; FW; LAIT 4; MTCW 1, 2; MTFW 2005; NFS 27; RGEL 2; RGSF 2; SFW 4; SSFS 1, 12, 20, 26; TEA; WLIT 2, 4

Lessing, Doris May
See Lessing, Doris

Lessing, Gotthold Ephraim 1729-1781 .... **DC 26; LC 8, 124, 162**
See also CDWLB 2; DLB 97; EW 4; RGWL 2, 3

Lester, Julius 1939- .... **BLC 2:2**
See also AAYA 12, 51; BW 2; BYA 3, 9, 11, 12; CA 17-20R; CANR 8, 23, 43, 129, 174; CLR 2, 41, 143; JRDA; MAICYA 1, 2; MAICYAS 1; MTFW 2005; SATA 12, 74, 112, 157; YAW

Lester, Richard 1932- .... **CLC 20**

Levenson, Jay .... **CLC 70**

Lever, Charles (James) 1806-1872 .... **NCLC 23**
See also DLB 21; RGEL 2

Leverson, Ada Esther 1862(?)-1933(?) .... **TCLC 18**
See also CA 117; 202; DLB 153; RGEL 2

Levertov, Denise 1923-1997 .. **CLC 1, 2, 3, 5, 8, 15, 28, 66; PC 11**
See also AMWS 3; CA 1-4R, 178; 163; CAAE 178; CAAS 19; CANR 3, 29, 50, 108; CDALBS; CP 1, 2, 3, 4, 5, 6; CWP; DAM POET; DLB 5, 165, 342; EWL 3; EXPP; FW; INT CANR-29; MAL 5; MTCW 1, 2; PAB; PFS 7, 17; RGAL 4; RGHL; TUS; WP

Levi, Carlo 1902-1975 .... **TCLC 125**
See also CA 65-68; 53-56; CANR 10; EWL 3; RGWL 2, 3

Levi, Jonathan .... **CLC 76**
See also CA 197

Levi, Peter (Chad Tigar) 1931-2000 .... **CLC 41**
See also CA 5-8R; 187; CANR 34, 80; CP 1, 2, 3, 4, 5, 6, 7; DLB 40

Levi, Primo 1919-1987 .... **CLC 37, 50; SSC 12, 122; TCLC 109**
See also CA 13-16R; 122; CANR 12, 33, 61, 70, 132, 171; DLB 177, 299; EWL 3; MTCW 1, 2; MTFW 2005; RGHL; RGWL 2, 3; WLIT 7

Levin, Ira 1929-2007 .... **CLC 3, 6**
See also CA 21-24R; 266; CANR 17, 44, 74, 139; CMW 4; CN 1, 2, 3, 4, 5, 6, 7; CPW; DA3; DAM POP; HGG; MTCW 1, 2; MTFW 2005; SATA 66; SATA-Obit 187; SFW 4

Levin, Ira Marvin
See Levin, Ira

Levin, Ira Marvin
See Levin, Ira

Levin, Meyer 1905-1981 .... **CLC 7**
See also AITN 1; CA 9-12R; 104; CANR 15; CN 1, 2, 3; DAM POP; DLB 9, 28; DLBY 1981; MAL 5; RGHL; SATA 21; SATA-Obit 27

Levine, Albert Norman
See Levine, Norman

Paterson, Katherine 1932- .... **CLC 12, 30**
See also AAYA 1, 31; BYA 1, 2, 7; CA 21-24R; CANR 28, 59, 111, 173; CLR 7, 50, 127; CWRI 5; DLB 52; JRDA; LAIT 4; MAICYA 1, 2; MAICYAS 1; MTCW 1; SATA 13, 53, 92, 133; WYA; YAW

Paterson, Katherine Womeldorf
See Paterson, Katherine

Patmore, Coventry Kersey Dighton
1823-1896 .... **NCLC 9; PC 59**
See also DLB 35, 98; RGEL 2; TEA

Paton, Alan 1903-1988 ..... **CLC 4, 10, 25, 55, 106; TCLC 165; WLC 4**
See also AAYA 26; AFW; BPFB 3; BRWS 2; BYA 1; CA 13-16; 125; CANR 22; CAP 1; CN 1, 2, 3, 4; DA; DA3; DAB; DAC; DAM MST, NOV; DLB 225; DLBD 17; EWL 3; EXPN; LAIT 4; MTCW 1, 2; MTFW 2005; NFS 3, 12; RGEL 2; SATA 11; SATA-Obit 56; TWA; WLIT 2; WWE 1

Paton Walsh, Gillian
See Paton Walsh, Jill

Paton Walsh, Jill 1937- .... **CLC 35**
See also AAYA 11, 47; BYA 1, 8; CA 262; CAAE 262; CANR 38, 83, 158; CLR 2, 6, 128; DLB 161; JRDA; MAICYA 1, 2; SAAS 3; SATA 4, 72, 109, 190; SATA-Essay 190; WYA; YAW

Patsauq, Markoosie 1942- .... **NNAL**
See also CA 101; CLR 23; CWRI 5; DAM MULT

Patterson, (Horace) Orlando (Lloyd)
1940- .... **BLCS**
See also BW 1; CA 65-68; CANR 27, 84; CN 1, 2, 3, 4, 5, 6

Patton, George S(mith), Jr.
1885-1945 .... **TCLC 79**
See also CA 189

Paulding, James Kirke 1778-1860 ... **NCLC 2**
See also DLB 3, 59, 74, 250; RGAL 4

Paulin, Thomas Neilson
See Paulin, Tom

Paulin, Tom 1949- .... **CLC 37, 177**
See also CA 123; 128; CANR 98; CP 3, 4, 5, 6, 7; DLB 40

Pausanias c. 1st cent. - .... **CMLC 36**

Paustovsky, Konstantin (Georgievich)
1892-1968 .... **CLC 40**
See also CA 93-96; 25-28R; DLB 272; EWL 3

Pavese, Cesare 1908-1950 .... **PC 13; SSC 19; TCLC 3**
See also CA 104; 169; DLB 128, 177; EW 12; EWL 3; PFS 20; RGSF 2; RGWL 2, 3; TWA; WLIT 7

Pavic, Milorad 1929- .... **CLC 60**
See also CA 136; CDWLB 4; CWW 2; DLB 181; EWL 3; RGWL 3

Pavlov, Ivan Petrovich 1849-1936 . **TCLC 91**
See also CA 118; 180

Pavlova, Karolina Karlovna
1807-1893 .... **NCLC 138**
See also DLB 205

Payne, Alan
See Jakes, John

Payne, Rachel Ann
See Jakes, John

Paz, Gil
See Lugones, Leopoldo

Paz, Octavio 1914-1998 . **CLC 3, 4, 6, 10, 19, 51, 65, 119; HLC 2; PC 1, 48; TCLC 211; WLC 4**
See also AAYA 50; CA 73-76; 165; CANR 32, 65, 104; CWW 2; DA; DA3; DAB; DAC; DAM MST, MULT, POET; DLB 290, 331; DLBY 1990, 1998; DNFS 1;

EWL 3; HW 1, 2; LAW; LAWS 1; MTCW 1, 2; MTFW 2005; PFS 18, 30; RGWL 2, 3; SSFS 13; TWA; WLIT 1

p'Bitek, Okot 1931-1982 . **BLC 1:3; CLC 96; TCLC 149**
See also AFW; BW 2, 3; CA 124; 107; CANR 82; CP 1, 2, 3; DAM MULT; DLB 125; EWL 3; MTCW 1, 2; MTFW 2005; RGEL 2; WLIT 2

Peabody, Elizabeth Palmer
1804-1894 .... **NCLC 169**
See also DLB 1, 223

Peacham, Henry 1578-1644(?) .... **LC 119**
See also DLB 151

Peacock, Molly 1947- .... **CLC 60**
See also CA 103, 262; CAAE 262; CAAS 21; CANR 52, 84; CP 5, 6, 7; CWP; DLB 120, 282

Peacock, Thomas Love
1785-1866 .... **NCLC 22; PC 87**
See also BRW 4; DLB 96, 116; RGEL 2; RGSF 2

Peake, Mervyn 1911-1968 .... **CLC 7, 54**
See also CA 5-8R; 25-28R; CANR 3; DLB 15, 160, 255; FANT; MTCW 1; RGEL 2; SATA 23; SFW 4

Pearce, Ann Philippa
See Pearce, Philippa

Pearce, Philippa 1920-2006 .... **CLC 21**
See also BYA 5; CA 5-8R; 255; CANR 4, 109; CLR 9; CWRI 5; DLB 161; FANT; MAICYA 1; SATA 1, 67, 129; SATA-Obit 179

Pearl, Eric
See Elman, Richard (Martin)

Pearson, Jean Mary
See Gardam, Jane

Pearson, Thomas Reid
See Pearson, T.R.

Pearson, T.R. 1956- .... **CLC 39**
See also CA 120; 130; CANR 97, 147, 185; CSW; INT CA-130

Peck, Dale 1967- .... **CLC 81**
See also CA 146; CANR 72, 127, 180; GLL 2

Peck, John (Frederick) 1941- .... **CLC 3**
See also CA 49-52; CANR 3, 100; CP 4, 5, 6, 7

Peck, Richard 1934- .... **CLC 21**
See also AAYA 1, 24; BYA 1, 6, 8, 11; CA 85-88; CANR 19, 38, 129, 178; CLR 15, 142; INT CANR-19; JRDA; MAICYA 1, 2; SAAS 2; SATA 18, 55, 97, 110, 158, 190; SATA-Essay 110; WYA; YAW

Peck, Richard Wayne
See Peck, Richard

Peck, Robert Newton 1928- .... **CLC 17**
See also AAYA 3, 43; BYA 1, 6; CA 81-84; 182; CAAE 182; CANR 31, 63, 127; CLR 45; DA; DAC; DAM MST; JRDA; LAIT 3; MAICYA 1, 2; NFS 29; SAAS 1; SATA 21, 62, 111, 156; SATA-Essay 108; WYA; YAW

Peckinpah, David Samuel
See Peckinpah, Sam

Peckinpah, Sam 1925-1984 .... **CLC 20**
See also CA 109; 114; CANR 82

Pedersen, Knut 1859-1952 .. **TCLC 2, 14, 49, 151, 203**
See also AAYA 79; CA 104; 119; CANR 63; DLB 297, 330; EW 8; EWL 8; MTCW 1, 2; RGWL 2, 3

Peele, George 1556-1596 .... **DC 27; LC 115**
See also BRW 1; DLB 62, 167; RGEL 2

Peeslake, Gaffer
See Durrell, Lawrence (George)

Peguy, Charles (Pierre)
1873-1914 .... **TCLC 10**
See also CA 107; 193; DLB 258; EWL 3; GFL 1789 to the Present

Peirce, Charles Sanders
1839-1914 .... **TCLC 81**
See also CA 194; DLB 270

Pelagius c. 350-c. 418 .... **CMLC 112**

Pelecanos, George P. 1957- .... **CLC 236**
See also CA 138; CANR 122, 165; DLB 306

Pelevin, Victor 1962- .... **CLC 238**
See also CA 154; CANR 88, 159; DLB 285

Pelevin, Viktor Olegovich
See Pelevin, Victor

Pellicer, Carlos 1897(?)-1977 .... **HLCS 2**
See also CA 153; 69-72; DLB 290; EWL 3; HW 1

Pena, Ramon del Valle y
See Valle-Inclan, Ramon (Maria) del

Pendennis, Arthur Esquir
See Thackeray, William Makepeace

Penn, Arthur
See Matthews, (James) Brander

Penn, William 1644-1718 .... **LC 25**
See also DLB 24

PEPECE
See Prado (Calvo), Pedro

Pepys, Samuel 1633-1703 ... **LC 11, 58; WLC 4**
See also BRW 2; CDBLB 1660-1789; DA; DA3; DAB; DAC; DAM MST; DLB 101, 213; NCFS 4; RGEL 2; TEA; WLIT 3

Percy, Thomas 1729-1811 .... **NCLC 95**
See also DLB 104

Percy, Walker 1916-1990 .... **CLC 2, 3, 6, 8, 14, 18, 47, 65**
See also AMWS 3; BPFB 3; CA 1-4R; 131; CANR 1, 23, 64; CN 1, 2, 3, 4; CPW; CSW; DA3; DAM NOV, POP; DLB 2; DLBY 1980, 1990; EWL 3; MAL 5; MTCW 1, 2; MTFW 2005; RGAL 4; TUS

Percy, William Alexander
1885-1942 .... **TCLC 84**
See also CA 163; MTCW 2

Perdurabo, Frater
See Crowley, Edward Alexander

Perec, Georges 1936-1982 .... **CLC 56, 116**
See also CA 141; DLB 83, 299; EWL 3; GFL 1789 to the Present; RGHL; RGWL 3

Pereda (y Sanchez de Porrua), Jose Maria de 1833-1906 .... **TCLC 16**
See also CA 117

Pereda y Porrua, Jose Maria de
See Pereda (y Sanchez de Porrua), Jose Maria de

Peregoy, George Weems
See Mencken, H(enry) L(ouis)

Perelman, S(idney) J(oseph)
1904-1979 .. **CLC 3, 5, 9, 15, 23, 44, 49; SSC 32**
See also AAYA 79; AITN 1, 2; BPFB 3; CA 73-76; 89-92; CANR 18; DAM DRAM; DLB 11, 44; MTCW 1, 2; MTFW 2005; RGAL 4

Peret, Benjamin 1899-1959 .... **PC 33; TCLC 20**
See also CA 117; 186; GFL 1789 to the Present

Peretz, Isaac Leib
See Peretz, Isaac Loeb

Peretz, Isaac Loeb 1851(?)-1915 ...... **SSC 26; TCLC 16**
See also CA 109; 201; DLB 333

Peretz, Yitzkhok Leibush
See Peretz, Isaac Loeb

Rado, James 1939- .... **CLC 17**
See also CA 105

Radvanyi, Netty 1900-1983 .... **CLC 7**
See also CA 85-88; 110; CANR 82; CD-
WLB 2; DLB 69; EWL 3

Rae, Ben
See Griffiths, Trevor

Raeburn, John (Hay) 1941- .... **CLC 34**
See also CA 57-60

Ragni, Gerome 1942-1991 .... **CLC 17**
See also CA 105; 134

Rahv, Philip
See Greenberg, Ivan

Rai, Navab
See Srivastava, Dhanpat Rai

Raimund, Ferdinand Jakob
1790-1836 .... **NCLC 69**
See also DLB 90

Raine, Craig 1944- .... **CLC 32, 103**
See also BRWS 13; CA 108; CANR 29, 51,
103, 171; CP 3, 4, 5, 6, 7; DLB 40; PFS 7

Raine, Craig Anthony
See Raine, Craig

Raine, Kathleen (Jessie) 1908-2003 .. **CLC 7,
45**
See also CA 85-88; 218; CANR 46, 109;
CP 1, 2, 3, 4, 5, 6, 7; DLB 20; EWL 3;
MTCW 1; RGEL 2

Rainis, Janis 1865-1929 .... **TCLC 29**
See also CA 170; CDWLB 4; DLB 220;
EWL 3

Rakosi, Carl
See Rawley, Callman

Ralegh, Sir Walter
See Raleigh, Sir Walter

Raleigh, Richard
See Lovecraft, H. P.

Raleigh, Sir Walter 1554(?)-1618 .... **LC 31,
39; PC 31**
See also BRW 1; CDBLB Before 1660;
DLB 172; EXPP; PFS 14; RGEL 2; TEA;
WP

Rallentando, H. P.
See Sayers, Dorothy L(eigh)

Ramal, Walter
See de la Mare, Walter (John)

Ramana Maharshi 1879-1950 .... **TCLC 84**

Ramoacn y Cajal, Santiago
1852-1934 .... **TCLC 93**

Ramon, Juan
See Jimenez (Mantecon), Juan Ramon

Ramos, Graciliano 1892-1953 .... **TCLC 32**
See also CA 167; DLB 307; EWL 3; HW 2;
LAW; WLIT 1

Rampersad, Arnold 1941- .... **CLC 44**
See also BW 2, 3; CA 127; 133; CANR 81;
DLB 111; INT CA-133

Rampling, Anne
See Rice, Anne

Ramsay, Allan 1686(?)-1758 .... **LC 29**
See also DLB 95; RGEL 2

Ramsay, Jay
See Campbell, Ramsey

Ramuz, Charles-Ferdinand
1878-1947 .... **TCLC 33**
See also CA 165; EWL 3

Rand, Ayn 1905-1982 ...... **CLC 3, 30, 44, 79;
SSC 116; WLC 5**
See also AAYA 10; AMWS 4; BPFB 3;
BYA 12; CA 13-16R; 105; CANR 27, 73;
CDALBS; CN 1, 2, 3; CPW; DA; DA3;
DAC; DAM MST, NOV, POP; DLB 227,
279; MTCW 1, 2; MTFW 2005; NFS 10,
16, 29; RGAL 4; SFW 4; TUS; YAW

Randall, Dudley (Felker)
1914-2000 .... **BLC 1:3; CLC 1, 135; PC
86**
See also BW 1, 3; CA 25-28R; 189; CANR
23, 82; CP 1, 2, 3, 4, 5; DAM MULT;
DLB 41; PFS 5

Randall, Robert
See Silverberg, Robert

Ranger, Ken
See Creasey, John

Rank, Otto 1884-1939 .... **TCLC 115**

Rankin, Ian 1960- .... **CLC 257**
See also BRWS 10; CA 148; CANR 81,
137, 171; DLB 267; MTFW 2005

Rankin, Ian James
See Rankin, Ian

Ransom, John Crowe 1888-1974 .. **CLC 2, 4,
5, 11, 24; PC 61**
See also AMW; CA 5-8R; 49-52; CANR 6,
34; CDALBS; CP 1, 2; DA3; DAM POET;
DLB 45, 63; EWL 3; EXPP; MAL 5;
MTCW 1, 2; MTFW 2005; RGAL 4; TUS

Rao, Raja 1908-2006 . **CLC 25, 56, 255; SSC
99**
See also CA 73-76; 252; CANR 51; CN 1,
2, 3, 4, 5, 6; DAM NOV; DLB 323; EWL
3; MTCW 1, 2; MTFW 2005; RGEL 2;
RGSF 2

Raphael, Frederic (Michael) 1931- ... **CLC 2,
14**
See also CA 1-4R; CANR 1, 86; CN 1, 2,
3, 4, 5, 6, 7; DLB 14, 319; TCLE 1:2

Raphael, Lev 1954- .... **CLC 232**
See also CA 134; CANR 72, 145; GLL 1

Ratcliffe, James P.
See Mencken, H(enry) L(ouis)

Rathbone, Julian 1935-2008 .... **CLC 41**
See also CA 101; 269; CANR 34, 73, 152

Rathbone, Julian Christopher
See Rathbone, Julian

Rattigan, Terence (Mervyn)
1911-1977 .... **CLC 7; DC 18**
See also BRWS 7; CA 85-88; 73-76; CBD;
CDBLB 1945-1960; DAM DRAM; DFS
8; DLB 13; IDFW 3, 4; MTCW 1, 2;
MTFW 2005; RGEL 2

Ratushinskaya, Irina 1954- .... **CLC 54**
See also CA 129; CANR 68; CWW 2

Raven, Simon (Arthur Noel)
1927-2001 .... **CLC 14**
See also CA 81-84; 197; CANR 86; CN 1,
2, 3, 4, 5, 6; DLB 271

Ravenna, Michael
See Welty, Eudora

Rawley, Callman 1903-2004 .... **CLC 47**
See also CA 21-24R; 228; CAAS 5; CANR
12, 32, 91; CP 1, 2, 3, 4, 5, 6, 7; DLB
193

Rawlings, Marjorie Kinnan
1896-1953 .... **TCLC 4**
See also AAYA 20; AMWS 10; ANW;
BPFB 3; BYA 3; CA 104; 137; CANR 74;
CLR 63; DLB 9, 22, 102; DLBD 17;
JRDA; MAICYA 1, 2; MAL 5; MTCW 2;
MTFW 2005; RGAL 4; SATA 100; WCH;
YABC 1; YAW

Ray, Satyajit 1921-1992 .... **CLC 16, 76**
See also CA 114; 137; DAM MULT

Read, Herbert Edward 1893-1968 ..... **CLC 4**
See also BRW 6; CA 85-88; 25-28R; DLB
20, 149; EWL 3; PAB; RGEL 2

Read, Piers Paul 1941- .... **CLC 4, 10, 25**
See also CA 21-24R; CANR 38, 86, 150;
CN 2, 3, 4, 5, 6, 7; DLB 14; SATA 21

Reade, Charles 1814-1884 .... **NCLC 2, 74**
See also DLB 21; RGEL 2

Reade, Hamish
See Gray, Simon

Reading, Peter 1946- .... **CLC 47**
See also BRWS 8; CA 103; CANR 46, 96;
CP 5, 6, 7; DLB 40

Reaney, James 1926-2008 .... **CLC 13**
See also CA 41-44R; CAAS 15; CANR 42;
CD 5, 6; CP 1, 2, 3, 4, 5, 6, 7; DAC;
DAM MST; DLB 68; RGEL 2; SATA 43

Reaney, James Crerar
See Reaney, James

Rebreanu, Liviu 1885-1944 .... **TCLC 28**
See also CA 165; DLB 220; EWL 3

Rechy, John 1934- ..... **CLC 1, 7, 14, 18, 107;
HLC 2**
See also CA 5-8R, 195; CAAE 195; CAAS
4; CANR 6, 32, 64, 152, 188; CN 1, 2, 3,
4, 5, 6, 7; DAM MULT; DLB 122, 278;
DLBY 1982; HW 1, 2; INT CANR-6;
LLW; MAL 5; RGAL 4

Rechy, John Francisco
See Rechy, John

Redcam, Tom 1870-1933 .... **TCLC 25**

Reddin, Keith 1956- .... **CLC 67**
See also CAD; CD 6

Redgrove, Peter (William)
1932-2003 .... **CLC 6, 41**
See also BRWS 6; CA 1-4R; 217; CANR 3,
39, 77; CP 1, 2, 3, 4, 5, 6, 7; DLB 40;
TCLE 1:2

Redmon, Anne
See Nightingale, Anne Redmon

Reed, Eliot
See Ambler, Eric

Reed, Ishmael 1938- . **BLC 1:3; CLC 2, 3, 5,
6, 13, 32, 60, 174; PC 68**
See also AFAW 1, 2; AMWS 10; BPFB 3;
BW 2, 3; CA 21-24R; CANR 25, 48, 74,
128; CN 1, 2, 3, 4, 5, 6, 7; CP 1, 2, 3, 4,
5, 6, 7; CSW; DA3; DAM MULT; DLB
2, 5, 33, 169, 227; DLBD 8; EWL 3;
LMFS 2; MAL 5; MSW; MTCW 1, 2;
MTFW 2005; PFS 6; RGAL 4; TCWW 2

Reed, John (Silas) 1887-1920 .... **TCLC 9**
See also CA 106; 195; MAL 5; TUS

Reed, Lou
See Firbank, Louis

Reese, Lizette Woodworth
1856-1935 .... **PC 29; TCLC 181**
See also CA 180; DLB 54

Reeve, Clara 1729-1807 .... **NCLC 19**
See also DLB 39; RGEL 2

Reich, Wilhelm 1897-1957 .... **TCLC 57**
See also CA 199

Reid, Christopher (John) 1949- .... **CLC 33**
See also CA 140; CANR 89; CP 4, 5, 6, 7;
DLB 40; EWL 3

Reid, Desmond
See Moorcock, Michael

Reid Banks, Lynne 1929- .... **CLC 23**
See also AAYA 6; BYA 7; CA 1-4R; CANR
6, 22, 38, 87; CLR 24, 86; CN 4, 5, 6;
JRDA; MAICYA 1, 2; SATA 22, 75, 111,
165; YAW

Reilly, William K.
See Creasey, John

Reiner, Max
See Caldwell, (Janet Miriam) Taylor
(Holland)

Reis, Ricardo
See Pessoa, Fernando

Reizenstein, Elmer Leopold
See Rice, Elmer (Leopold)

Remarque, Erich Maria 1898-1970 . **CLC 21**
See also AAYA 27; BPFB 3; CA 77-80; 29-
32R; CDWLB 2; DA; DA3; DAB; DAC;
DAM MST, NOV; DLB 56; EWL 3;
EXPN; LAIT 3; MTCW 1, 2; MTFW
2005; NFS 4; RGHL; RGWL 2, 3

Sidney, Sir Philip 1554-1586 .... **LC 19, 39, 131; PC 32**
See also BRW 1; BRWR 2; CDBLB Before 1660; DA; DA3; DAB; DAC; DAM MST, POET; DLB 167; EXPP; PAB; PFS 30; RGEL 2; TEA; WP

Sidney Herbert, Mary
See Sidney, Mary

Siegel, Jerome 1914-1996 .... **CLC 21**
See also AAYA 50; CA 116; 169; 151

Siegel, Jerry
See Siegel, Jerome

Sienkiewicz, Henryk (Adam Alexander Pius) 1846-1916 .... **TCLC 3**
See also CA 104; 134; CANR 84; DLB 332; EWL 3; RGSF 2; RGWL 2, 3

Sierra, Gregorio Martinez
See Martinez Sierra, Gregorio

Sierra, Maria de la O'LeJarraga Martinez
See Martinez Sierra, Maria

Sigal, Clancy 1926- .... **CLC 7**
See also CA 1-4R; CANR 85, 184; CN 1, 2, 3, 4, 5, 6, 7

Siger of Brabant 1240(?)-1284(?) . **CMLC 69**
See also DLB 115

Sigourney, Lydia H.
See Sigourney, Lydia Howard (Huntley)
See also DLB 73, 183

Sigourney, Lydia Howard (Huntley) 1791-1865 .... **NCLC 21, 87**
See Sigourney, Lydia H.
See also DLB 1, 42, 239, 243

Sigourney, Lydia Huntley
See Sigourney, Lydia Howard (Huntley)

Siguenza y Gongora, Carlos de 1645-1700 .... **HLCS 2; LC 8**
See also LAW

Sigurjonsson, Johann
See Sigurjonsson, Johann

Sigurjonsson, Johann 1880-1919 ... **TCLC 27**
See also CA 170; DLB 293; EWL 3

Sikelianos, Angelos 1884-1951 .... **PC 29; TCLC 39**
See also EWL 3; RGWL 2, 3

Silkin, Jon 1930-1997 .... **CLC 2, 6, 43**
See also CA 5-8R; CAAS 5; CANR 89; CP 1, 2, 3, 4, 5, 6; DLB 27

Silko, Leslie 1948- ...... **CLC 23, 74, 114, 211; NNAL; SSC 37, 66; WLCS**
See also AAYA 14; AMWS 4; ANW; BYA 12; CA 115; 122; CANR 45, 65, 118; CN 4, 5, 6, 7; CP 4, 5, 6, 7; CPW 1; CWP; DA; DA3; DAC; DAM MST, MULT, POP; DLB 143, 175, 256, 275; EWL 3; EXPP; EXPS; LAIT 4; MAL 5; MTCW 2; MTFW 2005; NFS 4; PFS 9, 16; RGAL 4; RGSF 2; SSFS 4, 8, 10, 11; TCWW 1, 2

Sillanpaa, Frans Eemil 1888-1964 ... **CLC 19**
See also CA 129; 93-96; DLB 332; EWL 3; MTCW 1

Sillitoe, Alan 1928- .. **CLC 1, 3, 6, 10, 19, 57, 148**
See also AITN 1; BRWS 5; CA 9-12R, 191; CAAE 191; CAAS 2; CANR 8, 26, 55, 139; CDBLB 1960 to Present; CN 1, 2, 3, 4, 5, 6; CP 1, 2, 3, 4, 5, 6; DLB 14, 139; EWL 3; MTCW 1, 2; MTFW 2005; RGEL 2; RGSF 2; SATA 61

Silone, Ignazio 1900-1978 .... **CLC 4**
See also CA 25-28; 81-84; CANR 34; CAP 2; DLB 264; EW 12; EWL 3; MTCW 1; RGSF 2; RGWL 2, 3

Silone, Ignazione
See Silone, Ignazio

Siluriensis, Leolinus
See Jones, Arthur Llewellyn

Silver, Joan Micklin 1935- .... **CLC 20**
See also CA 114; 121; INT CA-121

Silver, Nicholas
See Faust, Frederick (Schiller)

Silverberg, Robert 1935- .... **CLC 7, 140**
See also AAYA 24; BPFB 3; BYA 7, 9; CA 1-4R; 186; CAAE 186; CAAS 3; CANR 1, 20, 36, 85, 140, 175; CLR 59; CN 6, 7; CPW; DAM POP; DLB 8; INT CANR-20; MAICYA 1, 2; MTCW 1, 2; MTFW 2005; SATA 13, 91; SATA-Essay 104; SCFW 1, 2; SFW 4; SUFW 2

Silverstein, Alvin 1933- .... **CLC 17**
See also CA 49-52; CANR 2; CLR 25; JRDA; MAICYA 1, 2; SATA 8, 69, 124

Silverstein, Shel 1932-1999 .... **PC 49**
See also AAYA 40; BW 3; CA 107; 179; CANR 47, 74, 81; CLR 5, 96; CWRI 5; JRDA; MAICYA 1, 2; MTCW 2; MTFW 2005; SATA 33, 92; SATA-Brief 27; SATA-Obit 116

Silverstein, Virginia B(arbara Opshelor) 1937- .... **CLC 17**
See also CA 49-52; CANR 2; CLR 25; JRDA; MAICYA 1, 2; SATA 8, 69, 124

Sim, Georges
See Simenon, Georges (Jacques Christian)

Simak, Clifford D(onald) 1904-1988 . **CLC 1, 55**
See also CA 1-4R; 125; CANR 1, 35; DLB 8; MTCW 1; SATA-Obit 56; SCFW 1, 2; SFW 4

Simenon, Georges (Jacques Christian) 1903-1989 .... **CLC 1, 2, 3, 8, 18, 47**
See also BPFB 3; CA 85-88; 129; CANR 35; CMW 4; DA3; DAM POP; DLB 72; DLBY 1989; EW 12; EWL 3; GFL 1789 to the Present; MSW; MTCW 1, 2; MTFW 2005; RGWL 2, 3

Simic, Charles 1938- .... **CLC 6, 9, 22, 49, 68, 130, 256; PC 69**
See also AAYA 78; AMWS 8; CA 29-32R; CAAS 4; CANR 12, 33, 52, 61, 96, 140; CP 2, 3, 4, 5, 6, 7; DA3; DAM POET; DLB 105; MAL 5; MTCW 2; MTFW 2005; PFS 7; RGAL 4; WP

Simmel, Georg 1858-1918 .... **TCLC 64**
See also CA 157; DLB 296

Simmons, Charles (Paul) 1924- .... **CLC 57**
See also CA 89-92; INT CA-89-92

Simmons, Dan 1948- .... **CLC 44**
See also AAYA 16, 54; CA 138; CANR 53, 81, 126, 174; CPW; DAM POP; HGG; SUFW 2

Simmons, James (Stewart Alexander) 1933- .... **CLC 43**
See also CA 105; CAAS 21; CP 1, 2, 3, 4, 5, 6, 7; DLB 40

Simmons, Richard
See Simmons, Dan

Simms, William Gilmore 1806-1870 .... **NCLC 3**
See also DLB 3, 30, 59, 73, 248, 254; RGAL 4

Simon, Carly 1945- .... **CLC 26**
See also CA 105

Simon, Claude 1913-2005 ... **CLC 4, 9, 15, 39**
See also CA 89-92; 241; CANR 33, 117; CWW 2; DAM NOV; DLB 83, 332; EW 13; EWL 3; GFL 1789 to the Present; MTCW 1

Simon, Claude Eugene Henri
See Simon, Claude

Simon, Claude Henri Eugene
See Simon, Claude

Simon, Marvin Neil
See Simon, Neil

Simon, Myles
See Follett, Ken

Simon, Neil 1927- .... **CLC 6, 11, 31, 39, 70, 233; DC 14**
See also AAYA 32; AITN 1; AMWS 4; CA 21-24R; CAD; CANR 26, 54, 87, 126; CD 5, 6; DA3; DAM DRAM; DFS 2, 6, 12, 18,. 24; DLB 7, 266; LAIT 4; MAL 5; MTCW 1, 2; MTFW 2005; RGAL 4; TUS

Simon, Paul 1941(?)- .... **CLC 17**
See also CA 116; 153; CANR 152

Simon, Paul Frederick
See Simon, Paul

Simonon, Paul 1956(?)- .... **CLC 30**

Simonson, Rick .... **CLC 70**

Simpson, Harriette
See Arnow, Harriette (Louisa) Simpson

Simpson, Louis 1923- ... **CLC 4, 7, 9, 32, 149**
See also AMWS 9; CA 1-4R; CAAS 4; CANR 1, 61, 140; CP 1, 2, 3, 4, 5, 6, 7; DAM POET; DLB 5; MAL 5; MTCW 1, 2; MTFW 2005; PFS 7, 11, 14; RGAL 4

Simpson, Mona 1957- .... **CLC 44, 146**
See also CA 122; 135; CANR 68, 103; CN 6, 7; EWL 3

Simpson, Mona Elizabeth
See Simpson, Mona

Simpson, N(orman) F(rederick) 1919- .... **CLC 29**
See also CA 13-16R; CBD; DLB 13; RGEL 2

Sinclair, Andrew (Annandale) 1935- . **CLC 2, 14**
See also CA 9-12R; CAAS 5; CANR 14, 38, 91; CN 1, 2, 3, 4, 5, 6, 7; DLB 14; FANT; MTCW 1

Sinclair, Emil
See Hesse, Hermann

Sinclair, Iain 1943- .... **CLC 76**
See also BRWS 14; CA 132; CANR 81, 157; CP 5, 6, 7; HGG

Sinclair, Iain MacGregor
See Sinclair, Iain

Sinclair, Irene
See Griffith, D.W.

Sinclair, Julian
See Sinclair, May

Sinclair, Mary Amelia St. Clair (?)-
See Sinclair, May

Sinclair, May 1865-1946 .... **TCLC 3, 11**
See also CA 104; 166; DLB 36, 135; EWL 3; HGG; RGEL 2; RHW; SUFW

Sinclair, Roy
See Griffith, D.W.

Sinclair, Upton 1878-1968 ...... **CLC 1, 11, 15, 63; TCLC 160; WLC 5**
See also AAYA 63; AMWS 5; BPFB 3; BYA 2; CA 5-8R; 25-28R; CANR 7; CDALB 1929-1941; DA; DA3; DAB; DAC; DAM MST, NOV; DLB 9; EWL 3; INT CANR-7; LAIT 3; MAL 5; MTCW 1, 2; MTFW 2005; NFS 6; RGAL 4; SATA 9; TUS; YAW

Sinclair, Upton Beall
See Sinclair, Upton

Singe, (Edmund) J(ohn) M(illington) 1871-1909 .... **WLC**

Singer, Isaac
See Singer, Isaac Bashevis

Singer, Isaac Bashevis 1904-1991 .. **CLC 1, 3, 6, 9, 11, 15, 23, 38, 69, 111; SSC 3, 53, 80; WLC 5**
See also AAYA 32; AITN 1, 2; AMW; AMWR 2; BPFB 3; BYA 1, 4; CA 1-4R; 134; CANR 1, 39, 106; CDALB 1941-1968; CLR 1; CN 1, 2, 3, 4; CWRI 5; DA; DA3; DAB; DAC; DAM MST, NOV; DLB 6, 28, 52, 278, 332, 333; DLBY 1991; EWL 3; EXPS; HGG; JRDA; LAIT

3; MAICYA 1, 2; MAL 5; MTCW 1, 2; MTFW 2005; RGAL 4; RGHL; RGSF 2; SATA 3, 27; SATA-Obit 68; SSFS 2, 12, 16, 27; TUS; TWA

Singer, Israel Joshua 1893-1944 .... **TCLC 33**
See also CA 169; DLB 333; EWL 3

Singh, Khushwant 1915- .... **CLC 11**
See also CA 9-12R; CAAS 9; CANR 6, 84; CN 1, 2, 3, 4, 5, 6, 7; DLB 323; EWL 3; RGEL 2

Singleton, Ann
See Benedict, Ruth

Singleton, John 1968(?)- .... **CLC 156**
See also AAYA 50; BW 2, 3; CA 138; CANR 67, 82; DAM MULT

Siniavskii, Andrei
See Sinyavsky, Andrei (Donatevich)

Sinibaldi, Fosco
See Kacew, Romain

Sinjohn, John
See Galsworthy, John

Sinyavsky, Andrei (Donatevich)
1925-1997 .... **CLC 8**
See also CA 85-88; 159; CWW 2; EWL 3; RGSF 2

Sinyavsky, Andrey Donatovich
See Sinyavsky, Andrei (Donatevich)

Sirin, V.
See Nabokov, Vladimir (Vladimirovich)

Sissman, L(ouis) E(dward)
1928-1976 .... **CLC 9, 18**
See also CA 21-24R; 65-68; CANR 13; CP 2; DLB 5

Sisson, C(harles) H(ubert)
1914-2003 .... **CLC 8**
See also BRWS 11; CA 1-4R; 220; CAAS 3; CANR 3, 48, 84; CP 1, 2, 3, 4, 5, 6, 7; DLB 27

Sitting Bull 1831(?)-1890 .... **NNAL**
See also DA3; DAM MULT

Sitwell, Dame Edith 1887-1964 ..... **CLC 2, 9, 67; PC 3**
See also BRW 7; CA 9-12R; CANR 35; CDBLB 1945-1960; DAM POET; DLB 20; EWL 3; MTCW 1, 2; MTFW 2005; RGEL 2; TEA

Siwaarmill, H. P.
See Sharp, William

Sjoewall, Maj 1935- .... **CLC 7**
See also BPFB 3; CA 65-68; CANR 73; CMW 4; MSW

Sjowall, Maj
See Sjoewall, Maj

Skelton, John 1460(?)-1529 ..... **LC 71; PC 25**
See also BRW 1; DLB 136; RGEL 2

Skelton, Robin 1925-1997 .... **CLC 13**
See also AITN 2; CA 5-8R; 160; CAAS 5; CANR 28, 89; CCA 1; CP 1, 2, 3, 4, 5, 6; DLB 27, 53

Skolimowski, Jerzy 1938- .... **CLC 20**
See also CA 128

Skram, Amalie (Bertha)
1847-1905 .... **TCLC 25**
See also CA 165

Skvorecky, Josef 1924- . **CLC 15, 39, 69, 152**
See also CA 61-64; CAAS 1; CANR 10, 34, 63, 108; CDWLB 4; CWW 2; DA3; DAC; DAM NOV; DLB 232; EWL 3; MTCW 1, 2; MTFW 2005

Slade, Bernard 1930-
See Newbound, Bernard Slade

Slaughter, Carolyn 1946- .... **CLC 56**
See also CA 85-88; CANR 85, 169; CN 5, 6, 7

Slaughter, Frank G(ill) 1908-2001 ... **CLC 29**
See also AITN 2; CA 5-8R; 197; CANR 5, 85; INT CANR-5; RHW

Slavitt, David R. 1935- .... **CLC 5, 14**
See also CA 21-24R; CAAS 3; CANR 41, 83, 166; CN 1, 2; CP 1, 2, 3, 4, 5, 6, 7; DLB 5, 6

Slavitt, David Rytman
See Slavitt, David R.

Slesinger, Tess 1905-1945 .... **TCLC 10**
See also CA 107; 199; DLB 102

Slessor, Kenneth 1901-1971 .... **CLC 14**
See also CA 102; 89-92; DLB 260; RGEL 2

Slowacki, Juliusz 1809-1849 .... **NCLC 15**
See also RGWL 3

Smart, Christopher 1722-1771 .... **LC 3, 134; PC 13**
See also DAM POET; DLB 109; RGEL 2

Smart, Elizabeth 1913-1986 .... **CLC 54**
See also CA 81-84; 118; CN 4; DLB 88

Smiley, Jane 1949- ...... **CLC 53, 76, 144, 236**
See also AAYA 66; AMWS 6; BPFB 3; CA 104; CANR 30, 50, 74, 96, 158; CN 6, 7; CPW 1; DA3; DAM POP; DLB 227, 234; EWL 3; INT CANR-30; MAL 5; MTFW 2005; SSFS 19

Smiley, Jane Graves
See Smiley, Jane

Smith, A(rthur) J(ames) M(arshall)
1902-1980 .... **CLC 15**
See also CA 1-4R; 102; CANR 4; CP 1, 2, 3; DAC; DLB 88; RGEL 2

Smith, Adam 1723(?)-1790 .... **LC 36**
See also DLB 104, 252, 336; RGEL 2

Smith, Alexander 1829-1867 .... **NCLC 59**
See also DLB 32, 55

Smith, Alexander McCall 1948- ..... **CLC 268**
See also CA 215; CANR 154; SATA 73, 179

Smith, Anna Deavere 1950- ...... **CLC 86, 241**
See also CA 133; CANR 103; CD 5, 6; DFS 2, 22; DLB 341

Smith, Betty (Wehner) 1904-1972 .... **CLC 19**
See also AAYA 72; BPFB 3; BYA 3; CA 5-8R; 33-36R; DLBY 1982; LAIT 3; RGAL 4; SATA 6

Smith, Charlotte (Turner)
1749-1806 .... **NCLC 23, 115**
See also DLB 39, 109; RGEL 2; TEA

Smith, Clark Ashton 1893-1961 .... **CLC 43**
See also AAYA 76; CA 143; CANR 81; FANT; HGG; MTCW 2; SCFW 1, 2; SFW 4; SUFW

Smith, Dave
See Smith, David (Jeddie)

Smith, David (Jeddie) 1942- .... **CLC 22, 42**
See also CA 49-52; CAAS 7; CANR 1, 59, 120; CP 3, 4, 5, 6, 7; CSW; DAM POET; DLB 5

Smith, Iain Crichton 1928-1998 .... **CLC 64**
See also BRWS 9; CA 21-24R; 171; CN 1, 2, 3, 4, 5, 6; CP 1, 2, 3, 4, 5, 6; DLB 40, 139, 319; RGSF 2

Smith, John 1580(?)-1631 .... **LC 9**
See also DLB 24, 30; TUS

Smith, Johnston
See Crane, Stephen (Townley)

Smith, Joseph, Jr. 1805-1844 .... **NCLC 53**

Smith, Kevin 1970- .... **CLC 223**
See also AAYA 37; CA 166; CANR 131

Smith, Lee 1944- .... **CLC 25, 73, 258**
See also CA 114; 119; CANR 46, 118, 173; CN 7; CSW; DLB 143; DLBY 1983; EWL 3; INT CA-119; RGAL 4

Smith, Martin
See Smith, Martin Cruz

Smith, Martin Cruz 1942- .. **CLC 25; NNAL**
See Smith, Martin Cruz
See also BEST 89:4; BPFB 3; CA 85-88; CANR 6, 23, 43, 65, 119, 184; CMW 4; CPW; DAM MULT, POP; HGG; INT CANR-23; MTCW 2; MTFW 2005; RGAL 4

Smith, Patti 1946- .... **CLC 12**
See also CA 93-96; CANR 63, 168

Smith, Pauline (Urmson)
1882-1959 .... **TCLC 25**
See also DLB 225; EWL 3

Smith, R. Alexander McCall
See Smith, Alexander McCall

Smith, Rosamond
See Oates, Joyce Carol

Smith, Seba 1792-1868 .... **NCLC 187**
See also DLB 1, 11, 243

Smith, Sheila Kaye
See Kaye-Smith, Sheila

Smith, Stevie 1902-1971 .... **CLC 3, 8, 25, 44; PC 12**
See also BRWS 2; CA 17-18; 29-32R; CANR 35; CAP 2; CP 1; DAM POET; DLB 20; EWL 3; MTCW 1, 2; PAB; PFS 3; RGEL 2; TEA

Smith, Wilbur 1933- .... **CLC 33**
See also CA 13-16R; CANR 7, 46, 66, 134, 180; CPW; MTCW 1, 2; MTFW 2005

Smith, Wilbur Addison
See Smith, Wilbur

Smith, William Jay 1918- .... **CLC 6**
See also AMWS 13; CA 5-8R; CANR 44, 106; CP 1, 2, 3, 4, 5, 6, 7; CSW; CWRI 5; DLB 5; MAICYA 1, 2; SAAS 22; SATA 2, 68, 154; SATA-Essay 154; TCLE 1:2

Smith, Woodrow Wilson
See Kuttner, Henry

Smith, Zadie 1975- .... **CLC 158**
See also AAYA 50; CA 193; DLB 347; MTFW 2005

Smolenskin, Peretz 1842-1885 .... **NCLC 30**

Smollett, Tobias (George) 1721-1771 ... **LC 2, 46**
See also BRW 3; CDBLB 1660-1789; DLB 39, 104; RGEL 2; TEA

Snodgrass, Quentin Curtius
See Twain, Mark

Snodgrass, Thomas Jefferson
See Twain, Mark

Snodgrass, W. D. 1926-2009 .... **CLC 2, 6, 10, 18, 68; PC 74**
See also AMWS 6; CA 1-4R; CANR 6, 36, 65, 85, 185; CP 1, 2, 3, 4, 5, 6, 7; DAM POET; DLB 5; MAL 5; MTCW 1, 2; MTFW 2005; PFS 29; RGAL 4; TCLE 1:2

Snodgrass, William De Witt
See Snodgrass, W. D.

Snorri Sturluson 1179-1241 .... **CMLC 56**
See also RGWL 2, 3

Snow, C(harles) P(ercy) 1905-1980 ... **CLC 1, 4, 6, 9, 13, 19**
See also BRW 7; CA 5-8R; 101; CANR 28; CDBLB 1945-1960; CN 1, 2; DAM NOV; DLB 15, 77; DLBD 17; EWL 3; MTCW 1, 2; MTFW 2005; RGEL 2; TEA

Snow, Frances Compton
See Adams, Henry (Brooks)

Snyder, Gary 1930- . **CLC 1, 2, 5, 9, 32, 120; PC 21**
See also AAYA 72; AMWS 8; ANW; BG 1:3; CA 17-20R; CANR 30, 60, 125; CP 1, 2, 3, 4, 5, 6, 7; DA3; DAM POET; DLB 5, 16, 165, 212, 237, 275, 342; EWL 3; MAL 5; MTCW 2; MTFW 2005; PFS 9, 19; RGAL 4; WP

Snyder, Zilpha Keatley 1927- .... **CLC 17**
See also AAYA 15; BYA 1; CA 9-12R, 252; CAAE 252; CANR 38; CLR 31, 121; JRDA; MAICYA 1, 2; SAAS 2; SATA 1, 28, 75, 110, 163; SATA-Essay 112, 163; YAW

Soares, Bernardo
See Pessoa, Fernando

Sobh, A.
See Shamlu, Ahmad

Sobh, Alef
See Shamlu, Ahmad

Sobol, Joshua 1939- .... **CLC 60**
See also CA 200; CWW 2; RGHL

Sobol, Yehoshua 1939-
See Sobol, Joshua

Socrates 470B.C.-399B.C. .... **CMLC 27**

Soderberg, Hjalmar 1869-1941 ...... **TCLC 39**
See also DLB 259; EWL 3; RGSF 2

Soderbergh, Steven 1963- .... **CLC 154**
See also AAYA 43; CA 243

Soderbergh, Steven Andrew
See Soderbergh, Steven

Sodergran, Edith (Irene) 1892-1923
See Soedergran, Edith (Irene)

Soedergran, Edith (Irene)
1892-1923 .... **TCLC 31**
See also CA 202; DLB 259; EW 11; EWL 3; RGWL 2, 3

Softly, Edgar
See Lovecraft, H. P.

Softly, Edward
See Lovecraft, H. P.

Sokolov, Alexander V(sevolodovich)
1943- .... **CLC 59**
See also CA 73-76; CWW 2; DLB 285; EWL 3; RGWL 2, 3

Sokolov, Raymond 1941- .... **CLC 7**
See also CA 85-88

Sokolov, Sasha
See Sokolov, Alexander V(sevolodovich)

Solo, Jay
See Ellison, Harlan

Sologub, Fedor
See Teternikov, Fyodor Kuzmich

Sologub, Feodor
See Teternikov, Fyodor Kuzmich

Sologub, Fyodor
See Teternikov, Fyodor Kuzmich

Solomons, Ikey Esquir
See Thackeray, William Makepeace

Solomos, Dionysios 1798-1857 .... **NCLC 15**

Solwoska, Mara
See French, Marilyn

Solzhenitsyn, Aleksandr 1918-2008 ... **CLC 1, 2, 4, 7, 9, 10, 18, 26, 34, 78, 134, 235; SSC 32, 105; WLC 5**
See also AAYA 49; AITN 1; BPFB 3; CA 69-72; CANR 40, 65, 116; CWW 2; DA; DA3; DAB; DAC; DAM MST, NOV; DLB 302, 332; EW 13; EWL 3; EXPS; LAIT 4; MTCW 1, 2; MTFW 2005; NFS 6; RGSF 2; RGWL 2, 3; SSFS 9; TWA

Solzhenitsyn, Aleksandr I.
See Solzhenitsyn, Aleksandr

Solzhenitsyn, Aleksandr Isayevich
See Solzhenitsyn, Aleksandr

Somers, Jane
See Lessing, Doris

Somerville, Edith Oenone
1858-1949 .... **SSC 56; TCLC 51**
See also CA 196; DLB 135; RGEL 2; RGSF 2

Somerville & Ross
See Martin, Violet Florence; Somerville, Edith Oenone

Sommer, Scott 1951- .... **CLC 25**
See also CA 106

Sommers, Christina Hoff 1950- ...... **CLC 197**
See also CA 153; CANR 95

Sondheim, Stephen 1930- .. **CLC 30, 39, 147; DC 22**
See also AAYA 11, 66; CA 103; CANR 47, 67, 125; DAM DRAM; DFS 25; LAIT 4

Sondheim, Stephen Joshua
See Sondheim, Stephen

Sone, Monica 1919- .... **AAL**
See also DLB 312

Song, Cathy 1955- .... **AAL; PC 21**
See also CA 154; CANR 118; CWP; DLB 169, 312; EXPP; FW; PFS 5

Sontag, Susan 1933-2004 ... **CLC 1, 2, 10, 13, 31, 105, 195**
See also AMWS 3; CA 17-20R; 234; CANR 25, 51, 74, 97, 184; CN 1, 2, 3, 4, 5, 6, 7; CPW; DA3; DAM POP; DLB 2, 67; EWL 3; MAL 5; MBL; MTCW 1, 2; MTFW 2005; RGAL 4; RHW; SSFS 10

Sophocles 496(?)B.C.-406(?)B.C. .... **CMLC 2, 47, 51, 86; DC 1; WLCS**
See also AW 1; CDWLB 1; DA; DA3; DAB; DAC; DAM DRAM, MST; DFS 1, 4, 8, 24; DLB 176; LAIT 1; LATS 1:1; LMFS 1; RGWL 2, 3; TWA; WLIT 8

Sordello 1189-1269 .... **CMLC 15**

Sorel, Georges 1847-1922 .... **TCLC 91**
See also CA 118; 188

Sorel, Julia
See Drexler, Rosalyn

Sorokin, Vladimir .... **CLC 59**
See also CA 258; DLB 285

Sorokin, Vladimir Georgievich
See Sorokin, Vladimir

Sorrentino, Gilbert 1929-2006 .... **CLC 3, 7, 14, 22, 40, 247**
See also CA 77-80; 250; CANR 14, 33, 115, 157; CN 3, 4, 5, 6, 7; CP 1, 2, 3, 4, 5, 6, 7; DLB 5, 173; DLBY 1980; INT CANR-14

Soseki
See Natsume, Soseki

Soto, Gary 1952- ... **CLC 32, 80; HLC 2; PC 28**
See also AAYA 10, 37; BYA 11; CA 119; 125; CANR 50, 74, 107, 157; CLR 38; CP 4, 5, 6, 7; DAM MULT; DFS 26; DLB 82; EWL 3; EXPP; HW 1, 2; INT CA-125; JRDA; LLW; MAICYA 2; MAIC-YAS 1; MAL 5; MTCW 2; MTFW 2005; PFS 7, 30; RGAL 4; SATA 80, 120, 174; WYA; YAW

Soupault, Philippe 1897-1990 .... **CLC 68**
See also CA 116; 147; 131; EWL 3; GFL 1789 to the Present; LMFS 2

Souster, (Holmes) Raymond 1921- .... **CLC 5, 14**
See also CA 13-16R; CAAS 14; CANR 13, 29, 53; CP 1, 2, 3, 4, 5, 6, 7; DA3; DAC; DAM POET; DLB 88; RGEL 2; SATA 63

Southern, Terry 1924(?)-1995 .... **CLC 7**
See also AMWS 11; BPFB 3; CA 1-4R; 150; CANR 1, 55, 107; CN 1, 2, 3, 4, 5, 6; DLB 2; IDFW 3, 4

Southerne, Thomas 1660-1746 .... **LC 99**
See also DLB 80; RGEL 2

Southey, Robert 1774-1843 .... **NCLC 8, 97**
See also BRW 4; DLB 93, 107, 142; RGEL 2; SATA 54

Southwell, Robert 1561(?)-1595 .... **LC 108**
See also DLB 167; RGEL 2; TEA

Southworth, Emma Dorothy Eliza Nevitte
1819-1899 .... **NCLC 26**
See also DLB 239

Souza, Ernest
See Scott, Evelyn

Soyinka, Wole 1934- .. **BLC 1:3, 2:3; CLC 3, 5, 14, 36, 44, 179; DC 2; WLC 5**
See also AFW; BW 2, 3; CA 13-16R; CANR 27, 39, 82, 136; CD 5, 6; CDWLB 3; CN 6, 7; CP 1, 2, 3, 4, 6 ,7; DA; DA3; DAB; DAC; DAM DRAM, MST, MULT; DFS 10, 26; DLB 125, 332; EWL 3; MTCW 1, 2; MTFW 2005; PFS 27; RGEL 2; TWA; WLIT 2; WWE 1

Spackman, W(illiam) M(ode)
1905-1990 .... **CLC 46**
See also CA 81-84; 132

Spacks, Barry (Bernard) 1931- .... **CLC 14**
See also CA 154; CANR 33, 109; CP 3, 4, 5, 6, 7; DLB 105

Spanidou, Irini 1946- .... **CLC 44**
See also CA 185; CANR 179

Spark, Muriel 1918-2006 .... **CLC 2, 3, 5, 8, 13, 18, 40, 94, 242; PC 72; SSC 10, 115**
See also BRWS 1; CA 5-8R; 251; CANR 12, 36, 76, 89, 131; CDBLB 1945-1960; CN 1, 2, 3, 4, 5, 6, 7; CP 1, 2, 3, 4, 5, 6, 7; DA3; DAB; DAC; DAM MST, NOV; DLB 15, 139; EWL 3; FW; INT CANR-12; LAIT 4; MTCW 1, 2; MTFW 2005; NFS 22; RGEL 2; TEA; WLIT 4; YAW

Spark, Muriel Sarah
See Spark, Muriel

Spaulding, Douglas
See Bradbury, Ray

Spaulding, Leonard
See Bradbury, Ray

Speght, Rachel 1597-c. 1630 .... **LC 97**
See also DLB 126

Spence, J. A. D.
See Eliot, T(homas) S(tearns)

Spencer, Anne 1882-1975 ...... **HR 1:3; PC 77**
See also BW 2; CA 161; DLB 51, 54

Spencer, Elizabeth 1921- .... **CLC 22; SSC 57**
See also CA 13-16R; CANR 32, 65, 87; CN 1, 2, 3, 4, 5, 6, 7; CSW; DLB 6, 218; EWL 3; MTCW 1; RGAL 4; SATA 14

Spencer, Leonard G.
See Silverberg, Robert

Spencer, Scott 1945- .... **CLC 30**
See also CA 113; CANR 51, 148; DLBY 1986

Spender, Stephen 1909-1995 ..... **CLC 1, 2, 5, 10, 41, 91; PC 71**
See also BRWS 2; CA 9-12R; 149; CANR 31, 54; CDBLB 1945-1960; CP 1, 2, 3, 4, 5, 6; DA3; DAM POET; DLB 20; EWL 3; MTCW 1, 2; MTFW 2005; PAB; PFS 23; RGEL 2; TEA

Spengler, Oswald (Arnold Gottfried)
1880-1936 .... **TCLC 25**
See also CA 118; 189

Spenser, Edmund 1552(?)-1599 ...... **LC 5, 39, 117; PC 8, 42; WLC 5**
See also AAYA 60; BRW 1; CDBLB Before 1660; DA; DA3; DAB; DAC; DAM MST, POET; DLB 167; EFS 2; EXPP; PAB; RGEL 2; TEA; WLIT 3; WP

Spicer, Jack 1925-1965 .... **CLC 8, 18, 72**
See also BG 1:3; CA 85-88; DAM POET; DLB 5, 16, 193; GLL 1; WP

Spiegelman, Art 1948- .... **CLC 76, 178**
See also AAYA 10, 46; CA 125; CANR 41, 55, 74, 124; DLB 299; MTCW 2; MTFW 2005; RGHL; SATA 109, 158; YAW

Spielberg, Peter 1929- .... **CLC 6**
See also CA 5-8R; CANR 4, 48; DLBY 1981

Spielberg, Steven 1947- .... **CLC 20, 188**
See also AAYA 8, 24; CA 77-80; CANR 32; SATA 32

Spillane, Frank Morrison
See Spillane, Mickey

Stuart, Don A.
See Campbell, John W(ood, Jr.)
Stuart, Ian
See MacLean, Alistair (Stuart)
Stuart, Jesse (Hilton) 1906-1984 ... **CLC 1, 8, 11, 14, 34; SSC 31**
See also CA 5-8R; 112; CANR 31; CN 1, 2, 3; DLB 9, 48, 102; DLBY 1984; SATA 2; SATA-Obit 36
Stubblefield, Sally
See Trumbo, Dalton
Sturgeon, Theodore (Hamilton)
1918-1985 .... **CLC 22, 39**
See also AAYA 51; BPFB 3; BYA 9, 10; CA 81-84; 116; CANR 32, 103; DLB 8; DLBY 1985; HGG; MTCW 1, 2; MTFW 2005; SCFW; SFW 4; SUFW
Sturges, Preston 1898-1959 .... **TCLC 48**
See also CA 114; 149; DLB 26
Styron, William 1925-2006 .. **CLC 1, 3, 5, 11, 15, 60, 232, 244; SSC 25**
See also AMW; AMWC 2; BEST 90:4; BPFB 3; CA 5-8R; 255; CANR 6, 33, 74, 126; CDALB 1968-1988; CN 1, 2, 3, 4, 5, 6, 7; CPW; CSW; DA3; DAM NOV, POP; DLB 2, 143, 299; DLBY 1980; EWL 3; INT CANR-6; LAIT 2; MAL 5; MTCW 1, 2; MTFW 2005; NCFS 1; NFS 22; RGAL 4; RGHL; RHW; TUS
Styron, William Clark
See Styron, William
Su, Chien 1884-1918 .... **TCLC 24**
See also CA 123; EWL 3
Suarez Lynch, B.
See Bioy Casares, Adolfo; Borges, Jorge Luis
Suassuna, Ariano Vilar 1927- .... **HLCS 1**
See also CA 178; DLB 307; HW 2; LAW
Suckert, Kurt Erich
See Malaparte, Curzio
Suckling, Sir John 1609-1642 . **LC 75; PC 30**
See also BRW 2; DAM POET; DLB 58, 126; EXPP; PAB; RGEL 2
Suckow, Ruth 1892-1960 .... **SSC 18**
See also CA 193; 113; DLB 9, 102; RGAL 4; TCWW 2
Sudermann, Hermann 1857-1928 .. **TCLC 15**
See also CA 107; 201; DLB 118
Sue, Eugene 1804-1857 .... **NCLC 1**
See also DLB 119
Sueskind, Patrick 1949- .... **CLC 182**
See Suskind, Patrick
See also BPFB 3; CA 145; CWW 2
Suetonius c. 70-c. 130 .... **CMLC 60**
See also AW 2; DLB 211; RGWL 2, 3; WLIT 8
Su Hsuan-ying
See Su, Chien
Su Hsuean-ying
See Su, Chien
Sukenick, Ronald 1932-2004 ..... **CLC 3, 4, 6, 48**
See also CA 25-28R; 209; 229; CAAE 209; CAAS 8; CANR 32, 89; CN 3, 4, 5, 6, 7; DLB 173; DLBY 1981
Suknaski, Andrew 1942- .... **CLC 19**
See also CA 101; CP 3, 4, 5, 6, 7; DLB 53
Sullivan, Vernon
See Vian, Boris
Sully Prudhomme, Rene-Francois-Armand
1839-1907 .... **TCLC 31**
See also CA 170; DLB 332; GFL 1789 to the Present
Su Man-shu
See Su, Chien
Sumarokov, Aleksandr Petrovich
1717-1777 .... **LC 104**
See also DLB 150

Summerforest, Ivy B.
See Kirkup, James
Summers, Andrew James
See Summers, Andy
Summers, Andy 1942- .... **CLC 26**
See also CA 255
Summers, Hollis (Spurgeon, Jr.)
1916- .... **CLC 10**
See also CA 5-8R; CANR 3; CN 1, 2, 3; CP 1, 2, 3, 4; DLB 6; TCLE 1:2
Summers, (Alphonsus Joseph-Mary Augustus) Montague
1880-1948 .... **TCLC 16**
See also CA 118; 163
Sumner, Gordon Matthew
See Sting
Sun Tzu c. 400B.C.-c. 320B.C. ...... **CMLC 56**
Surdas c. 1478-c. 1583 .... **LC 163**
See also RGWL 2, 3
Surrey, Henry Howard 1517-1574 ... **LC 121; PC 59**
See also BRW 1; RGEL 2
Surtees, Robert Smith 1805-1864 .. **NCLC 14**
See also DLB 21; RGEL 2
Susann, Jacqueline 1921-1974 .... **CLC 3**
See also AITN 1; BPFB 3; CA 65-68; 53-56; MTCW 1, 2
Su Shi
See Su Shih
Su Shih 1036-1101 .... **CMLC 15**
See also RGWL 2, 3
Suskind, Patrick .... **CLC 182**
See Sueskind, Patrick
See also BPFB 3; CA 145; CWW 2
Suso, Heinrich c. 1295-1366 .... **CMLC 87**
Sutcliff, Rosemary 1920-1992 .... **CLC 26**
See also AAYA 10; BYA 1, 4; CA 5-8R; 139; CANR 37; CLR 1, 37, 138; CPW; DAB; DAC; DAM MST, POP; JRDA; LATS 1:1; MAICYA 1, 2; MAICYAS 1; RHW; SATA 6, 44, 78; SATA-Obit 73; WYA; YAW
Sutherland, Efua (Theodora Morgue)
1924-1996 .... **BLC 2:3**
See also AFW; BW 1; CA 105; CWD; DLB 117; EWL 3; IDTP; SATA 25
Sutro, Alfred 1863-1933 .... **TCLC 6**
See also CA 105; 185; DLB 10; RGEL 2
Sutton, Henry
See Slavitt, David R.
Su Yuan-ying
See Su, Chien
Su Yuean-ying
See Su, Chien
Suzuki, D. T.
See Suzuki, Daisetz Teitaro
Suzuki, Daisetz T.
See Suzuki, Daisetz Teitaro
Suzuki, Daisetz Teitaro
1870-1966 .... **TCLC 109**
See also CA 121; 111; MTCW 1, 2; MTFW 2005
Suzuki, Teitaro
See Suzuki, Daisetz Teitaro
Svareff, Count Vladimir
See Crowley, Edward Alexander
Svevo, Italo
See Schmitz, Aron Hector
Swados, Elizabeth 1951- .... **CLC 12**
See also CA 97-100; CANR 49, 163; INT CA-97-100
Swados, Elizabeth A.
See Swados, Elizabeth
Swados, Harvey 1920-1972 .... **CLC 5**
See also CA 5-8R; 37-40R; CANR 6; CN 1; DLB 2, 335; MAL 5
Swados, Liz
See Swados, Elizabeth

Swan, Gladys 1934- .... **CLC 69**
See also CA 101; CANR 17, 39; TCLE 1:2
Swanson, Logan
See Matheson, Richard
Swarthout, Glendon (Fred)
1918-1992 .... **CLC 35**
See also AAYA 55; CA 1-4R; 139; CANR 1, 47; CN 1, 2, 3, 4, 5; LAIT 5; NFS 29; SATA 26; TCWW 1, 2; YAW
Swedenborg, Emanuel 1688-1772 ..... **LC 105**
Sweet, Sarah C.
See Jewett, (Theodora) Sarah Orne
Swenson, May 1919-1989 ...... **CLC 4, 14, 61, 106; PC 14**
See also AMWS 4; CA 5-8R; 130; CANR 36, 61, 131; CP 1, 2, 3, 4; DA; DAB; DAC; DAM MST, POET; DLB 5; EXPP; GLL 2; MAL 5; MTCW 1, 2; MTFW 2005; PFS 16, 30; SATA 15; WP
Swift, Augustus
See Lovecraft, H. P.
Swift, Graham 1949- .... **CLC 41, 88, 233**
See also BRWC 2; BRWS 5; CA 117; 122; CANR 46, 71, 128, 181; CN 4, 5, 6, 7; DLB 194, 326; MTCW 2; MTFW 2005; NFS 18; RGSF 2
Swift, Jonathan 1667-1745 ..... **LC 1, 42, 101; PC 9; WLC 6**
See also AAYA 41; BRW 3; BRWC 1; BRWR 1; BYA 5, 14; CDBLB 1660-1789; CLR 53; DA; DA3; DAB; DAC; DAM MST, NOV, POET; DLB 39, 95, 101; EXPN; LAIT 1; NFS 6; PFS 27; RGEL 2; SATA 19; TEA; WCH; WLIT 3
Swinburne, Algernon Charles
1837-1909 ... **PC 24; TCLC 8, 36; WLC 6**
See also BRW 5; CA 105; 140; CDBLB 1832-1890; DA; DA3; DAB; DAC; DAM MST, POET; DLB 35, 57; PAB; RGEL 2; TEA
Swinfen, Ann .... **CLC 34**
See also CA 202
Swinnerton, Frank (Arthur)
1884-1982 .... **CLC 31**
See also CA 202; 108; CN 1, 2, 3; DLB 34
Swinnerton, Frank Arthur
1884-1982 .... **CLC 31**
See also CA 108; DLB 34
Swithen, John
See King, Stephen
Sylvia
See Ashton-Warner, Sylvia (Constance)
Symmes, Robert Edward
See Duncan, Robert
Symonds, John Addington
1840-1893 .... **NCLC 34**
See also BRWS 14; DLB 57, 144
Symons, Arthur 1865-1945 .... **TCLC 11**
See also BRWS 14; CA 107; 189; DLB 19, 57, 149; RGEL 2
Symons, Julian (Gustave)
1912-1994 .... **CLC 2, 14, 32**
See also CA 49-52; 147; CAAS 3; CANR 3, 33, 59; CMW 4; CN 1, 2, 3, 4, 5; CP 1, 3, 4; DLB 87, 155; DLBY 1992; MSW; MTCW 1
Synge, (Edmund) J(ohn) M(illington)
1871-1909 .... **DC 2; TCLC 6, 37**
See also BRW 6; BRWR 1; CA 104; 141; CDBLB 1890-1914; DAM DRAM; DFS 18; DLB 10, 19; EWL 3; RGEL 2; TEA; WLIT 4
Syruc, J.
See Milosz, Czeslaw
Szirtes, George 1948- .... **CLC 46; PC 51**
See also CA 109; CANR 27, 61, 117; CP 4, 5, 6, 7

Szymborska, Wisława 1923- ... **CLC 99, 190; PC 44**
See also AAYA 76; CA 154; CANR 91, 133, 181; CDWLB 4; CWP; CWW 2; DA3; DLB 232, 332; DLBY 1996; EWL 3; MTCW 2; MTFW 2005; PFS 15, 27; RGHL; RGWL 3

T. O., Nik
See Annensky, Innokenty (Fyodorovich)

Tabori, George 1914-2007 .... **CLC 19**
See also CA 49-52; 262; CANR 4, 69; CBD; CD 5, 6; DLB 245; RGHL

Tacitus c. 55-c. 117 .... **CMLC 56**
See also AW 2; CDWLB 1; DLB 211; RGWL 2, 3; WLIT 8

Tadjo, Veronique 1955- .... **BLC 2:3**
See also EWL 3

Tagore, Rabindranath 1861-1941 .... **PC 8; SSC 48; TCLC 3, 53**
See also CA 104; 120; DA3; DAM DRAM, POET; DFS 26; DLB 323, 332; EWL 3; MTCW 1, 2; MTFW 2005; PFS 18; RGEL 2; RGSF 2; RGWL 2, 3; TWA

Taine, Hippolyte Adolphe
1828-1893 .... **NCLC 15**
See also EW 7; GFL 1789 to the Present

Talayesva, Don C. 1890-(?) .... **NNAL**

Talese, Gay 1932- .... **CLC 37, 232**
See also AITN 1; AMWS 17; CA 1-4R; CANR 9, 58, 137, 177; DLB 185; INT CANR-9; MTCW 1, 2; MTFW 2005

Tallent, Elizabeth 1954- .... **CLC 45**
See also CA 117; CANR 72; DLB 130

Tallmountain, Mary 1918-1997 .... **NNAL**
See also CA 146; 161; DLB 193

Tally, Ted 1952- .... **CLC 42**
See also CA 120; 124; CAD; CANR 125; CD 5, 6; INT CA-124

Talvik, Heiti 1904-1947 .... **TCLC 87**
See also EWL 3

Tamayo y Baus, Manuel
1829-1898 .... **NCLC 1**

Tammsaare, A(nton) H(ansen)
1878-1940 .... **TCLC 27**
See also CA 164; CDWLB 4; DLB 220; EWL 3

Tam'si, Tchicaya U
See Tchicaya, Gerald Felix

Tan, Amy 1952- ..... **AAL; CLC 59, 120, 151, 257**
See also AAYA 9, 48; AMWS 10; BEST 89:3; BPFB 3; CA 136; CANR 54, 105, 132; CDALBS; CN 6, 7; CPW 1; DA3; DAM MULT, NOV, POP; DLB 173, 312; EXPN; FL 1:6; FW; LAIT 3, 5; MAL 5; MTCW 2; MTFW 2005; NFS 1, 13, 16; RGAL 4; SATA 75; SSFS 9; YAW

Tandem, Carl Felix
See Spitteler, Carl

Tandem, Felix
See Spitteler, Carl

Tania B.
See Blixen, Karen (Christentze Dinesen)

Tanizaki, Jun'ichiro 1886-1965 ... **CLC 8, 14, 28; SSC 21**
See also CA 93-96; 25-28R; DLB 180; EWL 3; MJW; MTCW 2; MTFW 2005; RGSF 2; RGWL 2

Tanizaki Jun'ichiro
See Tanizaki, Jun'ichiro

Tannen, Deborah 1945- .... **CLC 206**
See also CA 118; CANR 95

Tannen, Deborah Frances
See Tannen, Deborah

Tanner, William
See Amis, Kingsley

Tante, Dilly
See Kunitz, Stanley

Tao Lao
See Storni, Alfonsina

Tapahonso, Luci 1953- .... **NNAL; PC 65**
See also CA 145; CANR 72, 127; DLB 175

Tarantino, Quentin (Jerome)
1963- .... **CLC 125, 230**
See also AAYA 58; CA 171; CANR 125

Tarassoff, Lev
See Troyat, Henri

Tarbell, Ida M(inerva) 1857-1944 . **TCLC 40**
See also CA 122; 181; DLB 47

Tarchetti, Ugo 1839(?)-1869 .... **SSC 119**

Tardieu d'Esclavelles,
Louise-Florence-Petronille
See Epinay, Louise d'

Tarkington, (Newton) Booth
1869-1946 .... **TCLC 9**
See also BPFB 3; BYA 3; CA 110; 143; CWRI 5; DLB 9, 102; MAL 5; MTCW 2; RGAL 4; SATA 17

Tarkovskii, Andrei Arsen'evich
See Tarkovsky, Andrei (Arsenyevich)

Tarkovsky, Andrei (Arsenyevich)
1932-1986 .... **CLC 75**
See also CA 127

Tartt, Donna 1964(?)- .... **CLC 76**
See also AAYA 56; CA 142; CANR 135; MTFW 2005

Tasso, Torquato 1544-1595 .... **LC 5, 94**
See also EFS 2; EW 2; RGWL 2, 3; WLIT 7

Tate, (John Orley) Allen 1899-1979 .. **CLC 2, 4, 6, 9, 11, 14, 24; PC 50**
See also AMW; CA 5-8R; 85-88; CANR 32, 108; CN 1, 2; CP 1, 2; DLB 4, 45, 63; DLBD 17; EWL 3; MAL 5; MTCW 1, 2; MTFW 2005; RGAL 4; RHW

Tate, Ellalice
See Hibbert, Eleanor Alice Burford

Tate, James (Vincent) 1943- ..... **CLC 2, 6, 25**
See also CA 21-24R; CANR 29, 57, 114; CP 1, 2, 3, 4, 5, 6, 7; DLB 5, 169; EWL 3; PFS 10, 15; RGAL 4; WP

Tate, Nahum 1652(?)-1715 .... **LC 109**
See also DLB 80; RGEL 2

Tauler, Johannes c. 1300-1361 ...... **CMLC 37**
See also DLB 179; LMFS 1

Tavel, Ronald 1936-2009 .... **CLC 6**
See also CA 21-24R; CAD; CANR 33; CD 5, 6

Taviani, Paolo 1931- .... **CLC 70**
See also CA 153

Taylor, Bayard 1825-1878 .... **NCLC 89**
See also DLB 3, 189, 250, 254; RGAL 4

Taylor, C(ecil) P(hilip) 1929-1981 .... **CLC 27**
See also CA 25-28R; 105; CANR 47; CBD

Taylor, Edward 1642(?)-1729 ..... **LC 11, 163; PC 63**
See also AMW; DA; DAB; DAC; DAM MST, POET; DLB 24; EXPP; RGAL 4; TUS

Taylor, Eleanor Ross 1920- .... **CLC 5**
See also CA 81-84; CANR 70

Taylor, Elizabeth 1912-1975 .... **CLC 2, 4, 29; SSC 100**
See also CA 13-16R; CANR 9, 70; CN 1, 2; DLB 139; MTCW 1; RGEL 2; SATA 13

Taylor, Frederick Winslow
1856-1915 .... **TCLC 76**
See also CA 188

Taylor, Henry 1942- .... **CLC 44**
See also CA 33-36R; CAAS 7; CANR 31, 178; CP 6, 7; DLB 5; PFS 10

Taylor, Henry Splawn
See Taylor, Henry

Taylor, Kamala 1924-2004 .... **CLC 8, 38**
See also BYA 13; CA 77-80; 227; CN 1, 2, 3, 4, 5, 6, 7; DLB 323; EWL 3; MTFW 2005; NFS 13

Taylor, Mildred D. 1943- .... **CLC 21**
See also AAYA 10, 47; BW 1; BYA 3, 8; CA 85-88; CANR 25, 115, 136; CLR 9, 59, 90; CSW; DLB 52; JRDA; LAIT 3; MAICYA 1, 2; MTFW 2005; SAAS 5; SATA 135; WYA; YAW

Taylor, Peter (Hillsman) 1917-1994 .. **CLC 1, 4, 18, 37, 44, 50, 71; SSC 10, 84**
See also AMWS 5; BPFB 3; CA 13-16R; 147; CANR 9, 50; CN 1, 2, 3, 4, 5; CSW; DLB 218, 278; DLBY 1981, 1994; EWL 3; EXPS; INT CANR-9; MAL 5; MTCW 1, 2; MTFW 2005; RGSF 2; SSFS 9; TUS

Taylor, Robert Lewis 1912-1998 .... **CLC 14**
See also CA 1-4R; 170; CANR 3, 64; CN 1, 2; SATA 10; TCWW 1, 2

Tchekhov, Anton
See Chekhov, Anton (Pavlovich)

Tchicaya, Gerald Felix 1931-1988 .. **CLC 101**
See also CA 129; 125; CANR 81; EWL 3

Tchicaya U Tam'si
See Tchicaya, Gerald Felix

Teasdale, Sara 1884-1933 .... **PC 31; TCLC 4**
See also CA 104; 163; DLB 45; GLL 1; PFS 14; RGAL 4; SATA 32; TUS

Tecumseh 1768-1813 .... **NNAL**
See also DAM MULT

Tegner, Esaias 1782-1846 .... **NCLC 2**

Teilhard de Chardin, (Marie Joseph) Pierre
1881-1955 .... **TCLC 9**
See also CA 105; 210; GFL 1789 to the Present

Temple, Ann
See Mortimer, Penelope (Ruth)

Tennant, Emma 1937- .... **CLC 13, 52**
See also BRWS 9; CA 65-68; CAAS 9; CANR 10, 38, 59, 88, 177; CN 3, 4, 5, 6, 7; DLB 14; EWL 3; SFW 4

Tenneshaw, S.M.
See Silverberg, Robert

Tenney, Tabitha Gilman
1762-1837 .... **NCLC 122**
See also DLB 37, 200

Tennyson, Alfred 1809-1892 ... **NCLC 30, 65, 115, 202; PC 6; WLC 6**
See also AAYA 50; BRW 4; CDBLB 1832-1890; DA; DA3; DAB; DAC; DAM MST, POET; DLB 32; EXPP; PAB; PFS 1, 2, 4, 11, 15, 19; RGEL 2; TEA; WLIT 4; WP

Teran, Lisa St. Aubin de
See St. Aubin de Teran, Lisa

Terence c. 184B.C.-c. 159B.C. .... **CMLC 14; DC 7**
See also AW 1; CDWLB 1; DLB 211; RGWL 2, 3; TWA; WLIT 8

Teresa de Jesus, St. 1515-1582 .... **LC 18, 149**

Teresa of Avila, St.
See Teresa de Jesus, St.

Terkel, Louis
See Terkel, Studs

Terkel, Studs 1912-2008 .... **CLC 38**
See also AAYA 32; AITN 1; CA 57-60; 278; CANR 18, 45, 67, 132; DA3; MTCW 1, 2; MTFW 2005; TUS

Terkel, Studs Louis
See Terkel, Studs

Terry, C. V.
See Slaughter, Frank G(ill)

Terry, Megan 1932- .... **CLC 19; DC 13**
See also CA 77-80; CABS 3; CAD; CANR 43; CD 5, 6; CWD; DFS 18; DLB 7, 249; GLL 2

Tertullian c. 155-c. 245 .... **CMLC 29**

Tertz, Abram
See Sinyavsky, Andrei (Donatevich)

Tesich, Steve 1943(?)-1996 .... **CLC 40, 69**
See also CA 105; 152; CAD; DLBY 1983

Tesla, Nikola 1856-1943 .... **TCLC 88**

Teternikov, Fyodor Kuzmich
1863-1927 .... **TCLC 9**
See also CA 104; DLB 295; EWL 3

Tevis, Walter 1928-1984 .... **CLC 42**
See also CA 113; SFW 4

Tey, Josephine
See Mackintosh, Elizabeth

Thackeray, William Makepeace
1811-1863 ...... **NCLC 5, 14, 22, 43, 169;**
WLC 6
See also BRW 5; BRWC 2; CDBLB 1832-
1890; DA; DA3; DAB; DAC; DAM MST,
NOV; DLB 21, 55, 159, 163; NFS 13;
RGEL 2; SATA 23; TEA; WLIT 3

Thakura, Ravindranatha
See Tagore, Rabindranath

Thames, C. H.
See Marlowe, Stephen

Tharoor, Shashi 1956- .... **CLC 70**
See also CA 141; CANR 91; CN 6, 7

Thelwall, John 1764-1834 .... **NCLC 162**
See also DLB 93, 158

Thelwell, Michael Miles 1939- .... **CLC 22**
See also BW 2; CA 101

Theo, Ion
See Theodorescu, Ion N.

Theobald, Lewis, Jr.
See Lovecraft, H. P.

Theocritus c. 310B.C.- .... **CMLC 45**
See also AW 1; DLB 176; RGWL 2, 3

Theodorescu, Ion N. 1880-1967 .... **CLC 80**
See also CA 167; 116; CDWLB 4; DLB
220; EWL 3

Theriault, Yves 1915-1983 .... **CLC 79**
See also CA 102; CANR 150; CCA 1;
DAC; DAM MST; DLB 88; EWL 3

Therion, Master
See Crowley, Edward Alexander

Theroux, Alexander 1939- .... **CLC 2, 25**
See also CA 85-88; CANR 20, 63; CN 4, 5,
6, 7

Theroux, Alexander Louis
See Theroux, Alexander

Theroux, Paul 1941- .... **CLC 5, 8, 11, 15, 28,**
46, 159
See also AAYA 28; AMWS 8; BEST 89:4;
BPFB 3; CA 33-36R; CANR 20, 45, 74,
133, 179; CDALBS; CN 1, 2, 3, 4, 5, 6,
7; CP 1; CPW 1; DA3; DAM POP; DLB
2, 218; EWL 3; HGG; MAL 5; MTCW 1,
2; MTFW 2005; RGAL 4; SATA 44, 109;
TUS

Theroux, Paul Edward
See Theroux, Paul

Thesen, Sharon 1946- .... **CLC 56**
See also CA 163; CANR 125; CP 5, 6, 7;
CWP

Thespis fl. 6th cent. B.C.- .... **CMLC 51**
See also LMFS 1

Thevenin, Denis
See Duhamel, Georges

Thibault, Jacques Anatole Francois
1844-1924 .... **TCLC 9**
See also CA 106; 127; DA3; DAM NOV;
DLB 123, 330; EWL 3; GFL 1789 to the
Present; MTCW 1, 2; RGWL 2, 3; SUFW
1; TWA

Thiele, Colin 1920-2006 .... **CLC 17**
See also CA 29-32R; CANR 12, 28, 53,
105; CLR 27; CP 1, 2; DLB 289; MAI-
CYA 1, 2; SAAS 2; SATA 14, 72, 125;
YAW

Thiong'o, Ngugi Wa
See Ngugi wa Thiong'o

Thistlethwaite, Bel
See Wetherald, Agnes Ethelwyn

Thomas, Audrey (Callahan) 1935- .... **CLC 7,**
13, 37, 107; SSC 20
See also AITN 2; CA 21-24R, 237; CAAE
237; CAAS 19; CANR 36, 58; CN 2, 3,
4, 5, 6, 7; DLB 60; MTCW 1; RGSF 2

Thomas, Augustus 1857-1934 .... **TCLC 97**
See also MAL 5

Thomas, D.M. 1935- ..... **CLC 13, 22, 31, 132**
See also BPFB 3; BRWS 4; CA 61-64;
CAAS 11; CANR 17, 45, 75; CDBLB
1960 to Present; CN 4, 5, 6, 7; CP 1, 2, 3,
4, 5, 6, 7; DA3; DLB 40, 207, 299; HGG;
INT CANR-17; MTCW 1, 2; MTFW
2005; RGHL; SFW 4

Thomas, Dylan (Marlais) 1914-1953 .... **PC 2,**
52; SSC 3, 44; TCLC 1, 8, 45, 105;
WLC 6
See also AAYA 45; BRWS 1; CA 104; 120;
CANR 65; CDBLB 1945-1960; DA; DA3;
DAB; DAC; DAM DRAM, MST, POET;
DLB 13, 20, 139; EWL 3; EXPP; LAIT
3; MTCW 1, 2; MTFW 2005; PAB; PFS
1, 3, 8; RGEL 2; RGSF 2; SATA 60; TEA;
WLIT 4; WP

Thomas, (Philip) Edward 1878-1917 . **PC 53;**
TCLC 10
See also BRW 6; BRWS 3; CA 106; 153;
DAM POET; DLB 19, 98, 156, 216; EWL
3; PAB; RGEL 2

Thomas, J.F.
See Fleming, Thomas

Thomas, Joyce Carol 1938- .... **CLC 35**
See also AAYA 12, 54; BW 2, 3; CA 113;
116; CANR 48, 114, 135; CLR 19; DLB
33; INT CA-116; JRDA; MAICYA 1, 2;
MTCW 1, 2; MTFW 2005; SAAS 7;
SATA 40, 78, 123, 137; SATA-Essay 137;
WYA; YAW

Thomas, Lewis 1913-1993 .... **CLC 35**
See also ANW; CA 85-88; 143; CANR 38,
60; DLB 275; MTCW 1, 2

Thomas, M. Carey 1857-1935 .... **TCLC 89**
See also FW

Thomas, Paul
See Mann, (Paul) Thomas

Thomas, Piri 1928- .... **CLC 17; HLCS 2**
See also CA 73-76; HW 1; LLW

Thomas, R(onald) S(tuart)
1913-2000 .... **CLC 6, 13, 48**
See also BRWS 12; CA 89-92; 189; CAAS
4; CANR 30; CDBLB 1960 to Present;
CP 1, 2, 3, 4, 5, 6, 7; DAB; DAM POET;
DLB 27; EWL 3; MTCW 1; RGEL 2

Thomas, Ross (Elmore) 1926-1995 .. **CLC 39**
See also CA 33-36R; 150; CANR 22, 63;
CMW 4

Thompson, Francis (Joseph)
1859-1907 .... **TCLC 4**
See also BRW 5; CA 104; 189; CDBLB
1890-1914; DLB 19; RGEL 2; TEA

Thompson, Francis Clegg
See Mencken, H(enry) L(ouis)

Thompson, Hunter S. 1937(?)-2005 .. **CLC 9,**
17, 40, 104, 229
See also AAYA 45; BEST 89:1; BPFB 3;
CA 17-20R; 236; CANR 23, 46, 74, 77,
111, 133; CPW; CSW; DA3; DAM POP;
DLB 185; MTCW 1, 2; MTFW 2005;
TUS

Thompson, James Myers
See Thompson, Jim

Thompson, Jim 1906-1977 .... **CLC 69**
See also BPFB 3; CA 140; CMW 4; CPW;
DLB 226; MSW

Thompson, Judith (Clare Francesca)
1954- .... **CLC 39**
See also CA 143; CD 5, 6; CWD; DFS 22;
DLB 334

Thomson, James 1700-1748 .... **LC 16, 29, 40**
See also BRWS 3; DAM POET; DLB 95;
RGEL 2

Thomson, James 1834-1882 .... **NCLC 18**
See also DAM POET; DLB 35; RGEL 2

Thoreau, Henry David 1817-1862 .. **NCLC 7,**
21, 61, 138, 207; PC 30; WLC 6
See also AAYA 42; AMW; ANW; BYA 3;
CDALB 1640-1865; DA; DA3; DAB;
DAC; DAM MST; DLB 1, 183, 223, 270,
298; LAIT 2; LMFS 1; NCFS 3; RGAL
4; TUS

Thorndike, E. L.
See Thorndike, Edward L(ee)

Thorndike, Edward L(ee)
1874-1949 .... **TCLC 107**
See also CA 121

Thornton, Hall
See Silverberg, Robert

Thorpe, Adam 1956- .... **CLC 176**
See also CA 129; CANR 92, 160; DLB 231

Thorpe, Thomas Bangs
1815-1878 .... **NCLC 183**
See also DLB 3, 11, 248; RGAL 4

Thubron, Colin 1939- .... **CLC 163**
See also CA 25-28R; CANR 12, 29, 59, 95,
171; CN 5, 6, 7; DLB 204, 231

Thubron, Colin Gerald Dryden
See Thubron, Colin

Thucydides c. 455B.C.-c. 395B.C. . **CMLC 17**
See also AW 1; DLB 176; RGWL 2, 3;
WLIT 8

Thumboo, Edwin Nadason 1933- .... **PC 30**
See also CA 194; CP 1

Thurber, James (Grover)
1894-1961 .. **CLC 5, 11, 25, 125; SSC 1,**
47
See also AAYA 56; AMWS 1; BPFB 3;
BYA 5; CA 73-76; CANR 17, 39; CDALB
1929-1941; CWRI 5; DA; DA3; DAB;
DAC; DAM DRAM, MST, NOV; DLB 4,
11, 22, 102; EWL 3; EXPS; FANT; LAIT
3; MAICYA 1, 2; MAL 5; MTCW 1, 2;
MTFW 2005; RGAL 4; RGSF 2; SATA
13; SSFS 1, 10, 19; SUFW; TUS

Thurman, Wallace (Henry)
1902-1934 .. **BLC 1:3; HR 1:3; TCLC 6**
See also BW 1, 3; CA 104; 124; CANR 81;
DAM MULT; DLB 51

Tibullus c. 54B.C.-c. 18B.C. .... **CMLC 36**
See also AW 2; DLB 211; RGWL 2, 3;
WLIT 8

Ticheburn, Cheviot
See Ainsworth, William Harrison

Tieck, (Johann) Ludwig
1773-1853 ..... **NCLC 5, 46; SSC 31, 100**
See also CDWLB 2; DLB 90; EW 5; IDTP;
RGSF 2; RGWL 2, 3; SUFW

Tiger, Derry
See Ellison, Harlan

Tilghman, Christopher 1946- .... **CLC 65**
See also CA 159; CANR 135, 151; CSW;
DLB 244

Tillich, Paul (Johannes)
1886-1965 .... **CLC 131**
See also CA 5-8R; 25-28R; CANR 33;
MTCW 1, 2

Tillinghast, Richard (Williford)
1940- .... **CLC 29**
See also CA 29-32R; CAAS 23; CANR 26,
51, 96; CP 2, 3, 4, 5, 6, 7; CSW

Tillman, Lynne (?)- .... **CLC 231**
See also CA 173; CANR 144, 172

Timrod, Henry 1828-1867 .... **NCLC 25**
See also DLB 3, 248; RGAL 4

Tindall, Gillian (Elizabeth) 1938- ...... **CLC 7**
See also CA 21-24R; CANR 11, 65, 107;
CN 1, 2, 3, 4, 5, 6, 7

Vasilikos, Vasiles
See Vassilikos, Vassilis
Vasiliu, George
See Bacovia, George
Vasiliu, Gheorghe
See Bacovia, George
Vassa, Gustavus
See Equiano, Olaudah
Vassilikos, Vassilis 1933- .... **CLC 4, 8**
See also CA 81-84; CANR 75, 149; EWL 3
Vaughan, Henry 1621-1695 .... **LC 27; PC 81**
See also BRW 2; DLB 131; PAB; RGEL 2
Vaughn, Stephanie .... **CLC 62**
Vazov, Ivan (Minchov) 1850-1921 . **TCLC 25**
See also CA 121; 167; CDWLB 4; DLB 147
Veblen, Thorstein B(unde)
1857-1929 .... **TCLC 31**
See also AMWS 1; CA 115; 165; DLB 246; MAL 5
Vega, Lope de 1562-1635 ... **HLCS 2; LC 23, 119**
See also EW 2; RGWL 2, 3
Veldeke, Heinrich von c. 1145-c.
1190 .... **CMLC 85**
Vendler, Helen (Hennessy) 1933- ... **CLC 138**
See also CA 41-44R; CANR 25, 72, 136; MTCW 1, 2; MTFW 2005
Venison, Alfred
See Pound, Ezra (Weston Loomis)
Ventsel, Elena Sergeevna
1907-2002 .... **CLC 59**
See also CA 154; CWW 2; DLB 302
Venttsel', Elena Sergeevna
See Ventsel, Elena Sergeevna
Verdi, Marie de
See Mencken, H(enry) L(ouis)
Verdu, Matilde
See Cela, Camilo Jose
Verga, Giovanni (Carmelo)
1840-1922 .... **SSC 21, 87; TCLC 3**
See also CA 104; 123; CANR 101; EW 7; EWL 3; RGSF 2; RGWL 2, 3; WLIT 7
Vergil 70B.C.-19B.C. .. **CMLC 9, 40, 101; PC 12; WLCS**
See also AW 2; CDWLB 1; DA; DA3; DAB; DAC; DAM MST, POET; DLB 211; EFS 1; LAIT 1; LMFS 1; RGWL 2, 3; WLIT 8; WP
Vergil, Polydore c. 1470-1555 .... **LC 108**
See also DLB 132
Verhaeren, Emile (Adolphe Gustave)
1855-1916 .... **TCLC 12**
See also CA 109; EWL 3; GFL 1789 to the Present
Verlaine, Paul (Marie) 1844-1896 .. **NCLC 2, 51; PC 2, 32**
See also DAM POET; DLB 217; EW 7; GFL 1789 to the Present; LMFS 2; RGWL 2, 3; TWA
Verne, Jules (Gabriel) 1828-1905 ... **TCLC 6, 52**
See also AAYA 16; BYA 4; CA 110; 131; CLR 88; DA3; DLB 123; GFL 1789 to the Present; JRDA; LAIT 2; LMFS 2; MAICYA 1, 2; MTFW 2005; RGWL 2, 3; SATA 21; SCFW 1, 2; SFW 4; TWA; WCH
Verus, Marcus Annius
See Aurelius, Marcus
Very, Jones 1813-1880 .... **NCLC 9; PC 86**
See also DLB 1, 243; RGAL 4
Very, Rev. C.
See Crowley, Edward Alexander
Vesaas, Tarjei 1897-1970 .... **CLC 48**
See also CA 190; 29-32R; DLB 297; EW 11; EWL 3; RGWL 3
Vialis, Gaston
See Simenon, Georges (Jacques Christian)

Vian, Boris 1920-1959(?) .... **TCLC 9**
See also CA 106; 164; CANR 111; DLB 72, 321; EWL 3; GFL 1789 to the Present; MTCW 2; RGWL 2, 3
Viator, Vacuus
See Hughes, Thomas
Viaud, (Louis Marie) Julien
1850-1923 .... **TCLC 11**
See also CA 107; DLB 123; GFL 1789 to the Present
Vicar, Henry
See Felsen, Henry Gregor
Vicente, Gil 1465-c. 1536 .... **LC 99**
See also DLB 318; IDTP; RGWL 2, 3
Vicker, Angus
See Felsen, Henry Gregor
Vico, Giambattista
See Vico, Giovanni Battista
Vico, Giovanni Battista 1668-1744 .... **LC 138**
See also EW 3; WLIT 7
Vidal, Eugene Luther Gore
See Vidal, Gore
Vidal, Gore 1925- ...... **CLC 2, 4, 6, 8, 10, 22, 33, 72, 142**
See also AAYA 64; AITN 1; AMWS 4; BEST 90:2; BPFB 3; CA 5-8R; CAD; CANR 13, 45, 65, 100, 132, 167; CD 5, 6; CDALBS; CN 1, 2, 3, 4, 5, 6, 7; CPW; DA3; DAM NOV, POP; DFS 2; DLB 6, 152; EWL 3; GLL 1; INT CANR-13; MAL 5; MTCW 1, 2; MTFW 2005; RGAL 4; RHW; TUS
Viereck, Peter 1916-2006 .... **CLC 4; PC 27**
See also CA 1-4R; 250; CANR 1, 47; CP 1, 2, 3, 4, 5, 6, 7; DLB 5; MAL 5; PFS 9, 14
Viereck, Peter Robert Edwin
See Viereck, Peter
Vigny, Alfred (Victor) de
1797-1863 .... **NCLC 7, 102; PC 26**
See also DAM POET; DLB 119, 192, 217; EW 5; GFL 1789 to the Present; RGWL 2, 3
Vilakazi, Benedict Wallet
1906-1947 .... **TCLC 37**
See also CA 168
Vile, Curt
See Moore, Alan
Villa, Jose Garcia 1914-1997 ... **AAL; PC 22; TCLC 176**
See also CA 25-28R; CANR 12, 118; CP 1, 2, 3, 4; DLB 312; EWL 3; EXPP
Villard, Oswald Garrison
1872-1949 .... **TCLC 160**
See also CA 113; 162; DLB 25, 91
Villarreal, Jose Antonio 1924- .... **HLC 2**
See also CA 133; CANR 93; DAM MULT; DLB 82; HW 1; LAIT 4; RGAL 4
Villaurrutia, Xavier 1903-1950 ...... **TCLC 80**
See also CA 192; EWL 3; HW 1; LAW
Villaverde, Cirilo 1812-1894 .... **NCLC 121**
See also LAW
Villehardouin, Geoffroi de
1150(?)-1218(?) .... **CMLC 38**
Villiers, George 1628-1687 .... **LC 107**
See also DLB 80; RGEL 2
Villiers de l'Isle Adam, Jean Marie Mathias Philippe Auguste 1838-1889 ... **NCLC 3; SSC 14**
See also DLB 123, 192; GFL 1789 to the Present; RGSF 2
Villon, Francois 1431-1463(?) .... **LC 62, 166; PC 13**
See also DLB 208; EW 2; RGWL 2, 3; TWA
Vine, Barbara
See Rendell, Ruth

Vinge, Joan (Carol) D(ennison)
1948- .... **CLC 30; SSC 24**
See also AAYA 32; BPFB 3; CA 93-96; CANR 72; SATA 36, 113; SFW 4; YAW
Viola, Herman J(oseph) 1938- .... **CLC 70**
See also CA 61-64; CANR 8, 23, 48, 91; SATA 126
Violis, G.
See Simenon, Georges (Jacques Christian)
Viramontes, Helena Maria 1954- .... **HLCS 2**
See also CA 159; CANR 182; DLB 122; HW 2; LLW
Virgil
See Vergil
Visconti, Luchino 1906-1976 .... **CLC 16**
See also CA 81-84; 65-68; CANR 39
Vitry, Jacques de
See Jacques de Vitry
Vittorini, Elio 1908-1966 .... **CLC 6, 9, 14**
See also CA 133; 25-28R; DLB 264; EW 12; EWL 3; RGWL 2, 3
Vivekananda, Swami 1863-1902 .... **TCLC 88**
Vizenor, Gerald Robert 1934- .... **CLC 103, 263; NNAL**
See also CA 13-16R; 205; CAAE 205; CAAS 22; CANR 5, 21, 44, 67; DAM MULT; DLB 175, 227; MTCW 2; MTFW 2005; TCWW 2
Vizinczey, Stephen 1933- .... **CLC 40**
See also CA 128; CCA 1; INT CA-128
Vliet, R(ussell) G(ordon)
1929-1984 .... **CLC 22**
See also CA 37-40R; 112; CANR 18; CP 2, 3
Vogau, Boris Andreevich
See Vogau, Boris Andreyevich
Vogau, Boris Andreyevich
1894-1938 .... **SSC 48; TCLC 23**
See also CA 123; 218; DLB 272; EWL 3; RGSF 2; RGWL 2, 3
Vogel, Paula A. 1951- .... **CLC 76; DC 19**
See also CA 108; CAD; CANR 119, 140; CD 5, 6; CWD; DFS 14; DLB 341; MTFW 2005; RGAL 4
Voigt, Cynthia 1942- .... **CLC 30**
See also AAYA 3, 30; BYA 1, 3, 6, 7, 8; CA 106; CANR 18, 37, 40, 94, 145; CLR 13, 48, 141; INT CANR-18; JRDA; LAIT 5; MAICYA 1, 2; MAICYAS 1; MTFW 2005; SATA 48, 79, 116, 160; SATA-Brief 33; WYA; YAW
Voigt, Ellen Bryant 1943- .... **CLC 54**
See also CA 69-72; CANR 11, 29, 55, 115, 171; CP 5, 6, 7; CSW; CWP; DLB 120; PFS 23
Voinovich, Vladimir 1932- .. **CLC 10, 49, 147**
See also CA 81-84; CAAS 12; CANR 33, 67, 150; CWW 2; DLB 302; MTCW 1
Voinovich, Vladimir Nikolaevich
See Voinovich, Vladimir
Vollmann, William T. 1959- ...... **CLC 89, 227**
See also AMWS 17; CA 134; CANR 67, 116, 185; CN 7; CPW; DA3; DAM NOV, POP; MTCW 2; MTFW 2005
Voloshinov, V. N.
See Bakhtin, Mikhail Mikhailovich
Voltaire 1694-1778 .. **LC 14, 79, 110; SSC 12, 112; WLC 6**
See also BYA 13; DA; DA3; DAB; DAC; DAM DRAM, MST; DLB 314; EW 4; GFL Beginnings to 1789; LATS 1:1; LMFS 1; NFS 7; RGWL 2, 3; TWA
von Aschendrof, Baron Ignatz
See Ford, Ford Madox
von Chamisso, Adelbert
See Chamisso, Adelbert von
von Daeniken, Erich 1935- .... **CLC 30**
See also AITN 1; CA 37-40R; CANR 17, 44

Wambaugh, Joseph Aloysius
See Wambaugh, Joseph, Jr.
Wang Wei 699(?)-761(?) . **CMLC 100; PC 18**
See also TWA
Warburton, William 1698-1779 .... **LC 97**
See also DLB 104
Ward, Arthur Henry Sarsfield
1883-1959 .... **TCLC 28**
See also CA 108; 173; CMW 4; DLB 70;
HGG; MSW; SUFW
Ward, Douglas Turner 1930- .... **CLC 19**
See also BW 1; CA 81-84; CAD; CANR
27; CD 5, 6; DLB 7, 38
Ward, E. D.
See Lucas, E(dward) V(errall)
Ward, Mrs. Humphry 1851-1920
See Ward, Mary Augusta
See also RGEL 2
Ward, Mary Augusta 1851-1920 ... **TCLC 55**
See Ward, Mrs. Humphry
See also DLB 18
Ward, Nathaniel 1578(?)-1652 .... **LC 114**
See also DLB 24
Ward, Peter
See Faust, Frederick (Schiller)
Warhol, Andy 1928(?)-1987 .... **CLC 20**
See also AAYA 12; BEST 89:4; CA 89-92;
121; CANR 34
Warner, Francis (Robert Le Plastrier)
1937- .... **CLC 14**
See also CA 53-56; CANR 11; CP 1, 2, 3, 4
Warner, Marina 1946- .... **CLC 59, 231**
See also CA 65-68; CANR 21, 55, 118; CN
5, 6, 7; DLB 194; MTFW 2005
Warner, Rex (Ernest) 1905-1986 ...... **CLC 45**
See also CA 89-92; 119; CN 1, 2, 3, 4; CP
1, 2, 3, 4; DLB 15; RGEL 2; RHW
Warner, Susan (Bogert)
1819-1885 .... **NCLC 31, 146**
See also AMWS 18; DLB 3, 42, 239, 250,
254
Warner, Sylvia (Constance) Ashton
See Ashton-Warner, Sylvia (Constance)
Warner, Sylvia Townsend
1893-1978 .. **CLC 7, 19; SSC 23; TCLC**
131
See also BRWS 7; CA 61-64; 77-80; CANR
16, 60, 104; CN 1, 2; DLB 34, 139; EWL
3; FANT; FW; MTCW 1, 2; RGEL 2;
RGSF 2; RHW
Warren, Mercy Otis 1728-1814 ..... **NCLC 13**
See also DLB 31, 200; RGAL 4; TUS
Warren, Robert Penn 1905-1989 .. **CLC 1, 4,**
6, 8, 10, 13, 18, 39, 53, 59; PC 37; SSC
4, 58; WLC 6
See also AITN 1; AMW; AMWC 2; BPFB
3; BYA 1; CA 13-16R; 129; CANR 10,
47; CDALB 1968-1988; CN 1, 2, 3, 4;
CP 1, 2, 3, 4; DA; DA3; DAB; DAC;
DAM MST, NOV, POET; DLB 2, 48, 152,
320; DLBY 1980, 1989; EWL 3; INT
CANR-10; MAL 5; MTCW 1, 2; MTFW
2005; NFS 13; RGAL 4; RGSF 2; RHW;
SATA 46; SATA-Obit 63; SSFS 8; TUS
Warrigal, Jack
See Furphy, Joseph
Warshofsky, Isaac
See Singer, Isaac Bashevis
Warton, Joseph 1722-1800 ... **LC 128; NCLC**
118
See also DLB 104, 109; RGEL 2
Warton, Thomas 1728-1790 .... **LC 15, 82**
See also DAM POET; DLB 104, 109, 336;
RGEL 2
Waruk, Kona
See Harris, (Theodore) Wilson
Warung, Price
See Astley, William

Warwick, Jarvis
See Garner, Hugh
Washington, Alex
See Harris, Mark
Washington, Booker T(aliaferro)
1856-1915 .... **BLC 1:3; TCLC 10**
See also BW 1; CA 114; 125; DA3; DAM
MULT; DLB 345; LAIT 2; RGAL 4;
SATA 28
Washington, George 1732-1799 .... **LC 25**
See also DLB 31
Wassermann, (Karl) Jakob
1873-1934 .... **TCLC 6**
See also CA 104; 163; DLB 66; EWL 3
Wasserstein, Wendy 1950-2006 . **CLC 32, 59,**
90, 183; DC 4
See also AAYA 73; AMWS 15; CA 121;
129; 247; CABS 3; CAD; CANR 53, 75,
128; CD 5, 6; CWD; DA3; DAM DRAM;
DFS 5, 17; DLB 228; EWL 3; FW; INT
CA-129; MAL 5; MTCW 2; MTFW 2005;
SATA 94; SATA-Obit 174
Waterhouse, Keith (Spencer) 1929- . **CLC 47**
See also BRWS 13; CA 5-8R; CANR 38,
67, 109; CBD; CD 6; CN 1, 2, 3, 4, 5, 6,
7; DLB 13, 15; MTCW 1, 2; MTFW 2005
Waters, Frank (Joseph) 1902-1995 .. **CLC 88**
See also CA 5-8R; 149; CAAS 13; CANR
3, 18, 63, 121; DLB 212; DLBY 1986;
RGAL 4; TCWW 1, 2
Waters, Mary C. .... **CLC 70**
Waters, Roger 1944- .... **CLC 35**
Watkins, Frances Ellen
See Harper, Frances Ellen Watkins
Watkins, Gerrold
See Malzberg, Barry N(athaniel)
Watkins, Gloria Jean
See hooks, bell
Watkins, Paul 1964- .... **CLC 55**
See also CA 132; CANR 62, 98
Watkins, Vernon Phillips
1906-1967 .... **CLC 43**
See also CA 9-10; 25-28R; CAP 1; DLB
20; EWL 3; RGEL 2
Watson, Irving S.
See Mencken, H(enry) L(ouis)
Watson, John H.
See Farmer, Philip Jose
Watson, Richard F.
See Silverberg, Robert
Watts, Ephraim
See Horne, Richard Henry Hengist
Watts, Isaac 1674-1748 .... **LC 98**
See also DLB 95; RGEL 2; SATA 52
Waugh, Auberon (Alexander)
1939-2001 .... **CLC 7**
See also CA 45-48; 192; CANR 6, 22, 92;
CN 1, 2, 3; DLB 14, 194
Waugh, Evelyn 1903-1966 ... **CLC 1, 3, 8, 13,**
19, 27, 44, 107; SSC 41; WLC 6
See also AAYA 78; BPFB 3; BRW 7; CA
85-88; 25-28R; CANR 22; CDBLB 1914-
1945; DA; DA3; DAB; DAC; DAM MST,
NOV, POP; DLB 15, 162, 195; EWL 3;
MTCW 1, 2; MTFW 2005; NFS 13, 17;
RGEL 2; RGSF 2; TEA; WLIT 4
Waugh, Evelyn Arthur St. John
See Waugh, Evelyn
Waugh, Harriet 1944- .... **CLC 6**
See also CA 85-88; CANR 22
Ways, C.R.
See Blount, Roy, Jr.
Waystaff, Simon
See Swift, Jonathan
Webb, Beatrice (Martha Potter)
1858-1943 .... **TCLC 22**
See also CA 117; 162; DLB 190; FW
Webb, Charles 1939- .... **CLC 7**
See also CA 25-28R; CANR 114, 188

Webb, Charles Richard
See Webb, Charles
Webb, Frank J. .... **NCLC 143**
See also DLB 50
Webb, James, Jr.
See Webb, James
Webb, James 1946- .... **CLC 22**
See also CA 81-84; CANR 156
Webb, James H.
See Webb, James
Webb, James Henry
See Webb, James
Webb, Mary Gladys (Meredith)
1881-1927 .... **TCLC 24**
See also CA 182; 123; DLB 34; FW; RGEL
2
Webb, Mrs. Sidney
See Webb, Beatrice (Martha Potter)
Webb, Phyllis 1927- .... **CLC 18**
See also CA 104; CANR 23; CCA 1; CP 1,
2, 3, 4, 5, 6, 7; CWP; DLB 53
Webb, Sidney (James) 1859-1947 .. **TCLC 22**
See also CA 117; 163; DLB 190
Webber, Andrew Lloyd
See Lloyd Webber, Andrew
Weber, Lenora Mattingly
1895-1971 .... **CLC 12**
See also CA 19-20; 29-32R; CAP 1; SATA
2; SATA-Obit 26
Weber, Max 1864-1920 .... **TCLC 69**
See also CA 109; 189; DLB 296
Webster, John 1580(?)-1634(?) ...... **DC 2; LC**
33, 84, 124; WLC 6
See also BRW 2; CDBLB Before 1660; DA;
DAB; DAC; DAM DRAM, MST; DFS
17, 19; DLB 58; IDTP; RGEL 2; WLIT 3
Webster, Noah 1758-1843 .... **NCLC 30**
See also DLB 1, 37, 42, 43, 73, 243
Wedekind, Benjamin Franklin
See Wedekind, Frank
Wedekind, Frank 1864-1918 .... **TCLC 7**
See also CA 104; 153; CANR 121, 122;
CDWLB 2; DAM DRAM; DLB 118; EW
8; EWL 3; LMFS 2; RGWL 2, 3
Wehr, Demaris .... **CLC 65**
Weidman, Jerome 1913-1998 .... **CLC 7**
See also AITN 2; CA 1-4R; 171; CAD;
CANR 1; CD 1, 2, 3, 4, 5; DLB 28
Weil, Simone (Adolphine)
1909-1943 .... **TCLC 23**
See also CA 117; 159; EW 12; EWL 3; FW;
GFL 1789 to the Present; MTCW 2
Weininger, Otto 1880-1903 .... **TCLC 84**
Weinstein, Nathan
See West, Nathanael
Weinstein, Nathan von Wallenstein
See West, Nathanael
Weir, Peter (Lindsay) 1944- .... **CLC 20**
See also CA 113; 123
Weiss, Peter (Ulrich) 1916-1982 .. **CLC 3, 15,**
51; TCLC 152
See also CA 45-48; 106; CANR 3; DAM
DRAM; DFS 3; DLB 69, 124; EWL 3;
RGHL; RGWL 2, 3
Weiss, Theodore (Russell)
1916-2003 .... **CLC 3, 8, 14**
See also CA 9-12R; 189; 216; CAAE 189;
CAAS 2; CANR 46, 94; CP 1, 2, 3, 4, 5,
6, 7; DLB 5; TCLE 1:2
Welch, (Maurice) Denton
1915-1948 .... **TCLC 22**
See also BRWS 8, 9; CA 121; 148; RGEL
2
Welch, James (Phillip) 1940-2003 ..... **CLC 6,**
14, 52, 249; NNAL; PC 62
See also CA 85-88; 219; CANR 42, 66, 107;
CN 5, 6, 7; CP 2, 3, 4, 5, 6, 7; CPW;
DAM MULT, POP; DLB 175, 256; LATS
1:1; NFS 23; RGAL 4; TCWW 1, 2

Weldon, Fay 1931- . **CLC 6, 9, 11, 19, 36, 59, 122**
See also BRWS 4; CA 21-24R; CANR 16, 46, 63, 97, 137; CDBLB 1960 to Present; CN 3, 4, 5, 6, 7; CPW; DAM POP; DLB 14, 194, 319; EWL 3; FW; HGG; INT CANR-16; MTCW 1, 2; MTFW 2005; RGEL 2; RGSF 2

Wellek, Rene 1903-1995 .... **CLC 28**
See also CA 5-8R; 150; CAAS 7; CANR 8; DLB 63; EWL 3; INT CANR-8

Weller, Michael 1942- .... **CLC 10, 53**
See also CA 85-88; CAD; CD 5, 6

Weller, Paul 1958- .... **CLC 26**

Wellershoff, Dieter 1925- .... **CLC 46**
See also CA 89-92; CANR 16, 37

Welles, (George) Orson 1915-1985 .. **CLC 20, 80**
See also AAYA 40; CA 93-96; 117

Wellman, John McDowell 1945- ...... **CLC 65**
See also CA 166; CAD; CD 5, 6; RGAL 4

Wellman, Mac
See Wellman, John McDowell; Wellman, John McDowell

Wellman, Manly Wade 1903-1986 ... **CLC 49**
See also CA 1-4R; 118; CANR 6, 16, 44; FANT; SATA 6; SATA-Obit 47; SFW 4; SUFW

Wells, Carolyn 1869(?)-1942 .... **TCLC 35**
See also CA 113; 185; CMW 4; DLB 11

Wells, H(erbert) G(eorge) 1866-1946 . **SSC 6, 70; TCLC 6, 12, 19, 133; WLC 6**
See also AAYA 18; BPFB 3; BRW 6; CA 110; 121; CDBLB 1914-1945; CLR 64, 133; DA; DA3; DAB; DAC; DAM MST, NOV; DLB 34, 70, 156, 178; EWL 3; EXPS; HGG; LAIT 3; LMFS 2; MTCW 1, 2; MTFW 2005; NFS 17, 20; RGEL 2; RGSF 2; SATA 20; SCFW 1, 2; SFW 4; SSFS 3; SUFW; TEA; WCH; WLIT 4; YAW

Wells, Rosemary 1943- .... **CLC 12**
See also AAYA 13; BYA 7, 8; CA 85-88; CANR 48, 120, 179; CLR 16, 69; CWRI 5; MAICYA 1, 2; SAAS 1; SATA 18, 69, 114, 156; YAW

Wells-Barnett, Ida B(ell)
1862-1931 .... **TCLC 125**
See also CA 182; DLB 23, 221

Welsh, Irvine 1958- .... **CLC 144**
See also CA 173; CANR 146; CN 7; DLB 271

Welty, Eudora 1909-2001 .... **CLC 1, 2, 5, 14, 22, 33, 105, 220; SSC 1, 27, 51, 111; WLC 6**
See also AAYA 48; AMW; AMWR 1; BPFB 3; CA 9-12R; 199; CABS 1; CANR 32, 65, 128; CDALB 1941-1968; CN 1, 2, 3, 4, 5, 6, 7; CSW; DA; DA3; DAB; DAC; DAM MST, NOV; DFS 26; DLB 2, 102, 143; DLBD 12; DLBY 1987, 2001; EWL 3; EXPS; HGG; LAIT 3; MAL 5; MBL; MTCW 1, 2; MTFW 2005; NFS 13, 15; RGAL 4; RGSF 2; RHW; SSFS 2, 10, 26; TUS

Welty, Eudora Alice
See Welty, Eudora

Wen I-to 1899-1946 .... **TCLC 28**
See also EWL 3

Wentworth, Robert
See Hamilton, Edmond

Werewere Liking 1950- .... **BLC 2:2**
See also EWL 3

Werfel, Franz (Viktor) 1890-1945 ... **TCLC 8**
See also CA 104; 161; DLB 81, 124; EWL 3; RGWL 2, 3

Wergeland, Henrik Arnold
1808-1845 .... **NCLC 5**

Werner, Friedrich Ludwig Zacharias
1768-1823 .... **NCLC 189**
See also DLB 94

Werner, Zacharias
See Werner, Friedrich Ludwig Zacharias

Wersba, Barbara 1932- .... **CLC 30**
See also AAYA 2, 30; BYA 6, 12, 13; CA 29-32R, 182; CAAE 182; CANR 16, 38; CLR 3, 78; DLB 52; JRDA; MAICYA 1, 2; SAAS 2; SATA 1, 58; SATA-Essay 103; WYA; YAW

Wertmueller, Lina 1928- .... **CLC 16**
See also CA 97-100; CANR 39, 78

Wescott, Glenway 1901-1987 .. **CLC 13; SSC 35**
See also CA 13-16R; 121; CANR 23, 70; CN 1, 2, 3, 4; DLB 4, 9, 102; MAL 5; RGAL 4

Wesker, Arnold 1932- .... **CLC 3, 5, 42**
See also CA 1-4R; CAAS 7; CANR 1, 33; CBD; CD 5, 6; CDBLB 1960 to Present; DAB; DAM DRAM; DLB 13, 310, 319; EWL 3; MTCW 1; RGEL 2; TEA

Wesley, Charles 1707-1788 .... **LC 128**
See also DLB 95; RGEL 2

Wesley, John 1703-1791 .... **LC 88**
See also DLB 104

Wesley, Richard (Errol) 1945- .... **CLC 7**
See also BW 1; CA 57-60; CAD; CANR 27; CD 5, 6; DLB 38

Wessel, Johan Herman 1742-1785 .... **LC 7**
See also DLB 300

West, Anthony (Panther)
1914-1987 .... **CLC 50**
See also CA 45-48; 124; CANR 3, 19; CN 1, 2, 3, 4; DLB 15

West, C. P.
See Wodehouse, P(elham) G(renville)

West, Cornel 1953- .... **BLCS; CLC 134**
See also CA 144; CANR 91, 159; DLB 246

West, Cornel Ronald
See West, Cornel

West, Delno C(loyde), Jr. 1936- .... **CLC 70**
See also CA 57-60

West, Dorothy 1907-1998 ...... **HR 1:3; TCLC 108**
See also AMWS 18; BW 2; CA 143; 169; DLB 76

West, Edwin
See Westlake, Donald E.

West, (Mary) Jessamyn 1902-1984 ... **CLC 7, 17**
See also CA 9-12R; 112; CANR 27; CN 1, 2, 3; DLB 6; DLBY 1984; MTCW 1, 2; RGAL 4; RHW; SATA-Obit 37; TCWW 2; TUS; YAW

West, Morris L(anglo) 1916-1999 ..... **CLC 6, 33**
See also BPFB 3; CA 5-8R; 187; CANR 24, 49, 64; CN 1, 2, 3, 4, 5, 6; CPW; DLB 289; MTCW 1, 2; MTFW 2005

West, Nathanael 1903-1940 ...... **SSC 16, 116; TCLC 1, 14, 44**
See also AAYA 77; AMW; AMWR 2; BPFB 3; CA 104; 125; CDALB 1929-1941; DA3; DLB 4, 9, 28; EWL 3; MAL 5; MTCW 1, 2; MTFW 2005; NFS 16; RGAL 4; TUS

West, Owen
See Koontz, Dean R.

West, Paul 1930- .... **CLC 7, 14, 96, 226**
See also CA 13-16R; CAAS 7; CANR 22, 53, 76, 89, 136; CN 1, 2, 3, 4, 5, 6, 7; DLB 14; INT CANR-22; MTCW 2; MTFW 2005

West, Rebecca 1892-1983 ... **CLC 7, 9, 31, 50**
See also BPFB 3; BRWS 3; CA 5-8R; 109; CANR 19; CN 1, 2, 3; DLB 36; DLBY 1983; EWL 3; FW; MTCW 1, 2; MTFW 2005; NCFS 4; RGEL 2; TEA

Westall, Robert (Atkinson)
1929-1993 .... **CLC 17**
See also AAYA 12; BYA 2, 6, 7, 8, 9, 15; CA 69-72; 141; CANR 18, 68; CLR 13; FANT; JRDA; MAICYA 1, 2; MAICYAS 1; SAAS 2; SATA 23, 69; SATA-Obit 75; WYA; YAW

Westermarck, Edward 1862-1939 . **TCLC 87**

Westlake, Donald E. 1933-2008 ... **CLC 7, 33**
See also BPFB 3; CA 17-20R; 280; CAAS 13; CANR 16, 44, 65, 94, 137; CMW 4; CPW; DAM POP; INT CANR-16; MSW; MTCW 2; MTFW 2005

Westlake, Donald E. Edmund
See Westlake, Donald E.

Westlake, Donald Edwin
See Westlake, Donald E.

Westlake, Donald Edwin Edmund
See Westlake, Donald E.

Westmacott, Mary
See Christie, Agatha (Mary Clarissa)

Weston, Allen
See Norton, Andre

Wetcheek, J. L.
See Feuchtwanger, Lion

Wetering, Janwillem van de
See van de Wetering, Janwillem

Wetherald, Agnes Ethelwyn
1857-1940 .... **TCLC 81**
See also CA 202; DLB 99

Wetherell, Elizabeth
See Warner, Susan (Bogert)

Whale, James 1889-1957 .... **TCLC 63**
See also AAYA 75

Whalen, Philip (Glenn) 1923-2002 .... **CLC 6, 29**
See also BG 1:3; CA 9-12R; 209; CANR 5, 39; CP 1, 2, 3, 4, 5, 6, 7; DLB 16; WP

Wharton, Edith (Newbold Jones)
1862-1937 . **SSC 6, 84, 120; TCLC 3, 9, 27, 53, 129, 149; WLC 6**
See also AAYA 25; AMW; AMWC 2; AMWR 1; BPFB 3; CA 104; 132; CDALB 1865-1917; CLR 136; DA; DA3; DAB; DAC; DAM MST, NOV; DLB 4, 9, 12, 78, 189; DLBD 13; EWL 3; EXPS; FL 1:6; GL 3; HGG; LAIT 2, 3; LATS 1:1; MAL 5; MBL; MTCW 1, 2; MTFW 2005; NFS 5, 11, 15, 20; RGAL 4; RGSF 2; RHW; SSFS 6, 7; SUFW; TUS

Wharton, James
See Mencken, H(enry) L(ouis)

Wharton, William 1925-2008 ..... **CLC 18, 37**
See also CA 93-96; 278; CN 4, 5, 6, 7; DLBY 1980; INT CA-93-96

Wheatley (Peters), Phillis
1753(?)-1784 .... **BLC 1:3; LC 3, 50; PC 3; WLC 6**
See also AFAW 1, 2; CDALB 1640-1865; DA; DA3; DAC; DAM MST, MULT, POET; DLB 31, 50; EXPP; FL 1:1; PFS 13, 29; RGAL 4

Wheelock, John Hall 1886-1978 .... **CLC 14**
See also CA 13-16R; 77-80; CANR 14; CP 1, 2; DLB 45; MAL 5

Whim-Wham
See Curnow, (Thomas) Allen (Monro)

Whisp, Kennilworthy
See Rowling, J.K.

Whitaker, Rod 1931-2005 .... **CLC 29**
See also CA 29-32R; 246; CANR 45, 153; CMW 4

Whitaker, Rodney
See Whitaker, Rod

Whitaker, Rodney William
See Whitaker, Rod

White, Babington
See Braddon, Mary Elizabeth

White, E. B. 1899-1985 .... **CLC 10, 34, 39**
See also AAYA 62; AITN 2; AMWS 1; CA 13-16R; 116; CANR 16, 37; CDALBS; CLR 1, 21, 107; CPW; DA3; DAM POP; DLB 11, 22; EWL 3; FANT; MAICYA 1, 2; MAL 5; MTCW 1, 2; MTFW 2005; NCFS 5; RGAL 4; SATA 2, 29, 100; SATA-Obit 44; TUS

White, Edmund 1940- .... **CLC 27, 110**
See also AAYA 7; CA 45-48; CANR 3, 19, 36, 62, 107, 133, 172; CN 5, 6, 7; DA3; DAM POP; DLB 227; MTCW 1, 2; MTFW 2005

White, Edmund Valentine III
See White, Edmund

White, Elwyn Brooks
See White, E. B.

White, Hayden V. 1928- .... **CLC 148**
See also CA 128; CANR 135; DLB 246

White, Patrick (Victor Martindale)
1912-1990 ...... **CLC 3, 4, 5, 7, 9, 18, 65, 69; SSC 39; TCLC 176**
See also BRWS 1; CA 81-84; 132; CANR 43; CN 1, 2, 3, 4; DLB 260, 332; EWL 3; MTCW 1; RGEL 2; RGSF 2; RHW; TWA; WWE 1

White, Phyllis Dorothy James
1920- .... **CLC 18, 46, 122, 226**
See also BEST 90:2; BPFB 2; BRWS 4; CA 21-24R; CANR 17, 43, 65, 112; CD-BLB 1960 to Present; CMW 4; CN 4, 5, 6; CPW; DA3; DAM POP; DLB 87, 276; DLBD 17; MSW; MTCW 1, 2; MTFW 2005; TEA

White, T(erence) H(anbury)
1906-1964 .... **CLC 30**
See also AAYA 22; BPFB 3; BYA 4, 5; CA 73-76; CANR 37; CLR 139; DLB 160; FANT; JRDA; LAIT 1; MAICYA 1, 2; RGEL 2; SATA 12; SUFW 1; YAW

White, Terence de Vere 1912-1994 ... **CLC 49**
See also CA 49-52; 145; CANR 3

White, Walter
See White, Walter F(rancis)

White, Walter F(rancis)
1893-1955 ..... **BLC 1:3; HR 1:3; TCLC 15**
See also BW 1; CA 115; 124; DAM MULT; DLB 51

White, William Hale 1831-1913 ..... **TCLC 25**
See also CA 121; 189; DLB 18; RGEL 2

Whitehead, Alfred North
1861-1947 .... **TCLC 97**
See also CA 117; 165; DLB 100, 262

Whitehead, Colson 1969- ...... **BLC 2:3; CLC 232**
See also CA 202; CANR 162

Whitehead, E(dward) A(nthony)
1933- .... **CLC 5**
See also CA 65-68; CANR 58, 118; CBD; CD 5, 6; DLB 310

Whitehead, Ted
See Whitehead, E(dward) A(nthony)

Whiteman, Roberta J. Hill 1947- ...... **NNAL**
See also CA 146

Whitemore, Hugh (John) 1936- .... **CLC 37**
See also CA 132; CANR 77; CBD; CD 5, 6; INT CA-132

Whitman, Sarah Helen (Power)
1803-1878 .... **NCLC 19**
See also DLB 1, 243

Whitman, Walt(er) 1819-1892 .. **NCLC 4, 31, 81, 205; PC 3, 91; WLC 6**
See also AAYA 42; AMW; AMWR 1; CDALB 1640-1865; DA; DA3; DAB; DAC; DAM MST, POET; DLB 3, 64, 224, 250; EXPP; LAIT 2; LMFS 1; PAB; PFS 2, 3, 13, 22; RGAL 4; SATA 20; TUS; WP; WYAS 1

Whitney, Isabella fl. 1565-fl. 1575 ..... **LC 130**
See also DLB 136

Whitney, Phyllis A. 1903-2008 .... **CLC 42**
See also AAYA 36; AITN 2; BEST 90:3; CA 1-4R; 269; CANR 3, 25, 38, 60; CLR 59; CMW 4; CPW; DA3; DAM POP; JRDA; MAICYA 1, 2; MTCW 2; RHW; SATA 1, 30; SATA-Obit 189; YAW

Whitney, Phyllis Ayame
See Whitney, Phyllis A.

Whitney, Phyllis Ayame
See Whitney, Phyllis A.

Whittemore, (Edward) Reed, Jr.
1919- .... **CLC 4**
See also CA 9-12R, 219; CAAE 219; CAAS 8; CANR 4, 119; CP 1, 2, 3, 4, 5, 6, 7; DLB 5; MAL 5

Whittier, John Greenleaf
1807-1892 .... **NCLC 8, 59; PC 93**
See also AMWS 1; DLB 1, 243; RGAL 4

Whittlebot, Hernia
See Coward, Noel (Peirce)

Wicker, Thomas Grey
See Wicker, Tom

Wicker, Tom 1926- .... **CLC 7**
See also CA 65-68; CANR 21, 46, 141, 179

Wicomb, Zoe 1948- .... **BLC 2:3**
See also CA 127; CANR 106, 167; DLB 225

Wideman, John Edgar 1941- .. **BLC 1:3, 2:3; CLC 5, 34, 36, 67, 122; SSC 62**
See also AFAW 1, 2; AMWS 10; BPFB 4; BW 2, 3; CA 85-88; CANR 14, 42, 67, 109, 140, 187; CN 4, 5, 6, 7; DAM MULT; DLB 33, 143; MAL 5; MTCW 2; MTFW 2005; RGAL 4; RGSF 2; SSFS 6, 12, 24; TCLE 1:2

Wiebe, Rudy 1934- . **CLC 6, 11, 14, 138, 263**
See also CA 37-40R; CANR 42, 67, 123; CN 1, 2, 3, 4, 5, 6, 7; DAC; DAM MST; DLB 60; RHW; SATA 156

Wiebe, Rudy Henry
See Wiebe, Rudy

Wieland, Christoph Martin
1733-1813 .... **NCLC 17, 177**
See also DLB 97; EW 4; LMFS 1; RGWL 2, 3

Wiene, Robert 1881-1938 .... **TCLC 56**

Wieners, John 1934- .... **CLC 7**
See also BG 1:3; CA 13-16R; CP 1, 2, 3, 4, 5, 6, 7; DLB 16; WP

Wiesel, Elie 1928- ...... **CLC 3, 5, 11, 37, 165; WLCS**
See also AAYA 7, 54; AITN 1; CA 5-8R; CAAS 4; CANR 8, 40, 65, 125; CDALBS; CWW 2; DA; DA3; DAB; DAC; DAM MST, NOV; DLB 83, 299; DLBY 1987; EWL 3; INT CANR-8; LAIT 4; MTCW 1, 2; MTFW 2005; NCFS 4; NFS 4; RGHL; RGWL 3; SATA 56; YAW

Wiesel, Eliezer
See Wiesel, Elie

Wiggins, Marianne 1947- .... **CLC 57**
See also AAYA 70; BEST 89:3; CA 130; CANR 60, 139, 180; CN 7; DLB 335

Wigglesworth, Michael 1631-1705 .... **LC 106**
See also DLB 24; RGAL 4

Wiggs, Susan .... **CLC 70**
See also CA 201; CANR 173

Wight, James Alfred 1916-1995 .... **CLC 12**
See also AAYA 1, 54; BPFB 2; CA 77-80; 148; CANR 40; CLR 80; CPW; DAM POP; LAIT 3; MAICYA 2; MAICYAS 1; MTCW 2; SATA 86, 135; SATA-Brief 44; TEA; YAW

Wilbur, Richard 1921- .. **CLC 3, 6, 9, 14, 53, 110; PC 51**
See also AAYA 72; AMWS 3; CA 1-4R; CABS 2; CANR 2, 29, 76, 93, 139; CDALBS; CP 1, 2, 3, 4, 5, 6, 7; DA; DAB; DAC; DAM MST, POET; DLB 5, 169; EWL 3; EXPP; INT CANR-29; MAL 5; MTCW 1, 2; MTFW 2005; PAB; PFS 11, 12, 16, 29; RGAL 4; SATA 9, 108; WP

Wilbur, Richard Purdy
See Wilbur, Richard

Wild, Peter 1940- .... **CLC 14**
See also CA 37-40R; CP 1, 2, 3, 4, 5, 6, 7; DLB 5

Wilde, Oscar 1854(?)-1900 ... **DC 17; SSC 11, 77; TCLC 1, 8, 23, 41, 175; WLC 6**
See also AAYA 49; BRW 5; BRWC 1, 2; BRWR 2; BYA 15; CA 104; 119; CANR 112; CDBLB 1890-1914; CLR 114; DA; DA3; DAB; DAC; DAM DRAM, MST, NOV; DFS 4, 8, 9, 21; DLB 10, 19, 34, 57, 141, 156, 190, 344; EXPS; FANT; GL 3; LATS 1:1; NFS 20; RGEL 2; RGSF 2; SATA 24; SSFS 7; SUFW; TEA; WCH; WLIT 4

Wilde, Oscar Fingal O'Flahertie Willis
See Wilde, Oscar

Wilder, Billy
See Wilder, Samuel

Wilder, Samuel 1906-2002 .... **CLC 20**
See also AAYA 66; CA 89-92; 205; DLB 26

Wilder, Stephen
See Marlowe, Stephen

Wilder, Thornton (Niven)
1897-1975 .. **CLC 1, 5, 6, 10, 15, 35, 82; DC 1, 24; WLC 6**
See also AAYA 29; AITN 2; AMW; CA 13-16R; 61-64; CAD; CANR 40, 132; CDALBS; CN 1, 2; DA; DA3; DAB; DAC; DAM DRAM, MST, NOV; DFS 1, 4, 16; DLB 4, 7, 9, 228; DLBY 1997; EWL 3; LAIT 3; MAL 5; MTCW 1, 2; MTFW 2005; NFS 24; RGAL 4; RHW; WYAS 1

Wilding, Michael 1942- ...... **CLC 73; SSC 50**
See also CA 104; CANR 24, 49, 106; CN 4, 5, 6, 7; DLB 325; RGSF 2

Wiley, Richard 1944- .... **CLC 44**
See also CA 121; 129; CANR 71

Wilhelm, Kate
See Wilhelm, Katie

Wilhelm, Katie 1928- .... **CLC 7**
See also AAYA 20; BYA 16; CA 37-40R; CAAS 5; CANR 17, 36, 60, 94; DLB 8; INT CANR-17; MTCW 1; SCFW 2; SFW 4

Wilhelm, Katie Gertrude
See Wilhelm, Katie

Wilkins, Mary
See Freeman, Mary E(leanor) Wilkins

Willard, Nancy 1936- .... **CLC 7, 37**
See also BYA 5; CA 89-92; CANR 10, 39, 68, 107, 152, 186; CLR 5; CP 2, 3, 4, 5; CWP; CWRI 5; DLB 5, 52; FANT; MAICYA 1, 2; MTCW 1; SATA 37, 71, 127, 191; SATA-Brief 30; SUFW 2; TCLE 1:2

William of Malmesbury c. 1090B.C.-c. 1140B.C. .... **CMLC 57**

William of Moerbeke c. 1215-c. 1286 .... **CMLC 91**

William of Ockham 1290-1349 ..... **CMLC 32**

Williams, Ben Ames 1889-1953 ..... **TCLC 89**
See also CA 183; DLB 102

Williams, Charles
See Collier, James Lincoln

Williams, Charles (Walter Stansby)
1886-1945 .... **TCLC 1, 11**
See also BRWS 9; CA 104; 163; DLB 100, 153, 255; FANT; RGEL 2; SUFW 1

Williams, C.K. 1936- .... **CLC 33, 56, 148**
See also CA 37-40R; CAAS 26; CANR 57, 106; CP 1, 2, 3, 4, 5, 6, 7; DAM POET; DLB 5; MAL 5

Williams, Ella Gwendolen Rees
See Rhys, Jean

Williams, (George) Emlyn
1905-1987 .... **CLC 15**
See also CA 104; 123; CANR 36; DAM DRAM; DLB 10, 77; IDTP; MTCW 1

Williams, Hank 1923-1953 .... **TCLC 81**
See also CA 188

Williams, Helen Maria
1761-1827 .... **NCLC 135**
See also DLB 158

Williams, Hiram Hank
See Williams, Hank

Williams, Hiram King
See Williams, Hank

Williams, Hugo (Mordaunt) 1942- ... **CLC 42**
See also CA 17-20R; CANR 45, 119; CP 1, 2, 3, 4, 5, 6, 7; DLB 40

Williams, J. Walker
See Wodehouse, P(elham) G(renville)

Williams, John A(lfred) 1925- .... **BLC 1:3; CLC 5, 13**
See also AFAW 2; BW 2, 3; CA 53-56, 195; CAAE 195; CAAS 3; CANR 6, 26, 51, 118; CN 1, 2, 3, 4, 5, 6, 7; CSW; DAM MULT; DLB 2, 33; EWL 3; INT CANR-6; MAL 5; RGAL 4; SFW 4

Williams, Jonathan 1929-2008 .... **CLC 13**
See also CA 9-12R; 270; CAAS 12; CANR 8, 108; CP 1, 2, 3, 4, 5, 6, 7; DLB 5

Williams, Jonathan Chamberlain
See Williams, Jonathan

Williams, Joy 1944- .... **CLC 31**
See also CA 41-44R; CANR 22, 48, 97, 168; DLB 335; SSFS 25

Williams, Norman 1952- .... **CLC 39**
See also CA 118

Williams, Roger 1603(?)-1683 .... **LC 129**
See also DLB 24

Williams, Sherley Anne
1944-1999 .... **BLC 1:3; CLC 89**
See also AFAW 2; BW 2, 3; CA 73-76; 185; CANR 25, 82; DAM MULT, POET; DLB 41; INT CANR-25; SATA 78; SATA-Obit 116

Williams, Shirley
See Williams, Sherley Anne

Williams, Tennessee 1911-1983 . **CLC 1, 2, 5, 7, 8, 11, 15, 19, 30, 39, 45, 71, 111; DC 4; SSC 81; WLC 6**
See also AAYA 31; AITN 1, 2; AMW; AMWC 1; CA 5-8R; 108; CABS 3; CAD; CANR 31, 132, 174; CDALB 1941-1968; CN 1, 2, 3; DA; DA3; DAB; DAC; DAM DRAM, MST; DFS 17; DLB 7, 341; DLBD 4; DLBY 1983; EWL 3; GLL 1; LAIT 4; LATS 1:2; MAL 5; MTCW 1, 2; MTFW 2005; RGAL 4; TUS

Williams, Thomas (Alonzo)
1926-1990 .... **CLC 14**
See also CA 1-4R; 132; CANR 2

Williams, Thomas Lanier
See Williams, Tennessee

Williams, William C.
See Williams, William Carlos

Williams, William Carlos
1883-1963 .... **CLC 1, 2, 5, 9, 13, 22, 42, 67; PC 7; SSC 31; WLC 6**
See also AAYA 46; AMW; AMWR 1; CA 89-92; CANR 34; CDALB 1917-1929; DA; DA3; DAB; DAC; DAM MST, POET; DLB 4, 16, 54, 86; EWL 3; EXPP; MAL 5; MTCW 1, 2; MTFW 2005; NCFS 4; PAB; PFS 1, 6, 11; RGAL 4; RGSF 2; SSFS 27; TUS; WP

Williamson, David (Keith) 1942- ..... **CLC 56**
See also CA 103; CANR 41; CD 5, 6; DLB 289

Williamson, Jack
See Williamson, John Stewart

Williamson, John Stewart
1908-2006 .... **CLC 29**
See also AAYA 76; CA 17-20R; 255; CAAS 8; CANR 23, 70, 153; DLB 8; SCFW 1, 2; SFW 4

Willie, Frederick
See Lovecraft, H. P.

Willingham, Calder (Baynard, Jr.)
1922-1995 .... **CLC 5, 51**
See also CA 5-8R; 147; CANR 3; CN 1, 2, 3, 4, 5; CSW; DLB 2, 44; IDFW 3, 4; MTCW 1

Willis, Charles
See Clarke, Arthur C.

Willis, Nathaniel Parker
1806-1867 .... **NCLC 194**
See also DLB 3, 59, 73, 74, 183, 250; DLBD 13; RGAL 4

Willy
See Colette, (Sidonie-Gabrielle)

Willy, Colette
See Colette, (Sidonie-Gabrielle)

Wilmot, John 1647-1680 .... **LC 75; PC 66**
See also BRW 2; DLB 131; PAB; RGEL 2

Wilson, A.N. 1950- .... **CLC 33**
See also BRWS 6; CA 112; 122; CANR 156; CN 4, 5, 6, 7; DLB 14, 155, 194; MTCW 2

Wilson, Andrew Norman
See Wilson, A.N.

Wilson, Angus (Frank Johnstone)
1913-1991 . **CLC 2, 3, 5, 25, 34; SSC 21**
See also BRWS 1; CA 5-8R; 134; CANR 21; CN 1, 2, 3, 4; DLB 15, 139, 155; EWL 3; MTCW 1, 2; MTFW 2005; RGEL 2; RGSF 2

Wilson, August 1945-2005 .... **BLC 1:3, 2:3; CLC 39, 50, 63, 118, 222; DC 2, 31; WLCS**
See also AAYA 16; AFAW 2; AMWS 8; BW 2, 3; CA 115; 122; 244; CAD; CANR 42, 54, 76, 128; CD 5, 6; DA; DA3; DAB; DAC; DAM DRAM, MST, MULT; DFS 3, 7, 15, 17, 24; DLB 228; EWL 3; LAIT 4; LATS 1:2; MAL 5; MTCW 1, 2; MTFW 2005; RGAL 4

Wilson, Brian 1942- .... **CLC 12**

Wilson, Colin (Henry) 1931- .... **CLC 3, 14**
See also CA 1-4R; CAAS 5; CANR 1, 22, 33, 77; CMW 4; CN 1, 2, 3, 4, 5, 6; DLB 14, 194; HGG; MTCW 1; SFW 4

Wilson, Dirk
See Pohl, Frederik

Wilson, Edmund 1895-1972 .. **CLC 1, 2, 3, 8, 24**
See also AMW; CA 1-4R; 37-40R; CANR 1, 46, 110; CN 1; DLB 63; EWL 3; MAL 5; MTCW 1, 2; MTFW 2005; RGAL 4; TUS

Wilson, Ethel Davis (Bryant)
1888(?)-1980 .... **CLC 13**
See also CA 102; CN 1, 2; DAC; DAM POET; DLB 68; MTCW 1; RGEL 2

Wilson, Harriet
See Wilson, Harriet E. Adams

Wilson, Harriet E.
See Wilson, Harriet E. Adams

Wilson, Harriet E. Adams
1827(?)-1863(?) ...... **BLC 1:3; NCLC 78**
See also DAM MULT; DLB 50, 239, 243

Wilson, John 1785-1854 .... **NCLC 5**
See also DLB 110

Wilson, John (Anthony) Burgess
See Burgess, Anthony

Wilson, Katharina .... **CLC 65**

Wilson, Lanford 1937- .. **CLC 7, 14, 36, 197; DC 19**
See also CA 17-20R; CABS 3; CAD; CANR 45, 96; CD 5, 6; DAM DRAM; DFS 4, 9, 12, 16, 20; DLB 7, 341; EWL 3; MAL 5; TUS

Wilson, Robert M. 1941- .... **CLC 7, 9**
See also CA 49-52; CAD; CANR 2, 41; CD 5, 6; MTCW 1

Wilson, Robert McLiam 1964- .... **CLC 59**
See also CA 132; DLB 267

Wilson, Sloan 1920-2003 .... **CLC 32**
See also CA 1-4R; 216; CANR 1, 44; CN 1, 2, 3, 4, 5, 6

Wilson, Snoo 1948- .... **CLC 33**
See also CA 69-72; CBD; CD 5, 6

Wilson, William S(mith) 1932- .... **CLC 49**
See also CA 81-84

Wilson, (Thomas) Woodrow
1856-1924 .... **TCLC 79**
See also CA 166; DLB 47

Winchester, Simon 1944- .... **CLC 257**
See also AAYA 66; CA 107; CANR 90, 130

Winchilsea, Anne (Kingsmill) Finch
1661-1720
See Finch, Anne
See also RGEL 2

Winckelmann, Johann Joachim
1717-1768 .... **LC 129**
See also DLB 97

Windham, Basil
See Wodehouse, P(elham) G(renville)

Wingrove, David 1954- .... **CLC 68**
See also CA 133; SFW 4

Winnemucca, Sarah 1844-1891 .... **NCLC 79; NNAL**
See also DAM MULT; DLB 175; RGAL 4

Winstanley, Gerrard 1609-1676 .... **LC 52**

Wintergreen, Jane
See Duncan, Sara Jeannette

Winters, Arthur Yvor
See Winters, Yvor

Winters, Janet Lewis
See Lewis, Janet

Winters, Yvor 1900-1968 .. **CLC 4, 8, 32; PC 82**
See also AMWS 2; CA 11-12; 25-28R; CAP 1; DLB 48; EWL 3; MAL 5; MTCW 1; RGAL 4

Winterson, Jeanette 1959- .... **CLC 64, 158**
See also BRWS 4; CA 136; CANR 58, 116, 181; CN 5, 6, 7; CPW; DA3; DAM POP; DLB 207, 261; FANT; FW; GLL 1; MTCW 2; MTFW 2005; RHW; SATA 190

Winthrop, John 1588-1649 .... **LC 31, 107**
See also DLB 24, 30

Winthrop, Theodore 1828-1861 ... **NCLC 210**
See also DLB 202

Winton, Tim 1960- .... **CLC 251; SSC 119**
See also AAYA 34; CA 152; CANR 118; CN 6, 7; DLB 325; SATA 98

Wirth, Louis 1897-1952 .... **TCLC 92**
See also CA 210

Wiseman, Frederick 1930- .... **CLC 20**
See also CA 159

Literary Criticism Series
Cumulative Topic Index

This index lists all topic entries in Gale's *Children's Literature Review* (CLR), *Classical and Medieval Literature Criticism* (CMLC), *Contemporary Literary Criticism* (CLC), *Drama Criticism* (DC), *Literature Criticism from 1400 to 1800* (LC), *Nineteenth-Century Literature Criticism* (NCLC), *Short Story Criticism* (SSC), and *Twentieth-Century Literary Criticism* (TCLC). The index also lists topic entries in the Gale Critical Companion Collection, which includes the following publications: *The Beat Generation* (BG), *Feminism in Literature* (FL), *Gothic Literature* (GL), and *Harlem Renaissance* (HR).

Topic Index

NCLC Cumulative Nationality Index

Nationality Index

ISBN-13: 978-1-4144-3410-0
ISBN-10: 1-4144-3410-3

90000

9 781414 434100